Q
641.5636
S

T4-ADM-233

A Worldwide Vegetarian Journey to Discover the Foods That Nourish America's Immigrant Soul

Judith Ader Spinzia

VOLUME II

Virtualbookworm Publishing   College Station, Texas

2015

"A Worldwide Vegetarian Journey to Discover the Foods That Nourish America's Immigrant Soul: Volume 2," by Judith Ader Spinzia. ISBN 978-1-62137-732-0.

Library of Congress Control Number on file with Publisher.

Published 2015 by Virtualbookworm.com Publishing Inc., P.O. Box 9949, College Station, TX 77842, US.
© 2015 Judith Ader Spinzia. All rights reserved. No part of this publication may be reproduced, stored in a retrieval system, or transmitted in any form or by any means, electronic, mechanical, recording or otherwise, without the prior written permission of Raymond E. or Judith Ader Spinzia.

Table of Contents

Volume I

Introduction

Europe

Middle East

Caucasus

Central Asia

South Asia

Index (includes references to recipes in volumes I and II)

Volume II

Acknowledgment and Dedication	*iv*
Africa	1-302
Asia	303-444
Oceania	445-485
The Americas	486-673
Appendix of Basic Recipes	674-698
Index (includes references to recipes in volumes I and II)	699

An individual table of contents precedes each section.

I am sincerely grateful to my husband Raymond

for his never-ending support,

his ever-receptive palate for the new and unusual,

and for the considerable time and effort

needed to create the maps which accompany each section.

These two volumes are dedicated to the explorers who enabled this story

by carrying the foods of the Western Hemisphere around the globe

and to the generations of women who adopted these foods

and carried them back to the Western Hemisphere – our ethnic heritage.

Africa

Africa

Algeria	3	Madagascar	145
Angola	10	Mali	154
Botswana	17	Mauritania	160
Burundi	25	Morocco	169
Cameroon	31	Mozambique	178
Cape Verde	40	Namibia	188
Central African Republic	45	Niger	197
Chad	54	Nigeria	201
Cote d'Ivorie	61	Republic of the Congo	45
Democratic Republic of the Congo	45	São Tomé and Principe	209
Djibouti	70	Senegal	215
Egypt	77	Sierra Leone	225
Equatorial Guinea	45	Somalia	230
Eritrea	83	South Africa	242
Ethiopia	90	Sudan	250
Gabon	45	Tanzania	259
The Gambia	98	Togo	267
Ghana	109	Tunisia	270
Guinea	116	Uganda	281
Kenya	123	Western Sahara	160
Liberia	131	Zambia	290
Libya	137	Zimbabwe	298

Algeria

Forests have been cleared by humans for agriculture, to allow for expanding human populations, to supply industries such homebuilding and shipbuilding, and to eliminate obstacles to military advances. The World Wide Forest Report verifies that, during the Roman period, ninety percent of Europe's forests were cut or burned. The Romans not only savaged Europe's forests, they crossed the Mediterranean into Numidia, the land we now know as Algeria. North Africa became the "granary of the empire" and the clearing of land for agriculture and the harvesting of the standing forests allowed for desertification to proceed up from the Sahara into once-fertile North Africa. Since antiquity the extensive forests of Atlas cedar that stood on the Saharan Atlas have been over-harvested for fuel and timber, with a further fifty percent loss of the remaining woodlands since 1830. Four-fifths of the country of Algeria can now be classified as desert. In 594 BC the Athenian statesman Solon recorded that Greece had been experiencing soil erosion and loss of fertile land as early as 650 BC due to clean-cutting of forests. This surely stood as a clear lesson to Rome as to the unsustainability of their practices. Today we face the same lack of response to lessons learned in the rain forests of the planet.

The original occupants of the western shoulder of North Africa arrived in about 30,000 BC, migrating north from the central African cradle of human development. These people, who began the cultivation of wheat, were eventually known as the Magrhrib or Maghreb, and gave their name to the area although they were later known as Berbers. Invasions by Arab Muslims during the period from 642 to 669 AD led to the conversion of the Berbers to Islam. The Ottoman Empire extended across North Africa, including Algeria, and it was under the Ottomans that Algeria's northern border along the Mediterranean was established. They made it a base for Ottoman privateers, known as the Barbary pirates or the Ottoman corsairs, whose piracy against American vessels resulted in two wars against the United States. The First and Second Barbary Wars, 1801-1805 and 1815 respectively, were in retaliation against the Ottoman capture and enslavement of non-Islamic people who were removed from American vessels attacked by the pirates. The Barbary pirates had been making coastal attacks in southern and western Europe for centuries. From the sixteenth to the nineteenth century it is estimated that perhaps 1.25 million Europeans were sold into the Arab slave markets on the Barbary Coast or in Istanbul. Algiers was a center of Mediterranean piracy and privateering for three centuries.

The French invaded Algeria in 1830 but despite significant emigration from France to Algeria, the French did not secure control until the early twentieth century. Not only did the colonial government invite French immigration to Algeria, they welcomed Spanish, Italian, and Maltese settlers to whom confiscated land was made available. The ethics of this confiscation not withstanding, the new landowners took up modern agricultural techniques. Their practices increased the productivity of the once-fertile land again and increased the arable land available for agriculture. Independence from France was achieved when the National Liberation Front launched a guerrilla campaign, known as the Algerian War of Independence, in 1954. Decades of one-party rule dissolved with the elections of 1991 but military intervention interrupted the election forcing out the sitting president, banning all political parties based on religion, and precipitating a civil war which lasted until 2002. Europeans account for less than one percent of the population today.

Africa–Algeria

North African *Couscous* Salad with Chick Peas
Salade aux Couscous

~

Puréed Tomato – Squash Soup
Chorba bil Matisha

~

Anise-Scented Baked Beets
Chlada Bandjar

~~~~~~~~~~~~~~~~~~~~

Skillet Potato Cakes   or   **Potato Omelet with Parsley**
Galette de Pommes de Terre de Algeria   *Bata bil Beyd*

Steamed Beet Greens with Lemon Wedges

North African Thyme Breads
Manaish bi Zahter

~~~~~~~~~~~~~~~~~~~~

Toasted Semolina Dessert with Honey
Tamina

Grapefruit Sections with Honey

NORTH AFRICAN *COUSCOUS* SALAD WITH CHICK PEAS
Salade aux Couscous

TPT - 2 hours and 4 minutes;
45 minutes = absorption period;
1 hour = cooling period

Here is another way to complement the protein components of grains and legumes and we think this dish really has "pizzazz and then some!" It is not just a "macaroni salad!" A friend of ours always rejected restaurant meals if couscous was served as the accompaniment to her main course. We have never understood it since she then readily agrees to a helping of macaroni as a side dish instead.

1 1/2 cups water
1 cup dry, quick-cooking, whole wheat couscous*

1 tablespoon *extra virgin* olive oil
1 teaspoon sesame oil*
2 tablespoons freshly squeezed lemon juice
1 garlic clove—*finely* chopped
1/4 cup chopped fresh coriander *(cilantro)*
1/4 cup chopped fresh parsley
2 scallions—trimmed, well-rinsed, and sliced
1/2 cup canned chick peas *(garbanzos)*—well-drained
Freshly ground black pepper, to taste

6 large red lettuce leaves

In a saucepan set over *HIGH* heat, bring water to the boil. Reduce heat to *LOW* and stir in *couscous*. Cover tightly and allow to cook for about 5 minutes. Remove from heat and allow *couscous* to cool for about 45 minutes. *All water should be absorbed.* Fluff cooked *couscous* with a wooden fork. Refrigerate until *completely cooled*—about 1 hour.

Using the fork, stir in olive and sesame oils, lemon juice, *finely* chopped garlic, chopped coriander *(cilantro)* and parsley leaves, sliced scallions, and *well-drained* chick peas. Season with black pepper to taste. Toss *gently*. Refrigerate until serving time.

When ready to serve, arrange red lettuce leaves in serving bowl. Pile *couscous* mixture in the center.

Africa–Algeria

**NORTH AFRICAN *COUSCOUS* SALAD
WITH CHICK PEAS** (cont'd)

Serve at once.

Yields 6 servings
adequate for 4 people

Notes: **Couscous* is packaged by several companies and is now generally available in grocery stores and food specialty stores as well as in Middle Eastern groceries and in natural food stores. Whole wheat *couscous* is worth seeking out. Sesame oil may also be obtained from these same sources.

This recipe may be halved or doubled, when required.

1/6 SERVING – PROTEIN = 3.4 g.; FAT = 3.1 g.; CARBOHYDRATE = 16.5 g.;
CALORIES = 107; CALORIES FROM FAT = 26%

ALGERIAN PURÉED TOMATO – SQUASH SOUP
Charba bil Matisha

TPT - 1 hour and 6 minutes

If you live in the Northeast United States, you have undoubtedly searched cookbooks to find new ways to use the tomato and squash harvest. This Algerian soup was, for me, a new and different way to enjoy the autumn's plenty and it became a family favorite. I usually serve it as a simple puréed soup with freshly baked bread and a salad. If you want a heartier main course soup, add cooked angel hair pasta.

5 cups VEGETABLE STOCK FROM SOUP [see index] **or other vegetarian stock, of choice**
4 cups diced butternut squash
4 stalks celery—chopped
3 1/2 cups peeled, seeded, and chopped tomatoes, with juice
1 medium onion studded with 3 whole cloves
1 1/2 teaspoons ground coriander
1/2 teaspoon ground turmeric

3/4 cup *two-percent* milk
Freshly ground mixed peppercorns—red, white, and black—to taste

In a kettle set over *MEDIUM-HIGH* heat, combine vegetable stock, diced butternut squash, chopped celery, chopped tomatoes, the onion with the cloves, ground coriander, and ground turmeric. Allow to come to boil. *Reduce heat to MEDIUM-LOW* and allow to cook for about 40 minutes. Stir occasionally. Remove from heat. Remove onion with cloves.* Allow to cool slightly.

Using a food processor, fitted with steel knife, or an electric blender, purée the soup mixture. Press through a fine sieve or a FOOD MILL into a clean saucepan, discarding any fibrous residue.** Return to *LOW* heat.***

Turn into heated soup tureen and serve into heated soup plates.

Yields 8 servings
adequate for 6 people

Notes: *Remove and discard the cloves. The onion without the cloves can be frozen with other vegetables and trimmings for stock.

**The puréed soup base can be frozen at this point, if desired.

***This is the point at which you can add cooked *pasta*, if desired.

If required, this soup can be doubled.

1/8 SERVING (i. e., per cupful) –
PROTEIN = 3.5 g.; FAT = 0.8 g.; CARBOHYDRATE = 12.7 g.;
CALORIES = 83; CALORIES FROM FAT = 9%

Africa–Algeria

ALGERIAN ANISE – SCENTED BAKED BEETS
Chlada Bandjar

TPT - 56 minutes

Beets are said to have originated in North Africa and there is no better way to remember that bit of trivia than to add this to your repertoire. I guess this recipe came into our files because I love beets and Ray loves fennel, and, to me, cooking should be fun.

6 small-medium beets with root intact and 2-inches of leaf stem attached—well-washed
2 tablespoons *extra virgin* olive oil
3 whole star anise—halved*
Salt, to taste
Freshly ground black pepper, to taste

Preheat oven to 375 degrees F.

Cut six squares of aluminum foil. Place a well-washed beet on each square. Sprinkle 1/2 teaspoonful of oil over each. Place half of a star anise on each square and sprinkle each beet with salt and black pepper. Gather the corners of the aluminum foil up and twist to form a tightly-sealed package.

Set wrapped beets in a roasting pan in preheated 375 degree F. oven and bake for 45 minutes, or until beets are tender when pierced with a fork. (*Open a test package to be sure.*) Remove to counter top and allow to cool slightly until packages are cool enough to handle. Move aluminum foil back and forth until skins loosen and slip off. Open packages and discard foil, star anise pieces, and skins. Cut stem end and root end off, discarding both. Cut beets in wedges or slices. Place in a heated serving bowl.

Serve at room temperature.

Yields 6 servings
adequate for 4 people

Notes: *Star anise are available in Asian groceries and natural food stores, from mail-order spice firms, and, increasingly in grocery stores. If you are unable to locate this most interesting spice, a teaspoonful of anise seeds may be divided among the beets to be baked as a substitution. Fennel seeds may also be used to flavor beets in this manner for a very different taste.

Steamed beet greens, those tender young leaves that were attached to the fresh beets when purchased, may be steamed and served as a garnish to this dish or as a side dish with lemon wedges.

1/6 SERVING – PROTEIN = 0.6 g; FAT = 3.8 g; CARBOHYDRATE = 3.6 g;
CALORIES = 49; CALORIES FROM FAT = 70 %

ALGERIAN SKILLET POTATO CAKES
Galette de Pommes de Terre de Algeria

TPT - 2 hours;
1 hour and 30 minutes = chilling period

French influence upon Algerian cuisine is unquestionably apparent in this dish but what Algerians take from French cuisine, they give back with distinctly exciting and exotic flavors. These potato cakes are an excellent use for leftover potatoes or for planned leftovers. The potato cakes themselves can also become an intentionally planned leftover since they reheat well.

3 cups *cold* mashed potatoes—approximately 4 large potatoes
1 1/2 teaspoons ground cumin
3/4 teaspoon ground paprika—*sweet or hot*, as preferred
1/2 cup fresh coriander (*cilantro*) leaves—well-rinsed and chopped
1/2 cup *fat-free* pasteurized eggs (the equivalent of 2 eggs)*
1/2 teaspoon salt, or to taste
Freshly ground black pepper, to taste
Pinch ground red pepper (cayenne)

1 tablespoon safflower *or* sunflower oil
1 tablespoon butter

In a large mixing bowl, combine *cold* mashed potatoes, ground cumin and paprika, and chopped fresh coriander (*cilantro*) leaves. Stir to combine well. Add pasteurized eggs and blend thoroughly. Season with salt, black pepper, and ground red pepper (cayenne). Blend the seasonings into the potato mixture *thoroughly*.

Africa–Algeria

ALGERIAN SKILLET POTATO CAKES (cont'd)

Divide potato mixture into 8 equal portions. Place these on a platter or board and chill in the refrigerator for at least 1 1/2 hours.

In a large, non-stick-coated skillet set over *LOW-MEDIUM* heat, heat oil and butter.

Shape each potato portion into a round flat cake. Transfer potato cakes to skillet and cook until browned on both sides. Use a wide spatula to turn cakes. This avoids breakage. Remove to a warm plate, covered with paper toweling, and set on a warming tray or in a warm oven. Keep warm until ready to serve.

Transfer to a heated serving platter to serve.

Yields 10 potato cakes
adequate for 5 people

Notes: *Because raw eggs present the danger of *Salmonella* poisoning, commercially-available pasteurized eggs are recommended for use in preparing the potato cakes.

This recipe may be halved or doubled, when required.

1/10 SERVING (i. e., per potato cake) –
PROTEIN = 2.5 g.; FAT = 2.6 g.; CARBOHYDRATE = 13.3 g.;
CALORIES = 88; CALORIES FROM FAT = 27%

ALGERIAN POTATO OMELET WITH PARSLEY
Bata bil Beyd
TPT - 49 minutes

I grew up blithely thinking that the simple farmer's omelet, which had been handed down from my German great-grandmother was simply a German farmer's omelet. As I came to learn, the story of this omelet is far from simple as the idea traveled far and wide. It is, in fact, an Italian potato "frittata"; a Basque omelet or a "tortilla de batatas a la Española"; a German "bauernomette" or "bauernfrühstück," depending on the region of Germany; or a "tortilla Española a la Mexicana," and there are probably a dozen more . . . ! Then, I discovered another version in which the potatoes are deep-fried first, turmeric is added, and it is flipped in the pan like a pancake instead of spending a few minutes under a hot broiler. Well, of course, I wanted to try this one too.

3 medium all-purpose potatoes—well-scrubbed, peeled, and chopped into 1/4-inch cubes
2 quarts *boiling* water

Oil for *shallow* deep-frying

1 tablespoon butter
1 small onion—chopped
Freshly ground black pepper, to taste

3 large eggs—beaten
2 tablespoons water
3 tablespoons *finely* chopped fresh parsley
1/4 teaspoon ground turmeric, or to taste

Boil diced potato in *boiling* water for 5 minutes. Remove from water and dry *thoroughly* on paper toweling.

Heat oil in a large saucepan or deep skillet to about 365 degrees F. While *carefully* stirring, deep-fry potatoes in several batches *until they begin to brown*. Remove from oil with a skimmer and drain *thoroughly* on paper toweling.

In a 9-inch non-stick-coated skillet set over *MEDIUM* heat, combine butter and chopped onion. Sauté gently until onion are soft and translucent, *being careful not to allow onions to brown*. Season with black pepper. Add deep-fried potato.

Beat eggs and water together. Add parsley, and ground turmeric. Stir beaten eggs into vegetables in skillet, spreading evenly over pan surface. Cook, *undisturbed*, until set. Carefully turn omelet onto a plate and then slide it back into skillet to brown the other side—about 4 minutes. Slide out onto a heated round serving platter.

Serve at once, cutting into wedges to serve.

Yields 4-5 servings
adequate for 3-4 people

1/5 SERVING – PROTEIN = 5.5 g.; FAT = 7.6 g.; CARBOHYDRATE = 14.7 g.;
CALORIES = 149; CALORIES FROM FAT = 46%

Africa–Algeria

(BREAD MACHINE) NORTH AFRICAN THYME BREADS
Manaish bi Zahter

TPT - 3 hours and 16 minutes*;
2 hours = automated preparation period;
30 minutes = pre-baking rising period

The aroma of these breads as they are baking is just incredible and the taste is really quite indescribable, reminding us a great deal of the Italian garlic and olive oil bread that we make. Although a breakfast favorite in North Africa and the Middle East, we prefer them as accompaniment to our mid-day or evening meal.

1 1/4 cups water—*heated to about 95 degrees F.*

2 1/2 cups bread flour
1 cup whole wheat flour
1 tablespoon sugar
3/4 teaspoon salt

1 tablespoon (1 envelope) *preservative-free* **active dried yeast****

2 tablespoons *extra virgin* **olive oil**
1/3 cup NORTH AFRICAN SUMAC SEASONING MIXTURE (*Zahter* or *Za'atar*) [see index]***

Bring all ingredients except warm water to room temperature.

Put water into the BREAD MACHINE pan.

Add bread and whole wheat flours, sugar, and salt, spreading the ingredients over the liquid as you add them. *Do not stir.*

Using a spoon, create a depression in the dry ingredients, being very careful not to press down into the liquid layer below. Pour yeast into the depression.

Select MANUAL SETTING and push START.

Prepare two cookie sheets by coating with non-stick lecithin spray coating.

In 2 hours, when the automated preparation period is over, remove dough to a floured surface and knead until smooth and all trace of stickiness is gone, adding more bread flour as needed. Flatten into a single round circle about 1/4-inch in thickness. Using a floured 3-inch biscuit cutter, cut out bread rounds. Place on prepared baking sheets. Allow to rise in a warm, draft free kitchen until doubled in volume—about 30 minutes.

Mix olive oil and *zahter* together. Brush risen loaves/biscuits *gently* with mixture.

Preheat oven to 400 degrees F.

Bake in preheated oven for about 10-15 minutes. Each loaf should have a crisp, golden brown crust.

Serve warm with or without butter.

Yield 16 three-inch rounds

Notes: *Preparation time depends, of course, on the brand of bread machine which you are using.

**Some packaged dried yeast available in grocery stores contain a preservative. Natural food stores carry an additive-free dried yeast. In addition, *do not use so-called fast action yeasts*. The results will not please you.

***Zahter* (alternately spelled *zatore* or *zaatar*) is an intriguing mixture of thyme, sumac, marjoram, ground sesame seeds, and salt and is an essential ingredient in many dishes found in the eastern end of the Mediterranean. It is available in Middle Eastern markets and from mail order spice firms, if you choose to not make it yourself. *Za'atar*, an oregano–like herb (*Origanum cyriacum*) used in Morocco, is often confused with *zahter*. It is not a mixture and, therefore, can not be substituted.

1/16 SERVING (i. e., per biscuit) –
PROTEIN = 3.2 g.; FAT = 3.4 g.; CARBOHYDRATE = 20.8 g.;
CALORIES = 137; CALORIES FROM FAT = 22%

Africa–Algeria

ALGERIAN TOASTED SEMOLINA WITH HONEY
Tamina

TPT - 55 minutes;
30 minutes = solidifying period

This sweet traditionally celebrates the birth of child in Algeria but it need not be reserved for such celebratory moments. It is curiously neither a cake nor a cookie nor a pudding; it is thoroughly unique. Semolina, although not nearly as available here as it is in Europe, North Africa, and the Middle East, is generally available in well-stocked natural food stores, but I have prepared this dish with farina or Cream of Wheat when necessity requires that the winter store of cereal grains must be used up in the spring. Tamina is an unexpected taste and texture, a difference to be savored.

1 cup medium or coarse semolina*

1/4 cup butter

3 tablespoons honey, of choice

Cinnamon, for garnish
***Organic* rose petals, for garnish**

In a non-stick-coated skillet set over *LOW-MEDIUM* heat, toast semolina until it browns lightly. Stir constantly.

Add butter. Cook, stirring until butter is absorbed and semolina begins to stick together. Remove from heat.

Add honey. Stir to combine well. Turn into the middle of a plate. Using a knife, flatten into a cake round and press the edges tightly into the cake. Allow to stand at room temperature for about 30 minutes to solidify.

Sprinkle cinnamon on a saucer or in a small fruit dish. Press the rim of a small glass into the cinnamon. Lightly press the cinnamon-coated rim of the glass onto the *tamina* to make a ring. Go back for more cinnamon and repeat the process to make a decorative pattern. Sprinkle with rose petals.

Break into pieces. Use a small cheese or pastry server to serve.

Yields 6 servings
adequate for 4 people

Notes: *Farina can be substituted.

**We harvest and dry our own unsprayed rose petals but organic rose petals are available from several mail order firms that sell rose petals, rosebuds, and rose hips.

1/6 SERVING – PROTEIN = 3.9 g.; FAT = 7.8 g.; CARBOHYDRATE = 33.2 g.;
CALORIES = 219; CALORIES FROM FAT =32 %

GRAPEFRUIT SECTIONS WITH HONEY

TPT - 1 hour and 5 minutes;
1 hour = refrigeration period

Algerians grow and eat a great deal of fruit, especially citrus fruits. A bowlful of seasonal fruit is usually presented with a meal and, unlike western hospitality, Algerian hostesses often peel the fruit for guests. In addition, the residents of this North African nation are the second largest consumers of honey in the entire world so this dessert is a natural. How many, many times have I sectioned grapefruit halves and sweetened the fruit with fragrant, local honey but this westernized presentation would not be quite right for an Algerian meal nor would peeling the fruit for guests feel quite right for a western hostess. A compromise follows.

2 cans (15 ounces each) red grapefruit, canned in light syrup—well-drained*
2 tablespoons honey, of choice

Arrange grapefruit sections in a shallow serving bowl or on a plate. Drizzle honey over. Refrigerate for at least 1 hour.

Serve chilled.

Yields 6 servings
adequate for 4 people

Notes: *Fresh grapefruits can be peeled and sectioned, if preferred.

This recipe can be halved, when required.

1/6 SERVING – PROTEIN = 1.2 g.; FAT = 0.0 g.; CARBOHYDRATE = 30.0 g.;
CALORIES = 126; CALORIES FROM FAT = 0%

Angola

The upper branches of the great Zambezi River and several branches of the Congo River traverse Angola making the fertile river valleys attractive to peoples from earliest times. Somewhere around 1,000 AD Bantu-speaking tribes replaced earlier inhabitants, thought to be Khoisan speakers. The name for the nation comes from the Bantu word for king, *ngola*. The Portuguese explorer Diego Câo arrived in 1482 and, subsequently, this area became a trading post on the Portuguese trading route around the continent of Africa to Southeast Asia and a primary source of slaves for the Portuguese colony of Brazil. In 1641 the Dutch, with full support of the Ndongo Kingdom, occupied the capital of Luanda in an attempt to drive the Portuguese from the region. In 1648, Portuguese forces sailed from Brazil to Angola and retook the Angolan capital and embarked on a war to reclaim the Ndongo states and conquer the Congo. Victorious, Angola remained under Portuguese rule. In 1885 the Berlin Conference defined the borders of Angola which led to extensive European interest. Portuguese and British commercial investment resulted in profitable mining operations exploiting the subsoil rich in diamonds, oil, gold, and copper; railway development; and progressive agriculture as a result of irrigation of the extensive savannah landscape. Independence came in 1975 after a long war with the Portuguese which was followed by three decades of civil war. The fertile land was left a wasteland littered with landmines and desiccated by agricultural mismanagement. Agriculture and the once active export trade of bananas, coffee, and sisal, the durable white fiber derived from the leaves of the *agave* plant, no longer existed. Poorer Angolans became subsistence farmers; the wealthier Angolan depends upon imported food mostly from Portugal and South Africa.

In 1992, after a long and costly civil war, Angola transitioned from a one-party socialist state, aligned with Russia and Cuba, to a multiparty democracy. A peace treaty was finally signed with rebel forces in 2006. Despite its extraordinary oil resources, oil receipts have been siphoned off by corrupt government officials leaving Angolans among the poorest population in Africa. In addition, the province in which most of the oil resources are located has recently seceded from Angola putting further pressure on economic development.

An estimated eighteen and a half million people live in Angola, a nation about three times the size of California, but a definitive census has not been made since 1975. In addition to their continued attempt at post-civil war recovery, Angola had given refuge to an estimated 12,100 refugees and 2,900 asylum seekers by the end of 2007. Over 400,000 nationals from the Democratic Republic of the Congo resided in Angola until the government began to expel them in 2003. Of those DRC nationals, 11,400 were refugees and the remainder were migrant workers. The government has actively encouraged repatriation of Angolan nationals who sought refuge in other nations during these decades of war; the response has been understandably slow.

Although geographically close to the Democratic Republic of the Congo, the Republic of Congo, and Zambia, the Angolan cuisine resembles little of the cuisines of its Central African neighbors. Apart from the traditional cuisines of tribal areas outside the cities, Angolan cuisine reflects a strong Portuguese influence as do the cuisines of the other nations of Africa that were once part of Portugal's colonial empire. In addition, dishes that are popular in Brazil have found there way to Angola giving some dishes a Portuguese–Latino–African flair such as a passionfruit mousse, *mousse de maracuja*; shrimp and okra, *caruru*; and *farofa*, a rice and beans dish with a toasted manioc flour top crust.

Africa–Angola

Aromatic Vegetable Soup with *Couscous* and Chick Peas
Sopa de Legumes

~

Fennel Salad with Lemon and Cheese
Salada de Funcho com Limão

Cabbage Slaw with Corn and Fresh Dillweed
Salada de Repolho com Trigo e Endro

~~~~~~~~~~~~~~~~~~~~~~~

Vegetable Stew with Beans and *Chouriço* Sausage
Feijoada

Steamed Rice

~~~~~~~~~~

Rice Curry with Peanut Butter and Bananas
Mantiega de Amendoim e Bananas

~~~~~~~~~~~~~~~~~~~~~~~~~

Yellow Coconut Pudding   Pineapple Slices with Cinnamon and Ginger
Cocada Amarela   *Ananás com Canela e Gingebre*

Peanut Candy
Doce de Amendoim

ANGOLAN AROMATIC VEGETABLE SOUP WITH *COUSCOUS* AND CHICK PEAS
Sopa de Legumes
TPT - 34 minutes

At the same time that a North American child might be spelling out his or her name using the alphabet pasta in their bowl of vegetable soup, an African child might be chasing the pieces of couscous in his or her bowl. Vegetable soups made with diced vegetables are made all over the world. The vegetables may differ and the seasoning may differ but the objective is always the same. Nothing comforts or nourishes like a bowl of garden vegetables whether it contains alphabet pasta or couscous.

1 quart VEGETABLE STOCK FROM SOUP *[see index]*, vegetarian stock of choice, *or* water
1/4 cup *preservative-free dark* raisins
1/2 teaspoon ground coriander
1/2 teaspoon ground ginger
1/4 teaspoon ground cumin
1/4 teaspoon ground turmeric

1 medium kohlrabi—peeled and diced
1 medium sweetpotato—peeled and diced
1 small zucchini—well-washed and diced
1 small yellow summer squash—peeled, seeded, and diced
1 cup canned, *diced* tomatoes
1 cup canned chick peas (*garbanzos*)—well-drained
1 medium onion—chopped
1/2 cup dry *couscous*

Salt, to taste
Freshly ground black pepper, to taste

In a large saucepan set over *MEDIUM* heat, combine vegetable stock or water, raisins, and ground coriander, ginger, cumin, and turmeric. Allow to come to the boil. *Reduce the heat to LOW-MEDIUM.*

ANGOLAN AROMATIC VEGETABLE SOUP WITH *COUSCOUS* AND CHICK PEAS (cont'd)

Add diced kohlrabi, sweetpotato, zucchini, yellow summer squash, and tomatoes, chick peas, chopped onion, and *couscous*. Cover and allow to cook for about 20-25 minutes, or until vegetables are *crisp-tender*.

Taste and season with salt and pepper. Turn into a heated soup tureen.

Ladle into heated soup bowls.

Yields about 9 cupfuls

Note: This recipe can be halved, when required.

The crispness of the vegetables is compromised with freezing but leftovers can be gently reheated

1/9 SERVING (i. e., 1 cupful) –
PROTEIN = 3.9 g.; FAT = 0.4 g.; CARBOHYDRATE = 21.6 g.;
CALORIES = 100; CALORIES FROM FAT = 4%

ANGOLAN FENNEL SALAD WITH LEMON AND CHEESE
Salada de Funcho com Limão

TPT - 4 minutes

"Crudités" were a part of every formal or holiday dinner when I was young, but we certainly did not use the French designation back then. Before there were beautifully and deliciously adorned bruschetta, restaurants plunked down a relish dish, oh yes there are such things, with celery, scallions, and radishes. Celery does refresh the palate but fennel, which I discovered when I married into an Italian-American family, literally cleanses the palate. No holiday meal is complete without fennel, served in the resurrected relish dish of yore or in the form of this wonderful Angolan salad, which so clearly shows the influence of the Portuguese colonial period.

1 large fennel bulb—trimmed and *thinly* sliced*

2 tablespoons freshly squeezed lemon juice
1 tablespoon water
1 tablespoon *extra virgin* olive oil
Pinch salt

2 tablespoons grated Parmesan cheese
Long, peeled shreds of lemon zest, for garnish

Put fennel into a shallow serving bowl.

In a cruet or small jar, combined lemon juice, water, olive oil, and salt. Shake vigorously and pour over the *thinly* sliced fennel. Toss.

Sprinkle grated cheese over and garnish with lemon zest shreds.

Serve at once.

Yields 6 servings
adequate for 4-6 people

Note: *Use only the most tender sections of the bulb for the salad. Refrigerate the tougher pieces for family snacking.

1/6 SERVING – PROTEIN = 1.5 g.; FAT = 2.7 g.; CARBOHYDRATE = 1.3 g.;
CALORIES = 34; CALORIES FROM FAT = 71%

ANGOLAN CABBAGE SLAW WITH CORN AND FRESH DILLWEED
Salada de Repolho com Trigo e Endro

TPT - 46 minutes;
30 minutes = wilting period

The prominence of dillweed in this Angolan salad is clear evidence of European influence. The intensely sweet corn to which we are accustomed is not an African crop. In addition to field corn for livestock, however, corn for human consumption is grown but most is dried or ground for winter use. As a consequence, canned corn is most often used to make this salad in Angola. In the winter I opt for frozen corn but, in season, I will drive to a nearby farm because nothing but today's corn will do.

Africa–Angola

**ANGOLAN CABBAGE SLAW
WITH CORN AND FRESH DILLWEED** (cont'd)

6 cups *finely* shredded green cabbage
1/2 teaspoon salt
1/2 teaspoon sugar

2/3 cup chopped fresh dillweed—well washed and dried
1 1/2 cups green (fresh) corn kernels
1 tablespoon *extra virgin* olive oil
1 teaspoon pineapple juice *or* lemon juice, if preferred

In a mixing bowl, combine finely shredded cabbage, salt, and sugar. Toss to mix well. Set aside at room temperature for 30 minutes to allow the cabbage to wilt.

Add chopped dillweed, corn kernels, olive oil and pineapple juice. Toss to mix well. Turn into a serving bowl or salad bowl. Refrigerate until ready to serve.

Serve chilled.

Yields 6 servings
adequate for 4 people

Note: This recipe is easily halved or doubled, when required. Doubling is a bit unwieldy but it is a beautiful, unfussy salad for a buffet table.

1/6 SERVING – PROTEIN = 3.9 g.; FAT = 2.8 g.; CARBOHYDRATE = 21.2 g.;
CALORIES = 102; CALORIES FROM FAT = 1%

VEGETABLE STEW WITH BEANS AND *CHOURIÇO* SAUSAGE
Feijoada

TPT - 50 minutes

Chorizo (chouriço) sausages are found in many Portuguese dishes. A combination of tiny, tiny clams and sausage was a specialty of a bar we stumbled across in Lisbon, a bar that at that time would not permit me, as a woman, to cross the threshold. Instead of clams or beef or lamb, Angolans combine the spicy sausages with chicken in this feijoada. Soy chorizo sausages are available right along side soy hot dogs in grocery stores that cater to vegetarians so I am able to introduce you to this wonderful stew. Hot piri piri peppers are added in Angola but since I feel that tolerance of piri piri is very much an acquired taste, I have chosen to add mild green chilies and ground red pepper (cayenne). If you are fan of piri piri, do add them, finely chopped, with the vegetables and eliminate the green chilies and cayenne.

2 tablespoons canola oil*
1 medium onion—*finely* chopped
3 garlic cloves—*very finely* chopped

1/2 cup water
4 vegetarian *chouriço* (*chorizo*) sausages—sliced

1 can (15.5 ounces) *cannellini* beans—*well-drained*
1 cup canned, *diced* tomatoes
3 carrots—pared, quartered lengthwise, and chopped
4 cups shredded cabbage—as for slaw
3 tablespoons mild green *chilies*—chopped
2 large bay leaves—halved
1/8 teaspoon ground red pepper (cayenne), or to taste

1/2 cup coarsely chopped parsley
Salt, to taste
Freshly ground black pepper, to taste

In a small kettle set over *MEDIUM* heat, heat oil. Add *finely* chopped onion and *very finely* chopped garlic. Sauté until onion is soft and translucent, *being careful to allow neither the onion nor the garlic to brown.*

Add water and sliced sausages. Allow to cook for a few minutes.

Add well-drained beans, diced tomatoes, chopped carrots, shredded cabbage, chopped green *chilies*, bay leaf pieces, and ground red pepper (cayenne). Allow to come to the boil, stirring frequently. *Reduce heat to LOW-MEDIUM* and simmer for about 25 minutes. Stir frequently.

Add chopped parsley. Season with salt and black pepper to taste. Turn into a heated serving bowl. Remove and discard bay leaves.

*Serve hot.*** Refrigerate any leftovers and reheat over *LOW* heat.

Yields 8 servings
adequate for 6 people

Notes: *Angolan cooks usually finish off this dish with a generous amount of oil. They use red palm oil which gives it a very traditional taste. Red palm oil is high in saturated fats and quite difficult to find in the middle of America. I use canola oil for this dish.

Africa–Angola

VEGETABLE STEW WITH BEANS AND *CHOURIÇO* SAUSAGE (cont'd)

**This is usually served over rice or millet in Angola but we often just serve the stew into a soup plate and accompany it with big chunks of rustic bread.

Leftover can be frozen.

1/8 SERVING – PROTEIN = 9.7 g.; FAT = 7.8 g.; CARBOHYDRATE = 17.3 g.; CALORIES = 175; CALORIES FROM FAT = 40%

ANGOLAN RICE CURRY WITH PEANUT BUTTER AND BANANAS
Mantiega de Amendoim e Bananas
TPT - 39 minutes

This, to me, is a dish which typifies the taste of Central Africa, a taste, in this case, which does not reflect the period of European colonization. Piri piri is not generally added to this rice dish so it is a mild introduction to Angolan cuisine for the faint of heart. It is beautiful; it is delicious; it is a dish that you will turn to often.

1/2 cup tomato juice *or* tomato canning liquid
1/2 cup water

1 cup long grain brown *or* white rice

1 tablespoon water
2 tablespoons freshly ground, *unsalted, additive-free smooth* peanut butter—*brought to room temperature*

1 tablespoon peanut oil
1/2 medium onion—*thinly* sliced
1/2 medium green bell pepper—*thinly* sliced
1/2 medium red bell pepper—*thinly* sliced

3/4 teaspoon HOMEMADE CURRY POWDER
  [see index] *or* commercially-available curry powder of choice
1/4 teaspoon salt
Freshly ground black pepper, to taste

1/4 cup canned, *diced* tomatoes

1 tablespoon peanut oil
2 firm, medium bananas—cut into 1-inch chunks

In a saucepan set over *MEDIUM* heat, combine tomato juice and the 1/2 cupful water. Allow to come to the boil.

Add rice. Stir and cover. *Reduce heat to LOW.* Allow to cook, undisturbed, for 20-25 minutes, or until all of the liquid has been absorbed. Remove from heat and set aside briefly on a warming tray.

In a small bowl, combine the 1 tablespoonful water and peanut butter. Stir until well mixed and smooth. Set aside briefly.

In a skillet set over *MEDIUM* heat, heat 1 tablespoonful oil. Add *thinly* sliced onion and green pepper. Cook, stirring frequently, until the onion is soft and translucent, *being careful not to allow vegetables to brown.*

Add curry powder and black pepper. Cook, stirring constantly, for 1 minute.

Add diced tomatoes and peanut butter. Stir to combine well. *Reduce heat to LOW-MEDIUM* while frying the bananas.

In a non-stick-coated skillet set over *MEDIUM-HIGH* heat, heat the remaining 1 tablespoonful oil. Add banana pieces and cook until slices are golden brown. Turn as necessary.

Spoon rice onto a heated platter. Spoon onion–pepper–tomato sauce over. Top with fried bananas.

Serve at once.

Yields 6 servings
adequate for 4 people

Note: This recipe can be doubled, when required.

1/6 SERVING – PROTEIN = 2.6 g.; FAT = 6.7 g.; CARBOHYDRATE = 14.6 g.; CALORIES = 137; CALORIES FROM FAT = 44%

Africa–**Angola**

ANGOLAN YELLOW COCONUT PUDDING
Cocada Amarela

TPT - 1 hour and 10 minutes;
20 minutes = refrigeration period

I remember a birthday cake that my grandmother loved. It was a lemon cake which was frosted and then just absolutely covered in coconut. The saturated fats in coconut, albeit less deadly than those from animal sources or, for that matter, trans fats, still have kept my use of coconut to a minimum but my coconut blancmange and this Angolan recipe can tempt me way too easily. Do note that the Portuguese influence upon Portuguese West African, later Angolan, cuisine is very obvious in sweet, egg-rich desserts such as this. It has seemed to me that one could follow the Portuguese explorations around the world just by locating cuisines where egg yolks are used in abundance and "connecting the dots." That is not to say that the colonies which comprised the "Ultramar Português," as the Portuguese Overseas Empire was known, did not use egg yolks but I have always speculated that extra egg yolks may have followed the introduction of the Portuguese cuisine to these far-flung cultures. This Angolan dessert makes a strong case for this theory.

3/4 cup sugar
3 cups water
2 whole cloves

1 cup desiccated, shredded/grated unsweetened coconut*

1 1/4 cups *fat-free* pasteurized eggs (the equivalent of 5 eggs)**

1/2 teaspoon ground cinnamon

Attach a candy thermometer to the side of a large saucepan. Set over *MEDIUM-HIGH* heat and add sugar, water, and whole cloves. Allow to come to the boil while constantly stirring. *When it boils, stop stirring immediately.* Allow the mixture to reach 230 degrees F. (110 degrees C.). *It will take time, often 15-20 minutes.*

Reduce the heat to LOW. Remove and discard the cloves.

Gradually, two or three tablespoonfuls at a time, add the shredded/grated coconut to the syrup. Stir after each addition. Continue cooking and stirring until coconut becomes translucent. Remove from heat.

In a small bowl, using a small wire whisk, beat eggs until thick and lemony. While stirring, pour several tablespoonfuls of the coconut and syrup into the eggs. Whisk thoroughly before adding more syrup until about *one-half* of the coconut and syrup have been incorporated. Pour the egg–coconut mixture into the pan with the remaining coconut and syrup. Stir to combine well. Cook over *LOW-MEDIUM* heat, stirring frequently, until the pudding thickens and pulls away from the sides of the pan—about 10 minutes.

Spoon into individual dessert dishes or custard cups. Sprinkle with ground cinnamon. Refrigerate for about 20 minutes.***

Serve at room temperature.

Yields 6 servings
adequate for 4 people

Notes: *If you have a fresh coconut on hand, do use it. TO PREPARE FRESHLY GRATED COCONUT, make two holes in the coconut through the shiny black "eyes" using a sharp pointed tool such as a screwdriver or an awl. Drain the coconut water into a dish to be used as the replacement for liquid in recipes calling for fresh coconut. Using a hammer or metal meat mallet, break the coconut into 4-6 pieces. Rinse each piece under running water to loosen meat from shell. With the help of a paring knife, remove coconut from shell. Place pieces on a cookie sheet in preheated 325 degree F. oven for about 5 minutes. Remove from oven and pare rind from coconut meat using a vegetable peeler. Using a food processor fitted with fine shredding disk or by hand, shred coconut. Reserve 1 tablespoonful for garnish.

**Although we prefer to make this dish using fat-free pasteurized eggs, six egg yolks can be substituted.

***We prefer to serve this dessert chilled. In Angola and in Portugal, where it is also frequently served, it is more often served at room temperature.

This recipe may be doubled, when required.

1/6 SERVING – PROTEIN = 5.8 g.; FAT = 6.1 g.; CARBOHYDRATE = 41.3 g.;
CALORIES = 244; CALORIES FROM FAT = 23%

Africa–**Angola**

PINEAPPLE SLICES WITH CINNAMON AND GINGER
Ananás com Canela e Gingebre

TPT - 17 minutes

Nothing could be simpler; nothing could be more refreshing than is this dessert. Traveling in Portugal in 1977, we were most apt to pick up fruit, bread, and cheese from roadside stands or eat at the posadas in which we took lodging. Whenever we went into grocery stores, we found pineapples, almonds, and other produce from Angola and Mozambique, the Portuguese colonies which had broken away just two years before. Horrific reminders of the wars that had preceded the independence of their colonies, in the person of amputees, could be seen even in the small villages we visited but the tropical products in the grocery stores suggested that trade agreements had been reestablished.

12 pineapple slices—fresh *or* canned in juice

1 tablespoon cinnamon sugar
1 teaspoon ground ginger, or to taste

Arrange two slices of pineapple on each of six dessert plates

Sprinkle cinnamon sugar and ground ginger over each.* Allow to stand at room temperature for about 15 minutes.

Serve chilled or at room temperature.

Notes: *A tea strainer is useful for achieving a light sprinkling of both the cinnamon sugar and the ground ginger.

This recipe can be reduced or increased proportionately as required.

Yields 6 servings
adequate for 4 people

1/6 SERVING –   PROTEIN = 0.8 g.; FAT = 2.0 g.; CARBOHYDRATE = 30.2 g.;
CALORIES = 113; CALORIES FROM FAT = 16%

PEANUT CANDY
Doce de Amendoin

TPT - 1 hour;
25 minutes = first cooling period;
25 minutes = second cooling period

Unbroken, this candy makes a lovely gift presentation especially if it is placed on a round, straw plate holder which has been lined with a paper doily.

1 cup *roasted*, but *unsalted*, peanuts
1/2 cup (1 stick) butter
1/2 cup sugar
1 tablespoon light corn syrup

Line bottom and sides of a 9-inch glass pie plate with aluminum foil. Butter thoroughly.

In a non-stick-coated-skillet set over *MEDIUM* heat, combine all ingredients. Cook, stirring constantly, until candy mixture boils and turns a *light golden brown*—about 6 or 7 minutes.

Quickly and *evenly* spread candy mixture in prepared plate. Allow to cool for at least 25 minutes. Remove from pie plate, peel aluminum foil off, and place on an absorbent layer of paper toweling. Allow to cool completely—about 25 minutes.

When cool, cut into pieces by positioning a knife on top of hardened candy and striking it sharply with a hammer, if necessary.

Store in an airtight tin.

Yields about 3/4 pound
—about 44 pieces

1/44 SERVING (i. e., per piece) –
PROTEIN = 0.7 g.; FAT = 3.7 g.; CARBOHYDRATE = 3.4 g.;
CALORIES = 49; CALORIES FROM FAT = 68%

Botswana

Botswana, Africa's oldest democracy, is one of the wealthiest and politically stable countries on the continent. The population, predominantly Tswana, was challenged by the Zulu in the 1820s and by the Boers from the Transvaal area of South Africa in the 1870s and 1880s. The Batswana took refuge in the British Empire in 1885, becoming a British protectorate known as Bechuanaland. In 1910, the Union of South Africa emerged as a nation formed from British colonies in the region. Bechuanaland (now, Botswana), Basutoland (now, Lesotho), and Swaziland (known as the "High Commission Territories") were not released by Great Britain. South Africa's formation of an apartheid state within the British Commonwealth in 1948 and eventual withdrawal from the Commonwealth in 1961 put an end to any idea that the excluded territories would be incorporated into South Africa. However, as South Africa withdrew from the British Empire, Botswana was allowed to proceed on the road to independence. A constitution was created in 1961 and independence was granted in 1966. The southern territory of the former protectorate became part of Cape Colony and is now part of the northwest province of South Africa.

Botswana has profited from the lucrative diamond mining industry but also has significant deposits of copper, nickel, silver, salt, and coal. It has also profited from its close economic ties with South Africa. Since independence from Great Britain, emphasis has been placed on education. With a literacy rate of just seventy percent, Botswana's citizens frequently lose employment to guest workers. The educational goal is an effort to provide a national work force to service expanding tourism and manufacturing industries. Today expatriates make up a significant percentage of the skilled work force.

Rock paintings, dated to about twenty thousand years ago, depict human figures and the animals they hunted across the principal geological feature of Botswana, the famed Kalahari Desert. The desert covers approximately seventy-percent of the nation's land mass, a land mass about the size of the state of California within a country slightly smaller than the state of Texas. The sandy savannah, still populated by nomadic, cattle-herding Bushmen, extends into Namibia and into South Africa. Because the Kalahari Desert is considered to be a semi-desert climate, as is the Serengeti, the diversity of wildlife is spectacular.

Grain production is limited due to the fact that only one percent of the country's land is arable, requiring the importation of wheat, rice, barley, and other grains, but sorghum and maize grow well in this semi-arid climate. Vegetables such as spinach, carrots, squashes, cabbage, yams, potatoes, tomatoes, onions, cow peas, and peanuts are cultivated quite successfully but Botswanans must salt and dry foods to bridge the months between crops.

Africa – Botswana

Pan-grilled Appetizer *Kebabs*

~

Milk Soup with Corn
Mielieroomsop

~

South African Curried *Pasta* Salad

~~~~~~~~~~~~~~~~~~~~~~

Slow Cooker Vegetable Stew   Rice Balls
Potjie

~ ~ ~

Meat Pies

Sautéed Butternut Squash with Greens

~ ~ ~

Spaghetti with Broccoli and Garlic

Fried Loaves
Diphapta

~~~~~~~~~~~~~~~~~~~~~~

Basic Baked Honey Egg Custard

Watermelon

MILK SOUP WITH CORN
Mielieroomsop

TPT - 26 minutes

Found on menus in southern Botswana and in South Africa, this gruel-like corn soup probably came to Botswana from South Africa. In most locales it is still known by its Afrikaans name.

1 tablespoon butter
1/2 cup *finely* chopped onion

1 tablespoon *fine* corn flour
2 cups *two percent* milk

1 can (14 3/4 ounces) creamed corn
1/2 teaspoon *finely* ground celery seed*
Freshly ground black pepper, to taste

2 tablespoons light cream *or* half and half

In a saucepan set over LOW-MEDIUM heat, heat butter. Add *finely* chopped onion and sauté until onion is soft and translucent, *being careful not to allow onion to brown*.

Add *fine* corn flour and stir to form a *roux*. Gradually, *tablespoonful by tablespoonful*, add milk while stirring constantly. Stir until slightly thickened.

Add creamed corn, *finely* ground celery seed, and black pepper. Cook until heated through.

Add cream just before serving. Turn into a heated soup tureen.

Serve into heated soup bowls.

Yields 6 servings
adequate for 4 people

Notes: *Use a mortar and pestle to grind celery seed.

This recipe is easily doubled, when required.

1/6 SERVING – PROTEIN = 5.7 g.; FAT = 5.2 g.; CARBOHYDRATE = 26.2 g.;
CALORIES = 165; CALORIES FROM FAT = 28%

Africa—Botswana

SOUTH AFRICAN CURRIED *PASTA* SALAD
TPT - 2 hours and 47 minutes;
30 minutes = *pasta* chilling period;
2 hours = flavor development period

Noodles, introduced by German and Dutch colonial settlers, have morphed into a passion for pasta. In addition, decades of exposure to Indian cuisine and the seasoning of South Asia have allowed that passion a clearly unexpected route to a pasta salad that is truly unique. This pasta salad, with variations, has been passed from cook to cook and national borders have not impeded its travels. It is popular in Botswana, South Africa, and Namibia. My version contains much less oil than was used by the cooks who shared their recipes making it more appealing to the American palate.

3 quarts *boiling* water
1 tablespoon freshly squeezed lemon juice
1 3-inch strip lemon zest
1 1/2 cups macaroni *fusilli* (twists), *conchiglie* (shells), *or pipettes*

1/2 cup *finely* chopped sweet onion—Vidalia, Walla Walla, *or* Texas or Mayan Sweet
1/2 medium yellow sweet pepper—cored, seeded and *finely* chopped
1/3 cup chopped fresh parsley

2 tablespoons bottled *chili* sauce
1 tablespoon safflower *or* sunflower oil
2 teaspoons red wine vinegar
2 teaspoons SOUTH AFRICAN CURRY POWDER [see index]

In a large kettle set over *HIGH* heat, add lemon juice and lemon zest to *boiling* water. Add macaroni and cook, stirring occasionally, over *HIGH* heat according to package directions. Drain thoroughly, discarding lemon zest. Rinse in *cold* water. Drain again, thoroughly. Chill in refrigerator for about 30 minutes.

Add *finely* chopped onion and pepper, and chopped parsley. Toss.

In a small bowl, combine *chili* sauce, oil, vinegar, and curry powder. Using a small wire whisk, combine well. Add to *pasta* mixture. Stir to coat vegetables. Cover with plastic wrap and refrigerate for at least 2 hours to allow for flavor development.

Serve chilled.

Yields 6 servings
adequate for 4 people

Note: This recipe is easily doubled or tripled, when required.

1/6 SERVING – PROTEIN = 6.0 g.; FAT = 2.9 g.; CARBOHYDRATE = 21.6 g.;
CALORIES = 137; CALORIES FROM FAT = 19%

SLOW COOKER BATSWANA VEGETABLE STEW
Potjie
TPT - 4 hours and 25 minutes
[slow cooker: 19 minutes at *HIGH*;
4 hours at *LOW*]

I remember a stew that was popular at Iroquois celebrations in our area of New York State. It contained meat, often squirrel or rabbit, and the locally grown vegetables. The unique addition of "corn cuts," as those little corn-on-the-cob pieces are now known, always fascinated me. In the summer and fall, the sweet corn was fresh from the field; in the winter, the corn, which had been dried, was reconstituted during the long cooking period. When visiting an inn in the Williamsburg restoration, I found a similar stew on the menu, described as a Southern colonial stew. A meal featuring this surprisingly protein-rich vegetable stew from Botswana reminds me of the Iroquois meal at which I was first introduced to those little corn cuts. The slow cooker modernizes this stew considerably from the hanging iron pot; the result is succulent.

SLOW COOKER BATSWANA VEGETABLE STEW (cont'd)

1 tablespoon safflower *or* sunflower oil
1 medium onion—chopped
2 large garlic cloves—*finely* chopped

2 medium potatoes—well-scrubbed, peeled, and cut into chunks
1 1/2 cups cubed butternut squash
1 large carrot—scraped or pared and cut into chunks
1 small French turnip—peeled and chopped
1 stalk celery—trimmed and chopped into 1/2-inch pieces
1/2 cup fresh *or* frozen lima beans
1 teaspoon crushed, dried oregano
1 teaspoon crushed, dried basil
1 1/2 cups *boiling* VEGETABLE STOCK FROM SOUP [*see index*] *or* other vegetarian stock of choice
1/2 teaspoon salt, or to taste
1/4 teaspoon freshly ground mixed peppercorns —red, white, and black—or to taste
6 corn cuts—fresh *or* frozen

BATSWANA RICE BALLS [*see recipe which follows*]

In the bowl of the slow cooker set at *HIGH*, heat oil. Add chopped onion and *finely* chopped garlic. Cook, stirring frequently, until onion is soft and translucent, *being careful to allow neither the onion nor the garlic to brown.*

Add chopped potatoes, butternut squash, carrots, turnip, and celery with crushed dried oregano and basil. Pour *boiling* vegetarian stock over vegetables. Stir. Add salt and ground mixed peppercorns. Stir. Tuck corn cuts into the mixture, cover, and *reduce slow cooker setting to LOW*. Allow to cook for about 4 hours, or until vegetables are tender. Add more stock, if necessary.

Taste for seasoning and correct, if required. Turn into a heated serving bowl.

Serve over rice balls.

Yields 6 servings
adequate for 6 people

Note: This recipe can be halved, when required.

1/6 SERVING – PROTEIN = 7.0 g.; FAT = 2.9 g.; CARBOHYDRATE = 53.6 g.;
CALORIES = 275; CALORIES FROM FAT = <1%

BATSWANA RICE BALLS
TPT - 37 minutes

Instead of making these into the traditional balls, I sometimes use a spray-coated rice mold to prepare each serving. My mold creates a molded portion with a depressed center which will catch a portion of the stew as you ladle it onto the plate.

2 cups *boiling* water
1 cup Japanese short-grain rice*
1/4 teaspoon salt

Combine *boiling* water, rice, and salt in a saucepan set over *LOW-MEDIUM* heat. Cover tightly and allow to cook, undisturbed for 20 minutes, or until almost all the liquid has been absorbed by the rice. Remove cover, and remove from heat to allow steam to dissipate. Drain well. Turn into a mixing bowl.

Set a shallow serving bowl or platter on a warming tray set at HIGH.

Using a potato masher, mash rice until it begins to clump and form a mass. ∗ Spoon about 2 tablespoons into your hand and form into a tight ball. Place the ball in the heated serving bowl. Repeat from ∗ until all rice has been formed into balls.

Spoon hot stew over. *Serve hot.*

Yields 6 servings
adequate for 4 people

Note: *Japanese short-grained rice is available from most Asian groceries and in the international section of well-stocked grocery stores. It results in a sticky rice, when cooked, with a glutinous rice texture. *Do not rinse it first for this dish.*

1/6 SERVING (rice balls exclusive of stew) –
PROTEIN = 2.2 g.; FAT = 0.1 g.; CARBOHYDRATE = 26.3 g.;
CALORIES = 119; CALORIES FROM FAT = <1%

Africa–**Botswana**

BATSWANA MEAT PIES
TPT - 2 hours and 6 minutes;
30 minutes = gluten relaxation period

British emigrants who settled in the Americas came with a legacy of wrapping just about any edible mixture in pastry, a dish that most likely originated in Egypt and spread from the Middle East across Europe. The savory pie and the famed pasties of Northern Michigan are remnants of that heritage. If you have eaten meat pies or the more modern vegetable versions in Great Britain, as I have, you know that the modern version is more like Latin American empañadas. The original pastry container for meat pies, known as a "coffin" or "coffyn," a word which actually means a box, was shaped like a box with tall sides. It was filled with meat, sauce ingredients, and sometimes vegetables. It was meant as a container for baking, like a casserole, and serving food, eliminating the need for a bowl or plate, and, incidentally, was probably too tough to eat after a long baking period. Meat pies, usually made with ground lamb, are a popular pick-me-up street food in Botswana. The edible pastry casing functions just as did the pastry boxes of ancient times. You can make them with an assortment of vegetables or you can, as in this case, use soy meat analogue products in your filling.

FILLING:
  2 tablespoons **CLARIFIED BUTTER**
    or **GHEE** [see index]
  1/2 cup *finely* chopped onion

  1/4 cup diced apple
  1/4 cup diced potato
  1 1/2 cups *frozen* vegetarian ground beef*
  1/3 cup *preservative-free* currants
  1 teaspoon chili powder
  Pinch or two ground red pepper (cayenne)

  1/4 cup *well-drained*, canned, *petite diced*
    tomatoes

PASTRY:
  2 cups unbleached white flour
  1/4 teaspoon baking soda
  Pinch salt

  1/2 cup *cold, hard* butter

  1/4 cup *fat-free* pasteurized eggs (the
    equivalent of 1 egg)

  1 or 2 tablespoons *cold* water

EGG WASH:
  1 egg yolk
  1 tablespoon water

In a skillet set over *MEDIUM* heat, melt 2 tablespoons clarified butter. Add *finely* chopped onion and sauté until onion is soft and translucent, *being careful not to allow onion to brown.*

Add diced apple, diced potato, vegetarian ground beef, currants, chili powder, and ground red pepper (cayenne). Sauté for a minute or two. *Reduce heat to LOW-MEDIUM.*

Add tomatoes and cook, stirring frequently, until most of moisture has evaporated. Remove from heat and set aside until required.

Preheat oven to 350 degrees F. Prepare a baking sheet by lining it with culinary parchment.

Using a pastry blender, work *cold* butter into flour mixture until of the texture of coarse corn meal.

While stirring with a fork, sprinkle with *ice cold* water, 1 or 2 tablespoonfuls at a time, until mixture holds together and pulls away from the sides of the bowl. Gather into six balls, wrap tightly in plastic wrap, and refrigerate for about 30 minutes to allow the gluten to relax.

On a lightly floured surface, roll each ball of pastry in turn to form a circle about 6 inches in diameter. Spoon *one-sixth* of the filling onto one side of the pastry circle. Fold into a half-moon. Using the moistened tines of a fork, press the edge to seal. Stab the meat pie with the tines of the fork to create steam holes. Transfer to parchment-lined baking sheet. Prepare remaining meat pies.

Combine egg yolk and water. Beat well. Using a pastry brush, brush the egg wash over the top surface of each meat pie.

Bake in preheated 350 degree F. oven for 35 minutes or until golden brown.

Serve hot or cold, as preferred.

Yields 6 servings
adequate for 4 people

Notes: *If you do not include soy meat analogue in your vegetarian regime, a mixture of finely chopped vegetables will do nicely.

This recipe can be halved or doubled, when required

1/6 SERVING – PROTEIN = 9.9 g.; FAT = 21.8 g.; CARBOHYDRATE = 44.5 g.;
CALORIES = 413; CALORIES FROM FAT = 48%

Africa–Botswana

SAUTÉED BUTTERNUT SQUASH WITH GREENS
TPT - 10 minutes

The African slave trade brought the cooking of the continent to the plantations of the American South. Frying whatever greens can be found has become a Southern standby and an indisputable comfort food of the African-American soul food tradition. Sautéed greens are enjoyed in almost every country in sub-Sahararan Africa and when combined with other vegetables or meats, they feed a hungry family. This dish from Botswana satisfies the soul and cheers the mood.

1 tablespoon butter
1 tablespoon *extra virgin* olive oil
1 1/2 cups *diced* butternut squash

2 large scallions—trimmed, well-washed, and sliced
10 ounces spring lettuce mixture or a suitable mixture of lettuces and cooking greens —trimmed, well-washed, and well-dried— about 10 cups
2 tablespoons *finely* chopped *raw preservative-free* peanuts
Freshly ground mixed peppercorns—red, white, and black—to taste

In a non-stick-coated skillet set over *MEDIUM* heat, heat butter and oil. Add diced butternut squash. Sauté until squash begins to soften and brown.

Add scallion slices, greens, *finely* chopped peanuts, and ground mixed peppercorns. Continue cooking, stirring constantly, until greens are wilted. Turn out into a heated serving bowl. Keep warm on a warming tray until ready to serve.

Yields 6 servings
adequate for 4 people

Note: This recipe can be halved or doubled, when required.

1/6 SERVING – PROTEIN = 3.0 g.; FAT = 5.5 g.; CARBOHYDRATE = 7.5 g.;
CALORIES = 115; CALORIES FROM FAT = 43%

SPAGHETTI WITH BROCCOLI AND GARLIC
TPT - 21 minutes

The member of the cabbage family, which today we know as broccoli, is said to have been introduced into America from Calabria, Italy, although, according to colonial recipe collections and manuscripts, a variety of this vegetable was known to American colonists as "brockala," which was a vegetable perhaps more like broccoli-rabe. My mother-in-law spoke often about making spaghetti with broccoli leaves for my father-in-law, who was born in Calabria. I was surprised to find that spaghetti with broccoli is popular in Botswana but Europeans did introduce many foods to Africa during the colonial period exemplified by the enthusiasm for spaghetti and macaroni in many African countries and not just by those living in the former Italian colonies.

3 quarts *boiling* water
1 tablespoon lemon juice
3-inch piece lemon zest
1/2 pound high protein, whole wheat, *or* Jerusalem artichoke spaghetti *or* macaroni, of choice

1 tablespoon butter
1 tablespoon *extra virgin* olive oil
3 garlic cloves—*finely* chopped

2 cups tiny broccoli leaves and small florets*
Salt, to taste
Freshly ground black pepper, to taste

Freshly grated Parmesan *or* *pecorino* Romano cheese, as preferred

In a large kettle set over *HIGH* heat, add lemon juice and lemon zest to *boiling* water. Add spaghetti or macaroni and cook according to package directions. Drain thoroughly.

While spaghetti is cooking, in a skillet with cover set over *LOW-MEDIUM* heat, melt butter. Add olive oil and *finely* chopped garlic. Sauté until softened, *being careful not to allow garlic to brown.*

Add broccoli leaves and florets, salt, and black pepper. Reduce heat to *VERY LOW*. Cover tightly and cook until spaghetti is ready, stirring frequently.

Turn well-drained spaghetti or macaroni into skillet with broccoli and garlic. Stir to mix well. Turn out onto a heated platter or into a large serving bowl.

Serve at once, with or without grated cheese.

Yields 6 servings
adequate for 4 people

Africa – **Botswana**

SPAGHETTI WITH BROCCOLI AND GARLIC (cont'd)

Notes: *When processing broccoli spears for freezing and diagonally-cut broccoli stems for Chinese dishes and soup, the tiny leaves and small florets can be blanched for about 30 seconds and frozen in a plastic bag in which they can be accumulated until there is a cupful. Then, this dish can go on the menu!!

This recipe is easily doubled, when required.

1/6 SERVING (exclusive of grated cheese) –
PROTEIN = 6.1 g.; FAT = 4.5 g.; CARBOHYDRATE = 28.1 g.;
CALORIES = 185; CALORIES FROM FAT = 22%

BATSWANA FRIED LOAVES
Diphapta
TPT - 54 minutes

The refinement of the non-stick-coated skillet has introduced some remarkable products to those of us whose first non-stick pans were lightly-coated aluminum pans from which the coating quickly peeled. Safe products, on the market now, have made many of us put away our cast iron skillets in favor of lighter skillets with surfaces that do not allow skillet breads or tortillas to burn.

2 cups unbleached white flour
1/2 teaspoon baking powder
1/2 teaspoon sugar
About 1/3 – 1/2 cup *two percent* **milk**

Preheat a large, heavy, well-oiled skillet over *MEDIUM* heat.

In a mixing bowl, combine flour, baking powder, and sugar. Stir to mix. Add 1/3 cupful milk, or more if necessary, to form a dough. Knead the dough on a lightly floured surface. Roll with a rolling pin to about a thickness of 1/4 inch. Cut into rounds about 4 inches in diameter. Fry two or three at a time in hot skillet, turning once. This will take about 15-20 minutes. *The loaves will puff up as they fry.* Transfer to a bread basket or heated serving bowl.

Serve hot with stew or soup.

Yields 10 loaves
adequate for 5 people

Note: This recipe can be halved or doubled, when required.

1/10 SERVING – PROTEIN = 2.8 g.; FAT = 4.6 g.; CARBOHYDRATE = 17.8 g.;
CALORIES = 87; CALORIES FROM FAT = 48%

BASIC BAKED HONEY – EGG CUSTARD
TPT - 1 hour and 40 minutes;
1 hour = chilling period

With all the successful variations we have evolved using this basic recipe, we feel that this is a "custard recipe to treasure." Every family must have a custard recipe to treasure because custard offers nutrition and comfort, spanning a lifetime from infancy to old age. Every woman in Botswana comes to her marriage with a custard recipe and every contact I made shared a recipe and then mentioned a variation or two. The variations that I share here have served me well for sixty years or so.

BASIC BAKED HONEY – EGG CUSTARD (cont'd)

2 cups skimmed milk
1 cinnamon quill

3/4 cup *fat-free* **pasteurized eggs (the equivalent of 3 eggs)**
2 tablespoons wildflower, orange blossom, *or* **clover honey, as preferred**
1/4 cup *instant* **non-fat dry milk powder**

3/4 teaspoon pure vanilla extract

Preheat oven to 350 degrees F. Prepare five 4-ounce custard cups by coating with non-stick lecithin spray coating.

In a saucepan set over *MEDIUM* heat, combine milk and cinnamon quill. Cook until bubbles appear around the edges. Remove from heat and allow to cool slightly. Remove cinnamon quill.*

In a mixing bowl, combine pasteurized eggs, honey, and dry milk powder. Stir with a wire whisk to combine thoroughly. While still stirring, *slowly* add scalded milk to egg mixture. Stir with the wire whisk to again combine thoroughly.

Add vanilla extract. Stir well. Skim any foam which appears on surface.

Divide among prepared custard cups. Spoon off any foam which remains. Set in a baking pan in which a 1-inch water bath has been prepared. Bake in preheated 350 degree F. oven for about 25 to 30 minutes, or until a knife inserted into the center comes out clean. Check water level occasionally and add *cold* water, if needed. *Do not allow water bath to simmer or boil—add cold water or ice cubes, if necessary.*

Chill in the refrigerator for at least 1 hour before serving.

Yields 5 individual servings

Notes: *Rinse and dry cinnamon quill to reuse as needed or put it into your teapot for an interesting change in your next pot of tea.

A 1-quart baking dish or soufflé dish may be used, if preferred. Baking time should be increased to about 35 to 40 minutes.

This recipe may be doubled with ease, when necessary.

The following variations are recommended also:

SUBSTITUTE 1 1/2 tablespoonfuls brown sugar, maple sugar, or white sugar for each tablespoonful of honey;

SUBSTITUTE 1 tablespoonful unsulphured molasses for 1 tablespoonful of honey;

ADD 1/4 teaspoonful pure orange extract or other pure extract of choice;

ADD 1 tablespoonful cocoa with honey;

ADD 1/8 teaspoonful cardamom with honey (excellent with cocoa-flavored variation);

ADD 1 tablespoonful coconut to each cup;

ADD 2 teaspoonfuls decaffeinated instant coffee with honey;

SPRINKLE with nutmeg before baking;

SPRINKLE with crunchy topping, such as OUR GRANOLA *[see index],* before serving;

or SERVE with a chilled fruit sauce or a nut sauce.

1/5 SERVING (without topping) –
PROTEIN = 7.7 g.; FAT = 0.2 g.; CARBOHYDRATE = 10.3 g.;
CALORIES = 68; CALORIES FROM FAT = <1%

Burundi

European colonization of Africa resulted in the annexing of this area, now known as Burundi, into what was known as German East Africa. In 1923 Belgium took over Burundi under a League of Nations mandate. This mandate was renewed by the United Nations with Burundi, together with Rawanda, becoming a trust territory, administered by Belgium and known as Ruanda–Urundi.

Burundi has been home for the past five hundred years to the Twa, a Pygmy people who make up about one percent of the population; the Hutu, a short, squat agricultural people who make up about eighty-five percent of the population; and the Tutsi, characteristically tall, thin, land-owning cattle ranchers who now comprise just fourteen percent of a population that was estimated in 2012 to be about 8.7 million people.

In the late seventeenth century, the last monarchy in a two hundred-year succession came to power. These monarchies did not resemble modern-day Western monarchies but were instead loosely organized tribal governance systems. With the coming of Europeans to Africa, this society disintegrated. These peoples had functioned well without prejudice but the situation changed when the Belgian colonial administration conducted censuses requiring classification. The artificial defining elements of this classification created divisions and frictions relevant to class and ethnicity that had never existed before. In 1972 this led to genocide against the Hutus resulting in the death of an estimated 100,000 people. 500,000 Burundians died in 1993 as a result of violence sparked by the assassination by Tutsi officers of the first democratically elected president, a Hutu, and his successor. This racial genocide spread from here to Rwanda resulting in the Rwandan Genocide of 1994.

Generally it is difficult for vegetarians to travel in Africa. The Burundian cuisine, unlike other African cuisines, places little emphasis on meat; beans have become their most important protein source. To put this in perspective one must consider the economic challenges of this country. A bit larger than our state of Vermont but with a population fifteen times that of Vermont and a birth rate of about six live births per woman, Burundi is a densely-populated fledgling democracy. It is one of the four poorest countries on the planet. Burundi's GDP (PPP) is about $625 per capita. Compare this to that of Qatar at $102,943 per capita or that of the United States at $52,839 per capita. Thirty percent of their GDP is from agriculture despite the fact that ninety percent of their agriculture can be classified as subsistence. Coffee is the primary export, representing ninety-three percent of the country's exports.

One would, therefore, think that a vegetarian could eat quite comfortably in this country and that is probably the case. However, in a country where food decisions are not made by choice, but by availability, the vegetarian food you may be offered by your hosts may be all they can provide. I have included recipes from which you can select a beautifully complex main course salad or either of two rich, leguminous soups with a side salad. Burundians do not normally eat dessert but it has been my plan in this work to suggest a sweet dish or snack for each country we have been visiting. The brown sugar cookies, enjoyed by Burundians on special occasions, end this menu most deliciously.

Africa–Burundi

Lettuce Salad with Potatoes and Bacon
Salade avec Pomme de Terre et Lard

~~~~~~~~~~~~~~~~~~~~~

Bean Salad with Corn and Mango
Salade de Haricot Rouge, Maïs, et Mangue

~ ~ ~

Bean and Celery Soup with Bananas
Potage de Trois Haricot avec Banane

~ ~ ~

Lentil Soup with Vegetables
Potage aux Lentilles et Legumes
Bread

~~~~~~~~~~~~~~~~~~~~~~~~~

Brown Sugar Cut – Out Cookies

Compote of Mango and Banana

BURUNDIAN LETTUCE SALAD WITH POTATOES AND BACON
Salade avec Pomme de Terre et Lard
TPT - 12 minutes

Burundi's German and Belgian colonial heritage is apparent in this salad. I remember eating many salads in German–American homes and I also remember many of those salads had a garnish of bacon bits and were dressed with a vinaigrette that usually contained a touch of mustard. A salad such as this is a perfect meal maker when you choose to prepare a main course soup.

1 teaspoon safflower *or* sunflower oil
2 slices soy bacon—*finely* chopped

VINAIGRETTE WITH MUSTARD:
    1/4 cup *extra virgin* olive oil
    2 tablespoons white wine vinegar
    2 tablespoons *finely* chopped shallot
    1 teaspoon *Dijon* mustard with white wine
    1/4 teaspoon salt
    1/4 teaspoon freshly ground black pepper

12 cross slices of a Romaine lettuce head *or*
  6 wedges of iceberg lettuce—well-rinsed and well-drained
12 pee wee potatoes—well-scrubbed, boiled, chilled, and halved— *or* 4 salad potatoes
  —well-scrubbed, boiled, chilled, and sliced

In a small skillet set over *LOW-MEDIUM* heat, heat safflower oil. Add *finely* chopped soy bacon. Sauté until bacon is crisp, *being careful now to allow bacon to burn.* Remove from heat and set aside briefly.

In a jar with a tightly fitting lid or in a cruet with a tightly fitting top or cork, combine olive oil, *finely* chopped shallots, *Dijon* mustard, salt, and black pepper. Shake vigorously and set aside until required.

Place two rounds of Romaine lettuce or a single wedge of iceberg on each of six salad plates. Arrange four potato halves on each plate. Sprinkle fried soy bacon over.

When ready to serve, again shake salad dressing vigorously. Drizzle salad dressing over each salad.

Serve at once.

                        Yields 6 individual servings

Note: This recipe can be halved, when required.

1/6 SERVING – PROTEIN = 0.2 g.; FAT = 8.6 g.; CARBOHYDRATE = 8.1 g.;
CALORIES = 118; CALORIES FROM FAT = 66%

Africa–**Burundi**

BURUNDIAN BEAN SALAD WITH CORN AND MANGO
Salade de Haricot Rouge, Maïs, et Mangue

TPT - 1 hour and 11 minutes;
1 hour = flavor development period

Someone suggested that if you picked up the lid of every pot now simmering in Burundi, the odds were very high that red kidney beans would be in the pot. Perhaps an exaggeration, but Burundians do use a lot of red kidney beans in their cooking. This salad is a meal in itself and is often served that way in Burundi where grilled chicken is frequently added. Without the chicken, the beans and corn contribute the amino acids needed to provide complemented protein to the salad. On a hot summer evening, we love to find a bowl of this salad in the refrigerator all ready for dinner.

HONEY – PINEAPPLE *VINAIGRETTE*:
    2 tablespoons *extra virgin* olive oil
    1 1/2 tablespoons red wine vinegar
    1 teaspoon honey *or agave* nectar, if preferred
    1 tablespoon well-drained *crushed* pineapple
    1 small garlic clove—halved
    1 teaspoon *tamari* soy sauce
    Pinch ground red pepper (cayenne), or to taste
    Freshly ground black pepper, to taste

1 can (15 ounces) red kidney beans—*well-drained**
1 cup fresh *or frozen* corn kernels
1 large mango—peeled, pitted and cubed
1/2 cup *finely* chopped onion
1/4 cup diced green pepper
1/4 cup diced red pepper
1/4 cup *finely* chopped fresh coriander (*cilantro*)
2 tablespoons freshly squeezed lime juice

In a small jar with a tight fitting lid or a cruet, combine olive oil, red wine vinegar, honey or *agave* nectar, *crushed* pineapple, garlic clove, soy sauce, ground red pepper (cayenne), and black pepper. Shake vigorously and set aside for 1 hour to allow for flavor development.

Immediately, in a salad bowl, combine *well-drained* kidney beans, corn kernels, cubed mango, *finely* chopped onion, diced green and red pepper, *finely* chopped fresh coriander (*cilantro*), and lime juice. *Gently* fold ingredients together. Refrigerate for 1 hour.

Add prepared honey–garlic *vinaigrette* to the bean salad mixture. *Gently* combine ingredients. Refrigerate until ready to serve.

Serve chilled, with a slotted spoon. Refrigerate leftovers.

Yields 8 servings
adequate for 4-6 people

Notes: *Black beans can be substituted, if preferred.

1/6 SERVING – PROTEIN = 5.9 g.; FAT = 4.5 g.; CARBOHYDRATE = 35.6 g.;
CALORIES = 198; CALORIES FROM FAT = 20%

BURUNDIAN BEAN AND CELERY SOUP WITH BANANAS
Potage de Trois Haricot avec Banane

TPT - 12 hours and 5 minutes;
8 hours = bean soaking period

This protein-packed soup reminds me somewhat of Moroccan "bessara," a soup made from cranberry, Roman, or pinto beans, lentils, and chick peas. The perfume of cinnamon, turmeric, and cloves rises from a bessara while a base of crushed tomatoes makes for a thick, rich texture. Parsley, onions, basil, and cumin perfume this soup and lima beans, white beans, and red kidney beans are the beans one finds in the larder of a Burundian kitchen.

Africa—**Burundi**

BURUNDIAN BEAN AND CELERY SOUP WITH BANANAS (cont'd)

1/2 cup dry lima beans
1/2 cup dry Great Northern beans
1/2 cup dry red kidney beans
1 quart *cold* water

1 quart VEGETARIAN STOCK FROM SOUP
 [see index], VEGETARIAN BROWN STOCK
 [see index] or other vegetarian stock of choice

1 tablespoon safflower *or* sunflower oil
1 cup *finely* chopped onion
1/2 cup diced green pepper

1/8 teaspoon crushed red pepper flakes, or to taste

2 large stalks celery—trimmed, well-cleaned, and chopped
1/4 cup *finely* chopped parsley
1 tablespoon *finely* chopped fresh basil
1/2 teaspoon ground cumin
1 teaspoon salt
Freshly ground black pepper, to taste

2 medium, green bananas—sliced

Rinse dry beans in several changes of water. Remove and discard any of poor quality. Place in a bowl with 1 quartful of *cold* water and soak overnight in the refrigerator.

In the morning, drain legumes and place in a large kettle with the 1 quartful stock. Bring to the boil, reduce heat to *LOW*, cover tightly, and allow to simmer for 2 hours.

While beans are cooking, in a skillet set over *MEDIUM* heat, heat oil. Add *finely* chopped onion and diced green pepper. Sauté until onions are soft and translucent, *being careful not to allow onions to brown*.

Add crushed red pepper flakes. Allow to cook, while stirring, for a minute or two. Remove from heat.

When beans have completed the preliminary cooking period, add sautéed onions and green pepper, chopped celery, *finely* chopped parsley and basil, ground cumin, salt, and pepper. Allow to simmer for an additional 1 to 1 1/2 hours, or until beans are tender. Stir occasionally.

Add banana slices. Cook for 10 minutes more. Turn into a heated tureen.

Serve at once into heated soup bowls. Refrigerate leftovers.

Yields 9 cupfuls

Notes: I find the slow cooker to be a very useful tool for bean cooking and have applied it to this soup. When prepared in a kettle on a conventional stove, it must be attended much more frequently.

This recipe can be doubled, when required.

This soup freezes well.

1/9 SERVING (i. e., per cupful) –
PROTEIN = 6.5 g.; FAT = 2.1 g.; CARBOHYDRATE = 28.9 g.;
CALORIES = 141; CALORIES FROM FAT = 13%

BURUNDIAN LENTIL SOUP WITH VEGETABLES
Potage aux Lentilles et Legumes

TPT - 1 hour and 54 minutes;
1 hour = lentil soaking period

Burundi has an equatorial climate that can limit agriculture but with about forty-four percent of the land mass classified as arable, there is opportunity to pick and choose your crops. This has led to the success of many vegetables that other countries in Central Africa will buy. The farmer that grows lentils, sweetpotatoes, carrots, cabbage, and onions not only can make this nutritious soup but he can sell these vegetables.

Africa–Burundi

BURUNDIAN LENTIL SOUP WITH VEGETABLES (cont'd)

1/2 cup dried, brown (*or* green) lentils

1 tablespoon *extra virgin* olive oil
3/4 cup *thinly* sliced onion

2 1/2 cups VEGETABLE STOCK FROM SOUP
  [see index] or **other vegetarian stock of choice**
3/4 cup peeled and diced sweetpotato
3/4 cup peeled and diced carrot
3/4 cup *finely* shredded cabbage
1/2 cup cut green beans
1/4 cup canned, *diced* tomatoes
Salt, to taste
Freshly ground mixed peppercorns—red, black, and white—to taste

Pick over lentils and discard any of poor quality. Rinse thoroughly. Drain. Pour into a mixing bowl and add the *boiling* water. Set aside at room temperature for 1 hour. Drain.

In a small kettle set over *MEDIUM* heat, heat oil. Add drained lentils and onion slices. Sauté until onions are soft and translucent, *being careful not to allow onions to brown. Reduce heat to LOW.*

Add stock, diced sweetpotato, diced carrot, *finely* shredded cabbage, cut green beans, *diced* tomatoes, salt, and ground mixed peppercorns. Cover. Simmer, stirring frequently, until vegetables are tender—about 40 minutes. Add more stock if necessary. Adjust seasoning. Turn into a heated tureen.

Serve into heated soup plates. Accompany with warm, crusty bread chunks.

Yields 6 cupfuls

Notes: This recipe can be halved, when required.

1/6 SERVING (i. e., per cupful) –
PROTEIN = 5.7 g.; FAT = 2.2 g.; CARBOHYDRATE = 19.5 g.;
CALORIES = 118; CALORIES FROM FAT = 17%

BROWN SUGAR CUT – OUT COOKIES
TPT - 2 hours and 4 minutes;
1 hour = chilling period

Shortly after we moved to Pennsylvania, I created this cookie and was amazed to find, some years later, that similar cookies was popular in Cuba and in Burundi. It is meant to be a crisp cookie which has led Cubans to make this cookie with lard. Vegetable shortening will give you a similarly crisp cookie. We, however, prefer to use butter and sacrifice a bit of the traditional crispness as do Burundians. We also replace a portion of the white flour, traditionally used, with whole wheat flour.

1 cup unbleached white flour
1/2 cup whole wheat flour
1 3/4 teaspoons baking powder
1 teaspoon ground cinnamon
1/2 teaspoon ground ginger

7 tablespoons butter—*softened to room temperature*
2/3 cup firmly packed *light* brown sugar

1/4 cup *fat-free* pasteurized eggs (the equivalent of 1 egg)
2 teaspoons pure vanilla extract
1 teaspoon pure almond extract

Sift whole wheat and white flours with baking powder. Set aside.

Using an electric mixer or food processor fitted with steel knife, cream butter until light and fluffy. Add brown sugar and, again, cream until light and fluffy.

Add pasteurized eggs, vanilla extract, and almond extract. Mix well. Gradually beat in sifted dry ingredients until again well-combined. Wrap in plastic wrap and refrigerate for at least 1 hour to make dough easy to handle.*

Preheat oven to 325 degrees F. Line cookie sheets with culinary parchment paper.

BROWN SUGAR CUT – OUT COOKIES (cont'd)

Unwrap chilled dough and knead lightly on floured surface. Using a covered rolling pin, roll dough to about 1/8 inch thickness. Using a floured 2 1/2-inch scalloped cookie cutter, cut out cookies. With a spatula, transfer cookies to prepared cookie sheets, leaving about 2 inches between each cookie.

Bake one cookie sheetful at a time in preheated 325 degree F. oven for about 8-9 minutes, being watchful to prevent excessive browning. Transfer to a wire rack to cool completely.

Store in an airtight container or plastic bag.

Yields approximately 18 cookies

Notes: *A supply of this dough in the freezer can be a great convenience.

When required, this recipe may be doubled.

1/18 SERVING (i. e., per cookie) –
PROTEIN = 1.5 g.; FAT = 4.8 g.; CARBOHYDRATE = 15.6 g.;
CALORIES = 111; CALORIES FROM FAT = 34%

Cameroon

Although, as we will see, many tribes and nations have come and gone from this area of Africa since its first occupation by human population groups in the Neolithic Period, Pygmy tribes, such as the Baka of Cameroon, have continuously inhabited this region for as long as 60,000 years. An African population that is estimated to exceed half a million people lives in the rainforests, open swamps, and deserts in Angola, Botswana, Burundi, Cameroon, the Central Africa Republic, the Democratic Republic of the Congo, the Republic of Congo, Equatorial Guinea, Gabon, Namibia, Rwanda, Uganda, and Zambia. These family-oriented, hunter-gatherer societies, albeit still primitive, represent a population of enormous social stability that present-day Cameroon is still struggling to achieve. Principally an agricultural nation, with only about sixteen percent of its GDP factory-based industry, Cameroon has achieved little industrial or technological development to link it economically to the larger world economy. As a result, employment prospects are poor, promising little to a population where public education is not a priority and where over forty-one percent of the population is under the age of fifteen.

The name Cameroon derives from the name given this beautiful area of West-Central Africa in 1472 by Portuguese explorers who, amazed and impressed by the abundance of prawns in the Wouri River, called it *Rio dos Camarões*, that is "River of Prawns." By the nineteenth century Europeans were actively trading with the coastal population and missionaries were pushing inland to convert the native peoples to Christianity. In response to this missionary activity, Modibo Adama led a *jihad* early in the nineteenth century against those who were not Muslim and established the Adamawa Emirate in the north of the country. In 1884 the German Empire pushed into Cameroon and established the colony of Kamerun. The German record in Kamerun is a sad saga of exploitation and extensive use of slave labor. In 1914 an Allied Expeditionary Force reached Kamerun and attempted to wrest the colony from the Germans. Campaigns against the Germans continued until 1916 but resolution of the colony's fate waited until Germany's ultimate defeat in World War I. In 1919 Kamerun became a mandate territory under the League of Nations and was divided into French Cameroon and British Cameroon. The League of Nations mandates were taken over by the United Nations and in 1946 these mandate territories became trusteeships. Independence by the populations in both trusteeships became pressing goals due to continued exploitation in French Cameroon by the French and a lack of interest in British Cameroon by the British, who administered their trusteeship from Nigeria. French Cameroon became independent in 1960. British Cameroon declared its independence in 1961 and joined with French Cameroon to form the Federal Republic of Cameroon. In 1972 the united nation changed its name to the United Republic of Cameroon and in 1984 it became known as the Republic of Cameroon.

A population of about eighteen million includes an amazing two hundred different ethnic and linguistic groups. Diversity is also reflected in geography that features beaches, mountains, deserts, rainforests, savannas, and even an active volcano across a country about the size of Michigan and Minnesota combined.

What do they eat in Cameroon? Just wait until you taste this lunch which combines simple African staples in a most imaginative and delicious way and offers you a quartet of desserts to try.

Africa – Cameroon

**Pan-Grilled Soymeat Brochettes
in the Style of West Africa**
Suya Sur la Gril

Papaya Jam
Confitures de Papaye

~

| **Cabbage Slaw with Pineapple** | **Layered Fruit Salad** |
| *Salade de Chou aux Anana* | *Salade aux Fruits* |

~

Yellow Plantain and Corn Soup

Flatbread or *Nan*

~~~~~~~~~~~~~~~~~~~~~~

Fried Okra

or

Greens with Garlic
Légumes Verts aux Ail

over

Yam, Potato, and Corn *Fufu*   or   **Yam and Plantain *Fufu***

~~~~~~~~~~~~~~~~~~~~~~

Mango Whip
Crema Fouettée avec Mangue

African Molded Sweet Rice Cakes
Riz Moule avec Crème de Noix de Cacao

Sweet *Cassava* Dessert Fritters
Beignets de Manioc

Sliced Fresh Papaya with Coconut and Honey

PAN-GRILLED SOYMEAT BROCHETTES IN THE STYLE OF WEST AFRICA
Suya Sur la Gril

TPT - 2 hours and 22 minutes;
2 hours = flavor development period

The ancient human practice of grilling meat and vegetables on sticks is reflected today in Italian spiedini, Middle Eastern kebabs, and brochettes, such as those threaded with marinated beef and known as "suya," popular in both Cameroon and in Ghana. The spicy peanut rub, used in Cameroon, works perfectly well on strips of soymeat analogue that can then be lightly grilled on a grill pan or sautéed in a skillet.

Africa–Cameroon

**PAN-GRILLED SOYMEAT BROCHETTES
IN THE STYLE OF WEST AFRICA** (cont'd)

1/4 teaspoon sugar
1/2 teaspoon garlic powder
1/2 teaspoon onion powder
1/2 teaspoon ground ginger
1/2 teaspoon ground cinnamon
1/2 teaspoon paprika
Pinch chili powder
1 tablespoon ground *raw* peanuts

8 ounces *frozen* soy meat analogue strips
—*defrosted*
Olive oil cooking spray

2 teaspoons *high-heat* safflower *or* sunflower oil

In a small dish, combine sugar, garlic and onion powders, ground ginger and cinnamon, paprika, chili powder, and ground peanuts. Stir to combine.

Place *defrosted* soymeat strips in a pie plate. Spray the strips lightly on both sides with the olive oil cooking spray. Sprinkle *one-half* of the spice mixture over the soymeat pieces. Turn them over and sprinkle the remaining *one-half* of the spice mixture over. Thread the soy strips onto *satay* sticks or small wooden skewers. Return the brochettes to the pie plate. Cover the pie plate with aluminum foil and allow the spices to penetrate the soymeat for at least 2 hours.

Heat a grill pan or skillet over *MEDIUM* heat. Brush the pan with *high-heat* safflower oil. When pan is hot, place brochettes on the heated surface and allow to *quickly* grill to a light brown. Turn frequently. Transfer to a heated platter.

Serve at once.

Yields 6 servings
adequate for 4 people

Note: This recipe can be halved, when required.

1/6 SERVING – PROTEIN = 15.9 g.; FAT = 4.1 g.; CARBOHYDRATE = 4.6 g.;
CALORIES = 106; CALORIES FROM FAT = 35%

CAMEROONIAN PAPAYA JAM
Confitures de Papaye

TPT - 33 hours;
8 hours = maceration period;
24 hours = cooling period

I prefer to use the large, Brazilian- or Mexican-grown Maradol cultivar of the papaya or pawpaw for this jam because the flesh is red and the resulting jam is so beautiful. Other cultivars can be used for this jam but you may have to use two fruits because they are much smaller.

1 medium Maradol papaya—peeled, seeded,
 and *thinly* sliced
1/4 cup freshly squeezed lemon juice
4 1/2 cups sugar

Sterilize five 1/2-pint canning jars. Also sterilize lids and rings for jars.

In a mixing bowl, combine papaya slices, lemon juice, and sugar. Toss to expose all the papaya slices to the lemon juice and sugar. Cover the bowl and allow fruit to macerate for 8 hours, or overnight.

When the maceration period is completed, transfer the papaya mixture to the work bowl of food processor fitted with steel knife. Process until a uniform purée is produced. Transfer to a saucepan set over *MEDIUM* heat. Allow to simmer until the moisture has evaporated and the volume has been reduced to about one-half.

Ladle into five hot, sterilized 1/2-pint canning jars, leaving a 3/4-inch clearance to the rim of the jar. Carefully wipe lips of jars. Seal with hot, sterilized lids and rings. Process in hot-water-bath canner for 10 minutes, *timing from the moment the water reaches a full rolling boil.* Remove to surface covered with thick towels or newspapers. Allow to cool for 24 hours *undisturbed.* Check to be sure jars are sealed before labeling and storing in a dark, cool, dry place.* Loosen or remove rings before storing.

Yields five 1/2 pint jarfuls

Notes: *Any jars that do not seal can be stored in the refrigerator for about one month or resealed using a *new lid.*

This makes a wonderful dessert sauce.

CAMEROONIAN PAPAYA JAM (cont'd)

1/72 SERVING (i. e., per tablespoonful) –
PROTEIN = 0.05 g.; FAT = 0.8 g.; CARBOHYDRATE = 15.0 g.;
CALORIES = 59; CALORIES FROM FAT = 12%

CAMEROONIAN CABBAGE SLAW WITH PINEAPPLE
Salade de Chou aux Anana

TPT - 12 minutes

Coleslaw has always been a salad option in my family since "wintering-over" cabbages in root cellars or refrigerators was one of the ways we preserved the harvested produce. Today I can dash into town for an organic cabbage if those which I stored in October have been used up. My grandmother and mother did not have that option and the addition of pineapple to their salads was really only for quite special occasions. Here I have refined the mayonnaise dressing Grandma, Mom, and I used for decades; it provides a taste closer to that which you would find in Cameroon.

3 tablespoons *calorie-reduced or light* **mayonnaise**
1 tablespoon *fat-free* **dairy sour cream**
1 tablespoon PLAIN YOGURT *[see index]* **or commercially-available plain yogurt**
1 tablespoon *light, sulfite-free* **coconut milk**

4 cups *thinly* **sliced, "knife-slivered," green cabbage—well-washed and well-dried**
1/2 small green bell pepper—well-washed, cored, and *thinly* **slivered**
2 firm Italian plum tomatoes—well-washed, halved, seeded, and slivered

1 cup pineapple tidbits—fresh *or* **canned in juice**

Freshly ground black pepper, to taste
Pinch or two celery *or* **lovage seeds**

In a small bowl, combine mayonnaise, sour cream, yogurt, and coconut milk. Using a wire whisk, beat well. Set aside briefly.

In a mixing bowl, combine slivered green cabbage, green pepper, and tomato. Toss to mix well.

Add pineapple tidbits. Toss again.

Add prepared mayonnaise-based salad dressing. Toss to coat the vegetables well.

Season with black pepper. Toss again. Turn into a salad bowl. Refrigerate until required.

Yields 8 servings
adequate for 6 people

Note: This recipe can be halved, when required.

1/6 SERVING – PROTEIN = 1.9 g.; FAT = 3.0 g.; CARBOHYDRATE = 9.9 g.;
CALORIES = 68; CALORIES FROM FAT = 40%

CAMEROONIAN LAYERED FRUIT SALAD
Salade aux Fruits

TPT - 46 minutes;
20 minutes = coconut milk cooling period;
30 minutes = salad chilling period

Beautiful, fresh fruits are always available to the menu planner in Cameroon and this salad shows them off with style. I like to use a small trifle bowl.

Africa–Cameroon

CAMEROONIAN LAYERED FRUIT SALAD (cont'd)

3 tablespoons *calorie-reduced or light* mayonnaise
2 tablespoons *light, sulfite-free* coconut milk
1 tablespoon pineapple juice

2 firm, ripe bananas—peeled and sliced
2 firm, ripe tomatoes—*thinly* sliced
1 small pineapple—peeled, eyed, and *thinly* sliced*
2 large, firm avocados—peeled, pitted, and sliced

1 tablespoon *roasted, unsalted* peanuts—chopped

In a small bowl, combine mayonnaise, coconut, milk, and pineapple juice. Using a small wire whisk, blend thoroughly. Set aside until required.

In a small trifle bowl or large crystal serving bowl layer fruits, alternating so that the layers repeat attractively.

Sprinkle chopped peanuts over.

Spoon mayonnaise–coconut milk mixture over. Refrigerate for at least 30 minutes before serving.

Serve chilled.

Yields 8 servings
adequate for 6 people

Notes: *Small, peeled pineapples are generally available in well-stocked grocery stores. These are perfect for this salad and do save time.

This recipe can be halved, when required.

1/8 SERVING – PROTEIN = 2.1 g.; FAT = 9.8 g.; CARBOHYDRATE = 21.5 g.;
CALORIES = 165; CALORIES FROM FAT = 53%

CAMEROONIAN YELLOW PLANTAIN AND CORN SOUP
TPT - 35 minutes

Cutting the corn from the cobs just as it comes from the farm while a plantain sits waiting in my fruit bowl, ripened to perfection, is one of those culinary moments that making cooking from scratch so very satisfying to the soul. The incredible taste combination of a fully ripened plantain and green (fresh) corn is something to absolutely celebrate and enjoy for lunch or as a light supper. This is a soup that virtually reverses "continental drift," fitting South America and Africa snuggly back together again.

Searching for the name by which this truly unique and delicious soup is known in Cameroon led me to a dilemma. There are some 230 recognized languages in Cameroon. Since French and English are the official languages, reflecting the country's colonial past, I have chosen to use the English name only.

2 tablespoons butter
1 medium onion—*finely* chopped
1 garlic clove—*very finely* chopped

1/2 cup canned, *diced* tomatoes
1 large *yellow* plantain—peeled and sliced
1 cup green (fresh) *or frozen* corn kernels

1 teaspoon dried tarragon—crushed
1/2 teaspoon dried parsley—crushed
1 quart VEGETABLE STOCK FROM SOUP
  [see index] *or* other vegetarian stock of choice
2 teaspoons *finely* chopped mild green *chilies*
Freshly ground black pepper

Pinch ground mace*

In a large saucepan or small kettle set over *MEDIUM* heat, melt butter. Add *finely* chopped onion and *very finely* chopped garlic. Sauté until onion is soft and translucent, *being careful to allow neither vegetable to brown.*

Add tomatoes, plantain slices, and corn. Cook, stirring gently, for several minutes.

Add crushed, dried tarragon and parsley, stock, *finely* chopped green *chilies*, and black pepper. Allow to come to the simmer. *Reduce heat to LOW-MEDIUM* and simmer for about 15 minutes.

Add mace. Stir to integrate. Turn into a heated soup tureen.

Serve into heated soup bowls.

Yields 8 servings
adequate for 4-6 people

Notes: *Nutmeg may be substituted, if preferred.

This recipe can be doubled, when required.

1/8 SERVING – PROTEIN = 1.6 g.; FAT = 3.3 g.; CARBOHYDRATE = 16.7 g.;
CALORIES = 90; CALORIES FROM FAT = 33%

Africa—Cameroon

CAMEROONIAN GREENS WITH GARLIC
Légumes Verts aux Ail
TPT - 26 minutes

It is, of course, a fact that sautéed and braised greens are a meal component in most sub-Saharan countries. The types of greens may vary with availability, the amount of garlic and hot pepper seasoning may vary with taste but it is, very much, a staple. If there are leftovers, we stir them up the next day with sliced soy chorizo sausages for lunch, a lunch that is worthy of planned leftovers.

2 tablespoons *extra virgin* **olive oil**
4 large garlic cloves—*very finely* **chopped**
1 medium onion—*finely* **chopped**

8 cups kale, young turnip, mustard, Swiss chard, *or* **collard greens**—**well-washed, trimmed of stems and veins, and coarsely chopped**

1/8 teaspoon ground mixed peppercorns—black, red, and white—or to taste
1/2 cup VEGETABLE STOCK FROM SOUP *[see index]*, **other vegetarian stock of choice,** *or* **water**

Salt, to taste

In a large skillet set over *MEDIUM* heat, heat oil. Sauté *very finely* chopped garlic and *finely* chopped onion until soft, *being careful not to allow the garlic to brown. Reduce heat to LOW.*

Add chopped greens. Sauté until greens are wilted.

Add ground mixed peppercorns and vegetable stock. Cover and allow to simmer over *LOW-MEDIUM* heat for about 10 minutes. Remove greens to a heated serving bowl, using a skimmer or chopsticks to lift them from the liquid.

Season with salt.

Serve at once.

Yields 6 servings
adequate for 4 people

Note: This recipe can be halved. Doubling requires a very, very large skillet so when I do double this recipe, I use a wok.

1/6 SERVING – PROTEIN = 3.1 g.; FAT = 4.8 g.; CARBOHYDRATE = 11.7 g.;
CALORIES = 91; CALORIES FROM FAT = 47%

YAM, POTATO, AND CORN *FUFU*
Fufu
TPT - 36 minutes

Little did I know that the mashed sweetpotatoes that I have eaten literally all my life, since Gerber jarred them as baby food, were fufu. Chances are you have seen a picture or a film of an African lady pounding something in what looks like a giant mortar using a long handled pestle. What you have most probably witnessed is the making of fufu. Although cassava fufu is favored in Cameroon, it is less nutritious than are other combinations which can include white sweetpotatoes, which are more authentic for this recipe if you can find them, white potatoes, rice, plantains, corn, cassava or yuca root, semolina, and even corn meal. These starchy variations are all pounded until smooth and rolled into balls to accompany meat or vegetable stews. You use the balls to scoop up meat or vegetables and sauce or gravy and pop it into your mouth. Corn, yams, and white potatoes can be combined with coconut milk, butter or ghee, and a touch of spice to elevate this very everyday, subsistence food.

4 quarts *boiling* **water**
1 medium sweetpotato *or* **yam—peeled and chopped**
1 medium white potato—peeled and chopped
1 cup green (fresh) *or* *frozen* **corn kernels**

1/3 cup *light, sulfite-free* **coconut milk, or more as needed**
2 tablespoons CLARIFIED BUTTER *or* **GHEE** *[see index]*
1 teaspoon OUR *TANDOORI* **SPICE MIXTURE (Chaat Masala)** *[see index]* **or commercially-available mixture**

Salt, to taste

In a kettle set over *MEDIUM* heat, combine *boiling* water, chopped sweetpotato and white potato, and corn. Boil until potatoes are soft, about 20 minutes. Drain well. Turn into a large mixing bowl and using a potato masher or a hand mixer, mash until thoroughly combine and smooth.* Turn into a clean saucepan set over *LOW-MEDIUM* heat.

Add coconut milk, butter, and *tandoori* spice mixture. Mix well. Cook, stirring frequently, until heated through.

Season with salt. Turn into a heated serving dish. Keep warm on a warming tray until ready to serve.

Africa–Cameroon

YAM, POTATO, AND CORN *FUFU* (cont'd)

Yields 6 servings
adequate for 4 people

Notes: *A potato ricer gives a very uniform texture and may be used to make the *fufu*, if preferred.

This recipe can be halved or doubled, when required.

1/6 SERVING – PROTEIN = 2.4 g.; FAT = 4.8 g.; CARBOHYDRATE = 17.7 g.; CALORIES = 116; CALORIES FROM FAT = 37%

YAM AND PLANTAIN *FUFU*
Fufu

TPT - 40 minutes

The combination of cooked and mashed yam and plantain creates a smooth, somewhat sweet, satisfying starch accompaniment to a meal. Although some of the starch in the plantain will, of course, convert to sugar, this is not a sweet, sweet dish as it would be if one used the common, yellow Cavendish banana.

4 quarts *boiling* **water**
1 medium sweetpotato *or* **yam—peeled and chopped**
1 large, slightly ripened plantain—chopped

1/3 cup *light, sulfite-free* **coconut milk, or more as needed**
2 tablespoons CLARIFIED BUTTER *or* **GHEE**
[see index]
1 teaspoon OUR *TANDOORI* **SPICE MIXTURE (Chaat Masala)** [see index] *or* **commercially-available mixture**

Salt, to taste

In a kettle set over *MEDIUM* heat, combine *boiling* water, chopped sweetpotato and plantain. Boil until sweetpotato and plantain are soft. Drain well. Turn into a large mixing bowl and using a potato masher or a hand mixer, mash until thoroughly combined and smooth.* Turn into a clean saucepan set over *LOW-MEDIUM* heat.

Add coconut milk, butter, and *tandoori* spice mixture. Mix well. Cook, stirring frequently, until heated through.

Season with salt. Turn into a heated serving dish. Keep warm on a warming tray until ready to serve.

Yields 6 servings
adequate for 4 people

Notes: *A potato ricer gives a very uniform texture and may be used to make the *fufu*, if preferred.

This recipe can be halved or doubled, when required.

1/6 SERVING – PROTEIN = 0.7 g.; FAT = 4.4 g.; CARBOHYDRATE = 12.1 g.; CALORIES = 86; CALORIES FROM FAT = 46%

CAMEROONIAN MANGO WHIP
Crema Fouettée avec Mangue

TPT - 1 hour and 19 minutes;
1 hour = chilling period

Popular in Cameroon, this dessert illustrates well the fusion of the foods available in West Africa with the dishes, techniques, and subsequent refrigeration introduced via European colonialism. A dessert quite similar to this is often served in Cuban restaurants and may have evolved through similar influences. It is light, although it feels so very rich.

CAMEROONIAN MANGO WHIP (cont'd)

2 ripe red mangoes—peeled and sliced from
   pit—*or* an equal quantity of canned mangoes,
   if necessary
3 tablespoons confectioners' sugar

1 cup heavy whipping cream
2 teaspoons confectioners' sugar

1 tablespoon shredded coconut—fresh *or*
   desiccated—*toasted*
Fresh mint leaves, for garnish

Using a food processor fitted with steel blade, purée the mango and the 3 tablespoons confectioners' sugar until a thick pulp forms. Turn into a mixing bowl and set aside briefly.

Using the electric mixer fitted with *chilled* beaters or by hand using a *chilled* wire whisk, beat heavy cream in a *chilled* bowl until soft peaks form. While continuing to beat, add confectioners' sugar. Beat until stiff peaks form.

Fold whipped cream *gently*, but *thoroughly*, into mango mixture. Divide mixture among four sherbet glasses or other small dessert dishes.*

Refrigerate for no more than an hour before serving. Garnish each serving with some *toasted* coconut and with mint leaves.

                               Yields 4 individual servings

Notes: *This dessert makes a lovely presentation if spooned into wine glasses or champagne flutes.

        This recipe can be doubled when required.

1/4 SERVING –   PROTEIN = 1.2 g.; FAT = 13.7 g.; CARBOHYDRATE = 18.8 g.;
                       CALORIES = 197; CALORIES FROM FAT = 63%

AFRICAN MOLDED SWEET RICE CAKES
Riz Moulé avec Crème de Noix de Cocoa

TPT - 1 hour and 9 minutes;
30 minutes = cooling period

Cameroonians make small circular sweet rice cakes that are very tasty little treats. Using the same ingredients, I make small molded rice cakes that can be served for dessert. The subtle hint of lemon reminds me of a French lemon rice pudding I often make. This dessert helps to increase the protein in a vegetable meal such as this.

4 cups *cooked* rice—preferably short-grained rice
2 tablespoons rice flour
1 tablespoon freshly squeezed lemon juice

3 tablespoons light cream, half and half, *or* light,
   sulfite-free coconut milk, if preferred
1/2 cup sugar
1/2 cup *fat-free* pasteurized eggs (the equivalent
   of 2 eggs)
1/2 teaspoon pure vanilla extract

Preheat oven to 350 degrees F. Prepare six small, 8-ounce ramekins by coating with non-stick lecithin spray coating for baking.

In a mixing bowl combine rice, rice flour, and lemon juice. Mix well.

Add cream, sugar, pasteurized eggs, and vanilla extract. Mix well. Divide among ramekins, packing the rice mixture into each ramekin. Bake in preheated 350 degree F. oven for 25 minutes, or until firm and pulling slightly from the side of the dish. Remove to a wire rack to cool to room temperature or refrigerate for 30 minutes.

Run a knife around the edge of a ramekin. Place a dessert plate on top and invert. Shake to loosen the rice cake. Repeat with all servings.

Serve at room temperature.*

                                  Yields 6 servings
                                adequate for 4 people

Notes: *If desired, the baked rice cakes can be made in advance and refrigerated. Unmold and bring to room temperature to serve.

        This recipe can be halved, when required.

AFRICAN MOLDED RICE CAKES (cont'd)

1/6 SERVING – PROTEIN = 5.2 g.; FAT = 0.9 g.; CARBOHYDRATE = 53.3 g.;
CALORIES = 247; CALORIES FROM FAT = 3%

CAMEROONIAN SWEET *CASSAVA* FRITTERS
Beignets de Manioc

TPT - 1 hour and 33 minutes

Cassava fritters are quite obviously a tribute to French beignets and to the influence of the French colonial period in Cameroon. Yes, these are quite different from the delicate French version but they are still quite addictive. Cameroonians sprinkle these with salt or sugar. Since we greatly prefer the sweet version, we add sugar to the cassava–egg mixture as well as rolling the fried fritters in sugar.

1 pound *baton de manioc, cassava,* or *yuca* tuber—peeled and chopped
3 quarts *boiling* water

1/4 cup *fat-free* pasteurized eggs (the equivalent of 1 egg)
2 tablespoons sugar
1/2 teaspoon salt

2 tablespoons unbleached white flour

High-heat safflower *or* sunflower oil for deep-frying

1/4 cup granulated sugar

In a large kettle set over *MEDIUM-HIGH* heat, combine chopped *cassava* and *boiling* water. Cook until *cassava* is soft—about 30 minutes. Drain thoroughly and allow to cool for about 15 minutes. *Remove all bits of woody core.* Turn into a large mixing bowl and mash until you have a lump-free, smooth mass.

Add pasteurized eggs and salt. Combine thoroughly. Turn out onto a well-floured surface. Turn and turn to coat the cassava mixture with flour. Roll the cassava into a rectangle about 1/2-inch high. Cut dough into small rectangular or square cakes.

In a deep frying pan set over *MEDIUM-HIGH,* add oil to a depth of about 1/2 inch. When hot, fry *cassava* fritters/cakes, a few at a time, until golden brown, turning once. Transfer to paper toweling to drain excess oil.

Place a quantity of granulated sugar, as preferred, into a shallow dish. Roll each well-drained fritter in sugar. Transfer to a platter.

Yields about 12 fritters
adequate for 4-6 people

Note: This recipe can be doubled.

1/6 SERVING – PROTEIN = 1.1 g.; FAT = 1.2 g.; CARBOHYDRATE = 21.3 g.;
CALORIES = 100; CALORIES FROM FAT = 11%

Cape Verde

A group of eighteen islands, eight of which are so small that they are classified as islets, sit about three hundred miles off the west coast of Africa. This volcanically-formed archipelago, slightly larger than the state of Rhode Island, constitutes the Republic of Cape Verde. Of the ten islands in the Barlavento group, only Santa Luzia is uninhabited. This group of islands has an unusual geological history. The volcanism which formed the islands is attributed to a magma hotspot that is found in what is known as the Cape Verde Rise, a semi-circular rise 994 miles wide and about 1.4 miles high in the floor of the Atlantic Ocean, the result of a swell in the earth's crust. Pillow lavas, dating to about 128-131 million years ago, have been found on the Island of Maio and on the northern peninsula of Santiago. Igneous rocks, volcanic structures, and pyroclastic debris fields attest to a violent geologic history. Except for the Island of Fogo, volcanic activity in Cape Verde had ceased, for the most part, by the time of human settlement.

Antonio de Noli, a Genovese explorer sailing for Portugal, discovered these islands in 1456. The Portuguese established the first settlement on the Island of Santiago in 1462 and De Noli was appointed governor by King Afonso V. Cape Verde prospered due to its desirability as a safe harbor and resupply station for Portuguese traders and explorers. By the sixteenth century its prosperity was a direct result of the slave trade. With the outlawing of the lucrative transatlantic transport of slaves, the fortunes of Cape Verde declined considerably although it still remained a safe harbor and resupply station for shipping.

Rising nationalism in Cape Verde prompted Portugal to change the colony's status to that of an overseas province in 1951. This move satisfied neither the Cape Verdeans nor the Guineans with whom they joined to form PAIGC, the African Party for the Independence of Guinea and Cape Verde. PAIGC, backed by the Soviet-bloc, initiated an armed rebellion against Portugal in 1961. In 1973 Portuguese Guinea declared independence and two years later Cape Verde, under the African Party for the Independence of Cape Verde, PAICV, established a single-party system which ruled until 1990.

Today, having adopted a multi-party system, Cape Verde is making amazing strides despite its limited natural resources and the necessity to import over ninety percent of the food required to feed its population. It is a world leader in exploration of renewable energy with extensive wind farm and solar field development but the lack of employment opportunities has driven many Cape Verdeans to emigrate resulting in an expatriate population which actually exceeds the resident population. More than five hundred thousand of Cape Verdean ancestry live in the United States. Large communities of expatriates can be found in Portugal, The Netherlands, Italy, France, Senegal, and São Tomé and Principe.

The long rule by Portugal has clearly influenced both the cuisine and the language of Cape Verde but both owe much to the nation's proximity to Africa. The large African and Creole population have preserved the dishes of their mainland African heritage and this combined with those dishes introduced by the Portuguese results in a fascinating cuisine. In this country we also see a language amalgamation in the local language known as Cape Verdean Creole, a unique dialectic language based on an archaic Portuguese dialect modified by phrases from African and European languages, which is widely spoken although the official language of business and trade is Portuguese.

Avocado Halves with Honey
Abacates com Mel

~~~~~~~~~~~~~~~~~~~~~

Rice and Lima Beans   Mashed Yams
Jagacida   *Pure de Inhame*

Crusty French Bread

Preserved Mango
Conserva de Manga

~~~~~~~~~~~

Bean Stew with Hominy and *Chouriço*
Cachupa Rica

Basic Bean Preparation Using the Slow Cooker

~~~~~~~~~~~~~~~~~~~~~~~~

Bananas in Pastry
Banana Enrolada

CAPE VERDEAN RICE AND LIMA BEANS
Jagacida
TPT - 46 minutes

I have found that combining grain and legume protein in the same dish is a worldwide practice; it is almost instinctive, or so it would seem. Often called just "jag," this "rice and beans" dish can be made with or without sausages. The flavor is wonderful with the addition of spicy soy chouriço but the protein level of the dish without the sausages is more than satisfactory. This is a simple dish, this is a delicious dish, and it is another one of those dishes that can be made from your larder when a run into town is not possible.

2 tablespoons safflower *or* sunflower oil
1 medium onion—*finely* chopped
1 large garlic clove—*very finely* chopped

3 tablespoons canned, *crushed* tomatoes

1 quart *boiling* water
2 bay leaves—broken in half and secured in a tea ball
1 cup *frozen* baby lima beans
3/4 cup *converted* rice*
1/4 teaspoon salt, or to taste
Freshly ground black pepper, to taste
Pinch ground red pepper (cayenne)

In a kettle set over *MEDIUM* heat, heat oil. Add *finely* chopped onion and *very finely* chopped garlic. Sauté until onion is soft and translucent, *being careful not to allow vegetables to brown.*

Add *crushed* tomatoes and sauté for a minute or two more.

Add *boiling* water, bay leaf pieces, lima beans, rice, salt, black pepper, and ground red pepper (cayenne). Reduce the heat to *LOW-MEDIUM*, cover, and allow to simmer for about 30 minutes, or until the rice is tender. Stir occasionally. Remove tea ball containing bay leaves. Turn the rice and bean mixture into a heated soup tureen.

Serve into heated soup plates.

Yields 6 servings
adequate for 4 people

Notes: *I often use a wild rice and white rice mixture, which I buy in bulk from an online firm, to make this stew.

This recipe can be halved, when required.

1/6 SERVING – PROTEIN = 5.0 g.; FAT = 4.6 g.; CARBOHYDRATE = 32.7 g.; CALORIES = 195; CALORIES FROM FAT = 21%

Africa–Cape Verde

CAPE VERDEAN PRESERVED MANGO
Conserva de Manga

TPT - 3 days and 24 minutes;
  3 days = flavor development period

"Putting food by" for the winter has been a part of the routine of my life since I was very young. I helped my mother and grandmother can and pickle and then took up the task each summer and fall of my adulthood. My generation, I fear, is the last, to have the pleasure of preserving. Unripe mangoes give this pickle a sweet, but not too sweet, taste. This is a very simply prepared "sweet and sour" as my Mennonite neighbors might say; a perfect recipe to introduce to a new convert to home-preserving. It accompanies so many menus well that doubling this assures that when I run down to my basement refrigerator to retrieve a jar for a meal, there is a greater chance that there is one left.

2 cups *boiling* water
1 teaspoon salt

4 unripe mangos—peeled and diced

1 cup safflower *or* sunflower oil
1/2 cup distilled white vinegar
2 tablespoons sugar
2 teaspoons crushed red pepper flakes
2 teaspoons grated fresh gingerroot

Sterilize two 1-quart canning jars. Also sterilize lids and rings for jars.

In a large saucepan, combine *boiling* water and salt. Add diced mango and allow to come to the boil over *MEDIUM* heat. Immediately remove from heat. Using a slotted spoon, remove mango pieces and transfer to a mixing bowl.

Add vinegar, oil, sugar, crushed red pepper flakes, and grated gingerroot. Stir to immerse the mango pieces in the oil–vinegar mixture.

Ladle into the two sterilized quart canning jars. Carefully wipe lips of jars. Seal with hot, sterilized lids and rings.

Refrigerate for three days before using to allow for flavor development. Store jar in the refrigerator.

Yields two 1-quart jarfuls*

Note: *The yield may vary due to the size of fruits.

1/20 SERVING (i. e., per 1/4 cupful)* -
PROTEIN = 0.2 g.; FAT = 1.5 g.; CARBOHYDRATE = 7.9 g.;
CALORIES = 43; CALORIES FROM FAT = 31%

CAPE VERDEAN BEAN STEW WITH HOMINY AND *CHOURIÇO*
Cachupa Rica

TPT - 19 hours and 42 minutes;
  12 hours = dried bean soaking period;
  7 hours = slow cooker preparation of beans

One of the treasures I brought back from a trip to Portugal was a recipe for a complex bean stew with red kidney beans, chick peas, and rutabagas (sopa de feijao e graos de bico Portuguesa). This Cape Verdean version combines beans with fava beans and vegetables more common to African cooking. It expands on the Portuguese bean stew to an extent that was quite unexpected. If you cook dried beans and soak dried hominy and allow the flavors of the finished stew to develop for about three days, you will have a pot of the most deliciousness you can imagine. I have included my favorite method of cooking dried beans but if you can not work it into your schedule, you can substitute well-drained canned beans. Bay leaves are a must, just as they are in Portugal. If you grow your own bay leaves, add fresh bay leaves to this stew; the flavor that they impart is amazing.

Africa–Cape Verde

**CAPE VERDEAN BEAN STEW
WITH HOMINY AND *CHOURIÇO*** (cont'd)

1/4 cup dried *fava* beans
1/4 cup dried Navy beans *or* Great Northern beans

2 tablespoons *extra virgin* olive oil
1 medium onion—*thinly* sliced
1 large garlic clove—*very finely* chopped
2 large bay leaves—halved

1 cup canned, *diced* tomatoes
2 cups shredded green cabbage
1 medium sweetpotato—peeled and chopped into 1/2-inch cubes
1 cup butternut squash—peeled and chopped into 1/2-inch cubes

1 cup (about 6 ounces) hominy—well-drained*
1 cup water
Freshly ground black pepper, to taste
2 *frozen* vegetarian *chouriço (chorizo)* sausages —sliced
1 slice soy bacon—*finely* chopped

1 plantain—sliced

Following the recipe BASIC BEAN PREPARATION USING THE SLOW COOKER which follows, prepare *fava* beans and Navy or Great Northern beans by soaking overnight and cooking until tender in the slow cooker. Drain well.

In a large kettle set over *MEDIUM* heat, heat oil. Add *thinly* sliced onion, *very finely* chopped garlic, and bay leaf pieces. Sauté until onions are soft and translucent, *being careful to allow neither the onions nor the garlic to brown.*

Add diced tomatoes, shredded cabbage, sweetpotato cubes, and butternut squash cubes. Cook stirring frequently for about 5 minutes.

Add hominy, cooked *fava* and Navy or Great Northern beans, and water. Taste and season with black pepper. Then, add sliced chorizo (*chouriço*) sausages and *finely* chopped soy bacon. Reduce heat to *LOW-MEDIUM* and allow to simmer for about 20 minutes.

Add plantain slices. Allow to simmer for 5 minutes more. Turn into a heated serving dish.

Serve hot. Refrigerate or freeze leftovers.

Yields 8 servings
adequate for 6 people

Notes: *Dried hominy, if available, can be soaked overnight with the beans and cooked with the beans.

This recipe can be halved, when required.

1/10 SERVING – PROTEIN = 7.0 g.; FAT = 5.4 g.; CARBOHYDRATE = 23.9 g.;
CALORIES = 169; CALORIES FROM FAT = 29%

BASIC BEAN PREPARATION USING THE SLOW COOKER

TPT - 12 hours and 5 minutes;
12 hours = overnight soaking period
[slow cooker: 7 hours at HIGH]

The time that must be devoted to cooking dried beans can often drive people to the over-salted, canned beans that all of us keep on hand just in case we forget to "put the beans to soak" the night before. The slow cooker, I find, just cooks the beans and lets me get on with my life. If you want firm beans, the alternative method for cooking beans, which does not require overnight soaking, tends to produce beans that fall apart during the final slow cooking. If you are planning to purée the beans for your recipe, of course, this is not a problem.

1 cup dry beans*
3 cups water

5 cups *boiling* water

Rinse dry beans in several changes of water. Remove and discard any of poor quality. Place in a bowl with the 2 cupfuls of water and soak overnight in the refrigerator.

Preheat slow cooker to HIGH.

In the morning, drain beans and place in the bowl of the slow cooker. Add *boiling* water. Cover and cook in slow cooker for 7 hours at HIGH.**

Use cooked beans in any recipe that calls for beans or freeze, with a bit of liquid, for future menu plans.

Yields about 1 1/2 cupfuls

Notes: *The time needed to cook a particular bean may differ so attention is required the first time you use this method for a different legume.

BASIC BEAN PREPARATION USING THE SLOW COOKER (cont'd)

**A *bouquet garni*, stuffed with flavoring items such as herbs and vegetables, can be tucked into the beans as they cook to provide subtle flavoring. It is advisable to move it around during the cooking process to more evenly flavor the beans.

This recipe may be prepared well in advance, even the day before, if convenient, and refrigerated until required. Simply reheat over *LOW* heat.

When required, this recipe is easily doubled.

1/6 SERVING (about 1/2 cupful) –
PROTEIN = 3.7 g.; FAT = 0.3 g.; CARBOHYDRATE = 10.9 g.;
CALORIES = 68; CALORIES FROM FAT = 4%

BANANAS IN PASTRY IN THE STYLE OF CAPE VERDE
Banana Enrolada

TPT - 34 minutes

This is a very filling dessert, but a wonderful ending for a salad menu. In Cape Verde a whole banana is enclosed in a sweet pie-dough pastry. I halve the Cavendish bananas or choose small "baby" bananas. Don't omit the coffee; it adds an elusive nuance to what is really a very simple dessert.

1 sheet (9 x 14 inches) *frozen* puff pastry—brought to room temperature

4 ripe bananas—halved *or* 8 baby bananas
1 tablespoon cinnamon sugar
1/2 teaspoon *crushed* coffee granules

Preheat oven to 400 degrees F. Prepare a cookie sheet by lining it with culinary parchment paper.

Do not unfold the sheet of puff pastry. Cut the sheet crosswise into 8 slices about 3 1/2 inches wide. Using a rolling pin, roll one of the pastry slices out so that the banana can be enclosed in it.

Place a banana piece in the middle of the rolled pastry. Sprinkle with some of the cinnamon sugar and some of the crushed coffee crystals. Fold the pastry over and secure. Place, seam-side-down on the parchment-lined baking sheet. Prepare all bananas in the same manner.

Bake in preheated 400 degree F. oven for 15 minutes. The pastry will puff and be golden brown. Remove from oven and transfer to a serving platter.

Serve warm.

Yields 8 servings
adequate for 4-6 people

Note: This recipe can be halved or doubled easily when required.

1/8 SERVING – PROTEIN = 2.9 g.; FAT = 8.6 g.; CARBOHYDRATE = 25.6 g.;
CALORIES = 187; CALORIES FROM FAT = 41%

Africa–**Central African Republics**

Democratic Republic of the Congo
Republic of the Congo
Central African Republic
Gabon
Equatorial Guinea

Assignation of recipes for this section of the book was seriously complicated by the fact that the demonym Congolese is favored by both the Democratic Republic of the Congo, known as the Belgian Congo from 1908-1960, and the Republic of the Congo, formerly part of the French colony of Equatorial Africa from 1908-1960 although ruled by the French from 1880 and known then as the French Congo. The area of Central Africa, now known as the Central African Republic became a colony of France in 1894 and was named Ubangi–Shari for the two important rivers that traverse the area. Briefly united with Chad in 1905, it was joined with Gabon and the French Congo in 1910 to form French Equatorial Africa. One of the poorest nations on Earth, the Central African Republic has remained relatively isolated from outside influence and preserves a unique cuisine, albeit a subsistence cuisine which is severely impacted by the widespread poverty. Gabon, on the other hand has had greater success as a sovereign nation since its independence from France in 1960. Gabon has infinitely better soil conditions than its neighbors and a more consistent and predictable rainfall pattern allowing for extensive year-round cultivation of diverse food crops. With a comparatively small population, one and a half million, agricultural production allows for export.

The cuisines of the Sub-Sahara nations are based on a limited number of foods because agriculture and animal husbandry are impacted by the lack of water in the Sub-Sahara. This has come with climatic changes over the millennia that eliminated the vast surface water of this region and now allows for the Sahara's southward advance. Specifically, the shift in the Earth's axis which occurred in 1600 BC caused a change in the monsoon pattern which resulted in a decrease in precipitation, the drying up of the lakes and rivers that once spread across the Sahara, and an increase in temperature. Looking at the Sahara Desert today one can not even imagine a lush savannah teaming with animals but over 30,000 petroglyphs of river animals and fossils of dinosaurs attest to a very different environment. Today, the lack of organized large scale agricultural operations and the lack of soil management programs in areas of these countries where climate conditions are more stable, acerbate the constant pressure on the human condition.

In Gabon, the Democratic Republic of the Congo, the Republic of the Congo, and Equatorial Guinea, Pygmy populations were displaced or absorbed into the tribes of the Bantu-speaking people as they spread across the continent in the Neolithic period and well into the Iron Age. Beginning in the 1870s the drive by European nations to divide up the continent began, resulting in exploitation of the indigenous population and the natural resources of these nations for decades. Unprepared by their colonial masters for nationhood when independence came in 1960, each government in this region has struggled with incorporating disparate tribes and tribal customs into a national image with global goals.

Equatorial Guinea has the distinct advantage of an Atlantic coastline and massive oil reserves. The former Spanish Guinea is now the richest country per capita in Africa due to oil production but this wealth has not been evenly distributed nor has it been used to create a safe water supply, to pasteurize milk products, or to improve health services for its population. The cuisine of Equatorial Guinea is highly plant-based with, as some say, a Spanish flair.

Africa – Central African Republics

My choice to combine the cuisines of these nations may seem somewhat disrespectful of their sovereignty and I apologize for any perceived slight but I see a flow of ingredients, cooking techniques, and seasoning, and a historical commonality that is remarkably consistent in countries outwardly separated by tribal customs, colonial influences, and political differences.

Tapas in the Style of Equatorial Guinea

Sautéed Greens with Peanuts   Vegetarian Meatballs with Sauce

Hard-cooked Eggs with Tomato–Garlic–Hot Pepper Sauce

Soy *Chouriço* Sausage Simmered in Red Wine

Fried Plantains   Fried *Polenta*

Sautéed Peanuts   Assorted Olives

~

Congolese Pineapple and Avocado Salad
Salade de Ananas et Avocat

Central African Millet and Corn Salad with Avocado
Salade de Millet, Maïs, et Avocat

Cucumber Salad with Peanut – Lime Dressing
Salade de Concombre

~~~~~~~~~~~~~~~~~~~~

Gabonese "Chicken" Stew
Nyembwe
over
Steamed Brown Rice or Millet

Congolese Summer Squash with Peanuts and Garlic
Courge Jaune avec Broutilles et Ail

~~~~~~~~~~

Central African Eggplant with Tomato
Augergine et Tomate

Fried Eggs

~~~~~~~~~~

Central African Spinach Stew with Peanut Butter
Chilli um Bido
over
Rice, Pasta, Boiled Potatoes, or *Polenta*

~~~~~~~~~~~~~~~~~~~~

Congolese Banana *Phyllo* Tart   **Baked Bananas**
Filo Tarte Bananae   *Bananes*

Fruit Salad in the Style of the Congo
Salade de Fruits

Africa–Central African Republics

CONGOLESE PINEAPPLE AND AVOCADO SALAD
Salade de Ananas et Avocat
TPT - 8 minutes

After World War II avocados finally reached our upstate New York grocery stores. Yes, my mother and father had tasted avocado in restaurants but it was not something you wandered into the local Loblaws to find back then. Once we found them in grocery stores, special occasion dishes often included the soft, rich fruits. Mom taught me to use lemon juice to keep the avocado from turning brown from oxidation but pineapple juice works just as well and adds a wonderful flavor to this salad. Although the Sub-Saharan climate does not support a highly productive agriculture, tropical fruits such as pineapples and avocados are now grown and enjoyed along with bananas, guavas, melons, and citrus fruits. This is a refreshing addition to a meal.

2 tablespoons *calorie-reduced or light* **mayonnaise**
1 tablespoon pineapple juice
1 teaspoon GARLIC OIL [see index]

2 cups pineapple chunks—fresh *or* **canned in juice—well-drained**
1 large avocado—peeled, pitted, and chopped

3 cups shredded lettuce
Freshly ground black pepper, to taste

In a serving bowl, combine mayonnaise, pineapple juice, and garlic oil. Stir to combine.

Add well-drained pineapple chunks and chopped avocado. Toss gently to coat the avocado and pineapple pieces with the dressing.

Scatter shredded lettuce over the top. Grind black pepper over lettuce.

Serve at once.

Yields 6 servings
adequate for 4 people

1/6 SERVING –   PROTEIN = 1.5 g.; FAT = 10.5 g.; CARBOHYDRATE = 19.1 g.;
CALORIES = 166; CALORIES FROM FAT = 57%

CENTRAL AFRICAN MILLET AND CORN SALAD WITH AVOCADO
Salade de Millet, Maïs, et Avocat
TPT -   1 hour and 42 minutes;
   1 hour = minimum flavor development period

Millet is the collective name for a group of small-seeded grasses of several genera that are believed to have originated in Africa. From Africa it traveled, as did the human species, to all parts of the world. Millet's use as human food and fodder for domestic animals has been documented, by paleoethnobotanists through identification of pollen, as far back in history as 10,000 years. This grain was so treasured by the ancients that it is considered to be one of the five sacred grains of the ancient Chinese. Millets are one of the principal grasses identified to have been plentiful in the area now known as the Sahara Dessert. Because many of these grasses are highly drought tolerant, they established well in Sub-Saharan Africa providing a dependable source of grain for bread. Millets are low in gluten and are the perfect grain for flatbreads. Teff, for example, the grain used to make injera in Africa, principally in Ethiopia, Eritrea, and in Djibouti, is a millet. Millets have a nutty flavor, especially when pan-toasted, making this salad not only nutritious but also very delicious.

CENTRAL AFRICAN MILLET AND CORN SALAD WITH AVOCADO (cont'd)

1/4 cup dry millet—rinsed and drained

2 cups water
Pinch salt

1 1/2 cups green (fresh) corn kernels cut from cob (about 3 large ears)
1 medium tomato—chopped
1 small scallion—trimmed, well rinsed, and *finely* chopped
2 tablespoons chopped parsley
1 small garlic clove—*very finely* chopped
1/2 teaspoon *very finely* chopped fresh gingerroot

1 tablespoon freshly squeezed lime juice
1 tablespoon *extra virgin* olive oil
1/2 teaspoon ground cumin
1/8 teaspoon ground red pepper (cayenne), or to taste
1/8 teaspoon ground allspice
1/4 teaspoon *light* brown sugar

1 small avocado—peeled, pitted and chopped

In a saucepan set over *LOW* heat, dry-roast the millet until lightly browned. *Monitor carefully because the grain can brown easily.*

Add water and salt. Increase heat to *LOW-MEDIUM*. Cover and allow to cook for about 20 minutes, or until the grains are soft. Drain well. Turn into a mixing bowl.

Add corn kernels, chopped tomato, *finely* chopped scallion, chopped parsley, and *very finely* chopped garlic and gingerroot. Toss to mix well.

In a small bowl, combine lime juice, olive oil, ground cumin, red pepper (cayenne), and allspice, and brown sugar. Stir to mix well. Pour over millet–corn mixture. Toss to coat the salad with dressing. Refrigerate for at least 1 hour to allow for flavor development.

When ready to serve, add chopped avocado. Toss. Turn into a chilled serving bowl.

Serve at once.

Yields 6 servings
adequate for 4 people

Note: This recipe can be doubled, when required.

1/6 SERVING – PROTEIN = 6.4 g.; FAT = 8.9 g.; CARBOHYDRATE = 39.6 g.;
CALORIES = 156; CALORIES FROM FAT = 51%

CUCUMBER SALAD WITH PEANUT – LIME DRESSING
Salade de Concombre
TPT - 12 minutes

Cucumbers have been dubbed one of the "dirty dozen" with good reason since enormously large quantities of pesticides are used by most farming operations. Albeit expensive, organic cucumbers are increasingly available in grocery stores so a bit of scrubbing allows the skin to be eaten safely. The dressing for this simple salad reflects the tastes of Central Africa and is a delightful dressing for crisp cucumber slices.

CENTRAL AFRICAN PEANUT – LIME DRESSING:
5 tablespoons freshly squeezed lime juice
2 tablespoons freshly ground, *unsalted, additive-free, smooth* peanut butter—brought to room temperature
2 tablespoons *calorie-reduced* or *light* mayonnaise

1/4 cup peanut oil
2 tablespoon sesame oil
1/4 teaspoon salt
6 drops *jalapeño chili* sauce

2 large *organic* cucumbers—well scrubbed, scored lengthwise with tines of a fork, and *thinly* sliced

1/4 cup chopped fresh coriander (*cilantro*)

In a small bowl, combine lime juice, peanut butter, and mayonnaise. Using a small wire whisk, blend thoroughly.

Add peanut and sesame oil, salt, and *jalapeño* sauce. Whisk until smooth. Set aside briefly.

When ready to serve, arrange cucumber slices in a spiral on a large, chilled platter. Spoon prepared salad dressing over following the same spiral pattern. Garnish with chopped coriander (*cilantro*).

Serve at once.

Yields 6 servings
adequate for 4 people

CUCUMBER SALAD WITH PEANUT – LIME DRESSING (cont'd)

Note: This recipe can be halved when required.

1/6 SERVING –   PROTEIN = 1.6 g.; FAT = 16.4 g.; CARBOHYDRATE = 3.4 g.;
CALORIES = 169; CALORIES FROM FAT = 87%

GABON "CHICKEN" STEW
Nyembwe
TPT - 45 minutes

It is not surprising that the cuisine of Gabon has incorporated techniques and ingredient combinations that remind one of basic French cuisine since Gabon is one of the four nations which emerged from the colonial region known as French Equatorial Africa. In addition, Gabon sits on the Atlantic Ocean and, as a result, became a crossroad of commerce and travel in Central Africa which introduced the Gabonese to foods of the nations to the east. Stews in the style of Ethiopia and Eritrea, known as wats, and the fiercely hot red pepper sauce from the same region, known as berebere, are mainstays of Gabonese cuisine. However, this stew, made with chicken and ground palm nuts in Gabon and with vegetarian soymeat analogue and ground hazelnuts as presented here, is probably closer to the Gabon cooking that was there before the European colonization. What is most remarkable is that it survives today.

1/2 cup ground *preservative-free* hazelnuts *or* hazelnut meal
1 3/4 cups water
2 tablespoons safflower *or* sunflower oil*
1 large onion—*thinly* sliced
2 tablespoons chopped mild green *chilies*
1 large garlic clove—*very finely* chopped
1/2 teaspoon salt
Several dashes ground red pepper (cayenne), or more to taste
Freshly ground black pepper, to taste

6 ounces *frozen* soy meat analogue strips

In a large saucepan set over *MEDIUM* heat, combine ground hazelnuts, water, oil, onion slices, chopped green *chilies*, *very finely* chopped garlic, salt, ground red pepper (cayenne), and black pepper. Stir to combine. Allow to come to the boil. *Reduce heat to LOW-MEDIUM* and cook for about 20 minutes. Stir frequently to prevent the stew from sticking to the bottom of the saucepan and add water, if necessary.

Add soymeat strips and continue to cook for about 10-15 minutes more. Turn into a heated serving bowl.

Serve hot over steamed rice or *couscous*.

Yields 6 servings
adequate for 4 people

Notes: *Red palm oil is more probably the oil a Gabonese cook would use. It is a highly saturated oil but if you wish to try it for a more authentic taste, seek out the product. If you do not have the good fortune to have an African or well-stocked international grocery nearby, red palm oil can be purchased from online mail order firms.

This recipe can be halved or doubled, when required.

1/6 SERVING –   PROTEIN = 22.8 g.; FAT = 7.8 g.; CARBOHYDRATE = 10.3 g.;
CALORIES = 256; CALORIES FROM FAT = 27%

CONGOLESE SUMMER SQUASH WITH PEANUTS AND GARLIC
Courge Jaune avec Bratilles et Ail
TPT - 30 minutes

Either yellow summer squash or zucchini can be used to replicate this Central African specialty and it is so good that heat-numbed summer appetites perk up and take notice. I usually accompany it with sautéed greens, any greens my kitchen garden can offer, and either cornbread or corn-on-the-cob. The amino acids in the corn or other grain chosen for this meal complement the leguminous proteins provided by the peanuts and then, as they say, "life is good."

CONGOLESE SUMMER SQUASH WITH PEANUTS AND GARLIC (cont'd)

1/2 cup *raw* peanuts

1 1/2 teaspoons *high-heat* safflower *or* sunflower oil
1 tablespoon GARLIC OIL *[see index]*
2 firm, medium yellow summer squashes—peeled and chopped into small cubes

Salt, to taste
1/2 teaspoon *light* brown sugar

Freshly ground mixed peppercorns—red, white, and black—to taste

Spray a non-stick-coated skillet with lecithin spray coating with olive oil. Place over *LOW-MEDIUM* heat. Add peanuts and pan-roast peanuts, shaking frequently, until well-colored. Remove from heat and set aside until required.

In a second, large skillet set over *MEDIUM* heat, heat safflower and garlic oil. Add cubed squash and cook, stirring frequently, until squash becomes *crisp-tender*—about 10 minutes.

Add salt, brown sugar, and roasted peanuts. Cook, stirring frequently, for about 5 minutes more. Turn into serving bowl.

Grind mixed peppercorns over.

Serve at once.

Yields 6 servings
adequate for 4 people

Note: This recipe can be halved or doubled, when required.

1/6 SERVING – PROTEIN = 3.3 g.; FAT = 9.2 g.; CARBOHYDRATE = 5.2 g.;
CALORIES = 112; CALORIES FROM FAT = 73%

CENTRAL AFRICAN EGGPLANT WITH TOMATO
Aubergine et Tomate
TPT - 44 minutes

Central Africa has always seemed to epitomize the phrase "darkest Africa," the phrase that the nineteenth century British explorers and journalists used, the phrase used by my social studies teacher to whom it was a whole lot less compelling than were Greece, Persia, Egypt, and Rome, and the phrase used by those who just plain did not know anything about the people who have lived there for millennia. The phrase came back to me as I searched for material for this book in the writings from the tribal areas and the journals of travelers, writings that really did not shed a whole lot of light on the food from this part of the world. Food and water scarcity, nomadic life styles, and differing tribal customs have led, in the attempt to consume sufficient protein for survival, to some strange recipes by Western standards. This recipe is not strange; in fact it is very familiar and comfortable. Do note that African eggplants are more bitter than are the ones we find in our grocery stores. For that reason I do advise you to leave the skin on and not to salt and drain the eggplant slices. The bitterness of the skin will give you a closer match in flavor.

2 tablespoons *high heat* sunflower *or* safflower oil
1 small eggplant—well-washed and sliced into 1/4-inch round slices

1 medium onion—halved and *thinly* sliced

2 cups canned, *diced* tomatoes
Freshly ground mixed peppercorns—black, red, and white—to taste
Pinch ground red pepper (cayenne) or to taste

Preheat oven to 350 degrees F.

Pour oil onto a baking sheet. Arrange slices on the baking sheet and bake in the 350 degree F. oven until the eggplant slices brown. Turn over and lightly brown the other side of each slice. Remove from pan. Chop into chunks and transfer to a non-stick-coated skillet. Transfer any oil remaining on baking sheet to the skillet too.

CENTRAL AFRICAN EGGPLANT WITH TOMATO (cont'd)

Set the skillet over *MEDIUM* heat. Add onion slices and sauté until onion is soft and translucent, *being careful not to allow the onions to brown.*

Add diced tomatoes and season with ground mixed peppercorns and ground red pepper (cayenne). Cook, stirring frequently, until thickened. Transfer to a warmed serving bowl and keep warm on a warming tray until ready to serve.

Yields 6 servings
adequate for 4 people

1/6 SERVING – PROTEIN = 1.5 g.; FAT = 4.7 g.; CARBOHYDRATE = 6.6 g.;
CALORIES = 71; CALORIES FROM FAT = 60%

CENTRAL AFRICAN SPINACH STEW WITH PEANUT BUTTER
Chilli um Bido

TPT - 21 minutes

Um'bido is a dish popular in Eritrea, in Ethiopia, in Somalia, and across the African continent. Differences from East to West seem to be in the variety of greens chosen, whether or not hot peppers are added, the intensity of the heat fired by hot peppers of choice or ground red pepper, as I prefer, and whether finely ground peanuts or peanut butter are preferred. This version, popular in the nations of Central Africa, combines the spinach with tomatoes, onions, and green bell peppers. Do feel free to take the seasoning to the incendiary levels enjoyed in both East and West Africa. We serve it over rice, polenta, pasta, and boiled potatoes.

1 tablespoon *extra virgin* olive oil
1 medium onion—*finely* chopped
1 cup canned, *diced* tomatoes
1/2 green bell pepper—chopped

6 cups baby spinach—stemmed, well-washed*
3 tablespoons chopped mild green *chilies*

1/4 cup freshly ground, *unsalted, additive-free*
    peanut butter—*smooth or chunky*, as
    preferred—*brought to room temperature*
1/4 teaspoon freshly ground black pepper
Pinch ground red pepper (cayenne), or to taste
Salt, to taste

In a non-stick-coated skillet set over *MEDIUM* heat, heat oil. Add *finely* chopped onion, diced tomatoes, and chopped green pepper, Sauté until onion is soft and translucent, *being careful not to allow any of the vegetables to brown.*

Add spinach and chopped green *chilies*. Cover and allow greens to wilt for several minutes. Remove cover.

Add peanut butter, black pepper, ground red pepper (cayenne), and salt. Stir to evenly distribute the seasoning. Cook, stirring constantly, for several minutes. Add a tablespoon or two of water, if necessary. Remove from heat. Turn into a heated serving bowl.

Serve at once.

Yields 6 servings
adequate for 4 people

Notes: *I often combine the spinach with bitter greens like collards, endive, escarole, broccoli rabe, or *arugula* to give the sauté depth. Even kale that has been picked before the frost is a nice addition.

This recipe is easily doubled, when required.

1/6 SERVING – PROTEIN = 5.0 g.; FAT = 7.5 g.; CARBOHYDRATE = 10.1 g.;
CALORIES = 128; CALORIES FROM FAT = 53%

Africa–Central African Republics

CONGOLESE BANANA *PHYLLO* TART
Filo Tarte Bananae
TPT - 38 minutes

Instead of pie crust for this traditional dessert, I choose to borrow phyllo pastry from North Africa, whose cuisines are often visited by Congolese cooks. It is a carefree dessert that bakes while you are attending to other parts of the meal.

14 sheets (9 x 13 inches) *phyllo* **pastry**—*defrosted*
2 tablespoons dry breadcrumbs
1 teaspoon soft, whipped butter

4 large bananas—*sliced*
2 tablespoons sugar
1 tablespoon *cold* **butter**—*diced*

Preheat oven to 350 degrees F. Prepare a 10-inch pie plate by coating with non-stick lecithin spray coating.

Take one of the half-sheets of *phyllo* and place it on a dry work surface. Using a pastry brush, lightly brush the sheet with the soft butter spread. Place the buttered pastry sheet onto the pie plate, allowing it to hang over the edge of the plate. Take a pinch of the breadcrumbs and sprinkle them over the pastry surface. Take another half-sheet of *phyllo*, butter it, and place it on top of the first sheet at a 45-degree angle. Sprinkle with crumbs. Continue with four more half-sheets of *phyllo*, positioning each at a 45-degree angle from the previous sheet. Carefully, using both hands, tuck the flaps from these first six half-sheets of *phyllo* into the pie plate under the nest base. Continue adding buttered half-sheets of *phyllo* in the same manner with a sprinkling of breadcrumbs but do not tuck these under, instead roll them gently toward the center. Press the center down to form a nest.

Arrange sliced bananas in the center "nest" area. Sprinkle with sugar. Scatter diced butter over. Bake in preheated 350 degree F. oven for 17-20 minutes. When the pastry is baked and puffed, remove from oven and carefully transfer the crisp *phyllo* pastry tart to the heated serving platter. Use two spatulas to loosen the nest from the pie plate.

Serve at once. Cut with a very sharp knife into pie-shaped wedges and transfer to each diner's plate.

Yields 6 servings
adequate for 6 people

Notes: *Cover *phyllo* sheets with a damp cotton towel to keep them moist while you are working.

Recipe can be very successfully halved using a 7- or 8-inch pie plate.

1/6 SERVING – PROTEIN = 3.2 g.; FAT = 3.3 g.; CARBOHYDRATE = 45.0 g.;
CALORIES = 210; CALORIES FROM FAT = 19%

BAKED BANANAS
Bananes
TPT - about 35 minutes

This is one of the most uncomplicated recipes in the world which I evolved way back when we were first married. Believe me, then I really needed simple! Many years later I found that bananas were prepared in the same way in Gabon.

2 tablespoons CLARIFIED BUTTER *or* **GHEE**
[see index]—*melted*
2 tablespoons freshly squeezed lime juice

6 medium bananas—*green-tipped and very firm*

2 tablespoons chopped, *unsalted, preservative-free*
nuts—hazelnuts, almonds, *or* pecans*
2 tablespoons breadcrumbs

Freshly grated nutmeg, to taste

BAKED BANANAS (cont'd)

Preheat oven to 350 degrees F. Prepare an *au gratin* dish, pie plate, or other oven-to-table baking dish by coating with non-stick lecithin spray coating.

Pour melted butter and lime juice into the baking dish.

Peel bananas and score lightly lengthwise with tines of a fork.

Combine ground nuts and breadcrumbs on a plate.

Roll each banana in the butter–lime juice mixture and then in the nut–breadcrumb mixture. Arrange these in the prepared baking dish.

Sprinkle with nutmeg.

Bake in preheated 350 degree F. oven for 15 minutes, or until heated through, but *not soft*. Remove from oven and allow to cool for about 5 minutes.

Serve warm.

Yields 6 servings

Notes: *Any *preservative-free* nuts, of choice, may be substituted.

This dessert can be prepared with or before the remainder of the menu and held on a warming tray until ready to serve. If these are prepared ahead, be sure to undercook slightly.

When required, this recipe can be easily halved, doubled, or tripled.

1/6 SERVING – PROTEIN = 5.0 g.; FAT = 5.1 g.; CARBOHYDRATE = 30.1 g.; CALORIES = 186; CALORIES FROM FAT = 25%

FRUIT SALAD IN THE STYLE OF THE CONGO
Salade de Fruits

TPT - 1 hour and 8 minutes;
1 hour = flavor development period

My mother often made a huge fruit salad for Sunday Night Supper whether she used the winter fruits available combined with canned fruits or the sweet fruits of summer and, just as they do in the Congo, she added lots of shredded coconut. It was a treat. Admittedly, avocado and papaya were not among the fruits she mixed because exotic fruits were rarely seen in upstate New York during World War II and for sometime thereafter.

1 *firm* avocado—peeled, seeded and chopped
1 small papaya—peeled, seeded, and chopped
2 medium pears—peeled, cored, and chopped
  or 4 canned pear halves—chopped
2 teaspoons sugar
6 *finely* chopped fresh mint leaves

1 red grapefruit—sectioned and pitted *or*
  1 can (15 ounces) red grapefruit sections
  —well-drained
Pinch ground cinnamon

1/2 cup shredded coconut—fresh *or* desiccated*

In a mixing bowl, combine chopped avocado, slices, papaya, and pears, sugar, and *finely* chopped mint leaves.

Section halved grapefruit. Add to fruit in mixing bowl. Squeeze the empty grapefruit halves over the fruit mixture, being sure to extract as much liquid as you can. Add the pinch of ground cinnamon and gently fold the fruit and juice together. Refrigerate for at least 1 hour to allow for flavor development.

Turn into a serving bowl. Sprinkle shredded coconut over.

Serve well-chilled.

Yields 6 servings
adequate for 4 people

Notes: *If you have freshly shredded coconut, so much the better. If not, dried coconut will do.

This recipe can be doubled, when required. When I expand this recipe, instead of doubling the fruit ingredients listed above, I add sliced red bananas and navel orange sections.

1/6 SERVING – PROTEIN = 1.8 g.; FAT = 8.6 g.; CARBOHYDRATE = 30.2 g.; CALORIES = 201; CALORIES FROM FAT = 39%

Chad

I remember pictures of Lake Chad taken in the 1960s when I was teaching and studying the critical importance of the wetlands on Long Island that were being violated by development and by the practices of the Army Corps of Engineers, who in their wisdom and under pressure from politicians and developers, were trying to preserve beaches and were not allowing an island to be an island. Aerial pictures of Lake Chad today are even more disheartening. Some 7,000 years ago Lake Chad covered about 130,000 square miles, encompassing an area about three times the size of the Commonwealth of Pennsylvania. Each year it is shrinking as the desert encroaches with recent measurements showing that the lake in less than 7,000 square miles.

The West African nation of Chad, which encompasses 459,753 square miles and is twenty-first in the world in terms of land mass, is named for Lake Chad. It is dominated by desert in the North and relatively fertile savanna terrain in the South, between which is an arid region. For over 2,000 years the Chadian Basin has been home to agricultural societies. The earliest of these societies was the Sao, who were defeated by the Kanem who formed the first empire. The Kanem Empire developed at the end of the first millennium AD. It gave way to successive empires that controlled the trade routes that criss-crossed the Sahara but whose influence remained well north of the fertile southern grasslands.

During the colonial period France claimed Chad and incorporated it into French Equatorial Africa. After World War II, France granted Chad the status of overseas territory but inexperience in governing, the diversity of the population, and the priorities of the various segments of the population led to a civil war which began in 1965, a civil war of which Libyans, their neighbors to the North, took advantage. As the world stood by, Libyan troops moved into Chad and became involved in the conflict. In 1987 the Chadians finally forced Omar Kadaffi's forces out of Chad. Continued and widespread challenges to the present government have created more instability.

Peoples of over two hundred different ethnic groups now live in Chad bringing their own customs, religions, and languages to one of the poorest and most corrupt nations on the earth. Eighty percent of the population lives below the poverty level. Add to this burden the steady influx of refugees from the Sudan's Darfur region and those from the Central African Republic and you can understand the enormity of the crisis in this country. Living predominately as subsistence farmers or herders, the lack of a lavish, expansive cuisine is understandable. Meat, millet, and beans are very important to what is not a diverse cuisine; a few simple foods satisfy nutritional needs and a vegetarian has to be creative.

Africa–Chad

Soup of Greens with Corn and Peanut Butter

~

Yam Salad with Scallions
Batata Salade

~~~~~~~~~~~~~~~~~~~~~~

Beans in Coconut Milk
M'Baazi wa Nazi

Rice

Sautéed Squashes with Peanuts
Courgettes aux Arachides

~~~~~~~~~~~~~~~~~~~~~~

Tea - Infused Dried Fruits with Whipped Cream

Easy Ginger Ice Cream

Almond – Pistachio Sweet
Loz

SOUP OF GREENS WITH CORN AND PEANUT BUTTER IN THE STYLE OF CHAD
TPT - 18 minutes

This is a far cry from a Welsh lettuce soup but it is the same principle. This is also, I suppose, a far cry from "koko na nyama," a traditional Chadian soup which is made with beef and koko leaves. We find this soup serves well as a first course or as lunch for hungry gardeners who can bring the greens right from the garden as they come in for lunch. I always accompany it with hard rolls or chunks of French bread.

1 tablespoon peanut oil
1 medium onion—*finely* chopped

5 cups VEGETABLE STOCK FROM SOUP
 [see index] *or* other vegetarian stock of choice
1/4 cup freshly ground, *unsalted, additive-free*
 peanut butter—*smooth or chunky, as preferred*
 —*brought to room temperature*

8 cups well-washed mixed greens—spinach, lettuces, escarole, chard, collards, *or* whatever you have in abundance
1/2 cup green (fresh) *or frozen* **corn kernels**
Freshly ground mixed peppercorns—black, red, and white—to taste

In a small kettle set over *MEDIUM* heat, heat oil. Add *finely* chopped onion and sauté until onion is soft and translucent, *being careful not to allow the onion to brown.*

Add vegetable stock and peanut butter. Using a wire whisk, stir until peanut butter is integrated. Allow to come to the boil.

Add greens, corn, and ground mixed peppercorns. Stir frequently until greens are wilted. Turn into a heated tureen.

Serve into heated soup bowls.

Yields 6 servings
adequate for 4 people

Note: This recipe can be halved or doubled, when required.

1/6 SERVING – PROTEIN = 6.0 g.; FAT = 6.8 g.; CARBOHYDRATE = 11.7 g.;
CALORIES = 123; CALORIES FROM FAT = 50%

Africa–Chad

CHADIAN YAM SALAD WITH SCALLIONS
Batata Salade

TPT - 4 hours and 32 minutes;
30 minutes = potato chilling period;
3 hours = marination period

For many years we enjoyed this salad without knowing that it was native to the area of Africa now known as Chad. In Africa it would be made with true yams, a starchy tuber of Old World, not New World, origin popular in Europe, Asia, and Africa. They are scaly, hairy, and not at all sweet. The dry, pale-skinned members of the Morning Glory family, known as sweetpotatoes would be a good choice for this recipe since they are less sweet than are the southern grown sweet, moist variety misnamed yams in the 1930s by a Louisiana ad agency.

2 large sweetpotatoes

2 medium scallions—trimmed, well-rinsed, and *thinly* sliced
1/4 cup vegetable oil
2 tablespoons freshly squeezed lemon juice
1/4 teaspoon freshly ground black pepper

1 medium tomato—cut into small wedges—for garnish

Wash and scrub sweetpotatoes well. Boil, *unpeeled*, in a large quantity of water until *fork–tender*, but *not soft* —about 20 to 45 minutes depending upon size. Peel and refrigerate for about 30 minutes.

Slice *cooled* sweetpotatoes crosswise and arrange in an overlapping spiral in a large pie plate.

In a jar with tightly fitting lid, combine scallion slices, oil, lemon juice, and black pepper. Shake vigorously. Pour dressing over sliced sweetpotatoes. Cover with plastic wrap.

Refrigerate for at least 3 hours. *Carefully* turn sweetpotatoes slices occasionally during marination period.

Using a slotted pie server, transfer sweetpotatoes slices to serving dish; include scallion slices, if possible. Garnish with tomato wedges.

Serve well-chilled.

Yields 6 servings
adequate for 4-6 people

Note: This recipe is easily halved or doubled, when required.

1/6 SERVING (drained of marination oil) –
PROTEIN = 2.3 g.; FAT = 2.1 g.; CARBOHYDRATE = 20.7 g.;
CALORIES = 108; CALORIES FROM FAT = 18%

CHADIAN BEANS IN COCONUT MILK
M'Baazi wa Nazi

TPT - 40 minutes

The cuisines of East Africa, at times, are strikingly similar, but nuances can be observed and appreciated. A very similar preparation from Kenya, called simply "M'Baazi," borrows more from the Indian subcontinent when it comes to flavoring. Here, the amazing seasoning turmeric, prized for its anti-inflammatory properties, and green chilies are the major seasonings with cardamom, red pepper flakes, and black pepper.

I do encourage you to cook dried beans to prepare this dish; soak overnight before cooking or cook them using the same-day-method included here. Pigeon peas or black-eyed peas are generally used in Chad but some of the interesting heirloom beans, such as tiger eye beans, or red, black, and butterscotch calypso beans, and cranberry and pinto beans look beautiful in this curry too.

Africa–Chad

CHADIAN BEANS IN COCONUT MILK (cont'd)

1 cup dried pigeon peas/black-eyed peas, or other bean of choice
1 quart water

1 quart water

2 tablespoons safflower *or* sunflower oil
1 large onion—coarsely chopped

1/2 teaspoon ground turmeric
1 tablespoon *mild* green *chilies or hot* green *chilies*, as preferred
1/2 teaspoon red pepper flakes
Pinch ground cardamom
Freshly ground black pepper, to taste

1 cup *light, sulfite-free* coconut milk*

Put beans and the quart of water into a saucepan. Bring to the boil over *MEDIUM-HIGH* heat, reduced heat to *LOW*, and simmer for 5 minutes. Cover tightly and allow to stand at room temperature for 2 hours. Drain beans and return to the saucepan.

Add the second quartful of water to the beans and set over *MEDIUM-HIGH* heat. Allow to come to the boil and immediately reduce heat to *LOW-MEDIUM*. Allow beans to *simmer, not boil*, for 2 hours, or until tender. Drain.

In a saucepan set over *MEDIUM* heat, heat oil. Add chopped onion. Sauté until onion is soft and translucent, *being careful not to allow the onion to brown*.

Add *finely* ground turmeric, chopped green *chilies*, and red pepper flakes. Cook, stirring constantly, for about two minutes.

Add cooked beans and coconut milk. *Reduce the heat to LOW.* Cover and allow to simmer for about 15 minutes, or until the mixture thickens. Stir frequently. Remove from heat and allow to come to room temperature.

Serve at room temperature over rice.

Yields 6 servings
adequate for 4 people

Notes: *Chadians prefer to use the very thick coconut milk but we choose to use the low-fat, light coconut milk to reduce our intake of saturated fats.

Canned black-eyed peas are available, if you do not have time to soak and cook the beans. They are often available canned in what is called "Southern-style" in which bacon and bacon fat are used in the preparation. You, of course, do not want the "Southern style" for this dish.

This recipe can be halved or doubled, when required.

1/6 SERVING – PROTEIN = 7.7 g.; FAT = 6.4 g.; CARBOHYDRATE = 22.5 g.;
CALORIES = 172; CALORIES FROM FAT = 34%

CHADIAN SAUTÉED SQUASHES WITH PEANUTS
Courgettes aux Arachides
TPT - 20 minutes

One year I trained the zucchini up and around the pickets of the fence that separated my small suburban vegetable and herb garden from the yard of the neighbor who hated vegetable gardens, an attitude he assumed after an unsuccessful season of tomato growing. Although a sizable portion of the ripened zucchini disappeared, presumably to the kitchen next door, and a sizable portion were poked full of holes, presumably by the neighbors obstreperous son, the harvest was still sufficiently large enough to send me searching for different ways to use zucchini. This simple recipe turned up and has remained in my files.

The area of Pennsylvania to which we retired is still home to large farm families who select the larger squashes in the grocery stores and at the farmers' market, overlooking the small squashes. Truth be known, I would much rather prepare several small squashes, especially if they are to be sautéed as in this dish. The smaller squashes are usually firmer, because they contain less water, and the seeds are under-developed and need not be removed.

Africa–Chad

CHADIAN SAUTÉED SQUASHES WITH PEANUTS (cont'd)

1 tablespoon sunflower, safflower, *or* canola oil
1 tablespoon CLARIFIED BUTTER *[see index]*
2 small zucchini—trimmed and diced
2 small yellow summer squash—trimmed, peeled, and diced

1 tablespoon water
1/2 cup *roasted*, but *unsalted*, peanuts—coarsely chopped
1/4 teaspoon ground cumin
Pinch salt
Freshly ground black pepper, to taste

In a non-stick-coated skillet set over *LOW-MEDIUM* heat, combine oil and clarified butter. Add diced squashes. Cook, stirring frequently, for about 10 minutes, or until *crisp-tender*.

Add water, peanuts, ground cumin, salt, and pepper. Stir to distribute seasonings. Continue cooking, stirring frequently, for about 5 minutes. Turn into a heated serving bowl.

Serve at once.

Yields 6 servings
adequate for 4 people

Note: This recipe can be halved or doubled, when required.

1/6 SERVING – PROTEIN = 2.5 g.; FAT = 8.7 g.; CARBOHYDRATE = 2.9 g.;
CALORIES = 95; CALORIES FROM FAT = 82%

TEA – INFUSED DRIED FRUITS WITH WHIPPED CREAM IN THE STYLE OF CHAD
TPT - 1 hour and 23 minutes;
1 hour = rehydration period

Dried fruits have always had a place in our winter diet. We preserve the fresh flavor of many of our favorites by dehydrating in-season fruits during the summer and the fall. This recipe was evolved in an effort to find another way to enjoy our dried treasures and, at the same time, to capitalize on the health benefits of black tea. Chadians also reconstitute dried fruits using tea. This is a wonderful end to a dinner that has been inspired by the dishes of East Africa.

1 1/2 teaspoons English Breakfast tea leaves
2 cups *boiling* water

18 *preservative-free* dried whole apricots
6 *preservative-free* dried pineapple slices
12 pitted, *preservative-free* prunes
6 tablespoons *preservative-free dark* raisins

1/2 cup heavy whipping cream
1 tablespoon confectioners' sugar

8 teaspoons freshly squeezed orange juice

In a *warmed* teapot, combine tea and *boiling* water. Steep for about 10 minutes to form a strong tea. Pour brewed tea through a tea strainer into a pie plate.

Arrange dried fruits in the *hot* tea. Allow to rehydrate for at least 1 hour.

Using the electric mixer fitted with *chilled* beaters or by hand using a *chilled* wire whisk, beat heavy cream in a *chilled* bowl until soft peaks form. While continuing to beat, add confectioners' sugar. Beat until stiff peaks form. Refrigerate until required.

When ready to serve, arrange a rehydrated pineapple slice, three apricots, two prunes, and a tablespoonful of raisins attractively on each of four plates. Sprinkle 2 teaspoonfuls of orange juice over the fruits on each plate.

Divide the whipped cream among the plated fruits, placing a dollop on each.

Serve at once.

Yields 4 individual servings

Note: This recipe is easily halved or doubled, when required.

1/4 SERVING – PROTEIN = 2.4 g.; FAT = 11.3 g.; CARBOHYDRATE = 33.7 g.;
CALORIES = 235; CALORIES FROM FAT = 43%

Africa–Chad

EASY GINGER ICE CREAM

TPT - 8 hours and 12 minutes;
8 hours = freezing period

A creative hotel chef in the Admiral Hotel's Pinafore Restaurant in Copenhagen first introduced us to an exciting tasting ice cream on Christmas Eve Day, 1985. We came home and created this version. Years later we found that ginger ice cream is also enjoyed in Chad, albeit with lots of egg yolks and a fresh mint-leaf garnish.

1 cup heavy whipping cream

2/3 cup *fat-free* sweetened condensed milk
1 tablespoon AUSTRALIAN SWEET GINGER SYRUP *[see index]* **or the syrup from jarred stem ginger**
1/2 cup *fat-free* pasteurized eggs* (the equivalent of 2 eggs)
2 teaspoons pure vanilla extract

2 tablespoons *very finely* chopped *crystallized* ginger

Fresh mint leaves

Notes: *Because raw eggs present the danger of *Salmonella* poisoning, commercially-available pasteurized eggs are recommended for use in preparing this dish.

This recipe is easily doubled, when required. Use a 9 x 5 x 3-inch non-stick-coated loaf pan.

Prepare a 7 x 3 x 2-inch non-stick-coated loaf pan by placing it in the freezer until required.

Using an electric mixer fitted with *chilled* beaters or by hand, using a *chilled* wire whisk, beat heavy cream in a *chilled* bowl until stiff. Set aside.

In a large bowl, combine sweetened condensed milk, ginger syrup, pasteurized eggs, and vanilla extract. Stir to blend thoroughly. *Whisk-fold* stiffly whipped cream and *very finely* chopped *crystallized* ginger *gently*, but *thoroughly*, into egg–milk mixture.

Pour mixture into chilled loaf pan. Spread evenly. Cover tightly with aluminum foil. Freeze overnight, or until firm—about 8 hours.

Either scoop ice cream from pan to serve or remove entire block of ice cream from pan and slice. Garnish each serving with a mint leaf or two.

Leftovers should be returned to the freezer, tightly covered.

Yields about eight 1/2-cup servings

1/8 SERVING (i. e., per 1/2 cupful) –
PROTEIN = 4.2 g.; FAT = 9.8 g.; CARBOHYDRATE = 24.0 g.;
CALORIES = 202; CALORIES FROM FAT = 44%

CHADIAN ALMOND – PISTACHIO SWEET

Log

TPT - 37 minutes;
15 minutes = resting and absorption period

The fragrance that orange blossom water gives this confection makes this recipe one of my most treasured sweets. Chad is a country whose inhabitants "eat to live" and yet, this dessert reflects a suppressed "live to eat" spirit. We love these with tea or coffee in the afternoon.

CHADIAN ALMOND – PISTACHIO SWEET (cont'd)

1/4 cup shelled, *unsalted* pistachio nuts—*finely* chopped
3 tablespoons confectioners' sugar

1 cup ground, *preservative-free* almonds *or* almond meal
1/2 cup confectioners' sugar
2 tablespoons orange blossom water

In another small bowl, combine *finely* chopped pistachio nuts and the 2 tablespoonfuls confectioners' sugar. Stir to mix. Set aside until required.

In a mixing bowl, combine ground almonds and the 1/2 cupful confectioners' sugar. Stir to combine. *Gradually* add orange blossom water, stirring it with each addition until a stiff paste begins to form. Knead with your hands until it is smooth. Set aside for about 15 minutes to rest and allow for the orange blossom water to be evenly absorbed.

Form the almond mixture into small balls about the size of walnuts. Roll each ball in the reserved confectioners' sugar with pistachio nuts. Place on a serving plate to serve or into an airtight container until required.

Yields 16 confections

Note: This recipe can be doubled, when required.

1/16 SERVING (per confections) –
PROTEIN = 3.2 g.; FAT = 8.6 g.; CARBOHYDRATE = 8.8 g.; CALORIES = 118; CALORIES FROM FAT = 66%

Côte d'Ivoire

During the fifteenth century, when the Portuguese were the predominant traders to Africa, areas of the coast of West Africa were identified by their exports—that is, Gold Coast, Grain Coast (or Pepper Coast), Coast of the Five and Stripes (which referenced a much sought-after cotton fabric), and Slave Coast. Cote d'Ivoire, Ivory Coast, was also called Teeth Coast since the ivory obtained from this region was generally put to use in Europe to make false teeth.

France had moved early to stake its claims in Africa and in 1843 a treaty made Ivory Coast a protectorate of France. In 1892, coincident with the "scramble for Africa" by European nations, France secured its position in West Africa by declaring the protectorates it has established to be colonies, thus blocking other nations, notably the British, from moving into the region. Côte d'Ivoire has been one of the more successful and prosperous nations to be formed from the huge French colonial possession known as French West Africa. This colony included, in addition to Ivory Coast, the countries we know today as Senegal, Mali, Burkina Faso, Benin, and Guinea. The French made the decision not to assimilate the populations of their African colonies as French citizens but instead treated them harshly and used them as labor in their exploitation of natural resources. The indigenous population, although subjects of France, had no political rights and were subject to a unique and separate system of law known as the *indigénat*. As part of their tax liability, they worked in the mines, on plantations, as porters, and on public projects. They were also conscripted into the military. French citizens moved into the colony and used the native population to plant and harvest coffee, cocoa, bananas, and palm oil crops for export. One third of the cocoa, coffee, and banana plantations were owned by French citizens. By the end of World War II, the French colonials across West Africa were vocal in their desire for self-rule but it was not until 1960 that Côte d'Ivoire gained its independence.

The climate of Côte d'Ivoire ranges from equatorial at the southern coast to tropical in the central regions to semiarid in the far north. Despite the fact that only about eight percent of the land mass is considered arable, agriculture still drives the market-based economy of this country that is about twice the size of the state of Florida. It is the world's largest exporter of cocoa beans but hardwood exports have been increasing to the point that Côte d'Ivoire's exports surpass those of Brazil. Deforestation is an increasing concern since forest management has taken a backseat to profit.

With the fall in world coffee and cocoa prices, Ivory Coast has determined to move forward to bring education to all of its people and thus provide a work force to move to a more service- and manufacturing-based economy. It is estimated that perhaps forty percent of the population is illiterate which has resulted in a large influx of foreign workers. Approximately sixty-seven percent of the population is composed of foreigners, foreign workers, and refugees from neighboring nations. Social changes have been slowed due to political upheaval and two civil wars in recent years have resulted in the stationing of several thousand French and United Nation troops to help the Ivorians resolve their differences and execute the commitments made in the Linas–Marcoussis Peace Accord in 2003 and in the more recent Ouagadougou Political Agreement.

Food available in urban areas show a strong French influence but a native diet, common to most of this area of Africa, is consumed by rural families.

Africa – Côte d'Ivoire

Avocado and Pineapple Appetizer Spread
Mettre en Appetit de Poire d'Avocat et Ananas

Sliced Avocados
served with
Lime Mayonnaise with Hot Peppers and Ginger
Mayonnaise Pili Pili

~

Chilled Avocado Soup with Garlic
Soupe d'Avocat Abidjanaise

Cream of Sweetpotato Soup
Veloute d'Ignames

~

Egg and Potato Salad	Fruit Salad with Citrus *Vinaigrette*
Salad aux Oeufs et Pomme de Terre	*Salads de Fruits*

~~~~~~~~~~~~~~~~~~~~~

Tofu "Tuna" – Stuffed Cucumber Boats
Concombre Fourré avec Poisson

Sliced Tomatoes with Salt and Sugar

~~~~~

Spicy Sweetpotato and Tomato Stew
Igname et Tomate

over

Steamed Rice

~~~~~~~~~~~~~~~~~~~~~

Lime Pudding with Sweetened Condensed Milk
Dessert au Citrones Vertes

Pastry with Banana and Chocolate
Mille-feuille aux Banane et Chocolate

AVOCADO AND PINEAPPLE APPETIZER SPREAD IN THE STYLE OF THE *CÔTE D'IVOIRE*
Mettre en Appetit de Poire d'Avocat et Ananas
TPT - 7 minutes

Côte d'Ivoire in West Africa, known to American school children as the Ivory Coast, is the largest producer of pineapples in the world. Since pineapples are enjoyed, not just exported, many native dishes have found novel ways to include pineapple. This Ivoirian spread, popular in the "maquis," is an example of an extraordinarily simple and unusual way to use pineapple. Some people just use the pineapple bits as a garnish; we prefer to incorporate crushed pineapple into the spread. This is wonderful on crackers or as a dip for crudités. It is a welcome change from guacamole.

Africa – Côte d'Ivoire

**AVOCADO AND PINEAPPLE APPETIZER SPREAD
IN THE STYLE OF THE *CÔTE D'IVOIRE*** (cont'd)

**1 large, ripe avocado
1/2 teaspoon freshly squeezed lemon juice
Pinch salt**

**2 tablespoons *crushed* pineapple—very well-drained
Fresh pineapple *tidbits*, for garnish**

Halve the avocado and remove the pit. Using a spoon, scoop the flesh out and put it into a bowl.

Add lemon juice and salt. Mash well.

Add *well-drained crushed* pineapple. Mix well. Turn into a small chilled serving bowl.* Garnish with pineapple *tidbits*.

Serve with crackers, *crudités*, and/or chips.

Yields 3/4 cupful

Notes: *Serve within 30 minutes of preparation. Even with the lemon juice and pineapple you may get some browning from oxidation.

This recipe is easily doubled, when required.

1/12 SERVING (per tablespoonful) –
PROTEIN = 0.4 g.; FAT = 2.7 g.; CARBOHYDRATE = 1.5 g.;
CALORIES = 30; CALORIES FROM FAT = 81%

IVORIAN LIME MAYONNAISE
WITH HOT PEPPERS AND GINGER
Mayonnaise Pili Pili

TPT - 3 minutes

A portion of West African bordering on the Gulf of Guinea was traditionally referred to as the Grain Coast or the Pepper Coast during the period of exploration as trade was developed. The name derives from the pepper spice (Aframomum melegueto) known as "grain of paradise." During the early years of Portuguese trade, hot chilies, from this area of Africa, were introduced to Europe. I first encountered the super hot cultivar Capsicum frutescens, known as pili pili or piri piri, as seasoning for almonds in Portugal in 1977 and can attest to the fact that they can be very hot to the uninitiated. Mayonnaise, on the other hand, has a cooling effect. Mayonnaise with very finely diced chilies is a sauce/dressing often served in Côte d'Ivoire but even that is too hot for some. The following recipe can be adjusted to your taste by increasing the ground red pepper (cayenne) or brave on and try very finely chopped pili pili.

**1/2 cup *calorie-reduced or light* mayonnaise
    or BLENDER MAYONNAISE** *[see index]*
**1 tablespoon freshly squeezed lime juice
1/4 teaspoon ground red pepper (cayenne)
1/4 teaspoon ground ginger**

In a small bowl, combine mayonnaise, lime juice, ground red pepper (cayenne), and ground ginger. Stir to combine thoroughly. Taste and adjust seasoning when necessary. Turn into a dish for dipping or dress individual salads.

Serve as a sauce or dip.

Yields 12 servings

Note: This recipe can be doubled or tripled, when required.

1/12 SERVING (about 2 teaspoonfuls) –
PROTEIN = 0.0 g.; FAT = 3.3 g.; CARBOHYDRATE = 1.1 g.;
CALORIES = 35; CALORIES FROM FAT = 85%

Africa–Côte d'Ivorie

CHILLED AVOCADO SOUP WITH GARLIC IN THE STYLE OF THE IVORY COAST
Soupe d'Avocat Abidjanaise

TPT - 2 hours and 7 minutes;
2 hours = chilling period

This is a most refreshing and nutritious soup, easily made yet very elegant. It is a good choice for a summer dinner party or on a warm spring evening. We like to garnish it with chopped fresh tomato for color and interest.

2 large, *ripe* avocados—peeled and chopped
2 medium garlic clove—peeled and chopped

2 1/2 cups VEGETARIAN WHITE STOCK
  [see index]*
2 tablespoons freshly squeezed lime juice, or more to taste
2 tablespoons *fat-free* dairy sour cream *or* YOGURT CRÈME [see index]
2 dashes Tabasco Sauce, or to taste
Salt, to taste

Fat-free* dairy sour cream *or* YOGURT *CRÈME [see index], **for garnish**
Chopped fresh coriander (*cilantro*) leaves *and/or* chopped chives, for garnish
1 medium tomato—cored, seeded, and *finely* chopped—for garnish

In the work bowl of the food processor fitted with steel knife, combine chopped avocado and garlic. Process until smooth.

Add vegetable stock, lime juice, 2 tablespoonfuls sour cream or yogurt *crème*, Tabasco Sauce, and salt. Process until smooth.

Chill for at least 2 hours before serving.

Pour into a *chilled* soup tureen. Serve into *chilled* soup cups, garnishing each serving with a dollop of *fat-free* sour cream or yogurt *crème*, if desired, a sprinkling of chopped herbs, and a spoonful of diced tomato.

Yields 5 cupfuls which is adequate for 6 first-course servings

Notes: *Commercially-available vegetable stocks vary in flavor and are often quite salty. With this particular soup, you do not want strong vegetable flavors to overwhelm the fruit flavors. In addition, you do not want the color of the avocado soup ruined by a stock that has too much tomato. It is infinitely better to make your own stock for this soup.

This recipe can be halved or doubled, when required.

1/6 SERVING –   PROTEIN = 3.0 g.; FAT = 16.5 g.; CARBOHYDRATE = 9.7 g.;
CALORIES = 184; CALORIES FROM FAT = 81%

IVORIAN CREAM OF SWEETPOTATO SOUP
Velouté d'Ignames

TPT - 1 hour and 23 minutes

I have always been a fan of creamed soups. Perhaps it is the result of growing up in a family with roots all over northern Europe. The sweetpotato is not, to my recollection, a vegetable that my grandmother or mother ever turned into a cream soup despite the fact that there were bushel baskets of sweetpotatoes in our root cellars during the winter months. The first time I tasted this velvety soup, I wondered why they had not experimented with this vegetable; the recipe is strikingly similar to the creamy white potato and leek soup that was frequently on our table.

Do note that the dry, pale-skinned members of the Morning Glory family, known as sweetpotatoes, are the best choice for this recipe. As mentioned elsewhere in this volume, our stores also carry a southern grown sweet, moist variety. The name yam was given to this variety in the 1930s by a Louisiana ad agency. True yams are a starchy tuber of Old World, not New World, origin which is scaly, hairy, and not at all sweet. True yams are more popular in Europe, Asia, and Africa. World agricultural statistics reveal that the sweet, dark orange tubers which we call yams are favored by North Americans and Australians, but by few others. To further complicate this already complicated picture, please note that potatoes are members of the Nightshade family and, consequently, not even related to the wonderful misnamed New World vegetable popularly know as the sweetpotato or the yam.

IVORIAN CREAM OF SWEETPOTATO SOUP (cont'd)

2 *thinly* sliced leeks—*white and very light green portions only**

2 tablespoons butter
1/2 cup *finely* chopped onion

4 cups diced sweetpotato
5 cups water
1 teaspoon salt

1/4 teaspoon freshly ground *white* pepper
1 cup light cream *or* half and half, if preferred

Wash *thinly* sliced leeks in several changes of cold water and, using your fingers, remove all sand and grit. Drain thoroughly.

In a small kettle, with cover, set over *MEDIUM* heat, melt butter. Add *well-rinsed* leek slices and *finely* chopped onion. Sauté until onion is soft and translucent, *being careful not to allow vegetables to brown*.

Add diced sweetpotato, water, and salt. Allow to come to the boil. Reduce heat to *LOW-MEDIUM*, partially cover, and simmer for about 45 minutes, or until vegetables are *very tender*.

Purée two or three ladlefuls at a time in the electric blender, or in the food processor fitted with steel knife, or mash finely and press through a fine sieve or FOOD MILL.** Pour into a clean saucepan set over *LOW-MEDIUM* heat.

Stir in *white* pepper and cream. Allow to heat through. Turn into a heated soup tureen.

Serve into heated cream soup cups or bowls.

Yields 8 cupfuls

Notes: *Save green portions for use in preparing soup stocks.

**The base for this soup may be prepared ahead to this point and refrigerated for a day or two or frozen for future use. Defrost in the refrigerator, season, add milk, and heat.

1/8 SERVING (i. e., per cupful) –
PROTEIN = 2.0 g.; FAT = 5.7 g.; CARBOHYDRATE = 10.8 g.;
CALORIES = 103; CALORIES FROM FAT = 50%

IVORIAN EGG AND POTATO SALAD
Salad aux Oeufs et Pomme de Terre

TPT - 51 minutes;
30 minutes = potato chilling period

While attending a symposium some years ago, the vegetarian lunch option provided was an egg salad sandwich which included finely chopped onion. I have never made my egg salad with onion but the flavor it added was impressive. When I encountered this egg salad from Côte d'Ivoire, I again encountered onion but in this the onion flavor was contributed by scallions. The addition of diced potato was the big surprise this time. I was again impressed.

1 large potato—peeled and diced
3 cups *boiling* water

3 chilled, *hard-cooked* eggs—peeled and chopped
5 scallions—trimmed, well-rinsed, and sliced into 1/4-inch pieces
Freshly ground black pepper

3 tablespoons *reduced-calorie or light* mayonnaise
1 1/2 tablespoons PLAIN YOGURT *[see index]*
   or commercially-available plain yogurt
1 teaspoon *Dijon* mustard with white wine

In a saucepan set over *MEDIUM* heat, combine diced potato and *boiling* water. Boil for about 18 minutes, or until *crisp-tender*. Drain well. Chill for at least 30 minutes.

In a mixing bowl, combine cooked, *chilled* potato, chopped *hard-cooked* eggs, sliced scallions, and black pepper. Set aside briefly.

In a small dish, combine mayonnaise, yogurt, and mustard. Mix well. Add dressing to egg–potato mixture. *Gently* fold dressing into egg mixture. Turn into serving bowl. Refrigerate until ready to serve.

Serve chilled. Refrigerate leftovers.

Yields 6 servings
adequate for 4 people

1/6 SERVING – PROTEIN = 4.0 g.; FAT = 5.4 g.; CARBOHYDRATE = 7.0 g.;
CALORIES = 95; CALORIES FROM FAT = 51%

Africa–Côte d'Ivoire

IVORIAN FRUIT SALAD WITH CITRUS *VINAIGRETTE*
Salade de Fruits

TPT - 1 hour and 6 minutes;
1 hour = flavor development period

The beautiful color that will fill your salad bowl can only be matched by the beautiful flavor that will descend upon your taste buds.

CITRUS *VINAIGRETTE*:
- 2 tablespoons *extra virgin* olive oil
- 2 teaspoons freshly squeezed orange juice
- 2 teaspoons freshly squeezed lime juice
- 2 teaspoons guava nectar
- 2 drops *jalapeño* pepper sauce *or* Tabasco Sauce, if preferred*
- Salt, to taste
- Freshly ground black pepper, to taste

1 can (15 ounces) red grapefruit sections—well-drained and sliced in half crosswise
1 1/2 cups diced papaya
1 *ripe, but firm* avocado—peeled, pitted, and chopped into bite-sized pieces
1/4 cup *well-drained, crushed* pineapple

In a jar or cruet, combine olive oil, orange juice, lime juice, guava nectar, *jalapeño* sauce, salt, and pepper. Shake vigorously. Set aside briefly.

In a salad bowl, combine grapefruit pieces, diced papaya, chopped avocado, and *crushed* pineapple. Again, shake dressing vigorously. Pour dressing over fruit. Gently stir fruit to expose it to the dressing. Refrigerate for 1 hour to allow for flavor development.

Serve with a slotted spoon.

Yields 6 servings
adequate for 4 people

Note: If your taste buds are well-trained, you can increase the hot pepper seasoning. Ivorians appreciate the hot aftertaste.

1/6 SERVING – PROTEIN = 1.8 g.; FAT = 9.3 g.; CARBOHYDRATE = 22.0 g.;
CALORIES = 167; CALORIES FROM FAT = 50%

TOFU "TUNA" – STUFFED CUCUMBER BOATS
Concombre Fourré avec Poisson

TPT - 17 hours and 32 minutes;
8 hours = freezing period;
8 hours = beancurd draining period;
1 hour = refrigeration period

An Ivorian recipe in which flaked fish is used to stuff hollowed-out cucumber halves seemed to me to be a lovely summer entrée but we made a complete break with meat and fish in 1973 and assumed a vegetarian lifestyle that has satisfied us for over forty years. Probably one of the last non-vegetarian lunches I ate that April was a tuna fish salad sandwich on whole wheat toast. It was a favorite "take-to-work" lunch of mine for years. A mention of a vegan "tuna" product sparked my imagination and, believe it or not, the problem of texture was solved by a college student who posted her roommate's recipe online. After forty years I am quite sure that I can not be relied upon to compare the taste of this salad to albacore tuna but if not over-stirred and if it is served very cold, it is a satisfying approximation; good enough that when I served this appetizer to friends one evening, I was asked if it was tuna. On a summer evening, when the heat of the day has not yet dissipated but your enthusiasm for dinner preparation has dissipated, this salad entrée can be an option.

1 package (10.3 ounces) *extra firm silken tofu*

2 large stalks celery—diced
1/4 cup Italian red onion—*very finely* chopped

1/2 cup *calorie-reduced or light* mayonnaise
2 tablespoons *tamari* soy sauce
1 tablespoon freshly squeezed lemon juice
1/2 teaspoon kelp powder *or* ground sea vegetable
Freshly ground black pepper, to taste

3 medium cucumbers—scored with the tines of a fork *if organic*; peeled and scored with the tines of a fork *if not organic*

6 Boston lettuce leaves—well-washed and dried

TOFU "TUNA" – STUFFED CUCUMBER BOATS (cont'd)

Freeze the package of *tofu* overnight. The next day remove the frozen *tofu* from the package and wrap it in several cotton tea towels. Place a bread board on top and allow the *tofu* to drain for an additional 8 hours. Change the towels when they become too wet. Turn the block of soy beancurd into a bowl and, using a fork, shred to the consistency of tuna fish.

Add diced celery and *very finely* chopped red onion. Gently combine.

In a small bowl combine mayonnaise, soy sauce, lemon juice, kelp powder, and black pepper. Stir to combine well. Add to *tofu* mixture and gently stir until the mayonnaise is completely integrated. Refrigerate for at least 1 hour.

Slice scored cucumbers in half lengthwise. Hollow each to form a "boat." Spoon a portion of the *tofu* salad mixture into each of the six cucumber boats. Refrigerate until ready to serve.

Place a lettuce leaf on each dinner plate. Using two large spoons, transfer a stuffed cucumber boat onto each plate.

Serve chilled.

Yields 6 individual servings

Note: This recipe can be doubled, when required. If you only want two or four servings, save the rest of the "tuna" filling for tomorrow's lunch.

1/6 SERVING – PROTEIN = 4.6 g.; FAT = 7.4 g.; CARBOHYDRATE = 8.1 g.; CALORIES = 115; CALORIES FROM FAT = 58%

IVORIAN SPICY SWEETPOTATO AND TOMATO STEW
Igname et Tomate
TPT - 38 minutes

Home from the market I came with several of the large sweetpotatoes that always get left in the produce bin; the roots that would take too long to bake. I was on a week-long mission to test a slew of African recipes. This was one of those recipes and I was very glad I had chosen to try this Ivorian favorite. By the time we had tasted it as a sauce over rice and then over polenta, it was in our repertoire for good and always.

2 tablespoons safflower *or* sunflower oil
3 cups diced sweetpotato
1 medium onion—*finely* chopped
1 garlic clove—*very finely* chopped

2 cups canned, *diced* tomatoes
1/8 teaspoon ground ginger
1/8 teaspoon ground red pepper (cayenne), or
  to taste
Salt, to taste

In a large skillet set over *MEDIUM* heat, heat oil. Add diced sweetpotato, *finely* chopped onion, and *very finely* chopped garlic. Sauté until onions are soft and translucent, *being careful not to allow the vegetables to burn. Reduce heat to LOW*.

Add *diced* tomatoes, ground ginger, ground red pepper (cayenne), and salt. Cover and allow to cook until the sweetpotato is tender and the mixture has thickened to a sauce. Stir frequently. Turn into a serving bowl.

Serve over steamed rice or *polenta*.

Yields 6 servings
adequate for 4 people

Note: This recipe can be doubled, when required.

1/6 SERVING – PROTEIN = 2.3 g.; FAT = 4.7 g.; CARBOHYDRATE = 14.6 g.; CALORIES = 105; CALORIES FROM FAT = 40%

Africa – Côte d'Ivoire

LIME PUDDING WITH SWEETENED CONDENSED MILK
Dessert au Citrones Vertes

TPT - 10 minutes

Sweetened condensed milk and evaporated milk are products that have made their way around the world providing safe pasteurized and canned milk products to cooks. Try to seek out fat-free sweetened condensed milk; the difference in calories from the full-fat product will amaze you. This pudding can be made with either lemon or lime juice and it can be piled into baked pastry tarts or a pie crust if desired.

1/2 cup *fat-free* sweetened condensed milk
1/4 cup freshly squeezed lime juice
3 tablespoons *fat-free* pasteurized eggs
1/2 teaspoon pure vanilla extract

1 cup heavy whipping cream
1 tablespoon confectioners' sugar

In a small bowl, combine sweetened condensed milk, lime juice, and vanilla extract. Stir to combine thoroughly. Set aside briefly.

Using the electric mixer fitted with *chilled* beaters or by hand using a *chilled* wire whisk, beat heavy cream in a *chilled* bowl until soft peaks form. While continuing to beat, add confectioners' sugar. Beat until stiff peaks form.

Add condensed milk mixture and, using LOW speed, *gently* fold the milk mixture into the whipped cream. Divide among six small dessert dishes or wine glasses.

Serve at once.

Yields 6 individual servings

Note: This recipe can be halved or doubled, when required.

1/6 SERVING – PROTEIN = 3.6 g.; FAT = 13.1 g.; CARBOHYDRATE = 21.2 g.;
CALORIES = 217; CALORIES FROM FAT = 54%

IVORIAN PASTRY WITH BANANA AND CHOCOLATE
Mille-feuille aux Banane et Chocolate

TPT - 51 minutes

The French left many food traditions in Côte d'Ivoire such as the love of pastry. Delicious pastry like this simple dessert does not require a trip to the passterie or enrolling in a course in pastry making.

3 large *phyllo* pastry sheets
2 tablespoons *melted* butter

1/4 cup *fat-free* sweetened condensed milk
2 teaspoon unsweetened cocoa powder
1/2 teaspoon rum

1 cup heavy whipping cream

4 medium bananas

1 tablespoon grated or slivered bittersweet chocolate

Remove pastry from refrigerator or freezer and allow to come to room temperature.

Preheat oven to 400 degrees F.* Prepare two baking sheets by lining with culinary parchment paper.

Place one sheet of *phyllo* pastry on the work surface. Brush with *melted* butter. Place a second sheet of *phyllo* pastry on top of the first. Brush with *melted* butter. Top with the third sheet of *phyllo* pastry. Brush with *melted* butter. Cut the pastry into twelve squares. Transfer to parchment-line baking sheets. Bake at 400 degrees F. for about 12-15 minutes, *checking to be sure that the pastry does not over-brown*. Remove from oven and allow to cool for about 20 minutes on the baking sheets.*

IVORIAN PASTRY WITH BANANA AND CHOCOLATE (cont'd)

Meanwhile, in a small bowl combine sweetened condensed milk, cocoa powder, and rum. Mix well. Set aside until required.

Using the electric mixer fitted with *chilled* beaters or by hand using a *chilled* wire whisk, beat heavy cream in a *chilled* bowl until stiff peaks form. Reduce mixer speed to LOW and add condensed milk–cocoa–rum mixture. Continue beating until incorporated. *Do not overbeat.*

Spoon 1 tablespoonful of the cream mixture onto six of the baked *phyllo* squares.

Slice bananas and apportion to six dessert plates. Apportion the remaining cream mixture over the bananas. Place a baked *phyllo* pastry square with cream on top of the bananas on each of the plates. Top each serving with one of the remaining baked *phyllo* pastry squares.

Garnish each with a pinch of the grated bittersweet chocolate.

Serve at once.

Yields 6 individual servings

Notes: *If you do not have a convection oven, switch and turn baking sheets in the oven about 7 minutes into the baking to avoid over-browning.

This recipe can be halved or doubled, when required.

1/6 SERVING – PROTEIN = 3.1 g.; FAT = 19.2 g.; CARBOHYDRATE = 31.2 g.; CALORIES = 298; CALORIES FROM FAT = 58%

Djibouti

When I began this project, I knew only two things about the small country of Djibouti: It was a port on the sea of Aden and it hosted whale sharks from October to January. Whale sharks are solitary members of the same subclass of *Chondrichchtyes* as are other sharks, they are larger than most sharks, often reaching a length of forty feet, they filter feed as do whales, and their young are born live as are the young of mammals. I was to learn more, much more, about this stony, semi-desert nation, a country only slightly larger than our state of New Jersey.

Between 1883 and 1887, during the period of African colonization or "the grab for Africa" as it is sometimes called, France signed treaties with the local Sultans in Obock. They then renamed their colony French Somaliland which remained under French administration until 1967. A plebiscite confirmed the population's almost unanimous support for independence in 1977.

With no developed national resources other than salt and a desert terrain to their West, Djibouti turned to the magnificent harbor formed by the Gulf of Tadjoura as the focus for it economy, developing a service-oriented economy which has functioned for centuries. It serves as a secure transit and service port in the Horn of Africa and the chief outlet for Ethiopian export shipping since the secession of Eritrea from, now, land-locked Ethiopia. International transshipment and refueling services are provided for ships entering and leaving the Suez Canal. In an effort to reduce its high unemployment, which hovers close to fifty percent, the government has tried to attract industry. Djibouti has a strong, stable government and a stable currency. The lack of the danger of overwhelming inflation experienced by other African nations, due to the fact that the Djiboutian franc is fixed to the French franc and to the U. S. dollar, has been an attractive incentive to large international firms but their commitment is discouraged because of the lack of a skilled, educated work force. As a result, literacy and education have become primary concerns of the government that now dedicates over twenty percent of its budget to education since abandoning the French elitist education system previously in effect.

This equatorial nation can depend on very little rainfall in a good year, only about five inches. Summer temperatures range from 107 degrees F. down to 89 degrees F.; daytime winter temperatures range from highs of from 83 degrees F. to 70 degrees F. As a result of this severe climate, only about one-half of one percent of the total land mass is arable driving the Djiboutians to import most of their food needs. A remarkable cuisine has nonetheless evolved. The cuisine of Djibouti shows significant influence from its neighbors and by those who have traveled to and from its port. The Arabs introduced spices such as saffron and cinnamon. They also brought the pomegranate. In the sixteenth century the British brought their cuisine and, at the same time, the cuisine of India with its complex spicing arrived on these shores. The Portuguese also influenced this stunning melting pot cuisine, introducing the fruits from their African and Asian colonies as well as New World foods like peppers, tomatoes, and corn. The Portuguese, British, and French all shared their love of cheeses and even to this day a dollop of French Dijon mustard may be served by Djiboutians as a garniture. Dishes have been borrowed from its neighbors in the Horn of Africa so you will find many dishes of the Somali majority along with those of Eritrean and Ethiopian origin. Both *kebbeh* from Ethiopia and *ghee* from India have become staples of Djiboutian cooking. Foods from far-away lands are testimony to those who anchored in their harbor. *Fatira* is a popular omelet similar to a Greek tomato omelet called *omeletta me domatoes* and you do not have to go far to find a pizza.

Potable water is in seriously short supply in Djibouti and generally the drinking water has an alkali taste and is very salty. This has led to the wide availability and consumption of fruit juices. Although the Djibouti version of Indian *chai*, called *shaï* and containing the same cinnamon, clove, and cardamom seasoning, is widely available, the taste of the local water overwhelms the sweet seasoning.

Africa–Djibouti

*Below is an assortment of vegetarian soups popular in East Africa.
Anyone of them would make a great main course*

Spicy Bean Soup with Coconut Milk
Maharagwe

Groundnut and Vegetable Soup

East African Seasoning Mixture
Masala Mewsi

**Chick Pea and Kale Soup
with Peanut Butter and Tomatoes**
Zim Zim

~

Cornbread   French *Baguettes*   Ethiopian National Flatbread
Injera [see index]

~~~~~~~~~~~~~~~~~~~~

Lentils with Gingerroot
Lentilles

Spicy Rice with Tomatoes
Skoudehkaris

~~~~~~~~~~

Macaroni with *Kebbeh*, Black Pepper, and *Garam Masala*

Banana Slices

~~~~~~~~~~~~~~~~~~~

Fruit Juice—Pineapple, Orange, and Pomegranate Juices
or Banana Nectar

~

Banana Fritters
Beignets aux Banane

Pomegranate Halves

Africa–Djibouti

EAST AFRICAN SPICY BEAN SOUP WITH COCONUT MILK
Maharagwe
TPT - 38 minutes

A friend, whose daughter married a "cradle vegetarian," asked me how she and her daughter could "use" beans. I often turn to African recipes when I am looking for a complementary leguminous protein for a menu. African cooks employ peanuts and other legumes with so much more ease than do we in the United States. However, finding these recipes in a cookbook can be a challenge since there are few really good, non-Westernized African cookbooks. Young girls in East Africa learn to cook from parents, aunts, older siblings, and grandmothers and are expected to have mastered family recipes by the tender age of thirteen. The entire family would be embarrassed if a woman should consult a cookbook and, for this reason, cookbooks tend to be written for the tourist or for the Western kitchen. This bean dish, popular in the East African coastal cultures so very much influenced by Islam, is just wonderful with cornbread or a multi-grained country loaf of bread. I like to use red or black calypso beans or painted pony heirloom beans for this vegan soup/stew but pinto beans or even black-eyed peas will do.

2 tablespoons canola oil
1 medium onion—chopped

2 teaspoons ground turmeric, or to taste
2 teaspoons chili powder, or to taste

1 1/2 cups canned, *diced* tomatoes in purée
1/2 cup water
3 cups well-drained canned pinto beans *or* Roman beans *or* cooked, dried beans*
1 can (14.4 ounces) *light, sulfite-free* coconut milk
Salt, to taste*

In a large skillet set over *MEDIUM* heat, heat oil. Add onion and sauté until onion is soft and translucent, *being careful not to allow onion to brown.*

Add ground turmeric and chili powder. Sauté for another 30 seconds or so until the aroma is released.

Add diced tomatoes. Stir and allow to come to the boil. Cover, *reduce heat to LOW,* and allow to simmer for about 5 minutes.

Add beans, coconut milk, and salt, if necessary. Stir. Allow to cook for about 15 minutes, stirring occasionally. Turn into a heated serving bowl. Keep warm on warming tray until ready to serve.

Yields 6 cupfuls
adequate for 4-5 people

Notes: *Canned beans will require no further salting but you may want to taste for salt if you use cooked, dried beans.

This recipe is easily halved, when required.

1/8 SERVING (about 3/4 cupful) –
PROTEIN = 6.3 g.; FAT = 3.2 g.; CARBOHYDRATE = 20.2 g.;
CALORIES = 84; CALORIES FROM FAT = 34%

EAST AFRICAN GROUNDNUT AND VEGETABLE SOUP
TPT - 1 hour and 5 minutes

East African agriculture, to a great extent, is subsistence farming but commerce within Africa brings produce from adjacent countries especially those in West Africa where the land is more hospitable to agriculture. Everyone grows groundnuts but Senegal and Ghana are major producers of the legume which extends a protein lifeline to the less agriculturally successful nations and to vegetarians around the world. This is one of those recipes that not only satisfies the palate but it satisfies the soul of a cook. That such a joyously delicious meal can be the result of "this and that and a bit of this too" is amazing. I usually make this large batch because the complexity is even more enjoyable the next day.

Peanut butter was introduced to America and the world by the Kellogg brothers in the 1890s as a source of protein for patients in their Michigan sanatorium. It doesn't just spread well on peanut butter and jelly sandwiches, it enables the creation of a smooth base for soups like this.

Africa–Djibouti

EAST AFRICAN GROUNDNUT AND VEGETABLE SOUP (cont'd)

1 medium onion—chopped
1 cup VEGETARIAN BROWN STOCK *[see index]*, other vegetarian stock of choice, *or* water

2 1/2 teaspoons EAST AFRICAN SEASONING MIXTURE (*Masala Meusi*) *[see recipe which follows]*
1/4 teaspoon salt

3 1/2 cups VEGETARIAN BROWN STOCK *[see index]*
1 medium carrot—pared or scraped and sliced
1/2 cup canned, *diced* tomatoes
1/2 cup green (fresh) *or frozen* corn kernels
1 medium, all-purpose potato—peeled and cut into 1/4-inch dice

2 1/2 tablespoons freshly ground, *additive-free smooth* peanut butter
2 cups chopped green cabbage
1/2 cup fresh *or* frozen, cut green beans

1 sweet banana, peeled and sliced, for garnish

In a kettle, with cover, set over *MEDIUM-HIGH* heat, cook onion in the 1 cupful stock until softened—about 5 minutes.

Add EAST AFRICAN SEASONING MIXTURE and salt. Cook for 1 minute longer.

Add remaining 3 1/2 cupfuls stock, carrot slices, chopped tomatoes, corn, and cubed potato. Stir to combine well. Bring to the boil. Reduce heat to *LOW-MEDIUM* and simmer, covered, for 30 minutes, stirring occasionally.

In a small bowl, using a wire whisk, combine peanut butter and a couple of ladlefuls of the soup stock. Add to vegetables in kettle with chopped cabbage and cut green beans. Stir to integrate the peanut butter uniformly. Continue simmering, uncovered, for about 15 minutes more. Stir occasionally. Taste and adjust seasoning, if necessary.

Turn into a heated tureen and serve into heated soup plates. Garnish with banana slices.

Yields 7 cupfuls

Notes: This recipe may be doubled, when required.

Leftovers may be reheated most successfully. A chopped vegetarian *chorizo (chouriço)* sausage and/or greens help to extend leftovers, if needed, and are delicious additions to this soup.

1/7 SERVING (i. e., per cupful) –
PROTEIN = 3.4 g; FAT = 2.8 g; CARBOHYDRATE = 16.7 g;
CALORIES = 99; CALORIES FROM FAT = 25%

EAST AFRICAN SEASONING MIXTURE
Masala Meusi
TPT - 11 minutes

Berbere hot pepper seasoning is used throughout East Africa. However, our experience with piri piri chilies on a trip to Portugal and our lack of fortitude when introduced to hot peppers straight from the garden by our friend from Ethiopia, resulted in the search for a less fiery seasoning mixture. We found it in this mixture, undoubtedly influenced by Indian spice mixtures like garam masala and chaat masala. The heat in this mixture can be adjusted easily to your tolerance level.

1 1/2 tablespoons cumin seeds

5 cardamom seeds

1/2 teaspoon whole allspice

1/4 teaspoon fenugreek seeds

1 tablespoon paprika
1/2 freshly ground black pepper
1/2 teaspoon ground cinnamon
1/2 teaspoon ground ginger
1/8 teaspoon ground cloves

In a non-stick-coated skillet set over *MEDIUM* heat, heat cumin seeds. Dry-fry for several minutes.

Add cardamom seeds. Dry-fry for a minute.

Add whole allspice. Dry-fry for a minute.

Add fenugreek seeds. Dry-fry for a minute. Remove from heat. Pour into SPICE and COFFEE GRINDER.

Add paprika, black pepper, and ground cinnamon, ginger, and cloves.* Grind the mixture to a uniform powder. Turn into a clean glass jar. Store in a dry, cool place.

Africa–Djibouti

EAST AFRICAN SEASONING MIXTURE (cont'd)

Yields 6 servings
adequate for 4 people

Notes: *If dried hot peppers, crushed red pepper, or ground red pepper (cayenne) are to be added, add at this point.

This mixture will keep well without loss of potency for several months but you can easily halve or double the recipe.

FOOD VALUES for such spice mixtures are almost negligible.

EAST AFRICAN CHICK PEA AND KALE SOUP WITH PEANUT BUTTER AND TOMATOES

Zim Zim
TPT - 37 minutes

"Zim zim" best translates as "stew" and although I call this a soup, it is thick enough to be classified as zim zim. To complement the legume protein, we serve it with cornbread or corn fritters or with pancakes, as a sort-of a home-style flatbread. Normally made with spinach-like greens, we use kale to make a hearty, healthy winter soup.

1 3/4 cups VEGETABLE STOCK FROM SOUP [see index] or VEGETARIAN BROWN STOCK [see index]
1/4 cup freshly ground, *additive-free smooth* peanut butter

1 tablespoon *extra virgin* olive oil
1 large onion—chopped
1 large garlic clove—*very finely* chopped

1 teaspoon ground Hungarian paprika—*hot or sweet*, as preferred
1 teaspoon ground coriander
1/4 teaspoon ground ginger
Pinch ground cinnamon
1/4 teaspoon ground red pepper (cayenne)

1 can (15 ounces) chick peas (*garbanzos*)—well-drained and well-rinsed
1 3/4 cups canned, *diced* tomatoes

2 cups chopped kale—well-rinsed and drained*

In the electric blender, combine about 1/2 cupful stock with the peanut butter. Blend until smooth. *Gradually* add remaining vegetable stock, blending with each addition. Set aside until required.

In a kettle, with cover, set over *MEDIUM* heat, heat oil. Add chopped onion and *very finely* chopped garlic. Sauté until soft and translucent, *being careful to allow neither the onion nor the garlic to brown.*

Stir in ground paprika, coriander, ginger, cinnamon, and red pepper (cayenne). Cook, stirring constantly, for about 1 minute.

Add blended peanut butter–stock mixture, well-drained chick peas, and diced tomatoes. Stir to combine. Allow to come to the boil. *Reduce heat to LOW-MEDIUM* and allow to cook, stirring frequently, for about 15-20 minutes.

Just before serving, stir in chopped kale. Turn into a heated soup tureen or serving bowl.

Serve at once into heated soup plates.

Yields 6 servings
adequate for 4 people

Notes: *Substitute spinach, if preferred.

This recipe may be halved or doubled, when required.

Leftovers may be reheated most successfully.

1/6 SERVING – PROTEIN = 7.7 g.; FAT = 7.6 g.; CARBOHYDRATE = 14.6 g.;
CALORIES = 120; CALORIES FROM FAT = 57%

Africa—Djibouti

DJIBOUTI LENTILS WITH GINGERROOT
Lentilles au Gingembre

TPT - 2 hours and 20 minutes;
1 hour = lentil soaking period
[slow cooker: 3-4 hours at LOW]

Djiboutians add the hot, hot berbere sauce, so popular in East Africa, to this lentil dish. I have found that that fiery sauce tends to interfere with or obliterate appreciation of the onion, garlic, and ginger that make this lentil dish so very different and delicious.

3/4 cup dried, brown (*or* green) lentils
3 cups *boiling* water

2 tablespoons butter
2 garlic cloves—*very finely* chopped
3/4 cup *finely* chopped Italian red onion
3 tablespoons *finely* chopped mild green *chilies*

1 cup water
2 teaspoons grated fresh gingerroot
3 drops *jalapeño chili* sauce, or to taste

Salt, to taste
Freshly ground black pepper, to taste

Pick over lentils and discard any of poor quality. Rinse thoroughly. Drain. Pour into a mixing bowl and add the *boiling* water. Set aside at room temperature for 1 hour. Drain.

In a large *non-aluminum** kettle set over *LOW-MEDIUM* heat, melt butter. Add *very finely* chopped garlic, *finely* chopped red onion and green *chilies*. Sauté until soft and transparent, *being careful not to allow the vegetables to brown.*

Add soaked and drained lentils, water, grated gingerroot, and *jalapeño chili* sauce. Allow to come to the boil. *Reduce heat to LOW*, cover, and allow to simmer for 1 hour, stirring occasionally. Remove cover. Increase heat to *MEDIUM* and continue cooking until most of liquid has evaporated. *Stir frequently to prevent the lentils from sticking to the bottom of the pan.*

Season with salt and black pepper. Turn into a heated serving bowl.

Serve hot.

Yields 6 servings
adequate for 4-6 people

Notes: *Since aluminum discolors lentils rather unpleasantly, avoid using aluminum cookware or serving bowls in this case.

This recipe can be doubled, when required.

1/6 SERVING – PROTEIN = 7.2 g.; FAT = 4.1 g.; CARBOHYDRATE = 20.2 g.;
CALORIES = 144; CALORIES FROM FAT = 26%

DJIBOUTI SPICY RICE WITH TOMATOES
Skoudehkaris

TPT - 1 hour and 8 minutes;
[slow cooker: about 3 hours at LOW]

Skoudehkaris is a dish served in Djibouti in which lamb is slowly simmered with tomatoes, onions, and spices. Near the end of the cooking period, rice is added. We make this dish without the lamb, of course, and although you might think it sounds like the dish invented in America and called "Spanish rice," the nuances of East African seasoning make this quite different.

1 tablespoon *extra virgin* olive oil
1/2 cup *finely* chopped medium onion
1 small garlic clove—*very finely* chopped

1 cup dry converted rice

1 cup canned, *diced or* peeled, seeded, and chopped fresh tomatoes
1 cup bottled water *or* refrigerated water*
1 cup VEGETARIAN BROWN STOCK *[see index] or* other vegetarian stock of choice
1 tablespoon tomato paste
1/4 teaspoon ground cumin
1/4 teaspoon ground cloves
1/4 teaspoon ground cardamom
4 drops *jalapeño chili* sauce, or to taste
Salt, to taste
Freshly ground black pepper, to taste

DJIBOUTI SPICY RICE WITH TOMATOES (cont'd)

In a non-stick-coated skillet, with cover, set over *MEDIUM* heat, heat oil. When hot, add *finely* chopped onion and *very finely* chopped garlic. Sauté until onion is soft, *allowing neither the onion nor the garlic to brown*.

Add rice and continue to sauté until rice is *lightly browned*.

Stir in chopped tomatoes, water, stock, tomato paste, ground cumin, cloves, and cardamom, salt, and pepper. When thoroughly combined, cover and cook *undisturbed* over *very LOW* heat until all liquid is absorbed—about 45 minutes. *Do not stir during cooking period!* Add more water only if absolutely necessary. Turn into a heated serving bowl.

Serve hot.

Notes: *Since the chlorine in tap water destroys the B-vitamin thiamin in grains, it is advisable to cook grains in either bottled water or water that has been refrigerated uncovered for at least 24 hours.

If preferred, this dish can be prepared in a slow cooker set at LOW.

Yields 6 servings
adequate for 4 people

1/6 SERVING – PROTEIN = 1.0 g.; FAT = 2.0 g.; CARBOHYDRATE = 7.8 g.;
CALORIES = 50; CALORIES FROM FAT = 36%

DJIBOUTIAN BANANA FRITTERS
Beignets aux Banane
TPT - 37 minutes

Rarely do I deep-fry but when bananas over-ripen, I have several recipes which I use to salvage their sweetness and this is one of them.

1/2-1 cup high heat safflower or sunflower oil, depending upon size of skillet

3 tablespoons sugar
2 tablespoons *fat-free* pasteurized eggs

2 medium, *very ripe* bananas—peeled and chopped

1 1/3 cups white rice flour
1/2 teaspoon freshly grated nutmeg
1/4 teaspoon ground cinnamon

Confectioners' sugar

In a deep skillet set over *MEDIUM* heat, heat oil.

Meanwhile, in a small bowl combine sugar and pasteurized eggs. Mix well until sugar is dissolved.

Using a potato masher, mash bananas in a mixing bowl until a uniform pulp forms.

Add rice flour, grated nutmeg, and ground cinnamon. Mix thoroughly.

Add sugar–egg mixture. Mix to a pancake batter consistency, adding a bit of water, if necessary.

Using soup spoons, drop spoonfuls of batter into the hot oil in batches of three or four. Allow to brown on one side. Turn and brown the other side. Using a slotted spoon or skimmer, transfer fritters to paper towel-covered surface to drain excess oil.

Arrange on a serving platter. Dust with confectioners' sugar or provide granulated sugar in which the fritters can be dipped.

Serve warm.

Yields 18 fritters

Note: This recipe can be doubled, when required.

1/18 SERVING (i. e., per fritter exclusive of extra sugar) –
PROTEIN = 1.0 g.; FAT = 1.6 g.; CARBOHYDRATE = 11.7 g.;
CALORIES = 68; CALORIES FROM FAT = 21%

Egypt

One of my passions as a child was my treasured 1935 edition of *The Book of Knowledge* that gave me an understanding of poetry and mythology and led me through ancient history. Each time I dove into a volume I was confronted with a world beyond my small world and that is where I first discovered Egypt. Fascinated still, I've taken several courses on ancient Egypt and never miss a television program that celebrates that which the desert is still revealing to those of us who continue to wonder.

Egypt's approximately seventy-six million people live near the Nile River, the river that has given and still gives life to the ancient desert nation through annual flooding that replenishes the soil. Although Egypt encompasses about 387,000 square miles, only about 15,000 square miles is suitable for agriculture and that is where the vast majority of its population resides. The first Pharaonic dynasty was established in about 3150 BC but there is evidence that the land was occupied by a hunting and fishing culture before a culture of grain-growing peoples settled in the tenth century BC. About 10,000 years ago climate changes and overgrazing led to the formation of the Sahara desert in a manner similar to the formation of the Sonora desert in our own hemisphere. Neolithic cultures established independently in the upper and lower Nile Valley in about 6000 BC. These were unified under King Menes in the First Dynasty. To date some thirty native Pharaonic dynasties have been identified before the periods of foreign influence from the Persians, the Greco-Macedonians, and the Romans, all of whom added a layer of complexity influencing language, religion, and cuisine. More layers were added to the national identity as Egypt came under the control of the Byzantine Empire and in 639 AD it was absorbed into the Islamic Empire with Sunni Muslim rulers in control for the next six centuries. Later the Ottoman Empire left its imprint as did both the French and the British. A parliamentary representative system was established in 1923 which was overthrown in a *coup de-état* in 1952. King Farouk was forced to abdicate, leading to the formation of the Egyptian Republic in 1953. In 1956, two years after Gamal Abdel Nasser forced the resignation of the first president of the republic General Muhammad Naguib, full independence from the United Kingdom was declared and the Suez Canal, built in cooperation with the French in 1869, was nationalized precipitating the Suez Crisis.

Sometimes it seems that Egypt struggles with identity; sometimes it seems that Egypt must always manage the shifting sands.

~

Vegetables are not served in the same manner to which we in the West have become accustomed. I was considerably challenged to find vegetable side dishes to accompany the lentil and rice dish which I have included here and, thereby, make this menu comfortable to the western cook and the western diner. Beans are the first vegetable recommended by an Egyptian cook and, granted, there are more bean recipes than one could possibly desire but this was not necessary to balance this menu; another protein source was not needed. Artichokes, beetroots, cabbage, cauliflower, cucumbers, okra, pumpkin, spinach, tomatoes, and zucchini (marrow), are popular and are prepared in many ways to be served as *mezze*, the celebrated Egyptian version of the Spanish *tapas*. Vegetables are most often added to a stew or soup but they are occasionally prepared as side dishes for large meals too and fit very nicely into the western meal presentation. If you are looking for a vegetable dish, I suggest you search the "mezze" chapter of any cookbook; there you will find vegetarian possibilities for your Egyptian menu.

You will see Fig Newtons on this menu and will, no doubt, pause. Ancient Egyptians made a pastry filled with fig paste that is remarkably similar to the fig cookie we know today.

Africa–Egypt

Ground Legume and Spice Mixture
Dukka

Pita Bread Triangles

~

Watermelon, Tomato, and Feta Salad
Gibna wi Bateegh

~~~~~~~~~~~~~~~~~~~~~

Slow Cooker Lentils and Rice
Kusherie

Boiled Baby Artichokes with Lemon Dipping Sauce
Kharshuf Maslu'

Fried Spinach with Chickpeas and Grated Cheese
Sabanikh Mihammar

~~~~~~~~~~~~~~~~~~~~~

Whole Grain Pudding with Raisins
'Ashura

Palace Honey Bread
Esh es Seraya

Fig Newtons

EGYPTIAN GROUND LEGUME AND SPICE MIXTURE
Dukka
TPT – 7 minutes

Egyptians routinely use this ground mixture, albeit much saltier than the version presented here, as a breakfast dip with bread. This ancient custom observed amino acid complementation without knowing about such vegetarian needs long before we could all name the essential amino acids. Offered with bread, this mixture makes an interesting and nutritious snack or casual first course for a dinner.

1 tablespoon coriander seeds

3/4 teaspoon salt
1 tablespoon chopped, *roasted*, *unsalted* peanuts
1 tablespoon chopped dry chick peas (*garbanzos*)
1 1/2 teaspoons crushed, dried mint
1 1/2 teaspoons sesame seeds

In a dry skillet set over *MEDIUM* heat, toast coriander seeds for about 5 minutes. Set aside to cool briefly.

Using a SPICE and COFFEE GRINDER, or a mortar and pestle, grind the *toasted* coriander seeds with salt, chopped peanuts and chick peas (*garbanzos*), crushed mint leaves, and sesame seeds until a uniformly fine mixture is formed. Turn into a saucer.

Store in a cool, dry place for no more that a month. Use as a dry dip for bread.

Yields about 3 tablespoonfuls

Note: This recipe can be doubled, when required.

1/9 SERVING (per teaspoonful –
PROTEIN = 1.5 g.; FAT = 1.0 g.; CARBOHYDRATE = 0.7 g.;
CALORIES = 13; CALORIES FROM FAT = 69%

Africa–Egypt

EGYPTIAN WATERMELON, TOMATO, AND *FETA* SALAD
Gibna wi Bateegh

TPT - 5 minutes

Similar to a South African fruit salad, but with the addition of tomato, this salad also makes a wonderfully fresh pita stuffing or a topping for a flatbread sandwich. It is frequently served for breakfast and it is an interesting way to start the day especially as an adventure for visiting grandchildren. South Africans season with fresh mint but the Egyptian version is distinctive in that it is seasoned with a popular Middle Eastern seasoning mixture of sumac, thyme, sesame, and salt known as zahtar (za'atar or zatar). You can make your own zahtar or you can buy it at a Middle Eastern market or through a mail order spice firm.

1 cup crumbled *feta* cheese—preferably Woolrich *feta*, if available*

1 medium tomato—seeded and diced

1 tablespoon *extra virgin* olive oil
1 1/2 teaspoons NORTH AFRICAN SUMAC SEASONING MIXTURE (*Zahtar* or *Zaatar*)
[see index]

6 cups watermelon chunks

2 whole wheat *pita* bread loaves—cut into six triangles each and warmed

Place crumbled *feta* cheese in the center of a large shallow serving bowl or platter.

Surround the *feta* with diced tomato.

Drizzle olive oil over and sprinkle with the *zahtar*.

Surround the seasoned rings of cheese and tomato with watermelon chunks.

Serve well-chilled with warmed *pita* triangles.**

Yields 6 servings
adequate for 4 people

Notes: *Any *feta*, domestic or imported, which you prefer, can be used. We like the Canadian *feta*, for this particular dish, because it is very crumbly and very tangy. Greek herbed *feta* products are also interesting in this recipe if the herb mixture is compatible with your menu.

**If being served for breakfast or lunch, instead of cutting the *pita* loaves into triangles, cut them in half to provide a pocket for the salad mixture.

This dish can be halved or doubled, when required.

1/6 SERVING – PROTEIN = 9.2 g.; FAT = 11.9 g.; CARBOHYDRATE = 22.2 g.;
CALORIES = 224; CALORIES FROM FAT = 47%

SLOW COOKER EGYPTIAN LENTILS AND RICE
Kusherie

TPT - 2 hours and 21 minutes
[slow cooker: about 2 hours at *HIGH*:
about 6-8 hours at *LOW*

I often use a Moroccan tagine to make this dish and would suggest that, if you have one, you use it too. The crock-pot is a modern version of this ancient slow cooker and, in the summer especially, I use the electric slow cooker because it does not heat up the kitchen. As with risotto, I like a creamy texture for this dish so I use short-grained Arborio rice, grown in the northern Italian agricultural provinces of Piemonte, Tuscana, and Lombardia.

Macaroni is generally added to kusherie. Since the lentils and rice comprise a dish in which the amino acids are perfectly complemented, we do not feel that it is necessary to add more grain. Macaroni can be added if you prefer.

2 teaspoons *extra virgin* olive oil
2 teaspoons butter
1 medium onion—*finely* chopped

1/2 cup dry brown (*or* green) lentils—well-rinsed and sorted
1/2 cup dry short grain, Italian *Arborio* rice*
1 1/2 teaspoons ground cumin
1/4 teaspoon ground cinnamon
1/4 teaspoon salt
2 1/2 cups *boiling* water

SLOW COOKER EGYPTIAN LENTILS AND RICE (cont'd)

Preheat slow cooker to *HIGH*.

Add olive oil, butter, and *finely* chopped onion. Allow the onions to cook in the oil–butter mixture for about 15 minutes.

Add lentils, rice, ground cumin and cinnamon, salt, and *boiling* water. Cover and cook at *HIGH* for 2 hours, or until all of the liquid has been absorbed.** Stir occasionally and add more liquid, if necessary.

Turn into a heated serving bowl and keep warm on a warming tray until ready to serve. Refrigerate leftovers.

Notes: *Short grain *Arborio* rice is available in Italian groceries, food specialty stores, natural food stores, and from specialty mail order firms.

**If you wish to start this in the morning, set the slow cooker temperature at *LOW* after you add the lentils and rice and allow to cook for 6-8 hours.

This recipe can be doubled, when required. Timing and the amount of liquid may need to be adjusted, depending on your slow cooker.

Leftovers can be frozen.

Yields 8 servings
adequate for 4 people

1/6 SERVING – PROTEIN = 4.6 g.; FAT = 2.1 g.; CARBOHYDRATE = 19.6 g.;
CALORIES = 115; CALORIES FROM FAT = 16%

EGYPTIAN BOILED BABY ARTICHOKES WITH LEMON DIPPING SAUCE

Kharshuf Maslu'

TPT - 28 minutes

We make a special trip to a grocery store north of us to buy baby artichokes when they are in season. Divinely different from the big globe artichokes, they are so very easy to prepare since the irritating choke has not yet developed. They are very tender and can be prepared in many ways. The dipping sauce that accompanies the boiled artichokes in this recipe is light enough to allow the sweet flesh of the artichoke to be appreciated.

This recipe assumes that each of six diners will eat one baby artichoke but be advised this may not be sufficient if you have gathered artichoke lovers at your table.

6 baby artichokes—trimmed, if necessary, and well-rinsed
1/2 lemon

4 quarts *boiling* water

LEMON DIPPING SAUCE:
    1/4 cup freshly squeezed lemon juice
    2 tablespoons safflower oil *or* other very light oil
    1/4 teaspoon dried mustard
    Pinch salt
    Freshly ground black pepper, to taste

Prepare artichokes one at a time. Cut stem flush with base to form a flat "seat." Remove outer tough and discolored petals. Using a sharp knife, cut about 1/2 inch from the tops of the petals. Using a kitchen scissors, snip sharp tips from all petals. Rub all cut surfaces with lemon.

In a kettle set over *MEDIUM* heat, boil artichokes into *boiling* water until tender—about 20 minutes.

Meanwhile, in the electric blender, combine lemon juice, oil, dried mustard, salt, and black pepper. Blend until smooth.

Divide the sauce into six saucers and place a saucer above each dinner plate. Serve the artichokes directly onto the dinner plate as a side dish to the main meal. Encourage diners to peel the leaves, one at a time, from the thistles, dip them in the sauce, and scrape the sweet flesh with their teeth from the inside of the leaf. When the heart is reached, the immature choke can be scraped off, and the heart transferred to the saucer with the sauce where it can be cut and eaten in small sauce-drenched mouthfuls. Be sure to provide a bowl into which the discarded leaves can be placed.

Yields 6 servings
adequate for 4-6 people

Note: This recipe can be halved or doubled, when required.

Africa–Egypt

**EGYPTIAN BOILED BABY ARTICHOKES
WITH LEMON DIPPING SAUCE** (cont'd)

1/6 SERVING – PROTEIN = 1.4 g.; FAT = 4.5 g.; CARBOHYDRATE = 4.3 g.;
CALORIES = 75; CALORIES FROM FAT = 54%

FRIED SPINACH WITH CHICK PEAS AND GRATED CHEESE IN THE STYLE OF EGYPT
Sabanikh Mihammar

TPT - 10 minutes

Spinach is my solution to the fact that the Egyptian table often lacks color. Egyptians bake it with cheese and béchamel sauce; they purée and cream it. It is also baked and stewed with beef but, perhaps, my favorite way to prepare spinach for a side dish is to sauté it as in this recipe.

1 tablespoon *extra virgin* olive oil
1 tablespoon butter
10 ounces baby spinach—well-washed, stems trimmed, and well-dried

1/4 cup canned chick peas (*garbanzos*)—well-drained, seed coats removed, and halved

1 tablespoon grated Parmesan cheese

In a large skillet set over *LOW-MEDIUM* heat, heat oil and butter until butter is melted. Add spinach. Cover and allow spinach to wilt, stirring frequently to keep spinach in contact with the oil–butter sauté mixture. Remove cover.

Add chick pea halves and allow to heat through, stirring frequently. Turn into heated serving dish.

Sprinkle Parmesan cheese over.

Serve at once.

Yields 6 servings
adequate for 4 people

Note: This recipe can be halved, when required.

1/6 SERVING – PROTEIN = 2.4 g.; FAT = 4.4 g.; CARBOHYDRATE = 3.1 g.;
CALORIES = 59; CALORIES FROM FAT = 67%

EGYPTIAN WHOLE GRAIN PUDDING WITH RAISINS
'Ashura

TPT - 5 hour and 15 minutes;
4 hours = raisin rehydration period;
1 hour = refrigeration period

I have always enjoyed hot cereal in the morning but since my breakfast is often eaten at the computer, I rarely take the time to make cereal. A granola bar, more often than not, sits on my desk next to my tea, to be shared with one of our feline companions, leaving those precious grains of my favorite hot cereal to be incorporated into other dishes such as this simple dessert or a loaf of bread. Egyptians also enjoy whole grain cereal for breakfast and, as did my grandmother and her grandmother before her, utilize a single cooking process in the morning to provide a hot breakfast and a sweet pudding for supper. Traditionally, a whole grain sweet pudding, similar to this, is served on the 10th of Muharram, the first month of the Islamic calendar.

1/2 cup *preservative-free black* raisins
1 tablespoon sugar
1 1/2 cups *boiling* water

1 1/2 cups *two-percent* milk

3/4 cup ground whole grain hot cereal mixture*
3 tablespoons sugar
1 1/2 teaspoons butter

3/4 teaspoon rose water *or ma ward***

Cinnamon sugar

EGYPTIAN WHOLE GRAIN PUDDING WITH RAISINS (cont'd)

Put raisins and sugar into a small bowl. Pour *boiling* water over. Cover with a saucer and allow to sit at room temperature for 4 hours, or until the raisins are well-plumped. Drain thoroughly.

In a saucepan set over *MEDIUM* heat, heat milk until bubbles form around the perimeter.

Add cereal, sugar, and butter. Cook, stirring frequently, until thickened.

Stir in rose water. Apportion among six dessert dishes. Refrigerate for at least 1 hour before serving.

Divide the plumped raisins among the servings. Sprinkle cinnamon sugar over.

Serve chilled.

Yields 6 individual servings

Notes: *Seven-grain or eight-grain cereal mixtures available in natural food stores, are perfect for this dessert. There are wheatless mixtures and there are those that include a whole wheat portion. A whole wheat hot cereal, such as Wheatena, can also be used.

**Both French and Lebanese rose water products are available in food specialty stores.

One third of this recipe can be prepared for just two portions. Two thirds of the recipes will serve four.

1/6 SERVING (exclusive of cinnamon sugar) –
PROTEIN = 4.1 g.; FAT = 3.2 g.; CARBOHYDRATE = 34.7 g.;
CALORIES = 181; CALORIES FROM FAT = 15%

EGYPTIAN PALACE HONEY BREAD
Esh es Seraya

TPT - 2 hours and 8 minutes;
2 hours = refrigeration period

This is not a bread, per se, but a way of using bread instead. Overnight this dessert hardens into a sticky confection that is perfect for "high" tea. Adorn tiny slices with a rosette of whipped cream.

A grocery store in a nearby city has an excellent in-store bakery from which I often buy a large, round loaf of French or Italian bread, a pain de campagna. The first slices are lunch, accompanied by luscious slices of fresh mozzarella. Then, I collect the breadcrumbs necessary to make this most unusual dessert. The remainder of the loaf either gets sliced for British fried cheddar sandwiches or crumbed to bread eggplant for eggplant parmigiana.

1/2 cup honey
1/2 cup *light* brown sugar
1/2 cup butter—hard butter, *not whipped*
  —*softened to room temperature*
2 1/2 cups fresh whole wheat breadcrumbs
  from bread of choice
1 teaspoon pure vanilla extract

Whipped heavy cream, for garnish

Prepare a 9-inch two-piece tart tin with removable ring by coating with non-stick lecithin spray coating.

In a saucepan set over *LOW-MEDIUM* heat, combine honey, brown sugar, *softened* butter, breadcrumbs, and vanilla extract. Cook, stirring constantly, until butter is melted and mixture is thoroughly combined.

Pour mixture into prepared tart tin, spreading it evenly to the perimeter. Refrigerate for at least 2 hours until *cold and firm*—preferably overnight.

When ready to serve, remove tart pan ring. Slice into wedges and serve, garnished with whipped cream.

Yields 12 servings
adequate for 9-12 people

Notes: Leftovers keep well, if refrigerated.

This recipe can be halved if you have a suitable pan—a 6- or 7-inch tart pan.

1/12 SERVING (with 2 tablespoons whipped cream) –
PROTEIN = 1.3 g.; FAT = 5.9 g.; CARBOHYDRATE = 21.3 g.;
CALORIES = 135; CALORIES FROM FAT = 39%

Eritrea

Located literally on top of the juncture of three tectonic plates at the point known as the Danakil Depression or the Afar Triangle, the Arabian Plate, and Nubian and Somali plates of the large African Plate, Eritrea is dangerously situated since these plates are slowly, but steadily, pulling away from each other. The mountains of the Great Rift Valley bisect the country contributing to rainfall or the lack thereof. Fertile land lies to the West of the mountains; a desert lies to the East.

Eritrea is an active archeological area of the world as paleontologists search for information about the cradles of human evolution. Italian scientists unearthed a cranium in 1995 in Danakil whose carbon dating strongly suggests that hominids occupied or traversed this area more than one million years ago and that they could have been the transitional link between *Homo erectus* and an early proto-*Homo sapiens*. In 1999 an excavation of an incredible site dating from the Paleolithic period, over 125,000 years ago, showed that early humans were involved here in marine harvests and had developed tools to do so.

Geographic precariousness is mirrored by the long history of war and political instability. Eritrea was an Italian colony from 1890 to 1941, known as *Colonia Primigenia* by the Italians. In 1951 Eritrea became federated with Ethiopia but the parliament was dissolved by Emperor Haile Selassie's order and Eritrea was declared the fourteenth province of Ethiopia in 1962. After a long and bitter civil war, Eritrea declared independence in 1993 and the People's Front for Democracy and Justice formed a government creating a single-party, Marxist state in which a constitution has yet to be enacted.

Eritreans enjoy hot, spicy stews of meat and vegetables or of legumes and vegetables, served on *injera* as do the Ethiopians. Of all the different distinct groups that form the Eritrean population only the Soho seem to season their food at heat levels manageable by most Westerners. *Alicha*, made without *berbere*, and some *shiro*, legume purées which can generally be ordered "according to fire," can painlessly ease Westerners into the cuisine. Italian influences are substantial but Eritreans, in integrating dishes common to the colonial period, give familiar Italian recipes a very distinctive African touch. Because the Eritreans observe many religious fast days, every cook and every restaurant has a few standbys for the non-meat eater. Breakfasts are never a problem since cooked grain cereals, yogurt, eggs, and hard rolls with honey and *ricotta* cheese are the norm.

Africa – Eritrea

Papaya Juice

Garlic Dipping Oil with Yogurt
Sirsie

with

Breadsticks and Bran-rich Hard Rolls
Grissini   *Banni*

Roasted Chickpeas   Roasted Pumpkin Seeds

~

Ethiopian / Eritrean Seasoning Mixture

~

Noodle Soup
Capelli d'Angelo in Brodo

~

Finely Shredded Cabbage Slaw

with

Pepper *Vinaigrette*
Vinagreta con Pimiento

~~~~~~~~~~~~~~~~~~~~~~~

Lentils with Tomato and Garlic
Alitcha Birsen

Sautéed Greens

~~~~~~~~~~~~~~~~~~~~~~~

Coffee Ice Dessert
Graniti di Espresso con Crema

Italian-Style Baked Rusks
Biscotti

Espresso – Made with Ethiopian Coffee,
either Black, *Bün*, or with Milk, *Mucchiato*

ERITREAN PAPAYA JUICE
TPT - 5 minutes

Using perfectly ripened fresh papaya, Eritreans make a thick, sweet papaya drink that is delicious. Although occasionally we find giant papaya from South America in our markets, one small papaya is usually the only ripe papaya in the tropical produce section on any given morning. Consequently, I evolved this variation with papaya nectar and that one ripe papaya as a first course for a summer al fresco dinner. Since this can be doubled easily and since leftovers suffer none from refrigeration, those huge papayas from Belize, if you find them, can provide a large pitcher full of nutrition as a first course or as a refreshing afternoon break..

It is so pretty served in champagne flutes.

ERITREAN PAPAYA JUICE (cont'd)

1 ripe papaya—peeled, seeded, and chopped
2 tablespoons freshly squeezed lime juice
1 can (12 ounces) papaya nectar*

Lime wedges, for garnish

In the container of the electric blender, combine chopped papaya, lime juice, and about 1/2 of the papaya nectar. Blend for about 2 minutes until liquefied.**

Add the remaining papaya nectar and blend again. Divide among four wine glasses or champagne flutes. Garnish with a lime wedge.

Serve at once.

Notes: *Eritreans like this juice drink very sweet. The sugar in the papaya nectar is sufficient for our taste but additional sugar can be added, if desired.

**The juice can be prepared to this point and refrigerated in the blender container until you are ready to serve. Before serving, add remaining papaya nectar and blend until frothy.

This recipe can be doubled and served from a large pitcher or ladled from a punch bowl, when required.

Yields four 6-ounce servings

1/4 SERVING – PROTEIN = 2.0 g.; FAT = 1.6 g.; CARBOHYDRATE = 22.4 g.;
CALORIES = 89; CALORIES FROM FAT = 16%

ERITREAN GARLIC DIPPING OIL WITH YOGURT
Sirsie

TPT - 15 minutes

In much the same manner in which Italians sprinkle garlic- and herb-seasoned olive oil on bread, Eritreans enjoy this as a dip with bread, hard rolls, and breadsticks as an appetizer or as a snack. It can be a fiery affair, especially for the western palate. Since we serve this as an appetizer and we do want our guests to be able to taste the courses which follow, we greatly prefer this milder version. My own "berbere," which is considerable milder than would be customary in either Eritrea or Ethiopia, plus the tempering addition of tomato purée and yogurt, take the heat down several notches. Do not be afraid to adjust this to your own tolerance level.

1/2 cup *extra virgin* olive oil

2 large garlic cloves—*very finely* chopped

1 tablespoon ETHIOPIAN / ERITREAN SEASONING MIXTURE (Berbere) [see recipe which follows]
6 tablespoons tomato purée
3 tablespoons water

6 tablespoons PLAIN YOGURT [see index]
or commercially-available plain yogurt

In a small saucepan, heat oil over *LOW-MEDIUM* heat.

Add *very finely* chopped garlic. Sauté until garlic is soft and translucent, *being careful not to allow the garlic to brown.*

Add seasoning mixture, tomato purée, and water. Stir together thoroughly. Cook, stirring frequently, over the *LOW-MEDIUM* heat for about 8 minutes.

Divide the dipping sauce among six individual small bowls and serve while still warm. Pass yogurt, to be added by each diner, and bread to dunk and scoop up the dipping sauce.

Yields 6 individual servings

Note: The basic sauce recipe, exclusive of the yogurt, can be doubled and since it can be an exciting seasoning addition to East African dishes, we often do double it and store the extra in a condiment bottle in the refrigerator.

1/6 SERVING (with 1 tablespoonful yogurt) –
PROTEIN = 1.0 g.; FAT = 15.1 g.; CARBOHYDRATE = 2.4 g.;
CALORIES = 150; CALORIES FROM FAT = 91%

Africa–Eritrea

ETHIOPIAN / ERITREAN SEASONING MIXTURE
Berbere
TPT - 9 minutes

The level of "hot" that people of the Horn of Africa can tolerate is staggering. I used to think that the Thai were the world's champion in that regard but a friend from Ethiopia proved me wrong. Hot chilies straight from my garden, seeds and all, were a treat for him but my cooking remained too bland for his taste. I tasted berbere once at full strength and I could not imagine "getting used to it," as Hailu suggested I would. The version I present here is dramatically less hot and a bit more complex but I feel that I can taste my food through the heat which was impossible with the full strength version. Add more ground red pepper (cayenne) as your tolerance grows.

1 teaspoon ground ginger
1/2 teaspoon ground cardamom
1/2 teaspoon ground cinnamon
1/2 teaspoon ground coriander
1/2 teaspoon ground fenugreek seeds
1/2 teaspoon freshly grated nutmeg
1/4 teaspoon ground cloves

1/2 cup Hungarian sweet paprika
1 tablespoon salt
2 tablespoons ground red pepper (cayenne)
1/2 teaspoon freshly ground black pepper

In a non-stick-coated skillet set over *LOW* heat, combine ground ginger, cardamom, cinnamon, coriander, fenugreek, nutmeg, and cloves. Toast, stirring frequently, for about 4 minutes, *being careful not to allow the spices to burn. The aroma should be intense.* Remove from heat.

In a jar, with tightly fitting lid, combine paprika, salt, ground red pepper, cayenne and black pepper. Stir to combine well. Add the toasted spices. Again, stir to combine well.

Store, tightly covered, in a cool dry place.*

Notes: *This seasoning is best stored in the refrigerator where it will easily keep for 6 months.

Although I prefer to toast whole seeds and then grind them, most Americans have the ground spices on hand and, if carefully watched while toasting, a very respectable "berbere" can be made.

When required, this recipe can be halved or doubled.

Yields about 15 tablespoonfuls

FOOD VALUES for such spice mixtures are almost negligible.

ERITREAN NOODLE SOUP
Capelli d'Angelo in Brodo
TPT - 23 minutes

This Eritrean noodle soup quite obviously reflects the Italian influence. It is usually made with a chicken broth, but a complex vegetarian soup stock works just as well. I have often cooked up a noodle soup using a flavorful vegetarian soup stock and fettuccine for lunch on a cold winter's day, a soup that reminds me of the hot noodle soup my mom had waiting for us after we had walked home from school for lunch during those cold winters. This is another version of that comfort food and I suspect it is viewed with equal affection in Eritrea. Since angel hair pasta is readily available, fresh and dried; we do not have to go through the tedious, time-consuming process of making the long thin noodles.

We serve this in over-sized soup cups so that we can eat the noodles with a fork and drink the remaining broth.

Africa–Eritrea

ERITREAN NOODLE SOUP (cont'd)

6 cups VEGETABLE STOCK FROM SOUP *[see index]* **or other vegetarian stock of choice**
3/4 pound angel hair *pasta (capelli d'angelo)**

6 tablespoons freshly grated *pecorino Romano* **cheese**

In a large saucepan, heat vegetarian stock to the boil. Add *pasta* and allow soup to come back to the boil and simmer for about 5 minutes.

Turn into a heated tureen and serve into oversized soup cups. Pass grated cheese. Serve with forks.

Yields 6 serving
adequate for 4 people

Notes: *Nests of angel hair *pasta*, when available, make a particularly attractive presentation.

**The vegetable stock is, of course, nutritional but calculating its food values is difficult without chemical analyses techniques. For these reasons, we have chosen to treat these stocks merely as flavoring—omitting them from nutritional calculations but recognizing them as a food, quite rich in vitamins and minerals.

This recipe can be doubled, when required.

1/6 SERVING (with 1 tablespoonful grated cheese) –
PROTEIN = 8.6 g.; FAT = 2.4 g.; CARBOHYDRATE = 41.2 g.;
CALORIES = 230; CALORIES FROM FAT = 9%**

PEPPER *VINAIGRETTE* IN THE STYLE OF ERITREA
Vinagreta con Pimienta
TPT - 2 minutes

Eritreans enjoy a finely shredded cabbage slaw with a dressing which contains both black pepper and chopped fresh jalapeño pepper. Instead of mincing a hot pepper into the vinaigrette, I add jalapeño hot chili sauce. It gives the salad dressing a beautiful blush, just the right kick, and it keeps well in the refrigerator.

1/4 cup *extra virgin* **olive oil**
1/4 cup distilled white vinegar
1/4 teaspoon ground mixed peppercorns—black, red, and white
1/4 teaspoon red *jalapeño chili* **sauce, or to taste**

In a cruet, combine oil, vinegar, ground peppercorns, and *jalapeño chili* sauce. Shake vigorously.

Yields 1/2 cupful

Notes: *Jalapeño* sauce is available in Hispanic groceries, food specialty stores, and in most grocery stores throughout the Southwest.

This recipe can be halved or doubled, when required.

1/16 SERVING (i. e., about 1 1/2 teaspoonfuls) –
PROTEIN = 0.0 g.; FAT = 2.8 g.; CARBOHYDRATE = 0.0 g.;
CALORIES = 25; CALORIES FROM FAT = >99%

Africa–Eritrea

ERITREAN LENTILS WITH TOMATO AND GARLIC
Alitcha Birsen

TPT - 1 hour and 14 minutes

It is amazing how this little, protein-packed pulse has traveled the world from its ancient origins in the Middle East, where it was one of the first crops domesticated. An important element in the diet of Homo sapiens since Neolithic times, it is surpassed only by the soybean and hemp in protein content and, therefore, is important to vegetarian cultures and to diets in which soybean and animal protein is less available. Deficient in two essential amino acids, methionine and cystine, lentils must be complemented and since they readily supply the essential amino acids isoleucine and lysine, grain sources, such as bread or rice which are deficient in the isoleucine and lysine, are the sensible choices to accompany this dish.

As I traveled in this virtual circumnavigation of the world, I was fascinated with the number of lentil recipes I found. I was equally fascinated to see how many cultures had adapted the tomato as a main ingredient in a soup or a stew. This tomato-based dish from Eritrea clearly hints at Italian influences, as do many dishes and preparations in this former Italian colony. On occasion Eritrean cooks will top a bowl of pasta with butter in the form of "niter kebbeb" and even add the fiery berbere seasoning.

2 tablespoons canola oil
2 garlic cloves—crushed and *finely* chopped

3/4 cup canned, *diced* **tomatoes**—well-drained—
   or **1 large tomato**—peeled, seeded, and chopped

1/2 cup brown (*or* green) lentils

2 cups VEGETARIAN BROWN STOCK *[see index]*
   or **vegetarian stock of choice**
2 tablespoons *finely* **chopped mild green** *chilies**
3/4 teaspoon ground ginger
1/2 teaspoon *jalapeño chili* **sauce, or to taste***
1/4 teaspoon freshly ground black pepper, or to taste
Salt, to taste

In a non-aluminum saucepan** set over *MEDIUM* heat, heat oil. Add *very finely* chopped garlic and sauté until golden, *being careful not to allow the garlic to brown.*

Add tomatoes and simmer for about 5 minutes.

Sort lentils and discard those of poor quality. Rinse thoroughly. Add to tomato–garlic mixture.

Add vegetable stock, *finely* chopped green *chilies*, ground ginger, *jalapeño chili* sauce, black pepper, and salt. Allow to come to the boil. Reduce heat to *LOW*, cover, allow to cook for 55-60 minutes, or until the lentils are tender and the liquid has been absorbed. Stir occasionally.***

Serve into heated soup bowls with chunks of bread or *injera* or, if preferred, serve traditionally by ladling a portion over *injera* or other flatbread, of choice.

Notes: *Since fresh hot *chilies* would be customary in Eritrea, you may wish to replace the *jalapeño chili* sauce and the green *chilies* with fresh red *chilies*. The combination here appeals to the Western palate.

**Aluminum discolors lentils rather unpleasantly so it is advisable to avoid the use of aluminum cookware or serving bowls in this case.

***If desirable, this dish may be prepared in advance to this point and refrigerated until about an hour before serving time.

This recipe may be halved or doubled, when required.

Yields 6 servings
adequate for 4 people

1/6 SERVING – PROTEIN = 5.0 g.; FAT = 4.7 g.; CARBOHYDRATE = 13.2 g.;
CALORIES = 109; CALORIES FROM FAT = 39%

Africa–**Eritrea**

ERITREAN COFFEE ICE DESSERT
Graniti di Espresso con Crema

TPT - 8 hours and 20 minutes;
5 hours = first freezing period;
1 hour = second freezing period;
2 hours = third freezing period

A direct result of its years as an Italian colony, espresso coffee is the preferred coffee of Eritrea, "bün" or, if you add milk," mucchiato." When I tasted this dessert for the first time, I was convinced that it was an Italian ice but it was richer than any I had ever tasted. Eritreans have taken the "syrup-over-shaved-ice" Italian and New York street treat to a very cosmopolitan level making it the perfect ending for a meal Do not expect an ice cream; do expect an ice with cream!.

Be sure that the dessert dishes you choose will withstand the last freezing period.

1/4 cup *boiling* **water**
4 1/2 tablespoons *granulated* **sugar**

2 1/2 cups brewed *espresso* **coffee—***chilled*****

1 1/2 cups heavy whipping cream
1 1/2 tablespoons *confectioners'* **sugar**

3 tablespoons *crème de cacao* **liqueur** *or* **Kahlua**

In a small saucepan or Turkish coffee pot set over *MEDIUM* heat, combine *boiling* water and the *verifine* sugar. Cook for about 5 minutes, or until it begins to thicken. Remove from heat.

Add the *cold espresso* coffee. Stir to combine. Turn into a loaf pan and place in the freezer for about 5 hours, or overnight. Remove the coffee mixture from the freezer and using a fork, break the large ice crystals. Return to the freezer for 1 hour.

Meanwhile, using the electric mixer fitted with *chilled* beaters or by hand using a *chilled* wire whisk, beat heavy cream in a *chilled* bowl until soft peaks form. While continuing to beat, add confectioners' sugar. Beat until stiff peaks form. Set aside until required.

Remove the *graniti* slush from the freezer. Add *crème de cacao*. Stir it gently into the icy mixture.

Add whipped cream and fold it into the coffee mixture. Divide among six dessert dishes. Place the dessert dishes in the freezer for at least 2 hours.

Remove from the freezer no more than 5 minutes, before serving.

Yields 6 individual servings

Notes: Regular "American" coffee, characterized as "dishwater" in Italy, is too weak to use in this dish.

When required, this recipe can be halved.

1/6 SERVING –   PROTEIN = 1.2 g.; FAT = 19.6 g.; CARBOHYDRATE = 14.1 g.;
CALORIES = 253; CALORIES FROM FAT = 70%

Ethiopia

Remains of *Ardipithecus ramidus kadabba*, dated by various researchers to between 5.8 - 5.2 million years ago, and *Auralopithecus anamensis*, the pro-human ancestor that included the representative we know as "Lucy," dating to about 4.2 million years ago, have been found in Ethiopia. The history of this sub-Saharan country, originally called Abyssinia, is steeped in a traditional origin that is accepted but unconfirmed. Menelik I, who has been traditionally described as having been the son of the Queen of Sheba and King Solomon, is said to have been its first ruler. In the first century BC the Aksumite Empire united the smaller kingdoms that had established on the Ethiopian Plateau. Successive dynasties maintained an isolationist policy until the fifteenth century AD when diplomatic contact was made with European kingdoms. However, Ethiopia returned to isolationism for about one hundred years, from 1755 to 1855 in a period that has been called the "Age of Princes," *Zemene Mesafint*, during which the emperor was relegated to a powerless position and the country was controlled by warlords.

Ethiopia emerged finally under Emperor Menelik II, who repulsed an Italian invasion in 1896 and went on to expand his empire by conquering neighboring territories. He was succeeded by his daughter in 1917 with his cousin Ras Tafari Makoonen as regent. When the empress died in 1930, Ras Tafari Makoonen assumed the throne as Emperor Haile Selassie I. Italy took the opportunity during this period of succession and reorganization to once again try to conquer Ethiopia in 1935. On May 9, 1936, Italy's colonial ambitions led to formal annexation of Ethiopia into Italy, the incorporation of Ethiopia with Eritrea and Somalia (Italian Somaliland) into Italian East Africa, and the assumption of the title of Emperor of Ethiopia by the King of Italy. It was thought that emigration from Italy to its African colonies would solve the poverty in Italy's overpopulated southern provinces and although many did emigrate in the 1930s, their impact on Ethiopia was minimal since the majority of the emigrants chose to move to Libya. Nevertheless, about 200,000 Italians did move to Italian East Africa. The onset of World War II brought Italy's colonial ambitions to an end as the Allies drove into North Africa against the Axis Powers, which included Italy. By May 5, 1941, Haile Selassie I had reclaimed the Ethiopian throne in the wake of the British military action against the Italians in Italian East Africa.

Ethiopia experienced a period as a Socialist state under a military dictatorship after Haile Selassie was deposed in 1974. From 1977 to 1991, with the support of Soviet Russia, Lt. Col Mengistu Haile Mariam held onto power but this period was plagued by civil wars that resulted in the deaths of thousands. And, despite the fact that eighty-five percent of the Nile's total water flow originates in Ethiopia, thousands also died due to drought and famine while that astonishing potential water supply remained unexploited. Mariam fled into exile in Zimbabwe when the Soviet Union collapsed. Now a federal republic and still working toward political stability, Ethiopia is one of the fastest growing economies in the world.

Coptic Christianity was introduced to this area of Africa c. 341 AD and is considered to be the state religion with The Ethiopian Orthodox Church its official name. The church calendar requires fasting on Wednesdays, Fridays, and throughout the forty-days of Lent so Ethiopians have developed recipes to comply resulting in a fairly large selection of vegan dishes, mostly vegetable stews or *alechas* served directly onto the national bread *injera*. *Tef*, the flour used to make *injera*, is very difficult to obtain here but, if you wish to serve this menu traditionally, a recipe for *injera* has been included using pancake mixes, quite easily available all over the United States. Several of the side dishes that I have chosen to include here hint at an Italian influence in the preparation. You will note that olive oil is in common use in addition to sesame and safflower oils. Since coffee is said to have originated in Ethiopia, be sure to provide coffee at the end of this meal.

Africa–Ethiopia

Our dear friend from Ethiopia, Hailu, as is the case with most of his countrymen, could tolerate the fieriest seasoning. The fire in these recipes has been tempered to the toleration level of most Americans but feel free to add hot chilies to your heart's content.

Ethiopian National Flatbread for the Western Kitchen
Injera

~

Cheese Salad
Iab

~

White Eggplant and Red Kidney Bean Salad

~~~~~~~~~~~~~~~~~~~~

Vegetable Stew
Shiro Alecha

Spiced Clarified Butter
Niter Kebbeb

Kale with Onion and Spices
Zelbo Gomen

Beets with Oil and Lemon
Yeqey sir Qiqqil

~~~~~~~~~~~~~~~~~~~~

Prunes with Cardamom and Almonds in Red Wine Sauce
Garaza gar Wayn Taj

Stewed Figs with Cream

Dates Rolled in Cardamom–Sugar

Coffee with Cream

Africa–**Ethiopia**

ETHIOPIAN NATIONAL FLATBREAD
for the Western Kitchen

Injera

TPT - 41 minutes

A finely ground millet flour, known as tef, is used to make injera in Ethiopia. It is not easily found in the United States, as I have previously mentioned, although millet and millet flour are available in natural food stores, if you wish to experiment. Tef is used to prepare a batter which is fermented for a day or two. In Ethiopia, the baked injera is spread out to cover the table, as a "tablecloth," if you will. The food is then served onto the injera and the meal is consumed communally. A single loaf, placed on a dinner plate, can approximate the traditional serving method. We enjoy these injera breads for breakfast and serve them just as we would serve pancakes.

1 cup buckwheat pancake mix
1 cup *reduced-fat* **Bisquick baking mix**

2 cups water

In a large mixing bowl, combine pancake mix and baking mix. Stir to mix thoroughly.

Add water. Stir to form a pourable batter, adding more water if necessary.

Preheat a non-stick-coated skillet, with cover, over *MEDIUM* heat.*

[**] Pour about 1/3 cupful of batter onto the heated pan surface in a spiral, *beginning at the outside and working quickly into the center of a 7-inch circle.* Cover the skillet and cook the *injera* for 1 minute. The bread will rise slightly. The top should be slightly moist; the bottom, dry but *not crisp or browned.* Using a long spatula, remove the bread to a platter or wire rack to cool.

Repeat from [**] until all breads are prepared.

Pile loaves onto a serving platter.

Place a loaf on each diner's plate. Serve the food onto the bread. Small pieces of *injera,* torn from the loaf, are used as an utensil to scoop up the food.

Yields sixteen 7-inch loaves
adequate for 6 people

Notes: *A well-seasoned, griddle with cover, would be on-hand in every Ethiopian kitchen and reserved just for the preparation of the daily *injera.*

The combination of commercially-available buckwheat pancake and whole wheat biscuit mixes does give a texture similar to the original. However, the taste is quite different. This quick-mix combination is generally more acceptable to the Western palate.

This recipe may be doubled, when required. This bread should, however, be freshly made for each meal.

Leftovers are delicious with soft butter and sprinkling of sugar or honey.

1/16 SERVING (i. e., per 7-inch loaf) –
PROTEIN = 3.9 g.; FAT = 4.1 g.; CARBOHYDRATE = 27.4 g.;
CALORIES = 146; CALORIES FROM FAT = 25%

ETHIOPIAN CHEESE SALAD

Iab

TPT - 38 minutes;
30 minutes = flavor development period

Iab is made from an Ethiopian curd cheese that I have never found in the United States. Even our friend from Ethiopia had accepted cottage cheese in place of the unique cheese that is more of the consistency and saltiness of fresh feta cheese. Combining small curd farmers' cheese with feta gives an approximation. Put a refreshing serving of iab on your injera-covered table. You will find it to be an excellent flavor and texture counterpoint to Ethiopian wats or stews.

Africa–Ethiopia

ETHIOPIAN CHEESE SALAD (cont'd)

1/4 cup Greek *feta* cheese—*finely* crumbled
3/4 pound farmers' cheese *or low-fat, small curd* cottage cheese, if preferred
1/4 cup PLAIN YOGURT *[see index] or* commercially-available plain yogurt

3 tablespoons *finely* chopped fresh parsley leaves
2 tablespoons *finely* snipped chives
1 tablespoon freshly grated lemon zest
1 tablespoon *finely* chopped fresh basil leaves
1/4 teaspoon *white* pepper, or to taste

In a mixing bowl, work the *finely* crumbled *feta* cheese into curd cheese until the *feta* cheese is uniformly distributed throughout the mixture ingredients. Add the yogurt and mix thoroughly.

Add *finely* chopped parsley, *finely* snipped chives, grated lemon zest, *finely* chopped basil, and white pepper. Mix thoroughly.

Refrigerate for at least 30 minutes to allow flavors to marry.

Serve as a salad or relish with almost any menu, especially those which include vegetable stews. This cheese is also excellent with *crudités* and crackers as an appetizer.

Yields 2 cupfuls
adequate for 4-6 people

Note: This recipe is easily halved or doubled, when required.

1/6 SERVING (about 1/3 cupful) –
PROTEIN = 8.6 g.; FAT = 1.6 g.; CARBOHYDRATE = 3.5 g.;
CALORIES = 99; CALORIES FROM FAT = 15%

ETHIOPIAN WHITE EGGPLANT AND RED KIDNEY BEAN SALAD
TPT - 27 minutes

Small white eggplants hang from the plant like bunches of eggs and clearly show how this vegetable got its name. In our produce departments, we are usually presented with the purple eggplants or, occasionally, the mild, long, skinny Chinese/Asian eggplants. In Africa "garden eggs" usually refers to a small, light purple eggplant but the mild, firm white- or cream-colored eggplants are preferred for this recipe. Since the eggplant is neither salted nor cooked in this recipe, the mild white or galaxie eggplants are preferable. I usually buy two extra eggplants when I make this salad and put them in a fruit bowl to use as the centerpiece; it is easier than explaining. The sweet finish to a forkful is a surprise that always elicits comments. I serve it with big hunks of warm country-style bread.

2 white eggplants—peeled and diced to yield about 4 cups

2 tablespoon lemon juice
Salt, to taste
Freshly ground black pepper, to taste

1 cup canned red kidney beans—well-drained
1 large garlic clove—*very finely* chopped
2 tablespoons *extra virgin* olive oil

2 teaspoons sugar

Turn the diced eggplant into a mixing bowl.

In a small bowl, combine lemon juice, salt, and black pepper. Stir to combine and pour over the eggplant. Allow to stand for 20 minutes. Stir occasionally.

In another mixing bowl, combine kidney beans, *very finely* chopped garlic, and olive oil. Stir gently to mix. Add eggplant and the marinade in which it has been sitting. Toss gently. Turn into a serving dish.

Sprinkle sugar over.

Serve at once.

Yields 6 servings
adequate for 4 people

Notes: Any dried, boiled beans or well-drained canned beans you prefer can be used to make this salad. I used red kidney beans because the resulting color contrasts stimulate the appetite.

This recipe can be doubled, when required.

1/6 SERVING – PROTEIN = 2.9 g.; FAT = 4.0 g.; CARBOHYDRATE = 11.9 g.;
CALORIES = 94; CALORIES FROM FAT = 38%

Africa–Ethiopia

ETHIOPIAN VEGETABLE STEW
Shiro Alecha
TPT – 37 minutes

A significant portion of the Ethiopian population follows the tenants of the Coptic Christian Church and, therefore, observes many meatless fast days. As a consequence each household has vegetarian favorites for those observances, often very hotly seasoned. A version of "shiro alecha," known as" shiro wot," can be made as per these directions but with the addition of Berbere spice mix or, more simply, the addition of two or three finely chopped hot chilies. The recipe given here is a mild interpretation of this stew which should be more acceptable to Western palates.

Cabbage is often included in the alecha but it has been omitted here since kale is included elsewhere in this menu. However, if you chose to, you can allow small wedges of cabbage to steam gently on top of the alecha at the end of the cooking period.

2 quarts *boiling* **water**
12 small, "salad" potatoes—peeled and halved— *or* **3 medium potatoes—peeled and cut into chunks**
24 baby carrots—scraped or peeled

3 tablespoons water
1 medium onion—chopped
2 garlic cloves—chopped
1 tablespoon fresh gingerroot
1 small hot *chili* **pepper, of choice—seeded and** *finely* **chopped***

1 1/2 tablespoons ETHIOPIAN SPICED CLARIFIED BUTTER *(Niter Kebbeb)* [see recipe which follows]

2 cups water
1 tablespoon tomato paste
1/2 cup diced green bell pepper
1/2 cup diced red bell pepper
2 small ears of corn—cut into 1-inch cross-cob slices**
About 24 whole, *very thin* **green beans—well-washed and trimmed**
Freshly ground black pepper, to taste
1/2 teaspoon ground cardamom

In a large saucepan set over *MEDIUM* heat, parboil potatoes and carrots for about 10 minutes. Turn into a colander and drain thoroughly.

In the food processor fitted with steel knife, combine the 3 tablespoonfuls water with chopped onion, garlic, gingerroot, and hot pepper. Process until very smooth. Turn into a large kettle set over *LOW-MEDIUM* heat.

Add clarified butter and cook until most of the moisture has been evaporated, *being careful not to allow onion to brown.*

Add the 2 cupfuls water and tomato paste. Mix well. Add parboiled potatoes and carrots with chopped green and red pepper, corn slices, and whole green beans. Season with black pepper and cardamom. *Cover tightly and cook for 8 minutes. Uncover, stir gently.* Continue cooking until vegetables are *tender*, but *not soft.*

Carefully transfer vegetables to a heated serving bowl or deep platter. Spoon sauce over the vegetables.

Serve at once.

Yields 6 main-course servings
adequate for 4-6 people

Notes: *Be sure to use gloves when seeding and chopping the hot peppers. If you do not want to handle the hot *chili* peppers, *jalapeño* sauce, ground red pepper (cayenne), or even Tabasco sauce can be used.

**Corn, cut into small cross-cob slices, can often be found frozen in grocery stores, if fresh corn is out-of-season.

This recipe is easily halved or doubled, when required.

The vegetables chosen to make this stew may be modified based on preference or availability.

1/6 SERVING – PROTEIN = 3.9 g.; FAT = 4.1 g.; CARBOHYDRATE = 27.4 g.;
CALORIES = 146; CALORIES FROM FAT = 25%

Africa–Ethiopia

ETHIOPIAN SPICED CLARIFIED BUTTER
Niter Kebbeh
TPT - 55 minutes

This spiced clarified butter is every bit as essential to Ethiopian cooking as extra virgin olive oil is to Italian cooking. Refrigerators are not common in Ethiopian homes so cooking oils and butters become rancid quickly. Clarified and preseasoned, this butter can be stored on a pantry shelf for several months without ill effect. It does keep practically forever when refrigerated.

The food values are not significantly different from that of the butter with which you started. It has been flavored, but nothing really has been added.

1 pound sweet (*unsalted*) butter

1/4 cup coarsely chopped onion
1 large garlic clove—*finely* chopped
1 1/2 teaspoons *finely* chopped gingerroot
3/4 teaspoon ground turmeric
1 cardamom pod—crushed
1 one-inch piece cinnamon quill
1 whole clove
Pinch freshly grated nutmeg

In a heavy saucepan set over *MEDIUM* heat, allow butter to melt completely.

When the surface of the melted butter is completely covered with foam, stir in the chopped onion, *finely* chopped garlic and gingerroot, ground turmeric, crushed cardamom pod, cinnamon quill, whole clove, and grated nutmeg. *Reduce heat to LOW* and allow to simmer, *undisturbed,* for about 45 minutes. The milk solids which have settled to the bottom of the pan will be browned; the clarified butter on top will be transparent.

Strain by pouring through a sieve lined with a cotton tea towel. Discard the seasonings and *be sure to discard all milky residue remaining in the bottom of the pan* because elements of this are what cause butter to become rancid. *Strain again* through the sieve lined with a *clean* cotton tea towel.

Pour the *kebbeh* into a jar. Allow to *cool completely*. Cover tightly and store in the refrigerator until ready to use. The *kebbeh* will solidify when chilled, as does any clarified butter.

Yields about 2 cupfuls

Notes: ETHIOPIAN SPICED CLARIFIED BUTTER keeps for months when refrigerated, as do clarified butter and Indian *ghee*. Additionally, it does not burn at high temperatures as does regular butter so it can be used very successfully to flavor foods before outdoor or pan-grilling.

This recipe may be halved, if desired.

KALE WITH ONION AND SPICES IN THE STYLE OF ETHIOPIA
Gomen
TPT - 29 minutes

Huge, dark green heads of kale are one of the most beautiful sights at the farmers' market in the fall, sitting there beside the piles of gourds and squashes, the last harvest of potatoes, and the snowy heads of cauliflower. To many they are little more than decoration and people pass right by the vitamin-rich heads without a thought or with the thought that the kale may be bitter. Kale benefits from the light frosts that end the growing seasons of other leafy vegetables so if we have had a frost, I know that that freshly harvested head of kale will be sweet. Kale can be much more than just decoration on a salad bar or a late fall decoration in the garden. It is a good food, rich in beta carotene, vitamin K, and all the cancer-fighting sulforaphane for which the members of the cabbage family are to be valued. Anti-inflammatory and antioxidant properties are impressive. Kale and other member of the cabbage family enjoy popularity in Ethiopia and are frequently added to wats and alechas. This recipe, flavored in a way I had never, ever had kale, allows the deep green, nutritious vegetable to be served as a side dish.

If you must buy your kale from a grocery store or green grocer, refrigerate the head for several days. This treatment also results in a sweeter taste.

Africa—Ethiopia

**KALE WITH ONION AND SPICES
IN THE STYLE OF ETHIOPIA** (cont'd)

1 pound kale—about 10 cupfuls—trimmed of heavy stems and discolored leaf tips, coarsely chopped and well-washed to remove any sand*

2 cups *boiling* water
3/4 cup *finely* chopped Italian red onion
2 tablespoons ETHIOPIAN SPICED CLARIFIED BUTTER *(Niter kebbeb)* *[see recipe which precedes]*
1 garlic clove—*very finely* chopped
1 tablespoon *very finely* chopped gingerroot
1/2 teaspoon *jalapeño chili* sauce, or more to taste**

Salt, to taste
Freshly ground black pepper, to taste

Pour *boiling* water into a large saucepan or a deep skillet set over *MEDIUM* heat. Add kale, *finely* chopped onion, spiced clarified butter, *very finely* chopped garlic and gingerroot, and *jalapeño chili* sauce. Cook, stirring frequently, for 25 minutes.

Season with salt and pepper. Turn into a heated serving dish.

Serve hot or at room temperature. Refrigerate leftovers.

Yields 6 servings
adequate for 4 people

Notes: *Many grocery stores now carry tender, baby kale in prewashed packaging. It is a fine product and less bitter than mature kale.

**The *jalapeño* sauce is a great convenience but, if preferred, a small *jalapeño* chili can be used instead. With gloves on, remove seeds and membranes and chop *very finely* before adding.

This recipe can be halved, when required.

1/6 SERVING – PROTEIN = 3.6 g.; FAT = 6.1 g.; CARBOHYDRATE = 14.2 g.;
CALORIES = 112; CALORIES FROM FAT = 49%

BEETS WITH OIL AND LEMON
Yegey sir Qiggil
TPT - 8 minutes

Surprised? I was surprised too when I first encountered this recipe. Beets? I certainly did not expect beets to be a favorite in Ethiopia but I found that lots of "cold weather" vegetables are popular in this East African nation. There is little doubt that the years as an Italian colony influenced this preparation of beets. Although this dish is usually made with sliced or diced beets, I often choose to make it with tiny, baby beets.

6 large beets—boiled, peeled, and sliced— *or* the equivalent in well-drained, canned beets
2 tablespoons water*

2 tablespoons *extra virgin* olive oil
2 tablespoons freshly squeezed lemon juice

In a saucepan set over *MEDIUM* heat, combine sliced beets and water. Allow it to come to the boil. Reduce heat to *LOW*.

Add oil and lemon juice. Allow to heat through, stirring frequently to coat the slices with the oil and lemon juice. Turn into a heated serving dish.

Serve at once with a slotted spoon.

Yields 6 servings
adequate for 4-6 people

Notes: *If you are using canned beets, replace the water with 2 tablespoonfuls of the beet canning liquid.

This recipe can be halved, when required.

1/6 SERVING – PROTEIN = 0.8 g.; FAT = 3.8 g.; CARBOHYDRATE = 5.7 g.;
CALORIES = 59; CALORIES FROM FAT = 39%

Africa–**Ethiopia**

ETHIOPIAN PRUNES WITH CARDAMOM AND ALMONDS IN RED WINE SAUCE

Garaza gar Wayn Taj

TPT - 1 hour and 26 minutes;
30 minutes = cooling period

Although Ethiopian meals rarely include desserts or a sweet, westerners expect a dessert and Ethiopian restaurants in the United States and in Great Britain do serve pastries that may, in Ethiopia, be reserved for holidays. Dried fruits are often served with coffee and this unusual dessert is one of our favorite ways to finish off an Ethiopian meal. It reminds me of a dessert served in Italy's Piedmont where cherries are cooked in red wine and suggests to me that the preparation may have been introduced to Ethiopians by Italians who settled there in the 1930s. It really highlights the Ethiopian love of cardamom.

2 cups pitted *preservative-free* prunes
1/2 cup *preservative-free* almonds—*blanched* and chopped
1 cup red wine
1/4 cup sugar
1/2 teaspoon ground cardamom
2 whole cloves

In a saucepan set over *MEDIUM* heat, combine *pitted* prunes, chopped almonds, wine, sugar, ground cardamom, and whole cloves. Allow to come to the boil. *Reduce heat to LOW.* Cook, stirring frequently, until mixture thickens—about 45 minutes. Remove and discard whole cloves. Pour into a serving dish. Allow to come to room temperature.

Provide spoons to each diner and allow them to serve themselves from the common bowl. Refrigerate leftovers.

Yields 8 servings
adequate for 6 people

Note: This recipe can be doubled, when required.

1/6 SERVING – PROTEIN = 2.2 g.; FAT = 4.1 g.; CARBOHYDRATE = 28.8 g.;
CALORIES = 155; CALORIES FROM FAT = 24%

The Gambia

Hanno was chosen as the name for a small impact crater along the western edge of the lunar feature named Mare Australe. Thinking that it had been named for the Carthaginian King Hanno the Great, I was surprised to find out that it had been named for Hanno II, an early, nominal king who reigned from 480 to 440 BC, a king who was better known as Hanno the Navigator. You probably wonder what this has to do with the Gambia but it is Hanno who first explored this area along the northwestern coast of Africa in the fifth century BC. The consensus of scholars, upon studying the descriptions in Hanno's journals, is that his expedition to found colonies, which included some thirty thousand sailors and sixty ships, did reach the mouth of the Gambia River.

No written record of the peoples of this region appears until Arab traders began to travel through the region in the ninth and tenth centuries AD. By the thirteenth century they were under the rule of the Mali Empire until the empire collapsed in the sixteenth century and the territory was claimed by the Portuguese. In 1588 Antonio, Prior of Crato, who claimed legitimacy to the Portuguese throne, sold exclusive trade rights on the Gambia River to English merchant traders. The maintaining of a trade route to facilitate the slave trade by first the Portuguese and then by the British, led eventually to the small country that is now The Gambia. It is the smallest country on the mainland continent of Africa, occupying the Gambia River valley, and enclaved within Senegal. The Gambia River is the primary trade and shipping route in this region of West Africa with an outlet to the Atlantic Ocean from Gambia's small coastline border.

The French established a colonial government in 1840, making Senegal a part of French West Africa together with Mauritania, French Sudan (now, Mali) French Guinea, Côte d'Ivoire, Upper Volta (now, Burkina Faso), Dahomey (now, Benin), and Niger. Senegal literally surrounds Gambia on its three land borders and wanted the British trade arteries. By the end of the seventeenth and throughout the eighteenth century the French challenged the British for the Gambia and Senegal rivers. Finally in 1889 the present boundaries of Gambia were established and it was declared a British Crown Colony. Full independence was granted in 1965. The constitutional monarchy remained in the British Commonwealth until 2013.

Despite the difficulties during the British colonial period and the loss of their original land mass in an agreement between the British and the French Republic, Gambians did not reject all that was British as one might have well expected; they remain in the Commonwealth. They have also taken the opportunity to adopt many and adapt many more British foods. Crossover dishes found throughout West Africa such as yam, cassava, and plantain *fufu*, millet *couscous*, *chakeri*, and papaya jam are understandably found in Gambia since all of these nations were once part of the great tribal empires that dominated this part of Africa. You will find examples of all these regional food in recipes in this volume.

Thanks to the emphasis on tourism, vegetarians can do quite nicely in Gambia.

Africa–The Gambia

Deep-Fried Plantain Chips

Breaded and Deep-Fried Okra   **Tomato Dipping Sauce**

Guava Juice

~

Tomato Soup with Basil

French-Style *Baguettes*
Tapalapa

~

Banana and Mango Salad   Fresh Pineapple Slices with Honey

~ ~

Black Beans in Tomato – Garlic Sauce

Millet *Couscous* **with Vegetables**
Ruy

~ ~ ~ ~ ~ ~ ~ ~ ~ ~

Boiled Potatoes

Sautéed Soymeat

with

Peanut Butter and Tomato Sauce with Garlic
Domodo

~ ~ ~ ~ ~ ~ ~ ~ ~ ~

Toubab **Macaroni and Vegetables**

Mashed Yams, Cassava, or Plantains
Fufu

~ ~ ~ ~ ~ ~ ~ ~ ~ ~ ~ ~ ~ ~ ~ ~ ~ ~ ~ ~

Sweet Couscous Pudding
Caakiri

Bread and Butter Pudding with Coconut   **Maple Multigrain Bread**

Flax – Banana Cake

BREADED AND DEEP-FRIED OKRA
TPT - 36 minutes

Deep-fried okra is really quite delicious. When pre-treated with vinegar, the mucilaginous nature of okra is moderated and makes a very enjoyable appetizer.

Oil for deep-frying

6 tablespoons distilled white vinegar
1 teaspoon crushed red pepper flakes
2 teaspoons turmeric

15 firm okra—well-washed and trimmed

1/2 cup unbleached white flour
1/4 cup *very finely* **ground corn meal, such as** masa harina

Salt, to taste

Africa – The Gambia

BREADED AND DEEP – FRIED OKRA (cont'd)

Place an oven-proof dish in a warm oven to heat.

Pour oil into a deep frying pan or kettle to a depth of about 1/2 inch. Set over *MEDIUM* heat and allow to preheat to 365 degrees F.

In a mixing bowl, combine vinegar, crushed red pepper flakes, and turmeric.

Slice okra in half lengthwise. Add to vinegar mixture and allow to marinate for at least 10 minutes.

Put flour and corn meal in a mixing bowl. Form a paste by adding a tablespoonful of the vinegar mixture at a time.

Using a spatula, lift out the okra pieces and add to flour mixture. Using a spoon, gently stir to coat the okra with the flour mixture. Deep-fry in the hot oil in batches until crisp and browned. Transfer to paper toweling to drain off excess oil. Transfer to the dish in the warm oven and keep warm until ready to serve.

Sprinkle generously with salt.

Serve with a dipping sauce of choice.

Yields 30 pieces
adequate for 6 people

Note: This recipe can be halved, when required.

1/30 SERVING – PROTEIN = 0.5 g.; FAT = 0.8 g.; CARBOHYDRATE = 3.2 g.;
CALORIES = 21; CALORIES FROM FAT = 34%

GAMBIAN TOMATO DIPPING SAUCE
TPT - 42 minutes

"Akra" fritters are bean fritters that are frequently served as appetizers in The Gambia. They are accompanied by an assertive sauce that is useful as a dipping sauce for other foods such as French-fried potatoes or chips, fried plantains, and fried okra. I freeze this sauce in small batches so that it can be plucked from the freezer when we get the urge to indulge. You can make it as hot as you please or, if preferred, tone it down to a mild salsa.

1 tablespoon peanut oil
1 medium onion—*very finely* **chopped**

1 cup canned, *crushed* **tomatoes** *or* **tomato purée ***
1/2 cup water
2 tablespoons *finely* **chopped mild green** *chilies*
Ground red pepper (cayenne), to taste
Salt, to taste
1/4 teaspoon freshly ground mixed peppercorns
   —**red, black, and white—or to taste**

2 tablespoons freshly squeezed lemon juice

In a heavy, non-stick-coated saucepan set over *MEDIUM* heat, heat oil. Add very *finely* chopped onion and garlic. Sauté until onion is soft and translucent, *being careful to allow neither the onion nor the garlic to brown.*

Add tomatoes, water, *finely* chopped green *chilies*, ground red pepper (cayenne), salt, and ground mixed peppercorns. Allow to come to the boil. *Reduce heat to LOW-MEDIUM* and allow to simmer until sauce has reduced by *one-half*, stirring frequently.

Add lemon juice and continue cooking for about 5 minutes. Turn into a heated serving bowl.

Serve warm.

Yields 2 cupfuls

Notes: *If the brand of crushed tomatoes that you buy has chunks of tomato in it, purée it to uniformity first.

This recipe can be easily doubled, when required, and since it freezes well, this is a convenient feature.

1/32 SERVING (i. e., per tablespoonful) –
PROTEIN = 0.4 g.; FAT = 0.9 g.; CARBOHYDRATE = 1.9 g.;
CALORIES = 16; CALORIES FROM FAT = 51%

GAMBIAN TOMATO SOUP WITH BASIL
TPT - 36 minutes

In late summer, when the tomato harvest overwhelms Gambians, you can be sure that this soup will appear on many, many tables. Canned, crushed tomatoes can extend the pleasure of this soup.

Africa – The Gambia

GAMBIAN TOMATO SOUP WITH BASIL (cont'd)

2 tablespoons *extra virgin* olive oil
4 garlic cloves—*very finely* chopped
1 cup *very finely* chopped onion

4 cups canned, *crushed* tomatoes
1 cup VEGETABLE STOCK FROM SOUP
   [see index] or other vegetarian stock of choice
2 teaspoons crushed dried basil
Salt, to taste
Freshly ground black pepper, to taste

1/2 cup *finely* slivered fresh basil leaves, for garnish

In a large saucepan, set over *LOW-MEDIUM* heat, heat oil. Add *very finely* chopped garlic and onion. Sauté until onion is soft and translucent, *being careful to allow neither the garlic nor the onion to brown.*

Add tomatoes, vegetable stock, crushed basil, salt, and pepper. Simmer gently for at least 25 minutes. Turn into a heated soup tureen.

Garnish with the basil chiffonade.

Serve into heated soup plates.

Yields 7 cupfuls

Notes: When required, this recipe can be halved or doubled.

This soup freezes well.

1/7 SERVING (i. e., about 1 cupful) –
PROTEIN = 1.9 g.; FAT = 3.5 g.; CARBOHYDRATE = 8.9 g.;
CALORIES = 71; CALORIES FROM FAT = 44%

FRENCH – STYLE *BAGUETTES*
Tapalapa

TPT - 4 hours and 30 minutes;
   2 hours = automated preparation period;
   1 hour = cooling period

My French-style baguettes have a good, French-bread crust and are really not that hard to make. With a few additions you can approximate the taste of the tapalapa baguettes that would be found in Gambian bakeries. The addition of beaten egg whites lightens the texture and eliminates the need for extra baking powder that Gambian bakers add to lighten their multigrain loaves.

2 large egg whites

1 cup minus 1 tablespoon water—*heated to about 95 degrees F.*

2 3/4 cups bread flour
1/4 cup yellow corn meal
2 tablespoons whole wheat flour
2 tablespoons millet flour
1 1/2 tablespoons sugar
1/2 teaspoon salt
2 tablespoons butter
2 1/2 teaspoons *preservative-free* active dried yeast*

1/4 cup bread flour

1/2 large egg—well-beaten
1/2 teaspoon sugar
1 tablespoon water

Bring all remaining ingredients except for *warm* water to room temperature.

Using an electric mixer fitted with *grease-free* beaters, or by hand using a *grease-free* wire whisk, beat egg whites in a *grease-free* bowl until stiff. Set aside.

Pour water into the BREAD MACHINE pan.

Sprinkle bread flour, corn meal, whole wheat flour, millet flour, sugar, and salt. *Do not stir.* Leave an area at one end of loaf pan for the yeast. Scatter the butter chunks at the other end of the bread pan.

Using a spoon, create a depression in the dry ingredients, being very careful not to press down into the liquid layer below. Pour yeast into the depression.

Select MANUAL SETTING and push START. When all ingredients are moist, add stiffly-beaten egg whites and allow the automated cycle to continue.

Prepare a 16-inch non-stick-coated DOUBLE FRENCH BREAD PAN by coating with non-stick lecithin spray coating.

FRENCH-STYLE *BAGUETTES* (cont'd)

In 1 1/2 - 2 hours, when the automated preparation period is over, remove dough to a floured surface and knead until smooth and all trace of stickiness is gone.** Divide in half and form two 14-inch *baguettes* by pressing dough into an elongated rectangle, by hand or by using a rolling pin. Roll each rectangle, jelly-roll style, to form a French-style loaf.

Place one in each side of prepared French bread pan. Allow to rise in a warm, draft-free kitchen until doubled in volume—about 40 minutes.

Preheat oven to 375 degrees F. Place a pie plate filled with water onto the bottom rack of the oven.

Prepare egg wash by beating egg, sugar, and 1 tablespoonful water together thoroughly.

Using a French *lame*, a double-edged razor blade, or a very sharp knife, cut diagonal slashes into each risen loaf. Brush egg wash over top and ends of each loaf, *being careful not to allow it run down into baking pan.*

Bake in preheated 375 degree F. oven for about 30-35 minutes. Allow to cool completely on a wire rack before slicing and serving. This French bread loaf is best served the same day that it is baked.

Notes: *Some packaged dried yeast available in grocery stores contain a preservative. Natural food stores carry an additive-free dried yeast. In addition, *do not use so-called fast action yeasts.* The results will not please you.

**Preparation time depends, of course, on the brand of bread machine which you are using. I use a Zojirushi bread machine and this recipe is designed for the dough cycle of that manufacturer's product.

If preferred, this French bread dough may be baked in standard loaves. This, however, will produce a softer crust. Prepare two 9 x 5 x 3-inch non-stick-coated loaf pans by coating with non-stick lecithin spray coating. Divide kneaded dough in half and form two standard loaves. Place in prepared pans. Allow these to rise in a warm, draft-free kitchen until doubled in volume—about 45 minutes. Bake in preheated 350 degree F. oven for about 40-45 minutes. Turn out of baking pans and cool completely on a wire rack before slicing and serving.

Yields two 15-inch loaves

1/40 SERVING (i. e., per slice) –
PROTEIN = 1.5 g.; FAT = 0.9 g.; CARBOHYDRATE = 8.3 g.;
CALORIES = 46; CALORIES FROM FAT = 18%

BANANA AND MANGO SALAD
TPT - 8 minutes

Despite an area of only 4,007 square miles, The Gambia has the perfect tropical climate for cultivating fruits. Salads and desserts often feature fruits so very fresh that the taste has no relationship to that which we buy in our grocery stores. If you have ever bought a big wedge of fresh pineapple from one of the stands that spring up all over Hawaii, then you know what fresh fruit can do to your spirit after a long flight.

3 large mangoes—peeled and sliced into four large slices each*
3 bananas—peeled and quartered
6 tablespoons freshly made BLENDER MAYONNAISE [see index]
3 tablespoons orange pulp, for garnish**

On each of six salad plates, arrange two large slices of mango. Arrange two slices of banana on top of the mango slices. Spoon 1 tablespoonful of mayonnaise on top of the fruit. Garnish each serving with 1 1/2 teaspoonfuls orange pulp.

Serve chilled.

Notes: *Cut two slices of mango from either side of the flat seed.

**Often you will not have an orange in your refrigerator from which to obtain the pulp called for in this recipe. I sieve high pulp orange juice to get the garnish I need.

This recipe can be adjusted easily for two or four diners.

Yields 6 individual servings

1/6 SERVING – PROTEIN = 1.7 g.; FAT = 11.6 g.; CARBOHYDRATE = 31.9 g.;
CALORIES = 225; CALORIES FROM FAT = 46%

Africa – The Gambia

GAMBIAN BLACK BEANS IN TOMATO – GARLIC SAUCE
TPT - 49 minutes

Cooks in Gambia make good use of the tomato, introduced to Europe and, then to, Africa from the Americas. The beautifully flavored tomato–garlic sauce is the perfect host for the black beans. Although conventionally served over rice or millet couscous, this often appears at our table as a topping for a tostado, or a filling for a taco or burrito.

1 tablespoon *extra virgin* olive oil
3 garlic cloves—*very finely* chopped
1/4 cup *finely* chopped onion

2 cups canned, *diced* tomatoes
2 tablespoons commercially-available bottled *chili* sauce
2 tablespoon *finely* chopped mild green *chilies*

1 can (15.5 ounces) black beans—well-drained

In a non-stick-coated saucepan set over *LOW-MEDIUM* heat, heat oil. Add *very finely* chopped garlic and *finely* chopped onion. Sauté until onion is soft and translucent, *being careful to allow neither the garlic nor the onion to brown.*

Add tomatoes, *chili* sauce, and *finely* chopped green *chilies*. Cook, stirring frequently, for about 20 minutes. The sauce will thicken.

Add well-drained black beans. Stir to immerse the beans completely in the sauce. Cook for about 15 minutes, or until heated through.

Serve hot over rice or millet *couscous*.

Yields 6 servings
adequate for 4 people

Note: This recipe can be doubled, when required.

1/6 SERVING – PROTEIN = 9.5 g.; FAT = 2.3 g.; CARBOHYDRATE = 17.2 g.;
CALORIES = 97; CALORIES FROM FAT = 21%

MILLET *COUSCOUS* WITH VEGETABLES
Ruy
TPT - 45 minutes

The several species of grasses that are included under the umbrella referred to as millet provided our hunter/gatherer ancestors with nutritional options as floods and droughts challenged their existence. Today millet is still eaten and provides a delicious nutty source of grain amino acids for breakfast and for dinner. You will find it on family tables across Africa. When serving spicy vegetable dishes, we greatly prefer the taste of millet to the usual couscous or rice accompaniment.

1/2 cup dry millet—rinsed and drained

1 quart water
1/2 teaspoon salt

2 tablespoons *extra virgin* olive oil
1 cup diced onion
1 cup diced carrot
1 cup diced sweet red pepper
1/2 cup green beans cuts into small dice-sized pieces
1/2 cup green (fresh) *or frozen* corn kernels

1 1/2 tablespoons butter

In a saucepan set over *LOW* heat, dry-roast the millet until lightly browned. *Monitor carefully because the grain can brown easily.*

Add water and salt. Increase heat to *LOW-MEDIUM*. Cover and allow to cook for about 30-35 minutes, or until the grains are soft. Drain well.

While millet is cooking, in a non-stick coated skillet set over *LOW-MEDIUM* heat, heat oil. Add diced onion, carrot, and red pepper, chopped green beans, and corn. Cook, stirring frequently, until vegetables begin to soften. Reduce heat to *LOW* and keep warm until required.

Turn drained millet into a heated serving bowl. Add butter. Fluff with a wooden fork until butter melts. Spoon sautéed vegetables over.

Serve at once.

Yields 8 servings
adequate for 4 people

Note: Other vegetables, dried fruits, herbs, and spices can be added. One of the most uncomplicated ways to serve millet is to top it with a mixture of sautéed vegetables as in this recipe.

1/8 SERVING – PROTEIN = 5.9 g.; FAT = 6.4 g.; CARBOHYDRATE = 16.7 g.;
CALORIES = 147; CALORIES FROM FAT = 39%

Africa–The Gambia

GAMBIAN PEANUT BUTTER AND TOMATO SAUCE WITH GARLIC
Domado

TPT - 20 minutes

Because of their large and important tourist trade, Gambians are very accustomed to the European palate and very accommodating to vegetarians. Of course, this dish can be prepared with fiery hot peppers but this milder version will be appreciated just as much, especially by the younger members of your family. We serve this very useful and flavorful sauce over boiled potatoes, rice, millet, and couscous as a rule but, often, it becomes the sauce of choice for a soy patty or burger. Since it freezes well, it is there when we need it.

3/4 cup freshly ground, *unsalted, additive-free, smooth* peanut butter—*brought to room temperature*
1 1/2 cups *boiling* VEGETABLE STOCK FROM SOUP [see index], **other vegetarian stock of choice, *or* water**

1 tablespoon canola oil *or extra virgin* olive oil
2 medium onions—*finely* chopped
2 garlic cloves—*very finely* chopped

1 cup canned, *crushed* tomatoes
1/4 cup *very finely* chopped mild green *chilies*
1/4 teaspoon freshly ground black pepper

Put peanut butter into a mixing bowl. While stirring constantly, add *boiling* vegetable stock and stir until the peanut butter–stock mixture is smooth. Set aside until required.

In a large saucepan set over *MEDIUM* heat, heat oil. Add *finely* chopped onion and *very finely* chopped garlic. Sauté until onion is soft and translucent, *being careful not to allow onion to brown.*

Add tomato paste and cook, stirring constantly, for a minute.

Add crushed tomatoes, peanut butter, *very finely* chopped green *chilies*, and black pepper. Reduce heat to *LOW-MEDIUM.** Cover and cook, stirring frequently, for about 10 minutes, or until sauce is very thick.

Yields 8 servings
adequate for 6 people

Notes: *This sauce can be a very nice vehicle for shredded soy meat analogue, seitan, or tempeh. If desired, add at this point.

This recipe can be doubled, if desired.

1/8 SERVING – PROTEIN = 6.1 g.; FAT = 13.5 g.; CARBOHYDRATE = 8.9 g.;
CALORIES = 189; CALORIES FROM FAT = 64%

GAMBIAN *TOUBAB* MACARONI AND VEGETABLES
TPT - 1 hour and 3 minutes

Many dishes, popular in Gambia are referred to as "toubabs." These recipes survive from the British colonial period when Anglo street venders and small shops hawked their wares for two shillings, i. e., two "bobs." The phrase eventually referred not only to Anglo dishes but also to Caucasians in general. These dishes have maintained their popularity and are often included on restaurant menus. This macaroni dish can be attributed to that period and before you exclaim, "Macaroni . . . English?" consider the fact that the British adopted macaroni from the Romans and evolved the ever-popular macaroni and cheese.

1 tablespoon *extra virgin* olive oil
1/2 cup *finely* chopped onion
2 garlic cloves—*thinly* sliced

2 medium carrots—scraped or pared and diced
1 rib celery—trimmed and diced

1/4 cup full-bodied red wine such as a *Pinot Noir or* a Zinfandel

2 cups canned, *diced* tomatoes

4 quarts *boiling* water
2 cups *pipettes*, elbow, *penne*, or *fusilli* macaroni, as preferred

1 cup freshly shelled *or frozen* peas
1/2 cup light cream *or* half and half
1/4 cup slivered fresh basil leaves
Salt, to taste
Freshly ground mixed peppercorns—red, white, and black—to taste

Africa – The Gambia

GAMBIAN *TOUBAB* MACARONI AND VEGETABLES (cont'd)

In a large skillet set over *LOW-MEDIUM* heat, heat oil. Add *finely* chopped onion and sliced garlic. Sauté until onion is soft and translucent, *being careful to allow neither the onion nor the garlic to brown.*

Add diced carrots and celery. Cook for several minutes, stirring constantly.

Add the wine. *Increase the heat to MEDIUM-HIGH.* Stir for several minutes. *Reduce heat to LOW.*

Add diced tomatoes. Cover and allow to simmer for about 30 minutes.

Meanwhile, in a kettle set over *MEDIUM-HIGH* heat, cook macaroni in *boiling* water until *al dente*. Drain.

Add macaroni, peas, cream, and basil to tomato sauce. Thin with a tablespoonful or two of water, if necessary. Season with salt and ground mixed peppercorns. Turn into a heated serving bowl or pile onto a small platter.

Yields 6 servings
adequate for 4 people

Note: *This recipe can be halved or doubled, when required.

1/6 SERVING – PROTEIN = 8.3 g.; FAT = 6.4 g.; CARBOHYDRATE = 39.5 g.;
CALORIES = 254; CALORIES FROM FAT = 23%

GAMBIAN *SWEET COUSCOUS* PUDDING
Caakiri

TPT - basic preparation time = 33 minutes;
1 hour and 33 minutes = refrigeration period if to be served chilled;
8 hours = refrigeration period if to be molded

The evolution of a dish eaten throughout West Africa is an interesting illustration of how the world influences the foods we eat, no matter where we live. This dessert can be found under various names such as caakiri, chakery, chakrey, thikray, tiakri, and simply sweet couscous in the American South where it is made with molasses. Cooked grains are still eaten today with milk or cultured milk products as they have been down through history. The introduction of couscous, made from wheat, from North Africa and the greater availability of sugar has turned what may once have been a simple sustenance dish, made from whatever grains were available such as one of the many indigenous grasses collectively known as millet, into a very pleasing dessert, warm or chilled. Fruit, such as pineapple or plumped raisins, can be added to this dish if desired.

3/4 cup *two-percent* milk
1/2 cup dry, quick-cooking, whole wheat
  couscous**

1 tablespoon butter

1/2 cup PLAIN YOGURT *[see index] or*
  commercially-available plain yogurt
1/4 cup *fat-free* dairy sour cream
3 tablespoons light cream *or* half and half
3 tablespoons sugar
1/4 teaspoon pure vanilla extract

In a saucepan set over *MEDIUM* heat, bring milk to the boil. Reduce heat to *LOW* and stir in *couscous*. Cover tightly and allow to cook for about 5 minutes.

Remove from heat. Stir butter into hot *couscous*. Cover and allow *couscous* to steam for about 10 minutes. *All milk should be absorbed.*

In a mixing bowl, combine yogurt, sour cream, light cream, sugar, and vanilla extract. Using a wire whisk, combine well. Add to cooked *couscous*. Using a rubber spatula, *gently* stir the *couscous* into the dairy mixture. Turn into a serving bowl or into six individual dessert dishes.*

Serve warm or refrigerate and serve chilled.

Yields 6 servings
adequate for 4 people

Notes: *If you turn the dessert into a small mixing bowl or soup bowl, you can unmold it after an overnight refrigeration period. It looks very dramatic when centered on a black plate.

This recipe can be halved or doubled, when required.

1/6 SERVING – PROTEIN = 5.5 g.; FAT = 3.7 g.; CARBOHYDRATE = 25.4 g.;
CALORIES = 145; CALORIES FROM FAT = 23%

Africa–The Gambia

GAMBIAN BREAD AND BUTTER PUDDING WITH COCONUT

TPT - about 2 hours and 30 minutes;
30 minutes = soaking period;
1 hour = chilling period

The British colonial period in The Gambia introduced Gambians to bread pudding. Obviously they and the tourists who visit Gambia are as fond of bread pudding as my dad and I were. We often ordered it when we went out to eat. Mom, on the other hand, said that she had eaten enough of it during the Depression and considered it poor-man's food. I never understood since her mother made a super bread pudding and that or her rice pudding were always requested by grandchildren when we "stayed over." This Gambian recipe is less rich than Grandma's and I am quite sure that Grandma never thought of adding coconut milk..

3 thick slices (BREAD MACHINE) MAPLE MULTIGRAIN BREAD *[see recipe which follows]* or whole wheat bread—crusts removed*
1 tablespoon butter

1/2 cup *fat-free* pasteurized eggs (the equivalent of 2 eggs)
1/3 cup sugar
1 cup evaporated *skimmed* milk
2/3 cup *light, sulfite-free* coconut milk
1 cup *boiling* water
1 teaspoon pure vanilla extract

Cream

Prepare a 1- or 1 1/2-quart baking dish or soufflé dish by coating with non-stick lecithin spray coating.

Lightly toast bread slices. Butter each and cut into cubes. (There should be about 2 cupfuls.) Arrange bread cubes in the bottom of prepared baking dish. Set aside.

In a large mixing bowl, combine pasteurized eggs, sugar, evaporated milk, and coconut milk. Blend thoroughly. Stir in *boiling* water and vanilla extract. Pour custard mixture over bread cubes.

Allow to stand at room temperature for at least 30 minutes. Skim any remaining bubbles from the surface.

Preheat oven to 325 degrees F.

Place bread pudding in baking pan in which a 1-inch water bath has been prepared. Bake in preheated oven for 45 minutes to 1 hour, or until a knife inserted into the center comes out clean. *Do not allow water bath to simmer or boil—by adding cold water or ice cubes*, if necessary.

Chill for at least 1 hour before serving. Serve at room temperature or thoroughly chilled, as preferred.

Pass cream separately.

Yields 6 servings
adequate for 4 people

Note: *Reserve crusts to make breadcrumbs.

1/6 SERVING (exclusive of cream) –
PROTEIN = 5.7 g.; FAT = 2.8 g.; CARBOHYDRATE = 27.5 g.;
CALORIES = 150; CALORIES FROM FAT = 17%

(BREAD MACHINE) MAPLE MULTIGRAIN BREAD

TPT - about 3 hours and 34 minutes;
3 hours and 30 minutes = automated machine preparation period*

Multigrain breads are featured in the in-store bakeries of grocery stores across the country. A wonderful, albeit expensive, loaf is even delivered to our grocery store in central Pennsylvania twice-a-week from California. This bread machine version uses a non-wheat eight-grain hot cereal mixture, available in natural food stores, so that the cupboards, refrigerator, and freezer are not full of half-used flour and seed bags. It is based on our favorite maple oatmeal bread and is far less salty than are the in-store multigrain loaves.

1 cup plus 2 tablespoons water
1/3 cup pure maple syrup
1 tablespoon vegetable oil

2 3/4 cups bread flour
1/2 cup quick-cooking rolled oats *(not instant)*
1/2 cup *dry* eight-grain hot cereal mix
1/4 cup whole wheat flour
1/2 teaspoon salt

1 tablespoon (1 envelope) *preservative-free* active dried yeast**

Africa–The Gambia

(BREAD MACHINE) MAPLE MULTIGRAIN BREAD (cont'd)

Bring all ingredients except warm water to room temperature.

Put water, maple syrup, and oil into the BREAD MACHINE pan.

Add bread flour, oats, *dry* eight-grain hot cereal mix, whole wheat flour, and salt, spreading the ingredients over the liquid as you add them. *Do not stir.*

Using a spoon, create a depression in the dry ingredients, being very careful not to press down into the liquid layer below. Pour yeast into the depression.

Yields 1 large loaf
— about 20 slices

Notes: *Preparation time depends, of course, on the brand of bread machine which you are using. I use a Zojirushi bread making machine and these directions apply to that manufacturer's product.

**Some packaged dried yeast available in grocery stores contain a preservative. Natural food stores carry an additive-free dried yeast. In addition, *do not use so-called fast action yeasts*. The results will not please you.

If preferred, the MANUAL SETTING on your BREAD MACHINE may be selected. When the cycle has been completed, turn the dough out onto a floured surface and knead until smooth and all trace of stickiness is gone. Prepare a 9 x 5 x 3-inch non-stick-coated loaf pan by coating with non-stick lecithin spray coating. Form kneaded dough into a loaf. Place in prepared pan. Cover with a cotton tea towel and allow to rise in a warm, draft-free kitchen until doubled in volume—about 45 minutes. Bake in preheated 350 degree F. oven for about 40-45 minutes. Turn out of baking pan and cool completely on a wire rack before slicing and serving.

To make dinner rolls, prepare dough using manual setting. Coat a non-stick-coated 8 x 8-inch baking pan with non-stick lecithin spray coating. Divide dough into sixteen equal pieces. Roll dough into balls. Brush each lightly with oil and place side by side in prepared baking pan. Cover with a cotton tea towel and allow to rise in a warm, draft-free kitchen until doubled in volume—about 45 minutes. Bake in preheated 350 degree F. oven for about 40-45 minutes. Turn out of baking pan and cool completely on a wire rack before separating and serving.

1/20 SERVING (i. e., per slice) –
PROTEIN = 3.1 g.; FAT = 1.1 g.; CARBOHYDRATE = 20.4 g.;
CALORIES = 65; CALORIES FROM FAT = 10%

1/16 SERVING (i. e., per roll) –
PROTEIN = 3.8 g.; FAT = 1.4 g.; CARBOHYDRATE = 25.5 g.;
CALORIES = 130; CALORIES FROM FAT = 10%

FLAX – BANANA CAKE

TPT - 1 hour and 40 minutes;
15 minutes = initial in-pan cooling period;
30 minutes = final cooling period

Several times in history bananas have demonstrated clearly the importance of biodiversity, becoming the lumper potato of that decade. The dominance of a single variety of banana, the asexually-propagated Cavendish, led to a decrease in supply and increase in price in the 1990s-2000s when the 'Black Sigtoka" fungi first began to cause damage to the banana plants. Although we do not eat anywhere near the 26.2 pounds of bananas that Americans are estimated to eat each year, there was always a container of mashed bananas in the freezer, that is, before the days of the home dehydrator. That is what we did with overripe bananas back then rather than drying bananas for snacks. Now I let a couple of bananas over-ripen so that I can make this bread and enjoy the taste and the health advantage that flax seeds offer. Since we do not eat fish to obtain Omega-3, we include flax seeds in many recipes.

FLAX – BANANA CAKE (cont'd)

3/4 cup unbleached white flour
1/2 cup whole wheat flour
1/2 cup ground flax seed*
1 teaspoon baking powder
1 teaspoon baking soda

1/2 cup firmly packed *light* brown sugar
1/2 cup *unsalted, cultured* buttermilk
1/4 cup *fat-free* pasteurized eggs (the equivalent of 1 egg)
3 tablespoons canola oil

1 cup puréed *ripe* bananas

Preheat oven to 350 degrees F. Prepare a 9 x 5 x 3-inch non-stick-coated loaf pan by coating with non-stick lecithin spray coating.

In a mixing bowl, combine white and whole wheat flours, ground flax seed, baking powder, and baking soda. Mix well. Set aside.

In a large mixing bowl, combine brown sugar, buttermilk, pasteurized eggs, and oil. Stir to mix well. Add mixed dried ingredients. Stir only until moistened. *Do not overmix.*

Add the banana purée. Stir to mix. Again, *do not overmix*.

Pour into prepared loaf pan, spreading the mixture evenly to the side of the pan. Bake in preheated 350 degree F. oven for 40-45 minutes, or until a cake tester inserted in the center comes out clean. Set the bread, still in its baking pan, on a wire rack and allow it to cool for about 15 minutes. Remove the bread from the loaf pan and allow it to cool thoroughly.

Yields 12 slices

Note: *Flax seed is a slightly sweet and nut-flavored grain which is available in natural food stores. Store flax seed in the refrigerator or freezer to minimize the chance of rancidity.

1/12 SERVING (i. e., per slice)
PROTEIN = 3.6 g.; FAT = 5.8 g.; CARBOHYDRATE = 26.0 g.;
CALORIES = 179; CALORIES FROM FAT = 29%

Ghana

When a friend, who had searched for her African roots, concluded that her family had come as slaves from Ghana, I really understood something that is easily overlooked by most Americans, the sad truth that not all Americans can know where their ancestors came from. Being an African-American was not enough for my friend; she to had to keep searching. She was many generations from those who had come from that area of West Africa, an area that did not even have a name when her ancestors were shipped to the New World.

From the fifteenth through the seventeenth centuries many European nations tried to hold this gold-rich area of Africa by establishing presence, by building some forty fortresses, and continually trying to drive each other out. The Portuguese were the first but they were soon challenged by the Dutch. More Europeans came, notably the Spanish, the Danes, the Swedes, and the British. The Dutch finally withdrew and, in 1874, Great Britain established the Gold Coast Crown Colony, a colony which included most, but not all, of today's Republic of Ghana; British Togoland remained a separate entity.

In 1957 the colony achieved independence, the first of Europe's African colonies to do so, choosing the name of the ancient empire that occupied much of present-day Senegal, Mali, and Mauritania. Although a parliamentary republic, Ghana has a close relationship with the People's Republic of China, celebrating fifty years of diplomatic ties in 2010.

British interests in this colony had been strongly tied to its rich gold resources. Ghana is still one of the world's top producers of gold but today it is also a player in the world's demand for crude oil, with an estimated oil reserve of over five billion barrels and an export projection of 120,000 barrels per day by 2113. Diamonds, bauxite, timber, natural gas, manganese, and cocoa are also important export products while the development of an "off shore" banking system is attracting money from all over the world.

Although Ghana experiences two distinct seasons, a wet season and a dry season, the geography of Ghana allows for extensive and successful agriculture. Since its population is well-fed with a life expectancy of sixty-three years for both men and women and not a victim of the inter-ethnic strife so prevalent in other African nations, the Ghanaian government has been able to focus on what it considers to be its strongest asset, the education of its population. Although the adult literacy rate remains in the sixty percentile, ninety-five percent of Ghanaian children attend school which, in itself, is an astounding accomplishment for a nation comprised of about twenty-four million people of fifty-two distinct ethnic groups. There are six universities, the oldest, the University of Ghana, having been established in 1948. Since 2008 Kofi Annan, former secretary-general of the United Nations, has been the chancellor of the University of Ghana. English is the official language for business and commerce but most Ghanaians speak local languages as well with seventy-nine languages recognized within the population.

Africa–Ghana

Mashed Avocado and Mayonnaise Salad

~

Tomato – Groundnut Soup

~ ~

Layered Vegetable Salad

Fried Potato Cakes

~ ~ ~ ~ ~ ~ ~ ~ ~ ~

Gari with Eggs
Gari Foto

Stewed Corn with Coconut
Abrow ne Kokosi

Mashed Sweetpotato	or	Fried Yams with Onions
Fufu		*Yele*

~ ~ ~ ~ ~ ~ ~ ~ ~ ~ ~ ~ ~ ~ ~ ~ ~ ~ ~ ~

Rice Flour Pudding	Banana Nectar Beverage Dessert
Muhallabia	

Fresh Pineapple Spears
Sprinkled with Salt and Coarse Demerara Sugar

GHANAIAN MASHED AVOCADO AND MAYONNAISE SALAD
TPT - 19 minutes

This is often served in Ghana as an appetizer or first course but we like to serve it as a salad. It accompanies a myriad of dishes well and is a smooth, creamy contrast to a hot, spicy stew.

3 cups mixed salad greens of choice—trimmed, well-rinsed, and well-dried
3 cups baby spinach—trimmed, well-rinsed, and well-dried

2 ripe avocados—peeled, pitted, and chopped
4 teaspoons freshly squeezed lime juice

3 tablespoons *calorie-reduced or light* **mayonnaise**
1/4 cup *very finely* **chopped onion**
Freshly ground mixed peppercorns—red, black, and white—to taste

1 lime cut into 6 wedges, for garnish

Set up six salad plates. Arrange a cupful of salad greens on each.

In a mixing bowl, combine chopped avocados and lime juice. Mash until smooth.

Add mayonnaise, *very finely* chopped onion, and ground mixed peppercorns. Mix and mash until the mixture is uniform. Place *one-sixth* of the avocado mixture in the center of each salad plate.

Garnish each serving with a lime wedge.

Serve at once.

Yields 6 individual servings

Note: This recipe can be halved when required.

1/6 SERVING – PROTEIN = 2.0 g.; FAT = 13.6 g.; CARBOHYDRATE = 0.2 g.;
CALORIES = 156; CALORIES FROM FAT = 78%

Africa–Ghana

TOMATO – GROUNDNUT SOUP
TPT - 40 minutes

I based this soup on a chicken stew that is frequently eaten in Ghana. You will find the peanut butter flavor much more subtle than the original main-course stew making it a perfect first course for this menu. We especially like to serve this soup with the main-course layered vegetable salad, also included in this chapter. Note that Ghanaians use very little pepper in their cooking but the small amount of ground red pepper (cayenne) that we add to this soup gives it significant punch.

3 cups water
1 1/2 cups canned, *crushed* tomatoes
1/2 green bell pepper—seeded, membrane removed, and *finely* chopped
1 cup *finely* chopped onion
1/2 teaspoon salt
1/8 teaspoon ground red pepper (cayenne)

2 tablespoons *boiling* water
2 tablespoons freshly ground, *unsalted, additive-free, smooth* peanut butter—*brought to room temperature*

In a large saucepan set over *MEDIUM* heat, combine water, crushed tomatoes, *finely* chopped green pepper and onion, salt, and ground red pepper (cayenne). Allow to come to the boil. Cook for about 20 minutes, stirring frequently.

In a small bowl, combine *boiling* water and peanut butter. Using a small wire whisk, beat water into peanut butter.

Add peanut butter to the soup base. Using a large wire whisk, stir to integrate the peanut butter thoroughly into the soup. Do not allow the peanut butter to settle to the bottom of the pan and stick. Turn into a heated soup tureen.

Serve at once into heated soup plates.

Yields 5 cupfuls

Notes: When required, this recipe can be doubled or tripled.

This soup can be frozen quite successfully.

1/5 SERVING (i. e., per cupful) –
PROTEIN = 3.0 g.; FAT = 3.4 g.; CARBOHYDRATE = 10.9 g.;
CALORIES = 84; CALORIES FROM FAT = 36%

GHANAIAN LAYERED VEGETABLE SALAD
TPT - 42 minutes;
30 minutes = onion marinating period

My grandmother could always find something in the refrigerator and this and that in the kitchen garden to make a salad. I too learned that lettuce and tomato are not a salad, as most restaurants would seem to believe, but instead merely a starting point for a summer tossed salad. When a leftover cooked potato, fresh or frozen corn, cooked or canned kidney beans, an onion, a couple of hard cooked eggs, and an avocado are added to the lettuce and tomato, then you really have something. This salad, popular in Ghana, is a salad I have eaten all my life. I never wrote it down until now because it is a salad that just happens; it happens in Ghana just as it happens here and it is a meal in a bowl.

1/4 large Spanish onion—*thinly* sliced into rings
2 tablespoons red wine vinegar
Freshly ground black pepper, to taste

2 cups shredded lettuce—well-washed and well-dried
1 small cucumber—peeled, quartered, seeds, and chopped
1 small *cooked* and *chilled* potato—peeled and diced
1/2 cup green (fresh) *or* defrosted, frozen corn kernels
1/2 cup well-drained, canned *or* cooked, dry red kidney beans

1/3 cup *calorie-reduced or light* mayonnaise
2 tablespoons *light, sulfite-free* coconut milk *or* cow's milk, if preferred

1 tomato—*thinly* sliced into rounds
2 hard-cooked eggs—peeled and sliced
Freshly ground mixed peppercorns—black, white, and red—to taste

Place onion rings on in a shallow bowl or on a plate. Pour red wine vinegar over. Grind black pepper over. Toss to coat. Allow to sit at room temperature for about 30 minutes. Using a fork, turn once during the marination period to insure uniform marination.

GHANAIAN LAYERED VEGETABLE SALAD (cont'd)

Put shredded lettuce into a large salad bowl. Scatter chopped cucumber, diced potatoes, corn kernels, and kidney beans over.

In a small bowl, combine mayonnaise and coconut milk. Using a small wire whisk, combine thoroughly. *If necessary, add more coconut milk.* Spoon over vegetables in salad bowl.

Arrange tomato slices on top of the dressing. Arrange hard-cooked egg slices on top of the tomatoes. Grind mixed peppercorns over. Arrange marinated onion slices on top of the eggs.

Serve at once. Do not toss; let diners just serve themselves. The dressing will be scooped up with the vegetables.

Yields 8 servings
adequate for 4 people

Note: This recipe can be halved or doubled. It is a great salad for a buffet table.

1/8 SERVING – PROTEIN = 3.5 g.; FAT = 1.9 g.; CARBOHYDRATE = 11.6 g.;
CALORIES = 116; CALORIES FROM FAT = 15%

GHANAIAN FRIED POTATO CAKES
TPT - 1 hour and 25 minutes;
1 hour = refrigeration period

Sold by street vendors, fried potato cakes are an inexpensive pick-me-up food in Ghana. Ghanaians will argue over the merits of the product of each street vendor from the amount of garlic and/or salt added to the potatoes to the freshness of the oil used for frying but these criticisms not withstanding, Ghanaians never miss an opportunity to munch down a fried potato cake.

4 cups *warm, riced or mashed* **potatoes**
3 garlic cloves—**crushed and** *very finely* **chopped**
1/2 cup *thinly* **sliced scallion**—***both white and green portions***
1/2 cup *finely* **chopped fresh parsley**
1 teaspoon salt, or to taste
1/2 teaspoon freshly ground black pepper, or to taste

1/4 cup unbleached white flour

1/2 cup *high-heat* **safflower** *or* **sunflower oil**

In a mixing bowl, combine riced potatoes, *very finely* chopped garlic, *thinly* sliced scallion, *finely* chopped parsley, salt, and black pepper. Using your hands, mix the ingredients thoroughly. Form into ten balls. Press each into a patty.

Put flour into a soup plate. Carefully coat each patty with flour. Place on a plate. Refrigerate for 1 hour.

In a deep skillet set over *MEDIUM-HIGH* heat, heat oil. Fry potato patties until deeply browned, turning to insure even browning. Transfer to paper toweling to absorb excess oil. Place on a heated serving platter.

Serve at once.

Notes: This recipe can be halved or doubled, when required.

An egg or 1/4 cupful fat-free pasteurized eggs can be incorporated into the potato mixture, if desired. We prefer the vegan patty but an egg does help to bind the mixture.

Yields 10 potato cakes

1/10 SERVING – PROTEIN = 1.7 g.; FAT = 4.6 g.; CARBOHYDRATE = 15.7 g.;
CALORIES = 107; CALORIES FROM FAT = 39%

Africa–Ghana

GHANAIAN *GARI* WITH EGGS
Gari Foto
TPT - 19 minutes

This dish from Ghana is traditionally made with fermented and dried cassava, gari, but this product is only available in areas of the United States where there are grocery stores that cater to large African populations. Unless someone is very adventurous, the four days required to prepare, cook, ferment, and dry cassava may be discouraging. I have found that this dish can be made quite successfully with tapioca, which of course is made from the cassava or manioc, or with farina or Cream of Wheat. The unfermented taste is different but the texture is spot on for this dish. Typically served for breakfast in Ghana, it makes a savory light supper dish.

2 tablespoons safflower *or* sunflower oil
1 large onion—*finely* **chopped**
2 large garlic cloves—*very finely* **chopped**

1 cup canned, *diced* **tomatoes**

1/4 cup quick-cooking tapioca

3 eggs—beaten

Salt, to taste
Freshly ground black pepper, to taste

In a large skillet set over *MEDIUM* heat, heat oil. Add *finely* chopped onion and *very finely* chopped garlic. Sauté until onion is soft and translucent, *being careful to allow neither the onion nor the garlic to brown.*

Add tomatoes and cook for several minutes until liquid evaporates.

Add tapioca and stir into the tomato mixture. *Stir quickly to prevent clumping.*

Add beaten eggs and cook as for scrambled eggs.

Season with salt and pepper to taste. Turn onto a heated platter.

Serve at once.

Yields 4 servings
adequate for 3 people

Note: This recipe can be doubled, when required, but you will need a very large skillet.

1/6 SERVING – PROTEIN = 6.4 g.; FAT = 11.1 g.; CARBOHYDRATE = 20.2 g.;
CALORIES = 192; CALORIES FROM FAT = 52%

GHANAIAN STEWED CORN WITH COCONUT
Abrow ne Kokosi
TPT - 12 minutes

Dried corn is used to make this dish in Ghana when fresh corn is unavailable. I find frozen corn to be a perfectly adequate replacement. If I have a fresh coconut on hand, I add a cupful of chopped coconut to this dish; the chunks of coconut are a wonderful contrast to the corn kernels.

4 cups green (fresh) *or frozen* **corn kernels**
1 cup *light, sulfite-free* **coconut milk**

In a saucepan set over *MEDIUM* heat, combine corn and coconut milk. Cook for about 10 minutes, stirring occasionally, until the corn is tender. Turn into a heated serving bowl.

Serve hot or allow to cool to room temperature.

Note: This recipe can be halved or doubled, when required.

Yields 6 servings
adequate for 4 people

1/6 SERVING – PROTEIN = 6.7 g.; FAT = 3.4 g.; CARBOHYDRATE = 41.3 g.;
CALORIES = 193; CALORIES FROM FAT = 16%

Africa–Ghana

GHANAIAN FRIED YAMS WITH ONIONS
Yele

TPT - about 3 hours;
2 hours = potato chilling period

My mother's next door neighbor decided to do a missionary tour quite late in her life. Regina contacted me before she left to inquire about the food in Ghana. I continued to share my ideas with her through letters for the entire year of her tour. She had found yams over there was at loss what to do with them since the starchy, pale, bland tuber is so different from the soft, rich yams we have available in our grocery stores. The flesh of this relative of the honeysuckle is a mainstay in Africa because it is easily grown and is very filling but a constant diet of boiled yams can be very boring as Sister Regina related in her letters. Prepared as one would prepare lyonniase potatoes a very delicious dish akin to our hash-browned potatoes results.

3 small sweetpotatoes—well-scrubbed and peeled
4 quarts *boiling* water

1/4 cup butter
1 medium onion—chopped
Freshly ground mixed peppercorns—black, red, and white—to taste

In a large kettle set over *MEDIUM-HIGH* heat, combine *boiling* water and sweetpotatoes. Boil sweetpotatoes until *crisp-tender*, but *not mushy*—about 25 minutes. Drain and refrigerate for at least 2 hours until potatoes are *completely cold*. Slice sweetpotatoes into rounds.

In a large skillet set over *MEDIUM* heat, melt butter. Add sweetpotatoes slices and cook, folding over occasionally with a spatula, until potatoes are evenly browned—about 20 minutes. Add chopped onion and continue sautéing until onion is soft and translucent, *being careful not to allow onion to brown*. Season generously with ground mixed peppercorns. Turn out onto a heated serving platter.

Serve at once.

Yields 6 servings
adequate for 4 people

Note: This recipe may be halved or doubled, when required.

1/6 SERVING – PROTEIN = 1.0 g.; FAT = 7.6 g.; CARBOHYDRATE = 9.4 g.;
CALORIES = 108; CALORIES FROM FAT = 63%

RICE FLOUR PUDDING
Muhallabia

TPT - 2 hours and 32 minutes;
2 hours = refrigeration period

I first tasted this dessert in a Middle Eastern restaurant. Reminded by the appearance of the British nursery cornstarch pudding to which all small children on either side of the Atlantic have been exposed for centuries, I was delighted to find ground almonds and rose water flavoring which raised it to a whole new level. It is a popular dessert in North Africa and in West Africa and can be found in the cuisines of many Middle Eastern countries. This recipe comes from a Ghanaian newspaper. Instead of folding the nuts into the pudding before chilling, ground almonds are sprinkled on top before serving which maintains the pudding texture for those who still remember that nursery pud.

2 tablespoons rice flour
2 tablespoons corn starch
5 tablespoons sugar

1 quart *two-percent* milk

1 tablespoon rose water

3 tablespoons ground, *preservative-free* almonds
 or almond meal
1 tablespoon pine nuts (*pignoli*) *or* pistachio nuts

In a small bowl or cup combine rice flour, corn starch, and sugar. Add a few tablespoonfuls of the milk. Stir to form a smooth paste. Set aside until required.

In a large saucepan set over *MEDIUM* heat, bring milk to just below the boil.

Add the prepared paste of rice flour, corn starch, and sugar. Cook, stirring very frequently with a wire whisk, until pudding thickens. *This will take time so be patient and be sure to stir very frequently to prevent the pudding from burning.*

Africa–Ghana

RICE FLOUR PUDDING (cont'd)

When thickened, add rose water. Using a wire whisk stir well. Pour through a sieve into a serving bowl. Refrigerate for at least 2 hours.

Serve chilled pudding into dessert dishes. Sprinkle with a portion of the ground almonds and a few pine nuts (*pignoli*) or pistachio nuts, if you choose.

Yields 6 servings
adequate for 4-6 people

Note: This recipe can be halved, when required.

1/6 SERVING – PROTEIN = 7.4 g.; FAT = 7,8 g.; CARBOHYDRATE = 26.1 g.; CALORIES = 200; CALORIES FROM FAT = 35%

BANANA NECTAR BEVERAGE DESSERT
TPT - 6 minutes

A quality banana nectar exported from Belgium is available here in the United States. It is a convenient product for making this dessert beverage, popular in Ghana, but making your own banana nectar is infinitely simple. Brandy or white rum are added to the blended banana as an after-dinner cordial. By providing a few small, one serving "airline" bottles of rum and brandy, available in most liquor stores, diners can add a touch to their banana nectar.

6 ripe bananas—peeled and cut into chunks
1 teaspoon freshly squeezed lemon juice*
1 cup crushed ice

6 tablespoons *two-percent* milk
1 teaspoon pure vanilla extract
1 tablespoon *agave* nectar

White rum *or* brandy, to taste

In the container of the electric blender, combine bananas, lemon juice, and crushed ice. Blend until smooth.

Add milk, vanilla extract, and *agave* nectar. Again blend until smooth. Pour into four brandy snifters.

Serve at once. Allow diners to add white rum or brandy to taste.

Notes: *The lemon juice prevents the bananas from browning.

This recipe can be halved, when required, but most home blenders will not accommodate the ingredients if doubled.

Yields 4 individual servings

1/4 SERVING (without rum or brandy) –
PROTEIN = 2.6 g.; FAT = 1.4 g.; CARBOHYDRATE = 32.3 g.;
CALORIES = 132; CALORIES FROM FAT = 10%

Guinea

Medieval Ghana and, subsequently, the Mali Empire, controlled the plains in the northwest of what is now the Republic of Guinea. In the fifteenth century the coastal area was explored by the Portuguese. By the seventeenth century the British, the French, and the Portuguese were competing for trade with the local chieftains for slaves, palm oil, peanuts, gold, and diamonds. Arguments, which arose between the French traders and the chieftains, prompted the French to declare the coastal city of Boké a protectorate in 1849. Desirous of Guinea's rich bauxite deposits, the world's main source of aluminum, France then set out to claim all of Guinea, which was at the time a part of Senegal. In 1891 it became a separate French colony, eventually becoming part of French West Africa.

In 1958 Guinea, under the leadership of Sékou Touré, opted for independence. All financial and technical aid was withdrawn by France in retaliation for the move. Under Touré, Guinea adopted a Marxist model and moved into a close relationship with the Soviet Union, a relationship that was dissolved in 1961 by the Guineans, charging the Soviets with excessive interference in their governmental affairs. Touré, who ruled until his death in 1984, gradually moved toward a closer relationship with the West. Within hours after Touré's death, Lansana Conté became president as the result of a *coup d'etat* and remained so until his death in 2008. Guinea's political situation has remained unsettled since President Conté's death with *coup* attempts and civilian protests over the lack of transparency and the lack of return of economic profit to the welfare of the public.

About the size of our state of Michigan and with a population of about ten million people, roughly about the same population as that of Michigan, Guinea finds itself dealing with twenty-four different ethnic groups, not all of whom speak the official language of French. With one of the lowest rates of literacy in the world, the concern with education availability and enforcement of the mandatory eight-year school attendance requirement are not being addressed. Children are kept at home to help with the subsistence farming creating a never-ending cycle of illiteracy and struggle for survival.

Development and maintenance of the infrastructure has been ignored. Transportation in Guinea is abysmal. A case in point is the railway from Guinea's capital Conakry to Kankan which ceased operations in 1980s. The domestic air service can not be depended upon and most major roads are in serious need of repair. The taxis, the ubiquitous old cars that roam both city and country roads, must be depended upon for transportation since there are few private cars and no bus service.

Guinea is dependent upon agriculture and mining. Agriculture involves about eighty percent of the population. Before independence from France, Guinea was a major exporter of palm oil, coffee, peanuts, pineapples, and bananas. The economic opportunities that adequate soil fertility and water can provide have not been pursued and this too has resulted in an underdeveloped cuisine depending upon foods typical of rural West Africa. Today the emphasis is clearly on mining. An estimated twenty-five percent of the world bauxite reserves, diamonds, iron ore, gold, and uranium can be found within its borders. As in the days of "the scramble for Africa," there is no lack of international interest, both governmental and industrial, to partner in the extraction of Guinea's natural resources. Partnerships to develop Guinea's hydroelectric potential and off-shore oil reserves are being developed.

Africa–Guinea

Mango and Onion Soup
Mangoé Rafalari

~

Avocado Halves with Spicy Dressing
Salade de Poire d'Avoct

~~~~~~~~~~~~~~~~~~~~

Lentils with Groundnut Butter
Végétarien Kansiyé

over

Steamed Rice

~~~~~

Soft *Polenta* with Herbs
Polenta aux Herbes

Fried Plantains with Spicy Tomato – Onion Sauce
Banani Lako

or

Fried Sweetpotatoes
Patates Douces Fritas (Igname Frites)

~~~~~~~~~~~~~~~~~~~~

**Semolina Dessert with Bananas
in the Style of Guinea**
Docono

GUINEAN MANGO AND ONION SOUP
Mangoé Rafalari
TPT - 31 minutes

To extend the protein supply, both river and ocean fish and crustaceans (prawns) are dried by African homemakers and added to soups and stews. This is such a soup. Without the addition of fish or shellfish, the mangoes and onions give this soup exotic character that we really enjoy. When we first married, mangoes were a luxury, available occasionally from an upscale greengrocer; a fruit that I would buy to garnish a fruit salad. Mangoes are now available year round and they are reasonably priced. However, the heavily-saturated red palm oil, with which this soup is made in Guinea, is not readily available so I substitute canola oil, peanut oil, or safflower oil.

2 tablespoons canola, peanut, *or* safflower oil
1 large red onion—chopped

3 cups VEGETABLE STOCK FROM SOUP *[see index] or* other vegetarian stock of choice
4 medium, *ripe, but firm,* mangoes—peeled and cut into large chunks
3 tablespoons *finely* chopped mild green *chilies**
Salt, to taste

In a kettle set over *LOW-MEDIUM* heat, heat oil. Add onion and sauté until onion is soft and translucent, *being careful not to allow onion to brown.*

Add vegetable stock, mango chunks, *finely* chopped green *chilies*, and salt to taste. Cook, stirring occasionally, for about 20 minutes. Turn into a heated tureen.

Serve at once into heated soup bowls.

Africa–Guinea

GUINEAN MANGO AND ONION SOUP (cont'd)

Yields 6 servings
adequate for 4 people

Notes: *Guineans add hot *chilies* to this soup but since this volume has been designed to persuade Americans to try unusual dishes from around the world, I have toned down the *chilies* a bit. If you prefer, you can add hot red *chilies* instead.

This recipe can be doubled, when required.

1/6 SERVING – PROTEIN = 1.5 g.; FAT = 4.8 g.; CARBOHYDRATE = 27.2 g.;
CALORIES = 145; CALORIES FROM FAT = 30%

AVOCADO HALVES WITH SPICY DRESSING
Salade de Poire d'Avocat
TPT - 9 minutes

Guineans often garnish a dish with slices of avocado to cool the palate. In this salad spicy mango salsa and mayonnaise play off the soft texture and cool smoothness of an avocado half to make a dramatic salad presentation. This pairs well with Guinean mango and onion soup.

1 cup *calorie-reduced or light* **mayonnaise**
1/4 cup hot mango *salsa*
1 scallion—trimmed and *thinly* sliced

3 ripe avocados

In a small bowl, combine mayonnaise, *salsa,* and *thinly* sliced scallion. Stir to combine.

Just before you are ready to serve, halve and pit the avocados. Put one avocado half in each of six small dishes. Spoon mayonnaise–*salsa* mixture into the depression left by the pit in each.

Serve at once with a spoon.

Yields 6 individual servings

Note: This recipe can be adjusted to serve two or four diners, with ease.

1/6 SERVING – PROTEIN = 2.1 g.; FAT = 29.7 g.; CARBOHYDRATE = 10.5 g.;
CALORIES = 306; CALORIES FROM FAT = 87%

GUINEAN LENTILS WITH GROUNDNUT BUTTER
Végétarien Kansiyé
TPT - 3 hours and 2 minutes;
2 hours = lentil soaking period

Lentils have sustained human populations for centuries. The cultivation of this tiny pulse most probably originated in Central Asia and from there made its way to Europe and the Middle East. Discovery of lentils in the Franchthi Cave in Southern Greece, which was occupied for more than 20,000 years in prehistoric times, confirms the use of this legume in the Paleolithic Period, and excavations at the site of Mureybet, the ancient Euphrates settlement, uncovered lentils dating from the Late Mesolithic Period. Lentils were regarded as poor man's food and fell out of favor in Europe during the Middle Ages but excavations in and recipes from Africa and the Middle East confirm the continued dependence upon lentils.

Africa–Guinea

GUINEAN LENTILS WITH GROUNDNUT BUTTER (cont'd)

1/3 cup dry, brown (*or* green) lentils
2 cups water

1 1/2 tablespoons freshly ground, *unsalted, additive-free smooth* peanut butter—*brought to room temperature*
1 1/2 cups *boiling* VEGETABLE STOCK FROM SOUP *[see index]* *or* VEGETARIAN BROWN STOCK *[see index]*

1 tablespoon safflower *or* sunflower oil
3/4 cup *finely* chopped onion
1 large garlic clove—*very finely* chopped

2 tablespoons *finely* chopped fresh parsley
1/4 teaspoon crushed, dried thyme
1/4 teaspoon crushed, dried marjoram
1/8 teaspoon salt, or to taste
1/8 teaspoon freshly ground black pepper, or to taste
Pinch ground cloves

1/2 cup canned, *crushed* tomatoes

Sort lentils and discard those of poor quality. Rinse thoroughly. In a bowl, combine lentils and the 2 cupfuls water. Allow lentils to soak for 2 hours. Drain well.

In a small bowl, combine peanut butter and *boiling* vegetable stock. Using a wire whisk, stir peanut butter into the stock. Set aside until required.

In a non-aluminum saucepan* set over *MEDIUM* heat, combine oil, *finely* chopped onion and garlic. Sauté until soft and translucent, *allowing neither the onion nor the garlic to brown.*

Add *finely* chopped fresh parsley, crushed thyme and marjoram, salt, black pepper, and ground cloves. Stir to combine.

Add drained lentils, *crushed* tomatoes, and dissolved peanut butter–stock mixture. Stir to combine. Allow to come to the boil. Reduce heat to *LOW-MEDIUM* and continue cooking for about 40 minutes, or until lentils are soft. Stir frequently. Add more water if necessary to prevent sticking. Turn into a heated serving dish.

Serve over steamed rice.

Yields 6 servings
adequate for 4 people

Notes: *Since aluminum discolors lentils rather unpleasantly, avoid the use of aluminum cookware or serving bowls in this case.

This recipe may be doubled, when required.

1/6 SERVING – PROTEIN = 4.5 g.; FAT = 4.1 g.; CARBOHYDRATE = 11.2 g.;
CALORIES = 99; CALORIES FROM FAT = 37%

GUINEAN SOFT *POLENTA* WITH HERBS
Polenta aux Herbes
TPT - 28 minutes

Maize is an important food staple in West Africa and making polenta, under a variety of names, is an important talent. Many years ago our friend Mario taught me how his family made polenta and I have made it this way ever since. You will note that most recipes for polenta direct that the corn meal be added to boiling water. The method Mario taught me results in a lump-free porridge. Guineans serve this as a stiff porridge but if you prefer, it can be packed into a small loaf pan, refrigerated overnight, sliced, and then fried.

1 cup *cold* water
3/4 cup *fine* yellow corn meal – *masa harina* (*amarilla fina*)
1 cup *boiling* water
2 tablespoons butter

1/2 cup *finely* chopped red bell pepper
1/4 cup *finely* chopped fresh parsley
1 teaspoon crushed, dried marjoram
1 teaspoon crushed, dried basil
Freshly ground black pepper, to taste

3 tablespoons grated *pecorino* Romano *or* Parmesan cheese, as preferred

In the top half of the double boiler, combine *cold* water and corn meal. Place insert over simmering, *not boiling*, water. While stirring with a wooden spoon, add *boiling* water. Add butter and continue to stir until butter is melted and integrated. Cook, stirring frequently, until thickened and smooth.

GUINEAN SOFT *POLENTA* WITH HERBS (cont'd)

Add *finely* chopped red bell pepper, *finely* chopped parsley, crushed, dried marjoram and basil, and black pepper. Stir to integrate. Cover and allow to cook, stirring frequently, for about 10 minutes.

Stir grated cheese into the softly cooked *polenta*. Turn into a heated serving bowl. Keep warm on a warming tray.

Note: When required, this recipe may be halved or doubled.

Yields 6 servings

1/6 SERVING – PROTEIN = 3.7 g.; FAT = 4.3 g.; CARBOHYDRATE = 26.9 g.;
CALORIES = 158; CALORIES FROM FAT = 24%

FRIED PLANTAINS WITH SPICY TOMATO – ONION SAUCE
Banani Loko
TPT - 20 minutes

Plantains are members of the genus Musa as are the familiar sweet/dessert bananas. They are, however, a starchy cousin that requires cooking. Americans seem to have taken a long time to appreciate plantains. While living on Long Island, I often visited Hispanic groceries to pick up items which were not then available in our larger grocery stores just as we visited Chinatown groceries in New York City to pick up supplies for Asian recipes. The increase in Hispanic residents finally brought the plantain and other South American specialties to the produce department of our very conservative grocery stores in Pennsylvania. It has taken a very long time for people to understand the fruits and roots that are delightful alternatives to the mundane.

2 tablespoons sunflower oil
1 large onion—*thinly* sliced

2 tablespoons *finely*, diced green *chili or* a small, red, hot *chili*, if preferred

1 1/2 cups canned, *diced* tomatoes
1 teaspoon crushed, dried basil
1/4 teaspoon crushed, dried thyme
Dash or two of ground red pepper (cayenne), or to taste
Salt, to taste
Freshly ground black pepper, to taste

4 ripe, black-skinned plantains—peeled and cut into large slices
High-heat sunflower oil for deep-frying heated to 365 degrees F.

In a saucepan set over *MEDIUM* heat, heat the 1 tablespoonful of oil. Add onion slices and sauté until onion is soft and translucent, *being careful not to allow onion to brown.*

Add diced *chilies* and sauté for a minute or two more. *Reduce heat to LOW.*

Add *diced* tomatoes, crushed basil and thyme, ground red pepper (cayenne), salt, and black pepper. Cook, stirring frequently, until the sauce thickens.

Meanwhile, in a deep skillet or saucepan, deep-fry plantain slices in batches. Transfer to several layers of paper toweling to drain.

Turn the sauce into a small heated bowl. Set it on large, heated platter. Transfer the fried plantain slices to the platter.

Serve at once.

Yields 6 servings
adequate for 4 people

Note: This recipe can be halved or doubled, when required.

1/6 SERVING – PROTEIN = 2.0 g.; FAT = 4.8 g.; CARBOHYDRATE = 31.3 g.;
CALORIES = 185; CALORIES FROM FAT = 23%

Africa–**Guinea**

GUINEAN FRIED SWEETPOTATOES
Patates Douces Fritas (Igname Frites)
TPT - 18 minutes

We tend to ignore sweetpotatoes when we think of fried foods. People in West Africa stop at a street vendor for a bagful of fried sweetpotatoes when hunger strikes in much the same way Americans stop for French fries. Actually the fried sweetpotatoes on the streets of Guinea are a better bet for vegetarians since most fast-food chains fry potatoes in beef fat. Try these as an appetizer with a lovely fruit punch or with a sweet, sparkling wine. Guineans dip these tasty bits in a tomato–onion sauce flavored with dried fish sauce.

1 cup *high*-heat safflower *or* sunflower oil

2 medium sweetpotatoes—peeled and cut into
  3-inch by 1/2-inch slices

Salt, to taste

In a deep skillet set over *MEDIUM-HIGH* heat, heat oil until it reaches about 365 degrees F.

Fry sweetpotato wedges in small batches.* Using a skimmer, transfer them to several layers of paper toweling. When all the potato wedges have been fried, transfer them to a heated serving dish. Sprinkle with salt.

Serve at once.

Yields 6 servings
adequate for 4 people

Notes: *When done, the fries will be lightly browned but not crisp like American fast-food French fried potatoes.

This recipe can be doubled or tripled, when required.

1/6 SERVING –   PROTEIN = 0.7 g.; FAT = 4.5 g.; CARBOHYDRATE = 7.7 g.;
CALORIES = 74; CALORIES FROM FAT = 55%

SEMOLINA DESSERT WITH BANANAS
IN THE STYLE OF GUINEA
Docono
TPT - 1 hour and 45 minutes;
1 hour = cooling period

When I was a child, Cream of Wheat, leftover from breakfast, was often transformed into a sweet, after-school treat with sugar and cream, or with jam and cream. It filled you up and nourished in the rather starched British tradition, but it was sweet and, oh, how we craved a sweet during the rationing of World War II. We have found so many semolina desserts as we have made our journey. Wheat, one of the earliest cultivated grains, comes to our generation in many ways, not the least is bread which has been given the lofty designation of "staff of life." I think one gets closest to the "ancestors" and their recognition of wheat as an important survival food when one is presented with a simple dessert like this or a simple bowl of hot cereal in the morning. This is only cosmic seconds away from the gruel of early man and only a nano-second away from that after-school treat I remember.

Africa–Guinea

**SEMOLINA DESSERT WITH BANANAS
IN THE STYLE OF GUINEA** (cont'd)

3 1/4 cups skimmed milk

3/4 cup semolina, enriched quick-cooking farina *or* Cream of Wheat cereal—*not instant**

1/3 cup sugar

1/4 cup *cold* skimmed milk

1 teaspoon pure vanilla extract
1/2 teaspoon ground cinnamon
2 *firm* bananas—diced

Pour 3 1/4 cupfuls milk into a large saucepan. Set over *MEDIUM* heat and allow to come to a low boil.

In a mixing bowl, combine farina, sugar, and 1/2 cupful *cold* milk. Stir to form a paste. *Gradually*, while stirring constantly with a wire whisk, add hot milk to farina mixture. Return to saucepan and set over *LOW* heat. Cook, stirring constantly with a wooden spoon for about 10 minutes, or until thickened. *Press out any lumps with the back of the spoon.* Remove from heat and allow to cool to room temperature.

Add vanilla extract and ground cinnamon. Mix well. Add diced bananas and stir *gently* to integrate *without mashing the banana pieces*. Turn into a serving bowl or into individual serving dishes. Refrigerate for at least 1 hour.

Serve chilled. Refrigerate any leftovers.

Yields 6 servings
adequate for 4 people

1/6 SERVING – PROTEIN = 7.4 g.; FAT = 0.7 g.; CARBOHYDRATE = 46.0 g.;
CALORIES = 213; CALORIES FROM FAT = 3%

Notes: *Semolina, the hard wheat from which good quality *pasta* is made, is available in most grocery stores and natural food stores. It is also available from mail order firms. This would be the more traditional grain with which to make this dessert but we are more apt to have farina on hand.

This recipe can be halved, if required.

Kenya

Kenya is different from other countries in East Africa and these differences keep me from being comfortable, as are many authors, with the an all-encompassing consideration of "East Africa." The Italian colonization period in East Africa, after their conquering of Ethiopia in 1895; Somalia, known then as Italian Somaliland, in 1889 and the subsequent addition of the Kenyan territory of Jubaland in 1925; and Eritrea in 1890, does group those nations together under an influence that does persist today while other nations, such as Kenya, show little-to-no cross-fertilization from the Italian colonies.

Paleontological records indicate that this land, which lies both to the north and to the south of the equator, was home to nomadic primates perhaps as far back as twenty million years. Concentrations of remains of *Homo habilis* (1.8–2.5 million years ago) and *Homo erectus* (1.8 million–350,000 years ago) near Lake Turkana suggest some level of settlement in the area. These people and their *Homo sapiens* descendants, dating from about 1.6 million years ago, from the African cradle of human development reached Europe and East Asia in their wanderings. The evidence of migration is clearly evident in DNA studies. Our ancestors, who eventually carried these ancient genes from Europe to the New World, have given us, deep in the mitochondria inherited from our female progenitors, the story of the human race. With modern genetic technology we can now follow ancestral routes. How amazing that the routes that food traveled from continent to continent were at one time our only clue.

The culinary influence of its British colonial period from 1890 as a British protectorate and as a Crown Colony from 1920 to 1957 is more evident, more so than are the influences of seafaring Arabic settlement in the first century or of the Portuguese settlement in the fourteenth century, established to service its trade voyages to the Far East. Although one will observe a significant contrast in seasoning and the greater consumption of fish in coastal cities like Mombasa. A writer, commenting on Kenyan cuisine, quipped that her cuisine might be more interesting if they had been colonized by the French instead of the British but the influence of more than forty distinct ethnicities who now live in Kenya and the lack of diversity in agriculture combined with the lack of any extensive agricultural trade has limited the development of an elaborate cuisine in the western sense. Colonial farmers became wealthy farming coffee and tea but, to protect their economic interests, taxed the members of the Kikuyu tribe, who provided the labor required, and banned them from owning land hence changing in large part the ability of Kenya to "feed itself" after the departure of the plantation owners. Kenyans, it may be said, "eat to live," not "live to eat." This said, however, there are meatless dishes from which to choose for the vegetarian.

When the mother of a friend described her visit to Kenya, I was beyond fascinated. She had stayed at the fabulous Treetops Hotel that was built on stilts to enable a view of wildlife below. Oh, how I wished I could travel to that far away land in East Africa. Maybe I will some day . . .

Africa–Kenya

*I beg indulgence for the inclusion of three salads.
These are three of our favorite salads
and we are sure that you will add them to your repertoire.*

Poached Eggs with Vegetarian Gravy

~

Orange and Tomato Salad

Papaya, Avocado, and Grapefruit Salad

Banana Salad with Rice

~~~~~~~~~~~~~~~~~~~~~

Black-Eyed Peas in Coconut Milk
M'Baazi

Corn Meal Cake
Ugali

Green Squash with Warm *Vinaigrette*

Corn-on-the-Cob, Kenyan Style

~~~~~~~~~~~~~~~~~~~~~

Cake with **Kenyan Sour Cream and Honey Dessert Sauce**

KENYAN POACHED EGGS WITH VEGETARIAN GRAVY
TPT - 28 minutes

One of the first things my mother taught me to cook was gravy. We did not open cans; we did not use bouillon cubes or gravy powder; we did not use Bovril; we made honest gravy from the meat drippings. Since you could be judged by your gravy, you learned to make gravy by the "feel" and you cultivated a "taste" so that you knew it was the most perfect gravy you could put into your gravy boat. British vegetarians are always searching for "gravy" and as a result their food industry has actually created "vegetarian gravy" powders and mixes. American vegetarians, on the other hand, seem able to accept other sauces without the pangs of cultural withdrawal and have had no problem switching to the term "sauceboat." The vegetarian gravy I have included here, which we serve with lentil roasts and roasted potatoes, also works well in this dish.

GRAVY "WITHOUT THE SUNDAY ROAST":
1 tablespoon WILD MUSHROOM STOCK
  [see index]
1/2 teaspoon corn starch

2 tablespoons butter
1/4 cup *very finely* chopped onion

2 tablespoons unbleached white flour
About 1 cup BROWN VEGETABLE STOCK
  [see index], *or* VEGETABLE STOCK
  FROM SOUP [see index], *or* WILD
  MUSHROOM STOCK [see index]

1 tablespoon *tamari* soy sauce
Freshly ground black pepper, to taste

Additional vegetarian stock, as needed

6 slices bread—trimmed and cut into circles

6 eggs

2 tablespoons *dry* breadcrumbs

KENYAN POACHED EGGS WITH VEGETARIAN GRAVY (cont'd)

Place six salad or dessert plates on a warming tray or in a warming oven set at *MEDIUM*.

In a small bowl or cup, combine mushroom stock and corn starch. Stir until corn starch is in suspension. Set aside until required.

Set up egg poacher, adequate for six eggs, over *LOW-MEDIUM* heat.

In a saucepan set over *LOW* heat, melt butter. Add *very finely* chopped onion and sauté until onion is soft and translucent, *being careful not to allow onion to brown*.

Remove from heat and, using a wire whisk, make a *roux* by beating in flour. Return to heat and, stirring constantly, cook for 2 minutes, *being careful not to burn or overbrown the roux*. Remove from heat and gradually beat in vegetable broth. Return saucepan to heat and cook, stirring constantly, until thickened.

Add mushroom stock–corn starch suspension and stir to combine thoroughly.

Add soy sauce and black pepper. Thin with additional vegetable stock, if necessary to obtain desired consistency. Place on warming tray until ready to serve. Break each egg into a small Pyrex dish or cup, being sure that the yolk is intact with each egg. Transfer to egg poacher and allow to cook only until egg whites have set.

Meanwhile toast bread rounds and place one on each of the warmed plates.

When the egg whites have set, transfer a poached egg onto each of the bread rounds.

Apportion gravy over each egg and sprinkle with breadcrumbs.

Serve at once.

Yields 6 individual servings

Notes: This recipe can be halved, when required.

The GRAVY "WITHOUT THE SUNDAY ROAST" can be frozen if you prefer to make a double or triple recipe in advance of need.

1/6 SERVING – PROTEIN = 10.5 g.; FAT = 10.0 g.; CARBOHYDRATE = 27.0 g.;
CALORIES = 240; CALORIES FROM FAT = 37%

KENYAN ORANGE AND TOMATO SALAD
TPT - 1 hour and 13 minutes;
1 hour = marination period

If our garden presents us with a perfectly ripened tomato, we used to slice it as a salad or as a garnish or tuck it into a sandwich with mayonnaise, never thinking of combining it with orange slices. Sliced oranges are often used for salads in North Africa but paring the two gloriously colored fruits was a new experience. It is a feast for the eyes and for the palate.

2 tablespoons safflower *or* sunflower oil
1 tablespoon freshly squeezed lemon juice
1/8 teaspoon sugar
Salt, to taste
Freshly ground black pepper, to taste

2 quarts *boiling* water
2 medium tomatoes—peeled and sliced into rounds

2 *organic* navel oranges—*well-scrubbed**

1/4 Italian red onion—sliced into thin slices and separated into rings

In a cruet combine oil, lemon juice, sugar, salt, and pepper. Shake vigorously. Set aside until required.

Place tomatoes in *boiling* water until skins loosen. Peel and slice into rounds. Place the rounds around the perimeter of a shallow serving bowl.

Peel oranges, reserving the peel. Remove pith and slice into crosswise into rounds. Arrange orange slices to the center of the serving bowl overlapping the tomato slices.

Using a sharp knife, remove any remaining pith from the orange peel. Cut into matchstick pieces and scatter over the tomato and orange slices.

Shake the *vinaigrette* again and pour over the salad. Arrange onion rings over the top. Refrigerate for at least 1 hour to allow for flavor development.

Africa–Kenya

KENYAN ORANGE AND TOMATO SALAD (cont'd)

Serve chilled.

Yields 6 servings
adequate for 4 people

Notes: *Organic oranges are recommended since the peel is eaten in this salad.

This recipe can be halved or doubled, when required.

1/6 SERVING – PROTEIN = 0.9 g.; FAT = 4.6 g.; CARBOHYDRATE = 7.6 g.;
CALORIES = 73; CALORIES FROM FAT = 57%

KENYAN PAPAYA, AVOCADO, AND GRAPEFRUIT SALAD
TPT - 8 minutes

For years we have enjoyed a salad which simply combines avocado and grapefruit sections. The taste of the grapefruit and the avocado bounce off each other superbly and it accompanies almost any meal beautifully. That is initially why I had created it. I discovered a recipe from Kenya which added the extra layer of papaya and a vinaigrette. This is not just a salad to accompany a main course, the contrasting textures are noticed by the palate and the extra bonus is that it takes just minutes to prepare.

Similar salads, with the addition of fresh coriander (cilantro) or watercress and tomato, in some instances, can be found in the varied cuisines of the Caribbean.

1 tablespoon *extra virgin* olive oil
1 tablespoon freshly squeezed lemon juice
Freshly ground black pepper
Pinch of ground allspice

1 pink grapefruit—peeled and segmented

1 ripe papaya—peeled, seeded, and cut into 1-inch chunks
2 large avocados—peeled and cut into 1-inch chunks

12 large leaves Boston *or* Bibb lettuce—well-washed and well-dried

6 *thin* slices of lemon, for garnish

In a cruet, combine oil, lemon juice, black pepper and ground allspice. Shake well to combine thoroughly. Set aside.

Cut each grapefruit segment in half and turn into a mixing bowl.

Add papaya and avocado chunks. Toss *gently* to combine.

On a large plate or platter, arrange lettuce. Spoon fruit mixture over.

Shake *vinaigrette* vigorously and drizzle it over fruit mixture.

Garnish platter with lemon slices.

Serve at once.

Yields 6 servings
adequate for 4 people

Note: This recipe can easily be halved or doubled, when required.

1/6 SERVING – PROTEIN = 1.4 g.; FAT = 7.4 g.; CARBOHYDRATE = 11.0 g.;
CALORIES = 107; CALORIES FROM FAT = 62%

Africa–Kenya

KENYAN BANANA SALAD WITH RICE

TPT - 35 minutes;
30 minutes = flavor development period

Not being terribly fond of the seemingly tasteless, bananas in grocery stores today, I was surprised and amazed at the remarkable taste of this salad. I substitute firm, almost green, sweet baby bananas in this salad to add that divinely subtle pineapple nuance. Rice with coconut is a traditional Kenyan preparation but this carries the dish to a very different level. Basmati rice is popular in Kenya, especially in the Indian-influenced coastal region, but any rice can be used.

1 tablespoon light vegetable oil, such as safflower oil
1 tablespoon freshly squeezed lemon juice
1/4 teaspoon sugar
1/8 teaspoon chili powder, or to taste

6 *green-tipped* baby bananas—peeled and cut into 1/2-inch chunks*
1/4 cup *finely* chopped onion
1/4 cup cooked *brown basmati* rice
1 tablespoon grated coconut—fresh *or* desiccated

In a cruet, combine oil, lemon juice, sugar, and chili powder. Shake vigorously. Set aside until required.

In a mixing bowl, combine chopped bananas, *finely* chopped onion, cooked rice, and grated coconut. Toss gently to mix.

Add prepared *vinaigrette* and toss to coat all ingredients well. Allow to stand at room temperature to allow for flavor development. Turn into a serving bowl.

Serve at room temperature.

Yields 6 servings
adequate for 4 people

Notes: *Baby bananas have a sweet taste that the large, commercially-ripened bananas do not. Two regular bananas can be substituted but the flavor with be quite different.

This recipe can be halved or doubled, when required.

1/6 SERVING – PROTEIN = 5.4 g.; FAT = 3.0 g.; CARBOHYDRATE = 17.2 g.;
CALORIES = 93; CALORIES FROM FAT = 29%

KENYAN BLACK-EYED PEAS IN COCONUT MILK
M'Baazi

TPT - 40 minutes

The cuisine of the coastal areas of eastern Kenya has been very much influenced by its trade with India. Chapatis, raitas, and curries are common. Therefore, it was no surprise to find a dish such as this in Kenya. Black-eyed peas were introduced to Asia from Africa as much as three thousand years ago. They are a staple in the southwestern areas of India where they are added to soups and stews and ground into flour for crêpes and pancakes. In this dish we see the return of the black-eyed peas to Kenya from India in a coconut curry, albeit very much less spiced than is the Indian coconut curry with black-eyed peas and spinach that we have enjoyed for years. I add both garam masala and chili powder, *the same combination that I use in my Indian recipe, just to give it a bit more complexity. Although this dish is traditionally served on a lettuce leaf, I serve it over rice or with ugali.*

You might have the time to cook dried beans to prepare this dish. Some of the interesting heirloom beans, such as tiger eye beans, or red, black, and butterscotch calypso beans, and cranberry and pinto beans look beautiful in this curry too.

2 tablespoons safflower *or* sunflower oil
1/2 medium onion—*finely* chopped

1/2 cup *finely* chopped green bell pepper
1/4 teaspoon OUR INDIAN SPICE MIXTURE (Garam Masala) [see index] *or* commercially-available mixture
1/4 teaspoon chili powder—or to taste
Red pepper flakes, to taste

1 can (15 ounces) black-eyed peas—drained and well-rinsed*
1/2 cup *light, sulfite-free* coconut milk

In a saucepan set over *MEDIUM* heat, heat oil. Add *finely* chopped onion. Sauté until onion is soft and translucent, *being careful not to allow the onion to brown.*

Africa–Kenya

KENYAN BLACK-EYED PEAS IN COCONUT MILK (cont'd)

Add *finely* chopped green pepper, *garam masala*, chili powder, and red pepper flakes. Cook, stirring constantly, for about two minutes.

Add black-eyed peas and coconut milk, and water. *Reduce the heat to LOW*. Cover and allow to simmer for about 15 minutes, or until the mixture thickens. Stir frequently. Remove from heat and allow to come to room temperature.

Serve at room temperature over rice or with *ugali*.

Notes: *Canned black-eyed peas are often available canned in what is called "Southern-style" in which bacon and bacon fat are used in the preparation. Your vegetarian lifestyle not withstanding, you do not want the "Southern style" for this dish.

This recipe can be doubled, when required.

Yields 6 servings
adequate for 4 people

1/6 SERVING – PROTEIN = 5.6 g.; FAT = 5.2 g.; CARBOHYDRATE = 11.5 g.;
CALORIES = 107; CALORIES FROM FAT = 44%

KENYAN CORN MEAL CAKE
Ugali
TPT - 26 minutes

Corn meal has been in my larder since I had my first apartment. I was not all that impressed the first time I cooked "corn meal mush," as it was referred to on the box I had bought. It was pretty much tasteless, I concluded, and I returned to an oatmeal breakfast. Over the years I have met Romanian "mămăligă," Italian "polenta," and recipes like this traditional Kenyan recipe that form a base for and support the flavors of other dishes. You could use rice; you could use pasta; you could use potatoes; you could use corn meal.

Ugali is the name given this dish in the Kenyan language of Kirundi but it is also known as "sima," "sembe," "posho," "ngima," and, "kuon." In South Africa it is called "mealie pap," in Zimbabwe it is known as "sadza," in Zambia it is called "nshima," in Uganda it is called "posho," and Caribbean names range from "cou-cou" in Barbados, "funchi" in Curacao, "funjie" in the Virgin Islands, "funche" in Puerto Rico, and "mayi moulin" in Haiti. In Kenya it is generally gathered into a ball with a thumb-sized depression using the fingers and then dipped into a sauce or stew of vegetables. We cut it into wedges and serve it as base for a "sukuma wiki," a vegetable stew.

2 1/2 cups *boiling* water

1 cup yellow corn meal

Salt, to taste
Freshly ground black pepper, to taste

Coat a 7-inch non-stick-coated skillet with olive oil non-stick lecithin spray coating. Set aside until required.

Pour *boiling* water into a saucepan set over *LOW-MEDIUM* heat.

While stirring, *slowly* add corn meal. Cook, stirring constantly, for about 10 minutes, or until it becomes thick and smooth. Adjust heat lower, *being careful not to allow the corn meal to brown.**

Season with salt and pepper. Stir to combine well. Turn into the prepared skillet. Set over *MEDIUM-LOW* heat to keep warm and allow for further evaporation of the liquid for about 10 minutes. Remove from heat. Place a large plate or round platter on top of the skillet and invert the skillet over the plate to release the corn meal cake. Place on a warming tray until ready to serve.

Cut into wedges to serve. Refrigerate leftovers.

Yields 6 servings
adequate for 4 people

Notes: *If desired and if appropriate to the menu, a tablespoonful of butter can be added at this point. Leftovers are good for lunch with hot melted butter or grated cheese.

KENYAN CORN MEAL CAKE (cont'd)

This recipe can be halved or doubled, when desired. Be sure to choose a non-stick-coated skillet appropriate to the amount in which to mold the cake.

1/6 SERVING – PROTEIN = 2.0 g.; FAT = 0.8 g.; CARBOHYDRATE = 16.0 g.;
CALORIES = 79; CALORIES FROM FAT = 9%

KENYAN GREEN SQUASH WITH WARM *VINAIGRETTE*
TPT - 13 minutes

We call green summer squash zucchini and the British, among other Europeans, call them marrows, but Kenyans use the French "courgettes" to designate a squash quite similar to that which we can buy in any grocery store. We are blessed to have summer squash varieties available year round; not so for the Kenyan housewife who must relegate this recipe to the summer growing season.

2 tablespoons safflower *or* sunflower oil
1/4 teaspoon salt
1/4 teaspoon freshly ground black pepper

4 small zucchini—well washed and cut into round slices*

2 teaspoons freshly squeezed lemon juice
1/4 teaspoon sugar

In a large skillet set over *MEDIUM* heat, heat the 2 tablespoonfuls oil. Add salt and pepper.

Add zucchini slices and fry until golden brown on both sides. Remove to paper toweling and pat to remove excess oil.

Add lemon juice and sugar. Turn into a heated serving bowl.

Serve at once with a slotted spoon.

Yields 6 servings
adequate for 4 people

Notes: *Small zucchini have less water and retain a crisp texture when fried in this manner.

This recipe can be halved or doubled, when required.

1/6 SERVING – PROTEIN = 0.7 g.; FAT = 4.6 g.; CARBOHYDRATE = 2.4 g.;
CALORIES = 51; CALORIES FROM FAT = 81%

CORN-ON-THE-COB, KENYAN STYLE
TPT - 10 minutes

Native Americans have given two enormously important gifts to humanity that allowed the human species to prosper and multiply. The hundreds of varieties of potatoes that were developed by those who lived in the Andes were carried to Europe by the returning explorers. An easily grown food that grew safely below the ground and was therefore a source of food that legions, drought, and fires could not destroy, potatoes allowed for the population to survive and its numbers to grow. The carefully cultivated maize grown by the North and South American tribes, who added agriculture to their hunting and gathering lifestyle, was perhaps the first genetically engineered crop. They chose the best ears to dry for seed for next year's crop and selected for ear size, kernel size and uniformity, and sweetness. Corn too was introduced to Europe, in what has become known as the Columbian Exchange. Ultimately corn reached Africa as well. Corn is an important crop in Africa to feed both people and domesticated animals just as it is here, and just as it was in the Western Hemisphere before the period of European contact.

6 large ears of corn—shucked, ends trimmed, and silk removed

3 tablespoons butter
1/4 cup *high heat* safflower *or* sunflower oil

Salt, to taste
Freshly ground black pepper, to taste
1 tablespoon freshly squeezed lime juice

CORN-ON-THE-COB, KENYAN STYLE (cont'd)

Break or cut each ear in half.

In a large skillet set over *MEDIUM* heat, heat butter and oil. Add corn and cook until the entire ear is lightly browned. *Use tongs to constantly move the corn.* Remove to a heated platter.

Season with salt and pepper. Sprinkle lime juice over.

Serve at once. Provide each diner with corn holders to facilitate eating.

Notes: Keep the heat set at *MEDIUM*. If higher heat is used, the corn can pop right off the cob and cause dangerous oil spattering.

This recipe can be halved, when required.

Yields 12 servings
adequate for 6 people

1/12 SERVING – PROTEIN = 2.4 g.; FAT = 4.4 g.; CARBOHYDRATE = 15.3 g.;
CALORIES = 99; CALORIES FROM FAT = 40%

KENYAN SOUR CREAM AND HONEY DESSERT SAUCE
TPT - 1 minute

While in graduate school I shared an apartment with a young high school teacher. I was living on a small teaching stipend so our Christmas party was not a lavish affair. My roommate's sister gave me a melon baller, of all things. I mention this only because this dessert sauce is often served with fruit such as melon in Kenya and that melon baller, which is still in a kitchen drawer, actually comes in handy to create a very pretty dessert. Kenyans make good use of cultured and soured milk products, as do those in Germany and Eastern Europe. This simple, quickly prepared sauce, which is the perfect finish for a slice of unfrosted cake, I predict, will be a part of your repertoire once you have tried it.

1/4 cup *fat-free* dairy sour cream
1/4 cup honey, of choice
1 teaspoon *finely* grated fresh gingerroot

In a small bowl, combine sour cream, honey, and *finely* grated gingerroot. Stir to combine thoroughly. Turn into a serving bowl. Refrigerate until ready to serve.

Serve chilled.

Yields 8 tablespoonfuls

Note: This recipe can be halved or doubled, when required.

1/8 SERVING (i. e., per tablespoonful) –
PROTEIN = 1.1 g.; FAT = 0.1 g.; CARBOHYDRATE = 11.3 g.;
CALORIES = 47; CALORIES FROM FAT = 2%

Liberia

In 1773 a project which would "return" American Negroes to Africa was conceived by The Reverend Samuel Hopkins of Newport, RI. In the early 1800s Paul Cuffe, a Quaker ship owner transported free blacks to Sierra Leone at his own expense and then brought sellable cargoes back to North America. His plans to make one voyage a year were curtailed by his death in 1817. The same year the American Colonization Society was founded to facilitate the "repatriation" of both free-born and enslaved blacks and their American-born families. Among the supporters of the colonization project masterminded by Charles Fenton Mercer were Henry Clay, The Reverend Robert Finley, Richard Bland Lee, William Thornton, Francis Scott Key, President James Monroe, Maryland Governor John Eager Howard, John Randolph, Daniel Webster, Supreme Court Chief Justice John Marshall, and Associate Supreme Court Justice Bushrod Washington. Bushrod Washington, a nephew of George Washington, was the Society's first president and served in that capacity until his death in 1829. The success of Sierra Leone, England's Negro colony founded in 1787, gave impetus to this project that began in 1819 with emigration of the first group of individuals under the auspices of the American Colonization Society. On January 3, 1820, The "Liberian Mayflower," as the ship the *Elizabeth*, was nicknamed, set sail with eighty-eight individuals of thirty families only to be trapped in ice in New York Harbor. Finally, on February 6th they were on their way to begin the building of the nation of Liberia but twenty-two of those first settlers and the American Colonization Society agents died within weeks from yellow fever forcing them to return to Sierra Leone to await more colonists. The *Nautilus* brought two shiploads the next year and an island settlement was established at Mersurado Bay. Today Americo–Liberians, those who can trace their decadency to the American Colonization period, either from the United States or the Caribbean, are estimated to comprise only five-percent of the population of approximately three and a half million, who are members of sixteen different indigenous groups.

A colony of the United States, Liberia became an independent nation in 1847 when a government modeled after that of the United States was formed headed by Joseph Jenkins Roberts. The motto of the new nation was and is, "The love of freedom brought us here." It was formed and led by the Americo–Liberian minority with little consideration of the indigenous majority. Nevertheless, this government model successfully ruled until 1980 when it was overthrown in a military coup in which the then president William R. Tolbert, Jr. was murdered in the executive mansion. Two civil wars, the first 1989-1996 and the second 1999-2003, have led to displacement of hundreds of thousands of people into neighboring nations. Also as a result of the upheaval of these periods of war, the economy of Liberia all but collapsed. Despite the poverty and emigration from Liberia due to the decades of war, Liberia is now steadily recovering and is said to be presently experiencing economic growth.

Even today the food and flavors of the American South can be seen in the cuisine of Liberia but one must remember that many of the foods we designate as southern are the result of the recipes introduced to southern families by their cooks, slaves brought to the Colonies from Africa in the first place.

Africa–Liberia

Fresh Pineapple Drink with Fresh Gingerroot

~

Black-Eyed Pea and Tomato Soup

~

Cabbage Salad with Pineapple

~~~~~~~~~~~~~~~~~~~~~~

Spicy Stew with Bananas and Soymeat

Supa ya n Digi

Golden Buttermilk Cornbread *[see index]*

~~~~~~~~~~~~~~~~~~~~~~

Spiced Pumpkin Cake

"Stewed" Mangoes with Cloves

LIBERIAN FRESH PINEAPPLE DRINK WITH FRESH GINGERROOT

TPT - 8 hours and 25 minutes;
8 hours = flavor development period

My mother was joyous when the pineapple harvest would arrive from Hawaii. You could smell the fragrance across the produce department and we followed to the most enormous pineapples. Mom knocked them knowingly and chose one, which I must admit was always perfectly ripened and sweet beyond anything you could expect. I remember too the work it was to prepare that fresh pineapple. Rarely do we find the large Hawaiian pineapples in our produce departments today; the supply generally comes from Latin America, especially from Honduras. However, one of the great conveniences of this millennium is that the work of peeling and removing the eyes of the fresh pineapple can be avoided because peeled and cored whole pineapples, pineapple slices, and pineapple spears arrive at almost every grocery store each week. This is a refreshing drink like no other made easier not only because of the prepared pineapples in the produce department but also by the food processor. Imagine preparing the pineapple and then grinding the ginger and mashing the pineapple by hand . . .

1 ounce fresh gingerroot—peeled and chopped

1 small fresh, ripe, peeled, and cored pineapple

1/2 cup sugar

2 quarts *cold* water

In the work bowl of the food processor fitted with steel knife, process the chopped gingerroot until *very finely* chopped, scraping down the sides of the work bowl as necessary.

Set the pineapple on a platter and chop into small pieces. Put the pieces into the work bowl with the ginger. Add the pineapple juice that accumulates on the platter as well. Process until a fine purée results.

Add sugar. Again, process. Turn into a large pitcher, bowl, or kettle.

Add water. Stir well. Cover and refrigerate for 8 hours, or overnight.

Set a fine sieve over a large bowl. Line the sieve with a cotton tea towel. Pour the pineapple–ginger mixture into the towel-lined sieve and allow the liquid to strain through. Gather the tea towel and squeeze it tightly to recover as much liquid as possible.* Turn the strained juice into a serving pitcher. Refrigerate until required.

Serve chilled in champagne flutes.

Yields 8 cupfuls

Notes: *The gingered pineapple mixture which remains can be folded into whipped cream for a really wonderful dessert.

This is easily halved, when required.

1/16 SERVING (about 1/2 cupful) –
PROTEIN = 0.3 g.; FAT = 0.1 g.; CARBOHYDRATE = 17.0 g.;
CALORIES = 66; CALORIES FROM FAT = <1%

Africa–Liberia

LIBERIAN SPICY BLACK-EYED PEA AND TOMATO SOUP
TPT - 47 minutes

This soup is often prepared with a lot more fire than this in Liberia. If you really like it hot, add ground red pepper (cayenne), to taste, at the end. When I serve this as a main coarse offering, rather than a first course soup, I add one cupful of corn at the same time that I add the greens.

2 tablespoons canola oil
1 medium onion—chopped
1 cup diced celery
2 large garlic cloves—*finely* chopped

1 tablespoon crushed, dried thyme
2 teaspoons ground turmeric, or to taste
2 teaspoons chili powder, or to taste
1 teaspoon ground allspice

3 cups canned, *diced* tomatoes with liquid
1 quart water

1 can (14.5 ounces) black-eyed peas—*well-drained*— or cooked, dry beans*
1/2 cup chopped red bell pepper

2 cups chopped fresh collard greens—well-washed and drained**
1 cup green (fresh) *or frozen* corn kernels (optional)

In a large skillet set over *MEDIUM* heat, heat oil. Add chopped onion, diced celery, and *finely* chopped garlic. Sauté until onion and celery are soft and translucent, *being careful not to brown any of the vegetables.*

Add crushed, dried thyme, ground turmeric, chili powder, and ground allspice. Sauté for another 30 seconds or so until the aroma is released.

Add diced tomatoes and water. Stir and allow to come to the boil. Cover, *reduce heat to LOW*, and allow to simmer for about 5 minutes.

Add beans and chopped red pepper. Allow to cook for about 15 minutes, stirring occasionally.

Add chopped greens and corn, if desired. Stir the soup. Allow to cook until the greens have wilted.

Turn into a heated serving tureen. Keep warm on warming tray until ready to serve.

Yields about 9 cupfuls without corn;
yields 10 cupfuls with corn

Notes: *Canned beans will required no further salting but you may want to taste for salt if you use cooked, dried beans. Be careful when buying canned black-eyed peas. Canned black-eyed peas are often available canned in what is called "Southern-style" in which bacon and bacon fat are used in the preparation. Your vegetarian lifestyle not withstanding, you do not want the "Southern style" for this dish.

**Kale, escarole, Swiss chard, or spinach can be substituted.

This recipe is easily halved, when required, but since it freezes well we find a full recipe to be a true convenience.

1/9 SERVING without corn (i. e., per cupful) –
PROTEIN = 5.2 g.; FAT = 3.2 g.; CARBOHYDRATE = 12.9 g.;
CALORIES = 57; CALORIES FROM FAT = 50%

1/10 SERVING with corn (i. e., per cupful) –
PROTEIN = 5.6 g.; FAT = 3.2 g.; CARBOHYDRATE = 17.7 g.;
CALORIES = 88; CALORIES FROM FAT = 33%

LIBERIAN CABBAGE SALAD WITH PINEAPPLE
TPT - 47 minutes;
30 minutes = salting period

To our upstate New York family there was as clear a difference between coleslaw and cabbage salad as there was between store-bought bread and Grandma's bread. Coleslaw was the "shredded" cabbage salad with a sweet, creamy dressing that you got in a restaurant or a diner, not in a German home; cabbage salad, on the other hand, contained not only "knife-slivered, not shredded," cabbage but other ingredients such as green bell pepper, onion, caraway seeds, and pineapple. Cabbage salad as made in Liberia is amazingly similar, is it not?

Africa–Liberia

LIBERIAN CABBAGE SALAD WITH PINEAPPLE (cont'd)

1/4 cup PLAIN YOGURT *[see index]* or commercially-available plain yogurt
1 tablespoon *fat-free* dairy sour cream

1 tablespoon *skimmed* milk
Pinch or two ground ginger

4 cups *thinly* sliced, "knife-slivered," green cabbage—well-washed and well-dried
3/4 cup *thin, diagonally* sliced celery—well-washed and well-dried
1/4 cup *finely* slivered onion

1/2 teaspoon salt

1/2 small green bell pepper—well-washed, cored, and *thinly* slivered
2 firm Italian plum tomatoes—well-washed, halved, seeded, and slivered
1 cup cubed fresh pineapple
Freshly ground black pepper, to taste

2 tablespoons *finely* chopped fresh parsley
1 tablespoon *finely* chopped fresh marjoram

In a small dish, combine yogurt and sour cream. Mix thoroughly.

Gradually, teaspoon by teaspoon, add milk, beating well after each addition. Add ground ginger and beat that in as well. Set aside until required.

In a large mixing bowl, combine *thinly* slivered cabbage, *thinly* sliced celery, and *finely* slivered onion. Toss.

Sprinkle salt over and toss again. Turn into a salad spinner and allow vegetables to wilt at room temperature for about 30 minutes. Toss occasionally to distribute the salt. Rinse the vegetables well in *cold* water and spin to *dry thoroughly*. Turn into a clean mixing bowl.

Add slivered peppers, slivered tomatoes, and diced pineapple. Toss gently. Season with black pepper. Toss again. Add prepared yogurt–sour cream dressing. Toss to coat vegetables evenly. Turn into a serving bowl.

Sprinkle chopped parsley and marjoram over.

Serve chilled.

Yields 8 servings
adequate for 6 people

Note: This recipe can be halved, when required.

1/8 SERVING – PROTEIN = 2.4 g.; FAT = 0.5 g.; CARBOHYDRATE = 10.8 g.;
CALORIES = 53; CALORIES FROM FAT = 9%

SPICY STEW WITH BANANAS AND SOYMEAT IN THE LIBERIAN STYLE

Supa ya n Digi

TPT - 58 minutes

Liberians, of course, would use chicken and chicken stock in this classic stew. To the Western palate it is an odd, but fascinating, combination. Again, we can see the changes in cuisine as ideas cross and recross the ocean.

We generally accompany this stew with cornbread but it is also good over rice.

1 tablespoon *extra virgin* olive oil
3 large celery ribs, with leaves—chopped to yield about 1 1/2 cups
1/2 cup chopped Italian red onion

3 garlic cloves—*very finely* chopped

1 tablespoon OUR INDIAN SPICE MIXTURE (*Garam Masala*) *[see index]* or HOMEMADE CURRY POWDER *[see index]*
1/8 teaspoon ground red pepper (cayenne), or to taste
1/4 teaspoon salt, or to taste
1/4 teaspoon freshly ground black pepper, or to taste

2 cups VEGETARIAN BROWN STOCK *[see index]*, other vegetarian stock of choice, *or* water
3 cups canned, *diced* tomatoes in tomato purée
1/4 cup *unsweetened* shredded coconut—fresh *or* desiccated

5 ounces *frozen* soy meat analogue—chopped into large, bite-sized pieces*
3 large *green* bananas—*thickly* sliced

Africa–Liberia

SPICY STEW WITH BANANAS AND SOYMEAT IN THE LIBERIAN STYLE (cont'd)

In a kettle set over *MEDIUM* heat, heat oil. Add chopped celery and onion and sauté until onion begins to soften. *Be careful to allow neither the celery nor the onion to brown.*

Add *very finely* chopped garlic. Continue sautéing for a minute or two more.

Add *garam masala* or curry powder, ground red pepper (cayenne), salt, and black pepper. Stir for a minute or two to release the oils of the spices.

Add vegetable stock or water, tomatoes, and coconut. Allow to come to the boil. *Reduce heat to LOW-MEDIUM*, cover, and allow to simmer for about 30 minutes.**

Add frozen soymeat pieces and banana slices. Continue cooking, uncovered, for about 12 minutes. Turn into a heated serving bowl or soup tureen.

Serve at once into heated soup plates.

Yields 8 servings
adequate for 6 people

Notes: *Frozen meat substitutes are generally available in natural food stores and in the natural foods sections of large grocery stores.

**If convenient, the base for this stew can be made to this point and frozen. Defrost, heat, and add soymeat and bananas. The stew with soymeat and bananas does not freeze well nor does it reheat well.

This recipe can be halved or doubled, when required.

1/8 SERVING – PROTEIN = 6.8 g.; FAT = 4.0 g.; CARBOHYDRATE = 18.8 g.
CALORIES = 118; CALORIES FROM FAT = 30%

LIBERIAN SPICED PUMPKIN CAKE

TPT - 1 hour and 10 minutes*;
30 minutes = cooling period

Having collected pumpkin cake recipes for years in search of the perfect pumpkin cake, I finally settled on a recipe which calls for oil not butter. Then I found this recipe from Liberia and, naturally, I had to try it. Liberians grow pumpkins and make this cake using puréed *fresh pumpkin but I prefer canned pumpkin because it is a thicker, more flavorful purée and the texture of cakes is consistent. Also, white flour is used in Liberia but I have found that the combination of cake flour and whole wheat flour gives a texture which I prefer.*

Serve with a bowl of soup, this makes a delicious lunch with vegetable, bread, and dessert in one slice.

1/2 cup sifted cake flour
1/4 cup whole wheat flour
1/2 teaspoon baking powder
1/2 teaspoon baking soda
1/2 teaspoon ground cinnamon
1/4 teaspoon ground ginger
1/8 teaspoon ground cloves

1/4 cup butter—*softened to room temperature*
1/4 cup sugar
1/4 cup *fat-free* pasteurized eggs (the equivalent of 1 egg)
1/2 cup canned pumpkin—*unseasoned* and *unsweetened***
1/2 teaspoon pure vanilla extract

Confectioners' sugar, whipped cream *or* ice cream, as preferred

Preheat oven to 350 degrees F. Prepare a 9 x 5 x 3-inch square baking pan by coating with non-stick lecithin spray coating. Dust with cake flour.

Into a large mixing bowl, combine cake and whole wheat flours with baking powder, baking soda, and ground cinnamon, ginger, and cloves. Stir to mix well. Set aside.

Using the electric mixer, cream butter until light and fluffy. Add sugar and continue creaming until again light and fluffy. While beating, *gradually* add pasteurized eggs, pumpkin purée, and vanilla extract. Beat until mixture is thoroughly combined.

Gradually add spiced flour mixture and beat only until dry ingredients are incorporated. *Be careful not to overbeat.* Turn into prepared baking pan. Rap pan sharply on counter top to release any large bubbles.

Bake in preheated 350 degree F. oven for 22-25 minutes, or until a cake tester inserted in the center comes out clean. Cool *completely* on a wire rack.

LIBERIAN SPICED PUMPKIN CAKE (cont'd)

Sift confectioners' sugar over, or, if preferred, leave unfrosted and serve with a dollop of whipped cream or ice cream.

Yields 6 servings

Notes: *The batter for this cake is perfect for making small cakes or tartlets. Bake for about 9-10 minutes. Cool slightly before removing from tart pans.

**Cooked, puréed, and strained fresh pumpkin may be used but we recommend that you mix it half and half with cooked, puréed, and strained fresh Golden Nugget or Acorn squash.

This cake freezes well.

1/6 SERVING –
PROTEIN = 3.3 g.; FAT = 7.7 g.; CARBOHYDRATE = 21.3 g.;
CALORIES = 165; CALORIES FROM FAT = 42%

1/14 SERVING (i. e., per tartlet) –
PROTEIN = 1.4 g.; FAT = 3.3 g.; CARBOHYDRATE = 9.1 g.;
CALORIES = 71; CALORIES FROM FAT = 42%

LIBERIAN "STEWED" MANGOES WITH CLOVES
TPT - 1 hour

I originally tasted this very simple dessert at the 1963-64 New York World's Fair at the end of a lunch that had contained a few too many hot chilies for my unaccustomed taste buds. It soothed and excited the sweet receptors helping me to recover my sense of taste again, at least for a few hours. I remember stopping for ice cream at some point, when the "mango magic" had worn off. Either peach or mango nectar can be used but I do prefer the subtle contrast of the peach and the mango.

3 medium *ripe* mangoes

12 whole cloves
1 can (12 ounces) peach nectar

Peel the mangoes. Stand each mango upright on its flattest end with the large, flat pit perpendicular to you. Using a very sharp knife, cutting parallel to the pit, slice off large thin, flat slices. Place in a saucepan.

Scatter cloves among the mango slices. Pour peach nectar over. Place over *MEDIUM* heat and allow to come just to the boil. Remove from heat and allow to cool to room temperature. Transfer to the refrigerator for at least 45 minutes.

Transfer mango slices into a large soup plate. Scatter a few cloves over and remove the rest from the peach nectar remaining in the saucepan. Pour the remaining nectar over the mango slices.

To serve, spoon a few mango slices with juice into chilled fruit dishes. Garnish each with a single clove.

Yields 6 servings
adequate for 4-6 people

Note: This recipe can be reduced or increased proportionally for, say, one mango, two mangoes, four mangoes, etc.

1/6 SERVING – PROTEIN = 0.7 g.; FAT = 0.3 g.; CARBOHYDRATE = 26.6 g.;
CALORIES = 104; CALORIES FROM FAT = 2%

Libya

Phoenicians, also known as the "Sea People," spread their influence west to the area we now know as Libya in the first century BC driving the Berber tribes from the coastal areas south into the Sahara Dessert which covers much of the land mass of present-day Libya. The Phoenicians colonized the eastern section of Libya, known as Cyrenaica, while the western part of the country we know today as Libya, was colonized by the Greeks. This western section, known as Tripolitania, came under the Carthaginians and subsequently fell to the Romans in 46 BC. The area was part of the Roman Empire until 436 AD. By the sixteenth century Tripolitania was one of the outposts of the Barbary pirates who raided merchant ships as they came into the Mediterranean. The Pasha of Tripoli set the ransom/tribute and when his demand for tribute was increased, conflicts, known as the Barbary Wars, broke out with the United States. A peace was achieved in 1805 and United States vessels no longer were required to pay tribute. The era of the independent pashas was brought to an end when Libya was incorporated into the Ottoman Empire.

Italy moved troops into Tripoli in 1911 when conflict broke out between Italy and the Ottoman Empire. Libya and Ottoman forces fought the Italian occupation until 1914 by which time most of Libya was controlled by Italy. In 1934 Italy united Tripolitania and Cyrenaica as an Italian colony. Tripoli fell to Allied forces after the bitter dessert campaigns of World War II. In 1949 the United Nations voted to end Allied administration and allow Libya to become an independent nation. The United Kingdom of Libya was formerly declared in 1951.

In 1958 the discovery of oil changed Libya from a poor, backwater of North Africa into a player in the global economy but not without consequences. Libya was militarized by Muammar al-Qaddafi who came to power in 1969 when he, a twenty-seven-year old army officer, led a small group of military officers in a *coup d'etat* against King Idris. In 1977 Libya officially became the Socialist People's Libyan Arab *Jamahiriya*. Gaddafi, a clever but bizarrely irrational dictator, always challenged convention and the world order becoming one of the most egregious sponsors of international terrorism. Confrontation with the United States occurred when Gaddafi claimed two hundred miles of the Gulf of Sitre (alternately, Gulf of Sidra), banning international usage. He dared the world to cross his "line of death" and just as had been the case with the Barbary pirates, conflict ensued. A United States reconnaissance plane was hit by a missile, Gaddafi ordered the burning of the United States embassy, and engaged the ships of a United States naval fleet which had positioned just off the Libyan coast. Libyan-sponsored terrorism acts continued despite the pressure of world governments and the United States responded in 1986 by striking Tripoli and Bengahzi. Libya's unrelenting defiance resulted in sanctions which were put in place by the United Nations Security Council in 1993. Finally, in 1999 there seemed to be some change in Gaddafi's face to the world even to his public condemnation of the September 11, 2001, attacks on the World Trade Center. In 2011, emboldened by the uprisings in the Middle East and North Africa, dubbed the Arab Spring, anti-Gaddafi elements precipitated a civil war. It was successful with the help of United Nations forces who established a no-fly zone and whose planes bombed the Gaddafi loyalists "with all means necessary to protect the civilian population." The vicious dictatorship of the iron-fisted Gaddafi ended in 2011 when he was killed by soldiers of the popular uprising.

The National Transitional Council, which assumed power, renamed the country Libya again. It is the council's intention to oversee a transition to a constitutional democracy and to lead this nation of 5.7 million people forward.

Africa – Libya

The cuisine of Libya borrows from both the cuisines to the west, Tunisia and Morocco, and from cuisines in the Middle East, to the east. Borrowing bits from here and there does not necessarily result in a complex cuisine in this case but instead in what some refer to as a "tent cuisine," a healthy, well-flavored but unsophisticated cuisine with dishes often quite different from the source dish. For example, in the eastern part of Libya *couscous* is not the flour and water *pasta* pearls we expect in North Africa. It is, instead, a dish made from braised lamb which is served over steamed buckwheat, vegetables, and dried fruit. As you travel the world you observe the changes in the starch staple—potatoes, rice, macaroni or noodles, *couscous*, corn, and breads made of every grain imaginable. Libyan cuisine exhibits a rather unique approach to this important, cuisine-defining basic that can be illustrated by dividing the nation roughly in half at the Bay of Sirte. To the east of this imaginary line, a historical region designated Cyrenaica, a diet similar to that eaten in Egypt is found where *couscous* is eaten on occasion but can not be considered the staple carbohydrate source. To the west, historically Tripolitania, *couscous* is the staple starch. The influence of Italy, as part of the bread basket of the Roman Empire and/or its period as a colony of Italy, certainly account for the wheat-based staple *couscous* and for the Libyan passion for *pasta*. Many ingredients used on a daily basis in Libya strongly suggest an Italian influence—capers, bay leaves, and certainly olive oil; Libyans are said to consume twice as much olive oil per capita than do Italians.

Pumpkin Appetizer Dip
Kara'a

Goat Cheese and Yogurt Spread
Jibna Bayda

Pita Bread and Crackers
Deviled Eggs with Curry

~

Red Lentil Soup
Shurba

~

Lentil and Spinach Salad
Salata

Chick Pea Salad
Leblebi S'alalah

~ ~ ~ ~ ~ ~ ~ ~ ~ ~ ~ ~ ~ ~ ~ ~ ~ ~ ~ ~

Eggplant *Tagine*
Tagine bil Badhinjan

~ ~ ~ ~ ~ ~ ~ ~ ~ ~

Shirred Eggs and Vegetables
Shashouka

~ ~ ~ ~ ~ ~ ~ ~ ~ ~ ~ ~ ~ ~ ~ ~ ~ ~ ~ ~

Assorted Melon Slices Drizzled with Honey
Dates

Africa–Libya

LIBYAN PUMPKIN APPETIZER DIP
Kara'a
TPT - 8 minutes

Compare the texture and flavors of this dip to that ubiquitous sour cream–onion dip of the 1950s. Whatever were we thinking back then? We love this with crudités and corn chips or pita triangles for lunch. Although this dip can be made with fresh chopped pumpkin or a winter squash such as butternut or acorn, the canned, puréed product gives a wonderful texture.

2 tablespoons *extra virgin* olive oil
1/2 medium onion—*finely* chopped
2 garlic cloves—*very finely* chopped

1 teaspoon ground cumin
1/2 teaspoon paprika
1/4 teaspoon ground ginger
1/4 teaspoon OUR INDIAN SPICE MIXTURE (*Garam Masala*) *[see index] or* HOMEMADE CURRY POWDER *[see index]*, if preferred
1/8 teaspoon ground red pepper (cayenne), or to taste
1/8 teaspoon ground coriander
Pinch sugar

1 1/2 cups canned pumpkin—*unseasoned* and *unsweetened**
1/2 cup canned, *crushed* tomatoes
1 tablespoon freshly squeezed lemon juice

In a skillet set over *MEDIUM* heat, heat oil. Add *finely* chopped onion and *very finely* chopped garlic. Sauté until onion is soft and transparent, *allowing neither the onion nor the garlic to brown.*

Add ground cumin, paprika, ground ginger, *garam masala*, ground red pepper (cayenne), ground coriander, and sugar. Cook, stirring constantly, for a minute or two or until the spices release aroma. Remove from heat.

Add pumpkin, tomatoes, and lemon juice. Stir to combine thoroughly. Turn into serving dish. Refrigerate until required.

Serve chilled or at room temperature with an assortment of *crudités*, crackers, or hunks of bread. Refrigerate leftovers.

Yields 1 3/4 cupfuls

Notes: *Canned pumpkin is specified because it is a thicker, more flavorful purée. Cooked, puréed, and strained fresh pumpkin may be used but we recommend that you mix it half and half with cooked, puréed, and strained fresh Golden Nugget or Acorn squash.

This recipe can be halved or doubled, when required.

1/28 SERVING (i. e., per tablespoonful) –
PROTEIN = 0.2 g.; FAT = 0.8 g.; CARBOHYDRATE = 1.5 g.;
CALORIES = 14; CALORIES FROM FAT = 51%

LIBYAN GOAT CHEESE AND YOGURT SPREAD
Jibna Bayda
TPT - 3 minutes

At one point in my life, goat cheese was far from a joy to me. In the 1980s and 1990s every hostess, it seemed, placed a slice on top of a side salad. Some of these selections left you feeling that the goat was right there under the table—kind of the way my dad always felt when lamb was served because he had had way too much mutton as a boy. Your choice of "fromage de chèvre," goat cheese, can make all the difference in the world. Do not give up on goat cheese because if you taste a little of every selection you encounter, one day you will say, "Wow, I really do like this goat cheese."

4 ounces goat cheese with herbs *or* with honey —*brought to room temperature*
3 tablespoons PLAIN YOGURT *[see index] or* commercially-available plain yogurt*
1 tablespoons freshly squeezed lemon juice
1 tablespoon *finely* chopped fresh fennel fronds
1 tablespoon *finely* chopped fresh parsley

2 teaspoons *extra virgin* olive oil

In a small bowl combine *softened* goat cheese, yogurt, lemon juice, and *finely* chopped fresh fennel and parsley. Using the back of a spoon, work the mixture into a smooth spread. Turn it into a small serving dish.

Drizzle olive oil over.

Set the serving dish on a plate and surround the dish with crackers, pieces of *pita* bread, or *crudités*. Provide a spreader for the cheese.

Africa – Libya

LIBYAN GOAT CHEESE AND YOGURT SPREAD (cont'd)

Serve at room temperature.

Yields about 3/4 cupful

Notes: *If you prefer to serve this as a dip, add more yogurt until you get the desired consistency.

This recipe can be doubled, when required.

1/24 SERVING (i. e., about 1 1/2 teaspoonfuls) –
PROTEIN = 0.9 g.; FAT = 1.5 g.; CARBOHYDRATE = 0.3 g.;
CALORIES = 18; CALORIES FROM FAT = 75%

LIBYAN RED LENTIL SOUP
Shurba

TPT - 1 hour and 5 minutes

Soups are wonderful one-pot meals. How often have we sat down to a bowl of minestrone, bread, and fruit and left the table totally satisfied. Libyans love soup; one writer actually referenced soup as the national dish. Of course, his preference was for a soup made with beef or lamb. Punctuated with red vegetables bits, this is a very beautiful soup which can be as spicy as you wish. We serve this soup with a hard-crusted loaf of a rustic bread and fresh fruit or a chilled fruit pudding for dessert.

1 cup dry red lentils *or masur dal*
2 cups *boiling* **water**

2 tablespoons *extra virgin* **olive oil**
1/2 cup *finely* **chopped onion**

1/2 cup *finely* **chopped celery**
1 large garlic clove—*finely* **chopped**

1 medium tomato—**peeled, seeded, and diced** *or*
1 cup canned, *diced* **tomatoes**

2 cups VEGETARIAN BROWN STOCK *[see index]* **or VEGETABLE STOCK FROM SOUP** *[see index]*
2 cups water
1 teaspoon Tabasco Sauce, or to taste
1/2 teaspoon freshly ground black pepper, or to taste
1/8 teaspoon ground turmeric, or to taste
1/8 teaspoon ground cumin, or to taste
1/8 teaspoon chili powder, or to taste

2 tablespoons *cold* **water**
2 tablespoons corn starch

1 red bell pepper—**cored, seeded, and diced**

Pick over lentils and discard any of poor quality. Rinse thoroughly.

In a bowl, combine lentils and 2 cupfuls *boiling* water. Set over *MEDIUM* heat and cook for about 15 minutes.

Ladle half of the lentils and liquid into the work bowl of the food processor. Purée until smooth. Set both the puréed and unpuréed lentils aside until required.

In a *non-aluminum** kettle set over *LOW* heat, melt butter. Add onions. Place a piece of waxed paper on top of the *finely* chopped onions and allow them to sweat for about 2 minutes. *Do not allow vegetables to brown.***

Add *finely* chopped celery and garlic. Replace waxed paper and allow vegetables to continue sweating for about 5 minutes. *Do not allow vegetables to brown.* Remove and discard waxed paper.

Add diced tomatoes. Cook, stirring occasionally, for about 5 minutes.

Add vegetarian stock, 2 cupfuls water, Tabasco sauce, black pepper, turmeric, cumin, and chili powder. *Raise heat to MEDIUM.* Allow soup to come to the simmer.

Add both the puréed lentils and the reserved, unpuréed lentils and liquid. Allow to cook until lentils are tender—about 20 minutes.

In a small dish, add corn starch and 2 tablespoonfuls *cold* water. Stir to put the corn starch into suspension. Add to soup. Cook, stirring constantly, until soup thickens slightly. Remove from heat.

Add diced red pepper.

Turn into a heated soup tureen. Serve into heated soup plates.

Yields about 8 cupfuls

LIBYAN RED LENTIL SOUP (cont'd)

Notes: *Since aluminum discolors lentils rather unpleasantly, avoid using aluminum cookware or serving bowls in this case.

**This French technique of sweating vegetables works superbly, in this case. If preferred, you can sweat the vegetables in a small, covered saucepan over *LOW* heat.

Although this soup freezes beautifully, be sure to defrost completely. As you reheat, do not allow soup to boil because texture will be impacted.

1/8 SERVING (i. e., per cupful) -
PROTEIN = 7.8 g.; FAT = 3.2 g.; CARBOHYDRATE = 23.0 g.;
CALORIES = 160; CALORIES FROM FAT = 18%

LIBYAN LENTIL AND SPINACH SALAD
Salata

TPT - 1 hour and 51 minutes;
1 hour = flavor development period

When planning a tossed salad, you are not apt to think of lentils but this salad is not only unusual, it is a nutritious and very tasty combination. If you want to go vegan, just skip the grated cheese.

1 tablespoon *extra virgin* olive oil
1 1/2 teaspoons red wine vinegar
1/2 teaspoon *Dijon* mustard with white wine
1/4 teaspoon grated fresh, organic lemon zest
1/4 teaspoon ground cumin
Salt, to taste
Freshly ground black pepper, to taste

1/3 cup dry brown (*or* green) lentils
1 1/2 cups VEGETARIAN BROWN STOCK *[see index]* or other vegetarian stock of choice
1 bay leaf—broken

1/4 cup *finely* chopped celery
3 tablespoons *thinly* slivered onion
1 small garlic clove—*thinly* slivered

4 cups chopped fresh spinach—well-washed and well-dried
1/4 cup chopped fresh parsley
1 tablespoon chopped fresh thyme leaves

1 tablespoon grated Parmesan *or pecorino Romano* cheese, as preferred

In a mixing bowl, combine oil, vinegar, mustard, lemon zest, and ground cumin. Using a small wire whisk, combine thoroughly. Add salt and pepper to taste. Set aside until required.

Sort lentils and discard those of poor quality. Rinse thoroughly.

In a non-aluminum saucepan set over *MEDIUM* heat, combine lentils, stock, and broken bay leaf. Bring to the boil. Reduce heat to *LOW*, cover tightly, and simmer for about 30 minutes, or until lentils are tender. Drain, reserving liquid for soup stock and discarding bay leaf pieces. Add lentils to prepared *vinaigrette*.

Add *finely* chopped celery, and slivered onion and garlic. Stir. Refrigerate for at least 1 hour to chill and to allow for flavor development.

When ready to serve, put chopped spinach, parsley, and thyme into a salad bowl. Spoon lentil mixture over.

Sprinkle grated cheese over.

Toss at the table before serving onto salad plates.

Yields 6 servings
adequate for 4-6 people

Notes: This salad is a terrific choice for a picnic. Take the chilled lentil mixture in one container, the spinach mixture in a large container with a tightly fitting lid, and the grated cheese in a salt shaker. Assembly takes only minutes once your picnic table is set up. Seal up any leftovers in the spinach container and take them home for supper.

When required, this recipe can be halved or doubled.

1/6 SERVING – PROTEIN = 5.0 g.; FAT = 3.7 g.; CARBOHYDRATE = 10.2 g.;
CALORIES = 80; CALORIES FROM FAT = 42%

Africa–Libya

LIBYAN CHICK PEA SALAD
Leblebi S'alalah

TPT - 20 hours and 26 minutes;
　　8 hours = overnight soaking period;
　　8 hours = overnight flavor development period;
　　[slow cooker = 4 hours at HIGH]

Archeological evidence unearthed in Turkey and near Jericho indicates that chick peas (Cicer aretinum), also known as "ceci" in Italy and "garbanzos" in Spain and Spanish-speaking nations of the western hemisphere, were cultivated as early as 3500 BC. By the Bronze Age, the legume was known in Greece and in Italy. Just as we do, the Romans made a broth of chick peas and roasted them as a snack, both recipes for which I have included elsewhere in this book. They carried their passion for this sweet, useful bean across the Mediterranean. Although I have made this salad using drained, canned chick peas, I have found that the cooked, dry chick peas absorb more flavor from the marinade.

1/2 cup dry chick peas (*garbanzos*)
2 cups water

5 cups *boiling* water
1 large bay leaf—halved

2 tablespoons *extra virgin* olive oil
1 tablespoon red wine vinegar
1 teaspoon chopped fresh thyme
1/4 teaspoon ground cumin
Freshly ground black pepper, to taste

1/4 cup *finely* chopped Italian red onion
2 tablespoons chopped fresh parsley
1 small garlic clove—*very finely* chopped
1 tablespoon *well-rinsed* marinated capers

1 hard-cooked egg yolk

Rinse dry beans in several changes of water. Remove and discard any of poor quality. Place in a bowl with the 2 cupfuls of water and soak overnight in the refrigerator.

Preheat slow cooker to HIGH.*

In the morning, drain chick peas and place in the bowl of the slow cooker. Add *boiling* water and bay leaf pieces. Cover and cook in slow cooker for 4 hours at HIGH.* Drain. Discard bay leaf pieces. Turn drained chick peas into a plastic container with lid. Allow to come to room temperature.

In a small bowl, combine oil, vinegar, chopped thyme, ground cumin, and black pepper. Using a fork, stir well to combine. Add to chick peas.

Add *finely* chopped red onion, chopped fresh parsley, *very finely* chopped garlic, and capers. Cover tightly and slosh back and forth to coat the vegetables with the *vinaigrette*. Refrigerate for 8 hours or overnight. Slosh the container occasionally to insure uniform marination.

When ready to serve, turn salad into a chilled serving bowl.

Sieve the egg yolk over the salad through a fine sieve.

Serve chilled with a slotted spoon. Refrigerate leftovers.

　　　　　　　　　　Yields 8 servings
　　　　　　　　　　adequate for 6 people

Notes:　*A slow cooker is a marvelous tool for cooking dry beans but if you do not have a slow cooker, cook the chick peas in boiling water over direct heat for about 2 hours.

This recipe can be doubled, when required.

1/8 SERVING – PROTEIN = 1.8 g.; FAT = 3.8 g.; CARBOHYDRATE = 5.0 g.;
CALORIES = 61; CALORIES FROM FAT = 56%

EGGPLANT *TAGINE*
Tagine bil Badhinjan

TPT - 2 hours and 20 minutes

The tagine slaoui is a cooking pot of Moroccan origin, a round, shallow, earthenware casserole with a pointed, conical lid of ancient origin and a most efficient casserole for cooking over braziers. Libyans also use the tagine. Cooking baby eggplants slowly in a tagine produces a succulent eggplant taste infused with the garlic and added spices that is second only to eggplant parmigiana according to the eggplant lover in this family

Africa–Libya

EGGPLANT *TAGINE* (cont'd)

Bouquet garni:
    1 tablespoon whole coriander seeds—crushed
    1/2 cinnamon quill

1 tablespoon *extra virgin* olive oil
1 medium onion—*thinly* sliced
2 garlic cloves—*very finely* chopped

1 1/2 cups canned, *diced* tomatoes
1/2 cup VEGETARIAN BROWN STOCK *[see index]* or VEGETABLE STOCK FROM SOUP *[see index]*
1 teaspoon ground cumin
1/4 teaspoon ground ginger
1 teaspoon *agave* nectar *or* honey
1/8 teaspoon red pepper flakes, or more to taste
1/4 teaspoon HOMEMADE PAPRIKA *[see index]* or commercially-available Hungarian sweet paprika
1/8 teaspoon Hungarian *hot* paprika, or to taste

5 small, baby eggplants—trimmed, well-washed, and halved

Salt, to taste
Freshly ground black pepper, or to taste

1/4 cup shopped fresh coriander (*cilantro*), for garnish
Thick Greek-style yogurt

In a tea ball or in a cheesecloth *bouquet garni* bag, secure crushed coriander seeds and cinnamon quill. Set aside until required.

Preheat oven to 300 degrees F. Prepare a *tagine** or an oven-to-table baking dish, of choice, with non-stick lecithin spray coating.

In a skillet set over *MEDIUM* heat, heat oil. Add sliced onion and *very finely* minced garlic. Sauté until onion is soft and translucent, *being careful to allow neither the onion nor the garlic to brown*. Turn into prepared *tagine*.

Add diced tomatoes, vegetable stock, ground cumin and ginger, *agave* nectar or honey, red pepper flakes, and sweet and hot paprika. Stir to combine.

Nestle baby eggplant halves into the tomato–spice mixture. Nestle teaball with spices into the center.

Bake, covered, in preheated 300 degrees F. for 1 hour, or until eggplants are tender. Remove from oven.

Season with salt and pepper to taste.

Garnish with chopped fresh coriander (*cilantro*). Serve directly from *tagine* or oven casserole. Keep warm on a warming tray or in a warm oven until ready to serve. Pass yogurt to accommodate individual tastes. Serve with hot *pita* loaves and salads or serve over *couscous*. Refrigerate any leftovers and *gently* reheat or serve at room temperature, if preferred.

Yields 6 servings
adequate for 4 people

Notes: *If you do not have a *tagine*, use an oven-to-table casserole which is tolerant of direct heat.

This recipe may be halved, when required.

1/6 SERVING (exclusive of yogurt) –
PROTEIN = 1.9 g.; FAT = 2.2 g.; CARBOHYDRATE = 10.0 g.;
CALORIES = 64; CALORIES FROM FAT = 31%

LIBYAN SHIRRED EGGS AND VEGETABLES
Shashouka
TPT - 42 minutes

The incredible, edible egg—it is the perfect food that feeds the developing avian organism and can feed humans from birth to old age. Almost every cuisine seems to have a dish where eggs are slid into vegetables, rice, or cheese, sauced, and then baked or, as they say, shirred. This North African specialty has found its way into the kitchens of Southern Italian homes, where it is proudly claimed as a local dish and even referred to by its African name. The vegetables used do vary from place to place.

Since these eggs are soft, undercooked, be sure to use well-washed organic eggs.

LIBYAN SHIRRED EGGS AND VEGETABLES (cont'd)

2 tablespoons *extra virgin* olive oil
2 large (about 1 3/4 pounds) all-purpose potatoes
  —peeled and cut into 1/2-inch dice
1 medium red bell pepper—cored, seeded, and cut into 1/2- x 2-inch strips
1 medium green bell pepper—cored, seeded, and cut into 1/2- x 2-inch strips
1 medium onion—*thinly* sliced
4 Italian plum tomatoes—peeled, seeded, and chopped *or* 4 canned, *whole* tomatoes—seeded and chopped
1/8 teaspoon *Szechuan (Sichuan) chili* paste*
1/2 teaspoon dried basil—**crushed**
Pinch dried oregano—**crushed**

4 large eggs

In a large skillet, with cover, set over *MEDIUM* heat, heat oil. Add diced potato, pepper strips, and sliced onion. Cook, stirring constantly, for 4 minutes. Add tomatoes and cook, stirring constantly, for about 4 minutes.

Stir in *chili* paste and crushed basil and oregano leaves.

Reduce heat to *LOW*, cover, and cook, stirring very frequently, until vegetables are *very tender*, about 12 minutes.**

Preheat oven to 300 degrees F. Prepare four *au gratin* dishes by coating with non-stick lecithin spray coating with olive oil.

Divide vegetable mixture among prepared *au gratin* dishes. Make an indentation in the vegetable mixture in each dish. Break an egg into each indentation.

Bake in preheated 300 degree F. oven until egg whites are set.

Serve at once.

Notes: **Szechuan (Sichuan) chili* paste is available in Asian groceries and in some food specialty stores. It distributes its flavor through the vegetable mixture more evenly than would chopped hot *chilies*.

**This may be prepared to this point as much as a day in advance and refrigerated or frozen most successfully for several months. Bring to room temperature before proceeding.

When required, this recipe is easily halved or doubled. We often make several double batches of this recipe in the fall, when both peppers and plum tomatoes are available and reasonably priced, to freeze for winter menus.

Served without eggs, as a vegetable mélange, this is a valuable menu-maker.

Yields 4 individual servings

1/4 SERVING – PROTEIN = 9.6 g.; FAT = 11.6 g.; CARBOHYDRATE = 23.2 g.;
CALORIES = 235; CALORIES FROM FAT = 44%

Madagascar

Attached to India until about eighty-eight million years ago, this island, somewhat smaller than our state of Texas, broke from this attachment during the final throes of the continental drift event that broke up the supercontinent Gondwana. As a result of the long isolation it has experienced, about ninety percent of all plants and animals that inhabit the island are entirely endemic to this island, descended from the megaflora and megafauna that greeted the first settlers.

In 350 BC Philip of Macedon was warring against dissident factions; the four vassal kingdoms of the Phoenicians prospered as the Phoenicians dominated the Mediterranean; Artexerxes III ruled Persia; and the settlement of Madagascar by Austronesian peoples, most probably from Borneo, began what is the long history of the fourth largest island on our planet. This early ethnicity has persisted and most of today's population of twenty-two million are of Malay–Polynesian ancestry integrated with Indonesian ancestry from an influx of migrating peoples from about 700 BC and the introduction of the genes, cultural practices, and unique zebu cattle of Bantu immigrants in about 1000 AD.

The French colonized the island in 1885. In 1895 the French ended the Malagasy monarchy and exiled Queen Rànaàlona II, the last of the monarchal line that had begun with King Andrianampoinimerina in 1787 and continued with his son Radama I in 1810, who had unified the island. Except for a brief period during World War II when it was occupied by the British, the French continued to administer the island until 1958 at which time Madagascar became an autonomous republic. Governmental instability has been a serious impediment to Madagascar's progress with four republics having been formed since independence in 1960. Presently Madagascar is a constitutional democracy with a caretaker government formed after the resignation of the previous government in November 2011. During this period little has been done to deal with the very serious problems of the country, including the need to eliminate the abject poverty of the population, the need to provide a safe water supply, and the need to expand education. Political jockeying has been the main thrust of politicians in this interim government to the point of media censorship.

It is hoped that the long abandoned agenda of needed changes and progress will be addressed by the new administration and that they will also address the need for safe tourism. Bio-tourism is potentially a major industry for Madagascar because of its amazing biodiversity. Development of this and control of its impact on this fragile ecosystem and the endangered species will be a major project for this government. Memory of the massive famine of 1930-1931 should give pause to those who wish to develop this country and open it up to global ecotourism. The famine was caused by a French colonist's introduction in 1925 of the cochineal, an insect that destroyed the prickly pear cactuses which had become the major source of food and water for the zebu cattle.

Although there is a strong cultural influence from Indonesian and Malaysia, a uniquely Malagasy cuisine exists integrating elements of the cuisines of the French, Chinese, and Indians who have settled here. Curries are subtle and food, in general, is not over-spiced. However, hot spice mixtures like *sakay* are greatly appreciated but, unlike many other cuisines in Asia and in Africa, the Malagasy allow the diner to adjust the heat and spice to his or her own palate. *Ranonapango* is a unique and popular beverage in Madagascar that takes some getting used to. It is prepared from burned rice and it is drunk with meals instead of water.

Africa – Madagascar

Traditional Three-Salad First Course - *Composé*

Macaroni Salad
Salade de Macaroni

Grated Carrot Salad
Lasary Karoty

Vegetable Salad   **Potato Salad**
Macedoine de Legumes   *Salade de Pommes de Terre*

~~~~~~~~~~~~~~~~~~~~~

Curried Beans with Sausage
Saosisy sy Tsaramaso

Steamed Baby *Bok Choy*   or   Sautéed Mixed Greens

Steamed Rice

Mango Salad
Salade de Mangue

Curried Fritters with *Chilies*
Mofo Sakay

~~~~~~~~~~~

Macaroni

with

Zucchini and Rice in Tomato Sauce
Courge a la Moelle et Tomate avec Riz

or

Stir-Fried Vegetables

Tomato Condiment
Lasary Voatabia

Sliced Avocado with Lemon Juice and Black Pepper

~~~~~~~~~~~~~~~~~~~~~

Hot Pepper Seasoning
Sakay

~

Fruit Compote with Vanilla
Salady Voankazo

Farina Pudding with Coconut Milk and Spices
Godrogodro

Africa–**Madagascar**

MACARONI SALAD
Salade de Macaroni

TPT - 1 hour and 26 minutes;
1 hour = refrigeration period

A simple macaroni salad is part of the three-salad first course, served in Madagascar. It is so simple that I hesitate to present the recipe or to presume that it is necessary.

4 quarts *boiling* water
2 cups dry elbow macaroni

1/2 cup *very finely* chopped onion
2 tablespoons *calorie-reduced or light*
   mayonnaise with olive oil *or* BLENDER
   MAYONNAISE *[see index]*
Freshly ground black pepper, to taste

Prepare a bowl of ice water.

In a large kettle set over *MEDIUM-HIGH* heat, combine *boiling* water and macaroni. Cook according to package directions. Drain. Plunge the macaroni into the ice water to stop further cooking. When thoroughly chilled, drain well. Turn into mixing bowl.

Add *very finely* chopped onion, mayonnaise, and black pepper. Stir to distribute the onion and coat the macaroni with mayonnaise. Refrigerate for at least 1 hour.

When ready to serve, arrange the macaroni salad on the large serving platter together with the grated carrot and vegetable salads *[see recipes which follow]*.

Yields 8 servings
adequate for 4-6 people

Note: This recipe can be halved, when necessary.

1/8 SERVING – PROTEIN = 3.6 g.; FAT = 1.5 g.; CARBOHYDRATE = 21.8 g.;
CALORIES = 122; CALORIES FROM FAT = 11%

GRATED CARROT SLAW

TPT - 5 minutes

In Madagascar carrot slaw is usually served as a first course together with a mixed vegetable salad and a macaroni salad. They are arranged together on a platter and the diner takes as much or a little of each as they please.

2 tablespoons *extra virgin* olive oil
1 tablespoon freshly squeezed lemon juice
1/4 teaspoon HOMEMADE CURRY POWDER
   [see index] or commercially-available curry
   powder of choice
1/8 teaspoon *Dijon* mustard with white wine
1/8 teaspoon salt, or to taste
1/8 teaspoon freshly ground black pepper, or
   to taste

4 large carrots—scraped or pared and *coarsely grated**

In a mixing bowl, combine olive oil, lemon juice, curry powder, *Dijon* mustard, salt, and pepper. Using a wire whisk, combine thoroughly.

Add grated carrots.

Arrange on a platter, leaving room for the vegetable and macaroni salads. Chill until ready to serve.

Yields 6 servings
adequate for 4 people

Notes: *In choosing large carrots take care not to select them so large that they have become "woody."

This recipe is easily halved or doubled, when required.

1/6 SERVING – PROTEIN = 0.3 g.; FAT = 3.8 g.; CARBOHYDRATE = 3.4 g.;
CALORIES = 62; CALORIES FROM FAT = 55 %

Africa–**Madagascar**

VEGETABLE SALAD IN THE STYLE OF MADAGASCAR
Macedoine de Legumes

TPT - 1 hour and 21 minutes

The third salad in the three-salad first course called "composé," is easily assembled from frozen or fresh vegetables, whatever you like and whatever you happen to have on hand. All vegetables are cut to about the size of green peas and if I have frozen peas, I add them too. If you have ever been to Moscow, you may see a similarity to what is called Moscow salad or Russian salad.

3 cups diced vegetables—peas, potato, carrot, scallion, red or yellow pepper, zucchini, corn, and/or frozen artichoke hearts
5 cups *boiling* **water**

3 tablespoons *calorie-reduced or light* **mayonnaise** *or* **BLENDER MAYONNAISE** *[see index]*
Salt, to taste
Freshly ground black pepper, to taste

Put diced vegetables into a large saucepan. Pour *boiling* water over. Allow to stand for 8 minutes. Drain thoroughly. Turn vegetables into a mixing bowl. Allow to cool to room temperature.

Add mayonnaise. Gently fold mayonnaise into vegetables. Season with salt and pepper. Refrigerate for at least 1 hour.

Arrange chilled salad on a platter, leaving room for the carrot and macaroni salads. Chill until ready to serve.

Yields 6 servings
adequate for 4 people

Note: This recipe can be halved, when required.

1/6 SERVING – PROTEIN = 1.2 g.; FAT = 2.7 g.; CARBOHYDRATE = 7.3 g.;
CALORIES = 51; CALORIES FROM FAT = 48%

MALAGASY POTATO SALAD
Salade de Pommes de Terre

TPT - 9 minutes

Wherever the potato has traveled, the cooks of that land have created soups and salads. This may not be the potato salad in your recipe box but there is a familiarity about this salad that bridges the oceans and continents that separate us from Madagascar. Crushed, drained green peppercorns are usually added to this salad. Sans those, we increase the black pepper.

1 1/2 pounds tiny red potatoes—cooked and
cut into chunks while still warm
2 tablespoons distilled white vinegar

1/4 cup pitted *Kalamata* **olives—cut into lengthwise quarters**
1/4 cup chopped Italian red onion
2 tablespoons chopped, fresh parsley
1 garlic clove—*very finely* **chopped**
1/4 teaspoon salt, or to taste
1/4 teaspoon freshly ground black pepper, or to taste

1/4 cup *fat-free* **dairy sour cream**
2 tablespoons *calorie-reduced or light* **mayonnaise**

In a mixing bowl, combine *warm* potato chunks and vinegar. Toss *gently*.

Add quartered olives, chopped red onion and parsley, *very finely* chopped garlic, salt, and black pepper. Toss *gently,* but *thoroughly.*

In a small bowl, combine sour cream and mayonnaise. Mix well. Add to potato mixture, folding gently until thoroughly integrated. Turn into serving bowl.

Refrigerate until ready to serve.

Yields 6 servings
adequate for 4 people

Note: This recipe can be halved or doubled, when required.

1/6 SERVING – PROTEIN = 3.7 g.; FAT = 2.2 g.; CARBOHYDRATE = 19.5 g.;
CALORIES = 119; CALORIES FROM FAT = 17%

Africa–**Madagascar**

MALAGASY CURRIED BEANS WITH SAUSAGE
Saosisy sy Tsaramaso
TPT - 40 minutes

Many, many years ago my husband went surf casting for stripers and blues along the South Shore of Long Island with our friend Wally. They were at the beach at sunrise so breakfast had not been an option. Several hours later my daughter and I arrived with a pot of baked beans and sausages to sustain them. Memory of that event drew me to this dish the first time. In Madagascar almost any kind of canned bean can be used as the base and because Christian and native religions are practiced for the most part, pork sausage is their choice. I prefer to make it with the vegetarian baked beans marketed by Heinz in Europe. In addition to being fat-free they are not as sweet or salty and respond well to the classic additions popular in Madagascar.

1 tablespoon safflower *or* sunflower oil
1/2 cup chopped Italian red onion
1 teaspoon *very finely* chopped fresh gingerroot
2 large garlic cloves—*very finely* chopped

1/2 cup canned, *diced* tomatoes
1/4 cup water
1 1/2 teaspoons HOMEMADE CURRY POWDER *[see index] or* commercially-available mixture of choice
Salt, to taste
1/4 teaspoon freshly ground black pepper, or to taste

1 can (13.7 ounces) (blue-labeled) Heinz vegetarian baked beans

6 small, *frozen*, vegetarian soy breakfast sausages

In a saucepan set over *MEDIUM* heat, heat oil. Add chopped red onion and *very finely* chopped gingerroot and garlic. Sauté until onion is softened, *being careful not to allow any of the vegetables to brown.*

Add tomatoes, water, curry powder, salt, and pepper. Stir well.

Add baked beans. Stir well.

Add sausages. Cook, stirring frequently, for about 25 minutes, or until sausages and beans are heated through. Add more water, if necessary. Turn into a heated serving bowl.

Serve hot.

Yields 6 servings
adequate for 4 people

Note: This recipe can be doubled, when required.

1/6 SERVING – PROTEIN = 7.9 g.; FAT = 3.8 g.; CARBOHYDRATE = 12.6 g.;
CALORIES = 121; CALORIES FROM FAT = 28%

MALAGASY MANGO SALAD
Salade de Mangue
TPT - 1 hour and 7 minutes;
1 hour = refrigeration period

The first time I tried this salad, I ate one mouthful and apologized to my dinner companion as the tears ran down my face. It was so hot that I thought the top of my head would come off. Even the Thai, who also can remove the top of your head in one forkful, do not take their mango salad to this level. When I decided to include it in the book, I was torn between authenticity and acceptance. Acceptance won and you will find that this is a version where you can expect to finish every forkful.

2 tablespoons freshly squeezed lime juice
2 tablespoons *extra virgin* olive oil
6-8 drops *jalapeño chili* sauce

2 large underripe mangoes—peeled, pitted, and *julienned*
2 garlic cloves—*very finely* chopped
1/2 cup onion—*finely* chopped
1/4 cup *finely* chopped fresh parsley
1/4 cup *finely* chopped mild green *chilies**
Salt, to taste

In a mixing bowl, combine lime juice, oil, and *jalapeño chili* sauce. Using a small wire whisk, beat until thoroughly combined.

Add mango *julienne, very finely* chopped garlic, *finely* chopped onion, parsley, and *chilies*, and salt. Toss well. Turn into a serving bowl. Refrigerate for at least 1 hour.

Africa–*Madagascar*

MALAGASY MANGO SALAD (cont'd)

Serve chilled.

Yields 6 servings
adequate for 4 people

Notes: *Hotter peppers can be used, if tolerated.

This recipe can be halved.

1/6 SERVING – PROTEIN = 0.9 g.; FAT = 4.1 g.; CARBOHYDRATE = 21.9 g.;
CALORIES = 119; CALORIES FROM FAT = 31%

MALAGASY CURRIED FRITTERS WITH *CHILIES*
Mofo Sakay
TPT - 25 minutes

Curried fritters with chilies . . .? Oh yes, and they are not only a surprise to your taste buds, they are a delicious specialty of Madagascar that is well worth trying.

2 cups unbleached white flour
1 teaspoon salt
1 teaspoon HOMEMADE CURRY POWDER
  [see index] *or* commercially-available
  curry powder of choice
1 teaspoon baking powder
1/2 teaspoon freshly ground black pepper

2 scallions—*both green and white portions*
  —trimmed, well-rinsed, and *finely* chopped
3 tablespoons *finely* chopped mild green *chilies*
1/4 cup *finely* chopped and well-drained canned
  tomatoes
1/8 teaspoon *jalapeño chili* sauce, or to taste
1 - 1 1/2 cups water

Oil for deep-frying

In a mixing bowl, combine flour, salt, curry powder, baking powder, and black pepper. Stir to mix thoroughly.

Add *finely* chopped scallions, green *chilies*, tomato, and *jalapeño* sauce. Mix well. Gradually, while stirring, add water until you have smooth, thick batter. Set aside briefly.

In a kettle or deep skillet, heat oil.

Using two soup spoons, drop three tablespoonfuls of batter into the hot oil in small batches. Using two chopsticks, drag the batter into an elongated shape. Fry until golden brown, turning once. Transfer to a surface covered with several thicknesses of paper toweling to absorb excess oil. Continue until all fritters have been fried. Transfer to a serving platter.

Serve hot.

Yields 16-18 fritters

Note: This recipe can be halved.

1/16 SERVING – PROTEIN = 1.4 g.; FAT = 1.6 g.; CARBOHYDRATE = 9.8 g.;
CALORIES = 59; CALORIES FROM FAT = 24%

MALAGASY ZUCCHINI AND RICE IN TOMATO SAUCE
Courge a la Moelle et Tomate avec Riz
TPT - 51 minutes

Vegetable marrow, the vegetable we know on this side of the Atlantic as zucchini, can be a rather dull vegetable, to my way of thinking, and if you plant it in your garden you will usually have a large harvest to consume. A recommendation by a food writer some years ago suggested cutting zucchini halves into fans and then sprinkling them with herbs. Well, that did not really do much for the taste of the zucchini although the presentation was pleasing. This recipe from Madagascar, however, is quite a different story and the seasoning works well as a counterpoint to the rather tasteless squash.

Africa–Madagascar

MALAGASY ZUCCHINI AND RICE IN TOMATO SAUCE (cont'd)

1/2 cup *boiling* water
2 tablespoons dry long grain brown rice

1 tablespoon *extra virgin* olive oil
3 garlic cloves—*very finely* chopped
3 bay leaves

1/2 cup canned, *diced* tomatoes in tomato purée
3/4 cup water
2 medium zucchini—trimmed, quartered lengthwise, and chopped into bite-sized pieces

Salt, to taste
Freshly ground black pepper, to taste

In a saucepan set over *LOW-MEDIUM* heat, combine *boiling* water and brown rice. Stir, cover, and cook until rice is tender—about 20 minutes. Set aside until required.

In a large skillet set over *MEDIUM* heat, heat oil. Add *very finely* chopped garlic and bay leaves. Sauté for about 3 minutes.

Add tomatoes, water, chopped zucchini, and *cooked* rice. Stir to combine well.

Season with salt and pepper. *Reduce heat to LOW-MEDIUM.* Cover and cook for about 15-20 minutes. Stir occasionally. Turn into a heated serving bowl. Remove and discard bay leaves.

Serve at once.

Yields 6 servings
adequate for 4 people

Note: This recipe can be halved or doubled, when required.

1/6 SERVING – PROTEIN = 1.2 g.; FAT = 2.0 g.; CARBOHYDRATE = 6.1 g.;
CALORIES = 45; CALORIES FROM FAT = 40%

MALAGASY TOMATO CONDIMENT
Lasary Voatabia

TPT - 2 hours and 2 minutes;
2 hours = flavor development period

This is similar to a Zambian tomato and scallion salad except that fresh gingerroot is added to this one and sets it apart. A small spoonful is traditionally served on main dinner plate as a way to compliment the main course or cleanse the palate.

2 medium tomatoes—*finely* chopped
1 large scallion—trimmed, well-rinsed, and *finely* chopped
1 tablespoon freshly squeezed lime juice
1/4 teaspoon *very finely* chopped *or* grated fresh gingerroot
Salt, to taste

In a small serving bowl, combine all ingredients. Cover with plastic wrap and refrigerate for at least 2 hours.

Serve chilled.

Yields 6 servings
adequate for 6 people

Note: This recipe can be halved or doubled, when required.

1/6 SERVING – PROTEIN = 0.4 g.; FAT = 0.1 g.; CARBOHYDRATE = 2.7 g.;
CALORIES = 14; CALORIES FROM FAT = 6%

MALAGASY HOT PEPPER SEASONING
Sakay

TPT - 6 minutes

Malagasy can tolerate a sakay mixture that would blow the top of your head off. My version of this mixture contains much less ground red pepper and is, therefore, tolerated by more people who have not grown up with this intense seasoning mixture. Do pass it to allow your guests to take a little or a lot. And, do warn them upfront about its potency.

Africa—**Madagascar**

MALAGASY HOT PEPPER SEASONING (cont'd)

1 1/2 tablespoons light oil, such as safflower *or* sunflower
1 tablespoon ground red pepper (cayenne)
1 1/2 teaspoons ground ginger

1 garlic clove—crushed and *very finely* chopped

In a small bowl, combine oil, ground red pepper (cayenne), and ground ginger. Mix to a smooth paste.

Add *very finely* chopped garlic. Stir to combine. Turn into a small serving bowl.*

Yields 3 1/2 tablespoonfuls

Notes: *I serve it with a small wooden skewer and encourage people to try a dot or two until they want to come back for more.

This recipe can be halved.

1/84 SERVING (i. e., about 1/8 teaspoonful) –
PROTEIN = 0.2 g.; FAT = 0.0 g.; CARBOHYDRATE = 0.1 g.;
CALORIES = 2; CALORIES FROM FAT = 0%

MALAGASY FRUIT COMPOTE WITH VANILLA
Salady Vaankazo

TPT - 6 hours and 8 minutes;
6 hours = maceration period

Since Madagascar is a principal source of the world's supply of vanilla beans, Malagasy use whole vanilla beans, vanilla seeds, or the very best pure vanilla extract in all kinds of desserts. One finds custards and rice puddings and fruit compotes from which the aroma of vanilla rises like a genie, drawing you in.

3 tablespoons pineapple juice
1 teaspoon pure vanilla extract

1/2 vanilla bean

6 large fresh pineapple spears
1 can (11 ounces) mandarin orange sections —well-drained
1 cup canned *lychees*—well-drained
9 strawberries—hulled and halved
1 teaspoon sugar

In a shallow serving bowl, combine pineapple juice and vanilla extract. Stir.

Split the vanilla bean and scrape the seeds into the juice mixture.

Settle the fruits—pineapple spears, mandarin orange sections, *lychees*, and strawberry halves—into the liquid. Sprinkle sugar over the fruit. Cover the dish tightly with plastic wrap and refrigerate for 6 hours to allow for flavor development. Rearrange fruit every hour or so to get maximum exposure to the liquid.

Serve into dessert dishes. Spoon fragrant syrup over each serving.

Yields 6 servings
adequate for 4 people

Note: This recipe can be halved or doubled, when required. When doubling, use a large flat serving bowl in which all the fruit can sit in a single layer.

1/6 SERVING – PROTEIN = 0.9 g.; FAT = 0.2 g.; CARBOHYDRATE = 27.3 g.;
CALORIES = 108; CALORIES FROM FAT = 2%

Africa–**Madagascar**

MALAGASY FARINA PUDDING WITH COCONUT MILK AND SPICES

Godrogodro

TPT - 2 hours and 24 minutes;
2 hours = refrigeration period

It amazes me how many cooks in many different countries have been inspired by sweetened breakfast farina to create a dessert. Whether you call it farina or semolina, you will recognize it as the Cream of Wheat of your childhood. Easy access to spices and vanilla have created a most unusual wheat pudding from Madagascar. Malagasy also make a version of this that is much, much sweeter. Sugar is caramelized first and poured over the farina which had been cooked until it is very thick and then spread out in a pan to make a cake-like base. We prefer both the texture and the less sweet nature of the pudding version.

2 cups *light, sulfite-free* **coconut milk**
1/2 cup water
2/3 cup sugar
1/2 teaspoon ground cinnamon
1/2 teaspoon freshly grated nutmeg
1/8 teaspoon ground cloves

6 tablespoons farina *or* **Cream of Wheat cereal**

1 teaspoon pure vanilla extract

In a non-stick-coated saucepan set over *MEDIUM* heat, combine coconut milk, water, sugar, ground cinnamon, freshly grated nutmeg, and ground cloves. Stir well until thoroughly mixed. Cook, stirring frequently until sugar is dissolved and the coconut milk mixture begins to bubble.

While stirring, gradually add farina. Cook, stirring frequently, until the pudding thickens. *It will thicken further as it chills.*

Stir in vanilla extract. Turn into a serving bowl. Refrigerate until thoroughly chilled—about 2 hours.

Serve chilled.

Yields 6 servings
adequate for 4 people

Note: This recipe can be halved, when required.

1/6 SERVING – PROTEIN = 2.1 g.; FAT = 3.1 g.; CARBOHYDRATE = 35.8 g.;
CALORIES = 177; CALORIES FROM FAT = 16%

Africa–Mali

Mali

Three large and powerful empires once controlled the trans-Saharan trade route—The Ghana Empire, the Mali Empire, and the Songhai Empire. Present-day Mali was once part of each of those tribally-controlled Sahelian kingdoms.

During the period of African colonization by European nations, France took control of Mali in an effort to gain access to the vast natural resources including gold, uranium, phosphate, kaolinite, salt, and limestone. By 1905 virtually all of Mali had been incorporated into the French Sudan, or Sudanese Republic.

In 1960, with independence from France, Mali joined with Senegal to form the short-lived Mali Federation and then, after the withdrawal of Senegal from the federation, declared itself the Republic of Mali. After independence, Mali was ruled by a single party system until a *coup* in 1991 which established a democratic state with recognition of opposition parties and a new constitution that established a secular state with freedom of religion. The decade that followed was a period of relative political and social stability when the immediate and acute challenges of education, illiteracy, security, health care, water quality, and the long-term challenges of desertification, deforestation, and soil erosion were addressed. There was progress on all fronts with the help of the international community under the presidency of Amadou Toumani Toure until January 2012 when the concern for security took precedence.

In January 2012 the National Movement for the Liberation of Azawad staged a *coup d'état*. The NMLA, acting swiftly, took control of the north, declaring in to be the independent state of Azawad. The NMLA, however, was not strong enough to hold the region and Islamist groups including the Ansar Dine and Al-Qaeda have moved into northern Mali, driving out the NMLA and the sparse nomadic population, rejecting the declared independence, and declaring the region to be a Mali under *Sharia*. The regions of Kidal, Tombouctou, and Gao are no longer under the control of the central democratic government. In July 2012 President John Atta Mills, who has led the move to a two-party system and under whose presidency oil exportation has become a significant contribution to Mali's GDP, died during his first term as president. Mali's future is of concern to all nations.

Africa–Mali

African-Style Toasted Millet Salad
Salade de Millet

Cucumber and Tomato Slices
with Scallion Slices and French Dressing

~~~~~~~~~~~~~~~~~~~~~

Sweetpotato Soufflé
Soufflé de Patate

Skewered Soymeat and Peppers
Kyinkyinga

Steamed Whole Carrots

French Bread

~~~~~~~~~~

Okra and Tomato Stew
Gumbo aux Tomate

Steamed Rice   or   Steamed Dumplings

~~~~~~~~~~~~~~~~~~~~~~~

Watermelon Balls

Large Slices of Mango
with Fresh Orange Sections

Sweet Rice and Millet Pudding
Pouding de Riz et Millet

AFRICAN-STYLE TOASTED MILLET SALAD
Salade de Millet

TPT - 1 hour and 40 minutes;
1 hour = flavor development period

The dependence on millet by sub-Saharan nations is being threatened by the severe drought conditions now prevalent in the region. Millet is gathered from several grass species indigenous to the grasslands of Africa and has nourished Africans for millennia. Although millets do survive well in areas prone to drought, in the past there was less competition between grazing animals and harvesting for human consumption. If the seeds are cooked for a short period of time, a couscous-like texture results which is preferred for a salad like this. It can replace couscous or bulgur wheat in recipes and although some Malians prefer rice to millet, many still favor millet and have substituted rice only because it was readily available from relief agencies. This meal-in-a-bowl salad may well have originated in Morocco or Tunisia but versions of this salad have become an integral part of the cuisines of many African nations including Mali.

Africa–Mali

AFRICAN-STYLE TOASTED MILLET SALAD (cont'd)

1 tablespoon safflower *or* sunflower oil
1/2 cup millet—well-rinsed and well-drained

3 cups *boiling* water

1/2 cup green (fresh) *or frozen* corn kernels
1/2 cup *diced* onion
1/2 green bell pepper—*diced*
1 tomato—seeded and chopped
2 tablespoons chopped fresh parsley
1 medium garlic clove—*very finely* chopped
1 tablespoon *very finely* chopped fresh gingerroot

2 tablespoons *extra virgin* olive oil
2 tablespoons freshly squeezed lemon juice
1/2 teaspoon *light* brown sugar
1/2 teaspoon chili powder
1/8 teaspoon ground allspice
1/4 teaspoon salt *or* 1 teaspoon *tamari* soy sauce, if preferred
Pinch ground red pepper (cayenne)
1/4 teaspoon freshly ground black pepper, or to taste

2 tablespoons chopped *roasted*, but *unsalted*, peanuts

In a skillet set over *LOW-MEDIUM* heat, heat oil. Add millet and cook, stirring frequently until the seeds are dry and there is a fragrant aroma.

Add *boiling* water. *Reduce heat to LOW*, cover, and allow to cook for 15-18 minutes. Drain and rinse well in cold water. Drain well.

In a mixing bowl, combine drained millet, corn kernels, *diced* onion, *diced* green pepper, chopped tomato, and *very finely* chopped garlic and gingerroot. Toss gently with a large wooden salad fork to mix well.

In a small bowl, combine olive oil, lemon juice, brown sugar, chili powder, ground allspice, salt, ground red pepper (cayenne), and black pepper. Using a small wire whisk, whisk to mix well. Add to millet and vegetable mixture. Toss again with the fork to mix well. Turn into a serving bowl. Refrigerate for at least 1 hour to allow for flavor development.

Garnish with chopped peanuts.

Serve well-chilled.

Yields 8 servings
adequate for 6 people

Note: When required, this recipe may be halved or doubled.

1/8 SERVING – PROTEIN = 6.4 g.; FAT = 7.4 g.; CARBOHYDRATE = 15.2 g.;
CALORIES = 117; CALORIES FROM FAT = 57%

SWEETPOTATO *SOUFFLÉ*
Soufflé de Patate

TPT - 1 hour and 6 minutes

The Portuguese explorers found the sweetpotato in South America and the world-traveling Portuguese traders introduced the sweetpotato to other parts of the world. This tuber, which is not related to the white potato but was dubbed sweetpotato because of its physical and textural resemblance, grew well on the plantations of the volcanic island chain of São Tomé and Principe and from there, through trade, it was planted on the mainland where it has thrived ever since, becoming a staple in African cuisines. Then the French introduced food preparation techniques to their African colonies. We have all become the beneficiaries of the sweetpotato's adventure.

3 quarts *boiling* water
2 large sweetpotatoes—peeled and chopped

2 large egg yolks
1 small garlic clove—*very finely* chopped
1 teaspoon sugar
1/2 teaspoon salt
Freshly ground black pepper, to taste

2 large egg whites

Preheat oven to 350 degrees F. Prepare a 1 1/2 quart soufflé dish by coating with non-stick-lecithin spray coating.

In a large saucepan set over *MEDIUM* heat, boil sweetpotatoes in *boiling* water for 20 minutes. Drain well. Turn into a mixing bowl. Using a potato masher, mash well.

Add egg yolks, *very finely* chopped garlic, sugar, salt, and black pepper. Mash the added ingredients thoroughly into the sweetpotatoes. Set aside briefly.

Africa–Mali

SWEETPOTATO *SOUFFLÉ* (cont'd)

Using an electric mixer fitted with grease-free beaters or by hand, using a grease-free wire whisk, beat egg whites in a grease-free bowl until *stiff*, but *not dry*. Fold beaten egg whites into the sweetpotato mixture. Turn into prepared baking dish. Bake in preheated 350 degree F. oven for 25-30 minutes, or until puffed and golden.

Serve warm or at room temperature.

Yields 6 servings
adequate for 4 people

Note: This recipe can be halved, when required.

1/6 SERVING – PROTEIN = 4.2 g.; FAT = 2.9 g.; CARBOHYDRATE = 19.5 g.; CALORIES = 114; CALORIES FROM FAT = 23%

SKEWERED SOYMEAT AND PEPPERS IN THE STYLE OF MALI
Kyinkyinga

TPT - 1 hour and 17 minutes;
1 hour = marination period

Skewered meat and peppers are a common street food in Mali. The meat is marinated in a wonderful mixture of onion, garlic, ginger, and ground peanuts before being skewered with the peppers and then grilled. Entrepreneurial young men, often on bicycles, rush out at red lights to offer their wares to drivers and miraculously maneuver out of harm's way as the light changes and the traffic roars through the intersection. We find that there is no reason for vegetarians not to enjoy these kebab-like snacks because they can be prepared using the widely available frozen meat analogue products. We use them as an appetizer or as a fun main course for a light supper.

1 medium onion—*very finely* chopped
1 small garlic clove—*very finely* chopped
1 teaspoon *grated* fresh gingerroot
2 tablespoons *finely* ground *raw* peanuts
1/4 teaspoon salt

2 tablespoons tomato purée
1/2 teaspoon *jalapeño chili* sauce, or to taste

8 ounces *frozen* soy meat analogue strips—cut into uniform pieces

2 medium sweet green bell peppers—cut into 1-inch squares*

In the work bowl of the food processor fitted with steel knife, combine *very finely* chopped onion and garlic, *grated* gingerroot, *finely* ground peanuts, and salt. Process until uniform.

Add tomato purée and *jalapeño* sauce. Process again. Turn into a mixing bowl.

Add soymeat pieces. Cover with sauce. Refrigerate for at least 1 hour.

Preheat grill pan over *MEDIUM* heat.

Thread marinated soymeat pieces onto bamboo skewers alternately with pepper squares. Grill on grill pan, turning frequently, until evenly browned. Transfer to a heated serving platter.

Serve at once.

Yields 6 servings
adequate for 4-6 people

Notes: *The trimmings from the peppers can be diced, secured in a tightly sealed plastic bag, and frozen for use whenever a recipe calls for "finely chopped green pepper".

This recipe can be halved, when required.

1/6 SERVING – PROTEIN = 17.4 g.; FAT = 4.6 g.; CARBOHYDRATE = 8.9 g.; CALORIES = 137; CALORIES FROM FAT = 30%

Africa–Mali

MALIAN OKRA AND TOMATO STEW
Gumbo aux Tomate
TPT - 46 minutes

Okra is a member of the mallow family and of West African or Ethiopian origin although its popularity has spread worldwide and you find okra dishes in Brazil, Japan, and Vietnam. It is generally only known as okra in the United States. Okro is the spelling in the Caribbean, where it is very popular. This low-fat vegetable is often called "lady's fingers" or "gumbo" and "kimbgombo" in languages of Bantu derivation. The beautiful flower notwithstanding, its lack of popularity in the United States, with the exception of many dishes eaten in the American South, seems to be related to its mucilaginous texture, a characteristic common to many plants in this botanical family. This texture is minimized when cooked a long time with an acid food such as tomatoes. Malians add either fresh-caught river fish, akin to tilapia, or dried fish to this stew.

2 tablespoons safflower *or* sunflower oil
2 medium onions—*finely* chopped
2 garlic cloves—*very finely* chopped
2 tablespoons *finely* chopped mild green *chilies*

1 cup tomato juice
2 cups canned, *diced* tomatoes in tomato purée
10-15 okras—well-washed, trimmed and sliced
1 teaspoon crushed, dried thyme
1/2 teaspoon fennel seeds
Pinch ground red pepper (cayenne), or more
  to taste

In a deep skillet set over *MEDIUM* heat, heat oil. Add *finely* chopped onions, *very finely* chopped garlic, and *finely* chopped green *chilies*. Sauté until onions are soft and translucent, *being careful not to allow vegetables to brown.*

Add tomato juice, diced tomatoes, sliced okras, crushed thyme, fennel seeds, and ground red pepper (cayenne). *Reduce heat to LOW-MEDIUM.* Simmer for about 30 minutes. You may have to add water because of the thickening quality of the okra. Turn into a heated serving dish.

Serve over steamed rice, millet, or steamed dumplings made from a fine *semolina*.

Yields 6 servings
adequate for 4 people

Note: This recipe can be halved or doubled, when required.

1/6 SERVING – PROTEIN = 2.5 g.; FAT = 4.7 g.; CARBOHYDRATE = 10.5 g.;
CALORIES = 87; CALORIES FROM FAT = 49%

SWEET RICE AND MILLET PUDDING
Pouding de Riz et Millet
TPT - 41 minutes

With the long cycles of drought and the increase in desertification, millet is less available to the homemaker in Mali. A Malian women who was interviewed for a research project said that she greatly preferred the taste of millet for her recipes but was finding that she had to rely on imported rice and rice flour more and more. In Mali you will most often find millet served steamed as a couscous or made into wonderful sweet fritters sprinkled with confectioners' sugar for breakfast or as a snack offered by street vendors. I do not waste cooked millet, as I am sure that Malian lady understands, so leftover steamed millet is added to a rice base for a dessert pudding.

Malians use very little milk or cheese in their cooking so a pudding like this would be made with water in Mali. If you wish to make it with milk, do so.

SWEET RICE AND MILLET PUDDING (cont'd)

2 cups *boiling* water
6 tablespoons Cream of Rice cereal
5 tablespoons sugar

1/2 cup *steamed* millet
1 teaspoon pure vanilla extract

Light cream *or* half and half, to thin, if desired

Pour *boiling* water into a saucepan set over *LOW-MEDIUM* heat. Gradually, while stirring constantly, pour Cream of Rice cereal into the *boiling* water. Add sugar and cook, stirring constantly until the cereal base thickens. Remove from heat.

Stir in cooked millet and vanilla extract. Turn into a serving dish or individual dessert dishes, if preferred. Refrigerate for at least 30 minutes before serving.

If the consistency is too thick, thin with cream or serve with a pitcher of cream to allow diners to thin the pudding to the consistency they prefer.

Yields 6 servings
adequate for 4 people

Note: This recipe can be halved, when required.

1/6 SERVING (exclusive of cream) –
PROTEIN = 2.0 g.; FAT = 0.1 g.; CARBOHYDRATE = 33.2 g.;
CALORIES = 146; CALORIES FROM FAT = <1%

Mauritania
Western Sahara

One finds the cuisine of the Islamic nation of Mauritania (Mauretania) and that of the disputed Western Sahara, with its Spanish and Berber influences, surprisingly similar, due in part to the fact that both have a long Atlantic coastline with plentiful ocean fish. Perhaps the most important influence on this area is the severe equatorial climate modified by the ever-advancing Sahara Desert that dictates the crops that can be grown and the animals that can be raised. Recipes borrowed from neighboring nations and the nations under whom they lived in the colonial past, albeit quite different, do often influence the way cooks address the same ingredient.

Cuisine aside, these are two very different states.

The widely dispersed Sahrawi, a Bedouin tribal society who occupy the 103,000 square miles of arid, desert flatlands of the Western Sahara, still wait for a decision as to whether their fledgling government will be recognized and they will be restored to their homeland. They speak a dialect of Arabic also spoken in Mauritania, they too are mostly Sunni Moslems, and they are genetically indistinguishable from the Hassaniya-speaking peoples of Mauritania known as Moors. Until 1975 this was a clan-based, nomadic society that functioned as it had for hundreds of years. In 1975 part of the population was dispersed by the gorilla forces of the Polisario Front, which was formed in 1973 to militarily bring an end to Spanish interests in the area. Refugees took asylum in Algeria and formed a government in exile, the Sagrawi Arab Democratic Republic. In 1976 the Western Sahara was partitioned with two-thirds of the area ceded to Morocco, a territory the Moroccans called the "Southern Provinces." The Mauritanian-controlled area was known as *Tiris al-Gharbiyya*. In 1979 Mauritania was forced by the Polisario guerrillas to give up its claims to the territory and the Polisario moved in to take over administration of this area. They were subsequently recognized by the United Nations as the representatives of the people of Western Sahara although Morocco does not accept this declaration.

Mauritania, on the other hand, is a more progressive Islamic state. In the eleventh century it was the center for the Berber Almoravid movement in its effort to spread Islam through West and North Africa. During the period sometimes known as "the partition of Africa," the French took control of this huge country, a country as big as our states of Washington, Oregon, Idaho, and Nevada combined with room for Maine; a country that occupies close to one-fifth of the land mass of the continent of Africa. Mostly desert and sparsely populated, France nevertheless made it a territory in 1904 and combined this territory with its other colonies to form French West Africa. Mauritania was recognized as an independent Islamic republic in 1960 despite Morocco's claim to the territory. The next focus of Morocco was the territory known as the Spanish Sahara with its long coastline. In 1975, after the Spanish left, Mauritania and Morocco divided the territory, with Mauritania controlling the southern third of the territory now known as Western Sahara until 1979, as previously mentioned. A relaxation of the strict *Sharia* law in 1984 led to Mauritania's first multiparty elections in 1986 and in 1991 a constitution created a multiparty democracy. The fact that the only fertile area of Mauritania is the Senegal River valley in the South has led to conflict with Senegal and conflicts with Western Sahara have arisen over the grazing lands in the North.

Despite the Mauritanian proverb, shared by the author Jessica Harris. "Before one cooks one must have meat," I decided to delve into the literature and contact Mauritanians for help in finding a way to experience the tastes of this land as a vegetarian.

Pancakes with Vegetable Topping
Leksour

~

Couscous Salad with Chick Peas and Tomatoes
Salade aux Couscous

Avocado Slices with Lime Juice
and Slivered Red Onion

Cabbage and Carrot Salad with Yogurt Dressing
Ensalada Cocinarada con Berza y Zanahoria

~

Spiced Tomato Bouillon with Chick Peas
Bouillon de Tomate aux Pois Chiche

~~~~~~~~~~~~~~~~~~~~~

Millet *Couscous* with Chick Peas and Tomatoes
Cherchem

Mashed Sweetpotatoes or Yams

~~~~~~~~~~

Sweetpotato, Carrot, and Onion *Tagine* **with Prunes**
over

Angel Hair *Pasta*   or   Steamed *Couscous*   or   Rice

Spiced, Baked Eggplant Slices
with yogurt

Chilled Apricot Halves

~~~~~~~~~~~~~~~~~~~~

Millet and Yogurt Pudding
Lakh

Avocado Pudding   **Banana Pastry**
Abacate con Crema   *Pâtisserie aux Banane*

Assorted Dried Fruits
Fruits Séchés

MAURITANIAN PANCAKES WITH VEGETABLE TOPPING
Leksour

TPT - 1 hour and 3 minutes

This dish is a specialty of Quadane in Northern Mauritania where leksour are large, crêpe-like pancakes, generally made with a combination of wheat and millet flour. A combination of whole wheat and white flour makes very acceptable leksour. Because they include meat in the vegetable topping, it becomes a nutritious meal in a land where food options are few. The unorthodox addition of eggs to the pancakes fills the protein void left by removal of the meat. We find this to be a very satisfying vegetarian entrée or first course dish.

MAURITANIAN PANCAKES WITH VEGETABLE TOPPING (cont'd)

TOPPING:
- 4 quarts *boiling* water
- 2 medium carrots—scraped or pared and diced
- 2 medium potatoes—peeled and diced
- 2 tablespoons *extra virgin* olive oil
- 1 1/2 cups canned, *diced* tomatoes
- 1 large red *or* green bell pepper—well washed, cored, seeded, membranes removed, and diced
- 1/4 cup water
- 2 bay leaves—halved
- Salt, to taste
- Freshly ground mixed peppercorns—red, black, and white—to taste

LEKSOUR:
- 1/2 cup whole wheat pancake mix
- 1/2 cup white-flour pancake mix
- 1 1/2 cups water
- 1 tablespoon canola oil
- 1/4 cup *fat-free* pasteurized eggs (the equivalent of 1 egg)

Place a heat-resistant large plate or platter in a warm oven or on a warming tray.

In a kettle set over *MEDIUM* heat, combine *boiling* water and diced carrots and potatoes. Cook for about 10 minutes. Drain thoroughly. Turn into a large skillet set over *LOW-MEDIUM* heat.

Add olive oil. Sauté for several minutes until vegetables just begin to brown.

Add diced tomatoes and bell pepper, water, bay leaf pieces, salt, and ground mixed peppercorns. Cook, stirring frequently, for about 20 minutes, or until of sauce-like consistency.

Meanwhile set up non-stick-coated *crêpe* pan or griddle. In a mixing bowl, combine whole wheat and white-flour pancake mixes, water, canola oil, and pasteurized eggs. Stir just until moistened. Prepare large, thin, *crêpe*-like pancakes, turning once. Place prepared pancakes on heated platter while preparing the rest.

Turn sauce into a heated serving bowl. Remove and discard bay leaf pieces.

Serve at once, allowing diners to ladle sauce onto pancakes.

Yields 12 appetizer servings
adequate for 6 people

Note: This recipe can be halved, when required.

1/12 SERVING – PROTEIN = 8.5 g.; FAT = 3.1 g.; CARBOHYDRATE = 14.5 g.;
CALORIES = 95; CALORIES FROM FAT = 29%

MAURITANIAN *COUSCOUS* SALAD WITH CHICK PEAS AND TOMATOES
Salade aux Couscous

TPT - 2 hours and 4 minutes;
45 minutes = absorption period;
1 hour = cooling period

As in Algeria and Morocco and, in fact, across North Africa and into the Middle East, Mauritanians and those living in Western Sahara enjoy a couscous salad. Each nationality has a slightly different approach to the ingredients added or the presentation and you will note that this version differs from others in this volume. I have found that the flagging appetites of mid-summer revive a bit when a salad such as this is either served on the side, as an appetizer, or as a light supper main course. Yes, it is a versatile dish to add to your repertoire.

- 1 cup water
- 1/2 cup dry, quick-cooking, whole wheat *couscous**

- 1 tablespoon *extra virgin* olive oil
- 1 tablespoon freshly squeezed lemon juice
- 1 garlic clove—*very finely* chopped
- 2 tablespoons chopped fresh coriander (*cilantro*)
- 1/2 cup canned chick peas (*garbanzos*)—well-drained
- 2 medium tomatoes—seeded and chopped
- Freshly ground black pepper, to taste

- 10 *Kalamata* olives
- 10 *pitted* green olives
- 1/2 cup crumbled *feta* cheese

MAURITANIAN *COUSCOUS* SALAD
WITH CHICK PEAS AND TOMATOES (cont'd)

In a saucepan set over *HIGH* heat, bring water to the boil. Reduce heat to *LOW* and stir in *couscous*. Cover tightly and allow to cook for about 5 minutes. Remove from heat and allow *couscous* to cool for about 45 minutes. *All water should be absorbed.* Fluff cooked *couscous* with a wooden fork. Refrigerate until *completely cooled*—about 1 hour.

Using the fork, stir in olive oil, lemon juice, *finely* chopped garlic, chopped coriander *(cilantro)* and parsley leaves, *well-drained* chick peas, and chopped tomato. Season with black pepper to taste. Toss *gently*. Turn out onto a plate or small platter. Spread evenly. Refrigerate until serving time.

When ready to serve, arrange olives on top in a large **X** by nestling them down into the *couscous* salad. Scatter *feta* cheese over.

Serve at once.

Yields 6 servings
adequate for 4 people

Notes: *Couscous* is packaged by several companies and is now generally available in grocery stores and food specialty stores as well as in Middle Eastern groceries and in natural food stores. Whole wheat *couscous* is worth seeking out.

This recipe may be halved or doubled, when required.

1/6 SERVING – PROTEIN = 6.4 g.; FAT = 8.4 g.; CARBOHYDRATE = 16.8 g.;
CALORIES = 172; CALORIES FROM FAT = 44%

SAHARAN CABBAGE AND CARROT SALAD WITH YOGURT DRESSING
Ensalada Cocinarada con Berza y Zanahoria

TPT - 2 hours and 25 minutes;
2 hours = raisin soaking period

Unlike the mayonnaise-dressed cabbage and carrot salads most of us are accustomed to, salads are more frequently dressed with an oil and lemon or oil and lime vinaigrette in this part of the world. This salad recipe combines the carrot salads, so popular in Morocco, and cabbage slaw but in a unique way. The vegetables are sautéed in oil and then dressed. This can be served cold or at room temperature.

1/4 cup *preservative-free dark* raisins
1 cup *boiling* water

2 tablespoons water
1 1/2 tablespoons *extra virgin* olive oil
2 1/2 cups *very finely* sliced red *or* green cabbage,
   as preferred
2 medium carrots—scraped or pared and shredded
1/2 cup *finely* chopped red onion

DRESSING:
   2 tablespoons thick Greek-style yogurt *or*
   YOGURT *CRÈME* [see index]
   1 tablespoon freshly squeezed lemon juice
   1 teaspoon honey
   1/2 teaspoon ground cumin
   1/2 teaspoon ground coriander

In a small bowl or mixing cup, combine raisins and 1 cupful *boiling* water. Allow raisins to rehydrate for 2 hours. Drain. Set aside until required.

In a skillet set over *LOW-MEDIUM* heat, heat 2 tablespoonfuls water and oil. Add *very finely* sliced cabbage, shredded carrot, and *finely* chopped onion. Cover and allow to steam, stirring frequently, until the vegetables are soft. Turn into a mixing bowl.

Add raisins.

In a small bowl, combine yogurt, lemon juice, honey, and ground cumin and coriander. Blend thoroughly. Add to vegetables. Gently, integrate the dressing. Turn into a serving bowl. Refrigerate until ready to serve.

Yields 6 servings
adequate for 4 people

Note: This recipe can be doubled, when required.

1/6 SERVING – PROTEIN = 1.6 g.; FAT = 2.9 g.; CARBOHYDRATE = 13.0 g.;
CALORIES = 81; CALORIES FROM FAT = 32%

Africa–**Mauritania/Western Sahara**

SPICED TOMATO BOUILLON WITH CHICK PEAS
Bouillon de Tomate aux Pois Chiche

TPT - about 1 hour

Moslems across the Islamic world prepare a soup of meat, traditionally lamb or goat, and chickpeas in a tomato–meat stock to break the fast of Ramadan. Often they are thick stew-like soups. Using a number of recipes for "harira," I have created a vegetarian version that can easily be served as a first course or which can be retrieved from the freezer for a light lunch.

4 1/2 cups VEGETABLE STOCK FROM SOUP
  [see index] *or* **other vegetarian stock of choice**
2 cups tomato juice *or* **tomato-vegetable juice, if preferred**
1/4 cup chopped fresh parsley
1/4 cup chopped onion
2 garlic cloves—*smashed* but *not chopped*
1/8 teaspoon ground cumin
1/8 teaspoon ground coriander
2 pinches saffron
Freshly ground black pepper, to taste

1 cup canned chick peas (*garbanzos*)—well-drained and seed coats removed

In a small saucepan set over *MEDIUM-HIGH* heat, combine stock, tomato juice, chopped parsley, chopped onion, smashed garlic cloves, ground cumin and coriander, saffron, and black pepper. Bring to the boil, reduce heat to *LOW*, and simmer gently for 30 minutes. Remove and pour soup into a clean saucepan through a sieve that has been lined with a dampened cotton tea towel. *This may take some time. Do not try to hurry the process or your bouillon may not be clear.*

Once the bouillon has been recovered, set the saucepan over *LOW-MEDIUM* heat. Add chick peas. Allow soup to reheat. Turn into a heated soup tureen.

Serve into heated soup plates.

Yields about 6 cupfuls

Notes: This recipe is easily doubled or tripled, when required. Since it freezes well, this is a nice menu maker to freeze.

It is often more convenient to prepare this soup as much as two days in advance of serving. Refrigerate, covered, and reheat at serving time.

1/6 SERVING (i. e., per cupful) –
PROTEIN = 2.9 g.; FAT = 0.2 g.; CARBOHYDRATE = 11.8 g.;
CALORIES = 55; CALORIES FROM FAT = 3%

MAURITANIAN MILLET *COUSCOUS* WITH CHICK PEAS AND TOMATOES
Cherchem

TPT - 1 hour and 17 minutes

Meatless recipes, of course, are cooked in every cuisine; when there is no meat for the table the family must still be fed. As I have searched for these recipes all across the globe, I have been struck by the almost instinctive combination of grain and legume proteins. I remember my grandmother's instructions as we prepared a stew. "If you don't have meat, add beans. That will be OK because you are going to serve it with bread." My grandmother did not read nutrition books, she was not a vegetarian, but she had learned from her mother who had probably learned from her mother, and so on. Somehow they knew instinctively how to complement plant proteins. This is the Mauritanian version of a recipe that appears on menus all across this area of Africa. Elsewhere in this volume you will find a recipe for "ruy," a Gambian couscous also made with millet which has more of a vegetable "paella" feel to it. Mauritanians pay considerable attention to the seasoning of the dish which may well be a result of the nation's close ties with France.

MAURITANIAN MILLET *COUSCOUS* WITH CHICK PEAS AND TOMATOES (cont'd)

1/2 cup dry millet—rinsed and drained

1 quart water
1/2 teaspoon salt

2 teaspoons *extra virgin* olive oil
2 teaspoons butter
1 large garlic clove—crushed and *very finely* chopped

1/2 cup canned, *crushed* tomatoes*
1/2 teaspoon *hot* Hungarian paprika
1/4 teaspoon crushed, dried oregano
1/4 teaspoon crushed, dried mint
1/4 teaspoon crushed, dried thyme
1/4 teaspoon ground coriander
Several dashes ground red pepper (cayenne)
1 bay leaf—halved

1 cup canned chick peas (*garbanzos*)—well-drained and seed coats removed
Salt, to taste
Freshly ground black pepper, to taste

In a saucepan set over *LOW* heat, dry-roast the millet until lightly browned. *Monitor carefully because the grain can brown easily.*

Add water and salt. Increase heat to *LOW-MEDIUM*. Cover and allow to cook for about 30-35 minutes, or until the grains are soft. Drain well. Set aside until required.

In a clean saucepan set over *LOW-MEDIUM* heat, combine butter and oil. Add *very finely* chopped garlic. Sauté for several minutes, *being careful not to allow the garlic to brown.*

Add crushed tomatoes, hot paprika, crushed oregano, mint, and thyme, ground coriander, ground red pepper (cayenne), and bay leaf pieces. Stir to integrate seasoning.

Add cooked millet and chick peas (*garbanzos*). Season with salt and pepper. *Reduce heat to LOW.* Cover and allow to cook, stirring occasionally, for about 20 minutes.

Turn out onto a heated platter or into a heated serving bowl. Fluff with wooden fork. Remove and discard bay leaf pieces.

Serve at once.

Yields 6 servings
adequate for 4 people

Notes: *Some manufacturers market a crushed tomato product that is more like diced tomatoes in purée. A well-crushed, thick purée, of uniform texture, is appropriate for this dish.

Lots of people soak millet overnight prior to cooking. I have found that this dry-roasting technique works well, eliminating the need to soak overnight. In addition, I find the millet flavor is enhanced considerably by the dry-roasting.

This recipe can be doubled, when required.

1/6 SERVING – PROTEIN = 7.4 g.; FAT = 4.2 g.; CARBOHYDRATE = 14.9 g.;
CALORIES = 100; CALORIES FROM FAT = 38%

SWEETPOTATO, CARROT, AND ONION *TAGINE* WITH PRUNES
TPT - 1 hour and 5 minutes

If you have never cooked with a tagine, you are really missing something. I bought a Moroccan tagine years ago and after cooking several meals in it, I was completely sold on the cooking technique and the pot. The end result of the slow cooking, required by this clay cooking pot, was succulent. Tagine cooking is popular in Morocco and Algeria so it is no surprise that Mauritanians and those living out in the desert flatlands of the Western Sahara have also adopted this cooking utensil. Vegetables, such as the onions, sweetpotatoes, and carrots in this dish, are grown in the Atlas Mountains and these too enter into the commerce of the area.

Africa–Mauritania / Western Sahara

SWEETPOTATO, CARROT, AND ONION *TAGINE* WITH PRUNES (cont'd)

2 medium carrots—scraped or pared and cut into 1/2-inch pieces
12 pitted *preservative-free* prunes
1 cup VEGETABLE STOCK FROM SOUP *[see index]* or other vegetarian stock of choice
1 teaspoon honey
1/2 teaspoon ground cinnamon
1/2 teaspoon ground ginger

2 tablespoons *extra virgin* olive oil
1 tablespoon butter
12 *frozen* white boiling onions
1 1/2 pounds cooked sweetpotato—chopped

1/4 cup *finely* chopped fresh coriander (*cilantro*)
1/4 cup *finely* chopped fresh mint

Preheat oven to 300 degrees F.

In the bottom half of the *tagine* or casserole, combine carrot pieces, *pitted* prunes, vegetable stock, honey, and ground cinnamon and ginger. Place in preheated 300 degree F. oven. Cover *tagine* or casserole. Allow to cook, stirring occasionally for about 40 minutes.

In a non-stick-coated skillet set over *MEDIUM-HIGH* heat, combine oil and butter. When hot, add onions and chopped sweetpotatoes. Cook, stirring almost constantly, until vegetables brown and caramelize. Remove from heat and set aside until required.

When the cooking period for the carrots and prunes is completed, add caramelized onions and sweetpotatoes with any oil or butter remaining in the skillet. Stir. Return to the oven, cover, and allow to cook for 15 minutes more. Remove from oven.

Add *finely* chopped coriander and mint. Stir for a minute or two.

Serve at once directly from the *tagine* or casserole.

Yields 6 servings
adequate for 4 people

Note: This recipe can be doubled, when required.

1/6 SERVING – PROTEIN = 2.7 g.; FAT = 5.7 g.; CARBOHYDRATE = 27.8 g.;
CALORIES = 184; CALORIES FROM FAT = 28%

SPICED, BAKED EGGPLANT SLICES
TPT - 1 hour and 47 minutes;
1 hour = eggplant salting period

Frying eggplant in oil can be a caloric disaster so I bake eggplant this way. It gives you all the mouthfeel and all the flavor that you expect. The spiced oil–butter basting captures the flavor nuances of North Africa with aplomb.

1 medium eggplant—washed, trimmed, and sliced into 1/4-inch crosswise slices
Coarse or kosher salt

High-heat safflower *or* sunflower oil to coat baking pan

2 tablespoons *melted* butter
2 tablespoons GARLIC OIL *[see index]*
1/2 teaspoon ground cumin
1/2 teaspoon paprika
1/2 teaspoon ground coriander
1/4 teaspoon ground mixed peppercorns—red, black, and white

PLAIN YOGURT *[see index] or* commercially-available plain yogurt

Salt eggplant slices generously and place them in a sieve or colander set in the sink. Place a plate on top and a weight—a large can or a tea kettle filled with water—on top of the plate. Allow to stand for 1 hour. Rinse each slice of eggplant well to remove excess salt. Pat dry with paper toweling.

Line a large non-stick-coated cookie sheet with aluminum foil. Brush it lightly with *high-heat* safflower or sunflower oil. Place cookie sheet in oven to heat. Preheat oven to 350 degrees F.

Combine *melted* butter, garlic oil, ground cumin, paprika, ground coriander, and ground mixed peppercorns.

Africa–Mauritania / Western Sahara

SPICED, BAKED EGGPLANT SLICES (cont'd)

Remove preheated baking sheet from oven. Arrange eggplant slices on the prepared baking sheet. Brush each slice, both sides, with the spice butter–oil mixture. Bake in preheated 350 degree oven for 10 minutes. Rotate baking sheet. Continue baking for an additional 10 minutes. Remove baking sheet from oven. Turn each eggplant slice. Baste with remaining oil–butter mixture. Return to oven for about 10 minutes more, or until each slice is lightly browned. Transfer to a heated serving platter.

Serve with plain yogurt.

Yields 6 servings
adequate for 4 people

1/6 SERVING (exclusive of yogurt) –
PROTEIN = 0.7 g.; FAT = 7.6 g.; CARBOHYDRATE = 3.7 g.;
CALORIES = 86; CALORIES FROM FAT = 80%

MAURITANIAN MILLET AND YOGURT PUDDING
Lakh

TPT - 1 hour and 28 minutes;
1 hour = refrigeration period

Traditionally served to mark the end of Ramadan in both Mauritania and in Senegal, this sweet dessert can be a nutritious end to a meal. Millet flour is available in most natural food stores.

2 cups *boiling* water
1 cup fine millet flour

1/2 cup sugar
Pinch salt

2 cups Greek-style vanilla yogurt *or* sweetened YOGURT CRÈME [see index]
1 tablespoon grated coconut—fresh *or* desiccated

Pour *boiling* water into a large saucepan set over MEDIUM-HIGH heat. While stirring constantly, slowly pour millet flour into the *boiling* water. Boil and stir until mixture is smooth. *Reduce heat to LOW-MEDIUM.*

Add sugar and salt. Continue cooking, stirring frequently, for about 25 minutes, or until thick. Transfer thickened millet pudding to a sieve set over a bowl. Press pudding through. Transfer sieved pudding to a pie plate or large platter. Spread it evenly into a circle.

Pour the yogurt into the middle of the millet base. Using a spoon or knife, spread the yogurt out into a circle just slightly smaller than the millet circle. Sprinkle grated coconut over.

Refrigerate for at least 1 hour before serving.

Yields 6 servings
adequate for 4 people

Note: This recipe can be doubled or halved, when required.

1/6 SERVING – PROTEIN = 5.5 g.; FAT = 2.4 g.; CARBOHYDRATE = 43.8 g.;
CALORIES = 218; CALORIES FROM FAT = 10%

SAHARAN AVOCADO PUDDING
Abacate con Crema

TPT - 25 minutes

A dish similar to this is popular in Venezuela where the Spanish influence is reflected in the cuisine as it is in the cities of the Western Sahara. The dessert is eaten in Mauritania as well where it is referred to by its French name, pudim d'avocat. Since lime juice will minimize oxidation and the browning of this beautiful pudding, you can prepare this as much as an hour before serving.

SAHARAN AVOCADO PUDDING (cont'd)

4 ripe avocados—peeled, pitted, and sliced
1/4 cup confectioners' sugar
2 tablespoons freshly squeezed lime juice

6 tablespoons ground *preservative-free* almonds *or* almond meal

About 6 tablespoons half and half *or* light cream

Turn the avocado flesh into the mixing bowl of the electric mixer. Using the electric mixer fitted with the paddle, mash the avocado flesh and beat until fluffy. Add confectioners' sugar and lime juice and again beat until of a light and uniform consistency.

Add ground almonds. Blend well.

Gradually, tablespoonful by tablespoonful, add cream until you achieve a pudding consistency. Turn into a chilled serving bowl or divide among individual dessert dishes or sherbet glasses. Refrigerate for no more than one hour before serving.

Yields 6 individual servings

Note: The ingredients can be adjusted to make just two or four servings, when required.

1/6 SERVING – PROTEIN = 6.0 g.; FAT = 31.4 g.; CARBOHYDRATE = 17.8 g.;
CALORIES = 353; CALORIES FROM FAT = 80%

BANANA PASTRY
Pâtisserie aux Banane
TPT - 46 minutes

The long period of French colonization of Mauritania has resulted in a taste for pastries. Pastry shops are a permanent fixture in the cities and each afternoon you will see ladies going in and coming out with pastries destined for their dinner table. Fruit tarts and pastries, of course, make use of the fruits of Africa and here a sweet banana filling pairs with puff pastry. Frozen puff pastry makes this dessert a possibility for a quick and easy family dessert. Mauritanian cooks use what is called Parisienne essence, which is simply a brown sugar syrup. Honey, agave nectar, or brown corn syrup can be substituted.

2 tablespoons honey, *agave* nectar, brown corn syrup, *or* sugar syrup
1/4 teaspoon ground cinnamon

1/2 sheets *frozen* puff pastry—*brought to room temperature*

4 large bananas
2 tablespoons *fat-free* sweetened condensed milk

Remove pastry from refrigerator or freezer and allow to come to room temperature.

In a small dish, combine honey, or the sugar syrup you have selected, and ground cinnamon. Blend thoroughly. Set aside until required.

Preheat oven to 400 degrees F.* Prepare a baking sheet by lining it with culinary parchment paper.

Place puff pastry sheet on prepared baking sheet. Bake at 400 degrees F. for about 15 minutes, *checking to be sure that the pastry does not over-brown*. Remove from oven and allow to cool for about 10 minutes on the baking sheet.

Peel bananas and slice each into quarters lengthwise. Slice each banana quarter into wedge-shaped pieces. Turn into a mixing bowl. Add sweetened condensed milk. Stir gently. Set aside briefly.

Using a sharp, serrated knife, slice the puffed pastry lengthwise into two long rectangles. Remove the top layer and set aside. Transfer the bottom later to a bread board from which you can serve. Spoon the bananas over the bottom pastry later. Place the top layer on top.

Drizzle the honey–cinnamon mixture over the top.

Serve at once, cutting with the sharp knife. Transfer to dessert plates.

Yields 6 servings
adequate for 4 people

Note: This recipe can be halved, or doubled, when required.

1/6 SERVING – PROTEIN = 3.2 g.; FAT = 6.1 g.; CARBOHYDRATE = 43.3 g.;
CALORIES = 226; CALORIES FROM FAT = 24%

Morocco

The English name Morocco is believed to derive from either the Spanish word *Marruecos* or from the Portuguese word *Marrocos*. This entomology immediately suggests that many influences have shaped the nation which evokes such an emotional feeling to those in the West. Morocco, wrapped seductively around the western shoulder of Africa has always been a siren to Europeans and those in the western hemisphere, inviting one to an exotic exploration. The food of Morocco captures those who have wandered into its spell.

Morocco is a constitutional monarchy in which the king holds considerable executive powers unlike most European constitutional monarchs. About ninety-nine percent of the population are Arabs or Arabized Berbers, living primarily in an area west of the Atlas Mountains. The Berbers, originally known as Magrhrib or Maghred, descended from those who migrated north from the central African cradle of human development in about 30,000 BC. Archeological research confirms habitation by the Capsian culture about 2000 BC. The independent Berber Kingdom of Mauretania, occupying northern Morocco, dates to 110 BC. [Note: This Berber kingdom did not occupy the same territory as does present day (Mauritania) Mauretania.] In the seventh century AD the region was conquered by Arab Muslims, specifically the Umayyad Arabs from the region of Damascus, Syria. They not only brought Islam to this land so distant from their own they also brought their language and their system of government. By the eleventh century powerful Berber dynasties, which controlled the western Mediterranean, also controlled the wider region known as the Maghreb and Muslim Spain. The Moors, as they were known, were driven from Spain by the policies of the Catholic monarchs during the *Reconquista* in the fifteenth century. Large numbers of Islamic and Jewish Spaniards fled across the Mediterranean to Morocco. Although some Moroccan Jews continue to live in this religiously tolerate country, a significant number of the Jewish population, estimated at about 265,000 in 1948, emigrated from Morocco in 1948 to settle in Israel and now form the second largest ethnic group in the Jewish state.

In 1777 Morocco declared American merchant ships to be under the protection of the sultanate and thus assured the safety of the merchant ships from attacks by Barbary pirates. In 1787 Morocco became one of the first nations to recognize the United States as an independent nation.

Portions of present day Morocco became a Spanish protectorate in 1912 as Spanish Morocco; the rest of Morocco fell under French control, also in 1912, and was known as French Morocco. The French established an apartheid system which precipitated a nationalistic movement. France finally allowed the exiled Sultan Mohammed V to return to Morocco in 1955 and independence was declared in 1956 following what has become known as *Taourat al-malik wa shaab*, The Revolution of the King and the People. Both French and Spanish Morocco were returned to the sultanate in 1956.

The influence of these many encounters is clearly seen in the cuisine of Morocco. Elements of the native Berber cuisine and the Andalusian and Jewish cuisines brought by *Moriscos* who fled Spain blend with Turkish influences introduced by the Ottoman Turks and with that brought from the Middle East by Arabs from many different countries. These influences, blended with the spices so beloved by Moroccans and a flare for dramatic presentation, have created a unique cuisine that also seduces.

Africa–Morocco

Pomegranate Refresher
Sharab Rumman

Couscous Salad with Roasted Eggplant and Red Pepper
Salade de Couscous bil B'Dilgan

~

Mixed Legume Soup
Bessara

~

Artichoke Heart Salad with Preserved Lemons and Honey
Quartiers de Fonds d'Artichauts au Hamad Mrakad

Preserved Lemon Conserve
Hamad Mrakad

Orange and Date Salad
Salade de Oranges et Datte

~~~~~~~~~~~~~~~~~~~~

Swiss Chard and Rice *Tagine*
Marak Silk

Glazed Carrots with Mint
Sauté de Carottes au Menthe

Pita or Flatbread

~~~~~~~~~~~~~~~~~~~~

Whole Pan Pancake with Sweetened Mixed Berries and Honey
Beghrir

Pears in Honey – Lavender Syrup
Poire en Miel Liquide et Lavande

~

Green Tea with Mint

MOROCCAN POMEGRANATE REFRESHER
Sharab Rumman

TPT - 3 minutes

On a late spring evening, I was looking for an appetizer to precede dinner. I thought that pomegranate juice would taste good but it was June, not December, so there would be no pomegranates in my grocery store in the middle of Pennsylvania. Bottled juice was available so that is where this very refreshing, good-for-you, beverage began.

MOROCCAN POMEGRANATE REFRESHER (cont'd)

3 cups pure pomegranate juice
2 tablespoons freshly squeezed lemon juice
1 tablespoon sugar
2 teaspoons orange flower water

Chipped ice, if desired

In a pitcher, combine pomegranate and lemon juices, sugar, and orange flower water. Stir to mix well. Refrigerate until ready to serve.

Serve into champagne flutes over chipped ice, if desired.

Yields 6 servings
adequate for 4 people

Note: This recipe can be halved or doubled, when required.

1/6 SERVING (about 1/2 cupful) –
PROTEIN = 0.5 g.; FAT = 0.0 g.; CARBOHYDRATE = 26.7 g.;
CALORIES = 86; CALORIES FROM FAT = 0%

COUSCOUS SALAD WITH ROASTED EGGPLANT AND RED PEPPER IN THE MOROCCAN STYLE
Salade de Couscous bil B'Dilgan

TPT - 1 hour and 40 minutes;
20 minutes = roasted vegetable and *couscous* cooling period;
30 minutes = flavor development period

White or cream eggplants are more frequently used in African cooking, especially in the cuisines of countries south of the Sahara. If you prefer and have an available source, you may wish to use white eggplants in this dish rather than the purple eggplants more commonly available in our produce departments.

1 medium eggplant—well-washed and cut into
    3/4-inch chunks*
1 sweet red bell pepper—perfect, unblemished,
    and well-washed
1 tablespoon *extra virgin* olive oil

1 cup whole wheat *couscous*
Pinch salt
1 cup *boiling* water

1 medium yellow summer squash—peeled,
    quartered, seeded, and cut into thin slices
8 ripe, pitted black olives—preferably Greek *or*
    OLIVES IN GREEK MARINADE (*Elyes Meh
    Ladoxksitho*) [see index]—*thinly* sliced
1/4 cup chopped *fresh* basil leaves

1 tablespoon *extra virgin* olive oil
2 tablespoons GARLIC–BASIL VINEGAR
    [see index] *or* other vinegar of choice
1 teaspoon sugar
2 garlic cloves—forced through a garlic press
Freshly ground black pepper, to taste

2 tablespoons pine nuts (*pignoli*)—*toasted*

Preheat oven to 350 degrees F.

Remove seeds and membranes from pepper. Chop pepper into 1-inch-square pieces. Place on a cookie sheet. Place eggplant pieces on cookie sheet with pepper squares. Drizzle 1 tablespoon oil over and toss to coat vegetable pieces.

Bake in preheated 350 degree F. oven for about 50 minutes, until soft and evenly browned. *Turn each piece* every 15 minutes during roasting period to insure even browning. Remove from oven and allow to cool on the baking pan.

While eggplant and pepper are roasting, place *couscous* and salt in a mixing bowl. Pour the 1 cupful *boiling* water over. Cover and allow to steam for about 5 minutes, or until all water is absorbed. Fluff with a fork. Set aside to cool.

Cool all ingredients to room temperature—about 20 minutes.

Add roasted eggplant and red pepper, squash pieces, olive slices, and basil to *couscous*. Combine *gently*, but *thoroughly*. Turn into salad bowl or serving bowl, of choice.

In a small bowl, combine remaining 1 tablespoonful oil, vinegar, sugar, *pressed* garlic cloves, and black pepper.

VOLUME II - 171

COUSCOUS SALAD WITH ROASTED EGGPLANT AND RED PEPPER IN THE MOROCCAN STYLE (cont'd)

Using a wire whisk, beat to form an emulsion. Pour dressing over salad ingredients. Toss *gently* to combine. Refrigerate for 30 minutes to allow for flavor development.

Before serving, toss again to coat ingredients with dressing and garnish with *toasted* pine nuts *(pignoli)*.

Yields 6 servings
adequate for 4 people

Note: This recipe can be halved or doubled, as required.

1/6 SERVING – PROTEIN = 5.8 g.; FAT = 7.9 g.; CARBOHYDRATE = 28.7 g.; CALORIES = 205; CALORIES FROM FAT = 35%

MOROCCAN-STYLED MIXED LEGUME SOUP
Bessara

TPT - 16 hours and 12 minutes;
12 hours = overnight soaking period

"Bessara" is one of the most efficient and delicious ways of bringing leguminous protein to your table. As served in Morocco, bessara is quite different from this lovely soup and is served as a thick dip of fava beans. Large quantities of olive oil make the authentic version too high in fat to suit our Western ideas of nutrition. This adaptation brings the wonderful taste of Morocco to our table most pleasantly. It is also reminiscent of traditional Moroccan harira but without the meat stock, lamb, and egg/flour/yeast thickening.

1/2 cup dry *borlotti*, cranberry, Roman, *or* small pinto beans
1/2 cup dry brown (*or* green) lentils
1/2 cup dry chick peas (*garbanzos*)
1 quart *cold* water

1 quart VEGETARIAN BROWN STOCK *[see index]* or other vegetarian stock of choice
10 cups water
1/2 teaspoon dried red pepper flakes, or to taste
1/2 teaspoon ground turmeric
1/4 teaspoon ground cinnamon
4 whole cloves*

1 1/2 cups canned, *crushed* tomatoes
1/4 cup tomato paste

3/4 cup PLAIN YOGURT *[see index]* or commercially-available plain yogurt
1 tablespoon freshly squeezed lemon juice
1/2 teaspoon freshly grated lemon zest
1 1/2 tablespoons *finely* chopped fresh mint leaves

2 tablespoons chopped fresh coriander (*cilantro*) leaves, for garnish

Rinse dry beans, lentils, and chick peas in several changes of water. Remove and discard any of poor quality. Place in a bowl with the 1 quartful of *cold* water and soak overnight in the refrigerator.

In the morning, drain legumes and place in a large kettle with the 1 quartful stock, 10 cupfuls water, red pepper flakes, ground turmeric, ground cinnamon, and whole cloves. Bring to the boil, reduce heat to *LOW*, cover tightly, and allow to simmer for 2 hours.

When beans have completed the preliminary cooking period, add crushed tomatoes and tomato paste. Allow to simmer for an additional 1 to 1 1/2 hours, or until beans are tender. Remove and discard whole cloves.

Using an electric blender or food processor fitted with steel knife, purée *half* of the soup—beans and liquid. Return to the kettle and keep warm while preparing the sauce.

Combine yogurt, lemon juice and zest, and *finely* chopped fresh mint leaves. Stir to combine thoroughly. Turn into serving bowl.

Turn soup into heated soup tureen, garnish with chopped coriander (*cilantro*) leaves, and serve into heated soup bowls. Pass yogurt sauce separately.

Yields 8 servings
adequate for 4-6 people

Notes: *The whole cloves are most easily recovered if secured inside a tea ball during the simmering process.

If you have a slow cooker, preparation of *bessara* can be conveniently and easily adapted.

MOROCCAN- STYLED MIXED LEGUME SOUP (cont'd)

This recipe is easily doubled, if required, and freezes well.

1/8 SERVING – PROTEIN = 9.3 g.; FAT = 1.2 g.; CARBOHYDRATE = 24.4 g.; CALORIES = 142; CALORIES FROM FAT = 8%

MOROCCAN ARTICHOKE HEART SALAD WITH PRESERVED LEMONS AND HONEY
Quartiers de Fonds d'Artichauts au Hamad Mrakad

TPT - 46 minutes;
15 minutes = cooling period

The artichoke was originally found growing wild in the Mediterranean and there is evidence that artichokes were eaten in ancient Rome and in ancient Greece. It appears that the reintroduction in Europe of artichokes as food was a contribution of the Moors by way of Sicily and the Iberian Peninsula. Those who are fond of artichokes make every effort to consume them in season. Syrians and Lebanese enjoy "salatat khurshoof," a salad whose main ingredient is also artichoke hearts. Just as we search out the most perfect globes to prepare for Christmas, so Moroccans find every possible way to enjoy the divine thistles when they are available. Perfect whole artichokes are steamed and served whole, albeit not stuffed as in the Sicilian style. The hearts are poached, chopped, and served with garlic and herbs as an appetizer or as a salad. Here Moroccan preserved lemons are added. "Hamad mrakad," are available in Middle Eastern groceries if you do not choose to make them yourself. Because frozen artichoke hearts are now quite widely available, we do not have to wait for the artichoke harvest or pay the high price of off-season imports to enjoy this thoroughly unique and delicious salad.

2 tablespoons *extra virgin* **olive oil**
2 garlic cloves—*very finely* **chopped**

1 slice fresh gingerroot—**grated***
1 tablespoon freshly squeezed lemon juice
2 tablespoons honey, of choice
Pinch saffron threads

3 tablespoons MOROCCAN PRESERVED LEMON CONSERVE *(Hamad Mrakad)*
[see recipe which follows]
1/2 cup water

6 ounces *frozen* **artichoke hearts**—*defrosted*

In a skillet set over *LOW-MEDIUM* heat, heat oil. Add *very finely* chopped garlic and sauté for several minutes, *being careful not to allow the garlic to brown*. Reduce heat to *LOW*.

Add gingerroot, lemon juice, honey, and saffron threads. Stir to combine and allow to cook for a minute or two.

Add preserved lemon conserve and water. Stir to combine well.

Add *defrosted* artichoke hearts. Stir to coat with honey–preserved lemon mixture. Cover and allow to simmer for about 10 minutes. Remove cover and continue cooking, stirring frequently, until liquid is reduced to a syrup. Turn into a serving bowl and allow to cool to room temperature—about 15 minutes.

Serve at room temperature.

Yields 6 servings
adequate for 4 people

Notes: *If you do not have a ginger grater, chop the gingerroot as finely as possible.

This recipe can be halved or doubled, when required.

1/6 SERVING – PROTEIN = 1.0 g.; FAT = 3.9 g.; CARBOHYDRATE = 11.0 g.; CALORIES = 78; CALORIES FROM FAT = 45%

Africa – Morocco

MOROCCAN PRESERVED LEMON CONSERVE
Hamad Mrakad

TPT - 1 hour and 7 minutes

There is, unfortunately, little similarity between the small, thin-skinned lemons used to prepare this dish in Morocco and the common, thick-skinned lemons found in our supermarkets. This recipe seeks only to recreate the tangy, sweet taste of this African condiment, a taste which very much compliments the food of the region. The method of achieving this taste is vastly different from the classic preparation where a salt-based, fermentation technique is used to produce the thickened, lemon-flavored preserve. It is, we feel, quite pleasant to the Western palate while still being complimentary to North African cuisines.

5 lemons

1 tablespoon coarse (kosher) salt
2 cups sugar
2 cups water

Sterilize two one-pint canning jars. Also sterilize lids and rings for the jars.

Scrub lemons well with a brush, cut off ends, slice *thinly*, and remove pips.

In a large saucepan set over *MEDIUM* heat, combine *thinly* sliced lemons, coarse salt, sugar, and water. Bring to the boil. *Reduce heat to LOW.* Cook until the lemon slices are tender and the liquid is reduced to a thick syrup—about 50 minutes. Stir occasionally.

Ladle hot, preserved lemon conserve into the sterilized canning jars. Carefully wipe the lips of the jars. Seal each with a hot, sterilized lid and ring. Refrigerate for up to 3 months.

Serve the lemon slices, at room temperature or chilled, as a condiment for Middle Eastern menus.

Yields about 2 cupfuls of lemon slices*

Note: *The sweet, thick, lemon syrup in which the lemon slices are preserved can be used to make salad dressings, if desired.

1/10 SERVING – PROTEIN = 0.3 g.; FAT = 0.1 g.; CARBOHYDRATE = 14.0 g.;
CALORIES = 53; CALORIES FROM FAT = 2%

MOROCCAN ORANGE AND DATE SALAD
Salade de Oranges et Datte

TPT - 6 minutes

This is one of several versions of the much-loved Moroccan orange salad. Navel oranges will do but if you use blood oranges to make this salad, you will know to what heights it can go. The dates, in this version, are a counterpoint to the texture of the oranges and their sweetness plays on your tongue as a foil to the tartness of the lemon juice. We enjoy this as a salad, as a dessert, and as an appetizer.

4 large navel oranges—peeled, pith removed, and sliced
1/2 cup pitted *preservative-free* dates—chopped
1/4 cup chopped *toasted preservative-free* almonds

1 tablespoon freshly squeezed lemon juice
1 teaspoon confectioners' sugar
1 tablespoon orange flower water, if available
Pinch salt

Ground cinnamon, to taste

Arrange orange slices in a serving dish such as a quiche dish or decorative pie plate. Scatter chopped dates and *toasted* almond pieces over.

In a small bowl, combine lemon juice, sugar, orange flower water, and salt. Combine well. Pour over assembled salad. Refrigerate until ready to serve.

Serve chilled, garnished with a sprinkling of ground cinnamon.

Yields 6 servings
adequate for 4 people

Note: This recipe can easily be halved or doubled or tripled, when required.

1/6 SERVING – PROTEIN = 2.1 g.; FAT = 2.8 g.; CARBOHYDRATE = 22.6 g.;
CALORIES = 114; CALORIES FROM FAT = 22%

Africa–Morocco

MOROCCAN SWISS CHARD AND RICE *TAGINE***
Marak Silk

TPT - 1 hour and 15 minutes

Swiss chard, a relative of the common beet, grown for its leaves, is a common green in North Africa. It is underused in the United States today. My grandfather always planted it so that when the sweet spinach and the tender beet greens were finished, we would still have greens. The variety he planted, with its long red stalks and red-veined leaves, is still sold at our farmstand and in the produce departments of the large grocery chain stores nearby. When the Swiss chard was just at the end of its season, wonderful, curly, blue-gray kale was mature, touched by the first frost, and ready to grace our table on into the fall. Tagine cooking delivers tender chard and plump, flavorful rice. This is a real favorite of ours.

2 pounds young, thin-stalked Swiss chard
—trimmed, coarse stalk ends discarded, and *very* well-washed

1 1/2 tablespoons *extra virgin* olive oil
2 garlic cloves—*finely* chopped

1/2 teaspoon ground Hungarian *hot* paprika, or to taste

1 medium Italian red onion—coarsely *shredded**
2 tablespoons dry converted rice
1 tablespoon long grain brown rice
1/4 cup chopped fresh coriander (*cilantro*)
6 tablespoons water
3 threads saffron—crushed

1/8 teaspoon freshly ground black pepper, or to taste

Preheat oven to 325 degrees F. Prepare a *tagine*** or an oven-to-table baking dish, with cover, with non-stick lecithin spray coating.

Separate the leaves from the thick ribs of the Swiss chard. Coarsely chop the leaves and set aside until required. Slit the ribs open and sliced into strips about 1/2-inch wide by 1-inch long.

In a large skillet with cover, set over *LOW-MEDIUM* heat, heat oil. Add the sliced chard ribs and *finely* chopped garlic. Cover tightly and cook for about 10-12 minutes, stirring occasionally.

Stir in *hot* paprika and cook, while continuing to stir, for about 1 minute. Turn into prepared *tagine* or baking dish.

Add *shredded* onion, chopped Swiss chard leaves, white and brown rice, chopped fresh coriander (*cilantro*), water, and crushed saffron threads. Stir well.

Place vented cover on top and bake in preheated 325 degree F. oven for about 40-50 minutes, or until rice has absorbed the cooking liquid and is tender. *If necessary,* add a tablespoon or two more of water.

Serve directly from the *tagine* or oven casserole. Keep warm on a warming tray or in a warm oven until ready to serve. Serve with hot *pita* loaves and salads.

Yields 6 servings
adequate for 4 people

Notes: *Shredding a large onion can be a weepy affair. Freeze the peeled onion, *with the root end still attached,* for about 30 minutes before attempting to grate it. *Keep the root end attached until the very last minute!* It usually works.

**The *tagine slaoui* is Morocco's cooking pot, a round, shallow, earthenware casserole with a pointed, conical lid of ancient origin and a most efficient casserole for cooking over *braziers*. Failing this, use an oven-to-table casserole.

This recipe may be halved or doubled, when required.

1/6 SERVING – PROTEIN = 2.2 g.; FAT = 3.0 g.; CARBOHYDRATE = 10.1 g.;
CALORIES = 75; CALORIES FROM FAT = 36%

Africa—**Morocco**

MOROCCAN GLAZED CARROTS WITH MINT
Sauté de Carottes au Menthe
TPT - 38 minutes

Carrot salads are popular in Morocco and several Moroccan carrot salads have been favorites of ours for many years. This recipe approaches carrots in a different way and can be made with the packaged small carrots or with regular carrots that have been pared and cut into quarters but I, personally, love to make them with the perfect organic Belgian carrots that are carried in my grocery store. Leaving just a bit of the green on top seems to confirm that these are not carrots that traveled from the edges of the known world in a plastic bag.

1 pound whole, baby Belgian carrots—about 12 carrots

2 tablespoons *extra virgin* **olive oil**
1 tablespoon GARLIC OIL [*see index*]

1 garlic clove—*very finely* **chopped**

1 1/2 teaspoons sugar

1 teaspoon grated organic lemon zest
1 tablespoon freshly squeezed lemon juice
2 tablespoons chopped fresh mint
Freshly ground black pepper, to taste
Pinch salt

Cut all but 1/2 inch of green leaves from each carrot. Wash well. Peel carrots.

In a large skillet set over *LOW-MEDIUM* heat, heat olive oil and garlic oil. Place carrots in the skillet in a single layer. Cook, turning occasionally, for about 15 minutes.

Add *very finely* chopped garlic. Cook, stirring frequently, for another 5-8 minutes.

Add sugar and cook, stirring constantly, until sugar begins to caramelize.

Add grated lemon zest, lemon juice, chopped mint, black pepper, and salt. Stir to coat the carrots well. Turn into a heated serving dish.

Serve at once.

Yields 6 servings
adequate for 5 people

Note: This recipe can be halved when required.

1/6 SERVING – PROTEIN = 1.4 g.; FAT = 5.8 g.; CARBOHYDRATE = 14.4 g.;
CALORIES = 112; CALORIES FROM FAT = 47%

WHOLE-PAN PANCAKE WITH SWEETENED MIXED BERRIES AND HONEY IN THE STYLE OF MOROCCO
Beghrir
TPT - 17 minutes

I based this simple but rather spectacular presentation loosely on a favorite Moroccan pancake dessert ("beghrir"). We enjoy it as a dessert, for a weekend breakfast, for brunch, and even as an indulgent lunch.

1/3 cup butter
1/3 cup honey—*alfalfa or a wildflower honey would be our choice**

1 cup commercially-available pancake mix**
1/4 teaspoon ground ginger, or to taste
1 cup skimmed milk
1/4 cup *fat-free* **pasteurized eggs (the equivalent of 1 egg)**
2 teaspoons safflower, sunflower, *or* **corn oil**

2 cups mixed sweetened berries, of choice

Preheat oven to lowest temperature possible. Place a non-stick-coated baking sheet in the oven to heat. Also, place an oven-proof serving plate or pie plate in the oven to warm.

In a small saucepan or Turkish coffee pot, combine butter and honey. Allow to heat over *LOW* heat until required.

Prepare a 9-inch non-stick-coated skillet by coating with non-stick lecithin spray coating. Preheat over *MEDIUM-LOW* heat.

WHOLE-PAN PANCAKE WITH SWEETENED MIXED BERRIES AND HONEY IN THE STYLE OF MOROCCO (cont'd)

In a mixing bowl, combine pancake mix, ground ginger, milk, pasteurized eggs, and oil. Using a wire whisk, beat only until large lumps disappear. *Do not overbeat.*

Test the skillet with a drop or two of water. If ready, the water will sizzle and evaporate almost at once. Ladle enough batter into the skillet to form a thin 9-inch round, for each pancake. *Do not turn when bubbles form on the uncooked surface*, as you normally would when preparing pancakes. These pancakes *should not be browned*, instead, *pale-golden in color* on the cooked surface with craters on the uncooked surface. Transfer completed pancakes onto the warmed baking sheet in the oven. This will allow the uncooked surface to firm up. After making four large pancakes, transfer the pancakes from the baking sheet to the warm serving platter. Pile in overlapping layers on the serving platter to prevent sticking.

Stir honey and butter together. Pour over prepared pancakes.

Serve at once onto a dinner plate or fold and serve onto a dessert plate with a serving of berries on the side.

Yields 4 nine-inch pancakes
adequate for 4 people

Notes: *A drop or two of orange-flower water, available in food specialty stores and in Middle Eastern groceries, or pure orange extract may be added to the honey before serving.

**Whole wheat pancake mixes, although nutritionally superior, produce too dense a pancake, in this case.

***Turkish coffee pots are convenient for heating and serving both the butter and honey.

This recipe can be halved or doubled, when required.

1/4 SERVING – PROTEIN = 6.8 g.; FAT = 18.2 g.; CARBOHYDRATE = 60.0 g.;
CALORIES = 423; CALORIES FROM FAT = 39%

MOROCCAN PEARS IN HONEY – LAVENDER SYRUP
Poire en Miel Liquide et Lavande

TPT - 8 hours and 21 minutes;
8 hours = flavor development period

This recipe can turn a thoroughly mundane can of pears or a sliced orange into an exotic dessert when necessary. I always have canned pears in my pantry for a quick dessert or as insurance when the fresh pears I have purchased fail to ripen perfectly. And, a tiny canning jar filled with dried lavender flowers, a product of my herb gardens, is always on my herb and spice shelves. Although I do grow and dry lavender each summer, dried, organic lavender flowers are available in gourmet shops and from mail order firms.

2 cans (15 ounces each) sliced pears, packed in light syrup

3/4 cup canning liquid drained from pears
3 tablespoons wildflower honey
1 tablespoon freshly squeezed lemon juice

2 tablespoons dried *organic* lavender flowers
   —well-rinsed
1 cinnamon quill
Pinch saffron threads
A long strip of *organic* orange zest

Drain pear slices, retaining the canning liquid. Place pears in a shallow serving dish or pie plate. Set aside briefly.

In a saucepan set over *LOW* heat, combine 3/4 cupful of canning liquid drained from pears, wildflower honey, and lemon juice. Stir to combine thoroughly.

Add lavender flowers, cinnamon quill, saffron, and orange zest. Allow to heat, stirring occasionally, for about 5 minutes. Pour over pears. Allow to cool to room temperature. Cover and refrigerate for 8 hours, or overnight. Bathe the pears in syrup several times during this flavor development period. Remove cinnamon quill and orange zest.

Serve chilled.

Yields 6 servings
adequate for 4 people

Note: This recipe can be halved, when required.

1/6 SERVING – PROTEIN = 0.5 g.; FAT = 0.5 g.; CARBOHYDRATE = 32.1 g.;
CALORIES = 134; CALORIES FROM FAT = 3%

Africa–**Mozambique**

Mozambique

This area of southeastern Africa was named by the Portuguese after the Island of Mozambique. Prior to the arrival of the Portuguese led by the exploratory voyage of Vasco de Gama in 1498 this land was occupied by migrating Bantu-speaking people beginning in about the first century AD. Numbering over forty million Africans, the Bantu language group includes those who speak Swahili, Zula, and Kafir. Between 1500 and 1700 the Portuguese pushed inland, wresting much of the coastal trade from the Arabs and establishing trading posts along the Zambezi River which not only supported those using the trade routes to India but provided support for gold prospectors. By the late 1600s investment in this region of Africa began to diminish as Portugal became more focused on trade with India, the Far East, and Brazil. Contracts were granted to companies by the Portuguese government to establish concessions in the Mozambican colony. Lisbon's disinterest in the area persisted into the twentieth century until the *Estado Novo* regime of Oliveira Salazar during which the contracts of most of the company concessions were not renewed. Eventually, in 1942, Portuguese's African colonies, including Mozambique, were declared Overseas Provinces.

The Portuguese became wealthier; the tribal populations became poor. Deeply-felt resentment of the Portuguese by native communities led to the formation of the Front for the Liberation of Mozambique (*FRELIMO*) in 1964. This became part of the Portuguese Colonial War which had begun in 1961 and continued until 1974. It included movements in Angola and Portuguese Guinea whose native populations had also become restless. Independence from Portugal was declared in 1975 and was followed by a lengthy and violent civil war pitting the anti-Communist rebel opposition, *RENAMO*, against the Marxist regime formed by the *FRELIMO*. In 1986 Samora Machel, the Marxist leader of the Mozambican government, was killed in an airplane crash, a crash widely believed to have been caused by a false navigational beacon signal that had been intentionally positioned to divert the plane. Joaquim Chissano succeeded Machel and started reforms, the most dramatic of which was the move from a Marxist political philosophy to a market-based capitalist economy. The civil war which had begun in 1977 finally ended in 1992 after which an extraordinary repatriation of refuges was accomplished. By 1993 approximately 1.5 million refugees from the Mozambican civil war who had lived in exile in neighboring nations, returned to their country.

Although the official language of Mozambique is Portuguese, only about fifty percent of the population of about twenty-three million speaks Portuguese. Ninety-eight percent of the population can still be identified as Bantu with a minority white population of Portuguese descent. Government corruption and lack of education have hindered the Mozambicans but an economic growth rate in excess of seven percent per year since 2002 clearly shows that those who returned to Mozambique after the civil war are determined to make their free-market capitalism successful.

~

We visited Coimbra, Portugal, the historic university city in central Portugal in 1977, just two years after Mozambican independence. Mid-day hunger drove us into a grocery store. A couple of bags of almonds would assuage hunger until the evening but we, not conversant in Portuguese, were not aware that the almonds were seasoned with *piri-piri*. The almonds, exported from Mozambique, were so incredibly hot that I, to this day, am not a fan of *piri-piri*, the fiery hot pepper sauce used in so many dishes in Mozambique. In the following recipes, the heat can be raised to your toleration with *piri-piri*, *jalapeño* sauce, or hot peppers.

Africa–**Mozambique**

Assorted Cheeses
with
Tomato Jam
Doce de Tomate

~

Winter Squash Soup with Garlic
Sopa de Abóbora

~

Avocado, Peach, and Tomato Salad
Salada Pera de Abacate, Pessego, e Tomate
with
Lemon – Peach Salad Dressing
Milho de Limao e Pessego

~~~~~~~~~~~~~~~~~~~~~

Rice with Tomatoes and Coconut Milk
Arroz de Coco

Steamed Pumpkin or Winter Squash
with Butter and Fennel

~~~~~~~~~~

Meatballs and Fruit in Curry Sauce
Almôndegas em Molho de Caril
with
Kneaded Flour for Thickening
Buerre Manie
over
Steamed and Buttered Rice

Sautéed Cabbage, Carrot, and Onion with Cumin and Oregano
Caril de Repolho

~~~~~~~~~~~~~~~~~~~~~

Avocado and Tangerine Dessert
Sobremesa de Abacate

Banana Dessert
Bananas com Leite

Sweet Egg Dessert with Papaya
Ovos Moles de Papaia

Africa–Mozambique

MOZAMBICAN TOMATO JAM
Doce de Tomate

TPT - 40 hours and 5 minutes;
8 hours = first refrigeration period;
24 hours = cooling period

I was not surprised to find that this recipe was a specialty of Mozambican cooks since I had enjoyed it as a garnish in a restaurant in Portugal. This is another way to preserve the tomato harvest and enjoy the bounty if you wish to use peeled, freshly harvested tomatoes.

2 cans (1 pound, 12 ounces each) *whole* tomatoes

4 cups sugar

Sterilize six 1/2-pint canning jars. Also sterilize lids and rings for jars.

Place tomatoes in a kettle. Using a potato masher, crush tomatoes into small chunks, cover, and bring to the boil over *LOW-MEDIUM* heat. *Reduce heat to LOW* and allow to cook down for about 3 hours. Stir frequently and add a bit of water if tomatoes begin to stick. Cover and refrigerate for another 8 hours, or overnight.

The next day, bring the tomatoes to the boil. *Reduce heat to LOW.* Add sugar and allow to cook for 3 to 4 more hours. Stir frequently until very thick.

Ladle tomato jam into hot, sterilized 1/2-pint canning jars. Carefully wipe lips of jars. Seal with hot, sterilized lids and rings. Process in hot-water-bath canner for 10 minutes, *timing from the moment the water reaches a full rolling boil.* Remove to surface covered with thick towels or newspapers. Allow to cool for 24 hours *undisturbed.* Check to be sure jars are sealed before labeling and storing in a dark, cool, dry place. Loosen or remove rings before storing.

Yields six 1/2-pint jarfuls

1/96 SERVING (i. e., per tablespoonful) –
PROTEIN = 0.2 g.; FAT = 0.03 g.; CARBOHYDRATE = 10.0 g.;
CALORIES = 40; CALORIES FROM FAT = <1%

MOZAMBICAN WINTER SQUASH SOUP WITH GARLIC
Sopa de Abóbora

TPT - 1 hour and 40 minutes

Beautiful winter squashes are appreciated all over the world. Mozambicans would use a squash similar to what is most often known in our hemisphere as a calabaza, West Indian pumpkin, green pumpkin, Cuban or Jamaican squash, a toadback, or a crapaudback. Any one of these names will probably help you locate the variety of hard-shelled winter squash that would be appropriate for this soup. I often use butternut or acorn squashes since they are so plentiful throughout the year.

2 pound *calabaza* squash*

1 cup water

2 teaspoons butter
2 teaspoons *extra virgin* olive oil
1/2 cup *finely* chopped onion
3 large garlic cloves—*finely* chopped

1 teaspoon grated fresh gingerroot
1/4 teaspoon HOMEMADE CURRY POWDER
   [see index] or commercially-available curry powder mixture of choice
1/8 teaspoon ground turmeric
1/4 teaspoon HOMEMADE PAPRIKA [see index]
   or commercially-available Hungarian sweet paprika
1 large bay leaf—halved

3 cups *boiling* water

Ground red pepper (cayenne), for garnish, if desired

Preheat oven to 350 degrees F.

Cut the top of the squash all the way around the top as you would for a jack-o-lantern. Remove top and scoop out the seeds and stringy material. Replace the top and place the squash in a baking pan. Surround the squash with about 1 inch of water. Bake in preheated oven for 1 hour. Add more water to the pan as required. Remove from oven and scoop out the flesh of the squash. Mash well.

Put mashed squash into the work bowl of the food processor fitted with steel knife. Add the 1 cupful water. Process until very smooth.

VOLUME II - 180

Africa – Mozambique

MOZAMBICAN WINTER SQUASH SOUP (cont'd)

In a large saucepan, with cover, set over *MEDIUM* heat, heat butter and oil. Add *finely* chopped onion and garlic. Sauté until onion is soft and translucent, *being careful to allow neither the onion nor the garlic to brown.*

Add grated gingerroot, curry powder, ground turmeric, paprika, and bay leaf pieces. Sauté for a couple of minutes more. Remove and discard bay leaf pieces. Add spice mixture to puréed squash. Again, process until very smooth.

Pour into a fine sieve set over a clean saucepan. Discard residue.

Add the 3 cupfuls of *boiling* water. Allow to come to the boil again. Add more water if necessary. Taste and adjust seasoning, if necessary. When heated through, turn into a heated soup tureen.

Sprinkle ground red pepper (cayenne) over as a garnish.

Serve into heated soup plates.

Yields 6 cupfuls

Note: This recipe can be halved and half of the mashed squash can be frozen for another meal. Since the soup freezes well, I usually use all of the squash to make soup and then freeze the soup.

1/6 SERVING (i. e., per cupful) –
PROTEIN = 2.1 g.; FAT = 3.4 g.; CARBOHYDRATE = 15.9 g.;
CALORIES = 86; CALORIES FROM FAT = 36%

MOZAMBICAN AVOCADO, PEACH, AND TOMATO SALAD
Salada Pera de Abacate, Pessego, e Tomate
TPT - 8 minutes

I suppose describing a salad as soft and sensuous seems a bit bizarre but that is what makes this unusual and a delightful counterpoint to other foods.

6 large Boston lettuce leaves

2 medium, ripe tomatoes—cut into 3 slices each
1 ripe avocado—peeled, pitted, and cut into 18 uniform slices
24 large, canned peach slices—canning syrup can be reserved to prepare MOZAMBIQUE LEMON PEACH SALAD DRESSING *(Milho de Limao e Pessego)* [see recipe which follows]

8 tablespoons MOZAMBIQUE LEMON PEACH SALAD DRESSING *(Milho de Limao e Pessego)* [see recipe which follows]

On a large platter or tray, arrange lettuce leaves in such a manner that each becomes the base for a separate salad which can be lifted from the platter to an individual salad plate.

On each lettuce leaf, arrange one tomato slice, three avocado slices, and four peach slices. Moisten each salad with prepared salad dressing.

Serve at once, with the remaining salad dressing in a cruet or serving bowl.

Yields 6 individual servings

Note: This recipe may be halved or doubled, when required.

1/6 SERVING – PROTEIN = 1.4 g.; FAT = 9.3 g.; CARBOHYDRATE = 14.1 g.;
CALORIES = 137; CALORIES FROM FAT = 61%

MOZAMBIQUE LEMON – PEACH SALAD DRESSING
Milho de Limao e Pessego
TPT - 5 minutes

Sweet salad dressings are often more complimentary to a meal, especially when there is fruit in the salad that is served. This subtly spiced, yet sweet, dressing is an intriguing taste that always is analyzed by guests. No one has yet guessed that it contains dried chives!

MOZAMBIQUE LEMON PEACH SALAD DRESSING (cont'd)

Pinch dried chives
Pinch dried oregano
Pinch dried parsley
Pinch dried tarragon
1/8 teaspoon garlic powder
1/8 teaspoon freshly ground black pepper

2 tablespoons freshly squeezed lemon juice
1/4 cup peach nectar *or* peach syrup drained from canned peaches
2 tablespoons olive oil

In a mortar, combine dried chives, oregano, parsley, tarragon, garlic powder, and black pepper. Using a pestle, grind seasonings together. Set aside.

In the container of the electric blender, combine lemon juice and peach syrup. Blend at *LOW* speed. Remove cover insert, turn machine on, and add the olive oil *very slowly* in a thin, steady stream. Add ground seasonings. Turn off machine.

Pour into a cruet or serving bowl.

Serve at once, since the emulsion will eventually break down.

Yields about 8 tablespoonfuls

Note: This recipe may be halved or doubled, when required.

1/8 SERVING (i. e., per tablespoonful) –
PROTEIN = 0.01 g.; FAT = 2.8 g.; CARBOHYDRATE = 1.0 g.;
CALORIES = 29; CALORIES FROM FAT = 87%

RICE WITH TOMATOES AND COCONUT MILK IN THE STYLE OF MOZAMBIQUE
Arroz de Coco

TPT - 9 hours and 28 minutes;
8 hours and 30 minutes = coconut infusion period

I worked out a method for preparing coconut milk since finding coconut milk without added sulfiting agents or other preservatives was difficult until recent years. I still make my own because I love the fresh taste and the bonus of drying my own coconut is another bit of freshness in our cooking. This is a remarkably good-tasting dish. A friend once commented that she would never have ever thought of cooking rice this way; neither had I but I was glad I tried it.

1 medium coconut

2 cups *boiling* water

1 tablespoon peanut oil
1 medium onion—*finely* chopped
1 small sweet green pepper—well-washed, cored, seeded, and *finely* chopped

3/4 cup dry converted rice

1 1/2 cups freshly prepared coconut milk
  —*prepared as directed below*
2 medium, ripe tomatoes—peeled, seeded, and chopped *or* 2/3 cup canned, *diced* tomatoes
1/2 teaspoon salt

3 tablespoons chopped mild green *chilies**

Preheat oven to 325 degrees F.

TO PREPARE FRESHLY GRATED COCONUT, make two holes in the coconut through the shiny black "eyes" using a sharp pointed tool such as a screwdriver or an awl. Drain the coconut water into a dish to be used as the replacement for liquid in recipes calling for fresh coconut.

Using a hammer or metal meat mallet, break the coconut into 4-6 pieces. Rinse each piece under running water to loosen meat from shell. With the help of a paring knife, remove coconut from shell. Place pieces on a cookie sheet in preheated 325 degree F. oven for about 5 minutes. Remove from oven and pare rind from coconut meat using a vegetable peeler.

Using a food processor fitted with fine shredding disk or by hand, shred coconut.

TO PREPARE COCONUT MILK, place 1 1/2 cupfuls of freshly grated coconut in a large mixing bowl. Add the 2 cupfuls *boiling* water and allow to infuse for about 30 minutes at room temperature. Place in the refrigerator for 8 hours or overnight.

Africa–Mozambique

RICE WITH TOMATOES AND COCONUT MILK IN THE STYLE OF MOZAMBIQUE (cont'd)

The next morning, pour through a fine sieve set over a second mixing bowl or through several layers of culinary cheesecloth. Squeeze coconut well to release all possible coconut milk to yield the 1 1/2 cupfuls required.**

In a large skillet, with cover, set over *MEDIUM* heat, heat oil. Sauté *finely* chopped onion and green pepper until onion is soft and translucent, *allowing neither the onion nor the pepper to brown*.

Add rice and sauté for a minute or two, until the grains are coated.

Add coconut milk, chopped tomatoes, and salt. Stir to combine well. Cook, stirring constantly, until mixture begins to simmer. Reduce heat to *LOW*, cover tightly, and allow to cook, *undisturbed*, for about 30 minutes, or until all liquid has been absorbed.

Remove from heat and set skillet on a heat-proof surface. Stir in *chilies* and cover tightly again. Allow rice to sit at room temperature or on a warming tray for about 10 minutes before serving.

Turn rice out in a heated bowl or onto a heated serving platter. Fluff the rice with a fork before serving.

Notes: *The very hot *chilies* most often used in this dish have been replaced with the milder green *chilies*. If you would prefer a more fiery dish, substitute *very finely* chopped *chilies* of your preference.

**Reserve shredded coconut for snacks, fruit cup, cookies, breakfast cereal mixes, or any recipe calling for coconut. If coconut is to be kept for any length of time before serving, dry on a cookie sheet in oven set at *WARM*. Although considerable flavor has been released into the coconut cream, the remaining coconut is still superior, in our view, to the canned and packaged varieties.

An acceptable substitute for fresh coconut milk can be made using packaged *unsweetened* moist coconut. After infusion, the remaining coconut will not have much flavor. Use it for a textural ingredient rather than for the coconut flavor.

This recipe may be halved, when required. If you wish to double this recipe, cook the rice in two separate skillets for a better result.

Yields 6 servings
adequate for 4 people

1/6 SERVING – PROTEIN = 3.3 g.; FAT = 4.0 g.; CARBOHYDRATE = 28.1 g.;
CALORIES = 162; CALORIES FROM FAT = 22%

MOZAMBICAN MEATBALLS AND FRUIT IN CURRY SAUCE
Almôndegas em Molho de Caril
TPT - 46 minutes

Fruit, fruit and always a way to work fruit into a dish . . . this seems to be a reoccurring theme in Mozambican cooking. It is delicious fun to turn in a different direction when you are creating a dish. I have found that letting Mozambican cooks lead the way helps a lot in the courage department. Imagine the reaction I would get if another shopper in my rural grocery store asked me what I was going to do with one apple, one pear, one green banana, a pineapple, and a package of soy meatballs and I answered, "I'm making a curried meatball stew for dinner tonight." This is one of our very most favorite curried dishes.

3 cups VEGETABLE STOCK FROM SOUP *[see index]* or other vegetarian stock, of choice
1 cup sliced onions
1/2 teaspoon ground turmeric
1/2 teaspoon HOMEMADE CURRY POWDER
   [see index] or commercially-available curry powder mixture of choice
1/4 teaspoon sugar

1 large bay leaf—halved
4 whole cloves

1/2 cup light cream *or* half and half
3-4 balls *buerre manie*—each about 1 teaspoon
   [see recipe which follows]

1 apple—peeled, cored, and coarsely chopped
1 pear—peeled, cored, and coarsely chopped
1 under-ripe banana—peeled and sliced

2 slices pineapple—fresh or canned in juice—cut into large tidbits
18 *frozen* vegetarian "meatballs"

Slivered, *preservative-free* almonds, to garnish, if desired

Africa—Mozambique

MOZAMBICAN MEATBALLS AND FRUIT IN CURRY SAUCE (cont'd)

In a large saucepan or small kettle set over *MEDIUM* heat, combine vegetable stock, sliced onions, turmeric, curry powder, and sugar. Stir well.

Secure bay leaf pieces and whole cloves in a tea ball. Add to stock base. Allow to come to the boil. Reduce heat to *LOW-MEDIUM*. Allow to cook 15 minutes. Stir occasionally.

Gradually, tablespoonful by tablespoonful, beat cream into spiced stock base. Add *buerre manie*, a ball at a time, *stirring well after each addition and until the base thickens to your liking.*

Add coarsely chopped apple and pear, sliced banana, pineapple pieces, and soy meatballs. Cook, stirring frequently until meatballs are heated through. Remove tea ball. Turn into a heated serving bowl.

Serve at once, garnished with slivered almonds if desired.

Yields 6 servings
adequate for 4 people

Note: This recipe can be doubled, when required. When I want to halve this recipe, I make the full curried stock base and add half the fruit and half the meatballs. Any of the creamy curried sauce that is leftover can be used in another dish, for another meal.

1/6 SERVING – PROTEIN = 9.4 g.; FAT = 5.3 g.; CARBOHYDRATE = 20.3 g.;
CALORIES = 152; CALORIES FROM FAT = 31%

KNEADED FLOUR FOR THICKENING
Buerre Manie

TPT - 1 hour;
1 hour = refrigeration period

An absolute essential for the simplified thickening of soups and sauces, buerre manie is easily made. Tucked in a container in the refrigerator, it can be available whenever the need arises, that is, when you need just a little more thickening power. It is a unique way to thicken with flour since the combination of the fat with the flour means that you do not have to go through the process of making a roux to thicken and it also means there will be no lumps because the butter releases the starch grain by grain.

**1/4 cup whole wheat or unbleached white flour,
as preferred
1/4 cup butter**—*softened to room temperature*

Place a piece of waxed paper or plastic wrap on a plate. Refrigerate until required.

Put flour and butter into a mixing bowl. Using a wooden spoon or paddle, work the mixture until combined and smooth. Roll about a teaspoonful of the mixture into a ball and place on the cold plate. Continue until all the mixture has been formed into balls. Refrigerate for 1 hour.

Collect hardened *buerre manie* balls into a small plastic container. Cover tightly and refrigerate to use as needed.

Note: This recipe can be halved or doubled, when required.

Yields 48 one-teaspoonful balls

1/48 SERVING (i. e., per teaspoonful) –
PROTEIN = 0.1 g.; FAT = 1.0 g.; CARBOHYDRATE = 0.4 g.;
CALORIES = 11; CALORIES FROM FAT = 78%

Africa–**Mozambique**

SAUTÉED CABBAGE, CARROT, AND ONION WITH CUMIN AND OREGANO
Caril de Repolho

TPT - 1 hour and 7 minutes

This traditional vegetable dish of Mozambique is cooked until very thick. Its complex flavors make it a wonderful side dish. I find it to be one of those dishes which does not send me running to the store for this and that; I always have the necessary thises and thats on hand so it is often in our menu plans.

1 tablespoon *extra virgin* **olive oil**
1/2 cup sliced onion
3 garlic cloves—*very finely* **chopped**

1 cup canned, *diced* **tomatoes**
1/2 cup chopped green bell pepper
1 teaspoon HOMEMADE CURRY POWDER
   [see index] **or commercially-available mixture of choice**
1 teaspoon ground cumin
1 teaspoon crushed, dried oregano
1 large bay leaf—broken in half
1/2 teaspoon salt

3 cups cabbage shredded as for cabbage salad
1 carrot—peeled and cut into julienne pieces
1 cup VEGETABLE STOCK FROM SOUP *[see index]* **or other vegetarian stock of choice**

Freshly ground black pepper, to taste

In a large saucepan set over *LOW-MEDIUM* heat, heat oil. Add onions and garlic. Sauté until onions are soft and translucent, *being careful to allow neither the onions nor the garlic to brown.*

Add diced tomatoes, chopped green pepper, curry powder, ground cumin, crushed, dried oregano, bay leaf pieces, and salt. Cook, stirring, frequently, until very thick.

Add shredded cabbage, julienned carrot, and vegetable stock. Allow to come to simmer. Cook, stirring frequently for about 30 minutes, or until vegetables are tender and the sauce is thick.

Season with black pepper. Turn into a heated serving bowl.

Serve at once.

Yields 6 servings
adequate for 4 people

Notes: This recipe can be doubled, when required.

Leftovers make an interesting topping for soy burgers.

1/6 SERVING – PROTEIN = 1.5 g.; FAT = 2.1 g.; CARBOHYDRATE = 6.6 g.;
CALORIES = 47; CALORIES FROM FAT = 40%

MOZAMBICAN AVOCADO AND TANGERINE DESSERT
Sobremesa de Abacate

TPT - 10 minutes

In America avocados seem to be viewed either as a salad ingredient, a topping for tacos, or as an ingredients in guacamole. Few people that I know would make an avocado soup or an avocado dessert but avocados turn up in many unexpected dishes around the world. The avocado in this mousse-like dessert may be unexpected, but it is certainly appreciated. If you substitute orange juice for the tangerine juice, a necessity here at certain times of the year, do be sure to use juice with lots of pulp.

2 ripe avocados—peeled and pitted
3 tablespoons sugar

6 tablespoons tangerine juice

Ground cinnamon, to taste

In a mixing bowl, combine avocados and sugar. Using a potato masher or a fork, mash the avocado flesh well.

Add tangerine juice, *tablespoonful by tablespoonful*, working the juice into the avocado until you have a creamy mixture. Add more or less juice to achieve the texture you want. Divide among six tea cups or custard cups.

Sprinkle with ground cinnamon.

MOZAMBICAN AVOCADO AND TANGERINE DESSERT (cont'd)

Serve at once or refrigerate for no more than 30 minutes.

Yields 6 individual servings

Note: This recipe can be halved or doubled, when required.

1/6 SERVING – PROTEIN = 1.5 g.; FAT = 11.0 g.; CARBOHYDRATE = 12.8 g.; CALORIES = 146; CALORIES FROM FAT = 67%

MOZAMBICAN BANANA DESSERT
Bananas com Leite

TPT - 1 hour and 5 minutes (warm); 1 hour and 30 minutes (cold)

When a salad will satisfy for dinner, a dessert like this is added nutritional insurance. It satisfies too. The Portuguese certainly shared their love for rich desserts during the colonial period as this dish exemplifies. Sweetened condensed whole milk and egg yolks would be the preference of Mozambican cooks.

5 red bananas—peeled and sliced
2 teaspoons *finely* chopped lemon pulp*
1 tablespoon *cold* butter—*finely* chopped

1/2 can *fat-free* sweetened condensed milk
1/4 cup *fat-free* pasteurized eggs (the equivalent of 1 egg)

1 tablespoon grated coconut—fresh *or* desiccated
1/4 teaspoon ground cinnamon

Preheat oven to 300 degrees F. Prepare a pie plate or other oven proof plate by lightly coating with non-stick lecithin spray coating for baking.

Arrange banana slices in one layer on prepared plate. Scatter finely chopped lemon pulp as evenly over the bananas as possible. Scatter the chopped *cold* butter over the bananas.

In a small bowl, combine sweetened condensed milk and pasteurized eggs. Mix well. Pour over bananas.

Sprinkle with grated coconut and ground cinnamon. Bake in preheated 300 degree F. oven for 40 minutes, or until it is well set across the entire plate and lightly browned.

Serve warm or chilled, as preferred.

Notes: *We juice organic lemons and freeze the juice for our needs. If you drain the frozen juice, the lemon pulp called for in this recipe is easily obtained. Otherwise, juice a lemon and collect the pulp.

This recipe can be doubled when required. Be sure you have an oven-proof plate, such as a pie plate, that will accommodate the banana slices in a single layer.

Yields 6 servings
adequate for 4 people

1/6 SERVING – PROTEIN = 4.6 g.; FAT = 4.6 g.; CARBOHYDRATE = 43.9 g.; CALORIES = 211; CALORIES FROM FAT = 19%

Africa–**Mozambique**

SWEET EGG DESSERT WITH PAPAYA FROM MOZAMBIQUE
Ovos Moles de Papaia

TPT - 3 hours and 10 minutes;
30 minutes = cooling period, if to be served at room temperature;
2 hours = chilling period, if to be served cold

I am teased for taking a perfectly ripened slice of brie to make a brie paté. Blending a perfectly-ripened papaya to make this dessert takes some courage too but it is worth the sacrifice. If you have tasted the classic ovos moles in Portugal, you will be delighted to add this lower fat variation to your repertoire. This recipe is respectful of its historic origins but . . . so much more!

1 medium, ripe papaya (about 1 pound)—peeled, seeded, and coarsely chopped
3 tablespoons freshly squeezed lime juice—*strained*
3 tablespoons water

1 1/3 cups sugar
1 large cinnamon quill
4 whole cloves

3/4 cup *fat-free* **pasteurized eggs (the equivalent of 3 eggs)**

In the container of the electric blender or in the work bowl of the food processor fitted with steel knife, combine chopped papaya, *strained* lime juice, and water. Blend until a smooth purée is formed, scraping down the sides of the container as required. Press the purée through a fine sieve into a large, stainless steel saucepan.

Add sugar, cinnamon quill, and cloves. Mix well.

Attach a candy thermometer to the side of the pan set over *MEDIUM-HIGH* heat. Bring to the boil *while stirring constantly with a wire whisk*. Continue boiling and stirring until syrup reaches a temperature of 180 degrees F. on the candy thermometer. *Immediately remove syrup from heat.* Using a slotted spoon, remove and discard cinnamon quill and cloves.

Using the electric mixer, beat pasteurized eggs until slightly thickened—about 45 seconds. While continuing to beat, *pour hot papaya syrup into eggs in a very thin stream.* Continue beating until mixture is smooth and thickened.

Apportion the mixture among six dessert dishes or heat-resistant sherbet glasses. Allow to cool to room temperature for about 30 minutes, during which time it will continue to thicken.

Serve at room temperature or chill in the refrigerator for no more than 2 hours and serve well-chilled. This tends to separate so leftovers do not keep well.

Yields 6 individual servings

1/6 SERVING – PROTEIN = 3.3 g.; FAT = 0.7 g.; CARBOHYDRATE = 57.2 g.;
CALORIES = 237; CALORIES FROM FAT = 3%

Namibia

This large, sparsely populated country is named for the Namib Desert, a desert region dating from the Pleistocene Period thus making it one of the oldest desert regions on earth. In Namibia arable land is limited to less than one-percent of the land mass by two great deserts. The gravel plains and dunes of the Namib Desert stretch inland from the Atlantic Ocean along Namibia's entire coastline. The approximately 350,000-square-mile Kalahari Desert covers about one-third of Namibia, most of Botswana, and even extends into South Africa. Despite the lack of farm land, approximately fifty-percent of the Namibian population is involved in agriculture with a reported four thousand farmers owning half of that land. With very little rainfall, the least of any country in sub-Saharan Africa, subsistence farming is insufficient to sustain the population necessitating the importation of food; approximately fifty percent of the country's cereal requirements are imported. A land reform policy, similar to that executed in Zimbabwe, is planned through which land will be redistributed from the farmers who cultivate large farms for commercial sale to the landless black Namibians. Some say that this move may create a crisis and actually acerbate the lack of Nambian-grown food.

Namibia was first visited by the Portuguese in the 1400s, at about the same time that the Bantu drove out the remnants of existing tribes during the period of their great migration. Both Diogo Cão, in 1485, and Bartolomeu Dias, in 1486, came, explored, and moved on, not claiming the area for the Portuguese crown. It remained a loosely structured tribal region for centuries. In the nineteenth century, during "the grab for Africa," as it is sometimes called, Germany saw an opportunity to block Great Britain's acquisition of the land to the west of South Africa and to exploit the region's extensive non-petroleum mineral deposits, including diamonds. In 1884 Namibia became a German protectorate, known as German South-West Africa, and remained so until 1915 when the South Africans defeated the Germans garrisoned there and occupied German South-West Africa. After World War I, as with other German possessions, Namibia's fate fell to the League of Nations. Under Article 20 of the League of Nations the German colony was mandated to South Africa, then a dominion state under the British Crown. The mandate gave South African control of the territory, known then as South-West Africa. South Africa's racial policies were enforced in the territory and in 1948 the policy of apartheid was officially applied to Namibia. It was not until 1966 that the United Nations finally declared the League of Nations mandate terminated and the International Court of Justice declared South African presence in Namibia illegal. South Africa stubbornly continued its interference. In 1968 the United Nations acted to officially change the territory's name to Namibia. By 1973 the unrest in Namibia and the demands of its predominately black population were brought before the United Nations at which time the United Nations recognized the South West Africa People's Organization (SWAPO) as the official representative of the Namibian people. Full independence finally came in 1990 and Namibia made a complete transition from white minority apartheid rule.

Today fourteen and a half percent of GDP is contributed by tourism, especially ecotourism, which contributes over eighteen percent of all employment. Expanding education, now required through age sixteen, and curbing the widespread health issues associated with malaria and HIV/AIDS have become major objectives of this young parliamentary democracy.

Africa–Namibia

Goat Cheese

Black Olive *Tapenade* with Pine Nuts   or   Assorted Green and Black Olives

Dutch Oven Unkneaded Bread
Potbrod

~

Vegetable Soup with Chick Peas and Groundnut Butter

Rye Bread

~

Kiwi Slices

~~~~~~~~~~~~~~~~~~~~

**Oven – Roasted Root Vegetables
with Fresh Herbs and Mushrooms**
Braais

Mango Chutney

Pan-Grilled Asparagus Spears

~

Black-Eyed Peas
Oashingali
over

Rice or *Polenta*

Individual Sliced Bananas

Grilled Corn-on-the-Cob

~~~~~~~~~~~~~~~~~~~~

Banana *Strudel*
Bananestrudel

Orange Wedges with Prickly Pear Nectar or Kumquat Preserves

Guava – Cream Tapioca Pudding

Africa–**Namibia**

BLACK OLIVE *TAPENADE* WITH PINE NUTS
TPT - 24 hours and 7 minutes;
24 hours = flavor development period

In Namibia an assortment of olives or a tapenade is often served as part of a first course. A tapenade, made with black olives, can result in a delicious appetizer bruscheta but the typical mixture is made, not only with salty olives but also, with capers, and anchovy fillets. It is more than anybody's electrolyte balance should have to endure. We desalinated our life many years ago. A box of Salt Sense can last us several years. Instead of reaching for the myriad of salt varieties that challenge blood pressure levels today, I reach for grated Parmesan or pecorino Romano cheese if salt is needed. Granulated salt is useful to facilitate the shelling of hard-cooked eggs and for removing the bitterness from eggplant; it helps unwind the protein molecules when your goal is fluffy scrambled eggs; and it is a necessary addition to some potato dishes but reducing the sodium load is a worthy pursuit. This tapenade will amaze you because the addition of ground pine nuts gives it a creamy texture and moderates the sodium.

And, not only can this be served as an appetizer, it can be the taste sensation of a pasta entrée if a couple of tablespoonfuls is added to cooked and buttered fettucine. You will not soon forget that plate of fettucine.

1/3 cup pine nuts (*pignoli*)*

1 jar (5-6 ounces) pitted *Kalamata* olives—well-drained
2 tablespoons preserved capers—well-rinsed and well-drained
1 teaspoon *Dijon* mustard with white wine
1 teaspoon freshly squeezed lemon juice
1 garlic clove—*very finely* chopped

1 tablespoon *extra virgin* olive oil

In the work bowl of the food processor fitted with steel knife, process pine nuts (*pignoli*) until they form a paste, scraping down the bowl several times during the process.

Add well-drained olives and capers, mustard, lemon juice, and garlic. Process by pulsing the processor until the olive mixture is finely and uniformly chopped, scraping down the bowl several times as required.

Add olive oil and process only until oil has been mixed into the olive mixture. Transfer to a container or covered dish, cover, and refrigerate for at least 24 hours to allow for flavor development.**

Serve as a spread for dry toasts, bread, or crackers.

Notes: *When selecting pine nuts in your store or online, be sure to avoid the small, dull, oval nuts. These have been reported to leave an unpleasant aftertaste for days in those sensitive to a malady known as PNS, Pine Nut Syndrome. These generally are an export product of China, although they may be labeled as a product of Korea or Russia. Choose instead pine nuts grown in the Mediterranean. The large, elongated, brown-tipped pine nuts from the Italy are the most desirable, and, unfortunately, the most expensive.

**This will keep well for several weeks in the refrigerator.

If necessary, this recipe can be doubled.

Yields 24 servings
adequate for 6 people

1/24 SERVING – PROTEIN = 1.0 g.; FAT = 0.1 g.; CARBOHYDRATE = 0.5 g.;
CALORIES = 24; CALORIES FROM FAT = 79%

Africa–Namibia

DUTCH OVEN UNKNEADED BREAD
Potbrood

TPT - 21 hours and 2 minutes;
  18 hours = initial rising period;
  15 minutes = resting period;
  2 hours = second rising period

Potbrood are traditional South African breads first introduced by the Boer settlers. They were baked in cast iron pots, known as Dutch ovens, which were put into a pit in the ground and lined with hot coals. Today these pot breads are still baked in Dutch ovens but a barbecue has replaced the pit. The lid is turned upside down and filled with coals. An unkneaded pot or bowl bread has become popular in the United States which can be prepared in that old Dutch oven casserole that is probably in the back of your pantry. This recipe was adapted back in 2006 from Jim Lahey of the Sullivan Street Bakery; it requires only a small amount of quick-rise yeast and, yes, it really does not require kneading.

2 3/4 cups bread flour
1/4 cup whole wheat flour
1/4 teaspoon *instant or quick-rise* yeast*
1 1/4 teaspoons salt
1 1/2 cups plus 1 tablespoon water

Bread flour for dusting

In a mixing bowl, combine bread flour, whole wheat flour, instant or quick-rise yeast, and salt. Stir. Add water and stir until you have formed a sticky dough. Cover bowl with plastic wrap. Allow to rise for 18 hours at room temperature (about 70 degrees F.). Dough will be ready when the surface is covered with bubbles.

Dust a work surface with flour. Turn the dough out onto the floured surface. Sprinkle flour over the dough and fold it over itself several times. Cover with plastic wrap and allow the dough to rest for 15 minutes.

Place a cotton tea towel on the counter top. Dust it generously with flour*.

Dust hands and work surface with flour again and quickly shape the dough into a ball. Place it seam-side-down on the dusted tea towel. Cover with another tea towel. Allow to rise until doubled in size—about 2 hours.

About 1 1/2 hours into this rising, preheat oven to 425 degrees F. Place a 6-quart Dutch oven (cast iron, enamel, or ceramic) in oven as it heats.

When dough has risen and does not spring back when poked with a finger, carefully remove pot to a heat-resistant surface. Slide your hand under the towel and transfer the bread, seam-side-up into the *hot* pot. Shake pan a couple of times if dough is unevenly distributed. Cover pot with its lid and return to oven. Bake for 30 minutes. Remove lid and bake for about 20-30 minutes until loaf is evenly browned. Remove from oven and transfer loaf to a wire rack to cool.

Yields one 1 1/2-pound loaf

Notes: *This will not work with regular yeast.

**Corn meal or wheat bran can used to coat the tea towel, if preferred.

1/12 SERVING (i. e., per slice) –
PROTEIN = 3.5 g.; FAT = 0.025 g.; CARBOHYDRATE = 21.5 g.;
CALORIES = 100; CALORIES FROM FAT = <1%

Africa–**Namibia**

NAMIBIAN VEGETABLE SOUP WITH CHICK PEAS AND GROUNDNUT BUTTER
TPT - 51 minutes

Many African soups and stews get their protein punch from chick peas or groundnuts, the legume we know as the peanut. Nevertheless, every one of the dishes I have collected is slightly different, clearly reflective of agricultural availability. This is perhaps heartening to the hungry vegetarian who might visit Africa but close scrutiny of these dishes gives insight into the food crisis in Africa. So many times in our travels our vegetarian choice has been questioned with the logic that if you can afford to travel, then you can afford meat. Increased desertification, wars, drought, disease, and governmental mismanagement threaten the lives of Africans every day. To illustrate, just look at these statistics for Namibia—life expectancy as of 2012 was 52.2 years; infant mortality as of 2013 was 45.62 deaths in the first year of life per 1,000 live births. Here again, the ingenuity of the people with what is available, with vegetables that keep well through the year, must provide and sustain.

With freshly baked rye bread, this soup makes a very satisfying main course.

2 tablespoons *extra virgin* **olive oil**
3/4 cup *finely* **chopped onion**
1 large garlic clove—crushed and *very finely* chopped
1 slice fresh gingerroot—crushed and *very finely* chopped
1/4 teaspoon crushed red pepper flakes

1/2 teaspoon ground cinnamon
1/8 teaspoon freshly ground black pepper

1 quart VEGETABLE STOCK FROM SOUP *[see index] or* **other vegetarian stock of choice**
1 small potato—peeled and cubed
1 cup cubed pumpkin*
1/3 cup diced green pepper

1 cup *thinly* **sliced kale**—*well-rinsed*
1 cup canned chick peas (*garbanzos*)—*well-drained*
Salt, to taste

1 cup *boiling* **water**
2 tablespoons freshly ground, *unsalted, additive-free smooth* **peanut butter**

In a large kettle set over *MEDIUM* heat, heat oil. Add *finely* chopped onion, *very finely* chopped garlic and gingerroot, and crushed red pepper flakes. Sauté until onions are soft and translucent, *being careful not to allow vegetables to brown.*

Add cinnamon and black pepper. Sauté for 1 minute more.

Add vegetable stock, cubed potatoes and pumpkin, and diced green pepper. Stir and allow to come to boil. Reduce heat to *LOW-MEDIUM* and allow to cook for about 30 minutes, or until potatoes and pumpkin are tender. Stir occasionally.

Add *thinly* sliced kale and *well-drained* chick peas. Salt to taste. Cook, stirring frequently, until kale has wilted and chick peas have heated through.

In a small bowl, combine *boiling* water and peanut butter. Stir to combine well. Add to soup, stirring to integrate. Turn into a heated soup tureen.

Serve into heat soup bowls with large chunks of rye bread.

Yields 9 cupfuls

Notes: *If you do not have a fresh pumpkin, butternut or acorn winter squash can be substituted.

This recipe can be halved, but since it tastes even better the second day and it freezes well, I usually make a whole batch.

1/6 SERVING – PROTEIN = 3.1 g.; FAT = 4.3 g.; CARBOHYDRATE = 11.6 g.; CALORIES = 98; CALORIES FROM FAT = 39%

Africa—**Namibia**

OVEN – ROASTED ROOT VEGETABLES WITH FRESH HERBS AND MUSHROOMS
Braais

TPT - 1 hour and 5 minutes

Roasting vegetables in or by the fire is a technique that is probably as old as man's first cooked meal. Cooking over a camp fire or the barbecue grill is far less reliable than is oven–roasting. By including oven-roasted vegetables in a menu you can give even the simplest meals wonderful taste and genuine appeal. You will probably have to clean the oven after roasting, but the taste of this roasted feast is worth it.

1/2 large knob celery root (celeriac)—peeled and cut into 1/2-inch-thick slices
1 small rutabaga (yellow or Canadian turnip)—peeled and cut into 1/2-inch-thick slices
3 quarts *boiling* **water**

3 tablespoons *extra virgin* **olive oil**
8 small, red, new potatoes—well-scrubbed
3 medium carrots—scraped or pared and cut into 4-inch lengths
3 medium parsnips—peeled and cut into 4-inch lengths
2 large leeks—*white and light green portions only*—*very well-rinsed*, **and sliced into 3-inch pieces**
8 white boiling onions—dry, outside leaves removed and an X sliced into root end
4 shallots—outside, dry leaves removed
2 sprigs of fresh oregano—well-washed*
2 sprigs of fresh rosemary—well-washed**
5 or 6 whole sage leaves—well-washed***
2 sprigs of fresh thyme—well-washed****
Salt, to taste
Freshly ground mixed whole peppercorns—red, black, and white—to taste

10 ounces whole *crimini* **mushrooms—trimmed,** *well-rinsed and brushed to remove any foreign matter*
6 large garlic cloves—*unpeeled*

2 tablespoon grated Parmesan *or pecorino* **Romano cheese, as preferred**

Preheat oven to 350 degrees F. Prepare a 13 x 9 x 2-inch baking pan, preferably non-stick coated, by coating with non-stick lecithin spray coating.

Blanch knob celery root (celeriac) and rutabaga slices in *boiling* water for 3 minutes. Drain well and pat dry.

Drizzle olive oil over prepared pan surface. Add vegetables including blanched knob celery root and rutabaga slices. Toss and stir to coat vegetables with oil. *Remove leek pieces and set aside until required.* Add sprigs of oregano, rosemary, sage, and thyme. Toss again to coat herbs with oil. Spread vegetables out in baking pan to form one layer. Season lightly with salt and ground mixed peppercorns.

Bake in preheated 350 degree F. oven *undisturbed* for 30 minutes.

Using wooden spoons or spatulas, turn vegetables. *Add reserved leek pieces,* mushrooms, and garlic cloves. Continue roasting for an additional 25-30 minutes, stirring occasionally to encourage even roasting. The outer surfaces of the vegetables will become crisp and browned while the inside will become soft. Discard herb sprigs.

Turn roasted vegetables into a heated serving bowl or onto a serving platter.

Serve at once, allowing those who wish to squeeze out the roasted garlic flesh, to do so. Pass grated cheese.*****

Yields 6 servings
adequate for 4 people

Notes: *Once you have grown and dried your own oregano *(Oregano vulgare),* you will never again buy that which passes for dried oregano on the spice shelves of grocery stores! There are several varieties of oregano and all, with the exception of Mexican oregano, are prolific and very hardy perennials, thriving in Zones 5-9. Oregano taste varies from plant to plant. Find your favorite and propagate from the mother plant to maintain the flavor you want since seedlings do not always produce the same flavor of the mother plant. By keeping the oregano from going to seed you will not only maintain the consistent flavor you enjoy, but you will also keep the all-too-easily propagated plant under control. We have moved the variety we prefer several times, planting it in each new herb garden.

Africa–Namibia

**OVEN – ROASTED ROOT VEGETABLES
WITH FRESH HERBS AND MUSHROOMS** (cont'd)

**Upright Rosemary *(Rosemarinus officinalis)* is a highly scented, tender perennial in northern climates which can be brought indoors in the fall to provide both scent to your kitchen and leaves for seasoning well into the winter. It can be grown as an evergreen shrub in extreme southern zones. Both the leaves and flowers, which range from deep blue to pink to white depending upon the cultivar, are used in cooking and garnishing. Prostrate rosemary *(Rosemarinus prostratus)* is a creeping variety which is most attractive in the garden. The blue-flowered creeping cultivar is quite frost sensitive and it too must be treated as an annual in the North. However, a showy white-flowered prostrate variety is more hardy, if you can find it.

***Sage *(Salvia officinalis)* is an assertive and aromatic herb, rarely used in vegetarian dishes. It is, however, a delicious addition to herb breads and pasta dishes. Used judiciously, it also compliments both eggs and cheeses. Of the many varieties of this hardy and easily-grown perennial, a variety call 'Berggarten' is our usual choice for this dish. It will survive well into the winter, if mulched with evergreen boughs. If you plan to grow your own sage, rosemary, lavender, and thyme are good companion plantings and the close proximity of this combination seems to keep insect pests away. Dried sage can not be substituted in this recipe.

****Try lemon thyme, English thyme, French thyme, nutmeg thyme, or combinations of the many interesting varieties of thyme that please you.

*****If desired, this dish may be served with any of a myriad of sauces that please your palate.

Winter savory *(Satureja montana)* makes a nice addition to this herb mixture, if you find it available or if you grow it in your herb garden. It is a low-growing perennial, hardy in Zones 6-9, with a stronger, peppery taste which is best reserved for use in a mixed-vegetable/herb dish such as this or with stronger-tasting vegetables such as turnips and members of the cabbage family. Winter savory is not fussy about soil conditions, in fact preferring organically poor soil, but really requires full sun for best growing form. Summer savory *(Satureja* [the satyr] *hortensis),* on the other hand, is a quite different annual herb which can not be substituted in this dish.

When required, this recipe may be halved or doubled.

1/6 SERVING (with 1/2 teaspoonful grated cheese) –
PROTEIN = 8.2 g.; FAT = 6.7 g.; CARBOHYDRATE = 48.2 g;
CALORIES = 272; CALORIES FROM FAT = 23%

NAMIBIAN BLACK-EYED PEAS
Oashingali
TPT - 10 minutes

Sadly, I rarely find fresh black-eyed peas in my markets except in late December and early January. They are so crisp and so nutty that there is really no substitute for them. Canned black-eyed peas are, to my mind, a completely different vegetable. The nuttiness seems to be gone and they are generally mushy and salty. Nevertheless, I have to assume that most of my readers will have access to the canned version and do not want to wait around until New Year's to experience this Namibian dish, touted by many as the national dish of Namibia.

1 can (15 ounces) black-eyed peas—*well-drained**
1/4 cup VEGETABLE STOCK FROM SOUP
  [see index] *or* other vegetarian stock of choice
1/4 teaspoon ground red pepper (cayenne), or to taste *or* 1 hot, red *chili* pepper, crushed and *very finely* chopped**

In a saucepan set over *LOW* heat, combine the black-eyed peas, stock, and ground red pepper (cayenne). Allow to heat through.

Serve over rice or *polenta*.

Yields 6 servings
adequate for 4 people

NAMIBIAN BLACK-EYED PEAS (cont'd)

Notes: *When shopping for black-eyed peas, be sure not to select the item labeled "Southern style." It will most probably contain either ham or bacon and bacon fat.

**If you choose to use a fresh, hot *chili*, wear vinyl gloves when seeding and chopping the pepper.

This recipe can be doubled.

1/6 SERVING – PROTEIN = 5.2 g.; FAT = 0.0 g.; CARBOHYDRATE = 9.9 g.; CALORIES = 53; CALORIES FROM FAT = 0%

BANANA *STRUDEL*
Bananestrudel

TPT - 3 hours and 45 minutes;
2 hours = raisin soaking period;
30 minutes = pastry rising period

A mid-afternoon stroll in the urban centers of Namibia will help you find the best pastry shops because Namibians ritually stop for coffee or tea and a sustaining pastry. Introduced to apple strudel by German settlers, a small piece of strudel is still a satisfying choice. This is really an easily made dessert now that we have the availability of puff pastry in the freezer department of most grocery stores. My grandmother taught me to make puff pastry and I refined the technique with the helpful teaching of Julia Child's but today it seems like a very big production when there is an alternative.

1/4 orange juice
1/4 cup water
1/3 cup *preservative-free* raisins

1 sheet *frozen* puff pastry—*defrosted, but still cool*

2 medium bananas—diced
1 teaspoon cinnamon sugar
1 tablespoon *light* brown sugar

Sweetened whipped cream—for garnish—if desired

In a small saucepan set over *MEDIUM* heat, bring orange juice and water to the boil. Remove from heat. Add raisins. Cover and set aside for 2 hours to allow the raisins to plump. Drain thoroughly.

Preheat oven to 400 degrees F. Prepare a cookie sheet by lining with parchment paper.

On a cool surface, roll the puff pastry to double its size. Fold in half and roll again. Turn and roll the pastry again to double its size and then fold in half again. About *one inch* in from one of longest edges of the rolled pastry sheet spoon the diced bananas so that they are distributed from one end of the pastry to the other. Spread the bananas across the pastry, *leaving one inch all the way around*. Sprinkle the cinnamon sugar and brown sugar over the bananas from one end to the other. Turn the left and side margins toward the center. Press gently. Take the pastry edge nearest to you and roll it *tightly* over the fruit. Continue rolling until you have a tight roll. Moisten the edge and ends and secure. Place sealed-side-down on prepared baking sheet.

Allow to the pastry to rise at room temperature for 30 minutes.

Preheat oven to 400 degrees F. while pastry is rising.

Bake in preheated 400 degree F. oven for about 35-40 minutes, or until golden brown. Remove from baking sheet to a serving platter or cutting board. Allow to cool to room temperature—about 15 minutes.

Using a sharp knife, slice and transfer to a dessert plate.

Yields 12 slices

Note: This can be halved, using a half-sheet of puff pastry, if required.

Africa–**Namibia**

BANANA *STRUDEL* (cont'd)

1/12 SERVING (i. e., per slice exclusive of whipped cream garnish) –
PROTEIN = 1.8 g.; FAT = 5.7 g.; CARBOHYDRATE = 21.6 g.;
CALORIES = 144; CALORIES FROM FAT = 36%

GUAVA – CREAM TAPIOCA PUDDING

TPT - 1 hour and 40 minutes;
5 minutes = pre-cooking tapioca saturation period;
20 minutes = cooling period;
1 hour = refrigeration period

Both cassava (tapioca) and guava are ingredients used by Namibian cooks so I set out to create a dessert. It was late February and my options were going to be limited; fresh guavas are rare in the middle of Pennsylvania even in June when they are in season. Guava paste and guava juice, however, are generally available. The next thing I knew we were sitting down to bowls of a new version of an old comfort food. Trust me, this is not that old nursery pudding that everybody jokes about.

1/3 cup sugar
3 tablespoons *quick-cooking* tapioca
1 3/4 cups guava juice *or* nectar
1 cup light cream *or* half and half
1/4 cup *fat-free* pasteurized eggs (the equivalent
　of 1 egg) *or* 1 egg—well-beaten

In a saucepan, combine sugar, tapioca, guava nectar, cream, and pasteurized eggs. Stir to mix thoroughly. *Allow to stand for about 5 minutes* to allow tapioca to become saturated with the liquid.

Set over *LOW-MEDIUM* heat and, stirring frequently, cook pudding until it thickens. *Be careful not to allow the pudding to boil or you will risk curdling.* Remove from heat. Set aside for 20 minutes to cool slightly. Stir again.

Divide among six dessert dishes or sherbet glasses or, if preferred, turn into a serving bowl. Refrigerate for at least 1 hour to allow for firm setting.

Refrigerate leftovers.

Yields 6 servings
adequate for 4 people

1/6 SERVING – PROTEIN = 2.5 g.; FAT = 3.7 g.; CARBOHYDRATE = 29.4 g.;
CALORIES = 162; CALORIES FROM FAT = 21%

Niger

Thousands of years ago the northern portion of Niger, a country about twice the size of the state of Texas, was covered with fertile grasslands fed by abundant water. Archeological findings confirm that there was a culture of advanced complexity living there in 10,000 BC even before the period referenced by some as the Green Sahara period from about 7500 BC to 3000 BC. The area which is now so inhospitable was hospitable to humans and to the wildlife and plants upon which humans depend. Evidence of a huge freshwater lake, ample fish, and wetlands has been confirmed in the area now covered by the ever-advancing Sahara Dessert and satellite images reveal enormous subterranean lakes deep under the dessert that still hold water.

During the past two thousand years most of what is now Niger has been lost to the Sahara displacing the nomadic Tuaregs of Berber and Arab descent, one of Niger's earliest tribal groups and today one of its poorest. About eighty percent of their national territory is desert. Most of the population of this landlocked country lives in the south near the Niger River, the river for which the country is named. The almost sixteen million people known as Nigeriens, as contrasted with Nigerians who live in the neighboring country of Nigeria, have lived under five constitutions since their independence from France in 1960 and are now ruled by a military junta, the third such military government that has tried to bring this developing country from subsistence to prosperity. Niger's development is hampered by its landlocked geographical position, the lack of arable land, and the lack of an educated population. Niger's known deposits of gold and oil, being developed by a joint venture with China, represent potential income in the years to come. The deposits of uranium ore, now of decreased demand in the world and which have provided over seventy-percent of export revenues, and coal may still help the economy but little else is made or grown in quantities sufficient for export. Further, Niger's lack of a deep-water port limits their ability to export efficiently. The Nigerien government is seriously challenged to feed its population, much less consider exportation of agricultural products. Niger lacks grasslands to support even the most rudimentary animal husbandry and experiences frequent droughts and locust plagues, as in the period between 1968 and 1975 and then again in 2010. These drought periods precipitated wide-spread famine and increased the already high infant and child mortality rates. With almost fifty percent of the population under the age of fifteen today, Niger is seriously challenged to improve the overall nutrition of its population, provide improved health care and family planning information, expand its education system beyond the compulsory six years, and create jobs for this future workforce, jobs that do not degrade further their environment or natural resources.

I have chosen to include a menu from the country of Niger because women there have been challenged to feed their families for centuries. Recipes are passed orally from mother to daughter and, as a result, I have found few Nigerien recipes and not a single book to educate me. I resisted the collective "West African" approach, so convenient because Niger was part of French West Africa from 1896-1922, and the "similar to Nigeria" dismissal. This, thankfully, is where the Internet community of women has stepped forward and through their sharing we have learned together. By necessity, simplicity is the overriding characteristic of Nigerien cuisine but British, Portuguese, and French influences are apparent in some recipes as are influences brought from North Africa by traders, travelers and migrant workers, invaders, and immigrants. Dishes borrowed from neighboring cuisines and spices, such as nutmeg, cinnamon, ginger, cloves, and saffron, which were gifts of the Arabs, have created a truly international cuisine found today almost exclusively in the cities.

Africa–Niger

Mango, Pineapple, and Apricot Salad
Salad de Mangue aux Ananas et Abricot

~~~~~~~~~~~~~~~~~~~~~~

Meatballs and Vegetables Skillet Dinner
O Jo Jo

Deep-Fried Black-Eyed Peas with Bananas
Cecena

~~~~~~~~~~~~~~~~~~~~~~

Sweet *Couscous* Pudding with Raisins and Pineapple
Caakiri

MANGO, PINEAPPLE, AND APRICOT SALAD FROM NIGER
Salad de Mangue aux Ananas et Abricot

TPT - 34 minutes;
30 minutes = refrigeration period

This recipe celebrates the treasure of luscious tropical sweetness grown in the southern areas of the sub-Saharan nation of Niger. My mother often served a fruit salad on Sunday evening in the days when Sunday dinner was served at one-o'clock and Sunday night suppers were always light meals that inevitably featured comfort foods. This salad can be served as a lovely side salad or a refreshing dessert.

1/2 cup apricot nectar
2 1/2 tablespoons freshly squeezed lemon juice

1 ripe mango—cut into large chunks
1 cup fresh pineapple chunks
4 fresh, pitted apricots *or* firm, canned apricots, if necessary—quartered

In a small bowl, combine apricot nectar and lemon juice.

In a large, shallow mixing bowl, combine mango and pineapple chunks with quartered apricots. Pour juice–nectar mixture over. Refrigerate for at least 30 minutes, basting the fruits with juice frequently.

Serve into small fruit bowls if serving as a salad; serve into sherbet glasses or wine glasses if serving as a dessert.

Yields 6 servings
adequate for 6 people

Note: This recipe can be halved or doubled, when required.

1/6 SERVING – PROTEIN = 0.7 g.; FAT = 5.1 g.; CARBOHYDRATE = 14.8 g.;
CALORIES = 59; CALORIES FROM FAT = 9%

MEATBALLS AND VEGETABLES SKILLET DINNER IN THE STYLE OF NIGER
O Jo Jo

TPT - 40 minutes

When an online correspondent suggested this skillet meal to me she did not know that I was a vegetarian so she went to great lengths to describe how she made her meatballs from ground beef. She then said, "Add some vegetables," without specifying vegetables that would be appropriate to a dinner in Niger. I have, therefore, created this skillet supper with soy meatballs and an assortment of vegetables and all my thanks to the cook in Niamey who was so gracious and who called her dish "o jo jo."

Africa–Niger

MEATBALLS AND VEGETABLES SKILLET DINNER IN THE STYLE OF NIGER (cont'd)

2 quarts *boiling* water
1 1/2 cups quartered new or baby potatoes
 —well-scrubbed and unpeeled

1 tablespoon *extra virgin* olive oil
1 tablespoon butter
1 medium onion—chopped

1 package (9 ounces) vegetarian "meatballs"
1 cup whole green beans—well-washed and trimmed
1/4 cup diced green bell pepper

3/4 cup canned, *diced* tomatoes
Freshly ground black pepper, to taste
Several dashes ground red pepper (cayenne)

In a saucepan set over *MEDIUM-HIGH* heat, parboil potatoes in boiling water for 10-12 minutes. Drain.

In a large skillet set over *MEDIUM* heat, heat oil and butter. Add chopped onion and parboiled potatoes. Sauté until onion is soft and translucent, *being careful to allow neither the potatoes nor the onion to brown. Reduce heat to LOW-MEDIUM.*

Add soy meatballs, green beans, and diced green pepper. Cook, stirring frequently, until meatballs are heated through and vegetables are *crisp-tender*.

Add diced tomatoes, black pepper, and ground red pepper (cayenne). Cook, stirring frequently, until all is heated through and the tomato sauce has thickened. Turn into a heated, shallow serving bowl.

Serve at once.

Yields 6 servings
adequate for 4 people

Note: This recipe can be halved or doubled, when required.

1/6 SERVING – PROTEIN = 9.6 g.; FAT = 6.5 g.; CARBOHYDRATE = 13.0 g.;
CALORIES = 136; CALORIES FROM FAT = 43%

NIGERIEN DEEP-FRIED BLACK-EYED PEAS WITH BANANAS
Cecena
TPT - 17 minutes

This crumbled, crisp black-eyed preparation is so very different. It reminds me a bit of the texture of the fried clams served up at Howard Johnson restaurants for decades. Although you can certainly cook dried black-eyed peas to make this dish, I have found that very well-drained canned black-eyed peas are a great time saver. Since you are going to blend the bean and onion mixture, the soft texture of the canned beans is actually a plus. Be aware that canned black-eyed peas that are labeled "Southern style" contain bacon and bacon fat.

Be prepared to hear the question, "Are you sure this is made from black-eyed peas?"

Oil for deep-frying

1 can (15 ounces) black-eyed peas—*well-drained*
1 small onion—chopped
1/4 teaspoon *jalapeño chili* sauce

1 large egg

6 bananas

Heat oil for deep-frying in a wok to about 365 degrees F.*

In the food processor fitted with steel knife, process *well-drained* black-eyed peas, chopped onion, and *jalapeño chili* sauce until of uniform consistency.

Add egg. Process to integrate.

Deep-fry, a few tablespoonfuls at a time. Remove the oil with a skimmer. Transfer to paper toweling to drain.

Place a whole, peeled banana on each plate. Slice about eight diagonal cuts into each banana. Twist the bananas gently into a crescent. Serve fried black-eyed peas into the curve of the crescent. Accompany with extra hot sauce, of choice.

Yields 6 servings

Notes: *Using a wok to fry these fritters decreases considerably the amount of oil used.

This recipe can be halved when required.

Africa–Niger

**NIGERIEN DEEP-FRIED BLACK-EYED PEAS
WITH BANANAS** (cont'd)

1/6 SERVING – PROTEIN = 7.7 g.; FAT = 5.3 g.; CARBOHYDRATE = 38.0 g.;
CALORIES = 209; CALORIES FROM FAT = 23%

NIGERIEN SWEET *COUSCOUS* PUDDING
WITH RAISINS AND PINEAPPLE
Caakiri

TPT - 4 hours and 16 minutes;
3 hours = raisin soaking period;
1 hour = chilling period

I have seen this recipe called "chakery" and "thiakry"; the name seems to vary from region to region. I have also seen reference to this recipe made with rice instead of couscous. Everybody makes rice puddings but Nigeriens uniquely use couscous. It is luscious, nutritious, not too sweet, and very easy to make.

1/4 cup *preservative-free dark* raisins
1 cup *boiling* water

1/2 cup *whole wheat couscous*
1 cup *boiling* water

1 1/2 teaspoons butter

1/3 cup light cream *or* half and half
1/4 cup PLAIN YOGURT *[see index] or*
   commercially-available plain yogurt
1/4 cup *fat-free* dairy sour cream
3 tablespoons sugar
1/2 teaspoon pure vanilla extract
1/8 teaspoon freshly grated nutmeg

1 tablespoon crushed pineapple—fresh *or*
   canned in juice

In a small bowl or Pyrex measuring cup, soak raisins in 1 cupful *boiling* water for 3 hours. Drain thoroughly. Set aside until required.

In a saucepan set over *MEDIUM* heat, combine *couscous* and 1 cupful *boiling* water. Allow to come back to the boil, remove from heat, cover, and allow to steam for 10 minutes, or until all of liquid has been absorbed.

Add butter.

While *couscous* is steaming, in a mixing bowl, combine light cream, yogurt, sour cream, sugar, vanilla extract, and grated nutmeg. Using a wire whisk, blend thoroughly.

Add well-drained raisins, cooked *couscous*, and crushed pineapple. Stir to mix thoroughly. Turn into a serving dish. Refrigerate for at least 1 hour.

Serve well-chilled.

Yields 6 servings
adequate for 4 people

Note: This recipe can be halved or doubled, when required.

1/6 SERVING – PROTEIN = 4.5 g.; FAT = 2.7 g.; CARBOHYDRATE = 30.7 g.;
CALORIES = 162; CALORIES FROM FAT = 15%

Nigeria

The first Europeans to reach Nigeria were the Portuguese who established a slave trade in the 1400s. Many of the foods that are staples today returned with the Portuguese as ballast in the ships that carried enslaved people to the New World. Pepper, cinnamon, and nutmeg came to Nigeria in much the same way, with those who traded along the east coast of Africa, India, and Asia and chanced to drop anchor off the mangrove swamps that dominated Nigeria's coastline. The Portuguese were not the only traders who made port along the Nigerian coast. By the 1700s the British dominated the slave trade in Nigeria. The trafficking in slaves gradually was replaced with trade in commodities such as lumber and palm oil.

Today Nigeria is the seventh most populated country in the world. It has been confirmed by archaeologists that there was human habitation in this region since at least 9000 BC. The Bantu, who migrated to and settled in central and southern Africa in the first and second millennium BC, are believed to have begun their journey across Africa from a homeland that is now the Federal Republic of Nigeria. In the northern portion of the modern nation of Nigeria, near the cities of Kano and Kasina, the Hausa kingdoms and the Bornu Empire, near Lake Chad, operated as a destination for the north-south trade between the Berbers and the people of the tropical forests who sold slaves, ivory, and kola nuts as early as 1000 AD. The Berbers exchanged the important commodity of salt for these along with cloth, weapons, brass, cowrie shells, and glass beads.

The British expanded their trade into the interior after the Napoleonic Wars and in 1914 the area, including present-day Nigeria, became known as the Colony and Protectorate of Nigeria. The British ruled the colony in a unique manner. Until independence in 1960 the northern and southern regions were not administered as a single colony due to the difficulty of governing two populations with vastly different religious beliefs and the religiously-based governmental structures already in place. In 1963 Nigeria severed its ties with Great Britain altogether and declared the Nigerian First Republic. A military *coup* in 1966 ended the First Republic and the political climate dissolved into *coups* and counter-*coups* and internal strife that led to a war known as the Nigerian–Biafran War when Eastern Nigerian formed a break-away republic which they named Biafra. Finally in 1970 Biafra was reintegrated into Nigeria and in 1979 a Second Republic, patterned after the United States governing system, was declared. The Second Republic survived until overthrown in a palace *coup* in 1983. A second palace *coup* took place in 1985. In 1999 a Fourth Republic was formed through popular election, ending the brief Third Republic, but it too has been plagued with religious unrest. Nevertheless, the results of a popular election resulted in a smooth transfer of power in 2007.

Sweetpotatoes, plantains and other tropical fruits, peanuts, cassava, millet, rice, corn, black-eyed peas/beans, and tomatoes are basic staples here as they are in most of the cuisines of Central and West Africa but in each African cuisine a distinct signature of the nation of origin is apparent. For example, *jollop* rice, a rice dish with tomatoes in broth which is eaten all over West Africa, is also eaten in Nigeria and any Nigerian cook will confirm that their version is *the* authentic version.

Africa–Nigeria

*This is a wonderful soup-based menu that takes very basic foods
and really shows them off.
It is a satisfying menu that leaves just enough room
to sample some of Nigeria's sweet dishes.*

Tropical Fruit Salad

~

Puréed Potato and Sweetpotato Soup
Obe

Coconut – Bean Soup with Rice
Obe

Pan-Grilled Plantains with Peanuts
Boli – Bopa

~

Nigerian Seasoning Mixture
Suya

~

Ginger Cake

Tapioca Pudding with Cloves

Sweet Rice Clusters

Fried Dough Balls
Chin Chin

NIGERIAN TROPICAL FRUIT SALAD

TPT - 2 hours and 5 minutes;
2 hours = flavor development period

Large papayas from South America are now increasingly available in grocery stores. They are usually better priced than are the small ones that come from Hawaii but there is a trade-off because they are less sweet and there is always some papaya left over. This simple, quickly-prepared, and totally delicious salad is a perfect way to use up the other half of those giant papayas. We serve this as a salad or as a dessert.

**1/2 large South American "Maradol" papaya—
  peeled, seeded, and chopped into large chunks
2 medium bananas**—sliced into large chunks
1/2 cup pineapple tidbits—fresh *or* canned in juice
**1/2 cup freshly squeezed orange juice
1 tablespoon sugar
1 three-inch piece of cinnamon quill**

In a mixing bowl, combine papaya and banana chunks, pineapple tidbits, orange juice, sugar, and cinnamon quill. Stir gently to coat all the fruits with orange juice. Cover and refrigerate for 2 hours to allow for flavors to marry.

Serve chilled with a slotted spoon.

Yields 6 servings
adequate for 4 people

Note: This recipe can be halved, when required.

1/6 SERVING – PROTEIN = 0.9 g.; FAT = 0.4 g.; CARBOHYDRATE = 19.5 g.;
CALORIES = 77; CALORIES FROM FAT = 5%

Africa—**Nigeria**

NIGERIAN PURÉED POTATO AND SWEETPOTATO SOUP
Obe

TPT - 1 hour and 12 minutes;
10 minutes = cooling period

Cooks in the island nations of the Caribbean make a soup similar to this. The version from Nigeria, undoubtedly the model for many in the New World, is far more complex and is punctuated by hot chilies. The base for this soup includes both white potatoes, rhizomes of the Nightshade family, and sweetpotatoes, rhizomes of the Morning Glory family, and freezes beautifully, making it a treasured resource in our freezer.

2 tablespoons peanut oil
1 cup *finely* chopped onion
1 large clove garlic—crushed and *finely* chopped

1 large carrot—pared or scraped and chopped
1 large sweetpotato—peeled and chopped
2 medium white *or* Yukon gold potatoes
   —peeled and chopped
2 fresh *jalapeño* peppers—seeds and stems
   removed and *finely* chopped *or* 1 teaspoon
   jalapeño chili sauce, or to taste

1 1/2 cups canned, *crushed* tomatoes
3 cups VEGETABLE STOCK FROM SOUP
   [see index] *or* other vegetarian stock of choice
1 small slice fresh gingerroot
Pinch sugar
1/4 teaspoon salt
1/4 freshly ground black pepper, or to taste

1/2 cup light cream *or* half and half

In a kettle set over *MEDIUM* heat, heat oil. Add *finely* chopped onion and garlic. Sauté until onions *are soft and translucent, being careful not to allow any of the vegetables to brown.*

Add chopped carrot, sweetpotato, and potatoes with *finely* chopped hot peppers or *jalapeño* sauce. Sauté for several minutes.

Add crushed tomatoes, vegetable stock, gingerroot, sugar, salt, and black pepper. Allow to come to boil. *Reduce heat to LOW.* Allow to simmer for about 30 minutes. Remove from heat and allow to cool for about 10 minutes.

Using an electric blender or food processor fitted with steel knife, purée the soup in several batches until very smooth. Set a sieve over clean saucepan and pour the puréed soup into the saucepan.*

Pour cream into puréed soup and integrate it using a wire whisk. Place over *LOW* heat and allow to heat through.

When ready to serve, turn into a heated soup tureen and serve into heated soup bowls.

Yields about 7 1/2 cupfuls

Notes: *If desired, the soup base may be frozen at this point. Leftovers may also be frozen for a future menu.

This recipe is easily doubled, when required.

1/10 SERVING (i. e., about 3/4 cupful) –
PROTEIN = 2.0 g.; FAT = 3.5 g.; CARBOHYDRATE = 14.2 g.;
CALORIES = 97; CALORIES FROM FAT = 32%

NIGERIAN COCONUT – BEAN SOUP WITH RICE
Obe

TPT - 43 minutes

When a main course can be assembled as quickly as can this soup, the cook enjoys the meal as much as do the rest of the diners. Second helpings, I find, are generally the rule when this luscious and nutritious soup fills the tureen. It is a soup version of coconut rice with red beans, a thick main-course stew. I have found that this soup appeals more to the western palate than does the thick stew. Plan to make the rice early in the day and refrigerate it until you begin the soup preparation. If you choose to cook dry kidney beans rather than using canned beans, these too can be cooked early in the day or the day before.

Africa – Nigeria

NIGERIAN COCONUT – BEAN SOUP WITH RICE (cont'd)

3 tablespoons butter
1/2 cup *finely* chopped onion

1/2 cup *finely* chopped green bell pepper
1 1/2 teaspoons HOMEMADE CURRY POWDER
  [see index] or commercially-available curry powder mixture of choice
1/8 teaspoon ground red pepper (cayenne), or to taste

1 cup canned, *diced* tomatoes in purée

1 can (15.5 ounces) red kidney beans—well-drained
1 can (14.4 ounces) *light, preservative-free* coconut milk
2 cups water

1 cup *cooked*, long grain white *or* brown rice, as preferred
1/2 teaspoon salt
1/4 teaspoon freshly ground black pepper

In a kettle set over *MEDIUM* heat, melt butter. Add *finely* chopped onions and sauté until onion are soft and translucent, *being careful not to allow onions to brown*.

Add finely chopped green pepper and curry powder. Cook, stirring constantly, for several minutes.

Add diced tomatoes and cook, stirring constantly, for several more minutes.

Add kidney beans, coconut milk, and water. Allow to come to the simmer. Reduce heat to *LOW-MEDIUM* and simmer for about 12 minutes. *Do not allow to boil.*

Add *cooked* rice and simmer for another 5-7 minutes.

Season with salt and pepper. Turn into a heated soup tureen.

Serve into heated soup plates. Refrigerate leftovers and *reheat* gently for a second appearance.

Yields 8 cupfuls

Notes: This recipe can be halved, when required.

Dishes containing coconut milk do no lend themselves well to freezing.

1/8 SERVING (about 1 cupful) –
PROTEIN = 4.6 g.; FAT = 5.6 g.; CARBOHYDRATE = 18.3 g.;
CALORIES = 138; CALORIES FROM FAT = 37%

NIGERIAN PAN – GRILLED PLANTAINS WITH PEANUTS
Bali-Bapa
TPT - 36 minutes

Plantain (plantano in Spanish; banane in French) is a general name for a number of starchy, mild-tasting members of the banana family which must be cooked to be edible. Generally used as a vegetable and not as a fruit, they are increasingly available in grocery stores but can always be found in Latin American, Caribbean, and African groceries. Colors, when ripe, vary dramatically from greens and yellows to reds and blacks but at least one variety or another is usually available in our store.

Raw peanuts have generally been available only at natural food stores. They are now available from a national nut distributor in grocery stores, in the nut section, and in discount stores, in the snack section.

1/2 cup *raw* peanuts with skins

4 medium, *firm* plantains—peeled*
1/2 teaspoon olive oil

Preheat oven to 250 degrees F.

Spread peanuts out on pie plate. Bake peanuts in preheated oven for about 10 minutes, or until toasted and fragrant. Set aside until required.

Preheat GRILL PAN over *MEDIUM-HIGH* heat until hot.**

Brush peeled plantains with olive oil. Grill on hot grill pan until well-marked and heated through—about 7 minutes. Turn and grill on the other side for 7 minutes to be sure that plantains are heated through completely.

Cut into large chunks. Place on a heated serving dish and sprinkle *toasted* peanuts over.

Serve at once.

Yields 6 servings
adequate for 4 people

Africa–Nigeria

NIGERIAN PAN – GRILLED PLANTAINS WITH PEANUTS (cont'd)

Notes: *Ripe plantains yield to gentle pressure and can be stored in the refrigerator for several days after they have ripened. Wrap in plastic wrap if you choose refrigerator storage.

**If preferred, the plantains can be prepared under a hot broiler. Be sure to turn several times to insure that the plantains are cooked through.

This recipe may be halved or doubled, when required.

1/6 SERVING – PROTEIN = 4.8 g.; FAT = 4.9 g.; CARBOHYDRATE = 34.0 g.;
CALORIES = 175; CALORIES FROM FAT = 25%

NIGERIAN SEASONING MIXTURE
Suya
TPT - 4 minutes

The amount of ground red pepper used by Nigerians in their seasoning mixtures is astounding to the Western palate. The amount that we use in this version is "one-forty-eighth" of that called for in the master recipe, through which I was first introduced to suya. We feel that more can be added at the table by any one who wants more. To us it is much like our preference for cooler climates; you can always add another layer to keep warm but there is a decency factor that must be observed in hot climates. If you like the "heat," go for it.

1 tablespoon garlic powder
2 teaspoons onion powder
1 tablespoon ground ginger
1 tablespoon paprika
1/2 teaspoon ground red pepper (cayenne)
2 tablespoons *finely* ground *raw* peanuts

3 tablespoons peanut oil

In a jar, with tightly fitting lid, combine garlic and powders, ground ginger. paprika, red pepper (cayenne), and *finely* ground peanuts. Stir to combine well.

Store, tightly covered, in a cool dry place.*

When ready to use, mix 1 tablespoonful of seasoning mixture with about 1 teaspoonful of peanut oil. Use as a marinade and for basting foods to be grilled or oven–roasted.

Yields about 9 tablespoonfuls

Notes: *This seasoning can be stored for at least a month without rancidity.

When required, this recipe can be halved or doubled.

1/27 SERVING (i. e., per teaspoonful with oil added) –
PROTEIN = 0.1 g.; FAT = 1.6 g.; CARBOHYDRATE = 0.6 g.;
CALORIES = 17; CALORIES FROM FAT = 85%

NIGERIAN GINGER CAKE
TPT - 1 hour and 34 minutes;
20 minutes = cooling period

As you bite into the first forkful of this cake, the molasses and ginger will remind you of soft molasses cookies or gingerbread.

1 1/2 cups unbleached white flour
1/2 cup whole wheat flour
1/2 teaspoon baking powder
1/2 teaspoon baking soda

1/2 cup sugar
3/4 cup *unsulfured* molasses
6 tablespoons butter

1/4 cup *fat-free* pasteurized eggs (the equivalent of 1 egg)
Scant 3/4 cup *two-percent* milk
2 1/2 teaspoons ground ginger, or more to taste

Preheat oven to 325 degrees F. Prepare a 9-inch loaf/bread pan or a 9-inch round cake pan by coating with non-stick lecithin baking spray coating.

NIGERIAN GINGER CAKE (cont'd)

Sift together white and whole wheat flours, baking powder, and baking soda. Set aside.

In a saucepan set over *LOW-MEDIUM* heat, combine sugar, molasses, and butter. Heat, stirring occasionally, until sugar is melted. Remove from heat.

In a large mixing bowl, combine pasteurized eggs, milk, and ground ginger. Using a wire whisk, combine thoroughly. While stirring, gradually add hot sugar–molasses–butter mixture. Using a wooden spoon, stir in sifted dry ingredients. Mix batter well. Turn into prepared baking pan. Bake in preheated 325 degree F. oven for 50 minutes, or until a cake tester inserted into the center comes out clean.

Cool on a wire rack for at least 20 minutes. Serve while slightly warm or at room temperature as is or with:

PINEAPPLE–LEMON SAUCE *[see index]*,
CUSTARD SAUCE *[see index]*,
FRESH ORANGE CUSTARD SAUCE *[see index]*,
or LEMON SAUCE *[see index]*

garnishing with candied orange peel. Leftover cake, which has a crusty texture, is enjoyable with a scoop of ice cream.

Yields 10 servings
adequate for 6-8 people

1/10 SERVING – PROTEIN = 4.0 g.; FAT = 7.4 g.; CARBOHYDRATE = 54.9 g.;
CALORIES = 265; CALORIES FROM FAT = 25%

TAPIOCA PUDDING WITH CLOVES
TPT - 2 hours and 20 minutes;
2 hours = chilling period

Quick-cooking tapioca replaces grated cassava in this pudding that is very popular in Nigeria. Nigerians enjoy snacks throughout the day, as do those in many other nations in West Africa. A large variety of savory and sweet snacks are sold as street food by the ubiquitous vendors who work the streets of the big cities. No matter how many snacks the family has consumed during the day, a Nigerian homemaker can be sure that there will always be a positive reception when a bowl of this clove-flavored sweet is set down on the table.

3 cups skimmed milk
1/3 cup sugar
1/4 cup quick-cooking tapioca
6 whole cloves

1/4 cup *fat-free* **pasteurized eggs (the equivalent of 1 egg)**
1 teaspoon pure vanilla extract

In a large saucepan set over *LOW-MEDIUM* heat, combine milk, sugar, tapioca, and whole cloves. Using a wire whisk, combine well. Allow mixture to come to a boil, stirring *very* frequently. *Remove from heat.*

In a mixing bowl, combine pasteurized eggs and vanilla extract. Whisk to combine.

While stirring the eggs with a wire whisk, add two or three tablespoonfuls of the tapioca mixture. Beat well. Then, add two or three tablespoonfuls more of the tapioca mixture. Again, beat it into the egg mixture. *Gradually*, while stirring the tapioca mixture in the saucepan with a wire whisk, add the egg mixture to the tapioca pudding. Whisk until thoroughly combined. Place over *LOW* heat and cook, stirring constantly, until the pudding thickens. Remove and discard the cloves. Turn into a serving bowl. Refrigerate for at least 2 hours, until cold and firmly set.

Serve chilled.

Yields 6 servings
adequate for 4 people

Note: This recipe can be halved, but who would ever halve a tapioca pudding recipe?

1/6 SERVING – PROTEIN = 4.6 g.; FAT = 0.2 g.; CARBOHYDRATE = 26.0 g.;
CALORIES = 124; CALORIES FROM FAT = 1%

Africa–Nigeria

NIGERIAN SWEET RICE CLUSTERS
TPT - 23 minutes

When we have short grain rice leftover from a meal, there is usually rice pudding for dessert the next day. One day I stumbled upon this recipe from Nigeria, a street food eaten with enthusiasm as a snack. I promptly decided that there was an alternative to rice pudding. Since desserts are uncommon in West Africa and I, consequently, tend to opt for fruit at the end of meal, I was delighted to have an authentic sweet dish to share with guests. Occasionally we fry; sometimes we make corn fritters and sometimes we make these sweet rice clusters.

2 cups *cold, cooked,* short grain rice*
1/4 cup *fat-free* pasteurized eggs (the equivalent of 1 egg)
2 tablespoons freshly grated coconut, if available, *or* moist, dried coconut
1/4 cup *light* brown sugar

Oil for deep-frying preheated to 375 degrees F.

In a mixing bowl, combine *cold, cooked* rice, pasteurized eggs, coconut, and brown sugar. Mix well. The mixture should be firm enough to form small balls.** Form into small balls.

Deep-fry a few at a time until the balls are browned on both sides—about 3 minutes. *Be sure to bring the oil back to 375 degrees F. before each batch is fried.* Remove cooked rice balls using a slotted spoon or a Chinese skimmer and transfer to paper toweling to drain the excess oil. Transfer to a heated serving bowl.

Serve warm.

Yields about 24 rice clusters
adequate for 6 people

Notes: *Short grain rice is a starchy rice. Its stickiness is a definite advantage when making rice balls.

**If rice mixture is not firm enough to form the rice balls, add a bit of rice or wheat flour.

1/24 SERVING (per rice cluster) –
PROTEIN = 8.3 g.; FAT = 1.2 g.; CARBOHYDRATE = 9.3 g.;
CALORIES = 56; CALORIES FROM FAT = 19%

Africa–Nigeria

NIGERIAN FRIED DOUGH BALLS
Chin Chin

TPT - 30 minutes

There are many, many versions of "fried dough" translated into many, many languages in many, many cultures. The range goes from celebratory pastries to German friedcakes and Chinese honey bows all the way down to dough fried in lard that was shamefully introduced by the Bureau of Indian Affairs to the Native Americans of the United States Southwest. I grew up with the fried doughnuts known as friedcakes, prepared by my grandmother once-a-week. These Nigerian dough balls are very much like the friedcake "holes" my grandmother made for the grandchildren long before there were "munchkins." Although we all still celebrate those friedcakes, the first truly celebratory "fried dough" recipes that I encountered were honey balls, a holiday specialty in the Calabrese branch of my husband's family. "Struffoli" consists of balls of deep-fried dough which are mounded and drenched with honey and covered with colored sprinkles to resemble a Christmas tree. Chin chin are also sweet fried dough balls beloved by Nigerians and Nigeriens, too. They can be flavored with nutmeg or not, as preferred.

Oil for deep-frying

2 cups unbleached white flour
1 teaspoon baking powder
1/2 cup sugar
2 teaspoons freshly grated nutmeg

2 tablespoons *hard* butter—chopped into chunks

1/2 cup *fat-free* pasteurized eggs (the equivalent of 2 eggs)

In a wok set over *MEDIUM* heat, heat oil to 365 degrees F. Line a serving platter with paper towels.

Meanwhile, in a mixing bowl, combine flour, baking powder, sugar, and nutmeg. Using a pastry cutter, stir the mixture well.

Add the butter and, using the pastry cutter, cut the butter into the dry ingredients. The mixture should have the consistency of coarse corn meal.

Add pasteurized eggs. Using a fork, stir.

Gather the batter into small balls. Roll the batter between your palms and transfer the balls to a piece of waxed paper.

Fry a few balls at a time until golden, turning as necessary. Remove to paper toweling using a Chinese skimmer. *Allow the oil to reheat before frying the next batch.*

Transfer the *chin chin* to the serving platter lined with paper toweling.

Serve warm.

Yields about 30 fried dough balls

Note: This recipe can be halved, when required.

1/30 SERVING – PROTEIN = 1.2 g.; FAT = 1.2 g.; CARBOHYDRATE = 9.7 g.;
CALORIES = 54; CALORIES FROM FAT = 20%

São Tomé and Principe

The two islands which form this nation are part of a chain of islands off the western equatorial coast of Africa in the Gulf of Guinea known as the Cameroon volcanic mountain line, a now extinct volcanic mountain range. It is a small nation covering a total area of 372 square miles, about four times the size of the District of Columbia. The islands were uninhabited when the Portuguese arrived in about 1470. Beginning in 1493, the Portuguese established settlements on the islands which they had named for the explorers who discovered them, Joao de Santarem and Pedro Escboar. The larger southern island was subsequently named in honor of Saint Thomas. São Tomé came under the Portuguese Crown in 1522 while the neighboring island became part of the Portuguese sphere in 1573. Today know as Principe, the more northern of the two islands was originally named Santo Antão in honor of Saint Anthony. Principe changed its name to Ilha do Principe, Prince's Island, to honor the prince of Portugal to whom export duties were paid on agricultural production.

Early settlers delivered to the islands by the Portuguese crown including Jewish children, who had been taken from their parents in Portugal and converted to Christianity, and exiled convicts and prostitutes known as *degredados*. Free whites assumed the jobs as plantation managers, government officials, and soldiers. They found the volcanic soil especially suitable for producing sugar. By the middle of the sixteenth century these two islands were Africa's largest exporter of sugar but this came with a price because the labor required to produce the sugar was solved by the Portuguese with the importation of slave labor from the mainland. Sugar production in the western hemisphere surpassed that of this Portuguese colony and by the middle of the seventeenth century São Tomé and Principe were little more than a departure point for slaves being shipped to the West.

Independence from Portugal came, as it did for other Portuguese colonies, in 1975 but after the fifteen-year, Marxist-Leninist rule of Manuel Pinto da Costa ended in 1990, an unstable period of governance, albeit now multi-partied, has followed allowing for little development of infra-structure. Also there has been little expansion and management of agriculture after the breakdown of the plantation system which existed before independence. Education is compulsory at this point for only four years which limits the availability of a skilled work force available to companies looking to locate in the nation. It is a vicious and destructive circle since employment and globalization are limited by the education of the available indigenous work force and expansion of the education system requires a sizable investment by the government. Military *coups* as recently as 2003, in response to control of oil discoveries in the nations territorial waters, have continued the instability. In 2011 Pinto da Costa was re-elected and has vowed to eliminate corruption.

Coffee and cocoa, which both benefit from the mineral-rich volcanic soil, were introduced in the early nineteenth century and today cocoa exports represent about ninety-five percent of the nation's total imports. Insufficient food is produced by the island nation to feed its population of about 183,000, about that of Paterson, New Jersey, requiring importation of food, mostly from Portugal. Nevertheless, there are signature dishes which we enjoy, many of which hint strongly at the many years of Portuguese influence. One particular specialty, that all too clearly shows the Portuguese influence and is way to good not to mention, is the popular sausage rolls that can be picked up from a street vender for lunch or as an afternoon pick-me-up as you stroll through the city. Warm Portuguese *saloio* rolls stuffed with *chorizo* sausages fit right in your hand.

Africa–São Tomé and Principe

*The following menu offers suggestions
for a thoroughly satisfying luncheon or light supper.*

Eggplant and Tomato Salad with Goat Cheese
Salada de Beringela e Tomate com Queijo de Cabra

Avocado Slices Sprinkled with Pineapple Juice or Pineapple Nectar

~~~~~~~~~~~~~~~~~~~~~~

Banana Omelet
Omeleta de Banana

or

Sweetpotato Omelet
Omeleta com Batata Doce

Warm Portuguese *Saloio* Rolls
Stuffed with Soy *Chorizo (Chouriço)* Sausages

~~~~~~~~~~~~~~~~~~~~~~

Sweet Corn Meal Pudding
Canjica

Fresh Papaya, Bananas, or Pineapple
or Fruits, if preferred

Mochalata Cordial	or	Creamy Cocoa Cordial
Licor de Cacau		*Licor de Cacau*

EGGPLANT AND TOMATO SALAD WITH GOAT CHEESE
Salada de Beringela e Tomate com Queijo de Cabra
TPT - 45 minutes

The two small volcanic islands that form the nation of São Tomé and Principe have little arable land and consequently must import much of their food. Vegetable gardening and cheese making have become very important skills for the homemaker. Publications encourage and teach about home gardening, canning, animal husbandry, and cheese making in an attempt to decrease the national dependency upon imports. This salad could come right from your backyard...

3 small eggplants—well washed and sliced lengthwise

2 tablespoons *high heat* safflower *or* sunflower oil

1 tablespoon *extra virgin* olive oil
2 tablespoons GARLIC–BASIL VINEGAR *[see index] or* other vinegar of choice
1/4 teaspoon dried marjoram—crushed
Salt, to taste
Freshly ground mixed peppercorns—red, white, and black—to taste

3 ripe tomatoes—well-washed and sliced

2 ounces *dry* goat cheese—crumbled

A few large curls of *pecorino Romano* cheese, for garnish

Place a rimmed cookie sheet in the oven to heat. Preheat oven to 375 degrees F.

EGGPLANT AND TOMATO SALAD WITH GOAT CHEESE (cont'd)

Remove preheated baking sheets from oven. Pour about the two tablespoonfuls of oil on the pan; brush to edges. Arrange eggplant slices on each of prepared baking sheets. Bake in preheated 375 degree oven for 15 minutes. Remove baking sheets from oven. Turn each eggplant slice. Return to oven for about 15 minutes more, or until each slice is golden brown. Drain eggplant slices *thoroughly* on several thicknesses of paper toweling.

In a cruet or jar, combine olive oil, vinegar, crushed, dried marjoram, salt, and pepper. Shake vigorously.

On a large platter arrange baked and well-drained eggplant slices alternately with tomato slices.

Pour *vinaigrette* over.

Sprinkle with *dry* goat cheese and curls of hard cheese.

Serve at room temperature.

Yields 6 servings
adequate for 4 people

1/6 SERVING – PROTEIN = 2.7 g.; FAT = 8.9 g.; CARBOHYDRATE = 5.1 g.;
CALORIES = 109; CALORIES FROM FAT = 73%

BANANA OMELET FROM THE ISLANDS OF SÃO TOMÉ AND PRINCIPE
Omeleta de Banana
TPT - 23 minutes

When green bananas are used in dishes such as this omelet, the resultant dish does not have the cloying sweetness one would expect because the starch has not yet been converted to sugars. It is somewhat akin to the taste change when one eats a potato omelet. As your saliva encounters the starch the conversion of starch to sugar begins and your taste buds sense the sweetness.

6 eggs—beaten
2 tablespoons *two-percent* milk
2 tablespoons unbleached white flour

1 tablespoon *extra virgin* olive oil
5 medium *very green* bananas—peeled and cubed

Preheat broiler to about 350 degrees F.

In a mixing bowl, combine beaten eggs, milk, and flour. Using a wire whisk or a fork, combine well. Set aside briefly.

In a non-stick-coated, 10-inch skillet set over *LOW-MEDIUM* heat, heat olive oil. Add banana cubes and sauté until the pieces of banana are golden brown.

Add egg mixture and allow to cook, undisturbed, until set. *Be careful not to scorch eggs.* Wrap pan handle with aluminum foil, if necessary, to protect it from burning. Place under preheated broiler until *lightly browned.* Be careful not to scorch eggs.

Slide out of skillet onto a heated round serving platter.

Serve at once, cut into wedges.

Yields 6 servings
adequate for 4 people

Note: This recipe can be halved, using an 8-9-inch skillet, when required.

1/6 SERVING – PROTEIN = 7.8 g.; FAT = 8.2 g.; CARBOHYDRATE = 24.1 g.;
CALORIES = 192; CALORIES FROM FAT = 38%

SWEETPOTATO OMELET IN THE STYLE OF SÃO TOMÉ AND PRINCIPE
Omeleta com Batata Doce
TPT - 30 minutes

If you usually just bake sweetpotatoes or make that awful holiday casserole with marshmallows, a visit to the cuisines of Africa will fill your files with creative ideas. I must admit that I would never have thought of making an omelet with grated sweetpotato until I encountered a recipe from this former Portuguese colonial region. It is perfect for breakfast, lunch, and dinner. This is one of those very perfect recipes.

SWEETPOTATO OMELET
IN THE STYLE OF SÃO TOMÉ AND PRINCIPE (cont'd)

1 tablespoon butter—*melted*
1 tablespoon *extra virgin* olive oil

2 small sweetpotatoes—peeled and grated
2 large garlic cloves—*very finely* chopped
6 eggs—beaten
1/2 cup *two-percent* milk
1/4 teaspoon salt

Preheat oven to 325 degrees F. Prepare a 9-inch *au gratin* dish or deep-dish pie plate by coating with *melted* butter and olive oil.

In a mixing bowl, combine grated sweetpotato, *very finely* chopped garlic, beaten eggs, milk, and salt. Using a wire whisk or a fork, combine well. Pour into prepared pie plate.

Bake in preheated 325 degree F. oven until set—about 20-22 minutes. *Shake gently to be sure that center is not still liquid but is still quivering.*

Serve at once onto warmed plates. Cut into wedges as you would with a pie.*

Yields 6 servings
adequate for 4 people

Notes: *Leftovers can be served cold with a sprinkling of freshly grated cheese for an interesting breakfast or lunch.

This recipe can be halved, when required. Use an 8-inch *au gratin* dish or pie plate.

1/6 SERVING – PROTEIN = 8.2 g.; FAT = 9.9 g.; CARBOHYDRATE = 11.3 g.;
CALORIES = 167; CALORIES FROM FAT = 53%

SWEET CORN MEAL PUDDING
Canjica

TPT - 1 hour and 20 minutes;
1 hour = cooling period

Corn (maize) is used in dishes all over the world, having made its round-the-world journey from Mesoamerica very successfully, but one does not always find the yellow or white varieties with which we are familiar. If you have ever seen Indian corn, you know that the genes that determine color in corn can be lively creating a spectrum of colors that are so beautiful they are used more for decoration than as food. Ears of red kernels, blue, brown, black, and green are preferred in some cultures. The green variety, favored for this pudding, which is grown in the volcanic soils of São Tomé and Principe must be able to tolerate the salty ocean spray and the tropical climate. Our yellow or white corn meals are slightly sweeter grain flours and, when combined with the eggs, results in a very beautiful dessert. You may at first find corn meal to be an unusual base for a dessert but farina and rice are commonly used to make puddings. They are all grasses whose grains nourish.

1 1/4 cups *boiling* water
3/4 cup yellow *or* white corn meal

1/2 cup sugar
1 cinnamon quill

6 tablespoons *fat-free* pasteurized eggs

Put *boiling* water into a saucepan set over *LOW-MEDIUM* heat. While *stirring constantly, gradually* add the corn meal. Continue stirring until any lumps have been worked out.

Add sugar and cinnamon quill. Cook, *stirring constantly*, until the sugar is dissolved and mixture is thickened.

While stirring vigorously, *gradually* beat the pasteurized eggs into the pudding mixture. Continue cooking until the pudding's consistency is to your liking. Remove cinnamon quill. Turn into a small serving bowl. Allow to cool to room temperature for about an hour or so.

Serve at room temperature. Refrigerate leftovers.

Yields 6 servings
adequate for 4 people

Note: This recipe can be doubled, when required.

1/6 SERVING – PROTEIN = 3.0 g.; FAT = 0.6 g.; CARBOHYDRATE = 31.6 g.;
CALORIES = 143; CALORIES FROM FAT = 4%

Africa–São Tomé and Principe

MOCHALATA CORDIAL
Licor de Cacau

TPT - 4 weeks and 2 hours;
       1 hour = vodka–coffee infusion;
       30 minutes = syrup cooling period;
       4 weeks = flavor development period

Cocoa liqueurs are an export product of the island nation of São Tome and Principe. This version, with its mellow coffee–cocoa flavor, is reminiscent of Kahlua while the second version which follows is a milk-based beverage. Both are fun to make and very smooth.

1/2 cup freshly ground coffee beans
1 bottle (750 milliliters) (3 1/4 cups) 80-proof
  Russian *or* Finnish vodka

1 cup sugar
1 cup water
1 large vanilla pod—broken in half

1/2 cup honey

6 tablespoons *dark, unsweetened* cocoa powder
1/2 teaspoon pure vanilla extract
1/4 teaspoon freshly grated nutmeg

Add ground coffee beans to vodka. Allow to stand for 1 hour. Strain through a fine gold coffee filter or through dampened cheesecloth to remove coffee grounds.

In a saucepan, combine sugar, water, and vanilla bean pieces. Over *MEDIUM-HIGH* heat, bring sugar mixture to the boil while stirring constantly. Allow to boil for 2 minutes. *Immediately remove from heat* and allow to cool to room temperature—about 30 minutes. Remove vanilla bean pieces and reserve for future use.

Add honey. Stir to integrate.

In a large glass jar, combine the coffee-flavored vodka, the sugar–honey syrup with the vanilla bean, cocoa powder, vanilla extract, and grated nutmeg. Cover securely and place in a cool, dark place. Allow to stand for 4 weeks to allow for full flavor development. Stir the contents of the bottle gently every day.

Set a fine sieve, preferably a gold coffee filter, over a mixing bowl. Pour the liqueur mixture through, removing any residual coffee grounds or vanilla seeds.

Clean out the sieve and pour the liqueur mixture through the coffee filter again.

Sterilize decorative cordial bottles and corks.

Strain cordial through a paper coffee filter-lined sieve into sterilized bottles. Seal with a sterilized cork.

Store in the refrigerator.

Serve into cordial glasses. *This cordial should be icy cold when served.*

Yields about 4 1/2 cupfuls

1/24 SERVING (i. e., 3 tablespoonfuls) –
PROTEIN = 0.5 g.; FAT = 0.07 g.; CARBOHYDRATE = 20.0 g.;
CALORIES = 94; CALORIES FROM FAT = 0%;
CALORIES FROM ALCOHOL = 30.5

CREAMY COCOA CORDIAL
Licor de Cacau

TPT - 8 weeks and 64 minutes;
       2 weeks = first flavor development period;
       6 weeks = second flavor development period

This cordial is preferred by those who like a milk-based cocoa cordial such as Cadbury Cream Liqueur, Mozart Gold Chocolate Cream Liqueur, or Vermeer Dutch Chocolate Cream Liqueur.

1 tablespoon whole coffee beans

2 cups *whole* milk
1 cup sugar
6 tablespoons *dark, unsweetened* cocoa powder

1 cup 80-proof Russian *or* Finnish vodka
1/2 teaspoon pure vanilla extract

CREAMY COCOA CORDIAL (cont'd)

Secure the coffee beans in a tea ball.

In a saucepan, combine milk, sugar, water, the tea ball containing the coffee beans, and cocoa powder. Over *MEDIUM-HIGH* heat, bring sugar mixture to the boil while stirring constantly. Allow to boil for 2 minutes. *Immediately remove from heat* and allow to cool to room temperature—about 30 minutes. Remove tea ball and discard coffee beans.

In a large glass jar, combine the cocoa–milk mixture, vodka, and the vanilla extract. Cover securely and place in a cool, dark place. Allow to stand for 2 weeks.

Set a fine sieve, preferably a gold coffee filter, over a mixing bowl. Pour the liqueur mixture through. Clean out the sieve and pour the liqueur mixture through the coffee filter again.

Sterilize decorative cordial bottles or a one-quart wine bottle and corks.

Strain cordial through a paper coffee filter-lined sieve into sterilized bottles. Seal each with a sterilized cork.

Store in the refrigerator for at least 6 weeks for maximum flavor development.

Serve into cordial glasses. *This cordial should be icy cold when served.*

Yields about 4 cupfuls

Note: This recipe can be doubled, when required.

1/21 SERVING (i. e., 3 tablespoonfuls) –
PROTEIN = 1.2 g.; FAT = 0.8 g.; CARBOHYDRATE = 14.0 g.;
CALORIES = 74; CALORIES FROM FAT = 10%;
CALORIES FROM ALCOHOL = 11

Senegal

Senegal is a relatively stable West African country about the size of Nebraska with about seven times the population. Islam spread to this area of Africa in the eleventh century and the indigenous tribal population, the Toucouleur people, converted to Islam but modified their faith to incorporate the animistic beliefs practiced for centuries. Today about ninety-five percent of the population is Muslim. Senegal, however, is a secular Islamic republic with a representative democratic system and some eighty political parties.

In the thirteenth and fourteenth centuries this area came under the domination of the Mandingo or Mali Empire which included the modern-day countries of Mali, Senegal, southern Mauritania, northern Burkina Faso, western Niger, The Gambia, Guinea-Bissau, Guinea, Côte d'Ivoire, and northern Ghana. It is also during this period that the Jolof Empire of Senegal was established.

When the Portuguese began exploring the African coastline, the wide and deep estuaries of the Senegal and Gambia rivers were immediately of interest. The Senegal River was reached by the Portuguese in 1444 and the Gambia River was reached in 1455. The Portuguese found these river estuaries suitable anchorages on their voyages around Africa to their trade and colonial interests in Asia and had little competition for the ports until the seventeenth century when the British and French established trading posts and settlements in the area beginning in about 1638. In 1677 the French seized Gorée Island, just off Cape Verde, from the Dutch. What followed were years of disputes and overt military action by the British and the French to secure the territory for one side or the other. The French established a colonial government in 1840, making Senegal a part of French West Africa together with Mauritania, French Sudan (now, Mali) French Guinea, Côte d'Ivoire, Upper Volta (now, Burkina Faso), Dahomey (now, Benin), and Niger. Except for those who were citizens of the Four Communes of Senegal, the citizens of these colonies were considered "French subjects" and were denied legal rights, property rights, rights to travel, the right to dissent, and the right to vote.

In 1959 Senegal and the French Sudan (Soudan) joined to form the Mali Federation. The united nations became fully independent in June 1960 but the union dissolved in August of the same year. Senegal proclaimed independence from the Soudan and Soudan formed what is known today as the Republic of Mali. Although French is still the official language, it is spoken only by the educated elite. Most commerce outside of the cities is still conducted in indigenous languages of which Wolof is the most predominate.

Seventy-five percent of the 12.5 million population lives rurally. The food eaten in those areas has changed little over the decades with influences on preparation from West African neighbors and from North Africa. In the cities, however, one sees more reminders of the Portuguese and French colonial periods. The cuisine is very much like our Southern Creole cooking which is not at all surprising when we reflect on the fact that so many Senegalese were brought to our country as slaves. Their cooking became very much a part of our "American cooking" tradition. In addition, immigration of Vietnamese, beginning in the 1950s with the onset of the war in French Indochina and continuing through the American involvement in the Vietnam War, and the presence of Chinese traders have contributed to the Senegalese cuisine. One will find Vietnamese fish sauce and soy sauce added to traditional dishes along with the ubiquitous and very hot Scotch bonnet *chili* sauce condiment that accompanies most meals. Spring rolls and *tofu* can be found among the elements of Asian cuisine entering modern-day Senegalese cuisine.

Africa–Senegal

Winter Squash and Peanut Soup
Potage de Gourde et Buerre d'Arachilde or *Mafe*

Yam and Peanut Soup with Oven-Dried Tomatoes
Potage de Igname et Buerre d'Archilde or *Mafe*

Pita bread or Flatbread

~

Steamed and Chilled Greens *Vinaigrette*
with Sieved Hard-Cooked Eggs
Salade Verte

Avocado, Mango, and Orange Salad with Citrus Dressing
Salade Avocat et Mango

~~~~~~~~~~~~~~~~~~~~~~

Toasted Millet *Croquettes* **with Sour Cream**
Fondé

Sautéed Swiss Chard

~~~~~~~~~~~

Pasta **and Vegetable Salad with Peanut Butter Dressing**
Salade de Pasta et Légumes aux Buerre de Cacahuèle

Fried Yam *Croquettes*
Fufu

~~~~~~~~~~~~~~~~~~~~~

Milk Rice Pudding	**Groundnut Ice Cream**
Gossi	*Crème Glacee aux Beurre d'Arachide*

~

Fresh French *Baguettes*
with Pineapple Jam *[see index]*

~

Yogurt Drink
Toufam

SENEGALESE WINTER SQUASH AND PEANUT SOUP
Potage de Gourde et Buerre d'Arachilde or *Mafe*
TPT - 1 hour and 3 minutes

Soups like this are soups that thrill the taste buds. It is mildly spiced so that the diverse flavors can make their way to and fro over the tongue receptors. Our very young grandson just did not know what to make of peanut butter in a soup and said so. "Do you like it? I asked. "Yes, but it's different." "Good; that's just what I was looking for."

Africa–Senegal

SENEGALESE WINTER SQUASH AND PEANUT SOUP (cont'd)

1 tablespoon peanut oil
4 cups cubed, peeled butternut squash
1 medium onion—*finely* chopped
2 large garlic cloves—*very finely* chopped
1/2 teaspoon ground cumin
1/4 teaspoon ground coriander

1 quart VEGETARIAN STOCK FROM SOUP *[see index]* or other vegetarian stock of choice
3/4 cup freshly ground, *unsalted, additive-free smooth* peanut butter
1/4 cup canned, *crushed* tomatoes
1/2 teaspoon *crushed* red pepper flakes*

1/4 cup chopped fresh coriander (*cilantro*) leaves, for garnish

In a kettle set over *LOW-MEDIUM* heat, heat oil. Add cubed squash, *finely* chopped onions, *very finely* chopped garlic, and ground cumin and coriander. Sauté gently until onion is soft and translucent, *allowing neither the onion nor the garlic to brown.*

Add stock, peanut butter, tomato paste, and crushed red pepper flakes. Stir to combine. *Increase heat to MEDIUM-HIGH.* Stir constantly while allowing the soup to come to the boil. *Reduce heat to LOW* and allow to simmer for about 15 minutes, or until squash is tender. Stir occasionally. Remove from heat and turn into a heated tureen.

Serve into heated soup bowls, garnishing each serving with chopped coriander *(cilantro).*

Yields about 8 cupfuls

Notes: *These are most efficiently crushed using a mortar and pestle.

This recipe is easily doubled or halved, when required.

A variation of this soup can be made using sweetpotato instead of squash, SENEGALESE YAM AND PEANUT SOUP WITH OVEN-DRIED TOMATOES *(Potage de Igname et Buerre d'Archilde).* See recipe which follows for OVEN-DRIED TOMATOES. Add five or six slices of tomato at the beginning of the cooking procedure and they will be soft by the time the soup is done.

1/6 SERVING (i. e., per cupful) –
PROTEIN = 7.1 g.; FAT = 13.5 g.; CARBOHYDRATE = 13.4 g.;
CALORIES = 246; CALORIES FROM FAT = 49%

OVEN – DRIED TOMATOES
TPT - about 54 hours and 36 minutes;
48 hours = freezing period

Sun-dried tomatoes not only became all-the-rage, they presented a delicious convenience to add intense tomato flavor to winter stews, casseroles, and salads. Sun-drying was certainly not new. In the 1830s recipes appeared that described the procedures used by the Turks and Italians for sun-drying tomatoes and it is said that those migrating West along the Oregon Trail also sun-dried the fruit with sugar to be used as a confection. However, sun-drying and dehydrator-drying both take several days and invite mold development during the drying period on those hot, humid August and September days when the very freshest, best tasting local tomatoes are available, or when your harvest "comes in." We developed this reliable and efficient oven-drying method after a year when our harvest had to go into the compost pile when tray after tray molded in the dehydrator. It was such a disappointment.

We have found this rather unorthodox method to be reliable since the slices do not overbrown or, in truth, cook as they will do when drying is attempted using a cookie sheet in a constantly heated oven.

Extra virgin olive oil
Italian plum tomatoes—well-washed and sliced into 1/4–inch slices

Preheat oven to 150 degrees F., or *as low as you can set your oven.* Prepare a non-stick-coated ventilated rack* by brushing *lightly* with olive oil.

Africa–Senegal

OVEN – DRIED TOMATOES (cont'd)

Remove core and seeds from each slice and place on ventilated rack.

Dry in preheated oven for 1 hour. *Turn.*

Continue drying for 1 1/2 hours. *Turn* tomato rings.

> ~ Then, *turn oven off.* Place tray of tomatoes in *unheated oven* for 30 minutes. *Turn* tomato rings.
>
> ~ *Turn oven back on to lowest setting.* Place tray of tomatoes in heated oven for 30 minutes. *Turn* tomato rings.
>
> ~ *Turn oven off.* Place tray of tomatoes in *unheated oven* for 30 minutes. *Turn* tomato rings.
>
> ~ *Turn oven back on to lowest setting.* Place tray of tomatoes in heated oven for 30 minutes. *Turn* tomato rings.

Continue this on and off procedure, from ~ above, for about 6-7 hours, or until *dry* and *leathery*. Remove slices as they dry and place on paper toweling to absorb any residual moisture or oil.

When cold, place in a plastic bag and freeze for 48 hours to kill any undetectable insect larvae that may have been in the tomatoes.

Sterilize a quart canning jar. Also sterilize a lid and ring for the jar.

Remove oven-dried tomatoes from freezer. Transfer them to the sterilized canning jar. Tightly seal.

Oven-dried tomatoes can be stored in the pantry for about 6 months.**

Notes: *Several mail order firms offer ventilated racks which can be used to dry *biscotti* and such. These racks work well for tomato slices because they allow air to circulate. Inexpensive ventilated broiling pans also work well.

**If you prefer, oven-dried tomatoes can be stored in the refrigerator or freezer. Be sure the plastic bag or canning jar is tightly sealed.

STEAMED AND CHILLED GREENS *VINAIGRETTE* WITH SIEVED HARD-COOKED EGG
Salade Verte

TPT - 2 hours and 20 minutes;
2 hours = marination period

When you mention a green salad, most people, unfortunately, think of a bowl of iceberg lettuce with maybe a chopped tomato or cucumber and some onion. A very nice green salad can be made in the Senegalese style by steaming and chilling greens that are most often served as either a hot vegetable or added to a soup. We use beet greens, kale, escarole, spinach, curly endive (chicory), chard, and even young collard greens for this salad. Steamed greens are popular in Africa but this salad is somewhat out of the ordinary.

2 tablespoons *extra virgin* olive oil
1 tablespoon red wine vinegar
10 fresh tarragon leaves—well washed
Freshly ground black pepper, to taste
Pinch of sugar

6 cups greens of choice—trimmed, well-rinsed,
   and torn into pieces, if necessary
2 tablespoons water

1 hard-cooked egg—chopped and sieved

In a cruet or jar, combine oil, vinegar, tarragon leaves, black pepper, and sugar. Shake vigorously. Set aside briefly.

Put greens into a large saucepan or small kettle set over *LOW-MEDIUM* heat. Add water, cover, and allow greens to wilt. Remove from heat and drain thoroughly. Turn into a serving bowl or place on a small platter.

Shake *vinaigrette* vigorously again and pour over greens. Refrigerate for at least two hours.

Africa—Senegal

STEAMED AND CHILLED GREENS *VINAIGRETTE*
WITH SIEVED HARD-COOKED EGG (cont'd)

When ready to serve, sprinkle sieved hard-cooked eggs over.

Yields 6 servings
adequate for 4 people

Note: This recipe can be halved or doubled, when required.

1/6 SERVING (using beet greens) –
PROTEIN = 5.1 g.; FAT = 5.3 g.; CARBOHYDRATE = 11.4 g.;
CALORIES = 113; CALORIES FROM FAT = 42%

SENEGALESE AVOCADO, MANGO, AND ORANGE SALAD WITH CITRUS DRESSING
Salade Avocat et Mango

TPT - 1 hour and 10 minutes;
1 hour = flavor development period

In the market, in which I generally shop for produce, avocados and mangoes are always side by side at the end of one of the display tables. It had never occurred to me to combine them until I visited the cuisine of Senegal and discovered this salad gem. The textures of the avocado and the mango combine so well that you will wonder why you too probably brought them home together in the same bag but never combined them. Trust me it is a match made in heaven and the citrus dressing brings them to life.

Because of the many regional languages spoken in Senegal the avocado may turn up in a market labeled "awooka." Buy it; it's an avocado.

CITRUS DRESSING:
    3 tablespoons freshly squeezed orange juice
    3 tablespoons freshly squeezed lime juice
    1 tablespoon pineapple juice
    1 tablespoon peanut oil *or* safflower oil, as preferred
    1/4 cup *finely* chopped fresh parsley
    1/8 teaspoon *jalapeño chili* sauce, or to taste
    Freshly ground mixed peppercorns—black, red, and white—to taste
    Pinch salt

1 ripe mango—peeled and cut from the pit into 1/4-inch chunks
2 ripe avocados—peeled, pitted, and chopped into 1/4-inch chunks

1 navel orange—peeled and sectioned—for garnish

In a cruet or jar, combine orange, lime, and pineapple juices, oil, *finely* chopped parsley, *jalapeño* sauce, ground mixed peppercorns, and salt. Shake vigorously. Pour into a mixing bowl.

Add mango and avocado pieces. Toss gently. Refrigerate for at least 1 hour to allow for flavor development. Turn into a serving bowl.

Slice each orange section into 1/4-inch slices. Scatter the slices of orange over the marinated fruits.

Serve chilled.

Yields 6 servings
adequate for 4 people

Note: This recipe is easily halved, when required.

1/6 SERVING – PROTEIN = 2.0 g.; FAT = 12.9 g.; CARBOHYDRATE = 14.8 g.;
CALORIES = 168; CALORIES FROM FAT = 69%

Africa–Senegal

SENEGALESE TOASTED MILLET *CROQUETTES* WITH SOUR CREAM
Fondé

TPT - 1 hour and 13 minutes

Senegalese are inordinately fond of a snack called "fondé" which consists of balls of cooked millet served with sour cream. To create a vegetarian main course version of "fondé" I slightly redesigned the original, for which I hope I will be forgiven. It is very good way to celebrate this low-gluten grain. These delicate croquettes can be fried or baked; I prefer to bake them.

1 tablespoon safflower *or* sunflower oil
1/2 cup dry millet—well-rinsed and well-drained

3 cups *boiling* water

1/2 cup *very finely* chopped onion
1/2 carrot—scraped or pared and *grated*
1 large garlic clove—*very finely* chopped
3 tablespoons *finely* chopped parsley
1 tablespoon canned, *crushed* tomatoes
1 tablespoons *tamari* soy sauce
1 1/2 teaspoons ground ginger
1/2 teaspoon ground cinnamon
1 teaspoon ground cumin
1/2 teaspoon chili powder
1/2 teaspoon smoked paprika
1 tablespoon unbleached white flour

1 cup *fat-free* dairy sour cream
3 tablespoons *two-percent* milk

Preheat oven to 350 degrees F. Prepare a cookie sheet by lining it with aluminum foil and then spraying it with non-stick lecithin spray coating.

In a skillet set over *LOW-MEDIUM* heat, heat oil. Add millet and cook, stirring frequently until the seeds are dry and there is a fragrant aroma.

Add *boiling* water. Reduced heat to *LOW*, cover, and allow to cook for 15 minutes. Drain and rinse well in cold water. Drain well and turn into a mixing bowl.

Add *very finely* chopped onion, *grated* carrot, *very finely* chopped garlic, *finely* chopped parsley, crushed tomatoes, soy sauce, ground cinnamon, ginger, and cumin, chili powder, smoked paprika, and flour. Mix well and form into twelve small patties directly on the foil-lined baking sheet. *If you need more liquid to form the patties, add a little more of the crushed tomatoes.* Bake in preheated oven for about 20-30 minutes, or until lightly browned.

While *croquettes* are baking, in a small saucepan set over *LOW* heat, combine sour cream and milk. Using a small wire whisk, combine thoroughly. Allow to heat through, stirring frequently. Turn into a small sauceboat.

Using a spatula, carefully transfer *croquettes* to a heated serving platter. Serve with sour cream.

Yields 12 servings
adequate for 4-6 people

Note: This recipe can be halved, when required.

1/6 SERVING – PROTEIN = 4.8 g.; FAT = 2.0 g.; CARBOHYDRATE = 11.9 g.;
CALORIES = 69; CALORIES FROM FAT = 26%

Africa–**Senegal**

WEST AFRICAN *PASTA* AND VEGETABLE SALAD WITH PEANUT BUTTER DRESSING
Salade de Pasta et Légumes aux Buerre de Cacahuèle
TPT - 1 hour and 23 minutes

Rather recently I came across a" pastami" in Dakar that produced macaroni, cheveux d'ange (angel hair), langues d'oiseaux (orzo), and spaghetti. I had encountered many pasta dishes in my research and I knew that there were pasta firms in South Africa but I had always assumed that, except for couscous, most of the pasta eaten in West and Central and East Africa was imported as were the inspirations for many of pasta dishes one finds in Africa. Cross-fertilization occurred for centuries beginning with the Romans and carried over into the period of Italian colonization. The sauces in Africa, however, are entirely unique and would never be recognized as Italian. Peanut and garlic sauces, popular throughout Africa, really do wonders for bland bases like pasta or potatoes. The following is a salad combination which we often pack up and take to a nearby state forest for an afternoon of quiet and cool pleasures. Since peanuts are not nuts, but are instead legumes which contain the amino acids necessary to complement the amino acid deficiency in the grain-based pasta, protein complementation is achieved in one salad bowl. Oh, did I mention taste . . . ? This is not one of your run-of-the-mill pasta salads!

4 quarts *boiling* **water**
1/2 pound whole wheat spaghetti—broken in half

1 1/2 cups *thin* **carrot rounds**
1 1/2 cups *tiny* **broccoli florets—well-rinsed**
1/4 cup *finely* **chopped red onion**

WEST AFRICAN PEANUT BUTTER DRESSING:
    1/4 cup freshly ground, unsalted, additive-free smooth peanut butter—brought to room temperature
    1 small garlic clove—*very finely* chopped
    1/4 teaspoon ground ginger
    Freshly ground mixed peppercorns—red, white, and black—to taste
    1/4 cup *boiling* **water**
    2 tablespoons unseasoned rice wine vinegar
    2 tablespoons *tamari* **soy sauce**

1 tomato—cut into wedges—to garnish

In a kettle set over *MEDIUM-HIGH* heat, combine 4 quartfuls *boiling* water and broken spaghetti. Cook as directed on package.

During the last 2 minutes of the spaghetti cooking period, add carrot slices, broccoli florets, and *finely* chopped red onion. Drain thoroughly. Transfer to a mixing bowl.

In a small bowl, combine peanut butter, *very finely* chopped garlic, ground ginger, and ground pepper. Mix well. Gradually stir in the 1/4 cupful *boiling* water, rice wine vinegar, and soy sauce. Stir until smooth. Add to *pasta*-vegetable mixture, tossing to coat spaghetti. Turn into a serving bowl. Refrigerate for at least 1 hour before serving.

Garnish with tomato wedges.

Yields 6 servings
adequate for 4 people

Note: This recipe can be doubled, when required.

1/6 SERVING – PROTEIN = 7.8 g.; FAT = 6.5 g.; CARBOHYDRATE = 33.4 g.; CALORIES = 226; CALORIES FROM FAT = 26%

SENEGALESE FRIED YAM *CROQUETTES*
Fufu
TPT - 20 minutes

Fufu is a term used for mashed or pounded vegetables in many African countries. This is a fufu but this is not the simple mashed vegetable paste one routinely finds in a rural kitchen. Fufu may not be native to Senegal but this Senegalese version not only takes the extra step of adding other vegetables it also calls for frying the croquettes which, I think, makes them quite special. The starchy yam that grows in Africa is quite different from the yams or sweetpotatoes that we can buy in our markets here in the United States. Consequently, this delicious way of using the tuber will taste entirely different from that which you would be served on the other side of the Atlantic. This is considered a national specialty in several countries. Cooks from Nigeria, Sierra Leone, Ghana, and Senegal shared their recipes. To my amazement I also found that a similar yam cake can be enjoyed in Singapore.

SENEGALESE FRIED YAM *CROQUETTES* (cont'd)

1/2 cup unbleached white flour

1 cup *high heat* safflower *or* sunflower oil

1 cup mashed, cooked yams or sweetpotatoes
1/2 medium onion—*very finely* chopped
1/2 cup canned, *diced* tomatoes—well-drained
1/8 teaspoon ground red pepper (cayenne), or to taste
1/2 teaspoon crushed, dried thyme
1/4 teaspoon salt
1 egg—beaten

Place flour in a soup plate.

In a deep skillet set over *MEDIUM* heat, heat oil to about 350 degrees F.

In a mixing bowl, combine mashed yams, *very finely* chopped onion, *finely* chopped tomatoes, ground red pepper (cayenne), crushed thyme, salt, and beaten egg. Combine thoroughly.

Using two soup spoons, shape the yam mixture into *croquettes*, a few at a time. Place in flour and roll until coated. Slide into the hot oil. Fry yam *croquettes*, a few at a time, until golden brown. Drain on several layers of paper toweling until all are prepared.

Serve at once.

Yields about 20 yam *croquettes*

Note: This recipe can be doubled, when required.

1/20 SERVING (i. e., per *croquette*) –
PROTEIN = 1.5 g.; FAT = 1.7 g.; CARBOHYDRATE = 5.7 g.;
CALORIES = 41; CALORIES FROM FAT = 37%

SENEGALESE MILK RICE PUDDING

Gassi

TPT - 1 hour and 8 minutes;
[slow cooker: 2 hours and 51 minutes]

My mother and grandmother did not make rice pudding on top of the stove; they did not think deli rice pudding was, in fact, a proper rice pudding. Their recipe and mine, when I first began to cook, was a baked custard rice pudding. They did, however, often cook rice in milk and I just grew up assuming that it was a German dish "for children." Prepared for supper on evenings when my dad was working late and served with sugar and cinnamon, it was a favorite. I have found "milk rice" in the cuisines of many, many nations. It is surprisingly a much-loved dessert in Senegal as well, considering the fact that women in Senegal once associated barrenness with milk drinking. Dairy farming is important in northern areas of Senegal and milk, of course, finds its way into many dishes. Since rice is grown in the Casamance in southern Senegal, it is not surprising that "milk rice" also evolved in this cuisine. Here, instead of first cooking the rice in water, we cook it in milk for a richer flavor, the way it was cooked by my German great-grandmother, and all the generations that have followed.

3 1/2 cups skimmed milk
3/4 cup dry short grain white rice
1/2 vanilla bean

1/2 cup sugar, or to taste

In a saucepan set over *LOW-MEDIUM* heat, heat milk until just below the boiling point. Reduce heat to *LOW*. Stir in rice and vanilla bean, cover tightly, and cook, *undisturbed*, for 30 minutes.

Add sugar. Stir, replace cover, and cook, *undisturbed*, for another 30 minutes. If all milk is absorbed at this point, remove MILK RICE from heat. If all milk is not absorbed, return to heat and continue cooking until it is.

Remove vanilla bean.*

Turn into a serving bowl. Serve warm, at room temperature, or chilled, as preferred, with a pitcher of light cream, if desired.

Yields 6 servings
adequate for 4 people

Notes: *The vanilla bean will still have enough flavor in it to reuse. Rinse off, *dry thoroughly,* and tuck it into your sugar bowl or canister.

This pudding makes a nutritious and welcome breakfast offering which can easily be made the evening before. Reduce sugar to 1/4 cupful in this case.

When required, this recipe can be halved or doubled.

SENEGALESE MILK RICE PUDDING (cont'd)

If you chose the convenience of a slow cooker, heat milk in a saucepan to just below the boiling point before combining it with the rice and the vanilla bean in the cooking pot. Stir well. Cook for 2 hours at *LOW* setting. Add sugar. Stir and continue cooking at LOW setting for 45 minutes, or until milk has been absorbed by rice.

1/6 SERVING – PROTEIN = 6.2 g; FAT = 0.3 g; CARBOHYDRATE = 47.9 g; CALORIES = 221; CALORIES FROM FAT = 1%

SENEGALESE GROUNDNUT ICE CREAM
Crème Glacée aux Beurre d'Arachide

TPT - 8 hours and 12 minutes;
8 hours = freezing period

I have never been overly fond of just plain peanut butter as are so many others in my family but this use of peanut butter is real comfort food for me. This recipe is a bit different from that which you might find in homes or restaurants in Senegal where fresh heavy cream might be an unobtainable commodity. It does, we feel, do credit to the Senegalese use of this protein-rich legume which is a major cash crop in East Africa as it is in the southeastern United States. Incidentally, peanuts or groundnuts, as they are generally known in Africa, or "keur" as they are called in Wolof, are native to South America dating, at least, to the pre-Columbian Andean peoples but I had to go all the way to Senegal to find the custard frozen dessert that became the inspiration for this delicious frozen ice cream.

I have given the name for this luscious ice cream in French, for which I hope I will be excused. There are many languages spoken in Senegal, including Wolof to which I have alluded above, but French is generally spoken and used on menus, a throwback to colonial days.

1 cup heavy whipping cream

1/3 cup freshly ground, *additive-free*, smooth peanut butter—*brought to room temperature*
2/3 cup *fat-free* sweetened condensed milk
1 teaspoon pure vanilla extract

Prepare a 7 x 3 x 2-inch non-stick-coated loaf pan by placing it in the freezer until required.

Using an electric mixer fitted with *chilled* beaters or by hand, using a *chilled* wire whisk, beat heavy cream in a *chilled* bowl until stiff. Set aside.

Using the electric mixer, beat peanut butter until smooth. Gradually, *tablespoonful by tablespoonful*, beat sweetened condensed milk into peanut butter until thoroughly combined, scraping bowl as needed. Add vanilla extract. Mix well. *Whisk-fold* stiffly whipped cream *gently*, but *thoroughly*, into peanut butter mixture.

Pour mixture into chilled loaf pan. Spread evenly. Cover tightly with aluminum foil. Freeze overnight or until firm—about 8 hours.

Either scoop ice cream from pan to serve or remove entire block of ice cream from pan and slice.

Leftovers should be returned to the freezer, tightly covered.

Yields about eight 1/2-cup servings

Notes: When required, this recipe is easily doubled. Use a 9 x 5 x 3-inch non-stick-coated loaf pan.

A gilding of chocolate sauce, although not traditional or essential, is complimentary.

1/8 SERVING (i. e., per 1/2 cupful) –
PROTEIN = 3.8 g.; FAT = 14.3 g.; CARBOHYDRATE = 19.3 g.;
CALORIES = 227; CALORIES FROM FAT = 57%

Africa–Senegal

SENEGALESE YOGURT DRINK
Toufam

TPT - 50 minutes;
30 minutes = chilling period

Yogurt drinks such as kefir are enjoyed in North Africa and the Middle East. They not only refresh but they provide a delicious source of predigested protein. This Senegalese drink is enjoyed between meals or with meals and as a special welcome drink to a visitor or traveler.

3 cups water
3/4 cup sugar

1 1/2 cups PLAIN *or* VANILLA YOGURT, as preferred *[see index]* ***or* commercially-available yogurt of choice**

In a saucepan set over *MEDIUM* heat, combine water and sugar. Allow to come to a full boil. Boil for about 4 minutes to allow a light syrup to form. Refrigerate for at least 30 minutes.

In a carafe or pitcher, combine sugar syrup and yogurt. Using a long-handled spoon, stir until smooth or pour back and forth into another pitcher or measuring cup until well-mixed. Refrigerate until required.

Serve cold.

Yields 8 servings
adequate for 4-6 people

Note: This recipe can be halved or doubled, when required.

1/8 SERVING – PROTEIN = 2.1 g.; FAT = 0.7 g.; CARBOHYDRATE = 23.6 g.;
CALORIES = 109; CALORIES FROM FAT = 6%

Sierra Leone

Archaeological finds indicate that this area of West Africa has been continuously occupied since about 500 BC. Its dense forestation limited contact with the pre-colonial African empires to the North and East. The same natural barrier limited Islamic influence from the Mali Empire until much later than other countries in this coastal region of West Africa. Although Sierra Leone is a predominately Muslim country today, it is lauded for its religious tolerance. As was Liberia, Sierra Leone was originally founded as a homeland for freed slaves, many of whom had returned to Africa from the Americas after seeking refuge with the British army during the American Revolution and subsequently fleeing to Nova Scotia with other Loyalists.

Western contact had begun in 1462 with the arrival of the Portuguese explorer Pedro da Cintra. The Lion Mountains, *Serra Lyoa*, were named by da Cintra, as he mapped the mountains around what is now Freetown Harbour. The slave trade in Sierra Leone was the major commercial endeavor from the late fifteenth century through to the middle of the nineteenth century. Christopher Fyfe states in his 1962 book, *A History of Sierra Leone*, that an estimate in 1789 put the annual slave exportation at 74,000 persons. In 1792 Freetown was founded by the Sierra Leone Company and welcomed those who had been freed from slavery by the British throughout their empire but it must be noted than even after the 1807 British mandate forbidding transatlantic slave trading, illegal trafficking in slaves continued for several decades.

A colonial governor, situated in Freetown, the present-day capital of Sierra Leone, oversaw British interests in the African Gold Coast, now Ghana, Sierra Leone, and the settlements in what is today The Gambia. In 1808 Freetown became a British Crown Colony and in 1896 the interior of the country became a British Protectorate. Independence from Great Britain came in 1961 under the leadership of Sir Milton Margai, who made little display of his power or status nor was he corrupt. Unfortunately, he died suddenly in 1964 and was succeeded by his half brother Sir Albert Margai whose style of leadership was distinctly authoritarian leading to three military *coups* in 1967 and 1968. Sierra Leone declared itself a republic in 1971 but stability was elusive. From 1991 to 2002 the country was embroiled in a devastating civil war that put an end to agricultural and forest management systems, destroyed infrastructure, resulted in the deaths of an estimated fifty thousand people, and displaced an estimated two million people who fled as refugees to neighboring countries.

Sierra Leonean cuisine is a simple cuisine based on basic locally grown or gathered ingredients as are the cuisines of many of Africa's poorer countries. Agricultural production is challenged by the tropical climate pattern—from May to November there is a rainy season followed by a dry season from December to May during which cool, dry winds blow in from the Sahara Dessert. Decades of British influences are apparent in recipes. However, it is interesting to note that a significant number of Sierra Leoneans are immigrants from Lebanon or of Lebanese descent. Most live in the cities and are commercial traders. As a result of their presence in the country, Lebanese restaurants have become popular with both tourists and locals, and spices, previously unavailable to the Sierra Leonean cook, are now for sale in the open-air markets.

Africa–Sierra Leone

The white or orange flesh of the egusi, a watermelon variety popular in West Africa, will not be something you will be able to enjoy unless you travel to Sierra Leone. Our red-fleshed watermelon can be substituted in this menu.

Avocado Dip with Lime
with Warm Flatbread

~~~~~~~~~~~~~~~~~~~~

Black-Eyed Peas with Coconut Milk and Cocoa
Frejon

~~~~~~~~~~

Meatless "Chicken" Stew with Tomatoes and Garlic

Greens in Broth with Sesame Seeds

Steamed Rice

~~~~~~~~~~

Rice and Tomatoes with Coconut Milk
Kokosrijst

Mashed Sweetpotatoes with Ginger

~~~~~~~~~~~~~~~~~~~~

Watermelon

Sweet Rice Flour Balls
Foorah

SIERRA LEONEAN
AVOCADO DIP WITH LIME

TPT - 5 minutes

Avocados frequently are the base for a first course dip and those dips are frequently spicy. This version from Sierra Leone can be adjusted quite easily from gentle-gentle to hot-hot with the addition of more Tabasco sauce or jalapeño chili sauce. Actually everything is easy about this dip. We love it with warm flatbread or toasts, or even with crackers.

2 ripe avocados—peeled and pitted

2 tablespoons freshly squeezed lime juice
3 tablespoons *very finely* **chopped onion**
1/4 teaspoon salt
Freshly ground mixed peppercorns—red, white, and black—to taste
Several drops Tabasco sauce *or jalapeño chili* **sauce, or to taste**

In a shallow mixing bowl, mash avocados well.

Add lime juice, *very finely* chopped onion, salt, ground mixed peppercorns, and hot sauce. Mix well. Taste and adjust seasoning, if necessary. Turn into a serving bowl. Set on dinner plate and place breads, toasts, or crackers around the bowl.

Serve at once.

Yields 18 servings
adequate for 6 people

Note: This recipe can be halved or doubled, when required.

SIERRA LEONEAN
AVOCADO DIP WITH LIME (cont'd)

1/18 SERVING – PROTEIN = 0.5 g.; FAT = 3.6 g.; CARBOHYDRATE = 1.7 g.; CALORIES = 38; CALORIES FROM FAT = 85%

BLACK-EYED PEAS WITH COCONUT MILK AND COCOA IN THE STYLE OF SIERRA LEONE
Frejon
TPT - 24 minutes

Cocoa is another New World product that was introduced to Africa and has become an important export product due to the world's passion for chocolate. Although cocoa is not made into chocolate in Africa, unsweetened cocoa powder is added to stews and bean dishes, as is the case here. However, home consumption is not the purpose of this crop which is a major export crop for Ghana, Sierra Leone, and Côte d'Ivoire. This particular dish is traditionally served by Christians on Good Friday in Sierra Leone and in Nigeria.

1/8 teaspoon ground ginger
1/8 teaspoon ground cardamom
Pinch ground cinnamon
Pinch ground turmeric
Freshly ground black pepper, to taste

1 tablespoon unsweetened cocoa powder
1 tablespoon *hot* water

1 can (15 ounces) well-drained canned *or*
1 3/4 cups cooked, dry black-eyed peas (beans)*
1/2 cup *light, sulfite-free* coconut milk
1 tablespoon sugar
Salt, to taste**

In a small dish, combine ground ginger, cardamom, cinnamon, turmeric, and black pepper. Stir to mix. Set aside briefly.

In a second small dish, combine cocoa powder and hot water. Stir well until cocoa is dissolved.

In a saucepan set over *LOW-MEDIUM* heat, combine well-drained black-eyed peas, coconut milk, and sugar. Stir vigorously to slightly mash the beans.

Add spice mixture and dissolved cocoa powder. Stir to integrate the spices. Cook until thoroughly heated through.

Serve hot over *couscous* or steamed rice.

Yields 6 servings
adequate for 4 people

Notes: *Do not select "Southern-style" black-eyed peas if you choose to use canned beans. Southern-style denotes the addition of bacon or bacon fat.

**Beans canned without salt or beans prepared from dry beans may require additional salt.

This recipe can be halved, when required.

1/6 SERVING – PROTEIN = 5.6 g.; FAT = 0.9 g.; CARBOHYDRATE = 13.1 g.; CALORIES = 75; CALORIES FROM FAT = 75%

MEATLESS "CHICKEN" STEW WITH TOMATO AND GARLIC
TPT - 48 minutes

Although ocean fish and shellfish are generally the offering in coastal regions while meats and river fish will be found inland, a chicken stew, redolent with black pepper, and garlic, is a common dish served on holidays across Sierra Leone. It varies from area to area, from family to family. This vegetarian version, using soymeat "chicken" strips, allows us to enjoy the characteristic spicing of Sierra Leonean food.

1 1/2 teaspoons *extra virgin* olive oil
1 1/2 teaspoons butter
1 large onion—halved and *thinly* sliced
2 garlic cloves—*very finely* chopped

8 ounces *frozen* soymeat analogue strips
[see next page]

Africa—Sierra Leone

**MEATLESS "CHICKEN" STEW
WITH TOMATO AND GARLIC** (cont'd)

2 cups VEGETABLE STOCK FROM SOUP *[see index]* **or** other vegetarian stock of choice
1 cup canned, *whole* tomatoes with canning liquid
2 tablespoons freshly squeezed lime juice
1/4 teaspoon freshly ground black pepper, to more to taste
Ground red pepper (cayenne), to taste
Pinch crushed, dried marjoram
Pinch crushed, dried sage
Pinch dried thyme
Pinch powdered, dried rosemary
2 whole cloves

2 or 3 teaspoons KNEADED FLOUR FOR THICKENING *(Buerre Manie) [see index]*

In a small kettle set over *MEDIUM* heat, combine olive oil and butter. When the butter is melted, add *thinly* sliced onion and *very finely* chopped garlic. Sauté until onion is soft and translucent, *being careful to allow neither the onion nor garlic to brown*.

Add soymeat analogue strips. Sauté for a minute or two.

Add stock, whole tomatoes, lime juice, black pepper, ground red pepper (cayenne), crushed, dried marjoram, sage, and thyme, powdered rosemary, and cloves. Stir to integrate the herbs and spices.

Allow to come to the simmer. Reduce heat to *LOW* and allow to gently simmer for about 30 minutes, stirring frequently. Retrieve and discard cloves.

Add *buerre manie*, one at a time, and cook, stirring constantly, until the stew thickens. Turn into a heated serving bowl.

Serve over steamed rice.

*Yields 6 servings
adequate for 4 people*

Note: This dish can be frozen, defrosted, and slowly reheated for a subsequent appearance.

1/6 SERVING – PROTEIN = 9.8 g.; FAT = 2.7 g.; CARBOHYDRATE = 8.8 g.;
CALORIES = 136; CALORIES FROM FAT = 18%

SIERRA LEONEAN RICE AND TOMATOES WITH COCONUT MILK
Kokosrijst
TPT - 1 hour and 8 minutes

Sierra Leoneans cook rice in a way quite similar to a popular Indonesian specialty. Further they use a name for it that is unmistakably Dutch which suggests contact and adaptation although it is perhaps more often referred to as a "jollop" here and in other countries in West Africa. The addition of tomatoes, onions, and chili powder identifies this Sierra Leonean version. It is, to our way of thinking, a simple, comforting, and delicious main course for a family dinner.

2 cups VEGETABLE STOCK FROM SOUP *[see index]* **or** other vegetarian stock of choice
1 medium onion—*finely* chopped
1 1/2 cups canned, *diced* tomatoes canned in purée
1/2 teaspoon chili powder, or to taste
Salt, to taste

1 cup dry Japanese short grain white rice—*do not use precooked/converted variety*
1 tablespoon butter

3/4 cup canned *light, preservative-free* coconut milk*

In a saucepan set over *MEDIUM* heat, combine stock, *finely* chopped onion, diced tomatoes, chili powder, and salt. Allow to come to the boil, *reduce heat to LOW-MEDIUM*, cover, and cook for 10 minutes.

Add rice and butter. Stir to integrate the rice, cover, and allow to cook *undisturbed* for 20 minutes.

Add coconut milk. Taste and adjust chili powder and salt, if necessary. Cook, stirring frequently, for about 7-8 minutes more, or until heated through. Turn into a heated serving bowl. Keep warm on a warming tray until ready to serve.

Serve into heated soup plates. Refrigerate leftovers and reheat *gently* for another meal.

*Yields 6 servings
adequate for 4-6 people*

SIERRA LEONE RICE AND TOMATOES WITH COCONUT MILK (cont'd)

Notes: *Canned coconut milk is available in most grocery stores in either the international section or beverage section. Leftover coconut milk can be frozen.

This recipe may be have or doubled, when required.

1/6 SERVING – PROTEIN = 4.0 g.; FAT = 3.3 g.; CARBOHYDRATE = 35.6 g.; CALORIES = 189; CALORIES FROM FAT = 16%

SIERRA LEONEAN SWEET RICE FLOUR BALLS
Foorah

TPT - 1 hour and 53 minutes;
1 hour = chilling period

Friends, who are diner fans, were working on a truly monumental project to document and identify classic diners. We traveled with them to many diners where Mario often judged the diner on meatloaf, mashed potatoes, and lemon meringue pie and I ordered a grilled cheese sandwich with Swiss cheese on whole wheat bread and rice pudding. If it was a diner that served Greek items, the decision was made on their spinach pie. I related the diner story to another friend who knew about my fondness for rice pudding. She asked me if I had ever eaten these sweet rice flour balls and, of course, I had to try them.

1 cup *boiling* water
1/2 cup sugar

1 cup rice flour
1/2 cup *two-percent* milk*

1 tablespoon rice flour

Pour *boiling* water and sugar into a saucepan and set over *LOW-MEDIUM* heat. Cook, stirring frequently, until sugar is dissolved.

In a mixing bowl, combine the 1 cupful rice flour and milk. Stir until a paste is formed. Pour the flour paste into the simmering sugar syrup. Cook, stirring constantly, until it forms a thick paste. Remove from heat and allow to cool slightly.

With two spoons, remove a tablespoonful of the rice paste and form into a small ball. Coat with reserved tablespoonful of rice flour. Place on serving plate. Repeat until all the rice paste has been formed into balls. Refrigerate for at least 1 hour.

Serve chilled.

Yields 23 rice flour balls

Notes: *Milk is added in this instance to increase the nutrition and flavor of the rice balls. Water can be substituted if you prefer to make these as a vegan dessert.

This recipe can be doubled, when required.

1/23 SERVING (i. e., per rice flour ball) –
PROTEIN = 0.6 g.; FAT = 0.1 g.; CARBOHYDRATE = 9.8 g.;
CALORIES = 42; CALORIES FROM FAT = 2%

Somalia

Mogadishu, the capital of Somalia, was founded in the year 900 AD but archeological findings confirm that the land that is now Somalia had been inhabited continuously at least since about 500 BC; Paleolithic cave paintings in Laas Gaal, the oldest on the African continent, have been dated to 9000 BC. The founding of the capital city corresponds to the period when Islam took hold in this part of Africa. At that point in history the northwest area of the country was part of the Aksumit Empire which controlled the region from the third century to the seventh century AD. After the Aksumite Empire, tribal city-states and kingdoms were established, a system of governance which lasted until, and even into, the colonial period.

Colonization of Somalia was marked by bloody conflicts as Great Britain and Italy laid claims to Somalia beginning in the late 1880s after the Berlin Conference of 1884. The British created a protectorate known as British Somaliland; the Italians, after failing to win militarily in their bid for Ethiopia in 1895, eventually colonized the southern area of the region, which included the capital of Mogadishu. This Italian colony, known as Italian Somaliland, was established in 1925, and an estimated thirty-two thousand Italians immigrated to the colony.

Benito Mussolini set his sights on colonizing Abyssinia (now, Ethiopia) in 1935, resulting in the occupation of Ethiopia and its annexation into Italian East Africa. In 1940 Italy moved from Ethiopia into British Somaliland and in eleven days succeeded in occupying Berbera. In January 1941 British forces moved into the occupied territory from Kenya. By February most of Italian Somaliland had been captured. Moving in from the sea, British forces retook British Somaliland by March. In 1949, four years after the defeat of the Axis Powers in World War II, the United Nations returned Italian Somaliland to Italy as a trustee territory with the condition that Somalia be prepared for and be granted independence within ten years. British Somaliland was not granted independence until 1960.

By 1978 support for the ruling military dictatorship weakened as the people found no improvement in their lives that had been devastated by the Ogaden War with Ethiopia. In 1991 the northern region of the country, the former British Somaliland, declared itself Somaliland and set on a path to self governance. This region of the country, albeit not officially recognized by any nation or by the United Nations, established a government and achieved relative stability. This was not the case in the southern region, the former Italian Somaliland. The Somali Civil War, the continual conflicts that have followed especially with the Islamists of the South, and the lack of a strong central government have resulted in anarchy and a breakdown in society. The problems of crime, piracy, hyperinflation, fuel shortages, and forceful restrictive policies of the government have led to a mass emigration resulting in expatriate communities all over the world.

Somali enjoy meat and you will find that vegetarian dishes are few and far between. If you request a meatless dish, they will graciously leave the meat out of the dish but beware, the dish will be made with lamb, beef, or chicken stock and they will consider that meatless. All is not lost if you wish to explore Somali cooking; explore it at home and make the changes necessary for your lifestyle. In the following menu suggestions you will see hints of the many influences that have contributed to the Somali cuisine. These range from the adaptation of traditional East African dishes, such as thin pancakes and sautéed greens; to foods introduced during the Italian colonial period and taken to heart, such as *pasta*; and those introduced by Arab and Indian traders such as *halva* and *hummus*. Together with New World food staples like tomatoes, pumpkins, corn, and potatoes, these influences have led to thoroughly unique cuisine.

Africa–Somalia

Skillet Flatbread with *Hummus*
Muufo

Banana Nectar or other Nectar or Fruit Juice of choice

~

Puréed Lentil Soup

~

Saladh

Mushroom and Chick Pea Salad	*Couscous* **Salad** **with Tomato – Black Bean** *Vinaigrette*
Avocado and Grapefruit Salad	**Orange Salad with** *Calamarata*

~~~~~~~~~~~~~~~~~~~~~

Spaghetti

with

Tomato Sauce with Potatoes, Garlic, and Fresh Coriander

Sautéed Greens with Peanuts

~~~~~~~~~~

Baked Spaghetti with Two Sauces
Baasto Forno

Banana Slices

~~~~~~~~~~

Bean and Hominy *Chili*
Muthokoi

Skillet Flatbread *[see above]*
Muufo

~~~~~~~~~~~~~~~~~~~~~

Green Tomato Relish

~

Pineapple Dessert with Coconut and Cream
Sambusa

Creamsicle *Sorbet*
Jalaato

~

Chilled Coffee Milk with Cardamom and Cinnamon
Qahwe

Cinnamon Candies

Africa–**Somalia**

SOMALI SKILLET FLATBREAD
Muufo
TPT - 21 minutes

Unlike the "canjeero," which is more like the injera pancakes made from the millet grain tef which one finds in Ethiopia, this flatbread is perhaps more akin to flatbreads one would find in the Middle East. It is a skillet bread that can be prepared in minutes.

1/2 cup unbleached white flour
1/4 cup whole wheat flour
1/4 cup *fine* corn meal, such as *masa harina* used to make *tortillas*
1 teaspoon sugar
1 1/2 teaspoons baking powder
1/4 teaspoon salt

1 cup *two-percent* milk
2 tablespoons *fat-free* pasteurized eggs

Lightly coat a non-stick-coated skillet with lecithin spray coating. Preheat over *MEDIUM* heat.

In a mixing bowl, combine white and whole wheat flours, corn meal, sugar, baking powder, and salt. Stir to mix.

Add milk and pasteurized eggs. Stir to form a batter.

Starting in the middle of the pan and working in a circular clockwise motion, spread 1/4 cupful of batter in the preheated pan. When browned on the bottom surface, remove with a spatula to a serving plate. Continue until all the batter has been used.

Serve warm.

Yields 14 loaves

Note: This recipe can be doubled, when required.

1/14 SERVING (i. e., per loaf) –
PROTEIN = 1.8 g.; FAT = 0.4 g.; CARBOHYDRATE = 8.9 g.;
CALORIES = 46; CALORIES FROM FAT = 8%

SOMALI PURÉED LENTIL SOUP
TPT - 1 hour and 57 minutes;
1 hour = lentil soaking period

As I have traveled the world in search of culinary treasures that I have indeed found, lentil soups, stews, and casseroles have turned up as I crossed border after border. The small pulse nourishes every corner of our planet. This nicely seasoned soup needs nothing more than bread, a salad, and some fruit to satisfy and nourish well.

1/2 cup dry brown (*or* green) lentils
3 cups *boiling* water

1 tablespoon *extra virgin* olive oil
1 small onion—*finely* chopped

2 medium potatoes—peeled and diced
1 medium carrot—scraped or pared and diced

3 cups VEGETABLE STOCK FROM SOUP *[see index]*, VEGETARIAN BROWN STOCK *[see index]*, *or* other vegetarian stock of choice
1 large garlic clove—*very finely* chopped
1 cup canned, *diced* tomatoes
1/4 cup chopped fresh coriander (*cilantro*)
1/2 teaspoon ground cumin
3/4 teaspoon chili powder
Salt, to taste
Freshly ground black pepper, to taste

Pick over lentils and discard any of poor quality. Rinse thoroughly. Drain. Pour into a mixing bowl and add the *boiling* water. Set aside at room temperature for 1 hour. Drain.

In a small *non-aluminum** kettle set over *MEDIUM* heat, heat oil. Add *finely* chopped onion and sauté until soft and transparent, *being careful not to allow onion to brown.*

Add diced potatoes and carrot. Cook stirring constantly, for several minutes.

Add vegetable stock, *very finely* chopped garlic, diced tomatoes, chopped fresh coriander (*cilantro*), ground cumin, chili powder, salt, and black pepper. Add drained lentils. Cook, stirring frequently, until potatoes and carrots are tender—about 30 minutes.

Africa–Somalia

SOMALI PURÉED LENTIL SOUP (cont'd)

Using a food processor fitted with steel knife or an electric blender, process the soup in small batches until a smooth purée results. Turn into a clean, large saucepan set over *LOW-MEDIUM* heat. Allow puréed soup to heat through. Add more water if texture is too thick. Turn into a heated soup tureen.

Serve into heated soup plates.

Yields about 5 1/4 cupfuls

Notes: This recipe can be frozen very successfully.

When required, this recipe can be doubled.

1/7 SERVING (i. e., about 3/4 cupful) –
PROTEIN = 5.3 g.; FAT = 1.9 g.; CARBOHYDRATE = 19.2 g.;
CALORIES = 112; CALORIES FROM FAT = 15%

SOMALI MUSHROOM AND CHICK PEA SALAD
TPT - 5 minutes

I have made hundreds of salads in my lifetime and eaten hundreds more in my travels but the combination of vegetables and the unusual salad dressing ingredients in this popular Somali salad were a new experience for me, one that I have repeated many times since that very exciting first taste.

8 ounces fresh mushrooms of choice—trimmed, well-rinsed, and sliced
1 cup canned chick peas (*garbanzos*)—rinsed and well-drained
1/2 cup sliced *Kalamata* olives
3 large shallots—sliced
1/2 cup chopped red bell pepper
1 medium tomato—seeded and chopped

DRESSING:
    1/4 cup *light, sulfite-free* coconut milk
    1 garlic clove—*very finely* chopped
    1 tablespoon freshly squeezed lemon juice
    1/4 teaspoon ground cumin
    1/8 teaspoon ground turmeric
    1/2 teaspoon crushed, dried basil

In a serving bowl, combine sliced mushrooms, chick peas, sliced olives, sliced shallots, chopped red pepper, and chopped tomato. Toss gently.

Prepare salad dressing in a jar or cruet by combine coconut milk, *very finely* chopped garlic, lemon juice, ground cumin and turmeric, and crushed basil. Shake well to combine.

Just before serving, pour prepared dressing over vegetables. Toss to combine.

Serve at once.

Yields 6 servings
adequate for 4 people

Note: This recipe can be doubled, when required.

1/6 SERVING – PROTEIN = 3.3 g.; FAT = 1.5 g.; CARBOHYDRATE = 8.9 g.;
CALORIES = 59; CALORIES FROM FAT = 23%

Africa–**Somalia**

SOMALI *COUSCOUS* SALAD
WITH TOMATO – BLACK BEAN *VINAIGRETTE*
TPT - 8 hours and 38 minutes;
8 hours = flavor development period

The remarkably unique protein complementation concept first attracted me to this recipe. Putting the leguminous protein into a salad dressing just had never occurred to me and it is a useful recipe for using up the chick peas and black beans that have been squirreled away in the freezer. This wonderful one-dish meal is an opportunity for a cook to prepare a meal and actually enjoy it because it can be prepared early in the day or the day before. I often make this salad to take on a picnic, picking up some fresh pita or nan loaves en route to our favorite state forest site.

3 cups *boiling* **water**
1 1/2 cups whole wheat *couscous*

TOMATO–BEAN *VINAIGRETTE*:
  1/2 cup canned, *diced* **tomatoes plus about 1/4 cup of canning liquid** *or* **peeled and chopped fresh tomatoes**
  1/3 cup trimmed, well-rinsed, and chopped scallions
  1/3 cup canned black beans—well-drained
  1/4 cup canned chick peas (*garbanzos*) —well-drained with seed coats removed
  2 garlic cloves—chopped
  3 tablespoons chopped fresh coriander (*cilantro*)
  1/4 teaspoon freshly grated nutmeg
  1/8 teaspoon freshly ground black pepper
  1/8 teaspoon ground allspice
  Salt, to taste*

  2 tablespoons *extra virgin* olive oil

12 canned, baby corn ears—well-rinsed and chopped into 1/2-inch pieces

In a saucepan set over *LOW* heat, combine *boiling* water and *couscous*. Cover tightly and allow to cook for about 5 minutes. Remove from heat and allow *couscous* to steam for about 10 minutes. *All water should be absorbed.* Refrigerate while dressing is being prepared.

In the work bowl of the food processor fitted with steel knife or in the electric blender, combine diced tomatoes, chopped scallion, black beans, chick peas, garlic, fresh coriander (*cilantro*), grated nutmeg, black pepper, ground allspice, and salt. Process until a smooth purée results, scraping down the sides of the work bowl as needed.

While the processor or blender is still running, slowly pour the oil through the ingredient tube until thoroughly integrated. Pour *vinaigrette* mixture into a mixing bowl.

Add cooked *couscous* and baby corn slices. Stir to combine. Chill for at least 8 hours. Turn into a serving bowl or onto a platter.

Serve chilled.

Yields 8 servings
adequate for 6 people

Notes: *If you choose to cook dry beans for this recipe, salt may be required.

Served over baby spinach, this can be a very pleasant luncheon or light supper entrée.

This recipe can be halved or doubled, when required.

1/6 SERVING – PROTEIN = 7.5 g.; FAT = 4.0 g.; CARBOHYDRATE = 41.3 g.;
CALORIES = 218; CALORIES FROM FAT = 17%

AVOCADO AND GRAPEFRUIT SALAD
TPT - 15 minutes

Yes, the taste of the grapefruit and the avocado bounce off each other superbly and that is initially why I created this salad, but the textures of the three ingredients are what make it remarkable. It is not just a salad to accompany a main course, it is noticed by the palate. Years later I found that this is one of the combinations of fruits that often appear in fruit salads in Somalia. They gild what I consider to be a perfect salad with lemon juice and sugar and garnish the salad with coconut but I find these added adornments unnecessary. Other fruits are often added by Somali cooks including bananas, guavas, mangoes, melons, or oranges.

Africa–Somalia

AVOCADO AND GRAPEFRUIT SALAD (cont'd)

1 large white *or* pink grapefruit, as preferred

1 ripe avocado

6 Boston lettuce leaves—well-washed and dried

Slice grapefruit in half. Remove large seeds and section. Transfer sections to a mixing bowl. Drain off as much juice as possible, reserving it for another use, and remove any seeds.

Peel, halve, slice, and chop avocado. Add to grapefruit sections. Toss gently to mix.

Chill in the refrigerator until ready to serve.

Line a serving bowl with Boston lettuce leaves. Pile grapefruit–avocado mixture into center.

Serve at once.

Yields 6 servings
adequate for 4 people

Note: This recipe is easily doubled, when required.

1/6 SERVING – PROTEIN = 1.0 g.; FAT = 5.5 g.; CARBOHYDRATE = 5.4 g.;
CALORIES = 69; CALORIES FROM FAT = 77%

ORANGE SALAD WITH *CALAMARATA*
TPT - 39 minutes

Orange slices with olive oil is a classic Italian salad much loved by us any time but especially when my friend from childhood days sends us oranges from the tree in his California yard. This simple salad was introduced to Italy's African colonies and adapted by Somali cooks to the fruits available. Although fish are not widely eaten in Somalia except along the coast, a salad of sliced fruit with calamari, squid, is a popular salad often found on restaurant menus. Since Somali are very fond of pasta, I have evolved a vegetarian version of that salad using calamarata macaroni. It is usually available in stores that sell pasta imported from Italy and if the rings are cut into narrow rings after they are cooked, the effect is very much that of sliced squid tentacles with the same chewy texture.

1 1/2 ounces large *calamarata pasta*
3 quarts *boiling* water

6 *small* navel oranges—peeled and pith removed

1 1/2 tablespoons *extra virgin* olive oil*
Freshly ground black pepper, to taste

In a large kettle set over *MEDIUM* heat, cook *pasta* in *boiling* water until tender. Drain well. Using a scissors, cut each macaroni ring into two thinner rings. Set aside until required.

Using a sharp knife, slice each orange into thin slices. Arrange on six salad plates.

Apportion *calamarata* rings among the salad plates, scattering them over the oranges.

Sprinkle olive oil over each serving. Grind black pepper generously over each serving.

Serve chilled or at room temperature, as preferred.

Yields 6 servings

Notes: *Be sure to use the best tasting olive oil you can find.

This recipe can easily be increased or decreased to accommodate the number of servings required.

1/6 SERVING – PROTEIN = 2.3 g.; FAT = 3.0 g.; CARBOHYDRATE = 21.4 g.;
CALORIES = 116; CALORIES FROM FAT = 23%

Africa–Somalia

SOMALI TOMATO SAUCE WITH POTATOES, GARLIC, AND FRESH CORIANDER
TPT - 44 minutes

The influence of Italian colonization is firmly ensconced in the cuisine of Somalia to the point that lunch counters and street vendors often offer spaghetti and macaroni sauced with ketchup much the way French fries are offered as "walk-around-food" at our farmers' market. A marinara sauce, with quite different seasoning than that to which we are accustomed, is a common sauce for pasta as is this sauce. Whenever I make this sauce, my husband muses as to what his mother would have said. I very much suspect she would have said, ". . . not my style." Somali generally add ground beef to such a sauce; ground soymeat may be added, if desired.

2 tablespoon *extra virgin* olive oil
1/2 cup *finely* chopped onion
5 garlic cloves—*very finely* chopped

1 can (28 ounces) *diced* tomatoes
1 can (6 ounces) tomato paste

1 large potato—peeled and cubed

3/4 cup chopped fresh coriander (*cilantro*)
5 large basil leaves—*finely* chopped— *or*
   2 teaspoons dried, crushed basil
1 teaspoon ground coriander
1/4 teaspoon ground mixed peppercorns—red, black, and white—or to taste
Salt, to taste

In a small kettle set over *MEDIUM* heat, heat olive oil. Add *finely* chopped onion and *very finely* chopped garlic. Sauté until onion is soft and translucent, *being careful to allow neither the onion nor the garlic to brown.*

Add diced tomatoes and tomato paste. Cook, stirring frequently, for about 5 minutes.

Add potato cubes. *Reduce heat to LOW–MEDIUM* and cook for about 15 minutes, stirring frequently.

Add chopped fresh coriander (*cilantro*) and basil, ground coriander, ground mixed peppercorns, and salt. Stir to mix well. Cook, stirring frequently, for about 15 minutes more. Turn into a serving dish.

Serve hot over cooked spaghetti or macaroni, of choice.

Yields 8 servings
adequate for 6 people

Note: Since this sauce freezes well, I often make a double batch.

1/8 SERVING – PROTEIN = 2.6 g.; FAT = 3.1 g.; CARBOHYDRATE = 14.4 g.;
CALORIES = 93; CALORIES FROM FAT = 30%

BAKED SPAGHETTI WITH TWO SAUCES
Baasto Forno
TPT - 1 hour and 38 minutes

Years ago we had dinner with our close friend from graduate school days and her mother. They served a remarkable "lasagna al forno" which was made with two sauces, a tomato sauce and a béchamel. This Somali casserole was certainly adapted from such a dish. The adaptation of Italian macaroni and spaghetti dishes by the Somali is not surprising. Influences from the Italian colonial period are pervasive in the Somali cuisine and, as above, one finds Italian words, or versions of such words, incorporated into the vernacular speech of the population. This dish is quite different from any "pasta al forno" that one would find in Italy but there is no doubt as to the culinary origin. Somali usually add a layer of ground meat but it is just as satisfying a family meal without the meat. Also Somali generally serve bananas with pasta dishes which is not as obtuse a concept as once might think. During the Italian colonial period huge plantations of bananas were planted by Italian entrepreneurs; the mental connection of bananas and pasta is not forgotten by the Somali.

BAKED SPAGHETTI WITH TWO SAUCES (cont'd)

4 quarts *boiling* water
1/2 pound dry spaghetti

TOMATO SAUCE:
    2 tablespoons *extra virgin* olive oil
    1 medium onion—*finely* chopped
    2 large garlic cloves—*very finely* chopped

    2 cups canned, *diced* tomatoes
    1 teaspoon ground coriander
    Salt, to taste
    Freshly ground black pepper, to taste

BÊCHAMEL SAUCE:
    1/4 cup safflower *or* sunflower oil

    1/4 cup unbleached white flour

    3 cups *skimmed* milk
    1 teaspoon salt
    1/8 teaspoon freshly grated nutmeg, or
        to taste

3 tablespoons grated *pecorino Romano* cheese

3 tablespoons chopped fresh coriander (*cilantro*) leaves *or* parsley leaves, if preferred

Prepare a 2-quart soufflé dish or other oven-to table dish by spraying with non-stick lecithin spray coating.

In a kettle set over *MEDIUM* heat, combine *boiling* water and spaghetti. Cook spaghetti according to package directions. Drain thoroughly. Set aside until required.

In a saucepan set over *MEDIUM* heat, heat olive oil. Add *finely* chopped onion and *very finely* chopped garlic. Sauté until onion and garlic are soft and translucent, *being careful not to allow either vegetable to brown.*

Add tomatoes, ground coriander, salt, and pepper. Cook, stirring frequently for about 15 minutes. Adjust seasoning, if necessary.

Meanwhile, prepare the *bêchamel* sauce. In a non-stick-coated saucepan set over *LOW-MEDIUM* heat, heat safflower or sunflower oil. Remove from heat and, using a wire whisk, make a *roux* by beating in flour. Return to heat and, stirring constantly, cook for 2 minutes, *being careful not to burn or overbrown the roux.* Remove from heat and gradually beat in milk. Return saucepan to heat and cook, stirring constantly, until thickened.

Add salt and nutmeg. Stir well. Remove from heat.

Preheat oven to 350 degrees F.

Spoon about *one-third* of the tomato sauce into the bottom of the prepared baking dish. Spoon about *one third* of the *bêchamel* sauce over. Layer *one-half* of the cooked and drained spaghetti over. Spoon *one-half* of the remaining tomato sauce over followed by *one-half* of the remaining *bêchamel* sauce. Layer the remaining spaghetti over. Spoon the remaining tomato sauce over the spaghetti followed by the remaining *bêchamel* sauce.

Sprinkle grated cheese over.

Bake in preheated 350 degree F. oven for 25 minutes.

Sprinkle chopped fresh coriander (*cilantro*) or parsley over the casserole. Return to the oven to continue baking for about 7 minutes more.

Serve at once.

                              Yields 6 servings
                            adequate for 4 people

Note: This recipe can be halved, if required. Bake the halved portion in a 1-quart baking dish.

1/6 SERVING – PROTEIN = 7.6 g.; FAT = 14.3 g.; CARBOHYDRATE = 41.5 g.;
CALORIES = 342; CALORIES FROM FAT = 38%

Africa–Somalia

SOMALI BEAN AND HOMINY *CHILI*
Muthokoi

TPT - 55 minutes

Hominy, which is the name for maize in the Algonquian language, was first described by Captain John Smith in 1629 when he was introduced to it by the Powhatan Indian tribe. It is the result of a corn preservation process called nixtamalization during which corn is treated with alkali/lye to prevent the seed from sprouting during storage. In addition, it converts niacin into a form which is more absorbable by the body, it augments amino acid absorption, and improves the calcium to phosphorus ratio. If you have passed hominy by in your supermarket simply because you do not know how to prepare it, this very flavorful casserole is an excellent dish to acquaint you with the texture and flavor of hominy. Some recipes for muthokoi are as simple as beans, hominy, onion, and tomatoes but this one builds on the basics. It is a very flavorful way to complement leguminous and grain proteins.

2 tablespoons corn *or* peanut oil
1 medium onion—coarsely chopped about 1 cupful
1 garlic clove—*very finely* chopped

1 can (15.5 ounces) red kidney beans—*undrained*
  or* equivalent in cooked, dry beans
1 can (15.5 ounces) hominy—well-drained
2 cups canned, *diced* tomatoes packed in tomato purée *or* 2 cups peeled, seeded, and chopped fresh tomatoes
1 tablespoon tomato paste
1 teaspoon sugar
1 teaspoon chili powder, or more if desired
1/2 teaspoon ground cumin
3/4 teaspoon freshly ground black pepper
Pinch dried oregano leaves—crushed
Pinch freshly grated nutmeg

3 tablespoons chopped fresh coriander (*cilantro*)

***Fat-free* dairy sour cream, to garnish**

In a heavy kettle, with cover, set over *MEDIUM* heat, heat oil. Add chopped onion and garlic. Sauté gently until onion is soft and translucent, *being careful not to allow either vegetable to brown.*

Add *undrained* kidney beans, drained hominy, *diced* tomatoes, tomato paste, sugar, chili powder, ground cumin, black pepper, crushed oregano, and grated nutmeg to sautéed vegetables. Combine *gently*, but *thoroughly*. Bring to the boil, turn heat to *LOW*, cover tightly, and simmer for 40 minutes. Stir occasionally during cooking period. Remove cover and continue cooking, stirring frequently, until thickened to your liking.

Add chopped fresh coriander (*cilantro*). Stir. Allow to cook for about 5 minutes more.

Turn into heated serving bowl and serve into heated soup bowls with sour cream.

Yields 10 servings
adequate for 6 people

Notes: *Adzuki beans, very much favored in Somalia, may be substituted if preferred.

Flavor actually improves if this is prepared the day before serving.

This recipe may be doubled but increase cooking time to 1 1/4 hours. Since this dish freezes well, this is an excellent way to plan a "menu-maker" for a busy schedule.

1/10 SERVING (about 1 cupful exclusive of sour cream garnish) –
PROTEIN = 3.7 g.; FAT = 2.7 g.; CARBOHYDRATE = 16.3 g.;
CALORIES = 100; CALORIES FROM FAT = 24%

SOMALI GREEN TOMATO RELISH
TPT - 26 hours and 6 minutes;
24 hours = cooling period

The tomatoes that remain unripened as the first frost approaches have often been the subject of articles in which every conceivable suggestion is made as to how to get these stragglers to ripen before they rot. The women in my family solved that problem by making and canning green tomato mincemeat for holiday pies. This relish is also one of those "waste not" recipes. It can, be made with tomatillos, which are not small unripe tomatoes as many people think but members of a separate genus within the nightshade family. Originally called tomate (tomătl), "fat water" or "fat thing," the Spaniards confused it with the larger red fruit that was cultivated by the Aztecs and called jitomate, "fat water with navel" or "fat thing with navel." The Spaniards introduced the large red tomato to Europe as tomate and the true tomato has been all but forgotten except in central Mexico where the name tomate is still used for the tiny green fruits we call tomatillos.

Africa–Somalia

SOMALI GREEN TOMATO RELISH (cont'd)

1/2 pound *tomatillos*—husks removed, well-washed, and chopped *or* green tomatoes, if preferred
1 cup apple cider vinegar
1 1/2 cups sugar
1/2 teaspoon salt
1/2 teaspoon freshly grated nutmeg
1/2 teaspoon ground cinnamon
1/8 teaspoon ground cloves
1/8 teaspoon ground allspice

1 tablespoon *very finely* chopped mild green *chilies*

Sterilize three 1/2-pint canning jars or jelly jars. Also sterilize lids and rings for jars.

In a large kettle set over *LOW-MEDIUM* heat, combine chopped *tomatillos*, vinegar, sugar, salt, grated nutmeg, and ground cinnamon, cloves, and allspice. Mix thoroughly. Allow to come to the boil, stirring frequently. Boil for about 5 minutes until sugar is dissolved. Stir frequently.

Reduce heat to *LOW*. Cook stirring frequently, until mixture thickens—about 1 1/2 hours.

Add *very finely* chopped green *chilies*. Continue cooking for 5-10 minutes more.

Ladle into the three sterilized 1/2-pint canning jars. Carefully wipe rims of jars. Seal with hot, sterilized lids and rings. Process in hot–water–bath canner for 10 minutes, *timing from the moment the water comes to a full rolling boil.* Remove to surface covered with thick towels or newspapers. Allow to cool for 24 hours *undisturbed.* Check to be sure jars are sealed before labeling and storing in a dark, cool, dry place.* Loosen or remove rings before storing.

Yields three 1/2-pint jarfuls

Notes: *Any jars that do not seal can be stored in the refrigerator for several months or resealed using a *new lid.*

This recipe can be frozen, if preferred.

1/24 SERVING (i. e., 2 tablespoonfuls) –
PROTEIN = 0.1 g.; FAT = 0.017 g.; CARBOHYDRATE = 15.1 g.;
CALORIES = 59; CALORIES FROM FAT = <1%

PINEAPPLE DESSERT WITH COCONUT AND CREAM
Sambusa
TPT - 15 minutes

A slice of pineapple can be a sweet and refreshing end to a Somali meal but with few embellishments, it can be a bit more of a dessert. The tart sweetness of the pineapple is greatly complimented by the creamy cheese sauce.

1/4 cup *mascarpone* cheese
2 tablespoons light cream *or* half and half
1 tablespoon pineapple juice

3 tablespoons shredded coconut—fresh *or* desiccated

1 tablespoon sugar

6 chilled pineapple slices—fresh *or* canned in juice

Assemble six dessert plates.

In a small bowl, combine *mascarpone* cheese, cream, and pineapple juice. Beat well until smooth. Spoon about 1 tablespoonful of the cheese mixture into the middle of each dessert dish.

Sprinkle 1 tablespoon of coconut over the cheese on each dish.

Sprinkle about 1/4 teaspoonful of sugar over the coconut.

Settle a pineapple slice on top of the cheese base. Serve at once or chill in the refrigerator until ready to serve.

Serve chilled.

Yields 6 servings
adequate for 4 people

Notes: *Cream cheese can be used, if preferred, but the beautiful texture and richness of *mascarpone* is wonderful.

This recipe is easily adjusted to the number of diners.

1/6 SERVING – PROTEIN = 1.0 g.; FAT = 3.7 g.; CARBOHYDRATE = 20.0 g.;
CALORIES = 125; CALORIES FROM FAT = 27%

Africa–Somalia

CREAMSICLE *SORBET*
Jalaato

TPT - 8 hours and 13 minutes;
8 hours = freezing period

The childhood memory of the taste of vanilla ice cream encased in a sheath of orange ice on a wooden stick surfaces frequently. It was a terrific taste; the orange ice was refreshing, thirst-quenching, and throat-soothing, and then you broke through to the vanilla ice cream! I wonder if creamsicles taste as good today as they did sitting on the curb watching the "Good Humor" man drive on down Chadwell Road. Somali, who make frozen juice on a stick or popsicles as we know them, also add milk to these treats. I have converted a walk-around treat to a dessert that at once refreshes and evokes a fond memory.

1/2 cup water
1 cup freshly squeezed orange juice
1 1/2 tablespoons *frozen* orange juice concentrate*

3 tablespoons *fat-free* sweetened condensed milk

Chill six small ramekins thoroughly.

In a bowl, combine water, orange juice, and orange juice concentrate. Blend well. Turn into ice cube trays and freeze for at least 8 hours.**

Transfer ice cubes to the work bowl of the food processor, fitted with steel knife. Using the on-and-off pulsing technique, chop ice cubes, scraping down sides of work bowl several times.

Add sweetened condensed milk, *tablespoonful by tablespoonful,* pulsing after each addition until a *slushy* sorbet has formed. Divide among six *chilled* ramekins.***

Serve at once, with *demitasse* spoons. ****

Yields 6 individual servings

Notes: *If desired, orange–pineapple or orange–tangerine frozen concentrate can be substituted.

**The fruit juice base can be conveniently frozen for several weeks.

***For more formal presentation, the sorbet may be served in chilled sherbet glasses.

****If more convenient, the filled ramekins can be prepared several hours ahead of time and set on ice cube trays in the freezer until serving time.

1/6 SERVING – PROTEIN = 1.1 g.; FAT = 0.1 g.; CARBOHYDRATE = 10.6 g.;
CALORIES = 53; CALORIES FROM FAT = 2%

CHILLED COFFEE MILK
WITH CARDAMOM AND CINNAMON
Qahwe

TPT - 8 hours and 7 minutes;
8 hours = flavor development period

Somali are milk drinkers. They enjoy cows', ewes', goats', and camels' milk, which is drunk in large quantities by nomadic herdsmen. The afternoon or evening cup of coffee is sometimes spiced coffee milk accompanied by dates. I took this and carried it a bit further to make a beverage dessert that is really quite satisfying. It can be served quite elegantly in demitasse cups or in small brandy snifters.

1 cup freshly brewed coffee
1/4 cup sugar
1 large cinnamon quill—broken in half
4 crushed cardamom pods

3 cups light cream *or* half and half

Africa–Somalia

**CHILLED COFFEE MILK
WITH CARDAMOM AND CINNAMON** (cont'd)

In a large wine carafe or pitcher, combine coffee, sugar, cinnamon quill pieces, and crushed cardamom pods. Stir or swish to dissolve the sugar.

Add cream. Stir to mix. Refrigerate for 8 hours to allow for flavor development.

Set a strainer over a clean carafe or pitcher and pour coffee milk through. Discard cardamom pieces but retrieve, wash, and dry cinnamon quill pieces for reuse.

Serve chilled in *demitasse* cups or small glasses with dried fruits such as dates, dried apricots, or dried banana slices.

Yields 6 servings
adequate for 4 people

Note: This recipe can be halved, when required.

1/6 SERVING – PROTEIN = 2.3 g.; FAT = 7.5 g.; CARBOHYDRATE = 12.6 g.;
CALORIES = 127; CALORIES FROM FAT = 53%

SOMALI CINNAMON CANDIES
Kashata na Nazi

TPT - 2 hours and 36 minutes;
2 hours = cooling period

Candies are always served at weddings and very festive occasions in Somalia and they are often served at the end of meal or with tea in the afternoon. This creamy sweet is very simple to make.

1 1/2 cups sugar

1 can (14 ounces) *light, sulfite-free* coconut milk
3/4 teaspoon ground cinnamon
1/4 teaspoon salt

Prepare a 9-inch square baking pan by lightly coating it with butter.

In a cast iron or non-stick coated deep saucepan set over *MEDIUM* heat, heat sugar until it begins to melt.

Add coconut milk, ground cinnamon, and salt. *Attach a candy thermometer to the side of the pan.* Cook, stirring constantly, until the candy mixture reaches the hard-crack stage—300 degrees F. Immediately, turn the candy mixture into the prepared baking pan. Spread it to the sides of the pan.

While still warm, score the candy mixture into squares or diamonds, if preferred. Allow to cool completely—about 2 hours.

Break *kashatas* along scoring lines. Trim edges.

Store in an air-tight tin with waxed paper between the layers.

Yields 32 pieces

Note: The same ingredients can be used to make a sauce for ice cream, puddings, and cakes. Cook only until thickened for sauce.

1/32 SERVING – PROTEIN = 0.03 g.; FAT = 0.3 g.; CARBOHYDRATE = 10.8 g.;
CALORIES = 44; CALORIES FROM FAT = 6%

South Africa

Pursuit of the archeological record of this area of Africa has been a passion of the South Africans resulting in more active archaeological sites than anywhere in the world and the scientific confirmation that South Africa has been occupied by modern humans for at least 100,000 years. It has also revealed that *australopithecines* traveled this land about three million years ago. These prehumans were succeeded by various members of the genus *Homo*, including *Homo habilis* and *Homo erectus*, before the evolution of *Homo sapiens*.

European influences in South Africa first arrived with the Portuguese explorer Bartolomeu Dias in 1487. In 1652 a "refreshment station" for sailors rounding the Cape of Good Hope was established by Jan van Riebeeck on behalf of the Dutch East India Company. It soon became a trading post, a settlement, and a magnet for other nationalities. Germans came to work in the Cape, Malayan slaves arrived at the end of the seventeenth century, and French Huguenots, fleeing religious persecution, settled. In 1795 the British declared the Cape of Good Hope a colony and brought Indian indentured labor to work the gold and diamond mines while workers from Mozambique and Angola not only brought their families and the influences from their areas of Africa but also those of the Portuguese under whose colonial rule they had lived. In 1961 South Africa declared independence from Great Britain and has since struggled to meld the diverse population that is this complex country. Since the elimination of apartheid more and more native African influences have found their way quite comfortably into this thoroughly intercultural mix best seen from our distant position in the cuisine and its tremendous diversity.

The climate of this region has a strong influence on the food grown and, consequently, on the food eaten. Although the extremes of climatic diversity are present with desert conditions in the Northwest and a lush subtropical climate in the East along the Indian Ocean at the Mozambique border, South Africa can be said to have a temperate climate, cooler than most at its latitude due, in part, to the increasing elevation of the country as one moves inland and due, in part, to the moderation affected by the Atlantic and Indian oceans that bathe the coastline for approximately 1,500 miles. A fairly even rainfall pattern, reflected in a dependable growing season, is experienced along the south coast, an area known as the Garden Route. This is also the case in the area around Johannesburg, in the center of the Highvelt, the central plateau which sits at 5,700 feet above sea level. The Highvelt has reliable rainfall and does not experience the extremes of heat typical of subtropical regions. The cold winter explains the abundance of recipes which feature "cold weather" crops.

Granted, meat is the center of most meals and vegetable dishes are often an afterthought but I have found many dishes that thoroughly satisfy a vegetarian nutritionally and, at the same time, are enjoyable applications of the multitudinous influences present in South Africa.

Africa–South Africa

Brie with Apple – Raisin Compote

~

Watermelon and Feta Salad
Waatelmoen met Kas

~

Curried Corn Chowder

South African Curry Powder

~~~~~~~~~~~~~~~~~~~~~

Spiced Orange Lentils
Gebraaide Lensie

Steamed Rice

Carrots with Ginger and Dill
Wortel met Gemmer

Slow Cooker Dried Fruit Curry
Slaai Vrug

or

Apple Slices, home-canned in light syrup,
with **South African Curry Powder**

Sweet Onions with Dates
Dadel Slaai

~~~~~~~~~~~~~~~~~~~~~

Individual Coconut Custards
Klappertert

SOUTH AFRICAN *BRIE* WITH APPLE – RAISIN COMPOTE
TPT - 24 hours and 37 minutes;
24 hours = raisin rehydration period

Their justly respected wines are not the only way grapes are enjoyed by South Africans. Raisins are used extensively in cooking. Apples also, once only an import product from Europe and Australia, are widely cultivated. The Granny Smith apple, grown just about everywhere now, was an apple we were only able to get as an import from New Zealand and Australia until the late 1970s. In 1972 it was introduced into the United States and it is also successfully grown in South Africa. I first encountered this South African sweet-savory appetizer, which delightfully exploits both apples and raisins for the aggrandizement of a perfectly ripened piece of Brie, wrapped in pastry and baked. "Why not just warm the naked Brie," said I. With the sweet, textured compote, it is a delicious appetizer with a glass of wine.

1/2 cup *preservative-free dark* raisins
1 cup *boiling* water

2 large Granny Smith apples—well-washed,
 peeled, quartered, seeded, and *finely* chopped
1 tablespoon sugar
Pinch of ground cinnamon

A 15-ounce mini wheel, ripened *Brie**

1/2 cup *toasted preservative-free* pecan pieces
Dash or two of **OUR INDIAN SPICE
 MIXTURE *(Garam Masala)*** [see index]
 or commercially-available mixture

VOLUME II - 243

SOUTH AFRICAN *BRIE* WITH APPLE – RAISIN COMPOTE (cont'd)

In a small bowl, combine raisins and *boiling* water. Place a saucer over the bowl and allow the raisins to plump at room temperature for 24 hours. Refrigerate after that 24-hour period until required.

Set a sieve over a mixing bowl. Pour raisins into the sieve and allow to drain.

In a mixing bowl, combine raisins, *finely* chopped apples, sugar, and cinnamon. Set aside briefly.

Preheat oven to 200 degrees F.

Wrap the wheel of *Brie* in two layers of aluminum foil. Place on a cookie sheet and place in the oven for about 15-20 minutes. Remove from oven, unwrap, place on marble cheese board.

Add toasted pecan pieces and *garam masala* to the apple–raisin compote. Stir to combine. Spoon a tablespoonful or two on top of the *Brie*; put the remainder into a small serving dish next to the *Brie*.

Remove a thin wedge from the *Brie* to allow it to begin to flow. Serve the *Brie* and accompanying compote with crackers or toasts.

Yields 10 servings

Notes: *Every morning we take the wrapped wheel of *Brie* out of the refrigerator and leave it on the counter top in the kitchen. Every evening we replace it in the refrigerator. This process goes on day after day until the aroma of ripened *Brie* becomes evident. Some ripen quickly; some take a week. You can not rush a ripening *Brie* and the date on the package is, sadly, no guide.

A 7-ounce wedge of *Brie* can be prepared the same way, when less is required. Just halve the compote.

1/10 SERVING – PROTEIN = 9.8 g.; FAT = 15.5 g.; CARBOHYDRATE = 15.6 g.;
CALORIES = 234; CALORIES FROM FAT = 59%

SOUTH AFRICAN WATERMELON AND *FETA* SALAD
Waatlemoen met Kaas

TPT - 3 minutes

Even though our bodies need nourishment, our taste buds need encouragement in the middle of the summer. The thought of dinner preparation can make you feel more weary before you even get started. The contrast of the watermelon and the tangy Canadian Woolrich feta cheese is just perfect, the chiffonade of mint is beautiful and bright, and this dish takes no more that three minutes to assemble, even if you have to slice the mint leaves! It is, in our opinion, a perfect fruit and cheese course at the end of light summer meal or maybe as a salad for a menu featuring South African spiced lentils.

6 cups watermelon chunks
1/2 cup crumbled *feta* cheese—preferably Woolrich *feta*, if available*

3 tablespoons *very thinly* slivered fresh mint leaves

In a salad bowl or serving dish, combine watermelon and crumbled *feta* cheese. Toss.

Scatter the chiffonade of mint over the top.

Serve well-chilled.

Notes: *Any *feta*, domestic or imported, which you prefer, can be used. We like the Canadian *feta*, for this particular dish, because it is very crumbly and very tangy. Greek herbed *feta* products are also interesting in this recipe if the herb mixture is compatible with your menu.

This dish can be halved or doubled, when required.

Yields 6 servings
adequate for 4 people

1/6 SERVING – PROTEIN = 3.7 g.; FAT = 4.7 g.; CARBOHYDRATE = 12.3 g.;
CALORIES = 101; CALORIES FROM FAT = 42%

Africa–South Africa

SOUTH AFRICAN CURRIED CORN CHOWDER
TPT - 39 minutes

One of my most loved soups is a corn chowder that I have made since our daughter was a small child. It is, I suppose, just a potato soup, common to so many cultures, but with the addition of corn this potato soup seems to be at home again in the western hemisphere from whence it began its extraordinary worldwide journey. A similar soup, nuanced a bit with African and Asia ingredients is popular in South Africa and, yes, it too has returned to the western hemisphere and is enjoyed right here in Pennsylvania.

1 medium potato—peeled and diced
3 cups *boiling* **water**

1 tablespoon butter
1/2 cup *finely* **chopped onion**
1 bay leaf—halved

1/4 cup tomato purée —homemade, if possible

2 cups green (fresh) *or frozen* **corn kernels**
1 cup VEGETARIAN WHITE *or* **BROWN STOCK**
  [see index], **as preferred**
2 teaspoons SOUTH AFRICAN CURRY POWDER
  [see recipe which follows] or **commercially-available curry powder mixture of choice**

1 cup *light, sulfite-free* **coconut milk**

In a saucepan set over *HIGH* heat, cook diced potato in *boiling* water until *crisp-tender*—about 5 minutes. Drain and rinse with *cold* water to stop further cooking. Set aside until required.

In a 2-quart saucepan set over *MEDIUM* heat, melt butter. Sauté *finely* chopped onion with bay leaf pieces, until onion is soft and translucent, *being careful not to allow onion to brown.*

Add tomato purée and continue to sauté for 3-4 minutes. Remove bay leaf pieces and discard.

Add corn, stock, curry powder, and cooked, diced potato. Bring to the simmer over *MEDIUM-LOW* heat and simmer very gently for about 10 minutes.

Stir in coconut milk and allow to just heat through—*do not boil!* Taste and adjust seasoning, if necessary.

Turn into heated tureen and serve into heated soup bowls.

Yields 6 servings
adequate for 4 people

Note: This recipe is easily doubled, when required.

1/6 SERVING – PROTEIN = 4.5 g.; FAT = 5.1 g.; CARBOHYDRATE = 29.2 g.;
CALORIES = 163; CALORIES FROM FAT = 28%

SOUTH AFRICAN CURRY POWDER
TPT - 3 minutes

South Africa has become home to many from the Indian Subcontinent. They have contributed much to South Africa's diverse culinary matrix. Although Madras-style "curry powders" can be used to prepare African curried dishes, they distort the authentic taste of the true African curry. African curry mixtures are often much hotter than the version we present here, which we feel appeals more to North American taste buds. A version found in Malawi, containing ground piquin dried hot chilies, is fiery hot.

1 tablespoon coriander seeds
1 teaspoon black peppercorns
1 tablespoon poppy seeds
3/4 teaspoon mustard seeds
1 teaspoon cumin seeds
1 teaspoon ground turmeric
3 whole cloves
3/4 teaspoon ground cinnamon
1/8–1/4 ground red pepper (cayenne), or to taste*

Using a mortar and pestle or a SPICE and COFFEE GRINDER, grind spices to form a fine powder.

Store in a jar, tightly-sealed, away from light and heat.

Yields about 3 tablespoonfuls

Notes: *Any ground red *chili* can be used in this mixture—"firing it to the rooftops," if desired.

SOUTH AFRICAN CURRY POWDER (cont'd)

This recipe may be doubled or tripled, when required. It is easier to grind in a mortar if halved.

FOOD VALUES for such spice mixtures are almost negligible.

SOUTH AFRICAN SPICED ORANGE LENTILS
Gebraaide Lensie
TPT - 47 minutes

The presence of guest workers from areas of East Africa and the Indian Subcontinent have greatly influenced the cuisine of South Africa. Young and imaginative chefs have transformed a once often unexciting cuisine into a stimulating cuisine that utilizes African influences rather then serving the past; it now celebrates the fusion of cuisines. Gone are the timidly seasoned Dutch dishes of days gone by.

1 cup orange lentils *or* Egyptian lentils
5 cups *boiling* water

1 tablespoon canola oil
1 medium onion—*finely* chopped

1/2 teaspoon *grated* and crushed fresh gingerroot
1/2 teaspoon *finely* chopped and crushed garlic
1/2 teaspoon ground coriander
1/2 teaspoon ground turmeric
1/4 teaspoon ground cumin
1/2 teaspoon ground cardamom
1/2 teaspoon chili powder
1/2 cup canned, *diced* tomatoes

Pick over lentils and discard any of poor quality. Rinse thoroughly. Put lentils into a *non-aluminum** saucepan set over *LOW* heat. Add *boiling* water. (The water should cover the lentils.) Allow to cook for about 25 to 30 minutes, or until lentils are soft and most of liquid is absorbed. Drain any remaining liquid from lentils.

Turn *well-drained* lentils into a pie plate and mash slightly with a fork. Set aside until required.

In a skillet set over *MEDIUM* heat, heat oil. Add chopped onion and sauté until onions are soft and translucent, *being careful not to allow onions to brown.*

Add *grated* and crushed gingerroot, *finely* chopped and crushed garlic, ground coriander, turmeric, cumin, and cardamom, chili powder, and chopped tomato. Cook, stirring constantly, for several minutes to release flavors.

Add mashed lentils. Stir well to combine. Cook, stirring constantly, until liquid is evaporated and mixture is thick.

Turn into heated serving bowl.

Serve at once.

Yields 6 servings
adequate for 4 people

Notes: *Since aluminum discolors lentils rather unpleasantly, avoid using aluminum cookware or serving bowls in this case.

This recipe can be doubled, when required.

1/6 SERVING – PROTEIN = 10.0 g.; FAT = 2.7 g.; CARBOHYDRATE = 25.2 g.;
CALORIES = 159; CALORIES FROM FAT = 15%

Africa—South Africa

SOUTH AFRICAN CARROTS WITH GINGER AND DILL
Wortel met Gemmer
TPT - 18 minutes

Striking similar to the German "mohrruben mit ingwer," from which it may have evolved or to which it may have contributed, this dish clearly displays cultural differences. The assertive fresh ginger paste is in real contrast to the ground ginger or ginger preserves used by German cooks. Moderating it with honey and orange juice does not, however, address the bite of chili. I was amazed and rather pleased to see that South Africans added ground chili flakes to this carrot preparation, although, admittedly I do tone it down a bit.

2 quarts *boiling* water
30 Belgian baby carrots (approximately 3 cups),
   all about the same size*—pared or scraped

Fresh gingerroot

2 tablespoons butter
2 tablespoons honey
2 tablespoons water
2 tablespoons freshly squeezed orange juice
1/4–1/2 teaspoon *finely* ground red pepper flakes,
   to taste

2 tablespoons chopped fresh dillweed

In a large saucepan set over *MEDIUM* heat, combine *boiling* water and carrots. Parboil for 10 minutes. Drain.

Using a ginger grater, grate gingerroot finely to form about 1 tablespoonful. Using a sharp knife, chop the grated gingerroot into a paste. Turn into a non-stick-coated skillet.

Add *parboiled* carrots, butter, honey, water orange juice, *finely* ground red pepper flakes. Set over *LOW-MEDIUM* and allow to cook until carrots are *crisp-tender*—about 10 minutes. Stir frequently.

Turn into a heated serving bowl, spooning ginger sauce, remaining in the skillet, over carrots.

Serve at once, garnished with chopped dillweed.

Yields 6 servings
adequate for 4 people

Notes: *If you find that Belgian baby carrots are unavailable in your market, carve substitutes from large carrots. Reserve trimmings for soup stock.

This recipe is easily halved or doubled, when required.

1/6 SERVING – PROTEIN = 1.2 g.; FAT = 4.0 g.; CARBOHYDRATE = 14.6 g.
CALORIES = 84; CALORIES FROM FAT = 43%

SOUTH AFRICAN SLOW COOKER DRIED FRUIT CURRY
Slaai Vrug
TPT - 4 hours and 10 minutes;
   [slow cooker: 2 hours at HIGH and 2 hours at LOW]

This unusual sweet and sour dish is an authentic South African recipe which I have adapted to the convenience of the slow cooker. The resultant fruit texture is magnificent and the bananas are the perfect foil for the seasoning. As a side dish on an international buffet table, this can end up being the main topic of conversation as to which part of South Africa's rich history may have contributed what. We find it to be a good choice for a winter salad or as a main dish over rice.

1/4 cup chopped, pitted *preservative-free* dates
1/4 cup chopped, pitted *preservative-free* prunes
1/2 chopped *preservative-free dark* raisins
1 cup chopped, *preservative-free* dried apples

2 cups *boiling* water

1 tablespoon oil
1 cup chopped onion
2 tablespoons *raw* peanuts*

1 tablespoon SOUTH AFRICAN CURRY
   POWDER *[see recipe which precedes] or*
   commercially-available curry powder
   mixture of choice
2 tablespoons freshly squeezed lemon juice
2 tablespoons distilled white vinegar

2 firm, *under-ripe* bananas—sliced

SOUTH AFRICAN DRIED FRUIT CURRY (cont'd)

Preheat the slow cooker to HIGH.

Cook the bowl of the slow cooker with lecithin non-stick spray coating. Add dried dates, prunes, raisins, and apples. Pour *boiling* water over, cover, and allow to cook for 2 hours. *Reduce slow cooker temperature setting to LOW* and continue cooking for an additional 2 hours.

In a large skillet set over *LOW-MEDIUM* heat, heat oil. Add chopped onion and sauté until onion is soft and translucent, *being careful not to allow onion to brown*. Add raw peanuts as the onion begins to soften. Stir frequently for several minutes.

Add curry powder, cooked fruits, lemon juice, and vinegar. Simmer for 2-3 minutes, stirring occasionally.

Turn fruits onto a heated platter. Arrange sliced bananas around the perimeter.

Serve at once, over rice, if desired.

Yields 6 servings
adequate for 4 people

Notes: *Raw peanuts are available in most natural foods stores.

This recipe may be halved or doubled, when required.

Although not traditional to South African cuisine, dried blueberries and/or cranberries make a nice addition.

1/6 SERVING – PROTEIN = 2.0 g.; FAT = 3.6 g.; CARBOHYDRATE = 55.4 g.;
CALORIES = 244; CALORIES FROM FAT = 13%

SWEET ONIONS WITH DATES IN THE STYLE OF CAPE MALAY
Dadel Slaai

TPT - 4 minutes

Years ago I had unearthed a spicy, sugared onion dish, really a sambal, from Indonesia. Discovering the culinary juxtaposition of onions and sugared dates in reference to South Africa really got me thinking. Many popular dishes in South Africa and especially in the area known as Cape Malay show clear evidence of the influence of cuisines of Southeast Asia, brought to the table by guest workers and resettlement from the former Dutch colony, now Indonesia. This was all starting to fit together.

We like to prepare this using Vidalia or Walla Walla sweet onions since the milder onion taste accompanies more menus successfully. Date farms in Arizona used to package a date sugar which was really quite finely chopped date pieces with sugar. It was useful product for a dish like this. I have not seen the product since the 1970s but if you have access to such a product, do use it.

1/2 cup *finely* chopped, pitted, *preservative-free* dates
2 tablespoons sugar

1 1/2 cups *finely* slivered Vidalia, Texas or Mayan Sweet, *or* Walla Walla onions

In a small bowl, combine *finely* chopped dates and sugar. Stir to coat the date pieces with sugar. Set aside until required.

Put onion slivers into a serving dish. Add sugared date mixture. Toss.

Serve at once.

Yields 6 servings
adequate for 4 people

Note: This recipe can be halved or doubled, as required.

1/6 SERVING – PROTEIN = 0.8 g.; FAT = 0.1 g.; CARBOHYDRATE = 24.0 g.;
CALORIES = 91; CALORIES FROM FAT = <1%

Africa–South Africa

SOUTH AFRICAN INDIVIDUAL COCONUT CUSTARDS
Klappertert

TPT - 2 hours;
1 hour = chilling period

This custard dessert is based on kalappertert, a coconut pie much beloved by South Africans, who seem to be very, very fond of custards as am I. So . . .

4 teaspoons apricot jam
1/2 cup grated *or* shredded fresh coconut—fresh *or* desiccated

1 1/2 cups *two-percent* milk
2 tablespoon *unsalted* butter—chopped into small pieces
1/2 cup sugar

3/4 cup *fat-free* pasteurized eggs (the equivalent of 3 eggs)
1/2 teaspoon pure vanilla extract

Whipped heavy cream, for garnish, if desired

Preheat oven to 300 degrees F. Prepare four 8-ounce custard cups by coating with non-stick lecithin spray coating. Spoon 1 teaspoonful of apricot jam into the bottom of each custard cup. Spoon 2 tablespoonfuls of coconut on top of the jam. Set aside until required.

In a saucepan set over *LOW* heat, combine milk, butter, and sugar. While stirring frequently with a wire whisk, heat until bubbles form at the edge and the butter has melted.

Meanwhile, in a mixing bowl, using a wire whisk, combine pasteurized eggs and vanilla extract. Mix well. *Gradually—tablespoonful by tablespoonful—*whisk hot milk mixture into beaten eggs.

Apportion egg–butter–milk mixture among the four custard cups. Skim all bubbles from surface.

Set in a baking pan in which a 1-inch water bath has been prepared. Place a large square of aluminum foil over the custard cups.

Bake in preheated 300 degree F. oven for about 45 minutes, or until a knife inserted into the center comes out clean. *Do not allow water bath to simmer or boil,* by adding cold water or ice cubes, if necessary.

Refrigerate for at least 1 hour.

Serve garnished with whipped cream, if desired.

Yields 4 individual servings

Note: This recipe is easily doubled, when required.

1/4 SERVING (without garnish of whipped cream) –
PROTEIN = 8.1 g.; FAT = 12.0 g.; CARBOHYDRATE = 46.1 g.;
CALORIES = 326; CALORIES FROM FAT = 33%

Sudan

Nubia, or the Kush as it was known to Egyptians, was inhabited 70,000 years ago as our nomadic ancestors came and went through the continent of Africa. In the eighth century BC Upper Egypt was conquered by the forces of the Nubian/Kushite ruler Kashta. He ruled Thebes until 740 BC. His successor, Piankhy, reunited Egypt under the twenty-fifth dynasty and the line of kings that he founded ruled Egypt for one hundred years. A pharonic ruling tradition persisted when the last Nubian pharaoh, Taharque (688-663 BC) moved the Kushite court to Meroe, in the area known as the Sixth Cataract, after a war between Egypt and Assyria. A powerful African kingdom in the third and second centuries BC, Meroe ruled the land and peoples from the Third Cataract north to the present site of Khartoum. Pyramids and stelae that record the ancient civilization have survived to attest to the historical timeline and to its achievements. The ruins of temples, palaces, and baths have also given us a view of this complex early culture, which ended in 350 BC when the Abyssinians/Ethiopians captured and destroyed Meroe, effectively ending the Meroitic kingdom.

A soldier of fortune named Muhammad Mi rose to prominence in part because of Napoléon Bonaparte's victory in 1797 at the so-called Battle of the Pyramids which eliminated the control held by the Mamelukes. Mi sent one of his sons to conquer the "Lands of the Blacks," Sudan, and by 1821 the northern and central regions of the country were united. By 1884 all of Sudan except Khartoum was ruled by Mohammad Ahmad, a mystic who had declared himself the Mahdi, the second great prophet. The British, determining that Khartoum could not be held, sent General Charles Gordon to evacuate the city. Besieged for 317 days by the Mahdi's "whirling dervishes," the city was taken and destroyed. A period of civil war followed and in September 1898 Anglo-Egyptian forces under General Herbert Kitchener met and defeated the Sudanese forces outside of Omdurman. In 1899 Great Britain and Egypt signed an agreement to jointly administer the country. The Sudan became a fully independent state in 1955 but before it could get its government fully established a military *coup* overthrew the ruling council and suspended democracy. The struggles continued and in 1983 the then president Jaafer Mohammed al-Numeiry declared that the existing penal code be suspended, that the judicial system be reformed, and that all infractions be judged by *Sharia* Law, with Koranic penalties. This increased the unrest in the south where the majority of the population are either Christian or animists. Numeiry was ousted from power and succeeded by a democratic government but with the support of only one political party. In 1989 another military *coup* deposed the government. The Southern Sudanese were alarmed by the Islamic totalitarian single-party state instituted by Omar al-Bashir and by the fact that his government was inviting and encouraging Islamic fundamentalism. This resulted in a devastating twenty-year civil war with an estimated two million casualties. In 2011 voters in Southern Sudan voted in favor of independence and this part of the Sudan set off on its separate path on July 9, 2011.

Of course, as one would expect, there has been considerable culinary cross-fertilization from Egypt and this is most easily observed if one compares the preparation of bean dishes. Ethiopia too has influenced the food and cooking of the Sudan. During the period when Sudan was controlled by the Ottoman Empire, Arab traders and those who chose to settle also contributed to the cuisine. Sudanese dishes benefited from the red pepper and garlic introduced by the Arabs from the Eastern Mediterranean and Turkish influences can be seen in the wonderful, rich, nut- and honey-filled pastries, spice combinations, and the presence of meatballs in the cuisine. It will be interesting to watch the changes in Sudanese cuisine as the new country of South Sudan celebrates its differences and creates a separate identity.

Africa–Sudan

Archeological evidence suggests that the ancient Nubians were the first to discover the grass we know as wheat. Not withstanding the preference for wheat in the North of the country, I have chosen to include my recipe for gorraasa which calls for a fine corn flour.

Yogurt and Peanut Butter Appetizer Dip
Naeamia be Dakwa
with
Flatbread
Crackers
Crudités, of choice

~

Tossed Salad with Cheese
Salata ma Jibna

Shredded Cucumber Salad with Yogurt
Salatet Zabady bil Ajur

~~~~~~~~~~~~~~~~~~~~

Potato and Onion Stew
Dama be Potaatas
or
Broad Bean Patties
Tamaaya

Sudanese Rice with Butter
Rouz Malfulfel
or
Fried Corn Flatbreads
Gorraasa

~~~~~~~~~~~~~~~~~~~~

Sweet *Pasta*
Shaaria

Peanut Macaroons
Ful-Sudani

Africa–Sudan

SUDANESE YOGURT AND PEANUT BUTTER APPETIZER DIP
Naeamia be Dakwa

TPT - 33 minutes

Pennsylvania, after decades of clear-cut logging, stepped up to the environmental plate and has preserved enormous acreage for recreation. It is a joy as civilization encroaches on the treasured beauty in other parts of our country. Ever since we moved to rural Pennsylvania, I have chosen to pack up a lunch and celebrate my autumn birthday in one of the wonderful state forests nearby. This dip, with pieces of flatbread or pita loaves and a selection of crudités, is a satisfying and nutritious lunch and one that I have chosen for that special picnic.

1/4 cup *extra virgin* olive oil
2 large onions—*finely* chopped

1/2 cup canned, *crushed* tomatoes
1 large garlic clove—*very finely* chopped
1 cup water

3 tablespoons freshly ground, *unsalted, additive-free smooth* peanut butter—*brought to room temperature*
1 cup PLAIN YOGURT *[see index] or* commercially- available plain yogurt

1 1/2 tablespoons unbleached white flour
Freshly ground black pepper, to taste
Pinch salt

In a non-stick-coated skillet set over *MEDIUM* heat, heat oil. Add *finely* chopped onion and sauté until soft and translucent, *being careful not to allow onions to brown.*

Add crushed tomatoes, *very finely* chopped garlic, and water. *Reduce heat to LOW*, cover, and allow to simmer for about 15 minutes. Stir frequently.

While the onion–tomato mixture simmer, gradually work peanut butter and yogurt together in a mixing bowl with a wooden spoon until smooth.

Add flour, black pepper, and salt. Stir until thoroughly integrated. Add to onion–tomato mixture and cook, stirring constantly, until mixture boils. Remove from heat. Turn into a serving dish.

Serve warm with breads, toasts, crackers and/or *crudités*, of choice.

Yields 6 people as a first course

Note: This recipe can be halved, when required.

1/6 SERVING – PROTEIN = 5.2 g.; FAT = 11.5 g.; CARBOHYDRATE = 28.5 g.;
CALORIES = 175; CALORIES FROM FAT = 59%

SUDANESE TOSSED VEGETABLE SALAD WITH CHEESE
Salata ma Jibna

TPT - 10 minutes

The onions and cabbage are slivered as in "cabbage salad," not shredded as in deli "coleslaw." The carrot rounds and tomato dice, then, have substantial company. Although the French influence is visible in the Sudanese cuisine, this salad pushes the envelope. It is amazing to us how the humble cabbage salad can be varied. Wherever cabbage is grown and eaten, there is a cabbage salad and it will have its own distinctive personality.

1 tablespoon *extra virgin* olive oil
1 tablespoon freshly squeezed lemon juice
1 1/2 teaspoons distilled white vinegar
1/8 teaspoon freshly ground black pepper

1 garlic clove

2 medium onions—slivered
2 cups white cabbage—*slivered, not shredded*
1 large carrot—peeled or pared and cut into thin round slices
1 large tomato—peeled, quartered, juiced, seeded, and cut into 1/2-inch dice

1/4 cup slivers of *pecorino Romano* cheese *or* other ewe's milk cheese of choice—prepared by slivering with a vegetable peeler or with a cheese plane

In a cruet or bottle, combine oil, lemon juice, vinegar, and black pepper. Shake vigorously.

Press garlic clove through a GARLIC PRESS and add to dressing.* Again, shake dressing vigorously. Set aside until required.

In a salad bowl, combine onion and cabbage slivers, carrot slices, and diced tomato. Toss.**

Africa–Sudan

SUDANESE TOSSED SALAD WITH CHEESE (cont'd)

Just before serving, toss vegetables with prepared garlic *vinaigrette*. Sprinkle cheese slivers over.

Serve into individual salad bowls or onto salad plates.

Yields 6 servings
adequate for 4-6 people

Notes: *The garlic flavor released when the cell walls are broken down by the garlic press is intense and that is just what you want in this salad for authenticity.

**The salad may be prepared ahead to this point. Place in a plastic bag and refrigerate until ready to serve.

Leftovers do not keep well.

This recipe may be halved or doubled, when required.

1/6 SERVING – PROTEIN = 3.0 g.; FAT = 3.1 g.; CARBOHYDRATE = 7.2 g.;
CALORIES = 64; CALORIES FROM FAT = 44%

SUDANESE SHREDDED CUCUMBER SALAD WITH YOGURT
Salatet Zabady bil Ajur

TPT - 2 hours and 11 minutes;
2 hours = flavor development period

I first found this dish when I had half of a cucumber sitting in the crisper drawer which I did not want to see end up in the compost pile. Similar in concept to the Indian salad "kheere raita" but a world apart in taste and appearance, this tangy Sudanese cucumber salad serves well as a side dish in many, many menus. I always use the thick Greek-style yogurt or drain yogurt until it is thick (yogurt crème or yogurt cheese) for this dish since the shredded cucumber, no matter how well you try to dry it, will exude liquid and thin the salad during the flavor development period. Choose small cucumbers to minimize the watery release.

2 small cucumbers—peeled, seeded, and shredded

1 large garlic clove—*very finely* chopped
1/4 teaspoon salt

1 cup thick Greek-style yogurt *or* YOGURT CRÈME [see index]
2 tablespoons *finely* chopped fresh mint
Pinch sugar
Freshly ground black pepper, to taste

Sprinkling ground cumin, for garnish

Place shredded cucumber on several thicknesses of paper toweling and pat as dry as possible with paper toweling. Turn into a mixing bowl.

On a cutting board, chopped peeled garlic clove. Sprinkle salt over and continue to chop the garlic clove, working the salt into the garlic to create a paste. Add the garlic paste to the shredded cucumber in the mixing bowl.

Add yogurt, *finely* chopped mint, sugar, and pepper. Mix well. Cover and refrigerate for 2 hours.

Taste and adjust seasoning, if necessary. Turn into chilled serving bowl. Sprinkle just a little ground cumin over to garnish.

Serve at once.

Yields 6 servings
adequate for 4 people

Note: This recipe can be halved to use that cucumber half that was leftover from another dish. It can also be doubled.

1/6 SERVING – PROTEIN = 6.0 g.; FAT = 0.1 g.; CARBOHYDRATE = 10.0 g.;
CALORIES = 65; CALORIES FROM FAT = 1%

Africa–Sudan

SUDANESE POTATO AND ONION STEW
Dama be Potaatas
TPT - 42 minutes

You may look at the title of this recipe and dismiss such a plebian combination. But wait; please read it through. Potatoes, onion, garlic, tomatoes, and green pepper do, I admit, seem very familiar but have you ever added cardamom and cinnamon to such a dish? You end up with a dish that is, at once, familiar but, then, a difference is detected; your taste buds say, "Oh, not the same old, same old..."

3 quarts *boiling* water
3 medium potatoes—peeled and cut into chunks

2 tablespoons *extra virgin* olive oil
2 medium onions—chopped

1 cup water

1/4 chopped green bell pepper
1 tablespoon chopped mild green *chilies*
1/2 cup water
1 cup canned, *diced* tomatoes *or* peeled, seeded, and chopped fresh tomatoes
2 tablespoons tomato paste
2 large garlic cloves—*very finely* chopped
1/2 teaspoon salt, or to taste
1/2 teaspoon ground cardamom
1/2 teaspoon ground cinnamon

In a saucepan set over *MEDIUM* heat, cook chopped potatoes in *boiling* water for about 10 minutes. Drain and set aside until required.

In a large kettle set over *MEDIUM* heat, heat oil. Add chopped onions and sauté until onions begin to soften, *being careful not to allow the onions to brown*. Reduce heat to *LOW-MEDIUM*.

Add the 1 cupful water, cover, and allow the onions to cook until the most of the water has evaporated, stirring occasionally.

Add parboiled potatoes, chopped bell pepper and green *chilies*, and the 1/2 cupful water. Cook for several minutes, stirring frequently.

Add chopped tomatoes, tomato paste, *very finely* chopped garlic, salt, and ground cardamom and cinnamon. Cover and cook for about 10 minutes, stirring frequently. Turn into a heated serving bowl and keep warm on warming tray until ready to serve.

Refrigerate leftovers and add a bit of water to reheat, if necessary.

Yields 6 servings
adequate for 4 people

Notes: This recipe can be doubled, when required.

When more protein is necessary for a menu, soymeat analogue strips can be added to this stew just as Sudanese would add beef or chicken.

1/6 SERVING – PROTEIN = 2.4 g.; FAT = 3.9 g.; CARBOHYDRATE = 16.9 g.;
CALORIES = 109; CALORIES FROM FAT = 32%

SUDANESE BROAD BEAN PATTIES
Tamaaya
TPT - 10 hours;
8 hours = flavor development period

Broad beans or fava beans are huge meaty beans which can be found dry or canned in most grocery stores. Because of their substantial nature, they are the perfect base for tamaaya, the bean patties so popular in the Sudan. These bean patties get their color from fresh herbs and scallions. Tamaaya are stuffed into bread pockets just as falafel are stuffed into pita loaves along with shredded salad and fried vegetables like potatoes and eggplant. They are a popular street food for breakfast, lunch, and dinner. Although, admittedly, we do not deep-fry frequently, so we often serve this mixture as a spread with "gorraasa" or with pita.

SUDANESE BROAD BEAN PATTIES (cont'd)

1 cup dry *fava* beans*
3 cups *boiling* water

1/4 cup *finely* chopped parsley
1/4 cup *finely* chopped fresh coriander (*cilantro*)
1/4 cup *finely* chopped onion
2 large scallions—*white and green portions*—trimmed, well-rinsed, and chopped
1 small garlic clove—*very finely* chopped

1/2 teaspoon ground coriander
1/4 teaspoon freshly ground black pepper
1/4 teaspoon chili powder
Pinch baking soda

1 tablespoon sesame seeds

2 tablespoons *high heat* safflower *or* sunflower oil

3 cups shredded mixed greens—well-washed and well-dried

In a saucepan set over LOW-MEDIUM heat, combine dry *fava* beans and *boiling* water. Cook for about 40-45 minutes, or until tender.

In the work bowl of the food processor fitted with steel knife, combine *finely* chopped parsley, fresh coriander (*cilantro*), and onion, chopped scallions, and *very finely* chopped garlic. Process, scraping down the work bowl sides as needed.

Add well-drained *fava* beans. Process until the bean mixture looks green, scraping down the work bowl sides as needed. Turn into a mixing bowl.

Add ground coriander and black pepper, chili powder, and baking soda. Stir to integrate the seasoning well. Refrigerate for at least 8 hours to allow for flavor development and to allow the mixture to become firm.

Fill the bowl of a large serving spoon with some of the mixture. Form it into a tight patty and place it on a waxed-paper-covered plate. Repeat until all the mixture has been formed into patties.

Sprinkle sesame seeds on each patty.

In a skillet set over MEDIUM heat, heat oil. Slide six patties into the hot oil and cook for 2-3 minutes. Turn over and cook for an additional 2-3 minutes. Using a slotted spatula, remove patties and drain on several thicknesses of paper toweling. Repeat until all patties have been cooked and well-drained. Transfer to a warm serving plate.

Serve warm. Serve with warm Sudanese Fried Corn Flatbreads (*gorraasa*) and shredded mixed greens or, if preferred, serve as an entrée with vegetables and Sudanese rice.

Yields about 18 bean patties
adequate for 6 people

Notes: *Most natural food stores carry dry *fava* beans.

This recipe can be doubled, when required.

1/18 SERVING (per bean patty) –
PROTEIN = 9.3 g.; FAT = 5.8 g.; CARBOHYDRATE = 21.4 g.;
CALORIES = 172; CALORIES FROM FAT = 30%

SUDANESE RICE WITH BUTTER
Rouz Malfulfel
TPT - 38 minutes

I started collecting rice-cooking methods many years ago. It grew into an astonishingly large file. The greatest diversity, however, seemed to be among the countries circling the Mediterranean. My Chinese rice cooker and my Thai rice-steaming basket were of no help. This traditional rice preparation results in very flavorful rice.

1 tablespoon butter*
1 cup dry converted rice

Boiling bottled water *or* refrigerated water**
1/2 teaspoon salt
1/4 teaspoon ground turmeric *or* ground cardamom, or to taste***

SUDANESE RICE (cont'd)

In a large, heavy saucepan set over *MEDIUM* heat, melt butter. Add rice and sauté for several minutes.

Add *boiling* water to a level of about 1 inch above the rice. Add salt and turmeric or cardamom. Stir to combine. Reduce heat to *LOW-MEDIUM*. Cover and allow to cook, *undisturbed*, until water is evaporated—25-30 minutes. Turn into a heated serving bowl. Keep warm on warming tray until ready to serve.

****Since the chlorine in tap water destroys the B-vitamin thiamin in grains, it is advisable to cook grains in either bottled water or water that has been refrigerated for at least 24 hours.

***The choice of seasoning will depend on the remainder of the menu.

Yields 6 servings
adequate for 4 people

Notes: *Some people use oil; I do like the flavor of the butter.

1/6 SERVING – PROTEIN = 2.8 g.; FAT = 2.0 g.; CARBOHYDRATE = 31.1 g.;
CALORIES = 158; CALORIES FROM FAT = 11%

SUDANESE FRIED CORN FLATBREADS
Gorraasa
TPT - 39 minutes

Gorraasa can be made with corn flour, wheat flour, or a combination of wheat and rye flour. I make these in a large non-stick-coated skillet which is considerably different from the flat frying pan used in the Sudan but it works.

2 cups corn flour – masa harina *
1/2 teaspoon baking powder
1/4 teaspoon salt

2 cups water

In a mixing bowl, combine corn flour, baking powder, and salt. Stir to combine.

Add water and stir until it forms a thick batter.

Prepare a 10-inch non-stick-coated skillet by spraying with non-stick lecithin spray coating. Set over *MEDIUM* heat. Ladle a portion of the batter onto the pan surface, spreading it thinly and evenly across the hot surface. When golden on one side, using two spatulas, flip and fry on the remaining side until golden. Turn onto a heated platter set on a warming tray while preparing the remaining breads.

Serve hot.

Note: *Masa harina is a fine corn flour, made from dehydrated or roasted corn, which is usually found in Hispanic groceries or in the international aisle of most well-stocked grocery stores.

This recipe can be halved or doubled, when required.

Yields 16 small breads

1/16 SERVING – PROTEIN = 2.3 g.; FAT = 0.0 g.; CARBOHYDRATE = 19.5 g.;
CALORIES = 64; CALORIES FROM FAT = 0%

Africa–Sudan

SUDANESE SWEET *PASTA*
Shaaria

TPT - 57 minutes;
20 minutes = cooling period

The Italian colonial period introduced Italian cooking to areas of Africa that was in turn adapted to their tastes, their crops, and their way of life. Some are admittedly extreme such as the serving of spaghetti with ketchup that is popular in Somalia. Earlier in history the Roman introduction of macaroni and spaghetti to North Africa also led to some very interesting adaptations. There are no two ways about it; this is an unusual dessert. My Italian-born mother-in-law would never have believed it.

1/4 cup *high-heat* safflower *or* sunflower oil
1 tablespoon sesame oil
6 dry angel hair *pasta* nests

Boiling water

1 tablespoon butter

3/4 cup sugar

2 tablespoons *finely* shredded desiccated coconut

In a large, deep skillet with cover set over *LOW-MEDIUM* heat, heat safflower and sesame oils. Add *pasta* nests and fry until *lightly* browned. Turn over and allow the remaining surfaces to brown.

Add a little *boiling* water. *Cover immediately to avoid splattering.* Remove lid and allow steam to escape. Pour more *boiling* water over the *pasta* nests until almost covered. Cover again and allow to cook for about 10 minutes.

Add butter. Stir it into the remaining water as it melts.

Sprinkle sugar over. Cook, stirring the liquid *around the nests gently*, until sugar is dissolved.

Using a slotted spatula, lift the *pasta* nests from the liquid and transfer to a large platter. Keep them well separated from each other.

Increase temperature of liquid remaining in skillet to MEDIUM-HIGH. Boil liquid until reduced by about one-half and thickened. Pour remaining sweet liquid over.

Sprinkle each with 1 teaspoonful of shredded coconut. Allow to cool to room temperature—about 20 minutes.

To serve, transfer one of the nests to each of six dessert plates.

Yields 6 servings
adequate for 4 people

Note: This recipe can be halved, when required.

1/6 SERVING – PROTEIN = 3.1 g.; FAT = 14.4 g.; CARBOHYDRATE = 52.0 g.;
CALORIES = 341; CALORIES FROM FAT = 38 %

SUDANESE PEANUT MACAROONS
Ful – Sudani

TPT - about 56 minutes

Instead of adding beans to a menu when leguminous amino acids are required for complementation, I often use peanuts. These chewy, light cookies, popular in the Sudan, make a delicious dessert. If you have a well-stocked natural food store nearby, check to see if they stock organic peanuts.

1 cup *unsalted, raw* peanuts

2 large egg whites—*brought to room temperature*
2/3 cup superfine sugar*

1/2 teaspoon pure vanilla extract

SUDANESE PEANUT MACAROONS (cont'd)

Preheat oven to 325 degrees F. Prepare cookie sheets by lining with culinary parchment paper.**

In a non-stick-coated skillet set over *LOW-MEDIUM* heat, allow peanuts to lightly brown. Stir frequently. Cool completely and chop *finely*.

Using an electric mixer fitted with *grease-free* beaters or by hand, using a *grease-free* wire whisk, beat egg whites in a *grease-free* mixing bowl until soft peaks form. Gradually, *tablespoonful by tablespoonful*, beat in superfine sugar. Continue beating until a stiff and glossy meringue results.

Fold *finely* chopped, *pan-roasted* peanuts into meringue. Thoroughly fold in vanilla extract.

Drop by teaspoonfuls onto prepared cookie sheet.

Bake in preheated 325 degrees F. oven for about 20-22 minutes, or until *lightly browned*. Allow cookies to cool for about 5 minutes on the baking sheet. Remove cookies carefully to a wire rack to cool completely.

Store cookies in an airtight tin in a single layer, to prevent breakage.

Yields about 24 cookies

Notes: *It is very important to use superfine sugar only in this recipe. *Neither granulated sugar nor confectioners' sugar can be substituted.*

**Culinary parchment paper for baking is available in food specialty and housewares' stores, and from mail order firms, where it is now even available as an unbleached, environmentally friendly product. In the United States, unlike in Europe, you do not always find it on the shelves of grocery stores. Lining baking sheets and pans with parchment paper, instead of greasing, buttering, or oiling, not only protects your baking sheets from scorching, it encourages the even browning of cookies, scones, cakes, etc.

These cookies *can not* be frozen.

This recipe *can not* be doubled successfully.

1/24 SERVING (i. e., per cookie) –
PROTEIN = 1.6 g.; FAT = 3.3 g.; CARBOHYDRATE = 7.3 g.;
CALORIES = 61; CALORIES FROM FAT = 49%

Tanzania

Parts of Tanzania should be very familiar even if you have not visited East Africa. The Great Rift Valley in the North; Mount Kilimanjaro, Africa's highest peak; Lake Victoria, Africa's largest lake; Lane Tanganyika, Africa's deepest lake; the great Serengeti National Park; and Gombe National Park, where Dr. Jane Goodall conducted her studies of chimpanzees, are all within the borders of Tanzania. Eighty percent of the population, which represents some one hundred and twenty ethnic groups, lives outside of the cities. Swahili and English unify the communication of this diverse heritage. Over thirty-four million people call this country home today and Tanzania's archaeological excavations have confirmed that humans and pre-humans have occupied this land in East Africa for over two million years making it one the oldest known inhabited areas in the world.

Tanzania is not only a country of diverse beauty, it is a country that has digested and shaped the influences of the many other cultures with which its people have come into contact. It is known that Islam was introduced to coastal populations in the eighth or ninth centuries AD. Although a census of religious affiliations has not, however, been conducted since 1967, it is estimated that about one-third of the population is Islamic, living principally on the former Island of Zanzibar and along the coastal regions on the mainland. Those of the Christian faith, who also represent about one-third of the population, tend to live inland. Influenced by the Portuguese, British, and Germans, many Tanzanians became Christians, choosing to join a wide range of sects which survive.

Tanzania's Indian Ocean coastline became an important port for the Portuguese, who ruled the area for two hundred years beginning in 1498 as Vasco de Gama took control of the coastal regions and trade routes in East Africa. In 1698 the Portuguese were driven from the region by the Arabs, who enslaved the population and made Zanzibar the center for the Arab slave trade. Little of Portuguese culture and cuisine is apparent, although they did introduce cassava and peanuts (groundnuts) and both continue to be dietary staples.

In the late nineteenth century, Germany conquered the mainland, Rwanda, and Burundi, creating German East Africa. After World War I the area became a British Mandate, gaining independence in 1961. The name by which this area was known under the Germans, Tanganyika, became the basis of the new name Tanzania when Tanganyika and Zanzibar united in 1964 to form the United Republic of Tanzania.

At one time the economy of Tanzania was a thriving African economy due to the cultivation and export of cloves, cotton, and coffee. The importance of these agricultural exports diminished with the end of the plantation system after World War I. In an effort to jumpstart a faltering economy in the 1970s Tanzania formed an alliance with China. The conditions of the economic assistance, however, required that the Tanzanian projects be operated by a Chinese workforce resulting in a huge immigration of Chinese, thereby increasing the complexity of an already complex society. The government is struggling to create jobs and to create an education system that will transform a very undereducated rural population into a workforce to fill those jobs.

Tanzania's cuisine benefits not only from the rich and diverse encounters with those from Europe, the Middle East, and the Indian Subcontinent but also from the dramatic diversity of its climate. Along the coast and for some distance inland the climate is tropical providing a dizzying selection of fruits; the dry and hot plateau that provides one of the world's most interesting wildlife habitats; the rich grassland of the highlands which provide for herd animals, especially goats; and the high lake regions where a moderate climate with cool nights and seasonal changes allows for the cultivation of vegetables and cool-weather fruit orchards. Since meat in scarce and usually reserved for celebratory occasions, vegetarians actually have much to explore in the cuisine of Tanzania.

Africa–Tanzania

Curried Coconut – Bean Soup with Brown Basmati Rice
Supuya Nazi

Chilled Banana Soup
Mtori

~

Tomato and Onion Salad
Saladi ya Nyanya

Vegetable Relish
Kachumbali

~~~~~~~~~~~~~~~~~~~~~~

Bean and Corn Casserole
Makande

Steamed Papaya
Papai

Greens with Peanuts
Um'bido

~~~~~~~~~~~~~~~~~~~~~~

Easy Tanzanian Banana Ice Cream
Aiskrimu n'dizi

Papaya and Mango Dessert with Apricot Sauce
Papai na Embe

Fresh Pineapple Dessert
Nanasi Tamu

~

Chai

TANZANIAN CURRIED COCONUT – BEAN SOUP WITH BROWN BASMATI RICE
Supuya Nazi
TPT - 35 minutes

Curries are popular in Africa, having been introduced to the continent from India. Most curries are made with Madras-style curry mixtures but in many parts of Africa the seasoning has been modified. South African curry powder is quite different from the curry powder you buy in the grocery store and is, in our estimation, a good choice for this vegan soup. Since the kidney beans and rice provide amino acid complementation, this soup can be a nutritious entrée with little more than a salad and some fruit needed to round out the meal.

Africa–Tanzania

TANZANIAN CURRIED COCONUT – BEAN SOUP WITH BROWN BASMATI RICE (cont'd)

1 tablespoon safflower *or* sunflower oil
1/2 cup *finely* chopped onion

2 tablespoons butter
1/2 cup chopped green bell pepper
1 teaspoon SOUTH AFRICAN CURRY POWDER
   [see index] *or* curry powder mixture of choice
1/4 teaspoon salt
1/4 teaspoon freshly ground black pepper

1 cup canned, *diced* tomato
1 can (16 ounces) canned kidney beans with liquid
2 cups *light, sulfite-free* coconut milk
2 1/2 cups water

1/2 cup *cooked* brown, *basmati* rice

1/4 cup shredded coconut—fresh *or* desiccated—
   for garnish

In a large saucepan set over *MEDIUM* heat, heat oil. Add *finely* chopped onions and sauté until onions are soft and translucent, *being careful not to allow the onions to brown.*

Add butter, chopped green pepper, curry powder, salt, and pepper. Cook, stirring constantly for a minute or two.

Add diced tomato, kidney beans, coconut milk, and water. Cook, stirring frequently, until the mixture begins to bubble. *Reduce heat to LOW.* Simmer, stirring frequently, for about 15 minutes.

Add cooked rice and allow to heat through. Turn into heated soup tureen.

Serve into heated soup bowls, garnished with a sprinkling of coconut.

Yields 9 servings

Note: This recipe can be halved, when required.

1/9 SERVING – PROTEIN = 4.6 g.; FAT = 7.3 g.; CARBOHYDRATE = 18.0 g.;
CALORIES = 142; CALORIES FROM FAT = 46%

TANZANIAN CHILLED BANANA SOUP
Mtori

TPT -   2 hours and 23 minutes;
       2 hours = refrigeration period

Our version of this very delicious soup may seem rather pale to a Tanzanian but the original, made with beef and soup bones, is hardly fare for a vegetarian. Men in Tanzania who generally dismiss soup as women's food are said to make an exception for "mtori" because the smell of it cooking and the first spoonful are too much too resist. We greatly prefer this as a cold soup.

2 cups VEGETABLE STOCK FROM SOUP [see index] *or* other vegetarian stock of choice
1/2 cup WILD MUSHROOM STOCK [see index]
1 tablespoon *tamari* soy sauce

3 medium, *underripe* bananas—green, if possible—chopped
1/2 medium onion—*finely* chopped
1/2 cup canned, *petite diced* tomatoes

1 teaspoon CLARIFIED BUTTER *or* GHEE
   [see index]
Salt, to taste
Freshly ground mixed peppercorns—black, red, and white—to taste

Halved tomato slices, for garnish

In a large saucepan or small kettle set over *MEDIUM* heat, combine vegetable stock, mushroom stock, and soy sauce. Allow to come to the boil.

Add chopped bananas, *finely* chopped onion, and *petite* diced tomatoes. Cook, stirring frequently, until all ingredients are very soft. Using a potato masher, mash ingredients until of a uniform consistency.

Add butter, salt, and ground mixed peppercorns. Turn into a soup tureen and refrigerate for 2 hours.

Serve into soup plates. Nestle two tomato slice halves into each serving as a garnish.

Yields about 7 cupfuls

Africa–Tanzania

TANZANIAN CHILLED BANANA SOUP (cont'd)

1/7 SERVING (i. e., per cupful) –
PROTEIN = 1.0 g.; FAT = 0.9 g.; CARBOHYDRATE = 13.6 g.;
CALORIES = 60; CALORIES FROM FAT = 14%

TANZANIAN TOMATO AND ONION SALAD
Saladi ya Nyanya
TPT - 5 minutes

How very often do we just stick a slice of tomato into a sandwich or bury a couple of slices in mayonnaise on a salad plate? Perhaps we have just become numbed by the disappointing store-bought tomatoes, bred for shelf-life not flavor. No matter how early you get to our farmers' market, you will find a line in front of the stand of a family of local Mennonite farmers because their tomatoes and corn are picked just before they leave for market and the flavor is beyond wonderful. When the day's harvest is gone, sometimes by 9:30 AM, there is not a backroom supply and those who have missed out will vow to get up and out earlier the next Wednesday. Their intensely flavorful, heirloom tomatoes stand up to the flavoring of this dressing used by Tanzanians.

1 garlic clove—crushed and *very finely* chopped
2 tablespoons freshly squeezed lime juice
Salt, to taste
Freshly ground black pepper, to taste

3 large tomatoes—sliced*
1/2 cup *finely* chopped onion

In a small bowl, combine *very finely* chopped garlic, lime juice, salt, and pepper. Combine well.

On a serving plate or platter, arrange tomato slices. Sprinkle *finely* chopped onion over. Pour prepared dressing over.

Serve at room temperature.*

Yields 6 servings
adequate for 4 people

Notes: *Tomatoes stored and served at room temperature will have better flavor.

This recipe can be halved or doubled, when required.

1/6 SERVING – PROTEIN = 0.6 g.; FAT = 0.2 g.; CARBOHYDRATE = 3.9 g.;
CALORIES = 19; CALORIES FROM FAT = 10%

TANZANIAN VEGETABLE RELISH
Kachumbali
TPT - 4 minutes

We enjoy this relish as a relish garnish, as a salad, and in almost any pita sandwich. It also can be used as a salad filling for a flour tortilla or a chappatis to make a "Tanzanian vegetable wrap." It is an interesting change from the ordinary.

1 cup *finely* chopped red onion
1 1/4 cups canned, *diced* tomatoes
1 tablespoon *finely* chopped mild green *chilies*
1/3 of a large cucumber—peeled, seeded, and *finely* chopped
1 small carrot—peeled and *finely* chopped
1 1/2 teaspoons freshly squeezed lemon juice
Salt, to taste
Freshly ground black pepper, to taste

In a serving bowl, combine all *finely* chopped ingredients.* Stir to mix well.

Serve at once, with a slotted spoon, as a relish or salad or sandwich filling. Leftovers do not keep well since the relish tends to become too liquid.

Yields 3 cupfuls

Notes: *An Italian *mesa-luna* is very useful for chopping this relish into a uniform *finely* chopped consistency.

This recipe may be doubled, when required.

Africa–Tanzania

TANZANIAN VEGETABLE RELISH (cont'd)

1/16 SERVING (i. e., about 3 tablespoonfuls) –
PROTEIN = 0.3 g.; FAT = 0.05 g.; CARBOHYDRATE = 2.1 g.;
CALORIES = 9; CALORIES FROM FAT = 5%

TANZANIAN BEAN AND CORN CASSEROLE
Makande

TPT - 1 hour and 10 minutes

Almost every culture has a legume–grain dish. This classic Tanzanian protein-complemented casserole with coconut cream, admittedly less than would be traditional, is greatly enhanced if a well-flavored stock is used.

1 can (19 ounces) red kidney beans *or* **the equivalent in cooked, dry beans—well-drained**
1 medium onion—*finely* **chopped**
2 garlic cloves—*finely* **chopped**
1 cup green (fresh) *or frozen* **corn kernels**
1/4 cup *light, sulfite-free* **coconut cream***
1/3 cup VEGETARIAN BROWN STOCK [see index] *or* **VEGETABLE STOCK FROM SOUP** [see index]

Freshly ground black pepper, to taste

Preheat oven to 325 degrees F. Prepare a 2-quart oven casserole by coating with non-stick lecithin spray coating.

In a saucepan set over *MEDIUM* heat, combine well-drained beans, *finely* chopped onion and garlic, corn, coconut cream, and stock. Allow to come just to the boil, stirring frequently. Season, to taste, with black pepper.

Turn into prepared oven casserole and bake in preheated 325 degree F. oven for about 1 hour, or until most of liquid has either been absorbed or has evaporated.

Keep warm on a warming tray until ready to serve.

Yields 6 servings
adequate for 4 people

Notes: *Canned coconut cream is available in most grocery stores in either the international section or beverage section. Leftover coconut cream can be frozen.

This recipe may be doubled, when required.

1/6 SERVING – PROTEIN = 7.1 g.; FAT = 2.5 g.; CARBOHYDRATE = 34.0 g.;
CALORIES = 179; CALORIES FROM FAT = 13%

TANZANIAN STEAMED PAPAYA
Papai

TPT - 26 minutes

African menus often include fruits served as vegetables. Under-ripe papayas and bananas provide a starchy vegetable accompaniment that is a pleasant change from the ordinary.

1 pound *under-ripe* **papaya**

1 tablespoon butter—*melted*
Freshly grated nutmeg, to taste

Set up a steamer over *MEDIUM* heat.

Peel, seed, and cut the papaya into 1/2-inch cubes. Spread the papaya chunks out in the steamer and cover tightly. Allow to steam over simmering water for about 15-20 minutes, or until tender. Turn into a colander and drain thoroughly.

Turn drained papaya into a heated serving bowl. Pour butter over and toss *gently* to coat the papaya with butter. Season *lightly* with nutmeg.

Serve at once.

Yields 6 servings
adequate for 4 people

Note: This recipe can be halved or doubled, when required.

A f r i c a – **T a n z a n i a**

TANZANIAN STEAMED PAPAYA (cont'd)

1/6 SERVING – PROTEIN = 0.3 g.; FAT = 2.0 g.; CARBOHYDRATE = 5.0 g.
CALORIES = 37; CALORIES FROM FAT = 49%

TANZANIAN GREENS WITH PEANUTS
Um'bido
TPT - 13 minutes

When the crop of greens in our kitchen garden exceeds our salad consumption capabilities, we usually harvest a big skilletful and sauté them for dinner in a rich, fruity olive oil with garlic and lots of black pepper. In the winter we buy organic spring green mixtures and make a salad or two, reserving the rest for use as a sautéed vegetable side dish. Tanzanians enjoy spinach and other greens in the same manner but they add peanuts. What a delightful addition; what a delightful way to add leguminous protein to a menu!

2 tablespoons *extra virgin* **olive oil**
1/2 cup *blanched, raw* **peanuts**

1 garlic clove—*very finely* **chopped**

8 cups greens, of choice—**trimmed, well-washed and well-dried**

Freshly ground black pepper, to taste

In a large skillet set over *LOW-MEDIUM* heat, combine oil and peanuts. Sauté peanuts until they begin to brown.

Add garlic and sauté for several minutes, *being careful not to allow the garlic to brown.*

Add greens and sauté until greens wilt.

Season with black pepper. Turn into a heated serving bowl.

Serve at once.

Yields 6 servings
adequate for 4 people

Note: This recipe can be halved, when required.

1/6 SERVING – PROTEIN = 2.9 g.; FAT = 8.0 g.; CARBOHYDRATE = 5.1 g.;
CALORIES = 103; CALORIES FROM FAT = 70%

EASY TANZANIAN BANANA ICE CREAM
Aiskrimu n'dizi
TPT - 8 hours and 12 minutes;
8 hours = freezing period

In Tanzania, this delicious frozen dessert is prepared from a rich egg custard. The version given here, although not traditional, is also delicious with the added advantages of quick and easy preparation and lowered fat.

1 cup heavy whipping cream

2/3 cup *fat-free* **sweetened condensed milk**
1/2 cup *fat-free* **pasteurized eggs* (the equivalent of 1 egg)**
1 teaspoon pure vanilla extract

2 medium–large, *very ripe* **bananas**—**peeled and mashed**

Prepare a 7 x 3 x 2-inch non–stick–coated loaf pan by placing it in the freezer until required.

Using an electric mixer fitted with *chilled* beaters or by hand, using a *chilled* wire whisk, beat heavy cream in a *chilled* bowl until stiff. Set aside.

In a large bowl, combine sweetened condensed milk, pasteurized eggs, and vanilla extract. Stir to blend thoroughly.

Fold mashed bananas into milk–egg mixture.

Whisk-fold stiffly whipped cream *gently,* but *thoroughly,* into banana–milk–egg base.

EASY TANZANIAN BANANA ICE CREAM (cont'd)

Pour mixture into chilled loaf pan. Spread evenly. Cover tightly with aluminum foil. Freeze overnight or until firm—about 8 hours.

Either scoop ice cream from pan to serve or remove entire block of ice cream from pan and slice.

Leftovers should be returned to the freezer, tightly covered.

Yields about nine 1/2-cup servings

Notes: *Because raw eggs present the danger of *Salmonella* poisoning, commercially-available pasteurized eggs are recommended for use in preparing this dish.

This recipe is easily doubled, when required. Use a 9 x 5 x 3-inch non-stick-coated loaf pan.

1/9 SERVING (i. e., per 1/2 cupful) –
PROTEIN = 4.2 g.; FAT = 2.6 g.; CARBOHYDRATE = 22.2 g.;
CALORIES = 129; CALORIES FROM FAT = 18%

TANZANIAN PAPAYA AND MANGO DESSERT WITH APRICOT SAUCE
Papai na Embe

TPT - 41 minutes;
30 minutes = sauce cooling period

Matunda is the Swahili word for fruits and this dessert really delivers matunda. The tropical symphony is a wonderful way to end an African-inspired dinner.

1/2 cup apricot nectar*
2 tablespoons freshly squeezed orange juice
 —preferably blood orange juice, if available
1 tablespoon light cream *or* half and half
1 1/2 teaspoons corn starch

1 large ripe mango—peeled, pitted, and cut into
 1/2-inch cubes
1 ripe papaya—peeled, seeded, and cut into
 1/2-inch cubes

In a small saucepan, combine apricot nectar, orange juice, and cream. Add corn starch. Using a wire whisk, beat corn starch into liquid until it is thoroughly combined and in suspension. Place saucepan over *MEDIUM* heat and cook, stirring constantly, until sauce thickens. *Do not allow to boil hard or cream will curdle.*

Remove from heat and refrigerate for about 30 minutes.

In a shallow serving bowl, combine mango and papaya pieces. Pour chilled sauce over and stir *gently* to coat fruit with sauce.

Refrigerate until ready to serve.

Yields 6 servings
adequate for 4 people

Notes: *Apricot nectar may be replaced with either papaya or mango nectar, if preferred.

This recipe may be halved or doubled, when required.

1/6 SERVING – PROTEIN = 0.7 g.; FAT = 0.6 g.; CARBOHYDRATE = 14.6 g.;
CALORIES = 60; CALORIES FROM FAT = 9%

Africa–Tanzania

TANZANIAN FRESH PINEAPPLE DESSERT
Nanasi Tamu

TPT - 2 hours and 4 minutes;
2 hours = flavor development period

Tanzanians enjoy a dessert of fresh fruit with honey and coconut. Pineapple, in our opinion, is especially enhanced by the honey and the sprinkling of salt, as my dad so wisely taught me.

1 fresh, ripe pineapple—cored, peeled, eyes removed, and chopped into chunks *or* slices, if preferred
Salt
2 tablespoons papaya nectar*
3 tablespoons *wildflower* honey

Shredded coconut—fresh or desiccated—for garnish, if desired

Turn the pineapple chunks or slices into an attractive serving bowl or onto a plate or platter. Sprinkle *lightly* with salt. Toss *gently*. Drizzle the papaya nectar over. Toss. Drizzle the honey over.

Refrigerate for at least 2 hours to allow for flavor development.

Serve, garnished with shredded coconut, if desired.

Yields 6 servings
adequate for 4-6 people

Notes: *Papaya nectar is usually found in the international food section of grocery stores. Apricot nectar or mango nectar may be substituted, if necessary.

This recipe may be halved or doubled, when required.

1/6 SERVING – PROTEIN = 0.5 g.; FAT = 0.6 g.; CARBOHYDRATE = 20.6 g.;
CALORIES = 82; CALORIES FROM FAT = 7%

Togo

    The Togolese Republic is a small country, a little smaller than our state of West Virginia, but its port and river transportation made it an important part of Africa's so-called "Slave Coast." From the sixteenth to the eighteenth century Togo was a major trading center for the export of slaves to Europe and to the Americas.

    Although the Danish had originally claimed what is now Togo, in 1884 Germany signed a treaty with Togo's King Mlapa III giving Germany a stretch of territory along the coast. This foothold was quickly expanded bringing Togo under German rule. It was a German protectorate from 1884 to 1914, when it was awarded to both Great Britain and France by a League of Nations mandate. British Togoland voted to become part of the newly independent nation of Ghana in 1957. French Togoland became an autonomous republic within the French Republic and gained full independence from France in 1960. Several post-independence governments were toppled until Eyadéma Gnassingbé came to power in 1967, also by means of a *coup d'etat*. He held onto power for thirty-eight years until his sudden death in 2005. The constitution stipulated the succession of the President of the Parliament pending a special presidential election in sixty days. The military prevented the return of Fambaré Outtara Natchaba, the President of the Parliament, who was out of the country at the time of Gnassingbé's death, and immediately installed Faure Gnassingbé, Eyadéma's son. Despite widespread international condemnation, Faure Gnassingbé has continued as the head of the Togolese government, having been elected in a nation-wide election in 2010. The planned transition to democracy has, however, stalled.

    Togo, which straddles the Mono River has wonderfully fertile soil which allows for a wider variety of vegetables and fruits and, thus, a more sustaining cuisine than is found in other West African nations. Coffee and cocoa are major crops for export and these too profit from the soil fertility. Restaurant menus will always include a variety of ocean and river fish, chicken, turkey, guinea fowl, and bush meat, especially bush rat, but eggs, maize, beans, grilled vegetables, cassava, yams, *couscous*, and rice with spicy groundnut (peanut) sauces can keep a vegetarian sustained. Both German and French influences can be seen in the foods enjoyed by Togolese but the influences of the thirty-seven ethnic groups, who call Togo home, are far more evident.

Sliced Bananas with Lime Mayonnaise

Papaya and Corn Salad with Citrus *Vinaigrette*
Salade de Papaye

~~~~~~~~~~~~~~~~~~~~~~~

Eggs Fried in *Ghee*

Grilled vegetables
with
Spicy Sauce with Ginger and Peanut Butter
Azi Dessi

Steamed *Couscous* – Wheat or Millet

~~~~~~~~~~~~~~~~~~~~~~~

Mango Slices

Rice Pudding with Peanut Butter Cream
Riz au Lait avec Beurre de Arachide

Africa–Togo

TOGOLESE PAPAYA AND CORN SALAD WITH CITRUS *VINAIGRETTE*
Salade de Papaye
TPT - 33 minutes

Years ago, the only papaya available to us in the northeastern United States was the dried, sugared papaya found in the natural food stores. Gradually, papaya became more and more available. It was not until I visited Hawaii that I tasted papaya at their incredible best. Due to the papaya ringspot virus and the failure of the varieties that were the mainstay of the Hawaiian crop, a genetically-engineered papaya variety has been developed to help re-establish Hawaii's papaya industry. Now that papaya, both the small, super-sweet ones and the large 'Maradol' are generally available year round even here in central Pennsylvania, it helps one imagine what it must be like to live in countries where these beautiful fruits are grown. Desserts, salads, and stews made with fresh papaya are far more often on our winter menus.

2 teaspoons butter
1 cup fresh *or frozen* corn kernels

3 cups diced, *firm* papaya
2 ripe tomatoes—seeded and chopped
1 tablespoon *very finely* chopped fresh mint leaves

1 teaspoon freshly squeezed lemon juice
1 teaspoon freshly squeezed orange juice
1 1/2 tablespoons sunflower *or* safflower oil
Pinch salt
Freshly ground black pepper, to taste

In a small skillet set over *MEDIUM* heat, melt butter. Add corn kernels and cook, stirring frequently, until corn kernels are flecked with brown. Remove from heat. Chill for at least 20 minutes. Turn into mixing bowl.

Add diced papaya, tomatoes, and *very finely* chopped mint leaves. Gently mix ingredients.

In a small jar or cruet, combine lemon juice, orange juice, oil, salt, and black pepper. Shake vigorously. Add to papaya mixture. Gently, combine. Turn into a serving bowl. Refrigerate until ready to serve.

Serve chilled.

Yields 6 servings
adequate for 4 people

Note: This recipe can be halved or doubled, when required.

1/6 SERVING – PROTEIN = 2.6 g.; FAT = 4.6 g.; CARBOHYDRATE = 21.6 g.;
CALORIES = 156; CALORIES FROM FAT = 27%

SPICY TOGOLESE SAUCE WITH GINGER AND PEANUT BUTTER
Azi Dessi
TPT - 8 minutes

Some may find this spicy sauce, prepared with smoked dried shrimp and served with fried oysters in the West African Republic of Togo, to be too hot but it is not nearly as hot as "pili pili" which will blow the top of your head off. I can never truly understand the use of excessively hot sauces like "pili pili" and those that are often found in Southeast Asian cuisines. I have grown hot, hot peppers for a friend from Ethiopia who would stand in my garden and eat them with relish but I still did not learn to appreciate the fiery sensation. It is not that I could not learn to tolerate them, it is that I like to taste the other components of my meal. We find this sauce to be quite compatible with a supper of eggs, potatoes, and soy sausages on a busy day when it is suddenly dinner time. It is also a perfect compliment to grilled vegetables.

1 cup canned, *crushed* tomatoes in purée
1 medium onion—*finely* chopped
1 garlic clove—*very finely* chopped
1/2 teaspoon red *jalapeño chili* sauce, or to taste*
3/4 teaspoon ground ginger

2 tablespoons freshly ground, *unsalted, additive-free, chunky* peanut butter—brought to room temperature

In a saucepan set over *MEDIUM* heat, combine crushed tomatoes, *finely* chopped onion, *very finely* chopped garlic, *jalapeño chili* sauce, and ground ginger. Cook, stirring frequently, for about 20 minutes.** Keep warm on a warming tray until ready to serve.

Just before serving, stir the peanut butter into the sauce base.

SPICY TOGOLESE SAUCE WITH GINGER AND PEANUT BUTTER (cont'd)

Serve at once.

Yields about 1 cupful

Notes: *A habanera *chili* would be the choice of a Togolese cook. *Jalapeño* sauce is a convenient substitute. Use more or less, to your taste.

**The sauce base can be prepared early in the day to this point and refrigerated until required. Stir the peanut butter into the sauce after it has been reheated, just before you are ready to serve.

This recipe can be doubled, when required.

1/8 SERVING (about 2 tablespoonfuls) –
PROTEIN = 1.2 g.; FAT = 0.9 g.; CARBOHYDRATE = 4.2 g.;
CALORIES = 28; CALORIES FROM FAT = 29%

RICE PUDDING WITH PEANUT BUTTER CREAM
Riz au Lait avec Beurre de Arachide

TPT - 2 hours and 56 minutes;
2 hours = refrigeration period

Some people fold the whipped cream into the rice pudding; some people add the peanut butter to the rice pudding. The first time I encountered this Togolese rice pudding, it was made with rice, cooked in water, into which a small amount of coconut milk, brown rice syrup, and peanut butter were mixed. My version, I feel, creates a richer rice taste. Your appreciation is broadened by the difference from spoonful to spoonful as you taste either more rice or more peanut butter cream. This is a delicious and, some would say, clever way to get complemented protein into a vegetarian meal.

1 cup *light sulfite-free* coconut milk*

1/2 cup dry Japanese short grain rice**
3 tablespoons sugar

2 tablespoons freshly ground, *unsalted, additive-free smooth* peanut butter—*brought to room temperature*
2 tablespoons *fat-free* sweetened condensed milk
2 tablespoons *two-percent* milk

1 cup heavy whipping cream

In a saucepan set over *MEDIUM* heat, heat coconut milk until just below the boiling point. Reduce heat to *LOW*. Stir in rice and sugar, cover tightly, and cook, *undisturbed*, for 30 minutes, or until most of milk has been absorbed. Turn into a serving bowl. Refrigerate for at least 2 hours.

In a small bowl, combine peanut butter, sweetened condensed milk, and milk. Using a spoon blend the mixture until smooth. Allow it to remain at room temperature until ready to serve.

Using the electric mixer fitted with *chilled* beaters or by hand using a *chilled* wire whisk, beat heavy cream in a *clean, chilled* bowl until stiff peaks form.

Add the peanut butter mixture and whisk-fold it into the whipped cream. Spread over the rice pudding when you are ready to serve.

Serve into dessert dishes. Refrigerate any leftovers.

Yields 6 servings
adequate for 4 people

Notes: *Canned, *sulfite-free* coconut milk is available in most grocery stores in either the international section or beverage section. Canned *sulfite-free, low-fat* coconut milk is hard to find but it is available. The reduction in saturated fats is well worth the search for this more healthful product. Leftover coconut milk can be frozen.

**When cooked, Japanese short-grained rice results in a sticky rice with a glutinous rice texture. *Do not rinse it first.*

This recipe can be doubled, when required.

1/6 SERVING – PROTEIN = 4.4 g.; FAT = 17.0 g.; CARBOHYDRATE = 29.9 g.;
CALORIES = 282; CALORIES FROM FAT =54 %

Tunisia

The Atlas Mountains dominate North Africa and Tunisia is the smallest of the countries that sit along this mountain range. The great Phoenician city of Carthage, founded in the ninth century BC by settlers from the Phoenician city of Tyre in present-day Lebanon, sat along its coast. By the fifth century Carthage was the dominant power in the western Mediterranean and in a series of wars, known as the Punic Wars, the Carthaginians, in fact, delayed the rise of Roman power. Following the defeat of Carthage at the Battle of Carthage in 149 BC, the region became the Roman province of Africa, chosen for its fertile soil which could provide the Roman Empire with substantial grain harvests. Despite the fact that a portion of the Sahara Desert covers the southern part of the country, the northern part of the country is still enormously fertile and productive. In the fifth century AD Rome's influence ended when Tunisia was occupied by the Vandals, the group of Germanic tribes from Scandinavia who had settled in Silesia around 120 BC and who had established kingdoms in Spain and North Africa. The area was reconquered in the sixth century, during the rule of Emperor Justinian, but Roman dominance in Africa was challenged by the Byzantine Empire in the sixth century. By the late seventh century Arab Muslims had invaded and established the city of Kairouan, the first Islamic city in North Africa. In the late 1500s Spain conquered many of the cities along the coast but these were eventually lost to the Ottoman Turks, under whom Tunisia had the good fortune to retain a high degree of autonomy. As did other countries in the Maghreb, Tunisians suffered under the reoccurrence of bubonic and pneumonic plagues and the famines of the late 1700s into the early years of the nineteenth century forcing Tunisia into a downward financial spiral. In May of 1819 it was reported in *The* [London] *Examiner* that Tunis had lost half of its inhabitants to the plague and that it was threatened with an Arab insurrection. In 1869 Tunisia declared bankruptcy and struggled to recover only to be invaded by France in 1883, becoming a French protectorate and remaining so until independence in 1956 when it became known as the Kingdom of Tunisia. The following year it proclaimed itself a republic. The first president Habib Bourguiba remained in office for thirty years and was succeeded in a bloodless *coup d'etat* by his prime minister Zine El Abidine Ben Ali, who ruled for twenty-three years before being forced from office by a popular revolution which began in December of 2010. Ben Ali, accused of corruption and repression, stepped down. He and six of his relatives fled into exile.

Although Tunisia is predominately an Islamic nation, which greatly influences its culture and cuisine, Sephardic Jewish residents, many of whom fled to Tunisia from Spain during the *Reconquista*, have also contributed food traditions that have persisted despite the fact that the Jewish population has fallen from 105,000 in 1948 to about 1,500 today. The Jewish community on the Island of Djerba dates back 2,500 years and, although today the home of only about 1,000 Jewish Tunisians, it has thirty-nine synagogues. French-influenced dishes are very much in evidence, reflecting the years as a protectorate of France during which large numbers of French and Italians moved to Tunisia. However, since independence, most French and Italian residents have chosen to return to Europe. Nevertheless, Tunisia has continued a close economic cooperation with France.

Africa – Tunisia

To me a Tunisian meal of salads, a vegetable stew, a dessert, and a Tunisian pastry is a heavenly thought. I have, therefore, included several favorite salads, a stew for winter and a stew for summer, and a few Tunisian sweets.

Garlic – Yogurt Sauce with *Tahini*
Laban ma'Taheena
with *Pita* Bread

~

Roasted Tomato and Pepper Salad
Salata Mechouia

Potato and Egg Salad with *Feta* Cheese
Salatat Batata

Radish and Egg Salad
Salatat Fijil

Hot Spinach, Rice, and Chick Pea Bread Salad
Fattat Sabanich

~~~~~~~~~~~~~~~~~~~~

Chick Pea and Potato Vegetable Stew
Chorba

or

Summer Vegetable Stew
Chakchouka de Saiff
with
Tunisian Garlic-Yogurt Sauce with *Tahini* [see above]

~~~~~~~~~~~~~~~~~~~~

Dried Fruit Compote
Fakka

Chick Pea Flour Sweet
Ghriaba

Almond Ball Sweet
Boulettes d'Amandes

Basic Almond Paste for Confections
Pate d'Amande

~

Tunisian Rose Petal Spice Mix
Baharat

Tunisian Coriander Seasoning
Tabil

Africa–Tunisia

TUNISIAN GARLIC – YOGURT SAUCE WITH *TAHINI*
Laban ma' Taheena
TPT - 7 minutes

Although generally not mixed with foods as in European cuisines, sauces are important throughout North Africa and the Middle East as accompaniments and dips. Versions of this yogurt–garlic sauce are found in many cuisines, with and without tahini and with lemon juice or without, as in this Tunisian version.

2 medium garlic cloves—peeled
Pinch salt

1 tablespoon sesame *tahini* (sesame paste or sesame butter)*
1 cup **PLAIN YOGURT** *[see index]* or commercially-available plain yogurt

Place peeled garlic cloves on a cutting board. Using the flat side of a large chef's knife, smash garlic cloves. Sprinkle salt on crushed garlic cloves and continue to crush them using the knife blade. *Finely* chop crushed garlic cloves. Turn into a mixing bowl.

Add sesame *tahini* to *finely* chopped garlic. Stir to mix thoroughly. Add yogurt and mix well to create a smooth sauce.

Refrigerate until ready to serve.

Yields about 1 cupful

Notes: *Tahini* is readily available in natural food stores and in stores specializing in Middle Eastern products. It can also be made at home using a food processor.

This recipe can be halved or doubled, when required.

1/16 SERVING (i. e., per tablespoonful) –
PROTEIN = 0.9 g.; FAT = 0.6 g.; CARBOHYDRATE = 1.0 g.;
CALORIES = 13; CALORIES FROM FAT = 42%

TUNISIAN ROASTED TOMATO AND PEPPER SALAD
Salata Mechouia
TPT - 1 hour and 10 minutes

In Tunisia, this salad is generally served as an appetizer or first course. Served with pita bread or an Italian or French baguette, it is a most satisfying course. Our version reflects our taste with much less salt and oil used than is traditional. Feel free to modify this recipe to your own taste.

1 large, red bell pepper—perfect, unblemished, and well-washed
1 large, green bell pepper—perfect, unblemished, and well-washed

4 large, ripe, *but firm,* tomatoes—perfect, unblemished, and well-washed

1/2 cup *finely* chopped onion

1 tablespoon freshly squeezed lemon juice—strained
1/2 teaspoon salt
Freshly ground black pepper, to taste

1 1/2 teaspoons *extra virgin* olive oil

12 imported black, ripe olives—preferably Greek, if available

Preheat oven to 400 degrees F.

Place peppers on a cookie sheet. Roast in preheated oven for about 20 minutes, *turning frequently.*

Place tomatoes on the cookie sheet with roasting peppers and continue to roast vegetables for 20 minutes more. *Turn frequently.*

Place roasted peppers in a heavy brown paper bag in dry sink. Roll the top of the bag down and allow to steam for about 15 minutes.

Allow tomatoes to cool until they can be handled comfortably. Peel the tomatoes and slice them into quarters. Squeeze the tomato wedges to remove the juice and seeds. Chop tomatoes. Set aside until required.

Remove peppers from the paper bag. Remove stems, seeds, and membranes, peel, and chop. Add to tomatoes with chopped onion.

Africa–Tunisia

TUNISIAN ROASTED TOMATO AND PEPPER SALAD (cont'd)

In a shallow serving bowl, combine lemon juice, salt, and black pepper. Stir to combine well. Add chopped tomatoes, peppers, and onion. Toss to mix well.

Dribble the olive oil over the mixture, *but do not mix.* Scatter olives over the surface.

Serve with a slotted spoon, warm or chilled, as preferred. Refrigerate leftovers.

Note: This recipe may be halved or doubled, when required.

Yields 6 servings
adequate for 4 people

1/6 SERVING – PROTEIN = 1.0 g.; FAT = 3.9 g.; CARBOHYDRATE = 6.6 g.;
CALORIES = 67; CALORIES FROM FAT = 52%

TUNISIAN POTATO AND EGG SALAD WITH *FETA* CHEESE
Salatat Batata

TPT - 1 hour and 12 minutes;
30 minutes = potato chilling period

A potato and cheese salad from Northern Italy is a special favorite of ours but a "potato and cheese salad" can taste completely different as in this Tunisian version when the cheese is feta instead of Gruyère and a wonderful lemon vinaigrette is used to dress the salad instead of the lemony mayonnaise of the Italian version.

4 medium potatoes
4 quarts *boiling* water

2 hard-cooked eggs—chilled and peeled

Pinch or two salt

1 garlic clove—crushed and *very finely* chopped
2 tablespoons *finely* chopped fresh coriander (*cilantro*)
3/4 cup crumbled *feta* cheese

2 tablespoons freshly squeezed lemon juice
2 tablespoons *extra virgin* olive oil

Freshly ground black pepper, to taste
2 tablespoons halved, pitted green olives

Scrub potatoes thoroughly and place in *boiling* water. Boil until cooked through, but still *firm*—about 25 minutes. *(They will yield to a fork, but not crumble.)* Drain thoroughly and chill for at least 30 minutes. Peel and dice into 3/4-inch cubes.

Dice the hard-cooked eggs into uniform pieces.

In a mixing bowl, combine diced potatoes and hard-cooked egg pieces. Sprinkle a bit of salt over. Toss *gently*.

Add *very finely* chopped garlic, *finely* chopped fresh coriander (*cilantro*), and crumbled *feta* cheese. Toss to combine.

In a cruet or jar, combine lemon juice and olive oil. Shake vigorously. Pour over combined ingredients. Toss *gently* to coat each ingredient. Turn into a shallow serving bowl or onto a platter.

Grind black pepper over. Sprinkle the olive halves over.

Serve at once.

Yields about 6 servings
adequate for 4 people

Note: This recipe is easily doubled, when required.

1/6 SERVING – PROTEIN = 7.7 g.; FAT = 13.3 g.; CARBOHYDRATE = 16.7 g.;
CALORIES = 201; CALORIES FROM FAT = 60%

Africa–Tunisia

TUNISIAN RADISH AND EGG SALAD
Salatat Fijil
TPT - 6 minutes

Tunisian salads are many in number, fresh in taste, and very interesting. We tend to use radishes and celery as bit players in tossed salads. In a Tunisian salad, thinly sliced or diced vegetables become stars without greens and Tunisians combine these stars in the most tasteful ways. I always garnish this salad with radish slices just to give diners a heads up about what those little red and white cubes are.

2 bunches of radishes—well-washed, well-trimmed, and diced
1/4 cup *finely* chopped celery
1/4 cup *finely* chopped parsley

2 tablespoons freshly squeezed lemon juice
2 tablespoons *extra virgin* olive oil

Freshly ground black pepper, to taste
2 hard-cooked eggs—chilled, peeled, and chopped
2 tablespoons halved, pitted green olives

2 radishes—*very thinly* sliced into rounds—for garnish

In a mixing bowl, combine diced radishes and *finely* chopped celery and parsley. Toss to combine.

In a cruet or jar, combine lemon juice and olive oil. Shake vigorously. Pour over combined ingredients. Toss *gently* to coat each ingredient. Turn into a shallow serving bowl or onto a platter.

Grind black pepper over. Sprinkle the chopped eggs and olive halves over.

Serve at once.

Yields about 6 servings
adequate for 4 people

Note: This recipe is easily doubled, when required.

1/6 SERVING – PROTEIN = 3.1 g.; FAT = 3.6 g.; CARBOHYDRATE = 3.5 g.;
CALORIES = 58; CALORIES FROM FAT = 56%

TUNISIAN HOT SPINACH, RICE, AND CHICK PEA BREAD SALAD WITH TUNISIAN GARLIC–YOGURT SAUCE WITH *TAHINI*
Fattat Sabanich
TPT - 1 hour and 40 minutes;
30 minutes = rice soaking period

This salad, which actually translates to "broken sandwich," is another creative and delicious meal-in-a-bowl bread salad from Tunisia.

2 cups bottled water *or* refrigerated water**
1/2 cup raw Indian *basmati* rice*

2 quarts bottled water *or* refrigerated water**

3 tablespoons water

1 tablespoon *extra virgin* olive oil
1 medium onion—peeled and chopped
1 tablespoon water

1 teaspoon ground coriander
3/4 pound fresh spinach—trimmed with tough stems removed, torn into bite-sized pieces, and *very well-washed*

1 cup canned chick peas (*garbanzos*)—well-drained
2 tablespoons water
Freshly ground black pepper, to taste

1 *pita* bread loaf

TUNISIAN GARLIC – YOGURT SAUCE WITH
    TAHINI (Laban ma' Taheena) [see recipe which precedes]

1/4 cup *preservative-free* pine nuts (*pignoli*)

Africa—Tunisia

TUNISIAN HOT SPINACH, RICE, AND CHICK PEA BREAD SALAD WITH TUNISIAN GARLIC–YOGURT SAUCE WITH *TAHINI* (cont'd)

Pour rice into a sieve and wash rice in several changes of water until water is no longer milky. Put rice in a bowl with 2 cupfuls water. Allow to soak for 30 minutes. Turn into a sieve and drain well.

Bring the 2 quartfuls water to the boil in a large saucepan set over *MEDIUM-HIGH* heat. Stir the drained rice into the *boiling* water, being sure that it does not settle to the bottom of the pan. Cook the *basmati* rice in the rapidly boiling water for 10 minutes. Pour water and rice into a sieve. Drain thoroughly. Shake to remove any water which might adhere to the rice. Turn into a clean saucepan.

Add the 3 tablespoonfuls water, cover, and place on a warming burner or on a burner set at *LOW*.

In a kettle set over *MEDIUM* heat, heat oil. Add onion and sauté until soft and translucent, *being careful not to allow onion to brown. Reduce heat to LOW.* Add 1 tablespoonful water.

Add ground coriander and sauté for 1 minute more to allow for the release of the spice's flavor. Add torn spinach leaves, in batches if necessary. The water adhering to the leaves should be sufficient to steam the spinach.

When the spinach is wilted, add drained chick peas (*garbanzos*), the 2 tablespoonfuls water, and black pepper. Cover and simmer over *LOW* heat for about 20 minutes. *Add more water, if necessary.*

Preheat oven to 200 degrees F.

Place *pita* bread on oven rack to heat for about 5 minutes. Remove and tear into bite-sized pieces. Set aside until ready to assemble salad.

When ready to serve, place warm *pita* in the bottom of a large heated serving bowl, such as a large, shallow spaghetti bowl. Spoon hot rice over the bread. Spoon hot spinach–chick pea mixture over the rice. Spoon 2 tablespoonfuls of the garlic–yogurt sauce over the top. Garnish with pine nuts (*pignoli*).

Serve at once. Pass more of the TUNISIAN GARLIC–YOGURT SAUCE WITH *TAHINI* (*Laban ma' Taheena*) to accommodate individual tastes.

Yields 4 servings as a main course salad;
yields 6 servings as a side salad

Notes: *Basmati* rice is available in Indian groceries, food specialty stores, and natural food stores. It adds a remarkable fragrance to this dish.

**Since the chlorine in tap water destroys the B-vitamin thiamin in grains, it is advisable to cook grains in either bottled water or water that has been refrigerated for at least 24 hours.

This recipe may be halved or doubled, when required.

1/6 SERVING – PROTEIN = 8.6 g.; FAT = 6.8 g.; CARBOHYDRATE = 22.2 g.;
CALORIES = 179; CALORIES FROM FAT = 34%

TUNISIAN CHICK PEA AND POTATO VEGETABLE STEW
Chorba
TPT - 1 hour

"Chorba" simply means soup and diverse versions of this are found in both Tunisia and Morocco, usually made with meat, chicken, beef, or lamb. It is a wonderfully thick "meal-in-a-bowl" that satisfies completely and does not require a search through ethnic groceries or online sources for exotic ingredients. A friend, who claimed that she cooked "American" and did not have exotic ingredients on hand, had all these ingredients in her kitchen except for the Hungarian hot paprika. Regular paprika will do, if you are in the same situation.

1 tablespoon *extra virgin* olive oil
1 large onion—chopped
2 garlic cloves—*very finely* chopped

1 tablespoon Hungarian *hot* paprika *or* Spanish *smoked* paprika, if preferred
1 teaspoon ground turmeric
1/2 teaspoon freshly ground black pepper
Pinch of ground ginger

1 medium carrot—pared or scraped and diced

1 large potato—peeled and diced
1 celery rib—trimmed and diced
2 cups canned chick peas (*garbanzos*)—well-drained
3 tablespoons chopped parsley
1 1/2 cups water, more or less as preferred*
1 tablespoon freshly squeezed lemon juice

1 cup canned, *diced* tomatoes in purée

Africa – Tunisia

TUNISIAN CHICK PEA AND POTATO VEGETABLE STEW (cont'd)

In a kettle set over *LOW-MEDIUM* heat, heat oil. Add onion and garlic and sauté until onion is soft and translucent, *being careful to allow neither onion nor garlic to brown.*

Add paprika, ground turmeric, black pepper, and ground ginger. Continue to sauté for a minute or two to allow spices to brown and for oils to be released.

Add diced carrot and sauté for about a minute.

Add diced potato and celery, well-drained chick peas, chopped parsley, water, and lemon juice. *Increase heat to MEDIUM.* Allow to come to the boil, stirring frequently.

Using the electric blender, purée the diced tomatoes into a smooth purée. Add to ingredients in kettle. *Reduce heat to LOW*, cover, and allow to simmer for about 35 minutes, or until potatoes are crisp-tender. Stir occasionally. Turn into a heated serving bowl and keep warm until ready to serve.

Serve into heated soup plates with warm flatbread.

Yields 8 servings

Notes: *When reheating this soup for a reappearance, additional water may be required.

This recipe can conveniently be halved or doubled.

1/8 SERVING – PROTEIN = 3.7 g.; FAT = 2.3 g.; CARBOHYDRATE = 14.1 g.;
CALORIES = 91; CALORIES FROM FAT = 23%

TUNISIAN SUMMER VEGETABLE STEW
Chakchouka de Saif
TPT - 54 minutes

In Tunisia this is considered a summer dish since the concurrent availability of the vegetable ingredients is seasonal. In the United States we have a year-round supply of these ingredients and can, therefore, enjoy this dish year-round, although it is certainly at its best with the garden-fresh produce of the late summer harvests. Tunisian cuisine evidences significant influences from its French colonial period and this stew emphasizes that point, being remarkably similar in concept to the classic French ratatouille, tweaked by vegetable availability, preferences, and cooking techniques.

- 1 tablespoon *extra virgin* olive oil
- 2 medium onions—peeled and sliced
- 2 medium carrots—pared or scraped, halved lengthwise, and sliced into 3-inch-long thick julienne slices
- 1 green pepper—cored, seeded, and sliced into 2-inch-long slices
- 1 red pepper—cored, seeded, and sliced into 2-inch-long slices
- 10 *frozen* artichoke heart quarters—*defrosted* and sliced
- 2 ripe tomatoes—peeled, seeded, and chopped
- 2 cups fresh cauliflower florets—cut larger ones in half
- 1 tablespoon *finely* chopped mild green *chilies**
- 3 garlic cloves—coarsely chopped *or* sliced, as preferred

- 2 cups water
- 6 tablespoons tomato paste

- 3-4 small all-purpose potatoes—peeled and quartered
- 1/4 cup chopped fresh dillweed

- 1 teaspoon anise seed

- 1 teaspoon Hungarian paprika—sweet *or* hot, as preferred
- 1/2 teaspoon freshly ground *white* pepper
- Pinch salt

In a wok or large, deep skillet, with cover, set over *MEDIUM* heat, heat oil. Add sliced onions, carrots, green and red pepper, artichoke hearts, chopped tomatoes, cauliflower florets, *finely* chopped green *chilies*, and chopped or sliced garlic. *Stir-fry* for about 10 minutes, or until vegetables are beginning to soften.

Add water and stir in tomato paste. Cover the pan and allow it to come almost to the boil. Stir frequently to prevent vegetables from sticking.

Add quartered potatoes and chopped dillweed. Cook, stirring occasionally, until potatoes are *crisp-tender*—about 15 minutes.

Using a mortar, grind anise seeds with a pestle until quite fine. Set aside.

When potatoes are cooked, reduce heat to *LOW*. Stir in ground anise, paprika, *white* pepper, and salt. Continue to cook for about 10-15 minutes more, stirring frequently.

Africa–Tunisia

TUNISIAN SUMMER VEGETABLE STEW (cont'd)

Turn into a heated serving bowl or onto a heated, deep serving platter. Serve warm, into warmed soup plates, with the sauce that remains in the bottom of the cooking pan.

Chakchouka is often served with a poached egg nestled into each serving of the vegetable mélange.

This recipe may be halved but since leftovers reheat well, there seems little advantage in preparing the smaller amount. Reheated, it pairs well with *couscous*.

Yields about 8 servings
adequate for 4-6 people

Notes: *Hotter *chilies* may be used, if appreciated.

1/8 SERVING – PROTEIN = 3.8 g.; FAT = 1.8 g.; CARBOHYDRATE = 21.4 g.;
CALORIES = 111; CALORIES FROM FAT = 15%

TUNISIAN DRIED FRUIT COMPOTE
Fahka

TPT - 8 hours and 34 minutes;
30 minutes = sugar syrup cooling period;
8 hours = dried fruit soaking period

The store of dried fruits that "gets us through the winter" is not just nibbled upon like a trail mix. We have searched the world for interesting ways to use dried fruit as part of our "winter five-a-day." Fahka is a favorite. The overnight soaking results in firmer fruit than would be resultant from the boiling water reconstitution, so often recommended.

1 1/2 cups water
1/4 cup sugar

Zest of 1 lemon
1 tablespoons freshly squeezed lemon juice
1-inch piece of vanilla pod

3/4 pound assorted *preservative-free* dried fruits, of choice*

VANILLA YOGURT *[see index]*, **whipped heavy cream,** *or* **a sprinkling of toasted, chopped *preservative-free* walnuts, for garnish, as preferred**

In a saucepan over *MEDIUM-LOW* heat, combine water and sugar. Allow to come to a boil. Cook, stirring frequently, until is sugar is dissolved. *Remove from heat.*

Add lemon zest, lemon juice, and vanilla pod. Allow sugar syrup to cool for 30 minutes.

Add dried fruit. Stir *gently* to combine. Refrigerate 8 hours or overnight.

Remove large fruit pieces, such as apple and pineapple slices, from compote and cut these into bite-sized pieces. Turn all fruit and liquid into a serving bowl.

Serve into individual dessert dishes, garnished with yogurt or whipped cream, if desired.

Yields 6 servings
adequate for 4 people

Notes: *If prunes are chosen, be sure to select pitted ones.

This recipe can be halved or doubled, when required.

1/6 SERVING – PROTEIN = 1.7 g.; FAT = 0.6 g; CARBOHYDRATE = 48.6 g
CALORIES = 170; CALORIES FROM FAT = 3%

Africa–Tunisia

TUNISIAN CHICK PEA FLOUR SWEET
Ghriaba
TPT - 41 minutes

I first saw ghriaba in an ethnic bakery in London but when I tried to make them, I could not find chick pea flour and had to grind dried chick peas to make a flour. Chick pea (garbanzo or besan) flour is now usually available at Middle Eastern groceries and natural food stores so this unique treat is more easily made at home. The obvious nutritional bonus of legume protein aside, these sweets are very pleasant and a definite change from the excessively sweet, nut pastries most associated with this part of the world. Served with a plate of fresh fruit, ghriaba make a very pleasant light dessert.

2 tablespoons butter—*softened to room temperature*
1/4 cup *light* olive oil
1 teaspoon pure vanilla extract

1 cup chick pea (*garbanzo* or *besan*) flour
1 cup unbleached white flour
6 tablespoons confectioners' sugar
Up to 3 tablespoons water

2 tablespoons confectioners' sugar

Preheat oven to 300 degrees F. Prepare a cookie sheet by lining with culinary parchment paper.

In the work bowl of the food processor fitted with steel knife, combine *softened* butter, oil, and vanilla extract. Process just to mix.

In a mixing bowl, combine chick pea flour, white flour, and the 6 tablespoonfuls confectioners' sugar. Gradually work mixture into butter–oil mixture. *Machine-knead* until thoroughly blended, adding water until dough begins to stick together. Remove to a *cold*, smooth surface such as a pastry marble or Formica counter top or table and continue to knead until smooth, adding more water if necessary. Pinch about 2 teaspoonfuls of the dough and roll to form a ball. Place on parchment-lined cookie sheet.

Bake in preheated 300 degree F. oven for about 15-20 minutes, or until the bottom of the pastries become a *very light brown*. Transfer to a wire rack to cool completely.

Place on a serving platter. Sprinkle the remaining 2 tablespoonfuls of confectioners' sugar over.

Store in an airtight tin with waxed paper between layers.

Yields about 22 pieces

Note: Of course, this recipe may be prepared by hand if a food processor is unavailable. Be careful to knead thoroughly until mixture is very smooth.

1/22 SERVING (i. e., per piece) –
PROTEIN = 3.0 g.; FAT = 3.7 g.; CARBOHYDRATE = 14.3 g.;
CALORIES = 101; CALORIES FROM FAT = 33%

TUNISIAN ALMOND BALL SWEET
Boulettes d'Amandes
TPT - 16 hours and 30 minutes;
    8 hours = drying period;
    8 hours and 16 minutes = preparation time
         for BASIC ALMOND PASTE

Sweet shops and chocolatiers are few and far between now. Candy sits at the check-out of grocery stores and seems, though I do not know why, to satisfy. As a child I remember peeking up into the cases in sweet shops, wondering how those lovely candies, artfully pyramided on trays and plates, were made and what they tasted like. You did not buy them by the pound, but by the piece. You savored them and remembered them. There were still a few of those shops in suburban shopping malls when my daughter was little but now, where are they? I also remember the thrill of touring Fanny Farmer's factory in Rochester, New York, and being allowed to sample candies as they came off the conveyer belt. Even in Europe, packaged, assembly line candies are everywhere. If you too were fascinated by those handmade sweets of yesteryear, you might like to try this recipe. The work they entail is very satisfying in the end.

Africa–Tunisia

TUNISIAN ALMOND BALL SWEET (cont'd)

1/4 cup sugar
1/4 cup *preservative-free* almond meal *or finely ground almonds*

2 tablespoons water

1 prepared recipe for TUNISIAN ALMOND PASTE *(Pate d'Amandes)* [see recipe which follows]—i. e., twenty 1/2-inch balls

Place sugar and almond meal in a saucer or small fruit dish. Stir to combine well.

Place water in a saucer.

Roll the almond balls made from the almond paste, *one at time,* in the water. Then, roll the in the sugar–almond mixture until well coated. Place on a serving dish and allow to dry thoroughly—about 8 hours.

Store in an airtight container when thoroughly dry.

Yields about 20 1/2-inch sweets

Note: This recipe may be halved or doubled, when required.

1/20 SERVING – PROTEIN = 2.0 g.; FAT = 5.7 g.; CARBOHYDRATE = 12.4 g.;
CALORIES = 107; CALORIES FROM FAT = 48%

TUNISIAN BASIC ALMOND PASTE for CONFECTIONS
Pate d'Amande

TPT - 8 hours and 16 minutes;
8 hours = drying period

You can easily find almond paste, even in grocery stores, but there is challenge and pleasure in making your own. Although I very much like to get down to an entry level approach to food preparation in other cultures, I am not adverse to the use of a food processor to make almond paste! I use this paste to prepare TUNISIAN ALMOND BALLS (Boulettes d'Amandes) and TUNISIAN ALMOND–FILLED PASTRIES (Samsa).

1 1/4 cups *preservative-free* almonds
2/3 cup sugar
1 teaspoon freshly grated orange zest
1/4 teaspoon natural almond oil*
2 tablespoons rose water**

Using a food processor fitted with steel knife, grind the almonds and sugar into a paste. As the paste begins to form, add freshly grated orange zest, almond oil, and rose water. Continue processing until well-integrated.

Using about 1 teaspoonful of prepared almond paste, prepare a ball by rolling the almond paste between your palms. Set aside on waxed paper to dry for at least 8 hours, or overnight.

Use to prepare confections.

Notes: *Natural almond oil is available in stores specializing in candy-making supplies and, often, in groceries carrying Indian and Pakistani food items. Almond extract *can not* be substituted.

**Rose water, generally available as a French import, is available at many food specialty stores or in Middle Eastern groceries.

This recipe may be halved or doubled, when required.

Yields about thirty 1/2-inch balls

1/30 SERVING – PROTEIN = 0.9 g.; FAT = 2.7 g.; CARBOHYDRATE = 6.0 g.;
CALORIES = 52; CALORIES FROM FAT = 81%

Africa–**Tunisia**

TUNISIAN ROSE PETAL SPICE MIX
Baharat

TPT - 6 minutes

If tabil, the hot spice mixture of Tunisia, is too hot for your taste buds, the Tunisian version of baharat, Arabic for "mixed spices," might be more acceptable. I make up a double or triple batch of this as soon as the fragrant red roses in my herb garden bloom and use it in dishes that require "warm" spices.

2 tablespoons *dried* rose petals—*home-grown and spray-free*

1 teaspoon ground cinnamon
1 teaspoon freshly ground black pepper
1/4 teaspoon ground cloves

Using a SPICE and COFFEE GRINDER, grind dried rose petals until *evenly and finely ground.*

Add ground cinnamon, black pepper, and cloves. Grind the mixture to uniform consistency. Turn into a glass jar to store.*

Use to season *tuajen* [plural of *tagine*] and vegetables, or season oil with the mixture to spread on bread.

Yields 1 1/2 tablespoonfuls

Note: *This mixture stores well for 3 to 4 months before it begins to lose flavor. However, do check for rancidity if stored for an extended time period. If preferred, this mixture can be stored in the refrigerator or in the freezer to extend its shelf life.

FOOD VALUES for such spice mixtures are almost negligible.

TUNISIAN CORIANDER SEASONING
Tabil

TPT - 2 minutes

Tabil simply means "seasoning" in Tunisian but may well have been the word for the spice coriander in Moorish Andalusia. The spice is said to have been brought to Tunisia from Andalusia by Muslims fleeing forced conversion to Christianity in Spain beginning at the end of the fifteenth century after the collapse of the Muslim kingdom of Granada. The seasoning blend has also taken on the name of its primary ingredient. The addition of garlic cloves that have been allowed to "roast" in the African sun before drying and grinding and hot peppers aside, this is a rather nice way to give a rather mundane vegetable dish an exotically ethnic twist. Some westerners grind crushed dried red peppers, others use chili powder.

2 tablespoons coriander seeds
1 tablespoon caraway seeds
1 1/2 tablespoons ground garlic*
2 teaspoons crushed, dried red peppers

Using a SPICE and COFFEE GRINDER, grind until evenly pulverized. Turn into a glass jar for storage.**

Yields about 3 tablespoonfuls

Notes: *Note that we use ground garlic, which can be ordered from spice and baking firms. *You can not substitute garlic powder or garlic salt in this recipe.*

**This mixture stores well, almost indefinitely, but does begin to lose its pungency after about four months.

FOOD VALUES for such spice mixtures are almost negligible

Uganda

Bantu-speaking people, who migrated from central Africa about 2,300 years ago and who would eventually sweep across Africa, displaced the hunter-gathers who roamed the area of Africa we now know as Uganda. For centuries this part of Africa saw great tribal empires come and go. In about 120 AD Nilotic people began migrating into the area from the North. The migration and settlement of Ateker and Luo herdsmen and farmers led to loss of power by some tribal dynasties and the rise of others. The Empire of Kitara (Rwanda), also known as the Chwezi Empire, which achieved its zenith in the fourteenth and fifteenth centuries, covered most of what is known as the great lakes area from Lake Albert, Lake Tanganyika, and Lake Victoria to Lake Kyoga. The Luo migration and integration actually continued until the sixteenth century well after the Kitara had declined.

Cobalt and copper deposits attracted the European powers during the period of African colonization. In 1888 Uganda became a protectorate of Great Britain, not gaining independence until 1962 although it chose to remain within the British Commonwealth until 1967.

The British left behind a strong Indian influence in Ugandan cooking. This statement may confuse at first but if one looks back to the British colonial period, the reason becomes clearer. The British brought 32,000 Indians to Uganda to construct the Uganda Railway. Nearly seven thousand of those workers chose not to return to India when their indentured labor contracts expired. By the 1960s the Indian minority population was estimated to be about 80,000. Their presence is still apparent in the spicing of foods. The spice mixture called *garam masala* is found in the spice markets and the ingredients are readily available to the housewife who wishes to prepare her own mixture.

In 1967, after a brutal power struggle, Uganda declared itself a republic. Within a few years of independence, the country experienced a military *coup* through which the sadistic dictator Idi Amin seized power. An estimated 300,000 Ugandans were killed by the regime. The highly entrepreneurial Indians, who chose to remain after the British left, were expelled causing a collapse of the economy. The regime of Idi Amin finally ended in 1979 as a result of the invasion of a combined force of Tanzanian soldiers and Ugandan exiles. The years that followed did not, however, bring stability. Instead, Ugandans struggled through wars, *coups*, and governmental instability until the coming to power in 1986 of Yoweri Museveni. Museveni has been president ever since and was re-elected in 2006.

Uganda claims a large portion of Lake Victoria which it shares with Kenya and Tanzania. and is situated in the Nile basin. As a consequence, it experiences a rather regular and predictable rainfall pattern. It does not have the agricultural dilemmas that accompany the climate of other areas of Africa where seasonal extremes can swing between period of very wet weather and periods of virtual drought. Uganda, under Yoweri Museveni, has been encouraging agriculture and the replanting of the fertile soils with which it is blessed as well as rehabilitating infrastructure destroyed during the war years. Museveni has also allowed the return of the Indian population expelled by Idi Amin. Today, about 15,000 Ugandans identify themselves as Indian. In addition, plans are being developed to tap the reserves of crude oil and natural gas for export although transparency of these industries is a concern which has deterred foreign investment. Foreign investors have also balked at laws that require investments to pass through Uganda's national bank. An average annual growth figure of 2.5% between 2000 and 2003 was reported but an increase in poverty of 3.8% was reported for the same time period.

Africa – Uganda

Feta Cheese   Assorted Olives

Mango – Pineapple Chutney

Pan-Grilled Skewers Yam Chunks

~ ~ ~

Fruit Salad

Macaroni Salad with *Pesto* and *Chouriço*

~ ~

Potatoes with Yogurt Curds

Steamed Green Bananas or Plantains
Matooke

Steamed Rice with **Mung Bean Sauce with Tomatoes and Garlic**
Choroko

~ ~ ~ ~ ~

Rice with Potatoes

Stir-Fried Bamboo Shoots and Greens
Maleya

~ ~ ~ ~ ~

Slow Cooker Black-Eyed Pea *Chili*

or

Our *Chili*

Golden Buttermilk Cornbread *[see index]* or Corn Muffins

~ ~

Bananas with Cream

Ripe Mango Slices

MANGO – PINEAPPLE CHUTNEY
TPT - 26 hours and 6 minutes;
24 hours = cooling period

This is stupendous choice as an appetizer with goat cheese on a cracker or toasted bread. Some people use pineapple tidbits, I prefer to use crushed pineapple because the end result is easier to spread.

2 tablespoons safflower *or* sunflower oil
1 teaspoon crushed red pepper flakes

1 1/2 cup *finely* chopped sweet onion—Vidalia, Walla Walla, *or* Texas or Mayan Sweet

2-inch piece of fresh gingerroot—peeled and *very finely* chopped
1 large green, yellow, orange, *or* red bell pepper, as preferred—cored, seeded, and *finely* chopped

3 large ripe mangos—peeled, pitted, and diced
3 cups *crushed* pineapple—fresh or canned, as preferred—*well-drained*
1/2 cup apple cider vinegar
1/2 cup firmly-packed *light* brown sugar
1 1/2 tablespoons HOMEMADE CURRY POWDER *[see index]* or commercially-available curry powder mixture of choice

MANGO – PINEAPPLE CHUTNEY (cont'd)

Sterilize eight 1/2-pint canning jars. Also sterilize lids and rings for jars.

In a large kettle set over *LOW-MEDIUM* heat, heat oil. Add crushed red pepper flakes. Cook, stirring constantly, until the pepper flakes start to sizzle and spit.

Add *finely* chopped onion and sauté until onion is soft and translucent, *being careful not to allow onion to brown. Increase heat to MEDIUM.*

Add *very finely* chopped gingerroot and *finely* chopped bell pepper. Cook, stirring constantly, for several minutes.

Add diced mango, crushed pineapple, vinegar, brown sugar, and curry powder. Allow to come almost to the boil over *MEDIUM* heat. *Reduce heat to LOW.* Cook, uncovered, for about 30 minutes until thickened. Stir frequently.

Ladle into the sterilized 1/2-pint canning jars. Carefully wipe rims of jars. Seal with hot, sterilized lids and rings. Process in hot–water–bath canner for 10 minutes, *timing from the moment the water comes to a full rolling boil.* Remove to surface covered with thick towels or newspapers. Allow to cool for 24 hours *undisturbed*. Check to be sure jars are sealed before labeling and storing in a dark, cool, dry place.* Loosen or remove rings before storing.

Yields eight 1/2-pint jarfuls

Note: *Any jars that do not seal can be stored in the refrigerator for several months or resealed using a *new lid.*

1/64 SERVING (i. e., 2 tablespoonfuls) –
PROTEIN = 0.2 g.; FAT = 0.5 g.; CARBOHYDRATE = 5.5 g.;
CALORIES = 25; CALORIES FROM FAT = 2%

UGANDAN FRUIT SALAD
TPT - 1 hour and 9 minutes;
1 hour = flavor development period

Tropical fruits, grown in Uganda or in neighboring countries, are the basis of many salads. There are over twenty varieties of bananas grown in Uganda alone, some of which are strictly for cooking. In our stores we rarely see anything but Cavendish bananas thanks to the "Banana Wars" in the early part of the twentieth century which resulted from the effort by the United States and the United Fruit Company to maintain commercial interests in Latin America. Today the Cavendish is threatened by a variant of the disease that had wiped out the 'Gros Michels' banana, a disease to which resistance had been assured by its hybridizers. Assured of resistance and longevity, other varieties were replaced by a single banana variety, the Cavendish. Diversity such as one sees in the growing of this crop in Uganda insures a future. Ugandans are said to consume about five hundred pounds of bananas per year. Jackfruit and mangoes are also important fruits crops in this part of Africa and they too get added to this salad. Jackfruit, even canned, is not widely available in the United States so my version of this salad does not include a fruit that would most likely be included in Uganda.

2 ripe mangoes—peeled and cubed, *reserving flesh within skin and around pit for dressing*
2 large bananas—preferably Red Dacca— peeled and sliced
1 can (11-ounces) mandarin oranges—well-drained
1/4 cup chopped, dried, *preservative-free* apples
1/4 cup chopped, dried *preservative-free* apricots or peaches

1/3 cup bits and pieces leftover from mango preparation
1/4 cup shredded, desiccated *preservative-free* coconut
1/2 teaspoon OUR INDIAN SPICE MIXTURE (*Garam Masala*) [see index], or more to taste
1/2 teaspoon tamarind purée *
1/2 teaspoon honey *or agave* nectar
Pinch salt

UGANDAN FRUIT SALAD (cont'd)

In a mixing bowl combine mango cubes, banana slices, well-drained mandarin orange segments, and chopped, dried apples and apricots or peaches. Toss gently.

In the work bowl of the food processor fitted with steel knife, combine mango trimmings, coconut, *garam masala*, tamarind liquid concentrate, honey or *agave nectar*, and salt. Process until you have a smooth paste, scraping down the sides as required. Pour over fruits in mixing bowl. Toss to coat the vegetables with the seasoned dressing. Refrigerate for at least 1 hour to allow for flavor development.

Serve chilled as a salad or as an accompaniment to grilled vegetables.

Yields 6 servings
adequate for 4 people

Notes: *Tamarind liquid concentrate is often available in the international sections of well-stocked groceries or in Indian/Pakistani groceries. It can also be ordered online. Lemon juice can be substituted if you can obtain the tamarind.

This recipe can be halved or doubled, when required.

1/6 SERVING – PROTEIN = 1.4 g.; FAT = 2.1 g.; CARBOHYDRATE = 36.3 g.;
CALORIES = 155; CALORIES FROM FAT = 12%

UGANDAN MACARONI SALAD WITH *PESTO* AND *CHOURIÇO*

TPT - 1 hour and 22 minutes;
30 minutes = macaroni chilling period;
30 minutes = flavor development period

Admittedly, I was not prepared for a salad like this as I explored the cookbooks, articles, and menus I had collected when I began to explore the cuisine of Uganda. Everywhere I ran into pasta references. This one particularly fascinated; the pesto, the mayonnaise, and the chouriço (chorizo) sausage led directly to European influences. I make it with or without the sausage but since a vegetarian soy meat analogue manufacturer does produce a fully cooked vegetarian chouriço sausage that works quite nicely in this salad, I add the soy sausage to increase the available complemented protein, especially in the summer.

3 quarts *boiling* water
1 tablespoon freshly squeezed lemon juice
1 3-inch strip lemon zest
1 1/2 cups *tortiglioni* (or, *cavatappi* as it is sometimes known), elbows *or fusilli* macaroni

1 tablespoon **PESTO** SAUCE (*Pesto alla Genovese*) [see index]
1 tablespoon *calorie-reduced or light* mayonnaise
Freshly ground mixed peppercorns—black, red, and white—to taste

1/2 medium red bell pepper—peeled and *finely* chopped
1 scallion—*both green and white portions*—*thinly* sliced
1 soy *chouriço (chorizo)* sausage—defrosted and diced

In a large kettle set over *HIGH* heat, add lemon juice and lemon zest to *boiling* water. Add macaroni and cook, stirring occasionally, over *HIGH* heat according to package directions. Drain thoroughly, discarding lemon zest. Rinse in *cold* water. Drain again, thoroughly. Chill in refrigerator for about 30 minutes.

In a serving bowl, combine *pesto* sauce and mayonnaise. Stir well to combine.

Add *finely* sliced pepper, *thinly* sliced scallion, diced sausage, and slightly chilled macaroni. Toss. Season with ground mixed peppers. Toss again to coat vegetables and macaroni with dressing.

Chill in refrigerator, covered with plastic wrap, for 30 minutes before serving to allow for flavor development.

Yields 6 servings
adequate for 4 people

Note: This recipe can be halved or doubled, when required.

UGANDAN MACARONI SALAD
WITH *PESTO* AND *CHOURIÇO* (cont'd)

1/6 SERVING – PROTEIN = 5.8 g.; FAT = 3.6 g.; CARBOHYDRATE = 22.3 g.;
CALORIES = 142; CALORIES FROM FAT = 23%

UGANDAN POTATOES WITH YOGURT CURDS
TPT - 35 minutes

Potatoes are important to the subsistence farmer since they grow in almost any soil and can be added to meat dishes to extend them. The potato, the pepper, the tomato, and maize all made the journey from the Americas and can be found in many African dishes prepared by cooks, many of whom may have no idea that we share very directly in the meal they are preparing. This very tasty potato dish can also be made with vegetarian meatballs, as they do in Albania. African cuisines, including that of Uganda, reveal a great fondness for meatballs. I remember the incredibly detailed and enthusiastic email sent by a Nigerien cook from Niamey in which she conveyed her meatball making process to me, unaware that I was a vegetarian. I must confess, when all is said and done, I do prefer this potato version.

3 quarts *boiling* water
36 peewee or baby potatoes—well-scrubbed but *not peeled*

2 garlic cloves—crushed and *very finely* chopped
1/4 cup *very finely* chopped onion
1/2 teaspoon salt

1 tablespoon safflower *or* sunflower oil

3 cups PLAIN YOGURT *[see index]* *or* commercially-available plain yogurt
1/8 teaspoon ground red pepper (cayenne), or to taste
1/2 cup *finely* chopped fresh parsley

In a saucepan or small kettle, combine *boiling* water and potatoes. Cook until tender—about 20 minutes. Drain.

On a breadboard, combine *very finely* chopped garlic and onion. Sprinkle salt over and continue chopping until you have a paste.

In a non-stick-coated skillet set over LOW-MEDIUM heat, heat oil. Add garlic–onion mixture and potatoes. Sauté until onions are soft and translucent.

Add yogurt, ground red pepper (cayenne), and *finely* chopped parsley. Cook, stirring frequently, until yogurt curdles. Drain over the sink using a fine sieve. Turn into a heated serving bowl.

Serve at once.

Yields 6 servings
adequate for 4 people

Note: This recipe can be halved or doubled, when required.

1/6 SERVING – PROTEIN = 9.1 g.; FAT = 4.3 g.; CARBOHYDRATE = 39.8 g.;
CALORIES = 240; CALORIES FROM FAT = 16%

MUNG BEAN SAUCE WITH TOMATOES AND GARLIC
Choroko
TPT - 10 hours;
8 hours = soaking period

Mung beans need not be sprouted to be enjoyed. In Uganda a sauce is made from these tiny protein powerhouses and is served over rice or is used as a dip for chapattis. We use it as dip for tortilla chips or as a sandwich spread.

1/4 cup dried mung beans—well-rinsed and sorted to remove any extraneous material

2 cups *boiling* water

1 tablespoon sunflower oil
1/2 cup *finely* chopped onion
2 large garlic cloves—*very finely* chopped

3/4 cup canned, *crushed* tomatoes
Salt, to taste
Freshly ground black pepper, to taste

Africa–Uganda

MUNG BEAN SAUCE WITH TOMATOES AND GARLIC (cont'd)

Soak mung beans in water to cover for at least 8 hours. Drain. Turn into a saucepan set over *LOW-MEDIUM*. heat. Add *boiling* water. Allow beans to simmer for about 1 1/2 hours or until beans are soft, *adding more boiling water if necessary*. Drain. Turn into a mixing bowl. Using a fork, mash beans well.

In a skillet set over *MEDIUM* heat, heat oil. Add *finely* chopped onions and *very finely* chopped garlic. Sauté until onions are soft and translucent, *being carefully to allow neither the onions nor the garlic to brown*.

Add *mashed* mung beans, *crushed* tomatoes, salt, and black pepper. Cook, stirring frequently, for about 20 minutes. Turn into a heated serving bowl.

Yields 2 1/4 cupfuls

Note: This recipe can be doubled, when required.

1/9 SERVING (i. e., about 1/4 cupful) –
PROTEIN = 0.7 g.; FAT = 1.6 g.; CARBOHYDRATE = 3.1 g.;
CALORIES = 28; CALORIES FROM FAT = 51%

UGANDAN RICE WITH POTATOES
TPT - 1 hour and 4 minutes

This dish delivers ample protein from a vegetable combination that few Americans might consider. I showed the recipe to several friends and the response was almost unanimous—"Wow, all those carbs." Rice and potatoes contribute protein, albeit in the form of uncomplemented amino acids which can be combined with other foods such as beans to sustain human nutrition without any dairy or animal protein. People on this planet eat this way out of necessary; in America vegans eat this way out of choice. The potato and the tomato, New World foods, contribute to a diet in Uganda that could not have been possible without the Columbian Exchange.

1 tablespoon sunflower oil
1/2 cup *finely* chopped onions

2 medium potatoes—peeled and diced
1 cup canned, *diced* tomatoes

1 1/2 cups VEGETARIAN STOCK FROM SOUP
   [see index] *or* **other vegetarian stock**
3/4 cup dry converted rice
1/2 teaspoon SOUTH AFRICAN CURRY POWDER
   [see index]
1 tablespoon grated *pecorino Romano* cheese
Ground mixed peppercorns—red, white, and black—to taste

Preheat oven to 325 degrees F. Prepare a 1-quart soufflé dish or other oven-to-table baking dish by coating with non-stick lecithin spray coating.

In a large skillet set over *MEDIUM* heat, heat oil. Add *finely* chopped onions and sauté until onions are soft and translucent, *being careful not to allow onions to brown*.

Add *diced* potatoes and tomatoes. Cook, stirring frequently, for about 5 minutes.

Add stock, rice, curry powder, salt, and ground mixed peppercorns. Stir and allow to come to the boil. Turn into prepared baking dish. Bake in preheated 325 degree F. oven for 40 minutes, or until rice has absorbed liquid and potatoes are tender.

Serve at once.

Yields 6 servings
adequate for 4 people

Note: This recipe can be doubled, when required.

1/6 SERVING – PROTEIN = 3.6 g.; FAT = 2.7 g.; CARBOHYDRATE = 33.2 g.;
CALORIES = 174; CALORIES FROM FAT = 14%

Africa–Uganda

UGANDAN STIR-FRIED BAMBOO SHOOTS AND GREENS
Maleya
TPT - 11 minutes

I did not expect to find a passion for fresh bamboo shoots in Uganda any more than I could expect to find fresh bamboo shoots in central Pennsylvania. The smoked, dried bamboo shoots so easily available in Uganda are also not an option here. As a result, this recipe uses canned bamboo shoots. Since a can of bamboo shoots can go a long way, I plan an Asian stir-fry for half of the can and then cruise around the world to this stir-fry to use the rest of the bamboo shoots. If you have only used bamboo shoots for Asian stir-fries, then you will, as did I, find a very different way of enjoying the texture of this vegetable.

1 tablespoon sunflower oil
1/2 can whole bamboo shoots—well-drained and cut into chunks or sliced

10 cups mixed baby greens, of choice—trimmed, well-rinsed, and spun dry
Chili powder, to taste

1 tablespoon ground raw peanuts

In a large skillet set over *MEDIUM* heat, heat oil. Add chopped or sliced bamboo shoots. Sauté for a minute or two.

Add greens and chili powder. Stir-fry until greens are wilted.

Add ground peanuts and stir-fry for a minute or two more. Turn onto a small heated platter or plate.

Serve at once.

Yields 6 servings
adequate for 4 people

Note: This recipe can be halved, when required.

1/6 SERVING – PROTEIN = 2.2 g.; FAT = 3.3 g.; CARBOHYDRATE = 3.9 g.;
CALORIES = 68; CALORIES FROM FAT = 44%

SLOW COOKER BLACK-EYED PEA *CHILI*
TPT - 4 hours and 13 minutes;
[slow cooker: 2 hours on HIGH; and about 2 hours on LOW]

Beans are important in the diet of Ugandans, who are also quite fond of chilies. This bean chili surprises the expectant American taste buds with hints of turmeric, cumin, and ginger. We often choose to celebrate New Year's Day with lentil soup but many of our neighbors celebrate with black-eyed peas so every December I find fresh black-eyed peas in my market. Fresh black-eyed peas cook quickly without soaking. The first meal is usually to serve the cooked beans topped with caramelized onions so that their crunchy nuttiness can be enjoyed. The second appearance of the black-eyed peas is in this slow cooker chili. The inviting aroma fills the house and makes a January day a pleasant day indeed.

2 tablespoons *high heat* safflower *or* sunflower oil
1 large onion—coarsely chopped to yield about 1 1/2 cupfuls
1 medium green, bell pepper—coarsely chopped
1 large celery rib—sliced
1 large garlic clove—*very finely* chopped

2 cups fresh black-eyed peas—well-rinsed
2 cups canned, *diced* tomatoes, packed in tomato purée *or* 2 cups, peeled, seeded, and chopped fresh tomatoes
1 cup *boiling* water
1 tablespoon tomato paste
1 1/2 teaspoons chili powder, or more if desired
3/4 teaspoon freshly ground black pepper
1/2 teaspoon crushed, dried oregano leaves
1/4 teaspoon ground turmeric
1/4 teaspoon ground cumin
1/4 teaspoon ground ginger

In a slow cooker set at *HIGH*, heat oil. Add chopped onion and green pepper, sliced celery, and *very finely* chopped garlic. Sauté gently until onion is soft and translucent, *being careful not to allow onion to brown.*

Add well-rinsed black-eyed peas, *diced* tomatoes, water, sliced celery, tomato paste, chili powder, black pepper, crushed oregano, and ground turmeric, cumin, and ginger to sautéed vegetables. Combine *gently*, but *thoroughly*. Cover and allow to cook at *HIGH* for 2 hours. Turn cooker setting to *LOW* and allow to cook for about 2 hours more. Stir occasionally during cooking period and add more water, if necessary.

Turn into heated serving bowl and serve into heated soup bowls.

Yields 8 servings
adequate for 4-6 people

Africa–Uganda

SLOW COOKER BLACK-EYED PEA *CHILI* (cont'd)

Notes: Flavor actually improves if this is prepared the day before serving.

This recipe can be frozen very successfully.

> 1/8 SERVING (about 1 cupful) –
> PROTEIN = 5.5 g.; FAT = 4.9 g.; CARBOHYDRATE = 18.3 g.;
> CALORIES = 133; CALORIES FROM FAT = 33%

OUR *CHILI*
TPT - 55 minutes

. . . our favorite! There is nothing more welcome on a cool autumn evening or for lunch or supper after walking or skiing across snowy fields. Cumin, turmeric, and ginger are added to a bean chili in Uganda that is strikingly similar to this which evolved from my mother's chili con carne recipe as I tweaked it year by year beginning when I was in graduate school. Accompanying a bean chili such as this with "ugali" or polenta will compliment your legume amino acids with grain amino acids and, therefore, become, a meal-in-a-bowl.

2 tablespoons vegetable oil
1 large onion—coarsely chopped to yield about 1 1/2 cupfuls
1 medium green, bell pepper—coarsely chopped
12 ounces fresh mushrooms—trimmed, rinsed, cleaned well with a brush, and sliced

1 large celery rib—sliced
1 can (19 ounces) red kidney beans, *undrained or* **equivalent in cooked, dry beans**
2 cups canned, *diced* **tomatoes, preferably packed in tomato purée** *or* **2 cups peeled, seeded, and chopped fresh tomatoes**
1 tablespoon tomato paste
1 teaspoon chili powder, or more if desired
3/4 teaspoon freshly ground black pepper
Pinch dried oregano leaves—crushed

In a heavy kettle, with cover, set over *MEDIUM* heat, heat oil. Add chopped onion and green pepper and sliced mushrooms. Sauté gently until onion is soft and translucent, *being careful not to allow onion to brown.*

Add sliced celery, *undrained* kidney beans, tomatoes, tomato paste, chili powder, black pepper, and crushed oregano to sautéed vegetables. Combine *gently*, but *thoroughly*. Bring to the boil, turn heat to *LOW*, cover tightly, and simmer for 45 minutes. Stir occasionally during cooking period. Remove cover and continue cooking, stirring frequently, until thickened to your liking.

Turn into heated serving bowl and serve into heated soup bowls.

> Yields 8 servings
> adequate for 4-6 people

Notes: Flavor actually improves if this is prepared the day before serving.

This recipe may be doubled but increase cooking time to 1 1/4 hours. Since this dish freezes well, this is an excellent way to plan a "menu-maker" for a busy schedule.

Leftovers may also be frozen to reappear as filling for an omelet, *tacos,* or *burritos.*

> 1/8 SERVING (about 1 cupful) –
> PROTEIN = 6.1 g.; FAT = 3.3 g.; CARBOHYDRATE = 19.6 g.;
> CALORIES = 127; CALORIES FROM FAT = 23%

Africa–Uganda

BANANAS WITH CREAM
TPT - 7 minutes

Before a young Ugandan woman embarks on married life, she will traditionally be instructed on how to cook and how to manage a household by the older women in her family. Although the objective is to be sure she is competent in cooking basic recipes, the more creative attempts of her mother, grandmothers, aunts, and older cousins are also shared. Her desirability as a partner is often judged by her recipe repertoire. The food columns in urban newspapers are just beginning to publish recipes but few cookbooks are available to those of us outside of Uganda because of this oral transfer of recipes. Bananas are plentiful and inexpensive giving a Ugandan woman the opportunity to create. They are used in salads, steamed as a starch accompaniment to main courses, and made into luscious desserts. One dessert that I encountered layered bread and bananas, more like the banana sandwiches my mother use to make, but this combination was a bit too heavy for our taste. The following recipe captures the spirit of the Ugandan layered banana dessert with a modern twist.

Per serving:
   2 Maria biscuits* *or* British digestives*

   2 tablespoons light cream *or* half and half
   2 teaspoons *fat-free* sweetened
      condensed milk

   1 tablespoon apricot *or* peach jam
   1 ripe, medium banana—sliced
   2 Maria biscuits *or* British digestives
   2 tablespoons light cream *or* half and half

In the center of a soup plate, arrange two Maria biscuits.

Combine 2 tablespoonfuls cream with the sweetened condensed milk. Pour over the biscuits and allow it to soak in.

Spoon jam evenly over the cream-soaked biscuits. Scatter banana slices over. Place the remaining two Maria biscuits on top of the banana slices. Pour the remaining 2 tablespoonfuls cream over.

Serve at once.

Yields 1 serving

Note: *Maria biscuits are available in the United States under the Goya label.

1 SERVING –   PROTEIN = 5.5 g.; FAT = 8.6 g.; CARBOHYDRATE = 66.5 g.;
CALORIES = 355; CALORIES FROM FAT = 22%

Zambia

Early hunter-gatherer societies in the area of south-central Africa, known to us today as Zambia, were displaced during the Bantu expansion in the thirteenth century. Zambia remained isolated from European influence until the late eighteenth century when European explorers and adventurers arrived beginning with the Portuguese explorer Dr. Francisco José de Lacerda. Among these adventurers was David Livingston, who, in 1855 became the first European to view the famous and spectacular waterfalls on the Zambezi River called the *Mosi-o-Tunya* or "thundering smoke." These are the falls that Livingston renamed Victoria Falls in honor of Queen Victoria which are twice as wide as and one and a half times higher than Niagara Falls. Livingston had come to Zambia not as an explorer but with a plan to end the slave trade. His plan, called the 3Cs, involved the spread of Christianity and the development of civilization with expanded commerce displacing the trade of enslaved people to the nations of the Western Hemisphere.

In 1888 the British South Africa Company under Cecil Rhodes obtained the mineral rights to the area from the local tribal chieftain and a few years later large scale mining began in two areas designated North-Western Rhodesia and North-Eastern Rhodesia. In 1911 the two areas were merged into the British colony of Northern Rhodesia.

The period of self-governance began in 1964 with the declaration of independence from Great Britain. From 1964 to 1991 Zambia was led by Kenneth Kaunda of the socialist United National Independence Party (UNIP). In 1972 the Zambian governmental structure was altered to allow for only one political party, the UNIP. Kaunda and Saddam Hussein became close friends and the Zambian government developed strong ties to the communist regimes of the Soviet Union and the People's Republic of China. In 1991 Kaunda and the UNIP were defeated by Frederick Chiluba and the social-democratic Movement for Multi-Party Democracy. Since 1991 Zambia has seen a relatively peaceful succession of leaders, increased decentralization of the government, and a rise in social-economic growth with a concurrent increase in the standard of living for the population. Though the country is about three times the size of the state of Michigan, or to put it another way, about the size of Texas and California combined, the population of an estimated twelve million people is concentrated in the urban areas. Since the economy of this landlocked country has been largely dependent on the rise and fall of copper demand in the world since the discovery of and exploitation of the mineral riches during the Rhodes era, an economic diversification program is being instituted to expand agriculture, gemstone mining, and hydroelectric power generation for export while developing the country to attract tourism.

Education and healthcare have become major goals of the government. Although the literacy rate is said to be about 80.6%, opportunities for education beyond the secondary level are limited. In addition, education is free only up until the seventh year resulting in a precipitous drop in the student population once the family must pay tuition. Educating their people about HIV/AIDS has proven a challenge but there has been considerable progress shown by the 25% decline in new cases since 2001. Nevertheless, in 2009 an estimated 13.5% of those of reproductive age, aged fifteen to forty-nine, tested positive for HIV.

Although there are many regional languages spoken in Zambia, English is considered the official language which is helpful in identifying dishes that can vary from region to region, from tribe to tribe, dishes that can often have very different local names. Zambia's isolation from world influence has allowed for the survival of a more traditional cuisine based on a limited number of ingredients. Although *nshima*, maize or mealie meal, is the staple food, there are other dishes to please a visiting vegetarian since animal protein is often at a premium and Zambian cooks have learned to improvise. Peanuts also have become a staple food that provides the amino acids to compliment grains; an important nutritional tool where animal protein is scarce during the long dry season.

Africa–Zambia

| Spicy Potato Crisps | Mashed Avocado Dip with Tomato |

Roasted Pumpkin Seeds

~

Vegetable and Groundnut Soup

~

Tomato and Green Onion Salad

~~~~~~~~~~~~~~~~~~~~~

Tomato and Peanut Sauce

over

Steamed Rice

with

| Steamed Collard Greens or Pumpkin Leaves with Ground Peanuts | or | Steamed and Mashed Pumpkin with *Ghee* and Salt |

~~~~~~~~~~

Dried Mushrooms in Tomato Sauce

over

Steamed Rice

Skewered Fruits

Groundnut Biscuits

~~~~~~~~~~~~~~~~~~~~~

Sweetpotato Pudding with Coconut

Stove-Top Rice and Peanut Butter Pudding

SPICY POTATO CRISPS
TPT - 22 minutes

A journal entry by a blogger, who was visiting Zambia, referenced the spicy potato crisps he was served. Unfortunately he did not think to offer a recipe just his positive response to the eating experience. The recipe which follows is my version of his musings. These are not French-fried potatoes by any stretch of the imagination!

2 large potatoes—peeled and *very thinly* sliced into rounds and submerged in cold water

1/4 cup unbleached white flour
1/2 teaspoon ground cumin
1/2 teaspoon ground mixed peppercorns—black, red, and white—or to taste
1/2 teaspoon salt
1/4 teaspoon dry mustard powder
1/4 teaspoon chili powder

Oil for deep-frying

In a shallow bowl, combine flour, ground cumin, ground mixed peppercorns, salt, dry mustard powder, and chili powder. Stir to mix well. Set aside briefly.

Remove potato slices from cold water to clean, dry cotton tea towels or to paper toweling. Pat the potato slices dry. Put them into a plastic bag.

Add flour and spice mixture. Shake the bag until the potato slices are lightly coated with the flour mixture.

Heat the oil to 365 degrees F. in a deep skillet or saucepan.

Deep-fry the potatoes, a handful at a time, until golden. Using a skimmer, remove the potatoes to dry paper toweling to drain off excess oil.

When all potatoes have been fried and drained, turn them into a serving bowl.

Africa–Zambia

SPICY POTATO CRISPS (cont'd)

Serve with a *salsa* or dip, if desired.

adequate for 6 people

Note: This recipe can be doubled, when required.

1/6 SERVING – PROTEIN = 1.5 g.; FAT = 3.8 g.; CARBOHYDRATE = 14.0 g.;
CALORIES = 97; CALORIES FROM FAT = 35%

MASHED AVOCADO DIP WITH TOMATO
TPT - 4 minutes

Zambian cooks present good local food, simply prepared. It is as succinct a description as that and from that we can learn much. This avocado dip is a delicious example.

2 large, ripe avocados—peeled, pitted, and mashed
3 tablespoons peeled, seeded, and diced tomato *or* canned, *diced* tomato, if preferred
3/4 teaspoon chili powder, or to taste

In a mixing bowl, combine mashed avocados, diced tomato, and chili powder. Mix thoroughly. Turn into a serving bowl. Refrigerate until ready to serve.

Serve chilled as a dip.

Yields 18 servings
adequate for 6 people

Note: This recipe can be halved or doubled, when required.

1/18 SERVING – PROTEIN = 0.5 g.; FAT = 3.7 g.; CARBOHYDRATE = 1.5 g.;
CALORIES = 37; CALORIES FROM FAT = 90%

ZAMBIAN VEGETABLE AND GROUNDNUT SOUP
TPT - 1 hour and 5 minutes

Because groundnuts, or peanuts, are a staple of many African countries, soups can be found up and down the continent to which peanuts or peanut butter are added. This one is a bit different in that it calls for white potatoes, not yams, and corn. Corn is grown in Zambia but peanuts and peanut products must be imported from West African nations such as Senegal, the self-proclaimed peanut capital of the world, or from Zambia's close neighbor Zimbabwe, formerly Rhodesia, where peanuts are also an export crop.

1 large onion—chopped
1 cup VEGETARIAN BROWN STOCK *[see index]*, **other vegetarian stock of choice, *or* water**

1/2 teaspoon ground ginger
1/2 teaspoon ground cumin
1/4 teaspoon ground cinnamon
1/8 teaspoon ground red pepper (cayenne), or to taste
1/4 teaspoon salt, or to taste

3 cups VEGETARIAN BROWN STOCK *[see index] or* **other vegetarian stock of choice**
1 medium carrot—pared or scraped and sliced
3/4 cup canned, *diced* tomatoes
1 cup green (fresh) *or frozen* corn kernels
1 medium, all-purpose potato—peeled and cut into 1/2-inch cubes

2 tablespoons freshly ground, *additive-free, smooth* peanut butter
1/4 cup *boiling* water
2 cups chopped green cabbage
1 cup fresh *or frozen*, cut green beans

1 sweet banana, peeled and sliced, for garnish

Africa–Zambia

ZAMBIAN VEGETABLE AND GROUNDNUT SOUP (cont'd)

In a kettle, with cover, set over *MEDIUM-HIGH* heat, cook onion in the 1 cupful stock until softened—about 5 minutes.

Stir in ground ginger, cumin, cinnamon, and red pepper (cayenne), and salt. Cook for 1 minute longer.

Add remaining 3 cupfuls stock, carrot slices, chopped tomatoes, corn, and cubed potatoes. Stir to combine well. Bring to the boil. Reduce heat to *LOW-MEDIUM* and simmer, covered, for 30 minutes, stirring occasionally.

In a small bowl, using a wire whisk, combine peanut butter and *boiling* water. Add to vegetables in kettle with chopped cabbage and cut green beans. Stir to integrate the peanut butter uniformly. Continue simmering, uncovered, for about 15 minutes more. Stir occasionally. Taste and adjust seasoning, if necessary.

Add banana slices. Turn into a heated tureen and serve into heated soup plates. Garnish with banana slices.

Yields 8 servings

Notes: This recipe may be doubled, when required.

Leftovers may be reheated most successfully.

1/8 SERVING (i. e., about 1 cupful) –
PROTEIN = 3.5 g.; FAT = 3.7 g.; CARBOHYDRATE = 18.7 g.;
CALORIES = 100; CALORIES FROM FAT = 24%

TOMATO AND GREEN ONION SALAD
TPT - 6 minutes

Chopped fresh tomatoes and scallions are more often added to tossed greens in the West but the two vegetables, lightly dressed with a lemony vinaigrette, create a bright salad that Zambians enjoy often.

3 large tomatoes—*well-washed and coarsely chopped*
3 large scallions—*both white and green portions —trimmed, well-rinsed, and sliced*
1/4 teaspoon salt, or to taste
1/4 teaspoon ground mixed peppercorns—*black, red, and white*—or to taste

1 1/2 tablespoons peanut oil
1 tablespoon freshly squeezed lemon juice, of choice

In a serving bowl, combine coarsely chopped tomatoes, salt, and ground mixed peppercorns. Toss gently, but well, to distribute seasoning.

In a small bowl, combine peanut oil and lemon juice. Using a small wire whisk, beat well. Add to salad ingredients. Toss gently.

Refrigerate until ready to serve.

Yields 6 servings
adequate for 4 people

Note: This recipe can be halved or doubled, when required.

1/6 SERVING – PROTEIN = 0.6 g.; FAT = 2.9 g.; CARBOHYDRATE = 2.7 g.;
CALORIES = 39; CALORIES FROM FAT = 67%

Africa–Zambia

ZAMBIAN TOMATO AND PEANUT SAUCE
TPT - 22 minutes

Nshima is a corn meal dish found in Zambia, Malawi, Mozambique, and in areas of the Democratic Republic of the Congo. It is an inexpensive dish that is similar to the ugali one finds in East Africa or the fufu of West Africa and not unlike polenta. Zambians may be surprised if you request it in a restaurant and even more surprised if you request this tomato and peanut sauce or relish, but they take great pride in the texture and taste of their recipe and will be honored to share it with you. The popularity of this simple sauce has spread from Zambia to neighboring countries. When served over rice, the leguminous amino acids complement the amino acids contributed by the rice to provide a meatless main course that is enormously satisfying. We often serve it as a sauce with breaded soy analogue products that are available in the frozen food aisles of most grocery stores.

1 tablespoon *extra virgin* olive oil
1 large onion—*thinly* sliced

1 1/2 cups peeled, seeded, and chopped fresh tomatoes *or* canned, *diced* tomatoes

1/2 cup ground, *raw* peanuts
2 teaspoons *tamari* soy sauce
1/2 teaspoon chili powder

In a saucepan set over *MEDIUM* heat, heat oil. Add *thinly* sliced onion and sauté until onion is soft and translucent, *being careful not to allow onion to brown*. Reduce heat to *LOW-MEDIUM*.

Add chopped tomatoes. Cook, stirring frequently, until liquid has evaporated and the tomato–onion mixture has thickened, about 8-10 minutes.

Add peanuts, soy sauce, and chili powder. Cook, stirring frequently, until heated through. Turn into a heated serving dish.

Serve hot or at room temperature, if preferred. Refrigerate or freeze leftovers.

Yields 6 servings
adequate for 4 people

Note: This recipe can be halved, when required.

1/6 SERVING – PROTEIN = 2.6 g.; FAT = 5.0 g.; CARBOHYDRATE = 6.8 g.;
CALORIES = 77; CALORIES FROM FAT = 58%

ZAMBIAN DRIED MUSHROOMS IN TOMATO SAUCE
TPT - 51 minutes;
30 minutes = mushroom soaking period

I am very fortunate at this stage of my life to have access to a wider variety of fresh mushrooms than do most Americans. Sixty percent of mushrooms available in the United States are grown in Pennsylvania, where we chose to retire. Nevertheless, I dehydrate mushrooms for winter use for convenience, not that they are unavailable in my grocery stores. I also sauté and freeze mushrooms when they are specially-priced, again for cooking convenience. Mushrooms that have been dehydrated keep well in our pantry and add a distinctive taste to dishes. Although fresh mushrooms can be prepared in a similar manner, this easily prepared Zambian dish really excels when made from dried mushrooms.

Since I clean and dehydrate my own mushroom, I am assured of their quality. Commercially-available dried mushrooms should be well-brushed and rinsed before using to remove any clinging "mushroom soil."

2 cups *dried* mushrooms*
1 quart *boiling* water

1 tablespoon *extra virgin* olive oil
1/2 cup *finely* chopped onion

1/2 cup tomato purée

Salt, to taste
Freshly ground black pepper, to taste

In a large measuring cup, combine dried mushrooms and *boiling* water. Set a small custard cup in the top of the measuring cup to keep the mushroom pieces submerged. Allow mushrooms to rehydrate for at least 30 minutes. Drain well, *retaining the mushroom liquid*.**

In a non-stick-coated skillet set over *LOW-MEDIUM* heat, heat oil. Add onion and sauté until onion is soft and translucent, *being careful not to allow onion to brown*.

Africa–Zambia

ZAMBIAN DRIED MUSHROOMS IN TOMATO SAUCE (cont'd)

Add drained mushrooms and tomato purée. Cook, stirring frequently, until purée has thickened and mushrooms are soft. Thin with mushroom liquid as needed.

Season with salt and pepper. Turn into a heated serving dish.

Serve at once as a vegetable side dish or over rice, if preferred.

Notes: *A mixture of mushroom varieties gives this dish increased dimension.

**Freeze any leftover mushroom liquid to use in soups and stews.

When necessary, this dish can be halved or doubled.

Yields 6 servings
adequate for 4 people

1/6 SERVING – PROTEIN = 0.7 g.; FAT = 1.9 g.; CARBOHYDRATE = 3.4 g.;
CALORIES = 32; CALORIES FROM FAT = 53%

ZAMBIAN SKEWERED FRUITS
TPT - 24 minutes

In Africa and the Near East fruit often accompanies a main course or is added to the entrée. Fruit just completely changes the perception of the eating experience by your taste buds. Here, grilled fruit kebabs, a readily available street food snack in Zambia, accompany a more formal meal presentation.

24 large cubes of fresh mango
24 pineapple cubes *or* canned pineapple chunks, if necessary
Non-stick lecithin spray olive oil
1 tablespoon white sesame seeds

Preheat grill or grill pan to *MEDIUM-HIGH*.

Skewer mango and pineapple cubes alternately on six bamboo skewers that have been soaked in water. Spray each lightly with olive oil spray. Sprinkle each with sesame seeds. Place on preheated grill or grill pan. Allow to brown, turning as necessary. Transfer to a heated serving plate.

Serve at once, one skewer per diner.

Yields 6 servings
adequate for 4 people

Note: This recipe can be halved or doubled, when required.

1/6 SERVING – PROTEIN = 0.9 g.; FAT = 1.3 g.; CARBOHYDRATE = 18.4 g.;
CALORIES = 98; CALORIES FROM FAT = 12%

ZAMBIAN GROUNDNUT BISCUITS
TPT - 32 minutes

It is believed that the first people to domesticate and cultivate the peanut or groundnut were the native peoples of Paraguay. Portuguese traders carried the peanut to all parts of the world. These biscuits, which can be served as a snack, as an accompaniment to a salad meal, or as simply a bread with dinner, are another way in which Zambian cooks increase the protein intake of their families using the humble, but oh so useful, peanut.

3/4 cup unbleached white flour
1/4 cup whole wheat flour
2 teaspoons baking powder
2 tablespoons *finely* ground, *raw* peanuts
1 teaspoon sugar
1/4 teaspoon salt

1 1/2 tablespoons peanut oil

1/4 cup *fat-free* pasteurized eggs (the equivalent of 1 egg)
Water or milk, if necessary

Africa–Zambia

ZAMBIAN GROUNDNUT BISCUITS (cont'd)

Preheat oven to 400 degrees F. Prepare a baking sheet by lining it with culinary parchment paper.

Into a large mixing bowl, sift white and whole wheat flours with baking powder. Stir in *finely* ground peanuts, sugar, and salt.

Using a pastry blender or by pulsating the mixture in the food processor, fitted with steel knife, cut oil into dry ingredients until mixture is the consistency of coarse corn meal.

Make a well in the center, pour pasteurized eggs into the well and stir until mixture forms a soft dough and pulls from the sides of the bowl. Add a bit of water or milk, a little at a time, *only if necessary. (You do not want a sticky dough.)*

Turn dough out onto a *lightly* floured surface. Lightly flour your hands and knead dough for only about 30 seconds. Pat or roll dough to an even 1/2-inch thickness. Cut with a floured 2-inch biscuit cutter. Using a spatula, transfer biscuit rounds to an *ungreased* baking sheet, spacing them at least 1 1/2 inches apart to allow for expansion and even browning.

Bake in preheated 400 degree F. oven for 12-15 minutes, or until *golden brown.*

Serve hot.

Yields 8 biscuits

Note: This recipe can be doubled, when required.

1/6 SERVING – PROTEIN = 2.7 g.; FAT = 3.1 g.; CARBOHYDRATE = 9.2 g.;
CALORIES = 83; CALORIES FROM FAT = 34%

ZAMBIAN SWEETPOTATO PUDDING WITH COCONUT

TPT - 1 hour and 10 minutes;
20 minutes = minimum cooling period

Sweetpotatoes are one of the most important foods in Africa and they have been adapted to every phase of a menu. We are all familiar with sweetpotato pie, a Southern specialty that no doubt owes its origins to the cooking of African slaves during the colonial period. This is a chance for you too to bring the sweetpotato back to its origins in the Western Hemisphere and provide a very nutritious and delicious dessert for your family.

2 quarts *boiling* water
1 large sweetpotato—about 1 pound, peeled and chopped

1 1/2 cups *two-percent* milk
1/2 cup *fat-free* pasteurized eggs (the equivalent of 2 eggs)
1/4 cup grated coconut—fresh *or* desiccated
1/3 cup sugar
1 teaspoon baking powder

Preheat oven to 350 degrees F. Prepare a 1 1/2 quart soufflé dish or other baking dish by coating with non-stick lecithin spray coating.

In a saucepan set over *MEDIUM* heat, cook sweetpotato in *boiling* water until sweetpotato is soft—about 15 minutes. Drain. Turn sweetpotato into a mixing bowl. Mash well.

Add milk, pasteurized eggs, grated coconut, sugar, and baking powder. Mix well. Turn into prepared baking dish. Bake in preheated 350 degree F. oven for about 25 minutes, or until firm and lightly browned. Cool for at least 20 minutes before serving.

Serve warm, at room temperature, or chilled, as preferred.

Yields 6 servings
adequate for 4 people

Note: This recipe can be halved, when required.

1/6 SERVING – PROTEIN = 3.1 g.; FAT = 1.5 g.; CARBOHYDRATE = 17.7 g.;
CALORIES = 93; CALORIES FROM FAT = 15%

Africa–**Zambia**

ZAMBIAN STOVE-TOP RICE AND PEANUT BUTTER PUDDING
TPT - 1 hour and 38 minutes;
1 hour = refrigeration period

If you are fond of peanut butter cookies, you will probably put this pudding on your list of favorites. Nutritionally it is block-buster too. Zambians are very fond of peanut butter and generally put a much larger amount into this pudding.

1 cup *boiling* water
1/2 cup sugar
1/2 cup dry short grain rice

2 tablespoons freshly ground, *unsalted, additive-free, smooth* peanut butter—*brought to room temperature*

1/4 cup *fat-free* pasteurized eggs (the equivalent of 1 egg)
1/2 cup light cream *or* half and half

In a saucepan set over *LOW-MEDIUM* heat, combine *boiling* water, sugar, and rice. Stir to combine well. Cover and cook for about 20 minutes or until almost all liquid has been absorbed. *Remove from heat.*

Add peanut butter and stir until peanut butter has been thoroughly integrated.

Add pasteurized eggs and cream. Stir well. *Return to MEDIUM heat* and cook, stirring constantly, until mixture thickens. Turn into a serving bowl. Refrigerate for at least 1 hour before serving.

Serve at room temperature or chilled. Refrigerate leftovers.

Yields 6 servings
adequate for 4 people

1/6 SERVING –   PROTEIN = 5.6 g.; FAT = 4.2 g.; CARBOHYDRATE = 52.1 g.;
CALORIES = 269; CALORIES FROM FAT = 14%

Zimbabwe

The Khoisan established in this part of Africa as early as 200 BC. They were succeeded by the Bantu civilization, which left behind unique stone architecture built prior to the period of history we call the Middle Ages. They were succeeded by the Shona, the Nguni, the Zulu, and the Ndebele, a powerful warrior kingdom that controlled the area by the middle of the ninth century AD. In roughly the tenth century AD the inhabitants of this area of southern Africa bordering South Africa were known to have been trading gold, ivory, and copper for textiles and glass. For a very long period, from about 1250 to 1629 AD, they were part of the Mutapa Empire. After a series of wars with the Portuguese, the power of the Mutapa Empire was diminished to the point that the British gained a foothold. From the 1880s, with the establishment of Cecil Rhode's British South Africa Company, until 1923 the British controlled the area and an influx of foreigners, mostly white and largely of English, South African, and Portuguese origins, came to live in Rhodesia, as the nation was known from 1898 until 1980, when the ancient name Zimbabwe, meaning "stone house," was adopted as the nation's new name. English is still the official language of Zimbabwe and is the language of business and commerce. However, it is the first language of only two percent of the population.

Records show that about 1,000 white immigrants came to live in Rhodesia each year up until the mid-1970s but from 1976 to 1985 more than 150,000 white Zimbabweans left the country due to repressive governance, reform plans, and economic mismanagement. The large farming complexes have been replaced by small, family plots, a policy which decreased the land productivity to the level of subsistence farming since without large-scale, advanced farming techniques the land returns to the desert and savanna that characterizes most of the terrain. The farmland of Zimbabwe is fed by the Lipopo and Zambesi rivers, providing adequate irrigation during the growing season. However, the river levels drop during the winter. To survive this dry season, Zimbabweans plan ahead and dry meats, fish, and produce for winter meals. Corn and corn meal form a significant portion of the national diet. The national dish, *sadza*, is eaten just about everyday, made from corn meal in much the way Romanians enjoy *mamaliga* or Americans used to eat corn meal mush.

Life expectancy in Zimbabwe is among the lowest in the world with men expected to live no more than thirty-seven years and women rarely living past the age of thirty-four. War, hunger and poor nutrition, almost non-existent health care, and the excesses of horribly abusive governing in addition to the ravages of HIV/AIDS have prevented the Zimbabweans from turning their once high literacy rate, about 90% of the adult population in 1995, into productivity that could advance the nation.

Africa–Zimbabwe

Avocado Halves with Lemon Juice and Ground Peanuts

~

Sweet and Sour Bean Salad

~~~~~~~~~~~~~~~~~~~~~~

Vegetable Soup with Peanut Butter, Sweetpotato, and Greens

Dovi ne Bowara

Sweetpotato Biscuits

~~~~~~~~~~~~~~~~~~~~~~

Papaya Slices with Sugar Syrup and Crushed Fresh Mint Leaves

Custard Corn Meal Dessert

SWEET AND SOUR BEAN SALAD IN THE STYLE OF ZIMBABWE
TPT - 12 hours and 15 minutes;
12 hours = marination period

Food costs in Zimbabwe have made salads a luxury item leading wedding and restaurant menus to tout their salad offerings to entice customers. Bean salads and rice salads are frequently served and this, a salad I have made for many, many years, is similar to the bean salad enjoyed in Zimbabwe, with a few changes—brown sugar and basil have been added and the chick peas, which I always add to my bean salad, have been omitted here.

The mother of my dearest childhood friend, Joanne, often made a salad similar to this, a salad which still appears on the ubiquitous salad bars across America. "Three Bean Salad," as this was called, was popular in the 1950s and I guess everybody had a version but Mrs. Pritchard's, much sweeter than this, was the model for my own version. The salad really improves day by day so leftovers are not a problem. Other leftover beans and corn may be added to keep the "brew" going for as long as ten days. When I travel, I often leave a big bowlful of the mixture, to which corn has been added, in the refrigerator for Ray.

1 can (19 ounces) red kidney beans—well-drained*

1 cup *frozen* cut green beans *or* cut yellow wax beans
1 cup *frozen* baby lima beans
1/2 cup diced green pepper
1/2 cup *finely* chopped onion
1 large garlic clove—*finely* chopped
1 tablespoon *finely* chopped fresh basil

1/4 cup vegetable oil

2 tablespoons *light* brown sugar

1/4 cup red wine vinegar

1/4 teaspoon freshly ground black pepper

In a large shallow bowl, combine well-drained red kidney beans, *frozen* cut green beans or yellow wax beans, *frozen* lima beans, diced pepper, *finely* chopped onion and garlic, and *finely* chopped basil. Toss to mix thoroughly.

Add oil. Toss gently to coat.

Add sugar. Toss gently to coat.

Add vinegar. Toss gently to coat.

Season with black pepper. Again toss to mix thoroughly.

Cover dish with plastic wrap and refrigerate for *at least* 12 hours. Stir occasionally.

Serve with a slotted spoon.

Yields about 12 servings
adequate for 8 people

Africa – Zimbabwe

**SWEET AND SOUR BEAN SALAD
IN THE STYLE OF ZIMBABWE** (cont'd)

Notes: *Freshly cooked dry kidney beans, limas, or butter beans may be substituted and ratios of bean types may be varied to taste.

If desired, this recipe may be decreased proportionately to use up leftover beans in a most agreeable way.

1/12 SERVING – PROTEIN = 3.9 g.; FAT = 4.4 g.; CARBOHYDRATE = 14.8 g.;
CALORIES = 129; CALORIES FROM FAT = 31%

Please note, these values do not reflect the fact that most of the marinade remains after the salad has been eaten.

ZIMBABWEAN VEGETABLE SOUP
WITH PEANUT BUTTER, SWEETPOTATO, AND GREENS

Davine Bowara

TPT - 1 hour and 6 minutes

This is a vegetarian version of a classic Zimbabwean chicken stew. It is substantial and delicious as a first course or as a main course. Although "bowara," pumpkin leaves, are traditionally used in this stew, other greens can be substituted.

**1 tablespoon butter
1 medium onion**—*finely* **chopped
1 garlic clove**—*finely* **chopped
1/4 teaspoon freshly ground black pepper
1/8 teaspoon ground red pepper (cayenne), or to taste**

1 large green bell pepper—cored and diced

**3 cups water
1 1/2 cups canned,** *crushed* **tomatoes with liquid
1 medium carrot—peeled and diced
1/2 medium sweetpotato—peeled and diced**

3 tablespoons freshly ground, *unsalted, additive-free, smooth* **peanut butter**

6 cups fresh, young pumpkin, spinach, green leaf lettuce leaves, *or* **young collard greens —trimmed, tough stems removed,** *very well-washed* **and coarsely chopped**

In a kettle set over *MEDIUM-LOW* heat, melt butter. Add *finely* chopped onion and garlic. Sauté until onions are soft and translucent, *allowing neither the onion nor the garlic to brown.* Season with black pepper and ground red pepper (cayenne).

Add chopped green peppers and cook for about 5 minutes more, stirring constantly.

Add water, chopped tomatoes with liquid, and diced carrots and sweetpotato. Bring to the boil. Reduce heat and allow to simmer for about 20 minutes.

Put peanut butter into a bowl. Ladle about 1/2 cupful of broth into the peanut butter and, using a wire whisk, beat until the peanut butter has been thinned. Add to soup in kettle. Simmer for about 15 minutes, stirring frequently, until heated through.

Just before you are ready to serve, add chopped pumpkin or spinach leaves. Remove from heat.

Turn into a heated soup tureen or large serving bowl and serve into heated soup plates.

Yields 6 servings
adequate for 4 people

Notes: This recipe can be halved or doubled, when required.

Leftovers can be reheated, but not frozen, successfully.

1/6 SERVING – PROTEIN = 5.0 g; FAT = 5.7 g; CARBOHYDRATE = 11.3 g;
CALORIES = 110; CALORIES FROM FAT = 47%

Africa–**Zimbabwe**

SWEETPOTATO BISCUITS

TPT - 2 hours and 47 minutes;
        1 hour = sweetpotato baking period;
        1 hour = sweetpotato cooling period

The dry, pale-skinned members of the Morning Glory family, known as sweetpotatoes are a more traditional choice for this recipe than are the southern grown sweet, moist variety misnamed yams in the 1930s by a Louisiana ad agency. They were, no doubt, a specialty of the cooks of the plantation homes of the American South, who may have brought the recipe from Africa. It is, therefore, no surprise to find sweetpotato biscuits at the dinner tables in many countries in Africa. These low-fat biscuits derive from the Southern colonial tradition here in the United States and are just plain good.

1 large sweetpotato—washed and well-scrubbed

2/3 cup *unsalted*, cultured buttermilk *or* skimmed milk, as preferred
1 1/2 teaspoons grated *organic* lemon zest

2 cups unbleached white flour
1/2 cup whole wheat flour
2 tablespoons firmly packed *light* brown sugar
1 tablespoon baking powder
1/2 teaspoon freshly grated nutmeg

1/2 cup (4 ounces) *cold*, low-fat *Neufchâtel* cheese —chopped into pieces

Preheat oven to 400 degrees F.

Cut an **X** in the top of the sweetpotato. Place in preheated oven and allow to bake for about 1 hour, or until soft.

Scrape sweetpotato flesh into a mixing bowl and mash well. (You should have 3/4 cupful.) Refrigerate mashed sweetpotato for 1 hour, or until well-chilled. Combine 3/4 cupful of mashed, cooked sweetpotato, buttermilk, and grated lemon zest. Stir well to mix. Set aside until required.

Again, preheat oven to 400 degrees F. Prepare a baking sheet by coating with non-stick lecithin spray coating.

In a large mixing bowl, combine white and whole wheat flours, brown sugar, baking powder, and grated nutmeg. Stir well to combine. Using a pastry blender, work chopped *Neufchâtel* cheese into dry ingredients until of the consistency of coarse corn meal with lumps the size of small peas. Add sweetpotato–milk mixture and stir until just combined. (The dough will be a bit dry.)

Transfer the dough to a floured surface. Knead a few times and roll dough out to thickness of about 1/2 inch. Using a floured 2 1/2-inch biscuit cutter, cut out biscuits. Transfer to prepared baking sheet.*

Bake in preheated 400 degree F. oven for about 12-15 minutes, or until tops are *lightly browned* and firm to the touch.

Serve warm.

Yields 16 biscuits

Notes: *This recipe may be prepared to this point as much as 3 hours ahead of time. Cover cut-out biscuits with plastic wrap and refrigerate until ready to bake.

Baked biscuits may be frozen in a tightly sealed plastic bag. Wrap defrosted biscuits in aluminum foil and warm slightly before serving.

When required, this recipe may be doubled.

1/16 SERVING (per biscuit) –
PROTEIN = 3.1 g.; FAT = 1.8 g.; CARBOHYDRATE = 8.8 g.;
CALORIES = 100; CALORIES FROM FAT = 16%

Africa–Zimbabwe

ZIMBABWEAN CUSTARD CORN MEAL DESSERT
TPT - 1 hour and 4 minutes

Corn meal is not only used to make "sadzu," which is so widely consumed that it is now considered to be the national dish. This baked corn meal dessert is the perfect ending to a meal. We serve it warm with fruit. Refrigerated leftovers take on a completely different texture and are a real treat for breakfast.

1 1/2 tablespoons butter—*melted*

2 cups *two-percent* **milk**
1/4 cup sugar
1 1/2 tablespoons butter

1/2 cup yellow corn meal

1 large egg—*beaten*

2 teaspoons pure vanilla extract

1/4 cup *fat-free* **dairy sour cream**

Preheat oven to 350 degrees F. Prepare a 9 x 5 x 2-inch, non-stick-coated loaf pan by coating it well with the 1 1/2 tablespoonfuls butter. Set aside briefly.

In a saucepan set over *MEDIUM* heat, heat milk, sugar, and the remaining 1 1/2 tablespoons butter to just below the boiling point. Using a wire whisk, stir frequently. *Reduce heat to LOW.*

Put beaten egg into a small bowl. *Gradually, tablespoonful by tablespoonful*, whisk about 1/2 cupful of the hot milk into the beaten egg, being careful to keep beating to prevent curdling. *While whisking constantly, gradually* add the egg to milk in saucepan.

While stirring constantly, slowly add corn meal. Cook, *stirring constantly*, until mixture thickens.

Add vanilla extract. Stir well to integrate. Turn into prepared loaf pan. Bake in preheated oven for 30 minutes. Remove from oven.

Spread sour cream over the surface of the baked dessert. Return to the oven for about 15 minutes more, or until top is lightly browned. Transfer to a wire rack to cool slightly.

Cut into slices and remove with a wide spatula. *Serve while still warm.*

Yields 6 servings
adequate for 4 people

Note: This recipe can be doubled using an 8-inch-square baking pan.

1/6 SERVING – PROTEIN = 6.1 g.; FAT = 8.6 g.; CARBOHYDRATE = 25.5 g.;
CALORIES = 202; CALORIES FROM FAT = 38%

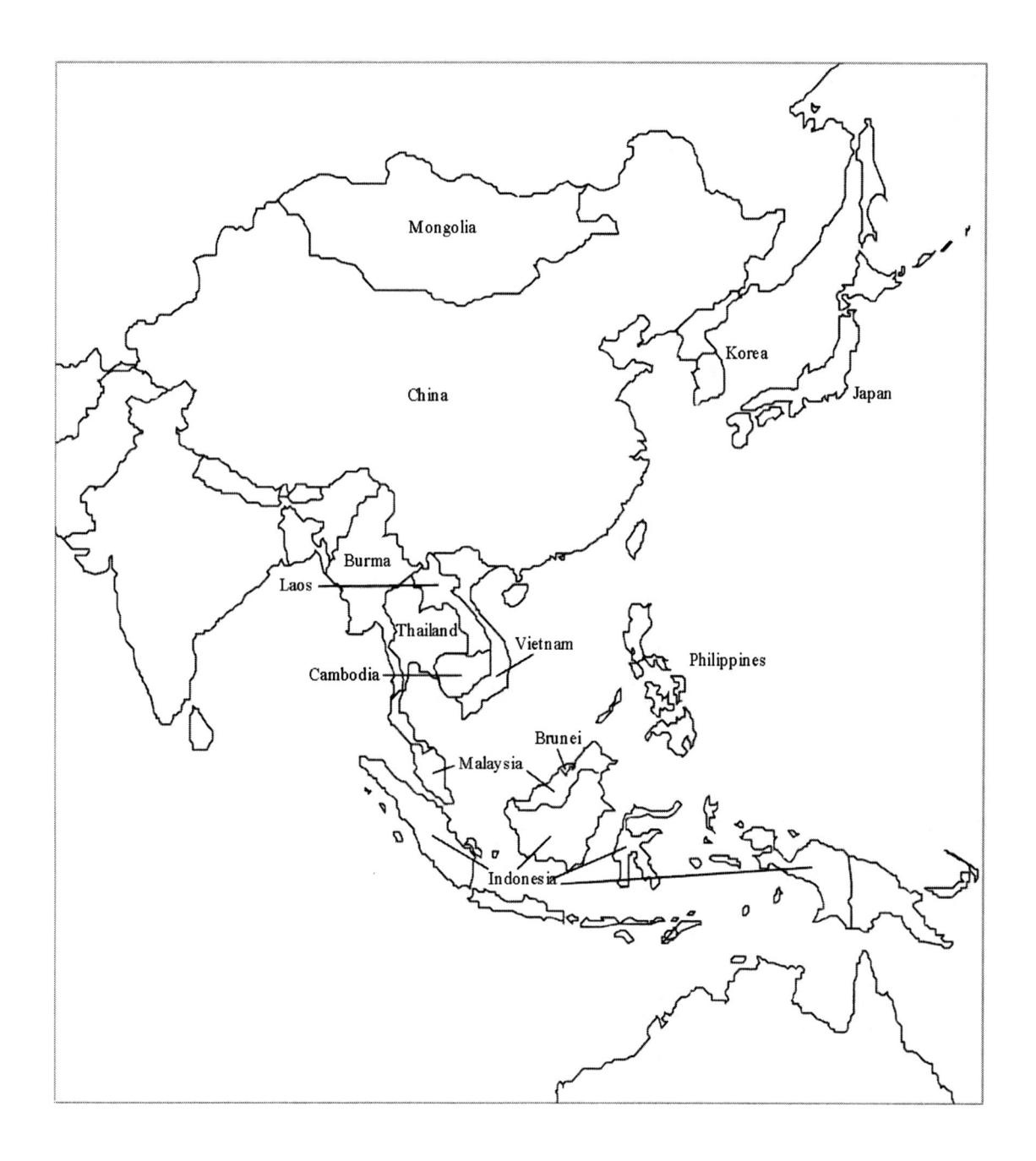

Asia

Asia

Brunei	. .	305
Cambodia	. .	314
China / Tibet	. .	322
Indonesia	. .	350
Japan	. .	359
Korea	. .	369
Laos	. .	381
Malaysia	. .	391
Mongolia	. .	398
Myanmar (Burma)	.	408
The Philippines	.	417
Thailand	.	428
Vietnam	.	437

Brunei

According to early Chinese records the area on the north coast of island of Borneo, now known as Brunei or Brunei Darassalm, was known as P'o-li in the sixth century AD. An account in the seventh century AD references the same areas as Vijayapura and say that they were ruled by the Chinese Funan dynasty's royal family. Few details are known about the intervening centuries other than the fact that Brunei became part of the Javanese Majapahit kingdom during the thirteenth and fourteenth centuries and that Hinduism was introduced at that time. By the fifteenth century the Majapahit kingdom had declined, Islam had been widely adopted, and Brunei had become the powerful Sultanate of Brunei. Until the seventeenth century and the arrival of European influences, Brunei had extensive influence in the South Pacific.

The relationship with the Portuguese was one of trade and mutual benefit but Brunei's relationship with Spain was not so benign. In 1578 Spain declared war but because the troops, a combined force from Spain, The Philippines, and Borneo, encountered cholera and dysentery as well as the Bruneians, the attempt to take over Brunei was abandoned and the survivors withdrew. Brunei continued as a sultanate with power in the area until the 1880s. In 1888 a treaty of protection was negotiated with Great Britain. Brunei remained a protectorate of the British government until 1905 when its status was changed to that of a dependency. Great Britain's influence in Brunei remained until 1984, interrupted only by Japanese occupation from 1941-1945. British attempts to free the Brunei from Japanese control were easily rebuffed.

The monarchy of Brunei, now five hundred years old, functions today as an Islamic constitutional monarchy. Oil was discovered in 1929 and the first off-shore well was drilled in 1957, allowing Brunei to maintain economic sufficiency. Today about ninety percent of the nation's GDP can be attributed to crude oil and natural gas exports which provide its population one of the highest per capita income in Asia.

Many recipes found in Brunei have their origins in Malaysia, after all Brunei borders Malaysia on three sides and sixty-seven percent of the population identify themselves as Malaysian. However, recipes from Thailand, Cambodia, Singapore, China, or Japan have become firmly implanted in the repertoire of Bruneian cooks. One example is a popular rice dessert with mango. It is made with cow's milk in some areas and coconut milk in other regions. The most beautiful version of this dessert is made with black or purple rice, often referred to as "Forbidden rice." This unusual rice pudding is found in both Brunei and Thailand. Bakeries of every imaginable ethnicity sell cakes, cupcakes, fruit tarts, Chinese cookies, French pastries, English custard tarts, a cake very similar to an Eccles cake, and other sweet treats that have been adopted by the Bruneians from the many cuisines of the region and from the cuisines of the colonial powers who came and went. Since Brunei must import a significant amount of the agricultural products needed by its population of about 409,000 and since Bruneian have taken to fast foods from the West with enthusiasm, an identifiable Bruneian cuisine is becoming harder and harder to find.

The durian is a fruit, or some might say a phenomenon, found in this part of Southeast Asia and it is popular in Brunei, which is amazing since the Bruneian taste preferences tend toward subtle complexity which is not a characteristic that the rancid-tasting durian can claim. They are shipped from Malaysia and, boy, do they take some getting used to. I prefer to end a Bruneian meal with one of the tropical fruits native to the island that grow well in the tropical equatorial climate but the durian would not be my choice.

Asia–Brunei

Fried *Tofu* with Dipping Sauce

~

Noodle and Mushroom Soup with Vegetables

~

Brilliantly Green Steamed Vegetable Salad
with Sweet Black Sesame Dressing

Fruit Salad with Tamarind Dressing
Rujak Brunei

~~~~~~~~~~~~~~~~~~~~~~

Stir-Fried Noodles and Vegetables

Sweet Soy Sauce
Kecap Manis

~~~~~~~~~~~

Stir-Fried Vegetables with Coconut

Spicy Eggplant with Tomato and *Chili* Sauce
Terong Belado

~~~~~~~~~~~~~~~~~~~~~~~

Sliced Bananas
with

Rose Water Syrup
Sirap Bandung

Black Rice Pudding with Mangoes
Bubur Ketan Hitam

FRIED *TOFU* WITH BRUNEIAN DIPPING SAUCE
TPT - 5 hours and 11 minutes;
5 hours = bean curd draining period

Many years ago, a friend, who was invited to a Chinese banquet meal that I put together, passed the grilled tofu dish on quickly. I wondered why and when we got to dessert, which was an almond custard float, I found out why. He abhorred custardy foods. He, however, had sampled the fried tofu appetizer several times and did not have the same reaction. Frying tofu results in a very different texture and mouth-feel so if you have family members who do not like tofu for one reason or another, try this. You might just find a tofu dish that they like.

BRUNEIAN DIPPING SAUCE:
    1 large garlic clove—*crushed and very finely* chopped
    3 tablespoons freshly squeezed lime juice
    2 tablespoons bottled *chili* sauce
    2 tablespoons *tamari* soy sauce
    1-2 teaspoons Thai red curry paste, or to taste

2 packages (12.3 ounces each) *extra firm silken tofu*

6 tablespoons *high heat* safflower *or* sunflower oil

In a small bowl, combine *very finely* chopped garlic, lime juice, *chili* sauce, soy sauce, and red curry paste. Stir to combine thoroughly. Turn into a serving bowl. Set aside until required.

Wrap soybean curd cakes in a cotton tea towel and place on the counter top. Place bread board or other flat weight on top. Allow to drain for 2 hours. Remove weight, unwrap beancurd, rewrap beancurd in a dry cotton tea towel, place again on the counter top and again press with weights—this time for 3 additional hours. Unwrap beancurd. Pat it dry. Cut into 1/2-inch cubes.

FRIED *TOFU* WITH SPICY SAUCE (cont'd)

In a deep skillet set over *MEDIUM* heat, heat oil. When hot, fry cubes of *tofu* until lightly browned on all sides. Remove from oil to paper toweling to drain excess oil. Transfer to a platter.

Serve at once, accompanied by the prepared sauce. Provide bamboo skewers or fondue forks for dipping.

Yields 6 servings
adequate for 4 people

Note: This recipe can be doubled, when required.

1/6 SERVING – PROTEIN = 8.3 g.; FAT = 7.2 g.; CARBOHYDRATE = 8.0 g.; CALORIES = 123; CALORIES FROM FAT = 52%

NOODLE AND MUSHROOM SOUP WITH VEGETABLES

TPT - 1 hour and 26 minutes;
1 hour = mushroom rehydration period

I like to think that little Asian children enjoyed this noodle soup for lunch like we enjoyed the "noodle-soup-in-the-red-can" when we were children and had just come in out of the snow. . . . those lucky children also had vegetables in their soup bowls! This is a terrific first course soup for an Asian menu.

1/2 cup dried mushroom slices—black *shiitake*, if available
1 cup *boiling* water

3 quarts *boiling* water
2 ounces *chuka soba* Japanese noodles—broken into thirds*

3 cups THAI DARK VEGETABLE STOCK *[see index]* or JAPANESE VEGETARIAN STOCK FROM *KOMBU* (**Kombu Dashi**) *[see index]*
1 small leek—*white and light green portions only*—trimmed, well-rinsed, and *thinly* sliced
2 large spinach leaves—*very well-washed*, stems removed, and torn into bite-sized pieces to yield about 2 cupfuls
10 small, whole snowpeas—ends trimmed

2 tablespoons fresh coriander *(cilantro)* leaves, for garnish

Tamari soy sauce

In a small bowl or measuring cup, pour the 1 cupful *boiling* water over the dried mushroom slices. Allow mushrooms to rehydrate for about 1 hour. Drain, *reserving mushroom liquid.*

In a large saucepan set over *MEDIUM* heat, combine 3 quartfuls *boiling* water with broken noodles. Allow to boil for 3 minutes. Drain and rinse well with *cold* water to stop further cooking. Set aside to drain until final assembly of soup.

In a large saucepan set over *MEDIUM* heat, combine stock and reserved mushroom soaking water. Allow to come to a *gentle boil.* Add rehydrated mushroom slices, leek slices, spinach, and snowpeas. Allow to cook for 5 minutes. Add drained noodles and allow to cook for an additional 2-3 minutes.

Turn into heated soup tureen. Garnish with fresh coriander *(cilantro)* leaves.

Serve at once, into heated soup bowls. Pass soy sauce for those who wish to add it.

Yields about 6 cupfuls

Notes: *These items are available in Asian markets.

This recipe can be halved or doubled, when required.

1/6 SERVING – PROTEIN = 2.3 g.; FAT = 0.6 g.; CARBOHYDRATE = 11.1 g.; CALORIES = 61; CALORIES FROM FAT = 8%

Asia—**Brunei**

BRILLIANTLY GREEN STEAMED VEGETABLE SALAD WITH SWEET BLACK SESAME DRESSING
TPT - 45 minutes

Lightly steamed green vegetables brighten to intense green and if they are quickly cooled, they retain that wonderful color. This salad takes advantage of that technique and the result is a vegetable salad that can not be resisted by even those who avoid a second helping of vegetables.

BRUNEIAN SWEET BLACK SESAME DRESSING:

    2 tablespoons black sesame seeds*

    2 tablespoons *tamari* soy sauce
    1 tablespoon water
    1 tablespoon honey
    1 1/2 teaspoons rice wine vinegar

2 baby *bok choy*—leaves separated, well-rinsed, and trimmed

4 ounces whole green beans—trimmed

1 cup small broccoli florets

18 whole edible pod peas, snowpeas, *or* sugar snap peas—trimmed

Set up steamer.

Set up bowl of ice water.

In a skillet set over *MEDIUM* heat, dry-roast sesame seeds for 1 minute. Turn into a mortar. Grind seeds with a pestle. Turn into a small bowl.

Add soy sauce, water, honey, and rice wine vinegar. Mix well.

Steam *bok choy* leaves until *bright green*—about 5 minutes. Remove leaves from steamer. Plunge leaves into ice water.

Steam green beans until *bright green*—about 5 minutes. Remove beans from steamer. Plunge beans into ice water.

Steam broccoli florets until bright green—about 5 minutes. Remove broccoli from steamer. Plunge florets into ice water.

Steam pea pods until bright green—about 3 minutes. Remove pea pods from steamer. Plunge pea pods into ice water. Remove and drain all vegetables.

Spread a cotton tea towel on the counter top. Spread drained vegetables on tea towel. Using a second tea towel, pat the vegetables dry. Cut large *bok choy* leaves into manageable pieces. Turn into a salad bowl.

Pour prepared sesame seed dressing over. Toss.

Serve at once.

                              Yields 8 servings
                           adequate for 4-6 people

Notes: *White sesame seeds can be substituted. I do consider the more intense flavor of the black sesame seeds to be a plus for this salad.

         This recipe can be halved or doubled, when required.

1/8 SERVING – PROTEIN = 2.0 g.; FAT = 1.5 g.; CARBOHYDRATE = 6.0 g.; CALORIES = 40; CALORIES FROM FAT = 34%

BRUNEIAN FRUIT SALAD WITH TAMARIND DRESSING
Rujak Brunei
TPT - 32 minutes

Texture and contrasting sensations of sweetness are important in Brunei when preparing a dish. This careful planning can be sensed in their salads perhaps most specifically. Pears, cucumbers, jicama, and even apples can add a nuance of texture to a fruit salad that is unexpected by the diner. The following recipe gives the cook latitude to choose from what is available and to choose fruits that he or she prefers. These ingredients can be combined, tossed, and dressed or, more traditionally, the fruits can be presented, beautifully arranged on a large platter, with the dressing on the side.

Asia–Brunei

BRUNEIAN FRUIT SALAD WITH TAMARIND DRESSING (cont'd)

BRUNEIAN TAMARIND DRESSING:
- 1/2 cup water
- 1 tablespoon tamarind paste*

- 1 small, green-tipped banana—peeled, seeded, and chopped
- 1/4 cup *light* brown sugar
- 3 tablespoons *ground, unsalted, roasted* peanuts
- 2 teaspoons Thai red curry paste
- 1/4 teaspoon *jalapeño chili* sauce

4 cups fruits—choose from:
- 1 small cucumber—peeled, seeded, and *thinly* sliced
- 1 cup *thinly* sliced *jicama*
- 1 *carambola* (starfruit)—sliced
- 1 cup cubed, firm papaya
- 1 firm, under-ripe pear—peeled, cored, and cubed

1 cup fresh pineapple chunks

In a small bowl combine water and tamarind paste. Stir to dissolve thoroughly. Pour through a fine strainer into the work bowl of the food processor.

Add chopped banana, brown sugar, ground peanuts, red curry paste, and *jalapeño* sauce. Process until smooth. Turn into a small serving bowl, suitable for dipping. Set aside until required.

On a large platter or attractive tray, arrange fruits chosen in separate piles leaving the center open to accommodate the bowl with the dressing. Add a pile of pineapple chunks. Place the bowl of dressing in the middle. Refrigerate until ready to serving.

Provide fondue forks, cocktail forks, or skewers and encourage diners to dip fruit in dressing.

Yields 6 servings
adequate for 4 people

Notes: *Tamarind paste can usually be found in Asian markets.

This recipe can be halved or doubled for a buffet table presentation, when required.

1/6 SERVING – PROTEIN = 1.3 g.; FAT = 2.4 g.; CARBOHYDRATE = 20.0 g.;
CALORIES = 130; CALORIES FROM FAT = 16%

BRUNEIAN STIR-FRIED NOODLES AND VEGETABLES
TPT - 23 minutes

Before the onset of fast food chains, my generation defined fast food as a take-out pizza, canned soup, or a stir-fry. We accepted the fact that you could buy salty canned soups or simmer homemade soups for hours but the fresh, crisp taste of the green, yellow, and red vegetables that we tossed into our woks soon had us convinced of an Asian method of cooking our mothers and grandmothers had not discovered. We did not and do not have to microwave or stop for take-out if a dinner must be on the table almost as soon as we arrive home; we take out our trusty woks and do a little fast chopping and before everybody has started snacking, we have dinner done. If you wish to serve this stir-fry as a vegan entrée, tofu or soymeat analogue strips can be added just as we have been doing now for over five decades.

- 2 tablespoons *high heat* safflower *or* sunflower oil
- 2 tablespoons SWEET SOY SAUCE *(Kecap Manis)* [see recipe which follows]
- 2 tablespoons water
- 1 tablespoon *light* brown sugar
- 1 teaspoon crushed red pepper flakes

- 1/2 cup *finely* chopped onion
- 1 large garlic clove—*very finely* chopped
- 2 teaspoons *finely* chopped fresh gingerroot

- 1/2 cup whole snowpeas—trimmed
- 3 scallions—trimmed, well-rinsed, and chopped into 1-inch pieces
- 2 Kaffir lime leaves*

- 1/2 cup fresh mung bean sprouts—trimmed of any brown areas and *very well-washed*
- 8 ounces *cooked* Chinese or Korean flat wheat noodles, such as *lo mein* noodles**
- 1 tablespoon freshly squeezed lime juice

Asia – **Brunei**

BRUNEIAN STIR-FRIED NOODLES AND VEGETABLES (cont'd)

In the wok or large non-stick coated skillet set over *LOW* heat, combine SWEET SOY SAUCE, water, brown sugar, and crushed red pepper flakes. Cook, stirring constantly, for several minutes.

Increase heat to MEDIUM. Add *finely* chopped onion, *very finely* chopped garlic, and *finely* chopped fresh gingerroot. Cook, stirring constantly, until onions are soft and translucent, *being careful not to allow any of the vegetables to brown.*

Add snowpeas, chopped scallions, and Kaffir lime leaves. Stir-fry for several minutes.

Add *very well-washed* mung bean sprouts, *cooked* noodles, and lime juice. Toss to mix. Cook, stirring constantly, until noodles are heated through. Turn out onto a heated platter.

Serve at once.

Yields 6 servings
adequate for 4 people

Notes: *Kaffir lime leaves are available in Thai and Chinese groceries and from mail order firms.

**Chinese and Korean flat wheat noodles are usually available at Asian groceries.

This recipe can be halved or doubled, when required.

1/6 SERVING –   PROTEIN = 6.0 g.; FAT = 5.2 g.; CARBOHYDRATE = 38.7 g.;
CALORIES = 228; CALORIES FROM FAT = 16%

SWEET SOY SAUCE
Kecap Manis
TPT - 18 minutes

This sweet soy sauce is a thick molasses-like condiment, popular in both Brunei and Indonesia. It is available commercially but I decided to make my own. It is not all that difficult a project but the first time I allowed it to thicken too much and I could only get it out of the jar with a butter knife. Purists will note that I have omitted salam leaves and laos which are generally used to make this unique soy sauce in Indonesia. They are unavailable in most parts of the United States so I do not worry about the nuances.

1/2 cup sugar

1/2 cup Chinese dark soy sauce
1 garlic clove—smashed
2 cloves/pods broken from a star anise bulb
2 tablespoons water

In a non-stick-coated skillet set over *LOW* heat, melt sugar. Stir frequently.

Add soy sauce, garlic, star anise pod, and the 2 tablespoonfuls water. Increase heat to *MEDIUM* and allow to come to the boil. Stir for about 5-8 minutes until it begins to thicken. Remove from heat and allow to cool. Transfer to a small, sterilized jelly jar so that any that is not used can be stored in the refrigerator for future use.

Add to recipes as directed and serve as a condiment at room temperature with Bruneian and Indonesian meals.

Yields 10 tablespoonfuls

Note: This recipe can be halved or doubled, as required.

1/10 SERVING (per tablespoonful) –
PROTEIN = 0.3 g.; FAT = 0.1 g.; CARBOHYDRATE = 12.4 g.;
CALORIES = 51; CALORIES FROM FAT = <1%

Asia–**Brunei**

BRUNEIAN STIR-FRIED VEGETABLES WITH COCONUT
Urap
TPT - 13 minutes

A stir-fry depends on the concept of "mise en place," the French technique to which I am very devoted. As a child I was taught to get everything out of the cupboard and refrigerator before beginning to bake. Grandma and Mom assured me that some day I would be ready to bake and I would find that I did not have a needed ingredient. " Mise en place" was just a short step from that baking regime. You saved time when you were not dashing here and there retrieving ingredients. The need for this cooking approach with stir-frying is another step, perhaps to some a giant step, but it is essential to have ingredients ready because stir-fried foods are cooked at high heat and only for a short time. If you have to run off and chop vegetables or shred coconut as you are going along, you will have an unevenly cooked presentation. Even stopping to get an herb or spice from the pantry can be fatal to the texture of a stir-fried dish.

SAUCE:
    2 tablespoons freshly squeezed lime juice
    1 tablespoon bottled *chili* sauce
    1 tablespoon *tamari* soy sauce
    1 teaspoon Thai red curry paste, or to taste

1 tablespoon *high heat* safflower *or* sunflower oil
6 ounces fresh green beans—cut into 2-inch pieces
2 carrots—scraped or pared and cut into 2-inch julienne pieces
3 cups shredded cabbage—well-washed and dried
1 medium scallion—*both white and green portions*—trimmed, well-rinsed, and *thinly* sliced
1/4 cup sliced, canned bamboo shoots—well-rinsed

4 ounces mung bean sprouts*

3 tablespoons shredded coconut—fresh *or* desiccated

In a small bowl, combine lime juice, *chili* sauce, soy sauce, and red curry paste. Stir to combine thoroughly. Set aside until required.

In a large, non-stick-coated skillet or wok set over *MEDIUM-HIGH* heat, heat oil. Add green bean and carrot pieces, shredded cabbage, *thinly* sliced scallion, and sliced bamboo shoots. Stir-fry for several minutes, or until cabbage is wilted.

Add bean sprouts and stir-fry for another minute or two.

Add sauce mixture. Stir-fry for another minute or two. Turn out onto a heated platter.

Sprinkle shredded coconut over.

Serve at once.

Yields 6 servings
adequate for 4 people

Notes: *Since sprouts can often deliver both bacteria and molds to your plate, be very sure to check carefully before using, i. e, smell for mold and look for any decay. If you think they are relatively clean, then rinse very well before using.

This recipe can be halved or doubled, when required.

1/6 SERVING – PROTEIN = 1.5 g.; FAT = 2.4 g.; CARBOHYDRATE = 7.4 g.; CALORIES = 53; CALORIES FROM FAT = 40%

SPICY EGGPLANT WITH TOMATO AND *CHILI* SAUCE IN THE BRUNEIAN STYLE
Terang Belado
TPT - 1 hour and 41 minutes;
1 hour = eggplant salting period

The first time I tasted this Bruneian specialty, I was overwhelmed by the amount of oil the eggplant was allowed to absorb. The spicy sauce or sambal that adorned it was delicious but all you could taste was the oil. Frying eggplant, I have come to believe, is a disgrace because the obliging vegetable just soaks up oil like a sponge. I bake the eggplant for my eggplant parmigiana, for my Armenia breaded eggplant, and I bake the eggplant for this dish too.

SPICY EGGPLANT IN THE BRUNEIAN STYLE (cont'd)

2 small eggplants—sliced
1/4 cup safflower *or* **sunflower oil**

SAUCE:
    1/2 cup canned, *crushed* **tomatoes**
    1 tablespoon *very finely* **chopped mild green chilies**
    3 small shallots—*very finely* **chopped**
    1/8 teaspoon ground red pepper (cayenne)

1 tablespoon freshly squeezed lime juice

Salt eggplant slices generously and place them in a sieve or colander set in the sink. Place a plate on top and a weight—a large can or a tea kettle filled with water—on top of the plate. Allow to stand for 1 hour.

Rinse eggplant slices well in cold water and pat dry.

Place rimmed cookie sheets in oven to heat. Preheat oven to 400 degrees F.

Remove preheated baking sheets from oven. Pour about 2 tablespoonfuls of oil on each pan; brush to edges. Arrange eggplant slices on each of prepared baking sheets. Bake in preheated 400 degree F. oven for 10 minutes. Rotate baking sheets and switch racks. Continue baking for an additional 10 minutes. Remove baking sheets from oven. Turn each eggplant slice. Return to oven for about 10 minutes more, or until each slice is crisp and well-browned. Drain eggplant slices *thoroughly* on several thicknesses of paper toweling.

While eggplant slices are baking, in the work bowl of the food processor, fitted with a steel knife, combine crushed tomatoes, *very finely* chopped green *chilies*, *very finely* chopped shallots, and ground red pepper (cayenne). Process until the ingredients are of uniform consistency. Transfer to a small skillet set over *LOW* heat. Allow to heat through. Remove from heat.

Add lime juice. Stir to mix well. Keep warm on a warming tray until ready to serve.

Arrange eggplants on a heated platter. Spoon the sauce over the eggplant slices, spreading it so that each slice has a portion of the spicy paste.

Serve hot.

                        Yields 6 servings
                     adequate for 4 people

Note: This recipe can be halved or doubled.

1/6 SERVING – PROTEIN = 0.9 g.; FAT = 9.1 g.; CARBOHYDRATE = 5.8 g.;
CALORIES = 108; CALORIES FROM FAT = 75%

BRUNEIAN ROSE WATER SYRUP
Sirap Bandung

TPT - 2 hours and 16 minutes;
2 hours = refrigeration period

"Air sirap bandung" is a popular drink in Brunei that, with a few adjustments makes a fabulous dessert sauce for tropical fruits. I do not color it red as is the tradition in Brunei and I use light cream rather than evaporated milk. This sauce compliments bananas providing a slightly exotic way to end the meal.

6 tablespoons sugar
1 cup *boiling* **water**

1/2 teaspoon rose water *or* **ma ward***
2 tablespoons light cream *or* **half and half**

In a heavy saucepan set over *HIGH* heat, combine sugar and *boiling* water. Attach a candy thermometer. Allow the syrup to boil until your thermometer reaches 210 degrees F. Remove from heat. Turn into heat resistant bowl.

While stirring with a small wire whisk, add rose water and cream. Refrigerate for at least 2 hours. Turn into a cream pitcher.

Serve chilled. Pass to allow diners to add to their serving of fruit. Refrigerate leftovers.

                    Yields about 18 tablespoonfuls

Asia–**Brunei**

BRUNEIAN ROSE WATER SYRUP (cont'd)

Notes: *Both French and Lebanese rose water products are available in food specialty stores.

This recipe can be halved or doubled, when required.

1/6 SERVING (about 3 tablespoonfuls) –
PROTEIN = 0.1 g.; FAT = 0.5 g.; CARBOHYDRATE = 14.3 g.;
CALORIES = 61; CALORIES FROM FAT = 7%

BLACK RICE PUDDING WITH MANGOES
Bubur Ketan Hitam

TPT - 1 hour and 53 minutes;
1 hour = refrigeration period

Bruneian cuisine borrows heavily from Thai cuisine and this classic dessert rice is a perfect example. Both countries make this with white rice and both countries make this with the treasured black rice. Our favorite Thai restaurant makes a "sticky rice" dessert similar to this and it is generally my choice if I choose to have dessert because it cools the palate so very, very perfectly after all the spices and sauces that have preceded it. My version takes the saturated fat in this dish down a bit and shortens the preparation time. As a result, it is a dish we can enjoy frequently. If you really want to introduce your family to an exotic moment, make this dessert with black rice; they surely will not dismiss dessert as "just rice pudding" and you will all feel as privileged as Chinese emperors for whom this rice was originally reserved.

1 1/2 cups *skimmed* milk

3/4 cup dry black (purple) rice*
3 tablespoons *agave* nectar**

1 cup *light, sulfite-free* coconut milk, or more if required

2 perfectly ripened mangoes

In a saucepan set over *MEDIUM* heat, heat skimmed milk until bubbles begin to appear around the edges.

Stir rice and *agave* nectar into the hot milk and cover. *Reduce heat to LOW-MEDIUM* and allow to simmer for about 40 minutes, or until most of the liquid is absorbed and rice is tender. Remove from heat.

Stir coconut milk into rice. Return to *LOW-MEDIUM* heat and cook for about 20 minutes more. Remove from heat. Refrigerate for at least 1 hour.***

When ready to serve, peel mangoes. Slice lengthwise, *with the pit*, into as many long full slices you can get from each side of the pit.

Apportion slices of mango on each of six dessert plates. Using an ice cream scoop or two large spoons, place a scoop of the cooked rice *attractively* on each of the six dessert plates beside the mango slices. Any leftover mango can be chopped and used as a garnish.

Yields 6 individual servings

Notes: *Black or purple rice is often marketed as "forbidden rice."

**Palm sugar syrup is used to make this pudding in Brunei. It is not easily found in our grocery stores so I have substituted *agave* nectar.

***If rice is too firm, stir a bit more coconut milk into the cooked, cooled rice.

This recipe can be halved, when required.

1/6 SERVING – PROTEIN = 3.0 g.; FAT = 1.8 g.; CARBOHYDRATE = 28.4 g.;
CALORIES = 135; CALORIES FROM FAT = 12%

Cambodia

A Neolithic farming culture dating from about the second century BC has been confirmed by archaeological evidence to have existed in this region of Southeast Asia. This was followed by settlements and a stable farming culture established in the first century AD by small kingdoms whose people it is believed migrated from southeastern China. An economy based on the cultivation of rice and fishing flourished. By the fourth century AD Indians had arrived and settled in Funan on the Mekong Delta. It is in this Indianized state that Cambodia has its roots. The influences seen in Khmer cuisine, architecture, and culture today were already taking shape. Funan was succeeded by the Angkor Empire and for six hundred years a succession of powerful Khmar kings dominated this region—from Myanmar east to the South China Sea and north to Laos. By the twelfth century AD the Khmer kingdom included present-day Cambodia, portions of Vietnam, Laos, Thailand, Burma (now Myanmar), and the Malay Peninsula. One of greatest gifts of the Khmer kings was their dedication to the development of irrigation and shipping canals that connected the regions of the kingdom and provided water where needed. Many of the canals and associated waterworks are still in use today.

The rise of the powerful Thai kingdoms and the simultaneous decline of the Khmer kingdom in the thirteenth and fourteenth centuries may well have been cause and effect but any statement on this is, at this point, speculative. However, the wide acceptance of Theravada Buddhism did impact the kingdom, at that time led by an elite Hindu minority. Buddhism played a significant role in the changes in the thinking of the Khmer people and the subsequent change in Cambodia's imperial aspirations. The hold on society by the ruling Hindu families was undermined by the expanding belief that anyone could achieve enlightenment, not just those who were born well.

Thailand eventually controlled Cambodia and installed King Norodom, who, fearing the rising conflict between Thailand and Vietnam, invited colonization by the French as a protective move. Cambodia remained a protectorate of France from 1863 to 1953 as part of French Indochina. Had the French not accepted the kingdom as a protectorate, it is entirely possible that Cambodia would have been overrun by one or both of its neighbors and would not exist as an independent nation today. With the death of King Norodom, France manipulated successors and finally installed King Norodom Sihanouk, a grandson of King Norodom's brother King Sisowth and a young man who was wrongly viewed by the French as completely controllable. Instead, he declared Cambodia independent in 1953. Two years later Sihanouk abdicated in favor of his father in order to become prime minister and once again assumed the role of head of state in 1960 at his father's death. While out of the country he was deposed by a *coup*. He encouraged loyalists to overthrow the "illegitimate" military government and the Khmer Rouge rebels found it convenient to link into the monarchial cause. At this time, the war we call the Vietnam War and they call the American War raged and Cambodia was bombed and briefly invaded by United States forces as they pursued the Viet Cong and the Khmer Rouge. At the end of the war the Khmer Rouge, led by Pol Pot, took power, established a communist rule, and changed the name of the country to Democratic Kampuchea. They attempted to reconstruct the country's agriculture with forced labor using an eleventh-century model. Priceless architecture was destroyed, literature and art were destroyed, Western medicine was abandoned, and mass killings, especially of minority populations, became the norm. This era of horror finally ended in 1993 when Norodom Sihanouk was restored as King of Cambodia. A *coup d'etat* in 1997 briefly interrupted the monarchy but stability returned when the political parties formed a coalition government and the constitution was amended to create a representative senate. Sihanouk officially abdicated his throne in 2004 and King Norodom Sihamoni now rules the constitutional monarchy.

Asia – Cambodia

Asian Buddhists do not consider fish to be a meat that is to be avoided in a vegetarian diet unlike Western Buddhists who generally add fish to the list of foods they do not eat. Khmer cuisine is unique in Southeast Asia in the fact that although they serve a version of the ubiquitous fermented fish sauce, they do not serve it with noodle dishes giving vegetarians a large number of divine dishes to sample. Also, in contrast to Thailand, the cuisine of Cambodia is well-spiced but not fiery hot. Hot sauce is always on the table as an optional condiment. Dipping sauces are designed to allow you to taste the ingredients in the food.

Vegetarian Spring or Egg Rolls
Num Chaui

Tamarind Dipping Sauce
Tamarin

~

Broth with Preserved Lemons, Snowpeas, and *Shiitake* Mushrooms
Ngam Nguo

Moroccan Preserved Lemon Conserve – *Hamad Mrakad*
[see index]

Baguette

~

***Pomelo* Salad**
Somo O

Rice Noodle Salad with Mango and Sweet *Cilantro* Dressing

~ ~

Vegetarian Curried Vegetables with *Tofu*
Salar Kari Sap

Homemade Curry Powder

Grilled Corn–on–Cob
Poat Dot

Thai Hot, Sweet *Chili* Sauce

~ ~

Sticky Rice and Banana Sweet   **Sweet, Coconut Rice with Mangoes**
Ansom Chek   *Kao Nieow Ponma – Muang*

Coffee with Sweetened Condensed Milk

Asia – Cambodia

TAMARIND DIPPING SAUCE
Tamarin
TPT - 17 minutes

The pulp around the seeds in the brown pod of the legume tamarind, a sour flavoring very popular throughout Asia and the Indian subcontinent, is available in jars as a concentrated pulp. Although I have made a usable liquid with the seed pods [see index – Indonesian Tamarind Water – Asam], the jarred concentrate is enormously convenient and it keeps well if refrigerated. Tamarind gives a rich, sour flavor to sauces and will be recognized as that illusive flavor in Worcestershire sauce. Some substitute double strength lemon juice for tamarind in recipes but I do not find the substitution satisfactory. I must admit that I have never found a dipping sauce as complex or as interesting as this in any Asian restaurant.

TAMARIND LIQUID:
    1 tablespoon tamarind concentrated pulp
    2 tablespoons *warm* water

1 tablespoon GARLIC OIL [see index]
1 tablespoon water
1 tablespoon freshly squeezed fresh lime juice
1 tablespoon Thai sweet *chili* sauce
2 tablespoons *very finely* chopped shallot
1 teaspoon *light* brown sugar

In a small bowl, combine tamarind pulp and warm water. With the back of a spoon, work the tamarind pulp into the liquid until no big chunks remain. Pour through a fine sieve into a small bowl.

Add garlic oil, water, lime juice, sweet *chili* sauce, *very finely* chopped shallot, and brown sugar. Stir until sugar is dissolved. Turn into a small serving bowl.

Serve into individual condiment dishes.

Yields about 9 tablespoonfuls

Notes: Thai hot *chili* sauce or a few drops of *jalapeño* sauce may be added when appropriate to the meal.

This recipe can be halved or doubled, when required.

1/27 SERVING (i. e., per teaspoonful) –
PROTEIN = 0.02 g.; FAT = 0.4 g.; CARBOHYDRATE = 1.0 g.;
CALORIES = 8; CALORIES FROM FAT = 5%

BROTH WITH PRESERVED LEMONS, SNOWPEAS, AND *SHIITAKE* MUSHROOMS IN THE STYLE OF CAMBODIA
Ngam Nguo
TPT - 2 hours and 15 minutes;
2 hours = mushroom soaking period

Our vegetarian version of "ngam nguo," I submit, does embody the spirit of the classic chicken soup. Ngam nguo includes one of the most unusual ingredients you would ever expect to find in Cambodia but, is it truly unexpected? When the French came to Cambodia, they not only brought the baguette, now a staple in Cambodian bakeries, they also brought their passion for the preserved lemon product which they had encountered in Morocco. Lemons are treasured in tropical countries and since they mold quickly, the Cambodians must have been all too pleased to learn another way to preserve lemons.

2 large, *dried shiitake* mushrooms*
2 cups warm water

6 cups THAI DARK VEGETABLE STOCK
    [see index]
2 tablespoons *finely* chopped MOROCCAN PRESERVED LEMON CONSERVE (*Hamad Mrakad*) [see index]

1/4 cup diced soy meat analogue slices
6 *thin* slices sweetpotato cut with a vegetable peeler or a cheese plane

12 small, whole snowpeas—well-washed and trimmed
Long thin shreds of *organic* lemon peel, for garnish

Asia–Cambodia

BROTH WITH PRESERVED LEMONS, SNOWPEAS, AND *SHIITAKE* MUSHROOMS IN THE STYLE OF CAMBODIA (cont'd)

In a small bowl or Pyrex measuring cup, soak dry mushrooms in warm water for 2 hours. Trim and slice each mushroom into six thin slices.

In a small kettle set over *MEDIUM* heat, bring vegetable stock to the boil. Add *finely* chopped preserved lemon conserve, diced soymeat, *thin* slices of sweetpotato, and mushroom slices. Allow to cook for about 5 minutes. Turn into a heated tureen.

Float snowpeas and lemon peel shreds on the top.

Serve into heated soup bowls, including two mushroom slices, two sweetpotato slices, and two snowpeas in each cupful.

Notes: *Although domestically-grown fresh *shiitake* mushrooms are generally available in grocery stores today, they do not have the rich earthy flavor or the substance of the dried, imported mushrooms.

This recipe can be halved or double, when required.

Yields 6 servings

1/6 SERVING – PROTEIN = 1.7 g.; FAT = 0.4 g.; CARBOHYDRATE = 3.3 g.; CALORIES = 21; CALORIES FROM FAT = 17%

CAMBODIAN *POMELO* SALAD
Somo O

TPT - 6 minutes

I was surprised to see recipes for grapefruit in Cambodian and Thai resources but soon realized that pomelo ('Citrus maxima'), known as "somo o" in Asia, would probably be the fruit of choice in Southeast Asia. Pomelo are larger and sweeter than grapefruit and do make a wonderful salad.

1 large *pomelo*—peeled, pith and seeds removed, heavy membranes removed, and shredded*
3 tablespoons *finely* chopped onion
1 tablespoon shredded lemongrass
1/2 cup chopped fresh coriander (*cilantro*)

2 teaspoons safflower *or* sunflower oil
2 teaspoons *tamari* soy sauce**

2 tablespoons chopped, *roasted, but unsalted, preservative-free* cashews

In a mixing bowl combine shredded *pomelo*, *finely* chopped onion, shredded lemongrass, chopped fresh coriander (*cilantro*). Toss to combine.

Add oil and soy sauce. Toss to combine. Turn into a serving bowl.

When ready to serve, sprinkle chopped peanuts over.

Notes: *The Chandler *pomelo*, grown in California, can be found in some produce departments.

**Tamari* soy sauce is available in Asian groceries and in most well-stocked grocery stores.

This recipe can be halved or doubled, when required.

Yields 6 servings
adequate for 4 people

1/6 SERVING – PROTEIN = 1.7 g.; FAT = 4.0 g.; CARBOHYDRATE = 8.8 g.; CALORIES = 75; CALORIES FROM FAT = 50%

Asia–Cambodia

RICE NOODLE SALAD WITH MANGO AND SWEET *CILANTRO* DRESSING

TPT - 2 hours;
45 minutes = rice noodle soaking period;
20 minutes = noodles chilling period;
30 minutes = flavor development period

Rice noodles are a staple of many Southeast Asian cuisines. They are called "mai-fun" or "mi-fun" in China; in Indonesia they are called "beehoon," " kalaksa," or "mihoon"; in Thailand they can be found labeled "senme," or simply Phad Thai rice sticks; in Vietnamese groceries they will be found as "ph'o' bhan-hoi"; and in the many Filipino markets across America you will find them labeled "pancit" or " pancit-bihon." Thai rice-stick noodles are now readily available in the international section of most grocery stores and mangoes from India are available year-round at reasonable prices, although I do prefer Haitian mangoes when I can get them. So, logically or illogically, this combination evolved and my summer menu plans often include this salad based generally on classic subcontinent cuisines.

3 quarts *hot, not boiling,* **water**
4 ounces wide rice sticks *or* **rice-stick noodles***

CAMBODIAN SWEET *CILANTRO* DRESSING:
    1 1/2 tablespoons *tamari* **soy sauce***
    1 1/2 tablespoons freshly squeezed lime juice
    1 tablespoon rice wine vinegar*
    1 tablespoon Chinese duck sauce
    1 small garlic clove—*very finely* **chopped**
    10 drops Tabasco sauce
    1/4 cup fresh coriander leaves (*cilantro***)**
    —firmly packed

3 quarts *boiling* **water**

3 quarts *ice* **water**

1/2 medium cucumber—peeled, seeded *(save pulp for soup stock),* **and cut into matchstick pieces**
8 snowpeas—trimmed and cut diagonally into matchstick pieces
1 large ripe mango—halved, pitted, and cubed
3 tablespoons slivered Vidalia sweet onion

In a large mixing bowl or kettle, soak rice sticks in hot water for about 45 minutes.

Meanwhile, prepare the dressing. In the container of the electric blender, combine soy sauce, lime juice, rice wine vinegar, duck sauce, *very finely* chopped garlic, Tabasco sauce, and fresh coriander leaves (*cilantro*). Blend until *cilantro* leaves are just tiny specks of color. Set aside briefly.

Drain soaked noodles. Add noodles to *boiling* water. Continue to cook at *LOW-MEDIUM* heat for about 8 minutes, or until tender. Turn into a sieve or colander and drain *thoroughly*. Plunge into *ice* water for a couple of minutes to stop further cooking. Again, turn into a sieve or colander and drain thoroughly. Turn into a mixing bowl. Chill for about 20 minutes.

Add prepared salad dressing, cucumber matchsticks, snowpea matchsticks, mango cubes, and slivered onion to rice noodles. Toss *very gently*, but *very thoroughly*.

Cover tightly and allow to marinate for at least 30 minutes in the refrigerator. Toss occasionally to insure uniform marination.

Turn onto a *chilled* noodle platter or into a large serving bowl.

        Yields 6 servings
adequate for 4 people as a side dish or
adequate for 3 people as a main course offering

Note: *These items are increasingly available in grocery stores. Asian markets and food specialty stores regularly stock all these items.

1/6 SERVING – PROTEIN = 5.0 g.; FAT = 0.5 g.; CARBOHYDRATE = 55.7 g.;
CALORIES = 232; CALORIES FROM FAT = 2%

Asia–Cambodia

CAMBODIAN VEGETARIAN CURRIED VEGETABLES WITH *TOFU*

Salor Kari Sap

TPT - 2 hours and 22 minutes;
2 hours = *tofu* draining period

Cambodian cuisine has been influenced by its neighbors as this stir-fry demonstrates. The technique of stir-frying was borrowed from the Chinese but the seasoning tells us that India's curry mixtures and wonderful Thai sauces have been borrowed also but with restraint. As you will sense, the ingredients are familiar, common to the region, but the result is quite amazingly unique.

8 ounces *extra firm* **soybean curd** *(tofu)*

1/4 cup water
1/2 teaspoon corn starch
2 tablespoons Thai sweet *chili* **sauce**
2 tablespoons *tamari* **soy sauce**
1 teaspoon INDIAN MANGO POWDER *(Amchur)* [see index]
1 teaspoon HOMEMADE CURRY POWDER [see recipe which follows] **or commercially-available curry powder, if necessary**

1 tablespoon *high heat* **safflower** *or* **sunflower oil**
2 large shallots—sliced
1 garlic clove—*very finely* **chopped**
1 slice fresh gingerroot—*shredded*

1 cup fresh mung bean sprouts—trimmed and very well-washed
2 baby *bok choy***—trimmed, well-rinsed, and chopped**
1/2 red sweet bell pepper—cored, seeds, and chopped into strips
1 medium *green* **mango—cut into large chunks***
2 cups fresh *enoki* **or beech mushrooms—well-rinsed and separated from the mycelium base to which they might be attached at purchase**
1/4 cup *unsalted* **whole,** *preservative-free* **cashews —split in half**
2 inches fresh lemongrass—shredded
2 Kaffir lime leaves**

Wrap soybean curd (*tofu*) in a cotton tea towel for at least 2 hours. Cut into chunks.

In a small dish, combine water, corn starch, sweet *chili* sauce, soy sauce, mango powder, and curry powder. Using a small whisk, beat until corn starch is in suspension and the mixture is thoroughly combined. Set aside until required.

In a wok set over *MEDIUM-HIGH* heat, heat oil. Add shallot slices, *very finely* chopped garlic, and *shredded* gingerroot. Stir-fry briefly.

Add bean sprouts, chopped *bok choy*, red pepper strips, mango chunks, mushrooms, cashew halves, lemongrass, and lime leaves. Stir-fry mixture until *bok choy* is wilted.

Add *tofu* chunks and stir-fry for a minute more.

Add sauce ingredients and keep stir-frying until sauce thickens and vegetables are coated.

Turn out onto a heated platter. Remove and discard Kaffir lime leaves.

Serve at once.

Yields 8 servings
adequate for 4-6 people

Notes: *If you are using mango elsewhere in your menu, as in that presented in this chapter, you may wish to omit the mango in this stir-fry.

**Kaffir lime leaves are available in most Asian markets.

This recipe can be halved or doubled, when required.

1/8 SERVING – PROTEIN = 4.4 g.; FAT = 5.7 g.; CARBOHYDRATE = 11.8 g.;
CALORIES = 107; CALORIES FROM FAT = 48%

Asia – Cambodia

HOMEMADE CURRY POWDER
TPT - 3 minutes

This is my own blend for a mild curry powder. If I want a warmer, sweeter blend, I use my South African curry powder blend. Both were evolved from the recipes of others, tweaked, added to, and finally accepted. Adjust it to your taste and to your menu needs.

1 tablespoon coriander seeds
1 teaspoon black peppercorns
3/4 teaspoon mustard seeds
1 teaspoon cumin seeds
1 tablespoon whole cardamom pods
1 teaspoon ground turmeric
1/4 teaspoon ground red pepper (cayenne)
1/4 teaspoon ground ginger

Using a mortar and pestle or a SPICE and COFFEE GRINDER, grind spices to form a fine powder.

Store in a jar, tightly-sealed, away from light and heat.

Yields about 3 1/2 tablespoonfuls

Note: This recipe may be doubled or tripled, when required, although it easier to grind in a mortar if a smaller amount is used.

FOOD VALUES for such spice mixtures are almost negligible.

GRILLED CORN – ON – THE – COB
IN THE STYLE OF CAMBODIA
Poat Dot
TPT - 33 minutes

Many people are astonished to find corn-on-the-cob eaten with enthusiasm in Southeast Asia. Introduced by Western traders, it is most often found as a street vendor food prepared with a hot, sweet, and salty oil to which the ubiquitous fish sauce is added. This recipe can be prepared over a charcoal fire but when cooked in a heavy iron skillet or a grill pan, the corn is rarely ever over-cooked nor is there the problem that arises when hot oil sets off flare-ups that char the corn ears.

3 tablespoons water
2 tablespoons sugar
1 1/2 teaspoons salt

3 tablespoons corn oil
4 scallions—*white portions only*—trimmed, well-rinsed, and *thinly* sliced

6 ears *freshly-picked* corn—shucked (or husked), rinsed, and all silks removed
Vegetable oil

Preheat grill pan over *MEDIUM-HIGH* heat.

In a small saucepan set over *LOW-MEDIUM* heat, combine water, sugar, and salt. Stir occasionally to encourage the dissolving of the sugar and salt. In another small saucepan set over *MEDIUM-HIGH* heat, heat oil until it is almost smoking. Add very hot oil to sugar mixture. Add scallion slices. Allow to boil for about a minute. *Remove from heat* and set aside while grilling the corn.

Using a sharp knife, cut tips and stem ends from each ear of corn. Brush corn lightly with oil.

Place corn ears on *hot* grill pan and grill, turning every 2-3 minutes, until corn is tender and lightly charred. Turn onto a heated platter. Brush with prepared hot oil sauce.

Serve at once, with hot oil sauce on the side.

Yields 6 servings
adequate for 4-6 people

Note: If you have tasted corn prepared in this fashion in Cambodia and miss the fish sauce, a liquid amino acid product, marketed by Braggs, gives a fair approximation and it is vegetarian.

1/6 SERVING (i. e., per ear) –
PROTEIN = 4.9 g.; FAT = 7.0 g.; CARBOHYDRATE = 35.9 g.;
CALORIES = 203; CALORIES FROM FAT = 28%

Asia – Cambodia

CAMBODIAN "STICKY" RICE AND BANANA SWEET
Ansam Chek
TPT - 15 minutes

A sweet-not-too-sweet dessert that is the perfect ending for a Cambodian meal or any meal, should be filed under "treasures: treasures for any night in the week."

3 baby bananas—mashed
1 tablespoon pineapple juice
1 tablespoon *fat-free* **sweetened condensed milk**

2 cups *steamed* **Japanese** *glutinous* **rice**

Line a cookie sheet with a dampened cotton tea towel.

In a small dish, combine mashed bananas, pineapple juice, and sweetened condensed milk. Combine thoroughly.

Take 1/3 cupful of rice and spread it out into a rectangle on the tea towel. Be sure the long side of the rectangle is toward you. Spread one-sixth of the banana filling on the rice. Roll, using the tea towel to help you, into a cylinder. Press the cylinder firmly and place on a chilled plate. Repeat until you have made six rice rolls. Refrigerate until ready to serve.

Yields 6 servings

Note: This recipe can be halved or doubled, when required.

1/6 SERVING (i. e., per rice roll) –
PROTEIN = 1.4 g.; FAT = 0.3 g.; CARBOHYDRATE = 19.0 g.;
CALORIES = 81; CALORIES FROM FAT = 3%

SWEET COCONUT RICE WITH MANGOES
Kao Nieow Panma – Muang
TPT - 1 hour and 53 minutes;
1 hour = refrigeration period

My version of this dessert, popular in Cambodia and Thailand, takes the saturated fat down a bit and shortens the preparation time. As a result, it is a dish we can enjoy frequently.

1 1/2 cups *skimmed* **milk**

3/4 cup dry Japanese *glutinous* **rice**
2 tablespoons sugar

1/2 cup *light, sulfite-free* **coconut milk, or more if required**

2 perfectly ripened mangoes

In a saucepan set over *MEDIUM* heat, heat skimmed milk until bubbles begin to appear around the edges.

Stir rice and sugar into the hot milk and cover. *Reduce heat to LOW* and allow to simmer for about 30 minutes, or until most of the liquid is absorbed and rice is tender. Remove from heat.

Stir coconut milk into rice. Return to *LOW* heat and cook for about 5-8 minutes more. Remove from heat. Refrigerate for at least 1 hour.*

When ready to serve, peel mangoes. Slice lengthwise, *parallel to the pit*, into as many long full slices as you can get from each side of the pit.

Place two of the large slices of mango on each of six dessert plates. Using an ice cream scoop or two large spoons, place a scoop of the cooked rice *attractively* on each of the six dessert plates beside the mango slices. Any leftover mango can be chopped and used as a garnish.

Yields 6 individual servings

Notes: *If rice is too firm, stir a bit more coconut milk into the cooked, cooled rice.

This recipe can be halved, when required.

1/6 SERVING – PROTEIN = 4.2 g.; FAT = 1.6 g.; CARBOHYDRATE = 58.5 g.;
CALORIES = 272; CALORIES FROM FAT = 5%

China

China was home to early hominids, as revealed by the fossil evidence, as early as 2.24 million years ago. The oldest evidence of *Homo sapiens* is dated to 67,000 years ago and was found in Guangxi.

The writing on oracle bones, radiocarbon-dated to 1500 BC, from the Shang (Yin) Dynasty (c. 1700 BC to c. 1046 BC), testifies to the existence of a Chinese dynasty along the Yellow River during this very early period. The beginnings of Chinese culture, literature, and philosophy came during the Zhou Dynasty (1045 BC to 256 BC). History records three sovereigns and five ancient emperors prior to the Imperial Period in Chinese history ushered in by Qin Shi Huang, who united the warring regional kingdoms in 221 BC, created the first Chinese empire, and declared himself to be the First Emperor. Successive dynasties met with greater or lesser success in their contributions to the cultural growth and expansion of China. Prior to the nineteenth century China could be said to be one of the most advanced societies in the world but China did not respond to the Industrial Revolution and began a decline. Imperialism and internal weakness led to the overthrow of the emperor and the political and social structures put in place by the centuries of dynastic rule. In 1912 The Republic of China, commonly now known as Taiwan, emerged under its first president Sun Yat-sen with control over Taiwan, Penghu, Kinmen, Matsu, and the Pratas Island group. In 1949, after the Sino-Japanese War (1937-1945) and the subsequent Chinese Civil War, The People's Republic of China was established with a system of Communist socialism led by Mao Zedong. No peace treaty has ever been signed and The Republic of China survives as a free and democratic China on the Island of Taiwan to which Chiang Kai-shek, Sun Yat-sen's successor, and supporters of the *Kuomintang* (the Nationalist Party) were forced to flee.

From the point of view of a child growing up in the United States, a comparatively young nation, China's 4,000 years of continuous civilization is an astonishing historical journey. Its influence in Asia and throughout the world is incalculable. Since China has always been challenged to feed its large population, it is here to which we can look for the first steps in food innovation. The soybean, "meat without a bone," was introduced in China in about 1000 BC. Once cultivated on a wide scale, it became an important part of the Chinese diet and an important contribution to the world, especially to the vegetarians of the world. At about the same time ice was being cut for refrigeration purposes. Evidence indicates that the Chinese were farming fish by about 850 BC. Records indicate that in 800 BC the Chinese Minister of Agriculture was teaching the peasants crop rotation which helped to increase crop productivity and especially that of rice which was becoming a significant part of the Chinese diet.

In the 1960s I put the canned gray chicken *chow mein* and the canned deep-fried "*chow mein*" noodles, that always accompanied it, behind me. That was a mainstay of the postwar kitchen and of every college cafeteria. I was learning to respect the food, its color and its texture. I can still see my dining room table covered with my yellow longevity china, each dish filled with beautiful food when I courageously cooked my first authentic Chinese banquet. My guide and mentor, our Chinese-American friend, was there and I guess I was too busy to be scared that my presentation would not measure up. It was a success; I served ten courses with the right sauce for the right dish.

I have included many vegetable side dishes for you to choose from but if you could have been with me as I selected these from the many, many that I have collected over these many years, you would appreciate the frustration of making arbitrary choices and my sincere desire to share.

Asia – China

Wonton Appetizers

Wonton Skins

Mustard – Soy Dip

Duck or Plum Sauce

Radish Appetizer

~

Rolled Noodle and Spring Onion Summer Salad

Chinese Spicing Mixture

Asian Eggplant Salad

~

Creamed Corn Soup with Egg Whites

~ ~

Almond Vegetables Mandarin *Mu Shu*   or   **Almond Vegetables Mandarin**
Mu Shu or *Moo Shoo*   with Steamed Rice

Deep-Fried Beancurd with Chinese Ginger and Sesame Sauces

"Foot Long" Beans with Black Mushrooms in Brown Garlic Sauce

or

Buddhist Asparagus with Three Mushrooms
"Fine Jade Meets Three Nuns"

~ ~ ~ ~ ~ ~ ~ ~ ~ ~

Beancurd and Mushrooms with Brown Sauce

Steamed Baby *Bok Choy* with Sautéed Mushrooms

Roasted Baby Peppers with Black Beans

Steamed White Rice   or   **Egg Fried Rice**

~ ~

Almond Junket

Almond Cookies

Tea with Rosebuds

WONTON APPETIZERS
TPT - about 1 hour and 52 minutes;
30 minutes = mushroom soaking period

When I evolved this appetizer back in the 1970s, I was convinced that these were the ultimate appetizers for a Chinese banquet. I am still convinced! So many of my guests have suggested that I take orders and sell them as "take-out"; they are that good. No, then they would become work instead of pleasure, for these are in that category of wonderful food to share with your family and friends.

Asia–China

WONTON APPETIZERS (cont'd)

2 medium, dried *shiitake* or black Chinese mushrooms
1 cup water

3/4 cup mung bean sprouts—*seed coats removed*
2 cups *boiling* water

1 tablespoon safflower *or* sunflower oil
1 thin slice fresh gingerroot—*finely* chopped
1 small garlic clove—*finely* chopped

1 cup coarsely chopped spinach pieces—well-washed
1 medium scallion—*thinly* sliced
2 tablespoons *shredded* bamboo shoot

30 *wonton* skins*

Oil for deep-frying

MUSTARD–SOY DIP *[see recipe which follows],*
   duck sauce, plum sauce, *or* other dipping sauce, of choice
Scallion fans, for garnish

Soak *shiitake* mushrooms in the *boiling* water for 30 minutes, or until soft. (Reserve soaking water for stock pot.) Cut off stems, reserving them also for the stock pot. Shred mushrooms. Set aside.

Blanch mung bean sprouts in *boiling* water to cover for 1 minute. Drain and rinse in *cold* water. Set aside.

In a wok or a skillet set over *MEDIUM-HIGH* heat, heat oil. Add *finely* chopped gingerroot and garlic. *Stir-fry* for about 1 minute. Add shredded *shiitake* mushrooms, blanched bean sprouts, spinach pieces, *thinly* sliced scallion, and shredded bamboo shoot. *Stir-fry* for about 3 minutes. Turn into a bowl and begin filling *wontons*.

Place a heaping teaspoonful of filling in the center of a *wonton* skin. Fold over and seal edge with water. Twist the ends around to form a kind of "turban." Again seal with water. Place on a cookie sheet covered with plastic wrap. Continue until all filling has been used.

Freeze until hard. Transfer to plastic bags and freeze until required or proceed immediately by deep-frying a few at a time in oil heated to 365 degrees F. until *evenly browned.*** Drain on paper toweling. These may be frozen in the same manner as the uncooked *wontons* for several weeks and then heated, while still frozen, in a preheated 375 degree F. oven for about 8-10 minutes before serving with dipping sauces of choice.

Garnish with scallion fans. Be sure to provide cocktail forks to facilitate dipping for those who are not too adept at using chopsticks.

Yields 30 *wontons*
adequate for 4-6 people

Notes: **wonton* skins are available in Asian groceries and even in some grocery stores. They freeze well. If you wish to take the trouble to make them yourself, see our more nutritious version for *WONTON* SKINS *[see recipe which follows].*

**These may also be boiled in stock or soup, if desired, for a vegetable-based *WONTON* SOUP.

When necessary, this recipe may be easily doubled.

1/30 SERVING (i. e., per *wonton* exclusive of dipping sauce) –
PROTEIN = 1.0 g.; FAT = 1.5 g.; CARBOHYDRATE = 4.4 g.;
CALORIES = 36; CALORIES FROM FAT = 38%

WONTON SKINS
TPT - about 2 hours and 45 minutes before final cooking;
30 minutes = dough resting period

Yes, these are a bit of work. Wonton skins, now readily available even in small midwestern chain grocery stores, were not nearly so obtainable when I first began to explore Chinese cooking. I had to travel to New York City's Chinatown or persuade a Chinese restaurant to sell me some. If you only make your own wonton skins once, there is a pride in the effort and the result; and most definitely, as also is the case with strudel pastry, a respect for the convenience product.

1 1/2 cups unbleached white flour
1/2 cup whole wheat flour
2 tablespoons soy flour
1/2 cup *fat-free* pasteurized eggs (the equivalent of 2 eggs)

Up to 4 tablespoons *cold* water

Unbleached white flour as required for kneading

Asia–China

WONTON SKINS (cont'd)

Into a mixing bowl, sift flours together. Stir in pasteurized eggs. *Gradually, tablespoonful by tablespoonful,* stir in as much *cold* water as needed to form a dough.

Turn out onto lightly floured surface and knead until *very smooth* using additional unbleached white flour as needed.* Divide dough into six balls. Cover these with a cotton tea towel and allow gluten to rest for about 30 minutes.

Roll out each ball, in turn, as thinly as possible.* Cut each into 3-inch squares. Stack, wrap well, and freeze until required or proceed by placing a heaping teaspoonful of filling in the center. Fold over and seal edges with water. Twist the ends around to form a kind of "turban." Again seal with water. Place on a cookie sheet and freeze until required or proceed with preparation by either boiling in soup stock for 3-4 minutes or deep-frying at 365 degrees F. for soups or appetizers.**

Yields about forty-six 3-inch-square skins

Notes: *A *pasta* machine is very helpful for these processes.

**Deep-fried *wontons* may also be frozen in the same manner as the uncooked "turbans" for several weeks and then warmed in a preheated 375 degree F. oven for about 8-10 minutes before serving in soup or as *WONTON* APPETIZERS with dipping sauce(s) of choice [see recipe which precedes].

1/46 SERVING (without filling) –
PROTEIN = 0.8 g.; FAT = 0.1 g.; CARBOHYDRATE = 4.0 g.;
CALORIES = 21; CALORIES FROM FAT = <1%

MUSTARD – SOY DIP
TPT - 1 minute

While eating lunch in a noodle house in Chinatown in New York City many, many years ago, my mentor on all foods Chinese and dear friend taught me to mix this simple sauce. I will always be in his debt. In a minute I learned about one of the best sauces you will ever taste. Take a minute . . . .

1/4 cup MUSTARD SAUCE [see index]
1/4 cup *tamari* soy sauce*

In a small bowl, combine MUSTARD SAUCE and soy sauce. Stir well to mix thoroughly. Turn into a serving bowl, adequate for serving and dipping.

Yields 1/2 cupful
adequate for 4-6 people

Notes: *Tamari* soy sauce is available in Asian groceries, natural food stores, and in many grocery stores.

MUSTARD–SOY DIP is excellent with *WONTON* APPETIZERS, *crudités*, deep-fried beancurd, and some cheeses.

This mixture is also a favorite condiment, especially with any wheat noodle *lo mein*.

Leftover portions keep well, if refrigerated.

1/8 SERVING (i. e., per tablespoonful) –
PROTEIN = 1.3 g.; FAT = 1.0 g.; CARBOHYDRATE = 5.1 g.;
CALORIES = 34; CALORIES FROM FAT = 26%

CHINESE RADISH APPETIZER
TPT - 12 hours and 21 minutes;
12 hours = refrigeration period;
15 minutes = soaking period

Radishes appeared thousands of years ago. Grown for food even then, they were especially popular in China, Egypt, and Greece. Traditional Asian medicine utilized radishes for gastric problems including cancer, constipation, parasites, arthritis, and whopping cough. . . . just a bowl of radishes and a dish of salt? This is so very much more interesting!

CHINESE RADISH APPETIZER (cont'd)

1/2 pound (about 20) blemish-free red radishes
1/4 teaspoon salt
2 teaspoons sugar

2 medium scallions—trimmed and well-rinsed

Trim the ends off each radish. Rinse radishes well. Put each radish between two chopsticks and cut down crosswise to make thin slices. (The chopsticks will stop your knife before it cuts all the way through.)

Put "sliced" radishes in a plastic container with cover. Sprinkle with salt and sugar. Toss gently to coat radishes. Refrigerate overnight.

When ready to serve, drain radishes. Soak in *cold* water for about 15 minutes, rinse well, and drain thoroughly. Press each radish gently to form a fan. Arrange on serving dish. Slice each end of each scallion lengthwise, leaving about 1/2 inch in the center. Strips will curl. Garnish radish serving dish with scallion fans.

Chill in refrigerator until ready to serve.

Yields 4 servings
of about 5 radishes each
adequate for 4 people

Note: This recipe is easily doubled, when required.

1/4 SERVING – PROTEIN = 0.5 g.; FAT = 0.05 g.; CARBOHYDRATE = 4.7 g.;
CALORIES = 20; CALORIES FROM FAT = 2%

CHINESE ROLLED NOODLE AND SPRING ONION SUMMER SALAD
TPT - 1 hour and 14 minutes;
1 hour = flavor development period

When we lived on Long Island, we shopped in New York's Chinatown for the ethnic ingredients we used. I was very spoiled with the variety of products available and have never been content with the selection of Asian products available in most grocery stores. Even Asian groceries carry a limited selection because Americans, except those of Asian descent, do not demand variety. There was a whole wall of shelving devoted to noodles in my favorite basement market in Chinatown. Noodle houses in Chinatowns across America and Canada do provide dishes made with more interesting noodles, which they probably have made right there in their kitchens, but rarely can you find these noodles in markets even in the same Asian communities. In China, noodle houses produce and serve noodles of all shapes and sizes, some even akin to Italian pasta and that is why, in frustration, I often substitute Italian pasta for the Chinese flour noodles that I can not obtain. The noodle used in this salad looks like a tiny rolled ear as do Italian "capelletti" or "gnocci" pastas allowing for a substitution that preserves the visual memory of this popular Chinese summer dish.

3 quarts *boiling* water
1 cup dry, tiny rolled Chinese noodles *or* dry, Italian capelletti, "little hats or *gnocci pasta*," if preferred

2 small spring onions (scallions)—trimmed, well-rinsed, and sliced

1 1/2 teaspoons rice wine vinegar
1 teaspoon *tamari* soy sauce
1 teaspoon tomato purée*
1 teaspoon CHINESE SPICING MIXTURE *[see recipe which follows]*

In a large saucepan set over *MEDIUM-HIGH* heat, cook noodles in *boiling* water according to package directions. Drain and plunge into *ice* water for about 10 minutes to eliminate further cooking. Drain thoroughly. Turn into a serving bowl.

Add scallion slices. Toss.

In a small bowl, combine vinegar, soy sauce, tomato purée, and seasoning mix. Stir to combine thoroughly. Pour over noodle mixture. Toss well to coat vegetables with dressing. Refrigerate for about 1 hour to allow for flavor development.

Asia–China

CHINESE ROLLED NOODLE AND SPRING ONION SUMMARY SALAD (cont'd)

Serve chilled as a side dish. Refrigerate leftovers.

Yields 6 servings
adequate for 4 people

Notes: *Even the small amount of tomato purée that is used in this recipe adds to the *unami* taste sensation so essential to the sense of satiety for a vegetarian.

This recipe can be doubled, when required.

1/6 SERVING – PROTEIN = 2.5 g.; FAT = 0.6 g.; CARBOHYDRATE = 14.2 g.;
CALORIES = 75; CALORIES FROM FAT = 7%

CHINESE SPICING MIXTURE
TPT - 3 minutes

A pinch of this mixture can really jazz up vegetables or a stir-fry. We greatly prefer the fresh flavor of the ground sesame seeds to that of sesame oil so this is always on hand.

2 one-inch pieces dried orange zest*
1/3 cup sesame seeds
1 tablespoon anise seed

1 tablespoon ground ginger
1 tablespoon ground, dehydrated garlic**
Pinch ground red pepper (cayenne)
1 teaspoon kosher salt

Using a SPICE and COFFEE GRINDER, grind orange zest with sesame and anise seeds.

When of relatively uniform consistency, add ground ginger, garlic, and red pepper (cayenne), and salt. Grind to a uniform consistency.

Turn into a small jelly or spice jar. Cover tightly and shake to mix thoroughly. Store in a cool, dark place.***

Yields about 8 tablespoonfuls

Notes: *A simple dehydrator is useful for drying orange peels. Be sure to remove the pith from inside the peels to eliminate the bitter taste.

**Ground, dehydrated garlic is readily available in the spice sections of grocery stores but can also be prepared using a dehydrator. Instead of air-drying all of the harvested garlic bulbs so that they will develop the papery protective covering, we dehydrate a portion and grind them.

***Refrigerator storage for this seasoning mixture is advisable to avoid rancidity.

This recipe can be doubled, when required, but since the flavor dissipates considerably due to the release of the volatile oils with crushing, it is advisable to replace the seasoning combination after about 6 months.

1/48 SERVING (i. e., per 1/2 teaspoonful) –
PROTEIN = 0.2 g; FAT = 0.6 g.; CARBOHYDRATE = 0.2 g.;
CALORIES = 7; CALORIES FROM FAT = 77%

ASIAN EGGPLANT SALAD
TPT - 2 hours and 25 minutes;
2 hours = marination period

As you circle the globe, the range of salads created using eggplant is amazing. This one is distinctly Chinese and is an especially good choice as a side dish with noodle dishes.

1/2 medium eggplant—*unpeeled*

1 tablespoon *tamari* soy sauce*
1 teaspoon sesame oil*
1 tablespoon firmly packed *light* brown sugar

1/2 teaspoon ground ginger

VOLUME II - 327

Asia–China

ASIAN EGGPLANT SALAD (cont'd)

Prepare steamer.

Cut eggplant in half. Steam until *tender*, but *not mushy*—about 15 minutes.

Using a very sharp knife, slice eggplant in serving wedges yielding about 12 slices. Arrange slices in a wheel pattern in a 9-inch pie plate.

In a small dish or measuring cup, combine soy sauce, sesame oil, brown sugar, and ground ginger. Pour over eggplant slices. Cover tightly with plastic wrap and refrigerate for 2 hours, turning eggplant slices once during marination period.

Using a slotted spatula, transfer eggplant slices carefully to a serving dish, allowing as much marination liquid as possible to drip off before transferring. Arrange attractively.

Serve *well-chilled*.

Yields 12 slices
adequate for 4 people

Notes: *Both *tamari* soy sauce and sesame oil are increasingly available in grocery stores. Asian markets and food specialty stores regularly stock both.

This recipe may be doubled, when required.

1/4 SERVING (i. e., 3 slices) –
PROTEIN = 0.4 g.; FAT = 0.5 g.; CARBOHYDRATE = 3.1 g.;
CALORIES = 18; CALORIES FROM FAT = 25%

CANTONESE CREAMED CORN SOUP WITH EGG WHITES
TPT - 24 minutes

Americans are often accused of being poor tourists, of expecting to find American food wherever they travel. We have seen it but we have also seen other nationalities demand and criticize. Not to belabor this imagery, Americans can expect American food when they travel to a far greater extent than one would think. If you take into account the global spread of foods which originated in the Americas, an overwhelming percentage of the cuisines of the world owe much to what is often referred to as the Columbian Exchange. Where would the world cuisines be today without potatoes, tomatoes, chocolate, vanilla, peanuts, pineapples, avocados, papayas, chili peppers, and corn? Corn may well have been introduced to Asia by explorers, missionaries, and traders visiting the Pearl River port of Canton, now Guangzhou. This soup has been around for centuries in one form or another and is popular in Guangzhou to this day, sometimes as a vehicle for seafood.

2 1/2 cups VEGETABLE STOCK FROM SOUP
   [see index] **or other vegetarian stock of choice**
3/4 cup *low-sodium* **canned creamed corn**
1/4 teaspoon sugar
Freshly ground black pepper, to taste

1 1/2 teaspoons corn starch
1 tablespoon water
1 teaspoon *tamari* **soy sauce**

1 *organic* **egg white—***lightly beaten*

1/4 teaspoon sesame oil

1 large scallion—trimmed, well-rinsed, and *thinly* **sliced**

In a saucepan set over *MEDIUM* heat, heat vegetable stock, creamed corn, sugar, and black pepper until it begins to boil. *Reduce heat to LOW-MEDIUM.*

In a small bowl, combine corn starch and water. Stir until the corn starch is thoroughly suspended. Add to the soup base and stir constantly until the soup thickens.

Add beaten egg white and using a fork, stir the egg white into the soup until it forms shreds.

Add sesame oil. Stir. Turn into a heated soup tureen.

Garnish with scallion slices.

Yields four 3/4-cupful servings

Note: This recipe is easily doubled, when required.

1/4 SERVING – PROTEIN = 2.2 g.; FAT = 0.9 g.; CARBOHYDRATE = 14.3 g.;
CALORIES = 64; CALORIES FROM FAT = 13%

Asia—China

ALMOND VEGETABLES MANDARIN *MU SHU*
Mu Shu or *Moo Shoo*
TPT - about 21 minutes

Peking doilies or pancakes are often available frozen in Asian groceries in areas of the country where there are large Asian communities. The substitution of flour tortillas for these lovely delicate Chinese pancakes makes these delicious ancestors of the sandwich a dish that everyone can try. The flour tortillas are also more substantial making this easier for the inexperienced to eat since Chinese doilies are fragile and by the time you dip them into the sauce, the distance to your mouth seems like miles.

8 commercially-available flour *tortillas*—preferably whole wheat, if available—*or* Peking doilies

1/2 cup VEGETARIAN BROWN STOCK [see index] or other vegetarian stock of choice
1 1/2 teaspoons *tamari* soy sauce*
1 tablespoon corn starch
1/8 teaspoon *chili* paste with garlic *or* Szechwan (Sichuan) paste,* or to taste

1 tablespoon safflower *or* sunflower oil
1 slice fresh gingerroot—*finely* shredded
1 garlic clove—smashed

3 tablespoons slivered, *unblanched, preservative-free* almonds

1 cup julienne-sliced carrots
1 cup cauliflower florets, *preferably raw but frozen may be used with a less crisp result*—chopped
2 medium scallions—*white and light green portions*—trimmed, well-rinsed, and cut into 2-inch shreds
1 cup coarsely chopped *bok choy*, broccoli rabe, *or* mustard greens
12 snowpea pods—cut lengthwise into julienne slices

Wrap flour *tortillas* or Peking doilies loosely in aluminum foil and then in a dampened cotton tea towel. Keep warm in oven set at *LOW*.

In a small bowl, combine stock, soy sauce, corn starch, and *chili* paste. Set aside.

In a wok or skillet set over *MEDIUM-HIGH* heat, heat oil. Add shredded gingerroot and smashed garlic. *Stir-fry* for about 1 minute. Remove with slotted spoon and discard.

Add slivered almonds and *stir-fry* for about 1 minute, or until *golden* and fragrant. Remove with slotted spoon and set aside until required.

Add carrot julienne. *Stir-fry* for about 2 minutes. Add chopped cauliflower and scallion shreds. *Stir-fry* for an additional minute. Add chopped *bok choy* or other green selected and snowpea pod julienne. Continue to *stir-fry* for only about 30 seconds.

Stir previously prepared sauce ingredients to keep corn starch in suspension and then add to stir-fried vegetables in wok. Continue cooking and stirring until thickened.

Turn stir-fried mixture into heated serving bowl. Fold soft, warm flour *tortillas* or Peking doilies into quarters, as you would for *crêpes,* and arrange on heated serving plate.

Serve at once. Each diner spoons a portion of the stir-fried mixture onto a *warm* flour *tortilla* or Peking doily and rolls it up. These are to be eaten much the way a hot dog is eaten. Accompany with sauce for "dipping" such as SOY–MUSTARD *DIP* [see recipe which precedes] or serve with commercially-available duck or plum sauces.

Yields 8 servings
adequate for 4 people

Notes: *Szechwan (Sichuan)* paste is a blend of hot peppers, salt, and garlic in the form of a *chili* ketchup. It is generally available in Asian groceries and in many food specialty stores as is *tamari* soy sauce.

The ALMOND VEGETABLES MANDARIN mixture can be served without the Peking doily wraps.

This recipe may be doubled easily, when required.

1/8 SERVING (i. e., per *mou shu*) –
PROTEIN = 3.8 g.; FAT = 4.8 g.; CARBOHYDRATE = 21.9 g.;
CALORIES = 145; CALORIES FROM FAT = 30%

Asia–**China**

DEEP – FRIED BEANCURD
WITH CHINESE GINGER AND SESAME SAUCE
TPT - 30 minutes

Crisp, deep-fried beancurd is always the perfect foil for a spicy, complex sauce. This concept is recognized all over Asia and is being introduced to the adventuresome palate here in the United States. Instead of offering a menu of mild-tasting Cantonese dishes, restaurants are including the exciting dishes that they enjoy in their own homes, from their home provinces. Recently I ate lunch with friends in a small, newly-opened strip-mall Chinese restaurant in Carmel, New York, the bulk of whose business was take-out. Never have I had such lightly fried and perfectly sauced tofu. It did not matter that it was served on paper plates or that the tea was served in paper cups or that the television was blaring out a Chinese-to-English children's program.

If you compare this to the Malaysian version we have included elsewhere in this volume, you will see both the obvious culinary cross-fertilization and the obvious differences between the two cultures and the interpretation of a dish as "it travels."

2 *firm, low-fat* beancurd cakes (*tofu*)

CHINESE GINGER AND SESAME SAUCE;
    2 1/2 tablespoons *tamari* soy sauce*
    1 tablespoon sugar
    1 tablespoon GARLIC OIL *[see index]*
    1 1/2 teaspoons sesame oil
    1/4 - 1 teaspoon Korean ground red pepper*
    2 teaspoons *finely* chopped fresh gingerroot
    1 teaspoon *toasted* sesame seeds

High-heat safflower *or* sunflower oil

1 scallion—*white and light green portions*—trimmed, well-rinsed, and *thinly* sliced

Cut the beancurd cake in half the long way. Cut each half crosswise into eight pieces. Place on paper toweling and pat dry.

In a shallow serving bowl, set on warming tray heated to MEDIUM, combine soy sauce, sugar, GARLIC OIL, sesame oil, Korean ground red pepper, *finely* chopped gingerroot, and *toasted* sesame seeds. Using a wire whisk, combine thoroughly.

Pour about 1/2 inch of oil into a wok or 1/4-inch of oil into a large, deep skillet set over *MEDIUM-HIGH* heat. Fry slices of beancurd, a few at a time, until crisp and browned. Transfer to *dry* paper toweling to dry. Place in a large, shallow serving bowl. Spoon sauce over fried beancurd.

Scatter scallion slices over.

Serve at once.

Notes: *Tamari soy sauce is available in most Asian groceries. Korean ground red pepper, also available in most Asian groceries, can often be too hot for Western taste. Start with 1/4 teaspoonful for this recipe and work up to your tolerance level. Ground red pepper (cayenne) can be substituted, if necessary.

This recipe can be halved, when required.

Yields 8 servings
adequate for 6 people

1/8 SERVING – PROTEIN = 5.3 g.; FAT = 6.7 g.; CARBOHYDRATE = 3.2 g.;
CALORIES = 93; CALORIES FROM FAT = 65%

Asia–**China**

CHINESE "FOOT LONG" BEANS WITH BLACK MUSHROOMS IN BROWN GARLIC SAUCE

TPT - 1 hour and 2 minutes;
45 minutes = mushroom rehydration period

I used to have to pick up Chinese long beans in Chinatown when we made our provisions trips into Manhattan. Today they are increasingly available in grocery stores and especially in stores that stock Asian vegetables. At the same time I would buy a large bag of dried Chinese black mushrooms (Lentinus edodes). They are distinctive and well worth adding to this recipe. As you search for these mushrooms you will find names such as black winter mushrooms, fragrant mushrooms, shiitake mushrooms, black forest mushrooms, brown oak mushrooms, or simply Chinese dried mushrooms, depending upon the area of Asia or Southeast Asia from which they have come. The best quality are usually dried for export. The fresh and dried shiitake mushrooms, now grown in the United States and widely available, are inferior in taste. Try to obtain dried black mushrooms which are thick and show deep, white fissures on the caps. Their taste is superior. If you are fortunate enough to find superior dried, Chinese black mushrooms in quantity, ignore the price, buy them, and store in a cool dry place. They keep well for years and, if well-sealed, can even be stored in the freezer. My mother-in-law called mushrooms wood and felt that they had no nutritional value. However, it is now known that mushrooms contain ergosterol, a substance which can be converted to vitamin D when exposed to UVB light, among other beneficial nutrients such as pantothenic acid, riboflavin, niacin, selenium, copper, potassium, antioxidants, and immunity-stimulating factors. Enjoy the unami taste sensation of mushrooms and know that you are not just indulging yourself; mushrooms are good for you!!

24 *small* dried *shiitake or* Chinese black mushrooms*
Warm water

CHINESE BROWN GARLIC SAUCE:
    1/2 cup mushroom soaking liquid
    2 tablespoons *tamari* soy sauce
    1 1/2 tablespoons *hoisin* sauce

2 tablespoons peanut oil
2 large garlic cloves— *finely* chopped
1 1/2 tablespoons *finely* chopped fresh gingerroot

1 pound Chinese long beans *or* whole green beans —trimmed but left whole

Freshly ground black pepper, to taste

Soak dried, *shiitake* mushrooms in *warm* water to cover for 45 minutes. When soft, drain well, *reserving mushroom soaking liquid,* and cut off hard stems. Set aside.

In a small bowl or measuring cup, combine 1/2 cupful mushroom soaking liquid, soy sauce, and *hoisin* sauce. Stir to combine. Set aside until needed.

In a large skillet, with cover, set over *MEDIUM* heat, heat oil. Add *finely* chopped garlic and gingerroot. Sauté for about 2 minutes, *being careful to allow neither the garlic nor the gingerroot to brown.* Reduce heat to *MEDIUM-LOW.* Add rehydrated mushrooms, green beans, and soy sauce mixture. Stir to coat vegetables with sauce mixture. Cover and cook for about 6 minutes, or until beans are *crisp-tender,* stirring frequently.

Season with black pepper. Transfer beans and mushrooms onto a heated serving platter. Invert the mushrooms so that the caps are up. Using a spatula, scrape the remaining sauce from the skillet over the vegetables.

Serve at once to preserve bright green color.

Yields 6 servings
adequate for 4 people

Note: This recipe can be halved, when required.

1/6 SERVING – PROTEIN = 3.9 g.; FAT = 4.4 g.; CARBOHYDRATE = 18.5 g.;
CALORIES = 125; CALORIES FROM FAT = 32%

BUDDHIST ASPARAGUS WITH THREE MUSHROOMS
"Fine Jade Meets Three Nuns"

TPT - 57 minutes;
30 minutes = mushroom soaking period

The names of Buddhist dishes translate into food images that are fascinatingly imaginative and fun. When our daughter Katy was little she always giggled when I served this dish because the image of mushrooms as Buddhist nuns was just so funny to her. I hear that giggle to this day as I prepare this simple dish.

BUDDHIST ASPARAGUS WITH THREE MUSHROOMS (cont'd)

12 dried, Chinese black mushrooms *or* ***shiitake*** **mushrooms, about 1 inch in diameter***

1 can (15 ounces) peeled, whole straw mushrooms—well-rinsed and well-drained*

16 whole, small, fresh ***crimini*** **mushrooms—trimmed, rinsed, and cleaned well with a brush**

1/2 cup VEGETARIAN WHITE STOCK *[see index]*
1 tablespoon *tamari* **soy sauce***
1 tablespoon corn starch

16 stalks fresh asparagus—trimmed and well-washed

2 tablespoons safflower *or* **sunflower oil**

1 teaspoon sesame oil*

Soak dried *shiitake* mushrooms in warm water for about 30 minutes, or until softened. Trim stems from each mushroom.

Combine softened and trimmed *shiitake* mushrooms with well-drained straw mushrooms and well-cleaned fresh *crimini* mushrooms. Set aside until required.

In a measuring cup or small bowl, combine stock, soy sauce, and corn starch. Stir well until starch is in suspension. Set aside.

Set up steamer. Steam asparagus until *crisp-tender*—about 12 minutes. Transfer to a heated platter and keep warm on a warming tray until sauce with mushrooms is prepared.

In a wok or large skillet, heat vegetable oil over *MEDIUM-HIGH* heat. Add prepared mushrooms and *stir-fry* for about 1 minute.

Stir sauce ingredients well. Add to mushrooms and continue to stir until sauce thickens. Remove from heat. Stir in sesame oil. Pour over hot asparagus.

Serve at once, with rice.

Yields 4 servings
adequate for 4 people

Notes: *Dried, Chinese black mushrooms *or* *shiitake* mushrooms, straw mushrooms, *tamari* soy sauce, and sesame oil are available in Asian groceries and, increasingly, in grocery stores.

This recipe may be doubled or halved, when required.

When fresh asparagus is not available, broccoli spears make a splendid substitute.

1/4 SERVING – PROTEIN = 6.0 g.; FAT = 7.1 g.; CARBOHYDRATE = 16.4 g.;
CALORIES = 152; CALORIES FROM FAT = 42%;
CALORIES FROM FAT when served with 3/4 cup rice = 21%

BEANCURD AND MUSHROOMS WITH CHINESE BROWN SAUCE

TPT - 4 hours and 45 minutes;
4 hours = beancurd pressing period

This is such an elegant juxtaposition of flavor and texture even those who turn their noses up at the mention of tofu will be very pleased.

15 small dried *shiitake* **or Chinese black mushrooms***

3 soybean curd (*tofu***) cakes (2 3/4 x 2 1/2 x 1 inch each)****

CHINESE BROWN SAUCE:
    3 tablespoons *hoisin* **sauce***
    3/4 cup VEGETARIAN BROWN STOCK
    [see index] **or other vegetarian stock of choice**
    1 tablespoon *tamari* **soy sauce***
    1 tablespoon corn starch
    2 or 3 drops Tabasco sauce

2 cups *boiling* **water**

Soak dried, *shiitake* mushrooms in water to cover for 30 minutes. When soft, drain well and cut off hard stems. Set aside.

Wrap the soybean curd cakes in a cotton tea towel and place on the counter top. Place bread board or other flat weight on top and weight this with cans or with a tea pot filled with water to a weight of about 3 pounds. Allow to stand for about 4 hours or until most of moisture has been pressed out of the cake and absorbed by the towel. (Change towel after 2 hours, if necessary.) Place *pressed* beancurd in a shallow pan or dish until required.

BEANCURD AND MUSHROOMS WITH BROWN SAUCE (cont'd)

In a saucepan, combine *hoisin* sauce, stock, soy sauce, corn starch, and Tabasco sauce. Stir to combine thoroughly. Place over *MEDIUM-LOW* heat and cook, stirring frequently, until thickened. Add drained mushroom caps.

Pour *boiling* water over soybean curd cakes and allow to stand for 4-5 minutes until beancurd is heated through. Remove cakes to a cutting board and slice each into five slices. Arrange slices side by side on a heated platter.

Spoon hot sauce and mushrooms over warm beancurd slices. Allow to stand for about 5 minutes, preferably on a warming tray, while remainder of meal is being completed. This allows the beancurd to absorb the flavors of the sauce.

Yields 5 servings***
adequate for 3-4 people

Notes: *These items are increasingly available in grocery stores. Asian markets and food specialty stores regularly stock all these items.

**Fresh soybean curd, soybean cakes, *tofu*, or *toufu* may be purchased at Asian groceries or restaurants, if not available in your grocery store. Refrigerate under water for not more than 3 days before using.

***The number of servings will, of course, depend upon accompanying dishes. The assumption is made with this calculation that this will be served as an entree with no more than two other dishes—one of which will be rice.

When necessary, this recipe is easily doubled.

1/5 SERVING – PROTEIN = 7.4 g.; FAT = 3.3 g.; CARBOHYDRATE = 11.7 g.;
CALORIES = 101; CALORIES FROM FAT = 29%

STEAMED BABY *BOK CHOY* WITH SAUTÉED MUSHROOMS
TPT - 30 minutes

The availability of tender, baby vegetables has increased in the last decade and we find that they present beautifully as individual servings. In addition, baby vegetables steam quickly and more evenly, especially if you steam using layered bamboo steamer baskets as I do.

1 tablespoon safflower or sunflower oil
1 tablespoon GARLIC OIL [see index]

1 pound *crimini* or baby bella mushrooms—stems removed, rinsed, cleaned well with a brush, and **thickly** sliced

3 baby *bok choy*—trimmed, if necessary, well-rinsed, and halved lengthwise

2 tablespoons *tamari* soy sauce
1/2 teaspoon sesame oil
1/4 teaspoon ground ginger
Freshly ground black pepper, to taste

Set up steamer.

In a large skillet set over *MEDIUM* heat, heat safflower or sunflower and garlic oils. Cook, stirring frequently, until liquid exuded by mushrooms has evaporated and the mushrooms begin to brown. Remove from heat.

Steam the *bok choy* until *crisp-tender*—about 12-15 minutes.

About 10 minutes into the steaming process, return mushrooms to *MEDIUM* heat. Add soy sauce, sesame oil, ground ginger, and black pepper. Allow to heat through, stirring frequently. Turn into the center of a heated round serving plate. Arrange steamed *bok choy* like the spokes of a wheel with the leaves draped over the mushroom center.

Serve at once.

Yields 6 servings
adequate for 4 people

Note: This recipe can be halved or doubled when required.

1/6 SERVING – PROTEIN = 2.9 g.; FAT = 4.9 g.; CARBOHYDRATE = 5.6 g.;
CALORIES = 54; CALORIES FROM FAT = 81%

Asia–China

CHINESE ROASTED BABY PEPPERS WITH BLACK BEANS
TPT - 17 minutes

A jar of fermented black beans can sit in the back of the refrigerator for years. Then, all of a sudden, you need it and there is nothing that can be substituted. The beans are preserved in the ancient way and ready to do their magic, enhancing that satisfying unami taste in any dish to which they are added. Although I first tasted green peppers prepared in this manner, I love to use the tiny, red, yellow, orange, and green peppers that are frequently available in the produce section of my grocery store. They are neat, they are charming, and the colors seem to improve the appetite.

1 1/2 tablespoons preserved black beans *or* **black bean sauce***
1 1/2 tablespoons rice wine
3 tablespoons *finely* **chopped onion**
1 1/2 tablespoons *high heat* **safflower** *or* **sunflower oil**
2 tablespoons *tamari* **soy sauce**

12 baby bell peppers—green, red, orange, and/or yellow—cored, seeded, well-rinsed, and well-dried

4 teaspoons rice wine vinegar

In a small bowl, combine black bean paste, rice wine, *finely* chopped onion, oil, and soy sauce. Using the back of a spoon, mash the ingredients together until well-blended. Set aside until required.

Heat a wok over *MEDIUM-HIGH* heat until it begins to smoke. *Working in two or three batches*, place peppers into the *hot* wok and allow them to scorch slightly. Use a spatula to turn them and press them down so that there are scorch marks here and there on each pepper. As soon as they are scorched and wilted, remove from wok and roast another batch. *Reduce heat to MEDIUM.*

Add black bean mixture to the wok. Return all the peppers to the wok and stir-fry to bring the peppers into contact with the black bean sauce.

Add rice wine vinegar. Continue stir-frying for about 30 seconds more. Turn into a heated serving bowl.

Yields 6 servings
adequate for 4-6 people

Notes: *This extraordinary condiment, often referred to by the ancient name of "*shi*" is made from black soybeans which are decomposed and fermented by a mold. In this manner, they have been preserved for centuries. They are available in Asian groceries and in the Asian section of well-stocked grocery stores.

This recipe can be halved, when required.

1/6 SERVING (i. e., two whole baby peppers) –
PROTEIN =1.6 g.; FAT = 3.8 g.; CARBOHYDRATE = 4.3 g.;
CALORIES = 56; CALORIES FROM FAT = 61%

EGG FRIED RICE
TPT - 12 minutes

This has always been a family favorite. I have never understood why people buy fried rice as "take-out" at Chinese restaurants where it is usually too salty and very oily. It need be neither salty nor oily and it is so quick and easy to make if you cook and chill your rice early in the day. Without the eggs, you have perfect fried rice. With the addition of about one-third cupful of sautéed, slivered almonds, you have a very tasty almond fried rice which is nicely accompanied by sweeter stir-fried dishes, such as those with fruits.

1 teaspoon *high heat* **safflower** *or* **sunflower oil**
2 large eggs—slightly beaten

1 tablespoon safflower *or* **sunflower oil**
1/4 cup *thinly* **sliced scallion—***both white and green portions*
2 cups *chilled, cooked* **long grain brown rice** *or* **converted rice**
2 teaspoons *tamari* **soy sauce***
1/8 teaspoon onion powder

Asia–**China**

EGG FRIED RICE (cont'd)

In a 9-inch non-stick-coated skillet set over *MEDIUM* heat, heat the 1 teaspoonful oil. Add slightly beaten eggs and scramble until *almost set*, but *not dry*. Set aside.

In a wok, set over *MEDIUM-HIGH* heat, heat the 1 tablespoonful oil. Add *thinly* sliced scallion and *stir-fry* for about 30 seconds. Add *cold* rice and *stir-fry* for about 3-4 minutes, or until heated through. Be sure to coat grains evenly with oil. Add soy sauce and onion powder. Mix well. Stir in cooked eggs, breaking into small pieces while stirring.

Turn out into heated serving bowl. *Serve at once.***

Yields four 1/2-cup servings
adequate for 2-4 people
depending upon remainder of menu

Notes: *Tamari* soy sauce is increasingly available in grocery stores. If not available in your store, it is available in Asian groceries.

**This may be made slightly in advance of serving and reheated at serving time in a casserole at 325 degrees F. for about 15 minutes or quickly stir-fried again, if preferred. Also, this dish may be frozen for 4-6 weeks in advance of serving with considerable success and reheated as previously described.

When required, this recipe is easily doubled.

1/4 SERVING – EGG FRIED RICE –
PROTEIN = 6.2 g.; FAT = 7.3 g.; CARBOHYDRATE = 29.8 g.;
CALORIES = 209; CALORIES FROM FAT = 31%

1/4 SERVING – ALMOND FRIED RICE –
PROTEIN = 4.8 g.; FAT = 9.8 g.; CARBOHYDRATE = 31.8 g.;
CALORIES = 177; CALORIES FROM FAT = 50%

CHINESE ALMOND JUNKET

TPT - 2 hours and 20 minutes;
2 hours = gelling period

Dairy products are little used in Chinese cooking which makes it difficult to manage proteins if soybeans or soybean curd are not on the menu. There are wonderful Chinese desserts but most are complicated, sweet, banquet affairs so one usually settles for fruit or ice cream for weekday meals. This gelatin version of a junket dessert always pleases and does contribute substantial dairy protein to a meal.

2 1/2 cups *cold* **water**
1 tablespoon (1 envelope) unflavored gelatin*

1/2 cup *fat-free* **sweetened condensed milk**
1 tablespoon pure almond extract

Slivered *preservative-free* **almonds, for garnish**

1 cup frozen, sliced strawberries in syrup—
defrosted—or other fruit, of choice, suggested below**

Pour *cold* water into a saucepan. Sprinkle gelatin over and allow to soften for about 5 minutes. Set pan over *LOW* heat and allow to heat until gelatin is completely dissolved and water is almost at the boil. Remove from heat and set aside to cool slightly—about 10 minutes.

Stir in sweetened condensed milk and almond extract.

Divide evenly among five lotus dessert dishes or shallow crystal dessert dishes, if available. Refrigerate for at least 2 hours before serving.

Garnish each serving with slivered almonds and pass sliced strawberries, or other fruit in syrup, separately to be spooned over.

Yields 5 individual servings

Notes: *Agar-agar or kosher gelatin may be substituted for plain gelatin, if preferred. Since preparation procedures differ for these products, be sure to follow package directions.

**Serve with canned kumquats; canned cherries; diced, canned peaches; canned plums; canned pineapple chunks or tidbits; canned lychees; or canned mandarin oranges. Choose fruit to suit your taste and menu.

This is often served as ALMOND FLOAT in which case combined ingredients are allowed to set in a square, flat pan or shallow serving bowl. When set, the junket is cut into diamond shapes or squares. These are floated with fruit in the sweet syrup from the canned fruit.

When required, this recipe is easily doubled.

1/5 SERVING – PROTEIN = 4.9 g.; FAT = 1.5 g.; CARBOHYDRATE = 32.9 g.;
CALORIES = 163; CALORIES FROM FAT = 8%

Asia–China

CHINESE ALMOND COOKIES
TPT - about 1 hour

Ducking into a bakery in New York's Chinatown, to buy honey bows and almond cookies, is one of those wonderful family food memories. This recipe helps to keep that warm memory alive.

1 1/2 cups unbleached white flour
3/4 cup whole wheat flour
1 1/2 teaspoons baking powder
1/2 cup sugar
1/2 cup *preservative-free* almond meal *or finely* ground almonds

2/3 cup butter—*softened to room temperature*
1 teaspoon pure almond extract
1 large egg—well-beaten

2 large egg yolks
2 teaspoons water
20 whole, blanched *preservative-free* almonds, for garnish

Preheat oven to 375 degrees F.

Into a large mixing bowl or into the work bowl of a food processor fitted with steel knife, sift white and whole wheat flours with baking powder. Stir in sugar and almond meal.

Using a pastry blender or the food processor, cut butter into combined dry ingredients. Stir in almond extract and beaten egg. Knead with your hands or *"machine-knead"* until a ball is formed. Turn out onto lightly floured surface and knead until smooth. Break off pieces and form into approximately twenty balls.* Flatten each into a small round cake. Place on *ungreased* cookie sheets allowing 2 inches between each.

Bake in preheated 375 degree F. oven for 7-9 minutes, or until *lightly browned.* Cool completely on wire rack. Store in an airtight container.

Yields 20 cookies

Notes: *It is most convenient to freeze formed balls on a plastic wrap covered cookie sheet. When frozen hard, place in a plastic bag and freeze until required.

Instead of twenty large, classic Chinese-style cookies you might prefer to make forty smaller ones. You will then, of course, need forty whole, blanched almonds.

1/20 SERVING (i. e., per large cookie) –
PROTEIN = 2.9 g.; FAT = 9.2 g.; CARBOHYDRATE = 16.4 g.;
CALORIES = 160; CALORIES FROM FAT = 52%

1/40 SERVING (i. e., per small cookies) –
PROTEIN = 1.6 g.; FAT = 4.9 g.; CARBOHYDRATE = 8.3 g.;
CALORIES = 84; CALORIES FROM FAT = 53%

CHINESE TEA WITH ROSEBUDS
TPT - 40 minutes
30 minutes = rosebud infusion period

Oh yes, I am tea drinker; the morning's first cup of freshly-brewed tea helps make the day possible and that afternoon cup of tea refreshes the wearied body and mind. Our Spencer used to say that, "Grandma drinks 'cream tea," but there are times when I would never put cream or milk or lemon into tea and this recipe would be one of those times. The subtleness of the flavoring contributed by the rosebuds is a rare pleasure. Much as I like to cook with the petals of our first flush of roses, I sacrifice blooms for several pots of this tea.

6 *flavorful, home-grown, spray-free* rosebuds—*very well-rinsed*
1/2 cup *boiling* water

1 pot (6-cup) *hot* tea, of choice, brewed over loose tea leaves *(our choice is Assam tea)*

Place *well-rinsed* rosebuds in a small, warmed bowl.*
Pour *boiling* water over rosebuds and allow to infuse for 30 minutes.

Pour rosebud infusion over tea leaves in the warmed teapot. Fill pot with *boiling* water. Allow to steep for 3-5 minutes.

Strain tea into teacups or tea glasses to serve.

Yields 6 cupfuls

Note: *If you have a Chinese tea pot in an insulated straw basket, it is the perfect system for making this tea since the rosebud infusion will then stay hot.

Tibet

The highest mountain on Earth, Mount Everest, rises to a height of 29,029 feet in the magnificent Himalayan Mountains dividing Tibet and Nepal. It is here that we find the headwaters of the great rivers of East Asia – the Yangtze, the Yellow, the Indus, the Mekong, the Ganges, the Salween, and the Yarlung Tsangpo. The Yarlung Tsangpo Grand Canyon, is the longest canyon on Earth, exceeding the Grand Canyon of Arizona by fifty kilometers (31.06 miles). The Tibetan Plateau has been recognized since ancient times as a vital water source in Asia. Today, without control of this water China could not function.

The conflicting territorial claims of Tibet and China were apparent from the earliest days of the Tibetan Empire in the seventh century AD. Unified by Songtsan Gampo, whose rule from 604 to 650 AD created a strong empire, Tibet set about aggressively incorporating territory across Central Asia. Considerable inroads were made into Chinese territory with the Tibetan Empire reaching the Tang's capital Chang'an, modern-day Xian in 763, from which they were repelled in very short order. By 750 AD all of the Tibetan territorial acquisitions had been lost to the Chinese but in 751 the Chinese were defeated at the Battle of Talas by the forces of Arba Abbasid Caliphate ending China's expansion west into Central Asia and giving the Tibetans the opportunity to expand their influence once again as China experienced a period of civil war. The Tibetan Empire remained strong until the middle of the ninth century when it became part of China under the Yuan Dynasty. Although Tibet had some control of religious and regional affairs, the Yuan emperor and his Mongol allies controlled the Himalayan region until their overthrow by the Ming Dynasty in the mid 1300s. It was not until the rise of China's Qing Dynasty in the early 1700s that the Dalai Lama was restored as ruler. In 1792 the Qing emperor eliminated the autonomy that Tibet had enjoyed, firmly evoking Chinese control of Tibet. By the middle of the nineteenth century the Qing Dynasty had begun to weaken and, as a result, so did its direct control of Tibet. Just prior to the Xinhai Revolution in 1911, the Qing government again deposed the Dalai Lama and exerted its repressive control of Tibet. The thirteenth Dalai Lama was forced into exile in India. After the overthrow of the Qing Dynasty, the succeeding Republic of China allowed the Dalai Lama to return and he and his regents ruled for thirty-six relatively uneventful years. However, through the 1930s and 1940s the Chinese used every opportunity to seize control of areas of Tibet. In 1950 the Chinese incorporated Tibet into the People's Republic of China and negotiated a Seventeen Point Agreement with the fourteenth Dalai Lama which granted Tibetan autonomy but reaffirmed Chinese sovereignty over Tibet. A rebellion in 1959 forced the Dalai Lama's government to flee to Dharamsalad, India, where it established a government in-exile. The Chinese renounced their agreement of autonomy and executed severe social and political policies. During this period as many as one million Tibetans died and an estimated six thousand monasteries were destroyed in the path of Mao Tse-tung's Chinese Cultural Revolution. Although a few monasteries have been rebuilt, the tyrannical repression of the Tibetan people and especially of the Buddhist monks has continued to this day.

It was under Songtsan Gampo that Buddhism established in Tibet. His first wife Bhrikuti, a Nepali princess, is credited with being a strong supporter of Buddhism. Under subsequent kings, the adherence to Buddhism led to the adoption of Buddhism as the state religion, albeit with tolerance of the Muslim and Christians minority, and the Dalai Lama, recognized by Buddhists as a direct descendant of The Buddha, as leader.

Living at an average elevation of 16,000 feet above sea level presents a food choice challenge to Tibetans that is far from the experiences, albeit varied as they may be, of most of the rest of those of us living on this planet. Tibet is in a high altitude desert with little precipitation or humidity for nine months of the year and an average snow fall of just eighteen inches. This together with a short growing season limits vegetable choices and long winters demand creative preserving.

Asia–China / Tibet

Soup with Roasted Potato
Shogo Tan

Tibetan Vegetable Broth
Tukpa

Tukpa Broth with *Soba* Noodles and *Bok Choy*
Tse Tentuk

~

Glass Noodle and Vegetable Slaw
Tangtsel

~~~~~~~~~~~~~~~~~~~~~

Stir-Fried Spinach with *Tofu* and Mushrooms
Tse Tofu

Steamed Bhutan Red Rice

~~~~~~~~~~

Eggs and Peas with Curried Tomato Sauce
Gonga Tsey

Stir-Fried Cabbage, Carrots, and Red Pepper
Logo Petse

Buddhist Stir-Fried Mushrooms and Bamboo Shoots
"Two Winters"
Tse Sesha

Green Onion Sesame Skillet Bread
Tsey Paley

~~~~~~~~~~~~~~~~~~~~

Daikon and Red Radish Pickle

Yogurt Condiment with Fresh Coriander, Garlic, and *Chilies*
Sonam Pensom Sibeh

or

Cheese and *Chili* Sauce
Chiru Sibeh

~

Sweet Creamed Rice with Cardamom
Khir

Baked Cheese Balls in Cream Sauce
Rasbari

Ceremonial Sweet, Saffron Rice
Deysi

Asia–China / Tibet

TIBETAN SOUP WITH ROASTED POTATO
Shogo Tang
TPT - 1 hour and 6 minutes

Potatoes keep well in root cellars in the Himalayans just as they did in my family's root cellars in upstate New York and any eyes that begin to sprout in the spring will become the seed for the next crop. The taste of potatoes cooked in the ashes of a campfire is a memory that is one of those almost perfect food memories. Oh, the taste of the smoky potato flesh was so good, so different. If it is possible to roast the potatoes for this soup in a wood fire instead of in the oven, by all means do it. You will find the smoky flavor will become a memory that you do not forget.

2 large potatoes—well-scrubbed, eyes removed, and cut into wedges
2 teaspoons *high-heat* safflower *or* sunflower oil

1 tablespoon butter
3 tablespoons *finely* chopped onion
3 garlic cloves—*finely* chopped
1 tablespoon *finely* chopped gingerroot

1 teaspoon crushed red pepper flakes
Freshly ground mixed peppercorns—red, white, and black—to taste
2 cups TIBETAN VEGETABLE BROTH (*Tukpa*)
    [see recipe which follows]
2 cups water

1 scallion—trimmed, well-rinsed, and chopped—for garnish

Preheat oven to 350 degrees F.

Place potato wedges in a roasting pan. Add safflower or sunflower oil. Toss to coat potato pieces with oil. Roast potatoes in preheated 350 degree F. oven for 45 minutes, stirring occasionally. Remove from oven until required. Remove to a cutting board and chop so that the dry, charred skins are in small pieces.

In a kettle set over *MEDIUM* heat, melt butter. Add *finely* chopped onion, garlic, and gingerroot. Sauté until onion is soft and translucent, *being careful not to allow vegetables to brown.*

Add potatoes. Using a potato masher, mash potatoes. Leave some small chunks for texture. Add red pepper flakes and ground mixed peppercorns to potatoes. Add vegetable broth and water. Stir to mix well. Allow to come to the boil while stirring frequently to prevent sticking. Turn into a heated soup tureen.

Sprinkle chopped scallion over.

Serve into heated soup plates or bowls.

Yields 6 cupfuls

Note: This recipe can be halved or doubled, when required.

1/6 SERVING (i. e., per cupful) –
PROTEIN = 1.2 g.; FAT = 3.5 g.; CARBOHYDRATE = 11.9 g.;
CALORIES = 85; CALORIES FROM FAT = 37%

TIBETAN VEGETABLE BROTH
Tukpa
TPT - 1 hour and 16 minutes

There are many vegetable broths that I have made over the years; many of those I still make on a regular basis. This one was evolved to serve as a base for Tibetan vegetarian dishes and will always be found on my canning shelves. Many Tibetan recipes I encountered did not purée and strain the tukpa. I find the incredibly complex flavor of this broth and the convenience of being able to can it important so if I want vegetables in the final dish, I add them as I cook.

TIBETAN VEGETABLE BROTH (cont'd)

1 tablespoon safflower *or* sunflower oil
1 large onion—*finely* chopped
1 1/2 tablespoons *finely* chopped gingerroot
3 garlic cloves—*finely* chopped

2 cups canned, *diced* tomatoes
1 small potato—peeled and cubed
1 teaspoon lovage seeds*
1/4 teaspoon ground turmeric
1/4 teaspoon **OUR INDIAN SPICE MIXTURE**
   (*Garam Masala*) [see index] *or* commercially-available mixture
1/4 teaspoon chili powder
9 cups water

In a kettle set over *MEDIUM* heat, heat oil. Add *finely* chopped onion, gingerroot, and garlic. Sauté until onion is soft and translucent, *being careful not to allow vegetables to brown.*

Add diced tomatoes, cubed potato, lovage seeds, ground turmeric, *garam masala*, and chili powder. Stir to combine well. Add water and allow to come to the boil. Reduce heat to *LOW-MEDIUM* and allow to simmer for about 40 minutes.

Using a fine sieve, strain vegetables from stock. Discard vegetables. Strain stock through a sieve lined with culinary cheesecloth or a cotton tea towel.

Refrigerate until ready to use or freeze in quantities appropriate for future use.

Yields about 9 cupfuls

Notes: *Since commercially-available celery seed is often, in reality, lovage seed, celery seed can be substituted in this recipe.

The calories available from vegetarian stocks are almost negligible. For these reasons, we have chosen to treat these stocks merely as flavoring—omitting them from nutritional calculations but recognizing them as a food, quite rich in vitamins and minerals.

This recipe may be halved or doubled, when required.

To save space in the freezer, the stock can be canned using a hot-water-bath canner. Ladle into hot, sterilized pint or quart canning jars. Carefully wipe lips of jars. Seal with hot, sterilized lids and rings. Process in hot-water-bath canner for 10 minutes, *timing from the moment the water reaches a full rolling boil.* Remove to surface covered with thick towels or newspapers. Allow to cool for 24 hours *undisturbed*. Check to be sure jars are sealed before labeling and storing in a dark, cool, dry place. Loosen or remove rings before storing. Any jars that do not seal can be stored in the refrigerator for about one week or resealed using a *new lid*.

TIBETAN *TUKPA* BROTH WITH *SOBA* NOODLES AND *BOK CHOY*
Tse Tentuk

TPT - 15 minutes

As I have noted, jars of Tibetan tukpa broth sit side-by-side on my canning shelves with other broths that I use for cooking. Canning soup stocks using a simple hot water bath canner can provide a varied canvas for soups and stews and a feeling of satisfying accomplishment as you stand before those shelves looking at those jars and planning the next experiment.

1 quart **TIBETAN VEGETABLE BROTH** (*Tukpa*)
[see recipe which precedes]

4 ounces buckwheat *soba* noodles—broken into thirds
2 baby *bok choy*—trimmed, chopped crosswise to yield about 4 cups, and *well-rinsed*

In a large saucepan set over *MEDIUM* heat, bring *tukpa* broth to the boil.

Add noodle pieces and chopped *bok choy* slices. Allow to simmer for about 8-10 minutes.* Turn into a heated soup tureen.
Serve into heated soup bowls.

Yields about 6 cupfuls

Notes: *Be careful not to overcook the soup; buckwheat *soba* noodles, if overcooked, will become mushy.

This recipe can be halved or doubled, when required.

Asia–China / Tibet

**TIBETAN *TUKPA* BROTH
WITH *SOBA* NOODLES AND *BOK CHOY*** (cont'd)

1/6 SERVING (i. e., per cupful) –
PROTEIN = 2.7 g.; FAT = 0.4 g.; CARBOHYDRATE = 15.4 g.;
CALORIES = 73; CALORIES FROM FAT = 4%

TIBETAN GLASS NOODLE AND VEGETABLE SLAW
Tangtsel

TPT - 1 hour and 19 minutes;
1 hour = flavor development period

The flavor of this simple salad will amaze you. It compliments other dishes, prepares the palate for tastes to come, and yet excites the taste buds all by itself.

1 1/2 ounces dry glass noodles, bean threads, *or*
   cellophane noodles
6 cups *boiling* **water**

1/4 cup freshly shelled *or frozen* **peas**

1 cup *finely* **shredded green cabbage**
1/2 cup *finely* **shredded carrot**
2 tablespoons thinly sliced scallion—*green portion only***—well-rinsed**

1 tablespoon sesame oil
2 tablespoons rice wine vinegar
1 teaspoon *tamari* **soy sauce**
1/4 teaspoon sugar

In a saucepan or mixing bowl, soak rice noodles in *boiling* water for about 5 minutes. When pliable, cut with a scissors.

Add *frozen* green peas. Allow the noodles and the peas to sit in the hot water until "glassy"—about 10 minutes. Drain thoroughly. Turn into a serving bowl.

Add *finely* shredded green cabbage and carrot and *thinly* sliced scallion.

In a small bowl, combine sesame oil, rice wine vinegar, *tamari* soy sauce, and sugar. Stir to combine well. Pour over noodles and vegetables. Mix well. Refrigerate for at least 1 hour to allow for flavor development. Stir occasionally to insure uniform marination.

Serve cold or at room temperature, as preferred. Use a slotted spoon to serve.

Yields 6 servings
adequate for 4 people

1/6 SERVING – PROTEIN = 0.8 g.; FAT = 2.4 g.; CARBOHYDRATE = 10.3 g.;
CALORIES = 66; CALORIES FROM FAT = 32%

TIBETAN STIR-FRIED SPINACH
WITH *TOFU* AND MUSHROOMS
Tse Tofu

TPT - 2 hours and 44 minutes;
2 hours = *tofu* pressing and mushroom soaking period

If you cook using the philosophy of "mise en place," that is, arranging your ingredients prior to beginning a recipe, than stir-fry cooking is as enjoyable a technique for you as it is for me. Sometimes, with everything ready to go, the cook actually gets to sit down for a bit or take a walk in the garden. An author I once encountered attributed "mise en place" to Auguste Escoffier but I am inclined to doubt that. There is not an Asian cook who has not prepared for cooking in this manner since long before there was a term for it. It just makes sense. Why be frazzled by the time you get the meal on the table?

Asia–China / Tibet

TIBETAN STIR-FRIED SPINACH WITH *TOFU* AND MUSHROOMS (cont'd)

1 package (10.5-ounces) *extra firm* silken soybean curd *(tofu)*

6 dried, Chinese black mushrooms *(shiitake)**
1 1/2 cups *boiling* water

2 bunches spinach—stems and hard ribs removed, *very well-washed*, and torn into pieces
1 tablespoon *high-heat* safflower *or* sunflower oil
1/4 teaspoon freshly ground black pepper, or to taste

2 scallions—trimmed, well-rinsed, and chopped
2 garlic cloves—*very finely* chopped
1 tablespoon *very finely* chopped fresh gingerroot
2 tablespoons *tamari* soy sauce
1/2 teaspoon HOMEMADE PAPRIKA [see index] *or* commercially-available Hungarian sweet paprika
1/4 teaspoon chili powder

2 teaspoons *high-heat* safflower *or* sunflower oil

1/4 cup freshly shelled *or* frozen peas

Wrap soybean curd *(tofu)* in a cotton tea towel for at least 2 hours. Cut into chunks.

In a bowl, soak dried black mushrooms in *boiling* water for about 40 minutes, or until soft and pliable. Drain softened mushrooms and cut stems from each. *(Reserve stems for soup stock.)* Slice mushroom caps in half. Set aside briefly.

Wash spinach pieces several times in cold water to be sure there is no sand left in the folds of the spinach leaves. Place the spinach pieces with the water adhering to the leaves in a large wok or skillet. Add oil and black pepper. Set aside until required.

In a bowl, combine chopped scallions, *very finely* chopped garlic and gingerroot, soy sauce, paprika, and chili powder.

When ready to proceed, toss spinach in skillet to coat with oil and black pepper. Set over *MEDIUM* heat, cover, and allow to steam while preparing the remainder of the dish.

Heat the 2 teaspoons oil in a second wok or skillet set over *MEDIUM-HIGH* heat. Add scallion mixture and stir-fry for several minutes. Add mushrooms and continue to stir-fry for several minutes. Add *tofu* chunks and green peas. Continue stir-frying until *tofu* begins to brown. Remove from heat.

Turn steamed spinach out onto a heated platter. Spoon stir-fried *tofu* mixture over.

Serve at once with rice. Bhutan red rice makes an especially beautiful presentation with this stir-fry.

Yields 6 servings
adequate for 4 people

Note: This recipe can be halved or doubled, when required.

1/6 SERVING – PROTEIN = 6.3 g.; FAT = 4.8 g.; CARBOHYDRATE = 5.8 g.; CALORIES = 85; CALORIES FROM FAT = 50%

EGGS AND PEAS WITH CURRIED TOMATO SAUCE
Ganga Tsey
TPT - 30 minutes

The tomato found its way from the Americas to Tibet too and in this dish only the curry and gingerroot in the sauce reminds you that you are a long way from home. Since the eggs and the curried tomato sauce can be prepared early in the day, a very nutritious lunch or supper can be on the table in no time at all.

EGGS AND PEAS WITH CURRIED TOMATO SAUCE (cont'd)

1 tablespoon safflower *or* sunflower oil
1 large onion—*finely* chopped
2 garlic cloves—*very finely* chopped
1 tablespoon *very finely* chopped fresh gingerroot

1 1/2 cups canned, *crushed* tomatoes
2 teaspoons HOMEMADE CURRY POWDER
  [see index] or commercially-available curry powder of choice
1/4 teaspoon salt

1/3 cup freshly shelled *or frozen* peas
2 scallions—trimmed, well-rinsed, and sliced

6 hard-cooked eggs—chilled, shelled, and halved

Set a shallow serving dish on a warming tray or in an oven set at *LOW*.

In a skillet set over *MEDIUM* heat, heat oil. Add *finely* chopped onion, and *very finely* chopped garlic and gingerroot. Sauté until onion is soft and translucent, *being careful not to all any of the vegetables to brown. Reduce heat to LOW*.

Add crushed tomatoes, curry powder, and salt. Cook, stirring frequently, for about 10 minutes.

Add peas and scallion slices. Allow to simmer for about 3 minutes more.

Place egg halves in the heated serving dish cut-side-up. Pour curried tomatoes sauce over the eggs. Set back on the warming tray or in the oven for about 5-7 minutes while finishing other dishes.

Serve hot.

Yields 6 servings
adequate for 4 people

Note: This dish can be halved, when required.

1/6 SERVING – PROTEIN = 8.3 g.; FAT = 8.1 g.; CARBOHYDRATE = 9.2 g.;
CALORIES = 139; CALORIES FROM FAT = 52%

TIBETAN STIR-FRIED CABBAGE, CARROTS, AND RED PEPPER
Logo Petse
TPT - 18 minutes

"Logo petse" is a cabbage dish to which meat is usually added. This vegetarian version is a delight as a side dish, a sort of stir-fried vegetable slaw. Tibetan cooks, not unlike cooks in neighboring China, give elaborate directions as to how the vegetables should be cut but there are no hard and fast rules.

1/2 cup chopped onion
1 large garlic clove—*very finely* chopped
1 tablespoon *very finely* chopped gingerroot

3 cups cabbage cut as for cabbage salad *or* in triangles if preferred
2 carrots—sliced into wide strips using a vegetable peeler and then cut into 1-inch rectangles

1 red bell pepper—cored, seeded, and sliced into thin strips

1 tablespoon *high-heat* safflower *or* sunflower oil
1 teaspoon HOMEMADE PAPRIKA *[see index] or* commercially-available Hungarian sweet paprika

2 tablespoons canned, *crushed* tomatoes

Prepare all vegetables and have in place.

In a wok or skillet set over *MEDIUM* heat, heat oil. Add paprika. Stir for a few seconds. Add chopped onion and *very finely* chopped garlic and gingerroot. Stir-fry until onion is soft and translucent, *being careful to allow none of the vegetables to brown.*

Add tomatoes. Stir.

Add cabbage and carrots slices. Cover and allow to steam for a minute or two. Stir.

Add red pepper strips. Stir for a minute or two. Turn into a heated serving dish.

Serve at once.

Yields 6 servings
adequate for 4 people

1/6 SERVING – PROTEIN = 1.3 g.; FAT = 2.4 g.; CARBOHYDRATE = 7.2 g.;
CALORIES = 52; CALORIES FROM FAT = 41

Asia–China / Tibet

BUDDHIST STIR-FRIED MUSHROOMS AND BAMBOO SHOOTS – "TWO WINTERS"

Tse Sesha

TPT - 58 minutes;
40 minutes = mushroom rehydration period

Straight from the winter larder shelves to the table, this provides an unusual "sauce" for grilled tofu. Sesha mushrooms are favored by Tibetans but I have found that shiitake or Chinese black mushrooms are worthy substitutes. We generally serve sautéed greens and a brightly-colored fruit garnish, such as mandarin orange sections or kiwi wedges, to brighten the presentation.

18 small, dried, Chinese black mushrooms (*shiitake*)*

1/2 can (5 ounces) bamboo shoots*

1/2 cup TIBETAN VEGETABLE BROTH (*Tukpa*)
  [see index]
2 teaspoons corn starch
1 tablespoon *tamari* soy sauce*

2 teaspoons vegetable oil

1 teaspoon sesame oil*

In a bowl, soak dried black mushrooms in water to cover for about 40 minutes, or until soft and pliable.

Meanwhile, cut bamboo shoots into pieces about the same size as the mushrooms selected. Soak in *cold* water to desalinate.

Drain softened mushrooms and cut stems from each. *(Reserve stems for soup stock.)*

Drain bamboo shoot pieces well.

In a small bowl, combine stock, corn starch, and soy sauce. Stir well and set aside.

In a wok set over *MEDIUM-HIGH* heat, heat vegetable oil. When hot, add drained mushrooms and bamboo shoot pieces. Stir-fry for about 2 minutes until *thoroughly* heated through.

While stirring, add sesame oil.

Stir sauce ingredients again to keep corn starch in suspension. Add to stir-fried vegetables and cook, stirring constantly, until sauce thickens.

Turn into heated serving dish and keep warm on a warming tray or in warm oven, if necessary, until served.

Yields 6 servings
adequate for 4 people

Notes: *These items are available in Asian groceries, specialty food stores, and in many natural food stores.

When required, this recipe is easily doubled.

1/6 SERVING – PROTEIN = 2.4 g.; FAT = 2.2 g.; CARBOHYDRATE = 10.1 g.;
CALORIES = 69; CALORIES FROM FAT = 28%

Asia–China / Tibet

GREEN ONION SESAME SKILLET BREAD
Tsey Paley

TPT - 1 hour and 45 minutes;
1 hour = gluten resting period

We visited several food stores in Moscow during our visit in December 1983 and marveled that sprouting onions were for sale. The base of the onion could still add flavor to a stew or soup but the green sprouts offered the fresh taste of scallions to the cook. When an onion sprouts in my larder, it is only an opportunity, an opportunity to add green onions to a salad. I have also found that grocery store scallions can be planted which avoids the slimy package of over-the-hill expensive organic scallions in the vegetable drawer of the refrigerator. I soak those that I am not using in a carafe for a few days to allow the roots to grow. Then I transplant them to the herb garden where they thrive providing me an endless supply of green tails when I need a bit of fresh onion flavor The first time I made this bread I was so delighted at the taste and texture that I wondered why I had not tried it before. Our trips into New York City's Chinatown always included a trip to a favorite bakery. The children wanted almond cookies and honey bows and although I saw the green onion loaves in the case, browned and salt incrusted, I never tried them. All these decades later a recipe fell into my hands. I made the skillet breads, popular in both China and Tibet, and have been hooked ever since.

1/3 cup unbleached white flour
1/3 cup whole wheat *pastry* flour
2 teaspoons sesame oil
1 tablespoon baking powder
Pinch salt
1/4 cup *ice* water

2 tablespoons rice flour—brown or white

1/4 cup *finely* chopped scallions—*both white and green portions*—well-rinsed
Pinch salt

In the work bowl of the food processor fitted with a steel knife, combine white flour, whole wheat *pastry* flour, sesame oil, baking powder, and salt. Add *ice* water. Pulse until the ingredients form a dough. Turn out onto a lightly floured surface. Knead until there is no evidence of stickiness and the dough is silky smooth. Cover with a cotton tea towel and allow the gluten in the dough to rest for about 1 hour.

Knead dough again until smooth. Spread rice flour across work surface. Roll dough out into a large 17-inch square to a thickness of about 1/8 inch.

Scatter *finely* chopped scallions over the pastry. Sprinkle with salt. Roll pastry jelly-roll style. Pinch ends and seam. Using the palms of your hand, work the dough into a long rope by rolling it back and forth. Lay the rope down on your work surface and coil it around itself. Tuck the end under. Using a rolling pin roll the coil into a nine-inch circle.

Spray a non-stick-coated griddle or large skillet with non-stick lecithin spray coating. Preheat over *MEDIUM-HIGH* heat. *Carefully* transfer the bread onto the hot surface and cook until lightly browned—about 2 minutes. *Firmly press down any areas that bubble up.* Turn bread over and brown the remaining side. Remove to a paper towel-covered plate and cover to keep it warm until you are ready to serve.

Serve warm. Cut into six wedges to serve.

Yields 6 servings
adequate for 3-4 people

Note: This recipe can easily be doubled or tripled, when required. After you have rolled it out and added the scallion pieces, divide it into two balls, if you are doubling, or into three balls, if you are tripling. Form each loaf separately.

1/6 SERVING – PROTEIN = 1.6 g.; FAT = 2.5 g.; CARBOHYDRATE = 12.0 g.;
CALORIES = 76; CALORIES FROM FAT = 30%

Asia–China / **Tibet**

TIBETAN *DAIKON* AND RED RADISH PICKLES
Tsang Lafu

TPT - 3 days and 26 minutes;
3 days = pickling period

Radishes are the first nibble that our garden offers in the spring. The seeds germinate quickly and grow to maturity in a few weeks. This quick maturation is an enormous advantage in Tibet, Nepal, and Bhutan where the growing season is short and food for winter eating must be a consideration of each and every acre planted. Many cuisines in Asia feature pickled vegetables that are not unlike the vegetable pickles of northern Europe that I learned to preserve.

1/2 teaspoon crushed red pepper
1/4 teaspoon *whole* mixed peppercorns—red, black, and white
2 tablespoons rice wine vinegar
1/2 teaspoon salt
1/4 teaspoon sugar

One 8-ounce *daikon* radish—about 6 inches long

1 bunch red radishes—leaves and tap root removed and well-rinsed

Water

Sterilize two pint canning jars, two lids, and two rings.

In each jar, put 1/4 teaspoon crushed red pepper, 1/8 teaspoon mixed peppercorns, 1 tablespoon rice wine vinegar, 1/4 teaspoon salt, and 1/8 teaspoon sugar. Set aside briefly.

Trim and peel the *daikon* radish by cutting it into a rectangle. Thinly slice the radish into crosswise rectangles. Rinse well and divide between the two jars.

Slice the red radishes crosswise into *thin* circular slices. Rinse well and divide between the two jars.

Add water to cover the radish slices. Seal with lids and rings. Slosh to encourage the salt, the crushed red pepper, and the peppercorns to distribute evenly.

Place on a window sill for three days. Slosh occasionally.

Once the pickling period is completed, keep refrigerated. These pickles keep well for several weeks in the refrigerator.

Yields 6 servings per pintful

Note: This recipe can be halved, if you do not think you will be able to eat them up in a month.

1/12 SERVING – PROTEIN = 0.3 g.; FAT = 0.5 g.; CARBOHYDRATE = 1.3 g.;
CALORIES = 10; CALORIES FROM FAT = 45%

TIBETAN YOGURT CONDIMENT WITH FRESH CORIANDER, GARLIC, AND *CHILIES*
Sonam Penzom Sibeh

TPT - 5 minutes

This condiment is often made with chopped tomatoes, rather than yogurt, but I am very partial to this version because it adds just a bit more protein to a meal. Unlike garlic–yogurt sauces found in the Middle East, this sauce has the bright taste of the fresh coriander (cilantro) and a kick from the chilies that one would never find served in the countries of the eastern Mediterranean. That said though, this condiment is a wonderful spread for a pita sandwich.

1 cup fresh coriander (*cilantro*) leaves—well-rinsed and coarsely chopped
2 tablespoons chopped mild green *chilies*
1/2 teaspoon crushed red pepper flakes, or to taste
2 large garlic cloves—coarsely chopped
1/2 teaspoon salt, or to taste
3 tablespoons water

1 cup PLAIN YOGURT *[see index]* or commercially-available plain yogurt

In the work bowl of food processor, fitted with steel knife, or in the container of the electric blender, combine chopped fresh coriander (*cilantro*), chopped green *chilies*, crushed red pepper flakes, chopped garlic, salt, and water. Process until all ingredients are evenly chopped.

TIBETAN YOGURT CONDIMENT WITH FRESH CORIANDER, GARLIC, AND *CHILIES* (cont'd)

Add yogurt and process until well-combined but only to a stage where bits of green and red are still visible. Turn into a small serving bowl. Refrigerate until required.

Yields 1 1/4 cupfuls

1/20 SERVING (per tablespoonful) –
PROTEIN = 0.7 g.; FAT = 0.2 g.; CARBOHYDRATE = 0.9 g.;
CALORIES = 9; CALORIES FROM FAT = 20%

Notes: The flavor of the *cilantro* fades quickly so I never keep this sauce in the refrigerator for more than three or four days.

The recipe, however, can be halved or doubled, when required.

TIBETAN CHEESE AND *CHILI* SAUCE
Churu Sibeh
TPT - 12 minutes

Many years ago I stumbled upon a Tibetan recipe which called for blue cheese. I, quite naturally, suspected that it was the westernization of a recipe but was amazed to find that blue-veined cheese is combined with garlic and chilies to create a condiment unique to Tibet. The taste is quite extraordinary cheese It reminded me somewhat of the famed chilies and cheese dish so popular in Bhutan but it did not contain whole chilies and feta cheese.

3 tablespoons *chili* garlic sauce*
2 garlic cloves—*finely* chopped

6 tablespoons blue-veined cheese such as blue *or* Gorgonzola
6 tablespoons cup *hot* water

In a stone mortar, combine *chili* garlic sauce and *finely* chopped garlic. Using a pestle, grind until no evidence of the garlic can be seen.

Add cheese. Continue grinding until combined with the garlic mixture. Then, pour a little *hot* water into the cheese mixture. Continue grinding until well mixed. Continue mixing and adding water until you have a relatively smooth sauce. Turn into a small serving bowl. Refrigerate until required.

Yields 9 tablespoonfuls

1/9 SERVING (i. e., per tablespoonful) –
PROTEIN = 1.1 g.; FAT = 1.4 g.; CARBOHYDRATE = 0.3 g.;
CALORIES = 18; CALORIES FROM FAT = 70%

Notes: **Chili* garlic sauce is commercially-available from several food companies that specialize in the export of Asian foods to the United States. You can easily find one that suits your taste. Check the international aisle of your grocery store and any Asian groceries in your area.

The recipe can be halved or doubled, when required.

TIBETAN SWEET CREAMED RICE WITH CARDAMOM
Khir
TPT - 8 hours and 14 minutes;
6 hours = refrigeration period

If you have ever eaten in an Indian restaurant, you have no doubt eaten the Indian version of this dessert, kheer. Tibetans are also fond of this rice dessert and their name suggests that there is a close connection between their khir and the Indian specialty kheer. However, there are several significant differences. Tibetans sauté basmati rice in butter before adding it to the simmering milk base and coconut is added near the end of the cooking. Our version of this classic rice pudding is a less sweet and less rich dessert than that generally made by Tibetans where a combination of cream and whole milk are used to prepare this sweet.

TIBETAN SWEET CREAMED RICE WITH CARDAMOM (cont'd)

1 quart *two-percent* milk
3/4 cup light cream *or* half and half
6 tablespoons sugar

3 tablespoons butter
6 tablespoons brown *basmati* rice

3 cardamom pods
3 tablespoons shredded coconut—fresh *or* desiccated
1/4 cup *preservative-free dark* raisins

In the top half of a double boiler set over direct *MEDIUM* heat combine milk, cream, and sugar. Bring to the boil, stirring frequently.

Meanwhile, in a non-stick-coated skillet set over *MEDIUM* heat, melt butter. Add rice and cook, stirring constantly, for about 3 minutes.

Add to simmering milk–butter–sugar mixture in top half of double boiler and place over *boiling* water. Allow to simmer, *stirring frequently*, until the rice is soft and the liquid is reduced—about 1 hour and 30 minutes. *Check occasionally to be sure that water in bottom of double boiler has not boiled away.*

Meanwhile, open cardamom pods *over a mortar* and remove the tiny black seeds. Remove and discard any pieces of the pods which might drop into the mortar. Using a pestle, crush the seeds. Add to rice mixture with coconut and raisins. Cook stirring frequently until the mixture has thickened to your liking—another 20-30 minutes, or so. Pour into a colorful, shallow serving bowl. Refrigerate for 6-8 hours or overnight.

Serve well-chilled.

Yields 6 servings

Note: This recipe may be halved or doubled, when required.

1/6 SERVING – PROTEIN = 7.5 g.; FAT = 18.5 g.; CARBOHYDRATE = 42.9 g.;
CALORIES = 370; CALORIES FROM FAT = 45%

TIBETAN BAKED CHEESE BALLS IN CREAM SAUCE
Rasbari

TPT - 9 hours and 13 minutes;
8 hours = chilling period

It was great fun to inform the family that we were having rasbari for dessert and watch the looks on their faces when these creamy white Tibetan cheese balls were served. Trans-lingual homonyms aside, with the availability of ricotta and cream cheeses to substitute for Tibetan cheeses these lovely, sweet cheese balls are easily made and very, very delicious. I have made this specialty from the "the top of the world" in several ways, including making my own cheese and boiling them like dumplings as they do in Nepal, but this Tibetan recipe, in which the cheese balls are baked, is far and away my favorite.

1 cup *part-skimmed milk ricotta* cheese
4 ounces *fat-free* cream cheese

1/3 cup *fat-free* sweetened condensed milk
6 tablespoons sugar
6 tablespoons unbleached white flour

1 1/2 cups light cream *or* half and half
1/2 teaspoon ground cardamom

1 teaspoon rose water
1 tablespoon slivered *preservative-free* almonds

Preheat oven to 325 degrees F. Prepare a 9-inch *au gratin, quiche* dish, or deep-dish pie plate by lining with culinary parchment. Coat the parchment with non-stick lecithin spray coating for baking.

Using the electric mixer fitted with paddle, work *ricotta* and cream cheeses together until well-combined and smooth.

Add sweetened condensed milk, sugar, and flour. Mix until a stiff, smooth mixture forms.

Using two soup spoons, gather cheese mixture into 1-inch balls and place them in the prepared baking dish side-by-side, circle-within-circle. Bake in preheated oven for about 30 minutes, or until lightly browned. Transfer to a wide-based serving bowl.

In a saucepan set over *MEDIUM* heat, combine cream and ground cardamom. Cook, stirring frequently, until the milk has thickened to a syrupy consistency.

Asia–China / Tibet

TIBETAN BAKED CHEESE BALLS IN CREAM SAUCE (cont'd)

Add rose water. Pour over cheese balls. Sprinkle with slivered almonds. Refrigerate for 8 hours, or overnight.

Serve chilled into small desert dishes. Refrigerate leftovers.

Yields about 24 cheese balls
adequate for 6 people

Note: This recipe can be halved or doubled, when required.

1/6 SERVING – PROTEIN = 10.9 g.; FAT = 8.3 g.; CARBOHYDRATE = 36.0 g.;
CALORIES = 269; CALORIES FROM FAT = 27%

CEREMONIAL SWEET, SAFFRON RICE
Deysi

TPT - 2 hours and 40 minutes;
2 hours = raisin soaking period

Also known as dresti, dresil, desi, and dreysi, this sweet rice is traditionally served on the morning of Losar (New Year's), at weddings, and as a welcome-home dish when someone is returning from a long trip. This is a breakfast option for me. I love to take a bowlful and sit in the arbor up on the ridge at the back of our property and just enjoy the morning. It is, however, a bit sweet for some people's taste, albeit far less sweet than are the sweet, commercial cereals. When served for dessert, the response at our table has always been, "Oh, this is not a rice pudding, is it?" Short grain basmati rice is the preferred base for this dish but we rarely find the short-grained variety available in our grocery stores so I generally use Japanese short grain rice.

1/2 cup *preservative-free dark* **raisins***
1 cup *boiling* **water**

1/2 cup dry Japanese short grain rice
1 cup *boiling* **water**

1/4 cup butter—*melted*
1/4 cup *light* **brown sugar**
Pinch saffron threads

1/4 cup chopped, *unsalted, raw preservative-free*
  cashews

In a small bowl or measuring cup, combine raisins and 1 cupful *boiling* water. Set aside at room temperature and allow the raisins to plump for about 2 hours. Drain thoroughly.

In a saucepan set over *LOW* heat, combine rice and the remaining 1 cupful *boiling* water. Cover and allow to cook for about 20-25 minutes, or until the liquid has evaporated or has been absorbed by the rice. The rice grains should be *soft, but dry and separate*. Remove from heat.

In a small saucepan set over *LOW-MEDIUM* heat, combine *melted* butter, brown sugar, and saffron threads. Cook, stirring constantly, until sugar has dissolved and the butter mixture has turned a bright yellow. Add to cooked rice. Stir to coat the rice grains with the sweet butter mixture.

Add chopped cashews. Stir to integrate.

Using a meatball or ice cream scoop, place a scoop of the *deysi* in the bottom of each of six rice bowls or soup bowls.

Serve warm.

Yields 6 individual servings

Notes: *If you use bleached, golden raisins, which we do not, this dish would be more traditional.

This recipe can be halved or doubled, when required.

1/6 SERVING – PROTEIN = 2.8 g.; FAT = 11.9 g.; CARBOHYDRATE = 39.0 g.;
CALORIES = 265; CALORIES FROM FAT = 40%

Indonesia

Dana Toba is an enormous lake on the Indonesian island of Sumatra that lies at an elevation of 2,953 feet above sea level and which is 1,666 feet at its deepest point. The lake is the caldera of a great supervolcano that erupted about 73,000 years ago (± 4,000 years) and is said to have been the largest explosive eruption anywhere on the planet in the last twenty-five million years. It led to a volcanic winter which lasted for about six to ten years, a cooling period of close to 1,000 years confirmed by ice core and ash samples in Greenland, and the near extinction of the human species. It is theorized that human evolution was seriously slowed as the remaining population of perhaps 1,000 to 10,000 became responsible for the survival and success of the human species. The island nation of Indonesia is the result of the volcanoes formed in the subduction zones between the Eurasian and Indo-Australian tectonic plates. Part of the Pacific Ring of Fire, Indonesia is composed of about 17,508 islands. There are thirty-five active volcanoes on Sumatra; there are forty-five active volcanoes and some twenty small craters and cones on the small island of Java, with Krakatau, which erupted violently in 1883 and last erupted in 2001, in the Sunda Strait between Sumatra and Java along with its parasitic cones Anak Krakatau, Serturn, Panjan, and Rakata. It is estimated that there are presently about one hundred and fifty active volcanoes in the archipelago nation.

During the 1980s several volcanic eruptions in Indonesia sent us to the beaches of Long Island during the summer at sunset to experience the extraordinarily dramatic sunsets resulting from those eruptions as the particulates circled the planet.

Homo erectus, popularized as "Java Man," inhabited this archipelago between five hundred thousand and two million years ago. As species recovered after the extinction and cooling period, animals and humans again found these fertile volcanic islands. About 2000 BC a group of people, referred to as Austronesian, began to migrate from the island we know as Taiwan and pushed the indigenous Melanesian peoples to the far eastern islands. During the first century AD trade and Hindu missionary work brought Indian culture and spices to the islands and by the seventh century Indonesia was actively involved in world trade absorbing, as it traded, the foods, the religions, and political models of those with whom they traded. Dutch influence, first in the form of the Dutch East India Company (VOC), formed in 1602 and dissolved in 1800, and then as the colonial ruler of the Dutch East Indies, is still apparent in architecture and in the cuisine. Dutch rule ended with the occupation by the Japanese during World War II and their inability to regain a foothold after the war. Indonesian independence was formally declared in 1949.

Geographic isolation has led to an enormous list of endemic species putting the Indonesia archipelago second only to Australia in this regard; thirty-six percent of its 1,531 avian species and thirty-nine percent of its mammalian species are endemic. That is, however, changing as the population increases accompanied by rapid industrialization. Indonesia is the fourth most populous nation on Earth, with a population of about 238 million people of three hundred identifiable ethnic groups, with over eighty-six percent of that population of the Islamic faith. The intensely volcanic island of Java is the most densely populated island on Earth.

Indonesians honor mountains as the home of the ancestors and the gods. On special occasions a buffet table is offered on which a cone-shaped mound of steamed plain rice or steamed rice with coconut milk takes a central and honored position. The mountain of rice, symbolizing the holy mountain, is surrounded by choice dishes to please the guests, to celebrate the occasion, and to show the abundance affordable by the host. On a smaller scale this makes a rather exotic first course with which you can be very creative.

Asia – Indonesia

(Mountain-Shaped) Indonesian Rice Cooked with Coconut Milk
Nasi Udak
surrounded by an assortment of dishes:

Steamed and Seasoned Vegetables
Urap

Roasted Peanuts

Pickled Eggs
Atjar Telur

Shredded Omelet

Corn Fritters
Perkedel Jagung

Rice Crackers

Mango Slices

| Orange Juice | Guava Juice | Mango Juice |
| *Jus Jeruk* | *Jus Jambu* | *Jus Mangga* |

~

Cauliflower and Noodle Soup
Sop mie Bloemkool

~~~~~~~~~~~~~~~~~~~~~

Fruit and Vegetable Salad
Rujak
with
Peanut Butter Salad Dressing
Kuah Selada Kacang Tanah

~~~~~~~~~~

Eggplant and Brown Rice
Masak Djeruk Terong Nasi

Baked Acorn Squash with Chutney
Labu Sambal

Braised Chinese Black Mushrooms with Garlic
Tumis Djamur Kering

Sweet Pineapple Relish   **Sweet Soy Sauce** *[see index]*
Petjili Nanas   *Kecap Manis*

~~~~~~~~~~~~~~~~~~~~

Avocado – Ice Cream Dessert
Eskrim Pokat

Asia–Indonesia

INDONESIAN RICE COOKED WITH COCONUT MILK
Nasi Udak

TPT - 1 hour and 8 minutes

Traditionally "lontong" rice was cooked in banana leaves but this method of par-boiling and then steaming after an absorption period is a typical Javanese cooking method and an easy route in the modern western kitchen. Cooking rice in cheesecloth bags is another modern Indonesian procedure for cooking rice which you might like to try.

1 cup dry Japanese short grain white rice
    —do not use precooked/converted variety
1 1/2 cups *light, preservative-free* **coconut milk***
1 salam leaf *or* **1 curry leaf, if available**
Pinch salt

Home-grown, spray-free **daylilies, for garnish, if desired**

In a saucepan set over *MEDIUM* heat, combine rice, coconut milk, salam or curry leaf, and salt. Allow to come to the boil. *Reduce heat to LOW.* Remove from heat, cover and allow to cook for 20 minutes, or until coconut milk has been absorbed.

Set up a bamboo steamer. Line steamer basket with aluminum foil.

Spoon rice onto the aluminum foil. Cover and steam for about 25-30 minutes.

Turn rice out into the center of a platter or tray onto banana leaves, if you have them. Mold it into a cone shape.

Serve at once, garnished with daylilies.

Yields 6 servings
adequate for 4-6 people

Notes: *Canned coconut milk is available in most grocery stores in either the international section or beverage section. Leftover coconut milk can be frozen.

This recipe may be doubled, when required.

1/6 SERVING – PROTEIN = 3.3 g.; FAT = 0.4 g.; CARBOHYDRATE = 32.1 g.;
CALORIES = 165; CALORIES FROM FAT = 2%

INDONESIAN PICKLED EGGS
Atjar Telur

TPT - 2 hours and 5 minutes;
    1 hour = room temperature marination period;
    1 hour = refrigerator marination period

When sliced with an egg slicer, these eggs make a particularly attractive presentation as part of salad or as an appetizer. The taste is subtle, but exciting.

1 cup *boiling* **water**
1/2 cup rice wine vinegar
3 slices gingerroot
1 small onion—sliced
1 tablespoon sugar
1 teaspoon ground turmeric
1 hot, red pepper—of choice—cut lengthwise
    or **1/2 teaspoon** *jalapeño chili* **sauce***

6 large eggs—hard-cooked and shelled

In a saucepan set over *MEDIUM* heat, combine *boiling* water, vinegar, gingerroot slices, onion slices, sugar, ground turmeric, and hot pepper or *jalapeño* sauce. Stir to combine. Bring to the boil. Remove from heat.

Using a sharp knife, cut a deep 1/2-inch cross into the top of each *shelled* egg. Add eggs to marinade mixture and set on a protected surface at room temperature for about 1 hour. Turn eggs frequently to insure even marination. Transfer eggs in the marinade to the refrigerator and continue marinating and turning eggs for at least 1 more hour. Drain marinade from eggs.

Serve at room temperature or chilled, as preferred. Serve as an appetizer or as an accompaniment to other dishes as part of a main course offering. INDONESIAN SWEET PINEAPPLE RELISH *(Petjili Nanas)* [see recipe which follows] accompanies these eggs well.

Yields 6 pickled eggs
adequate for 4 people

Asia – **Indonesia**

INDONESIAN PICKLED EGGS (cont'd)

Note: *Jalapeño* sauce is available in Hispanic groceries, food specialty stores, and in most grocery stores throughout the Southwest.

1/6 SERVING (i. e., per egg) –
PROTEIN = 6.4 g.; FAT = 5.7 g.; CARBOHYDRATE = 0.0 g.;
CALORIES = 78; CALORIES FROM FAT = 66%

INDONESIAN CAULIFLOWER AND NOODLE SOUP
Sop mie Bloemkool
TPT - 41 minutes

A serving of this white soup with a garnish of chopped fresh coriander is a beautiful presentation to set before adventurous diners. Although some dishes we have tasted from the various cuisines of Southeast Asia could cauterize your mouth and throat and deter you from even considering the next course, the seasoning in this soup is mild, clearly reflective of the Dutch colonial period which most probably accounts for both the cauliflower and the noodles also.

Note: Be sure to choose a white cauliflower to make this soup and not the yellow cauliflower, now increasingly available.

1 tablespoon peanut oil
2 garlic cloves—*finely* **chopped**
1 small onion—*finely* **chopped**
2 1/2 teaspoons ground cumin
1 1/2 teaspoons ground coriander
1/2 teaspoon salt
1/4 teaspoon freshly ground *white* **pepper, or to taste**

7 cups VEGETARIAN WHITE STOCK *[see index]**
6 cups (about 1 pound) *uniformly-cut white*
   cauliflower florets

1/4 pound dry, *fine* **egg noodles**

1 tablespoon *finely* **chopped fresh coriander**
   (*cilantro***), for garnish**

In a kettle or a large wok set over *MEDIUM* heat, heat oil. Add *finely* chopped garlic and onion, ground cumin, ground coriander, salt, and *white* pepper. Sauté until onion is soft and translucent, *being careful to allow neither the onion nor the garlic to brown.*

Add stock and cauliflower florets. Simmer, stirring occasionally, for about 20 minutes, or until the cauliflower is *crisp-tender.*

Add dry egg noodles and continue to cook until noodles are done—about 8-10 minutes.

Turn into a heated soup tureen. Serve into heated soup bowls, garnishing each serving with a sprinkling of *finely* chopped fresh coriander (*cilantro*).

Yields about 10 cupfuls

Notes: *Be sure that you used a light-colored vegetable *stock made without tomatoes.* The reddish color of a stock made with tomatoes would ruin the look of this soup.

When required, this recipe may be halved or doubled.

This soup can not be successfully frozen.

1/10 SERVING (i. e., per cupful) –
PROTEIN = 3.4 g; FAT = 2.2 g; CARBOHYDRATE = 12.1 g;
CALORIES = 74; CALORIES FROM FAT = 27%

Asia–Indonesia

INDONESIAN FRUIT AND VEGETABLE SALAD
Rujak
TPT - 10 minutes

"Rujack" is a widely popular salad in Southeast Asia. Mayalsians and Singaporian, who call it "Rojack," as well as Indonesians add their own touches with ingredients differing from country to country, from home to home, from street vender to street vender. We occasionally add beancurd, potatoes, or sweetpotatoes to this vegetarian version when it becomes a main course salad. I have seen recipes in which sliced hard-cooked eggs, sliced fish cakes, cuttlefish, octopus, sea cucumber, and prawns are added but the most unusual addition that I have seen, not tasted but seen, is the addition of slices of buffalo or cow lips. Jicama is a common ingredient and when I can find a small one, I do include it. Asian pears give a similar texture and their sweetness contributes another element to a salad that is full of texture and surprises. It is like an Italian composed salad—every forkful is different and interesting. I do not use hot peppers nor, of course, do I use "hae ko" sauce, a prawn sauce popularly used to make this salad. Hot peppers instead of Szechwan (Sichuan) chili paste can be added to the dressing.

1 Asian pear *or* a small *jicama*—peeled and *finely* sliced
1 small cucumber—peeled and *finely* sliced
1 *unripe or green* mango—peeled and *finely* sliced
1 *carambola* (starfruit)—well-washed, trimmed, and *finely* sliced
1 cup fresh pineapple chunks—each chunk sliced into 3 slices
1/2 *pomelo or* grapefruit, as preferred—separated into segments
1 cup fresh soybean sprouts—trimmed of any brown ends, well-rinsed and well-drained
1 tablespoon fresh mint—well-washed and slivered
2 tablespoons chopped, roasted peanuts

7 tablespoons INDONESIAN PEANUT BUTTER SALAD DRESSING *(Kuah Selada Kacang Tanah)* [see recipe which follows]

Scatter slices of Asian pear or *jicama*, cucumber, mango, *carambola*, and pineapple onto a large serving platter. Scatter *pomelo* or grapefruit sections over the fruit and vegetable slices. Scatter the soybean sprouts, fresh mint slivers, and chopped peanuts over all.

Serve at once with the peanut butter salad dressing.

Yields 8 servings
adequate for 6 people

Note: This recipe can be halved, when required. Since leftovers do not keep well, be sure that you will be consuming this at one sitting.

1/8 SERVING (with about 3/4 tablespoonful dressing) –
PROTEIN = 3.0 g.; FAT = 4.3 g.; CARBOHYDRATE = 1.4 g.;
CALORIES = 99; CALORIES FROM FAT = 39%

INDONESIAN PEANUT BUTTER SALAD DRESSING
Kuah Selada Kacang Tanah
TPT - 3 minutes

By making this salad dressing for an Indonesian meal, the essential tastes of Indonesia can be added to a meal where a more Western, less Southeast Asian, menu format is planned. Since we often make a meal out of a complex tossed salad mixture, to which we add well-drained tofu or cheese and toasted nuts, this dressing is a mainstay in our summer menu plans.

3 tablespoons freshly ground, *unsalted, additive-free, smooth* peanut butter—*brought to room temperature*
1 tablespoon tamarind paste
3 tablespoons rice wine vinegar
1 tablespoon *tamari* soy sauce
1/2 teaspoon sesame oil
1 teaspoon *very finely* chopped fresh gingerroot
1/8 teaspoon *Szechwan (Sichuan) chili* paste

In a mixing bowl, combine peanut butter, tamarind paste, vinegar, soy sauce, sesame oil, *very finely* chopped gingerroot, and *chili* paste. Using a wire whisk, whisk until *thoroughly* combined.

Yields about 7 tablespoonfuls

Asia–Indonesia

INDONESIAN PEANUT BUTTER SALAD DRESSING (cont'd)

Notes: *Szechwan (Sichuan) chili* paste is a blend of hot peppers, salt, and garlic in the form of a thick *chili* ketchup. It is generally available in Asian groceries and in many food specialty stores. *Be judicious* in the addition of this condiment.

This recipe can be doubled, when required.

1/7 SERVING (i. e., per tablespoonful) –
PROTEIN = 1.4 g.; FAT = 3.5 g.; CARBOHYDRATE = 2.2 g.;
CALORIES = 44; CALORIES FROM FAT = 72%

INDONESIAN EGGPLANT AND BROWN RICE
Masak Djeruk Terang Nasi
TPT - 39 minutes

The influence of India is unmistakable in the foods and spicing recognized as traditional in Indonesia. Considerable vegetarianism reflects the Indian influence also introduced to the islands through the religious practices of Buddhism and Hinduism long before Islam became the principle religion. This one-dish vegan meal is a flavorful alternative for my menu planning when I have turned up a nice firm eggplant. It is one of the first hot dishes we turn to in the fall and rather than serving the eggplant in coconut milk over the rice, which would be more traditional, we add the rice to the mélange and serve it with flatbread or lavash and fruit. We even use this as a filling for a wrap.

3 tablespoons peanut oil
1 medium-sized eggplant—*peeled* and cut into 1-inch cubes to yield about 4 cupfuls
1 large leek—*white part only*—trimmed, *well-cleaned,* and sliced into crosswise 1/4-inch slices
3 garlic cloves—*very finely* chopped

2 tablespoons water

1/2 cup coarsely chopped *raw* peanuts
1 tablespoon freshly grated gingerroot
1 tablespoon tamarind paste*
Dried red pepper flakes, to taste
1/2 teaspoon sesame seeds
1/2 teaspoon coriander seeds

1 cup *sulfite-free* coconut cream
Salt, to taste
Freshly ground black pepper, to taste

1 cup *cooked,* long grain brown rice

In a large skillet, with cover, set over *MEDIUM* heat, heat oil. Add eggplant cubes, leek slices, and *very finely* chopped garlic. Sauté for about 7 minutes.

Add water. Stir to integrate water and remove any bits that have adhered to the pan surface.

Add peanuts, grated gingerroot, tamarind paste, red pepper flakes, and sesame and coriander seeds. Stir to mix well.

Add coconut milk, salt, and pepper. Allow to come to the boil, while stirring. *Reduce heat to LOW,* cover, and simmer for about 20 minutes, or until leeks are very soft and transparent. Stir occasionally to prevent sticking.

Add *cooked* rice. Allow to heat through for a minute or two. Turn into a heated serving bowl.

Serve at once.

Yields 6 servings
adequate for 4 people

Notes: *Asian groceries and food specialty stores generally stock the product as, of course, do stores that specialize in Indian food items. The pulp can also be extracted from fresh tamarinds or from preserved tamarind, available in compressed cakes, which must be soaked in warm water until soft. These are not extensively available in the United States.

This recipe can be halved, when required.

1/6 SERVING – PROTEIN = 3.7 g.; FAT = 16.7 g.; CARBOHYDRATE = 45.1 g.;
CALORIES = 352; CALORIES FROM FAT = 43%

Asia–Indonesia

INDONESIAN BAKED ACORN SQUASH WITH CHUTNEY
Labu Sambal

TPT - 1 hour and 8 minutes
[slow cooker: 3 hours at HIGH]

Squashes and pumpkins are very much a part of Indonesian cuisine. Maybe our acorn squash is not the same winter-type squash available in Jakarta, but we can enjoy our acorn squash for dinner tonight just the way an Indonesian family might be enjoying their particular variety of squash a few hours from now.

2 medium-large acorn squash—well-washed

1/4 cup *melted* butter
1/4 cup Major Grey's chutney

Preheat oven to 350 degrees F.

Cut squash in half lengthwise and remove seeds. Place cut-side-down on a jelly roll pan or in a shallow baking pan with about 1/2-inch of water. Bake in preheated 350 degree F. oven for about 30 minutes. Turn each squash half cut-side-up and continue baking for an additional 30 minutes. Remove from oven.

Combine *melted* butter and chutney. Divide among the four squash halves.

Serve at once.

Yields 4 individual servings

Notes: This recipe can be halved or doubled, when required.

If you are halving this recipe, and therefore using just one acorn squash, the slow cooker is a convenient tool. Set the halves, cut-side-up, into about 1 inch of *boiling* water. Cover and allow to steam at *HIGH* for about 3 hours.

1/4 SERVING (with 1/2 teaspoonful cheese) –
PROTEIN = 2.9 g.; FAT = 11.5 g.; CARBOHYDRATE = 33.0 g.;
CALORIES = 235; CALORIES FROM FAT = 44%

INDONESIAN BRAISED CHINESE BLACK MUSHROOMS WITH GARLIC
Tumis Djamur Kering

TPT - 1 hour and 7 minutes;
30 minutes = dried mushroom soaking period

We are very fond of the earthy taste that dried mushrooms give to a dish and, as a consequence, often make sauces and soups from those that we have dried, adding a few of the more exotic varieties to the more common. The first time I tested this Indonesian mushroom dish, I plated a few as dramatic garnish beside a slice of a humble lentil loaf with a simple mushroom gravy and fresh asparagus spears. It was such a beautiful combination that I still remember.

24 small dried *shiitake* or Chinese black mushrooms*
***Warm* water**

2 teaspoons peanut oil *or* other vegetable oil, of choice
2 large garlic cloves—*thinly* sliced

1 cup *boiling* water
1 teaspoon *light* brown sugar
1/2 teaspoon ground cinnamon
Salt, to taste
Freshly ground black pepper, to taste

Soak dried, *shiitake* mushrooms in *warm* water to cover for 30 minutes. When soft, drain well and cut off hard stems. Set aside.

In a skillet with cover or in a wok set over *MEDIUM* heat, heat oil. Add *thinly* sliced garlic and stir-fry for about 1 minute, *being careful not to allow garlic to brown*.

Add *boiling* water, brown sugar, ground cinnamon, salt, black pepper, and *reconstituted* mushrooms. Reduce heat to *LOW*. Cover and simmer for 30 minutes.

Using a skimmer, remove mushrooms to a heated serving bowl. Keep warm on a *warming tray* until ready to serve.

Yields 6 servings
adequate for 4 people

INDONESIAN BRAISED CHINESE BLACK MUSHROOMS WITH GARLIC (cont'd)

Notes: *Dried Chinese black, *shiitake* mushrooms are available in Asian markets and food specialty stores. Fresh shiitake mushrooms can be substituted if available and if preferred; they will not require soaking. Be sure the fresh mushrooms are well-washed and that the stems have been removed.

This recipe can be halved or doubled, when required.

1/6 SERVING – PROTEIN = 2.2 g.; FAT = 1.4 g.; CARBOHYDRATE = 11.1 g.;
CALORIES = 66; CALORIES FROM FAT = 19%

INDONESIAN SWEET PINEAPPLE RELISH
Petjili Nanas
TPT - 17 minutes

In Indonesian kitchens, fresh hot, red peppers are fried with the onions to make this petjili or sweet relish, and you may prefer to use them too. We fine jalapeño sauce or Tabasco sauce more convenient and more to our " less tolerant Western taste" preference. The pineapple is a smashing sensation to pit against the hot sauce and tempering it all with cinnamon and sugar is genus.

1 tablespoon safflower *or* sunflower oil
1 small onion—sliced

1/8 – 1/2 teaspoon *jalapeño chili* sauce—green or red, as preferred— *or* Tabasco sauce, to taste*

1 small whole pineapple—trimmed, cored, and cut into wedges / chunks *or* a 20-ounce can of juice-packed pineapple chunks—well-drained, but juice reserved
1/2 cup *unsweetened* pineapple juice
1 teaspoon ground cinnamon (*preferably Vietnamese Cassia cinnamon**)
1 tablespoon sugar
Pinch salt, or to taste

In a skillet set over *MEDIUM* heat, heat oil. Sauté onion slices until soft and translucent, *being careful not to allow onions to brown.*

Season with hot pepper sauce, stirring to combine well.

Add pineapple chunks, ground cinnamon, pineapple juice, sugar, and salt. Cook, stirring frequently, for 10 minutes.

Serve at room temperature. Refrigerate any leftovers.

Yields 1 3/4 cupfuls

Notes: *Jalapeño* sauce is available in Hispanic groceries, food specialty stores, and in most grocery stores throughout the Southwest.

**Vietnamese Cassia cinnamon is the strongest cinnamon presently available. Formerly known as "Saigon cinnamon," it is again available from mail order spice firms. China Cassia cinnamon is also a good choice for this recipe.

This recipe can be halved or doubled, when required.

1/7 SERVING (i. e., per 1/4 cupful) –
PROTEIN = 0.5 g.; FAT = 1.7 g.; CARBOHYDRATE = 13.2 g.;
CALORIES = 65; CALORIES FROM FAT = 24%

Asia–Indonesia

INDONESIAN AVOCADO – ICE CREAM DESSERT
Eskrim Pokat

TPT - 1 hour and 8 minutes;
1 hour = freezing period

While I was picking out a perfectly ripened avocado for this dessert, another shopper cheerfully inquired if I was planning to make a salad or was it to be tacos on the menu that evening. When I told her that I was making this Indonesian dessert, the look on her face and the stammering response were priceless. Actually the ice cream is a wonderful vehicle for the soft, rich flesh of the avocado. You really have to try it to appreciate the splendor.

2 large, *very ripe* avocados
2 tablespoons freshly squeezed lemon juice
1/4 cup sugar

2 cups *low fat* (4.4%) vanilla ice cream of choice
  —slightly softened

Peel and pit avocados. In a small bowl, mash the avocado flesh.

Using the electric mixer or a wand blender, purée mashed avocado flesh with lemon juice and sugar until smooth.

Add ice cream and beat until smooth. Turn into a small bowl and place in the freezer for about 1 hour. Stir every twenty minutes. *You want the dessert mixture to be very cold but you do not want it to refreeze.*

Apportion into six dessert dishes or sherbet glasses.

Serve at once.

Yields 6 individual servings

Note: This recipe can be halved, if required.

1/6 SERVING – PROTEIN = 3.4 g.; FAT = 13.0 g.; CARBOHYDRATE = 27.0 g.;
CALORIES = 223; CALORIES FROM FAT = 53%

Japan

Japan, officially *Nippon* – "the sun's origin," is an ancient island nation comprised of 6,852 islands, most of which are small and mountainous. Situated at the juncture of three tectonic plates in a highly earthquake-active area of the so-called "ring of fire," the islands of the archipelago are volcanic in origin with active volcanoes and large inactive calderas. Archeological evidence reveals a Paleolithic culture dating to 30,000 BC followed by more sedentary hunter-gatherer cultures from the Mesolithic Period to the Neolithic Period. The world's second largest economy by nominal gross domestic product, Japan is, today, the world's fourth largest exporter and the sixth largest importer. *Nihonjin* have the longest life expectancy of the inhabitants of any nation on earth.

Nihon ryōri is the modern term for Japanese cuisine, referring to the traditional food eaten prior to the end of "national seclusion," that is before 1868, some fourteen years after the visit Commodore Matthew Perry's visit in 1854, which initiated the "opening of Japan to the West." However, ingredients and cooking methods that modified the pre-seclusion cuisine are now included in the definition of that term.

There are three rules that should be followed as you approach Japanese food. The presentation must be artistic and inviting, the choice of ingredients should be seasonal, and the quality of each ingredient should be as close to perfection as you can find.

We, as lacto-ovo vegetarians, do not eat meat or fish and, as a consequence, sauces, seasonings, and soups have had to be modified as we explored this cuisine. As you will see, *kombu* (kelp) *dashi* or vegetarian stock replaces that made with dried bonito or dried sardines; we do not use fish paste; and we have evolved several rather pleasing vegetarian *sushi* fillings. Many vegetables are enjoyed in Japan including sea vegetables and noodle dishes abound.

Small cakes and a variety of fruits and nuts are served as a sweet ending to a meal, when dessert is served. We enjoy a small mound of pine nuts, dried chestnuts, or almonds with a peeled and halved peach, or an apricot, or orange slices. Artfully arranged on *sushi* plate, they make a beautiful ending to a meal.

Asia–Japan

Vegetarian Meatballs with Sweet and Sour Glaze
Niku Dango

Steamed Japanese Short-Grained Rice
Gohan

~

Clear Soup with *Soba* Noodles and Vegetables
Dashi Yasai

Winter Squash in Sweet Vegetarian Stock
Kabocha no Nimono

Vegetarian Stock from *Kombu*
Dashi Kombu

~

Sweet and Sour Cucumber Salad
Kyuri no Sunomono

~~~~~~~~~~~~~~~~~~~~

Asparagus and *Wonton* Noodles with Egg Sauce
Asuparagasu Menrui kimi Shuyu

Broiled *Tofu* with Two *Miso* Sauces
Tofu Dengaku

~

Sesame Salt
Goma – Shio

~~~~~~~~~~~~~~~~~~~~

Green Tea Ice Cream
Aisukuriimu Ocha

or

Plum and Orange Ice Cream
Aisukuriimu Ume Orenji

Pine Nuts
Nattsu

Peeled, Halved, and Stoned Peaches
Momo

Provide sharp-pointed Japanese chopsticks and a spoon, if you can, although Western eating utensils are totally acceptable in your own dining room as they are in Japanese hotel restaurants that cater to Westerners.

Asia-**Japan**

VEGETARIAN MEATBALLS WITH SWEET AND SOUR GLAZE IN THE STYLE OF JAPAN
Niku Dango
TPT - 21 minutes

A bentō box is a container into which a single portion picnic or take-out meal or a home-packed lunch is packed in Japan. The origin of this delightful tradition can be traced back to the Kamakura Period (1185-1333) but the decorated lacquered boxes, the bentō box as we know it, did not appear until the Azuchi–Momoyam Period (1568-1600). Traditionally, the beautifully arranged meal is composed of fish or meat, rice, one or two portions of cooked or pickled vegetables, and, maybe, some fruit. This unique "boxed lunch," if you will, has been adopted by other Asian cultures. Filipinos call is "baon"; Koreans pack a similar takeout lunch which they call "dosirak"; it is "biandang" in Taiwan; and, of course, we have all heard the British talk about the "tiffin" boxes they enjoyed during the Indian colonial period. The beautifully decorated, lacquered, Japanese bentō box I was given as a Christmas gift many years ago is usually used as a table centerpiece for a meal such as this and has never been used for food although I did almost choose it to carry my lunch when I had to make a four-hour drive to help out my best friend who was to have surgery. A disposable takeout container from a fast-food restaurant does not really help to refresh the hungry traveler the way a thoughtfully presented bentō box meal does. Skewered, highly seasoned beef or pork meatballs are frequently a component of one section in a bentō box, with a serving of short-grained rice on the side. Here I have presented a vegetarian version that can be served with rice and vegetables as a light supper or lunch or as an appetizer for a dinner party.

JAPANESE SWEET AND SOUR GLAZE:
    1 teaspoon corn starch *or* potato starch
    1 teaspoon water

    1/2 cup WILD MUSHROOM STOCK
      [see index]
    2 tablespoons sugar
    1 tablespoon *very finely* chopped onion
    1 tablespoon plum sauce
    1 tablespoon *tamari* soy sauce
    3 tablespoons rice wine vinegar
    1/8 teaspoon MUSTARD SAUCE [see index]

1 package (9 ounces) *frozen* vegetarian "meatballs" —*defrosted*

Blades of Chinese garlic chives, if available, for garnish

In a small dish, combine cornstarch and water. Stir until cornstarch is in suspension. Set aside until required.

In a saucepan set over *MEDIUM* heat, combine mushroom stock, sugar, *very finely* chopped onion, plum sauce, soy sauce, vinegar, and mustard. Cook, stirring frequently, until the stock mixture comes to the boil. Reduce heat to *LOW*.

Add cornstarch suspension and cook, stirring constantly, until the glaze mixture thickens.

Add *defrosted* vegetarian meatballs and cook, stirring frequently, for about 10 minutes, or until meatballs are heated through. Place a skewer through each meatball and transfer to a serving platter. Garnish with garlic chives.

Serve at once with hot, steamed short grain Japanese rice as an appetizer or as a supper entrée.

                    Yields 9 servings
                    adequate for 4 people

Note: This recipe can be halved or doubled, when required.

1/9 SERVING (i. e., per meatball) –
PROTEIN = 5.4 g.; FAT = 1.5 g.; CARBOHYDRATE = 7.4 g.;
CALORIES = 60; CALORIES FROM FAT = 22%

CLEAR SOUP WITH *SOBA* NOODLES AND VEGETABLES IN THE JAPANESE STYLE
Dashi Yasai
TPT - 17 minutes

Making a Japanese dashi stock without meat or fish is a simple process. The stock can be made and frozen or even canned using a water-bath canner. The dashi I make has a subtle taste of the sea which I think compliments the added vegetables perfectly. This recipe can be made for one or for a crowd with amazing ease.

CLEAR SOUP WITH *SOBA* NOODLES AND VEGETABLES IN THE JAPANESE STYLE (cont'd)

Per serving:
- 1 quart water
- 4 pieces *soba* noodles—broken in half

- 1 cup JAPANESE VEGETARIAN STOCK FROM *KOMBU* (*Kombu Dashi*) *[see recipe which follows]*

- 2 fresh snowpeas—trimmed and well-washed
- 3 strips of carrot peeled from one-half carrot using a vegetable peeler
- 1 fresh *shiitake* mushroom—well-washed, stem removed, and sliced*
- 6 shelled fresh soybeans (*edamame*)

Freshly ground black pepper, to taste

In a kettle set over *MEDIUM-HIGH* heat, bring water to the boil. *Slowly* add *soba* noodles. *When water begins to boil again, add 1/4 cupful cold water. Each time water returns to the boil, add another 1/4 cupful of cold water.* Continue this process until noodles are tender—about 7 minutes. Drain and rinse well under cold water to stop further cooking. To avoid a sticky mass of noodles, separate the noodles by running your fingers through them as you drain the noodles. Set aside until required.

In a saucepan set over *MEDIUM* heat, bring *dashi* stock to the boil.

Put snowpeas, carrot strips, mushroom slices, *edamame*, and cooked *soba* noodle pieces into a heated soup bowl. Pour *boiling* stock over.

Season with black pepper.

Serve at once.

Yields 1 serving

Note: *A rehydrated, dried *shiitake* mushroom can also be used.

1 SERVING – PROTEIN = 3.2 g.; FAT = 1.5 g.; CARBOHYDRATE = 8.6 g.; CALORIES = 60; CALORIES FROM FAT = 22%

JAPANESE WINTER SQUASH IN SWEET VEGETARIAN STOCK
Kabocha no Nimono
TPT - 24 minutes

Kabocha squashes are increasingly available in produce departments. The green, spotted rind is distinctive and the sweet orange flesh is more akin to that of sweetpotatoes than of squash. We use butternut squash for this recipe with great success when we can't get a kabocha squash.

- 1 pound *kabocha* or butternut squash

- 3 cups JAPANESE VEGETARIAN STOCK FROM *KOMBU* (*Dashi Kombu*) *[see recipe which follows]* or SEA BROTH *[see index]*
- 2 tablespoons sugar

- 2 tablespoons *tamari* soy sauce

Cut squash crosswise into 1/2-inch slices. Using metal cookie cutters, cut the squash slices into attractive leaf and flower shapes. (Save trimmings for soup stock.) Cut off any peels still adhering.

In a large skillet set over *MEDIUM* heat, heat the Japanese vegetarian stock and sugar to the boil. Reduce heat to *LOW*. Add squash pieces *in a single layer* and simmer for 7 minutes. Using chopsticks, turn each squash piece. Add soy sauce, using a chopstick to agitate the soy sauce into the simmering stock. Allow squash pieces to cook for an additional 5 minutes, or until tender.

Turn squash pieces into a heated serving bowl. Ladle some of cooking liquid into individual soup bowls for each of those dining.

Serve bowl with soup to diners. Pass squash and allow diners to add the squash pieces to the stock in their soup bowl.

Yields 6 individual servings

The calories available from vegetarian stocks are almost negligible. For that reason, we have chosen to treat these stocks merely as flavoring—omitting them from nutritional calculations but recognizing them as a food, quite rich in vitamins and minerals.

Asia–**Japan**

JAPANESE WINTER SQUASH IN SWEET VEGETARIAN STOCK (cont'd)

1/6 SERVING – PROTEIN = 1.0 g.; FAT = 0.1 g.; CARBOHYDRATE = 9.5 g.;
CALORIES = 55; CALORIES FROM FAT = 2%

JAPANESE VEGETARIAN STOCK FROM *KOMBU*
Kombu Dashi

TPT - 3 hours and 28 minutes;
3 hours = soaking period

Brown soybean sauce and toasted rice give this version of the classic Japanese stock the complexity and smoky flavor that one finds in traditional "dashi" stocks in which bonito has been used.

4-inch piece *kombu* seaweed*

6 fresh Chinese black, *shiitake* mushrooms**
1 slice fresh gingerroot—peeled
2 scallions—*both white and green portions*—
   trimmed, well-rinsed, and chopped
1 quart water

1 tablespoon dry brown rice

1 teaspoon canned brown soybean sauce**

2 teaspoons *tamari* soy sauce**

Wipe *kombu* with a damp cloth to remove any foreign matter. *(The white powder on the surface of the kelp should not be washed off.)*

In a non-aluminum saucepan, combine the dried *kombu*, *shiitake* mushrooms, gingerroot, scallions, and water. Allow to soak at room temperature for at least 3 hours.

In a heavy skillet set over *MEDIUM* heat, toast rice kernels *just until they start to brown*. Remove from heat.

Add *toasted* rice kernels and brown bean sauce to soaked ingredients in saucepan. Set over *LOW-MEDIUM* heat and allow to *slowly* come to the boil. Remove from heat. Strain the stock through a fine sieve into a mixing bowl or clean saucepan.

Add soy sauce to the strained *dashi kombu* stock.***

Set a sieve over a clean mixing bowl. Line the sieve with a cotton tea towel. Pour the stock through the towel-lined sieve.

Use the clear stock to make soups, stews, and sauces for stir-fries.

Yields 7 1/2 cupfuls

Notes: *Kombu is a kelp of the *Laminaria* genus, popular in Japanese cooking. It is available, dried, in Asian groceries and natural food stores, and must be soaked for at least 30 minutes before cooking.

**Dried Chinese black, *shiitake* mushrooms, *tamari* soy sauce, and brown bean sauce are available in Asian markets and food specialty stores.

***This stock can be frozen in quantities appropriate to menu needs. It can also be canned in sterilized pint or quart canning jars by using a hot water-bath canner. Process the sealed jars for at least 15 minutes.

The calories available from vegetarian stocks are almost negligible. For these reasons, we have chosen to treat these stocks merely as flavoring—omitting them from nutritional calculations but recognizing them as a food, quite rich in vitamins and minerals.

JAPANESE SWEET AND SOUR CUCUMBER SALAD
Kyuri no Sunomono

TPT - 31 minutes;
15 minutes = wilting period

Serving a pickled vegetable is very much a part of a Japanese meal. For years I thought I would have to switch my "German" thinking about pickles and learn to pickle in the Japanese way until I discovered Japanese overnight pickling and salads like this. Wilting the cucumbers as I might for any European sweet and sour wilted cucumber salad was familiar, but then came the adventure.

JAPANESE SWEET AND SOUR CUCUMBER SALAD (cont'd)

3 medium *or*, preferably, 4 small cucumbers
—peeled, halved lengthwise, and seeded
1/2 teaspoon salt

1 thin slice fresh gingerroot—peeled and *very finely* shredded

2 tablespoons *light* brown sugar
2 tablespoons rice wine vinegar*
1/2 teaspoon *tamari* soy sauce*

1 teaspoon white sesame seeds—*toasted*—for garnish

Using a mandolin or a vegetable peeler, slice cucumber halves into *thin lengthwise strips.* Turn into a mixing bowl. Sprinkle with salt and toss to distribute the salt. Allow to stand for 15 minutes to allow vegetables to wilt *slightly.*

Put *very finely* shredded gingerroot into ice water to crisp.

Meanwhile, in a small bowl, combine brown sugar, vinegar, and soy sauce. Stir well. Set aside until required.

When cucumbers have wilted, put the mixing bowl under the faucet and run cold water over the cucumbers to rinse away the salt. Drain thoroughly or spin the *well-rinsed* vegetables in a salad spinner.

Drain ice water from shredded gingerroot.

When ready to serve, place *one sixth* of the *wilted* and *drained* cucumber on a *sushi* dish or other small serving dish. Sprinkle *one-sixth* of *very finely* shredded gingerroot over. Pour *one-sixth* of the prepared dressing over vegetables. Garnish with *toasted* sesame seeds. Prepare remainder of individual servings.

Serve at once.

Yields 6 individual servings

Notes: *These items can be found in any Asian grocery store and in most natural food stores, if not available in your grocery stores.

When required, this recipe can be halved or doubled. Since refrigerated leftovers lose their unique texture, it is recommended that you prepare only what will be consumed at one meal.

1/6 SERVING – PROTEIN = 0.5 g.; FAT = 0.4 g.; CARBOHYDRATE = 7.2 g.;
CALORIES = 32; CALORIES FROM FAT = 11%

JAPANESE ASPARAGUS AND *WONTON* NOODLES WITH EGG SAUCE
Asuparagasu Menrui Kimi Shoyu
TPT - 9 minutes

The number of noodle houses found in every Japanese city attests to the Japanese love of noodles. Each small family-run restaurant boasts its own specialties. Thin and delicate fresh wonton skin "noodles," prepared as in this recipe, can contribute a complimentary texture contrast when paired with crisp-cooked or stir-fried vegetables.

3 tablespoons *fat-free* pasteurized eggs (the equivalent of 1 egg yolk)*
1 tablespoon *tamari* soy sauce

2 pounds fresh asparagus spears—trimmed and well-washed**

3 quarts *boiling* water
12 commercially-available fresh *wonton* skins or *wonton* wrappers

JAPANESE SESAME SALT (*Goma–Shio*) [see recipe which follows]

Set up steamer.

In a small mixing bowl, using a wire whisk, combine pasteurized eggs and soy sauce. Whisk until well-combined. Set aside at room temperature.

Just before you are ready to serve. Steam asparagus spears until bright green and *crisp-tender*—about 5-7 minutes. Cut steamed asparagus into 1-inch pieces. Apportion steamed asparagus among four heated bowls.

JAPANESE ASPARAGUS AND *WONTON* NOODLES WITH EGG SAUCE (cont'd)

While the asparagus is steaming, drop *wonton* noodles one at a time into the *boiling* water in a kettle set over *MEDIUM-HIGH* heat. As they boil, *be sure to keep noodles separated.* Cook until white and transparent—about 2-3 minutes. *Remove from heat.* Using a large slotted spoon or spatula, lift the cooked *wonton* noodles from the water *one at a time.* Drain thoroughly. Using chopsticks, pick up a cooked and drained *noodle* and "scrunch" it into a heap on top of the asparagus pieces. Repeat with remaining cooked noodles apportioning three "scrunched up" *noodles* on top of each portion. Drizzle a portion of the egg–soy sauce mixture over each serving.

Serve at once, with the condiment JAPANESE SESAME SALT *(Goma–Shio).*

Notes: *Because raw eggs present the danger of *Salmonella* poisoning, commercially-available pasteurized eggs are recommended for use in preparing this dish.

**Allow about six asparagus spears per diner.

This recipe is easily increased or decreased proportionately, as required.

Yields 4 servings

1/4 SERVING (with 1 teaspoonful sesame seed seasoning) –
PROTEIN = 7.0 g.; FAT = 3.3 g.; CARBOHYDRATE = 17.3 g.;
CALORIES = 124; CALORIES FROM FAT = 24%

JAPANESE BROILED *TOFU* WITH TWO *MISO* SAUCES
Tofu Miso

TPT - 4 hours and 29 minutes;
4 hours = dehydration period;
15 minutes = marination period

This is an excellent way to introduce tofu to the skeptic. We find that if it is cut into smaller pieces after broiling, it makes a rather attractive first course presentation or cocktail party appetizer. Halved toothpicks may be inserted for serving.

1 package (16 ounces) *firm* soybean curd (*tofu*) containing 1 large cake*

MISO SAUCE #1:
    2 tablespoons *kome miso**
    1/2 teaspoon grated orange, lemon, or tangerine zest, as preferred
    1 teaspoon *frozen* orange juice concentrate —*thawed*
    1 teaspoon water

MISO SAUCE #2:
    about 1/2 cup watercress leaves—well-washed, chopped, and dried

    2 tablespoons *kome miso**
    1/2 teaspoon sugar
    1 1/2 teaspoons water

Watercress sprigs, for garnish
1 small turnip, carved into a rose, if possible

Wrap soybean curd cake in a cotton tea towel and place on the counter top. Place a bread board or other flat weight on top and weight this with cans or with a tea pot filled with water to a weight of about 3 pounds. Allow to stand for about 4 hours, or until most of moisture has been pressed out of the cake and absorbed by the towel. (Change towel after 2 hours, if necessary.)

Slice soybean curd cake into two equal halves. Then, slice each half into pieces about 2 inches long by 1 inch wide by 1/4 inch thick.

Prepare *MISO* SAUCE #1 by combining 1/4 cupful *miso*, grated citrus zest, of choice, *thawed* orange juice concentrate, and 1 teaspoonful water in a large pie plate. Stir to combine well and spread across the bottom of the pie plate. Place half of the rectangles of *tofu* into the marinade mixture and allow to marinate for 15 minutes. *Do not turn bean curd pieces over in the marinade.* Only one side should display the sauce.

Asia–**Japan**

JAPANESE BROILED *TOFU* WITH TWO *MISO* SAUCES (cont'd)

To **prepare** *MISO* SAUCE #2, place chopped watercress leaves into a mortar. Using a pestle, grind watercress until puréed and liquid has been extracted. Scrape puréed watercress and liquid into a small bowl. Add 1/4 cupful *miso*, sugar, and 1 1/2 teaspoonfuls water. Stir to combine well. Spread across the bottom of a large pie plate. Place the remaining rectangles of *tofu* into the marinade mixture and allow to marinate for 15 minutes. *Do not turn bean curd pieces over in the marinade.* Only one side should display the sauce.

Preheat broiler to 400 degrees F. Prepare a broiling pan by covering it with aluminum foil.

Using a wide spatula, transfer marinated *tofu* slices to prepared broiler pan. Brush residual marinade onto *tofu* pieces so that each piece has an even brown coating. Broil 6 inches from heat source until browned on one side and heated through—about 5-6 minutes.

Arrange broiled *tofu* pieces attractively on a heated platter. Garnish with watercress leaves and the turnip rose.

Serve at once.

Yields 5 servings of two pieces each adequate for 4 people as a main course offering or adequate for 8 people as an appetizer

Notes: *Fresh soybean curd, soybean cakes, *tofu*, or *toufu* may be purchased at Asian groceries or restaurants, if not available in your grocery store. Refrigerate under water for not more than three days before using.

**Mugi miso is a paste of soybeans, barley, seaweed, and salt, aged to develop flavor. It is available in Asian groceries and in natural food stores. *Kome miso* is milder in taste, made from brown rice instead of barley. *Hacho miso* is stronger in taste since it is made from soybeans without the mellowing effect of grains.

This recipe may be doubled, when required.

1/10 SERVING (i. e., per *tofu* rectangle) –
PROTEIN = 4.2 g.; FAT = 2.2 g.; CARBOHYDRATE = 3.0 g.;
CALORIES = 44; CALORIES FROM FAT = 45%

JAPANESE SESAME SALT
Goma – Shio
TPT - 6 minutes

The Japanese cuisine is most dramatic in its simplicity. Here the simple combination of sesame seeds with salt produces a condiment that can be used with cooked vegetables, salads, eggs, and rice to enhance flavor, not disguise food. It is usually made with black sesame seeds, which are available from mail order spice firms but frequently stocked in natural food stores and food specialty stores. I, however, often make it with white sesame seeds when the black specs of the dark goma-shio would ruin the appeal of a presentation.

5 teaspoons sesame seeds—black *or* white— as preferred

2 teaspoons course kosher salt

In a dry, non-stick-coated skillet set over *MEDIUM-LOW* heat, lightly toast sesame seeds for several minutes, stirring frequently. Remove from heat and allow to cool.

Using a SPICE and COFFEE GRINDER or a mortar and pestle, grind *toasted* sesame seeds with salt until they are well pulverized and resemble coarse corn meal. Turn into an airtight container and store in the refrigerator.

Yields 4 teaspoonfuls

Note: This recipe can be halved or doubled, when required.

1/16 SERVING (i. e. 1/4 teaspoonful) –
PROTEIN = 0.2 g.; FAT = 0.5 g.; CARBOHYDRATE = 0.1 g.;
CALORIES = 6; CALORIES FROM FAT = 75%

Asia–**Japan**

JAPANESE GREEN TEA ICE CREAM
Aisukuriimu Ocha

TPT - 8 hours and 9 minutes;
8 hours = freezing period

Although this is not the way it would be prepared in Japan, the flavor and essence of the popular ice cream is certainly captured in this version.

1 cup heavy whipping cream

1 tablespoon *boiling* **water**
2-3 teaspoons green tea *(matcha or* **gold** *sencha)* **leaves or to taste**—*ground to a fine powder**

2/3 cup *fat-free* **sweetened condensed milk**
1/4 cup *fat-free* **pasteurized eggs (the equivalent of 1 egg)****
2 teaspoons pure vanilla extract

Thinly **sliced ripe kiwifruit—for garnish—if desired**

Prepare a 7 x 3 x 2-inch non-stick-coated loaf pan by placing it in the freezer until required.

Using an electric mixer fitted with *chilled* beaters or by hand, using a *chilled* wire whisk, beat heavy cream in a *chilled* bowl until stiff. Set aside.

In a large bowl, combine the *boiling* water and powdered green tea. Stir to form a green paste.

Add sweetened condensed milk, pasteurized eggs, and vanilla extract. Stir to blend thoroughly. *Whisk-fold* stiffly whipped cream *gently*, but *thoroughly*, into milk mixture.

Pour mixture into chilled loaf pan. Spread evenly. Cover tightly with aluminum foil. Freeze overnight or until firm—about 8 hours.

Either scoop ice cream from pan to serve or remove entire block of ice cream from pan and slice. Garnish each serving with 2 slices of kiwifruit, if desired.

Leftovers should be returned to the freezer, tightly covered.

Yields about eight 1/2-cup servings

Notes: *Touted for its antioxidant properties, *matcha* is now widely available. Since it is high in caffeine and the taste of the green tea leaves, especially in ice cream, is most definitely an acquired taste, you may need to experiment with the amount that pleases you.

**Because raw eggs present the danger of *Salmonella* poisoning, commercially-available pasteurized eggs are recommended for use in preparing this dish. Eggs may be eliminated from this recipe, if a less rich ice cream is preferred. However, the eggs do help to modify the taste of the green tea for those who do not regularly detoxify with green tea and are, therefore, not accustomed to the taste.

This recipe is easily doubled, when required. Use a 9 x 5 x 3-inch non-stick-coated loaf pan.

1/8 SERVING (i. e., per 1/2 cupful with eggs and kiwifruit) –
PROTEIN = 3.6 g.; FAT = 9.9 g.; CARBOHYDRATE = 20.5 g.;
CALORIES = 185; CALORIES FROM FAT = 48%

1/8 SERVING (i. e., per 1/2 cupful with kiwifruit and without eggs) –
PROTEIN = 2.8 g.; FAT = 9.9 g.; CARBOHYDRATE = 20.1 g.;
CALORIES = 180; CALORIES FROM FAT = 50%

JAPANESE PLUM AND ORANGE ICE CREAM

TPT - 8 hours and 11 minutes;
8 hours = freezing period

This ice cream can undoubtedly be attributed to the increasing fusion of East and West. It beautifully compliments most Japanese menus while satisfying the Western desire for dessert and the Eastern love of fruit.

Asia–Japan

JAPANESE PLUM AND ORANGE ICE CREAM (cont'd)

5-6 large plums, canned in light syrup—peeled and pitted
2 tablespoons *frozen* orange juice concentrate —*defrosted*
1 tablespoon freshly squeezed lemon juice

1 cup heavy whipping cream

2/3 cup *fat-free* sweetened condensed milk
1 teaspoon pure vanilla extract
1 teaspoon pure almond extract

Japanese plum wine—for garnish—if desired
Canned mandarin orange sections—for garnish—if desired

Prepare a 7 x 3 x 2-inch non-stick-coated loaf pan by placing in the freezer until required.

In the work bowl of a food processor fitted with steel knife or into the container of the electric blender, combine plum flesh, *defrosted* orange juice concentrate, and lemon juice. Process until a smooth purée is formed. Scrape down sides of the container as necessary. Set aside.

Using an electric mixer fitted with *chilled* beaters or by hand, using a *chilled* wire whisk, beat heavy cream in a *chilled* bowl until stiff. Set aside.

In a large bowl, combine prepared plum purée, sweetened condensed milk, and vanilla and almond extracts. Stir to blend thoroughly. *Whisk-fold* stiffly whipped cream *gently*, but *thoroughly*, into plum–milk mixture.

Pour mixture into the chilled loaf pan. Spread evenly. Cover tightly with aluminum foil. Freeze overnight or until firm—about 8 hours.

Either scoop ice cream from pan to serve or remove entire block of ice cream from pan and slice. Serve garnished with a drizzle of plum wine and/or a single mandarin orange section, if desired.

Leftovers should be returned to the freezer, tightly covered.

Yields about eight 1/2-cup servings

Note: This recipe is easily doubled, when required. Use a 9 x 5 x 3-inch non-stick-coated loaf pan.

1/8 SERVING (i. e., per 1/2 cupful without garnish) –
PROTEIN = 2.8 g.; FAT = 9.8 g.; CARBOHYDRATE = 18.7 g.;
CALORIES = 173; CALORIES FROM FAT = 51%

Korea

Human fossil remains that have been discovered in the volcanic lava in the peninsula we know as Korea suggest that pre-humans passed this way somewhere between 100,000 and 300,000 BC. Early hunter-gathers, believed to have migrated from south-central Siberia, settled as early as 10,000 BC forming societies that evolved into agricultural communities. Although continuing to hunt and fish, evidence of the cultivation of millet, barley, wheat, legumes, and rice has been found. The remains of fermented beans, still an important Korean food, were also found by archaeologists in these very early settlements.

Through Mongol invasions in the thirteenth century period of the Goryea dynasty and Japanese invasions in the sixteenth century, Korea remarkably maintained political and cultural independence. Even while Korea was occupied by Japan from 1910 to 1945 after the fall of the Joseon dynasty, cultural integrity was preserved. The cultural unity enjoyed by Koreans for millennia was seriously impacted by the partitioning of the peninsula at the 38th parallel in 1945. The Soviet Union disarmed the Japanese occupiers in the North and the United States disarmed the Japanese in the South which led to a painfully divided Korea where the Republic of Korea, or South Korean, with its progressive western-style twenty-first century economy, presents the mirror image of the oppressive communist dictatorship know as the People's Republic of Korea in the North. The border is still a demilitarized zone that has remained guarded by United Nations forces since the end of the Korean War in 1953.

Vegetarians do not have to search too hard to find vegetarian restaurants in the Republic of Korea due to the considerable and continued influence of Buddhist traditions. Street stalls offer almost every dish you can imagine including oh-so-satisfying bowls of cellophane noodles with vegetables (*chapchae*). Vegetarian buffets with tempting rice, noodle, and *tofu* dishes accompanied by a plethora of wonderfully seasoned vegetable side dishes (*banchan*) can be found easily in Korean cities. Soup is a must at every Korean meal and sometimes it is the meal. As a result, restaurants and food stands that specialize only in soups abound; the variety is breathtaking.

Asia – Korea

Dumpling Soup
Manduguk

~~~~~~~~~~~~~~~~~~~~~~~

Broiled *Tofu* with Sweet Korean Sesame Marinade

with

Assorted *Banchan*:

Sweet Soy-Glazed Pumpkin or Squash
Yachaejorim

Sesame Spinach
Shiumchi Bokum

Watercress Salad with Sesame Dressing
Sang Meenari Muchim

Stir-Fried Dried Mushrooms
Beuseus Namul

Steamed Eggplant and Scallion Salad
Kajui Namul

Cabbage Pickle *Kimchi*
Baechu Kimchi

Kirby Cucumber Salad
Oee Namul Muchim

Lettuce Wraps with Rice
Sangchussam

~~~~~~~~~~~~~~~~~~~~

Oranges in Cinnamon – Orange Syrup

Poached Asian Pears with Black Peppercorns
Baesook

Asia–**Korea**

KOREAN DUMPLING SOUP
Manduguk

TPT - 1 hour and 43 minutes;
       30 minutes = mushroom soaking period;
       30 minutes = cabbage salting period

Many, many years ago we visited a noodle house in New York's Chinatown and, to our delight, sampled "dim sum" of every size and shape under the careful tutelage of our dear friends Merle and Wally. From then on wonton skins, spring roll (or egg roll) wrappers, and dumpling wrappers became a part of the experimental life of my kitchen world. The deep-fried wontons I made for Chinese banquets were a source of great pride, after all I had grown up in world of European noodles. Mandu, Korean dumplings, are more often than not referred to as "potstickers," a name I just adore. There are commercially-available frozen vegetarian potstickers and some are quite good but dumplings are simple and rather fun to make and the little bundles you can create are so much more appealing that the pierogi-style frozen versions.

2 medium, dried *shiitake or* black Chinese mushrooms
1 cup water

3 cups *finely shredded napa* cabbage *or* green cabbage, if preferred—well-washed
1/2 teaspoon salt

2 cups mung *or* soybean sprouts—trimmed, well-washed, and chopped
1 cup chopped spinach pieces—well-washed
2 medium scallions—*both white and green portions*—trimmed, well-rinsed, and *thinly* sliced
1/2 medium carrot—scraped or pared and shredded
2 tablespoons *shredded daikon* radish
1 thin slice fresh gingerroot—*finely* chopped
1 small garlic clove—*finely* chopped

1 tablespoon *tamari* soy sauce
2 teaspoons rice wine *or* a dry white wine
1/2 teaspoon sugar
3 drops sesame oil
Pinch of Korean chili powder*

48 dumpling wrappers (*gyōza* in Japanese) or wonton wrappers or skins*

2 quarts vegetarian stock, of choice
1 tablespoon *tamari* soy sauce
Korean chili powder *or* ground red pepper (*cayenne*), to taste

Soak *shiitake* mushrooms in the *boiling* water for 30 minutes, or until soft. (Reserve soaking water for stock pot.) Cut off stems, reserving them also for the stock pot. *Finely* chop mushrooms. Set aside.

Turn shredded cabbage into a mixing bowl. Add salt and stir to mix well. Turn into a sieve and set over the sink to drain for about 30 minutes. Rinse well, drain well, and pat dry. Turn into a clean mixing bowl.

Add chopped soybean sprouts and spinach pieces, sliced scallion, shredded carrot and daikon radish, and *finely* chopped gingerroot and garlic.

In a small bowl, combine soy sauce, rice wine, sugar, sesame oil, and Korean chili powder. Mix well and add to vegetable mixture.

Place a heaping teaspoonful of filling in the center of each dumpling wrapper. Fold over and seal edge with water. Twist the ends around to form a kind of "turban" or "beggar's bundle." Again seal with water. Wrap a second dumpling wrapper around each bundle and seal with water. Place on a cookie sheet covered with plastic wrap. Continue until all filling has been used.**

In a large kettle set over *MEDIUM* heat, bring the vegetable stock to the boil. Add dumplings and simmer for about 10 minutes. Turn into a heated soup tureen.

Serve into heated rice bowls. Provide soy sauce and Korean chili powder for those who wish to enhance their portion.

Yields 6 servings of soup with four dumplings

Notes: *Korean chili powder can be approximated by adding a tiny pinch of cayenne pepper and a tiny pinch of paprika with the chili powder on your spicerack.

**If convenient, the dumplings can be frozen at this point. Freeze on the cookie sheet and then transfer to plastic bags for extended storage..

This recipe can, of course, be halved or doubled, when required. Doubling is little work one you are into chopping and shredding and those potstickers in the freezer will be available for making more soup or frying for a snack or extra vegetable serving.

KOREAN DUMPLING SOUP (cont'd)

> 1/6 SERVING (i. e., broth with four dumplings) –
> PROTEIN = 5.2 g.; FAT = 0.7 g.; CARBOHYDRATE = 17.2 g.;
> CALORIES = 97; CALORIES FROM FAT = 7 %
>
> 1/24 SERVING (per *mundu*) –
> PROTEIN = 1.3 g.; FAT = 0.7 g.; CARBOHYDRATE = 4.3 g.;
> CALORIES = 24; CALORIES FROM FAT = 5%

BROILED *TOFU* WITH SWEET KOREAN SESAME MARINADE

TPT - 4 hours and 42 minutes;
4 hours = soybean curd pressing period;
30 minutes = marinating period

Marinated soybean curd was a special dinner when our daughter was young. Special because tofu was not available in every produce department as it is now and had to be purchased from either an Asian grocery several towns away or from a Chinese restaurant. Ray often stopped on his way home from work to pick up the tofu, which was unceremoniously scooped out of a pail of water in a restaurant kitchen. Then, I pressed it overnight and marinated it all the next day. With the drier, firm tofu, now available, the pressing takes just a few hours. This Korean marinade is one of my favorite ways to prepare tofu.

1 package (10.5 ounces) *firm* soybean curd (*tofu*) containing 1 large cake*

SWEET KOREAN SESAME MARINADE:
   1/4 cup *tamari* soy sauce**
   1 tablespoon honey
   1 teaspoon sesame oil
   1/8 teaspoon Asian hot *chili* paste, or to taste**
   1 tablespoon freshly squeezed orange juice
   1 1/2 teaspoons freshly squeezed lime juice

   2 tablespoons sesame seeds—*toasted*
   2 garlic cloves—*finely* chopped
   1 tablespoon *finely* chopped fresh gingerroot
   1 scallion—*white portion only*—trimmed, well-rinsed, and *finely* chopped

Wrap soybean curd cake in a cotton tea towel and place on the counter top. Place a bread board or other flat weight on top and weight this with cans or with a tea pot filled with water to a weight of about 3 pounds. Allow to stand for about 4 hours, or until most of moisture has been pressed out of the cake and absorbed by the towel. (Change towel after 2 hours, if necessary.)

Slice soybean curd cake on the diagonal to form a large triangle. Slice each of these triangles in half crosswise to create four 1-inch thick identical triangles.

In a measuring cup or small bowl, combine soy sauce, honey, sesame oil, Asian *chili* paste, orange juice, and lime juice. Stir to mix thoroughly.

In a pie plate or other shallow bowl, combine *toasted* sesame seeds, *finely* chopped garlic, gingerroot, and scallion. Add soy sauce mixture. Combine well.

Place the four triangles of *tofu* into the marinade mixture and allow to marinate for 30 minutes, turning after 15 minutes.

Preheat broiler to 400 degrees F. Prepare a broiling pan by covering it with aluminum foil.

Using a wide spatula, transfer marinated *tofu* slices to prepared broiler pan. Broil 6 inches from heat source until browned on one side. Turn each slice and brown the remaining side. Using a spoon, baste occasionally while slices are broiling.

Serve at once.

Yields 4 servings

Notes: *Fresh soybean curd, soybean cakes, *tofu*, or *toufu* may be purchased at Asian groceries or restaurants, if not available in your grocery store. Refrigerate under water for not more than three days before using.

**Tamari* soy sauce is increasingly available in grocery stores. If not in yours, seek out an Asian grocery or a natural food store. Asian *chili* paste will be found in Asian groceries.

This recipe may be doubled, when required.

1/4 SERVING – PROTEIN = 6.9 g.; FAT = 8.5 g.; CARBOHYDRATE = 8.9 g.;
CALORIES = 124; CALORIES FROM FAT = 62%

Asia–**Korea**

KOREAN SWEET SOY-GLAZED PUMPKIN OR SQUASH
Yachaejorim
TPT - 35 minutes

Somehow, as a small child who saw the world almost exclusively through my immediate environment, I just concluded that pumpkins were pretty exclusively for pumpkin pie and that they were something that grew Up North in abundance and not in the South and certainly not in other countries. I had been strongly influenced by Iroquois lore and the concept of "the three sisters"—squash, corn, and beans. Although I accepted the fact that indigenous peoples of Central and South America also grew these crops, I just never thought that I would ever find recipes from Africa or Asia that called for pumpkin. This impression was further complicated by the fact that my Italian-born mother-in-law was unfamiliar with squash/pumpkin purée and that I had sent cans of pumpkin purée to a friend in England, at her request, because she could not buy the dense purée that I used to bake a pumpkin pie when she visited us. Once you discover that gourds of all kinds and all sizes are found throughout the world and are used in dishes like this rather unique Korean dish, the autumn harvest Up North has enormous potential.

Although pumpkin would be the Korean choice for this dish, butternut squash is less watery and, I think, preferable. The fact that it is available year round makes this recipe less seasonal for us.

3 quarts *boiling* **water**
8 ounces peeled and seeded pumpkin *or*
  butternut squash—cut into 3/4-inch cubes

6 tablespoons water
1/2 cup sugar
1 tablespoon grated fresh gingerroot
6 tablespoons *tamari* **soy sauce**
Freshly ground mixed peppercorns—black, red,
  and white—to taste

Toasted sesame seeds, to garnish, if desired
Sprigs of garlic chives (Chinese chives), to garnish,
  if available

Parboil pumpkin or squash pieces in *boiling* water for 2-3 minutes. Drain well. Turn into skillet set over LOW-MEDIUM heat.

Add the 6 tablespoonfuls water, sugar, grated fresh gingerroot, *tamari* soy sauce, and pepper. Cook, stirring frequently, until the sugar dissolves. Cover and simmer, stirring occasionally, until the squash is tender and glazed with the thickened sweet soy syrup—about 25 minutes. Using a slotted spoon, transfer the squash into a heated shallow serving bowl.

Bring the syrup remaining in the skillet to the boil over MEDIUM-HIGH heat and allow to boil until thickened a bit more. Pour over the squash.

Serve at once or keep for a few minutes on a warming tray, if necessary.

Yields 6 servings
adequate for 4 people

Note: This recipe can be halved or doubled, when required.

1/6 SERVING – PROTEIN = 0.8 g.; FAT = 0.2 g.; CARBOHYDRATE = 22.5 g.;
CALORIES = 99; CALORIES FROM FAT = 2%

KOREAN SESAME SPINACH
Skiumchi Bokum
TPT - 43 minutes;
30 minutes = chilling period

A classic Korean treatment of spinach, which we have enjoyed since the 1960s, this dish never fails to please the palate. It is equally good when made with Swiss chard or Good King Henry (Chenopodium bonus–henricus), also known as goosefoot and eaten by humans since Neolithic times.

1 1/4 pounds fresh spinach—stems removed,
  leaves, thoroughly washed, and torn into
  bite-sized pieces

1 teaspoon sesame oil*
2 teaspoons rice wine vinegar*
1 teaspoon *tamari* **soy sauce***

1 tablespoon sesame seeds—*lightly toasted*

Asia–**Korea**

KOREAN SESAME SPINACH (cont'd)

In a saucepan set over *MEDIUM* heat, cook spinach until just wilted. *The water adhering to the spinach leaves after washing should be sufficient.* Turn into a sieve or colander and drain *very thoroughly.* Press out as much remaining liquid as possible and coarsely chop.

In a bowl, combine sesame oil, rice wine vinegar, and soy sauce. Add *well-drained* spinach. Toss to dress greens *thoroughly*.

Turn into a serving bowl or spread evenly onto a small platter. Sprinkle *toasted* sesame seeds evenly over. Refrigerate for at least 30 minutes before serving.

Serve at room temperature with a fork or chopsticks.

Yields 6 servings
adequate for 4 people

Notes: *These items are increasingly available in well-stocked grocery stores. Asian markets and food specialty stores regularly stock such items.

When necessary, this recipe may be halved or doubled.

1/6 SERVING – PROTEIN = 3.9 g.; FAT = 2.0 g.; CARBOHYDRATE = 5.3 g.;
CALORIES = 48; CALORIES FROM FAT = 38%

KOREAN WATERCRESS SALAD WITH SESAME DRESSING
Sang Meenari Muchim
TPT - 6 minutes

This is another" banchan" in our collection of which we are very fond. The peppery watercress leaves and Korean seasoning offer an exclamation mark every once and a while as you move from dish to dish. Some people blanch the watercress to reduce the peppery flavor but I definitely do not. I am reminded of the joyous gathering of watercress in Ireland as it leaps to life along melting streams in the spring. Here again, all the way over on the other side of the planet, watercress is valued for its freshness, its nutrition, and most of all for its extraordinary wake-up-the-appetite flavor.

2 cups of watercress—thick ends trimmed,
  halved into 3-inch segments, well-washed,
  and well-dried

KOREAN SESAME DRESSING:
  1 teaspoon *toasted* sesame seeds

  2 tablespoons *tamari* soy sauce
  1 tablespoon rice wine vinegar
  1/2 teaspoon sugar
  1/4 teaspoon Korean sesame oil
  1/8 teaspoon ground red pepper (cayenne),
    or to taste*

Place *well-trimmed, well-washed,* and *well-dried* watercress in a mixing bowl.

In a mortar, grind sesame seeds with a pestle to form a uniform powder. Pour into a cruet.

Add soy sauce, vinegar, ground, roasted sesame seeds, sugar, sesame oil, and ground red pepper (cayenne). Shake vigorously. Add to watercress. Toss well. Refrigerate until ready to serve. Turn into a serving bowl.

Serve either chilled or at room temperature.

Yields 6 servings
adequate for 4 people

Notes: *Chili powder can also be substituted, if preferred.

This recipe can be halved or doubled, when required.

1/6 SERVING – PROTEIN = 0.3 g.; FAT = 0.5 g.; CARBOHYDRATE = 1.3 g.;
CALORIES = 12; CALORIES FROM FAT = 37%

KOREAN STIR-FRIED DRIED MUSHROOMS
Beuseus Namul

TPT - 4 hours and 12 minutes;
4 hours = mushroom soaking period

Western taste is defined by the classic and valid "sweet, sour (or acid), salt, and bitter." Definable areas of the taste buds on the tongue are sensitive to these sensations. However, there is another nuance of taste that is considered in all Asian cuisines. If you think about it, the flavor of mushrooms does not fall into any of the classic western categories and you are hard-pressed to define it, but you can taste it. That earthy, fleshy or meaty flavor, known in Japanese as "umami," is a wonderful tool for the vegetarian cook. I have always thought a skillet of sautéed mushrooms is one of the most divine treats available to a cook with a fork in his or her hand. Our winter larder is always stocked with dried mushrooms, some that I dry myself, and wild and unusual mushrooms from around the world that I obtain from mail order firms. We rehydrate them to sauté and use in stews and sauces but this Korean side dish presents the western palate with a new experience.

2 ounces *dried*, wild mushrooms—well-rinsed and brushed to remove any foreign matter*
3 quarts *boiling* water

1 teaspoon safflower *or* sunflower oil
1/2 teaspoon Korean sesame oil

1 tablespoon *tamari* soy sauce
1 garlic clove—crushed
1/4 teaspoon sugar
1/8 teaspoon freshly ground black pepper

1 teaspoon *toasted* sesame seeds

Put *well-cleaned* mushrooms into a small bowl or measuring cup. Pour *boiling* water over. Weight the mushrooms down into the liquid using a small Pyrex dish. Allow to soak for at least 4 hours. Drain thoroughly, *reserving the soaking liquid*. Strain the soaking liquid, now mushroom stock, to remove any bits of the mushrooms that remain. This stock can be used in any dishes that need an assertive stock. [*see index* – WILD MUSHROOM STOCK]

Squeeze the rehydrated mushrooms to eliminate excessive liquid. Remove and discard hard stems. Slice mushrooms into thick slices or leave whole, if preferred.

In a skillet set over *MEDIUM* heat, heat safflower and sesame oil. Add mushroom slices and *stir-fry* for *only about 1 minute*.

Add soy sauce and crushed garlic clove, sugar, and black pepper. Continue stir-frying for about 1 minute.

Sprinkle sugar and black pepper over. Cook for just 15 seconds more. Remove and discard garlic clove. Pour the mixture into a serving bowl.

Garnish with *toasted* sesame seeds.

Serve warm or at room temperature, as preferred.

Yields 6 servings
adequate for 4 people

Notes: *Although the discerning Korean cook would prefer to make this with the wonderful mushrooms gathered from the mountains on the east coast of Korea, we rarely find such wonderful fungi available. A mixture of any flavorful dried mushrooms can be substituted.

This recipe can be halved or doubled, when required.

1/6 SERVING – PROTEIN = 1.5 g.; FAT = 1.7 g.; CARBOHYDRATE = 7.2 g.;
CALORIES = 50; CALORIES FROM FAT = 30%

KOREAN STEAMED EGGPLANT AND SCALLION SALAD
Kaji Namul

TPT - 42 minutes

Finding a firm, long, skinny Asian eggplant in my local grocery store was the joy of that day since I was planning a Korean meal and it would be perfect for a side dish salad. The cashier could not identify the lavender vegetable and went into gales of laughter when she found out that its code number identified it as a mini eggplant. I was so amused by the clerk's response to my treasured purchase. A minimum of five lovely and very diverse side dishes, known collectively as "banchan," accompany Korean meals, even in the home. If you are not in the mood for a rolled lettuce sandwich, "sangchussam," or a watercress salad, there are always other choices. This is one of our very most favorites.

Asia–Korea

KOREAN STEAMED EGGPLANT AND SCALLION SALAD (cont'd)

1 Asian eggplant—about 1/2 pound

2 medium scallions—*both white and green portions*—trimmed, well-rinsed, and sliced

1 teaspoon *tamari* soy sauce
1/2 teaspoon *toasted* sesame seeds
1/4 teaspoon Korean sesame oil
Freshly ground black pepper, or to taste
Pinch salt

Set up a steamer.

Wash the eggplant well and trim the ends. Place in the steamer and steam over simmering water for about 10-12 minutes, or until tender. Remove to the counter top and allow to cool for at least 20 minutes.

Slice the steamed eggplant into three lengthwise segments. Tear or slice the flesh into strips about 3-4 inches in length. Put into a mixing bowl.

Add scallions. Toss to combine.

In a small bowl, combine soy sauce, *toasted* sesame seeds, sesame oil, black pepper, and salt. Mix well. Add to eggplant–scallion mixture. Cover and refrigerate until ready to serve.

Serve at room temperature.

Yields 4 servings*

Notes: *When served as one of several side dishes, this will easily serve three or four people.

This recipe can be doubled, when required.

1/4 SERVING – PROTEIN = 0.9 g.; FAT = 0.7 g.; CARBOHYDRATE = 5.8 g.;
CALORIES = 29; CALORIES FROM FAT = 22%

KOREAN CABBAGE PICKLE *KIMCHI*
Baechu Kimchi

TPT - 10 days, 16 hours, and 35 minutes;
16 hours = brining period;
about 5 days = fermentation period;
5 days = refrigeration period

Koreans are very fond of fermented foods with fermented bean paste and kimchi present at almost every meal. Kimchi could be called the national dish if there could be national agreement as to how to make it. We favored a particular commercially available brand until it was reformulated with the addition of anchovies and shrimp. Another, found in an Asian market, proudly touted the ingredient "fish heads." Hot kimchi has been a staple in our house and we did not want to have to eliminate it from our pleasures so we set out to make our own. Pickled vegetables were and are winter salads in Korea just as they are in so many other parts of the world.

1 large Napa or Chinese cabbage—about 1 pound

5 quarts water
1/2 cup coarse salt

2/3 cup commercially-available garlic *chili* sauce*
2 inches fresh gingerroot—peeled and *very finely* chopped
2 teaspoons sugar
2 tablespoons water

6 scallions—trimmed and well-rinsed

1 small *daikon* radish—about 5 ounces— *or*
  1 cupful—peeled and coarsely grated
2 pickling cucumbers (Kirbys)—peeled, seeded, and cut into thin lengthwise strips using a vegetable peeler
10 fresh radish leaves—well-washed

Cut cabbage in half lengthwise. Trim core end but do not separate leaves from core. Cut each half into three lengthwise wedges. Rinse well.

In a large bowl or stainless steel kettle combine water and coarse salt. Swish back and forth to encourage the salt to dissolve in the water. Add cabbage wedges. Place a plate or platter with a weight such as a can on top of the cabbage to keep the cabbage in the brine. Set aside for about 16 hours, or until cabbage becomes limp in the brine.

Sterilize three or four quart canning jars. Also sterilize lids and rings. Set aside until required.

Drain the cabbage thoroughly. Rinse well in several changes of cool water. Squeeze the cabbage to remove as much water as possible. Place the cabbage in a mixing bowl.

Asia–Korea

KOREAN CABBAGE PICKLE *KIMCHI* (cont'd)

PUT ON UNPOWDERED VINYL GLOVES.

In a separate mixing bowl, combine garlic *chili* sauce, *very finely* chopped gingerroot, sugar, and the 2 tablespoonfuls water. Mix together thoroughly. Add to cabbage wedges and work the sauce mixture between the cabbage leaves with your *gloved* hands. Using a scissors, cut the cabbage wedges into about four pieces.

Slice scallions into 1-inch pieces, halve the cut pieces, and add to the cabbage mixture.

Add grated daikon radish and cucumber strips. *Using your gloved hands, again* mix until everything is coated with some of the sauce. Stuff the mixture into sterilized canning jars, pressing down hard to remove any air bubbles. Carefully wipe the rim of each jar. Seal with a lid and a ring. Using a marking pen, write the time and date on the side of the jars. Place at room temperature until you see fermentation bubbles begin to appear in the jars—5 days in cool weather or in the winter; several hours or up to 2 days in the hot summer. At this point refrigerate the jars for 5 days after which you can taste the *kimchi*.**

Yields about 16 servings

Notes: *A variety of garlic *chili* sauces can be found in the Asian section of most grocery stores. Finding one you like may take some experimentation but it does make the whole process a bit simpler. If the commercial sauce is too mild for your taste, experiment with the addition of Korean chili powder or ground red pepper (cayenne).

**The *kimchi* can be enjoyed as a pickle or garnish just as it is for about 3 weeks. After 3 weeks it becomes very strong and will be most appreciated when accompanied by food such as rice or dumplings or with bread on a sandwich.

This recipe can be halved, if necessary.

1/16 SERVING – PROTEIN = 0.7 g.; FAT = 0.3 g.; CARBOHYDRATE = 4.0 g.; CALORIES = 15; CALORIES FROM FAT = 18%

KOREAN KIRBY CUCUMBER SALAD
Oee Namul Muchim

TPT - 6 minutes

Unlike the cucumber salads I grew up with, this sweet and sour salad is not wilted. In fact, to allow it to wilt would be, according to any Korean cook, to ruin the crisp texture that this salad should have. In Korea, cucumber salads are not made with the English cucumbers most commonly used for salads in the United States. Kirby cucumbers are the choice of Korean cooks and are generally available in our produce departments for pickling.

1/2 teaspoon Korean sesame oil
1 teaspoon rice wine vinegar
Pinch Korean chili powder, or to taste*
Pinch salt
1/4 teaspoon sugar
1 small sliver of fresh garlic

2 *organic* Kirby cucumbers—well-washed
1 medium scallion—*white and light green portions*—trimmed, well-rinsed, and *thinly* sliced

Asia – Korea

KOREAN KIRBY CUCUMBER SALAD (cont'd)

In a cruet, combine sesame oil, vinegar, chili powder, salt, sugar, and garlic sliver. Shake to combine.

If you have been fortunate enough to find organic cucumbers, score them attractively using the tines of a fork, a vegetable peeler, and/or a lemon zester. If you are only able to find cucumbers whose peel may contain pesticide residue, peel these cucumbers and then decorate the flesh using the tines of a fork. Slice the cucumbers *very thinly*. Turn into a bowl filled with ice water. Refrigerate until ready to serve. Drain thoroughly. Turn into a serving bowl.

Add scallion slices.

Pour dressing over. *Remove and discard garlic sliver.* Toss.

Serve at once.

Yields 4 servings

Notes: *If Korean chili powder is not available, ground red pepper (cayenne) with a touch of Hungarian hot paprika or chili powder can be substituted.

This recipe can be halved or doubled, when required.

1/4 SERVING – PROTEIN = 0.3 g.; FAT = 0.4 g.; CARBOHYDRATE = 2.4 g.;
CALORIES = 12; CALORIES FROM FAT = 30%

KOREAN LETTUCE WRAPS WITH RICE
Sangchussam
TPT - 26 minutes

Korean food is, above all, beautiful. A display of perfect lettuce leaves, piled with rice and inviting the addition of bit of this or that, says almost more than any other dish, "I care about those who are dining with me." The transfer of a small portion of another "banchan" makes each wrap unique and assures the hostess that her guests are satisfied. A transfer by the hostess of a choice "banchan," say a beautiful mushroom, would say honor.

Failing glutinous rice, generally available in grocery stores today, use Japanese short grain rice. It will be sticky enough to easily be contained within the lettuce rolls.

1 cup *boiling* **water**
1/2 cup dry *glutinous* **rice**

2 tablespoons preserved black bean paste
  (*denjang* **paste)**
1 teaspoon Korean hot fermented *chili* **paste**
  (*gochu jang***)***
1 garlic clove—*very thinly* **sliced**
1/4 teaspoon *toasted* **sesame seeds**
1/4 teaspoon Korean sesame oil

12 perfect lettuce leaves, of choice, well-washed
  and well-dried

In a saucepan set over *LOW* heat, stir *glutinous* rice into *boiling* water. Cover and allow to cook, undisturbed for about 20 minutes. Remove from heat, but keep warm.

While the rice is cooking, in a small bowl, combine black bean paste, *chili* paste or sauce, *very thinly* sliced garlic, *toasted* sesame seeds, and sesame oil. Stir to combine well.

When ready to serve, spread each lettuce leaf with a portion of the seasoning paste. Add a portion of the cooked rice and arrange on a large platter or tray. Each diner can roll and eat a lettuce wrap as is or, using chopsticks, add a small portion of one of the other side dishes being offered.

Yields 12 servings
adequate for 4-6 people

Notes: *There are many hot or sweet sauces and pastes that can be used in this side dish if Korean hot fermented *chili* paste (*gochu jang*) is not available or too hot for your taste. Thai sweet *chili* sauce or other Asian-style *chili* sauces such as yellow or red curry paste can be substituted. Plum and duck sauces can be used and are a particularly good choice when this dish is being introduced to children.

This recipe can be halved, when required.

1/12 SERVING – PROTEIN = 1.0 g.; FAT = 0.4 g.; CARBOHYDRATE = 7.1 g.;
CALORIES = 37; CALORIES FROM FAT = 10%

Asia–Korea

KOREAN ORANGES IN CINNAMON – ORANGE SYRUP

TPT - 2 hours and 6 minutes;
15 minutes = syrup cooling period;
1 hour = flavor development period

Since all dishes to be served are traditionally placed on the table at the beginning of the meal in Korea, fruits to end the meal or cleanse the palate would also make their appearance at the beginning of the meal. This refreshingly sweet dessert can be anticipated throughout the meal and greatly appreciated on a hot Korean summer evening after a meal that has included some of the hot and spicy dishes of the South.

KOREAN CINNAMON – ORANGE SYRUP:
   1 cup freshly squeezed orange juice
   1 cup water
   1/2 cup sugar
   1/2 teaspoon ground cinnamon*

6 mandarin oranges *or* **clementines—peeled and divided into sections****

In a saucepan set over *MEDIUM* heat, combine orange juice, water, sugar, and ground cinnamon. Allow to come to the boil. *Reduce heat to MEDIUM-LOW.* Cook for about 40-45 minutes or until the syrup thickens and is reduced by about half. Remove from heat and allow to cool at room temperature for about 15 minutes.

Place orange sections into a serving bowl. Add the KOREAN CINNAMON – ORANGE SYRUP and mix gently.

Refrigerate for at least 1 hour before serving. *Serve chilled.*

Yields 6 servings
adequate for 4 people

Notes: *This recipe presents an opportunity to explore the many kinds of cinnamon available, but unfortunately available only through spice mail order firms. Korintje Cassia cinnamon is the mellow variety similar to that found in grocery stores. China Cassia cinnamon is a spicier variety, stronger than Korintje. Vietnamese Cassia cinnamon is the superb cinnamon formerly known as "Saigon cinnamon," which is now again available in the United States. It is much stronger than either Korintje or China Cassia, so strong, in fact, that it is advisable to reduce the amount called for in a recipe by about one-third. Ceylon cinnamon, from Sri Lanka, is another variety. It is light in color and mellow with a discernible citrus fragrance and taste.

**Tangerine and navel orange sections can be substituted, if desired.

This syrup is a fantastic sauce for a simple dish of vanilla or chocolate ice cream.

When required, this recipe can be doubled.

1/6 SERVING – PROTEIN = 0.1 g.; FAT = 0.2 g.; CARBOHYDRATE = 29.8 g.;
CALORIES = 122; CALORIES FROM FAT = 2%

KOREAN POACHED ASIAN PEARS WITH BLACK PEPPERCORNS

Baesook

TPT - 1 hour and 21 minutes;
1 hour = flavor development period

One very fortuitous day I happened upon a basket full of Asian pears ("Pyrus pyrifolia") in the produce section of a grocery store and said, "Why not?" No one was there to explain when I would know if they were ripe or whether you peeled them or just ate them out of hand or cooked them. Until I found this recipe from Korea, I never thought to poach them; we just peeled the thick, dark skin from the ripened fruit and ate it as we would an apple. Asian pears are fragrant and crisp, more like a grainy apple in texture than the pears we are used to. They are exported to the United States by Korea and by Australia and, although, quite pricey, it is considered an honor to be served or gifted with an Asian pear.

KOREAN POACHED ASIAN PEARS WITH BLACK PEPPERCORNS (cont'd)

2 Asian pears—peeled, cored, and quartered
24 black peppercorns
1/4 cup sugar
3 cups water

1/4 cup pine nuts (*pignoli*)

Using a sharp knife, round the edges of each quarter. Press three peppercorns into the outer side of each piece of fruit. Place in a saucepan.

Add sugar and water. Bring to the boil over *MEDIUM* heat. *Immediately reduce heat to LOW*. Allow to cook for 5 minutes. Transfer to a bowl and refrigerate for about 1 hour to allow for cooling and flavor development.*

Transfer two fruit pieces and several spoonfuls of syrup to each of four serving dishes. Sprinkle with pine nuts (*pignoli*).

Once you have added the pine nuts, serve immediately to preserve the texture of the seeds.** Provide a fruit knife and spoon to each diner.

Yields 4 servings

Notes: *The peeled Asian pear sections will brown if left exposed for too long. Try to serve them as soon after the flavor development period as possible.

**Warn your honored guests to remove the peppercorns before eating the fruit.

This recipe can be halved or doubled, when required.

1/4 SERVING – PROTEIN = 2.7 g.; FAT = 3.7 g.; CARBOHYDRATE = 21.5 g.; CALORIES = 122; CALORIES FROM FAT = 27%

Laos

The country in Southeast Asia which occupies the northwest portion of the Indochinese Peninsula, known today as Laos, can be traced to the Kingdom of Lan Xang, a kingdom founded in the fourteenth century. Lan Xang, which translates from Lao to mean "million elephants," gave way to three distinct kingdoms. Between 1763 and 1769 the northern part of present day Laos came under Burmese rule while Champasak, in the South, came under Siamese rule. The monarch of Luang Phrabang was rescued by French forces when the kingdom was overrun by the Chinese Black Flag Army. The kingdom became a French protectorate within the territory known as French Indochina. Luang Phrabang was joined shortly after by the Kingdoms of Champasak and Vietiane. Present-day Laos is a nation formed from these three kingdoms in 1893 as a French protectorate and remained so until it was occupied by the Japanese during World War II. It returned to French rule after the period of Japanese occupation in 1945 and remained part of French Indochina until 1954 when it gained independence and formed a constitutional monarchy. A protracted civil war ended the monarchy and a single-party socialist republic known as the Lao People's Democratic Republic was established in 1975 under the Communist Pathet Lao.

About twice the size of our Commonwealth of Pennsylvania, it too enjoys a wealth of natural resources. Once heavily forested, its logging industry is poorly managed with large portions of the trees that are cut going to Vietnam through illegal channels to feed the furniture industry. In addition there is a lack of national commitment to reforestation. As with Pennsylvania, Laos is rich in coal deposits but gold and copper are its greatest assets for the present world economy. Water resources have enabled the development of hydroelectric power in excess of national need and the market for exported power to Thailand and to Vietnam has grown. As this power generation has expanded there is well-founded concern by environmentalists and Laos' neighbors Vietnam and Cambodia, who share the Mekong River, that fishing resources and the hugely important eco-tourism may be adversely impacted as will the homes and livelihood of downstream populations.

Many families, totaling as much as ten percent of the population, fled into Thailand during the civil war and that together with the horrific casualties of the wars that decimated the adult male population in French Indochina and a low infant survival rate have resulted in a significant drop in population. Today the population is growing at a phenomenal rate with the result that two-fifths of the population is under the age of fifteen.

Sixty-seven percent of the population adheres to Theravada Buddhism, based on the earliest teachings of the Buddha. This is the same form of Buddhism that is practiced in Thailand and in Cambodia. In Laos, Buddhism has been and is a strong influence upon all aspects of life, politics, and cuisine to the extent that since 1975 the communist government has tried to use Buddhism for political purposes, rather than oppose the deeply embedded religion of the overwhelming majority of the population. Buddhism, as practiced in Southeast Asia, respects life as does Buddhism as practiced in the West. However, Eastern Buddhism does not generally view fish or poultry as meat which presents a formidable challenge to the western vegetarian when traveling. Lao have traditionally preferred raw foods which also can be a concern to the western digestive system but are gradually moving from a cuisine of principally raw foods to cooked dishes. Rice and soups are good options for the traveler as they are important elements of any meal in Laos. Although Asian cuisines are a result of borrowing and adapting, some elements of each are distinctive, identifying a menus nationality. Rice vermicelli (*klao poun*), glutinous rice (*klao niaw*), and fermented fish sauce (*pa daek*) are ubiquitous to the tables across Laos to the extent that one Lao author said that these foods should identify Laos not the slogan "Land of a Million Elephants."

Asia–Laos

Mushroom *Wontons* Appetizers   with   Lao Plum Sauce
Jeune Wonton   *Gail Plum*

Hard-cooked Eggs with Tomato – Coriander Sauce
Jaew Mak Len

~

Kohlrabi and Papaya Salad with Tamarind Dressing
Tam Mack Su Hao Houng

~

Rice Noodle and Meatball Soup
Feu

~ ~

Pineapple Fried Rice
Kore Kao Mock Nut

Stir-fried Eggplant
Maak Keu Ah

~ ~ ~ ~ ~ ~ ~ ~ ~ ~

Stir-Fried Long Beans and Mushrooms with Garlic
Kore Mock Tore Kack Hit

and / or

Bamboo Shoots with Sesame Seeds
Supe Nall Mike

"Sticky" Rice

~ ~ ~ ~ ~ ~ ~ ~ ~ ~ ~ ~ ~ ~ ~ ~ ~ ~ ~ ~

Tapioca Pudding with Sweetpotato
Num Wan Mun Gail

Sweet Oranges with Orange Flower Water

LAO MUSHROOM *WONTON* APPETIZERS
Jeune Wonton

TPT -   about 2 hours and 20 minutes;
1 hour = mushroom soaking period

Borrowed from Chinese cuisine, which has very strongly influenced the cuisine of Laos, these wontons are a wonderful way to begin a Lao meal or as a snack for an open house.

Asia – Laos

LAO MUSHROOM *WONTON* APPETIZERS (cont'd)

1 tablespoon *high heat* safflower *or* sunflower oil
1 cup fresh *enoki or* beech mushrooms
— trimmed well of any attached mycelium, well-rinsed, and brushed well with a brush
2 garlic cloves—*finely* chopped

2 large scallions—trimmed, well-rinsed and chopped
1 tablespoon *tamari* soy sauce
1 teaspoon sugar

24 *wonton* skins*

Oil for deep-frying

LAO PLUM SAUCE (*Jail Plum*) [see recipe which follows] *or* other dipping sauce, of choice

In a wok or a skillet set over *MEDIUM-HIGH* heat, heat oil. Add *enoki* or beech mushrooms and *finely chopped* garlic. *Stir-fry* for about 1 minute. Turn into the work bowl of the food processor.

Add chopped scallions, soy sauce, and sugar. Process until uniformly chopped. Turn into a bowl and begin filling *wontons*.

Place a heaping teaspoonful of filling in the center of a *wonton* skin. Fold over and seal edge with water. Twist the ends around to form a kind of "turban." Again seal with water. Place on a cookie sheet covered with plastic wrap. Continue until all filling has been used.

Freeze until hard. Transfer to plastic bags and freeze until required or proceed immediately by deep-frying a few at a time in oil heated to 365 degrees F. until *evenly browned.*** Drain on paper toweling. These may be frozen in the same manner as the uncooked *wontons* for several weeks and then heated, while still frozen, in a preheated 375 degree F. oven for about 8-10 minutes before serving with dipping sauces of choice.

Be sure to provide cocktail forks to facilitate dipping for those who are not too adept with chopsticks.

Yields 24 *wontons*
adequate for 4-6 people

Notes: **Wonton* skins are available in Asian groceries and in most well-stocked grocery stores. They freeze well. If you wish to take the trouble to make them yourself, see our more nutritious version for *WONTON* SKINS [see index].

**These may also be boiled in stock or soup, if desired.

When necessary, this recipe may be easily doubled.

1/24 SERVING (i. e., per *wonton* exclusive of dipping sauce) –
PROTEIN = 0.6 g.; FAT = 0.6 g.; CARBOHYDRATE = 3.7 g.;
CALORIES = 26; CALORIES FROM FAT = 21%

LAO PLUM SAUCE
Jail Plum
TPT - 21 minutes

I have often been asked if plum sauce and duck sauce are two names for the same sauce; believe me, they are different. Plum sauce really does contain plums and is a common condiment in Asia, so common that is now readily available in grocery stores all over the United States. You could just pick up your favorite brand on your next shopping trip or, instead, you could make this quick and easy version. If you are planning to serve this with Lao or Thai spring rolls, omit the gingerroot.

1/2 cup honey
2 dark plums—peeled, seeded, and *finely* chopped

2 tablespoons *tamari* soy sauce
6 tablespoons water

2 teaspoons corn starch
2 tablespoons *cold* water

2 tablespoons *finely* shredded fresh gingerroot

LAO PLUM SAUCE (cont'd)

In a saucepan set over *LOW-MEDIUM* heat, combine honey and *finely* chopped plums. Allow to come to the boil, stirring constantly.

Add soy sauce and 6 tablespoonfuls water. Allow to simmer for about 5 minutes.

In a small dish, combine corn starch and the 2 tablespoonfuls of *cold* water. Mix well until corn starch is in suspension. Add to honey–plum mixture. Stir and allow to cook for a minute or two.

Add shredded gingerroot. Mix well. Remove from heat. Turn into a small serving bowl or into a jar, if you are making it in advance of serving.

Serve at room temperature. Refrigerate leftovers.

Yields about 1 1/2 cupfuls

Note: This recipe can be doubled, when required.

1/10 SERVING (i. e., about 2 tablespoonfuls) –
PROTEIN = 0.3 g.; FAT = 0.2 g.; CARBOHYDRATE = 16.1 g.;
CALORIES = 62; CALORIES FROM FAT = 3%

LAO TOMATO – CORIANDER SAUCE
Jaew Mak Len
TPT - 20 minutes

Jaews are wonderful little sauces that are delicious scooped up with just a ball of cold "sticky" rice, added to a sandwich, or used as a condiment for a main course. We found this combination so complementary to eggs and cheese, I could not believe how quickly it became a passion for us. How often have I heard at lunchtime, "Is there any of that hot sauce from Laos left?" You can make it as hot as you wish; Lao do love to "fire it up." A mini-chop food processor makes this paste in seconds while a Lao cook might spend considerable time using a mortar and pestle to achieve an uniform texture.

2 large shallots—chopped
3 large garlic cloves—chopped
2 tablespoons chopped mild green *chilies**
1/2 teaspoon *jalapeño* sauce, or to taste*
2 scallions—*green and white portions*—trimmed, well-rinsed, and chopped
2/3 cup canned, *diced* tomatoes

1/4 cup chopped fresh coriander (*cilantro*)—well-washed
1 scallion—*white portion only*—trimmed, well-rinsed, and chopped
Salt, to taste

In a non-stick-coated skillet set over *MEDIUM* heat, combine chopped shallot, garlic, and green *chilies*, *jalapeño* sauce, the two chopped scallions, and chopped tomatoes. Sauté until vegetables just begin to color. Remove from heat. Turn into the work bowl of food processor. Process until it forms a paste, scraping down the sides of the work bowl as required.

Add chopped fresh coriander (*cilantro*), chopped white portion of the third scallion, and salt. Process on and off *only until integrated*. Turn into a serving dish. Refrigerate until required.

Serve at room temperature. Refrigerate leftovers.

Yields about 1 1/4 cupfuls

Notes: *Hot Thai *chilies* can be substituted. The combination we have offered usually satisfies our tolerance for "hot."

This recipe can be halved or doubled, when required.

1/20 SERVING (i. e., per tablespoonful) –
PROTEIN = 0.2 g.; FAT = 0.2 g.; CARBOHYDRATE = 0.8 g.;
CALORIES = 4; CALORIES FROM FAT = 45%

KOHLRABI AND PAPAYA SALAD WITH TAMARIND DRESSING
Tam Mack Su Hao Houng

TPT - 10 minutes

The Southeast Asian love of kohlrabi positively stunned me when I first encountered a recipe from North Vietnam and, of course, I pursued the thread. An off-hand comment on a travel show to the effect that the traveler, an Aussie, had never seen a people so mad for kohlrabi really set me back. Introduced by the Dutch during the days of exploration and trade, Vietnamese, Lao, Indonesians, Indians, and Japanese have all discovered that the crisp kohlrabi flesh adds taste, a slight sweetness, and a crunchy texture to salads and stir-fries. The beautiful leaves need not be discarded; they are a good substitute for bok choy in stir-fries and soups.

TAMARIND DRESSING:
- 2 tablespoons **TAMARIND LIQUID** *[see index]*
- 2 tablespoons **GARLIC OIL** *[see index]*
- 1 tablespoon freshly squeezed lime juice
- Several drops *jalapeño chili* sauce, or to taste*
- 1 tablespoon *very finely* chopped fresh Vietnamese mint**
- 1/4 teaspoon *light* brown sugar
- Two or three drops sesame oil

1 large, smooth kohlrabi—peeled and slivered into long matchstick pieces
1 medium *under-ripe* (i. e., *green*) papaya—peeled, seeded, and slivered into long matchstick pieces
1/2 small onion—slivered
1 large carrot—scraped or pared and sliced into long shreds using a vegetable peeler
1/2 cup fresh coriander (*cilantro*) leaves—chopped
3 tablespoons chopped fresh Vietnamese mint**
Zest of 1/2 large lemon—slivered into long thin shreds
Freshly ground mixed peppercorns—white, red, and black—to taste
Salt, to taste

In a small bowl prepare the dressing by combining tamarind water, garlic oil, lime juice, *jalapeño chili* sauce, *very finely* chopped Vietnamese mint, brown sugar, and sesame oil. Mix well. Set aside briefly.

In a large mixing bowl, combine slivered kohlrabi, papaya, and onion, carrot shreds, chopped fresh coriander (*cilantro*) and Vietnamese mint, and lemon shreds. Season with ground mixed peppercorns. Sprinkle a bit of salt over. Toss well. Turn into a salad bowl.

When ready to serve, add 2 tablespoonfuls of the prepared tamarind dressing. Toss. Pass remaining dressing.

Serve at once.

Yields 6 servings
adequate for 4 people

Notes: *Finely chopped fresh hot *chili* pepper may be substituted.

**Vietnamese mint grows as prolifically in the herb garden as does any true mint; it too needs to be contained. Even though we must treat it as an annual at our latitude, we plant it in a container which is then sunk into the ground and discourage its constant attempt to put down roots when it touches the ground. Vietnamese mint, *Polygonum adoratum*, is not a true mint. The leaves are smooth unlike common mints, with a reddish, brown patterns of anthocyanin pigmentation that forms an eye on each leaf. The unique peppery mint flavor is a useful cooking tool. Note that this herb is not a good candidate for drying or freezing. In the winter I rub a bit of dried regular mint over this salad.

This recipe can be halved or doubled, when required, and makes a very good addition to a buffet table.

1/6 SERVING – PROTEIN = 1.1 g.; FAT = 4.0 g.; CARBOHYDRATE = 9.6 g.;
CALORIES = 78; CALORIES FROM FAT = 46%

Asia–Laos

LAO RICE NOODLE AND MEATBALL SOUP
Feu
TPT - 23 minutes

While attending a baseball awards' dinner with my grandson, somebody asked me, "When you have spaghetti, what ever do you use for meatballs?" There are so many ways to prepare pasta that I never thought about meatballs; I don't think I ever made spaghetti with meatballs, so, quite frankly, I never missed them. As I thought about the absence of meatballs to the average "new vegetarian," I remembered a Spanish meatball soup called "Sopa Albóndigas" and a Persian meatball and rice soup and then I remembered this noodle and meatball soup from Laos. Although this more than likely originated in Vietnam, it is hugely popular in Laos and often is the only noon-time offering of small restaurants and street stalls. Lao add pa daek, the ubiquitous fish sauce of Laos, chili sauce, and sugar.

2 quarts *boiling* **water**
2 ounces rice *vermicelli* **or pea starch noodles***

5 cups VEGETABLE STOCK FROM SOUP
   [*see index*] *or* **other vegetarian stock of choice****
2 tablespoons Thai sweet *chili* **sauce**
1 teaspoon *tamari* **soy sauce**

18 small, *frozen* **vegetarian "meatballs"**
2 bamboo shoots—cut into julienne pieces
1/4 cup chopped fresh coriander (*cilantro***)**
2 scallions—trimmed, well-rinsed, and *thinly* **sliced**

A bowl of well-washed and trimmed baby spinach *or* other vegetable leaf of choice—about 3 cups

In a saucepan or mixing bowl, soak rice noodles in *boiling* water for about 5 minutes. Drain thoroughly. Cut noodles into 4-5-inch lengths

In a large saucepan, combine stock, *chili* sauce, and soy sauce. Allow to come to the boil.

Add drained *rice vermicelli*, "meatballs," bamboo shoot pieces, chopped fresh coriander (*cilantro*), and scallion slices. Allow soup to come back to the boil and simmer for about 5 minutes.

Turn into a heated tureen and serve into heated soup bowls. Pass spinach and allow diners to stir spinach into their soup.

Yields 6 servings
adequate for 4 people

Notes: *These items are increasingly available in grocery stores. Asian markets and food specialty stores regularly stock all these items.

**The vegetable stock is, of course, nutritional but calculating its food values is difficult without chemical analyses techniques. For these reasons, we have chosen to treat these stocks merely as flavoring—omitting them from nutritional calculations but recognizing them as a food, quite rich in vitamins and minerals.

This recipe can be halved or doubled, when required.

1/6 SERVING (with about 1/2 cupful of greens) –
PROTEIN = 9.2 g.; FAT = 2.8 g.; CARBOHYDRATE = 23.2 g.;
CALORIES =145; CALORIES FROM FAT = 17%**

PINEAPPLE FRIED RICE IN THE STYLE OF LAOS
Kore Kao Mack Nut
TPT - 12 minutes

Borrowed from Chinese cuisine, as are many dishes in Laos, fried rice is a popular accompaniment to meals or, in some cases, the base for a meal in itself.

PINEAPPLE FRIED RICE IN THE STYLE OF LAOS (cont'd)

1 tablespoon safflower *or* sunflower oil
1/4 cup *thinly* sliced scallion—*using both white and green portions*
2 garlic cloves—sliced
2 cups *cold, cooked* long grain brown rice *or* converted rice
1 tablespoon *tamari* soy sauce*
1/8 teaspoon onion powder

1 cup juice-packed canned *or* fresh pineapple chunks

In a wok, set over *MEDIUM-HIGH* heat, heat the 1 tablespoonful oil. Add *thinly* sliced scallion and garlic, and *stir-fry* for about 30 seconds. Add *cold* rice and *stir-fry* for about 3-4 minutes, or until heated through. Be sure to coat grains evenly with oil. Add soy sauce and onion powder. Mix well.

Stir in pineapple chunks. Turn out into heated serving bowl.

*Serve at once.***

Yields four 1/2-cup servings
adequate for 2-4 people
depending upon remainder of menu

Notes: *Tamari* soy sauce is increasingly available in grocery stores. If not available in your store, it is available in Asian groceries.

**This may be made slightly in advance of serving and reheated at serving time in a casserole at 325 degrees F. for about 15 minutes or quickly stir-fried again, if preferred. Also, this dish may be frozen for 4-6 weeks in advance of serving with considerable success and reheated as previously described.

When required, this recipe is easily doubled.

1/4 SERVING – PROTEIN = 2.4 g.; FAT = 3.1 g.; CARBOHYDRATE = 29.4 g.;
CALORIES = 157; CALORIES FROM FAT = 18%

LAO STIR-FRIED EGGPLANT
Maak Keu Ah

TPT - 50 minutes;
30 minutes = eggplant salting period

Oh sure, we have all fried eggplant but this Lao version is a very, very long way from the breaded Armenian eggplant that fits so nicely into a sandwich or eggplant parmigiana. Quickly stir-frying eggplant prevents it from soaking up the frying oil. It is sweet and salty, yes, but the crushed red pepper flakes and the ginger give it a wonderful bite. The Lao eggplant, a variety of the Kermit eggplant, is generally used in Laos. I have never found the 'Lao Green Stripe,' the 'Lao Purple Stripe,' the 'Lao Lavender,' or the 'Lao White" in my markets but the 'Galaxy' and lavender Japanese eggplants are frequently available. They have less seeds that do the more common eggplants and a milder taste.

2 small firm eggplants—preferably a Galaxy or a Japanese eggplant—well-washed and chopped into bite-sized pieces
Coarse or kosher salt

1/4 cup white distilled vinegar
1/4 cup water
1/4 cup *tamari* soy sauce
1 tablespoon corn starch
1 1/2 tablespoons sugar

1 tablespoon *high heat* safflower *or* sunflower oil
1 teaspoon crushed, dried red pepper flakes, or to taste
4 slices fresh gingerroot—*shredded or very thinly slivered*

2 scallions—trimmed, well-rinsed, and chopped into 1/2-inch diagonal slices

Put chopped eggplant into a coriander or sieve set over the sink. Sprinkle with salt. Toss. Allow to stand for about 30 minutes. Rinse very well to remove salt. Squeeze dry. Set aside until required.

In a small bowl combine vinegar, water, soy sauce, corn starch, and sugar. Stir until the corn starch is in suspension. Set aside until required.

In a large wok set over *MEDIUM-HIGH* heat, heat oil. Add crushed dried red pepper flakes and shredded gingerroot. Stir-fry for about 1 minute.

Add eggplant and scallion slices. Stir-fry until eggplant begins to brown. *Turn heat down to LOW-MEDIUM.*

Stir sauce mixture again. Add to eggplant. Stir until sauce forms and eggplant is glistening. Turn into a heated serving bowl.

LAO STIR-FRIED EGGPLANT (cont'd)

Serve at once.

Yields 8 servings
adequate for 6 people

Note: This recipe can be halved, when required.

1/8 SERVING – PROTEIN = 0.8 g.; FAT = 1.9 g.; CARBOHYDRATE = 8.7 g.;
CALORIES = 54; CALORIES FROM FAT = 32%

STIR-FRIED LONG BEANS AND MUSHROOMS WITH GARLIC
Kare Mack Tare Kack Hit
TPT - 18 minutes

If I am so fortunate as to find Chinese long beans in a market, I face the dilemma as to how to prepare them. These long beans are popular all over Asia and prepared in many different ways but always in a way that quickly cooks them and preserves the intense color. A friend once said that a dish of stir-fried long beans is probably the only stir-fried recipe that requires a knife. This simple, intensely garlicky recipe from Laos is divine, if you like garlic.

1 tablespoon *high-heat* safflower *or* sunflower oil
4 garlic cloves—sliced

1 1/2 pounds Chinese "foot long" beans—trimmed and well-washed*
3 tablespoons *tamari* soy sauce
1/4 teaspoon sugar
Pinch crushed, dried basil

2 cups fresh *enoki* or beech mushrooms—well-rinsed and cleaned well with a brush
Several dashes ground red pepper (cayenne), or to taste

In a large wok set over *MEDIUM-HIGH* heat, heat oil. Add garlic slices. Stir-fry for a minute or two, being careful not to allow the garlic to brown.

Add beans, soy sauce, sugar, and crushed basil. Stir-fry for a minute or two.

Add mushrooms and stir-fry for a minute or two. Cover and allow to steam for about 3 minutes. Remove cover.

Add ground red pepper (cayenne) and continue stir-frying until dry. Turn onto a heated platter.

Serve at once.

Yields 6 servings
adequate for 4 people

Notes: *If long beans are unavailable, you can substitute the wonderfully uniform green beans that are packaged for "in-the-bag" steaming.

This recipe can be halved, when required, but doubling is unwieldy.

1/6 SERVING – PROTEIN = 1.7 g.; FAT = 2.5 g.; CARBOHYDRATE = 6.4 g.;
CALORIES = 51; CALORIES FROM FAT = 44%

BAMBOO SHOOTS WITH SESAME SEEDS IN THE STYLE OF LAOS
Supe Nall Mike
TPT - 6 minutes

Fresh bamboo shoots ... oh, how I would love to be able to find them in our markets. I have never found them, even in Asian markets. As a result, we make this dish with canned bamboo shoots despite the slightly tinny taste which distorts the flavor somewhat but fortunately, not the crispness. Lao cooks cook extensively with bamboo shoots and this is, perhaps, my favorite of the Lao bamboo shoot recipes in my collection because it offers a mild, palate-soothing sensation in the midst of a meal that includes hot and spicy dishes.

Asia–Laos

**STIR-FRIED BAMBOO SHOOTS WITH SESAME SEEDS
IN THE STYLE OF LAOS** (cont'd)

4 teaspoons *high-heat* safflower *or* sunflower oil
2 cans (8 ounces each) sliced, bamboo shoots
   —drained, well-rinsed to remove brine

3/4 teaspoon sesame oil

4 scallions—trimmed, well-rinsed, and sliced into
   1/2-inch diagonal pieces
1/2 cup chopped fresh coriander (*cilantro*)
1 tablespoon *tamari* soy sauce
1/2 teaspoon sesame seeds

In a wok set over *MEDIUM-HIGH* heat, heat oil. Add sliced bamboo shoots. Stir-fry for a minute or two.

Add sesame oil. Stir-fry to coat the bamboo shoot slices.

Add sliced scallions, chopped fresh coriander (*cilantro*), soy sauce, and sesame seeds. Stir-fry until the sesame seeds begin to brown. Turn into heated serving dish.

Serve at once over steamed short grain ("sticky") rice.

Yields 6 servings
adequate for 4 people

Notes: *If you open a can of bamboo shoots and need only a couple of pieces for a dish, store the remainder covered with cold water in the refrigerator. If you change the water every couple of days, the shoots with retain their fresh crispness for about 2 weeks.

This same recipe can be used to prepare waterchestnuts.

This recipe can be halved, when required.

1/6 SERVING –   PROTEIN = 1.4 g.; FAT = 4.2 g.; CARBOHYDRATE = 3.4 g.;
CALORIES = 51; CALORIES FROM FAT = 74%

LAO TAPIOCA PUDDING WITH SWEETPOTATO
Num Wan Mun Gail

TPT - 2 hours and 20 minutes;
2 hours = chilling period

Although very similar to a dessert pudding popular in Thailand, this Lao version has an unexpected ingredient. The usual reaction as the pudding is served is, "Oh good, mango" or "Where did you get the apricots?" The surprised response when the first piece of sweetpotato is eaten is usually, "What is this? Interesting. . ..." It is a good way to add another bright colored vegetable to the day's menu.

1 1/4 cups diced sweetpotato*
3 cups *boiling* water

1 1/4 cups skimmed milk
1 1/4 cups *light, sulfite-free* coconut milk
5 tablespoons quick-cooking tapioca
1/2 cup sugar

1 teaspoon pure vanilla extract

In a saucepan set over *MEDIUM* heat, cook diced sweetpotato in *boiling* water for about 12 minutes. Drain thoroughly and set aside until required. *Do not overcook sweetpotato*; it should be *crisp-cooked*.

In a large saucepan set over *LOW-MEDIUM* heat, combine milk, coconut milk, tapioca, and sugar. Using a wire whisk, combine well. Allow mixture to come to a boil, stirring *very* frequently until the pudding thickens, *being careful not to allow the pudding to stick to the bottom of the saucepan or scorch*.

Add vanilla extract. Stir well. Add cooked sweetpotato. Turn into a six small dessert dishes. Refrigerate for at least 2 hours, until cold and firmly set.

Serve chilled.

Yields 6 individual servings

Notes: *Asians prefer the less-sweet, pale sweetpotato, the true yam, but the sweetpotatoes we can buy here in the United States can be used in this recipe.

This recipe can be doubled, when required.

LAO TAPIOCA PUDDING WITH SWEETPOTATO (cont'd)

1/6 SERVING – PROTEIN = 5.5 g.; FAT = 2.0 g.; CARBOHYDRATE = 35.7 g.;
CALORIES = 167; CALORIES FROM FAT = 11%

LAO SWEET ORANGES WITH ORANGE FLOWER WATER

TPT - 1 hour and 28 minutes;
1 hour = flavor development period

When we visited the Soviet Union in 1983, we heard a stream of "we invented" declarations that eventually became ludicrous. But I suspect that most Americans think the orange is either native to California or to Florida. After all the big decision when you are in the produce section is whether you want California navel or Florida juice oranges. In reality, oranges are believed to have originated in Southeast Asia; we did not "invent" them.

2 large oranges—peeled, seeded, and segmented

1/2 cup sugar
1 1/2 cups water
1 whole star anise

1 1/2 teaspoons orange flower water

Place the orange sections in a serving bowl.

In a saucepan set over *MEDIUM* heat, combine sugar, water, and star anise. Allow to come to a gentle boil. Stir to dissolve the sugar. Reduce heat to *LOW-MEDIUM* and allow to boil for about 12-15 minutes, or until a thin syrup forms. Remove from heat. Remove and discard star anise.

Add orange flower water. Stir. Pour over orange sections. Refrigerate for at least 1 hour, or until thoroughly chilled.

To serve, fill a large bowl with chopped ice. Set your serving bowl on top of the ice to insure that the orange sections and the syrup will be *very cold when serving*.

Serve into dessert dishes.

Yields 8 servings
adequate for 6 people

Note: This recipe can be doubled and served in a large glass bowl. This is a dramatic presentation for a holiday meal.

1/6 SERVING – PROTEIN = 0.5 g.; FAT = 0.04 g.; CARBOHYDRATE = 20.2 g.;
CALORIES = 79; CALORIES FROM FAT = <1%

Malaysia

Malaysia gained its independence in 1957 from the British Empire, one of the last of Great Britain's possessions to do so. In 1963 the independent federation, which included British Malaya and numerous small island kingdoms, was joined by Sarawak and British North Borneo. Today it a federation composed of thirteen states, based on the historical Malay Kingdoms, and three federal territories united under a constitutional monarchy in which a king is elected the federal head of state for a five-year term. Executive power, however, is vested in the cabinet headed by a prime minister.

Archaeology in the Malay Peninsula, referenced as "*Suvarnadvipa*" or the "Golden Peninsula" in ancient Indian documents and by Ptolemy as the "Golden *Khersonese*," shows habitation by humans dating back almost 40,000 years. Trading posts and ports were established by traders and settlers from India and China as early as the second century. These people brought their cultures and their religions. Although a majority of the population is Muslim, Buddhism and Hinduism, practiced by these early settlers, are still practiced today. Many also still follow the Christian faith introduced by the British and the Dutch who also left their influences when they controlled the area under the Anglo-Dutch Treaty of 1824.

Over fifty percent of the population is Malay with about twenty-four percent of Chinese ethnicity and about seven percent of the population claiming to be of Indian descent. In addition, Malaysia shares land borders with Thailand, Indonesia, and Brunei and maritime boundaries with the Philippines, Vietnam, and Singapore, which was once a part of the Federation of Malaysia. As a result, the cuisine is diverse and fascinating with interpretations of many "nearby" cuisines including Chinese, Indian, Thai, and Sumatran traditions from Indonesia.

What follows is a light summer supper menu that samples the taste of the island nation. Traditionally a meal consists of rice, one meat dish or seafood dish, and a vegetable dish. All dishes are presented at the beginning of the meal.

Asia–**Malaysia**

Cucumber and Shallot Salad

Fried Potatoes with Yogurt and *Chilies*
Rajam Partheeban

~~~~~~~~~~~~~~~~~~~~~

Potato and Green Bean Curry
Kari

~~~~~~~~~~

Stir-fried Chinese Cabbage, Pepper, and Eggs
Orak Arik

~~~~~~~~~~

Stir-fried Chive Buds with Beancurd in Spicy Sauce

or

**Deep-Fried Beancurd
with *Chili* and Garlic Sauce**

~~~~~~~~~~~~~~~~~~~~~~~

Tapioca in Coconut Milk with Fruit
Sago

MALAYSIAN CUCUMBER AND SHALLOT SALAD

TPT - 46 minutes;
30 minutes = cucumber salting period

When an organic, unwaxed cucumber comes to hand, this salad springs to mind. Malaysians carve the green skin of the cucumber when they make this salad so that when the cucumber is cut, bits of the pattern remain. Although a refreshing salad, it does not sidestep the Malaysian passion for seasoning. Contrasts in texture and seasoning are very characteristic of this cuisine borrowed from many travelers.

1 large cucumber—*organic* and *unwaxed*, if possible*
Salt

2 large shallots—peeled and halved through the root end

1/4 cup *light, sulfite-free* coconut milk
1/4 teaspoon ground cumin, or to taste
2 tablespoons chopped mild green *chilies*
1/2 teaspoon freshly squeezed lime juice

Lime wedges, for garnish

Using the tines of a fork and/or a vegetable peeler and/or a sharp knife, cut patterns into the skin of the cucumber. Halve the cucumber the long way and then halve each half. Remove seeds. Cut the four strips into bite-sized chunks. Turn into a strainer. Salt generously and toss to coat each slice of cucumber with salt. Allow to stand for 30 minutes. Rinse several times and drain well. Turn into a mixing bowl.

Slice the shallots in half through the root end. Using a sharp knife, slice each shallot into long thin slices. Add to the cucumber pieces.

Add coconut milk, ground cumin, chopped green *chilies*, and lime juice. Toss to distribute the seasoning. Turn into a shallow serving bowl. Refrigerate until required.

Garnish with lime wedges before serving.

Yields 6 servings
adequate for 4 people

Notes: *If you can not find an unwaxed, organic cucumber, peel and carve the inner flesh.

This salad can be doubled, when required.

Asia–**Malaysia**

MALAYSIAN CUCUMBER AND SHALLOT SALAD (cont'd)

1/6 SERVING –   PROTEIN = 0.4 g.; FAT = 0.4 g.; CARBOHYDRATE = 2.0 g.;
CALORIES = 12; CALORIES FROM FAT = 30%

MALAYSIAN FRIED POTATOES WITH YOGURT AND *CHILIES*
Rajam Partheeban
TPT - 22 minutes

This side dish or salad is reminiscent of an Indian potato raita but in Malaysia the potatoes are traditionally fried. It is distinctively flavored to the taste of the Malaysian palate and quite an enjoyable vegetable dish to serve over rice or with a loaf or two of warm nan.

I have most often seen this dish prepared by deep-frying the potatoes. You can minimize the amount of oil used and fat transferred to the potatoes by frying the potatoes in a wok set over high heat.

4 medium potatoes—peeled and cut into small cubes

3 quarts *boiling* water

3 tablespoons *high-heat* safflower *or* sunflower oil

3 large shallots—*finely* chopped

3 tablespoons *finely* chopped mild green *chilies*

1 slice fresh gingerroot—*finely* chopped

1 tablespoon chopped fresh coriander (*cilantro*) leaves, for garnish

Salt, to taste

1/4 cup YOGURT *CRÈME* [see index] *or* thick, Greek-style yogurt

In a large saucepan set over *MEDIUM* heat, combine potato cubes and *boiling* water. Cook for about 5 minutes. Drain well.

In a wok set over *MEDIUM-HIGH* heat, heat oil. Add par-boiled potato cubes and sauté until potatoes brown. Using a slotted spoon, remove fried potatoes to paper toweling to allow excess oil to be absorbed.

In a bowl combine *finely* chopped shallots, *chilies*, and gingerroot. Add fried potatoes and chopped fresh coriander (*cilantro*). Toss to combine.

Salt to taste. *Set aside until ready to serve.*

Just before serving, add yogurt and stir to combine.

Serve at room temperature. Refrigerate leftovers.

Yields 6 servings
adequate for 4 people

Note: This dish can be halved or doubled, when necessary.

1/6 SERVING – PROTEIN = 3.0 g.; FAT = 6.8 g.; CARBOHYDRATE = 19.5 g.;
CALORIES = 155; CALORIES FROM FAT = 40%

MALAYSIAN POTATO AND GREEN BEAN CURRY
Kari
TPT - 47 minutes

Spices and certain foods have health-maintaining or health-restoring properties in the view of Eastern healers. A study of Ayruvedic medicine is an amazing revelation as are the writings of Chinese herbal healers. An evaluation of the ingredients in this recipe praise the spices of garam masala, black pepper, onions, garlic, and gingerroot as having roles in the health of the body. This vegetable dish is not only an example of the incorporation of Eastern healing elements but it is also an illustration of the fusion cuisine of the multi-island nation now known as Malaysia. A wok is actually one of the most perfectly designed cooking pots in the world. Do not settle for a skillet, if there is wok in the back of your cupboard! And, please do not settle for just boiled potatoes and steamed green beans, if this recipe can be fitted into your menu plans!

VOLUME II - 393

MALAYSIAN POTATO AND GREEN BEAN CURRY (cont'd)

2 pounds all-purpose potatoes (not Idaho)
—peeled and cut into 1-inch cubes

1 tablespoon *high-heat* safflower *or* sunflower oil
2 tablespoons *finely* chopped shallots
1 small onion—chopped
2 garlic cloves—*very finely* chopped
1 tablespoon fresh gingerroot—*finely* chopped

1 tablespoon OUR INDIAN SPICE MIXTURE (*Garam Masala*) [see index] *or* Madras curry powder, as preferred

1 cup *light, sulfite-free* coconut milk
2 cups VEGETARIAN WHITE BROTH [see index] *or* THAI CLEAR or DARK VEGETABLE STOCK [see index]
Freshly ground black pepper, to taste

1 pound fresh, young, *small* green beans—trimmed

Place the peeled and cubed potatoes in *cold* water. Set aside until required.

In a wok set over *MEDIUM* heat, heat oil until hot. Add *finely* chopped shallots, chopped onion, *very finely* chopped garlic, and *finely* chopped gingerroot. Stir-fry until the onion is soft and translucent, *being carefully not to allow any of the vegetables to brown.*

Add the *garam masala* or curry powder and continue stir-frying for about 5 minutes or until the mixture becomes aromatic.

Meanwhile, drain the potatoes.

Add coconut milk, vegetable stock, drained potatoes, and black pepper. Reduce heat to *LOW* and allow potatoes to simmer for about 20 minutes, or until tender. Stir occasionally.

Add green beans and cook, stirring occasionally for about 10 minutes more. Using a skimmer or slotted spoon, transfer the vegetables to a heated serving bowl.

Serve at once.

Yields 6 servings
adequate for 4 people

Note: This recipe can be halved, when required.

1/6 SERVING – PROTEIN = 4.1 g.; FAT = 4.4 g.; CARBOHYDRATE = 28.5 g.;
CALORIES = 148; CALORIES FROM FAT = 27%

MALAYSIAN STIR-FRIED CHINESE CABBAGE, PEPPERS, AND EGGS
Orak Arik

TPT - 14 minutes

Unlike China, where dishes are delivered to the table in courses but all remain on the table to the end of the meal, all dishes are placed on the table at once in Malaysia. This stir-fried dish can be just one more side dish or it can be the centerpiece for lunch on one of those days when "what shall we eat for lunch" springs to mind and there just happens to be a napa or Chinese cabbage in the refrigerator. The first time I made this I announced that we were having peppers and eggs for lunch. Imagine the surprised look I elicited when this, far from his expectation of a favorite Italian dish, appeared on the table.

2 tablespoons vegetarian stock of choice *or* water
2 teaspoons preserved black bean sauce

2 tablespoons *high-heat* safflower *or* sunflower oil
2 garlic cloves—*very finely* chopped
1 red, orange, or yellow pepper—cored, seeded, and *thinly* sliced

1/2 large head (about 1 pound) *napa* or Chinese cabbage—*thinly* sliced as for slaw
2 scallions—*both white and green portions*—trimmed, well-rinsed, and diagonally sliced

3 eggs—*well-beaten*
Freshly ground black pepper

Combine vegetable stock and black bean sauce. Stir. Set aside until required.

In a wok set over *MEDIUM-HIGH* heat, heat oil. Add *very finely* chopped garlic and *thinly* sliced peppers. Stir fry for about 2 minutes.

Add *thinly* sliced cabbage and scallions. Stir-fry for 3 minutes.

Asia–Malaysia

MALAYSIAN STIR-FRIED CHINESE CABBAGE, PEPPER, AND EGGS (cont'd)

Add vegetable stock and black bean sauce to wok and stir-fry for another minute.

Add eggs and black pepper. Stir-fry quickly and turn out onto a heated platter when eggs have congealed.

Serve at once.

Yields 6 servings
adequate for 4 people

Note: This recipe can be halved, when required.

1/6 SERVING – PROTEIN = 4.7 g.; FAT = 7.6 g.; CARBOHYDRATE = 3.7 g.;
CALORIES = 99; CALORIES FROM FAT = 69%

STIR-FRIED CHIVE BUDS WITH BEANCURD IN SPICY SAUCE IN THE STYLE OF MALAYSIA

TPT - 2 hours and 21 minutes;
2 hours = beancurd dehydration period

Garlic scapes are usually used for this recipe in Southeast Asia. The scapes are tall bolts from which garlic flowers open and I, personally, think they are a beautiful bonus to growing garlic. I have never found garlic scapes for sale in any greengrocer anywhere that we have lived and I will not sacrifice the few bolts that I get each season. As a consequence, I make this Malaysian dish with chive flower buds that appear in my herb beds early in the spring or with those now frequently available in my grocery store.

1 package (16 ounces) *very firm* soybean curd (*tofu*) containing 1 large cake*

6 tablespoons water
2 teaspoons corn starch

2 tablespoons *tamari* soy sauce
1/4 teaspoon *Szechuan (Sichuan) chili* paste, or to taste *or* 1/4 teaspoon *jalapeño* green *chili* sauce, or to taste
Freshly ground mixed peppercorns—white, black, and red—to taste

2 tablespoons *high heat* safflower *or* sunflower oil
About 30 chive flower bud stems—well-washed, hard ends trimmed, and chopped into 1-inch lengths
2 large garlic cloves—*very finely* chopped

Wrap soybean curd cake (*tofu*) in a cotton tea towel and place on the counter top. Place a bread board or other flat weight on top and weight this with cans or with a tea pot filled with water to a weight of about 3 pounds. Allow to stand for about 2 hours, or until most of moisture has been pressed out of the cake and absorbed by the towel.

Slice soybean curd cake in half lengthwise and then into 1/2-inch cubes. Set aside until required.

In a small dish, combine water and corn starch. Stir until corn starch is in suspension.

Add soy sauce, *chili* paste, and ground mixed peppercorns. Stir well. Set aside until required.

In a wok set over MEDIUM heat, heat oil. Add chopped chive flower buds and stems and *very finely* chopped garlic. Stir fry for 2 minutes.

Add beancurd cubes. Continue stir-frying for 2 minutes more. *Reduce heat to LOW.*

Stir sauce ingredients and add to wok. *Gently* stir to coat vegetables with sauce. When it has thickened, turn into a heated serving bowl.

Serve at once.

Yields 6 servings
adequate for 4 people

Note: This recipe can be halved, when required.

1/6 SERVING – PROTEIN = 4.8 g.; FAT = 7.1 g.; CARBOHYDRATE = 6.1 g.;
CALORIES = 88; CALORIES FROM FAT = 73%

Asia – **Malaysia**

DEEP-FRIED BEANCURD WITH MALAYSIAN *CHILI* AND GARLIC SAUCE

TPT - 30 minutes

Deep-fried beancurd appears in many dishes, in many Asian cuisines. Its crisp texture is a wonderful contrast with other foods. My favorite Thai restaurant presents a vegetable dish in a rich, enjoyable sauce over large pillows of deep-fried beancurd; an Indonesian acquaintance, perhaps somewhat put off by our vegetarian lifestyle, said she clung to the idea that fried beancurd would be something she could serve us when we came to dinner; and I do not think I have ever been to Chinese banquet where deep-fried beancurd was not one of the courses. I do not use the intense combination of hot red and Thai bird's eye chilies so favored by Malaysians. It is a simple Malaysian recipe that can be made just as hot as you want it to be.

High-heat safflower *or* sunflower oil for deep-frying

2 *firm, low-fat* beancurd cakes (*tofu*)—cut into cubes

MALAYSIAN *CHILI* AND GARLIC SAUCE:
    2 tablespoons of oil used for deep-frying
    2 garlic cloves—*very finely* chopped
    2 tablespoons *very finely* chopped mild green *chilies**

    1 tablespoon *tamari* soy sauce *or* INDONESIAN SWEET SOY SAUCE (Kecap Manis) [see index]
    2 scallions—*both white and green portions*—trimmed, well-rinsed, and sliced diagonally into 1/4-inch slices
    Ground red pepper (cayenne), to taste

In a wok set over *MEDIUM-HIGH* heat, heat oil to a depth of about 2 inches.

Deep-fry cubes of beancurd, a few at a time, until crisp and browned. Transfer to paper toweling to dry.

Transfer 2 tablespoonfuls of the deep-frying oil to a non-stick-coated skillet set over *LOW* heat. Add *very finely* chopped garlic and green *chilies*. Sauté until garlic is softened, *allowing neither the garlic nor the chilies to brown.*

Add soy sauce and scallions. Season with ground red pepper (cayenne). Allow to heat through while stirring constantly.

Pour fried beancurd into a heated serving bowl. Spoon garlic–*chili* sauce over.

Serve at once.

Yields 8 servings
adequate for 6 people

Notes: *Red *chilies* or bird's eye *chilies* can be substituted.

        This recipe can be halved, when required.

1/8 SERVING – PROTEIN = 1.6 g.; FAT = 5.3 g.; CARBOHYDRATE = 1.1 g.;
CALORIES = 58; CALORIES FROM FAT = 82%

TAPIOCA IN COCONUT MILK WITH FRUIT IN THE MALAYSIAN STYLE

Sago

TPT - 2 hours and 17 minutes;
2 hours = chilling period

In Asia, sago, extracted from the pith of the stems of the sago palm, is readily available to the cook. Although sago is usually available in Asian groceries. Manioc or cassava is the source of what is known in the West as tapioca and since it is more readily available than is sago, I choose to use it for this dessert. The nursery room pudding of childhood is the base for sophisticated desserts in the Far East and in South America. Tapioca, interestingly enough, was introduced from South America to Africa by the Portuguese in the 1600s, after their return voyages from the Western Hemisphere. The not-too-sweet tapioca pudding is a perfect foil for the luscious tropical fruits.

TAPIOCA IN COCONUT MILK WITH FRUIT IN THE MALAYSIAN STYLE (cont'd)

3 tablespoons quick-cooking tapioca
1 cup *light, sulfite-free* coconut milk
1 cup *skimmed* milk
2 tablespoons sugar

1 teaspoon pure vanilla extract

Chunks or balls of fresh honeydew melon, chunks of fresh pineapple, baby banana slices, *carambola* (starfruit) slices, and/or sliced, fresh papaya

In a saucepan set over *MEDIUM* heat, combine granulated tapioca, coconut milk, skimmed milk, and sugar. Cook, stirring frequently, until the pudding base begins to simmer. *Reduce heat to LOW.* Continue to cook, *stirring constantly*, for about 5 minutes more.

Stir in vanilla extract.

Turn the tapioca mixture into a large shallow serving bowl, such as a noodle platter. Refrigerate for at least 2 hours.

When ready to serve, arrange fruits of choice on the soft pudding.

Serve at once. Spoon pudding with fruits into chilled fruit dishes. Cover and refrigerate any leftovers.

Yields 6 servings
adequate for 4-6 people

Note: This recipe may be halved or doubled, when required. Be sure to use an appropriately sized serving dish when decreasing or increasing.

1/6 SERVING (exclusive of the fruits chosen) –
PROTEIN = 1.5 g.; FAT = 1.6 g.; CARBOHYDRATE = 11.3 g.;
CALORIES = 65; CALORIES FROM FAT = 22%

Mongolia

Homo erectus had inhabited the region we know as Mongolia for almost 800,000 years before the arrival of *Homo sapiens*, who reached Mongolia about 40,000 years ago. Neolithic settlements have been identified that date from c. 5500-3500 BC. These peoples attempted to sustain themselves through agriculture and, as today, they too found this area of Asia a difficult environment for agricultural success. Copper and Bronze Age excavations evidence the introduction of non-agricultural, herding cultures of nomadic, horse-riding family groups. This nomadic lifestyle continued until well into the eighteenth century AD.

In 1206 AD a chieftain named Temüjin rose to power who took the name Chinggis Khan, although he is more often referred to by his Persian name Genghis Khan. He ended illiteracy among the disparate tribes, united these tribes, and adopted a form of writing known as the Uighur script. He is probably most know for his legendary conquests forming the Mongol Empire which spread from present-day Poland across the vast land of the Asian steppe to Korea and down to Vietnam, an empire encompassing over 13,000,000 square miles—twenty-two percent of the land mass of the planet. The power of the Khans reached its zenith in the third century AD. Kulai Khan, the last Mongol Khan, who had little Mongol tribal following and who was in retreat from the Manchus, set out to invade Tibet and to destroy the Yellow Hat sect of Buddhism. He died in 1634 on his way to Tibet ending the period of Khan rule. Mongolia subsequently came under the control of China's Qing Dynasty in 1689 and remained so until the end of the Chinese Revolution in 1911 and the collapse of the Manchus in 1912 when Mongolia declared its independence, a declaration not recognized by the Republic of China who claimed the territory known as Inner Mongolia. The Soviet Union turned its sights on Mongolia in 1920 to prevent the Chinese from moving West. In 1924 Outer Mongolia became a Soviet republic. A new constitution uniting the two Mongolias was introduced in 1992 with a multi-party system and a market economy.

Cooking across the wide expanse we know as Mongolia contains the elements of the lands conquered by the Mongols and the cuisines brought by those who conquered and ruled this land. We find understandably strong Chinese influence in Inner Mongolia. On the other hand, the cuisine and culture of the area once controlled by the Soviets reflects little Chinese influence. Islamic influence is strong but the centuries of contact with Tibetan Buddhism in the sixteenth and seventeenth centuries can be seen in cultural practices and, yes, in the cuisine. Mongolia's unique interpretation of Buddhism, which is practiced by fifty-three percent of the population, does not prohibit taking the life of a living thing for food. The eating of fish, rejected prior to the contact with Tibet, has not replaced the tremendous dependence upon meat, especially mutton, but is now acceptable as an alternative. Cheeses made from the milk of dri (female yaks), ewes, goats, camels, mares, and cows have been part of the cuisine for centuries but these cheeses are often acidic and rock hard.

A growing vegetarian movement resulted in the opening of the first vegetarian restaurant in 2006 starting a trend which has resulted in more than twenty vegetarian and vegan restaurants in the capital Ulan Bator (alternately, Ulaanbaatar) alone. Mongolian vegetarian restaurants use *tofu* and soy meat analogue products to mimic traditional meat ingredients in many dishes just as we do. A recent travel article warned that a vegan visitor would probably starve in this country but veganism is also on the rise in Mongolia with over 2,500 people identifying themselves as vegan and one percent of the population of nearly three million describing themselves as vegetarian. Campaigns have been in effect to promote the eating of salads, which admittedly have been borrowed from neighbors for the most part, and to encourage filling half the dinner plate with vegetables and fruits. This is somewhat of an uphill battle with homemakers since most vegetables are trucked in from China.

Asia – Mongolia

Green Onion Pancakes with *Feta* Cheese
Gambir

Ewe's Milk Cheese such as *Toscano* or a Young *Pecorino Romano*
or
Goat's Cheese
or
Feta Cheese in Brine

Black Tea with Milk

~

Sesame Noodle Salad with Corn   **Tossed Salad with Noodles
and Onion *Vinaigrette***

Eggplant Salad with Herb Dressing
Simpoog Aghtsa

Three-Bean Salad with Creamy Dressing

~

Chick Pea and Rice Soup

~ ~ ~ ~ ~ ~ ~ ~ ~ ~ ~ ~ ~ ~ ~ ~ ~ ~ ~ ~

Tea-Smoked *Tofu* with Ginger

Oven-Roasted or Grilled Mixed Vegetables
Leeks,
Potatoes,
Eggplants,
Carrots
with
Yogurt

and

***Hoisin* Barbecue Sauce**
Su Jeung

Flatbread or *Nan*

~ ~ ~ ~ ~ ~ ~ ~ ~ ~

Meatball and Vegetable Pastry Bundles
Buuz

Grilled Leeks

~ ~ ~ ~ ~ ~ ~ ~ ~ ~ ~ ~ ~ ~ ~ ~ ~ ~ ~ ~

Sweet Barley Porridge

over

Stewed Apple Slices

Yogurt Cream Whip with Ginger

Asia–**Mongolia**

MONGOLIAN GREEN ONION PANCAKES WITH *FETA* CHEESE
Gambir

TPT - 32 minutes

Elsewhere in this volume you find a recipe for "tsey paley," a Tibetan green onion skillet bread. Borrowed perhaps from the Tibetans, this pancake is filled with a local cheese but we use feta because it is easily available. In addition, instead of making pancakes from scratch, we use whole wheat pancake mix, thinning the batter down to make a thin crepe-like pancake that can be rolled easily. By adding whey, this appetizer becomes a super-protein food.

1 cup *whole wheat* pancake mix
1 1/2 cups whey, drained from cheese making, *or* the equivalent in reconstituted dry whey
2 teaspoons canola oil
1/4 cup *fat-free* pasteurized eggs (the equivalent of 1 egg)

1/4 cup *finely* chopped scallions—*both white and green portions*

3/4 cup crumbled *feta* cheese

Preheat a non-stick-coated griddle or large skillet over LOW-MEDIUM heat. Preheat oven to 170 degrees F.

In a mixing bowl, combine pancake mix, whey, canola oil, and pasteurized eggs. Stir to combine thoroughly.

Add *finely* chopped scallions. Stir.

Pour 1/4 cupful batter onto preheated griddle. Turn when the pancake bubbles and bottom is browned. Remove to a plate when cooked. Prepare all twelve pancakes.

Spoon 1 tablespoonful of *feta* cheese onto each pancake. Roll tightly. Place on an oven-proof serving dish. and place in the warm oven until ready to serve.

Serve warm.

Yields 12 servings
adequate for 6 people

Note: This recipe can easily be doubled or tripled, when required.

1/12 SERVING – PROTEIN = 4.1 g.; FAT = 3.6 g.; CARBOHYDRATE = 11.0 g.;
CALORIES = 96; CALORIES FROM FAT = 34%

MONGOLIAN SESAME NOODLE SALAD WITH CORN

TPT - 1 hour and 12 minutes;
1 hour = marination period

This kind of noodle salad, adapted from a popular Chinese salad, is a salad that is easily prepared and requires no fresh vegetables. It makes a very good side dish. Those who live at the edge of the Gobi desert have even less access to vegetables than do those in the cities who must frequent the markets supplied by the daily delivery of fresh produce from China.

1 tablespoon *tamari* soy sauce**
1 tablespoon sesame oil**
1 tablespoon rice wine vinegar**
1 tablespoon sesame seeds—*lightly toasted*
1/4 teaspoon sugar

1/2 cup green (fresh) *or frozen* corn kernels

2 quarts *boiling* water
2 cups Chinese curly wheat noodles

In a large plastic container with tightly fitting lid, combine soy sauce, sesame oil, rice wine vinegar, and *toasted* sesame seeds.

Add corn. Set aside briefly.

Add noodles to *boiling* water. Continue to boil for about 7 minutes, or until tender. Turn into a sieve or colander and toss *very gently*, but *very thoroughly*. Add to ingredients in plastic container. Cover tightly and allow to marinate for at least 1 hour in the refrigerator. Toss occasionally to insure uniform marination.

Turn into serving bowl.

Yields 6 servings
adequate for 4 people

Notes: *These items are increasingly available in grocery stores. Asian markets and food specialty stores regularly stock all these items.

This recipe can be halved, when required.

Asia – **Mongolia**

MONGOLIAN SESAME NOODLE SALAD WITH CORN (cont'd)

1/6 SERVING – PROTEIN = 3.5 g.; FAT = 3.8 g.; CARBOHYDRATE = 19.6 g.;
CALORIES = 126; CALORIES FROM FAT = 27%

MONGOLIAN TOSSED SALAD WITH NOODLES AND ONION *VINAIGRETTE*
TPT - 6 minutes

My mother's sister and her husband hosted my mother and me when we flew in to attend the funeral of my grandmother. Their usual meals of meat and potatoes were prepared and my uncle's not-too-subtle joke was to suggest to me that I go out in the backyard and graze. A piece of cheese was provided and a dressing-soaked salad became my dinner for several days. I could commiserate with a young, progressive Mongolian when I heard the story of his elderly Mongolian grandfather who would not eat greens, saying, "Don't feed me leaves. I'm not a goat." This salad is of Chinese origin but such salads are becoming more and more popular in Mongolia among those who do eat leaves.

MONGOLIAN ONION *VINAIGRETTE*:
    2 tablespoons safflower *or* sunflower oil
    1 1/2 tablespoons rice wine vinegar
    1 teaspoon sugar
    1 tablespoon grated onion
    1/2 teaspoon *tamari* soy sauce
    1/8 teaspoon lovage *or* celery seeds
    Pinch salt

2 cups *thinly* sliced *bok choy* leaves and stems
  —well-washed and well-dried
1 large scallion—trimmed, well-rinsed, and sliced diagonally into thin slices
1 cup *cooked* Chinese curly wheat noodles—*well-chilled*

2 tablespoons slivered, *toasted preservative-free* almonds

In a cruet or small jar, combine oil, vinegar, sugar, grated onion, soy sauce, lovage seeds, and salt. Shake vigorously. Set aside until required.

In a salad bowl, combine *thinly* sliced *bok choy*, thinly sliced scallions, and *cooked* curly wheat noodles. Toss.

Sprinkle *toasted* almond slices over.

Serve with onion *vinaigrette*.

Yields 6 servings
adequate for 4 people

Note: This recipe can be halved or doubled, when required.

1/6 SERVING – PROTEIN = 2.0 g.; FAT = 6.0 g.; CARBOHYDRATE = 9.3 g.;
CALORIES = 100; CALORIES FROM FAT = 54%

MONGOLIAN EGGPLANT SALAD WITH HERB DRESSING
Simpoog Aghtsa
TPT -   1 hour and 33 minutes;
        1 hour = marination period

As you circle the globe, the range of salads created using eggplant is amazing. This one, I suspect, owes homage to the cuisines of the Near East, encountered during the period of empire building by the Mongols under Chinggis Khan in the 1200s. It, however, has its own distinctive twist with the wonderful addition of rosemary, basil, and mint. It usually contains lamb but is a substantial, interesting salad without the meat addition. It is an especially good choice as a side dish with noodle dishes.

MONGOLIAN HERB DRESSING:
    1 tablespoon *extra virgin* olive oil
    3 tablespoons freshly squeezed lime juice
    1/2 cup *finely* chopped Italian red onion
    2 tablespoons chopped fresh mint leaves
    1/4 cup chopped fresh basil leaves
    1/4 cup chopped fresh parsley

1 medium eggplant—unpeeled

1 tablespoon *extra virgin* olive oil
2 garlic cloves—sliced
1/8 teaspoon powdered rosemary
Salt, to taste
Freshly ground mixed peppercorns—red, black, and white—to taste

1 medium tomato—chopped

MONGOLIAN EGGPLANT SALAD WITH HERB DRESSING (cont'd)

In a mixing bowl, combine 1 tablespoonful oil, lime juice, *finely* chopped onion, and chopped mint, basil, and parsley. Toss to mix well. Set aside until required.

Prepare steamer.

Cut eggplant in half. Steam until almost *tender*, but *not mushy*—about 10-12 minutes. *Using a very sharp knife*, cut eggplant into chunks. Turn into a non-stick-coated skillet.

Add remaining 1 tablespoonful oil, garlic slices, powdered rosemary, salt, and ground mixed peppercorns. Set over *MEDIUM* heat and cook, stirring frequently, until garlic and eggplant begin to brown.

Turn into the mixing bowl with the herb dressing. Stir to mix well. Cover with plastic wrap and refrigerate for at least 1 hour. Sir occasionally. Turn into a serving bowl or onto a small platter.

Garnish with chopped tomato.

Serve *well-chilled*.

Yields 6 servings
adequate for 4 people

Note: This recipe may be halved or doubled, when required.

1/6 SERVING – PROTEIN = 1.4 g.; FAT = 3.9 g.; CARBOHYDRATE = 8.0 g.;
CALORIES = 74; CALORIES FROM FAT = 47%

MONGOLIAN THREE-BEAN SALAD WITH CREAMY DRESSING
TPT - 2 hours and 6 minutes;
2 hours = flavor development period

Oh no, this is not the ubiquitous deli three-bean salad we find in the United States. The creamy dressing and salty chunks of cheese quickly alert you to a different country of origin. Mongolians often add meat chunks such as ham to this salad much the way Pennsylvanians add ham to a potato salad.

3/4 cup canned chick peas (*garbanzos*)—well-drained and seed coats removed
3/4 cup canned red kidney beans—well-drained
3/4 cup diagonally-cut fresh yellow wax beans
   or green beans, if preferred
6 tablespoons diced *feta* cheese in brine

6 tablespoons *calorie-reduced or light* mayonnaise
3 tablespoons *fat-free* dairy sour cream
1 1/2 teaspoons MUSTARD SAUCE [see index]
2 1/4 teaspoons freshly squeezed lemon juice
1 1/2 teaspoons crushed, dried dillweed
Freshly ground mixed peppercorns—red, white, and black—to taste

In a mixing bowl, combine chick peas (*garbanzos*), kidney beans, sliced yellow wax beans, and diced *feta* cheese. Toss to mix.

In a small bowl, combine mayonnaise, sour cream, mustard, lemon juice, crushed dillweed, and ground mixed peppercorns. Mix thoroughly. Add to bean mixture and fold the two mixtures thoroughly together. Turn into a serving bowl. Cover and refrigerate for at least 2 hours before serving.

Serve chilled.

Yields 6 servings
adequate for 4 people

Note: This recipe can be doubled, when required.

1/6 SERVING – PROTEIN = 6.3 g.; FAT = 14.4 g.; CARBOHYDRATE = 12.9 g.;
CALORIES = 202; CALORIES FROM FAT = 64%

MONGOLIAN CHICK PEA AND RICE SOUP
TPT - 34 minutes

Mongolians enjoy thick stew-like soups filled with meat; we prefer meatless soups that are more liquid. With only a few changes this popular Mongolian soup became a balanced protein vegan meal for six.

Asia – Mongolia

MONGOLIAN CHICK PEA AND RICE SOUP (cont'd)

1 quart VEGETABLE STOCK FROM SOUP *[see index]* or other vegetarian stock of choice
4 cardamom pods

3/4 cup dry converted *or* long grain rice—white or brown, as preferred

1 can (15.5 ounces) chick peas (*garbanzos*)—well–drained
1 tablespoons rice wine vinegar
1 teaspoon ground turmeric
1 teaspoon ground ginger
1/2 teaspoon ground coriander
1/2 teaspoon saffron

3 tablespoons chopped fresh coriander (*cilantro*) leaves

In a kettle set over *MEDIUM* heat, combine vegetable stock and cardamom pods. Bring to the boil. Reduce heat to *LOW-MEDIUM*.

Add rice. Stir. Cover and allow to simmer for 20 minutes until rice is tender. Remove cardamom pods.

Add well-drained chick peas, rice wine vinegar, ground turmeric, ginger, and coriander, and saffron. Cook, stirring frequently, until heated through. Add more stock if too thick for your taste.

Add chopped fresh coriander (*cilantro*). Adjust seasoning, if necessary. Turn into a heated soup tureen.

Serve into heated soup bowls.

Yields 7 cupfuls

Note: This soup freezes well.

1/7 SERVING (i. e., per cupful) –
PROTEIN = 3.5 g.; FAT = 2.5 g.; CARBOHYDRATE = 15.2 g.;
CALORIES = 74; CALORIES FROM FAT = 24%

TEA – SMOKED *TOFU* WITH GINGER
TPT - 9 hours and 28 minutes;
8 hours = bean curd pressing period;
1 hour = marination period

Soybean curd is extremely bland, which to some is reason to shun it. I, on the other hand, have always looked at tofu as an opportunity since it has the incredible ability to take on the flavors I introduce. We have the fantastic soy protein with the opportunity to experiment. You couldn't ask for more.

Be sure to experiment with this smoking technique when you can open the windows.

3 *firm, low-fat, silken* beancurd cakes (*tofu*)
—2 3/4 x 2 1/2 x 1 inch each

1/4 cup loose black tea leaves, such as English Breakfast, Earl Grey, or Assam
1/2 cup *boiling* water

1/2 cup *cold* water

2 tablespoons ginger preserves
Salt, to taste
Freshly ground black pepper, to taste

2 tablespoons ginger preserves
3 or 4 drops "liquid smoke"

2 scallions—*both white and green portions*—trimmed, well-washed, and cut into shreds

Wrap the soybean curd cakes in a cotton tea towel and place on the counter top. Place a bread board or other flat weight on top and weight this with cans or with a tea pot filled with water to a weight of about 3 pounds. Allow to stand for about 8 hours or until most of moisture has been pressed out of the cake and absorbed by the towel. (Change towel after 1 hour, if necessary.) Cut each pressed soybean cake into four triangles. Place *pressed* beancurd in a flat, high-sided dish until required.

Steep tea leaves in *boiling* water for 1 minute.

Add *cold* water. Steep for an additional 1 minute. Strain the liquid from the tea leaves into a flat, high-sided dish. *Reserve the tea leaves.*

Mix 2 tablespoonfuls of ginger preserves into the strained liquid, mixing well. Season with salt and pepper. Marinate the pressed beancurd cakes into the tea–ginger marinade for 1 hour, *turning four times during the marination period.*

Asia – Mongolia

TEA – SMOKED *TOFU* WITH GINGER (cont'd)

Mix 2 tablespoons of ginger preserves and "liquid smoke" into the reserved tea leaves.

Prepare a broiler pan by covering it with aluminum foil. Spread the reserved ginger preserve–tea leaf mixture onto the center of the aluminum foil-covered pan. Set a broiler rack above the "smoking mixture." Set oven rack about 6 inches below the broiler unit. Preheat broiler to about 375 degrees F.

When ready to broil, preheat broiler to get the "smoking mixture" smoking. Place the marinated beancurd wedges on a lightly oiled broiler pan above the "smoking mixture" and broil for about 5 minutes on each side. Transfer to a heated serving platter.

Garnish with scallion shreds.

Serve at once, accompanied by steamed rice.

Yields 6 servings

Notes: If you decrease the number of beancurd cakes being smoked, do not decrease the amount of tea or ginger preserves you use for the process.

If preferred, the beancurd cakes can be prepared over a charcoal grill. Place the aluminum foil with ginger preserves and tea leaves directly on the *glowing coals*. Grill the beancurd cakes about 4 inches above the smoking mixture.

1/6 SERVING – PROTEIN = 12.0 g.; FAT = 3.0 g.; CARBOHYDRATE = 13.6 g.;
CALORIES = 125; CALORIES FROM FAT = 22%

HOISIN BARBECUE SAUCE
Su Jeung
TPT - 4 minutes

Hoisin sauce is a sweet, spicy, garlicky sauce from southern China, popular now in the West, and embraced by Mongolians as well. This hoisin barbecue sauce is a wonderful flavor enhancer for grilled tofu and it is also a good choice for basting roasted or grilled vegetables such as asparagus, broccoli, red peppers, leeks, and carrots.

4 scallions—*white portions only*—trimmed, well-rinsed, and *very finely* chopped
1/4 cup *hoisin* sauce*
1 tablespoon *tamari* soy sauce*
1 tablespoon safflower *or* sunflower oil
1/4 teaspoon sesame oil*
1 tablespoon *very finely* chopped fresh gingerroot
1 tablespoon *very finely* chopped garlic
1/2 teaspoon Szechwan garlic–*chili* paste, or to taste*
1/4 teaspoon CHINESE FIVE – SPICE POWDER
  [see index]

Notes: *Szechwan *chili* paste is available in Asian groceries. *Hoisin* sauce, *tamari* soy sauce, and sesame oil are now available in most grocery stores.

This recipe can be halved or doubled, when required.

In a small bowl, combine *very finely* chopped scallions, *hoisin* sauce, soy sauce, safflower and sesame oils, *very finely* chopped gingerroot and garlic, Szechwan *chili* paste, and five-spice powder. Stir to thoroughly combine.

Use to spread on *tofu* for grilling or brush on roasted or grilled vegetables. Refrigerate leftovers.

Yields about 16 tablespoonfuls

1/16 SERVING (i. e., per tablespoonful) –
PROTEIN = 0.3 g.; FAT = 1.1 g.; CARBOHYDRATE = 2.9 g.;
CALORIES = 23; CALORIES FROM FAT = 43%

Asia–**Mongolia**

ASIAN MEATBALL AND VEGETABLE PASTRY BUNDLES
Buuz

TPT - 3 hours and 18 minutes;
2 hours = mushroom soaking period

If you have ever visited a Chinatown bakery or a dim sum restaurant, you will probably have seen or tasted lotus- or pork-stuffed bao. These buns may well be the inspiration for buuz, a Mongolian dumpling which is stuffed with any and all varieties of shredded and chopped food in sauce. Inspired by the "beggar's bundles," a pastry bundle with vegetables which was offered as a vegetarian entrée by a French restaurant we frequented, I created this. A refined interpretation of buuz, admittedly, but a descendant undoubtedly of such packets of meat and vegetables cooked over open fires. Today these bundles are often enclosed in aluminum foil or bread dough or a dumpling mixture. They are then cooked in an oven or over a fire pit. I prefer to wrap this Mongolian inspired mixture, sans the lamb, in puff pastry and bake it.

12 dried *shiitake* or black mushroom caps
2 cups *boiling* water

3 tablespoons *tamari* soy sauce
2 tablespoons red wine vinegar
2 tablespoons *hoisin* sauce
1/4 teaspoon ground ginger
1 garlic clove—*very finely* chopped
Pinch ground red pepper (cayenne)

2 teaspoons corn starch

1 tablespoon CLARIFIED BUTTER *or* GHEE
[see index]
1 cup corn kernels cut from the cob, *frozen* kernels, *or* the equivalent in thinly sliced baby corn, as preferred
1/2 cup diced potato
1/2 cup diced zucchini squash
1/2 cup diced red bell pepper
1/2 cup *finely* chopped leeks—*green portion only*
—well-rinsed

12 6 x 6-inch squares *frozen* puff pastry—*brought to room temperature*

12 *frozen* vegetarian "meatballs"

In a small bowl, soak mushrooms in *boiling* water. Allow to soak for 2 hours until soft. Cut stems from caps, squeeze water from caps, and set aside until required.

Preheat oven to 400 degrees F. Line a cookie sheet with culinary parchment.

In a mixing bowl, combine soy sauce, vinegar, *hoisin* sauce, ground ginger, *very finely* chopped garlic, and ground red pepper (cayenne). Stir to mix.

Add corn starch and, using a wire whisk, combine thoroughly. Set aside until required.

In a skillet set over *MEDIUM* heat, heat butter. Add corn, diced potato, squash, and red pepper, and *finely* chopped onion. Cook, stirring frequently, until vegetables just begin to soften. Remove from heat. Add to sauce ingredients in mixing bowl.

Roll out the 6-inch puff pastry square into an 8-inch square. Tuck the square into a large Pyrex dish so that the edges of the pastry drape over the side of the dish. Place a mushroom cap in the center of the square. Place a meatball in the center of the mushroom cap. Using a ladle, scoop out *one-twelfth* of the sauced vegetable mixture and pour it over the meatball. Gather the sides of the pastry together and twist into a "topknot." A couple of drops of water can be smeared at the top to secure the seal. Place on prepared baking sheet. Repeat until all twelve bundles have been prepared.

Bake in preheated 400 degree F. oven until pastry is puffed and golden.

Serve at once.

Yields 12 servings
adequate for 6-8 people

Note: This recipe can be reduced or increased to accommodate the number of diners.

1/12 SERVING – PROTEIN = 9.1 g.; FAT = 19.0 g.; CARBOHYDRATE = 60.3 g.;
CALORIES = 340; CALORIES FROM FAT = 50%

Asia–**Mongolia**

MONGOLIAN SWEET BARLEY PORRIDGE
Belila

TPT - 1 hour and 39 minutes

Barley is a super food in my view. It is said to lower cholesterol and, with that, the risk of coronary heart disease. It is also a great source of fiber, a much better source of fiber than is rice for which it can be substituted. Since pearled barley, the form most commonly available in grocery stores, cooks in about 10-20 minutes, it can be a useful tool to the busy homemaker. Barley was one of the first grains domesticated in the Fertile Crescent and wild barley can be found from North Africa all the way to Tibet where it became a staple food in the fifth century AD. A bowl of barley porridge makes a wonderful breakfast and a delicious dessert pudding as well.

1/2 cup dry pearl barley
1 cup *two-percent* milk
1 cup light cream *or* half and half
1 star anise pod

3 tablespoons honey
1 teaspoon pure vanilla extract

In a non-stick-coated saucepan set over *MEDIUM* heat, combine barley, milk, cream, and the star anise pod. Allow to come to a low boil. *Reduce heat to LOW* and cook, stirring frequently, until the barley becomes soft and the pudding thickens. Thin with more milk, if necessary. Remove from heat.

Add honey and vanilla extract. Stir to combine well. Remove star anise pod. Turn into a serving bowl. Refrigerate for at least 1 hour to cool.

Serve chilled.

Notes: This recipe can be halved or doubled, when required.

Cinnamon sugar can be provided at the table for those who like their pudding a bit sweeter.

This porridge is delicious served over stewed apples.

Yields 6 servings
adequate for 4 people

1/6 SERVING – PROTEIN = 4.1 g.; FAT = 4.7 g.; CARBOHYDRATE = 26.7 g.;
CALORIES = 162; CALORIES FROM FAT = 26%

YOGURT CREAM WHIP WITH GINGER

TPT - 4 hours and 8 minutes;
4 hours = yogurt draining period

Cheeses and cultured dairy products, such as sour cream and yogurt, extend the viability of the milk collected from herds in Mongolia. If you love the taste of ginger, as we do, you will find this dessert the perfect ending to a spicy meal when you want something cooling and satisfying, but not innocuous and forgettable.

3/4 cup VANILLA YOGURT *[see index] or*
  commercially-available vanilla yogurt

3/4 cup *fat-free* dairy sour cream

1/2 vanilla bean

3/4 cup heavy whipping cream

3 tablespoons *light* brown sugar
1/4 teaspoon ground ginger
1/2 teaspoon pure vanilla extract

2 tablespoons demerara, coarse sugar

YOGURT CREAM WHIP WITH GINGER (cont'd)

Prepare VANILLA YOGURT *CRÈME* by setting two automatic drip coffeemaker filters into a sieve over a medium-sized bowl or a yogurt filter over a 2-cup measuring cup. Pour the vanilla yogurt into the filters and set in the refrigerator. Allow to drain for about 4 hours.

Split the vanilla bean in half and scrape the seeds into the drained yogurt. Using a wire whisk, beat the seeds into the yogurt *crème*, until the *crème* is very smooth.

Add sour cream and again whisk until very smooth. Set aside briefly.

Using the electric mixer fitted with *chilled* beaters or by hand using a *chilled* wire whisk, beat heavy cream in a *clean, chilled* bowl until stiff peaks form.

Add yogurt–sour cream mixture, brown sugar, ground ginger, and vanilla extract. *Whisk-fold* the whipped cream into the yogurt.

Divide among six dessert dishes. Garnish each serving by sprinkling it with about 1/2 teaspoonful of demerara sugar. Refrigerate until ready to serve.

Yields 6 individual servings

Note: This recipe may be halved or doubled, when required.

1/6 SERVING – PROTEIN = 5.9 g.; FAT = 10.2 g.; CARBOHYDRATE = 28.1 g.;
CALORIES = 227; CALORIES FROM FAT = 40%

Myanmar
formerly Burma

Cave paintings and an archaeological site in Padah Lin in Myanmar's Shan State date a hunter-gatherer settlement to the Holocene period. Immigrants from the neighboring nations of Cambodia, Thailand, China, and India have contributed significantly to this true Asian melting pot nation. The residents of today's Union of Myanmar derive historically from the Indo-Aryans who moved into the Indochinese peninsular region in about 700 BC where they formed small kingdoms. The first unification in the eleventh century, known as the Bagan Empire, ended in the thirteenth century with the invasion of the Mongolian marauders under Kublai Khan. The Mongols did not stay long but the Tai-Shan people from Yunnan, who arrived with the Mongols, did stay. Burma became a land of warring ethnicities who again established kingdoms throughout the peninsula. In 1853 Rangoon and southern Burma became a part of British India after a long period of wars begun in 1824 when the Burmese tried to invade India. All of the country came under British India rule with the expansion of the British East India Company. In 1937, just prior to World War II, Burma became a separate colony. Just a few years later, as the Japanese war machine moved across Asia, Burma found itself occupied by the Japanese. Independence was finally achieved in 1948 but the resulting Union of Burma, a democratic republic, dissolved in 1962 after a military *coup*. With a succession of unstable governments, the country underwent *coups* and several name changes in recent years becoming known as the Socialist Republic of the Union of Burma in 1974, the Union of Burma, again, in 1988, and the Union of Myanmar in 1989.

Prior to the overthrow of the government of U Nu in 1962, Buddhism had been the state religion with about ninety percent of the population favoring Theravada Buddhism, certainly a result of the repeated introduction of Buddhism to Burma over the centuries. The 1974 constitution does assure religious freedom but Burma has always been comfortable with it religious diversity.

Myanmar's relatively large Buddhist population approach the vegetarian tenants of Buddhism somewhat differently than do western Buddhists and most western vegetarians. The extensive use of fish sauce and seafood in dishes the Myanmarese considered to be vegetarian can be a frustration to the vegetarian, who expects "meatless" options. The problem is a definition of "meat." Burmese Buddhists do not eat four-footed animals but do not have the same reverence for two-footed animals or for finned animals. As a result, chicken and fish are consumed by most who follow the Buddhist traditions with chicken and fish stocks used as soup bases. Those who follow the ancient Indian religion of Jainism have extreme reverence for all living things and do not eat root vegetables or even walk on grass for fear of destroying insects and soil organisms. In contrast, Burmese of Chinese descent enjoy pork and practice a mixture of Mahayana Buddhism, Taoism, Confucianism, and ancestor worship. Additionally, Hindus from India, Muslims from Pakistan, and a small population of Christians, mostly of European and Indian origin, influence what is eaten in a cuisine that is quite complex and, as a result, fascinating.

Asia – Myanmar / Burma

Cauliflower and Eggs
with **Dried Mushroom Condiment**
Ngapi Kywa

~

Sea Broth with Glass Noodles   Sea Broth
Rakhine Moti

~

Cabbage and Green Mango Salad
Thayat Thee Thoke

Lemon and Red Onion Salad in Lettuce Rolls

Radish and Garlic Relish/Salad
Monlar oo Thoke

~ ~ ~ ~ ~ ~ ~ ~ ~ ~ ~ ~ ~ ~ ~ ~ ~ ~ ~ ~

Curried Soymeat and Onions with Coconut Milk

Steamed Eggplant

Steamed Rice

~ ~ ~ ~ ~ ~ ~ ~ ~ ~ ~ ~ ~ ~ ~ ~ ~ ~ ~ ~

Lychees in Coconut Milk
Lai Nga

Coconut – Rice Porridge

CAULIFLOWER AND EGGS IN THE BURMESE STYLE
TPT - 25 minutes

This quickly-prepared entrée is appropriate as a luncheon dish, a first course offering, or the entrée served with rice for a light supper. If you, as did I, express surprise at finding cauliflower in the cuisines of Southeast Asia, wait until you taste how cauliflower and soy sauce play off each other. Broccoli works well in this recipe too.

2 tablespoons peanut *or* canola oil
1 medium onion—*finely* chopped
1 medium garlic clove—*very finely* chopped

4 cups frozen *or* fresh white cauliflower—cut into *small* florets*
1 1/2 tablespoons *tamari* soy sauce

4 large eggs—*well-beaten***

Thai sweet *chili* sauce

In a 9-inch skillet,*** set over *MEDIUM* heat, heat oil. Add *finely* chopped onion and *very finely* chopped garlic. Sauté until onion is soft and translucent, *being careful to allow neither the onion nor the garlic to brown.*

Add cauliflower florets and soy sauce. Cook, stirring frequently, until cauliflower is heated through.

Stir in beaten eggs, spreading evenly over the pan surface. Scramble *gently*. Turn out onto a heated round serving platter.

Serve at once. Pass sweet *chili* sauce to accommodate individual tastes.

Yields 6 first-course servings
or 4 main-course servings

Notes: *Raw cauliflower florets will take several minutes longer to cook. The frozen cauliflower will defrost quickly.

VOLUME II - 409

CAULIFLOWER AND EGGS IN THE BURMESE STYLE (cont'd)

****Four eggs are quite adequate for six people as a first course. This is easily increased proportionately as needed using the same 9-inch or a 10-inch skillet although it will require a longer cooking period.

***We use a non-stick-coated skillet which we further coat with a non-stick lecithin spray coating.

1/6 SERVING – PROTEIN = 6.5 g.; FAT = 7.7 g.; CARBOHYDRATE = 5.5 g.; CALORIES = 113; CALORIES FROM FAT = 61%

BURMESE DRIED MUSHROOM CONDIMENT
Ngapi Kywa

TPT - 12 hours and 25 minutes;
4 hours = mushroom stalk rehydration;
8 hours = mushroom stalk dehydration

Buddhist nuns devised a use for the stems of dried mushrooms that are often cut away and discarded. I too felt that discarding mushroom stems year after year was a dreadful waste but I did not know how to recoup this loss. Now I do. This condiment, a vegetarian adaptation of "ngapi kywa," is a really wonderful way to enhance plain noodles or rice or turn a simple vegetable side dish into a special vegetable side dish. Collecting the mushroom stems called for in this recipe can take time, although I always wash and dry the stems also when I dehydrate mushrooms. If you do not use a lot of dried mushrooms or if you do not dry mushrooms, dried mushroom kibble is available from several mushroom growers. This can be rehydrated and then dehydrated again to use in place of the stems. A dehydrator is indispensable for this dish but a slow oven can also be used, if necessary.

2 cups *dried* mushrooms
3 cups *cool* water

1 tablespoon peanut oil
4 large garlic cloves—sliced and, then, slivered into long strips
2 shallots—sliced and, then, slivered into long strips

1/2 teaspoon sugar
Pinch salt
1 1/2 teaspoons Thai sweet *chili* sauce
1/4 teaspoon *jalapeño chili* sauce, or to taste*

Prepare a pint canning jar by sterilizing thoroughly. Sterilize a lid and a ring.

In a mixing bowl, rehydrate mushroom stems in *cool* water—about 4 hours.

Once mushrooms have been rehydrated, dry them again in a dehydrator overnight. Once dry, shred the mushrooms in a mortar with a pestle until they are shredded into strands.** Set aside briefly.

In a non-stick-coated skillet set over *MEDIUM* heat, heat oil. Add garlic and shallot slivers. While stirring constantly, sauté until *lightly* browned.

Add mushroom strands and continue sautéing until the mushrooms begin to brown.

Add sugar, salt, Thai sweet *chili* sauce, and *jalapeño chili* sauce. Mix thoroughly. Turn into the sterilized canning jar. Refrigerate until required.

Yields 1 cupful

Notes: *Dried *chilies* can be substituted, if preferred.

**The texture required can only be achieved when the dehydrated mushrooms are rehydrated and dehydrated again.

1/16 SERVING (per tablespoonful) –
PROTEIN = 0.2 g.; FAT = 0.7 g.; CARBOHYDRATE = 1.0 g.;
CALORIES = 11; CALORIES FROM FAT = 57%

Asia—Myanmar / Burma

SEA BROTH WITH GLASS NOODLES
Rakhine Moti

TPT - 14 minutes

Several of the vegetarian soups in my files that are popular in Myanmar (Burma) are meals in themselves and too heavy to be served as a first course. Since fish or seafood stocks are not a violation of Buddhist tenants, many Burmese soups call for fish- or seafood-based stock. Years ago I evolved a broth using a sea vegetable, a seaweed called kombu which is readily available dried. This soup stimulates the appetite instead of satiating. Bean threads or cellophane noodles are made from mung beans and cook in just minutes when added to boiling stock.

1 quart SEA BROTH [see recipe which follows]

4 ounces dried glass noodles, bean threads, or cellophane noodles

Thin scallion slices—*green portion only*—**for garnish**

In a large saucepan set over MEDIUM heat, bring the broth to the boil. *Remove from heat.*

Add noodles, pushing them down into the broth. When pliable, cut with a scissors. Allow the noodles to sit in the hot broth until "glassy"—about 10 minutes. Set over LOW heat and allow to heat through. Ladle into serving bowls. Garnish with a few thin slices of scallion.

Serve at once.

Yields 6 first-course servings

Note: This recipe can be halved or doubled, when required.

1/6 SERVING – PROTEIN = 0.04 g.; FAT = 0.01 g.; CARBOHYDRATE = 66 g.; CALORIES = 66; CALORIES FROM FAT = >1%

SEA BROTH

TPT - 36 minutes

As a replacement for the fish stock that I used to make when we lived on the coast and for Asian soups that required a fish broth, this sea vegetable stock is a pleasant variation from the land vegetable stock I usually make.

1 quart water
About 1/4 cup dried *kombu*
2 scallions—trimmed, well rinsed, and chopped

1 teaspoon fresh tarragon
1 teaspoon freshly squeezed lemon juice

In a saucepan set over MEDIUM heat, combine water, dried seaweed, and scallions. Bring to the boil. Reduce heat to LOW and simmer for about 20 minutes. Remove seaweed and set aside to add to a stir-fry or the stock pot.

Add the tarragon and lemon, return to the heat, and simmer for 10 minutes more. Strain through a fine sieve before using as a clear broth soup or as an ingredient in a recipe.

Yields 3 cupfuls

Notes: *Dried *kombu* seaweed is available in most natural food stores and in food specialty stores. It should be well-rinsed and wiped dry before use. *Dulse* may be substituted if more readily available.

When required, this recipe can be doubled.

The broth can be frozen quite successfully. It can also be canned using a water-bath canner. Process for about 15 minutes.

The calories available from vegetarian stocks are almost negligible. For these reasons, we have chosen to treat these stocks merely as flavoring—omitting them from nutritional calculations but recognizing them as a food, quite rich in vitamins and minerals.

Asia–**Myanmar / Burma**

BURMESE CABBAGE AND GREEN MANGO SALAD
Thayat thee Thoke

TPT - 40 minutes;
30 minutes = onion soaking period

Whenever I find mangoes on sale and thus have several in the house ripening at inconvenient intervals, I remember to make this salad from one of the hard, green mangoes sitting in the fruit bowl. This salad from the country now known as Myanmar can be a very refreshing addition to an Asian menu. It can be spiked with hot chilies, as hot as you might please, or it can be a mild counterpoint to other spiced dishes.

Really unripe mangoes are rarely available in produce departments in the United States. The unripe mangoes used by the Burmese and the Thai are green, really green inside and out, and they are not sweet. Your best bet is to just use the hardest, most unripe, mango you can find.

1/2 cup diced *sweet* onion—Vidalia, Walla Walla, *or* Texas or Mayan Sweet
1 cup water

2 tablespoons safflower *or* sunflower oil
2 garlic cloves—sliced into long *very thin* slices
2 large shallot cloves—sliced into crosswise slices

1 *green* (*unripe*) mango—peeled and slivered
2 cups shredded green cabbage
1/4 cup chopped *fresh* coriander (*cilantro*)

2 teaspoons *tamari* soy sauce *or* "white" soy sauce, if preferred

1/2 teaspoon crushed, *roasted* red *chilies*, or to taste*
2 tablespoons crushed, *roasted*, *unsalted* peanuts
2 teaspoons chick pea flour**

In a small mixing bowl combined diced onion and water. Allow onion to soak for at least 30 minutes to mellow the taste. Drain well.

Meanwhile, in a small skillet set over *LOW-MEDIUM* heat, heat oil. Add garlic and shallot slices and sauté until golden, *being careful not to allow either vegetable to overbrown or burn*. Remove from heat. Add soy sauce. Set aside until required.

In a large, shallow serving bowl, such as a noodle bowl, combine shredded mango, shredded cabbage, chopped fresh coriander (*cilantro*), and drained, diced onion. Toss to mix.

Just before serving, add sautéed garlic and shallots with oil and soy sauce to vegetables in serving bowl. Toss to disperse dressing evenly.

Garnish with crushed, roasted red *chilies*, crushed, roasted peanuts, and chick pea flour.

Toss at the table and *serve at once*.

Yields 6 servings
adequate for 4 people

Notes: *Including more or less or none of the roasted *chilies* will still result in a wonderful salad. Manage the "fire" of the red *chilies* to be used in this salad to suit your taste.

**Chick pea flour is available in Asian and Middle Eastern markets, natural food stores, and, often, in the international sections of grocery stores. If you do not have chick pea flour, grind a few dry chick peas into flour using a SPICE and COFFEE GRINDER.

This recipe can be halved or doubled, when required.

1/6 SERVING – PROTEIN = 1.7 g.; FAT = 5.7 g.; CARBOHYDRATE = 10.9 g.;
CALORIES = 96; CALORIES FROM FAT = 53%

Asia–Myanmar / Burma

LEMON AND RED ONION SALAD IN LETTUCE ROLLS

TPT - 1 hour and 7 minutes;
1 hour = onion marination period

This salad is an adaptation of a classic Burmese salad which is refreshing but punctuated by flavors. Burmese Buddhists do not eat four-footed animals, considering them to be closely related to humans. As previously mentioned, most Asian Buddhists will, however, eat birds and fish. As a result, the interpretation of vegetarianism and the resultant dishes considered appropriate to present to a vegetarian can seriously challenge a western vegetarian, Buddhist or not. This dish, for example, is usually made with dried shrimp and fish paste but we have created this version to compliment our vegetarian dishes.

1 medium Italian red onion—peeled and *thinly* sliced into rings
1 tablespoon sugar
1 teaspoon safflower *or* sunflower oil

1 large lemon—peeled, pitted, and *thinly* sliced
1/4 teaspoon sugar
1/4 cup *finely* chopped fresh coriander (*cilantro*)

Freshly ground mixed peppercorns—red, white, and black—to taste

12 small red Boston lettuce leaves—well-washed and dried

In a plastic bowl with cover, combine onion rings, sugar, and oil. Shake gently to coat onion rings with the 1 tablespoonful sugar and oil. Refrigerate for at least 1 hour, turning gently every 10 minutes to insure uniform marination.

In a shallow serving bowl or on a plate, arrange lemon slices. Sprinkle the 1/4 teaspoonful sugar and chopped fresh coriander (*cilantro*) over.

Drain onion rings through a sieve. Pour over lemon slices.

Grind mixed peppercorns generously over.

Refrigerate until required.

Serve with lettuce leaves. Urge diners to create lettuce rolls by tucking some of the salad onto a lettuce leaf and rolling it tightly.

Yields 12 servings
adequate for 6 people

Note: This recipe can be doubled, when required.

1/12 SERVING – PROTEIN = 0.3 g.; FAT = 0.4 g.; CARBOHYDRATE = 2.4 g.;
CALORIES = 12; CALORIES FROM FAT = 30%

BURMESE RADISH AND GARLIC RELISH/SALAD
Monlar oo Thoke

TPT - 26 minutes

Burmese salads, I suppose, should more appropriately be called relishes since their importance is to enhance and counter other flavors in a meal. The ingredients are prepared, seasoned, and arranged on a board or platter. Diners, using their fingers, a technique called "a-thoke," mix together a salad of their choosing from the ingredients presented.

2 slices onion—separated into rings
2 cups *cold* water

3 tablespoons *raw* peanuts

1 tablespoons *toasted* sesame seeds

2 inches of a *daikon* radish—about 3 ounces—cut into *paper-thin* slices using a vegetable peeler

1 tablespoon peanut oil
3 garlic cloves—*finely* chopped

2 tablespoons fresh coriander (*cilantro*) leaves —chopped

In a mixing bowl, submerge onion rings in cold water. Set aside until required.

In a non-stick-coated skillet, dry-fry peanuts until golden. Cool for about 10 minutes. Using a nut grinder or a mortar and pestle, grind to a uniform meal.

Add *toasted* sesame seeds to ground peanuts. Set aside until required.

BURMESE RADISH AND GARLIC RELISH/SALAD (cont'd)

In a skillet set over *LOW* heat, heat oil. Add *finely* chopped garlic. Sauté until garlic is golden, *being careful not to allow garlic to burn.*

Drain onion rings and place in a pile on a serving board or platter.

Pile radish slices on the serving board or platter.

Arrange the ground peanut and sesame seed mixture, fried garlic, and chopped fresh coriander (*cilantro*) leaves, in piles on the same serving surface, being careful to place these components away from any residual moisture that may seep from onions.

*Serve at once.**

Yields 6 servings
adequate for 4 people

Notes: *In a more western fashion, we accompany the ingredients with *demitasse* spoons to facilitate serving.

If preferred, the ingredients may all be mixed together to make a composed salad.

This recipe can be halved or doubled, when required.

1/6 SERVING – PROTEIN = 1.7 g.; FAT = 5.1 g.; CARBOHYDRATE = 2.6 g.;
CALORIES = 61; CALORIES FROM FAT = 75%

BURMESE CURRIED SOYMEAT AND ONIONS WITH COCONUT MILK
TPT - 32 minutes

Every Burmese cook has a version of this recipe, essentially a chicken recipe with a sauce that delights the taste buds. Made with frozen soy meat products that not only mimic the texture of the original but also provide the complemented amino acids that all vegetarians seek, you can experience the taste of Burma (Myanmar) without the long flight and the difficulty of conveying the phrase, "I do not eat meat." This version contains neither the fish sauce nor the fiery hot chilies that would be traditionally incorporated. I add a little "hot" and let family and friends up the heat as they desire.

1 large garlic clove—*very finely* chopped
1 thin slice fresh gingerroot— *very finely* chopped

1/2 teaspoon *jalapeño chili* sauce* *or* a fresh *chili* pepper—seeded and chopped

1 tablespoon canola oil
1 large onion—*thinly* sliced

8 ounces *frozen* soy meat analogue—cut into strips
1/4 cup *light, sulfite-free* coconut milk
6 tablespoons water
1/4 teaspoon paprika
1/8 teaspoon ground turmeric

Combine *very finely* chopped garlic and gingerroot on a bread board and, using a chef's knife, chop together until *very, very finely* chopped. Turn into a marble mortar.

Add *jalapeño chili* sauce. Using the pestle, grind the mixture to a paste. Set aside briefly.

In a skillet set over *LOW-MEDIUM* heat, heat oil. Add *thinly* sliced onion and sauté until onion is soft and translucent, *being careful not to allow onion to brown.*

Add garlic–*chili* paste. Stir to blend.

Add chopped soy meat analogue, coconut milk, water, paprika, and ground turmeric. Stir to blend well and simmer gently for about 10 minutes, or until the soymeat is heated through.

Serve over steamed rice with extra *jalapeño* sauce to accommodate individual tastes.

Yields 4 servings
adequate for 3 people

Note: *Jalapeño* sauce is available in Hispanic groceries, food specialty stores, and in most groceries throughout the Southwest.

1/4 SERVING (exclusive of rice) –
PROTEIN = 11.3 g.; FAT = 5.5 g.; CARBOHYDRATE = 6.0 g.;
CALORIES = 114; CALORIES FROM FAT = 44%

Asia–Myanmar / Burma

BURMESE STEAMED EGGPLANT

TPT - 1 hour and 17 minutes;
1 hour = flavor development period for sauce

Long, thin, lavender Chinese eggplants are generally available from a well-supplied greengrocer although just finding any kind of eggplant in our very German area of Pennsylvania was a challenge when we first moved out here. The Chinese eggplant has a more delicate flavor, thinner skin, and fewer seeds than the dark purple globe eggplant. My mother never liked eggplants, hence I grew up not knowing too much about this fruit and I married into a family where eggplants were beloved and were very frequently on the menu. Mom disliked the skin, a problem easily solved by peeling, and she disliked the seeds claiming they were bitter, a problem that can be addressed by sexing the eggplant before buying it. Male eggplants tend to have fewer seeds, making them less bitter than are the female fruits. Examination of the base of eggplant can give you a clue. Male eggplants have a shallow round base; female eggplants have a deep indentation in the base. Small eggplants are always a good choice since the flavor is inevitably more mellow. Japanese eggplants, labeled as Asian eggplants, are often the only Asian eggplant choice. The Japanese variety is generally more bitter than is the Chinese variety.

3 tablespoons *tamari* **soy sauce**
1 tablespoon GARLIC OIL [see index]
1 tablespoon sesame oil
1 teaspoon Thai sweet *chili* **sauce**
3/4 teaspoon *jalapeño chili* **sauce**
1 scallion—trimmed, well-rinsed, and *finely* **chopped**
2 garlic cloves—*very finely* **chopped garlic**

4 Chinese eggplants—well-washed

In a small bowl combine soy sauce, garlic oil, sesame oil, Thai sweet *chili* sauce, *jalapeño chili* sauce, *finely* chopped scallion, and *very finely* chopped garlic. Stir to combine. Set aside at room temperature for about 1 hour to allow for flavor development.

Set up steamer over *MEDIUM* heat.

Steam eggplants for about 12-15 minutes, or until tender. Trim ends from eggplants and cut eggplants into 3/4-inch-thick rounds. Place on a heated platter. Spoon sauce over.

Serve at once.

Yields 8 servings
adequate for 4-6 people

Note: This recipe can be halved, when required.

1/8 SERVING – PROTEIN = 0.7 g.; FAT = 3.3 g.; CARBOHYDRATE = 4.1 g.;
CALORIES = 49; CALORIES FROM FAT = 61%

LYCHEES IN COCONUT MILK
Lai Nga

TPT - 1 hour and 3 minutes;
1 hour = refrigeration period

Although we generally end a meal from Burma with a fresh, tropical fruit selection, this is a simple dessert that perfectly ends a meal with the feeling of both fruit and pudding. A friend refers to that as a comfort ending! Lychees ("Litchi chinensis"), which are readily available shelled, pitted, and canned, are unique, so unique in fact that it is the sole member of the genus "Litchi" in the family "Sapindaceae." The evergreen from which this fruit is harvested has been cultivated since 2000 BC in China and is often no more than ten-feet tall. Because it requires a tropical to frost-free subtropical climate, the bulk of commercial supplies come from Southeast Asia and China but commercial growers in Hawaii, California, Texas, Florida, South Africa, and Israel have begun to cultivate the small evergreen whose fruit at one time was enjoyed only by the Chinese Imperial Court.

Asia – **Myanmar / Burma**

LYCHEES IN COCONUT MILK (cont'd)

1/2 cup *light, sulfite-free* coconut milk
1 tablespoon sugar

1 can (20 ounces) lychees (about 48 fruits)—well-drained

In a serving bowl, combine coconut milk and sugar. Stir to dissolve sugar.

Add well-drained lychees. Stir gently to coat the lychees with the sweet coconut. Refrigerate for at least 30 minutes.

Serve chilled or at room temperature, as preferred.

Yields 6 servings
adequate for 4 people

Note: This recipe can be easily doubled, when required.

1/6 SERVING – PROTEIN = 0.8 g.; FAT = 0.8 g.; CARBOHYDRATE = 20.7 g.;
CALORIES = 92; CALORIES FROM FAT = 8%

BURMESE COCONUT – RICE PORRIDGE

TPT - 50 minutes;
45 minutes = refrigeration period

There always seems to be leftover coconut milk, which, if not frozen, will mold quickly. I suspect that Burmese cooks avail themselves of extra coconut milk and leftover rice from the previous meal to prepare rice dishes with coconut milk as do I. Rice with coconut milk and fried onions is popular in Myanmar, as is this dessert. Unlike the Filipino version, which is a rice cake, this rice pudding is a porridge. Far less sweet than that usually prepared in Myanmar, it is more to our taste in the West.

Yes, add the salt; it is requisite for an authentic Burmese taste.

2 cups *steamed* short grain white rice
1 cup *light, sulfite-free* coconut milk, or more if necessary
1/2 cup sugar

1/2 teaspoon salt

In a saucepan set over *LOW-MEDIUM* heat, combine *cooked* rice, coconut milk, and sugar. Stir to combine. Cook, stirring frequently, until sugar is dissolved. Remove from heat.

Add salt. Stir to integrate. Transfer to a serving dish or individual dessert dishes, if preferred. Refrigerate for at least 45 minutes.

Serve chilled or at room temperature, as preferred.

Yields 6 servings
adequate for 4 people

Note: This recipe can be halved, when required.

1/6 SERVING – PROTEIN = 1.7 g.; FAT = 1.6 g.; CARBOHYDRATE = 35.0 g.;
CALORIES = 161; CALORIES FROM FAT = 9%

The Philippines

The "Dawnmen," as the first inhabitants of the Philippines are known, moved presumably from Southeast Asia across the land bridges that connected The Philippines to the Indonesian archipelago. Archaeological evidence suggests that these cave-dwelling people lived here as early as 250,000 years ago. They did not remain but moved on. They were followed by other peoples whose journey became less and less easy as the polar glaciers melted and the sea level rose. When the people who are referred to as the Aetnas arrived from Malaya, Borneo, and Australia approximately 27,000 years ago, although this date is disputed, they too used land bridges and settled in Palawan, Mindoro, and Mindanao. The rise of the ocean and formation of islands discouraged the further migration of these dark-skinned pigmies and they stayed, becoming the first permanent residents of this island nation, a nation which now consists of approximately 7,100 islands with a land mass roughly the size of Arizona. Most of these islands are volcanic in origin, sitting as they do over a very active subsidence area of the earth's crust known as the "Pacific ring of fire." Indonesians and Malays, emigrating from their homelands about 2,000 years ago, constitute the third wave of immigration.

The coat of arms of The Philippines perhaps says more than words can say about the history of The Philippines and the passion for their nation that dwells within Filipinos. The sun, positioned centrally on the coat of arms, symbolizes independence. The three golden stars at the top represent the three principal areas of the country, Luzon, The Visayas, and Mindanao. The lower part of the of the shield is divided into two portions—the right side, containing a lion, represents the Spanish occupation (1542-1899) and the left side, containing an eagle, represents the American occupation (1899-1946). The period of American occupation was interrupted during World War II when the Japanese invaded in 1942 and held the country until the end of the war in 1945. On July 4, 1946, the Commonwealth of The Philippines declared itself to be the Republic of The Philippines.

At the beginning of the third century AD the inhabitants of Luzon had made contact with Asia and entered into a vigorous trade with the East, especially with the Chinese. Trade with Southeast Asia, the Chinese, and, later, Japan, have greatly influenced the art, architecture, and cuisine of The Philippines as did the 356-year rule by Spain. One can also see the residual influence of the forty-four-year governance by the United States, which began at the end of the Spanish–American War. All of these influences meld to create a country different from all others in Southeast Asia.

We are indebted to our close, personal relationship with a former classmate from The Philippines who introduced us to their beautiful country, its culture, its struggles, and its cuisine in a way that few are privileged to explore. We will always be grateful to those friends whose friendship we treasure.

Asia – The Philippines

Hard-Cooked (unfertilized) Duck Eggs or **Preserved Sweet and Sour Eggs**
with salt and vinegar *Itlóg Preserbahin*

Baked or Fried Vegetable Egg Rolls with Soy Sauce
Lumpia Frito Shanghai

~

Cabbage Soup with Clear Cilantro Stock
Sopa de Pechay

Clear Cilantro Stock with Garlic
Sopa

~

Baby Banana Salad with Peanuts   Hearts of Palm Salad
Ensalada de Saging   *Ubod ng Niyog*

~~~~~~~~~~~~~~~~~~~~~~

Eggplant *Adobo*
Adobong Talong

Baby Spinach with Gingerroot and *Chilies*
in Coconut Milk
Laing

Fried Rice with Shallots and Garlic
Sinangag

~~~~~~~~~~~~~~~~~~~~~~

Creamed Pearl Tapioca Pudding
Yuca Bibingka

Lychees and *Macapuno* Balls in Sweet Cream
Letsiyas at Macapuno

Fried Rice Sweets
Dulce de Frito Arroz

Homemade Vanilla Extract

Coconut Brittle
Kendi Nyóg

Asia–The Philippines

FILIPINO PRESERVED SWEET AND SOUR EGGS
Itlóg Preserbahin
TPT - 24 hours and 53 minutes;
24 hours = cooling period

My grandmother told me about "putting down" eggs in sodium silicate, also known as "water glass," before the days of widespread refrigeration. The eggs kept for about six months because the sodium silicate kept air and bacteria from passing through the egg shell. By the time you ran out of eggs, the hens would again be laying and the price of eggs would have dropped. Another technique that Grandma told me about was the use of sulfuric acid, not under any condition a task to be undertaken by the average homemaker nor do I suspect that the average homemaker knew then that the sulfuric acid turned the lime in the shell to lime sulfite, thereby making the shell less permeable. Preserving eggs has been an obsession of man since ancient days. Anyone who has tasted a Chinese salted and preserved duck egg or a "thousand-year-old egg" buried in a huge jar in a Chinatown grocery will attest to the more extreme preservation methods; anyone who went to boarding school, college, or was in the military during World War II or in the 1950s will attest to tasteless results of powdered eggs, although that technique provided us a way to preserve egg whites for meringues and such. Pasteurized eggs, a useful and Salmonella-negative product, are available today as we still search for the perfect preservation technique. Natural egg-laying is considerably reduced during the period of the year when there are fewer hours of sunlight providing fewer and smaller eggs. Solved today by artificial lighting, hens do seem to keep up with the demand. During the early years of our marriage candled duck eggs were always available from the many duck farms then on Long Island; these rich, deeply flavored eggs were a special treat. Years later I learned that Filipinos also enjoy duck eggs but as an extremely bizarre street food known as "balut." The steamed fertilized duck eggs have become something of "an item" and are now served as appetizers in restaurants, often served adobo style or fried in omelets. No, this recipe for preserved sweet and sour eggs is nothing like "balut" nor are these preserved eggs anything like Chinese "thousand-year-old eggs." They are more like one of the "sweet and sours" that might be served by our Mennonite neighbors.

6 cups distilled white vinegar
2 3/4 cups sugar
1 teaspoon salt

1 tablespoon pickled spice mixture

9 *hard-cooked* eggs—cooled and peeled

Prepare three one-pint canning jars by sterilizing. Also sterilize lids and rings.

In a large saucepan set over *MEDIUM* heat, combine vinegar, sugar, and salt. Stir to dissolve the sugar.

Secure the pickling spices in a tea ball and attach to the side of the saucepan. Allow to come to the boil.

Add peeled eggs. Allow to simmer for about 5 minutes. Remove from heat.

Scoop three eggs into each of the sterilized jars. Cover the eggs with the boiling liquid. Wipe rim of jars and seal with hot, sterilized lids and rings. Process in hot-water-bath canner for 25 minutes, *timing from the moment the water reaches a full rolling boil.* Remove to surface covered with thick towels or newspapers. Allow to cool for 24 hours *undisturbed*. Check to be sure jars are sealed before labeling. Loosen or remove rings before storing. Store in refrigerator.

Yields 9 pickled eggs

1/9 SERVING (i. e., per egg) –
PROTEIN = 6.4 g.; FAT = 5.7 g.; CARBOHYDRATE = 1.6 g.;
CALORIES = 84; CALORIES FROM FAT = 61%

FILIPINO CABBAGE SOUP WITH CLEAR *CILANTRO* STOCK
Sopa de Pechay
TPT - 45 minutes

The February day, when we first tasted the prototype for this soup, the meal also included deep-fried vegetable fritters and a wonderful macaroon-like coconut cake a la mode for dessert. It was a very delicious lunch. This soup is rather unique in that most soups served in The Philippines are filled with either fish or meat.

Asia – The Philippines

FILIPINO CABBAGE SOUP WITH CLEAR *CILANTRO* STOCK (cont'd)

6 cups FILIPINO *CILANTRO* STOCK WITH GARLIC *[see recipe which follows]*
6 cups Chinese *napa* cabbage *or* celery cabbage if preferred, chopped and well-washed
1 medium garlic clove—*very finely* chopped
1/4 teaspoon ground sweet paprika
Pinch of salt

In a kettle set over *MEDIUM* heat, combine stock, chopped cabbage, *very finely* chopped garlic, ground paprika, and salt. Allow to come to the boil.

Reduce heat to LOW. Simmer, stirring frequently, for about 30 minutes, or until cabbage is cooked and slightly translucent. Turn into a heated soup tureen.

Serve into heated soup bowls.

Yields 6 servings
adequate for 4-6 people

Note: This recipe can be halved or doubled, when required.

1/6 SERVING – PROTEIN = 0.8 g.; FAT = 0.07 g.; CARBOHYDRATE = 2.2 g.;
CALORIES = 10: CALORIES FROM FAT = 1%

FILIPINO CLEAR *CILANTRO* STOCK WITH GARLIC
Sopa

TPT - 2 hours and 10 minutes

This is a gentle vegetarian stock, which we refer to as just plain "sopa," from which we can build very flavorful soups with just a hint of the exotic.

4 quarts water

2 bunches coriander *(cilantro)* sprigs—well-washed, trimmed, and *coarsely* chopped
2 large garlic cloves—peeled and *coarsely* chopped
2 scallions—trimmed, well-washed, and chopped
2 large slices fresh gingerroot—shredded

In a kettle set over *MEDIUM-HIGH* heat, bring water to the boil.

Reduce heat to LOW. Add *coarsely* chopped coriander *(cilantro)* stems and leaves and garlic, chopped scallions, and shredded gingerroot. Simmer, stirring frequently, for about 2 hours.

Using a fine sieve, strain vegetables from stock. Discard vegetables. Strain stock through a sieve lined with culinary cheesecloth or a cotton tea towel.

Refrigerate until ready to use or freeze in quantities appropriate for future use.

Yields 15 cupfuls

Notes: This recipe can be halved or doubled, when required.

The calories available from vegetarian stocks, such as this, are almost negligible.

FILIPINO BABY BANANA SALAD WITH PEANUTS
Ensalada de Saging

TPT - 8 minutes

Back in the 1940s a salad called a "candle salad" became all the rage I was recently reminded of this salad when my mother sent me all her old cookbooks and wartime pamphlets and there it was, that most peculiar salad in which a peeled banana stood vertically in a mayonnaise base on a salad plate. A maraschino cherry was attached to the top of the banana to simulate a flame, I guess. It was too much, too weird; I have never served it but I have never forgotten it. Baby bananas have a wonderful pineapple nuance that makes them head and shoulders above the almost tasteless Cavendish bananas we find in abundance in our grocery stores. They have been hybridized from the Cavendish banana but small as they might be, they are not small on flavor. They make a beautiful salad presentation.

FILIPINO BABY BANANA SALAD WITH PEANUTS (cont'd)

DRESSING:
    1/4 cup *light or calorie-reduced* mayonnaise
    2 tablespoons pineapple juice
    2 tablespoons *light, sulfite-free* coconut milk

6 small red lettuce leaves *or* **Boston lettuce leaves, if preferred**—*well-washed* and *well-dried*

6 *baby* bananas—sliced in half longitudinally

1/4 cup chopped, *roasted, but unsalted*, peanuts

In a small bowl, combine mayonnaise, pineapple juice, and coconut milk. Using a small wire whisk, beat until smooth. Set aside until required.

When ready to serve, place a red lettuce leaf on each of six salad plates. Arrange two halves of a banana attractively on the leaves on each plate. Sprinkle a portion of chopped peanuts over. Spoon a portion of the prepared salad dressing onto each plate.

Serve at once.

                                             Yields 6 individual servings

Note: This recipe can be halved or doubled easily, when required.

1/6 SERVING – PROTEIN = 1.5 g.; FAT = 7.2 g.; CARBOHYDRATE = 29.2 g.;
CALORIES = 178; CALORIES FROM FAT = 36%

FILIPINO HEARTS OF PALM SALAD
Ubad ng Niyog
TPT - 6 minutes

Enjoying a salad of hearts of palm always comes with a downside to me. Since a palmetto tree has to be sacrificed just to harvest the heart to satisfy my graving for this silky treasure, it seems a tremendous environmental extravagance. This Filipino salad is much simpler than that from Ecuador which I have included elsewhere in this book. But it gives an opportunity to appreciate the taste and texture that is so very unique to this vegetable.

***VINAIGRETTE*:**
    2 tablespoons safflower *or* sunflower oil
    1 tablespoon white wine vinegar
    1/4 teaspoon honey
    Tiny pinch dry mustard
    Freshly ground black pepper, to taste

2 cups *shredded* red Romaine lettuce
1 can (14 ounces) hearts of palm—drained, *well-rinsed*, and sliced into rounds
1 cup *finely* chopped sweet onion—Vidalia, Walla Walla, *or* Texas or Mayan Sweet

In a small bowl, combine oil, vinegar, honey, dry mustard, and black pepper. Whisk to blend well.

On a plate or serving platter, layer shredded lettuce, sliced hearts of palm, and *finely* chopped sweet onion.

Pour prepared *vinaigrette* over.

Serve at once. Toss salad at table as you serve.

                                             Yields 6 servings
                                            adequate for 4 people

Note: This recipe can be halved or doubled, when required.

1/6 SERVING – PROTEIN = 2.3 g.; FAT = 5.1 g.; CARBOHYDRATE = 7.0 g.;
CALORIES = 73; CALORIES FROM FAT = 63%

Asia—The Philippines

EGGPLANT *ADOBO*
Adobong Talong

TPT - 1 hour and 45 minutes;
1 hour = eggplant salting period

The adobo could safely be called the national dish of The Philippines if it were a dish but it really is more of a preparation technique. The variations are endless since chicken, pork, fish, and vegetables can be sauced with the traditional combination of vinegar, soy sauce, garlic, and ground peppercorns. It is distinctive; it is flavorful. An added bonus is that the vinegar, which acts as a preservative, enables foods cooked adobo-style to be kept for several days so leftovers can survive in the tropical climate.

Traditionally the eggplant is fried in oil but eggplant soaks up so much oil that I prefer to bake thick eggplant slices which can be cut into chunks and quickly sautéed and sauced.

1 medium eggplant—well-washed, ends trimmed, and cut into 1-inch-thick slices
1/2 teaspoon salt

2 tablespoons corn oil *or* peanut oil

1/2 cup distilled white vinegar
1/4 cup *tamari* soy sauce
1 large garlic clove—*very finely* chopped

Freshly ground black pepper, to taste

Salt eggplant slices generously and place them in a sieve or colander set in the sink. Place a plate on top and a weight—a large can or a tea kettle filled with water—on top of the plate. Allow to stand for 1 hour.

Place a rimmed cookie sheet in oven to heat. Preheat oven to 350 degrees F.

Remove preheated baking sheets from oven. Pour the 3 tablespoons of oil on the pan; brush to edges. Arrange eggplant slices on the prepared baking sheet. Bake in preheated 350 degree F. oven for 10 minutes. Remove baking sheet from oven. Turn each eggplant slice. Return to oven for about 10 minutes more, or until each slice is browned. Drain eggplant slices *thoroughly* on several thicknesses of paper toweling. Chop into 1/2-inch square pieces. Set aside briefly.

In a non-stick-coated skillet set over *MEDIUM* heat, combine vinegar, soy sauce, and *very finely* chopped garlic. Allow to come to the boil. Simmer for about 6 minutes.

Add baked eggplant pieces. Stir to coat with vinegar mixture. Allow to simmer for an additional 5 minutes. Stir and turn frequently.

Season with black pepper. Turn into a heated serving bowl.

Serve over steamed rice.

Yields 6 servings
adequate for 4 people

Note: This recipe can be halved or doubled, when required.

1/6 SERVING (exclusive of rice) –
PROTEIN = 0.7 g.; FAT = 3.9 g.; CARBOHYDRATE = 3.8 g.;
CALORIES = 55; CALORIES FROM FAT = 64%

BABY SPINACH WITH GINGERROOT AND *CHILIES* IN COCONUT MILK
Laing

TPT - 14 minutes

In The Philippines laing is made with kangkong, a native tropical green that is milder that spinach. For this reason and because I can not grow kangkong in my northern temperate climate, I use baby spinach for this dish and for my "adobong kangkong." Those who have tasted laing will immediately wonder how it can be made without the traditional addition of pork and shrimps. Letting the spinach star, unimpeded, is really not a bad idea.

BABY SPINACH WITH GINGERROOT AND *CHILIES* IN COCONUT MILK (cont'd)

1/2 cup *thick, sulfite-free* coconut milk
2 teaspoons *very finely* chopped gingerroot
1 garlic clove—*very finely* chopped
1/4 teaspoon salt
10 ounces baby spinach—well-washed and trimmed
2 tablespoons *finely* chopped mild green *chilies*

In a non-stick-coated skillet set over *LOW-MEDIUM* heat, combine coconut milk, *very finely* chopped gingerroot and garlic, and salt. Allow to come to the simmer, stirring occasionally.

Add spinach and *finely* chopped green *chilies*. Simmer until spinach is wilted—about 5-8 minutes. Stir frequently.

Serve at once.

Yields 6 servings
adequate for 4 people

Note: This recipe can be halved, when required.

1/6 SERVING – PROTEIN = 1.8 g.; FAT = 1.0 g.; CARBOHYDRATE = 2.9 g.; CALORIES = 23; CALORIES FROM FAT = 39%

FILIPINO FRIED RICE WITH SHALLOTS AND GARLIC
Sinangag
TPT - 17 minutes

A high school friend of Ray's from Manila and his wife often visited us when they made one of their frequent visits to the United States. On one occasion they actually trotted all the ingredients for a Filipino dinner from Manhattan out to our Long Island home. The whole day was spent in preparations; we finally ate about 9 PM. On another visit Marilen brought me a cookbook that had belonged to her mother. The small, well-used book has been a treasure ever since as a memory of a treasured friendship. There are many versions of fried rice, some are authentically Filipino and some are influenced by other Southeast Asian cuisines. This is authentically Filipino, a dish often eaten for breakfast, and it is brings thoughts of distant friends every time we serve it.

2 tablespoons safflower *or* sunflower oil
2 tablespoons *finely* chopped garlic
1/4 cup *finely* chopped shallots

3 cups *cold, cooked,* converted rice
1 1/2 tablespoons *tamari* soy sauce
Freshly ground black pepper, to taste

In a large non-stick-coated skillet set over *MEDIUM* heat, heat oil. Add *finely* chopped garlic and shallots and cook until soft and translucent, *being careful to allow neither the garlic nor the shallots to brown.*

Add *cold* rice, soy sauce, and black pepper. Cook, stirring constantly, until thoroughly heated through—about 10 minutes. Turn into a serving bowl.

Serve at once.

Yields 6 servings
adequate for 4 people

Note: This recipe can be halved or doubled, when required.

1/6 SERVING – PROTEIN = 3.7 g.; FAT = 4.6 g.; CARBOHYDRATE = 24.9 g.; CALORIES = 154; CALORIES FROM FAT = 27%

Asia—The Philippines

FILIPINO CREAMED PEARL TAPIOCA PUDDING
Yuca Bibingka

TPT - 12 hours and 26 minutes;
8 hours = tapioca soaking period;
30 minutes = cooling period

Although sago is an edible starch extracted from East Indian palms of the genus "Metrosylon," and tapioca or manioc comes from the root of the cassava, "Manihot esculenta," Filipinos still refer to and label any tapioca product as sago, albeit in parentheses now. This dessert is similar to "cassava bibingka," a classic Filipino custard pudding made from grated cassava. Such a pudding is usually served from a round bibingka mold lined with banana leaves.

1/3 cup pearl tapioca*
2 cups *cold* water

1/2 cup *fat-free* sweetened condensed milk
2 1/2 cups skimmed milk**

1/2 cup *fat-free* pasteurized eggs (the equivalent of 2 eggs)

TOPPING:
   3 tablespoons *fat-free* sweetened condensed milk
   3 tablespoons *light, sulfite-free* coconut milk***
   3 tablespoons *fat-free* pasteurized eggs

Soak pearl tapioca in *cold* water for at least 8 hours. Drain thoroughly.

In the top half of a double boiler set directly over *LOW* heat, combine sweetened condensed milk and skimmed milk. Using a wire whisk, combine well. Bring milk combination just to the boiling point. Place double boiler inset, containing scalded milks, over *simmering*, but *not boiling*, water. Add drained tapioca pearls. Cook, stirring frequently and *gently* with a wooden spoon, until tapioca are *translucent*—about 2 1/2 to 3 hours. *Check sample pearls carefully to be sure that tapioca is completely cooked.***** Remove from heat.

Pour eggs into a large mixing bowl. *Gradually, tablespoonful by tablespoonful*, stir hot tapioca mixture into eggs. Continue stirring until mixture begins to thicken.

Preheat oven to 350 degrees F. Prepare a 9-inch square baking pan or pie plate or, if preferred, a 1 1/2-quart soufflé dish by coating with non-stick lecithin spray coating.

Pour tapioca–milk–egg mixture into prepared baking dish.

In a mixing bowl, combine the 3 tablespoonfuls each of sweetened condensed milk, coconut milk, and pasteurized eggs to form the TOPPING. *Gently* spread prepared topping mixture evenly over the top of the pudding. Bake in 350 degree F. oven for 25 minutes.

Remove from oven and allow to cool for about 30 minutes, or until pudding is at room temperature.

Serve a room temperature or slightly chilled. Chilled leftovers are disappointing. Nevertheless, do be sure to refrigerate any leftovers.

Yields 6 servings
adequate for 4 people

Notes: *Pearl tapioca is available in Asian groceries and in specialty food stores if not available in your grocery store.

**Fresh cow's milk is a rarity in The Philippines, where a combination of evaporated milk and coconut milk would more often be used to prepare this type of dish.

***Canned, *sulfite-free* coconut milk is available in most grocery stores in either the international section or beverage section. Canned *sulfite-free, low-fat* coconut milk is hard to find but it is available. The reduction in saturated fats is well worth the search for this more healthful product. Leftover coconut milk can be frozen.

****The pearls stiffen as they cool so do not be alarmed if they seem quite soft at this stage. In addition, the entire mixture sets as it chills resulting in an adequately firm pudding.

When required, this recipe may be halved. If double this amount is required, make two separate batches.

1/6 SERVING – PROTEIN = 8.8 g.; FAT = 1.4 g.; CARBOHYDRATE = 46.1 g.;
CALORIES = 247; CALORIES FROM FAT = 5%

Asia—The Philippines

FILIPINO *LYCHEES* AND *MACAPUNA* BALLS IN SWEET CREAM
Letsiyas at Macapuno

TPT - 1 hour and 6 minutes;
1 hour = flavor development period

My mother often made a fruit salad for our Sunday night supper, a ritual, for the most part, now lost as an American tradition. In the winter, canned fruit might be supplemented with a storage apple. It was all bound together with whipped cream and occasionally a sprinkling of coconut transformed it to what was called "ambrosia." Filipinos also enjoy this salad but instead of dried coconut, they have access to macapuno balls, balls formed from the soft flesh that does not solidify in coconuts referred to as "sports." Macapuno balls are available, packed in heavy syrup, in Filipino groceries and from mail order firms. Fresh lychees are rarely available in regional grocery stores in the heartland of the United States, especially when you need them for a recipe. Canned lychees are readily available, convenient, and oh so sweet. The combination is a most unusual dessert.

1 can (20 ounces) *lychees* in syrup—well-drained
1/2 cup preserved *macapuno* balls—well drained

2 tablespoons *fat-free* Neufchâtel cheese *or low-fat* cream cheese, if preferred
3 tablespoons heavy whipping cream

In a mixing bowl, combine well-drained *lychees* and well-drained *macapuno* balls.

In a small bowl combine, Neufchâtel or cream cheese and cream. Work together until smooth. Pour over fruit and gently stir to coat the fruit. Turn into a serving bowl. Refrigerate for at least 1 hour to allow for flavor development.

Yields 6 servings
adequate for 3-4 people

Note: This recipe can be doubled, when required.

1/6 SERVING – PROTEIN = 0.6 g.; FAT = 3.3 g.; CARBOHYDRATE = 19.5 g.;
CALORIES = 112; CALORIES FROM FAT = 27%

FILIPINO FRIED RICE SWEETS
Dulce de Frito Arroz

TPT - 23 minutes

The very best pure vanilla extract will reward you more than you could ever anticipate when you make this unusual rice dessert. Any sweet sauce or syrup can be served over these delicious dessert morsels but ginger syrup is my favorite adornment. It is the perfect partner to the warm vanilla flavoring.

1 cup unbleached white flour
2 teaspoons baking powder
1/4 cup sugar
1/4 teaspoon salt

1/2 cup *fat-free* pasteurized eggs (the equivalent of 2 eggs)
6 tablespoons *thick, sulfite-free* coconut milk
1 1/2 teaspoons HOMEMADE VANILLA EXTRACT *[see recipe which follows]* **or** pure vanilla extract

1 cup *steamed* Japanese short grain rice

1/4 cup *high-heat* safflower *or* sunflower oil

AUSTRALIAN SWEET GINGER SYRUP *[see index]* **or** dessert syrup of choice

In a mixing bowl combine flour, baking powder, sugar, and salt. Stir to distribute the baking powder and salt evenly.

Add pasteurized eggs, coconut milk, and vanilla extract. Mix well.

Add cooked rice. Mix well.

In a non-stick-coated skillet set over *LOW-MEDIUM* heat, heat oil until it just begins to spit if a drop of water is dropped into the skillet. Using two soup spoons, form spoonfuls of the rice batter into four small patties, just as you would for corn oysters. Drop into the hot oil. Fry for a couple of minutes until the bottom is light browned. Turn over and allow the other side to brown.

FILIPINO FRIED RICE SWEETS (cont'd)

Transfer to paper toweling to drain. Repeat until all of the batter has been used and all the pastries have been fried. Place on a serving plate.

Serve at room temperature with sweet syrup.

Yields 24 pastries
adequate for 6 people

Note: This recipe can be halved or doubled, when required.

1/6 SERVING (exclusive of syrup) –
PROTEIN = 1.2 g.; FAT = 0.8 g.; CARBOHYDRATE = 8.2 g.;
CALORIES = 40; CALORIES FROM FAT = 2%

HOMEMADE VANILLA EXTRACT
TPT - 2 weeks and 55 minutes;
45 minutes = cooling period;
2 weeks = flavor development period

I have always added half of a vanilla bean to a bottle of pure vanilla extract. It is a useful way to use up a slightly too-dry vanilla bean that has lost its way in a spice storage bin. It is also an economical way to create a double-strength vanilla extract from a single-strength product. Making your own vanilla extract is simple and satisfying but there is an extra bonus since it will cost you about half the price.

1 fresh vanilla bean

3/4 cup vodka

Prepare a Pyrex measuring cup and a small condiment jar with lid by washing and drying well. Set a canning funnel into the measuring cup. Set a funnel into the condiment jar.

Split the vanilla bean and scrape all the seeds into the measuring cup. Set aside briefly.

In a saucepan set over *MEDIUM* heat, heat vodka until *hot,* but *not boiling*. Pour into measuring cup with vanilla seeds. Allow to cool to room temperature, about 45 minutes. Transfer the cooled vodka and vanilla seeds into the condiment jar. Seal and store at room temperature for two weeks, agitating gently each day to continue the release of flavor from the seeds.

Set a sieve over a clean measuring cup. Agitate infusion vigorously and pour into the sieve to remove any pod pieces. Return strained vanilla extract to condiment jar. *Don't worry about small seeds*, they will continue to flavor.*

Store in cupboard, away from heat. The extract will keep indefinitely.

Yields 3/4 cupful

Notes: *The seeds can be strained from the extract, if desired, but the seeds continue to increase the intensity of the extract for some time if left in the jar.

Calories from the alcohol are lost when the vodka is boiled. Therefore, the residual carbohydrate value of the vanilla extract, albeit small, will vary from batch to batch.

Asia–The Philippines

COCONUT BRITTLE
Kendi Nyóg
TPT - 26 minutes

When I was in high school I worked in the stationery department of a large department store, back when people chose their stationery and had it personalized, bought embossed notes on which to respond to invitations and write thank you notes, and chose their invitations and Christmas cards from large books. On a summer Saturday I was "loaned" to the candy department. I could sample all I wanted to, presumably so that I could describe the handmade confections accurately to customers, but very soon my taste buds and stomach wearied and I began to pray for 5PM to come. I did, however, come to know a great deal about summer coatings and the types of candy that could withstand the summer heat buildup in an era and a store without air conditioning. This brittle, from a recipe found in a 1973 reprint of an old Filipino cookbook, is simple to make. It was a welcome addition to our Christmas holidays and looks so pretty nestled between truffles and buttercreams and Christmas fudge and nut balls.

1 tablespoon butter—*soften to room temperature*

1 cup sugar

1 cup dried, shredded coconut

Using a brush, prepare a marble slab or a well-cleaned counter top by generously buttering.

In a heavy non-stick-coated skillet set over *MEDIUM* heat, melt sugar. Stir constantly until melted and golden in color. Remove from heat.

Add coconut. Stir to mix. Turn out onto buttered surface. Using a butter knife, spread the candy mixture into as thin a sheet as you can. Allow to cool slightly. Lift onto a board and break or cut into small pieces.

Wrap the pieces in waxed paper and store in a cool place.

Yields about 30 pieces

1/30 SERVING – PROTEIN = 0.2 g.; FAT = 1.4 g.; CARBOHYDRATE = 9.7 g.;
CALORIES = 51; CALORIES FROM FAT = 25%

Thailand

The beauty of the traditional architecture can only be matched by the beauty of the flowers and fruits fed by the monsoons in this tropical climate. The beautiful food of Thailand reflects this lush and varied climate but also displays the beauty and sensitivity of the Thai soul in the everyday activity of nourishing the body.

Thailand is a constitutional monarchy which dates its kingdom from 1238 AD. Known as Siam until 1939, and then again from 1945-1949, Thailand has struggled through many *coups* as it has evolved its democratic state. From 1992 until a military *coup* in 2006 Thailand was a functioning democracy. Elections held in 2007 restored the democratic system once again and Thailand has stepped forward under a new constitution. About ninety-three percent of the population are Buddhists, mostly of the Theravada tradition, with a Muslim minority of about six percent living throughout the country. Muslim enclaves in the southern border region with Malaysia, comprised mostly of ethnic Malayans, harbor an increasingly organized and violent Islamic secessionist movement.

Cooking traditions vary across Thailand creating, in essence, four regional cuisines, influenced by their Asian neighbors. For example, curries from the South contain coconut milk and fresh turmeric while Laotian influences can be seen in the northeastern area known as Isan where lime juice is used more extensively than it is elsewhere in the country. The adaptation of Chinese dishes is extensive, which is to be expected in a culture where approximately twelve percent of the population is of Chinese descent. Since Thailand was never colonized, any Western influence on the cuisines is minimal which we suspect might be the reason that it takes courage for some people to try one of the most beautiful and divinely complex cuisines in the world. Thai restaurants, increasingly convenient in any metropolitan area, introduce the supreme freshness and taste contrasts of this cuisine to the western palate, always with choices for the vegetarian, with only two accommodations, as we see it—dishes can be ordered according to "heat" and there is less use of the strongly-flavored fish sauce so ubiquitous in Thai cooking. Who would ever think that the small population of our middle-of-Pennsylvania-meat-and-potatoes culture could support four Thai restaurants where we can enjoy a spicy stir-fry with deep-fried *tofu* and cashews or an authentic vegetarian *pad Thai*, a green mango salad, a phenomenal sticky rice and mango pudding, and the best, bar none, Thai spring rolls ever?

Rice has been and is important to Thailand. Although Jasmine rice is eaten at just about every meal in Thailand, the Thai have come to recognize the danger posed by the loss of biodiversity. More than five thousand varieties of rice from Thailand alone are preserved in the rice gene bank of the International Rice Research Institute, located in The Philippines. You will note that I have included a recipe for sticky black rice, also known as Thai purple rice, in the following menu. If you are going to visit this exotic land, even for a few minutes, it seems to me enjoying this most exotic of grains is a very good point to start.

Asia – **Thailand**

**Vegetarian Appetizer on Mango Slices
in the Style of "Galloping Horses"**
Ma Har

Whole, Roasted Cashews

~

Corn and Sweetpotato Soup

Thai Clear Vegetable Stock

Thai Dark Vegetable Stock

~

Purple Rice and Mango Salad with Mint
Kao Neaw Dam Ma-Muang

Red Grapefruit Salad with Soymeat and Soy Sprouts
Som o Nam Jim

~~~~~~~~~~~~~~~~~~~~

Vegetables in Curried Coconut Milk
Pud Puk Sai

Stir-fried Rice Stick Noodles with Garlic and Thai Basil
Senmee Horapa

~~~~~~~~~~~~~~~~~~~~

Ginger Cream Pudding   Bananas in Coconut Milk

THAI VEGETARIAN APPETIZER ON MANGO SLICES IN THE STYLE OF "GALLOPING HORSES"
Ma Har

TPT - 58 minutes;
30 minutes = mushroom soaking period

I do wonder where this appetizer got the name "galloping horses"; it is such a delightful name. When you are putting together a Thai menu, this recipe can give you a very flexible first course since the "horse" can be almost any fruit that would compliment your meal and the topping can be adjusted to your taste and to the dishes that are to follow. Although generally made with pork by meat-eaters and with tofu by vegetarians, we prefer to create a spicy topping with mushrooms. Additional chili paste, such as "sambal ulek," can be served as a dot at the extreme edge of the "horse" to be added by those who wish.

8 large, whole, dried *shiitake* mushrooms
   —rinsed and cleaned well with a brush*
3 cups *boiling* water

1 tablespoon safflower *or* sunflower oil
2 large shallots—sliced into large flat pieces
1 garlic clove—sliced into large, thin flat pieces

1 tablespoon *tamari* soy sauce*
1 teaspoon Thai sweet *chili* sauce*

2 large ripe mangoes—peeled

Tiny Thai basil leaves, for garnish, if available

VOLUME II - 429

Asia–Thailand

THAI VEGETARIAN APPETIZER ON MANGO SLICES IN THE STYLE OF "GALLOPING HORSES" (cont'd)

In a mixing bowl, combine dried *shiitake* mushrooms and *boiling* water. Set a soup plate or bowl on top of the mushrooms to keep them submerged. Allow the mushrooms to rehydrate for about 30 minutes. Remove from water. Squeeze to remove excess water, cut off stems, and slice caps into large slices.

In a small non-stick-coated skillet set over *LOW-MEDIUM* heat, heat oil. Add mushroom, shallot, and garlic slices. Allow to gently cook, stirring frequently, until shallot and garlic slices have *softened*, but *not browned*.

Add soy sauce and sweet *chili* sauce. Stir into the mushroom mixture to coat the vegetables. Reduce heat to *LOW*.

Slice each peeled mango into large, flat slices by slicing straight down, parallel to the pit, to create two slices on each side of the pit. Lay two slices, overlapping, on each of six salad plates.

Slice the remaining bits of mango off the pit. Chop coarsely and add to the mushroom mixture. Allow to cook for a minute or two.

Spoon *one-sixth* of the sweet, spicy mushroom mixture in a mound on top of the mango slices on each plate. Garnish with a basil leaf or two.

Serve at once as an appetizer or salad, with or without the additional "dot" of hot *chili* paste.

Yields 6 individual first course servings

Notes: *These items are available in Asian groceries and some well-stocked grocery stores in the international aisle.

This recipe can be halved or doubled, when required.

1/6 SERVING – PROTEIN = 0.6 g.; FAT = 2.5 g.; CARBOHYDRATE = 17.2 g.;
CALORIES = 71; CALORIES FROM FAT = 32%

THAI CORN AND SWEETPOTATO SOUP
TPT - 36 minutes

This corn chowder is worlds apart from the corn and potato chowder I usually make but it too represents a comfort factor and has become one of our favorites. A meal in itself, it is short on preparation time but very long on very satisfying flavor; a most perfect combination, a most perfect soup.

1 tablespoon peanut oil
2 slices soy bacon—*finely* chopped
2 shallots—*finely* chopped
2 garlic cloves—*very finely* chopped

3 cups THAI CLEAR VEGETABLE STOCK
 [see index] *or* VEGETARIAN WHITE
 STOCK [see index]
2 Kaffir lime leaves*
1 medium sweetpotato—peeled and cubed

2 cans (16 ounces each) *low-sodium* canned
 creamed corn
1/2 cup *light, sulfite-free* coconut milk
1 tablespoon *tamari* soy sauce
1/8 teaspoon ground red pepper (cayenne), or
 to taste**

3 tablespoons shredded fresh basil leaves,
 preferably Thai basil if available
3 tablespoons ground, *toasted, preservative-free*
 cashews

In a non-stick-coated skillet set over *LOW-MEDIUM* heat, heat oil. Add *finely* chopped soy bacon, *finely* chopped shallots, and *very finely* chopped garlic. Sauté until shallots begin to soften. Turn in a large saucepan or small kettle set over *MEDIUM* heat.

Add stock, kaffir lime leaves, and cubed sweetpotato. Allow to come to the boil. Reduce heat to *LOW* and cook for 6-8 minutes, or until the sweetpotato cubes are *tender*, but *not falling apart*.

Add creamed corn, coconut milk, soy sauce, and ground red pepper (cayenne). Stir to integrate. Increase heat to *MEDIUM*. Allow soup to come back to the boil again. Remove from heat.** Taste and adjust seasoning, if necessary. Turn into a heated soup tureen. *Remove and discard Kaffir lime leaves.*

Serve hot into soup bowls with a garnish of shredded basil leaves and ground, *toasted* cashews over each serving.

Yields about 7 cupfuls

Asia–Thailand

THAI CORN AND SWEETPOTATO SOUP (cont'd)

Notes: *Kaffir lime leaves are available in most Asian markets.

**This soup can be cooled and frozen at this point. Defrost completely and heat over *LOW* heat. Do taste to see if seasoning has been altered by freezing before serving.

Hot red *chilies* are added to this soup in Thailand. If you appreciate the addition, by all means add one—*very finely* chopped.

1/7 SERVING (i. e., per cupful) –
PROTEIN = 6.2 g.; FAT = 8.8 g.; CARBOHYDRATE = 34.3 g.;
CALORIES = 222; CALORIES FROM FAT = 36%

THAI CLEAR VEGETABLE STOCK
TPT - 30 minutes

For the more delicate soups of Thailand, this should be your choice.

3 quarts water

Stems *only* from 20 fresh coriander (*cilantro*) sprigs
Stems *only* from 10 fresh basil sprigs
12 thin slices fresh gingerroot
2 large garlic cloves—peeled and halved
2 scallions—*white portions only*—trimmed, well-rinsed, and coarsely chopped
2 cups peeled and cubed Japanese white *daikon* radish*
2 cups peeled and cubed Chinese winter melon*

In a kettle set over *MEDIUM-HIGH* heat, bring water to the boil.

Reduce heat to LOW. Add coriander (*cilantro*) and basil stems, gingerroot slices, garlic halves, chopped scallions, and cubed *daikon* radish and winter melon. Simmer, stirring frequently, for about 20 minutes.

Using a fine sieve, strain vegetables from stock. Discard vegetables. Strain stock through a sieve lined with culinary cheesecloth or a cotton tea towel.

Refrigerate until ready to use or freeze in quantities appropriate for future use.

Yields 12 cupfuls

Notes: *Although always available in Asian groceries, these items are also available in many greengrocers and grocery stores.

This recipe can be halved or doubled, when required.

The calories available from vegetarian stocks, such as this, are almost negligible and the nutritional analyses will vary, quite naturally, with the choice of ingredients. For these reasons, we have chosen to treat these stocks merely as flavoring—omitting them from nutritional calculations but recognizing them as a food, quite rich in vitamins and minerals.

THAI DARK VEGETABLE STOCK
TPT - 2 hours

This is a dark-colored stock with exotic nuances and an overall smoky flavor.

2 medium onions—well-washed, but *unpeeled* and quartered
2 tomatoes—well-washed, cored, and quartered*
5 garlic cloves—well-washed, but *unpeeled*
1 large carrot—scraped or pared and chopped
3 cups peeled and cubed butternut squash *or* pumpkin

3 quarts water

2 cups peeled and cubed Japanese white *daikon* radish**
Stems *only* from 10 fresh coriander (*cilantro*) sprigs
Stems *only* from 10 fresh basil sprigs
10 thin slices fresh gingerroot—peeled

Asia–Thailand

THAI CLEAR VEGETABLE STOCK (cont'd)

Preheat oven to 350 degrees F.

On a cookie sheet, combine onion and tomato quarters, garlic cloves, and chopped carrot and pumpkin. Roast in preheated oven until the vegetables are browned—about 1 1/4 hours. Stir several times during the roasting period.

In a kettle set over *MEDIUM-HIGH* heat, bring water to the boil.

Reduce heat to LOW. Add the roasted vegetable pieces, cubed *daikon* radish, coriander and basil stems, and gingerroot slices. Simmer, stirring frequently, for about 20 minutes.

Using a fine sieve, strain vegetables from stock. Discard vegetables. Strain stock through a sieve lined with culinary cheesecloth or a cotton tea towel.

Refrigerate until ready to use or freeze in quantities appropriate for future use.

Yields 10 cupfuls

Notes: *Whole, canned tomatoes may be substituted for fresh tomatoes. Add to the roasting vegetables about 30 minutes into the roasting period.

**Although always available in Asian groceries, *daikon* radish is also available in many greengroceries and grocery stores.

This recipe can be halved or doubled, when required.

The calories available from vegetarian stocks, such as this, are almost negligible and the nutritional analyses will vary, quite naturally, with the choice of ingredients. For these reasons, we have chosen to treat these stocks merely as flavoring—omitting them from nutritional calculations but recognizing them as a food, quite rich in vitamins and minerals.

THAI PURPLE RICE AND MANGO SALAD WITH MINT
Kao Neaw Dam má Múang

TPT - 1 hour and 37 minutes;
45 minutes = rice chilling period

Unlike many Thai recipes, this is a cool and refreshing dish that we find a welcome side dish with the hot and spicy dishes that challenge the Western taste buds.

3/4 cup bottled water *or* refrigerated water*
**1/4 cup freshly squeezed tangerine juice *or*
    orange juice, if preferred**
1/2 cup dry Thai purple rice**
1 teaspoon butter
Pinch salt

**3/4 cup diced, peeled ripe mango—the flesh of
    1 medium mango*****
1/4 cup diced ROASTED RED PEPPER [see index]
2 tablespoons *finely* chopped Italian red onion
2 tablespoons *finely* chopped fresh mint leaves

2 tablespoons freshly squeezed lime juice
**1 tablespoon sunflower oil *or* other light-
    tasting oil**

Bring water and tangerine juice to the boil in a large saucepan set over *MEDIUM-HIGH* heat. Stir the rice into the *boiling* liquid, being sure that it does not settle to the bottom of the pan. Add butter and salt. *Reduce heat to low,* cover, and allow to simmer for 30 minutes, or until most of the liquid is absorbed and rice is tender. Remove from heat and allow to stand for 10 minutes.

Pour rice into a sieve. Rinse with cold water and allow to drain thoroughly.

Place rice in sieve over a mixing bowl and refrigerate for about 45 minutes, or until thoroughly cooled and dry.

To chilled rice, add diced mango, diced roasted red pepper, *finely* chopped red onion, and mint leaves. Toss well.

Add lime juice and oil. Again, toss to mix thoroughly.

Turn into a chilled serving bowl. Chill until ready to serve.

Asia–**Thailand**

THAI PURPLE RICE AND MANGO SALAD WITH MINT (cont'd)

Serve chilled or *at room temperature,* as preferred.

Yields 6 servings
adequate for 4 people

Notes: *Since the chlorine in tap water destroys the B-vitamin thiamin in grains, it is advisable to cook grains in either bottled water or water that has been refrigerated for at least 24 hours.

**Thai purple rice is also known as black sticky rice or "forbidden rice."

***To prepare mango dice, slice across the flat side of the mango, near center, following the curve of the large, flat pit. Repeat for the other side. Using a paring knife, score each slice into small dice. Penetrate the flesh until the knife point touches the skin but does not break through. Press the skin with your thumbs, turning the mango slice inside out. Cut the diced flesh away from the skin and cut each small piece of mango in half again to uniform size.

1/6 SERVING – PROTEIN = 1.0 g.; FAT = 3.0 g.; CARBOHYDRATE = 15.0 g.;
CALORIES = 90; CALORIES FROM FAT = 30%

THAI RED GRAPEFRUIT SALAD WITH SOYMEAT AND SOY SPROUTS
Som o Nam Jim

TPT - 1 hour and 10 minutes;
1 hour = soymeat marination period

I was surprised to see recipes for grapefruit in Thai resources but soon realized that pomelo ('Citrus maxima') would more probably be the fruit of choice of a Thai cook. Pomelo are less widely available in the United States although California surpassed even China in production in 2008. Pomelo are sweeter but canned, red grapefruit give a taste that is familiar enough to encourage exploration of the world of Thai salads, a world of unusual combinations that re-educate your thinking when it comes to the word "salad."

NAM JIM DRESSING:
  1 tablespoon GARLIC OIL [see index]
  2 tablespoons freshly squeezed lime juice
  2 tablespoons freshly squeezed orange juice
  2 tablespoons *tamari* soy sauce*
  1/4 teaspoon red *jalapeño chili* sauce, or to taste**
  1 two-inch piece lemongrass
  3 tablespoons *finely* chopped Italian red onion
  Pinch ground coriander***

3 ounces chopped *or* slivered *frozen* soy meat analogue

1 can (15 1/2 ounces) *ruby red* grapefruit sections—packed in light syrup—*well chilled*****

3 cups shredded *bok choy*—well-washed and well-dried
3 cups shredded romaine lettuce—well-washed and dried
2 cups fresh soybean sprouts—trimmed and well-washed*****
3 tablespoons fresh mint leaves—*finely* slivered

2 tablespoons *toasted, preservative-free* coconut —for garnish

In a cruet or jar, combine garlic oil, lime juice, orange juice, soy sauce, *jalapeño* chili sauce, lemongrass, *finely* chopped red onion, and ground coriander. Shake vigorously.

Put chopped or slivered frozen soy meat analogue into a shallow bowl. Pour prepared dressing over. Cover dish with a plate and allow the soymeat to marinate for about 1 hour.

Set a sieve over a mixing bowl. Pour grapefruit and juice into the sieve. Add grapefruit to marinating soymeat.

When ready to serve, put shredded *boy choy* and romaine lettuce, soybean sprouts, and mint into a salad bowl. Toss to mix well. Spoon marinated grapefruit and soymeat over the greens. Remove lemongrass from marinade and discard. Pour any remaining marinade over the salad.

Sprinkle toasted coconut over the salad.

Serve at once.

Yields 6 servings
adequate for 4 people

Asia–Thailand

THAI RED GRAPEFRUIT SALAD WITH "SOYMEAT" AND SOY SPROUTS (cont'd)

Notes: *Tamari* soy sauce is available in Asian groceries and in most well-stocked grocery stores.

***Jalapeño* sauce is available in Hispanic groceries, food specialty stores, and in chain groceries throughout the Southwest.

***Two very finely chopped fresh coriander (*cilantro*) roots can be added instead of the ground coriander, if available.

****The Chandler pomelo, grown in California, can be found in some produce departments.

*****Because of the possibility of *Salmonella* contamination, be sure to seek out the freshest supply of soybean sprouts possible, trim them well, and be sure to *rinse them very, very well.*

This recipe can be halved when required.

1/6 SERVING – PROTEIN = 7.9 g.; FAT = 4.1 g.; CARBOHYDRATE = 19.5 g.;
CALORIES = 141; CALORIES FROM FAT = 26%

THAI VEGETABLES IN CURRIED COCONUT MILK
Pud Puk Sai
TPT - 31 minutes

This can be a clean-out-your-sinuses kind of dish if you are heavy handed with the Thai red curry paste or it can be a mild vegetable- and tonsil-respectful side dish if you use a milder yellow curry paste. It is a marvelous meld of flavors. I am reminded of our first visit to a Thai restaurant. I ordered things I knew and asked for them to be mildly seasoned; Ray did not. He was on fire in moments and still says he remembers tasting nothing after his first bite. A cooling carrot and grain dessert ended that meal. I have never found a version of that recipe to show him what he missed. Since those days, Thai restaurants have "cooled the hot" and have adjusted their recipes from the fiery level which they tolerate to the mild levels tolerated by westerners. Thai concern for the preservation of vegetable freshness is so satisfying; the objective of the sauce is to compliment the vegetables, not bury them.

In between visits to our favorite Thai restaurant where their broccoli and tofu dishes delight us and their vegetable spring rolls are to die for, this dish has become an in-home favorite.

3 quarts *boiling* water
1 cup small cauliflower florets
1 cup green beans—trimmed, and cut into 2-inch pieces

1 tablespoon *high-heat* safflower *or* sunflower oil
1/2 cup fresh *shiitake* mushrooms—well-washed, trimmed, and cut into large slices

1/2 cup *light, sulfite-free* coconut milk
2 tablespoons WILD MUSHROOM STOCK *[see index]*
2 tablespoons water
2 tablespoons mild Thai yellow curry paste, or to taste*
2 tablespoons *tamari* soy sauce
1 tablespoon sugar

1/2 small red bell pepper—cored, seeded, and cut into slivers

1 cup baby spinach leaves—well-washed and trimmed
30 fresh Thai basil leaves

Pour *boiling* water into a saucepan set over *MEDIUM* heat. Add cauliflower florets and green bean pieces. Blanch for just 4 minutes. Drain and plunge vegetables into *ice water* to stop all further cooking.

In a skillet set over *MEDIUM* heat, heat oil. Add mushroom slices and sauté for about 7 minutes, or until mushrooms are browned. Remove mushrooms from skillet and set aside briefly.

In the same skillet set over *MEDIUM* heat, combine coconut milk, mushroom stock, water, curry paste, soy sauce, and sugar. Stir to combine thoroughly.

Add blanched cauliflower florets and green bean pieces, sautéed mushrooms, and bell pepper slivers. Simmer for about 10 minutes.

Add spinach leaves and basil leaves. Cook only until they begin to wilt. Turn into a serving bowl.

Serve at once with *sticky* rice or noodles.**

Yields 6 servings
adequate for 4 people

Asia – **Thailand**

THAI VEGETABLES IN CURRIED COCONUT MILK (cont'd)

Notes: *Red curry paste can also be used in this dish but do experiment, adding a little at a time, to get the right level of "hot."

**Choose glutinous or short grain Japanese rice or Thai noodles, as preferred.

This recipe is easily halved to serve two or doubled, to serve eight, when required.

1/6 SERVING – PROTEIN = 2.2 g.; FAT = 6.8 g.; CARBOHYDRATE = 10.1 g.;
CALORIES = 105; CALORIES FROM FAT = 58%

THAI STIR-FRIED RICE STICK NOODLES WITH GARLIC AND THAI BASIL
Senmee Horapa

TPT - 55 minutes
40 minutes = noodle soaking period

There are three varieties of basil used extensively in Thai cooking, all of which can be easily grown in our herb gardens. Thai holy basil ("kra phao"), Thai lemon basil "(manglak"), and the variety referred to simply as Thai basil ("horapa"). These have a more assertive flavor than do the sweet basils most of us grow. 'Queen of Siam' is a cultivar I particularly like because of the very small leaves and the ease with which it grows in my Pennsylvania herb beds. It is perhaps the most widely grown of the Thai basil cultivars here in the United States. Italian basils can be substituted, if you do not grow the Asian variety. Thai cooks use basil in many curry recipes and in stir-fries, as in this rice noodle recipe. Rice noodles or rice sticks or pad Thai noodles, as they are often called, are available in almost every grocery chain store in the Asian section of the international food aisle. They are often the basis for a vegetable and tofu stir-fry but I have found that they are the perfect accompaniment, contrasting in texture and taste, to complex Thai vegetable dishes or soups.

6 ounces *medium* **or** *wide* **rice stick noodles***

1/4 cup THAI CLEAR VEGETABLE STOCK [see index] **or THAI DARK VEGETABLE STOCK** [see index]**, as preferred**
1 tablespoon GARLIC OIL [see index]
1 tablespoon *tamari* **soy sauce***
1 teaspoon vegetarian oyster sauce, if available*
1/2 teaspoon corn starch

2 tablespoons Thai sweet *chili* **sauce***

1 tablespoon vegetable oil

3 tablespoons chopped fresh Thai basil
Freshly ground black pepper, to taste

Soak rice sticks in *warm, not hot,* water for 40 minutes. Drain well. Set aside until required.

In a small bowl, combine Thai stock, garlic oil, soy sauce, vegetarian oyster sauce, and corn starch. Stir until corn starch is in suspension.

Add sweet *chili* sauce. Stir well. Set aside until required.

In a wok set over *MEDIUM* heat, heat oil. Add *soaked* rice sticks and stir-fry for about 4 minutes.

Add sauce mixture. Stir to combine well. *Cook only long enough for sauce to begin to boil.*

Turn out onto heated serving platter. Garnish with chopped Thai basil and black pepper.

Serve at once.

Yields 6 servings
adequate for 4 people

Notes: *These items are available in Asian groceries.

This recipe can be halved or doubled, when required.

1/6 SERVING – PROTEIN = 1.7 g.; FAT = 3.7 g.; CARBOHYDRATE = 2.7 g.;
CALORIES = 154; CALORIES FROM FAT = 22%

Asia–Thailand

THAI GINGER CREAM PUDDING
TPT - 2 hours and 9 minutes;
2 hours = flavor development period

If you have a source of preserved gingerroot, then the sweet ginger syrup in which the gingerroot has been preserved is perfect for this dessert. The ginger syrup which I evolved from Australian sources is not a heavy syrup and more to our liking. This pudding is a perfect ending to a menu that features a hot, curried dish or even one that features a simple vegetable stir-fry. One warning: You do have to like ginger as we do or this may be wasted on you.

1 3/4 cups heavy whipping cream

2/3 cup PLAIN YOGURT *[see index]* **or commercially-available plain yogurt**
6 tablespoons AUSTRALIAN SWEET GINGER SYRUP *[see index]*

6 tablespoons *light* **brown sugar**
1/4 teaspoon ground ginger

2 tablespoons *finely chopped* **crystallized gingerroot**

Using the electric mixer fitted with *chilled* beaters or by hand using a *chilled* wire whisk, beat heavy cream in a *clean, chilled* bowl until stiff peaks form.

Using a wire whisk, beat ginger syrup into yogurt. Add to whipped cream and *gently* fold the yogurt into the beaten cream.

Divide among six sherbet glasses or champagne flutes.

In a small bowl, combine brown sugar and ground ginger. Sprinkle 1 tablespoonful of brown sugar–ginger mixture over each serving. Garnish each with about 1 teaspoon *finely chopped* crystallized gingerroot. Refrigerate for at least 2 hours to allow for flavor development.

Serve chilled.

Yields 6 individual servings

Note: This recipe can be halved or doubled, when required.

1/6 SERVING – PROTEIN = 2.9 g.; FAT = 22.9 g.; CARBOHYDRATE = 36.6 g.;
CALORIES = 364; CALORIES FROM FAT = 57%

THAI BANANAS IN COCONUT MILK
TPT - 11 minutes

When I find red bananas, which are far tastier than are the ubiquitous big, yellow Cavendish bananas, I always plan a dessert like this Thai dish, if, that is, I can hide a couple of bananas from the snackers. You would be surprised how the red bananas and the pineapple-flavored baby bananas are consumed by those of us who have come to view bananas generally as tasteless.

A few drops of mali essence, an intense jasmine essence, can be added if you can find the product. It is traditional but quite hard to find in the United States unless you have access to a well-stocked Thai or Asian grocery.

4 large, *firm, but ripe,* **red bananas**
1 cup *light, sulfite-free* **coconut milk**
3 tablespoons sugar
1/4 teaspoon salt

Peel bananas. Cut in half lengthwise and then cut each half crosswise into three pieces. Place bananas in a non-stick-coated skillet. Set aside briefly.

In a saucepan set over *MEDIUM* heat, combine coconut milk, sugar, and salt. Allow to come to boil. Boil for about 2 minutes.

Place skillet with bananas over *LOW* heat. Add coconut milk mixture. Cook until bananas are heated through. Turn into a serving dish.

Serve at once into warm dessert dishes allowing four pieces of banana per serving.

Yields 6 servings

Note: This recipe can be halved or doubled, when required.

1/6 SERVING – PROTEIN = 1.4 g.; FAT = 1.4 g.; CARBOHYDRATE = 34.1 g.;
CALORIES = 138; CALORIES FROM FAT = 9%

Vietnam

Vietnam, located on the Indochinese Peninsula, is a country most Americans only came to know in a most difficult period in our history, during the war we know as the Vietnam War, the war they know as the Resistance War Against America; the war that profoundly scarred every American and Vietnamese family. People have been here for several thousand years; archaeologists trace this culture to the Phung Nguyen culture of the late Neolithic Period. Boat-shaped coffins and burial jars and the evidence of stilt dwellings have been found as have small copper mine sites in North Vietnam that date to an ancient, flourishing social structure. Today, known as the Socialist Republic of Vietnam, it is home to over eighty-six million people making it the thirteenth most populous country on earth.

Beginning in the third century BC and for a thousand years thereafter, the land we know as Vietnam was under Chinese rule. They gained their independence in 938 AD with defeat of the Chinese forces at Bạch Dăng River and remained an independent nation for nine hundred years with Buddhism as the state religion until colonization by the French beginning in 1884. Colonial status as part of French Indochina (Indonchine) continued until 1954, interrupted only by Japanese occupation during World War II. With defeat of the French at the siege of Dien Bien Phu, two Vietnams emerged due to a coalition of nationalist and communist groups who resisted French governance. Communist rule was established in the North under Ho Chi Minh, ironically known after this partition as the Democratic Republic of Vietnam, and the bloody struggle for unity began with the United States forces entering as military advisors in 1950 on the side of the South Vietnamese, then known as the Republic of Vietnam. By 1965 United States involvement, which numbered more than 500,000 combat personnel at its peak, had become a ground combat operation. South Vietnam fell to the Chinese-supported Communist forces of North Vietnam in 1975, after which a socialist republic was declared.

As one might suspect, Chinese influences in custom and cuisine are entrenched but the years under the French have certainly left their mark. A Vietnamese bakery in Stony Brook, Long Island, introduced me to pastries that were the result of a phenomenal fusion that Vietnamese baking had achieved under the influence of the French. Foods never seen before French colonization, such as white potatoes, cauliflower, asparagus, dillweed, European sweet basil, and French bread, have now become just part of the cuisine. The extensive use of fresh herbs and the use of *nuoc mam*, the ubiquitous fermented fish sauce, do set this cuisine apart from the cuisines of neighboring countries. Despite these constants, regional food differences emerge as one travels through Vietnam. In the north there is a pronounced Chinese influence in the dishes and in preparation techniques with far less use of fresh fruits, vegetables, and herbs due, in part, to the much colder climate. The hot and spicy seasoning of the central area of Vietnam is a dramatic contrast to the north where black pepper is the primary seasoning. In the south one sees a stronger reference to the sophisticated influences of both France and the United States. Fruits, vegetables, and herbs grow well in the south and are in evidence in the regional cuisine. Sugar is used far more in the south than in any other region of the country. In addition, curried dishes have been adopted from India and are found in most restaurants. Buddhist dishes are still in evidence but usually with the addition of *nuoc mam*.

Asia – Vietnam

Beancurd and Chinese Chive Bud Soup
Canh Day Phu He

~

Watermelon and Cucumber Salad
with *Hoisin* – Lime Dressing and Roasted Peanuts
Rau Xàlách Dưa Hâu Cây Dưa Chôt

Roasted Eggplant Salad with Onion Dressing
Thit Quay Voi Ca Tim Cu Hanh

~~~~~~~~~~~~~~~~~~~~~~

Sweet Sweetpotatoes with Gingerroot
Cu Tu

Stir-Fried Cauliflower and Straw Mushrooms
with Spinach Garnish
Bong Cai Xao Nam Rom

Vietnamese Spicing Mixture

Pickled Mustard Greens

~~~~~~~~~~~~~~~~~~~~~~

Easy French Vanilla Ice Cream with Star Anise
Kem Cây Anit

Sweet Rice Balls
Xôi Nêp Dua

Fresh Fruit Platter – Pineapple Chunks, Mango Slices, Baby Banana Chunks,
and Peeled and Pitted Lychees, garnished with Lime Wedges

VIETNAMESE BEANCURD AND CHINESE CHIVE BUD SOUP
Canh Dau Phu He

TPT - 7 minutes

One day in November I found bunches of chive buds in a middle-of-Pennsylvania grocery store. I was delighted because there would be no chive buds from my garden for many, many months. I was a bit disappointed that I could not find Chinese or garlic chive buds but I took what I could get and home I went to make this most unusual soup. A sea broth, made from seaweed, substituted for the Vietnamese soup base traditionally seasoned with "nuoc mam."

1 quart SEA BROTH [see index]
1 tablespoon *tamari* soy sauce
1/4 teaspoon sugar
Freshly ground black pepper, to taste

1/4 pound well-washed chive buds—tough ends removed and cut into 2-inch lengths*
4 ounces *firm* beancurd (*tofu*)—cut into 1-inch cubes

In a large saucepan set over MEDIUM heat, combine broth, soy sauce, sugar, and black pepper. Allow to come to boil. Reduce heat to LOW-MEDIUM.

Add the chive buds and beancurd cubes. Allow to return to the boil. Turn into a heated tureen.

Asia–Vietnam

VIETNAMESE BEAN CURD AND CHINESE CHIVE BUD SOUP (cont'd)

Serve at once into heated soup or rice bowls.

Yields 6 servings
adequate for 4 people

Notes: *If Chinese or garlic chive buds are available, do use them.

This recipe can be halved or doubled, when required.

1/6 SERVING – PROTEIN = 1.8 g.; FAT = 0.9 g.; CARBOHYDRATE = 1.8 g.; CALORIES = 20; CALORIES FROM FAT = 41%

VIETNAMESE WATERMELON AND CUCUMBER SALAD WITH *HOISIN* – LIME DRESSING AND ROASTED PEANUTS
Rau Xàlách Dưa Hâu Cây Dưa Chất
TPT - 15 minutes

One very warm evening a wedge of watermelon sitting in the refrigerator, like an elephant in the room, which I moved each time I removed another ingredient for the stir-fry I was preparing, seemed to call and this salad is the result of that encounter. It is delicious and very refreshing on a summer's evening and goes perfectly with an Asian meal.

1/4 cup *raw* peanuts

2 tablespoons freshly squeezed lime juice
2 teaspoons *hoisin* sauce

2 cups seeded and diced watermelon
1 medium English cucumber—peeled, quartered, seeded, and sliced
3 tablespoons fresh parsley florets

Freshly ground black pepper, to taste

Roast raw peanuts in a 250 degree F. oven—about 8 minutes. Set aside until required.

In a small dish, combine lime juice and *hoisin* sauce. Stir to combine thoroughly.

In a *chilled* serving bowl, combine diced watermelon and sliced cucumber. Toss gently. Scatter parsley florets over.

Pour *hoisin* – lime dressing over. Season with black pepper. Toss gently.

Garnish with the previously prepared *roasted* peanuts.

Serve at once.*

Yields 6 servings
adequate for 4 people

Notes: *Both watermelon and cucumber will extrude a great deal of water and dilute the dressing so serving the salad immediately is essential.

This recipe can be halved or doubled, when required.

1/6 SERVING – PROTEIN = 1.7 g.; FAT = 2.4 g.; CARBOHYDRATE = 6.8 g.; CALORIES = 51; CALORIES FROM FAT = 42%

Asia–Vietnam

ROASTED EGGPLANT SALAD WITH ONION DRESSING IN THE VIETNAMESE STYLE
Thit Quay Vai Ca Tim Cu Hanh

TPT - 30 minutes

On a December afternoon, many, many years ago, I sat in the car in the parking lot of the IRS facility where our daughter was interviewing for a summer job. While waiting, I evolved a Vietnamese salad for a New Year's Eve dinner. The onion dressing was one of those perfect recipes. Obviously influenced by the years under the French, it is a good choice when you want a beautiful, assertive salad dressing. It was, all in all, a successful day because she got the job and we added an excellent dressing to our repertoire. Years later I realized how well that onion dressing complimented grilled Asian eggplants, so often served in Vietnam with a pork stuffing and seasoned, of course, with fish sauce or shrimp paste. I found beautiful Asian eggplants in the produce section and I remembered that perfect salad dressing...

VIETNAMESE ONION SALAD DRESSING:
    6 tablespoons safflower *or* sunflower oil
    3 tablespoons white wine vinegar
    1 *very small* garlic clove
    1/2 small yellow onion—coarsely chopped
    1/2 teaspoon sugar
    2 teaspoons *Dijon* country-style mustard
    1 tablespoon chopped fresh dillweed*

3 long lavender Asian eggplants *or* galaxy eggplants, if necessary—well-washed

1 1/2 cups mixed greens—well-washed and dried
1/2 cup chopped watercress—well-washed and dried with thick stems removed
Freshly ground black pepper, to taste

6 lime wedges

In the container of the electric blender, combine oil, vinegar, garlic, onion, sugar, mustard, and dillweed. Blend until *very smooth*—about 1 minute. Set aside in the refrigerator until required.**

Using a grill pan preheated over *MEDIUM-HIGH* heat, grill the eggplants until charred on the outside and soft on the inside.*** Turn frequently. Remove to a rack and allow to cool to room temperature.

Mix greens with watercress. Divide among six salad plates.

Slice each cooled eggplant into round slices. Apportion the slices among the individual salad plates on top of the greens. Grind black pepper over each serving.

Remove prepared onion dressing from refrigerator. Blend again. Pour some over each eggplant half. Put remainder into a small serving bowl.

Garnish with a lime wedge.

Serve at once.

Yields 6 individual servings

Notes: *When fresh dillweed is unavailable, 1/4 teaspoonful of dried dillweed may be substituted.

**Refrigerate leftover salad dressing for no more than a week. Blend again before serving.

***If you have the availability of a charcoal fire, set over hot coals. If you have a gas range, char directly over gas flames.

This recipe is easily halved or doubled, when required.

1/6 SERVING – PROTEIN = 0.9 g.; FAT = 11.4 g.; CARBOHYDRATE = 4.9 g.; CALORIES = 120; CALORIES FROM FAT = 85%

Asia – Vietnam

VIETNAMESE SWEET SWEETPOTATOES WITH GINGERROOT
Cu Tu

TPT - 21 minutes

Yes, sweetpotatoes thrive in Vietnam and are an important component of the diet especially for those who live in the country, eaten, as they are, even for breakfast. The Vietnamese are a part of the world's majority that prefer the starchy tuberous member of the Morning Glory family known as the true yam of Old World origin which is scaly, hairy, and not at all sweet. Only in recent years have Vietnamese restaurants in the United States included sweetpotato dishes on their menus. Made with the sweeter sweetpotatoes available and preferred in the United States and Australia, these dishes have great appeal and should certainly not be dismissed as "just peasant food," as yams have been labeled by one Vietnamese writer.

2 cups water
1/4 cup sugar
1 teaspoon grated fresh gingerroot

2 large sweetpotatoes—peeled and cut into 1-inch chunks

Freshly ground black pepper, to taste
2 tablespoons coarsely chopped *honey–roasted* peanuts

In a wok, with cover, or saucepan, set over *MEDIUM* heat, combine water, sugar, and grated gingerroot. Bring to the boil. Stir until sugar is dissolved.

Reduce heat to LOW. Add sweetpotato pieces. Cover and cook for 12 minutes, or until sweetpotatoes are *tender*, but *not mushy*. Stir occasionally to prevent sweetpotato chunks from sticking to the wok. Turn into a colander and drain thoroughly.

Turn drained sweetpotato chunks into a heated serving bowl. Season with black pepper. Garnish with chopped peanuts.

Serve at once.

Yields 5 servings
adequate for 3-4 people

Note: This recipe may be halved or doubled, when required.

1/5 SERVING – PROTEIN = 3.9 g.; FAT = 2.7 g.; CARBOHYDRATE = 35.6 g.;
CALORIES = 175; CALORIES FROM FAT = 14%

VIETNAMESE STIR – FRIED CAULIFLOWER
AND STRAW MUSHROOMS WITH SPINACH GARNISH
Bong Cai Xao Nam Rom

TPT - 14 minutes

The soy sauce used in Southeast Asia is thicker and sweeter than that which we use so we have added a bit more sugar to this classic dish. We have also added the spinach garnish to brighten the presentation since, as with so many Vietnamese dishes, the color palate would be quite dull. This cooks quickly and tastes wonderful.

2 tablespoons *tamari* soy sauce*
1/2 teaspoon sugar

1 tablespoon vegetable oil
2 leeks—*white and light green portions only*—trimmed, well-rinsed, and *thinly* sliced
1 1/2 cups cauliflower florets—sliced into thin lengthwise slices
2 tablespoons water

1 can (15 ounces) whole, peeled straw mushrooms —well-drained*

3/4 cup shredded fresh spinach—well-washed and well-drained

In a small bowl, combine soy sauce and sugar. Set sauce ingredients aside until required.

In a wok set over *MEDIUM-HIGH* heat, heat oil. Add leek slices and stir-fry for 1 minute. Add cauliflower slices and continue to stir-fry for 2 minutes. *Move wok to a burner set on LOW.* Add remaining 2 tablespoonfuls of water and *cover wok.* Allow vegetables to steam for 2 minutes.

VOLUME II - 441

VIETNAMESE STIR–FRIED CAULIFLOWER AND STRAW MUSHROOMS WITH SPINACH GARNISH (cont'd)

Remove cover. *Increase heat to MEDIUM-HIGH.* Add straw mushrooms and sauce mixture. Cook, stirring constantly, for 2 minutes more until thoroughly heated through.

Add shredded spinach. Remove from heat and turn into heated serving bowl.

Serve at once, with rice.

Notes: *These items are increasingly available in most well-stocked grocery stores. If not in yours, they are available in Asian groceries.

This recipe can be halved or doubled, when required.

Yields 6 servings
adequate for 4 people

1/6 SERVING – PROTEIN = 2.9 g.; FAT = 2.1 g.; CARBOHYDRATE = 16.1 g.;
CALORIES = 88; CALORIES FROM FAT = 18%

VIETNAMESE SPICING MIXTURE
TPT - 3 minutes

This mixture of spices is typical of the complex flavors employed by Vietnamese cooks. Personalizing the spicing mixture to control the fire or to compliment the ingredients is acceptable but using commercial curry powder in the preparation of dishes from Southeast Asia and the countries of the Indian Subcontinent is a travesty and an insult, in our opinion.

2 teaspoons cumin seeds
1 teaspoon coriander seeds
1 teaspoon chopped, dried lemongrass

2 teaspoons ground sweet paprika
1 teaspoon ground turmeric
1/2 teaspoon ground ginger
1/4 teaspoon ground cinnamon *(preferably Vietnamese Cassia cinnamon, if available)*
1/4 teaspoon salt

Using a SPICE and COFFEE GRINDER, grind cumin and coriander seeds with dried lemongrass.

When of relatively uniform consistency, add ground paprika, turmeric, ginger, and cinnamon, and salt.* Grind to a uniform consistency.

Turn into a small jelly or spice jar. Cover tightly and shake to mix thoroughly. Store in a cool, dark place.

Yields about 5 teaspoonfuls

Notes: *If desired, ground red pepper (cayenne) or hot Hungarian paprika may be added to this mixture. We, however, prefer to add hot elements directly to the dish being prepared since some vegetable dishes are more enjoyable with less "hot."

This recipe can be doubled, when required, but since the flavor dissipates considerably due to the release of the volatile oils with crushing, it is advisable to replace the seasoning combination after about 6 months.

FOOD VALUES for such herb mixtures are almost negligible.

VIETNAMESE PICKLED MUSTARD GREENS
Dua Cai Chua

TPT - 5 days and 8 minutes;
2 days = vegetable drying period;
3 days = vegetable pickling period

Pickled vegetables are very much a part of the cuisine of Vietnam as they are in Japanese cuisine and in the cuisines of many countries in Asia. Vegetables prepared this way keep well and are a convenience to the cook who finds good vegetables but knows full well that that supply may not be there the next time he or she shops.

Asia–Vietnam

VIETNAMESE PICKLED MUSTARD GREENS (cont'd)

2 pounds mustard greens or turnip greens, as preferred—well-washed and trimmed
6 scallions—trimmed and well-rinsed

1 quart water
5 teaspoons salt
1 1/2 teaspoons sugar

Sterilize two one-quart canning jars. Also sterilize lids and rings for the jars.

After trimming the mustard greens and scallions, cut into 2-inch lengths. Spread out on an herb-drying screen or other surface where the liquid will drain from the vegetables and the air can circulate. Allow to dry for a day or two. They will appear slightly shrunken.

In a large mixing bowl, combine water, salt, and sugar. Place the dried and shrunken vegetable pieces in the pickling liquid. Place a soup plate or another bowl into the bowl to keep the vegetables submerged. Cover the bowl and allow to sit on the counter top at room temperature for 3 days.

Ladle the greens and the pickling liquid into the sterilized jars. Refrigerate.*

Yields about 20 servings

Notes: *This pickle will keep, refrigerated, for several months.

When required, this recipe can be halved.

1/20 SERVING – PROTEIN = 0.5 g.; FAT = 0.06 g.; CARBOHYDRATE = 1.4 g.;
CALORIES = 7; CALORIES FROM FAT = 8%

EASY FRENCH VANILLA ICE CREAM WITH STAR ANISE, THE TASTE OF VIETNAM

Kem Cây Anit

TPT - 10 hours and 12 minutes;
2 hours = star anise infusion;
8 hours = freezing period

Although desserts are not served with every meal in Vietnam, sweet fruit endings to a meal and sweet celebratory dishes are part of their culinary tradition. As in India, mango ice cream, known in Vietnam as "Kem Xoai," is enormously popular. Not only are fruits welcome in ice cream but many herbs and spices work wonderfully too, complimenting the flavors in your menu. We have used lemon thyme, cinnamon basil with a dash or two of Vietnamese cinnamon or cardamom, lemon verbena, and pineapple sage. Here the infusion of star anise creates a rich, but very easily prepared, reminder of the French influence upon this Southeast Asian cuisine.

2 tablespoons *boiling* water
6 star anise cloves *or* 1 whole star anise bulb

1 cup heavy whipping cream

2/3 cup *fat-free* sweetened condensed milk
1/2 cup *fat-free* pasteurized eggs* (the equivalent of 2 eggs)
2 teaspoons pure vanilla extract

Prepare a 7 x 3 x 2-inch non-stick-coated loaf pan by placing it in the freezer until required.

In a small dish, combine star anise cloves and *boiling* water. Cover the dish with a saucer and allow to infuse for 2 hours. Pour the star anise and water through a fine tea strainer set over another small bowl. Set the water aside briefly; dry the star anise cloves to use in another dish, retaining one clove for garnish.

Using an electric mixer fitted with *chilled* beaters or by hand, using a *chilled* wire whisk, beat heavy cream in a *chilled* bowl until stiff. Set aside.

In a large bowl, combine sweetened condensed milk, star anise-infused water, pasteurized eggs, and vanilla extract. Stir to blend thoroughly. *Whisk-fold* stiffly whipped cream *gently*, but *thoroughly*, into egg–milk mixture.

Pour mixture into chilled loaf pan. Spread evenly. Cover tightly with aluminum foil. Freeze overnight or until firm—about 8 hours.

Asia – Vietnam

EASY FRENCH VANILLA ICE CREAM WITH STAR ANISE, THE TASTE OF VIETNAM (cont'd)

Grind one of the star anise cloves, which you dried after infusion, to a fine powder.

Either scoop ice cream from pan to serve or remove entire block of ice cream from pan and slice. Sprinkle just a pinch of the ground star anise over each serving.

Leftovers should be returned to the freezer, tightly covered.

Notes: *Because raw eggs present the danger of *Salmonella* poisoning, commercially-available pasteurized eggs are recommended for use in preparing this dish.

This recipe is easily doubled, when required. Use a 9 x 5 x 3-inch non-stick-coated loaf pan.

Yields about eight 1/2-cup servings

1/8 SERVING (i. e., per 1/2 cupful) –
PROTEIN = 4.1 g.; FAT = 9.8 g.; CARBOHYDRATE = 18.1 g.;
CALORIES = 179; CALORIES FROM FAT = 49%

SWEET RICE BALLS IN THE SPIRIT OF VIETNAM
Xôi Nếp Dừa

TPT - 1 hour;
15 minutes = rice cooling period

As a young family, we made regular trips into New York's Chinatown to get those very special ingredients that were not even available in the few ethnic groceries that existed on Long Island at the time. Glutinous rice was one of those very special items. Now it is found in practically every grocery store. The nuances of the grain varieties available, that are actually cultivars of rice and some called rice that are actually the seeds of other grasses, are known to an increasingly number of consumers who once only wrote "rice" on their shopping lists.

Vietnamese often celebrate special events with puréed rice balls rolled in sugar and fresh coconut. I created this recipe in the spirit of that treat to provide a dessert more recognizable as a dessert to Americans which can be made with either the traditional glutinous rice or with Japanese short grain rice. Glutinous rice, known as "gao nếp" in Vietnamese, is similar to Japanese short grain rice in that both are starchy and, hence, sticky when cooked. The starch in glutinous rice or sweet rice is low in amylose and high in amylopectin, the starch component responsible for the prized stickiness. It can be steamed or boiled but generally requires pre-soaking so check your package for instructions. Note that glutinous rice, the name not withstanding, is gluten-free.

5 1/2 cups *boiling* water
1 1/2 cups dry Japanese short grain rice

9 tablespoons sugar
3/4 cup freshly grated coconut meat

In a large saucepan set over *LOW* heat, combine *boiling* water and rice. Cover tightly and cook, *undisturbed*, for 25 minutes or until water has been absorbed. Remove from heat and allow to stand for 15 minutes. Remove cover and allow to stand for an additional 15 minutes to cool.

Take a spoonful and form into a ball with your hands. Squeeze tightly to make a compact ball. Repeat forming twelve small balls. Place two rice balls on each of six dessert plates.

Sprinkle 1 1/2 tablespoonfuls of sugar over each serving. Sprinkle 2 tablespoonfuls of coconut over each serving.

Serve at room temperature with a fork.*

Yields 12 rice balls
adequate for 6 people

Notes: *Refrigerate any leftovers.

This recipe can be halved or doubled, when required.

1/12 SERVING (i. e., per rice ball) –
PROTEIN = 1.7 g.; FAT = 2.6 g.; CARBOHYDRATE = 34.5 g.;
CALORIES = 169; CALORIES FROM FAT = 14%

Oceania

Oceania
including
Australasia

The Pacific Ocean is populated by island-dwelling people from the Aleutians in the North to New Zealand in the South. Four terms have been characteristically used to define the islands of this region of the world:

- Australasia includes Australia and New Zealand plus the smaller islands of the area;
- Melanesia, which extends from the western side of the Pacific Ocean eastward to Fiji, includes Vanuatu in the New Hebrides, the Solomon Islands, Fiji, Papua New Guinea, New Caledonia, and West Papua, which encompasses two provinces of Indonesia;
- Micronesia is a term used for the thousands of small islands which stand outside of Melanesia and Polynesia including United States territories Guam and Wake islands, the Marianas, the Caroline, Marshall, and Gilbert islands;
- Polynesia comprises over 1,000 islands and includes American Samoa, the Cook Islands, Easter Island, Fiji, French Polynesia, Hawaii, New Zealand, Niue, Norfolk Island, Pitcairn Islands, Samoa, Tonga, Tuvalu, Wallis and Futuna, and Rotoma.

Even Australia, New Zealand, Indonesia, Malaysia, Brunei, The Philippines, Borneo, and the Aluetians, states that really lie outside the geopolitical definition of Oceania, are included in Oceania by some authors while others use the term Oceania, as do I, to organize a groups of nations and cuisines that are disparate across a wide ocean.

Settled by seafarers who undertook the most difficult migrations perhaps since the migration of *Homo erectus* and *Homo sapiens* across the great expanses out of Africa, these islands, where people settled and established socially coherent communities as early as thirty thousand years ago, were only discovered by western explorers beginning in the fifteenth century.

Cooks on most of these islands find themselves with the same basic foods—yam, taro root, breadfruit, coconut, cassava, fish, a variety of green leaves, plantains, and tropical fruits. It is what these cooks manage to do with local foods that is amazing. Few cattle, sheep, goats, or pigs are raised on these small islands so people turn to canned corned beef and Spam and expensive, imported meat products, when affordable. Trade with the West and with South Asia introduced beans and pulses, melons, carrots, tomatoes, cucumbers, *chili* peppers, and pineapples, all of which thrived in the volcanic soils. Coffee beans turned out to be a successful crop in New Guinea where the microclimate at the higher elevations proved receptive.

Evidence of historical contact is still obvious in the cuisines of these islands although westernization in response to tourism sometimes blurs these clues. For example, bread and butter pudding is found on the islands which had prolonged contact with the British; *soubise*, albeit usually without cheese, and *baguettes* are found on the islands which had prolonged contact with the French. The spice pantheon of India is prevalent in some island cuisines and nonexistent in others. A Chinese stir-fry, a Japanese *bento* box, or an American hamburger may be offered on lunch menus but there will always be a "touch of the Pacific," often in the addition of fruit or with the side of a fruit drink.

Australia

With the severance of land bridges as the land we know as Australia separated from the ancient continent of Pangaea some 250 million years ago, the stage was set for a unique biological isolation on this, the flattest and least fertile of the Earth's continents. Speciation in this isolated land mass resulted in a most fascinating fauna evolution, allowing for animals found nowhere else on the planet. In dug-out canoes, using the remainders of the land bridges, now small islands, ancient peoples from Southeast Asia and the Indian subcontinent found this isolated island nation and its unique animal population. Evidence suggests that the indigenous, hunter-gather peoples of Australia preceded European arrival by some 40,000 years but, interestingly, land rights of the indigenous people were not recognized until 1992 when the High Court overturned *terra nullis* ("land belonging to no one"), the generally-accepted policy applying to the pre-European period.

The eastern half of Australia was claimed by the British in 1770 and the colony of New South Wales was settled as an Anglo-Celtic penal colony in 1788. It became the first of five Crown Colonies, which in 1901 joined to form the Commonwealth of Australia, a federal parliamentary democracy and constitutional monarchy, with the British monarch as titular head. Today Australia is the thirteenth largest world economy with a population of twenty-two million.

Those who emigrated from Britain and Ireland late in the 18th century strongly influenced the crops grown and the food eaten until recent decades and the ties to Great Britain can still be seen in Christmas traditions that persist as they do in the northern hemisphere despite the fact that Australians are at the height of their summer in December. The full English breakfast is still enjoyed as is the morning bowl of oatmeal porridge. Take-away shops abound in Australia as in England and traditional British meat pies and fish and chips are still popular, right along side the international fast food franchise stores and Asian take-out shops.

Perhaps the impetus to the change in Australian eating habits that enabled the cuisine we see today came with refrigeration. In 1805 Oliver Evans, an American inventor, designed the first refrigeration machine with the first practical version being developed by Jacob Perkins in 1834, using ether in a vapor compression cycle. Refrigeration, although originally explored by William Cullen at the University of Glasgow in 1748, was slow to find its way across the ocean and into the Australian home. James Harrison, an Australian, is credited, however, with adapting the technology in 1851 to create shipping containers to facilitate the transportation of food from the distant outback agricultural areas to the population centers.

The 1975 Racial Discrimination Act replaced the white Australian policy, whereby proof was required to confirm that an applicant for immigration had at least seventy-five-percent European ancestry, facilitating extensive immigration into Australia from Asia. This more open immigration policy brought the culture and food of China, Japan, Malaysia, Thailand, and Vietnam to the island continent. During the same period, emigrants arrived from southern Europe and the Middle East, especially from Greece, Italy, Lebanon, Syria, and Turkey. Since 1947, alone, the population has doubled due to immigration. The integration of immigrants led Australia gracefully into a globalization of attitude that is unique and a fusion cuisine that is exciting, fresh, and complex, referred to some writers as "Modern Australian."

Oceania–Australia

Winter Squash, Red Pepper, and Scallion Stir-Fry

~

| **Fresh Tomato Soup with Avocado and Shallots – Hot or Chilled** | **Celeriac and Apple Soup** |

~

| **Mesclun Salad with Shaved Macadamia Nuts** | **Hot Asparagus Salad with Raspberry *Vinaigrette*** |

Raspberry Vinegar

~ ~

**Pan-Grilled *Halloumi* Cheese with *Edamame*,
Peas, Roasted Red Peppers, and Mint**

or

Grainburger on Vegetable Spaghetti

Baked Red Onions with Raspberry *Vinaigrette*

~ ~ ~ ~ ~ ~ ~ ~ ~ ~

Grilled Mixed Vegetables
with **Eggplant Relish**

Oven-Roasted or Boiled Potatoes
with

Cream Sauce with Roasted Shallots and Fresh Thyme

or

***Chili* and Ginger Sauce**

~ ~ ~ ~ ~ ~ ~ ~ ~ ~

Lentil and *Pasta* Salad with Nasturtium

Sautéed Artichoke Hearts

~ ~

Puff Pastry "Pillows" with Raspberry Purée and Peaches

Fruit Spiders

Ginger – Steeped Prunes   with   Sweet Ginger Syrup

AUSTRALIAN WINTER SQUASH, RED PEPPER, AND SCALLION STIR-FRY
TPT - 12 minutes

It certainly will not surprise anyone that stir-fries are popular in Australia. A nation located in the South Pacific whose modern fusion cuisine is global in its reach and appreciation, tends to really do things "its own way." This vegetable stir-fry, which makes a truly unusual first course, can be made with any winter squash including pumpkin. We choose to make it with butternut or acorn squash, which are available to us throughout the year, or with the small jack-be-little pumpkins that appear in our markets in late September.

1 tablespoon *high heat* safflower *or* sunflower oil

1 pound butternut, acorn squash, *or* "jack-be-little" pumpkins—peeled, seeded, and cut into "sticks" as you would for carrots

1 small red bell pepper—seeded, cored, and cut into "sticks"

5 scallions—*both white and green portions*—trimmed, well-rinsed, and cut into pieces about the same size as the other vegetables

3 tablespoons water

1/4 teaspoon chili powder

[see next page]

AUSTRALIAN WINTER SQUASH, RED PEPPER, AND SCALLION STIR-FRY (cont'd)

1/2 cup *unsalted, roasted, preservative-free* cashews
1/4 teaspoon sesame oil
2 teaspoons Thai sweet *chili* sauce

In a wok set over *MEDIUM* heat, heat oil. Add squash pieces and stir-fry for about 2 minutes. *Reduce heat to LOW-MEDIUM.*

Add red pepper strips, scallion pieces, water, and chili powder. Stir to mix well, cover, and allow to cook for another 4 minutes, stirring occasionally.

Uncover. Add cashews, sesame oil, and sweet *chili* sauce. Cook, stirring constantly, until heated through. Turn into a heated serving dish.

Serve at once.*

Yields 6 small servings
adequate for 6 people as first course
adequate for 3-4 people as entrée serving

Notes: *Use heated salad plates for first-course service.

This can be an interesting entrée for a light supper or lunch when served over rice or noodles.

1/6 SERVING – PROTEIN = 3.6 g.; FAT = 8.9 g.; CARBOHYDRATE = 11.6 g.;
CALORIES = 149; CALORIES FROM FAT = 54%

AUSTRALIAN FRESH TOMATO SOUP WITH AVOCADO AND SHALLOTS — HOT OR CHILLED

TPT - 46 minutes = to serve hot;
1 hour and 46 minutes = to serve chilled

It would be a sin to make this soup with any tomatoes or tomato product other than the freshest tomatoes of the local fall harvest. The tomato and avocado harvests come into Australian markets at about the same time in March so the combination is an anticipated seasonal treat "down under." This is really a low-calorie soup which can be served as a main course with a salad, bread, cheese, and fruit or a protein-rich dessert on a late summer's evening.

1 tablespoon *light* olive oil
3 large shallots—*finely* chopped

1 teaspoon sugar
About 1/4 teaspoon chopped, fresh, red *chili*, of choice, *or* 1/8 teaspoon *Szechuan (Sichuan) chili paste*

6 medium, *fresh*, ripe tomatoes (about 1 1/2 pounds) —peeled and chopped
1 1/2 cups water

Salt, to taste
Freshly ground black pepper, to taste

1 *firm*, but *ripe*, avocado*

1 shallot—*finely* chopped—for garnish

In a saucepan set over *LOW-MEDIUM* heat, combine olive oil and the *finely* chopped shallots. Sauté until shallots are soft and translucent, *being careful not to allow the shallots to brown.*

Add sugar and hot *chili* or *chili* paste. Continue to sauté for about 1 minute more.

Stir in chopped tomatoes and water. Partially cover and cook for 20 minutes, stirring occasionally. Remove from heat and allow to cool briefly.

Using an electric blender or food processor fitted with steel knife, purée tomato mixture. Put purée through a FOOD MILL or a sieve into a clean saucepan. Season to taste with salt and pepper. Place over *LOW* heat to keep warm.**

Turn soup into a heated soup tureen, if it is to be served hot, or into a chilled soup tureen, if it is to be served cold.

Peel and slice the avocado. Apportion avocado slices among four soup plates. Centrally position the avocado slices in a fan and sprinkle each with a portion of chopped raw shallot.

At the table, ladle the soup *around* the centrally-positioned avocado slices.

Yields 1 quartful
or four 1-cup servings

AUSTRALIAN FRESH TOMATO SOUP WITH AVOCADO AND SHALLOTS — HOT OR CHILLED (cont'd)

Notes: *Avocados are, granted, high in calories and high in fat, albeit unsaturated, but the contribution of vitamin A, potassium, folic acid, magnesium, and protein are not to be ignored. All varieties of alligator pears or avocado pears, as they are also known, ripen well at room temperature and should not be refrigerated, if at all possible. To hurry the ripening process, place the avocados in a brown paper bag. The confinement concentrates the gases which are released from the fruit. Do not slice the avocado until you are ready to serve the soup since it will brown and for this recipe you should not brush it with lemon juice, the standard prevention technique. The acid of the tomatoes will keep it from browning at the table.

**If you are planning to serve this soup chilled, cover and chill the soup in the refrigerator for at least 1 hour.

This recipe is easily increased proportionately, as required.

1/4 SERVING – PROTEIN = 2.7 g.; FAT = 11.4 g.; CARBOHYDRATE = 10.9 g.;
CALORIES = 140; CALORIES FROM FAT = 73%

AUSTRALIAN CELERIAC AND APPLE SOUP
TPT - 43 minutes

The Granny Smith apple, now available throughout the world, originated in Australia, developed, according to tradition, by an accidental cross-breeding by a lady named Smith. When we were first married, we looked forward to the late winter day on which our Long Island greengrocer offered the first Granny Smiths of the "down-under" harvest, then, imported from Australia and New Zealand.

1 tablespoon butter
3/4 pound knob celery (celeriac)—peeled and diced

1 small-medium cooking apple—peeled, cored, and diced—*a Cortland apple is our preference, although a Granny Smith apple might be appropriate*
3 cups VEGETARIAN WHITE STOCK [*see index*]

Salt, to taste
Freshly ground *white* pepper, to taste

2 tablespoons *toasted* pine nuts (*pignoli*), for garnish
Chopped fresh parsley, for garnish

In a large saucepan set over *LOW-MEDIUM* heat, melt butter. Add diced knob celery (celeriac) and cook, stirring frequently, until *softened* and *golden in color*—about 15 minutes.

Add diced apple and stock. Cook for about 10 minutes more, or until apple has softened.

Purée two or three ladlefuls at a time in the electric blender, or in the food processor fitted with steel knife, or mash finely and press through a fine sieve or FOOD MILL. Turn into a clean saucepan. Season with salt and *white* pepper, to taste. Cook over *LOW-MEDIUM* heat until hot.

Turn into a heated soup tureen and serve into heated soup plates. Garnish each serving with *toasted* pine nuts (*pignoli*) and chopped parsley.

Yields six 3/4-cup servings
adequate for 4 people

Notes: When required, this recipe may be doubled or tripled.

This soup freeze well.

1/6 SERVING – PROTEIN = 1.1 g.; FAT = 3.1 g.; CARBOHYDRATE = 4.1 g.;
CALORIES = 47; CALORIES FROM FAT = 60%

Oceania–Australia

AUSTRALIAN *MESCLUN* SALAD WITH SHAVED MACADAMIA NUTS
TPT - 10 minutes

In 1996 I began to explore the cooking of Australia in anticipation of a trip to the Southern Hemisphere and, although the trip had to be canceled, my interest in their unusual combination of fresh ingredients continued. The rich, soft macadamia nuts are delicious counterpoints to the bits of mesclun and the vinaigrette enhances the total sensation.

6 cups *mesclun* or tiny "spring salad mix" and *fresh*, *baby* spinach leaves—well-washed and well-dried

1/4–1/3 cup large, *unsalted* macadamia nuts

AUSTRALIAN RASPBERRY *VINAIGRETTE* [see recipe which follows]

Turn well-washed and well-dried *mesclun* mixture into a salad bowl.

Using the food processor fitted with a slicing or coarse grating disk, shave macadamia nuts into large shreds.* Set aside until ready to serve.

Scatter shaved macadamia nuts over *mesclun* mixture. Serve into salad bowls or onto salad plates. Pass raspberry *vinaigrette* to accommodate individual tastes.

Yields 6 servings
adequate for 4-6 people

Notes: *The macadamia nuts may also be shaved using a sharp knife or a hand grater.

This recipe may be halved or doubled, when required.

1/6 SERVING (with 1 tablespoonful dressing) –
PROTEIN = 1.7 g.; FAT = 13.9 g.; CARBOHYDRATE = 2.3 g.;
CALORIES = 171; CALORIES FROM FAT = 73%

AUSTRALIAN HOT ASPARAGUS SALAD WITH RASPBERRY *VINAIGRETTE*
TPT - 8 minutes

In Australia, in September and October, this lovely, fresh combination of springtime flavors is frequently served as an appetizer or simply as a side vegetable. Enjoy it here in April and May!

2 pounds fresh asparagus spears—trimmed and well-washed, with spears cut to about equal lengths*

2 tablespoons AUSTRALIAN RASPBERRY *VINAIGRETTE* [see recipe which follows]
Freshly ground black pepper, to taste

Set up steamer.

Just before you are ready to serve, steam asparagus spears until bright green and *crisp-tender*—about 5-7 minutes.

Apportion steamed asparagus among four heated serving plates, such as elongated *au gratin* dishes. Drizzle raspberry *vinaigrette* over each serving. Grind black pepper over each.

Serve at once.

Yields 4 servings

Notes: *Allow about six asparagus spears per diner.

This recipe is easily increased or decreased proportionately, as required.

1/4 SERVING – PROTEIN = 3.2 g.; FAT = 4.7 g.; CARBOHYDRATE = 6.5 g.;
CALORIES = 74; CALORIES FROM FAT = 57%

Oceania–**Australia**

AUSTRALIAN RASPBERRY *VINAIGRETTE*
TPT - 1 hour and 2 minutes;
1 hour = flavor development period

The fresh, fresh, spontaneous taste of the fusion cuisine of Australia reflects the lifestyle. This vinaigrette is fresh, quickly-prepared, and has just the right sparkle for fresh, fresh ingredients. It is one of our favorite salad dressings.

1/2 cup *extra virgin* olive oil
2 1/2 tablespoons RASPBERRY VINEGAR *[see recipe which follows]* **or commercially-available, *preservative-free* raspberry vinegar**
2 tablespoons freshly squeezed lime juice
1/8 teaspoon freshly ground black pepper
Pinch salt

In a jar with a tightly fitting lid or in a cruet with a tightly fitting top or cork, combine all ingredients. Shake vigorously and set aside for about 1 hour to allow for development of flavor.

Alternately, the electric blender or the food processor fitted with steel knife may be used to produce a dressing which separates more slowly.

Always shake vigorously before serving.

Yields about 2/3 cupful

Note: This recipe is easily doubled or tripled, when required.

1/10 SERVING (i. e., per tablespoonful) –
PROTEIN = 0.08 g.; FAT = 8.9 g.; CARBOHYDRATE = 0.2 g.;
CALORIES = 81; CALORIES FROM FAT = 99%

RASPBERRY VINEGAR
TPT - 1 week and 4 minutes;
1 week = flavor development period

I can not quite remember when we Americans became entranced with raspberry vinaigrette but I do know that in the 1990s you rarely found an upscale restaurant that would not spritz it on just about everything. Bottles of raspberry vinegar and vinaigrette appeared on gourmet shelves at gourmet prices and mail order firms insulted you further by offering bottles at gourmet prices plus shipping and handling. Usually these had preservatives and other unnecessary additives. Raspberry vinegar is simpler to prepare at home than almost any other vinegar; it does not even require a trip to the herb garden. I evolved this to prove the point.

1 cup fresh *or unsweetened* frozen raspberries
 —well-washed and drained
1 small garlic clove—peeled
3 1/2 cups rice wine vinegar

Sterilize a 1-quart bottle or jar.

Coarsely chop raspberries. Put into sterilized 1-quart bottle or jar. Add peeled garlic clove. Pour rice wine vinegar over chopped raspberries and garlic clove, being sure to cover completely. Cap.

Allow to stand at room temperature in a dark cupboard for 1 week to allow for both flavor and color development.

Sterilize a clear, condiment bottle.

Using a fine sieve or a sieve lined with culinary cheesecloth, strain vinegar from raspberries into sterilized condiment bottle.

Store vinegar at cool room temperature away from light for up to three months.

Yields 3 1/2 cupfuls

Note: This recipe may be doubled or tripled or quadrupled with ease; helpful if you should want to give bottles as gifts.

1/56 SERVING (i. e., per tablespoonful) –
PROTEIN = 0.0 g.; FAT = 0.0 g.; CARBOHYDRATE = 0.0 g.;
CALORIES = 0.0; CALORIES FROM FAT = 0%

AUSTRALIAN PAN – GRILLED *HALLOUMI* CHEESE WITH *EDAMAME*, PEAS, ROASTED RED PEPPERS, AND MINT
TPT - 9 minutes

Halloumi cheese from Cyprus, made from ewes' milk with a hint of mint, is a favorite of ours since it can be planed, sliced, cubed, fried and, yes, pan-grilled. It makes a very striking presentation when it is pan-grilled. This entrée is quickly prepared and is a good choice when the day is hot and you want to keep preparation time to a minimum. I retrieve roasted red peppers from the freezer in the morning and head out into the garden for the mint and some Ruby Red or Red Ruffle basil just before I start to cook the cheese. Frozen edamame are fully cooked and need only be heated. Frozen green peas benefit greatly from undercooking so they can be cooked with the edamame in boiling water for just a few minutes. Add to this a baguette of fresh French bread or warm Soloio rolls and you have dinner.

This does reflect the Australian spontaneity but the influence of layers and layers of immigrant cultures is also clearly apparent.

3 cups *boiling* **water**
1 cup *frozen, shelled* **edamame***
1 cup freshly shelled *or frozen* **peas**

1 package (8.8 ounces) *Halloumi* **cheese**

1 1/2 teaspoons *finely slivered* **fresh mint leaves**
1 teaspoon *slivered* **red basil leaves**

Freshly ground peppercorn—black, white, and red—to taste

6 large pieces of ROASTED RED PEPPER *[see index]*—**well-drained if stored in oil**
Lemon wedges, for garnish

Preheat grill pan over *MEDIUM* heat.

Place saucepan containing *boiling* water over *LOW* heat. Add *edamame* and green peas. Allow to heat through while grilling cheese.

Using a sharp knife and holding the cheese firmly, cut the cheese crosswise into ten slices. Place on heated grill. When hot and marked on one side, turn over and cook until that side is marked. Transfer to a heated platter.

Drain beans and peas. Add mint and basil leaves. Toss and turn out on top of the grilled cheese.

Grind pepper mixture over.

Arrange roasted red pepper pieces on the platter and garnish with lemon wedges.
Serve at once.

Yields 10 servings
adequate for 4-5 people

Notes: *Fava beans or lima beans can be substituted, if preferred. They will, however, have to be cooked according to package directions. The complete protein available from soybeans and the incredible ease of preparation of the frozen *edamame* makes them our choice for this dish.

*Halloumi is now widely available in grocery stores that have a good selection of specialty cheeses. The secure plastic box in which it is packaged is unique and the bright blue label makes it easy to spot. If not available in your grocery store, it can be purchased online from purveyors of Greek and Cypriot foods.

This recipe can be halved or doubled, when required.

1/10 SERVING – PROTEIN = 7.5 g.; FAT = 8.1 g.; CARBOHYDRATE = 4.1 g.;
CALORIES = 113; CALORIES FROM FAT = 65%

GRAINBURGER ON VEGETABLE SPAGHETTI IN THE AUSTRALIAN STYLE
TPT - 33 minutes

Long shreds of vegetables, combined with spaghettini, provide a base for a burger that, without the exciting vegetable shreds, would be somewhat ho-hum. You can make your own grainburger or buy frozen ones that are available in most well-stocked grocery stores.

Oceania–Australia

GRAINBURGER ON VEGETABLE SPAGHETTI IN THE AUSTRALIAN STYLE (cont'd)

1 large carrot—peeled
1 large parsnip—peeled
1 red bell pepper—cored and seeded with membranes removed
1 green bell pepper—cored and seeded with membranes removed
1 medium leek—*white portion only*—trimmed and *very well-rinsed*

3 quarts *boiling* water
1 tablespoon freshly squeezed lemon juice
One 3-inch strip lemon zest
2 ounces whole wheat *or* high protein *spaghettini* (thin spaghetti)*

4 grainburgers**

2 tablespoons butter
3 tablespoons *fat-free* dairy sour cream
1/2 teaspoon freshly squeezed lemon juice

2 tablespoons grated Parmesan cheese***
8 well-washed and trimmed snowpeas

Australian tomato chutney, if available *or* **ROASTED TOMATO AND CITRUS CHUTNEY** *[see index]*, for garnish****

Using a sharp knife, a vegetable peeler, or any tool that will produce long, thin shreds similar to spaghetti, cut the carrot and parsnip. Sliver the red and green bell pepper halves into *thin* slices, similar to spaghetti. Slice the white portion of the well-washed leek into long, thin shreds, similar to spaghetti. Set aside until required.

In a large kettle set over *HIGH* heat, add lemon juice and lemon zest to *boiling* water. Add *spaghettini* and cook, stirring occasionally, according to package directions. Drain thoroughly, discarding lemon zest.

Add the shredded vegetables *in the last two minutes* of the *pasta* cooking process. Drain and transfer to a heated serving bowl.

At the same time, in a skillet set over *MEDIUM* heat, sauté the grainburgers according to package directions.

Add butter, sour cream, and lemon juice to the skillet. With a wooden spoon, stir it to form a sauce.

Apportion vegetable–spaghetti mixture among four heated plates. Sprinkle each serving with about 1 1/2 teaspoonfuls grated cheese. Nestle a grainburger into the vegetable mixture and spoon a bit of sauce from the skillet over each.

Garnish with two snowpeas and a spoonful of chutney on the side.

Serve at once.

Yields 4 individual serving

Notes: *If you are able to find spinach *spaghettini*, add it half-and-half with the "white" *spaghettini*.

**Grain and bean patties and grain-based sausages, that need only be sautéed, are marketed by several firms. They work well in this vegetarian version of a dish more often served with salmon patties in Australia.

***The grated cheese may be omitted, if you prefer a vegan entrée.

****Australian tomato chutney is a difficult product to find. If unavailable, substitute a chutney of your own preference.

This recipe can be halved or doubled, when required.

1/4 SERVING (exclusive of chutney) –
PROTEIN = 11.8 g.; FAT = 9.0 g.; CARBOHYDRATE = 48.1 g.;
CALORIES = 324; CALORIES FROM FAT = 25%

AUSTRALIAN BAKED RED ONIONS WITH RASPBERRY *VINAIGRETTE*
TPT - 40 minutes

Americans have never cooked with red onions much until recent years, favoring those everyday white or yellow onions, boiling and creaming some tiny white onions at holidays, venturing into the joy of a Spanish onion for a burger, and then settling on sweet Vidalia and Walla Walla onions as chic. Roasting an onion brings out such a wonderful taste and roasting red onions brings out flavors that you would never guess were there. This recipe proves that an onion does not have to breaded and fried to be special.

3 medium Italian red onions—with dry, outer skins removed
1 tablespoon *extra virgin* olive oil
Freshly ground black pepper, to taste

2 tablespoons **RASPBERRY VINEGAR** *[see recipe which precedes]*

AUSTRALIAN RASPBERRY *VINAIGRETTE* *[see recipe which precedes]*

AUSTRALIAN BAKED RED ONIONS WITH RASPBERRY *VINAIGRETTE* (cont'd)

Preheat oven to 375 degrees F. Prepare a cookie sheet or roasting pan by covering with aluminum foil and coating with non-stick lecithin spray coating.

Trim the root end of each onion flat *without cutting into it.* Slice about 1/8 inch across the stem end of each onion. Cut each onion in half lengthwise, i. e., from the top through the root end. Then, cut each half from the top through the root end to form quarter wedges.

Using a brush, coat each onion quarter with a thin coating of olive oil. Place onion wedges on prepared cookie sheet. Grind black pepper *generously* over each onion.

Bake in preheated 375 degree F. oven for about 25-30 minutes, or until tender. Remove onions from oven. Transfer to a heated serving platter.

Pour about 1/2 teaspoonful of the raspberry vinegar over each roasted onion wedge.

Allow to stand for a minute or two to allow the vinegar to penetrate. Then, *serve at once,* with a cruet of AUSTRALIAN RASPBERRY *VINAIGRETTE* to accommodate individual tastes.

Yields 6 servings
adequate for 4-6 people

Note: When required, this recipe can be decreased or increased proportionately.

1/8 SERVING (without added *vinaigrette*) –
PROTEIN = 1.0 g.; FAT = 1.9 g.; CARBOHYDRATE = 5.0 g.;
CALORIES = 37; CALORIES FROM FAT = 46%

AUSTRALIAN EGGPLANT RELISH
TPT - 35 minutes

A super accompaniment to grilled vegetables and veggie burgers for the eggplant lover in the family, this relish has enough flavor complexity to appeal to everyone. The lime juice, chopped fennel seeds, and Thai basil are an astonishingly inviting combination. Asian eggplants or the relatively new Graffiti eggplants, with sweeter flesh and fewer seeds, are perfect for this extra vegetable dish. Instead of frying the eggplant, which absorbs astonishing amounts of oil in the process, we prepare the eggplant by baking slices. When chopped and added to the rest of the relish ingredients, they take along a lot less oil.

1 medium eggplant—washed, trimmed, and sliced into 1/4-inch crosswise slices
Coarse or kosher salt

2 tablespoons *high heat* safflower *or* sunflower oil

1 tablespoon *extra virgin* olive oil
2 garlic cloves—*very finely* chopped
1 large shallot—cut into 1/4 inch dice
1 large celery rib—cut into 1/4-inch dice

1/2 cup canned, *diced* tomatoes

1 tablespoon freshly squeezed lime juice
4 pitted *Kalamata* olives—*finely* chopped
2 tablespoons *finely* chopped fresh Thai basil*
1/4 teaspoon fennel seeds—chopped

Salt, to taste
Freshly ground black pepper, to taste

Place rimmed cookie sheets in the oven to heat. Preheat oven to 335 degrees F.

Remove preheated baking sheets from oven. Pour about 2 tablespoons of oil into each pan; brush to edges. Arrange eggplant slices on each of prepared baking sheets. Bake in preheated 335 degree F. oven for 10 minutes. Rotate baking sheets and switch racks. Continue baking for an additional 10 minutes. Remove baking sheets from oven. Turn each eggplant slice. Return to oven for about 10 minutes more, or until each slice is lightly-browned. Drain eggplant slices *thoroughly* on several thicknesses of paper toweling. Peel eggplant slices and chop into small dice. Set aside on dry paper toweling until required.

In a large non-stick-coated skillet set over *MEDIUM* heat, heat olive oil. Add *very finely* chopped garlic, and diced shallot and celery. Sauté until garlic and shallot are soft, *being careful not to allow any of the vegetables to brown.*

Add diced tomato and stir for about 3 minutes.

Add baked and chopped eggplant, lime juice, *finely* chopped olives and fresh basil, and chopped fennel seeds. Stir-fry for several minutes.

Season with salt and pepper. Turn into a heated serving bowl.

AUSTRALIAN EGGPLANT RELISH (cont'd)

*Serve warm.***

Yields 8 servings
adequate for 6 people

Note: *If Thai basil is not available, use Italian basil.

**The relish can be made ahead and refrigerated for at least a day before serving. Reheat gently.

This recipe can be halved, when required.

1/8 SERVING – PROTEIN = 0.5 g.; FAT = 5.0 g.; CARBOHYDRATE = 2.9 g.;
CALORIES = 59; CALORIES FROM FAT = 76%

AUSTRALIAN CREAM SAUCE WITH ROASTED SHALLOTS AND FRESH THYME
TPT - 1 hour and 20 minutes

Variations of this sauce turn up in fine restaurants all over Australia but it is not at all like the flour-thickened French sauces of the 1950s and 1960s that buried fish and fowl alike. Sometimes you really do want to use a cream sauce and this sauce is beautifully fluid and well-flavored. The roasted shallots a remarkable flavor as does the infusion of fresh thyme. Try this French-inspired Australian sauce with boiled or oven-roasted new potatoes.

6 medium shallots—*well-washed* but *unpeeled*

1/4 cup heavy whipping cream
1/4 cup light cream *or* half and half
1 teaspoon freshly squeezed lemon juice
1 1/2 teaspoons *Dijon* mustard with wine
1/2 teaspoon fresh thyme leaves

Freshly ground black pepper, to taste

Preheat oven to 300 degrees F.

Place unpeeled shallots in either an onion baker or a garlic baker. Roast in preheated 350 degree F. oven for 50-55 minutes, or until the shallots are soft. Remove from oven and allow to cool.

When cool, peel the shallots and put into the blender with heavy and light cream, lemon juice, *Dijon* mustard, and thyme leaves. Blend until very smooth. Turn into a small saucepan set over *LOW* heat. Cook, stirring frequently, until heated through.

Season with black pepper. Turn into a sauceboat.

Serve at once.

Yields 3/4 cupful

Note: This recipe may be doubled, when required.

1/6 SERVING (about 2 tablespoonfuls) –
PROTEIN = 0.6 g.; FAT = 4.3 g.; CARBOHYDRATE = 2.2 g.;
CALORIES = 93; CALORIES FROM FAT = 42%

AUSTRALIAN *CHILI* AND GINGER SAUCE
TPT - 35 minutes

A most unusual flavor combination from Australia . . . Unusual, not withstanding, this is an interesting sauce for lentil loaves, grainburgers, soy sausages, and roasted vegetables, or as an appetizer dip–hot or cold.

1 tablespoon canola oil
1 medium onion—*finely* chopped
1 tablespoon shredded fresh gingerroot
1/4 teaspoon chili powder

2 cups canned, *diced* tomatoes—well-drained
1/3 cup apple juice
1/2 teaspoon honey
1 teaspoon apple cider vinegar

In a large skillet set over *MEDIUM-LOW* heat, heat oil. Sauté *finely* chopped onion, grated gingerroot, and chili powder until the onion soft and translucent, *being careful not to allow onion to brown.*

Add chopped tomatoes and apple juice. Stir to combine well. *Reduce heat to LOW.* Cover skillet and allow to simmer for 20 minutes, stirring occasionally. Remove from heat. Stir in honey and vinegar.

AUSTRALIAN *CHILI* AND GINGER SAUCE (cont'd)

Using the food processor fitted with steel blade, process tomato mixture until *finely chopped,* but *not smooth.* Press the puréed mixture through a fine sieve into a clean saucepan.*

Return to *MEDIUM* heat and cook, stirring frequently, until reduced to the desired consistency.

Serve either hot or cold, as dictated by your menu needs.

Yields about 1 cupful

Note: This recipe can be halved or doubled, when required.

1/8 SERVING (about 2 tablespoonfuls) –
PROTEIN = 0.9 g.; FAT = 1.9 g.; CARBOHYDRATE = 5.3 g.;
CALORIES = 38; CALORIES FROM FAT = 45%

AUSTRALIAN LENTIL AND *PASTA* SALAD WITH NASTURTIUM
TPT - 1 hour and 8 minutes

This is a simple salad that makes it appearance on our table from mid-August until the first frost takes the nasturtiums from the container at our northern hemisphere doorstep. The bay leaves from the herb bed are so full of flavor that as long as there is a bay leaf still in the garden, I use a fresh one to flavor the lentils. Italian and Greek influences are hinted at in this salad and are certainly homage to the ethnic diversity of Australia; the peppery nasturtium leaves and the colorful nasturtium petals are just the right touch to make it all sing.

3/4 cup dry brown (*or* green) lentils
2 cups *boiling* water
1 bay leaf–halved

1 tablespoon GARLIC–BASIL VINEGAR *[see index] or* other herb vinegar of choice
Freshly ground black pepper, to taste

1 cup *tiny pasta* shells
2 quarts *boiling* water

1 tablespoon *extra virgin* olive oil
1 teaspoon freshly squeezed lemon juice
1/4 cup *finely* shredded, well-washed nasturtium leaves
2 tablespoons snipped chives
1 teaspoon fresh lemon thyme leaves
Freshly ground black pepper, to taste

Home-grown, spray-free nasturtium petals, for garnish

Grated *pecorino Romano* cheese

Sort lentils and discard those of poor quality. Rinse thoroughly.

In a non-aluminum saucepan set over *MEDIUM* heat, combine lentils, 3 cupfuls *boiling* water, and broken bay leaf. Bring to the boil. Reduce heat to *LOW,* cover tightly, and simmer for about 30 minutes, or until lentils are tender. Drain, reserving liquid for soup stock and discarding bay leaf pieces.

Turn cooked lentils into a mixing bowl. Add 1 tablespoonful of vinegar and black pepper. Stir *gently* to mix and set aside to cool.

At the same time, in a saucepan set over *MEDIUM* heat, combine the 2 quartfuls *boiling* water and the *pasta* shells. Cook according to package directions. Drain and plunge into ice water to prevent further cooking. Drain well. Add to cooked lentils. Toss gently.

Add olive oil, lemon juice, *finely* shredded nasturtium leaves, snipped chives, and lemon thyme leaves. Toss gently. Taste and season with black pepper. Turn into a serving bowl. Refrigerate until required.

Serve chilled or at room temperature. Garnish with nasturtium petals before serving. Pass grated cheese.

Yields 6 servings
adequate for 4 people

Note: This recipe can be halved, when required.

1/6 SERVING (with 1 teaspoonful grated cheese) –
PROTEIN = 10.0 g.; FAT = 3.0 g.; CARBOHYDRATE = 31.3 g.;
CALORIES = 191; CALORIES FROM FAT = 14%

Oceania–Australia

PUFF PASTRY "PILLOWS" WITH RASPBERRY PURÉE AND PEACHES
TPT - 38 minutes

I was inspired to create this quite simple but divine dessert by the famous dessert Peach Melba, named for the Australian-born opera soprano Dame Nellie Melba, a dessert in which peaches and ice cream were topped with a corn starch-thickened raspberry sauce. Peach Melba was enormously chic when I was a teenager. One wonders if the peach and raspberry combination would have been named for her if she had not taken a stage name to honor the city of her birth, Melbourne; her real name was Helen Porter Mitchell. This version is a very bright, fresh finish to a meal and, I hope, an appropriate tribute to the taste of "down under."

1 package (10 ounces) frozen raspberries in syrup —*defrosted*

3 cups sliced peaches canned in light syrup

1 sheet *frozen* puff pastry—*brought to room temperature*

2 tablespoons honey, of choice—*clover honey is our choice*

Press *defrosted* raspberries through a fine sieve into a clean sauceboat. Refrigerate until required.

Set a sieve over a mixing bowl. Pour peaches into the sieve and allow them to drain *in the refrigerator* until required.

Preheat oven to 400 degrees F.* Prepare a baking sheet by lining with culinary parchment paper.

Cut the puff pastry sheet into twelve 2 x 3-inch pieces. Transfer it to the parchment-lined baking sheets. Bake at 400 degrees F. for about 15 minutes, checking to be sure that the pastry does not over brown. Remove from oven and allow to cool for about 5 minutes on the baking sheets.

Just before you are ready to serve, arrange two puff pastry "pillows" in each of six soup plates, propping one up against the other. Scatter 1/2 cupful drained peaches over. Ladle a couple of tablespoons of the crushed and strained raspberries over.

Drizzle honey in a zigzag pattern dramatically from edge to edge of each dish.

Serve at once.

Yields 6 individual servings

Note: This recipe can be halved, when required.

1/6 SERVING – PROTEIN = 3.9 g.; FAT = 11.2 g.; CARBOHYDRATE = 49.4 g.; CALORIES = 305; CALORIES FROM FAT = 33%

AUSTRALIAN FRUIT SPIDERS
TPT - 2 minutes

This is similar to the phenomenon know as a "root beer float" in the United States. Root beer is not available in Australia but this delicious, and very simple, dessert or beverage cooler is found throughout the island continent.

1 quart fruit juice *or non-carbonated* fruit drink or a mixture of choice—*chilled**
2 cups *low-fat* (4.4%) vanilla ice cream—*slightly softened*

Fill each of four clear drinking glasses about two-thirds full of fruit juice. *Gently* float about 1/2 cupful of *softened* ice cream on the fruit juice.

Serve at once and watch the "spider's legs" extend down into the juice.

Yields 4 individual servings

Notes: *A combination of orange juice, peach nectar, and lemonade is especially refreshing.

When required, this recipe may be easily halved or doubled.

1/4 SERVING – PROTEIN = 3.8 g.; FAT = 3.3 g.; CARBOHYDRATE = 47.2 g.; CALORIES = 228; CALORIES FROM FAT = 13%

Oceania–**Australia**

AUSTRALIAN GINGER – STEEPED PRUNES
TPT - 24 hours and 2 minutes;
24 hours = marination period

These are not your ordinary breakfast prunes. Each wrinkled plum becomes infused with the sweet ginger syrup. You will be tempted to serve them as a confection with teas as they do in Australia.

15 pitted *preservative-free* prunes
1/3 cup AUSTRALIAN SWEET GINGER SYRUP
[see recipe which follows]

Light cream *or* half and half, if desired

Place prunes in a bowl with a flat bottom which is small enough to tightly accommodate the prunes in a single layer or place the prunes in a plastic container with a tightly fitting lid. Pour ginger syrup over. Cover tightly and place the container in the refrigerator to allow prunes to marinate for at least 24 hours. Baste the prunes every 6 hours, or so, with the ginger syrup to insure even marination.

Drain extra ginger syrup from prunes, *saving it to reuse in other recipes.* Arrange prunes in a shallow fruit dish or in a crystal sherbet glass to serve. Pass a pitcher of cream and allow diners to add a splash of cream, if they desire.

Yields 15 ginger–steeped prunes

Note: This recipe may be doubled, when required.

1/15 SERVING (i. e., per prune with syrup) –
PROTEIN = 0.2 g.; FAT = 0.0 g.; CARBOHYDRATE = 9.8 g.;
CALORIES = 39; CALORIES FROM FAT = 0%

AUSTRALIAN SWEET GINGER SYRUP
TPT - 1 hour and 17 minutes;
1 hour = cooling period

If you love the taste of gingerroot, as we do, there is no need to mail order for the imported syrup when you can easily make your own. It has scores of delicious uses.

2 cups sugar
2 cups water
6 slices fresh gingerroot—peeled

In a large saucepan set over *MEDIUM-HIGH* heat, combine sugar, water, and gingerroot slices. Stir to combine well. Allow to come to the boil, stirring frequently. Continue to boil for a full 10 minutes. *Mixture will become syrupy and the volume will be reduced to about 2 1/4 cupfuls. Do not allow to boil longer than 10 minutes.**

Set aside at room temperature and allow to cool to room temperature—about 1 hour. Remove and discard gingerroot slices.

Turn into a glass jar with a tightly fitting lid and refrigerate until required.

Notes: **The syrup will thicken somewhat as it cools. If the ginger syrup is allowed to boil too long, it will crystallize!*

A most pleasing HOMEMADE GINGER ALE can be prepared by mixing about 1/4 cupful of SWEET GINGER SYRUP into 1 cupful *chilled* club soda.

Yields about 2 1/4 cupfuls

1/36 SERVING (i. e., per tablespoon) –
PROTEIN = 0.0 g.; FAT = 0.0 g.; CARBOHYDRATE = 12.5 g.;
CALORIES = 49; CALORIES FROM FAT = 0%

New Zealand

The island nation of New Zealand consists of two main islands, North and South islands, five inhabited smaller islands, and a group of outlying islands. This group of islands, volcanic in origin, extends south from the subtropical zone into the temperate zone of the southern hemisphere straddling the Pacific and Indo-Australian tectonic plates placing it in an active subduction region. Additionally, the nation lies above one of the planet's largest, active supervolcanoes which has erupted twenty-eight times in the past 27,000 years, the last time in 210 AD just thirty years after a massive eruption had occurred that is noted in the literature as having turned the skies red across China to Rome. Lake Taupo, on North Island, is in the remains of the caldera formed during the eruption about 26,500 years ago, an eruption referred to as the Oruanui eruption which may have contributed significantly to the last major glaciation period. Once part of a microcontinent about half the size of Australia which gradually submerged, the islands remained geographically isolated from other land masses for an estimated 80 million years resulting in a catalog of flora and fauna unique and unevolved.

New Zealand is one of the last land masses to have been settled by humans. By 1000 AD the seafaring people referred to as Ancestral East Polynesians had established on most of the islands of East Polynesia. These were adventuresome travelers who sailed not just to explore but to colonize as we have seen in the Hawaiian Islands. They appeared to have arrived and settled in New Zealand in the thirteenth century. This is supported by evidence that the Polynesian rat was well-established by 1280 AD. The Maori are descendants of those Polynesian explorers from the area known as East Polynesia.

The food traditions of the Maori were all but lost as English cooking traditions began to dominate and the immigrants from many nations brought and adapted their signature dishes to the food resources of the islands. English food customs are still very much in evidence in New Zealand—the Sunday roast, pub food, lamb broth, fish pies, nutburgers, mashed vegetable purées, roasted potatoes, celery, cauliflower, pasties, scones, summer puddings, apple crumble, all of these and many more form an ethnic core that has been integrated by the foods and seasoning of Southeast Asia with curried vegetable and meat dishes very much a part of the cuisine today. Only recently is there evidence of a more global palate as New Zealanders enjoy *lasagne*, albeit with cottage cheese, pizzas, flans, quiches, and *spanokopitta*. Nevertheless, the sweetpotato (*kumara*), treasured as the supreme source of carbohydrate, "*kai*," by the Maori, is still today an important part of the New Zealand diet. The starchy portion, *kai*, upon which a meal was built was all important to Polynesians; the rest of the meal rounded out the nutrition and provided the necessary protein, "*kinaki*"—a classic vegan life plan. Little that was native could provide that all important starchy component to the founding settlers. Instead the ocean teemed with animal protein, which up until then had not been the central focus of meal planning, but instead a secondary consideration. Even today the importance of New Zealand's marine resources can not be minimized and a marine economic zone is claimed that is approximately fifteen times the country's land area.

In truth, the founding settlers had become a meat-based society and craved the *kai* of the tropical islands from which they had come. As a result, they became dependent upon root crops like *kumara*, breadfruit, and fern roots and, subsequently, upon the wheat- and corn-based foods introduced to them by early European settlers who came in the wake of the exploratory voyages of Captain James Cook. Cook first visited the group of islands that are today known as New Zealand (*Aotearoa* in Māori) in 1769 and mapped the coastline. From that point on, other Europeans and North Americans came as they pursued whaling, sealing, and trading. By 1840 the British declared sovereignty over all of New Zealand incorporating it into the colony of New South Wales. The following year New Zealand was declared a separate Crown colony, remaining such until 1907 when New Zealand declared itself a Dominion within the British Empire. In 1947, after World War II, New Zealand became a Commonwealth nation.

Oceania–New Zealand

Kiwifruit *Frappé* Appetizer

Grilled *Pesto* Toasts
with
***Pesto* Sauce with Macadamia Nuts**

~

Avocado Halves Stuffed with Tomato Salad

Melon and Peach Salad with Fresh *Mozzarella*

**Roasted Sweetpotato (*Kumara*) Salad
with Macadamia Nuts**

Mixed Greens
with
Kiwifruit *Vinaigrette* with Honey

~

Puréed Carrot and *Kumara* Soup   Cream of Spinach and Potato Soup
with Gingerroot

~~~~~~~~~~~~~~~~~~~~~

Vegetable Pasties

or

***Hunza* Pie – New Zealand Potato and Spinach Pie**

with
Whole Wheat Pie Crusts

Buttered Green Peas

~~~~~~~~~~~~~~~~~~~~~

Peanut – Apple Crumble

Stewed Rhubarb with Tapioca

NEW ZEALAND KIWIFRUIT *FRAPPÉ* APPETIZER
TPT - 4 minutes

Kiwifruit and Granny Smith apples first appeared in our grocery stores when our daughter was still a toddler; now we would be surprised if a store did not have an ample supply of both. Fuzzy, brown-skinned kiwifruit with rich green flesh and dramatic black seeds and the now-so-familiar Granny Smith apples were only available to us "in season." Both bore little elliptical stickers identifying them as "Product of New Zealand." Soon there was another season as the Granny Smith apple was established in France and shipped to the United States. Today both kiwifruit and Granny Smith apples are grown in the United States. Kiwifruit, known by many names like Chinese gooseberry, wood berry, hairy bush fruit, vine pear, and Macaque peach, is native to the Yangtze River valley of China. The fruit was introduced to New Zealand by Mary Isabel Fraser, the principal of Wanganui Girl's School. Just as Thomas Jefferson introduced rice to the colonies by bringing seeds to Virginia, Mary Fraser gave the seeds of the Macaque peach or yang tao, as the fruit was commonly called, to a local nurseryman. The seeds produced their first fruit in 1910. A gold, smooth-skinned kiwifruit, developed from a variety found in India, is now also being marketed. Today New Zealand ranks second to Italy in kiwifruit production, with Chile a distant third.

6 kiwifruits—peeled and coarsely chopped*
3/4 cup ice cubes
2/3 cup *two-percent* milk
2 tablespoons organic *agave* nectar**

1 lime—well-washed and cut into 6 thin slices

Just before you are ready to serve, combine peeled and chopped kiwifruits, ice cubes, milk, and *agave* nectar in the container of the electric blender. Process until smooth. Divide among six wine glasses. Hang a slice of lime on each glass.

NEW ZEALAND KIWIFRUIT *FRAPPÉ* APPETIZER (cont'd)

Serve at once.***

Yields 6 individual servings

Notes: *There is a concentration of vitamins right under the skin of the kiwifruit. When peeling, remove as little of the brown, fiber-rich, and edible skin as absolutely necessary.

**Agave nectar is available at natural food stores and in well-stocked grocery stores. Organic nectar is recommended since the *agave* plants, grown for *tequila* production from which this is a byproduct, are heavily sprayed by Mexican growers.

***The enzyme actinidin in kiwifruit digests the protein in milk so this recipe must be served as soon as it is prepared. Actinidin will also dissolve the collagen proteins in gelatin very quickly, preventing gelling.

This recipe can be halved, when required.

1/6 SERVING – PROTEIN = 1.8 g.; FAT = 0.8 g.; CARBOHYDRATE = 19.0 g.;
CALORIES = 83; CALORIES FROM FAT = 9%

NEW ZEALAND *PESTO* SAUCE WITH MACADAMIA NUTS
TPT - 27 minutes

I never thought that I would be smitten with any variation of my beloved "pesto alla Genovese" but it happened. Instead of pine nuts (pignoli) New Zealanders use the macadamia nut, native to both Australia and New Zealand. It is a relatively expensive nut and that is partially because the kernel yield from one hundred pounds once the husk and shells have been removed is only about seven pounds. It is generally used in its raw state to make this sauce but we are rarely privileged to find macadamia nuts that have not been roasted, salted, and jarred so we must make some accommodations. This useful, flavorful paste does freeze well so we find it convenient to double or triple this recipe when fresh basil is available and to freeze the resultant sauce in small portions from which we can scoop a tablespoonful or so when needed.

1/3 cup macadamia nuts

1/3 cup loosely packed fresh basil leaves—well-washed and *thoroughly dried**
1/4 cup chopped fresh Italian flat-leafed parsley
2 large garlic cloves—peeled and coarsely chopped
1/2 cup freshly grated Parmesan *or* pecorino Romano cheese, as preferred

1/3 cup *extra virgin* olive oil

Wash the salt from the macadamia nuts and pat dry using several layers of paper toweling. Chop the nuts and set aside briefly.

In the work bowl of the food processor, fitted with steel knife, or in the container of the electric blender, combine fresh basil leaves, chopped fresh parsley leaves, chopped garlic cloves, and grated cheese. Process or blend to chop *finely*. Carefully, stir ingredients down with a spatula.

Add oil and blend until a smooth, thick paste is formed.

Add nuts and process just enough to chop the nuts finely. Scrape paste into a small mixing bowl.

Use as condiment in soups, stews, sauces. Refrigerate or freeze leftovers.

Yields about 1 1/4 cupfuls

Notes: *Use fresh basil only!

Since this sauce is used in small amounts to enhance the flavor of dishes, we have not reduced the fat content. Be aware that this is a high-fat condiment and, since the flavor is powerful, a little goes a long way.

This recipe may be increased or decreased proportionately as required.

1/20 SERVING (i. e., per tablespoonful) –
PROTEIN = 1.6 g.; FAT = 4.7 g.; CARBOHYDRATE = 1.2 g.;
CALORIES = 61; CALORIES FROM FAT = 69%

AVOCADO HALVES STUFFED WITH TOMATO SALAD

TPT - 1 hour and 12 minutes;
1 hour = flavor development period

Avocados were introduced to New Zealand and established well. In this recipe, the soft texture literally embraces the acidity of the tomato filling. New Zealanders really have the opportunity for a lovely, simple but dramatic presentation for a Christmas dinner in the southern hemisphere where the tomatoes are ripening in the summer sun and the chives are spilling over in their herb beds.

2 large ripe tomatoes—peeled, seeded, and chopped*
1 tablespoon NEW ZEALAND *PESTO* SAUCE WITH MACADAMIA NUTS [see recipe which precedes]
1 tablespoon *finely* chopped fresh basil
1 tablespoon *extra virgin* olive oil
1 teaspoon freshly squeezed lemon juice
Salt, to taste
Freshly ground black pepper, to taste

3 small avocados

1 1/2 teaspoons snipped chives
12 large chive blades

In a mixing bowl, combine chopped tomatoes, *pesto* sauce, *finely* chopped basil, oil, lemon juice, salt, and pepper. Toss to combine thoroughly. Cover and refrigerate for at least 1 hour to allow for flavors to meld.

When ready to serve, halve and pit avocados. Spoon *one-sixth* of prepared tomato–garlic filling into the depression left by the pit. Place each on a salad plate. Sprinkle 1/2 teaspoonful of snipped chives. Garnish with 2 large chive blades.

Serve at once.

Yields 6 individual servings

Notes: *Chopped oranges, tangerines, or clementines can be substituted for the tomatoes, if preferred.

This recipe can be increased or decreased proportionately to accommodate more or fewer diners.

1/6 SERVING – PROTEIN = 2.9 g.; FAT = 19.2 g.; CARBOHYDRATE = 8.7 g.;
CALORIES = 209; CALORIES FROM FAT = 83%

NEW ZEALAND MELON AND PEACH SALAD WITH FRESH *MOZZARELLA*

TPT - 25 minutes;
15 minutes = marination period

Every element of this summer salad is so very, very refreshing but to enjoy it fully you must have locally-grown, tree-ripened peaches and a perfectly ripened honeydew melon. I notice people pressing and squeezing honeydew melons in the produce section of our stores and truly wonder what they are learning about that sphere they are holding. I think that the most successful way to get a perfectly ripened, sweetened-to-perfection melon is to educate your nose. I kid you not, both honeydew melons and cantaloupes can be chosen just by the intensity and sweetness of their aroma. They should smell the way you want them to taste and with a little practice you will be able to confidently say, "today," "tomorrow," "three days."

2 tablespoons *extra virgin* olive oil
2 tablespoons RASPBERRY VINEGAR [see index], PEAR – ANISE HYSSOP VINEGAR [see index], MIXED FLOWER VINEGAR WITH OREGANO [see index], *or* other herb vinegar of choice
Pinch salt

1/2 ripe honeydew melon—peeled, seeded, and sliced into 3- or 4-inch thin slices
2 ripe peaches—peeled, pitted and sliced
Freshly ground black pepper, to taste

3 ounces *fresh mozzarella* cheese—chopped
1 tablespoon chopped *fresh* basil
1 tablespoon chopped *fresh* marjoram

NEW ZEALAND MELON AND PEACH SALAD WITH FRESH *MOZZARELLA* (cont'd)

In a cruet or jar with lid, combine oil, vinegar, and salt. Shake vigorously. Set aside briefly.

In a shallow bowl, spread out melon and peach slices. Season with black pepper. Pour prepared *vinaigrette* over. Allow to stand for 15 minutes at room temperature. Spoon *vinaigrette* over fruit slices to insure even coverage.

Add chopped cheese, basil, and marjoram. Toss gently. Immediately, using a slotted spoon and allowing excess *vinaigrette* to drain off, transfer salad mixture to a platter or large, shallow serving dish.

*Serve at once.**

Yields 8 servings
adequate for 6 people

Notes: *It may be tempting to make this salad early in the day and refrigerate it until dinnertime but we find that it is best served at room temperature right after it is prepared.

This recipe may be halved or doubled, when required.

1/6 SERVING – PROTEIN = 3.5 g.; FAT = 2.2 g.; CARBOHYDRATE = 7.7 g.;
CALORIES = 70; CALORIES FROM FAT = 26%

NEW ZEALAND ROASTED SWEETPOTATO (*KUMARA*) SALAD WITH MACADAMIA NUTS
TPT - 40 minutes

The constant confusion as to the sweetpotato, which is not a potato but a member of the morning glory family instead, is not at all confusing in New Zealand. There the sweet yellow root vegetable is called "kumara" and nobody muses when discussing potatoes, "Should I bake whites or sweets?" Kudos to the New Zealanders!! This salad is an absolute delight. You will marvel at flavor and texture that you never, ever thought to combine.

1 large sweetpotato (*kumara*)—cut into 1/2-inch cubes
1 tablespoon *extra virgin* olive oil
Pinch salt

2 tablespoons *extra virgin* olive oil
1 1/2 tablespoons white wine vinegar
1/4 teaspoon freshly squeezed lemon juice

4 large romaine lettuce leaves—well-washed and coarsely chopped
18 small grape tomatoes—well washed*

2 tablespoons crumbled *feta* cheese
1/4 cup halved macadamia nuts
1 red radish—trimmed and *finely* chopped
Freshly ground black pepper, to taste

Preheat oven to 350 degrees F.

Place the sweetpotato cubes in a roasting pan. Drizzle with the 1 tablespoonful olive oil. Sprinkle with salt. Roast for about 25-30 minutes, stirring occasionally. Remove from oven and allow to cool to room temperature.

In a cruet, combine oil, vinegar, and lemon juice. Shake vigorously and set aside until required.

In a salad bowl, combine chopped lettuce, tomatoes, and *cooled, roasted* sweetpotato pieces. *Gently* toss.

Sprinkle *feta* cheese over. Scatter macadamia nut halves over. Scatter *finely* chopped radish over. Grind black pepper over.

Serve at once. Pass the *vinaigrette* separately for those who wish to dress their salad.

Yields 6 servings
adequate for 4 people

Notes: *If small grape tomatoes are not available, halve large ones or choose cherry tomatoes and halve those.

This recipe can be halved or double, when required.

1/6 SERVING – PROTEIN = 3.3 g.; FAT = 16.6 g.; CARBOHYDRATE = 12.2 g.;
CALORIES = 218; CALORIES FROM FAT = 69%

Oceania–**New Zealand**

NEW ZEALAND KIWIFRUIT *VINAIGRETTE* WITH HONEY

TPT - 1 hour and 3 minutes;
1 hour = flavor development period

Kiwifruit, vine-grown berries also called Chinese gooseberries, were introduced into New Zealand from China in 1906 and became an important export crop. Called "yang tao" in Chinese, the fruit was renamed kiwifruit by the New Zealand Marketing Board, presumably after the native flightless kiwi bird. The diverse touches of flavor in this vinaigrette really perk up a salad. Although the less acidic gold variety is now widely available, I prefer to use green kiwifruits for this vinaigrette.

2 ripe kiwifruits—peeled and chopped
1 small garlic clove—crushed
2 1/2 tablespoons SPICED ORANGE VINEGAR [see index], SWEET AND TART CRANBERRY VINEGAR [see index], *or* RASPBERRY VINEGAR [see index], as preferred
2 tablespoons freshly squeezed lime juice
2 teaspoons wildflower honey
1 tablespoon *extra virgin* olive oil

In the container of the electric blender or in the work bowl of the food processor fitted with steel knife, combine all ingredients. Process until smoothly puréed.

Pour puréed *vinaigrette* mixture into a jar with a tightly fitting lid or in a cruet with a tightly fitting top or cork. Set aside for about 1 hour to allow for development of flavor.

Always shake vigorously before serving. To avoid rancidity, try to prepare dressing within an hour or two of serving.

Refrigerate any leftovers.

Yields about 1 cupful

Note: This recipe may be halved or doubled, when required.

1/16 SERVING (i. e., per tablespoonful) –
PROTEIN = 0.1 g.; FAT = 0.7 g.; CARBOHYDRATE = 1.9 g.;
CALORIES = 14; CALORIES FROM FAT = 45%

NEW ZEALAND PURÉED CARROT AND *KUMARA* SOUP WITH GINGERROOT

TPT - 6 hours and 27 minutes)
[slow cooker: 3 hours at HIGH;
3 hours at LOW]

Slow cooking the vegetables to make this soup gives a depth of flavor that is head and shoulders above some of the New Zealand soups I have tasted. Soup was an important remnant of the British colonial period in New Zealand. Today, with less dependence upon Great Britain, a more modern cuisine has been pursued and, sadly, soups seem to have little place in that cuisine. New Zealanders could have just turned the first course soup into a main course or a lunch option as Americans had done. It appears that the answer is in the egalitarian culture they created which eschewed all that represented a class system. Soup was considered an upperclass menu element. But meat as the main menu item was very upperclass in Britain and New Zealanders took to that with enthusiasm. That was different, everyone could eat all the meat they wanted; it was a sort of equality. I suppose the lack of convenient canned soups may also have played a role in the demise of soups in their cuisine as women entered the workforce and the time allotted to cooking a meal was reduced. This soup, presented by a radio personality and author, can be served as a first course or as a main course soup for a light supper or lunch. It is a wonderfully flavored soup and certainly a cut or two above the bland Victorian British soups that dominated the soup sections of old New Zealand cookbooks.

5 cups VEGETABLE STOCK FROM SOUP [see index] *or* other vegetarian stock of choice

1 tablespoon *extra virgin* olive oil
1 large onion—*finely* chopped
2 garlic cloves—*finely* chopped
1 large sweetpotato (*kumara*)—peeled and *finely* chopped
4 medium carrots—scraped or pared and *finely* chopped

1 tablespoon *finely* chopped fresh gingerroot
1 tablespoon chopped mild green *chilies*

Salt, to taste
Freshly ground black pepper, to taste

3 tablespoons chopped fresh coriander (*cilantro*) *or* parsley, if preferred

NEW ZEALAND PURÉED CARROT AND *KUMARA* SOUP WITH GINGERROOT (cont'd)

Preheat slow cooker at HIGH.

In a saucepan set over *MEDIUM-HIGH* heat, bring stock to the boil. Pour into slow cooker.

In a large skillet set over *MEDIUM* heat, heat oil. Add *finely* chopped onion, garlic, sweetpotato, and carrots. Sauté until the onion is soft and translucent, *being careful not to allow vegetables to brown.*

Add *finely* chopped gingerroot and green *chilies*. Continue sautéing for about 5 minutes more. Add to stock in slow cooker. Cover. Allow to cook for about 3 hours. *Reduce slow cooker setting to LOW.* Cook for an additional 3 hours.

Using the food processor fitted with steel knife or the electric blender, purée the cooked soup bases in batches until very finely puréed. Pour into clean saucepan set over *MEDIUM* heat.

Season, to taste, with salt and pepper. Allow to heat through. Turn into heated soup tureen.

Add chopped fresh coriander (*cilantro*) or parsley.

Serve into heated soup plates.

Yields 8 cupfuls

Note: This soup freezes well but can be halved, if desired.

1/8 SERVING (i. e., per cupful) –
PROTEIN = 1.5 g.; FAT = 1.6 g.; CARBOHYDRATE = 11.5 g.;
CALORIES = 63; CALORIES FROM FAT = 23%

CREAM OF SPINACH AND POTATO SOUP
TPT - 47 minutes

Greens have served man well. The emergence of spinach and sorrel in the spring here in the northern hemisphere and in the autumn in the southern hemisphere have always been greeted with celebratory dishes. A fourteenth century British cookbook, reportedly used by the household of King Richard II gives a recipe for "spinoches." Early residents of New Zealand found and used a spinach variation known as New Zealand spinach which grew wild. It was identified by Captain James Cook in 1770 and introduced into Europe the same year. It is still grown by some but the larger-leafed varieties and baby spinach have gained the public's favor. Most British recipes for spinach soup call for a flour and butter roux for thickening. A boiled potato can provide the thickening necessary and add a bit of vitamin C for good measure. European settlers, who brought the sheep whose wool was so valuable as an export, continued the meat-based eating habits of the Maori but introduced the foods of their homeland including the white potato. An indigenous purple potato, now a sought-after gourmet variety, and the kumara (sweetpotato) were rejected by the British settlers. Today the move away from animal products is apparent in an increased interest in vegetarianism, albeit a vegetarianism more akin to the movement found in Britain and the United States in the 1970s.

If a vegan soup is desired, replace the cream with low-fat coconut milk and omit the yogurt in the garnish.

1 1/2 teaspoons CLARIFIED BUTTER or *GHEE*
  [see index]
1 1/2 teaspoons *extra virgin* olive oil
2 medium onions—chopped
4 scallions—*green portions only*—trimmed, well-rinsed, and chopped

1 large potato—peeled and diced
6 cups VEGETARIAN WHITE STOCK *[see index]* or other vegetarian stock of choice

6 cups spinach—hard ribs removed, torn into small pieces, and *very well-rinsed**
1/2 cup fresh parsley leaves—well-washed
1/2 teaspoon chili powder, or to taste
1/4 teaspoon ground cumin

1/2 cup light cream *or* half and half

Salt, to taste

2 tablespoons PLAIN YOGURT *[see index]* or commercially-available plain yogurt
1 tablespoon light cream *or* half and half

In a kettle set over *MEDIUM* heat, heat clarified butter and oil. Add chopped onions and scallion greens. Sauté until onions are soft and translucent, *being careful not to allow onions to brown.*

Add diced potato and vegetable stock. Allow to come to the boil. Cook, stirring frequently, until the potato pieces are tender.

CREAM OF SPINACH AND POTATO SOUP (cont'd)

Add spinach, parsley, chili powder, and ground cumin. Allow to come to the boil again. Reduce heat to *LOW-MEDIUM* and cook until spinach is soft. Remove from heat.

Using the electric blender, purée the spinach soup base in batches until very smooth. Pour into a clean saucepan set over *LOW* heat.

Add cream. Allow to heat over *LOW* heat until hot.

Taste and season with salt. Turn into a heated soup tureen.

Mix yogurt with the remaining 1 tablespoonful cream.

Serve into heated soup plates. Garnish each serving with a "swiggle" of the cream–yogurt mixture.

Yields about 7 cupfuls

Notes: *In the spring we add a handful of sorrel leaves to this recipe.

This recipe can be halved, when required.

1/7 SERVING (i. e., per cupful) –
PROTEIN = 3.5 g.; FAT = 3.9 g.; CARBOHYDRATE = 11.3 g.;
CALORIES = 89; CALORIES FROM FAT = 39%

NEW ZEALAND VEGETABLE PASTIES
TPT - 47 minutes

Hand-held pies called pasties can be found in Great Britain, New Zealand, Australia, and on the Upper Peninsula of Michigan, where I first tasted one filled with potatoes, leeks, and rutabagas quite unlike the New Zealand version that follows. Much like the empanadas of Latin American and Italian calzone, pasties can be made with almost any filling. It is usually contained in a pie pastry wrap before baking but puff pastry definitely gives a lighter result.

1 tablespoon butter

1/2 cup diced carrot
1 large potato—peeled and diced
1/2 cup diced pumpkin *or* **winter squash, such as butternut** *or* **acorn**
1 large leek—*white and light green portions only*—**trimmed, well-rinsed, and sliced**

1/4 cup freshly shelled *or frozen* **peas**
Salt
Freshly ground black pepper

1 1/2 sheets *frozen* **puff pastry**—*brought to room temperature*

About 3 ounces *extra sharp* **Cheddar cheese—diced**
2 tablespoons *fat-free* **pasteurized eggs**

In a small skillet set over *MEDIUM* heat, melt butter. Add diced carrot, potato, and pumpkin or squash, and sliced leek. Sauté until vegetables have softened and begin to color. Remove from heat.

Add peas, salt, and pepper.* Set aside until required.

Preheat oven to 400 degrees F. Prepare a cookie sheet by lining it with culinary parchment.

Unroll the puff pastry and cut into large circles—two circles per half sheet.** Spoon *one-sixth* of the sautéed vegetables into the center of the circle of puff pastry. Scatter *one-sixth* of the diced cheese on top of the vegetables. Fold the circle over to form a half-moon. Roll and crimp edges to seal the filling in. *Be sure to seal any tears in the pastry.* Brush with the pasteurized eggs. Place on the prepared cookie sheet. Repeat until all pasties have been made. Bake in preheated 400 degree F. oven for about 15-20 minutes, or until evenly browned. Transfer to a heated serving platter.

Serve at once.

Yields 6 individual pies

Notes: *1/2 teaspoonful of curry powder can be added, if desired.

**The scraps of puff pastry left over from cutting the circles can be gathered, wrapped in plastic wrap, and refrozen for future use.

Although this makes six large pasties, if preferred, smaller pies may be more to your liking. Proceed just as described above except make four pastry circles per half sheet and spoon *one-twelfth* of the filling into each.

This recipe can be increased or decreased, as required.

1/6 SERVING – PROTEIN = 9.7 g.; FAT = 23.0 g.; CARBOHYDRATE = 32.5 g.;
CALORIES = 377; CALORIES FROM FAT = 55%

Oceania–New Zealand

HUNZA PIE – NEW ZEALAND POTATO AND SPINACH PIE
TPT - 1 hour and 26 minutes

The early British settlers of New Zealand, known as Pākehā, found that the foods with which they were familiar just did not exist or could not be grown in their new homeland, not unlike the plight of the first settlers from Polynesia. The foods and the methods of preparation of the Maori were too foreign. Many of the new crops introduced such as corn and wheat were from American seed brought by traders, the metal boxes used by the American colonists called "colonial ovens" were manufactured in America and exported to New Zealand; and eventually New Zealanders looked to the colonial American cuisine for recipe inspiration. Americans after all had learned to adapt that which they knew to that which they found with the help of the indigenous population. Newspapers of late 1870s reprinted recipes from American magazines to help homemakers and in those we find much reference to dishes made with corn meal such as corn puddings and corn bread and recipes for pumpkins, squash, and melons, easily grown in their climate but unfamiliar. British traditional cooking, however, was favored and continues. Meat pies, such as shepherd's pie, and puddings are still very much a part of the New Zealand cuisine. The following savory pie is based on a New Zealand specialty known as Hunza pie.

2 tablespoons butter
1 large leek—*white and light green portions only*— trimmed, well-rinsed, and sliced

3 quarts *boiling* **water**
1 large potato—peeled and chopped

2 cups baby spinach leaves, tightly packed —trimmed, well-washed, and slivered
1 large egg
Freshly ground black pepper, to taste
1 1/2 ounces *extra-sharp* **Cheddar cheese**—*shredded*

1/2 WHOLE WHEAT CRUST recipe *[see recipe which follows]*

1 tablespoon grated *pecorino Romano* **cheese** *or* **Parmesan cheese, if preferred**

Preheat oven to 350 degrees F.

In a skillet set over *MEDIUM* heat, melt butter. Sauté sliced leeks until soft and translucent, *being careful not allow leeks to brown*. Set aside until required.

In a large saucepan set over *MEDIUM* heat, boil chopped potato in *boiling* water. Cook, until potato is soft. Drain thoroughly.

Using a RICER, rice potato into a mixing bowl.

Add sautéed leeks, slivered spinach, egg, butter, black pepper, and shredded Cheddar cheese. Mix well. Pour into prepared pie shell and spread the filling evenly to the edge of the pie shell. Bake in preheated 350 degree F. oven for about 30 minutes.

Sprinkle grated cheese evenly over the pie. Return to the oven and bake for an additional 10-15 minutes, or until firm and lightly browned. Allow to stand for 10 minutes before serving.

To serve, cut pie into wedges.

Yields 6 servings
adequate for 4 people

Note: This recipe can be doubled and baked in a 10-inch pie shell.

1/6 SERVING – PROTEIN = 7.3 g.; FAT = 12.8 g.; CARBOHYDRATE = 24.1 g.;
CALORIES = 239; CALORIES FROM FAT = 48%

WHOLE WHEAT PIE CRUSTS
TPT - about 1 hour and 9 minutes;
30 minutes = gluten relaxation period;
15 minutes = second gluten relaxation period

Although we feel solid vegetable shortenings should be avoided, the quality of pie crusts made with oils is poor, in our opinion. There are always compromises in this life and platitudes to support them. This recipe produces two pie crusts. In this case only one is required. The second pie crust can be wrapped, unbaked, in plastic wrap and frozen for a future pie.

1 cup whole wheat flour
3/4 cup unbleached white flour
1/4 cup soy flour
2 tablespoons *toasted* **wheat germ**

1/4 cup *cold* **butter**
1/4 cup solid *trans-fat-free* **vegetable shortening**

6-8 tablespoons *ice cold* **water**

WHOLE WHEAT PIE CRUSTS (cont'd)

Sift flours into a large mixing bowl. Stir in wheat germ.

Using a pastry blender, work *cold* butter and shortening into flour mixture until of the texture of coarse corn meal.

While stirring with a fork, sprinkle with *ice cold* water, 1 or 2 tablespoonfuls at a time, until mixture holds together and pulls away from the sides of the bowl. Gather into two balls, wrap tightly in plastic wrap, and refrigerate for about 30 minutes to allow the gluten to relax.

Preheat oven to 425 degrees F. Prepare two 9-inch pie plates by generously buttering or by spraying with non-stick lecithin spray coating.

On a lightly floured surface, roll each ball of pastry in turn to form a circle about 10-11 inches in diameter. Fold in quarters (bottom to top; then right to left), lay in upper left quadrant of prepared 9-inch pie plate, and unfold. Trim around edge leaving about 1/2 inch beyond rim. Turn excess under and crimp—pressing down slightly as you go to give a rather firm attachment and thus reduce shrinkage somewhat. If time permits, freeze prepared crust for about 15 minutes. This too helps reduce shrinkage.

If pie crust is to be filled without prebaking, as in this recipe, simply fill the pie crust and bake according to recipe directions.

If a baked pie crust is required, cut two 12-inch squares of aluminum foil and fit lightly into crusts. Cover bottom surfaces with dried beans, peas, or raw rice (reserved for this purpose), or aluminum pastry weights, if preferred.

Bake in preheated 425 degree F. oven for 10 minutes. Remove aluminum foil and weights. Return crusts to oven for an additional 5 minutes. Remove from oven and set on wire racks to cool.

Fill as desired, following individual recipes from this point or wrap in aluminum foil, seal tightly, and freeze until required.

Yields two 9-inch pie crusts

Notes: This recipe may be halved, if desired, but we always make two crusts and freeze one as a convenience for a future menu. Freeze either baked or unbaked in accord with anticipated needs.

For variety, 1/2 cupful shredded cheese or 2 tablespoonfuls *toasted* sesame seeds may be rolled into each pastry ball.

1/2 recipe (i. e., one pie crust) –
PROTEIN = 19.5 g.; FAT = 50.0 g.; CARBOHYDRATE = 86.5 g.;
CALORIES = 863; CALORIES FROM FAT = 52%

PEANUT – APPLE CRUMBLE
TPT - about 1 hour and 5 minutes

The beloved apple crumble of which Brits are so fond is very much a favorite of New Zealanders who, as do their ancestors, make the crumble with rolled oats. I could share that version with you but I have chosen to include here an apple crumble that never ceases to please. This dessert recipe, originally a longtime family favorite from my mom's collection, is a recipe I copied and took with me when I moved to Michigan to take a research job in 1961. It still ranks among my most favorite desserts and I have yet to find anyone, to whom I have served it, that did not want seconds and a copy of the recipe.

6 medium, tart cooking apples—Cortland or Granny Smith apples are our choices

1/3 cup sugar
1/4 cup unbleached white flour
1/4 cup whole wheat flour
3 tablespoons freshly ground, *unsalted, additive-free smooth* peanut butter
3 tablespoons *cold* butter

Light cream *or* half and half

Preheat oven to 350 degrees F. Prepare a 9-inch square baking dish or pan or a 9-inch deep dish pie plate by coating with non-stick lecithin spray coating.

Wash, peel, core, and slice apples. Arrange evenly in prepared dish.

In a large mixing bowl, combine sugar and flours. Using a pastry blender, work peanut butter and *cold* butter into sugar–flour mixture until of the texture of coarse corn meal. Sprinkle resultant mixture evenly over sliced apples.

Bake in preheated 350 degree F. oven for about 50 minutes, or until apples are soft and *top is browned and slightly crunchy.*

PEANUT – APPLE CRUMBLE (cont'd)

Serve at room temperature or refrigerate and serve chilled, as preferred. Pass cream.

Notes: This freezes beautifully and may easily be doubled, when required.

Both vanilla and coffee ice cream compliment this dessert well.

Yields 6 servings
adequate for 4-6 people

1/6 SERVING (without cream) –
PROTEIN = 3.3 g.; FAT = 7.6 g.; CARBOHYDRATE = 53.3 g.;
CALORIES = 217; CALORIES FROM FAT = 32%

STEWED RHUBARB WITH TAPIOCA

TPT - 1 hour and 41 minutes;
30 minutes = tapioca softening period;
1 hour = chilling period

My grandmother's generation called rhubarb "pie plant" and, admittedly, they made lots of pies. Once you have established a crown or two of rhubarb in a northern hemisphere herb bed, you will find that it can be the gift that gives from May to September. The edible stalks can be used in savory stews, cut up in salads, preserved in jams and sauces, and frozen for mid-winter use. Mennonite cooks in our area of Pennsylvania make it into a sweet and sour relish and serve it as vegetable. However, rhubarb, the vegetable that "would be a fruit," is most often sweetened and used in desserts, alone or paired with other fruits. European settlers in Australia and in New Zealand introduced rhubarb and desserts like this are enjoyed there just as they are here in Pennsylvania, also settled by emigrants from Great Britain.

1 cup water
2 tablespoons quick-cooking tapioca

2 pounds young rhubarb—cut into 3/4-inch pieces
   to yield about 4 cupfuls
2/3 cup sugar
Thin lemon slice

Pour water into a large kettle, with cover. Sprinkle tapioca over water and allow to stand for 30 minutes to allow tapioca to soften.

Add chopped rhubarb, sugar, and lemon slice. Stir to combine ingredients. Bring to the boil over *MEDIUM* heat. Reduce heat to *LOW-MEDIUM* and simmer, *tightly covered*, for about 8 minutes, or until *tender*, but *not mushy*. Stir occasionally. Remove from heat. Remove and discard lemon slice.

Refrigerate until completely cooled, at least 1 hour.

Turn into serving dish or into individual sherbet glasses. Serve plain or with light cream or LEMON CURD *[see index]*, if desired.

Notes: Rhubarb freezes so easily that we secret a store throughout the spring and early summer. Simply remove and discard leaves, which incidentally are poisonous, and any tough strands or "strings." Wash and dry stems thoroughly. Chop into 3/4-inch pieces. Bag in freezer bags, label, and freeze.

For variety, 1 cupful sliced strawberries may be added with the rhubarb. Add an extra 1/4 cupful water if strawberries are to be added. Rhubarb and strawberries are ready for spring harvest at approximately the same time. This encourages this old-fashioned combination that is very pleasant to the palate. It is still popular throughout the Mid-Atlantic and Midwestern states of our diverse nation.

This recipe is easily increased or decreased proportionately, when required.

Yields about 3 cupfuls
adequate for 4 people

1/6 SERVING (i. e., 1/2 cupful) –
PROTEIN = 0.4 g.; FAT = 0.07 g.; CARBOHYDRATE = 32.0 g.;
CALORIES = 128; CALORIES FROM FAT = >1%

Pacific Islands

Papaya Punch (Hawaii)
Ono-Ono

Carambola **and Mango Appetizer with** ***Limoncello***
Faiakorn na Manggo Salatt

Ray's ***Limoncello*** **in the Style of Calabria**
Limoncello

~

Papaya Salad with Curried Island Dressing (Vanuatu)
Hearts of Palm, ***Jicama,*** **and Papaya Salad with Lime** ***Vinaigrette*** (Polynesia)
Curried Yam and Banana Salad with Hard-Cooked Egg Slices (Saipan)

~

Puréed ***Dhal*** **Soup** (Fiji)
with
Banana Biscuits (Fiji)

~

Cantaloupe Soup (Polynesia)

Cream of Hearts of Palm Soup (Papua New Guinea, Cook Islands, Hawaii)

~~~~~~~~~~~~~~~~~~~~

Vegetarian Reubens (Cook Islands)

Mashed Pumpkin with Coconut Garnish (French Polynesia)

~~~~~~~~~~

Caramelized Sweetpotatoes with Mandarin Oranges (Hawaii)

Pan-Grilled Pineapple Slices with Fresh Coriander

~~~~~~~~~~

Fried Rice with Pineapple (Cook Islands)   **Baked Beans with Pineapple** (Hawaii)

with

Pan-Grilled Bananas (Tahiti)

Roasted Eggplant (Fiji)

~~~~~~~~~~

Baked ***Tofu*** **with Citrus – Shallot Sauce** (Polynesia)

Carrots with Pineapple (Samoa)   or   Grilled Leeks, *Bok Choy*, and Red Onions
with Soy Sauce

Noodles with Onions (Solomon Islands)

~~~~~~~~~~~~~~~~~~~~~

Banana – Lime Whip (Cook Islands)
Banana with Uncooked Coconut Cream (Papua New Guinea)
Sweetpotato Pudding (Palau)
Koele Palau

Oceania–**Pacific Islands**

HAWAIIAN PAPAYA PUNCH
Ono-Ono
TPT - 15 minutes

An animated character gallops across your television screen and asks you if you want a Hawaiian punch. Well, that is one kind of Hawaiian punch, I guess. The commercial product advertised by this character is also called Hawaiian punch but it bears little resemblance to this fruit punch that is not only enjoyed in Hawaii but also throughout the Pacific. Starting a Pacific Island-inspired meal with a fruit drink can really set the mood. This is my favorite fruit juice combination but it can be adjusted to your taste.

**9 ounces pineapple–guava nectar
9 ounces pineapple–passion fruit nectar
1 cup freshly squeezed orange juice
1/4 cup freshly squeezed lime juice**

**3 cups (1 medium) chopped, ripe papaya
2 1/2 tablespoons crushed pineapple—fresh *or*
 canned in juice
1/4 cup sugar**

In a pitcher, combine pineapple–guava nectar, pineapple–passion fruit nectar, orange juice, and lime juice.

In the container of the electric blender, combine chopped papaya, crushed pineapple, and sugar. Add a couple of cups of the combined juices. Blend until smooth and frothy. Turn into a clean pitcher or decanter. Blend the remaining juice for several minutes and add to the papaya mixture. Stir. Refrigerate until ready to serve.

Serve chilled in a champagne flute or serve in a brandy snifter or old-fashioned glass over cracked ice.

Yields about 5 1/2 cupfuls

1/6 SERVING – PROTEIN = 0.3 g.; FAT = 0.08 g.; CARBOHYDRATE = 20.0 g.;
CALORIES = 62; CALORIES FROM FAT = 1%

CARAMBOLA AND MANGO APPETIZER WITH *LIMONCELLO*
Faiakorn na Manggo Salatt
TPT - 25 minutes

A friend shared this recipe with me but seeking out a starfuit and a perfectly ripened mango may sound like child's play to someone in the South Pacific or someone in California or New York. Just try to find a carambola and a ripe mango in central Pennsylvania. Rock-hard, underripe mangoes arrive at our markets and you are very much on your own to ripen the fruit before it spoils. Most produce managers in our area just dismiss a request for a carambola or starfruit, stating that there is no demand for them or they are too expensive to carry. However, once in a while the "stars do align" and both fruits appear in a store. This is an interesting and very delicious first course compote from Papua New Guinea; a far cry from the canned fruit cocktail served in the 1940s and '50s.

The carambola may have been introduced from Indonesia where it was grown long before it appeared in New Guinea. We use limoncello in this compote because we make our own and its smoothness is very complimentary. Cointreau can be substituted; it came to Southeast Asia with the French. Gin can also be substituted; it arrived there with the British. Schnapps is another liqueur that is found in the South Pacific which adds dimension to this compote; it was introduced by the Germans.

CARAMBOLA AND MANGO APPETIZER WITH *LIMONCELLO* (cont'd)

1/4 cup sugar
1/4 cup freshly squeezed orange juice
1/4 cup water

2 tablespoons freshly squeezed lime juice

1 tablespoon RAY'S *LIMONCELLO* IN THE STYLE OF CALABRIA (*Limocello*) *[see recipe which follows]* or *cointreau*, if preferred

2 large mangoes—peeled and sliced into long slices against the pit
2 small or 1 large *carambola* (starfruit)—peeled and sliced into star-shaped slices

In a saucepan set over *MEDIUM* heat, combine sugar, orange juice, water, and lime juice. Bring to the boil and allow to cook until a thin syrup forms. Remove from heat.

Add *limoncello* or *cointreau*, as preferred. Allow to cool to room temperature.

In a serving bowl, combine mango and *carambola* slices. Pour cooled syrup over. Toss gently. Refrigerate until required.

Serve into sherbet glasses or small dessert dishes.

Yields 6 servings
adequate for 4 people

Notes: This also makes an interesting dessert.

When required, this recipe can be doubled.

1/6 SERVING – PROTEIN = 0.9 g.; FAT = 0.4 g.; CARBOHYDRATE = 28.5 g.;
CALORIES = 114; CALORIES FROM FAT = 3%

RAY'S *LIMONCELLO* IN THE STYLE OF CALABRIA
Limoncello

TPT - 80 days, 1 hour, and 24 minutes;
40 days = first flavor development period;
30 minutes = syrup cooling period;
40 days = second flavor development period

This is the smoothest, most beautiful liqueur in the civilized world. Use only the best Russian or Finnish vodka. It makes a difference, so please do not take a chance with a cheap vodka.

15 thick-skinned *organic* lemons

1 bottle (750 milliliters) (3 1/4 cups) 80-proof
   Russian *or* Finnish vodka

3 1/2 cups sugar
5 cups water

1 bottle (750 milliliters) (3 1/4 cups) 80-proof
   Russian *or* Finnish vodka

Using a sharp vegetable peeler, peel the zest from each lemon. Then, using a sharp paring knife, cut all of the bitter, white pith off the zest peelings. Turn into a large jar, with cover, that will hold about 12-13 cupfuls.

Add one bottle of vodka, cover, and store in a dark, cool cabinet at room temperature for 40 days.

In a saucepan set over *MEDIUM-HIGH* heat, combine sugar and water. Allow sugar mixture to come to the boil while stirring constantly. Allow to boil for 2 minutes. *Immediately remove from heat* and allow to cool to room temperature—about 30 minutes.

Add cooled sugar syrup and remaining bottle of vodka to the lemon vodka in the jar. Stir with a long-handled spoon. Cover and return to the dark, cool cabinet for another 40 days.

Strain lemon zest from *limoncello* through a sieve set over a large mixing bowl.

Sterilize decorative cordial bottles and corks.

Strain cordial through culinary cheesecloth into sterilized bottles. Seal each bottle with a sterilized cork.

Store in the refrigerator or freezer, if preferred.

Serve into cordial glasses. *This cordial should be icy cold when served.*

Yields about 6 1/4 cupfuls

Oceania–Pacific Islands

RAY'S *LIMONCELLO* IN THE STYLE OF CALABRIA (cont'd)

1/33 SERVING (i. e., 3 tablespoonfuls) –
PROTEIN = 0.0 g.; FAT = 0.0 g.; CARBOHYDRATE = 30.1 g.;
CALORIES = 138; CALORIES FROM FAT = 0%;
CALORIES FROM ALCOHOL = 32%

PAPAYA SALAD WITH CURRIED ISLAND DRESSING
TPT - 10 minutes

This is a most enjoyable version of a salad popular in the Republic of Vanuatu, an archipelago consisting of a total of about eighty-two volcanic islands. Part of a larger group of islands known as the New Hebrides, administered by France and Great Britain, Vanuatu became independent in 1980.

CURRIED ISLAND DRESSING:
1 tablespoon *finely* chopped onion
1 garlic clove—smashed and *very finely* chopped
1 1/2 tablespoons crushed pineapple
 —fresh *or* canned in juice
1/2 firm, medium banana—*finely* chopped
1 1/2 teaspoons SRI LANKAN CURRY POWDER *[see index] or* curry powder mixture of choice
2 teaspoons mango chutney
2 tablespoons *thick* coconut milk
2 tablespoons *calorie-reduced or light* mayonnaise

Salt, to taste
Freshly ground black pepper
Water, to thin, if necessary

2 small ripe papaya *or* 1/2 medium Maradol papaya—peeled, seeded, and sliced
1/4 cup diced celery
2 scallions—trimmed, well-rinsed, and *thinly* sliced

In a mixing bowl, combine *finely* chopped onion, *very finely* chopped garlic, crushed pineapple, *finely* chopped banana, curry powder, mango chutney, coconut milk, and mayonnaise. Using a wire whisk, combine thoroughly.

Season with salt and pepper. Thin with water, if necessary. Turn into a serving bowl.

Arrange papaya slices on a small platter. Scatter diced celery and *thinly* sliced scallion over. Toss.

Serve at once with the prepared curried dressing.

Yields 6 servings
adequate for 4 people

Note: This recipe can be doubled, when required.

1/6 SERVING – PROTEIN = 1.1 g.; FAT = 2.0 g.; CARBOHYDRATE = 18.5 g.;
CALORIES = 76; CALORIES FROM FAT = 23%

HEARTS OF PALM, *JICAMA*, AND PAPAYA SALAD WITH LIME *VINAIGRETTE*
TPT -   1 hour and 17 minutes;
   1 hour = refrigeration period

I think you may find this to be one of the more perfect food combinations that you have encountered. The flavor and textural juxtapositions dance on the taste buds but compliment the rest of the menu without taking center stage.

1 can (14 ounces) hearts of palm—soaked in cold water, well-drained, and sliced
1/2 cup chopped Italian red onion
1 cup thin *jicama* strips about 1-inch long
1 1/2 cups cubed, ripe papaya

LIME *VINAIGRETTE* WITH CUMIN:
2 tablespoons safflower *or* sunflower oil
2 tablespoons freshly squeezed lime juice
1/8 teaspoon ground cumin
1/8 teaspoon salt, or to taste

HEARTS OF PALM, *JICAMA*, AND PAPAYA SALAD WITH LIME *VINAIGRETTE* (cont'd)

In a serving bowl, combine hearts of palm slices, chopped onion, *jicama* strips, and cubed papaya.

In a cruet or small jar, combine oil, lime juice, ground cumin, and salt. Shake vigorously. Pour over vegetables and fruit. Toss *gently*. Refrigerate for 1 hour to allow for flavor development.

Serve chilled.

Yields 6 servings
adequate for 4 people

Note: This recipe can be halved or doubled, when required.

1/6 SERVING – PROTEIN = 3.0 g.; FAT = 5.3 g.; CARBOHYDRATE = 33.5 g.;
CALORIES = 187; CALORIES FROM FAT = 25%

CURRIED YAM AND BANANA SALAD WITH HARD-COOKED EGG SLICES

TPT - 1 hour and 12 minutes;
30 minutes = sweetpotato chilling period

Northward from Guam stretches a string of islands know as the Marianas. Saipan lies in this chain and students of the Pacific campaigns of World War II will remember the Battle of Saipan when a combined force of United States Marine and Army troops invaded the island. The island, claimed and held by the Japanese during World War II, was taken resulting in the deaths of almost all the 30,000 Japanese defenders. The Navy Seabees, including one of my favorite college professors, moved onto the island to construct airfields and to establish a behind-the-lines hydroponic gardening system that provided fresh produce to U. S. troops. Today Saipan hosts tourists who probably know little of the origin of the rusting ordinance and military vehicles, both Japanese and American.

2 small or 1 large sweetpotato—peeled and cubed
4 quarts *boiling* **water**

CURRIED MAYONNAISE DRESSING:
    1/3 cup *calorie-reduced or light* **mayonnaise**
    2 tablespoons *finely* **chopped onion**
    1 1/2 teaspoons SRI LANKAN CURRY POWDER [see index] **or curry powder mixture of choice**
    1/2 teaspoon *very finely* **chopped fresh gingerroot**

1 large banana—peeled and sliced

1 *chilled* **hard-cooked egg—sliced**

In a kettle set over *MEDIUM* heat, combine cubed sweetpotatoes and *boiling* water. Cook for about 25 minutes or until *crisp-tender*. Drain thoroughly. Turn into a mixing bowl and refrigerate for at least 30 minutes.

While sweetpotatoes are chilling, prepare dressing. In a small bowl, combine mayonnaise, *finely* chopped onion, curry powder, and *very finely* chopped gingerroot. Stir. Set aside until required.

When ready to serve, add banana slices to chilled sweetpotato pieces. Add prepared dressing. *Gently* fold the dressing into the sweetpotato–banana mixture. Pile in the middle of a serving plate.

Garnish with egg slices.

Serve chilled.

Yields 6 servings
adequate for 4 people

Note: This recipe can be halved, when required.

1/6 SERVING – PROTEIN = 2.4 g.; FAT = 5.6 g.; CARBOHYDRATE = 17.6 g.;
CALORIES = 126; CALORIES FROM FAT = 40%

Oceania–Pacific Islands

FIJIAN PURÉED *DHAL* SOUP
TPT - 2 hours and 30 minutes;
1 hour = lentil and seed soaking period;
15 minutes = cooling period

Fijian cuisine is more complex than are those of most of the Pacific islands reflecting the interesting multicultural society and the demands of the tourists who are drawn to this republic which has been inhabited since the second century BC. Classic Polynesian and Melanesian dishes sit side by side with Indian, Chinese, and dishes introduced from the West. Indi-Fijian adaptations have been particularly transformative. Spicing, characteristic of Indian cuisine, has enlivened many "old" dishes and the use of lentils and pulses in cooking and the cultivation of these protein-rich legumes have expanded Fijian nutrition.

3/4 cup dry brown (*or* green) lentils

2 cups water
1/2 teaspoon fenugreek seeds
1/2 teaspoon yellow mustard seeds

1 tablespoon GARLIC OIL *[see index]*
1 tablespoon safflower *or* sunflower oil
2 large garlic cloves—chopped
1 cup chopped onion

5 cups VEGETABLE STOCK FROM SOUP
   [see index] or **other vegetarian stock of choice**

2 large carrots—scraped or pared and chopped
1/2 cup chopped celery
2 tablespoons *tamari* soy sauce
1 teaspoon SRI LANKAN CURRY POWDER
   [see index] or **curry powder mixture of choice**
1/2 teaspoon ground turmeric
1/4 teaspoon crushed red pepper flakes, or more to taste

Pick over lentils and discard any of poor quality. Rinse thoroughly. Put lentils into a mixing bowl.

Add fenugreek and mustard seeds. Allow to soak for 1 hour. Drain thoroughly.

In a large non-aluminum* kettle set over *MEDIUM* heat, heat garlic oil and safflower oil. Add chopped garlic and onion. Sauté until onion begins to soften, *being careful not to allow either vegetable to brown.*

Add drained lentils and seeds and vegetable stock. Allow to come to the boil. *Reduce heat to LOW-MEDIUM* and allow lentils to simmer for about 30 minutes.

Add chopped carrots and celery, soy sauce, curry powder, ground turmeric, and crushed red pepper flakes. Continue cooking for about 20 minutes or until carrots are softened. Remove from heat to cool for about 15 minutes.

Using the electric blender or food processor fitted with steel knife, purée the soup in batches. Turn into a clean kettle set over *LOW* heat. Allow to heat through. Turn into heated soup tureen.

Serve into heated soup bowls.

Yields about 7 cupfuls

Notes: *Since aluminum discolors lentils rather unpleasantly, avoid use of aluminum cookware or serving bowls in this case.

When required, this recipe can be halved or doubled.

This soup freezes well.

1/7 SERVING (i. e., per cupful) –
PROTEIN = 6.6 g.; FAT = 3.8 g.; CARBOHYDRATE = 6.1 g.;
CALORIES = 140; CALORIES FROM FAT = 24%

FIJIAN BANANA BISCUITS
TPT - 37 minutes

We did not have biscuits for dinner when I was a child. Biscuits were for shortbread desserts; bread was for family dinner; and rolls, such as Parker House rolls and croissants, were for formal dinners. I was young when we first visited the American South and I was amazed to find a basket of biscuits on the breakfast table in the restaurants we visited. If you were raised in the American South, these biscuits will be a whole new adventure.

FIJIAN BANANA BISCUITS (cont'd)

2 cups unbleached white flour
2 teaspoons baking powder

1 medium, ripe banana—peeled and chopped

1/2 cup *two-percent* **milk**
1 1/2 tablespoons safflower *or* **sunflower oil**

Butter or honey

Preheat oven to 385 degrees F. Line a cookie sheet with culinary parchment paper.

In a small bowl combine flour and baking powder. Stir to distribute the baking powder evenly. Set aside briefly.

In a large bowl, mash banana with a potato masher until of uniform consistency.

Add milk and oil. Mix well.

Gradually stir the flour mixture into the banana mixture until a workable, non-sticky dough results. *Add more flour as needed.* Turn out on a floured surface. Roll out to a thickness of about 1/2 inch. Using a 2-inch biscuit cutter, cut circles and transfer the biscuits to the prepared baking sheet. Bake in preheated 385 degree F. oven until lightly browned—about 20 minutes. Turn out into a bread basket.

Serve hot with butter or honey.

Yields 12 biscuits
adequate for 4 people

Note: This recipe can be doubled, when required.

1/6 SERVING (exclusive of butter) –
PROTEIN = 2.5 g.; FAT = 2.1 g.; CARBOHYDRATE = 17.0 g.;
CALORIES = 96; CALORIES FROM FAT = 19%

POLYNESIAN CANTALOUPE SOUP
TPT - 4 minutes

I guess I am an old-fashioned vegetable soup person; the fruit soups of Central Europe have never been my thing, as they say. When soup was proposed for dinner in my family, potatoes, carrots, onions or leeks, tomatoes, herbs, and stock were gathered; no one even thought about orange juice and cantaloupe. In fact, when we chose a vegetarian lifestyle, one of the first recipes I evolved was a good vegetarian stock. Live long enough and learn . . . This Polynesian soup is remarkably refreshing and it, as do all soups, stimulates the appetite.

2 cups freshly squeezed orange juice
1/4 cup freshly squeezed lime juice
1/4 teaspoon ground cinnamon
1/8 teaspoon ground ginger

4 cups diced cantaloupe

6 tablespoons PLAIN YOGURT *[see index]*
   or **commercially-available plain yogurt, for garnish**

In a soup tureen, combine orange and lime juices with ground cinnamon and ginger. Stir to mix.

Add diced cantaloupe. Refrigerate until ready to serve.

Serve well-chilled with a dollop of yogurt.

Yields about 6 cupfuls

Note: This recipe can be halved or doubled, when required.

1/6 SERVING (i. e., per cupful) –
PROTEIN = 2.1 g.; FAT = 0.7 g.; CARBOHYDRATE = 19.1 g.;
CALORIES = 89; CALORIES FROM FAT = 7%

Oceania–*Pacific Islands*

CREAM OF HEARTS OF PALM SOUP
TPT - 36 minutes

Hearts of palm, the heart of the palmetto coconut palm, have a lush, soft texture that takes beautifully to a partnership with cream. Why just slice a few hearts of palm over greens in a salad when you can enjoy a soup like this? Well, you could save out a few slices of the palm hearts to put in a salad to accompany this soup. Fresh hearts of palm are readily available in greengrocers throughout the Pacific so it is no surprise that this absolutely delicious soup can often be found on menus in Papau New Guinea, the Cook Islands, and in Hawaii. Unfortunately we have to settle for canned hearts of palm. If you ever get a chance to taste a fresh heart, your taste buds will just melt away with the sensation.

1 can (14 ounces) hearts of palm—soaked in cold water and then well-drained
3/4 cup *two-percent* milk

3 tablespoons butter
1/4 cup unbleached white flour
2 cups vegetarian stock, of choice

1 cup light cream *or* half and half
1/4 teaspoon freshly ground white pepper, or to taste

Place well-drained hearts of palm in the work bowl of the food processor, fitted with steel knife. Process, scraping down sides of work bowl as needed. Add milk. Process until a smooth purée results. Set aside briefly.

In a small kettle set over *LOW* heat, melt butter. Remove from heat and, using a wire whisk, make a *roux* by beating in flour. Return to heat and, stirring constantly, cook for 2 minutes, *being careful not to burn or overbrown the roux.* Remove from heat and gradually beat in vegetable stock.

Increase heat to MEDIUM. Return saucepan to heat and cook, stirring constantly, until thickened.

Add puréed hearts of palm and cook, stirring frequently, until heated through.

While stirring with a wire whisk, gradually beat in cream and white pepper. Cook, stirring constantly, for about 4 minutes. Turn into a heated soup tureen.

Serve at once into heated soup bowls.

Yields about 6 cupfuls

Note: This recipe can be halved or doubled, when required.

1/6 SERVING (i. e., per cupful) –
PROTEIN = 4.7 g.; FAT = 10.5 g.; CARBOHYDRATE = 9.9 g.;
CALORIES = 141; CALORIES FROM FAT = 67%

VEGETARIAN REUBENS
TPT - 22 minutes

Reubens can always be found on menus in New York City and on Long Island, despite the astronomical level of their saturated fat content. They are also amazingly popular in the Cook Islands where islanders prefer to use Swiss cheese and Thousand Island dressing, and where they even make breakfast versions on English muffins. For some unexplainable reason, we missed a good reuben when we became vegetarians although we had rarely indulged and had avoided altogether such things as corned beef or pastrami long, long before our vegetarian commitment. This open-faced version was created to capture some of the fun taste of the sandwich which was so very popular when we were young.

1 pound canned, *preservative-free* sweet and sour red cabbage—*thoroughly rinsed* and *well-drained*— or *well-rinsed* and *well-drained* sauerkraut*

2 tablespoons *calorie-reduced or light* mayonnaise
2 teaspoons HOMEMADE TOMATO KETCHUP
  [see index] *or* commercially-available *chili* sauce
1 small dill pickle—*finely* chopped

6 slices rye bread, of choice
3 ounces Swiss *Emmentaler*, Monterey Jack, *or* dilled *Havarti* cheese—*thinly* sliced and divided into six 1/2-ounce portions

6 sprigs of fresh dillweed, for garnish

VEGETARIAN REUBENS (cont'd)

Adjust oven rack to a position 4 inches from broiler element. Preheat broiler to 375 degrees F.

In a saucepan set over *LOW* heat, heat sweet and sour red cabbage or sauerkraut until warmed through.

Meanwhile, in a small bowl, prepare a dill Russian dressing by thoroughly combining mayonnaise, ketchup or chili sauce, and *finely* chopped dill pickle.

Lightly toast rye bread. Spread each slice with prepared dill Russian dressing. Place on a baking sheet. Divide *warmed* cabbage into 6 portions and pile on prepared toast slices. Top each open-faced sandwich with a 1/2-ounce portion of sliced cheese, *keeping cheese carefully away from edge.*

Place under preheated broiler and broil until cheese melts and bubbles.

Serve at once, garnished with sprigs of dillweed.

Yields 6 servings
adequate for 4-6 people

Notes: *Sulfite-free sauerkraut is packaged by several food processing firms and is available in natural food stores and in many grocery stores. If preferred, one pound of fresh or canned, *preservative-free* sauerkraut can be substituted.

This recipe may be halved or doubled, when required.

1/6 SERVING (made with sweet and sour red cabbage) –
PROTEIN = 6.7 g.; FAT = 6.7 g.; CARBOHYDRATE = 32.3 g.;
CALORIES = 209; CALORIES FROM FAT = 29%

1/6 SERVING (made with sauerkraut) –
PROTEIN = 6.5 g.; FAT = 6.9 g.; CARBOHYDRATE = 19.2 g.;
CALORIES = 156; CALORIES FROM FAT = 40%

CARAMELIZED SWEETPOTATOES WITH MANDARIN ORANGES

TPT - 2 hours and 9 minutes;
1 hour = sweetpotato cooling period

Caramelized sweetpotatoes, often topped with marshmallows, was one of those dishes that you came to expect at Thanksgiving gatherings of my family; somebody always brought candied sweetpotatoes, as they called them. The dish is said to have been introduced by the manufacturer of Cracker Jacks in a recipe campaign to increase flagging sales of marshmallows. They were gooey and sweet, and once you grew up, you said, "Never again . . ." However, when we were in Hawaii, I saw caramelized sweetpotatoes offered as one of the vegetable dishes at a luau. Upon analysis, I decided that taking a northeastern harvest dish to a luau was not all that strange; food influences do migrate . . .

3 medium sweetpotatoes—well-scrubbed
4 quarts *boiling* water

1/2 cup butter
1/2 cup *light* brown sugar
1/2 cup water

1 cup well-drained, canned mandarin orange sections
2 tablespoons shredded coconut—fresh *or* desiccated

In a large kettle set over *MEDIUM* heat, combine sweetpotatoes and *boiling* water. Allow sweetpotatoes to boil for about 30 minutes, or until *tender, but firm.* Refrigerate for at least 1 hour.

Peel and slice sweetpotatoes into thick slices. Set aside until required.

In a large skillet set over *LOW-MEDIUM* heat, melt butter. Add brown sugar and water. Stir to combine. Cook, stirring frequently, for 3-4 minutes.

Using a spatula, gently slide sweetpotato slices into the skillet, being carefully not to allow the slices to break. Simmer for about 20 minutes. Spoon the syrup over the potatoes during the cooking period. Transfer to a heated serving platter or shallow serving bowl.

Scatter mandarin orange sections over. Sprinkle shredded coconut over. Keep warm on a warming tray until ready to serve.

Yields 6 servings
adequate for 4 people

Note: This recipe can be halved or doubled, when required.

1/6 SERVING – PROTEIN = 1.4 g.; FAT = 16.0 g.; CARBOHYDRATE = 38.0 g.;
CALORIES = 322; CALORIES FROM FAT = 44%

Oceania–*Pacific Islands*

FRIED RICE WITH PINEAPPLE IN THE STYLE OF THE COOK ISLANDS
TPT - 9 minutes

Islanders are apt to add sausage or Spam to a fried rice preparation but this is a simplified version that accompanies a meal beautifully. It is not salty or oily as are "take–out" versions, available at Chinese restaurants, but its Chinese roots are apparent.

1 tablespoon safflower *or* **sunflower oil**
1/4 cup *thinly* **sliced scallion—***both white and green portions***—well-rinsed**
2 cups fragrant rice, jasmine rice, *or Makong* **rice**
2 teaspoons *tamari* **soy sauce**
1/8 teaspoon onion powder

1 cup pineapple tidbits—fresh *or* **canned in juice**

In a wok, set over *MEDIUM-HIGH* heat, heat oil. Add *thinly* sliced scallion and stir-fry for about 30 seconds. Add *cold* rice and stir-fry for about 3-4 minutes, or until heated through. Be sure to coat grains evenly with oil. Add soy sauce and onion powder. Mix well.

Add pineapple tidbits. Stir-fry for a minute or two more. Turn out into heated serving bowl.

*Serve at once.**

Notes: *This may be made slightly in advance of serving and reheated at serving time in a casserole at 325 degrees F. for about 15 minutes or briefly stir-fried again, if preferred. Also, this dish may be frozen for 4-6 weeks in advance of serving with considerable success and reheated as previously described.

When required, this recipe is easily doubled.

Yields four 1/2-cup servings
adequate for 2-4 people
depending upon remainder of menu

1/4 SERVING – PROTEIN = 2.4 g.; FAT = 3.6 g.; CARBOHYDRATE = 29.4 g.;
CALORIES = 161; CALORIES FROM FAT = 20%

HAWAIIAN BAKED BEANS WITH PINEAPPLE
TPT - 1 hour and 5 minutes

Heinz blue-labeled vegetarian baked beans, which are produced and canned in Australia, are distributed throughout the Pacific and shipped to the U. S. and Europe as well. They are low in fat, low in sodium, and lightly seasoned and sauced, allowing the experimental cook to jazz them up with anything that appeals; I often add peaches or apricots, and chunks of mozzarella cheese. In this version, you do not expect the pineapple but this taste is very good indeed.

1 can (blue-labeled) (13.7 ounces) Heinz vegetarian baked beans
1/4 cup chopped onion
2 tablespoons commercial *chili* **sauce**
2 tablespoon *light* **brown sugar**
3/4 cup well-drained pineapple chunks—fresh *or* **canned in juice**

Preheat oven to 325 degrees F. Prepare a bean pot or 1-quart oven-to-table casserole by coating with non-stick lecithin spray coating.

In the bean pot or casserole, combine beans, chopped onion, *chili* sauce, and brown sugar. Stir to combine well. Then, add pineapple chunks. Again, stir to combine.

Bake in preheated 325 degree F. oven for about 1 hour, or until hot and bubbling.

Yields 5 servings
adequate for 3 people

HAWAIIAN BAKED BEANS WITH PINEAPPLE (cont'd)

Note: This recipe is easily doubled or tripled, when required.

1/5 SERVING – PROTEIN = 3.9 g.; FAT = 0.1 g.; CARBOHYDRATE = 21.2 g.;
CALORIES = 103; CALORIES FROM FAT = <1%

FIJIAN ROASTED EGGPLANT
TPT - 1 hour and 5 minutes

If your family likes eggplant, I am sure you will enjoy adding another very tasty eggplant recipe to your repertoire. It reminds me somewhat of a dish popular in the American South where eggplant slices are baked in rich milk or light cream but in the Pacific where dairy products are at a premium, the coconut again comes to the rescue. For most recipes I try to find the lavender Asian eggplants because they are milder and the skin is less bitter. In this case, I look for the large purple eggplants because the skin holds up better when roasted and since it is peeled before finishing the dish, the bitterness of the skin is not an issue here.

2 medium, firm eggplants—well-washed

1/4 cup *light, sulfite-free* coconut milk
2 tablespoons *finely* chopped onion
2 tablespoons *finely* chopped canned, *diced* tomatoes
1 1/2 teaspoons *finely* chopped mild green *chilies*, or to taste
1 1/2 teaspoons freshly grated lemon juice
1/4 teaspoon salt
4-6 drops *jalapeño chili* sauce, or to taste

Preheat oven to 350 degrees F.

Pierce the eggplants and place them on a baking sheet. Bake in preheated 350 degree F. oven for about 50 minutes, or until soft. Turn occasionally during the baking period. When the eggplants are soft, transfer to a board. Remove skin. Turn flesh into a mixing bowl. Using a fork, shred the eggplant in thin, uniform strips.

Add coconut milk, *finely* chopped onion, tomatoes, and green *chilies*, lemon juice, salt, and *jalapeño* sauce. Gently fold the mixture together. If you want to serve this as a warm vegetable dish, turn into a saucepan set over *LOW* heat and allow to heat through. If you want to serve this as a cold vegetable dish, salad, or appetizer, refrigerate until ready to serve.

Serve warm, at room temperature, or chilled, as preferred.

Yields 8 servings
adequate for 6 people

Note: This recipe can be halved, when required.

1/6 SERVING – PROTEIN = 0.5 g.; FAT = 0.3 g.; CARBOHYDRATE = 2.0 g.;
CALORIES = 12; CALORIES FROM FAT = 22%

POLYNESIAN BAKED *TOFU* WITH CITRUS – SHALLOT SAUCE
TPT - 5 hours and 48 minutes;
4 hours = bean curd pressing period;
1 hour = bean curd marination period

There are always packages of tofu in our emergency boxes; its shelf life is long and it can be used in so many nutritious ways. Each year our boxes are refreshed and dated food items are replaced. This is one of my favorite ways to use up the firm tofu. The sauce used in this particular recipe was evolved from a sauce that included fish sauce, commonly used in the preparation of Southeast Asian sauces. This is an excellent sauce that makes something as bland as tofu taste exciting.

**POLYNESIA BAKED *TOFU*
WITH CITRUS – SHALLOT SAUCE** (cont'd)

2 packages (12.3 ounces each) *extra firm silken tofu*

POLYNESIAN CITRUS – SHALLOT SAUCE:
    1/4 cup *boiling* water
    1 tablespoon tamarind paste

    1 garlic clove—crushed and *very finely* chopped
    2 large shallots—crushed and *very finely* chopped
    1 tablespoon *tamari* soy sauce
    1 tablespoon freshly squeezed lemon juice
    1 tablespoon freshly squeezed lime juice
    1 teaspoon freshly grated lemon zest
    1 teaspoon freshly grated lime zest

    1/3 cup *light, sulfite-free* coconut milk*
    1/8 teaspoon *jalopeño chili* sauce, or more to taste—green or red, as preferred**
    1 tablespoon freshly ground, *unsalted, additive-free smooth* peanut butter
    1 tablespoon sesame *tahini* (sesame paste or sesame butter)***

Watercress sprigs, for garnish

Wrap soybean curd cakes in a cotton tea towel and place on the counter top. Place bread board or other flat weight on top and weight this with cans or with a tea pot filled with water to a weight of about 3 pounds. Allow to stand for about 4 hours or until most of moisture has been pressed out of the cakes and absorbed by the towel. (Change towel after 2 hours, if necessary.)

In a small bowl combine *boiling* water and tamarind paste. Stir until most of tamarind is dissolved. Set a fine strainer over a non-aluminum pan set over *MEDIUM* heat. Strain tamarind bits from liquid. Discard bits.

To tamarind liquid, add *very finely* chopped garlic and shallots with lemon and lime juices, and lemon and lime zests. Cook, stirring constantly, for 3-4 minutes.

Add coconut milk, *jalopeño chili* sauce, peanut butter, and *tahini*. Using a wire whisk, stir until smooth. Cook, stirring frequently, until the sauce thickens. Thin with water, if necessary. Turn into a large pie plate.

Cut each *tofu* cake diagonally into four large wedges. Place in a pie plate.

Pour prepared sauce over. Marinate for 1 hour, turning the *tofu* wedges every 15 minutes.*

Preheat oven to 350 degrees F.

Place pressed and marinated soy beancurd cake pieces on a baking sheet. Bake at 350 degrees F. for about 20 minutes.

Serve hot, garnished with watercress sprigs.

                     Yields 8 servings
                 adequate for 4-6 people

Notes: *Canned, *sulfite-free* coconut milk is available in well-stocked grocery stores in either the international section or beverage section. Leftover coconut milk can be frozen.

          **Although not generally used in Southeast Asian cooking, *jalopeño* sauce gives this sauce an authentic flavor and can be adjusted to Western taste preferences more easily than can fresh, hot peppers. The sauce is available in Hispanic groceries, food specialty stores, and in most grocery stores throughout the Southwest.

          ****Tahini* is readily available in natural food stores and in stores specializing in Middle Eastern products. It can also be made at home using a food processor.

Leftovers can be saved, if refrigerated. Use in two days.

This recipe can be halved or doubled, when required.

        1/8 SERVING – PROTEIN = 3.9 g.; FAT = 3.9 g.; CARBOHYDRATE = 5.7 g.;
                      CALORIES = 74; CALORIES FROM FAT = 47%

Oceania–Pacific Islands

SAMOAN CARROTS WITH PINEAPPLE
TPT - 9 minutes

The introduction of foods by European traders and settlers expanded the previously simple and restricted diet of Pacific Islanders. Carrots take well to a touch of sweetness and an herb garnish other than the usual parsley. One summer we grew a mixture of purple, white, and orange carrots and applied this recipe to the harvest for a little more exciting, a little more exotic presentation. I recommend the experience.

6 large carrots—scraped or pared and trimmed

1/2 cup *finely* **chopped onion**
1 teaspoon *very finely* **chopped gingerroot**
1/4 cup *unsweetened* **pineapple juice**
1 1/2 tablespoons butter

Freshly ground black pepper, to taste
2 tablespoons chopped fresh coriander (*cilantro***)**

Set up steamer.

Steam carrots for about 25 minutes.

Meanwhile, in a large skillet set over *LOW-MEDIUM* heat, combine *finely* chopped onion, *very finely* chopped gingerroot, pineapple juice, and butter. Cook, stirring frequently, until onion softens.

Transfer steamed carrots to skillet. Baste with pineapple mixture. Transfer to a long platter.

Grind black pepper over. Sprinkle with chopped fresh coriander (*cilantro*).

Serve at once.

Yields 6 servings
adequate for 4 people

Note: This recipe can be halved or doubled, when required.

1/6 SERVING – PROTEIN = 0.7 g.; FAT = 3.0 g.; CARBOHYDRATE = 7.6 g.;
CALORIES = 78; CALORIES FROM FAT = 34%

NOODLES WITH ONIONS IN THE STYLE OF THE SOLOMON ISLANDS
TPT - 16 minutes

In 1568 the Spanish navigator Alvaro de Mendaña was the first European to see these islands, just east of Papua New Guinea. He named them "Islas Salomón." The capital of the Solomon Islands is on the island of Guadalcanal on which was fought one of the bloodiest battles of World War II.

Chinese noodles have found a place in the cuisine of these islands and this is a favorite way of preparing them.

4 quarts *boiling* **water**
6 ounces Chinese *Yang Chung* **wheat noodles**
1/2 cup sliced onion

1 1/2 tablespoons *tamari* **soy sauce**
1 1/2 tablespoons Thai sweet *chili* **sauce**
1 scallion—*both white and green portions*—
  trimmed, well-rinsed, and *thinly* **sliced**

Cook wheat noodles and onion slices in *boiling* water according to package directions *but subtract two full minutes from cooking time.* Drain quickly. Turn into a large skillet set over *LOW-MEDIUM* heat.

Add soy sauce and sweet *chili* sauce. Toss and cook for several minutes, stirring frequently. Turn into a heated serving dish.

Serve at once with extra soy sauce and extra Thai sweet *chili* sauce.

Yields 6 servings
adequate for 4 people

Note: This recipe can be halved, when required.

1/6 SERVING – PROTEIN = 4.4 g.; FAT = 1.5 g.; CARBOHYDRATE = 22.2 g.;
CALORIES = 120; CALORIES FROM FAT = 11%

Oceania–Pacific Islands

COOK ISLANDS BANANA – LIME WHIP
TPT - 20 minutes

During World War II my grandmother came across town once a week to mind us while my mother went out to shop and pay bills. Grandma had to change bus lines in the middle of Rochester, New York. While she waited for the connecting bus, she always visited the bookstore in Sibley, Lindsay, and Curr, Co. in downtown Rochester. On one occasion she brought me a book with a genie-like lady in a pinafore who carried a magic spoon. From page to page the reader was whisked from country to country and, at each stop, a simple recipe was taught. The first one I tried, and the one I remember most vividly, was something called Banana Snow. This recipe from the Cook Islands reminds me a great deal of the experiment of that small child so many years ago.

Although the approximately nineteen thousand residents of the fifteen volcanic islands that form the small parliamentary democracy officially known as the Cook Islands are citizens of New Zealand, their cuisine is quite distinct and very unlike that of New Zealand.

4 ripe red bananas—peeled and chopped
3 tablespoons freshly squeezed lime juice
1/4 cup *agave* nectar *or* wildflower honey, as preferred

1 1/2 cups heavy whipping cream
3 teaspoons confectioners' sugar

Shredded coconut, for garnish
Freshly grated lime zest, for garnish

Using a food processor fitted with steel knife, process the banana, lime juice, and *agave* nectar until a smooth purée forms. Turn into a mixing bowl and set aside briefly.

Using the electric mixer fitted with *chilled* beaters or by hand using a *chilled* wire whisk, beat heavy cream in a *chilled* bowl until soft peaks form. While continuing to beat, add confectioners' sugar. Beat until stiff peaks form.

Fold whipped cream *gently*, but *thoroughly*, into the banana mixture. Divide mixture among six sherbet glasses or other small dessert dishes.*

Garnish each serving with a sprinkling of shredded coconut and grated lime zest.

Refrigerate for no more than an hour before serving.

Yields 6 individual servings

Notes: *This dessert makes a lovely presentation if spooned into wine glasses or champagne flutes.

This recipe can be halved or doubled, when required.

1/6 SERVING – PROTEIN = 2.0 g.; FAT = 20.2 g.; CARBOHYDRATE = 37.4 g.;
CALORIES = 327; CALORIES FROM FAT = 56%

BANANAS WITH UNCOOKED COCONUT CREAM SAUCE
TPT - 35 minutes;
30 minutes = refrigeration period

There are many versions of this recipe throughout South America, in Asia, and across the Pacific. Some cooks simply put the bananas in coconut milk or coconut cream. Cooks in French Polynesia tend to make a rich egg-based coconut cream. This is my favorite version. Pineapple can also be prepared in this manner to make "talautu," another dessert you will find in Papua New Guinea.

1/2 cup *fat-free* sweetened condensed milk
1/2 cup *light, sulfite-free* coconut milk
1/2 teaspoon pure vanilla extract

3 large bananas *or* 7 baby bananas—peeled and *thickly sliced*

VOLUME II - 484

Oceania–Pacific Islands

BANANAS WITH UNCOOKED COCONUT CREAM SAUCE (cont'd)

In a serving bowl, combine sweetened condensed milk, coconut milk, and vanilla extract. Using a wire whisk, combine thoroughly.

Add banana slices. Immerse the banana slices in the milk base. Refrigerate for at least 30 minutes.

Serve chilled.

Notes: *Baby bananas have a completely different flavor from the large Cavendish bananas, even though they are a Cavendish cultivar. I detect a slight pineapple nuance and I really like it.

This recipe can be halved or doubled, when required.

Yields 6 servings
adequate for 4 people

1/6 SERVING – PROTEIN = 3.1 g.; FAT = 1.2 g.; CARBOHYDRATE = 36.9 g.;
CALORIES = 160; CALORIES FROM FAT = 6%

PALAUAN SWEETPOTATO PUDDING
Kaele Palau

TPT - 2 hours and 25 minutes;
2 hours = refrigeration period

Palau is a presidential republic which maintains a free association with the United States, assuring defense, funding, and access to social services by this treaty association. It has a population of about twenty-one thousand who live on the 250 islands occupying the western chain of the Caroline Islands. The heritage of the population represents a blending of Micronesian, Melanesian, Austronesian, Filipino, and Japanese. Korean and Chinese food are favored on Koror, the largest island, but young people are very fond of western dishes such as burgers, pizza, and pasta.

Sweetpotatoes and yams were introduced into Asia from South America by the Spanish and Portuguese explorers. The bright, rich, sweet yams are favored in the United States and in Australia while most of Europe, Africa, and Asia prefer the starchy, pale-fleshed yam. I greatly prefer the dark orange-fleshed yams for desserts such as this.

3 quarts *boiling* **water**
1 large sweetpotato—peeled and chopped

1/2 cup *light, sulfite-free* **coconut milk**
3/4 cup *fat-free* **sweetened condensed milk**
1 teaspoon pure vanilla extract

2 teaspoons corn starch
1/4 cup *light, sulfite-free* **coconut milk**

In a large saucepan set over *MEDIUM* heat, combine *boiling* water and chopped sweetpotato. Cook until sweetpotato is soft—about 25 minutes. Drain thoroughly. Turn into the work bowl of the food processor fitted with steel knife.

Add 1/2 cupful coconut milk, sweetened condensed milk, and vanilla extract. Process until of uniform consistency, scraping down the sides of the work bowl as needed.

In a large saucepan set over *LOW-MEDIUM* heat, combine corn starch and the 1/4 cupful coconut milk. With a wooden spoon, stir until corn starch is thoroughly suspended. Add puréed sweetpotato mixture. Cook, stirring frequently, until mixture thickens. Reduce heat if mixture begins to stick. Turn into a serving bowl. Refrigerate for at least 2 hours.

Serve chilled.

Yields 6 servings
adequate for 4 people

Note: This recipe can be doubled, when required.

1/6 SERVING – PROTEIN = 4.4 g.; FAT = 1.2 g.; CARBOHYDRATE = 35.6 g.;
CALORIES = 172; CALORIES FROM FAT = 6%

The Americas

The Caribbean 487

Latin America:

Argentina	. .	507	Honduras	. .	571
Bolivia	. .	514	Mexico	. .	577
Brazil	. .	519	Nicaragua	. .	589
Chile .	. .	530	Panama	. .	596
Colombia	. .	536	Paraguay	. .	604
Costa Rica	. .	541	Peru .	. .	610
Ecuador	. .	547	Uruguay	. .	621
El Salvador	. .	558	Venezuela	. .	628
Guatemala	. .	565			

North America:

Canada 639

The Spirit of the Earth
  – the Native American Gift . . 650

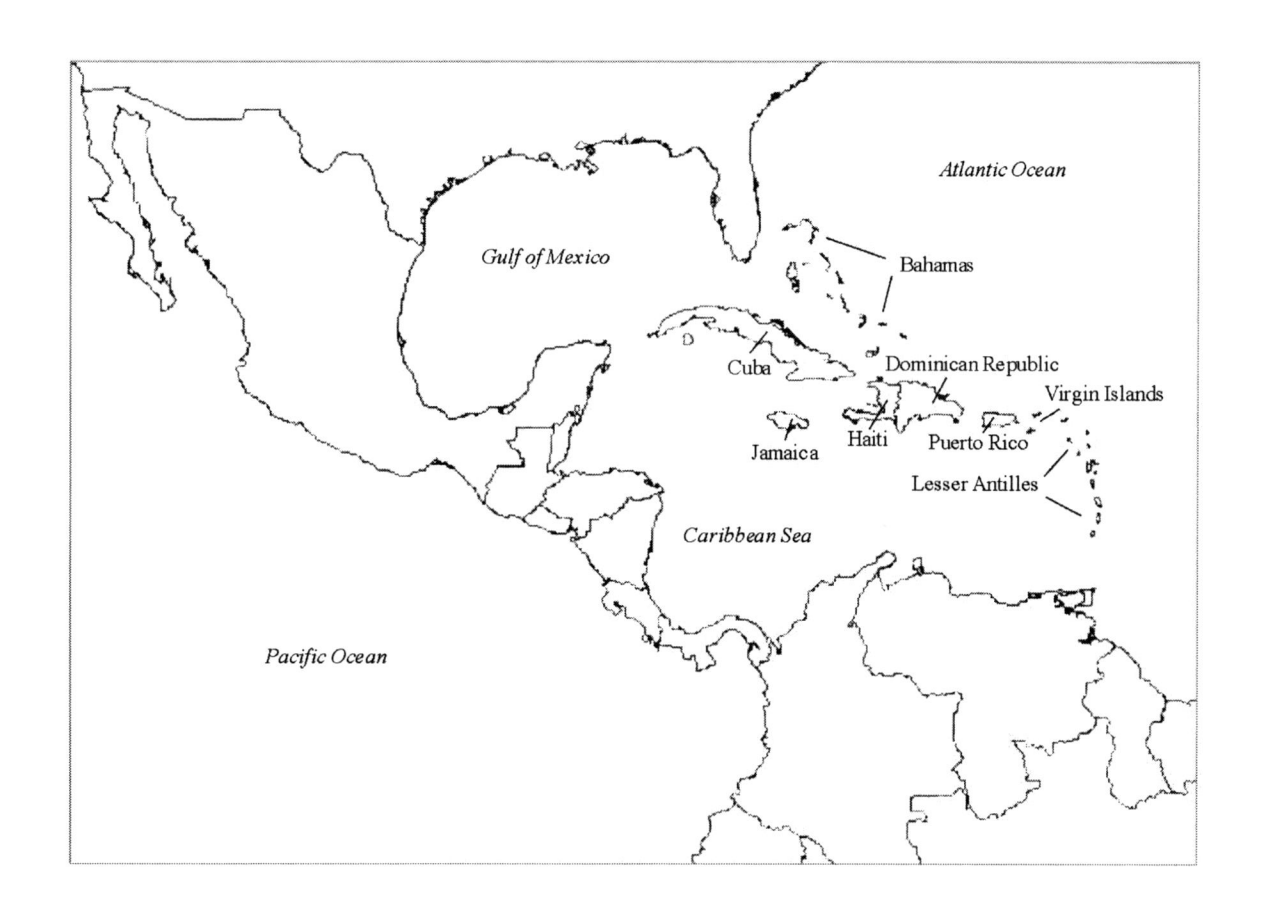

The Americas–Caribbean

The Caribbean

A tropical getaway from the pace of life for many people, the Caribbean is really a caldron of geologic and meteorological activity. Situated in the intertropical convergence zone, seen from space as a band of clouds often containing thunderstorms that circles the planet, these islands benefit from the convergence of wind fields from the northern and southern hemispheres with trade winds to offset potentially withering equatorial temperatures but when the earth's axis tips as we enter later summer in the North, this zone supports the weather systems moving west from Africa allowing for the development of cyclonic storm systems.

Further, the tectonic plates upon which we float are constantly moving and plate movements play a big role in this area of the western hemisphere. The Caribbean Plate abuts the North American and South American plates and extends west to the Cocos Plate, located in the Pacific Ocean to the west of the Isthmus of Panama. Geologic activity at the boundaries of these plates is responsible for frequent earthquakes. In addition, this is a geological environment which encourages volcanic activity. Seventeen active volcanoes lie along the plate boundaries. Both the western end of the plate in the Pacific and the eastern end of the plate are tectonic subduction regions. Port au Prince, Haiti, sits right over plate intersections and experiences frequent and often disastrous earthquakes as in 2010. Other islands have to worry about active volcanoes. Dominica has nine active stratovolcanoes and yet has not had an eruption since Columbus's visit to the island. The British Overseas Territory of Montserrat was left virtually uninhabitable by the 1995 Soufriere Hills volcanic eruption; it had been recovering from the destruction caused by the full force encounter with category-four Hurricane Hugo in 1989.

The collective land mass of 92,541 square miles, known as the Caribbean, is a group of more than 7,000 islands, islets, reefs, and cays that extends more than 2,000 miles between the Gulf of Mexico and the Caribbean Sea to the West and the Atlantic Ocean to the East. A large number of these islands sit on the Caribbean Plate which lies between the North and South American plates. More correctly designated as the West Indies, the region includes independent republics like Cuba, Dominica, the Dominican Republic, Haiti, and Trinidad and Tobago; the constitutional monarchies of Bahamas, Barbados, Grenada, Jamaica, Saint Kitts and Nevis, Saint Lucia, Saint Vincent and the Grenadines; the United States Commonwealth of Puerto Rico and the United States Virgin Islands, formerly the Danish West Indies, located in the Leeward Islands of the Lesser Antilles; British territories, French collectivities and departments, Dutch monarchal territories and municipalities; and islands within the territorial waters of South American and Central America nations. The Florida Keys are, in actuality, islands of the Caribbean. Panama alone claims more than thirteen hundred islands including the Kuna Yala Islands and three hundred more in the Bocas del Toro Archipelago.

An estimated 750,000 Amerindian lived in the Caribbean prior to European contact in the last decade of the 1400s but the introduction of diseases to which they had no natural immunity and social disruption depleted the population just as it did in Central America and in South America. The population grew from 1500 to 1800 not from recovery of the Amerindian population but by the introduction of slaves from West Africa, military prisoners, and slaves deported from Ireland by the Cromwellian reign in England. With the end of the trans-Atlantic slave trade the population of the Caribbean has gradually but steadily increased to over thirty-nine million as of 2009 census statistics.

~

The Americas – Caribbean

The nation islands of the Caribbean represent to me one over-riding passion and that is fruit. How many ways can you use fruit in a menu? It is a joy to see the fruits of the tropics in every course served. The decision to create a huge buffet of dishes from these islands was born out of the frustration to assign dishes to a specific island since overlapping due to borrowing is very wide-spread. I suppose that is precisely how the menus on cruise ships are created. The menus of hotel chain restaurants, especially on the so-called resort islands, can be so similar from island to island that assigning a recipe to St. Croix or St. Lucia or St. John's or Jamaica is near to impossible and misleading. In addition, creative chefs from all over the world arrive in the islands with their knives and their ideas, not to mention their sworn allegiances to the old and the new. Their interpretations further distort the concept of "Caribbean cuisine."

Frothy Passion Fruit Appetizer Drink

Sweetpotato – Bean Appetizer Rolls and **Curried Cashews**
with **Papaya and Grilled Pineapple Salsa**
Salsa de Papaya y Piña

~

Papaya and Garlic Soup   **Creamy Baked Sweetpotato Soup**
Sopa de Batata Calcinado con Leche
with Goat Cheese garnish

Bahamian Pumpkin Soup with Coconut Milk and Banana

~

Sweetpotato, *Jicama*, and Mango Salad in Citrus Dressing
Ensalada de Batata, Jicama, y Mango

Puerto Rican Papaya and Tomato Salad
Ensalada de Papaya y Tomate

Fruit Platter with Hearts of Palm and Lime *Vinaigrette*

Seasoned Salt from St. Croix

Haitian Bean Salad
Salade de Feve

~ ~

Grilled *Tofu* with **Cuban Lime Marinade for *Tofu***
Salsa de Ajo con Lima

Rice with Tomatoes
Arroz con Tomate Espanole

**Mashed Plantains with Tomato and Thyme
in the Style of the Dominican Republic**
Puré de Llantén con Tomate y Tomillo

~ ~ ~ ~ ~ ~ ~ ~ ~ ~

The Americas – Caribbean

Cuban Black Beans with Rice and Mango Relish
Moros y Cristianos con Salsa de Mango

**Baked *Christophenes* (*Chayote*) and Onions
as Prepared in Martinique**

Banana Custard Cornbread

~~~~~~~~~~

**"*Taro*" Greens and Vegetables
in the Style of the Virgin Islands**
Callaloo

~~~~~~~~~~~~~~~~~~~~~~

Nutmeg Ice Cream with **Sweet Coffee *Coulis***

Mango Pudding
Postre de Mango

Low-Fat Cuban Anise-   Scented Sweet Egg Custard
Natilla Cubana con Sirup con Anis

Spiced Sugar

Carambola **and Orange Dessert**

CARIBBEAN FROTHY PASSION FRUIT APPETIZER DRINK
TPT - 3 minutes

Commercials, promoting travel to the Caribbean, always show happy people drinking exotic fruit drinks; people who visit the Islands always relay the newest drink, never remembering the island where they tasted it. Even the blog of proprietors of a favorite Pennsylvania restaurant, who relocated to the Caribbean, encouraged you to come to taste their drink concoctions. As a first course for a Caribbean-inspired meal, one of these drinks, sans the alcohol, can be a real mood-setter.

For four servings:

1/2 cup passion fruit nectar
1/4 cup mango nectar
1/2 cup *light, sulfite-free* coconut milk
1 cup *two-percent* milk
1 1/2 tablespoons *agave* nectar
2 tablespoons freshly squeezed orange juice with pulp
1/8 teaspoon pure vanilla extract

1/4 cup crushed ice

4 well-washed, *home-grown and unsprayed* edible flowers, of choice, for garnish
4 long spiral threads of *organic* lime zest, for garnish

In the container of the electric blender, combine passion fruit and mango nectars, coconut milk, *two-percent* milk, *agave* nectar, orange juice, and vanilla extract.* Blend at HIGH speed until frothy.

Add crushed ice. Blend at HIGH speed for about 10 seconds. Pour into four large wine glasses.

Serve at once, each garnished with a flower and lime zest spiral.

Yields 4 servings

Note: *When I have a crowd, I prepare batches of the ingredients in measuring cups, large glasses, or whatever I have available so that the first course servings can be served together.

1/4 SERVING – PROTEIN = 2.5 g.; FAT = 2.4 g.; CARBOHYDRATE = 15.2 g.;
CALORIES = 102; CALORIES FROM FAT = 21%

CARIBBEAN SWEETPOTATO AND BLACK BEAN APPETIZERS
TPT - 54 minutes

One late autumn day I stood next to a shopper who was bemoaning the small sweetpotatoes in the vegetable bin. There were many small sweetpotatoes that were just the right size for a single serving. She picked up three humungous roots; she was determined to get her money's worth, that is, more sweetpotato, less peeling. If she was planning to bake them, I wondered how long it would have taken.

1 small sweetpotato—well-scrubbed

1/3 cup canned black beans—well-rinsed and well-drained
1/4 cup *finely* chopped Italian red onion
2 tablespoons *finely* chopped fresh coriander (*cilantro*)
1 garlic clove—*very finely* chopped
1 1/2 teaspoons freshly squeezed lime juice
1 1/2 teaspoons freshly squeezed orange juice
1/2 teaspoon ground cumin
1/4 teaspoon *jalapeño chili* sauce, or to taste

6 egg roll wrappers

High-heat safflower *or* sunflower oil

Preheat oven to 350 degrees F. Prepare a cookie sheet by lining with culinary parchment paper.

Cut an **X** in the top of the sweetpotato. Bake in preheated oven until soft—about 30 minutes. Remove from the oven and allow to cool until it can be handled.

While the sweetpotato is cooling, in a mixing bowl, combine black beans, *finely* chopped onion and fresh coriander (*cilantro*), *very finely* chopped garlic, lime and orange juices, ground cumin, and *jalapeño chili* sauce. Mix well.

Cut sweetpotato in half and scoop out the cooked flesh and add it to the ingredients in the mixing bowl. Stir to combine well.

Dip your finger in water and lightly moisten all four edges of a *wonton* wrapper. Spoon *one-sixth* of filling down one side of the *egg roll* wrapper. Roll tightly and pinch ends to seal. Place seam-side down on parchment-lined cookie sheet. Repeat until six rolls have been made and all of the filling has been used up.

Brush each roll lightly with safflower oil. Bake in preheated 350 degree F. oven for 12-15 minutes, or until golden brown. Transfer to a heated serving plate.

Serve hot with PAPAYA AND GRILLED PINEAPPLE SALSA *[see recipe which follows] or other salsa of choice.*

Yields 6 servings
adequate for 4-6 people

Note: This recipe can be doubled, when required.

1/12 SERVING – PROTEIN = 3.4 g.; FAT = 0.9 g.; CARBOHYDRATE = 16.6 g.; CALORIES = 86; CALORIES FROM FAT = 9%

PAPAYA AND GRILLED PINEAPPLE *SALSA*
Salsa de Papaya y Piña
TPT - 5 minutes

Do you remember when every plate served in a restaurant or at a formal dinner was garnished with a sprig of parsley? If you do not remember, then you did not live through the culinary "dull ages" that I remember well, the period right after World War II. Today, a small serving of a fruit- or vegetable-based salsa can elevate the entire presentation and this is one of my favorites.

1 cup pineapple chunks

1/2 ripe papaya (about 8 ounces)—peeled, seeded, and cut into small uniform cubes to yield about 1 cupful
1/4 cup chopped fresh coriander (*cilantro*)
1/4 cup *finely* chopped Italian red onion
2 tablespoons freshly squeezed lime juice
1/4 teaspoon *jalapeño chili* sauce, or more to taste*

Spray a non-stick-coated skillet with olive oil spray and set over *LOW-MEDIUM* heat. Add pineapple and cook, turning frequently until each side has browned. Remove from heat and chop into small, uniform pieces. Turn into a mixing bowl.

Add chopped papaya and fresh coriander (*cilantro*), *finely* chopped onion, lime juice, and *jalapeño* sauce. Toss gently. Cover and refrigerate for no more than 1 hour before serving to preserve fresh taste.

The Americas – Caribbean

PAPAYA AND GRILLED PINEAPPLE SALSA (cont'd)

Yields 6 servings
adequate for 4 people

Notes: *Jalopeño chili* sauce is available in Hispanic groceries, food specialty stores, and in most grocery stores throughout the Southwest.

This recipe can be doubled, when required.

1/6 SERVING – PROTEIN = 0.4 g.; FAT = 0.2 g.; CARBOHYDRATE = 8.4 g.;
CALORIES = 34; CALORIES FROM FAT = 5%

CURRIED CASHEWS
TPT - 9 minutes

Tastes of Africa and tastes of Asia abound in the Caribbean. Here cashews, which are the seeds of a fruit native to the Americas, are given a flavor with the spices that the explorers had set out to find. How interesting that this all should come full circle.

2 tablespoons butter
1 1/2 cups *raw, unsalted, preservative-free* cashews

1/2 teaspoon salt
1 teaspoon HOMEMADE CURRY POWDER *[see index]* **or commercially-available curry powder of choice**

In a non-stick-coated skillet set over *MEDIUM* heat, combine butter and cashews. Cook, stirring frequently, until the cashews are lightly browned. Remove from heat.

Sprinkle salt and curry powder over. Transfer to a serving dish. Allow to cool.

Yields 1 1/2 cupfuls

Note: This recipe can be halved or doubled, when required.

1/12 SERVING (about 2 tablespoonfuls) –
PROTEIN = 4.8 g.; FAT = 14.7 g.; CARBOHYDRATE = 8.2 g.;
CALORIES = 174; CALORIES FROM FAT = 76%

CARIBBEAN PAPAYA AND GARLIC SOUP
TPT - 1 hour

Fruit soups are popular in Scandinavia, Hungary, France, the Balkans, and in Eastern Europe. Brazilians took to fruit soups in the 1960s with enthusiasm but I dare say that this soup will entice even those who tend who dismiss fruit soups as fads, as desserts, as silly or pretentious. Three or four small, perfectly ripe papaya or one large Maradol papaya, if you are lucky enough to find one, should provide the three cupfuls of pulp needed to make this unusual soup. It is simple to make and delicious to eat. If you want to really surprise your guests, this is the soup with which to do it.

1 quart VEGETABLE STOCK FROM SOUP *[see index]* **or other vegetarian stock of choice**
3 1/2 cups chopped papaya pulp
6 garlic cloves—chopped

1 cup light cream *or* half and half

Salt, to taste
Freshly ground black pepper, to taste

In a kettle set over *MEDIUM* heat, combine stock, chopped papaya, and chopped garlic. Allow to come to the boil. Reduce heat to *LOW-MEDIUM* and allow to simmer for about 45 minutes. Remove from heat.

Add cream and stir to integrate.

Using the food processor fitted with steel knife or the electric blender, purée the soup in batches and pour into a clean saucepan. Return to *LOW-MEDIUM* heat and allow to heat through.

CARIBBEAN PAPAYA AND GARLIC SOUP (cont'd)

Taste and season with salt and black pepper. Turn into a heated tureen.

Serve at once into heated soup plates.

Yields 6 cupfuls

Note: This recipe can be halved or doubled, when required.

1/6 SERVING (about 1 cupful) –
PROTEIN = 2.3 g.; FAT = 3.9 g.; CARBOHYDRATE = 17.5 g.;
CALORIES = 109; CALORIES FROM FAT = 32%

CARIBBEAN CREAMY BAKED SWEETPOTATO SOUP
Sopa de Batata Calcinado con Leche

TPT - 1 hour and 45 minutes;
20 minutes = sweetpotato cooling period

Years ago, during the nutrition craze of the 1970s, a nutrition guru applauded the sweetpotato to extreme. He cooked perhaps a dozen sweetpotatoes each week, wrapped them, and took them with him for breakfast and lunch and snacks; he even packed sweetpotatoes into his suitcase when he had to travel. I am very fond of sweetpotatoes but somehow this seems just too extreme. I do think you will find that this sweetpotato soup, creamy and with an elusive sweetness, is far more appealing than is an aluminum foil-wrapped rhizome.

3 medium sweetpotatoes (about 1 3/4 pounds)
—well-scrubbed

1 tablespoon safflower *or* corn oil
1/2 cup *finely* chopped onion
1/2 cup *finely* chopped celery with leaves
1 large clove garlic—crushed and *finely* chopped
1 teaspoon *crushed*, dried basil

2 1/4 cups *whole* milk*

Pinch sugar
Pinch salt
1/4 freshly ground black pepper, or to taste
1/8 teaspoon ground allspice

Preheat oven to 350 degrees F.

Cut an **X** in each well-scrubbed sweetpotato and bake in preheated oven for 1 hour, or until tender. Allow to cool for at least 20 minutes before peeling. Using a ricer, rice sweetpotatoes into a large mixing bowl.

In a large saucepan or small kettle, heat oil over *MEDIUM* heat. Add *finely* chopped onion, celery, and garlic with *crushed*, dried basil. Sauté until onions are soft and translucent, *being careful not to allow any of the vegetables to brown.*

While stirring with a wire whisk, add milk. Add riced sweetpotatoes. Stir to mix well.

Season with sugar, salt, black pepper, and ground allspice. Cook, stirring frequently, until heated through. Thin with a bit more milk, if necessary. Turn into a heated soup tureen and keep hot on a warming tray until ready to serve.

Yields 4 cupfuls

Notes: *Skimmed or one-percent milk can be substituted, if desired.

Since this soup freezes well, we double the recipe for convenient menu planning.

1/4 SERVING (i. e., per cupful) –
PROTEIN = 4.1 g.; FAT = 5.9 g.; CARBOHYDRATE = 23.8 g.;
CALORIES = 176; CALORIES FROM FAT = 30%

The Americas–Caribbean

BAHAMIAN PUMPKIN SOUP WITH COCONUT MILK AND BANANA
TPT - 38 minutes

Pumpkin always pairs well with sweet accents and here the banana and coconut milk give it a rich, mellow smoothness. My first encounter with this soup was a version that was way too sweet for my taste where cinnamon, nutmeg, and allspice plus too much sweetened condensed milk overwhelmed the soup making it more of a dessert than a soup. We love this soup and serve it often on cool spring or autumn evenings with a complex green salad and tropically-inspired fruit dessert.

1 1/2 tablespoons butter
3/4 cup chopped carrot
3/4 cup chopped celery
2 ripe, medium bananas—chopped
1 garlic clove—*finely* chopped
1 bay leaf—broken
2 whole cloves

5 cups VEGETARIAN WHITE STOCK *[see index]*
1 can (15 ounces) pumpkin—*unseasoned* and *unsweetened*
2/3 cup *light, sulfite-free* **coconut milk**
1 tablespoon *fat-free* **sweetened condensed milk**
1 teaspoon crushed, *dried* **sage**
Pinch or two SOUTH AFRICAN CURRY POWDER *[see index] or* **commercially-available curry powder mixture of choice**
Pinch ground coriander
Freshly ground black pepper, to taste

Thin lime slices, for garnish
Cracked black peppercorns *or* **mixed peppercorns, for garnish**

In a skillet set over *LOW-MEDIUM* heat, melt butter. Add chopped carrot, celery, and banana, *finely* chopped garlic, bay leaf, and whole cloves. Sauté until vegetables have softened. Remove and discard bay leaf and whole cloves. Turn into the container of the electric blender and blend until mixture is *totally puréed* and *very smooth*. Scrape mixture into a kettle.

Add vegetable stock, pumpkin purée, coconut milk, sweetened condensed milk, dried sage, curry powder, ground coriander, and black pepper. Stir to combine. Increase temperature to *MEDIUM* and allow to come to the simmer. Cook, stirring frequently, for about 15 minutes. Turn into a heated soup tureen.

Serve into heated soup bowls, garnished with a lime slice and freshly cracked pepper.

Yields 8 servings

Notes: This soup can be make a day or two ahead and gently reheated when required.

Although this recipe can be halved, if necessary, it freezes well enough to make the whole batch for now and a plan-ahead meal. Once defrosted, blend again to restore the texture before reheating.

1/8 SERVING – PROTEIN = 1.2 g.; FAT = 5.8 g.; CARBOHYDRATE = 26.5 g.;
CALORIES = 165; CALORIES FROM FAT = 32%

SWEETPOTATO, *JICAMA*, AND MANGO SALAD IN CITRUS DRESSING IN THE STYLE OF THE CARIBBEAN
Ensalada de Batata, Jicama, y Mango
TPT - 4 hours and 18 minutes;
4 hours = minimum flavor development period

This salad, which evolved from a Cuban salad I had tasted years ago, sparkles with savory and sweet flavors. Since every ingredient is easily available summer or winter, there is no reason to put this aside as a summer salad or for a special occasion. The first time I made it I served it with a pizza. Believe it or not, it paired wonderfully.

The Americas–Caribbean

SWEETPOTATO, *JICAMA*, AND MANGO SALAD IN CITRUS DRESSING IN THE STYLE OF THE CARIBBEAN (cont'd)

2 cups sweetpotato chunks
1 tablespoons *extra virgin* olive oil
Sprinkling of salt

2 quarts *boiling* water
1 small *jicama*—about 3/4 pound—peeled and cut into thin strips

1 large *under-ripe* mango—peeled and chopped into large chunks
1/4 chopped fresh coriander (*cilantro*)

CITRUS DRESSING:
    2 tablespoons freshly squeezed orange juice
    2 tablespoons freshly squeezed lime juice
    1 tablespoon freshly squeezed lemon juice
    1 medium shallot clove—*very finely* chopped
    1 *very small* garlic clove—*very finely* chopped
    1 teaspoon safflower *or* sunflower oil
    1/2 teaspoon dried and crushed oregano
    1/8 teaspoon ground allspice
    Pinch ground cumin

Home-grown, spray-free daylilies, if in-season—well-washed with pistils, stamen, and sepals removed—for garnish

In a non-stick-coated skillet set over *LOW-MEDIUM* heat, heat olive oil. Add sweetpotato chunks and cook, stirring frequently, until they are *crisp-tender* and lightly browned. Remove from heat. Sprinkle with salt. Turn sweetpotato chunks and any remaining oil into a mixing bowl.

Cook *jicama* strips in *boiling* water for 2 minutes. Drain well. Rinse with cold water and drain again. Add to sweetpotato chunks.

Add mango chunks and chopped fresh coriander (*cilantro*). Toss gently.

In a small bowl, combine orange, lime, and lemon juices, *very finely* chopped shallot and garlic cloves, safflower oil, crushed oregano, and ground allspice and cumin. Mix well. Pour over the sweetpotato–*jicama*–mango mixture. Toss gently. Cover bowl with plastic wrap and refrigerate for at least 4 hours to allow flavors to marry.*

Turn into a serving bowl. *Serve chilled*. Refrigerate leftovers.

                              Yields 8 servings
                            adequate for 6 people

Notes: *The flavor of this salad greatly benefits from an overnight marination period, if convenient.

        This recipe can be halved or doubled, when required.

1/8 SERVING – PROTEIN = 0.9 g.; FAT = 2.2 g.; CARBOHYDRATE = 13.9 g.;
CALORIES = 74; CALORIES FROM FAT = 27%

PUERTO RICAN PAPAYA AND TOMATO SALAD
Ensalada de Papaya y Tomate
TPT - 6 minutes

The tomato is said to have originated somewhere in the region of South American south of Mexico. As it spread throughout the world, cooks have combined it with a multitude of other ingredients, claiming it as their own. Here, it is back to it origins, paired with the papaya which was also first encountered by the explorers in South America and, with them, traveled the world. Papayas and tomatoes are really soul mates; they do travel well together too. This, is from the "La Isla del Encanto," the Commonwealth of Puerto Rico. The self-governing unincorporated United States territory, is a melting pot of diverse influences but is in the Caribbean and that influence is unavoidably strong.

1/4 cup *calorie-reduced or light* mayonnaise
2 tablespoons freshly squeezed lime juice
1 tablespoon HOMEMADE TOMATO KETCHUP *[see index] or* commercially-available *chili* sauce, if preferred
1/2 teaspoon HOMEMADE VEGAN WORCESTERSHIRE-STYLE SAUCE *[see index] or vegetarian* Worcestershire sauce

2 large tomatoes—well-washed and chopped
1 large papaya—peeled, seeded, and cubed
2 tablespoons chopped fresh coriander (*cilantro*) leaves

Lime wedges, for garnish

PUERTO RICAN PAPAYA AND TOMATO SALAD (cont'd)

In a small bowl, combine mayonnaise and lime juice. Blend well. Add *chili* sauce and Worcestershire sauce. Set aside briefly.

In a large bowl, combine chopped tomatoes, cubed papaya, and chopped fresh coriander (*cilantro*). Add prepared dressing. Turn into a serving bowl. Refrigerate until ready to serve.

Serve chilled, garnished with lime wedges.

Notes: Refrigerate and cover any leftovers. Use within two days.

This recipe may be halved or doubled, when required.

Yields 6 servings
adequate for 4 people

1/6 SERVING – PROTEIN = 0.7 g.; FAT = 3.7 g.; CARBOHYDRATE = 8.0 g.;
CALORIES = 66; CALORIES FROM FAT = 50%

CARIBBEAN FRUIT PLATTER WITH HEARTS OF PALM AND LIME *VINAIGRETTE*
TPT - 14 minutes

Although this salad begs for summer-ripened cantaloupe and cucumber and my mantra of "eat foods only in season" haunts my subconscious, I have been known to buy a grocery store cucumber and a piece of South American melon to enliven a winter meal. The lime vinaigrette hides the dullness of the out-of-season melon and cucumber. Since the soul is refreshed with this salad it makes it a good choice for the Winter Solstice.

LIME *VINAIGRETTE*:
    3 tablespoons freshly squeezed lime juice
    3 tablespoons *extra virgin* olive oil
    1 teaspoon sugar

    1/4 teaspoon dry mustard
    Salt, to taste
    Freshly ground black pepper, to taste

1 half cucumber—peeled and *thinly* sliced
1 avocado—sliced
1/4 cantaloupe melon—peeled and *thinly* sliced
1 ripe mango—*thinly* sliced
2/3 cup sliced hearts of palm—well-rinsed and well-drained*

SEASONED SALT FROM ST. CROIX *[see recipe which follows]*, **to taste**

In a cruet, combine lime juice, olive oil, sugar, dry mustard, and black pepper. Shake vigorously. Set aside until required.

On a large platter, arrange cucumber slices in an overlapping semi-circle that covers about the half the serving platter. Arrange, avocado slices in a fan-shaped arrangement at one side of platter. Arrange melon slices so that they overlap the avocado slices. Arrange mango slices so that they overlap the melon slices. Scatter slices of hearts of palm over.

Shake *vinaigrette* vigorously again. Pour over fruits.

Sprinkle the seasoned salt over. Refrigerate until ready to serve.

Pass platter to allow diners to choose "favorites." Refrigerate leftovers.

Yields 8 servings
adequate for 6 people

Notes: *The taste of hearts of palm is greatly benefited by a presoaking in cold water.

This recipe can be halved or doubled, when required.

1/8 SERVING – PROTEIN = 1.5 g.; FAT = 8.6 g.; CARBOHYDRATE = 12.5 g.;
CALORIES = 124; CALORIES FROM FAT = 62%

The Americas–**Caribbean**

SEASONED SALT FROM ST. CROIX
TPT - 4 minutes

Someone, who had visited the Caribbean, told me about this salt substitute which appears to be used for literally everything including salads and as a dry marinade for grilling. We use very little salt in our cooking but occasionally, on a very, very hot summer's evening, this salt substitute comes off the spice rack to do its job. Commercial salt substitutes just do not substitute; this seasoned salt cuts the sodium and provides flavor, which is just what you are looking for, "c'est vrai?"

1 tablespoon salt*
1 teaspoon dried thyme—crushed
1 teaspoon dried parsley—crushed
1 teaspoons dried chives
1/2 teaspoon freshly ground black pepper
Pinch sugar
Pinch ground allspice

In a mortar, combine salt, crushed, dried thyme and parsley, dried chives, black pepper, sugar, and ground allspice. Using a pestle, grind until of uniform consistency.

In a jar with tightly fitting lid, combine all ingredients. Shake well to mix thoroughly. Store, tightly covered, in a dark, dry place.

Yields about 2 1/2 tablespoonfuls

Notes: *I prefer to use the product known as Salt Sense since it reduces the amount of sodium but still provides adequate flavor.

This seasoned salt may be doubled or tripled and kept on hand on your spice rack.

HAITIAN BEAN SALAD
Salade de Feve
TPT - 8 hours and 12 minutes;
8 hours = flavor development period

There are probably as many versions of this salad as there are Haitian cooks since it adapts well to variations that reflect your available larder. Some people mix the eggs right into the bean mixture, I prefer to use them as a garnish; some add garlic, I do not; while some add cheeses like Parmesan and Romano, others add nuts, which reminds me fondly of Georgian salads I have enjoyed; and so on and so on. It was much the same with the" three" bean salads of my youth; the variations could fill a recipe book on their own. Eventually even the requirement of three beans was abandoned and this salad too has flexibility. On warm summer evenings, we often serve this salad as a main course with bread and fresh fruit.

1 can (15 ounces) *low-sodium*, red kidney beans
  —well-drained
1 cup crisp-cooked cut green beans—well-drained
  and cooled
1/2 cup chopped celery
2 tablespoons chopped sweet gherkins or
  cornichones
1/4 cup *very finely* chopped onion
Freshly ground black pepper, to taste

2 tablespoons *extra virgin* olive oil
2 tablespoons freshly squeezed lemon juice

2 hard-cooked eggs—peeled and sliced
1 teaspoon grated *pecorino Romano* cheese
1/2 ounce *pecorino Romano* cheese—shaved into
  large, thin pieces using a cheese plane

In a mixing bowl, combine well-drained kidney beans, cut green beans, chopped celery, chopped pickle, *very finely* chopped onion, and black pepper. Toss gently.

In a cruet, combine oil and lemon juice. Shake vigorously and pour over vegetable mixture. Toss gently. Cover and refrigerate for at least 8 hours, or overnight, to allow for flavor development. Stir a couple of times during this period to keep the vegetables in contact with the *vinaigrette*.

Spoon salad into a shallow serving bowl or onto a platter or plate, mounding it in the middle of the serving dish. Arrange egg slices over the top, overlapping the slices attractively. Sprinkle grated cheese over the eggs. Scatter shaved cheese pieces over the top.

Serve chilled.

Yields 6 servings as a side salad
adequate for 4 people

Note: This recipe can be doubled, when required.

1/6 SERVING – PROTEIN = 7.7 g.; FAT = 6.7 g.; CARBOHYDRATE = 15.1 g
CALORIES = 150; CALORIES FROM FAT = 40%

CUBAN LIME MARINADE FOR *TOFU*
Salsa de Ajo con Lima

TPT - 8 hours and 10 minutes;
8 hours = *tofu* marination period

If my plans are to broil or stir-fry tofu, I find myself drawn to the sweet, but not too sweet, and spicy, but not too spicy, flavor of this garlicky sauce. It is similar to "mojo" which is referred to by some as "Cuba's national table sauce," albeit without the addition of olive oil. For all I know, they may be right. I have noticed that it is so often a part of a Cuban meal, it might well be the table sauce of choice of all Cubans. The touch of citrus makes this sauce different from all others but it is often difficult to find the traditional "Naranja agria," sour oranges so we substitute lime juice. We love it.

4 large garlic cloves from prepared GARLIC WITH THYME AND BAY IN OIL *[see index]*—*very finely* **chopped to yield about 2 tablespoonfuls**
2 medium shallots—*very finely* **chopped**
1 1/2 teaspoons salt

4 teaspoons ground cumin
2 teaspoons dried and crushed oregano
1/2 teaspoon freshly ground black pepper

1 cup freshly squeezed lime juice

In mortar, combine *very finely* chopped garlic and shallot with salt. Using a pestle, grind to a smooth paste.

Add ground cumin, crushed oregano, and black pepper. Continue grinding with the pestle until well-blended. Turn into a shallow bowl.

Add lime juice. Stir to combine.

Marinate *tofu* in the marinade for 8 hours, or overnight, for maximum flavor penetration before grilling or stir-frying.

Yields about 1 cupful

Note: This recipe is easily doubled, when required. Leftover marinade can not, however, be stored in the refrigerator for more than a day or two without significant flavor and quality loss.

1/16 SERVING (i. e., per tablespoonful) -
PROTEIN = 0.1 g.; FAT = 0.01 g.; CARBOHYDRATE = 1.5 g.;
CALORIES = 5; CALORIES FROM FAT = 2%

RICE WITH TOMATOES IN THE STYLE OF THE CARIBBEAN
Arroz con Tomate

TPT - 37 minutes

Probably of French origin, rice and tomatoes cooked in this manner have become a specialty of island cooks who would probably never admit to the European origin. It reminds me of a dish my mother cooked often during the rationing years of World War II. She added a bit of chopped green pepper, if she had it, and called it Spanish rice. Years later I found a treasure of wartime recipes that had been distributed by the Rochester Gas and Electric Company and there was that "Spanish rice" recipe.

1 tablespoon butter
1/2 cup onion—*finely* **chopped**

1 cup dry converted rice*
2 cups *boiling* water
Pinch salt

1 tablespoon butter
3/4 cup canned, *diced* tomatoes *or* **the equivalent in fresh tomatoes which have been peeled, seeded, and diced**
1 tablespoon *light, sulfite-free* coconut milk

In a saucepan set over *MEDIUM* heat, melt 1 tablespoonful butter. Add *finely* chopped onion and sauté until onion is soft and translucent, *being careful not to allow onions to brown*.

Add rice, *boiling* water, and salt. Reduce heat to *LOW*. Cover and cook for about 20 minutes, or until water is absorbed. *Remove cover and remove from heat.*

In a non-stick-coated skillet set over MEDIUM heat, melt remaining tablespoonful butter. Add diced tomatoes and sauté for several minutes. Add coconut milk and allow to heat for another minute or two. Add tomatoes to rice and cook, stirring frequently, until all moisture is evaporated. Turn into a heated serving bowl.

RICE WITH TOMATOES IN THE STYLE OF THE CARIBBEAN (cont'd)

Serve at once. Refrigerate any leftovers. Reheat over *LOW* heat.

Yields 6 servings
adequate for 4 people

Notes: *I also make this dish using brown rice.

This recipe can be halved or doubled, when required.

1/6 SERVING – PROTEIN = 3.3 g.; FAT = 4.1 g.; CARBOHYDRATE = 33.6 g.;
CALORIES = 188; CALORIES FROM FAT = 20%

MASHED PLANTAINS WITH TOMATO AND THYME IN THE STYLE OF THE DOMINICAN REPUBLIC
Puré de Llantén con Tomate y Tomillo
TPT - 40 minutes

The texture and the sweetness of this simple dish, so obviously related to the African dish known as "fufu," is a real change from mashed potatoes. Topping each serving with a poached egg would be traditional but we like to serve it as a side dish with a variety of entrees.

3 large, ripe plantains—peeled and cut into chunks
4 quarts *boiling* water

2 tablespoons butter

1 tablespoon *extra virgin* olive oil
1 small onion—*finely* chopped
1 large garlic clove—*very finely* chopped

1 large, ripe tomato—peeled, seeded, and chopped— *or* 1 1/2 cups canned, *diced* tomatoes
1 tablespoon *finely* chopped fresh thyme

Freshly ground black pepper, to taste
1 tablespoon GARLIC–BASIL VINEGAR [see index] *or* other herb vinegar of choice

1/4 cup *thinly* sliced Vidalia salad onion—*both white and green portions*

6 tablespoons *fat-free* dairy sour cream

Put a shallow serving bowl on a warming tray set at MEDIUM.

Cook plantain chunks in *boiling* water, set over *MEDIUM* heat, for about 20 minutes, or until tender. Drain. Transfer drained plantains to a mixing bowl.

Add butter and mash until of uniform consistency. Transfer to the center of heated serving bowl and keep warm until ready to serve.

In a skillet set over *MEDIUM* heat, heat olive oil. Add *finely* chopped onion and *very finely* chopped garlic. Sauté until soft and translucent, *allowing neither the onion nor the garlic to brown.*

Add chopped tomato and chopped thyme. Cook, stirring constantly, until liquid cooks off and sauce thickens. Season with black pepper. Add vinegar. Spoon over the top of the mashed plantains. Garnish with *thinly* sliced Vidalia salad onion.

Serve at once. Pass sour cream.

Yields 6 servings
adequate for 4 people

Note: This recipe can be halved or increased proportionately, when required

1/6 SERVING – PROTEIN = 3.3 g.; FAT = 5.8 g.; CARBOHYDRATE = 34.7 g.;
CALORIES = 193; CALORIES FROM FAT = 27%

CUBAN BLACK BEANS WITH RICE AND MANGO RELISH
Moros y Cristianos con Salsa de Mango
TPT - 21 minutes

Although the Cuban name for this dish may not be very politically correct in this day and age, our version of this classic dish is worth the political transgression. We find the mango relish, although not traditionally served with rice and beans to be a delicious garnish for this and a whole host of dishes. Whenever I make Cuban black beans, I always reserve a bit of the mango relish to serve with tostados at lunch the next day.

CUBAN BLACK BEANS WITH RICE AND MANGO RELISH (cont'd)

CUBAN MANGO RELISH:
    2 ripe mangoes—peeled and diced
    1/2 cup diced sweet red pepper
    4 medium scallions—*white and light green portions only*—trimmed, well-rinsed, and *thinly* sliced
    1/4 cup freshly squeezed lime juice

1 tablespoon *extra virgin* olive oil
2 garlic cloves—*finely* chopped
1/2 cup chopped onion

2 cans (15-ounce each) black beans—well-drained
1 medium green bell pepper—cored, seeded, and diced
1 tablespoon red wine vinegar
1 tablespoon grated *fresh* orange zest
1/2 teaspoon ground cinnamon
1/2 teaspoon ground cumin
2 teaspoons dried oregano—crushed
1/3 cup chopped fresh coriander (*cilantro*)

1/4 teaspoon ground red pepper (cayenne), or to taste

4 cups *hot, cooked*, converted rice

Prepare CUBAN MANGO RELISH first by combining diced mango and red pepper, sliced scallions, and lime juice. Toss. Refrigerate until required.*

To prepare CUBAN BLACK BEANS, in a saucepan set over *MEDIUM* heat, heat oil. Add *finely* chopped garlic and chopped onion. Sauté until onion is soft and translucent, *being careful to allow neither the garlic nor onion to brown.*

Reduce heat to LOW. Add *well-drained* black beans, diced green pepper, vinegar, grated orange zest, ground cinnamon and cumin, oregano, and chopped fresh coriander (*cilantro*). Stir in ground red pepper (cayenne) to taste. Cook, stirring frequently, for about 10 minutes or until heated through.

Keep warm on a warming tray until ready to serve.

Serve black beans and rice with chilled CUBAN MANGO RELISH.

                          Yields 8 servings
                        adequate for 6 people

Notes: *The mango relish really tastes better if it is made early in the day.

          When required, this recipe may be halved.

1/8 SERVING – PROTEIN = 9.2 g.; FAT = 2.2 g.; CARBOHYDRATE = 53.5 g.;
CALORIES = 248; CALORIES FROM FAT = 8%

BAKED *CHRISTOPHENES* (*CHAYOTE*) AND ONIONS *AU GRATIN* AS PREPARED IN MARTINIQUE
TPT - 50 minutes

Christophenes may not be as well known as they should be because they have a real identity problem. The small tropical squash is known as christophene in the Caribbean, mango squash, vegetable pear, chuchu, pepinello, choco in Australia, xuxu in Brazil, cho-cho in Great Britain, and brionne in France. If you are still trying to find it, try looking for it as chayote, which is the name most often used in Latin America and in greengrocers in the United States except those in Louisiana where it is called mirleton. Christophenes have a delicate flavor and a firm flesh, and every part of the squash is edible as are the shoots, leaves, and roots.

2 *christophenes* (*chayote*)—peeled and chopped into small pieces*
1 cup *boiling* water
Pinch salt

1 small onion—chopped
1 tablespoon butter
Freshly ground black pepper, to taste
Tiny pinch ground red pepper (cayenne)

2 tablespoons multigrain breadcrumbs
1 tablespoon grated Parmesan cheese

Preheat oven to 350 degrees F. Prepare a 1-quart soufflé dish or other oven-to-table baking dish by coating with non-stick lecithin spray coating.

In a saucepan set over *MEDIUM* heat, combine chopped *christophenes* (*chayote*), *boiling* water, and salt. Cook until squash is soft—about 20 minutes. Drain thoroughly. Turn into a mixing bowl. Mash with a potato masher or fork until squash is well-mashed.

Add chopped onion, butter, black pepper, and ground red pepper (cayenne). Mix well. Turn into prepared baking dish.

BAKED *CHRISTOPHENES* (*CHAYOTE*) AND ONIONS *AU GRATIN* AS PREPARED IN MARTINIQUE (cont'd)

Sprinkle the top with breadcrumbs and grated cheese. Bake in preheated 350 degree F. oven for about 15 minutes, or until the top is lightly browned.

Serve at once.

Notes: *The darker the color, the better the taste.

This recipe can be doubled, when required.

Yields 6 servings
adequate for 4 people

1/6 SERVING – PROTEIN = 1.6 g.; FAT = 2.4 g.; CARBOHYDRATE = 5.9 g.;
CALORIES = 48; CALORIES FROM FAT = 45%

CARIBBEAN BANANA CUSTARD CORNBREAD
TPT - 1 hour and 13 minutes

Please do not pass this by as just another cornbread recipe. It is anything but an ordinary accompaniment to a fruit salad or as a breakfast or brunch offering . . . warm, soft, creamy, and really quite special. Leftovers can reappear for lunch as an unusual base for chili.

3/4 cup unbleached white flour
1/4 cup whole wheat flour
3/4 cup yellow corn meal
1 teaspoon baking powder
1/2 teaspoon baking soda

1/2 cup *fat-free* pasteurized eggs (the equivalent of 2 eggs)
2 tablespoons butter—*melted*

1 1/2 tablespoons sugar
2 cups skimmed milk
1 1/2 tablespoons white distilled vinegar

1 *very ripe* banana—*well-mashed*

1 cup light cream *or* half and half

Preheat oven to 350 degrees F. Prepare an 8- or 9-inch non-stick-coated round cake pan by coating with non-stick lecithin spray coating.

Into a large mixing bowl, sift white and whole wheat flours, corn meal, baking powder, and baking soda. Set aside until required.

In a mixing bowl, using a wire whisk, beat pasteurized eggs lightly. *Gradually* beat in *melted* butter and continue beating until well-combined.

Add sugar, milk, and vinegar. Beat well.

Using a wooden spoon, stir sifted dry ingredients and mashed bananas into egg mixture. Stir until the batter is free of lumps but *do not overstir*. Pour batter into prepared cake pan.

Pour cream into the center of the batter. *Do not stir!*

Bake in preheated 350 degree F. oven for 55 minutes, or until *lightly browned*.

Serve warm. Cut into wedges as with a pie or cake.

Yields 8 servings
adequate for 5-6 people

Notes: This recipe may be halved in a 9 x 5 x 3-inch loaf pan. Baking time will have to be reduced to about 35 minutes.

Leftovers *can not* be successfully reheated.

1/8 SERVING – PROTEIN = 7.0 g.; FAT = 6.5 g.; CARBOHYDRATE = 30.4 g.;
CALORIES = 190; CALORIES FROM FAT = 31%

The Americas–Caribbean

"TARO" GREENS AND VEGETABLES IN THE STYLE OF THE VIRGIN ISLANDS
Callaloo

TPT - 31 minutes

If you have had poi in Hawaii then you are acquainted with the corm of the taro plant, Colocasia esculenta. Historically this tropical plant has nurtured many cultures who learned to process every part of the plant so has to avoid its ill effects. The root contains high levels of calcium oxalate and therefore can contribute to kidney stones so it must be cooked. The huge elephant-shaped ears, known in the Caribbean as callaloo, are toxic when eaten raw but quite safe after cooking especially if a pinch of baking soda is added to the cooking water. Collected by the explorers, the dramatic plant must have been quite a topic of conversation when it was introduced to Europeans. It is no less a topic of conversation when it is planted in American gardens. Only three plants, rice, the lotus, and taro can be grown successfully in flooded areas. Actually taro corms require much water to survive and are therefore only a novelty for most gardeners and a challenge to professional growers. An approximation of the taste of the taro leaves can be achieved by using a combination of spinach and Swiss chard which is what I have done in this version of the popular Caribbean stew.

3 cups *boiling* water
1 medium sweetpotato—peeled and diced
1 small eggplant—peeled, and diced
5 ounces fresh spinach—well-rinsed, stems removed, and chopped
5 ounces red-stalked Swiss chard—trimmed, well-rinsed, and chopped
3/4 cup *finely* chopped onion
2 large garlic cloves—*finely* chopped
1 tablespoon chopped fresh thyme *or* 1/2 teaspoon crumbled dried thyme
3 tablespoons chopped fresh parsley

2 tablespoons GARLIC–BASIL VINEGAR *[see index]* or **vinegar of choice**
1/2 teaspoon *jalapeño chili* sauce
1/2 teaspoon sugar
Salt, to taste
Freshly ground black pepper, to taste

In a small kettle set over *MEDIUM* heat, combine *boiling* water, diced sweetpotato and eggplant, chopped spinach, chopped Swiss chard, *finely* chopped onion and garlic, and chopped thyme and parsley. *Reduce heat to LOW-MEDIUM*, cover, and simmer for 15-20 minutes. Stir occasionally.

Add vinegar, *jalapeño* sauce, sugar, salt, and pepper.* Allow to simmer for 5-7 minutes more. Turn into a heated serving bowl.

Serve hot.

Yields 6 servings
adequate for 4 people

Notes: *About 1/4 cupful chopped green or red bell pepper can be added at this point, if desired.

This recipe can be halved, or doubled, when required.

1/6 SERVING – PROTEIN = 2.9 g.; FAT = 0.4 g.; CARBOHYDRATE = 9.2 g.;
CALORIES = 65; CALORIES FROM FAT = 2%

NUTMEG ICE CREAM
TPT - 8 hours and 12 minutes;
8 hours = freezing period

French vanilla ice cream takes on a whole new character when nutmeg is added. This recipe can be found on menus all over the Caribbean. It is a wonderful menu maker anytime but we especially like to enjoy this with a late-season peach to celebrate the coming of autumn.

2/3 cup *fat-free* sweetened condensed milk
1 tablespoon water
1/2 cup *fat-free* pasteurized eggs* (the equivalent of 2 eggs)
2 teaspoons pure vanilla extract
3/4 teaspoon freshly grated nutmeg

1 cup heavy whipping cream

Prepare a 7 x 3 x 2-inch non-stick-coated loaf pan by placing it in the freezer until required.

In a large bowl, combine sweetened condensed milk, water, pasteurized eggs, vanilla extract, and grated nutmeg. Stir to blend thoroughly.

NUTMEG ICE CREAM (cont'd)

Using an electric mixer fitted with *chilled* beaters or by hand, using a *chilled* wire whisk, beat heavy cream in a *chilled* bowl until stiff. Set aside.

Whisk-fold stiffly whipped cream *gently*, but *thoroughly*, into egg–milk mixture.

Pour mixture into chilled loaf pan. Spread evenly. Cover tightly with aluminum foil. Freeze overnight or until firm—about 8 hours.

Either scoop ice cream from pan to serve or remove entire block of ice cream from pan and slice.

Leftovers should be returned to the freezer, tightly covered.

Yields about eight 1/2-cup serving

Notes: *Because raw eggs present the danger of *Salmonella* poisoning, commercially-available pasteurized eggs are recommended for use in preparing this dish.

This recipe is easily doubled, when required. Use a 9 x 5 x 3-inch non-stick-coated loaf pan.

1/8 SERVING (i. e., per 1/2 cupful) –
PROTEIN = 4.1 g.; FAT = 9.8 g.; CARBOHYDRATE = 17.6 g.;
CALORIES = 179; CALORIES FROM FAT = 49%

CARIBBEAN SWEET COFFEE *COULIS*
TPT - 8 minutes

I have never had tiramisu as good as that that I had in a small restaurant we frequented in Rome during our stay. A pool of coffee coulis decorated the plate at lunch time and was quickly absorbed by the bottom cake layer; later in the day a liqueur was used . . . Oh, what a memory . . . This assertive coffee coulis, to which Tia Maria or Kahlua is added is delicious with ice cream, cakes, molded puddings, and scoops of ricotta cheese.

1 1/2 tablespoons freeze-dried coffee granules
1/4 cup *boiling* water

1 1/2 tablespoons *Tia Maria or Kahlua* liqueur
1/8 teaspoon corn starch
1/2 teaspoon pure vanilla extract
3 tablespoons sugar

In a saucepan set over *LOW-MEDIUM* heat, combine coffee granules and *boiling* water. Stir to dissolve coffee thoroughly.

In a small bowl, combine liqueur, corn starch, vanilla extract, and sugar. Stir until corn starch is in suspension. Add to coffee and cook, stirring constantly with a wire whisk, until sugar is dissolved and sauce has thickened. Pour into a small pitcher. Refrigerate until required.

Yields about 6 tablespoonfuls

Note: This recipe can be halved or doubled, when required.

1/9 SERVING (i. e., 2 teaspoonfuls) –
PROTEIN = 0.0 g.; FAT = 0.0 g.; CARBOHYDRATE = 5.3 g.;
CALORIES = 25; CALORIES FROM FAT = 0%

CARIBBEAN MANGO PUDDING
Pastre de Mango
TPT - 1 hour and 19 minutes;
1 hour = chilling period

This version of a far richer Caribbean specialty is a refreshing end to a tropical or Asian meal.

2 cups chopped fresh *or* canned mango
2 tablespoons freshly squeezed lime juice
2 tablespoons *light, sulfite-free* coconut milk*

3/4 cup *cold* skimmed milk
2 tablespoons *fat-free* sweetened condensed milk
1/4 cup corn starch
1 tablespoon firmly packed *light* brown sugar

In the container of the electric blender or in the work bowl of the food processor, combine chopped mango, lime juice, and coconut milk. Process to form a *very* smooth purée.

CARIBBEAN MANGO PUDDING (cont'd)

In the top half of a double boiler, combine *cold* skimmed milk and sweetened condensed milk. Using a wire whisk, stir until well-combined. Add corn starch and brown sugar. Whisk well *until corn starch is completely in suspension.* Stir in puréed mango mixture. Place over simmering water.

Bring pudding mixture to a boil. Continue cooking, stirring almost constantly with a wire whisk, until pudding is uniformly thickened—about 2-3 minutes. Remove from heat and turn pudding into a 1-quart soufflé dish or other shallow serving bowl. Refrigerate for at least 1 hour, or until thoroughly chilled.**

Notes: *Canned, *sulfite-free* coconut milk is available in well-stocked grocery stores in either the international section or beverage section. Leftover coconut milk can be frozen.

**This dessert makes a lovely presentation if spooned into wine glasses or champagne flutes. Allow the cooked pudding to cool slightly before spooning it into the glasses.

This recipe can be doubled when required.

Yields 4 servings
adequate for 3-4 people

1/4 SERVING – PROTEIN = 2.6 g.; FAT = 1.7 g.; CARBOHYDRATE = 46.1 g.;
CALORIES = 204; CALORIES FROM FAT = 8%

LOW-FAT CUBAN ANISE-SCENTED SWEET EGG CUSTARD
Natilla Cubana con Sirup con Anis

TPT - 8 hours and 53 minutes;
       4 hours = anise infusion period;
       10 minutes = cooling period;
       4 hours = refrigeration period

The natilla and flans, rich in egg yolks, that we enjoyed in Spain and Portugal were inevitably made with a caramelized topping. The Cuban versions we have sampled range from those with the traditional caramelized topping to firm, spice-scented pastry-like squares or diamonds dispatched from delis and bakeries in cupcake papers.

Although most natilla are either made from milk in which a cinnamon quill has been allowed to infuse or are garnished with a sprinkling of cinnamon, I find this anise-infused version a change and a pleasure. We do not begin with a caramelized base but we do occasionally sprinkle anise-scented granulated sugar over the chilled custard just before serving.

3 cups skimmed milk
2 star anise

16 ounces *fat-free* **pasteurized eggs (the equivalent of 8 eggs)**

1 cup skimmed milk
1/4 corn starch
1 cup sugar

1 teaspoon pure vanilla extract

1 tablespoon ANISE–SPICED SUGAR *[see recipe which follows]*

In a large saucepan set over *MEDIUM* heat, combine the 3 cupfuls milk and whole star anise. Heat to just below the boiling boil. Remove from heat and set aside at room temperature for 4 hours to allow for flavor infusion.

In a large measuring cup, combine the remaining 1 cupful milk with corn starch and sugar. Using a wire whisk, beat until corn starch is completely in suspension. Set aside until required.

Remove star anise from the milk.* Place the saucepan with the anise-scented milk over *LOW-MEDIUM* heat. Using a wire whisk, gradually beat in pasteurized eggs. Cook, stirring constantly with a wire whisk, until mixture begins to thicken.

Add milk–corn starch–sugar suspension and cook, stirring constantly with a wire whisk, until mixture thickens.

Remove from heat and allow to cool for about 10 minutes.

Whisk in vanilla extract.

LOW-FAT CUBAN ANISE-SCENTED SWEET EGG CUSTARD (cont'd)

Divide among eight dessert cups or sherbet glasses. Refrigerate for at least four hours, or overnight, if preferred.

Serve chilled, sprinkled with ANISE–SPICED SUGAR, if desired.

Notes: *Washed and dried thoroughly, the cloves of the star anise can be stored and then used again.

This recipe can be halved, when required.

Yields 8 individual servings

1/8 SERVING – PROTEIN = 9.5 g.; FAT = 0.2 g.; CARBOHYDRATE = 48.3 g.; CALORIES = 210; CALORIES FROM FAT = <1%

SPICED SUGAR
TPT - 2 weeks and 2 minutes;
2 weeks = flavor development period

In addition to the lavender sugar, which we always had on hand, I have found that other spices can be used to produce spiced sugars that can add a little excitement to a dish. Below is a basic recipe in which whole spices can be interchanged according to your sugar-and-spice mood. Spiced sugars can be used as part of the sugar required to make cakes, cookies, custards, or to flavor a frosting or glaze, and you can just sprinkle the scented sugar over a dessert of fresh fruit. . . or . . . or . . . .

1/2 cup sugar
8 whole anise cloves
   or 10 whole cloves
   or 2 two-inch cinnamon quill pieces
   or 1 or 2 slices crystallized ginger
   or 2 two-inch vanilla bean pieces
   or 8 whole cardamom pods
   or 2 whole nutmegs, halved

In a glass jelly jar, combine sugar and the desired whole spices. Cover tightly and store in a cool, dry place. Store for about 2 weeks before using to allow the flavor of the spice to thoroughly penetrate the sugar. Shake occasionally to expose the sugar to the spice for a more uniform taste.

Yields 8 tablespoonfuls

Notes: This recipe can be doubled, when required.

Leftover spices can, of course, be used for other purposes.

1/24 SERVING (i. e., per teaspoonful) –
PROTEIN = 0.0 g.; FAT = 0.0 g.; CARBOHYDRATE = 4.7 g.;
CALORIES =18; CALORIES FROM FAT = 0%

CARIBBEAN *CARAMBOLA* AND ORANGE DESSERT
TPT - 5 minutes

How often I pass someone in my grocery store musing over starfruit (carambola) wondering out loud what to do with them. When the pulp is combined with orange pulp, the result is an amazing marriage of flavors. That is why, I assume, this dessert is called "matrimony" in the Caribbean where you will often find it on a menu.

Pulp of 6 ripe starfruit (*carambola*)*
3 navel oranges—peeled and chopped
6 tablespoonfuls *fat-free* sweetened condensed milk

Freshly grated nutmeg

In a mixing bowl, combine starfruit pulp and chopped oranges. Toss to mix. Add sweetened condensed milk. Stir to coat the fruit uniformly. Divide among six wine glasses.

Sprinkle each serving with nutmeg. Keep refrigerated until ready to serve.

Yields 6 individual servings.

Notes: *To get at the pulp of a starfruit, cut off the bottom less than halfway down. The pulp can then be easily scooped out.

This recipe can be halved or doubled, when required.

1/6 SERVING – PROTEIN = 3.6 g.; FAT = 0.5 g.; CARBOHYDRATE = 29.5 g.;
CALORIES = 130; CALORIES FROM FAT = 4%

The Americas

Argentina

The first use of the name Argentina, derived from the Latin word *argentum* meaning silver, was found in the logs of sixteenth century explorations at the mouth of the Rio de la Plata, the "Silver River." The explorers did not know that the land they "discovered" had been occupied for centuries prior to its conquest by the Incas in 1480 but today we do know, as a result of archeological evidence in Patagonia, that human habitation dates to 11,000 BC. The Argentine Republic, the second largest nation in South America and the eighth largest nation in the world, is home to an estimated 40.5 million people.

Wilma, a college freshman housemate with whom I drank cocoa every morning, was my earliest introduction to Argentine food. Hot chocolate was what she drank every morning at home and she was homesick that first semester as were we all. Her German ancestors had emigrated to Argentina so until I met my husband, I erroneously assumed that Germany was the major European influence in that country so far from my own, at the southern tip of South America so close to Antarctica. Because quotas closely controlled immigration into the United States in the early part of the twentieth century, many Europeans, including some that would eventually marry into my husband's family, chose to immigrate to South American countries and then immigrate into the United States under more liberal quotas assigned to those countries. Italians poured into Argentina. Many stayed on and influenced the cuisine mightily but others eventually did make their way to the United States.

Food of the Argentine, thus influenced by successive waves of European immigration, does indeed pay homage to Italy and to Germany but food and eating patterns in Argentina are far more global. Yes, you find rabbit in red wine as in Calabria, breaded veal cutlet with cheese and ham in the style of Milan, pizza and pasta dishes as in Sicily, gelato, and espresso; apple pancakes, potato dumplings, and roast suckling pig introduced from Germany; and a quite different version of the famous Moscow salad known here simply as Russian salad or *Ensalada Rusa*. This nation of meat eaters, with an average annual consumption of 220 pounds per capita, consumes beef stew and *chartcuterie* in the French style, corn pie with meat, and seafood stews, also with meat, and, of course, *empananadas* stuffed with meat and barbecued meats with a *chimichuri* marinade, similar to that seen in Nicaragua. The gauchos of the Pampas really have their work cut out for them because the demand for meat, especially for beef, is high. In a country where soybeans represent a major crop, a vegetarian is challenged in the large cosmopolitan city of Buenos Aires unless the plan is to eat cheese and bread or *pasta* and visit *heladerias*, ice cream parlors, frequently. However, in provincial areas one finds increased consumption of the "three sisters" of my childhood, the same vegetables so valued by the Iroquois Nation. More use is made of corn, beans, pumpkins and squashes, the staples of native cooking in both hemispheres of the Americas. Game and wonderful fruits are abundant and are served without the European-influenced embellishment seen in the city.

The Americas – Argentina

Please note that *Ensalada Rusa* is presented in this menu as a first course, as it often is in Moscow, and the tossed salad is served after the main course, as it is in Italy.

Argentine-Styled Russian Salad
Ensalada Rusa

~~~~~~~~~~~~~~~~~~~~

Soymeat with *Chimichuri* and Herb Seasoning Over *Pasta*
Soya y Pasta Chimichuri

~~~~~~~~~~

Baked Corn and Cheese Pudding
Cazuela con Maize y Queso

Steamed Swiss chard

~~~~~~~~~~~~~~~~~~~~~~

Mixed Greens

with

Summer Fruit Dressing

Salad Burnet and Shallot Vinegar with Pepper

~

Puffed Pastry with Argentine Sweet Milk
Milhojas con Dulce de Leche
and

Grilled Pineapple with Honey – Lime Glaze
Piña Parillada con Lima

ARGENTINE-STYLED RUSSIAN SALAD
Ensalada Rusa

TPT - about 3 hours;
30 minutes = vegetable chilling period;
2 hours = marination period

Patterned after the Russian specialty known as "Salat Moscovski," or Moscow Salad, this colorful and popular salad is known in Argentina as "Ensalada Rusa," or Russian Salad. Would that all recipes would lead one back to its origins so easily. Every Argentine version of this salad that I have encountered eliminates the cucumber, celery, mushrooms, pickle, scallion, and capers of the traditional Moscow Salad, adding sweetpotatoes, beets, and, sometimes, chopped eggs. For convenience, I often prepare and chill the beets and potatoes with the evening meal the night before.

Note that every element should be the same size; nothing should be larger than a pea.

2 medium beets with root intact and 2-inches of
   leaf stem attached—well-washed

4 quarts *boiling* water
2 medium potatoes—peeled
1 large sweetpotato—peeled

1 large carrot—peeled or scraped and diced

1/3 cup freshly shelled *or frozen* peas
1/4 cup CLASSIC FRENCH DRESSING *[see index]*
Salt, to taste
Freshly ground black pepper, to taste

2 tablespoons *calorie-reduced or light* mayonnaise
1/4 teaspoon freshly squeezed lemon juice

ARGENTINE-STYLED RUSSIAN SALAD (cont'd)

Preheat oven to 375 degrees F.

Cut six squares of aluminum foil. Place a well-washed beet on each foil square. Gather the corners of the aluminum foil up and twist to form a tightly-sealed package.

Set wrapped beets in a roasting pan in preheated 375 degree F. oven and bake for 45 minutes, or until beets are tender when pierced with a fork. *(Open a test package to be sure.)* Remove to the counter top and allow to cool slightly until packages are cool enough to handle. Move aluminum foil back and forth until skins loosen and slip off. Open packages and discard foil. Cut stem end and root end off, discarding both. Chill for at least 30 minutes. Peel and dice.

In a large kettle set over *MEDIUM* heat, combine *boiling* water, potatoes, and sweetpotato. Boil until cooked through, but still *firm*—about 20-22 minutes. *(They will yield to a fork, but not crumble.)* Drain thoroughly and chill for at least 30 minutes. Peel and dice.

Cook diced carrot in *boiling* water to cover until cooked through, but *still firm*—about 8 minutes. Drain thoroughly.

In a large bowl with cover, combine diced beets, potatoes, sweetpotatoes, and carrot with *frozen* peas. Toss gently to combine.

Add French dressing, salt, and black pepper. Toss gently to coat thoroughly. Cover bowl and marinate in the refrigerator for at least 2 hours, occasionally tossing to redistribute settled marinade.

Just before serving, turn salad into a fine sieve and allow to drain *very thoroughly*. *(About 2 tablespoonfuls of marinade should drain off.)* Turn drained vegetables into a large mixing bowl.

In a small bowl, combine mayonnaise and lemon juice. Blend well. Add to vegetables. Toss *gently*, but *thoroughly*. Turn into a serving dish. Chill until required.

Serve into individual lettuce leaf cups, if desired.

Yields about 8 servings
adequate for 4-6 people

Note: This recipe is easily doubled, when required.

1/8 SERVING – PROTEIN = 1.2 g.; FAT = 3.6 g.; CARBOHYDRATE = 12.1 g.;
CALORIES = 88; CALORIES FROM FAT = 37%

SOYMEAT WITH *CHIMICHURI* AND HERB SEASONING OVER *PASTA* WITH THE TASTE OF ARGENTINA
Soya y Pasta Chimichuri

TPT - 24 minutes

When I took Spanish back in high school and college, the word for pasta was either "macaroni" or "alimentos." Now pasta has comfortably entered my Spanish dictionary. The combination of Italian seasoning and chimichuri sauce, used extensively in Argentina and other South American countries, gives this a taste you can neither imagine nor forget. The long shell pasta known as "castellane" is perfect for this dish since it scoops up the seasoned topping beautifully, but it is less widely available than are "orecchiette" ("little ears") and "campanelle" ("bells"), both of which work well too.

3 quarts *boiling* water
3/4 pound *castellane, orecchiette, or campanelle pasta*, as preferred

1 tablespoon *extra virgin* olive oil
8 ounces *frozen* vegetarian "ground beef"*

2 tablespoons NICARAGUAN GARLIC AND PARSLEY SAUCE *(Salsa Chimichuri)* [see index], or to taste**
1 teaspoon HERBED ITALIAN SEASONING MIX *(Miscuglio di Erbas Italiano)* [see index], or to taste

In a kettle set over *MEDIUM-HIGH* heat, cook *pasta* in *boiling* water according to package directions. Drain thoroughly, shaking residual water from the *pasta*.

While the *pasta* is cooking, in a large skillet set over *LOW-MEDIUM* heat, heat oil. Add ground soymeat and cook, stirring frequently, until soymeat is defrosted.

Add *chimichuri* sauce and Italian seasoning mixture. Cook, stirring frequently, until soymeat is well-coated with the seasoning mixtures and is heated through. Add well-drained, cooked *pasta*. Toss and cook, stirring constantly, for a few minutes, or until heated through. Turn into a heated serving bowl.

SOYMEAT WITH *CHIMICHURI* AND HERB SEASONING OVER *PASTA* WITH THE TASTE OF ARGENTINA (cont'd)

Serve at once.

Yields 6 servings
adequate for 4 people

Notes: *Several meat analogue products exist, both frozen and dried, which can be used to replace ground beef in dishes such as this. When using the dehydrated products such as "So Soya," follow the package directions for rehydration before proceeding.

**There are probably as many versions of *chimichuri* sauce as there are cooks who make it. The Nicaraguan version, which is included elsewhere in this volume, just happens to be our favorite.

This recipe can be halved or doubled.

1/6 SERVING – PROTEIN = 13.7 g.; FAT = 7.5 g.; CARBOHYDRATE = 44.6 g.;
CALORIES = 294; CALORIES FROM FAT = 23%

ARGENTINE BAKED CORN AND CHEESE PUDDING
Cazuela con Maize y Queso
TPT - 1 hour and 7 minutes

This casserole is so very reminiscent in flavor to a top-of-the-stove corn custard with cheddar cheese that was frequently served over noodles when I was a child during World War II, but it is flavored much more assertively with chilies and a salty, dry cheese much like pecorino Romano. The corn custard mixture is often baked as a pie instead of as a pudding.

1 tablespoon butter
1 pound green (fresh) or *frozen* corn kernels

1 cup *two-percent* milk

1 tablespoon butter
1 cup *finely* chopped onion

1 tablespoon *finely* chopped mild green *chilies**
1 teaspoon *jalapeño chili* sauce*

1/2 cup *fat-free* pasteurized eggs (the equivalent of 2 eggs)
1 tablespoon unbleached white flour
1/4 teaspoon freshly ground black pepper
1/4 cup grated *pecorino Romano* cheese

1/4 cup *pecorino Romano* cheese

Preheat oven to 325 degrees F. Prepare a 2-quart soufflé dish or other oven-to-table baking dish by coating generously with non-stick lecithin spray coating.

In a skillet set over *MEDIUM* heat, melt 1 tablespoonful butter and *thawed* corn. Sauté for about 5 minutes. *Reduce heat to LOW-MEDIUM.*

Add milk, cover, and simmer until corn is tender— about 8 minutes. Using the food processor fitted with steel knife, process the corn and milk to a coarse purée. Set aside briefly.

In the same skillet set over *MEDIUM* heat, melt the remaining 1 tablespoonful butter. Add onion and sauté until onion is soft and translucent, *being careful not to allow onion to brown.*

Add green *chilies* and *jalapeño chili* sauce. Continue sautéing for 2 minutes more. *Remove from heat.*

Add corn purée. Set aside briefly.

In a mixing bowl, combine pasteurized eggs, flour, black pepper, and 1/4 cupful of grated cheese. Stir to combine.

While stirring constantly, add corn mixture to egg mixture. Pour into prepared baking dish. Sprinkle remaining 1/4 cupful grated cheese over. Bake in preheated 325 degree F. oven for about 35 minutes, or until golden.

Serve at once.

Yields 6 servings
adequate for 4 people

Notes: *Hot peppers, such as *jalapeños* or *serranos* can replace this combination of green *chilies* and *jalapeño* sauce.

If desired, the filling can be used to fill a baked pie crust.

The Americas – Argentina

ARGENTINE BAKED CORN AND CHEESE PUDDING (cont'd)

This recipe can be halved or doubled. Be sure to choose an appropriately smaller or larger baking dish when necessary.

1/6 SERVING – PROTEIN = 8.3 g.; FAT = 6.8 g.; CARBOHYDRATE = 21.8 g.; CALORIES = 173; CALORIES FROM FAT = 35%

SUMMER FRUIT DRESSING
TPT - 30 minutes

This salad dressing is one that I turn to in the summer, especially when we have spent hours in the garden and the prospect of lifting the dinner fork to the mouth seems like almost as much work as pushing the gardening fork into the dense clay soil. Popular in Argentina and throughout Latin America and the Caribbean, it is a good dressing for tossed greens, garden-fresh tomatoes, and pasta or fruit salads.

1/4 cup apricot or peach nectar
1/4 cup freshly squeezed orange juice
3 tablespoons SALAD BURNET AND SHALLOT VINEGAR WITH PEPPER *[see recipe which follows]*, **rice wine vinegar,** *or* **distilled white vinegar, if preferred**
1 tablespoon freshly squeezed lime juice
1 tablespoon *extra virgin* **olive oil**
1 teaspoon wildflower honey
Freshly ground black pepper, to taste

In the container of the electric blender, combine apricot nectar, orange juice, vinegar, lime juice, olive oil, honey, and black pepper. Blend until smooth. Turn into a cruet.

Shake vigorously before serving. Refrigerate leftovers.

Yields 3/4 cupful

Note: This recipe can be doubled, when required.

1/12 SERVING (i. e., per tablespoonful) –
PROTEIN = 0.04 g.; FAT = 0.9 g.; CARBOHYDRATE = 1.5 g.;
CALORIES = 14; CALORIES FROM FAT = 68%

SALAD BURNET AND SHALLOT VINEGAR WITH PEPPER
TPT - 4 weeks and 14 minutes;
4 weeks = flavor development period

This is a variation of a classic British herbed vinegar. Rice wine vinegar provides a mellow base for the somewhat cucumber-like taste of the salad burnet and shallots add a few exclamation points.

1 quart rice wine vinegar

2 cups freshly picked and *well-washed* **salad burnet leaves***
2 large shallot bulbs—peeled, root end removed, and separated into cloves
1 tablespoon whole black, pink, white, and red peppercorns

Salad burnet sprigs, well-washed, for garnish
Chive blades, for garnish

Sterilize a one-quart canning jar, lid, and ring.

Pack *well-washed* salad burnet leaves, shallot cloves, and mixed peppercorns into the sterilized canning jar.

Pour vinegar over the salad burnet leaves. Using a chopstick, stir leaves for about 30 seconds to start the infusion. Seal the jar and place in a cool, dark place for 4 weeks.

Sterilize a clear, condiment bottle, or several if you are planning to give the vinegar as gifts.

Place a fine sieve over a one-quart measuring cup or mixing bowl. Strain the vinegar, discarding the salad burnet leaves, shallot cloves, and peppercorns recovered.

Pour vinegar into sterilized condiment bottle or bottles. Insert a sprig of salad burnet and a couple of blades of chives, for garnish. Cap and label.

Store at cool room temperature for up to three months.

Yields 3 cupfuls

The Americas–Argentina

SALAD BURNET AND SHALLOT VINEGAR WITH PEPPER

Notes: *Salad burnet *(Poterium sanguisorba)* is an easily grown herb of the rose family which has a fascinating cucumber taste, a beautiful fountain-like growing form, and graceful, serrated leaves. In dry, limestone soil and with full sun, it is an aggressive biennial which readily self-seeds. It actually does not do well in very rich soil and it does prefer low humidity. Pinch the flower heads which appear the second year to control its spreading and to prevent the leaves from becoming bitter. Encourage a new plant or two every few years since older plants do tend to become woody and lose their tender, fresh taste. Salad burnet is a wonderful addition to salads and cold drinks, greatly prized by Italian cooks who call it *pimpinella*.

Insects often lay their eggs on the underside of leaves so be careful to wash herb leaves well.

1/48 SERVING (i. e., per tablespoonful) – PROTEIN = 0.0 g.; FAT = 0.0 g.; CARBOHYDRATE = 0.9 g.; CALORIES = 2; CALORIES FROM FAT = 0%

ARGENTINE PUFFED PASTRY WITH ARGENTINE SWEET MILK
Milhojas con Dulce de Leche

TPT - 1 hour and 22 minutes;
40 minutes = pastry room temperature adjustment;
20 minutes = cooling period

Years and years ago, after little more than a half hour's instruction through a television program with the remarkable Julia Child, I attempted to make my own puffed pastry. It was so very much work that I abandoned the project for all eternity and chose to use the convenience and consistent quality of frozen puff pastry. I had tried making my own strudel and phyllo dough and had also turned to the frozen products. Frozen puff pastry is very good and easy to work with. On the other hand, canned "dulce de leche" is a product that I would sooner avoid since making a non-fat version is quite simple.

1 sheet *frozen* puff pastry—*brought to room temperature*

18 tablespoonfuls prepared ARGENTINE SWEET MILK *(Dulce de Leche)* [see recipe which follows]

Remove pastry from refrigerator or freezer and allow to come to room temperature.

Preheat oven to 400 degrees F.* Prepare two baking sheets by lining with culinary parchment paper.

Cut pastry in half. Cut each half into six equal rectangular slices. Using a sharp knife, make shallow cuts in the pastry to create a diamond pattern. Transfer it to one of the culinary-lined baking sheets. Bake at 400 degrees F. for about 15 minutes, *checking to be sure that the pastry does not over-brown*. Remove from oven and allow to cool for about 20 minutes on the baking sheets.

Transfer two baked pastry "pillows" to each of six dessert plates. Set one pillow in the center and set the second pastry pillow askew, partially on the plate and partially up on the first pastry pillow. Drizzle 3 tablespoonfuls of *dulce de leche* over the two pastry pieces.

Serve immediately to preserve crispness of baked pastry.

Yields 6 individual servings

Note: This recipe can be halved, when required.

1/6 SERVING – PROTEIN = 5.1 g.; FAT = 11.0 g.; CARBOHYDRATE = 30.4 g.; CALORIES = 245; CALORIES FROM FAT = 40%

The Americas–Argentina

ARGENTINE SWEET MILK
Dulce de Leche

TPT - 1 hour and 20 minutes

Just think about a milk caramel melting in your mouth and you pretty much have the feel of "dulce de leche." It is used in a zillion ways. South Americans usually take the label off a can of sweetened condensed milk and boil the whole can for a couple of hours but this technique has the potential for injury should the can explode so I set out to find a safer way to get this sweet wonderfulness. I did not want to have to make it from scratch because sweetened condensed milk is, oh, so very convenient.

1 1/2 cups *fat-free* sweetened condensed milk

Put the sweetened condensed milk into the top half of the double boiler set over simmering water, partially covered. Allow to cook over *LOW-MEDIUM* heat for about 1 1/4 hours. It will thicken and caramelize to a golden brown. *Be careful not to allow the water to boil away.**

Notes: *Should the water level get to low, a metal jar top or canning ring placed in the water in the bottom of the double boiler will alert you.

This recipe can be doubled or tripled, as required.

Yields about 18 tablespoonfuls

1/18 SERVING (per tablespoonful) –
PROTEIN = 2.1 g.; FAT = 0.0 g.; CARBOHYDRATE = 16.4 g.;
CALORIES = 75; CALORIES FROM FAT = 0%

GRILLED PINEAPPLE WITH HONEY – LIME GLAZE
Piña Parillada con Lima

TPT - 2 hours and 14 minutes;
2 hours = marination period

These pineapple slices can just as easily be prepared on top of the stove using a grill pan or, if preferred, on an outdoor grill, even at a picnic site. The grill marks really look quite attractive. We serve these as a side or dramatic garnish with grilled or roasted vegetables or as a dessert with cookies, plain cake squares, or baked puff pastry.

**1/2 cup honey
1 tablespoon freshly grated lime zest
1/4 cup freshly squeezed lime juice
2 tablespoons freshly squeezed orange juice with pulp**

1 large ripe, peeled and cored pineapple—cut into 6 crosswise ring slices*

Fresh mint leaves, for garnish

In a *glass* baking dish, large enough to hold the six pineapple slices in a single layer, combine honey, lime zest, and lime and orange juices. Using a wire whisk, combine thoroughly.

Place cored pineapple slices into the marinade, turning to cover both sides. Cover dish with plastic wrap and allow to stand at room temperature for 1 hour. Turn each pineapple slice over, recover, and allow to stand at room temperature for an additional hour. Remove pineapple slices to a broiler pan. *Reserve marinade to serve as sauce.*

Preheat broiler to about 350 degrees F.

Broil pineapple slices on a broiler pan set about six inches below the heat source. Turn when the pineapple slices *just begin to color. Watch carefully since the sugars can char quite quickly.*

Transfer broiled pineapple to a serving platter. Pour reserved marinade over.

Serve warm or chilled, as preferred. Garnish with mint leaves before serving.

Yields 6 servings

Notes: *Many grocery stores carry fresh, peeled and cored pineapples. It saves a great deal of time.

This may be doubled if you have two large glass baking dishes in which to marinate the pineapple.

1/6 SERVING (i. e., per slice) –
PROTEIN = 0.7 g.; FAT = 0.3 g.; CARBOHYDRATE = 43.3 g.;
CALORIES = 165; CALORIES FROM FAT = 2%

Bolivia

To many, I'm sure, Lake Titicaca, South America's largest lake bordered by Bolivia and Peru and the world's highest navigable lake, is the answer to several "Trivial Pursuits" questions and the indigenous giant frogs, unique to this deep, salty lake that thrive at 12,507 feet above sea level, fascinate but tell us little about the nation of Bolivia, officially know as Plurinational State of Bolivia. The Tiahuanaco kingdom was established around Lake Titicaca in about 600 BC. Conquered by the Incas in the thirteenth century, it remained part of the Inca Empire until European colonization in the sixteenth century, during which period it was known as "*Alto Peru*" and administered by the Viceroyalty of Peru. Independence was declared in 1809 but it was followed by war and instability, with one *coup d'eta* after another from 1809 to 1981 for a total of 193 governmental changes. Neighboring countries have used this instability to appropriate Bolivian territory: Chile annexed the nitrate rich costal areas along the Pacific Ocean as a result of The Pacific War (1879-1883); Brazil took the rubber producing regions in 1903; The Chaco Wars with Paraguay (1928-30, 1933-1935) and the treaty agreements negotiated with Argentina, Brazil, and Peru. resulted in further loss of territory.

About fifteen percent of the population is descended, unmixed, from the Spanish colonists. In addition to this *criollos* population, about fifty-five percent are still designated as Amerindian while thirty percent are labeled *mestizo*. About 40,000 Mennonites have settled and thrive in eastern Bolivia bringing not only their language, an uniquely archaic German dialect, but also their farming practices. Their influence on the general population and their influence upon the principally Roman Catholic religious practices of the nation are minimal as it is here in central Pennsylvania but they have lived in harmony with the land and with their neighbors for decades.

Anyone who visits Bolivia quickly learns that Bolivians eat meat, and a lot of it. There is little hope for vegetarian tourists, who wish to eat safely, unless they are willing to eat cheese, bread, and fruit at every meal. I am reminded of the resistance of the Portuguese and Spanish as we traveled in Europe. The Portuguese kept saying things like, "You are rich Americans; you can certainly afford meat. Why would you choose to eat as do the poor?" The Spanish were more practical when we refused the meat courses, saying " . . . but the meat is included; you are paying for it whether we serve it or not." The Russians, quoting a recent article in Pravda, just denied that our sixteen-year old would reach adulthood without meat and, in essence, accused us of parental cruelty. Eating in Bolivia is definitely challenging to the vegetarian. About 1,290 different potatoes are grown in Bolivia but vegetarians do not live by potatoes alone. Meat or meat stock is added to almost everything and the consumption of protein is excessive, both for human health and the health of the planet. Even beans with rice or corn, a protein balanced combination quite sufficient for a meal, are customarily served with meat. Consequently, Bolivian restaurants that do have vegetarian entrees have begun to use soy meat analogue products to "imitate" the "look" to which Bolivians are accustomed. Since soybeans are a major cash crop of Bolivia, this is advantageous to both vegetarians and the economy.

You will note that I have included, as a first course, a rather substantial stew, a wonderful combination of flavors that I could not allow myself to exclude. Soups, such as tomato, peanut, and vegetable purées and even wheat may have been a more balanced approach to this menu but once you have tried *locoro*, you will understand why it is one of our favorite supper entrées and why we felt that it must be included.

Bolivian chocolate is a superior chocolate often compared with that of Switzerland. It would be a wonderful ending to a Bolivian meal.

Vegetable Stew
Locoro

~

Fried Tomato and Onion Salad with Brown Rice
Ensalada de Tomate y Cebolla Fritos con Arroz Integral

~~~~~~~~~~~~~~~~~~~~~

Baked Macaroni Casserole
Pastel de Macarones al Horno

Baked Beets   Oven-Roasted Cauliflower
Betarraga   *Coliflowr*

with

Chili and Tomato Sauce
Uchu Llajwa

~~~~~~~~~~~~~~~~~~~~~

Sweet Baby Bananas
Guineos

BOLIVIAN VEGETABLE STEW
Locoro

TPT - 1 hour

This hearty, peasant vegetable stew is just crammed full of good food. Where else can you find such an extraordinary harvest in a bowl? The flavor of the vegetables is accented by the cheese and the touch of fresh oregano but it needs little else save, perhaps, a bit of black pepper. We serve it with cornbread or a wheat flatbread.

Bolivians use a dense, green-skinned squash that is as big as a pumpkin for this stew. We prefer to use acorn or butternut squash but the small, meaty pumpkins or even sweetpotatoes can be substituted. The additions of tomato paste and sun-dried tomatoes give this nuances of flavor that you would never anticipate.

1 pound *small* potatoes—new or salad potatoes
   —scrubbed, peeled, and quartered
1/2 cup *fresh* lima beans*
2 quarts *boiling* water

1 pound peeled and seeded acorn *or* butternut
   squash—cut into 1-inch chunks
1 1/2 cups VEGETABLE STOCK FROM SOUP
   [see index] *or* other vegetarian stock of choice

1 tablespoon *high-heat* safflower *or* sunflower oil
1/2 medium onion—*finely* chopped
2 medium canned, *diced* tomatoes
1 tablespoon tomato paste

3 tablespoons chopped sun-dried tomatoes *or*
   OVEN–DRIED TOMATOES [see index]
1 teaspoon *finely* chopped fresh oregano
Freshly ground black pepper, to taste

1 small cob of corn—shucked, silk removed, and
   cut into 2-inch rounds

1/2 cup freshly shelled *or frozen* peas

1/2 cup diced *feta* cheese**

2 tablespoons chopped, fresh parsley

BOLIVIAN VEGETABLE STEW (cont'd)

In a large saucepan set over *MEDIUM-HIGH* heat, combine peeled and quartered potatoes, lima beans, and *boiling* water. Parboil potato and lima beans for about 20 minutes. Drain and set aside until required.

In the large saucepan set over *MEDIUM* heat, combine squash chunks and vegetable stock. Cook, stirring often and *gently*, for about 10 minutes or until squash begins to soften. Remove from heat briefly.

Meanwhile, in a skillet set over *MEDIUM* heat, heat oil. Add onion and sauté until onion is soft and translucent, *being careful not to allow onion to brown.*

Add chopped tomatoes, tomato paste, sun-dried tomatoes, oregano, and black pepper. Stir to combine. Add to squash and vegetable stock. Stir to combine well. Add parboiled potato quarters and lima beans, and corn rounds. Allow to cook for about 10 minutes, *gently* stirring every now and then.

Add peas.

When corn and peas are cooked, add cheese. Stir gently until cheese begins to melt. Turn into a heated serving bowl.

Serve at once, garnished with parsley.

Yields 6-8 servings
adequate for 4-6 people

Notes: *If using frozen lima beans, add them at the point when you add the corn rounds.

**If you prefer to serve this vegan, pass the cheese for those who may which to add it instead of stirring into the hot stew.

1/8 SERVING – PROTEIN = 3.7 g.; FAT = 2.8 g.; CARBOHYDRATE = 15.2 g.;
CALORIES = 101; CALORIES FROM FAT = 25%

BOLIVIAN FRIED TOMATO AND ONION SALAD WITH BROWN RICE

Ensalada de Tomate y Cebolla Fritas con Arroz

TPT - 1 hour and 13 minutes;
1 hour = refrigeration period

Americans visiting Bolivia are often challenged when food is cooked in excessive amounts of oil. This vegetable dish, served as a cold salad, is a case in point. If you have tasted this dish in Bolivia, you will probably not recognize my version because the oil used to fry the tomatoes and onions is considerably less, allowing for the taste of the vegetables to dominate.

1 tablespoon *extra virgin* olive oil
1/2 cup slivered onions

8 canned, *whole* tomatoes—well-drained and
 coarsely chopped
Pinch sugar
1/4 teaspoon chili powder, or to taste
1 cup *cold, steamed* long grain *brown* rice

1/4 cup crumbled *feta* cheese*

In a skillet set over *MEDIUM* heat, heat oil. Add slivered onions and sauté until onions are soft and translucent, *being careful not to allow onions to brown.*

Add tomatoes, sugar, and chili powder. Cook, stirring frequently, until most of the liquid exuded from the tomatoes has been evaporated. Turn into a mixing bowl.

Add *cold, cooked* rice. Stir to mix. Refrigerate for at least 1 hour to allow for flavor development. Turn into a serving bowl.

Garnish with crumbled *feta* cheese.

Serve chilled. Refrigerate leftovers.

Yields 6 servings
adequate for 4 people

Notes: *Feta* cheese is a good substitute for Bolivian *quesillo*, which is rarely available outside of Bolivia. For a vegan salad, just eliminate the cheese.

This recipe can be doubled, when required.

1/6 SERVING – PROTEIN = 2.5 g.; FAT = 7.9 g.; CARBOHYDRATE = 12.7 g.;
CALORIES = 131; CALORIES FROM FAT = 54%

The Americas – Bolivia

BOLIVIAN BAKED MACARONI CASSEROLE
Pastel de Macarones al Horno

TPT - 1 hour and 4 minutes

I discovered this Bolivian oven casserole and was struck by the similarity of it to the classic Greek "pastitso" and, to boot, it calls for a "quesillo" cheese which can most efficiently be replaced with feta cheese. Although usually made with beef broth, it is easily transformed into a meatless entrée and I often replace the simple tomato sauce with my marinara sauce or pizza sauce to save a few minutes preparation time on a busy day. This is a good family supper dish.

4 quarts water
1 tablespoon lemon juice
1 3-inch strip lemon zest
1/2 pound high-protein or whole wheat macaroni
—elbow or other shape of choice

1 tablespoon *extra virgin* olive oil
3/4 cup *finely* chopped onion

1/4 cup *finely* chopped peeled, seeded fresh tomato
 or canned tomatoes, if preferred
3 tablespoons tomato purée
2 teaspoons *very finely* chopped fresh parsley
Freshly ground black pepper, to taste
1/4 cup VEGETARIAN BROWN STOCK *[see index]* or VEGETABLE STOCK FROM SOUP *[see index]*

6 tablespoons *fat-free* pasteurized eggs*
1/4 cup *skimmed* milk

2 hard-cooked eggs—sliced

3 ounces *crumbled* Greek *feta* cheese**

1 tablespoon butter—melted

Preheat oven to 325 degrees F. Prepare a 1 1/2-quart soufflé dish or other oven-to-table casserole by coating with non-stick lecithin spray coating.

In a large kettle set over *HIGH* heat, bring water to the boil. Add lemon juice and zest. Add macaroni. Boil for about 10-12 minutes. Pour into a strainer and allow to drain thoroughly. Discard lemon zest.

In a skillet set over *MEDIUM* heat, heat oil. Add *finely* chopped onion. Sauté until onion is soft and translucent, *being careful not to allow the onion to brown.*

Add *finely* chopped tomato, tomato purée, *very finely* chopped parsley, black pepper, and vegetable stock. Allow to cook for about 10 minutes, stirring frequently. Remove from heat.

In a mixing bowl, combine *drained, cooked* macaroni, pasteurized eggs, and milk.
~ Pour *one-half* of the macaroni mixture into the prepared baking dish.

~ Spread *one-half* of the tomato sauce over the macaroni.

~ Layer one of the sliced, hard-cooked eggs over the tomato sauce.

~ Layer *one-half* of the crumbled cheese over the eggs.

~ Spoon the remaining macaroni over the cheese.

~ Top with the remaining tomato sauce.

~ Layer the remaining egg slices over.

~ Sprinkle the remaining cheese evenly over all.

~ Pour the melted butter over the top of the casserole.***

Bake in preheated 325 degree F. oven for about 20-25 minutes.

Serve hot.

Yields 6 servings
adequate for 4 people

BOLIVIAN BAKED MACARONI CASSEROLE (cont'd)

Notes: *Pasteurized eggs are especially useful since this version would normally require an awkward 1 1/2 whole eggs.

**If you have the availability of a good "*quesillo*," by all means use it.

***The casserole can be prepared to this point early in the day and brought to room temperature just before baking.

This recipe can be doubled, when required.

1/6 SERVING –   PROTEIN = 13.0 g.; FAT = 12.4 g.; CARBOHYDRATE = 32.5 g.;
CALORIES = 301; CALORIES FROM FAT = 37%

BOLIVIAN *CHILI* AND TOMATO SAUCE
Uchu Llajwa
TPT - 4 minutes

Uchu Llagwa is the Quechua Indian name for a hot sauce made with locoto hot pepper, a pepper similar in "fire" to the more familiar jalapeño pepper. Bolivians add this as a seasoning to soups and stews and provide it as a table sauce. This can be a fiery hot sauce or it can be adjusted to your taste by using bottled jalapeño chili sauce.

1 cup canned, *diced* tomatoes—drained
3 tablespoons chopped red bell pepper
2 tablespoons *finely* chopped onion
1 tablespoon *finely* chopped fresh coriander (*cilantro*)
1/2 teaspoon *jalapeño chili* sauce, or to taste
   —green or red, as preferred*
Pinch salt

In the work bowl of the food processor, combine tomatoes, chopped red pepper, *finely* chopped onion and fresh coriander (*cilantro*), *jalapeño chili* sauce, and salt. Process until very smooth. Transfer to a condiment bottle.

Keep refrigerated.

Yields 1 cupful

Notes: *Jalapeno* sauce is available in Hispanic groceries, food specialty stores, and in most grocery stores throughout the Southwest.

This recipe can be halved or doubled, when required.

1/16 SERVING (i. e., per tablespoonful) –
PROTEIN = 0.2 g.; FAT = 0.03 g.; CARBOHYDRATE = 0.8 g.;
CALORIES = 4; CALORIES FROM FAT = 6%

Brazil

First settled by exiled men in 1543, some forty years after Pedro Alvares Cabral claimed the land for Portugal, a voluntary immigration policy was enacted in 1549 that carried with it the promise of prosperity based then on sugar cane and later on gold. It brought families to what is now the fifth largest country in the world. Brazil occupies almost one-half of the continent of South American. A colony of Portugal from 1500 until 1822, it is no surprise that Brazilians speak Portuguese and that the cuisine strongly reflects that of Portugal but with divine contributions of a population as diverse as is the geography. Here one finds the world's largest wetlands, the Pantanal, and the important and endangered equatorial rain forest that surrounds the Amazon River, semiarid deserts in the northeast, forests filled with conifers in the temperate south, and tropical savannas in the central region of the country. One finds native peoples almost untouched by the twenty-first century world and bustling metropolitan coastal populations attune to that which is current and trendy. Brazil is a study in contrasts.

From colony, to empire, to fascist dictatorship, to federated republic, Brazil has progressed always carrying the influences of Amerindian and European settlers, not as a burden but with the pride of diversity. The importation of slaves from West Africa strongly influenced the culture and the cuisine, adding another layer of complexity. Germans, Italians, Lebanese, Syrians, and Poles brought their traditions and quite unlike our "melting pot" tradition of absorption these influences are still apparent in a cuisine which is really a collection of regional and immigrant traditions rather than an amalgam. Japanese, who immigrated, brought their farming practices, introducing the concept known as "night soil" in which human waste is used to fertilize. The gorgeous array of fruits available in Brazil can be quite deadly to the unconditioned tourist. The "night soil" system was introduced also into Portugal to increase crop yield to the everlasting chagrin of this author.

Wars with the native peoples, wars among the native peoples, wars with neighboring countries as the Portuguese forced expansion into lands claimed by the Spanish, and wars against the French fill the history books as Brazil struggled to secure a huge land mass and unite a diverse population. Brazil, specifically Rio de Janeiro, actually became the seat of the Portuguese Empire in 1808 for a period of time as the Portuguese royal family fled Lisbon in advance of Napoléon Bonaparte's invasion of Portugal. Cisplatine, now occupied by the present country of Uruguay, was lost in one of these wars, the Argentina–Brazil War. After decades of dictatorship and military rule, a civilian government has been in power only since 1985.

Brazilian food is not highly seasoned, unlike the cuisines of many Latin American countries where the garlic or the hot sauce have to be adjusted. As a consequence, North American and European palates adapt quite quickly and quite easily to the tastes of Brazil and I wager to guess that you will find, as have we, Brazilian recipes will become part of your repertoire.

Broccoli and Potato Salad with Hollandaise Sauce
Salada de Bróccolos e Batatas

Blender Hollandaise Sauce
Sauce Hollandaise

Cashew Appetizer Toasts
Torradinhas de Castanho de Cajú

Colonial-Style Bread

~

Cream of Artichoke Hearts Soup
Sopa de Crème de Alcachôras

~

Vegetable Salad with Hearts of Palm
Salada de Vegetal com Palmito

~~~~~~~~~~~~~~~~~~~~

Corn and Lima Bean Custard Pudding
Milho e Fava Cozado em Crème

Fried Rice with Fried Garlic
Arroz Frito com Alho Frito

Sautéed Greens

Tomato and Peanut Sauce with Cream
Molho de Tomate com Amendoim

~~~~~~~~~~~~~~~~~~~~

Sweet Scrambled Eggs
Doce Ovos Mexidos

Coconut Tapioca Sweet
Cuscuz de Coco e Tapioca

The Americas – **Brazil**

BRAZILIAN BROCCOLI AND POTATO SALAD WITH HOLLANDAISE SAUCE
Salada de Brócolos e Batatas

TPT - 2 hours and 25 minutes;
1 hour = potato chilling period;
30 minutes = broccoli chilling period

Hollandaise sauce is not native to this hemisphere but it is a favorite in both the United States and in Brazil where the passion for egg yolk-filled pastries and sauces is a natural consequence of the Portuguese colonial period. Would that the Portuguese whom we met in Portugal had returned the favor and adopted this broccoli and potato salad. I had to wait over thirty years to discover what the Brazilians can do with broccoli. It is totally different from any broccoli or potato salad I have ever tasted and, yet, it strikes very familiar cords.

The ingredients for this salad can be prepared early in the day and assembled at the last minute. This is especially helpful if you chose to double this recipe for a buffet table salad or if you chose to serve it as a luncheon entrée. It also makes a different and enjoyable first course, a sort of Brazilian "antipasta" if you will.

1/2 cup BLENDER HOLLANDAISE SAUCE
(Sauce Hollandaise) [see recipe which follows]

3 quarts *boiling* **water**

2 medium-sized all-purpose waxy potatoes
— well-scrubbed, but *unpeeled*

2 cups small, fresh broccoli florets—trimmed and well-washed

2 medium-sized tomatoes—well-washed and cut into thin round slices

1 hard-cooked egg

Prepare and chill BLENDER HOLLANDAISE SAUCE.

Set up a steamer.

Pour *boiling* water into a saucepan set over *MEDIUM* heat. Add potatoes and cook until potatoes are tender. Drain and refrigerate potatoes for at least 1 hour.

Steam broccoli florets for about 10 minutes, or until *crisp-tender*. Remove from steamer and chill for at least 30 minutes.

Peel and slice cold, cooked potatoes and place around the outer perimeter of an attractive round platter. Place a ring of tomato slices within the ring of potato slices, overlapping slightly. Pile chilled, cooked broccoli florets in the center of platter.

Pour the prepared Hollandaise sauce over the broccoli.

Shell the hard-cooked egg. Separate the egg yolk from the egg white. Chop the egg white and scatter over the Hollandaise-topped broccoli. Press the egg yolk through a sieve set over a small bowl. Spoon the sieved egg yolk evenly over the tomato and potato slices, "mimosa style."

Serve chilled.

Yields 6 servings
adequate for 4 people

Note: This recipe can be doubled, when required.

1/6 SERVING – PROTEIN = 4.3 g.; FAT = 8.8 g.; CARBOHYDRATE = 10.9 g.;
CALORIES = 136; CALORIES FROM FAT = 58%

The Americas–Brazil

BLENDER HOLLANDAISE SAUCE
Sauce Hollandaise

TPT - 8 minutes

This recipe has never failed us!! What more could you ask of a Hollandaise sauce recipe?

1/2 cup *fat-free* **pasteurized eggs*** *(the equivalent of 2 eggs)—brought to room temperature*
2 tablespoons freshly squeezed lemon juice
   —strained **and** *brought to room temperature*
Several dashes ground red pepper (cayenne)

1/2 cup *hot* **melted butter**

1 tablespoon *boiling* **water**

Just before you are ready to serve, put pasteurized eggs, *strained* lemon juice, and ground red pepper (cayenne) into the container of the electric blender or into the work bowl of the food processor, fitted with steel knife. Cover, turn machine on, *and then turn it off immediately.*

Remove cover insert, turn machine on, and *very slowly* add *hot* melted butter in a thin, steady stream.

Very slowly add *boiling* water in the same manner. Turn off machine. Pour into heated sauceboat.

*Serve at once.***

Yields 1 cupful

Notes: *Because raw eggs present the danger of *Salmonella* poisoning, commercially-available pasteurized eggs are recommended for use in preparing this dish.

**Since the sulfur in egg yolks tarnishes silver, remember to use a stainless steel gravy ladle to serve egg sauces.

If required, this recipe may be doubled with ease.

1/16 SERVING (i. e., per tablespoonful) –
PROTEIN = 0.8 g.; FAT = 5.7 g.; CARBOHYDRATE = 0.5 g.;
CALORIES = 57; CALORIES FROM FAT = 90%

BRAZILIAN CASHEW APPETIZER TOASTS
Torradinhas de Castanho de Cajú

TPT - 18 minutes;
   10 minutes = dough cooling period

The Brazilians enjoy savory appetizers, salgadinos, with the same enthusiasm as we found in their mother country on a tour of Portugal many years ago. The taste and form do differ as a reflection of the ingredients available. Cashews were a rather expensive luxury when we were in Portugal but here they are plentiful because they are a major crop of northwestern Brazil. These are a great accompaniment to a mug of soup for lunch. Minas Gerais is a semi-hard cheese that is not often found in the United States but other cheeses can be substituted. Although white bread is most often used in Brazil, our Colonial-style bread reminds us of a corn meal-based, coarse country bread, we enjoyed in Portugal, albeit somewhat more refined.

6 slices bread such as COLONIAL-STYLE BREAD
   [see recipe which follows]

1/2 cup *grated or finely shredded* **Minas Gerais cheese, if available***
2 tablespoons grated Parmesan cheese
3 tablespoons *finely* **chopped scallion—***white portion only*—**or** *finely* **chopped onion, if preferred**
1 teaspoon paprika
Freshly ground black pepper, to taste

1/4 cup chopped *preservative-free* **cashews**

Preheat broiler to 350 degrees F.

Toast bread, trim crusts from bread, and cut diagonally into quarters to create triangles.

In a small bowl, combine grated cheeses, *finely* chopped scallion, paprika, and black pepper. Mix well. Using a spreader or butter knife, spread a portion of cheese mixture on each of the twenty-four toast triangles. Place toasts on a cookie sheet and place about 6 inches under broiler unit for about 5 minutes or until cheese melts. Remove from oven.

The Americas – **Brazil**

BRAZILIAN CASHEW APPETIZER TOASTS (cont'd)

Sprinkle chopped cashews over each toast. Return to oven for about 2 minutes. Remove from oven and transfer to a heated serving dish.

Serve hot.

Notes: *Dutch *Leyden* or *Delft*, Portuguese *Coimbra*, or Swiss *Gruyère* may be substituted.

This recipe can be halved or doubled, when required.

Yields 24 appetizer toasts

1/24 SERVING – PROTEIN = 1.8 g.; FAT = 2.2 g.; CARBOHYDRATE = 5.1 g.;
CALORIES = 39; CALORIES FROM FAT = 51%

(BREAD MACHINE) COLONIAL–STYLE BREAD

TPT - 4 hours and 2 minutes;
30 minutes = corn meal soaking period;
3 hours and 30 minutes = automated preparation period*

This is a good daily bread, American through and through, with a slightly sweet flavor . . . and good texture, color, and crumb.

1/3 cup yellow corn meal
1 1/2 cups water *heated to about 95 degrees F.*

1/3 cup pure maple syrup**

2 1/2 cups plus 1 tablespoon bread flour
1 cup whole wheat flour
1/2 teaspoon salt
1 tablespoon butter

1 1/2 teaspoons *preservative-free* **active dried yeast*****

Bring all remaining ingredients to room temperature.

Combine corn meal and *hot* water in a bowl. Stir to combine well. Allow to stand for 30 minutes. Turn into bread pan.

Add maple syrup.

Add bread and whole wheat flours, and salt, spreading the ingredients over the liquid as you add them. *Do not stir.* Leave an area at one end of loaf pan for the yeast. Scatter the butter chunks at the other end of the bread pan.

Using a spoon, create a depression in the dry ingredients, being very careful not to press down into the liquid layer below. Pour yeast into the depression.

Select BASIC SETTING. Set CRUST CONTROL at medium. Push START.

Yields on 1 1/2-pound loaf
—approximately 24 slices

Notes: *Preparation time depends, of course, on the brand of bread machine that you are using. I use a Zojirushi bread machine and this recipe is designed for that manufacturer's product.

**Molasses or honey can be substituted for maple syrup, if preferred.

***Some packaged dried yeast available in grocery stores contain a preservative. Natural food stores carry an additive-free dried yeast. In addition, *do not use so-called fast action yeasts.* The results will not please you.

If preferred, the MANUAL SETTING on your BREAD MACHINE may be selected. When the cycle has been completed, turn the dough out onto a floured surface and knead until smooth and all trace of stickiness is gone. Prepare a 9 x 5 x 3-inch non-stick-coated loaf pan by coating with non-stick lecithin spray coating. Form kneaded dough into a loaf. Place in prepared pan. Cover with a cotton tea towel and allow to rise in a warm, draft-free kitchen until doubled in volume—about 45 minutes. Bake in preheated 350 degree F. oven for about 40-45 minutes. Turn out of baking pan and cool completely on a wire rack before slicing and serving.

(BREAD MACHINE) COLONIAL–STYLE BREAD (cont'd)

1/24 SERVING (i. e., per slice) –
PROTEIN = 2.4 g.; FAT = 0.8 g.; CARBOHYDRATE = 17.3 g.;
CALORIES = 86; CALORIES FROM FAT = 8%

BRAZILIAN CREAM OF ARTICHOKE HEARTS SOUP
Sopa de Crème de Alcachôfras

TPT - 50 minutes

I wish I had a dollar for every artichoke I trimmed and "dechoked" in my married life; I would be a wealthy woman. Artichokes are work to prepare and just using the hearts for a soup would be like using a perfectly ripened brie for a cheese ball. Frozen artichoke hearts were available only from one specialty frozen food company and our local grocery did not feel what they considered to be an ethnic product was worth stocking, even though we bought them out each time they tested the demand. Finally a large grocery chain located north of us and they package artichoke hearts in large poly bags under their house name so we are never without sweet, wonderful artichoke hearts.

One Brazilian author resorted to jarred artichoke hearts which would change this soup completely. Please seek out frozen artichoke hearts or trim and "dechoke" the fresh thistles yourself. The inner leaves are very tender and should be included with the hearts. We prefer to have the chunks of artichoke hearts and pieces of the inner leaves floating in the soup but it can be puréed and sieved for a very different consistency.

2 tablespoons butter
30 *frozen* **artichoke hearts quarters with small leaves attached—about 4 ounces—defrosted and chopped**
1 small onion—*finely* **chopped**

1 quart *boiling* **water**

1 cup *whole* **milk**
1 tablespoon yellow corn meal

1/2 cup light cream *or* **half and half**
6 tablespoons grated *pecorino Romano or* **Parmesan cheese, as preferred**

Freshly grated nutmeg, to taste

1/2 cup small croutons, for garnish, if desired

In a skillet set over *MEDIUM* heat, melt butter. Add chopped artichoke hearts and onion. Sauté until onion is soft and translucent, *allowing neither vegetable to brown.* Remove from heat.

Set kettle with *boiling* water over *LOW-MEDIUM* heat. Add sautéed artichoke hearts and onion. Allow to cook for about 15 minutes.

In a measuring cup, combine milk and corn meal. Stir to mix well. Add to kettle. Cook, stirring frequently, until it thickens—about 20 minutes.

Add cream and grated cheese. Allow to heat through but *do not allow to boil once the cream has been added.* Turn into heated soup tureen.

Sprinkle a little nutmeg over the soup as a garnish.

Serve into heated soup cups or cream soup bowls with a few croutons floating on top, if desired.

Yields 7 cupfuls

Notes: When required, this recipe can be halved or doubled.

This recipe does not freeze well but leftovers can be reheated over *LOW* heat with success.

1/7 SERVING (i. e., per cupful) –
PROTEIN = 3.5 g.; FAT = 7.3 g.; CARBOHYDRATE = 5.2 g.;
CALORIES = 99; CALORIES FROM FAT = 66%

BRAZILIAN VEGETABLE SALAD WITH HEARTS OF PALM
Salada de Vegetal com Palmito

TPT - 44 minutes;
30 minutes = cooked pea chilling period

What a wonderful, exotic taste the heart of a palm tree can add to a salad. The peach palm, "Bactris gasipaes," is now the principal commercial source of this delicacy and is cultivated for its central core so the loss of wild palms in the Amazon region is no longer the galloping environmental concern it had been. Because the tree must be sacrificed to harvest its core, a salad prepared from it was often referred to as "millionaires' salad" and boycotted by environmentalists concerned about the deforestation of the equatorial rain forests and the consequent climate change the earth would suffer. We have found salads similar to this throughout Europe, in Russia, and in North America but the addition of the hearts of palm signals a definitive destination and you are transported to Brazil where food traditions of Europe meet the tropics.

2 cups *boiling* **water**
1/2 cup freshly shelled *or frozen* **peas**

1/2 can (i. e., 7 ounces) hearts of palm—rinsed and well-drained*

1 cup chopped canned beets—well-drained
1/2 cup chopped cucumber—seeded
1/4 cup chopped Vidalia salad onion—*white portion only*****
Freshly ground black pepper, to taste

3 tablespoons BLENDER MAYONNAISE *[see index]* **or commercially-available mayonnaise**
1 tablespoon freshly squeezed orange juice

1 tablespoon grated Parmesan cheese

Notes: *Hearts of palm are an important export product of Costa Rica and are available canned in most grocery stores. Fresh hearts of palm are much harder to find unless you have a Latin American greengrocer or a very well-stocked Latino grocery nearby.

**Vidalia salad onions, looking like enormous bulbous, scallions are generally available only in the fall and winter. If unavailable, use any sweet onion that is available.

This recipe can be halved or doubled, when required.

In a saucepan or mixing bowl, combine *boiling* water and peas. Allow peas to sit in hot water for about 5 minutes. Drain and refrigerate for about 30 minutes while preparing the remaining ingredients.

Slice palm hearts into bite-sized slices. Turn into a mixing bowl.

Add chopped beets, cucumber, and onion, and chilled peas. Season with black pepper.

In a small bowl, combine mayonnaise and orange juice. Blend well. Add to vegetables and toss *gently*. Turn into serving bowl.

Refrigerate until ready to serve.

Garnish with grated cheese before serving.

Yields 6 servings
adequate for 4 people

1/6 SERVING – PROTEIN = 2.8 g.; FAT = 6.2 g.; CARBOHYDRATE = 6.4 g.;
CALORIES = 82; CALORIES FROM FAT = 68%

The Americas – Brazil

BRAZILIAN CORN AND LIMA BEAN CUSTARD PUDDING
Milho e Fava Cozado em Crème

TPT - 1 hour and 12 minutes

This recipe, entirely typical of Brazil, is an example of a dish that could well have been created by my grandmothers and great grandmothers in upstate New York. At first I thought this was simply a harvest pudding but later found that it dates back to the Jewish communities of the sixteenth and seventeenth century, who, in an effort to maintain their kosher eating practices but still enjoy a meal at the home of Roman Catholic friends, would bring dishes like this grain and bean casserole with its beautiful nutmeg-scented custard to be served with the non-kosher meal prepared by their host. It was not considered in any way an affront to contribute in such a manner to the meal and is still practiced today. It can be a gracious way for a vegetarian to provide a dish which they can eat and, at the same time, share in the preparation.

3 tablespoons unbleached white flour
1 tablespoon sugar
1/4 teaspoon salt, or to taste
1/4 teaspoon freshly ground black pepper, or to taste
1/4 teaspoon freshly grated nutmeg

1 1/2 cups *frozen* lima beans—*defrosted*
1 1/2 cups frozen corn kernels—*defrosted*
3/4 cup *fat-free* pasteurized eggs (the equivalent of 3 eggs)

3 tablespoons butter
1 medium onion—*very finely* chopped
1 red bell pepper—*finely* chopped
1/8 teaspoon ground red pepper (cayenne), or to taste

2 cups *whole* milk

Preheat oven to 325 degrees F. Prepare a 2-quart soufflé dish or other oven-to-table baking dish by coating with non-stick lecithin spray coating.

In a small dish, combine flour, sugar, salt, black pepper, and nutmeg. Set aside briefly.

In a mixing bowl, combine *thawed* lima beans and corn with pasteurized eggs. Stir to combine and set aside until required.

In a saucepan set over *MEDIUM* heat, melt butter. Add *very finely* chopped onion and *finely* chopped red pepper. Sauté until onion is soft and translucent, *allowing neither vegetable to brown. Reduce heat to LOW.* Add ground red pepper (cayenne) and cook, stirring constantly, for about 1 minute.

While still stirring constantly, add flour–sugar–spice mixture and stir for several minutes to form a *roux*.

Gradually add milk, stirring as you do with a wooden spoon. Increase heat to *MEDIUM* again and cook, stirring constantly, until the mixture comes to the boil and thickens slightly.

Add lima bean–corn–egg mixture, stirring it into the milk with a wooden spoon. Turn into prepared baking dish. Set in a baking pan in which a 1-inch water bath has been prepared. Bake in preheated 325 degree F. oven for about 50 minutes, or until a knife inserted into the center comes out clean. Check water level occasionally and add *cold* water, if needed. *Do not allow water bath to simmer or boil—add cold water or ice cubes,* if necessary. Remove baking dish from water and allow to stand for about 5 minutes to allow for custard to firm before serving.

Serve hot.

Yields 8 servings
adequate for 6 people

Note: This recipe can be halved, when required.

1/8 SERVING – PROTEIN = 9.2 g.; FAT = 6.9 g.; CARBOHYDRATE = 28.7 g.;
CALORIES = 218; CALORIES FROM FAT = 29%

BRAZILIAN FRIED RICE WITH FRIED GARLIC
Arroz Frito com Alho Frito

TPT - 45 minutes

If you say you are serving "fried rice," it may immediately be assumed that you are serving an Asian meal but certainly not a dish from a South American country whose cuisine has strong Portuguese colonial influences. Brazilians do not usually cook the rice before adding it to the skillet but we find that too much oil is then absorbed by the rice and, thus, prefer to make it this way. Do not be put off by the amount of garlic in this dish, it sweetens as it fries and it is so good for you.

BRAZILIAN FRIED RICE WITH FRIED GARLIC (cont'd)

1 tablespoon *roasted* pumpkin seeds *or* shelled pumpkin seeds (*pepitas*), if available

2 cups *boiling* water
1 cup dry long grain *brown* rice *or* converted rice, if preferred

1 tablespoon *extra virgin* olive oil
3 large garlic cloves—peeled and *thinly* sliced

1 tablespoon *extra virgin* olive oil
1/4 cup *very finely* chopped onion

3 tablespoons *light, sulfite-free* coconut milk

Jalapeño chili sauce *or* other hot sauce of choice*

Using a SPICE and COFFEE GRINDER, grind roasted pumpkin seeds or *pepitas*. Set aside until required.

In a saucepan set over *LOW* heat, combine *boiling* water and rice. Cover and allow to cook for 20 minutes, or until the water has been evaporated. Remove from heat.

While the rice is cooking, in a skillet set over *MEDIUM* heat, heat 1 tablespoonful of the oil. Add garlic slices and sauté until lightly browned, *being careful not to allow garlic to burn*. Remove from heat and set aside briefly.

In a large skillet set over *MEDIUM* heat, heat remaining tablespoonful of oil. Add onion and sauté until onion is soft and translucent, *being careful not to allow onion to brown*.

Add *cooked* rice and continue cooking, while stirring constantly, until onion and rice just "begin to color."

Add coconut milk and continue cooking, while stirring constantly, until liquid from coconut milk has been absorbed or evaporated and the rice has a creamy consistency. Turn into a heated serving bowl. Scatter sautéed garlic slices and ground pumpkin seeds over.

Serve at once. Allow diners to add hot sauce, according to their own tolerance.

Yields 6 servings**
adequate for 4 people

Notes: *Molho apimentado*, a hot, hot sauce made with bird *chilies*, is traditionally used. *Jalapeño chili* sauce, found in most United States grocery stores, is an adequate substitute.

**Brazilians really like their rice and this would probably serve only three hungry Brazilians.

This recipe can be doubled, when required.

1/6 SERVING – PROTEIN = 2.1 g.; FAT = 3.4 g.; CARBOHYDRATE = 18.6 g.;
CALORIES = 114; CALORIES FROM FAT = 27%

BRAZILIAN TOMATO AND PEANUT SAUCE WITH CREAM
Molho de Tomate com Amendoim
TPT - 8 minutes

Although most often served over vegetables in Brazil, this is an excellent sauce for protein complementation over grain loaves and veggie burgers.

1 cup canned, *diced* tomatoes

1 tablespoon butter
Pinch of sugar
1/4 cup light cream *or* half and half
3 tablespoons ground, *roasted* peanuts—salted *or* unsalted, as preferred
Freshly ground black pepper, to taste

Turn chopped tomatoes into the work bowl of the food processor, fitted with steel knife. Process to create a coarse purée.

Turn purée into a coarse sieve set over a mixing bowl. Press purée through the sieve to remove seeds and to create a sauce base of uniform consistency.

BRAZILIAN TOMATO AND PEANUT SAUCE WITH CREAM (cont'd)

In a saucepan set over *LOW-MEDIUM* heat, melt butter. Add tomato purée, sugar, cream, ground peanuts, and black pepper. Heat until sauce comes to a gentle boil.

Turn into a heated sauceboat and serve over vegetables.

Yields 1 1/2 cupfuls

Notes: When required, this recipe can be halved or doubled.

Leftovers freeze well.

1/12 SERVING (i. e., 2 tablespoonfuls) –
PROTEIN = 1.4 g.; FAT = 3.5 g.; CARBOHYDRATE = 1.9 g.;
CALORIES = 42; CALORIES FROM FAT = 75%

BRAZILIAN SWEET SCRAMBLED EGGS
Doce Ovos Mexidos

TPT - 15 minutes

The confections of Brazil are strikingly similar to those of Portugal; the influence of the colonial period is strongly evident in the sweet, sweet mouthfuls made with dozens of eggs. However, who would ever dream that a Brazilian cook would get up in the morning, get out the eggs, and then reach for the sugar? Although, Russians do often add a bit of honey to their shirred eggs . . . The unexpected nuances of the flavor of this sweet version of scrambled eggs tastes wonderful with fresh fruit and a coffeecake for brunch or for an unusual dessert. Please note that I have decreased the amount of sugar to one-quarter of the sugar called for in the original recipe.

2 tablespoons sugar
2 tablespoons lemon juice
1 tablespoon orange flower water*

4 large eggs**

1 teaspoon butter

Home-grown, spray-free **daylilies, well-washed with pistil, stamen, and sepals removed—for garnish—if desired**

In a mixing bowl, combine sugar, lemon juice, and orange flower water. Mix well.

Add eggs. Using a wire whisk, combine well.

Place a non-stick-coated skillet over *MEDIUM* heat. Brush heated pan with butter. Pour egg mixture into pan and stir gently until eggs are coagulated.

Transfer scrambled eggs to a heated platter set on a warming tray.

Serve at once, garnished with daylilies.

Yields 3 servings
adequate for 2 people

Notes: *Orange flower water is available in food specialty stores.

**1/2 cupful fat-free pasteurized eggs may be substituted for two of the eggs, if preferred.

This recipe may be doubled, when required.

1/3 SERVING – PROTEIN = 8.5 g.; FAT = 8.9 g.; CARBOHYDRATE = 10.1 g.;
CALORIES = 155; CALORIES FROM FAT = 52%

The Americas–**Brazil**

BRAZILIAN COCONUT TAPIOCA SWEET
Cuscuz de Coco e Tapioca

TPT - 4 hours and 26 minutes;
4 hours = chilling period

"Couscous," introduced to Brazil from North Africa by African immigrants, became corrupted as "cuscuz." A sweet version of what is generally a grain-based main course dish evolved in northern Brazil utilizing native regional plenty—manioc or cassava and coconuts. This low-fat, not-too-sweet version of that northern Brazilian treat replaces coconut milk with vanilla-scented cows' milk and is served in small, snack portions rather than in cake-sized wedges or squares.

Tapioca, interestingly enough, became part of the African cuisine when cassava was introduced to Africa by the Portuguese in the 1600s after their return voyages from the Western Hemisphere.

1 cup quick-cooking tapioca
1/2 cup *preservative-free, unsweetened* **flaked**
  or shredded coconut
2 cups skimmed milk
6 tablespoons sugar

1 1/2 teaspoons pure vanilla extract

In a saucepan set over *MEDIUM* heat, combine granulated tapioca, flaked or shredded coconut, milk, and sugar. Cook, stirring frequently, until the pudding base begins to simmer. *Reduce heat to LOW.* Continue to cook, *stirring constantly*, for about 5 minutes more.

Stir in vanilla extract.

Turn the tapioca mixture into a non-stick-coated, 8-inch square baking pan, spreading it evenly to the sides of the pan. Set aside and allow to come to room temperature. Cover with plastic wrap and refrigerate for at least 4 hours, or overnight.

To serve, unmold onto a cutting board or other flat surface. Cut into squares or diamonds and transfer to a serving plate.*

Cover and refrigerate any leftovers.

Yields 16 servings
adequate for 4-6 people

Notes: *When this dish is served for dessert, thick, sweetened coconut milk, COCONUT CREAM *[see index]*, or cream-thinned *fat-free* sweetened condensed milk can be served if a sauce is desired.

This recipe may be halved or doubled, when required. Be sure to use an appropriately sized pan when decreasing or increasing.

1/16 SERVING – PROTEIN = 1.5 g.; FAT = 1.2 g.; CARBOHYDRATE = 21.7 g.;
CALORIES = 98; CALORIES FROM FAT = 11%

Chile

The incredible climatic diversity of this ribbon of land between the Andes Mountains and the Pacific Ocean gave the Inca chieftains the resources to feed their nation prior to contact in the sixteenth century. From the world's driest desert in the north, the Atacama, one travels southward to an Alpine climate complete with glaciers and fjords. The central area is more Mediterranean-like in climate and provides a long, effective crop-growing season, allowing for the cultivation of many fruits, vegetables, and grains.

The mixture of Native American recipes and Spanish recipes presents a puzzle as complex as a Rubix cube but creates a unique and very interesting cuisine. Initially, the vegetarian is very definitely challenged because one finds fish or meat added to almost everything. Although menus in the cities are dominated by meat and fish dishes, once you move out to the countryside or to the mountains, as in so many countries in South America, a world of vegetarian options opens up, options to you but food that has been eaten there for centuries. For example, quinoa, only introduced to health-conscious Anglos in recent years, has been an important grain here for six thousand years. Wonderful dishes are created with eggs, two of which I have chosen to include, and their one-pot stews are as comforting as the stew that your grandmother extended with a potato or two. Foods are not heavily seasoned so the good food just tastes like good food. Hot *chilies* are not as widely used in Chile as they are in other South American cuisines.

The mountains have provided an exceptional climate for growing "cold weather" crops giving Chileans immense choice. Fruits have become economically important crops for export with the cultivation of grapes for wine leading the way in the competition for North American markets.

Omelet on Omelet
Tortilla de Huevos

~

Puréed Cream of Corn and Basil Soup with Tomato
Crema de Choclo y Albhaca con Tomate

~~~~~~~~~~~~~~~~~~~~

Roasted Winter Squash with Corn and Eggs
Asada de Calabza con Maix y Huevos

Roasted Potatoes
~~~~~~~~~~~~~~~~~~~~~~~

Latin American Spice Mix
Condimento Latino Americano

~

Cherimoya with Orange Sauce   **Poached Papaya**
Chirimoya Alegre   *Papayas al Jugo*

The Americas–Chile

CHILEAN OMELET ON OMELET
Tortilla de Huevos

TPT - 27 minutes

The presentation of this Chilean appetizer omelet is unusual; no one could mistake it for a classic French omelet. So, it is fun, fresh, and a new experience. We have found it to be pleasant change from the ordinary, especially as a light supper entree. Unless you live in the Southwest or on the West Coast, finding queso blanco may present a problem. Mozzarella cheese is an adequate substitution.

1 medium scallion—trimmed, well-rinsed, and *slivered* into 4-6-inch pieces
1/4 small zucchini—well-washed and *slivered* into 4-6 inch pieces*
1/4 small yellow summer squash—well-washed, peeled, seeded, and *slivered* into 4-6-inch pieces*
1/2 small carrot—well-washed, peeled, and *slivered* into 4-5-inch pieces*

4 ounces *queso blanco* or *fresh mozzarella* cheese

2 large eggs
1 tablespoon water

6 large eggs
2 tablespoons water

Freshly ground black pepper, to taste

Put dinner plates on a warming tray set at *MEDIUM* or in a warming oven to heat.**

Toss vegetables together and put in a mixing bowl. Set aside until required.

Shred cheese and set it aside until required.

Break the two eggs into a cup. Add 1 tablespoonful water and mix vigorously with a fork.

In a non-stick-coated skillet set over *MEDIUM* heat, spoon about *one-sixth* of the beaten egg into the center of the hot skillet. Using a spoon to guide the liquid egg, make a small flat omelet disk about 4 inches in diameter. Transfer the omelet disk to a heated plate. Continue in the same manner to make five more of the small omelet disks.

Take one of the remaining six eggs and break it into a cup. Add 1 teaspoonful water and mix vigorously with a fork. Using a 7-inch non-stick-coated, make a 7-inch omelet disk. Turn out onto a heated dinner plate.

Continue to make the remaining five omelets in the same manner.

Put a portion of the shredded cheese in the middle of each warm omelet. Place a small omelet disk on top. Spoon a portion of the shredded vegetables on top of each small disk. Grind black pepper over.

Serve as soon as the cheese begins to melt.

Yields 6 individual servings

Notes: *The easiest way I have found to prepare the vegetable garnish is to peel long, thin slices using a vegetable peeler. I then lay these thin slices out a cutting board and, using a sharp chef's knife, cut these into the thin *spaghettini*-like shreds that I need for the garnish.

**Be sure to keep all you plates warm, *not hot*, so that your diners can eat together.

This recipe can be decreased to accommodate two or three diners, when required.

1/6 SERVING – PROTEIN = 14.2 g.; FAT = 11.0 g.; CARBOHYDRATE = 2.9 g.;
CALORIES = 164; CALORIES FROM FAT = 60%

The Americas–Chile

CHILEAN PURÉED CREAM OF CORN AND BASIL SOUP WITH TOMATO
Crema de Choclo y Albahaca con Tomate
TPT - 1 hour and 10 minutes

When I was young, my mother frequently made a dish she called "shrimp corn Creole." I, of course, assumed it had come from New Orleans and was a dish of the beautiful fusion cuisine in which the elements of Spanish, French, and African become unidentifiable as the dishes evolve and evolve. One August day, years and years after I had even thought of Mom's dish, I tasted elements of it in a cream soup from Chile. This is very much a summer soup for us because it is best when the corn and basil come right from the garden so it is a soup that is on my radar when a cold front heads south in August.

2 tablespoons butter
1 medium onion, chopped

3 cups green (fresh) *or frozen* **corn kernels**
1 1/2 cups VEGETABLE STOCK FROM SOUP *[see index]***, VEGETARIAN BROWN STOCK** *[see index], or* **other vegetarian stock, as preferred**
1 1/2 cups *whole* **milk**
8 large, fresh basil leaves
1 teaspoon sugar
1/2 teaspoon LATIN AMERICAN SPICE MIX (*Condimento Latino Americano***)** *[see index]***, or to taste**
Salt, to taste

12 canned, *whole* **tomatoes**
Finely chopped fresh basil, for garnish

In a kettle with cover, set over *MEDIUM* heat, melt butter. Add chopped onion and sauté until onion is soft and translucent, *being careful not to allow the onion to brown.*

Add corn, vegetable stock, milk, basil leaves, sugar, salt, and the spice mix. Bring to the boil. *Reduce heat to LOW-MEDIUM.* Cover and simmer for about 25-30 minutes. Stir occasionally and adjust heat if necessary. Remove from heat and allow to cool for about 15 minutes.

Using the electric blender or the food processor fitted with steel knife, purée soup mixture in small batches *until very smooth*. Turn into a clean kettle. Set over *LOW* heat and allow to heat through. Turn into a heated soup tureen. If the soup is too thick, thin with a bit more milk.

Place two whole, canned tomatoes into each heated soup bowl. Ladle soup over the tomatoes. Garnish each serving with *finely* chopped basil.

Serve at once.

Yields 6 cupfuls

Note: Although this soup is really at its best when served the day it is prepared, leftovers can be refrigerated and reheated and it can also be frozen for a future menu appearance.

1/6 SERVING (i. e., per cupful) –
PROTEIN = 5.8 g.; FAT = 6.8 g.; CARBOHYDRATE = 27.4 g.;
CALORIES = 177; CALORIES FROM FAT = 35%

CHILEAN ROASTED WINTER SQUASH WITH CORN AND EGGS
Asado de Calabaza con Maiz y Huevos
TPT - 55 minutes

The Native American staples squash and corn come together in this protein-packed casserole in which roasted squash pieces, infused with spices, contrast perfectly with the softness of the eggs and cheese. It is a symphony of texture and taste sensation. Our spice mixture shortens the preparation time and delivers just the right combination of "WOW" and "m-m-m."

The Americas – Chile

**CHILEAN ROASTED WINTER SQUASH
WITH CORN AND EGGS** (cont'd)

1 teaspoon LATIN AMERICAN SPICE MIX
 (Condimento Latino Americano) [see index]
Dash or two ground red pepper (cayenne), or to taste

1 pound butternut squash—peeled, seeded, and cut into 1-inch cubes
1 tablespoon canola oil

2 teaspoons butter
Paprika
1/2 medium onion—*thinly* sliced

1 cup green (fresh) *or frozen* corn kernels

2 large eggs—well-beaten
1 tablespoon *cold* water
1/2 cup diced (about 2 ounces) *queso blanco, mozzarella, or* Monterey Jack cheese

Preheat oven to 400 degrees F.

In a mixing bowl, combine spice mix and ground red pepper (cayenne). Stir to mix thoroughly.

Add butternut squash pieces and oil. Toss until squash pieces are evenly coated with the oil and seasoning mixture. Turn out onto a jelly roll pan, spreading the squash pieces apart from each other as much as possible.

Bake in preheated 400 degree F. oven for about 40 minutes, or until squash is tender and beginning to brown. Stirring frequently to insure even browning.

Just before squash is ready, in a skillet with cover set over *LOW-MEDIUM* heat, melt butter. Stir in enough paprika to color the butter pink. Add sliced onion and sauté until onion is soft and translucent, *being careful not to allow onion to brown.*

Reduce temperature to LOW. Add corn and roasted squash.

Using a wire whisk, beat eggs with *cold* water until quite light. Add diced cheese and stir to combine. Pour this egg–cheese mixture over vegetables in skillet and stir lightly to combine. Cook over *LOW* heat, lightly stirring as needed, until eggs are set—about 4 minutes.

Turn onto a heated serving platter or serve directly from the skillet.

Serve at once.

Yields 6 servings
adequate for 4 people

Note: This recipe may be easily halved or doubled, when required.

1/6 SERVING – PROTEIN = 7.0 g.; FAT = 9.4 g.; CARBOHYDRATE = 15.9 g.;
CALORIES = 158; CALORIES FROM FAT = 54%

LATIN AMERICAN SPICE MIX
Condimento Latino Americano

TPT - 12 minutes

A smidgen or a pinch of this mixture can give a pronounced Latin American flavor to almost any dish.

1/4 cup cumin seeds
3 tablespoons whole black peppercorns
1 tablespoon whole coriander seeds
1 tablespoon whole allspice berries

2 tablespoons sugar
1 teaspoon salt

In a heavy skillet set over *MEDIUM* heat, combine cumin seeds, whole peppercorns, whole coriander seeds, and whole allspice berries. Cook, stirring constantly, for about 8 minutes, or until toasted and fragrant. Remove from heat and set aside to cool briefly.

Pour toasted spices into a SPICE and COFFEE GRINDER, or into the container of the electric blender. Process until finely ground. Pass blended spices through a sieve into a bowl. Discard residue.

Add sugar and salt. Pour into a jar with a tightly fitting lid. Shake to mix thoroughly.

Yields about 2/3 cupful

Note: This spice mixture may be halved or doubled and kept on hand on your spice rack.

1/11 SERVING (i. e., per tablespoonful) –
PROTEIN = 1.9 g.; FAT = 2.4 g.; CARBOHYDRATE = 7.5 g.;
CALORIES = 49; CALORIES FROM FAT = 44%

CHILEAN *CHERIMOYA* WITH ORANGE SAUCE
Chirimoya Alegre

TPT - 2 hours and 4 minutes;
2 hours = refrigeration period

Cherimoya, also known as custard apple, is one of the most beautiful fruits I have ever seen. The creamy sweet fruit is covered by a scale-like rind that is akin to no other. The first time I found them in a market, I was entranced; the first time I tasted one, I was devoted. If you think that you have tasted it all and you have not tasted a cherimoya, you are in for a treat. When I find a couple of them in a produce section, I gather them up and take them home probably much like a "cavewife" celebrated the discovery of such a treat. Grand Marnier is often sprinkled over this Chilean specialty but I prefer a drizzle of honey since it compliments the taste so beautifully.

2 small, ripe *cherimoyas*—peeled, seeded, and cut into large chunks

1 cup freshly squeezed orange juice*

2 tablespoons honey, of choice

In a mixing bowl, combine orange juice and *cherimoya* chunks. Toss to coat the fruit with the orange juice. Refrigerate for about an hour, turning the fruit frequently to keep it well-coated with orange juice. Turn into a serving bowl.

Drizzle honey over.

Serve at once into small dessert dishes, sherbet glasses, or wine glasses.

Notes: *Orange juice not only helps to show off the taste of *cherimoyas* by contrasting with the honeyed taste, it also prevents the flesh from browning once cut.

This recipe can be halved or doubled, when required.

Yields 6 servings
adequate for 4 people

1/6 SERVING – PROTEIN = 2.9 g.; FAT = 0.9 g.; CARBOHYDRATE = 56.8 g.;
CALORIES = 225; CALORIES FROM FAT = 4%

CHILEAN POACHED PAPAYA
Papaya al Jugo

TPT - 5 hours and 32 minutes;
3 hours = soaking period;
1 hour = cooling period

We always loved the taste of papaya but it was not until we visited Hawaii that we really tasted a papaya, if you know what I mean. A friend turned her Honolulu apartment over to us to use as a base and left a basket of papayas on the kitchen counter as a gift. We enjoyed every one. Ever since our trip to Hawaii we have kept searching again for the perfect papaya. Until recently only Hawaiian papayas were available in our produce departments but now the large South American varieties are appearing on a regular basis. Although less sweet than are the Hawaiian variety, they are, in my opinion, perfect for this Chilean specialty.

Chileans usually prepare the poaching syrup by adding the seeds to the water with sugar and then draining the seeds from the resultant syrup. The seeds are edible and have a sharp, peppery taste. In fact, they are sometimes dried and used as a substitute for black pepper. However, phytochemicals in papaya, concentrated in the seeds, appear to suppress progesterone and are, as a consequence, used in some cultures as a contraceptive and abortifacient. You may or may not wish to add the seeds to your poaching liquid.

CHILEAN POACHED PAPAYA (cont'd)

1/2 large, *underripe*, South American papaya

6 cups water

2 cups sugar

1 cup sweetened whipped cream

To make the papaya easy to peel, wash the papaya well and put it into a large kettle of cold water with the cut surface above the water line. Set aside for 3 hours. Remove the papaya from the water and peel using a sharp paring knife. Transfer the peels to a saucepan. Cut the papaya in half longitudinally. Remove any seeds and either add them to the peels in the saucepan or discard them, as preferred. Add water to the saucepan, being sure that peels are completely covered. Place over *MEDIUM* heat. Bring to the simmer and cook for 20 minutes. Remove from heat. Set a sieve over a large measuring cup and pour the liquid through the sieve. Discard the peelings and seeds.

Cut the papaya into large chunks. Set aside until required.

Pour four cupfuls of the liquid into a clean saucepan set over *MEDIUM* heat. Add sugar and allow it to come to the boil. Cook, stirring frequently, until sugar is dissolved. *Reduce heat to LOW-MEDIUM.*

Add papaya chunks and poach for about 40-50 minutes.* Set aside at room temperature to cool. Refrigerate the papaya in the heavy syrup until thoroughly chilled, about 1 hour.

Serve cold with whipped cream. The syrup, known as "*mile de papayas*" can be refrigerated and used as a dessert syrup.

Yields 8 servings
adequate for 6 people

Note: *Poaching time will vary according to the ripeness of the papaya. Test with a fork.

1/8 SERVING – PROTEIN = 0.2 g.; FAT = 1.6 g.; CARBOHYDRATE = 61.0 g.;
CALORIES = 250; CALORIES FROM FAT = 6%

Colombia

Colombia, which claims islands in both the Caribbean Sea and in the Pacific Ocean, is the only country in South America to border on both bodies of water. Its geography is dominated by the Andes Mountains and its climate, hospitable to a wide range of agriculture at the lower altitudes, benefits from the trade winds and the rainfall patterns common to the Intertropical Convergence Zone. Hunter-gathers recognized the bio-diversity created by the topography and climate, establishing communities as early as 10,000 BC. Colombia's position on the earth's tectonic plates places it in the precarious and often violent "ring of fire" where earthquakes and volcanic eruptions are not uncommon. Fifteen major volcanoes are monitored constantly to forestall the extensive loss of life suffered with the Armero eruption in 1985.

The Spanish, who came in 1499, established the Viceroyalty of New Granada which included the territory of the nations we know as Colombia, Panama, Venezuela, and Ecuador. In 1830 the Republic of *Nueva Granada* was formed after Venezuela and Ecuador formed independent states. In 1858 the name was changed to the *Confederación Granadina,* the Grenedine Confederation, followed in 1863 by the United States of Colombia and, finally, in 1886 the present name, Republic of Colombia, became the official name. Cristoforo Colombo gave his Italian last name to a Spanish speaking country where he is, ironically, known as Cristóbal Colón and which, also ironically, he may never have explored if analysis of his diaries and maps is accurate. After the Thousand Days Civil War (1899-1902) Panama also became an independent nation, a move strongly influenced by the United States which was about to begin construction of the Panama canal, a project begun by the French in 1880 and abandoned due to the difficulty of the project.

The present government has worked to establish strong anti-narcotic laws in an effort to put the decades of control and violence by the drug cartels behind them and encourage tourism. Historic Bogotá and the beaches of Cartagena have become popular and much safer destinations for tourists due in no small part to the increased emphasis on security. Extraordinarily diverse national parks have attracted ecotourism and introduced people to diverse areas from those along the Caribbean coast to those in the spectacular Sierra Nevada de Santa Marta mountain range to the Tatacoa Desert in the central Andes and to the Amacayacu National Park in the Amazon River basin.

The cuisine of Colombia owes less to the traditions of its indigenous peoples than to other nations in South America and more to the cuisines of its neighbors and to those of the European countries with whom it has come into contact. As one would expect, the Spanish have contributed much to Colombian cuisine but strong influences can also be discerned from France, the Caribbean, Italy, and United States but preferences and preparations vary so widely from region to region that it would be inviting a heated discussion to suggest that there is a national cuisine; it is instead a nation of regional cuisines with regional specialties.

Egg and Avocado Salad
Ensalada de Huevos y Aguacates
with Tostados

~

Cream of Potato Soup with Corn
Ajiaco

~

Jicama and Carrot Salad with Mango
Ensalada de Jicama y Zanahoria con Mango

~~~~~~~~~~~~~~~~~~~~~~~

Beans and Tomatoes with Plantains
Habas y Tomates con Llanténos

Steamed Rice

~~~~~~~~~~~~~~~~~~~~~~~

Coconut Custard Crustless Pie
Pastel de Coco

COLOMBIAN EGG AND AVOCADO SALAD
Ensalada de Huevos y Aguacates
TPT - 10 minutes

As a salad or as an appetizer, this combination produces a rich yet cooling effect on the tongue punctuated by a tingle of hot. The more ground red pepper you add, the more the tingle. It is most enjoyable it as a counterpoint to really hot, spicy dishes.

4 hard-cooked eggs—well-chilled and *finely* chopped
2 firm avocados—peeled, pitted, and chopped
1/2 cup *finely* chopped onion
1/4 cup chopped fresh parsley
1/4 teaspoon ground red pepper (cayenne), or to taste
Pinch salt

2 tablespoons GARLIC–BASIL VINEGAR *[see index] or* a white wine vinegar of choice

Tiny red lettuce leaves—well-washed and dried

In a mixing bowl, combine *finely* chopped hard-cooked eggs, chopped avocados, *finely* chopped onion, and chopped fresh parsley. Toss gently to mix. While continuing to toss, sprinkle the ground red pepper (cayenne) and salt over the mixture. Toss *gently* to distribute the seasonings.

Add vinegar. Fold gently to integrate the vinegar. Turn into a serving bowl. Place the bowl in the center of a dinner plate. Refrigerate until required.

When ready to serve, arrange the lettuce leaves on the dinner plate, around the bowl containing the salad.

Yields 6 servings
adequate for 4 people

Note: This recipe can be halved, when required.

1/6 SERVING – PROTEIN = 5.9 g.; FAT = 14.8 g.; CARBOHYDRATE = 5.7 g.;
CALORIES = 170; CALORIES FROM FAT = 78%

The Americas—Colombia

COLOMBIAN CREAM OF POTATO SOUP WITH CORN
Ajiaco

TPT - 2 hours and 7 minutes

Sundays in Colombia are occasions for a potato and chicken soup called "ajiaco." This version, exclusive, of course, of the chicken and chicken stock, is, for us, an enjoyable Sunday night supper. Although Colombians frequently place cooked corn-on-the-cob in the bottom of a soup plate, over which they dramatically ladle the potato soup, we find that presentation a bit awkward to eat. Fresh or green corn kernels give this a beautiful finish and a fresh taste.

1 tablespoon GARLIC OIL *[see index]*
1 tablespoon butter
1/2 cup chopped onion
2 garlic cloves—*finely* chopped

3 cups diced potato—about 3 medium potatoes
3 cups VEGETARIAN WHITE STOCK *[see index]* or VEGETABLE STOCK FROM SOUP *[see index]*
1 teaspoon salt

1/8 teaspoon freshly ground *white* pepper, or to taste
1/2 cup light cream *or* half and half

1 1/2 cups green (fresh) corn kernels cut from cobs

In a skillet set over *MEDIUM* heat, combine garlic oil and butter. Add chopped onion and *very finely* chopped garlic. Sauté until the onion is soft and translucent, *being careful to allow neither the onion nor the garlic to brown.* Remove from heat and set aside until required.

In the small kettle with cover, combine diced potatoes, vegetable stock, and salt. Set over *MEDIUM-HIGH* heat and bring to the boil. Reduce heat to *MEDIUM-LOW*, partially cover, and simmer for about 14 minutes, or until vegetables are *crisp-tender*. Using a skimmer or slotted spoon, remove about 1 1/2 cups of cooked potatoes to a bowl and reserve.

Purée the rest of the potatoes and stock, two or three ladlefuls at a time, in the electric blender or in the food processor fitted with steel knife. Add the sautéed onion and garlic. Purée again until smooth. Pour into a large, clean saucepan or kettle.

Using a wire whisk, stir in *white* pepper and cream.

Add the corn kernels and the reserved potatoes. Return to *LOW* heat and allow to heat through. Pour into a *heated* soup tureen.

Serve into heated soup bowls.

Yields 6 servings

Note: This recipe can be halved or doubled, when required.

1/6 SERVING – PROTEIN = 4.2 g.; FAT = 6.4 g.; CARBOHYDRATE = 28.1 g.;
CALORIES = 176; CALORIES FROM FAT = 33%

COLOMBIAN *JICAMA* AND CARROT SALAD WITH MANGO
Ensalada de Jicama y Zanahoria con Mango

TPT - 35 minutes;
30 minutes = refrigeration period

Oh, how my dad loved the taste of mangoes. I do not, however, remember ever tasting a mango, or jicama for that matter, as a child and I do think those are tastes that would have remained in my memory. Mangoes often appear in our produce department at bargain prices now that they are imported from South America, Southeast Asia, and the Indian Subcontinent. I see people just pass them by to buy oh-hum bananas or storage apples. I, however, pounce and buy a few green ones and a few ripe ones and home I go to savor one of the most beautiful fruits on the planet. If I have found a firm, but not too green, mango and a small jicama then this quite simple, but dramatic, slaw goes on the menu. The contrasting flavors and textures of jicama, carrot, and mango play beautifully against each other; the red bell pepper, which may not be traditional, does add a bit of drama.

COLOMBIAN *JICAMA* AND CARROT SALAD WITH MANGO (cont'd)

1 1/2 cups *jicama*—peeled and cut into julienne pieces
1 firm mango—peeled and cut into julienne pieces
1/2 cup julienned carrot
1/4 cup chopped fresh coriander (*cilantro*)
1/4 cup chopped red bell pepper

1/4 cup freshly squeezed lime juice
Freshly ground black pepper, to taste
Several dashes of ground red pepper (cayenne)

In a mixing bowl, combine julienned *jicama*, mango, red bell pepper, and carrot, with chopped fresh coriander (*cilantro*) and red pepper. Toss.

Add lime juice, black pepper, and ground red pepper (cayenne). Again, toss. Refrigerate for at least 30 minutes to allow the flavors to marry. Turn into a serving bowl.

Serve chilled.

Yields 8 servings
adequate for 6 people

Note: This recipe can be halved or doubled, when required.

1/8 SERVING – PROTEIN = 0.6 g.; FAT = 0.4 g.; CARBOHYDRATE = 6.1 g.;
CALORIES = 40; CALORIES FROM FAT = 9%

COLOMBIAN BEANS AND TOMATOES WITH PLANTAINS
Habas y Tomates con Llantenes

TPT - 50 minutes

There is a sweetness to this bean dish that intrigues and satisfies totally. When I first encountered the taste, the dish had been made with an unripened plantain and so that is how I made it. One day, with nothing but a very ripe plantain in the house, I made the dish and was hooked from that day forward on the flavor that the ripened plantain contributes. It is a rich, sweet flavor that is so very complimentary to other dishes.

1 tablespoon *extra virgin* olive oil
1 medium onion—*finely* chopped
1 garlic clove—*very finely* chopped

1 1/2 cups canned, *diced* tomatoes
1 can (14.5 ounces) kidney beans *or* cooked, dry beans—well drained

1 ripe plantain—*finely* chopped
1/2 slice soy bacon—*finely* chopped
Freshly ground mixed peppercorns—red, black, and white—to taste

In a skillet set over *MEDIUM* heat, heat oil. Add *finely* chopped onion and *very finely* chopped garlic. Sauté until onion is soft and translucent, *being careful to allow neither the onion nor the garlic to brown.* Transfer to a saucepan.

Set saucepan over *MEDIUM-LOW* heat. Add diced tomatoes, well-drained kidney beans, *finely* chopped plantain, *finely* chopped soy bacon, and ground mixed peppercorns. Allow to come to the simmer. Cook, stirring frequently for about 30-40 minutes.

Turn into a heated serving bowl. Keep warm on warming tray until ready to serve.*

Yields 6 servings
adequate for 4 people

Notes: *This bean dish is even more flavorful if made the day before it is to be served. Reheat over *LOW* heat.

When required, this recipe can be doubled.

1/6 SERVING – PROTEIN = 6.0 g.; FAT = 2.5 g.; CARBOHYDRATE = 24.7 g.;
CALORIES = 137; CALORIES FROM FAT = 16%

The Americas–Colombia

COCONUT CUSTARD CRUSTLESS PIE
Pastel de Coco

TPT - 1 hour and 10 minutes

Pies and tarts filled with rich coconut custard are popular in Colombia. This pie, which makes its own crust, has all that wonderful taste and texture but with a few less calories. I prefer the taste of fresh coconut in many dishes and often have leftover coconut. Since coconut molds quite quickly, I shred it and dry it either in a slow oven or in my dehydrator. Then, when the urge to have this sweet delight overcomes me, I do not have to rush to the natural food store and I have the wonderful excuse that the coconut should be used up.

1/4 cup unbleached white flour
1/2 teaspoon baking powder

1/4 cup butter—*melted*
3/4 cup sugar

2 large eggs

1 cup *unsweetened*, shredded desiccated coconut
1 cup *two-percent* milk

Preheat oven to 325 degrees F. Prepare a 9-inch pie plate by coating well with non-stick lecithin spray coating.

In a small bowl combine flour and baking powder. Stir to combine thoroughly. Set aside until required.

In a mixing bowl, combine *melted* butter and sugar. Using a wire whisk, whisk until well-mixed.

Add eggs. Whisk until smooth.

Add flour–baking powder mixture, shredded coconut, and milk. Whisk to mix thoroughly. Turn into prepared pie plate. Bake in the middle of the preheated 325 degree F. oven for 1 hour, or until the surface is firm to the touch. Transfer to wire rack and allow to cool to room temperature before serving.

Cut into wedges as with any pie. Refrigerate leftovers.

Yields 8 servings

Note: This pie can be made a day or two in advance of serving and refrigerated. Bring to room temperature before serving.

1/8 SERVING – PROTEIN = 3.6 g.; FAT = 12.3 g.; CARBOHYDRATE = 33.2 g.;
CALORIES = 256; CALORIES FROM FAT = 43%

Costa Rica

Christopher Columbus' visit to this coast during his fourth and final voyage in 1502 led to colonization by the Spanish, who brought their culture and their diseases, just as did the Europeans who colonized North America. Costa Rica is unique in Latin America in that pre-Columbian influences are minimal owing to an almost complete eradication of the native populations by epidemics and war.

Although not a wealthy nation, Costa Rica is rich in many ways that the statisticians fail to take into account. Costa Rica has enjoyed a more politically stable and peaceful history than have neighboring countries and has one of the highest literacy rates in Latin America. The constitutional republic abolished its standing army in an amendment to its constitution, making it the first country in the world to do so. It was ranked first in the Americas and fifth in the world on the 2008 Environmental Performance Index prepared by Yale University and in 2007 declared its intention to achieve carbon neutrality by 2021. Its efforts have earned it acclaim as the "greenest country in the world." Some twenty-three percent of the national territory is included in the Protected Areas system providing habitat stability to its large and diverse plant and animal populations. It is said to have the greatest density of species in the world, encouraging bio- or eco-tourism.

A concerted effort aimed at multi-national manufacturers has created employment opportunities as the likes of Intel, GlaxoSmithKline, and Procter and Gamble have accepted the tax exemptions offered and have established manufacturing facilities. A remarkable spurt in economic growth of five percent was recorded in 2006 but despite the steadily improving economy, sixteen percent of the four and a half million residents remain below the poverty level. A welfare system, with spending as high as is seen in Scandinavia, was implemented to bridge the gap as the government works toward full employment.

Although rice, eaten at almost every meal, and beans are the staples of the cuisine, a reciprocal flow of influences with the islands of the Caribbean to their east has had remarkable influence on the cuisine of Costa Rica. For example, the salad I have included here, although served and enjoyed in Costa Rica, will be found in one form or another on the menus of the many hotels and resorts throughout the Caribbean.

The Americas – Costa Rica

Green Banana and Vegetable Salad
Ensalada de Banana y Vegetales

~~~~~~~~~~~~~~~~~~~~~

Soymeat Meatballs with Tomato and Onion Sauce
Albóndigas de Soya con Salsa de Tomate y Cebolla

Spiced Oven – Browned Potato Wedges
Patatas Bravas

~~~~~~~~~~

Rice Casserole with Tomatoes and Hearts of Palm
Cacerola de Arroz, Tomate, y Palmito

~~~~~~~~~~~~~~~~~~~~~~~

Fresh fruit platter: Blackberries *Moras;* Passion Fruit *Guayaba;* Guava *Granadilla;* Mango; Papaya; Pineapple *Piña;* Cantaloupe *Melon;* Starfruit *Carambola*

garnished with Roasted Cashews
Maranon

Brown Sugar Pound Cake
Queque de Azúcar Moreno, Matequilla, Huevos, y Harina a Partes Iguales

~

Iced Mocha
Café Moca con Helo

GREEN BANANA AND VEGETABLE SALAD IN THE STYLE OF COSTA RICA
Ensalada de Banana y Vegetales

TPT - 1 hour and 20 minutes;
1 hour = marination period

Growing up in a family to whom a potato salad was a picnic, it took some time to consider this recipe which is popular in the Caribbean as well as in Costa Rica. I remember my mother saying, "No, you can't have a banana; they aren't ripe yet." I guess those kind of admonitions get planted, take root, and really are hard to abandon. In this salad the green bananas take the place of another starch, such as a potato, in a salad I could never have imagined as a child.

The Americas – Costa Rica

**GREEN BANANA AND VEGETABLE SALAD
IN THE STYLE OF COSTA RICA** (cont'd)

3 *very green* bananas—peeled

1/4 medium Italian red onion—*thinly* slivered
  to yield about 1 cup
1 cup grape tomato halves
1/4 cup *thinly* sliced red radishes
2 tablespoons light-tasting oil such as safflower
  or sunflower oil
1 tablespoon white wine vinegar
2 tablespoons freshly squeezed lime juice

Salt, to taste
Freshly ground black pepper, to taste

Cut each banana in half lengthwise; then cut each half into half again; and then into 1/2-inch chunks.

In a shallow bowl, combine banana chunks, *thinly* slivered onion, grape tomato halves, and radish slices. Set aside briefly.

In a cruet, combine oil, vinegar, and lime juice. Shake vigorously. Pour over banana–vegetable mixture.

Season with salt and black pepper. Toss to combine well. Set aside for at least 1 hour to allow for flavor development. Turn into a serving bowl.

Serve at room temperature with a slotted spoon.

Yields 6 servings
adequate for 4 people

Notes: *Green-tipped bananas that are just under-ripe for eating are too ripe for this salad. Try to find green bananas or ask your greengrocer. They usually have green bananas ripening in "the back room."

One banana is sufficient for a side salad for two people.

1/6 SERVING – PROTEIN = 1.4 g.; FAT = 2.6 g.; CARBOHYDRATE = 18.6 g.;
CALORIES = 95; CALORIES FROM FAT = 25%

SOYMEAT MEATBALLS IN THE STYLE OF COSTA RICA
WITH TOMATO AND ONION SAUCE

Albondigas de Soya con Salsa de Tomate y Ceboll

TPT - 20 minutes

We had no difficulty giving up meatballs when we became vegetarians, as do some, because neither of our families ate meatballs with their spaghetti. The meat analogue meatballs just became another shape for soy and I tried to find ways to give us variety. This is a really nice sauce for soymeat meatballs. The flavor of the sauce gives them character and although Costa Rican purists might shudder that I have replaced their traditional veal meatballs, we more than appreciate a vegan entrée like this inspired by our neighbors to the South.

2 tablespoons *extra virgin* olive oil
1 cup chopped onion
2 garlic cloves—*finely* chopped

1/2 cup canned, *diced* tomatoes
3 tablespoons tomato purée
1/4 cup red wine
2 tablespoons vegetarian stock of choice
1/2 teaspoon LATIN AMERICAN SPICE MIX
  (Condimento Latino Americano) [see index], or
  to taste

1 package (9 ounces) vegetarian "meatballs"

In a skillet set over *MEDIUM* heat, heat oil. Add chopped onions and *finely* chopped garlic. Sauté until onions are soft and translucent, *being careful to allow neither the onions nor the garlic to brown.*

Add tomatoes, tomato purée, wine, vegetable stock, and spice mixture. Stir to combine well. Cook, stirring frequently, for about 5 minutes.

Add frozen meatballs and cook, stirring frequently, until heated through and liquid is considerably reduced.

Serve at once.

Yields 4 servings
of three meatballs each

Note: This recipe can be double, when required.

1/4 SERVING – PROTEIN = 13.0 g.; FAT = 9.0 g.; CARBOHYDRATE = 11.9 g.;
CALORIES = 169; CALORIES FROM FAT = 48%

COSTA RICAN SPICED OVEN – BROWNED POTATO WEDGES
Patatas Bravas
TPT - 57 minutes

Oven–browned potato wedges have always been a favorite of ours. When we found that Latin Americans roasted potato wedges in much the same way we did but with an exciting mixture of spices, we were on the trail of a new favorite. Although you will find rice at almost every Costa Rica meal, potatoes, especially roasted potato wedges, are an alternative appreciated by all.

Zacapa, a prized Guatemalan cheese, would be just perfect for this dish. However, it is rarely, if ever, available outside of Guatemala. Parmesan and Romano cheeses substitute adequately.

4 large Idaho baking potatoes—well-scrubbed but *unpeeled*

1/2 cup *high heat* safflower *or* sunflower oil
1/4 cup grated Parmesan *or* pecorino Romano cheese, as preferred
2 teaspoons LATIN AMERICAN SPICE MIX *(Condimento Latino Americano)* [see index]

Preheat oven to 375 degrees F. Prepare a large, shallow baking pan by oiling.

Cut potatoes into six wedges each. Stand wedges peel-side-down in prepared baking pan.

In a 2-cup liquid measuring cup, combine oil, grated cheese, and spice mixture. Stir well to combine thoroughly. Using a pastry brush, brush each potato wedge with mixture.

Bake in preheated 375 degree F. oven for about 45 minutes, until golden brown and fork-tender. Baste one or two times during the baking period until oil mixture is used up. Remove from oven. Transfer to heated serving platter.

Serve at once.

Yields 6 servings
adequate for 4-5 people

Note: This recipe may be halved or doubled, when required.

1/6 SERVING (i. e., 6 wedges) –
PROTEIN = 4.5 g.; FAT = 11.1 g.; CARBOHYDRATE = 30.4 g.;
CALORIES = 238; CALORIES FROM FAT = 42%

COSTA RICAN RICE CASSEROLE WITH TOMATOES AND HEARTS OF PALM
Cacerola de Arroz, Tomate, y Palmito
TPT - 45 minutes

Hearts of palm are expensive and deservedly so since a palmetto palm is sacrificed for the heart to give us this delicious and texturally unique vegetable. Palmetto trees are grown on large plantations in Costa Rica to supply the worldwide demand. Some plantations do grow the palms organically so search your grocery stores and natural food stores. This casserole is a meal in itself and easily prepared.

2 cups *cooked* converted rice
1/2 cup *fat-free* dairy sour cream
1 cup diced *low-moisture, part-skimmed milk* mozzarella, Muenster, *or* Monterey Jack cheese, as preferred
3 tablespoons *finely* chopped onion
1/2 cup canned, *crushed* tomatoes
1 cup *thinly* sliced hearts of palm

1 tablespoon butter—diced

Preheat oven to 375 degrees F. Prepare a 1 quart oven-to-table casserole, such as a soufflé dish by coating with non-stick lecithin spray coating.

COSTA RICAN RICE CASSEROLE WITH TOMATOES AND HEARTS OF PALM (cont'd)

Arrange ingredients in casserole as follows:

~ Layer *one-half* of the cooked rice into the prepared baking dish.

~ Layer *one-half* of sour cream over the rice in dollops.

~ Layer *one-half* of the diced cheese over the sour cream layer.

~ Sprinkle *all* of the *finely* chopped onion over the cheese.

~ Layer *one-half* of the crushed tomatoes over the onions.

~ Layer *one-half* of the thinly sliced hearts of palm over the tomatoes.

Repeat the layers, omitting the onion this time.

Dot the top with the diced butter.* Bake in preheated 375 degree oven for 20 minutes, or until heated through and lightly browned on top.

Serve at once using a slotted spoon.

Yields 6 servings
adequate for 4 people

Notes: *The casserole can be prepared ahead to this point and refrigerated until ready to bake.

This recipe can be doubled, when required.

1/6 SERVING – PROTEIN = 8.0 g.; FAT = 5.6 g.; CARBOHYDRATE = 28.1 g.;
CALORIES = 179; CALORIES FROM FAT = 28%

BROWN SUGAR POUND CAKE
Qeuque de Azúcar Moreno, Mantequilla, Huevos, y Harina a Partes Iguales

TPT - 1 hour and 42 minutes;
30 minutes = cooling period

I shall always remember the blandly flavored and too sweet, slices of pound cake, wrapped in plastic and offered as emergency sustenance in gas stations and next to the cash register at restaurants along my route as I drove back and forth from Michigan to my family home on Long Island and to my grandmother's home in Rochester, New York. Pound cake became popular as a tea cake or dessert base because it kept well and responded well to a myriad of flavors, such as orange, lemon, rum, brandy, and almond, making every baking session a creative experience. I found the Spanish name for pound cake amusing but it could not have been more descriptive or more accurate. Pound cake actually did get its name because it was originally made with a pound each of butter, sugar, eggs, and flour. Although the ingredients below do not reflect tradition, our pound cake is still popular in our household as a tea cake and as a dessert base.

2 cups sifted cake flour
1 cup whole wheat flour
1/4 teaspoon baking soda
1/4 teaspoon freshly grated nutmeg

1 1/4 cups (2 1/2 sticks) butter—*softened to room temperature*
1 1/4 cups firmly packed *light* brown sugar
[see next page]

BROWN SUGAR POUND CAKE (cont'd)

1 1/4 cups *fat-free* pasteurized eggs (the equivalent of 5 eggs)
1 1/2 teaspoons pure vanilla extract

1/2 cup *unsalted* buttermilk

Preheat oven to 350 degrees F. Prepare two 7 x 3 x 2-inch loaf pans by coating with non-stick lecithin spray coating. Dust with cake flour.

Into a large mixing bowl, sift cake and whole wheat flours with baking soda and nutmeg. Set aside.

Using the electric mixer or food processor fitted with steel knife, cream butter until light and fluffy. Add sugar and continue to cream for 5-7 minutes until again light and fluffy.

Reduce mixer speed. Beat in pasteurized eggs and vanilla extract. Continue beating until thoroughly combined.

Add sifted flours alternately with the buttermilk, beating until batter is very smooth.

Divide between prepared cake pans. Rap each sharply on the counter top to release any large bubbles.

Bake in preheated 350 degree F. oven for 40-50 minutes, or until a cake tester inserted in the center comes our clean.

Cool on wire rack for 10 minutes. Remove cakes from baking pans and cool *completely* on wire racks.*

Yields two small loaves
each yielding about 10 slices

Note: *The texture of this cake and the ease with which it can be sliced greatly improve if it is wrapped after it has cooled completely and allowed to rest overnight.

1/2 SERVING (i. e., per cake) –
PROTEIN = 33.0 g.; FAT = 115.2 g.; CARBOHYDRATE = 273.8 g;
CALORIES = 2269; CALORIES FROM FAT = 46%

1/20 SERVING (i. e., per slice) –
PROTEIN = 3.3 g.; FAT = 11.5 g.; CARBOHYDRATE = 27.4 g.;
CALORIES = 227; CALORIES FROM FAT = 46%

COSTA RICAN ICED MOCHA
Café Moca con Helo

TPT - 1 hour and 3 minutes;
1 hour = coffee chilling period

This is a smashing and unexpected, sweet ending to a meal and even those who generally drink tea are thoroughly satisfied. I serve this at the end of a Latin American menu with a plate of cookies or small cakes. It never fails to please.

1 1/2 cups freshly brewed Costa Rican coffee

1/2 cup light cream *or* half and half*
1 teaspoon sugar
1 1/2 teaspoons BASIC CHOCOLATE SYRUP
[see index]
1 teaspoon honey

4 large ice cubes

Chill brewed coffee for at least 1 hour.

In a pitcher, combine *chilled* coffee, cream, sugar, chocolate syrup, and honey. Stir to mix thoroughly. Refrigerate until ready to serve.

For each serving, place a large ice cube in each of four wine glasses. For each serving, pour 1/2 cupful of coffee mixture over ice cube.

Serve at once.

Yields 4 servings

Notes: *Cream makes this a rich and satisfying dessert but whole milk can be substituted, if desired.

This recipe can be doubled, when required.

1/4 SERVING – PROTEIN = 0.9 g.; FAT = 2.8 g.; CARBOHYDRATE = 4.1 g.;
CALORIES = 38; CALORIES FROM FAT = 66%

Ecuador

The country that we know as Ecuador began with scattered tribal civilizations. The Valdivia Culture and the Machalilla Culture established on the coast of the Pacific Ocean. The people referred to as the Cañari settled near the present city of Cuenca in the province of Azuay. The Quitus Culture established about 1000 AD near the present-day capital of Ecuador, Quito. These distinct tribes with different pottery styles, architecture, and religious practices were eventually absorbed into the great Inca Empire in the 1400s.

The Spanish conquistador Francisco Pizzarro conquered Peru and in 1563 Quito became the administrative seat of Spain and part of the Viceroyalty of Peru, which was later known as the Viceroyalty of New Granada. The Spanish rule was long and brutal. In 1820 Guayaquil became the first city in Ecuador to achieve independence from Spain but it took until 1822 for the rest of Ecuador to gain independence and this only after the Royalist forces were defeated by the forces under Antonio José de Sucre at the Battle of Pichincha. After the defeat of Spain, Ecuador joined Venezuela and Colombia in Simon Bolivar's Republic of Gran Colombia. Ecuador became a republic in 1830 but the period that followed was marked by great instability. War broke out with Peru in 1941 and a tentative peace agreement over the disputed border regions, where hostilities continued, was not signed until October 1998.

Ecuador has had forty-eight dictators in one hundred and thirty-one years but is today a democratic state having adopted a new constitution in 2007. Its challenges are enormous. Approximately sixty-five percent of the population of over fifteen million are of mixed Amerindian and white, *mestizo*, and twenty-five percent are Amerindian. Thirty-five percent of the population, live below the poverty line and these statistics have stayed relatively constant due in part to the fluctuation of crude oil prices since the late 1990s. Crude oil exportation is the country's biggest export and the impact on the economy could not be counter-balanced by agricultural exports since this drop in oil revenues coincided with the beginning of an *El Niño* period. The loss of fish and seafood for consumption and for export during this cyclic phenomenon, when the ocean temperature increases, greatly impacts the population. Ecuador is the primary exporter of bananas in world and an important exporter of cocoa and coffee. Flowers, especially roses, are exported from Ecuador to the United States. Timber, sugar, tropical oils, hearts of palm, rice, and corn are exported but the torrential rain events that accompany an *El Niño* weather pattern reduced harvest of these exportable products.

Ecuador is categorized as a megadiverse country of which there are only seventeen so categorized. Its biodiversity is astounding and it is said to have the greatest biodiversity of any nation on Earth. Environmental and human factors are, however, threatening this extraordinary ecosystem, especially that of the unique Galapagos Islands. The oil industry which is bringing wealth to Ecuador is doing so at a price. Although Ecuador is about the size of Nevada, the population of over fifteen million is concentrated in the region known as *La Costa*, along the Pacific Ocean, and in *La Sierra*, the Andeans highlands. The Galapagos Islands, *The Archipiélago de Colón or the Región Insular*, off the coast of the country and the Amazonic area to the East which comprises slightly under fifty-percent of the country's total land mass, *La Amazonia* or *El Oriente*, are relatively unpopulated. Two parallel ranges of the Andes Mountains run through Ecuador and many of those mountains are volcanic. Actively volcanic Mount Chimborozo at 6,310 meters (over 18,000 feet) above sea level is considered the point most distant from the center of the planet.

Many dishes found in Ecuador are understandably also found, with some variation, in Peru and Colombia. However, you will detect, in the menu suggestions that follow, the considerable influence of *mestizo* heritage in the cuisine.

The Americas—Ecuador

Steamed Corn- and Cheese-Stuffed Corn Husks
Humitas
or
Fried Corn and Cheese Fritters
Arepas
with *Crème Fraîche* or Sour Cream

~

Hearts of Palm Salad with Cheese
Ensalada de Palmito y Queso

Cabbage Salad with Avocado and Pickled Red Onion Relish
Ensalada de Repollo y Aguacate
and
Pickled Red Onion Relish with Lime Juice
Cebollas Encurtidas

~

Potato and Cheese Soup   **Vegetarian Vegetable Soup**
Locro   *Sopa de Vegetales*

~~~~~~~~~~~~~~~~~~~~~

Potato Cakes with Peanut Sauce
Llapingachos

Creamy Quinoa
Quinoto

Sautéed Artichoke Hearts

~~~~~~~~~~~~~~~~~~~~~

Dulce de Leche Soufflé   **Milk Cake**
Soufflé de Dulce de Leche   *Pastel de Leche*

Dulce de Leche
Dulce de Leche

Demitasse Cups of Hot Chocolate

Slices of Fresh Pineapple, Red Bananas, and Papaya

ECUADORIAN STEAMED CORN- AND CHEESE-STUFFED CORN HUSKS
Humitas

TPT - 1 hour and 30 minutes

I had not made these for many years because I could not find a source for pesticide-free corn husks. Living, as we do, in farm country alerts you to the way the food supply is grown and how easily it is adulterated by farming techniques. I had tried to grow a few rows of corn to provide the needed husks but unless you do a sizable planting, you do not get efficient cross fertilization and ear formation . . . therefore, no great big lovely husks to stuff. Several organic cooperative farms in our area now provide organically-grown corn. The husks can be dried during the summer and stored so that these wonderful tamales can surprise for a winter breakfast. I prefer to make them the Ecuadorian way because they are steamed, unlike those make in Argentina, Chili, and Peru where they are generally fried in oil. In Mexico and Central America they are known as "tamales," in Venezuela they are known as "hallacas," and you will find them in Peru and Chile where they are also called "humitas." This version, which includes baking powder, is light and sweet.

2/3 cup yellow corn meal
1/2 teaspoon baking powder

2 cups green (fresh) *or frozen* corn kernels
1 1/2 cups *finely* chopped (about 6 ounces) *low-moisture, part-skimmed milk mozzarella* cheese or *queso blanco**
1/2 cup *finely* chopped onion
1 large garlic clove—*crushed and finely* chopped
1/2 teaspoon ground coriander

1/2 cup *fat-free* pasteurized eggs (the equivalent of 2 eggs)
1 tablespoon *melted* butter
2 tablespoons light cream *or* half and half

Fresh, well-washed corn husks *or* well-soaked dried corn husks

Set up steamer.

In a small bowl, combine corn meal and baking powder. Stir to combine. Set aside until required.

In the work bowl of the food processor fitted with steel knife, combine corn kernels, *finely* chopped cheese, onion, and garlic, and ground coriander. Process until finely and uniformly chopped, scraping down the sides of the work bowl as necessary.

Add corn meal and baking powder. Process until well-combined.

Add pasteurized eggs, *melted* butter, and cream. Process until well-integrated. Turn into a mixing bowl.

Use two corn husks for each *humita*. Place them one inside the other and pull the inside one to the side to form a pocket. Spoon a tablespoonful or two, depending on the size of corn husk pocket, into the center. Fold the sides of the husk toward the center and fold each end over and toward the middle of the bundle. Tie each bundle with a strip of corn husk torn from one of the smaller husks which you probably would not use otherwise. Continue filling and wrapping the bundles until you have run out of corn husks or filling.** Place in steamer set over *MEDIUM* heat and steam for about 40 minutes. Transfer to a heated serving platter.

Serve at once with hot sauce or *salsa* of choice, if desired. Diners untie the bundle and, using a spoon or a fork, scoop out the corn and cheese cake.

Yields about 12 *humitas*

Notes: *Other cheeses, such as farmers' cheese, a drained *ricotta*, Muenster, or Monterey Jack, can be substituted. *Mozzarella*, however, gives a very gooey result that is fun.

**In our experience, this makes about twelve *humitas*. Smaller corn husks can be tucked one on top of the other to finish off the filling, if need be.

This recipe can be halved or doubled, when required.

1/12 SERVING – PROTEIN = 7.3 g.; FAT = 4.4 g.; CARBOHYDRATE = 17.3 g.; CALORIES = 126; CALORIES FROM FAT = 10%

ECUADORIAN FRIED CORN AND CHEESE FRITTERS
Arepas
TPT - 51 minutes

A recent grocery store purchase brought me face to face with a frozen convenience product that sent me right back to my recipe files. The arepas that I found frozen were dense and heavy with little evidence of the cheesy wonderfulness I remembered. I prepared this old friend and sighed. Yes, arepas can be light, running with cheesiness, and thoroughly addictive.

2 cups green (fresh) *or* frozen corn—*thawed and well-drained*
2 tablespoons *melted* butter
2 tablespoons *fat-free* pasteurized eggs
1 tablespoon milk

1/2 cup *masa harina**
1 tablespoon sugar

1 tablespoon grated *pecorino Romano* cheese
1/4 cup shredded, *low-moisture, part-skimmed milk* mozzarella cheese *or* queso blanco

1 tablespoon *high heat* safflower *or* sunflower oil
1 tablespoon butter

Fat-free dairy sour cream *or* crème fraîche

In the work bowl of the food processor fitted with steel knife, combine thawed and well-drained frozen corn, 2 tablespoonfuls melted butter, pasteurized eggs, and milk. Process until puréed and smooth.

Add *masa harina* and sugar. Pulse the mixture until the corn meal has been integrated. Allow to stand for about 30 minutes.

Add grated *Romano* cheese and shredded *mozzarella* to the batter in the food processor work bowl. Process until integrated.

In a large, non-stick-coated skillet set over *MEDIUM* heat, heat oil and the remaining tablespoonful of butter. When the oil and butter are hot and the foam has subsided, drop the batter by tablespoonfuls onto the hot surface. Press each down and fry. *Be careful not to allow the cakes to burn.* Turn and flatten the fritter. Fry until evenly browned—about 8 minutes total. Remove to a heated serving platter set on a warming tray or in a warm oven. Repeat until all are prepared.

Serve hot with sour cream or *crème fraîche*.

Yields about 24 small fritters

Notes: *Masa harina* is a corn meal that is milled to a fine texture, perfect for making *tortillas*. It is generally available in the international aisle of most well-stocked grocery stores.

This recipe can be halved, when required.

1/15 SERVING (per fritter exclusive of sour cream or *crème fraîche*) –
PROTEIN = 1.7 g.; FAT = 2.5 g.; CARBOHYDRATE = 9.1 g.;
CALORIES = 61; CALORIES FROM FAT = 37%

ECUADORIAN HEARTS OF PALM SALAD WITH CHEESE
Ensalada de Palmito y Queso
TPT - 7 minutes

The gorgeous ivory spears that are the interior, the heart, of the palmetto tree, the official state tree of Florida, have a taste and silky texture that is unique. The tree must be sacrificed to extract the heart, accounting therefore for the high retail price, but it is worth the expense to taste it in this Ecuadorian salad.

1 can (14 ounces) hearts of palm—*drained, well-rinsed and sliced into rounds*
1 medium tomato—*peeled, seeded, and chopped*
1/2 cup pitted *Kalamata* olives—*sliced*
1 large garlic clove—*very finely* chopped
1 tablespoon chopped mild green *chilies*

1 1/2 tablespoons *extra virgin* olive oil
1 tablespoon GARLIC–BASIL VINEGAR *[see index] or* other white or herb vinegar of choice
1 teaspoon honey
1 teaspoon freshly squeezed lime juice

2 teaspoons capers—*drained and well-rinsed*
1/2 cup *slivered, low-moisture, part-skimmed milk* mozzarella cheese

ECUADORIAN HEARTS OF PALM SALAD WITH CHEESE (cont'd)

In a large mixing bowl, combine palm heart slices, chopped tomato, sliced olives, *very finely* chopped garlic, and chopped green *chilies*.

In a small bowl, combine oil, vinegar, honey, and lime juice. Whisk to blend well. Add to hearts of palm mixture and toss to mix.

Add capers and *slivered* cheese and, again, toss.

Refrigerate until ready to serve.

Yields 6 servings
adequate for 4 people

Note: This recipe can be halved, when required.

1/6 SERVING – PROTEIN = 4.9 g.; FAT = 6.3 g.; CARBOHYDRATE = 5.9 g.;
CALORIES = 88; CALORIES FROM FAT = 64%

CABBAGE SALAD WITH AVOCADO AND ECUADORIAN PICKLED RED ONION RELISH WITH LIME JUICE
Ensalada de Repollo y Aguacate
TPT - 12 minutes

Shredded cabbage salads and sautéed cabbage are often found as part of Ecuadorian meals. Here the tartness of the red onion relish with lime juice, unique to Ecuador, plays off the mayonnaise and avocado for a very different salad, a salad that really compliments an Ecuadorian menu.

4 cups *finely* shredded white/green cabbage—well-rinsed and well-dried
3 tablespoons *calorie reduced or light* mayonnaise with olive oil
Freshly ground black pepper, to taste

9 tablespoons ECUADORIAN PICKLED RED ONION RELISH WITH LIME JUICE *[see recipe which follows]*

2 ripe avocados—sliced

In a mixing bowl, combine *finely* shredded cabbage and mayonnaise. Combine very thoroughly. Season with black pepper. Again, combine well. Refrigerate until ready to serve.

Apportion cabbage salad onto six salad plates. Using a slotted spoon, spoon about 1 1/2 tablespoonfuls of the red onion relish beside it on each plate. Arrange a portion of the avocado slices attractively over the cabbage salad on each salad plate.

Serve at once.

Yields 6 individual servings

Note: This recipe can be increased or decreased proportionately, as required.

1/6 SERVING – PROTEIN = 2.4 g.; FAT = 13.6 g.; CARBOHYDRATE = 9.2 g.;
CALORIES = 155; CALORIES FROM FAT = 79%

The Americas – Ecuador

ECUADORIAN PICKLED RED ONION RELISH WITH LIME JUICE
Cebollas Encurtidas

TPT - 3 hours and 22 minutes;
 3 hours = minimum flavor development period

Red onions are used extensively in Ecuador. This relish is popular from Mexico right down to Peru; some make it with vinegar and / or lemon juice or orange juice but lime juice does wonderful things to the onion taste and the color will astound you. You will often hear this called the "purple sauce."

1 medium Italian red onion—peeled, halved, and *thinly* sliced
***Boiling* water**

1/4 cup freshly squeezed lime juice
Pinch of sugar
1/4 teaspoon crushed, dried oregano*
Salt, to taste
Freshly ground black pepper, to taste

Prepare a 1 pint canning jar by sterilizing. Sterilize a lid and a ring too.

Put sliced onions in a mixing bowl and cover with *boiling* water. Allow to stand for about 15 minutes. Drain well. Turn onion slices into a dry bowl.

Add lime juice, sugar, crushed oregano, salt and black pepper. Turn into sterilized canning jar and seal. Refrigerate for at least 3 hours or, preferably, overnight to allow for flavor development.

This keeps well for about 1 week.

Yields 1 1/2 cupfuls

Notes: *Rub the oregano between your palms to produce a uniformly fine powder.

This recipe can be doubled, when required.

1/20 SERVING (i. e., per tablespoonful) –
PROTEIN = 0.1 g.; FAT = 0.0 g.; CARBOHYDRATE = 0.6 g.;
CALORIES = 2; CALORIES FROM FAT = <1%

ECUADORIAN POTATO AND CHEESE SOUP
Locro

TPT - 1 hour and 23 minutes

Venezuelans and Peruvians both enjoy this simple, comforting soup. But do not expect a bland potato soup because this one has character. It may seem like a lot of garlic but, in our opinion, it is the garlic that gives it a taste to remember. The celery leaves, although not authentic, add an almost unidentifiable flavor and since celery is one vegetable that is high in sodium, its sodium contribution is absorbed by the potatoes and you will find that you do not need to add much salt.

1 tablespoon butter
1 small onion—*very finely* chopped
2 large garlic cloves—*very finely* chopped

2 cups VEGETABLE STOCK FROM SOUP
 [see index] *or* other vegetarian stock of choice
1/2 cup *two-percent* milk
2 medium potatoes—peeled and diced
1 tablespoon celery leaves—*very finely* chopped

Salt, to taste
Freshly ground black pepper, to taste

3/4 cup shredded *queso fresco*, if available, Muenster, *or* low-moisture, part-skimmed milk mozzarella cheese

1 ripe avocado—peeled and chopped*

In a small kettle set over *MEDIUM* heat, melt butter. Add *very finely* chopped onion and garlic. Sauté until onion is soft and translucent, *being careful to allow neither the onion nor the garlic to brown.*

Add vegetable stock, milk, diced potatoes, and *very finely* chopped celery leaves. Allow to come to the boil. Reduce heat to *MEDIUM-LOW* and simmer soup for about 50 minutes until potatoes are very soft. Using a potato masher, mash the potatoes a few times to thicken the soup. *Do not mash too much; the soup should have chunks of potato in it.*

Season with salt and pepper.

Add shredded cheese. Stir until cheese begins to melt. Transfer the soup to a heated soup tureen.

Garnish with chopped avocado.

ECUADORIAN POTATO AND CHEESE SOUP (cont'd)

Serve at once into heated soup bowls.

Yields 6 cupfuls

Notes: *If you have avocado elsewhere in the menu, you may wish to omit this garnish.

This recipe can be doubled, when required.

1/6 SERVING (i. e., about 1 cupful) –
PROTEIN = 6.8 g.; FAT = 12.1 g.; CARBOHYDRATE = 9.5 g.;
CALORIES = 154; CALORIES FROM FAT = 71%

ECUADORIAN VEGETARIAN VEGETABLE SOUP
Sopa de Vegetables
TPT - 50 minutes

During World War II oleomargarine was introduced to replace butter. It was white like lard and thoroughly unappealing so food coloring was placed in a sealed button in the package. You broke the button and kneaded the package until the fat took on a "yellowish" color; I guess it was supposed to console you but it added red dye #3, now banned, to every meal. Today achiote or annatto seeds are used to color butter and margarines. The achiote shrub (Bixa orellana), native to tropical region of the Americas, produces a large spiny, red fruit filled with red seeds which can be added to dishes to augment the color and is a staple in the larders of Latin American cooks. It should also be noted that this seed is one of the richest natural sources of vitamin E in the form of delta-tocotrienol and gamma tocotrienol. The plant is also found in Southeast Asia and is used extensively in Filipino cooking. This vegetable soup is a truly beautiful soup.

ACHIOTE OIL:
    3 or 4 *achiote / annatto* seeds
    2 tablespoons *hot* olive oil

1 quart VEGETABLE STOCK FROM SOUP *[see index]* or other vegetarian stock of choice
1 medium potato—peeled and diced

1 tablespoon *extra virgin* olive oil
1 teaspoon *achiote* oil *[see above]*
1 medium yellow summer squash—peeled, seeded, and diced
1 medium zucchini—well-washed and diced
1/2 cup *finely* chopped Italian red onion
1 cup green (fresh) *or* frozen corn kernels

Freshly ground black pepper, to taste

2 tablespoons grated *pecorino Romano* cheese

In a small Pyrex dish combine *achiote / annatto* seeds in hot olive oil. Stir to encourage the release of the coloring into the oil. Place on a warming tray and, stirring frequently, allow the oil to color.

In a large saucepan set over *MEDIUM-HIGH* heat, combine vegetable stock and diced potato. Allow to come to the boil. Reduce heat to *MEDIUM*. Simmer until potatoes are soft. Remove from heat and allow to cool for about 10 minutes.

Using an electric blender, purée the potatoes and stock until smooth. Turn into a clean saucepan.

In a skillet set over *MEDIUM* heat, heat oil and *achiote* oil. Add diced yellow squash, and zucchini, *finely* chopped red onion, and corn. Sauté until onion is soft. Turn vegetables into the saucepan with puréed potatoes and stock. Place over *MEDIUM* heat and allow to come to the simmer. Cook, stirring frequently, for 5 minutes.

Season with black pepper. Turn into a heated soup tureen.

Serve into heated soup bowls. Sprinkle a teaspoonful of grated cheese over each serving.

Yields 6 cupfuls

Note: This recipe can be halved or doubled, when required, but note that is does not freeze well..

1/6 SERVING – PROTEIN = 3.3 g.; FAT = 3.7 g.; CARBOHYDRATE = 16.5 g.;
CALORIES = 101; CALORIES FROM FAT = 33%

The Americas—Ecuador

ECUADORIAN POTATO CAKES WITH PEANUT SAUCE
Llapingachos
TPT - 40 minutes

The Incas in the Andes of South America had been using the potato for food long before the arrival of the Spanish conquistadors. Although the Spanish are said to have brought the first potato from Quito, Ecuador, to Spain in 1539, the first written reference to this food was made in 1553 and the rest, as they say, is history. Potatoes are still important to the cuisines of South America. Their continued cultivation of old varieties is a practical science which we too should practice. In Ecuador a fried or poached egg is usually served on top of each potato cake. We have chosen to omit the eggs.

1/2 cup VEGETARIAN BROWN *or* WHITE STOCK, as preferred *[see index]*
2 medium onions—chopped

2 cups *cold* mashed potatoes*
2 medium scallions—trimmed, well-rinsed, and *finely* chopped
2 tablespoons chopped fresh parsley
2 tablespoons *fat-free* pasteurized eggs**

1 ounce *queso blanco or* Monterey Jack cheese —cut into 4 squares about 1/4 inch thick

About 3 tablespoons yellow corn meal

2 tablespoons butter

3 tablespoons *unsalted, additive-free, smooth* peanut butter

1 cup VEGETARIAN BROWN *or* WHITE STOCK, as preferred *[see index]*—**heated to boiling**

4 large lettuce leaves

2 tablespoons freshly shelled, *unsalted, additive-free* peanut halves

In a large skillet set over *LOW* heat, combine 1/2 cupful stock and chopped onions. Sauté until onions are soft and translucent, *being careful not to allow onions to brown.* Add more stock, if necessary to prevent browning. Remove from heat.

While onions are cooking, combine *cold* mashed potatoes with chopped scallions and parsley in a mixing bowl. Stir to combine well. Add pasteurized eggs and blend thoroughly.

Divide potato mixture into four equal portions and shape each portion around a piece of cheese, forming four 1-inch-thick cakes. Lightly coat each cake with corn meal.

In a large skillet set over *LOW-MEDIUM* heat, melt 2 tablespoonfuls of butter. Add potato cakes and cook until browned on both sides. Use a wide spatula to turn cakes. This avoids breakage. Remove to a warm plate set on a warming tray or in a warm oven. Keep warm until ready to serve.

Meanwhile, stir peanut butter into sautéed onions. Gradually, while stirring constantly, stir the remaining 1 cupful *hot* stock into mixture. Continue stirring until sauce is smooth and thickened. Add water, if necessary, to obtain the desired consistency.

Transfer peanut sauce into warmed sauceboat. Keep warm on a warming tray, also, until ready to serve.

To serve, place a lettuce leaf on each of four plates. Place a potato cake on each lettuce leaf. Garnish each serving with peanut halves.

Serve at once. Pass prepared peanut sauce to accommodate individual tastes.

Yields 4 individual servings

Notes: *This is an excellent use for leftover potatoes or for *planned leftovers.*

**Because raw eggs present the danger of *Salmonella* poisoning, commercially-available pasteurized eggs are recommended for use in preparing the potato cakes.

This recipe may be halved or doubled, when required.

1/4 SERVING – PROTEIN = 9.1 g.; FAT = 15.0 g.; CARBOHYDRATE = 29.3 g.;
CALORIES = 282; CALORIES FROM FAT = 48%

ECUADORIAN CREAMY *QUINOA*
Quinoto

TPT - 46 minutes

Quinoa is an ancient, ancient grain, cultivated by the Incas and rediscovered in the 1980s by two Americans who reestablished it as a specialty grain here in the United States. It is increasingly used to boost the protein in commercial foods. Referred to by the Incas as the "mother grain," it is called a super grain by nutritionist because the amino acids it contains require no complementation. In this spectacular recipe quinoa is cooked in a manner similar to risotto creating a creamy and most delicious dish.

1 cup *quinoa*—well-rinsed*
2 quarts *boiling* water

1 1/2 tablespoons butter
2 teaspoons *extra virgin* olive oil
1/4 cup *finely* chopped onion
1 garlic clove—*very finely* chopped

1/2 – 1 cup VEGETARIAN WHITE STOCK *[see index]* or other vegetarian stock of choice

1/4 cup light cream or half and half
Freshly ground black pepper
2 tablespoons grated *pecorino Romano* cheese

In a saucepan set over *LOW* heat, combine *quinoa* and *boiling* water. Cover and allow quinoa to cook for about 25 minutes, stirring occasionally. It should be soft and creamy and most of the water should have been absorbed. Drain well.

In a large non-stick-coated skillet set over *MEDIUM* heat, combine butter and oil. Add *finely* chopped onion and *very finely* chopped garlic. Sauté until onion is soft and translucent, *being careful to allow neither the onion nor the garlic to brown. Reduce heat to LOW.*

Add *cooked quinoa. Gradually, tablespoonful by tablespoonful*, add vegetable stock *while stirring constantly*. Cook, *stirring constantly*, until *quinoa* absorbs the liquid and expands. Set aside on a warming tray if not quite ready to serve.

When ready to serve, set over *LOW-MEDIUM* heat and allow to reheat while *stirring constantly*. Stir cream, black pepper, and grated cheese into the cooked grain. Turn into a heated serving bowl. Sprinkle with grated cheese.

Serve at once.

Yields 6 servings
adequate for 4 people

Note: *Quinoa, punto graneado*, is generally available in well-stocked natural food stores. Refrigeration, after you purchase a supply, will lengthen its shelf life. The seeds are naturally coated with saponins, most of which are removed by washing and rubbing after harvest. However, it is advisable to rinse well before cooking.

1/8 SERVING – PROTEIN = 3.9 g.; FAT = 6.6 g.; CARBOHYDRATE = 15.3 g.;
CALORIES = 139; CALORIES FROM FAT = 43%

DULCE DE LECHE SOUFFLÉ
Souffle con Dulce de Leche

TPT - 22 minutes

Yes, this is called a soufflé in Ecuador. And, yes, it shows very little resemblance to the French soufflés I learned to make. It is an unusual, traditional dessert using the much-loved dulce de leche. It is wonderfully dramatic as it rises to impressive heights, but very, very simple to make.

3/4 cup prepared *dulce de leche* [see recipe which follows]

4 large egg whites

4 large egg yolks
1/4 cup sugar

Sweetened whipped cream, for garnish, if desired
1 teaspoon ground, *preservative-free* almonds, for garnish

Preheat oven to 385 degree F. Prepare a 2 1/2-cup *soufflé* dish by coating the dish with the lecithin spray coating for baking.

DULCE DE LECHE SOUFFLÉ (cont'd)

Using a rubber spatula, spread the prepared *dulce de leche* over the bottom of the prepared *soufflé* dish.

Using an electric mixer fitted with *grease-free* beaters or by hand, using a *grease-free* wire whisk, beat egg whites in a *grease-free* bowl until *stiff*, but *not dry*. Spread beaten egg whites over the *dulce de leche* layer.

In the mixer bowl, combine egg yolks and sugar. Beat until very creamy. Spread over the egg whites. Bake in preheated 385 degree F. oven for 11-12 minutes.

Serve at once. Garnish each serving with a dollop of whipped cream, if desired, and a sprinkling of ground almonds.

Yields 6 servings
adequate for 4 people

1/6 SERVING (exclusive of whipped cream garnish) –
PROTEIN = 4.5 g.; FAT = 2.4 g.; CARBOHYDRATE = 17.6 g.;
CALORIES = 111; CALORIES FROM FAT = 20%

DULCE DE LECHE
Dulce de Leche

TPT - about 4 hours and 6 minutes

Over the years I have tried many recipes for dulce de leche including the dangerous and not recommended method of boiling cans of sweetened condensed milk. An oven experiment ended with an oven-cleaning; a top of the stove ended with burned bits in the bottom of the pan. This double boiler method is much more reliable and the combination of fat-free sweetened condensed milk and skimmed evaporated milk results in a less sweet, low-fat, caramelized "milk sweet" that works well in recipes calling for dulce de leche and is not so sweet as to make your teeth hurt when you dip your tasting spoon into the final product.

1 can (14 ounces) *fat-free* **sweetened condensed milk**
1 can (12 ounces) evaporated *skimmed* **milk**
1/2 teaspoon baking soda

1 tablespoon corn syrup
1/2 teaspoon pure vanilla extract

In the top half of a double boiler set over *boiling* water, combine sweetened condensed milk, evaporated milk, and baking soda. Using a wire whisk, stir to combine thoroughly. Set over *LOW-MEDIUM* heat and allow to cook for about 3-4 hours, or until the mixture is thick and brown. *Stir frequently.*

When thickened, remove from heat and beat until very smooth.

Add corn syrup and vanilla extract. Beat again until very smooth. Pour through a fine sieve into a clean bowl two or three times to remove any lumps. Allow to cool slightly. Turn into a stone crock or jar and refrigerate.

Yields about 1 1/2 cupfuls

Note: This recipe can not be doubled.

1/20 SERVING (i. e., per tablespoonful) –
PROTEIN = 2.7 g.; FAT = 0.0 g.; CARBOHYDRATE = 15.3 g.;
CALORIES = 74; CALORIES FROM FAT = 0%

ECUADORIAN MILK CAKE
Pastel de Leche

TPT - 2 hours and 30 minutes;
    30 minutes = cake cooling period;
    1 hour = cake flavoring period

Sometimes a piece of cake would seem the perfect ending to a meal but you think that you just do not have time to bake it. You will note that I have tirelessly tried to present recipes throughout this book that you will try, recipes that do not overwhelm the family cook or the hostess. This recipe is no exception. It is a dessert that I often prepare in the afternoon because it takes little time to prepare and provides sufficient protein when a vegetable or salad menu is planned. A traditional unbaked meringue topping has been omitted in this version because of the danger of Salmonella exposure in uncooked eggs.

3/4 cup unbleached white flour
1 1/2 teaspoons baking powder

2 egg whites
3/4 cup sugar

2 egg yolks
1/4 cup skimmed milk

TOPPING:
    1/3 cup *evaporated skimmed* milk
    1/3 cup *fat-free* sweetened condensed milk
    1 cup skimmed milk
    1 cup *fat-free* dairy sour cream

Fresh raspberries, strawberries, or cherries, for garnish, if desired.

Preheat oven to 350 degrees F. Prepare an 8-inch-square baking pan by coating with non-stick lecithin spray coating especially for baking.

In a small bowl, combine flour and baking powder. Stir to combine thoroughly. Set aside briefly.

Using an electric mixer fitted with *grease-free* beaters or by hand, using a *grease-free* wire whisk, beat egg whites in a *grease-free* bowl until *soft peaks form*. Gradually, tablespoonful by tablespoonful, beat sugar into egg whites. Continue beating until stiff.

Beat yolks into the batter, one at a time. Then slowly add flour and the 1/4 cupful milk. Pour batter into prepared pan. Bake in preheated 350 degree F. oven for about 40 minutes, or until the edges of the cake are golden brown. Transfer to a wire rack and allow to cool.

While the cake is cooling, combine evaporated milk, sweetened condensed milk, the 1 cupful milk, and sour cream. Stir to combine *but do not beat*. Spoon over cooled sponge cake and allow the topping to soak into the cake for at least 1 hour before serving.

Cut into squares to serve, garnishing each plate with a few berries. Refrigerate leftovers.

Yields 9 servings

Note: This recipe can be doubled, if desired. Use a 13 x 9 x 2-inch baking pan.

1/9 SERVING – PROTEIN = 8.5 g.; FAT = 1.4 g.; CARBOHYDRATE = 46.4 g.;
CALORIES = 232; CALORIES FROM FAT = 5%

El Salvador

El Salvador is the smallest country in Central America, about the size of New Jersey, with a considerable population today of 5.7 million people. The population is estimated to be as high as ninety percent *mestizo* with approximately forty-two percent still living in rural areas. Its turbulent political history dates back to repulsed invasions by the Spanish under Pedro de Alvarado in 1524 and in 1526. In 1528 the Spanish succeeded in conquering the area we now know as El Salvador. In 1811 an insurrection began against the Spanish crown resulting in the *Acta de Independencia* in 1921. This was followed by more unrest when an attempt was made to diminish their independence by adding them to Mexico. The following year the five Central American states formed the United Provinces of Central America but it was not a comfortable union and dissolved in 1839 after which El Salvador became an independent republic. Since then a sustained internal struggle for power has been experienced by the population. The left-of-center FMLN party, led by journalist Mauicio Funes, is now in power. Increased economic stability and a battle to reveal and eliminate the corruptive practices of past governments have brought a period of relative peace and increased prosperity.

El Salvador's geological history has also been turbulent. Located in a tectonically active area with active volcanoes, severe and destructive earthquakes and volcanic eruptions are commonplace. The instability of its weather results in cycles of torrential rains contrasted with long period of extreme droughts and the resulting consequences to crops and national prosperity. In 2001 El Salvador adopted the United States dollar as its currency. With a steadily growing economy today, El Salvador's greatest enemy to prosperity is the ever repeating cycle of natural disasters and political unrest and the "brain drain" created as educated El Salvadorans move to *El Norte*, relocating to the United States and Canada in search of economic opportunity.

The following menu suggestions will be viewed as arbitrary, I suppose, since I have not chosen to include the very, very traditional, thick corn tortillas called *papusas*. Stuffed with all kinds of wonderfulness, they are meals onto themselves. *Frijoles colorados*, red beans, another very traditional El Salvadoran dish, has been included because it too is heaven to vegetarians and can be served as a side dish or main dish depending on additions or subtractions.

The Americas – El Salvador

Avocado, Egg, and Cheese Appetizer
Guacamole con Huevos y Queso

Baked Corn *Tortilla* Chips
Tostaditas

~

Vegetable Slaw
Curido de Repollo

~~~~~~~~~~~~~~~~~~~~~

**Soymeat with Onions in the Style
of El Salvadoran "Chicken with Onions"**
"Pollo" Encebollado

Red Beans with Grated Cheese
Frijoles Colorados con Queso

Fried Plantains
Plátanos Fritos

~~~~~~~~~~~~~~~~~~~~~

Pineapple Pastry, a Tribute to El Salvador
Pastel de Piña

Pineapple Jam

EL SALVADORAN AVOCADO, EGG, AND CHEESE APPETIZER
Guacamole con Huevos y Queso
TPT - 9 minutes

Guacamole has become the American appetizer dip of choice to the point that it comes prepared and packed in plastic containers for picnics and football events with nary an avocado in sight. There are many versions of this in the countries south of our border where avocados grow in abundance but, for some unknown reason, the Tex-Mex version is the only one with which people seem to be familiar. This El Salvadoran guacamole is an appetizer/salad of much more complexity.

2 ripe avocados—peeled and pitted
1/2 teaspoon freshly squeezed lemon juice

1 hard-cooked egg—shelled and *finely* chopped

1/3 cup shredded *low-moisture, part-skimmed milk mozzarella* cheese or *queso blanco*, if available
2 tablespoons *very finely* chopped onion
1/2 teaspoon grated Parmesan cheese
Freshly ground black pepper, to taste

Large lettuce leaves—well-washed and dried
1 hard-cooked egg—sliced
BAKED CORN *TORTILLA* CHIPS (*Tostaditas*)
  [see recipe which follows], *tostado* triangles,
  or crackers

In a mixing bowl, mash avocados and lemon juice until of uniform consistency.

Add *finely* chopped hard-cooked egg and continue to mash.

Add shredded cheese, *very finely* chopped onion, grated cheese, and black pepper. Mix well.

Arrange lettuce leaves on an attractive plate or platter. Scoop prepared *guacamole* into the center of the serving dish. Arrange egg slices across the center of the *guacamole*.

The Americas—El Salvador

EL SALVADORAN AVOCADO, EGG, AND CHEESE APPETIZER (cont'd)

Serve guacamole chilled with *tostado* triangles, *tortilla* chips, or crackers.

Yields 12 servings
adequate for 6 people

Note: This recipe can be halved, when required.

1/12 SERVING (about 2 tablespoonfuls exclusive of chips or crackers) –
PROTEIN = 2.8 g.; FAT = 7.1 g.; CARBOHYDRATE = 0.6 g.;
CALORIES = 79; CALORIES FROM FAT = 80%

BAKED CORN *TORTILLA* CHIPS
Tostaditas

TPT - 13 minutes

No, these do not taste like the salty, oily commercially-produced tortilla chips. Their clean taste actually allows the food they accompany to be tasted.

10 five– or six–inch corn *tortillas*

Preheat oven to 400 degrees F.

Using a scissors or a sharp knife, cut the *tortillas, two or three at a time,* to yield four wedges each. Arrange *tortilla* chips in single layers on *ungreased* cookie sheets.

Bake in preheated 400 degree F. oven for 7-9 minutes, or until chips are crisp. *Be careful not to allow them to overbrown.** Turn out onto a large wire rack to cool.

Store in an airtight container for no more than 2 weeks.

Yields 40 chips

Notes: *A convection oven gives a perfectly browned result.

The chips may be salted, if desired. Salt while still warm.

This recipe may be halved or doubled, when required.

1/40 SERVING (i. e., per chip) –
PROTEIN = 0.5 g.; FAT = 0.3 g.; CARBOHYDRATE = 3.2 g.;
CALORIES = 17; CALORIES FROM FAT = 16%

EL SALVADORAN VEGETABLE SLAW
Curido de Repollo

TPT - 8 hours and 17 minutes
8 hours = flavor development period

Delis on Long Island that had a significant Latin American clientele always had coleslaw with shredded carrots and onion, which I, in my naiveté, simply attributed to the fact that most delis have coleslaw. It was sweeter and had a bit of a bite but it never occurred to me that coleslaw might be popular in South America and not just popular with the customers of Long Island delis. Yes, this is, I suppose, a surprise because one does not associate cabbage salads with Mesoamerica but Dutch colonial influences are still apparent in the cuisines of the Caribbean and many Islanders have migrated to Central America, taking their food specialties with them. Adopted by El Salvadoran cooks as a good and inexpensive way to add nutrition to meals, this coleslaw is found throughout the country in one form or another. It is not only an enjoyable salad, it is also a good alternative to shredded lettuce as a topping for tacos and tostados.

Although I prefer to allow this to marinate in the refrigerator, Salvadorans allow it to marinate at room temperature until it begins to ferment. If you prepare it, put it in a jar, and allow it to ferment at room temperature, you can make your own decision.

EL SALVADORAN VEGETABLE SLAW (cont'd)

3 cups shredded cabbage—well-rinsed
1 quart *boiling* water
1 quart *ice* water

1 large carrot—scraped or pared and coarsely shredded
1/4 cup *finely* slivered onion

1/2 teaspoon *dried* oregano—crushed
Dash or two ground red pepper (cayenne), or to taste
Pinch salt, or to taste

2 tablespoons apple cider vinegar *or* PINEAPPLE VINEGAR (*Vinagre de Piña*) [see index]*
1 tablespoon water
1 teaspoon *extra virgin* olive oil
1 teaspoon *light* brown sugar

Put shredded cabbage into a mixing bowl. Pour *boiling* water over. Allow to stand for only 1 minute. Drain thoroughly. Put cabbage back into bowl. Pour *ice* water over and allow to stand for 5 minutes. Drain thoroughly. Return cabbage to bowl.

Add shredded carrot and *finely* slivered onion. Toss.

Add crushed oregano, ground red pepper (cayenne), and salt. Toss. Set aside briefly.

In a cruet, combine vinegar, water, oil, and brown sugar. Shake vigorously. Pour over slaw. Toss very well to coat the vegetables and distribute the seasoning. Cover. Refrigerate for at least 8 hours, or overnight, to allow for flavor development. Toss several times during the refrigeration period. Turn into a serving bowl.

Serve chilled.

Yields 6 servings
adequate for 4 people

Notes: *A fermented vinegar taste, such as that which you get from apple cider vinegar or pineapple vinegar, a Latin American specialty, is important to this salad. Other vinegars do not contribute the same earthy flavor.

This recipe is easily halved or doubled, when required.

1/6 SERVING – PROTEIN = 0.8 g.; FAT = 0.7 g.; CARBOHYDRATE = 5.2 g.;
CALORIES = 31; CALORIES FROM FAT = 20%

SOYMEAT WITH ONIONS IN THE STYLE OF EL SALVADORAN "CHICKEN WITH ONIONS"
"Pollo" Encebollado
TPT - 19 minutes

Long before our 1973 commitment to a meatless lifestyle, the classic chicken and onions dish, so popular in El Salvadoran homes in Central American and on Long Island too, was a part of our life. Years later, after adapting it to the meat analogue products now available and after creating my own vegan Worcestershire sauce, it returned to our repertoire. Quick, easy, and flavorful, it is an excellent family meal choice.

3 tablespoons water
1 1/2 teaspoons MUSTARD SAUCE [see index] *or* a prepared, English-style mustard
1 teaspoon HOMEMADE VEGAN WORCESTERSHIRE-STYLE SAUCE [see index] *or* commercially-available vegetarian Worcestershire sauce
1/2 teaspoon crushed, dried thyme

1 1/2 tablespoons corn oil
4 ounces *frozen* soy meat analogue strips
About 24 *frozen* small white onions—halved

Freshly ground black pepper, to taste

In a small bowl, combine water, mustard, vegan Worcestershire-style sauce, and crushed thyme. Mix well and set aside briefly.

In a skillet set over *LOW-MEDIUM* heat, heat oil. Add frozen soymeat strips and onion halves. Sauté gently, being careful not to allow analogue product to overbrown. Reduce heat to *LOW*.

Add sauce mixture and stir to coat soymeat and onions uniformly. Cook, stirring frequently, until heated through.

Generously season with black pepper. Turn into a heated serving dish.

SOYMEAT WITH ONIONS IN THE STYLE OF EL SALVADORAN "CHICKEN WITH ONIONS" (cont'd)

Serve at once.

Yields 4-5 servings
adequate for 3-4 people

Note: This recipe can be halved or doubled, when required.

1/5 SERVING – PROTEIN = 9.6 g.; FAT = 4.9 g.; CARBOHYDRATE = 6.3 g.;
CALORIES = 101; CALORIES FROM FAT = 44%

EL SALVADORAN RED BEANS WITH GRATED CHEESE
Frijoles Coloradas con Queso
TPT - 13 minutes

Although El Salvadorans base their menus around meat, when available, beans accompany most meals including breakfast. This vegetarian recipe for red beans is filling, nutritious, and has a complex taste that can be served as a side dish or as a main course presentation with a salad and bread or soft, warm tortillas.

1 tablespoon corn oil
1/2 cup *thinly* sliced green bell pepper
1/2 cup *thinly* sliced red bell pepper
1/2 cup *thinly* sliced onion
1 garlic clove—*very thinly* sliced

1 can (15 ounces) red kidney beans *or* cooked, dried red kidney beans—*well-drained*
3 tablespoons tomato purée
Freshly ground black pepper, to taste
1/4 teaspoon sugar

2 teaspoons *finely* chopped fresh oregano *or*
 1 teaspoon crushed dried oregano

2 tablespoons *grated pecorino Romano* cheese, for garnish
About 6 tablespoons *fat-free* dairy sour cream, for garnish

In a saucepan set over *LOW-MEDIUM* heat, heat oil. Add *thinly* sliced green pepper, red pepper, and onion and *very thinly* sliced garlic. Sauté until vegetables soften, *being careful not to allow vegetables to brown.*

Add *well-drained* cooked or canned beans, tomato purée, black pepper, and sugar. Cook, stirring frequently, until heated through.

Add *finely* chopped oregano. Stir to combine. Turn into a heated serving bowl.

Sprinkle grated cheese over.

Serve with a dollop of sour cream.

Yields 6 servings
adequate for 4 people

Notes: This recipe can be doubled, when required.

A vegan entrée can easily be prepared by omitted the grated cheese and sour cream.

1/6 SERVING – PROTEIN = 7.4 g.; FAT = 2.7 g.; CARBOHYDRATE = 21.8 g.;
CALORIES = 138; CALORIES FROM FAT = 18%

FRIED PLANTAINS
Plátanos Fritos
TPT - 10 minutes

Fried plantains accompany meals all over Latin America. This starchy cousin of the banana can not be eaten raw as can the bananas we generally see in our groceries. The fruit of the "Musa acuminate" is starchy when green and sweet when ripe, but not too sweet, and is a significant source of carbohydrate calories in El Salvador. It adds variety to menus and I find that plantains often replace potatoes and noodles in my menus. Plantains must be ripe if you are going to fry them so, if you can only find green plantains in the grocery, allow them to ripen at room temperature before using; the skin will turn black.

FRIED PLANTAINS (cont'd)

3 tablespoons butter*
3 *ripe* plantains—peeled and cut into 1-inch chunks

In a large skillet set over *LOW-MEDIUM* heat, heat butter. Add plantain slices and allow to brown. Turn each chunk and allow to brown on the other side. Turn into a heated bowl.

Serve at once.

Notes: *Butter may be replaced with oil, if preferred.

One plantain is sufficient for two people.

Yields 6 servings
adequate for 6 people

1/6 SERVING – PROTEIN = 0.6 g.; FAT = 5.8 g.; CARBOHYDRATE = 24.0 g.;
CALORIES = 141; CALORIES FROM FAT = 37%

PINEAPPLE PASTRY, A TRIBUTE TO EL SALVADOR
Pastel de Piña

TPT - 43 minutes;
5 minutes = cooling period

A pineapple torte known as "la semita" is immensely popular in the restaurants and bakeries of El Salvador. The recipe I was given makes a very large, very sweet cake—way, way more than would be required for a family meal and much too sweet for our taste. I had found a lighter, flaky version of this dessert in a Central American bakery on Long Island and have tried to duplicate that here. Frozen puff pastry and home-canned or commercially-available pineapple jam make this a quick and easy dessert for a Central American meal.

Please see my recipe for pineapple jam, which is included, if you are unable to find pineapple preserves in your food specialty store.

1 sheet *frozen* puff pastry—*brought to room temperature*

3/4 cup PINEAPPLE JAM [*see recipe which follows*] **or commercially-available pineapple preserves**

Preheat oven to 400 degrees F.* Prepare two baking sheets by lining with culinary parchment paper.

Cut pastry in half. Cover one half with a damp cotton towel until required. On a cold surface, roll out one of the pastry halves until thin. Using a sharp knife, make shallow cuts in the pastry to create a diamond pattern. Transfer it to one of the culinary-lined baking sheets. Repeat with the second half of the puff pastry sheet. Bake at 400 degrees F. for about 15 minutes, checking to be sure that the pastry does not over brown. Remove from oven and allow to cool for about 5 minutes on the baking sheets.

Transfer one of the baked pastry halves to a serving dish or to an attractive bread board. Spread the pineapple preserves evenly over the pastry. Top with the second piece of baked pastry. Set aside to allow the pineapple preserves to melt across the surface.

Serve within an hour to preserve crispness of baked pastry. Cut with a very sharp knife.

Yields 8 servings
adequate for 4-6 people

Notes: *If you have a convection oven or a convection oven function in your range, use it for this pastry. It will allow for even rising and even browning without the necessity to turn the baking sheets during the baking process.

**A marble pastry slab is ideal to roll out the pastry.

This recipe can be halved or doubled, when required.

1/8 SERVING – PROTEIN = 2.3 g.; FAT = 8.3 g.; CARBOHYDRATE = 29.4 g.;
CALORIES = 203; CALORIES FROM FAT = 37%

The Americas–El Salvador

PINEAPPLE JAM
TPT - 25 hours and 3 minutes;
24 hours = cooling period

This is an old-fashioned favorite that became popular in the 1950s. Hawaii had become a state, canned pineapple was available, and the post-war economy was booming. We splurged on things like this. It is a nice jam for an afternoon tea in the winter or breakfast in the summer, a jam I often make in the winter if our fresh-fruit jam supply gets a little low.

4 cups crushed pineapple—canned in juice
—well-drained
1/4 cup lemon juice
1 teaspoon butter*
7 1/2 cups sugar

1 pouch (3 ounces) liquid pectin

Sterilize nine 1/2-pint canning jars. Also sterilize lids and rings for jars.

In a large, non-aluminum kettle, combine *well-drained* crushed pineapple, lemon juice, and butter. Stir in sugar. Place over *MEDIUM-HIGH* heat and bring to a *full boil—a boil which can not be stirred down.*

While stirring with a metal spoon, add fruit pectin. Continue stirring constantly while allowing mixture to return to the boil. *Boil for 1 minute. Immediately,* remove from heat. Stir and skim off all foam.

Ladle into nine hot, sterilized 1/2-pint canning jars. Carefully wipe lips of jars. Seal with hot, sterilized lids and rings. Process in hot-water-bath canner for 10 minutes, *timing from the moment the water reaches a full rolling boil.* Remove to surface covered with thick towels or newspapers. Allow to cool for 24 hours *undisturbed.* Check to be sure jars are sealed before labeling and storing in a dark, cool, dry place.** Loosen or remove rings before storing.

Notes: *The addition of butter prevents a foam or scum from forming at the surface. The butter can be omitted but, if omitted, it is recommended that the surface be skimmed with a metal spoon before pouring into jars.

**Any jars that do not seal can be stored in the refrigerator for about one month or resealed using a *new lid.*

Yields nine 1/2-pint jarfuls

1/144 SERVING (i. e., per tablespoonful) –
PROTEIN = 0.03 g.; FAT = 0.03 g.; CARBOHYDRATE = 12.6 g.;
CALORIES = 50; CALORIES FROM FAT = <1%

Guatemala

Nestled just below the Yucatan Peninsula, the Mayan world we know as Guatemala is one of the most intensely biodiverse nations in our hemisphere with fourteen distinct bioregions. The complex and significant ecosystems of this small nation, which is about the size of the state of Ohio, invite many and all to travel south to this land of natural wonders and incredible *tamales*. Yes, the variety of *tamales* eaten throughout Guatemala is comparable in diversity to that of the environment. Delicious and complex, *tamales* vary based on the "*masa*" which can be ground field corn, potatoes, or rice and the filling which can be meat, fruits, nuts, and vegetables. Wrapped in leaves or husks or *tortillas*, *tamales* can be sweet or savory.

The so-called Classic Period in Guatemala's 14,000-year human history is the period from 250 to 900 AD when the complex city-state structure of the Mayan civilization dominated. Mayan influences on cuisine are still evident in the foods eaten by the Indians of mountainous regions. Such indigenous ingredients as corn, beans, peppers, and the tomato grow well in the highlands and form the core of this cuisine as they have for centuries. It goes without saying, the visiting vegetarian is gratified. However, the ubiquitous *tamales* are usually filled with meat, especially to impress the visitor, and pleas of "*No carne, por favor*" result in a quizzical expression as do other versions of the phrase in so many other countries.

Although a study of the pre-Columbian historical influence on cuisine in Guatemala is compelling, the influence of European contact is unmistakable especially in the cuisine developed in the cities. It was in these population centers of the Spanish colonial period that a unique cuisine was developed by the *Ladinos*, the curious designation given to descendants of both Indians and Europeans. Of course the indigenous ingredients of the pre-Columbian Mayan cultures were used in this more urban cuisine but in ways learned from Europe with the additional of tropical ingredients which are easily cultivated in the lowlands. In a way, there are two Guatemalan cuisines still very much in place and unlike other cuisines of Central America, especially that of Costa Rica, the influence of their Mayan predecessors is still considerable.

I offer two soups with this menu to allow you to enjoy the edible flowers of the *yucca* plant, when in bloom. It is a short-lived display and this soup is one very delicious way of taking advantage of this perennial that we in the North do share with our Mesoamerican neighbors.

The Americas–**Guatemala**

Cream of Chick Pea Soup
Puré de Garbanzos con Crema

Yucca Soup
Sopa de Flor de Izote

~

Sliced Radish Salad with Mint
Picado de Rabano

~~~~~~~~~~~~~~~~~~~~~~~

Baked Garlic and Bread Pudding with Cheese
Sopa de Ajo con Queso

Chick Peas in Tomato Sauce
Garbanzos en Salsa de Tomate

~~~~~~~~~~~~~~~~~~~~~~~

Sweet Egg Sponge Cakes
Quesadillas de Huevos y Arroz

Sliced Baby Bananas
with Cinnamon Sugar and Cream

GUATEMALAN CREAM OF CHICK PEA SOUP
Puré de Garbanzos con Crema
TPT - 1 hour and 16 minutes

Although chick peas (garbanzos) are found in many, many dishes in many, many countries in Central and South America, cream is a more unusual ingredient in soups. Guatemalans also combine puréed chick peas (garbanzos) but with beef stock and add greens such as spinach or Swiss chard. This more elaborate creamed version, however, is a beautiful, nutritious, and delicious soup, to which very fine noodles can be added to complete protein complementation. I usually double or triple the recipe and freeze the base so that it is available throughout the winter.

2 tablespoons *extra virgin* olive oil
1 large onion—chopped

2 large garlic cloves—chopped
1/2 yellow *or* orange bell pepper—chopped*
1 carrot—*thinly* sliced
1 teaspoon dried oregano—crushed
1/2 teaspoon ground cumin
1/8 teaspoon ground red pepper (cayenne), or to taste
Pinch of crushed, dried mint

6 cupfuls VEGETABLE STOCK FROM SOUP
 [see index] *or* water
2 cans (16 ounces each) chick peas (*garbanzos*)
 —drained, rinsed, and *seed coats removed*

1 cup light cream *or* half and half

In a large kettle set over *MEDIUM* heat, heat oil. Sauté until onion is soft and translucent, *being careful not to allow onion to brown.*

Add chopped garlic and pepper, *thinly* sliced carrot, dried oregano, ground cumin, ground red pepper (cayenne), and dried mint. Cook, stirring frequently, for about 5 minutes.

Add vegetable stock or water and drained chick peas. Bring to the simmer. *Reduce heat to LOW-MEDIUM* and cook for about 45 minutes. Stir occasionally. Remove from heat.

Using the electric blender, purée the soup in batches.** Return the purée to a clean kettle set over *LOW-MEDIUM* heat.***

GUATEMALAN CREAM OF CHICK PEA SOUP (cont'd)

Stir in cream and allow to heat through. Turn into a heated soup tureen.

Serve into heated soup bowls.

Yields 8 servings
adequate for 4-6 people

Notes: *Choose a yellow or orange bell pepper because you want the final color of the soup to be a golden brown.

**The puréed soup base, when cooled, can be frozen at this point.

***A cupful of fine egg noodles can be added at this point if desired. Cook soup for an additional 3-4 minutes. The addition of the noodles provides, in one bowl, a meal of fully complemented proteins.

This recipe can be doubled, when required.

1/6 SERVING (without noodles) –
PROTEIN = 5.5 g.; FAT = 7.0 g.; CARBOHYDRATE = 13.3 g.;
CALORIES = 92; CALORIES FROM FAT = 89%

GUATEMALAN *YUCCA* SOUP
Sopa de Flor de Izote

TPT - 2 hours and 50 minutes

Many wonderful yucca species thrive in the gardens of "El Norte." This ornamental flower is a member of the agave family unlike the yuca plant, also known as the manioc or cassava, which is grown for its tuber. We have to wait for the yuccas in our gardens to bloom since we can not just buy them by the kilo at market, as you can in Guatemala and other countries south of our border. The pistil and stamen are bitter but the petals are sweet and have sufficient texture for salads, soups, and even omelets.

Use of a green pepper, the unripened fruit, here is typical of Latin American recipes. Most of the world's cuisines wait for peppers to ripen yet, fascinatingly, the use of green peppers in the United States was widespread even before the late twentieth century influence of Latin American immigration.

3 cups *boiling* water
2 cups **fresh, *home-grown, spray-free* yucca petals—well-washed**
2 1/2 cups **canned, *diced* tomatoes with canning liquid**
1 **green bell pepper**—*finely* **chopped**
1 **large onion**—*thinly* **sliced**
1 **large garlic clove**—*very finely* **chopped**
2 **tablespoons fresh basil**—*very finely* **chopped***
1 **tablespoon sugar**
1/4 **teaspoon freshly ground black pepper, or to taste**

1 **cup freshly shelled** *or* **frozen green peas**

In a kettle set over *LOW-MEDIUM* heat, combine *boiling* water, well-washed *yucca* petals, diced tomato, *finely* chopped green pepper, *thinly* sliced onion, *very finely* chopped garlic and basil, sugar, and black pepper. Cover and cook for about 40 minutes, stirring occasionally.**

Add green peas. Continue cooking for an additional 10 minutes.

Turn into a heated soup tureen. *Serve at once* into heated soup plates.

Yields 6 servings
adequate for 4 people

Notes: *We prefer to use lemon basil for this soup, if we have it growing in our herb bed.

**If you wish to prepare this soup early in the day, prepare it only to this point and refrigerate. Reheat and add peas just before serving. If you wish to freeze a portion of this soup for future use, freeze it at this point, that is, before you have added the green peas.

This recipe can be doubled or halved, when required.

1/6 SERVING – PROTEIN = 2.5 g.; FAT = 0.3 g.; CARBOHYDRATE = 11.6 g.;
CALORIES = 55; CALORIES FROM FAT = 5%

The Americas—Guatemala

SLICED RADISH SALAD WITH MINT IN THE STYLE OF GUATEMALA
Picado de Rabano

TPT - 33 minutes;
30 minutes = marination period

This delightful salad was a wonderful find as far as I was concerned because there are always tiny fresh mint leaves, bursting with flavor, in our herb garden when the radishes are ready to harvest. If you have ever grown radishes, you know that every radish seems to be ready to pull at the same time even when the seed planting has been staggered and the race to bring up radishes that have not been invaded by the subterranean pests is often a race that is lost by the gardener. There are just so many radishes you can slice into a tossed salad or present as a side dish with salt before the family says "enough." My mother is the only person I have ever known who could keep eating radishes without complaint until each row was empty as long as there was a salt seller at hand.

15 large, *fresh* mint leaves—well-washed and *finely* chopped
Salt, to taste
3 tablespoons freshly squeezed orange juice
1 1/2 tablespoons freshly squeezed lemon juice

30 red radishes—leaves removed, well-washed, and *thinly* sliced

In a serving bowl, combine *finely* slivered mint leaves, salt, orange juice, and lemon juice. Stir to combine.

Add radish slices. Toss to mix. Refrigerate for at least 30 minutes to allow for flavor development.

Serve chilled.

Yields 6 servings
adequate for 4 people

Note: This recipe can be halved or doubled, when required.

1/6 SERVING – PROTEIN = 0.9 g.; FAT = 0.1 g.; CARBOHYDRATE = 2.6 g.;
CALORIES = 9; CALORIES FROM FAT = 1%

GUATEMALAN BAKED GARLIC AND BREAD PUDDING WITH CHEESE
Sopa de Ajo con Queso

TPT - 54 minutes;
20 minutes = garlic infusion period

Both bread soups and garlic soups are popular throughout the Spanish- and Portuguese-speaking world. This baked Guatemalan version seems little like a soup nor is it a bread pudding, as we know them. It is, however, a very pleasant side dish or luncheon dish.

2 tablespoons safflower *or* sunflower oil
3 large garlic cloves—*crushed*
1/2 cup chopped onion

12 one-inch-thick slices of day-old, *unseeded* French bread
2 cups VEGETARIAN BROWN STOCK *[see index]* or VEGETABLE STOCK FROM SOUP *[see index]*

2 tablespoons grated *pecorino Romano* cheese

In a skillet set over *LOW* heat, heat oil. Add *crushed* garlic cloves and chopped onion. Sauté until garlic begins to brown and onion is soft and translucent. Remove from heat and set aside for about 20 minutes to allow the garlic flavor to infuse the oil. Stir occasionally. Remove and discard garlic cloves.

Scrape garlic-infused oil and onion from skillet into a shallow baking dish sufficiently large enough to hold the bread slices snugly in a single layer. Spread the oil evenly across the bottom of the dish.

Preheat oven to 350 degrees F.

Arrange bread slices in a large shallow baking pan or even in pie plates. Pour vegetable stock over bread slices. Allow the stock to be absorbed by the bread, turning once. Using a wide spatula, transfer the stock-soaked bread slices into the prepared baking dish. Sprinkle grated cheese evenly over the bread slices.

Bake in preheated 350 degree F. oven for about 20 minutes, or until most of liquid has been evaporated and the top is *lightly browned.*

The Americas–Guatemala

GUATEMALAN BAKED GARLIC AND BREAD PUDDING WITH CHEESE (cont'd)

Serve at once.

Yields 6 servings
adequate for 4 people

Note: This recipe may be halved or doubled, when required.

1/8 SERVING – PROTEIN = 6.0 g.; FAT = 5.1 g.; CARBOHYDRATE = 32.4 g.;
CALORIES = 198; CALORIES FROM FAT = 23%

GUATEMALAN CHICK PEAS IN TOMATO SAUCE
Garbanzos en Salsa de Tomate

TPT - 28 minutes

This is a straight forward vegan rendition of a classic Guatemalan dish where the vegetables would be sautéed with the fat rendered from bacon or sausages. We use this as a side dish with a complementing grain source such as rice, noodles, or pasta or with soy or grain sausages. Whenever possible I use the flavorful heirloom tomatoes and fresh bay leaves from our garden for the freshest possible taste.

1 1/2 tablespoons corn oil
1/2 cup chopped onion
2 garlic cloves—*finely* **chopped**
2 large bay leaves—**halved***
1/2 teaspoon crushed, dried thyme
1 cup chopped red bell pepper

1 can (15 ounces) canned chick peas (*garbanzos***)**
   —**well-drained**
1/4 cup tomato purée

In a skillet set over *MEDIUM* heat, heat oil. Add chopped onion, *finely* chopped garlic, bay leaf pieces, crushed thyme, and chopped red, sweet pepper. Sauté until onion is softened, *being careful not to allow any vegetables to brown.*

Add well-drained chick peas and tomato purée. Cook, stirring frequently, for about 15 minutes, or until thickened. Remove and discard bay leaf pieces.

Serve warm as a side dish or with rice, noodles, or pasta.

Yields 6 servings
adequate for 4 people

Notes: *Fresh bay leaves have an incredible flavor and will enhance the flavor of this dish considerably, if you have access to them.

This recipe can be halved, when required.

1/6 SERVING (exclusive of the rice or noodles) –
PROTEIN = 3.3 g.; FAT = 2.8 g.; CARBOHYDRATE = 10.0 g.;
CALORIES = 44; CALORIES FROM FAT = 57%

GUATEMALAN SWEET EGG SPONGE CAKES
Quesadillas de Huevos y Arroz

TPT - 1 hour and 6 minutes

Quesadillas, loosely translated as "small cheese things," appear in the cuisines of many Latin-American countries. This version is certainly different from the tortilla turnover "sandwiches," known by the same name, found in Mexico and now so much a part of our southwestern border cuisine, generally referred to as "Tex-Mex."

GUATEMALAN SWEET EGG SPONGE CAKES (cont'd)

1/2 pound (2 sticks) sweet *(unsalted)* butter
—*softened to room temperature**
1 cup sugar
1 cup *fat-free* pasteurized eggs (the equivalent of 4 eggs)
1 1/2 cups brown rice flour**
1/4 cup light cream *or* half and half

3/4 cup *white* corn meal
1 1/2 teaspoons baking powder

1/3 cup grated Parmesan cheese***

1/2 cup skimmed milk

Confectioners' sugar

Prepare two non-stick-coated cupcake pans by coating with non-stick lecithin spray coating.**** Dust lightly with rice flour.

Using the electric mixer, cream *softened* butter until light and fluffy. Add sugar and continue creaming until again light and fluffy. *Alternately*, add pasteurized eggs and rice flour, beating well after each addition. Add cream and continue to beat.

Sift *white* corn meal and baking powder together into a mixing bowl.

While continuing to beat the batter, add the sifted ingredients and the grated cheese. When integrated, *gradually* add milk. When milk has been thoroughly integrated, increase mixer speed to *MEDIUM-HIGH* and beat for about 10-12 minutes to create as light a sponge as possible.

Meanwhile, preheat oven to 325 degrees F.

Fill prepared cupcake pans about two-thirds full. Rap each sharply on the counter top to release any large bubbles.

Bake in preheated oven for about 20-22 minutes, or until *lightly browned* and a cake tester inserted in the center comes out clean. Cool in pan for 5-10 minutes before turning out onto a wire rack to cool completely.

Store in an airtight container. To serve, arrange cakes on a cake plate. Sift confectioners' sugar generously over.

Yields 22 small cakes

Notes: *Be sure to use *unsalted* butter in this recipe. Salted butter would make the sponge cake too salty since both the baking powder and the grated cheese contribute significant sodium.

**Brown rice flour is available in natural food stores and Asian groceries. Rice flours are standard thickening agents in many cuisines, used as we use corn starch. Here it is used as a flour.

***Parmesan cheese is about as close to the Guatemalan cheese used for this cake as you are likely to find. The cheese of *Zacapa*, prized for this cake, is rarely, if ever, available outside of Guatemala.

****If preferred, a single 9-inch square cake or two 9 x 5 x 3-inch loaves can be prepared using this recipe. Bake for 40-50 minutes for the larger cakes. Two 9-inch round cake layers would need to bake for only about 30-35 minutes.

These cakes, well-wrapped, may be frozen with considerable success.

1/22 SERVING (i. e., per small cake) –
PROTEIN = 3.1 g.; FAT = 9.2 g.; CARBOHYDRATE = 21.9 g.;
CALORIES = 181; CALORIES FROM FAT = 46%

Honduras

Honduras, another of the small nations that occupy the isthmus south of Mexico and north of South America, was formerly known as British Honduras to distinguish it from Spanish Honduras, now known as Belize. The delightful, but more than likely apocryphal, legion of the origin of the name "Honduras" is too wonderful not to share here. Honduras means "depths" in Spanish and it is said that, in referring to the northeastern coastal area which later would become known as Honduras, Columbus, who reached this area on his fourth and final voyage to the New World in 1502, is said to have written *"Gracias a Dios que hemos salido de esas Honduras,"* which translated into English as "Thank God we have come out of the depths."

Mayan influence is less in Honduras than in neighboring Guatemala. However, in western Honduras near the border with Guatemala, there was a major Mayan presence with a flourishing city state at Copán, in a kingdom know as *rtyu*, from the fifth to the early ninth century AD. As a result of the continued presence of small Mayan settlements into the thirteenth century and the fact that ninety percent of the population are of mixed Indian and European ancestry and a further seven percent are described as Amerindian, the influence of this heritage is still apparent in the cuisine.

The tropical lowland and temperate mountain climates range from sea level rain forests to cloud forests in the mountains, which rise to 9,943 feet (3,000 meters) above sea level. These climate extremes provide the opportunity for dramatic biodiversity which enhances the cuisine with both tropical fruits, such as pineapple, plantains, *chayotes*, avocados, *yuca*, passion fruits, and coconuts; "cold climate" crops such as beets, potatoes, and cabbage; and crops familiar to our temperate climate, are grown as well. Here is a cuisine in which beets with pineapple and corn tortillas are just "local foods."

Fried "Meat"
"Carne" Achorizada
on *Tostados* with Shredded Lettuce

Authentic Honduran Fermented Pineapple Vinegar *or* **My Pineapple Vinegar**
Vinagre de Piña

~

Puréed Banana, *Yuca*, and Coconut Soup
Sopa de Banana, Yucca, y Coco

~~~~~~~~~~~~~~~~~~~~

Tortilla Skillet
Chilaquilas en Sarten

Beets in Cream
Remolachas en Crema

~~~~~~~~~~~~~~~~~~~~

Easy Coconut Ice Cream
Helado de Coco

The Americas–**Honduras**

HONDURAN FRIED "MEAT"
"Carne" Achorizada

TPT - 49 minutes;
30 minutes = *achiote* (*annatto*) dissolving period

Several meat analogue products exist, both frozen and dried, that ably replace ground beef in dishes such as this. Actually the traditional seasoning of this Honduran recipe gives the soymeat products a tremendous boost. We serve this with soft, warm tortillas or tostados as a luncheon dish with a topping of cheese and lettuce, as a side dish in the summer with a big tossed salad or as an appetizer with tostados or toast.

The intense color of the "carne achorizada" is achieved by using achiote. Many, many years ago, a friend from the Philippines decided to prepare a traditional meal and arrived with all the ingredients in tow. Eight hours later we ate dinner after a day of considerable adventure. She brought a jar of red granules called annatto, a reddish orange food coloring made from the seeds of a small tree, "Bixa orellano." I still have some of that from my original introduction squirreled away in a baby food jar. To my amazement I was to discover that annatto is another name for achiote, used extensively in Latin American cooking and widely available in nuggets, as a paste, and as a liquid.

1/8 teaspoon *achiote* (*annatto*) **granules** *or* **paste**

2 teaspoons *hot* **corn oil**

2 teaspoons corn oil
8 ounces *frozen* **vegetarian "ground beef"***
1 tablespoon PINEAPPLE VINEGAR (*Vinagre de Piña***)** [*see recipes which follow*] *or* **apple cider vinegar**
1/2 teaspoon ground coriander, or to taste
Freshly ground black pepper, to taste

2 garlic cloves—pressed through a garlic press
1/4 cup *finely* **chopped onion**
1/2 cup chopped red bell pepper

2 tablespoons *finely* **chopped fresh parsley** *or* **coriander (***cilantro***), if preferred**

If using *achiote* (*annatto*) granules, grind in a mortar with a pestle.

Place *achiote* (*annatto*) granules or paste in a small Pyrex dish. Add hot corn oil and allow to stand for about 30 minutes. Stir frequently to dissolve. Strain the oil into a skillet. Discard granular residue of the *achiote*.

Set skillet over *MEDIUM* heat. Add an additional 2 teaspoonfuls of oil and allow to heat.

Add ground soymeat, vinegar, and black pepper to the oil remaining in the skillet. Stir-fry for several minutes.

Add garlic, *finely* chopped onion, and chopped red pepper. Continue to cook, stirring frequently for about 7-8 minutes. Any liquid should be evaporated.

Add parsley or fresh coriander (*cilantro*). Stir to integrate.

Serve warm with warm *tortillas, tostados*, or toast as a luncheon dish or as an appetizer

Yields 6 appetizer servings
adequate for 4 people

Notes: *When using the dehydrated products such as "So Soya," follow the package directions for rehydration before proceeding.

This recipe can be halved or doubled.

1/6 SERVING (exclusive of *tortillas, tostados*, or toast) –
PROTEIN = 6.9 g.; FAT = 3.1 g.; CARBOHYDRATE = 6.4 g.;
CALORIES = 72; CALORIES FROM FAT = 39%

The Americas–**Honduras**

AUTHENTIC HONDURAN FERMENTED PINEAPPLE VINEGAR
Vinegre de Piña

TPT - 1 week and 10 minutes;
1 week = fermentation and flavor development period

Latin Americans make a distinctively flavored pineapple vinegar using wild fermentation and the trimmings from a fresh pineapple. Without the added vinegar, the wild fermentation can be used to make an alcoholic beverage called "tepache." The vinegar is a popular condiment and salad dressing ingredient throughout Mexico and Central America and an economical way to use up the trimmings from a pineapple in a most natural way.

1/2 cup sugar
2 cups water
2 cups apple cider vinegar

Trimmings from a fresh *organic* pineapple
  —coarsely chopped

In a mixing bowl, combine sugar, water, and vinegar. Stir to dissolve the sugar.

Add pineapple peelings. Cover the bowl with culinary cheesecloth. Allow to stand at room temperature for about a week or until the liquid begins to darken. Remove pineapple trimmings and strain vinegar into a condiment jar.

Refrigerate and use as needed.

Yields 4 cupfuls

Note: This recipe can be halved, when required.

1/16 SERVING (i. e., 2 tablespoonfuls) –
PROTEIN = 0.0 g.; FAT = 0.0 g.; CARBOHYDRATE = 4.3 g.;
CALORIES = 16; CALORIES FROM FAT = 0%

MY PINEAPPLE VINEGAR
Vinegre de Piña

TPT - 96 hours and 5 minutes;
96 hours = flavor development period

Let's face it, you do not always have a fresh pineapple that will provide the trimmings needed to make an authentic batch of "vinegre de piña." Cored fresh pineapple is available in the produce section of most grocery stores and works perfectly for this less sweet version.

1 slice and the core of a fresh, cored pineapple
2 cups apple cider vinegar

Cut pineapple slice in four pieces; cut the core into four pieces and place in a wide, shallow dish. Pour vinegar over. Cover the dish with culinary cheesecloth. Allow to stand at room temperature for 96 hours, four days. Remove pineapple pieces and strain vinegar into a condiment jar.

Refrigerate and use as needed.

Yields 2 cupfuls

Note: This recipe can be halved, when required.

1/8 SERVING (i. e., 2 tablespoonfuls) –
PROTEIN = 0.0 g.; FAT = 0.0 g.; CARBOHYDRATE = 1.6 g.;
CALORIES = 4; CALORIES FROM FAT = 0%

PURÉED BANANA, *YUCA*, AND COCONUT SOUP IN THE STYLE OF HONDURAS
Sopa de Banana, Yuca, y Coco

TPT - 1 hour

Hondurans enjoy a conch soup called "Sopa de Caracol." I never had the pleasure of tasting the authentic soup and that I do regret but I thought that the ingredients of the broth deserved recognition. Without the conch meat and with the addition of green bananas, this becomes a creamy vegan soup that really satisfies.

PURÉED BANANA, *YUCA*, AND COCONUT SOUP IN THE STYLE OF HONDURAS (cont'd)

1 quart VEGETARIAN BROWN STOCK *[see index]* **or vegetarian stock of choice**

1 1/2 cupfuls (about 3/4 pound) *yuca* root
  —peeled and chopped
2 *green, unripe* bananas—peeled and chopped*
2 fresh Roma-style tomatoes—peeled, seeded, and chopped— *or* 1/2 cup canned, *diced* tomatoes

1 tablespoon corn oil
1/4 cup *finely* chopped onion
2 large cloves—*finely* chopped

1 1/2 cups *light, sulfite-free* coconut milk
1/4 cup chopped fresh coriander (*cilantro*)
1/2 teaspoon *jalapeño* red *chili* sauce, or more to taste**
1/2 teaspoon ground cumin

Salt, to taste
Freshly ground black pepper, to taste

VEGETARIAN BROWN STOCK *[see index]* **or water to thin, if necessary**

In a kettle set over *MEDIUM* heat, heat stock. Allow it to come to the boil. *Reduce heat to LOW-MEDIUM.*

Add chopped *yuca*, bananas, and tomato. Stir to mix well.

In a skillet set over *MEDIUM* heat, heat oil. Add *finely* chopped onion and garlic. Sauté until onions are soft and translucent, *being careful to allow neither the onions nor the garlic to brown.* Add to ingredients in kettle over *LOW-MEDIUM* heat. Cook, stirring occasionally, until *yuca* is soft, about 30 minutes.

Add coconut milk, chopped fresh coriander (*cilantro*), jalapeño chili sauce, and ground cumin. *Do not allow this to boil.* Remove from heat and allow to stand for about 10 minutes.

Using the food processor fitted with steel knife or the electric blender, process the soup in small batches until very smooth. Set a sieve over a clean kettle. Pour the puréed soup through the sieve. Discard residue. Set kettle over *LOW* heat.

Taste and season with salt and black pepper. Allow to reheat. Thin, if necessary with extra vegetable stock.

Turn into a heated soup tureen.

Serve into heated soup cups.

Yields about 8 cupfuls

Notes: *Green-tipped bananas will result in a soup that is too sweet. Be sure to choose hard, green, unripe bananas.

**Jalapeno chili* sauce is available in Hispanic groceries, food specialty stores, and in most grocery stores throughout the Southwest.

This recipe can be doubled, when required.

1/8 SERVING (i. e., per cupful) –
PROTEIN = 2.8 g.; FAT = 3.3 g.; CARBOHYDRATE = 20.3 g.;
CALORIES = 115; CALORIES FROM FAT = 6%

HONDURAN *TORTILLA* SKILLET
Chilaquiles en Sarten
TPT - 18 minutes

This is our skillet version of a traditional Honduran casserole which can be made with either corn or flour tortillas and is a good way to use up tortillas that have been sitting in the refrigerator for awhile. It can be a high-fat disaster but this version reduces that possibility. If you have had this with the traditional full-fat sour cream garnish and prefer that garnish, try serving it with a garnish of yogurt crème or fat-free sour cream to keep the fat calories under control. Waning appetites will perk up when this dish is on the menu.

HONDURAN *TORTILLA* SKILLET (cont'd)

8 ten-inch flour *tortillas* or 12 six-inch corn *tortillas*, as preferred

Oil for deep-frying

4 medium tomatoes—peeled, seeded, and chopped— *or* 2 cups canned, *diced*, and drained tomatoes
2 garlic cloves
2 tablespoons light cream *or* half and half
1/2 teaspoon dried oregano—crushed
1/4 teaspoon ground coriander
1/4 teaspoon freshly ground black pepper

4 medium scallions—trimmed, well-rinsed, and sliced
1/2 cup shredded (about 2 ounces) Monterey Jack cheese

Lime wedges, for garnish

Jalapeño chili sauce**

Using kitchen scissors, cut *tortillas* into 1/4-inch strips.

In a wok or deep-fryer, heat oil to 365 degrees F.*** Deep-fry *tortilla* strips in small batches until they are *lightly golden. Do not allow them to become browned and crisp!* Transfer to paper toweling to *thoroughly* drain.

Preheat broiler to about 400 degrees F.

Meanwhile, in the container of the electric blender or in the work bowl of the food processor, fitted with steel knife, combine tomatoes, garlic, light cream, crushed oregano, ground coriander, and black pepper. Blend or process until smooth.

In a 10-inch non-stick-coated skillet set over *LOW-MEDIUM* heat, arrange well-drained *tortilla* strips. Pour prepared sauce over. Sprinkle sliced scallions over and then top with shredded cheese.

If necessary, wrap skillet handle with aluminum foil to protect handle. Set pan 6 inches below broiler element. Broil only until cheese has melted.

Serve at once, directly from skillet, with lime wedges and *jalapeño chili* sauce for those who wish to enliven their serving.

Yields 6 servings
adequate for 4 people

Notes: *Commercially-available *tortillas* are more substantial and, consequently, are preferable to use for preparing this dish.

**Jalapeño chili* sauce is available in Hispanic groceries, food specialty stores, and in any grocery store in the Southwest.

***If preferred, *tortilla* strips can be fried in 1 inch of oil in a skillet.

This recipe is easily halved, when required.

1/6 SERVING (using flour *tortillas* and assuming only 1 tablespoonful of oil is retained) –
PROTEIN = 9.7 g.; FAT = 9.3 g.; CARBOHYDRATE = 24.6 g.;
CALORIES = 213; CALORIES FROM FAT = 39%

1/6 SERVING (using corn *tortillas* and assuming only 1 tablespoonful of oil is retained) –
PROTEIN = 8.3 g.; FAT = 10.6 g.; CARBOHYDRATE = 24.6 g.;
CALORIES = 193; CALORIES FROM FAT = 49%

HONDURAN BEETS IN CREAM
Remolachas en Crema
TPT - 51 minutes

When I first tasted this recipe, I was incredulous when I found that it was native to Honduras. I can tick off a dozen or so beet recipes and they are mostly from Europe and Russia. This is not only a delicious way to eat beets, it is a truly beautiful dish to serve since the cream is turned a gorgeous pink color.

3 quarts *boiling* water
1 1/2 pounds fresh beets—well-scrubbed, with roots intact and 2 inches of leaf stem attached*

1/4 cup light cream *or* half and half
1 hard-cooked egg yolk—*finely* chopped *or sieved*
1/2 teaspoon salt
1/4 teaspoon freshly ground *white* pepper
1 tablespoon *finely* chopped onion

The Americas—**Honduras**

HONDURAN BEETS IN CREAM (cont'd)

In a large kettle, cook beets in *boiling* water until tender—about 45 minutes. Drain. Rinse in *cold* water until they can be handled. Cut off root ends and stem ends. Slip off skins and cut into quarters.

In a saucepan set over *LOW* heat, combine cream, *finely* chopped or *sieved* egg yolk, salt, *white* pepper, and *finely* chopped onion. Stir to combine. Add beets. Cook until heated through. Stir frequently, spooning cream mixture over beets. *Do not allow the cream to boil.*

Turn into heated serving bowl.

Yields 6 servings
adequate for 4 people

Notes: *Although this dish may be prepared with canned, whole beets, the taste of fresh beets is infinitely superior.

This recipe may be halved or doubled, when required.

1/6 SERVING – PROTEIN = 1.2 g.; FAT = 1.9 g.; CARBOHYDRATE = 3.6 g.;
CALORIES = 36; CALORIES FROM FAT = 48%

EASY COCONUT ICE CREAM
Helado de Coco

TPT - 8 hours and 13 minutes;
8 hours = freezing period

Hondurans are said to consume more coconut than do any other Latin Americans so my favorite coconut ice cream seemed to be perfect for this menu. This is a nice dessert choice for Easter brunch for which you can decorate each dessert plate with a nest of finely shredded fresh coconut. Place a few chocolate eggs into the center of the nest. When ready to serve dessert, place a slice of this scrumptious coconut ice cream on each plate beside the nest.

1 cup heavy whipping cream

2/3 cup *fat-free* sweetened condensed milk
1/4 cup *fat-free* pasteurized eggs* (the equivalent of 1 egg)
1 tablespoon water
2 teaspoons pure vanilla extract

1 cup *finely* shredded fresh coconut**

Prepare a 7 x 3 x 2-inch non-stick-coated loaf pan by placing it in the freezer until required.

Using an electric mixer fitted with *chilled* beaters or by hand, using a *chilled* wire whisk, beat heavy cream in a *chilled* bowl until stiff. Set aside.

In a large bowl, combine sweetened condensed milk, pasteurized eggs, water, and vanilla extract. Stir to blend thoroughly. *Whisk-fold* stiffly whipped cream and shredded coconut *gently*, but *thoroughly*, into milk mixture.

Pour mixture into chilled loaf pan. Spread evenly. Cover tightly with aluminum foil. Freeze overnight, or until firm—about 8 hours.

Either scoop ice cream from pan to serve or remove entire block of ice cream from pan and slice.

Leftovers should be returned to the freezer, tightly covered.

Yields about eight 1/2-cup servings

Notes: *Because raw eggs present the danger of *Salmonella* poisoning, commercially-available pasteurized eggs are recommended for use in preparing this dish.

**The procedure for preparation of fresh coconut is described in the recipe for NICARAGUAN COCONUT PUDDING *(Antecoco)* [see index]. Commercially-available *unsweetened* shredded coconut may be substituted, if necessary.

This recipe is easily doubled, when required. Use a 9 x 5 x 3-inch non-stick-coated loaf pan.

1/8 SERVING (i. e., per 1/2 cupful) –
PROTEIN = 4.0 g.; FAT = 14.4 g.; CARBOHYDRATE = 25.6 g.;
CALORIES = 249; CALORIES FROM FAT = 52%

Mexico

Mexican cuisine is a fusion cuisine of much greater complexity than most people are aware. It, of course, owes much to the arrival of the Spanish conquistadors in 1519. Their introduction of pigs, sheep, goats, chickens, and the art of animal husbandry to the basic Aztec diet of corn, beans, tomatoes, *chilies*, herbs, and *nopales* changed the cuisine almost instantly. Who could imagine Mexican cuisine without cheese, olive oil, cinnamon, parsley, coriander, oregano, black pepper, rice, wheat, barley, and almonds, all of which were also introduced by the Spanish? The Spaniards carried influences to Mexico from the South, from areas which already had felt the swords of the conquistadors, introducing to Mexico the cultivation of fruits, potatoes, cauliflowers, lettuce, carrots, and sugarcane.

Evidence that humans passed through this area as early as 21,000 BC has been found in the Valley of Mexico. We do know the names of many of those who stayed and prospered and then were replaced by the civilization of others. Many cultures reached their zeniths here such as the Olmec, the first Mesoamerican civilization that endured from 1400 BC to about 400 BC; the Toltec, established between the sixth and eight centuries AD; the Teotihuacan with their distinctive large pyramids; the Zapotec, who lived in the Valley of Oaxaca in the sixth century; the Mixtec, remnants of whose extensive civilization can be found in Oaxaca, Guerrero, and Puebla; the Mayan, the very advanced civilization about whose accomplishments in mathematics and astronomy we have learned so much in recent years; and the Aztec, of Mixtec descent, who ended their nomadic lifestyle and created a complex and successful civilization based on the earlier Toltec only to fall to the Spanish in 1521. In 1821 the viceroyalty of New Spain gained independence and the independent nation of Mexico ventured forth through economic instability, civil wars, two empires, and dictatorships. In 1910 the Mexican Revolution began, seeking to shake off the chains of the dictatorship of Profiro Diaz. It culminated in a new constitution in 1917 and the emergence of today's political system.

From 1864 to 1867 the French added another layer to the complex matrix that is Mexico during the brief, tragic reign of Ferdinand Maximillian. Mayonnaise, cream and nut sauces, classic omelets, and such dishes as *conejo en mostaza* (rabbit in mustard sauce), *pollo en nogada* (chicken in nut sauce), and *pollo con ciruelas* (chicken with prunes), are often found on restaurant menus. These clearly reflect the French influence of those few short years and how quickly and completely modifying influences can be integrated.

I have regretfully never traveled deep into Mexico. As a result, my exposure to Mexican food has been "border food," mostly Tex-Mex, that I had encountered on forays from Arizona into Mexico after my parents moved to the Southwest. What surprises I encountered as I began to explore a cuisine I was sure I would find familiar. You will see that the usual Mexican restaurant menu has been side-stepped to introduce a very different Mexican cuisine. It is cuisine, for instance, where the beans and rice, which more often than not are found as part of a meal, need not be eaten as the ubiquitous pile of rice and refried beans found in most Mexican restaurants up here in the North. Just as we, by way of the Tex-Mex phenomenon, have lost perspective on the truly complex and exciting cuisine of Mexico, the tremendous inroads of American food, especially American fast food, into Mexico is blurring recognition by the developing middle class of their own national treasure.

Each course in the following menu can be a meal in itself but if you decide to have a party, this can be quite a party. You may wish to accompany this menu with *atole*, the classic chocolate beverage which can be traced back to the courts of the Aztecs. Stirred until it is frothy with a *molinillo*, its popularity survives but it takes some getting used to if you are the "rich, milky hot chocolate" kind of person. Instead I prefer to offer a fresh fruit drink such as the *trolebús de frutas* which follows.

The Americas – Mexico

Appetizer Dip with Corn and Walnuts
Salsa de Elote con Nueces
with *Tostados*

Corn Relish

Squash and Cheese *Quesadillas* with **Homemade Thickened Cream**
Quesadillas con Calabacita y Queso   *Crema Espeso*

Grilled Fresh Pineapple Slices

Prickly Pear Salad with **Apricot – Raspberry Dressing**
Salsa de Nopalitos

~

Cream of Peanut Butter Soup garnished with *pepitas*
Sopa de Cacahuate con Leche

Puréed Corn Soup with Sweet Red Peppers
Sopa de Elote con Pimientos

~~~~~~~~~~~~~~~~~~~~

Cheese – Stuffed Zucchini with Lentils and Fruit
Calabacitas Rellenas y Lentejas con Frutas

~~~~~~~~~~

Lima Beans with Tomatoes and Eggs
Habas Verdes con Tomates y Huevos Cocidos

Carved Cucumber Flower Garnishes
Ensalada de Cohombro

Grilled Vegetables, of choice

~~~~~~~~~~~~~~~~~~~~~

Baked Plantains with Cinnamon   Pound Cake and Vanilla Ice Cream
Plantanos con Cañela   with **Mocha – Cinnamon Dessert Sauce**
   Salsa de Chocolate y Café con Canela

~

Fresh Fruit Refresher
Trolebús de Frutas

MEXICAN APPETIZER DIP WITH CORN AND WALNUTS
Salsa de Elote con Nueces

TPT - 24 hours and 4 minutes;
24 hours = draining period

This, with a few dippables, could be a meal in itself and you can entice almost anybody, who insists they are too tired or too hot or too whatever, to consume a pretty complete dinner just dipping this and that into this dip. In the 1970s a friend used to make an appetizer using blocks of cream cheese over which she piled a seasoned corn–onion mixture. Gayle's appetizer has, after all these years, now evolved into a dip.

1 cup *part-skimmed milk ricotta* cheese
1 cup *fat-free* dairy sour cream *or* MEXICAN HOMEMADE THICKENED CREAM *(Crema Espeso)* [see recipe which follows]

1 tablespoon freshly squeezed lime juice
1 teaspoon chili powder
1 teaspoon ground cumin
1/4 teaspoon freshly ground mixed peppercorns
—white, black, and red

1 cup CORN RELISH—*well drained* [see recipe which follows]*

1/4 cup *toasted*, chopped *preservative-free* walnuts

In a mixing bowl, combine *ricotta* and sour cream. Mix well.

Set two automatic drip coffeemaker filters into a sieve over a medium-sized bowl or a yogurt filter over a 2-cup measuring cup. Pour the *ricotta*–sour cream mixture into the filters. Place a piece of plastic wrap on top of yogurt mixture and place a weight such as a jar of water set on a saucer on top. Allow to drain in the refrigerator for about 4 hours. Turn into a mixing bowl.

Add lime juice, chili powder, ground cumin, and pepper. Mix well.

Add well-drained CORN RELISH. Stir well. Refrigerate until required.

When ready to serve, sprinkle chopped, *toasted* walnuts over. Serve with a spreading knife as a communal first course with BAKED CORN *TORTILLA* CHIPS (*Tostaditas*) [see index], crackers, dry toasts, or *crudités*. Refrigerate leftovers.

Yields 1 1/2 cupfuls

Notes: *If you do not make CORN RELISH, it is available at farm markets and food specialty stores.

This recipe can be doubled, when required.

1/24 SERVING (i. e., per tablespoonful) –
PROTEIN = 2.9 g.; FAT = 1.5 g.; CARBOHYDRATE = 7.4 g.;
CALORIES = 56; CALORIES FROM FAT = 24%

CORN RELISH
TPT - 25 hours and 20 minutes;
24 hours = cooling period

Almost as far back as I can remember, the sight of a jar of corn relish coming up from my mother's or my grandmother's fruit cellar was a moment filled with anticipation. Every fall we canned it and the row of jars lined up on the shelf promised a winter vegetable alternative that could be depended upon to "please the troops." I spent years tweaking this one until it tastes, to the best of my memory, like their recipe.

10 cups green (fresh) corn cut from cob
—about 18-20 small-medium ears
3 large onions—chopped
6 large, red bell peppers—chopped
6 large, green bell peppers—chopped
1 small head cabbage—chopped
2 cups sugar
2 tablespoons dry mustard
2 tablespoons celery seed
2 tablespoons course (kosher) salt
2 tablespoons turmeric
1 quart apple cider vinegar
1 cup water

CORN RELISH (cont'd)

Sterilize ten 1-pint jars.* Also sterilize lids and rings for jars.

In a large kettle, combine all ingredients. Bring to the boil over *MEDIUM* heat. Reduce heat to *LOW* and simmer, uncovered, for about 25 minutes. Stir frequently.

Ladle into ten sterilized 1-pint canning jars. Carefully wipe lips of jars. Seal with hot, sterilized lids and rings. Process in hot-water-bath canner for 15 minutes, *timing from the moment the water reaches a full rolling boil.* Remove to surface covered with thick towels or newspapers. Allow to cool for 24 hours *undisturbed.*

Check to be sure jars are sealed before labeling and storing in a dark, cool, dry place.** Loosen or remove rings before storing.

Yields ten 1-pint jarfuls*

Notes: *The yield may vary due to the size of vegetables chosen so it is a good idea to sterilize an extra jar or two in anticipation.

**Any jars that do not seal can be stored in the refrigerator for several months or resealed using a *new lid.*

1/80 SERVING (i. e., per 1/4 cupful) –
PROTEIN = 1.6 g.; FAT = 0.4 g.; CARBOHYDRATE = 15.6 g.;
CALORIES = 64; CALORIES FROM FAT = 6%

<h2 align="center">MEXICAN SQUASH AND CHEESE QUESADILLAS</h2>
Quesadillas con Calabacita y Queso
TPT - 30 minutes;
10 minutes = squash draining period

Quesadillas means, roughly, "little cheese things." There are host of different interpretations of "little cheese things" throughout Latin America, from cakes to sandwiches. This is but one.

2 medium zucchini—well-washed and trimmed
Generous pinch coarse salt (or kosher salt)

8 eight-inch flour *tortillas*—whole wheat, if available
3/4 cup shredded (about 3 ounces) *queso blanco* or Monterey Jack cheese
3 tablespoons *finely* chopped Italian red onion
1 tablespoon *finely* chopped mild green *chilies*
2 tablespoons chopped fresh coriander (*cilantro*)

Shredded lettuce, for garnish
***Fat-free* dairy sour cream, for garnish**

Preheat oven to 450 degrees F. Prepare two baking sheets by coating with non-stick lecithin spray coating.

Using a food processor, fitted with medium shredding blade, or using the coarse side of a hand grater, grate zucchini. Place grated squash in a sieve or colander. Sprinkle coarse salt over and toss well. Set over sink and allow to drain for about 10 minutes. Squeeze as much liquid as possible from squash.

Place four *tortillas* on prepared baking sheet. Divide drained zucchini shreds among the four *tortillas,* spreading the squash evenly over the *tortilla* surface. Sprinkle *one-quarter* each of the shredded cheese, *finely* chopped red onion, diced green *chilies,* and chopped coriander (*cilantro*) over each of zucchini-spread *tortillas.* Place one of the remaining four *tortillas* on top of each prepared *tortilla,* pressing down firmly.

Bake in 450 degree F. oven for about 7 minutes, or until cheese is melted and *tortillas* begin to brown. Remove from oven and transfer to a cutting board. Using a large, sharp knife or a pizza cutter, cut each *quesadilla* into quarters. Arrange on heated plates.

Garnish with shredded lettuce and a dollop of sour cream or HOMEMADE THICKENED CREAM *[see recipe which follows]* before serving.

Yields 4 servings

Note: This recipe is easily halved or doubled, when required.

1/4 SERVING – PROTEIN = 10.8 g.; FAT = 10.4 g.; CARBOHYDRATE = 37.5 g.;
CALORIES = 280; CALORIES FROM FAT = 33%

MEXICAN HOMEMADE THICKENED CREAM
Crema Espeso

TPT - 18 hours and 2 minutes;
about 10 hours = culturing period*;
8 hours = final thickening period

Better than sour cream; more like French "crème fraîche."

3/4 cup heavy whipping cream
4 teaspoons fresh *cultured* dairy buttermilk

In a *sterile* glass container, stir the buttermilk into the cream. Cover with plastic wrap and set aside at room temperature until well-thickened.

Transfer to the refrigerator and allow to further thicken overnight.

Store in the refrigerator for up to 10 days.

Yields about 3/4 cupful

Notes: *The room temperature and the degree to which the cream has been pasteurized effect the activity of the culture and, therefore, the length of the thickening period.

This recipe may be doubled, when required.

1/12 SERVING (i. e., per tablespoonful) –
PROTEIN = 0.9 g; FAT = 4.9 g; CARBOHYDRATE = 0.5 g;
CALORIES = 53; CALORIES FROM FAT = 83%

MEXICAN PRICKLY PEAR SALAD WITH APRICOT – RASPBERRY DRESSING
Ensalada de Nopalitos

TPT - 38 minutes;
30 minutes = flavor development period

Nopalitos are the smallest and most tender prickly pear cactus paddles. Here they are combined with vinegar–infused onion rings and salty cheese, and then dressed with an exciting salad dressing. This is a super salad with all kinds of mouth-pleasing textures and tastes.

1/3 cup RASPBERRY VINEGAR [see index]
1 teaspoon sugar

1 small-medium Italian red onion—halved and *thinly* sliced

1 jar (15 ounces) *nopalitos* (prickly pear cactus paddles)—well-drained*
1/4 cup APRICOT – RASPBERRY SALAD DRESSING [see index]
1 tablespoon chopped fresh coriander (*cilantro*)
2 teaspoons chopped fresh oregano *or* 1 teaspoon dried oregano—crushed

1/4 cup crumbled *feta* cheese *or* Mexican *queso freso*, if available

In a saucepan set over *MEDIUM* heat, combine raspberry vinegar and sugar. Stir to combine well while allowing to come to the boil.

Add red onion slices and toss to coat with hot vinegar. Remove from heat and set aside to marinate for 30 minutes. Drain well.

When ready to serve, in a mixing bowl, combine well-drained *nopalitos*, APRICOT – RASPBERRY SALAD DRESSING, and chopped oregano and fresh coriander (*cilantro*). Toss to mix well. Turn out onto a serving plate or platter.

Arrange marinated onions over the dressed *nopalitos*. Sprinkle crumbled cheese over the top.

Serve at once.

Yields 6 servings
adequate for 4 people

Notes: *Nopalitos* are sliced and jarred by several firms in Arizona and California. They are available in Hispanic groceries, food specialty stores, and in grocery stores throughout the Southwest.

This recipe can be halved or doubled, when required.

1/6 SERVING – PROTEIN = 1.7 g.; FAT = 5.7 g.; CARBOHYDRATE = 7.4 g.;
CALORIES = 89; CALORIES FROM FAT = 58%

The Americas—Mexico

MEXICAN CREAM OF PEANUT BUTTER SOUP
Sopa de Cacahuate con Leche

TPT - 21 minutes

Complex flavored peanut-based soups also appear in cuisines of African nations, to which the peanut was exported from South America. Wherever the peanut is grown, whether it is called goober or groundnut or peanut, its versatility is explored with wonderful results such as this soup.

3 tablespoons butter
1/2 cup *finely* chopped onion
1 garlic clove—*very finely* chopped
3 tablespoons whole wheat flour
1 cup *one-percent* milk

1/2 cup freshly ground *unsalted, additive-free, smooth* peanut butter—*brought to room temperature*
2 1/2 cups *one-percent* milk
1/2 teaspoon freshly grated lemon zest
1/2 teaspoon *finely* crushed dried basil
1/2 teaspoon *finely* crushed dried parsley
1/4 teaspoon ground mace

Salt, to taste
Freshly ground black pepper, to taste

2 tablespoons *toasted,* slivered *preservative-free* almonds—for garnish

In a large saucepan set over *LOW-MEDIUM* heat, melt butter. Add *finely* chopped onion and *very finely* chopped garlic. Sauté for just a minute or two. Stir in flour. Cook, stirring constantly, for several minutes until a *roux* is formed. *Remove from heat.*

Using a wire whisk, beat the 1 cupful milk—*tablespoonful by tablespoonful*—into the *roux*. Return to *MEDIUM* heat. Stir for several minutes until the milk mixture begins to thicken. Add smooth peanut butter. Using a wire whisk, beat until smooth.

Gradually beat in remaining milk. Add grated lemon zest, crushed basil and parsley, and ground mace. Whisk until well-integrated. Cook, stirring frequently, until hot and thickened. Season with salt and black pepper, to taste. Thin with additional milk, *if necessary.*

Turn into a *heated* soup tureen. Serve into *heated* soup cups, garnishing each with *toasted* almond slivers.

Yields 4 servings

Note: This recipe is easily halved or doubled, when required.

1/4 SERVING –   PROTEIN = 15.3 g.; FAT = 24.4 g.; CARBOHYDRATE = 20.9 g.;
CALORIES = 369; CALORIES FROM FAT = 60%

MEXICAN PURÉED CORN SOUP WITH SWEET RED PEPPERS
Sopa de Elote con Pimientos

TPT - 1 hour and 5 minutes

We think the texture of this soup is fantastic and the play of flavors is just about perfect.

1 1/2 tablespoons safflower *or* sunflower oil
1 large onion—*finely* chopped

1 1/2 large, sweet red bell peppers—cored, seeded, and chopped
1 1/2 tablespoons *finely* chopped mild green chilies
3 garlic cloves—*finely* chopped
1/4 teaspoon ground cumin

7 1/2 cups green (fresh) *or frozen* corn kernels

5 cups VEGETARIAN BROWN STOCK *[see index]*, **VEGETABLE STOCK FROM SOUP** *[see index] or* **vegetarian stock of choice**
Pinch salt

6 tablespoons *fat-free* dairy sour cream, for garnish
Pinch dried and crushed *epazote*, for garnish, if available*
Commercially-available *tostados*, lightly toasted and broken into pieces—for garnish, if desired**
Lime wedges, for garnish

In a kettle or Dutch oven set over *MEDIUM* heat, heat oil. Add *finely* chopped onion. Sauté until onion is soft and translucent, *being careful not to allow onion to brown.*

Add chopped red pepper, diced *chilies, finely* chopped garlic, and cumin. Continue to sauté until vegetables soften, again *being careful not to allow vegetables to brown.*

MEXICAN PURÉED CORN SOUP WITH SWEET RED PEPPERS (cont'd)

Add corn kernels and continue to sauté for about 2 minutes more, to give the corn a slightly roasted flavor.

Add stock and salt. Bring to the simmer and allow soup to continue simmering for about 30 minutes.

Using a food processor fitted with steel knife or an electric blender, purée *only one-half* of soup mixture. Return purée to kettle and reheat soup over *LOW-MEDIUM* heat.

Turn into a heated soup tureen and serve into heated soup plates. Garnish each serving with a dollop of *fat-free* sour cream, a pinch of *epazote*, and a few pieces of a *toasted tostado*, if desired. Place a lime wedge on the side.

Yields 6 servings
adequate for 4 people

Notes: *Epazote (Chenopodium ambrosioides)*, available dried from spice specialty firms, is a rather unusual but mild-tasting green herb used extensively in Latin American and South American cooking. This large, easily-grown, but invasive, annual is also known as wormseed, goosefoot, Mexican tea, and Jerusalem oak and has a strong camphor-like odor which repels insects and protects other insect-susceptible plants. It is said to reduce the gassiness from legume dishes. To prevent the transfer of a bitterness, the leaves should be added during the last 15 minutes of a cooking period. If you choose to grow it in your herb garden, be sure to harvest the seeds before they disperse or you will have many, too many, *epazote* plants the next season than you could ever want. It is so tenacious that a handful scattered on a city sidewalk will produce a sizable crop firmly established in the sidewalk cracks!

**Tostados* are available in the Mexican food section of grocery stores. Although you might be tempted to use *tortilla* chips for garnish, we find them too salty for this soup.

This recipe may be doubled, when required.

Leftovers may be reheated with little loss of flavor. Therefore, this soup may be prepared a day in advance for convenience, reheated, and garnished just before serving.

1/6 SERVING (with 1 tablespoonful *fat-free* sour cream) –
PROTEIN = 9.2 g.; FAT = 4.7 g.; CARBOHYDRATE = 50.0 g.;
CALORIES = 305; CALORIES FROM FAT = 14%

MEXICAN CHEESE–STUFFED ZUCCHINI WITH LENTILS AND FRUIT
Calabacitas Rellenas y Lentejas con Frutas
TPT - 1 hour and 25 minutes

Cooking lentils with pork and fruits is a Mexican classic, prepared sometimes without the pork and sometimes without the fruits. Here, we have tried to maintain the spirit of this remarkable lentil dish by pairing it with the subtle, but complex, flavors of zucchini squash, another Mexican favorite.

MEXICAN CHEESE–STUFFED ZUCCHINI WITH LENTILS AND FRUIT (cont'd)

2/3 cup dry, brown (*or* green) lentils
3 cups VEGETARIAN BROWN STOCK *[see index]* or other vegetarian stock of choice
1 bay leaf—halved*

1 tablespoon safflower *or* sunflower oil
1/2 large onion—*finely* chopped
1 garlic clove—*finely* chopped

1 slice fresh *or* canned pineapple—cut into small wedges
1 apple—peeled, cored, seeded, and diced
1 firm, *green-tipped* banana—sliced
1 cup shredded (about 4 ounces) *sharp* Cheddar cheese
1 cup *fresh* whole wheat breadcrumbs
1/2 teaspoon chili powder
1/2 teaspoon ground allspice
Freshly ground black pepper, to taste

3 medium zucchini squashes

6 tablespoons *fat-free* dairy sour cream, for garnish

Prepare a 9-inch ceramic quiche dish, pie plate, or *au gratin* dish by coating with non-stick lecithin spray coating.**

Sort lentils and discard those of poor quality. Rinse thoroughly.

In a non-aluminum saucepan** set over *MEDIUM* heat, combine lentils, stock, and bay leaf halves. Bring to the boil. Reduce heat to *LOW*, cover tightly, and simmer for about 30 minutes, or until lentils are tender. Drain, reserving liquid for soup stock and discarding bay leaf pieces. Set aside briefly.

In a skillet set over *LOW-MEDIUM* heat, combine oil, *finely* chopped onion, and *finely* chopped garlic. Sauté until soft and translucent, *allowing neither the onion nor the garlic to brown.* Remove from heat. Add lentils and 2 tablespoons of the liquid drained from the lentils. Stir to combine well. Add pineapple wedges, diced apple, and banana slices. Stir to combine. Spoon into prepared baking dish. Set aside.

Preheat oven to 325 degrees F.

In a large bowl, combine shredded Cheddar cheese, *fresh* breadcrumbs, chili powder, ground allspice, and black pepper. Stir to combine well. Set aside.

Trim ends from zucchini. Wash thoroughly, but *do not peel*. Cut in half lengthwise and, using a small spoon, scoop out pulp to form "boats."***

Apportion prepared cheese filling among zucchini "boats," packing the filling down slightly to secure it.

Arrange filled "boats" in lentil–filled baking dish, nestling the zucchini into the lentils.**** Bake in preheated 325 degree F. oven for 25 minutes. Although the apples should become rather mushy, creating a creamy texture, *be careful not to overcook*.

Serve at once, garnished with sour cream.

Yields 6 servings
adequate for 4-6 people

Notes: *The bay leaf pieces are most easily recovered if secured inside a tea ball during the simmering process.

**Since aluminum discolors lentils rather unpleasantly, avoid the use of aluminum cookware or serving bowls in this case.

***Reserve pulp for soup stock or make MEXICAN SQUASH AND CHEESE QUESADILLAS [see recipe which precedes.].

****The entire dish may be prepared and assembled ahead to this point, covered, and refrigerated. Remove from the refrigerator about 35 minutes before serving time, allow to come to room temperature, and bake as directed.

This recipe is easily halved or doubled, when required.

1/6 SERVING – PROTEIN = 14.8 g.; FAT = 8.5 g.; CARBOHYDRATE = 39.5 g.; CALORIES = 279; CALORIES FROM FAT = 27%

The Americas – Mexico

MEXICAN LIMA BEANS WITH TOMATOES AND EGGS
Habas Verdes con Tomates y Huevos Cocidos
TPT - 34 minutes

When the freshly harvested lima beans appear in the farmers' market, we usually buy four quarts. They are yummy and tender so some just get snacked on raw. Two quarts are quickly frozen for winter eating and the rest end up in dishes like this. If there are also tiny, freshly dug, salad potatoes at market, then we know that we will have for dinner that evening.

Peruvians enjoy a dish similar to this but without the egg garnish and jalapeño bite. Their version is seasoned with chili powder and lemon.

2 cups *fresh* lima beans—well-rinsed
2 quarts *boiling* water

2 tablespoons butter
1 small onion—*finely* chopped
1 garlic clove—*very finely* chopped

2 medium tomatoes—peeled, seeded, and chopped— *or* 1 cup canned, *diced* tomatoes
1/2 teaspoon *jalapeño chili* sauce, or to taste*
1/2 teaspoon dried *epazote*
Freshly ground black pepper, to taste

3 hard-cooked eggs—sliced
Chopped fresh coriander (*cilantro*) *or* parsley, to garnish

In a saucepan set over *MEDIUM* heat, combine fresh lima beans and *boiling* water. Cook for about 20 minutes, or until tender. Drain. Turn into heated serving bowl and keep warm on a warming tray.

While lima beans are cooking, melt butter in a skillet set over *MEDIUM* heat. Add onion and garlic. Sauté until soft and translucent, *allowing neither the onion nor the garlic to brown*.

Add chopped tomatoes, *jalapeño chili* sauce, *epazote*, and black pepper. Cook, stirring frequently, until heated through and a sauce has formed. Pour tomato mixture over cooked beans.

Arrange sliced eggs on top and sprinkle with chopped fresh coriander (*cilantro*) or parsley.

Serve at once.

Yields 6 servings
adequate for 4 people

Notes: *Chopped fresh, hot peppers can be substituted but the *jalapeño chili* sauce is a convenient product. It is available in Hispanic groceries, food specialty stores, and in grocery stores throughout the Southwest.

This recipe can be halved or doubled, when required.

1/6 SERVING – PROTEIN = 9.2 g.; FAT = 6.8 g.; CARBOHYDRATE = 18.9 g.;
CALORIES = 172; CALORIES FROM FAT = 35%

MEXICAN CARVED CUCUMBER FLOWER GARNISHES
Ensalada de Cohombro
TPT - 1 hour and 12 minutes;
1 hour = marination period

Many, many years ago I picked up a small book that promised to make every meal presentation look like a garden of flowers. Vegetable and fruit garniture was all the rage and like Japanese paper folding it was often harder than it looked despite the promises of those that sold the "handy dandy" assortment of tools that "every hostess had to have." Oh well, its popularity gradually disappeared so I was content with radish roses, scallion fans, and this Mexican cucumber "flower" street food that doubles as a salad. Resembling flowers, the cucumber sections are beautiful as a garnish and provide a fresh, textural contrast.

1 teaspoon *jalapeño chili* sauce*
2 tablespoons freshly squeezed lime juice

1 cucumber—peeled

1 well-scrubbed lime—cut into 6 wedges

In a shallow bowl combine *jalapeño chili* sauce and lime juice. Stir to mix. Set aside briefly.

MEXICAN CARVED CUCUMBER FLOWER GARNISHES (cont'd)

Cut ends of cucumber straight across. Run the tines of a fork lengthwise down the cucumber. Repeat the scoring all the way around the cucumber. Using a sharp knife, cut the cucumber into six "flowers" of equal dimension by inserting the knife halfway through the cucumber forming V-shaped incisions. When the V-shaped incisions have been made all the way around the first flower segment, twist sharply and separate. Continue until all the flowers have been formed. Sculpture the end surfaces to match. Place the flowers into the *chili-lime* mixture, allowing one sculptured surface to be exposed to the marinade. Refrigerate for 1 hour.

Serve chilled with a wedge of lime tucked up against each "flower."

Yields 6 servings

1/6 SERVING – PROTEIN = 0.3 g.; FAT = 0.05 g.; CARBOHYDRATE = 2.4 g.; CALORIES = 8; CALORIES FROM FAT = 6%

MEXICAN BAKED PLANTAINS WITH CINNAMON
Plantanos con Cañela
TPT - 46 minutes

Years ago it was difficult to find plantains in my local produce department. As a consequence, my files contain many banana recipes adapted from plantain recipes. As plantains became "the other banana in the store," as a friend referred to them, I started trying to get those old banana recipes back to authenticity. This is one of those recipes that has now come to life again. It is a simple and special recipe that reveals the Mexican love of vanilla and plantains which can be served a dessert with a multitude of sauces or it can become a sauce, if baked for an extra 10-15 minutes, to serve over ice cream, puddings, or cakes.

1 tablespoon canola oil

3 ripened plantains—peeled and sliced lengthwise

1/2 vanilla bean

1/2 cup *light* brown sugar
2 teaspoons ground cinnamon
1/4 cup skimmed milk
1 tablespoon pure vanilla extract

Dessert sauce, of choice

Preheat oven to 300 degrees F.

Prepare a baking dish large enough to hold plantain halves by generously spraying with lecithin non-stick coating. Pour oil into dish and swish from side to side to spread oil over the bottom of the pan.

Arrange plantains in the bottom of the pan.

Split vanilla bean in half and scrape seeds into a small dish. (Save vanilla bean to flavor other desserts or sugar.)

Add brown sugar, ground cinnamon, water, and vanilla extract. Stir to mix well. Sprinkle over the plantains. Bake in preheated 300 degree F. oven for about 30-35 minutes, or until plantains are very soft. Using two serving spoons or a wide spatula, transfer a plantain half to each of six dessert dishes.

Spoon a little sauce over each. Choose sweetened whipped cream, sweetened sour cream, sweetened MEXICAN HOMEMADE THICKENED CREAM (*Crema Espeso*) [see recipe which precedes], or a simple CUSTARD SAUCE (*Crème Anglaise*) [see index], as preferred.

Serve warm.

Yields 6 individual servings

Note: This recipe can be halved, when required.

1/6 SERVING (exclusive of sauce) –
PROTEIN = 0.9 g.; FAT = 2.5 g.; CARBOHYDRATE = 33.6 g.;
CALORIES = 146; CALORIES FROM FAT = 15%

MEXICAN MOCHA – CINNAMON DESSERT SAUCE
Salsa de Chocolate y Café con Cañela
TPT - 12 minutes

Sometimes at Christmas, we serve a dessert, such as homemade ice cream or cake tartlets, with several sauces. This is a special sauce for such an occasion. When presented with French raspberry fig sauce or English toffee sauce, nobody can choose and, consequently, everybody has second helpings. So, why not a third sauce? Although most Mexican sauces are less sweet and Mexicans do prefer to use bittersweet chocolate, this sweeter, less fat-laden sauce can take it place right along side those other sweet Christmas dessert sauces we love.

3/4 cup light cream *or* **half and half**
6 tablespoons sugar
2 tablespoons *unsweetened* **dark cocoa**
2 teaspoons instant *espresso* **coffee powder**

1/4 cup light cream *or* **half and half**
1 teaspoon corn starch
1/4 teaspoon ground cinnamon

In a saucepan set over *LOW-MEDIUM* heat, combine the 3/4 cupful cream, sugar, cocoa, and *espresso* powder. Using a wire whisk, blend thoroughly. Cook, stirring frequently, until mixture is *just below* the boiling point.

In a small bowl, combine remaining 1/4 cupful cream, corn starch, and ground cinnamon. Using a wire whisk, blend thoroughly until corn starch is completely in suspension. Add to saucepan and cook, stirring constantly, until the mixture thickens. *Remove from heat* and allow to cool slightly.

Serve warm.

Yields about 18 tablespoonfuls

Notes: Conveniently, this sauce can be make several days ahead if covered and refrigerated. Reheat the sauce over *LOW* heat before serving.

This recipe can be halved or doubled, when required.

1/18 SERVING (i. e., per tablespoonful) –
PROTEIN = 0.6 g.; FAT = 1.4 g.; CARBOHYDRATE = 5.7 g.;
CALORIES = 37; CALORIES FROM FAT = 34%

MEXICAN FRESH FRUIT REFRESHER
Trolebús de Frutas
TPT – 5 minutes

This delightful refresher has the most fascinating name. Quite literally," trolebús" means trolley-bus. It can probably best be described as a frappé, the kind that I would order as a teenager at a soda shop which was near the bus stop at which I had to catch my bus after work. The first truly Mexican "trolebús" I ever tasted was made with honeydew melon, pineapple, and tangerine juice. You can see from this recipe, I am not slavish to first impressions.

1/2 cup chopped cantaloupe
1/2 cup chopped watermelon
1/2 cup chopped pineapple
1/2 cup chopped mango
1/2 cup chopped or sliced strawberries
1/2 cup tangerine juice, clementine juice, *or*
   orange juice
2 tablespoons sugar

Crushed ice

MEXICAN FRESH FRUIT REFRESHER (cont'd)

In the container of the electric blender, combine fruits, orange juice, and sugar.

Add crushed ice to about an inch from the top of the blender container. Process at high speed to create an uniform purée.

Serve at once in wine glasses.

Yields about 3 1/2 cupfuls

Notes: This is my favorite combination of fruits but you can easily adopt it to your favorites or to what is available.

This recipe can not be doubled. However, if you have your fruit prepared in advance and crushed ice in the freezer, you can easily make several batches for a crowd.

1/7 SERVING (i. e., 1/2 cupful) –
PROTEIN = 0.4 g.; FAT = 0.6 g.; CARBOHYDRATE = 11.8 g.;
CALORIES = 48; CALORIES FROM FAT = 11%

Nicaragua

What is now Nicaragua, the largest country in Central America, is another of the areas visited by Christopher Columbus on his fourth voyage in 1502. His journals show that he explored the Mosquito Coast. Gil González Dávila, who arrived in Panama in 1520 and launched an expedition in search of gold in this region, began the period of conquest which was shortly followed by permanent settlements in 1524. Granada on Lake Nicaragua, the first settlement, followed by León, near Lake Managua, were founded and defended by Francisco Hernández de Cordoba. By 1529 Nicaragua had been conquered and the civilization of the indigenous population had been destroyed. These peoples had been, for the most part, either enslaved by their conquerors or had died of the diseases introduced by the Europeans.

Often ignored is the influence upon the cuisine and the gene pool of Nicaragua that occurred with the European immigration that took place in 1800s. Germans, Italians, French, Belgians, and, of course, Spanish found a welcome in Nicaragua as they brought their wealth to the New World this time with intentions of starting up businesses.

Although the foundation of this blend of indigenous and Spanish cuisines is without doubt corn, inevitably, a discussion of Nicaraguan cuisine must come to the ubiquitous *gallo pinto* ("painted rooster"). In this unique Nicaraguan dish, rice is fried with onions and combined with boiled red beans and garlic, often with the addition of chopped peppers or other vegetables, and eaten in the morning with scrambled eggs and cheese, *tortillas*, and sweet plantains. At noon and in the evening *gallo pinto* is served with a variety of meats and/or seafood, and a salad. The complemented legume and grain proteins provide perfect protein nutrition so the poor, who can only afford to put the "painted rooster" on their table, are as well-fed as are those who add eggs and meat or seafood to their menu. *Gallo pinto* is increasingly popular in Costa Rica as more and more Nicaraguan expatriates take up residence to avoid political and economic instability.

The Americas–**Nicaragua**

Grapefruit with Honey
Toronja en Miel

~

Avocado Slices with Lime Juice
Aguacate con Zumo de Lima

~~~~~~~~~~~~~~~~~~~~~~

Grits with Cheese
Cazuela de Sémola de Maíz con Queso

Tomatoes and Squash with Pumpkin Seeds
Tomate y Calabacín con Chimichuri Pipian

Garlic and Parsley Sauce
Salsa Chimichuri

Mashed Sweetpotatoes and Pineapple
Puré de Camote y Piña

~~~~~~~~~~~~~~~~~~~~~~

Coconut Pudding
Antecoco

Coconut Corn Starch Pudding
Postre de Coco

NICARAGUAN GRAPEFRUIT WITH HONEY
Toronja en Miel

TPT - 2 hours and 3 minutes;
2 hours = flavor development period

Early in the spring I stock up on the canned red grapefruit sections that are available from a nearby grocery store as part of their generic line. Only this store carries these wonderful, sweet grapefruit sections and when they are gone, they are gone until the following winter crop of red grapefruits has grown and is again available for canning. They make such an easy, delicious dessert or appetizer in the summer too.

Cherimoya and papaya can be prepared using this same recipe.

1 can (15 ounces) red grapefruit sections—well-drained*
2 tablespoons wildflower honey
1 tablespoon freshly squeezed lime juice

4 *very thin* slices fresh, organic lime

In a serving bowl, combine well-drained grapefruit sections, honey, and lime juice. Stir to mix thoroughly. Refrigerate for at least 2 hours to allow for flavors to meld.

Serve chilled in small dessert dishes or sherbet glasses as a dessert or as an appetizer. Garnish each serving with a twisted lime slice.

Yields 4 servings

Notes: *Fresh grapefruits can be sectioned and used in this dish, if preferred.

This recipe can be doubled, when required.

1/4 SERVING – PROTEIN = 1.0 g.; FAT = 0.06 g.; CARBOHYDRATE = 28.9 g.;
CALORIES = 118; CALORIES FROM FAT = <1%

The Americas–Nicaragua

GRITS WITH CHEESE
Cazuela de Sémola de Maíz con Queso
TPT - about 40 minutes

This is a cheesy grits dish which became our very, very favorite ways to prepare grits back in the 1970s. Prepared all over Central and South America, this casserole is satisfying and easy to prepare. Nicaraguan cooks often add eggs and milk and turn it into a custard. We enjoy it without the eggs and milk as a side dish, as in this menu, or as a main course for a light supper. If someone asks, "What are we having for dinner?" and the answer is, "Grits," they know that this is what they can anticipate.

1 1/2 teaspoons butter
1/2 cup *finely* **chopped onion**

3 cups bottled water *or* **refrigerated water***
3/4 cup quick-cooking hominy grits

1/4 teaspoon Tabasco sauce, or more to taste
1/4 teaspoon freshly ground black pepper, or to taste

1/2 cup (about 2 ounces) shredded *sharp or extra-sharp* **Cheddar cheese**
1 tablespoon butter—*softened to room temperature*

2 tablespoons (about 1/2 ounce) shredded *sharp or extra-sharp* **Cheddar cheese**

Preheat oven to 325 degrees F. Prepare a 1 1/2-quart soufflé dish or other oven-to-table casserole by coating with non-stick lecithin spray coating.

In a non-stick-coated skillet set over *MEDIUM* heat, melt the 1 1/2 teaspoonfuls butter. Add *finely* chopped onion. Sauté, stirring constantly, until onion is soft and translucent, *being careful not to allow onion to brown.*

Meanwhile, bring the water to the boil in a saucepan. Add grits, *being careful not to allow water to stop boiling.* Continue to boil for 1 minute, *stirring constantly.* Reduce heat to *MEDIUM-LOW* and cook for an additional 4 minutes, or until thickened.

Using a rubber spatula, combine sautéed onions and grits. Stir in Tabasco sauce and black pepper.

Blend the 1/2 cupful shredded cheese with the remaining 1 tablespoonful of *softened* butter. Fold this mixture thoroughly into the grits–onion mixture. Turn into prepared casserole and sprinkle the remaining 2 tablespoonfuls of shredded cheese evenly over the top.

Bake in preheated 325 degree F. oven for about 20 minutes, or until cheese is melted and bubbling.

Serve at once.

Yields 6 servings
adequate for 3-4 people

Notes: *Since the chlorine in tap water destroys the B-vitamin thiamin in grains, it is advisable to cook grains in either bottled water or water that has been refrigerated uncovered for at least 24 hours.

This recipe is easily halved or doubled, when required.

1/6 SERVING – PROTEIN = 4.7 g.; FAT = 6.8 g.; CARBOHYDRATE = 15.6 g.;
CALORIES = 143; CALORIES FROM FAT = 43%

TOMATOES AND SUMMER SQUASH WITH PUMPKIN SEEDS IN THE STYLE OF NICARAGUA
Tomate y Calabacín con Chimichuri Pipian
TPT - 16 minutes

Pipian, roasted pumpkin seeds, are added to many dishes in Latin America. Their nutrition is not wasted as just a compost ingredient. When our daughter was young and the annual Halloween pumpkin was carved, she and I would clean the seeds off and roast them to snack on or add to dishes like this. Although perhaps not absolutely authentic, this very flavorful vegetable side dish is, as they say, "in the style of Nicaragua."

TOMATOES AND SUMMER SQUASH WITH PUMPKIN SEEDS IN THE STYLE OF NICARAGUA (cont'd)

2 cups canned, *diced or whole* tomatoes—drained
1 small yellow summer squash—peeled and diced

1 1/2 tablespoons NICARAGUAN GARLIC AND PARSLEY SAUCE *(Salsa Chimichuri)* [*see recipe which follows*], or to taste
3 tablespoons *unsalted, roasted* pumpkin seeds —*ground**
Pinch of chili powder, if desired

In a saucepan set over *LOW-MEDIUM* heat, combine tomatoes and diced squash. Cook, stirring frequently, until the squash softens and the tomatoes are bubbling.

Add *chimichuri* sauce, ground pumpkin seeds, and chili powder. Continue to cook, stirring frequently, for about 5 minutes more. Turn into a heated serving bowl.

Using a slotted spoon, s*erve at once.*

Notes: *If you do not have roasted pumpkin seeds available, gently toast raw, dried pumpkin seeds in a dry skillet over *LOW* heat. A SPICE and COFFEE GRINDER is the best tool to grind pumpkin seeds.

This recipe may be halved or doubled, when required.

Yields 6 servings
adequate for 4 people

1/6 SERVING – PROTEIN = 2.0 g.; FAT = 3.8 g.; CARBOHYDRATE = 4.4 g.;
CALORIES = 54; CALORIES FROM FAT = 63%

NICARAGUAN GARLIC AND PARSLEY SAUCE
Salsa Chimichuri

TPT - 48 hours and 5 minutes;
48 hours = flavor development period

Sort of a Nicaraguan pesto," chimichuri" is a bright, fresh, and useful condiment. We use it with vegetables and veggie burgers but it really shines, in my estimation, in a taco or tortilla wrap. How many times have I heard a lunchtime request from the kitchen, "Is there any of that sauce left?"

1 cup *very finely* chopped, *well-washed* and *well-dried*, curly parsley
3 large garlic cloves—*very finely* chopped
1/2 cup *extra virgin* olive oil
1 tablespoon freshly squeezed lemon juice
2 teaspoons freshly squeezed lime juice
1/2 teaspoon *jalapeño chili* sauce—green or red, as preferred—or to taste*

Pinch salt, or to taste
Freshly ground black pepper, to taste

In the work bowl of the food processor, combine *very finely* chopped parsley and garlic, olive oil, lemon and lime juices, and *jalapeño* hot pepper sauce. Process to a uniform consistency, scrapping down the sides of the work bowl as required.

Add salt and black pepper. Process again. Turn into a small condiment jar, cover, and refrigerate for 48 hours before using for optimum flavor development.

Serve at room temperature. Refrigerated leftovers will keep for about a week.

Yields about 12 tablespoonfuls

Notes: *Jalapeno chili* sauce is available in Hispanic groceries, food specialty stores, and in grocery stores throughout the Southwest.

This recipe can be doubled, when required.

1/12 SERVING (i. e., per tablespoonful) –
PROTEIN = 0.2 g.; FAT = 7.4 g.; CARBOHYDRATE = 0.7 g.;
CALORIES = 71; CALORIES FROM FAT = 94%

The Americas—**Nicaragua**

NICARAGUAN MASHED SWEETPOTATOES AND PINEAPPLE
Puréde Camote y Piña

TPT - 1 hour and 18 minutes

Every year, without fail, the ultimate Thanksgiving dinner is published in each and every food magazine. Even magazines with small recipe sections, online blogs, and television cooking programs assert their expertise. And, every year, without fail, somebody asks us, "Whatever do you eat for Thanksgiving?" To which, every year, without fail, I respond, "Think about it, how much of that traditional Thanksgiving meal is turkey?" There is so much for a vegetarian to choose from and so much to enjoy." This recipe, popular in Nicaragua, published frequently at Thanksgiving in the United States in some form or another, is a simple beautiful pairing of "sweets."

4 medium sweetpotatoes—well-scrubbed

1 teaspoon butter—*softened to room temperature*

1/2 cup *well-drained, crushed* pineapple—fresh
　or canned, as preferred
2 tablespoons light cream *or* half and half
1 tablespoon butter—*softened to room temperature*
1 tablespoon *light* brown sugar
1/2 teaspoon ground cinnamon

2 tablespoonfuls *well-drained* pineapple tidbits *or*
　large pieces of crushed pineapple

Preheat oven to 375 degrees F. Prepare an oven-to-table serving dish by lightly coating with the 1 teaspoonful softened butter.

Cut an **X** in the top of each sweetpotato. Bake in preheated oven for about 1 hour, or until the potatoes are soft. *Reduce oven temperature to 200 degrees F.*

Scoop potato flesh from the baked sweetpotatoes and put in a mixing bowl. Mash thoroughly.

Add well-drained crushed pineapple, cream, 1 tablespoonful softened butter, brown sugar, and ground cinnamon. Stir to mix well. Turn into prepared baking dish. Bake at 200 degrees F. until heated through and remainder of meal is prepared.

Garnish with pineapple tidbits.

Serve hot.

Yields 6 servings
adequate for 4 people

Note: This recipe can be halved or doubled, when required.

1/6 SERVING – PROTEIN = 1.6 g.; FAT = 3.0 g.; CARBOHYDRATE = 21.7 g.;
CALORIES = 121; CALORIES FROM FAT = 22%

NICARAGUAN COCONUT PUDDING
Antecoco

TPT - 11 hours and 25 minutes;
　　　8 hours and 30 minutes = coconut infusion period;
　　　2 hours = setting period

This version of the classic coconut pudding enjoyed in Nicaragua takes considerable time and effort, and most diners will never appreciate your efforts fully. It is a beautiful dessert which I have always enjoyed and in which I have always taken pride. I remember taking a hammer to a coconut on the garden walkway in front of my parents' Tucson house to prepare this pudding and I remember that my mom and dad enjoyed it immensely that Christmas. Be sure not to serve it after a very spicy meal since your taste buds will not fully appreciate the subtlety if they have been bombarded for a course or two.

The addition of commercially-available coconut milk enhances the flavor considerably.

1 medium coconut

2 1/2 cups *hot* skimmed milk—*hot, but not scalded*

2 tablespoons sugar

3 tablespoons corn starch
1/2 cup *cold* skimmed milk

1/4 cup *light, sulfite-free* coconut milk

1 teaspoon pure vanilla extract

2 tablespoons shredded, fresh coconut,
　for garnish

NICARAGUAN COCONUT PUDDING (cont'd)

Preheat oven to 325 degrees F.

TO PREPARE FRESHLY GRATED COCONUT, make two holes in the coconut through the shiny black "eyes" using a sharp pointed tool such as a screwdriver or an awl. Drain the coconut water into a dish to be used as the replacement for liquid in recipes calling for fresh coconut.

Using a hammer or metal meat mallet, break the coconut into 4-6 pieces. Rinse each piece under running water to loosen meat from shell. With the help of a paring knife, remove coconut from shell. Place pieces on a cookie sheet in preheated 325 degree F. oven for about 5 minutes. Remove from oven and pare rind from coconut meat using a vegetable peeler.

Using a food processor fitted with fine shredding disk or by hand, shred coconut. Reserve 1 tablespoonful for garnish.

TO PREPARE COCONUT CREAM, place 2 cupfuls of freshly grated coconut in a large mixing bowl. Add *hot* milk and allow to infuse for about 30 minutes at room temperature. Place in the refrigerator for 8 hours or overnight.

The next morning, pour through a fine sieve set over a second mixing bowl or through several layers of culinary cheesecloth. Squeeze coconut well to release all possible coconut cream.* Add milk to bring liquid to a full 2 cupfuls, if necessary.

Pour coconut cream into the top half of a double boiler set over simmering water. Stir in sugar using a wooden spoon.

In a small bowl, combine corn starch, *cold* milk, and canned coconut milk. Stir until corn starch is in suspension.

When coconut cream is hot, stir in corn starch suspension. Cook, stirring constantly, until mixture thickens—about 20 minutes. Continue cooking for an additional 10 minutes, stirring frequently.

Set aside to cool for about 10 minutes. Stir in vanilla extract. Turn into single serving dish or into five individual sherbet glasses.

Chill for at least 2 hours before serving. Garnish with reserved shredded, fresh coconut, if desired.

Yields 5 servings
adequate for 3-5 people

Notes: *Reserve shredded coconut for snacks, a fruit compote, cookies, breakfast cereal mixes, or any recipe calling for coconut. If coconut is to be kept for any length of time before serving, dry on a cookie sheet in oven set at *WARM*. Although considerable flavor has been released into the coconut cream, the remaining coconut is still superior, in our view, to the canned and packaged varieties.

An acceptable substitute for fresh coconut cream can be made using packaged *unsweetened* moist coconut. After infusion, the remaining coconut will not have much flavor. Use it for a textural ingredient rather than for the coconut flavor.

This recipe may be doubled, when required. Cooking time will have to be increased.

1/5 SERVING – PROTEIN = 5.4 g.*; FAT = 8.9 g.*; CARBOHYDRATE = 31.4 g.*;
CALORIES = 227*; CALORIES FROM FAT = 35%*

*These figures must be considered approximate since shredded coconut is recovered and reusable at the end of preparation. We have estimated that about one-half of the calories are transferred during infusion.

The Americas–**Nicaragua**

COCONUT CORN STARCH PUDDING
Postre de Coco

TPT - 1 hour and 27 minutes;
1 hour = chilling period

Although I do prefer to make a coconut pudding starting with a session that involves putting hammer to coconut, this version, made with canned coconut milk, is delicious and as comforting as is any corn starch pudding. If you have tasted "haupia," served at almost every restaurant in Hawaii, this is very different; it is soft and creamy. The coconut flavor is actually enhanced by the touch of vanilla.

1/2 cup sugar
6 tablespoons corn starch
1 1/2 cups *cold* **skimmed milk**

1 1/2 cups *light, sulfite-free* **coconut milk**

1/2 teaspoon pure vanilla extract

3 tablespoons shredded, unsweetened coconut,
 for garnish

In a saucepan, combine sugar, corn starch, and *cold* milk. Using a wire whisk, stir until corn starch is thoroughly dissolved. Place over *MEDIUM* heat. Cook, stirring frequently, until pudding begins to thicken. *Reduce heat to LOW-MEDIUM.*

Gradually, stir in coconut milk. Continue cooking, stirring almost constantly with a wire whisk, until pudding is uniformly thickened. Set aside to cool slightly.

Add vanilla extract, stirring to integrate thoroughly.

Divide among six sherbet glasses. Refrigerate for at least 1 hour before serving.

Yields 6 individual servings

Notes: This recipe *can not* be doubled successfully but it can be halved, when necessary.

Occasionally, even though you are very conscientious about stirring, corn starch puddings can become lumpy. Press through a sieve into a clean saucepan and continue cooking over hot water until uniformly thickened.

1/6 SERVING – PROTEIN = 2.4 g.; FAT = 3.5 g.; CARBOHYDRATE = 33.0 g.;
CALORIES = 170; CALORIES FROM FAT = 19%

Panama

Panama was first explored by Rodrigo de Bastidas in 1501. A year later Christopher Columbus arrived and established a settlement on the isthmus at the Gulf of Darien whose history was brief and ill-documented. Vasco Nuñez de Balboa, who first visited the New World as a crew member of the 1501 Bastidas expedition, became the first European to see the Pacific Ocean from the west coast of Central America. Balboa's 1513 expedition did discover that this strip of land could be transversed and that the two great bodies of water were separated by this narrow land mass. It was welcome news to the Spanish who made this their commercial crossroads, hauling gold, silver, foods, and plants from the Spanish New World Empire across the isthmus, on a route known as the *Camino Real*, to be loaded onto ships which then sailed to Spain. For three hundred years, Panama, an area only slightly larger than our state of West Virginia, was a keystone in the trade structure of the Spanish Empire. The importance of the *Camino Real* waned once navigation advanced to the point that merchant travel around Cape Horn, albeit longer, became preferable to the labor intensive trek across the isthmus, with its need for unloading and reloading cargo and its vulnerability to pirates.

In 1821 Panama became independent from Spain but then, and for eighty years thereafter, was administered by Colombia. The Thousand Days War, which lasted from 1899 to 1902 and ended with the Hay–Herran Treaty, finally brought the United States openly into Panama's fight for independence when the treaty was rejected by Colombia. In 1903 the Hay/Bunau–Varilla Treaty established Panamanian independence and granted the United States sovereignty in what came to be known as the Canal Zone, a zone about ten miles wide and fifty miles long in which a canal would be built and which the United States would then administer, fortify, and defend in perpetuity.

Since Balboa's trek across the narrow isthmus, Panama has been important for its geographic position separating the Pacific Ocean on the West and the Caribbean on the East. It is not surprising that ocean commerce became important nor is it surprising that the world would turn to Panama to explore the idea of transporting goods from east to west without traveling around hazardous Cape Horn at the southernmost tip of South America. In 1881 the first attempt to build a canal was begun under Ferdinand de Lesseps, the architect of the Suez Canal. De Lesseps' plan proceeded at sea level for 103 miles with no locks but was finally abandoned in 1890 when bankruptcy had to be declared. In 1914 the United States completed the present fifty-two-mile canal, half the length of the abandoned French canal, with three locks up and three locks down.

By 1988 a contentious relationship between the United States and the corrupt and repressive military regime of Manuel Antonio Noriega resulted in the invoking of the International Emergency Economic Powers Acts through which President Reagan froze all assets of the Panamanian government in the United States after sanctions proved ineffective. Noriega annulled the results of the 1989 election which had overwhelmingly elected anti-Noriega candidates. In December of that year, then President George H. W. Bush authorized an invasion of Panama to secure the canal. Manuel Noriega surrendered to United States authorities and was convicted of drug trafficking. Through the Torrijos–Carter Treaties, the canal and the Canal Zone were ceded to Panama in 1998.

The oldest samples of corn, *chilies*, and yams in Mesoamerica, dating from about 6000 BC, were found at Ladrones Cave in Panama. Whether or not these foods were cultivated, is still a subject of considerable speculation. The international cuisine of Panama is influenced first and foremost by pre-Columbian inhabitants and by the West Indies/Caribbean, Spain, and Portugal. Today one sees considerable evidence of influence from the United States, England, Holland, France, Portugal, Africa, China, and India as well as from neighboring countries in Latin America. It is a "melting pot cuisine," if you will, much like our own cuisine. Despite a healthy manufacturing and agricultural climate, Panama still needs to import about twenty-five percent of the population's domestic needs.

The Americas—Panama

Olive and Caper *Tapanade*
Alcaparrago

Toasts, Corn Chips, or Crackers

~

***Chayote* and Pepper Slaw**	**Pink Potato Salad**
Ensalada de Chayote	*Ensalada de Papas*

~~~~~~~~~~~~~~~~~~~~

Smoky Lentils with Vegetables
Sopa de Lentejas

Steamed Rice

~~~~~~~~~~

**Red Kidney Bean *Tacos*, or *Tostados*
with Sautéed Greens and Goat Cheese**
Tacos con Judia Pinta, Lechuga, y Queso de Cabra

Pickled Vegetables
Encuritido

~~~~~~~~~~~~~~~~~~~~~~

Sweet Hominy Dessert	**Bread Pudding**
Chichome	*Mamallena*

Tapioca Pudding

with

***Crème Fraîche* with Jam**
Crema Fresca con Conserva

PANAMANIAN OLIVE AND CAPER *TAPANADE*
Alcaparrago
TPT - 8 minutes

This salty condiment is served on the side in Spain and throughout the Latino world in the Western Hemisphere. A commercially-available version can occasionally be found in Latino markets or in the international aisles of gourmet groceries. It is very simple to make your own version which allows you to adjust seasoning to your family's taste.

4 ounces, *pitted, pimiento-stuffed* green olives
2 ounces *pitted* black olives
2 ounces marinated capers
1/2 cup well-washed and chopped fresh coriander
  leaves (*cilantro*)
1 large garlic clove—*finely* chopped
1/2 teaspoon *achiote* paste, or to taste
Freshly ground black pepper, to taste

The Americas – Panama

PANAMANIAN OLIVE AND CAPER *TAPANADE* (cont'd)

In the work bowl of the food processor fitted with steel knife, combine pitted green olives with pimiento, pitted black olives, capers, chopped fresh coriander (*cilantro*), *finely* chopped garlic, *achiote* paste, and black pepper. Process until uniformly chopped. Turn into a small serving bowl. Refrigerate until required.

Refrigerate leftovers.

Yields 10 servings
adequate for 6 people

Note: This recipe can be halved, when required.

1/10 SERVING – PROTEIN = 0.4 g.; FAT = 3.3 g.; CARBOHYDRATE = 1.0 g.;
CALORIES = 36; CALORIES FROM FAT = 83%

CHAYOTE AND PEPPER SLAW
Ensalada de Chayote
TPT - 7 minutes

Chayote are small tropical squashes, rarely more that a pound in weight, that are now found in most produce departments. Select the smallest and the darkest green squash you can find. They are often referred to as vegetable pears or "mirleton" in Louisiana where they are baked and filled with stuffing. The Australians call them "chokos" and use them very imaginatively. Although they can be substituted for other squashes in many recipes, we enjoy them most as part of a complex slaw because the delicate flavor of the crisp flesh is refreshing, especially when this salad accompanies dishes with strong sauces and lots of cheese such as enchiladas.

1 small red bell pepper—well-washed, peeled, and cut into slivers
1 small green bell pepper—well-washed, peeled, and cut into slivers
2 small *chayote* (about 1 pound)—peeled, pitted, and cut into matchstick pieces

Freshly ground mixed peppercorns—black, red, and white—to taste

1 tablespoon *extra virgin* olive oil
1 tablespoon GARLIC–BASIL VINEGAR *[see index]* **or OREGANO FLOWER VINEGAR** *[see index]*
1 teaspoon LATIN AMERICAN SPICE MIX (*Condimento Latino Americano*) *[see index]*

In a serving bowl, combine slivered red and green pepper slivers with *chayote* matchsticks. Toss to mix.

Grind pepper over.

In a small cruet, combine olive oil, vinegar, and spice mixture. Shake vigorously. Pour over slivered vegetables. Toss to distribute the *vinaigrette* evenly.

Serve at once.

Yields 6 servings
adequate for 4 people

Note: This recipe can be doubled, when required.

1/6 SERVING – PROTEIN = 0.8 g.; FAT = 2.0 g.; CARBOHYDRATE = 5.1 g.;
CALORIES = 40; CALORIES FROM FAT = 45%

PANAMANIAN PINK POTATO SALAD
Ensalada de Papas
TPT - 29 minutes

This is really a very pretty, not to mention nutritious, salad served at Christmas time in Panama. For those who might worry about the taste of beet in a potato salad, the color is the major contribution of the little beets; you hardly know they are there.

PANAMANIAN PINK POTATO SALAD (cont'd)

2 large all-purpose potatoes—peeled and diced
4 quarts *boiling* water

1 tablespoon white distilled vinegar

2 hard-cooked eggs—peeled and chopped
2 canned baby beets—diced
1/2 cup diced onion
2 medium celery ribs—trimmed and diced

1/2 cup *calorie-reduced or light* mayonnaise
1 tablespoon MUSTARD SAUCE *[see index]*
2 tablespoons beet canning liquid

1/4 teaspoon freshly ground black pepper, or to taste
Salt, to taste

In a kettle set over *MEDIUM* heat, combine diced potatoes and *boiling* water. Boil until potatoes are crisp-tender—about 12-15 minutes. Drain. Plunge potatoes into cold water to stop further cooking. When cold, drain well. Turn into a mixing bowl.

Sprinkle vinegar over. Toss.

Add chopped eggs, and diced beets, onion, and celery. Toss.

In a small dish, combine mayonnaise, mustard, and beet canning liquid. Stir to combine thoroughly. Add to vegetables. *Gently* combine.

Season with black pepper and salt. Gently combine. Turn into a serving bowl. Refrigerate until ready to serve.

Serve chilled.

Yields 6 servings
adequate for 4 people

Note: This recipe can be halved or doubled, when required.

1/6 SERVING – PROTEIN = 3.9 g.; FAT = 8.9 g.; CARBOHYDRATE = 16.0 g.;
CALORIES = 161; CALORIES FROM FAT = 50%

SMOKY LENTILS WITH VEGETABLES IN THE STYLE OF PANAMA
Sopa de Lentejas
TPT - 54 minutes

Panamanians add smoked meats to cooked lentils and serve this thick soup or stew over rice. By adding soy bacon or liquid smoke, you can achieve a similar taste. Although I do serve these lentils over rice, I also just make them to serve as a side dish.

2/3 cup dry, brown (*or* green) lentils
3 cups water

1 tablespoon *extra virgin* olive oil
1/2 cup *finely* chopped onion
1/4 cup *finely* chopped celery
1/4 cup *finely* chopped green bell pepper
2 tablespoons *finely* chopped mild green *chilies*

1 slice soy bacon—*finely* chopped*

1/4 cup liquid drained from cooking lentils
1/4 cup tomato purée
1/4 teaspoon crushed, dried oregano

Sort lentils and discard any of poor quality. Rinse well.

In a non-aluminum saucepan set over *MEDIUM* heat, combine washed lentils, and 3 cupfuls water. Bring to the boil. Reduce heat to *LOW*, cover tightly, and simmer for about 30 minutes, or until lentils are tender. Drain, reserving the liquid.

In a saucepan set over *MEDIUM* heat, heat oil. Add *finely* chopped onion, celery, green bell pepper, and green *chilies*. Sauté until onion is soft and translucent, *being careful not to allow any of the vegetables to brown. Reduce heat to LOW.*

Add *finely* chopped soy bacon and sauté for several more minutes.

SMOKY LENTILS WITH VEGETABLES IN THE STYLE OF PANAMA (cont'd)

Add 1/4 cupful of liquid drained from cooking lentils and tomato purée. Stir to combine well.

Add drained, cooked lentils and cook until heated through. Turn into a heated serving bowl.

Serve at once.

Yields 6 servings
adequate for 4 people

Notes: *If you do not use meat analogue products, a drop or two of liquid smoke can be used instead of the soy bacon.

This recipe can be halved, when required.

1/6 SERVING – PROTEIN = 7.1 g.; FAT = 2.3 g.; CARBOHYDRATE = 18.1 g.;
CALORIES = 118; CALORIES FROM FAT = 18%

RED KIDNEY BEAN *TACOS* OR *TOSTADOS* WITH SAUTÉED GREENS AND GOAT CHEESE
Tacos con Judia Pinta, Lechuga, y Queso de Cabra

TPT - 30 minutes

A young friend brought supper to the crew that worked with me to recover the Tiffany glass which hid everywhere in the debris of our burned-out church and there we sat that December night discussing food as the charred oak of the old structure filled our lungs and her good food filled empty stomachs. Jackie had lived in the North all of her life but had been born in Charleston, South Carolina, and her food showed her roots. Instead of a tossed salad that night, she brought a "mess of greens." We have all sprinkled shredded lettuce over our tacos, I, instead, add sautéed greens to this taco filling and remember a night when people cared very much about each other and a corn chip dipped in a "mess of greens" became a taste to remember.

6 pre-made corn *taco* shells or *tostados*, as preferred*

2 tablespoons *extra virgin* olive oil
1 large red onion—sliced into thick rings

3 garlic cloves—*thinly* sliced into large slices

6 cups mixed greens—trimmed, coarsely chopped, and *very well-washed* and *well-dried*
1 cup canned red kidney beans—rinsed and *well-drained*
1/4 cup VEGETABLE STOCK FROM SOUP
  [see index] or vegetarian stock of choice

Freshly ground black pepper, to taste

1/4 cup soft goat cheese—crumbled
2 tablespoons chopped fresh coriander (*cilantro*)

Preheat oven to about 170 degrees. Place the *taco* shells or *tostados* on a baking sheet and put in the oven to heat.

In a large non-stick-coated skillet set over *MEDIUM* heat, heat oil. Add onion rings and sauté until onions are soft and translucent, *being carefully not to allow onions to brown*.

Add garlic slices and sauté for several minutes more. Add chopped greens, kidney beans, and vegetable stock. Cook, stirring constantly to prevent the mixture from sticking to the bottom of the skillet until the greens are wilted.

Season generously with black pepper.

Remove the *taco* shells from the oven. Divide the filling among the *taco* shells. Sprinkle goat cheese and chopped fresh coriander (*cilantro*) over each.

Serve at once.

Yields 6 servings
adequate for 4 people

**RED KIDNEY BEAN *TACOS* OR *TOSTADOS*
WITH SAUTÉED GREENS AND GOAT CHEESE** (cont'd)

Notes: *If preferred, the filling can be used to fill warm *tortillas*.

This recipe can be halved or doubled, when required.

1/6 SERVING – PROTEIN = 9.5 g.; FAT = 8.5 g.; CARBOHYDRATE = 31.8 g.; CALORIES = 234; CALORIES FROM FAT = 33%

PANAMANIAN PICKLED VEGETABLES
Encuritido

TPT - 25 hours;
24 hours = post-canning flavor development period

When I was young, I thought that only people in northern climates pickled vegetables for winter salads because that is what my family, of northern European heritage, did. I know better now ... I found the Japanese passion for pickles an eye-opener and the attempt to curtail spoilage and mold in tropical climates by pickling, a complete and absolute surprise. Encuritido can be made from any variety of vegetables you find in over-supply and that you just like. It reminds me very much of a mixture called chow chow that my mother cold-pack canned and stored in our fruit cellar for the winter.

1 quart distilled white vinegar
1/2 cup orange juice*
1/2 cup freshly squeezed lime juice

3 tablespoons gingerroot slices
1 teaspoon allspice berries
1 teaspoon whole cloves
3-inch stick cinnamon
1 1/2 tablespoons mixed whole peppercorns—red, white, and black
1 tablespoon dried oregano
1/4 cup *very finely* chopped fresh coriander (*cilantro*)
1/4 cup sugar

1 cup small cauliflower florets—well-washed
1 large carrot—peeled and sliced
1/4 cup chopped Italian red onion
1 leek *or* Vidalia salad onion—*white and light green portions only*—trimmed, well-rinsed, and sliced
1 small Japanese eggplant—trimmed and chopped
1 cup baby red, yellow, and orange sweet bell peppers—sliced into rings
1 cup diced *chayote*
1 cup diced mango
3 whole mild green *chilies***

Sterilize 3 one-quart canning jars. Also sterilize lids and rings for jars.

In a large kettle set over *MEDIUM* heat, combine vinegar, orange juice, and lime juice. Allow to come to the boil.

Add gingerroot slices, allspice berries, whole cloves, cinnamon quill, mixed peppercorns, oregano, fresh coriander (*cilantro*), and sugar. Allow to return to the boil.

Add cauliflower florets, carrot slices, chopped red onion, sliced leek or sweet salad onion, chopped eggplant, pepper rings, diced *chayote*, diced mango, and whole *chilies*. Remove from heat. Remove cinnamon quill. Using a slotted spoon, divide vegetables among sterilized jars. Ladle liquid plus spices into jars. *Be sure that there is one green chili in each jar.* Carefully wipe rims of jars. Seal with hot, sterilized lids and rings. Process in hot-water-bath canner for 30 minutes, *timing from the moment the water reaches a full rolling boil.* Remove to surface covered with thick towels or newspapers. Allow to cool for 24 hours *undisturbed*. Check to be sure jars are sealed before labeling and storing in a dark, cool, dry place or in the refrigerator.*** Loosen or remove rings before storing.

Allow flavors to meld for at least 1 month before serving.

Yields 3 quartfuls
with about 10 servings per quart

The Americas – **Panama**

PANAMANIAN PICKLED VEGETABLES (cont'd)

Notes: *Use bitter or blood orange juice if available.

**Put one whole *chili* in each jar. If your mixture fills more than three quart canning jars, add more whole green *chilies*.

***Any jars that do not seal can be stored in the refrigerator for several months or resealed using a *new lid*.

1/30 SERVING – PROTEIN = 0.5 g.; FAT = 0.2 g.; CARBOHYDRATE = 7.8 g.;
CALORIES = 32; CALORIES FROM FAT = 6%

PANAMANIAN SWEET HOMINY DESSERT
Chichome
TPT - 10 minutes

Dried hominy, when available, is an inexpensive, nutritious food but the convenience and soft texture of the canned product is perfect for this dish. Chichome is most often served for breakfast but we find it to be a quickly-prepared dessert that nourishes and satisfies.

1 can (15 ounces) hominy (*posolo*)—*well-drained*
1/2 cup sugar
3/4 cup *two-percent* milk

1 tablespoon light cream *or* half and half
1/4 teaspoon pure vanilla extract
1/4 teaspoon ground cinnamon

In a saucepan set over LOW-MEDIUM heat, combine well-drained hominy, sugar, and milk. Cook, stirring frequently, until sugar is dissolved. Remove from heat.

Add cream, vanilla extract, and ground cinnamon. Stir to combine well. Turn into a serving bowl.

Serve chilled or at room temperature.

Yields 6 servings
adequate for 4 people

Note: This recipe can be halved or doubled, when required.

1/6 SERVING – PROTEIN = 1.8 g.; FAT = 1.1 g.; CARBOHYDRATE = 28.8 g.;
CALORIES = 135; CALORIES FROM FAT = 7%

PANAMANIAN BREAD PUDDING
Mamallena
TPT - 1 hour and 50 minutes;
30 minutes = bread absorption period;
15 minutes = minimum cooling period

Leftover breakfast rolls are sliced and dried to reappear at dinner in the bread basket in Portugal. In Italy the day's loaf is sliced and crostini with savory toppings appear at your table as an appetizer. Bread puddings are also an economic way to use up dinner rolls and day-old bread as cooks all over the world have found.

PANAMANIAN BREAD PUDDING (cont'd)

3 thick slices bread*

1 1/2 cups *two-percent* milk
1/2 cup *fat-free* pasteurized eggs (the equivalent of 2 eggs)
1/2 cup sugar
1/4 cup *preservative-free dark* raisins
1/4 cup butter—*melted*
1 teaspoon pure vanilla extract

Cream

Prepare an 8-inch square baking pan by coating with non-stick lecithin spray coating.

Lightly toast bread slices. Cut into cubes. (There should be about 2 cupfuls.) Set aside briefly.

In a large mixing bowl, combine milk, pasteurized eggs, sugar, raisins, *melted* butter, and vanilla extract. Add bread cubes and gently fold ingredients together. Turn into prepared baking pan. Spread evenly to the sides.

Allow to stand at room temperature for at least 30 minutes.

Preheat oven to 325 degrees F.

Place bread pudding in baking pan in which a 1-inch water bath has been prepared. Bake in preheated oven for about 50 minutes, or until a knife inserted into the center comes out clean. *Do not allow water bath to simmer or boil—by adding cold water or ice cubes*, if necessary. Remove from oven to a heat-resistant surface or wire rack. Allow to stand for at least 15 minutes before serving.

Serve warm, at room temperature, or thoroughly chilled, as preferred. Cut into squares and lift with a spatula to serve.

Pass cream separately.

Refrigerate leftovers.

Yields 8 servings
adequate for 4 people

Note: *I prefer to use my homemade multigrain bread or an oatmeal loaf that I also make.

1/8 SERVING (exclusive of added cream) –
PROTEIN = 3.9 g.; FAT = 6.6 g.; CARBOHYDRATE = 26.2 g.;
CALORIES = 181; CALORIES FROM FAT = 33%

PANAMANIAN *CRÈME FRAÎCHE* WITH JAM
Crema Fresca con Conserva

TPT -   24 hours and 3 minutes;
24 hours = thickening period

Although it is temping to use sour cream instead of crème fraîche, the freshly soured cream is richer, much softer, and less sour than commercial sour cream available in the United States. Panamanians mix the crème fraîche with mango jam and serve it over fruited rice as a dessert. I like this best with peach jam and I prefer to serve it over tapioca pudding. Raspberry, strawberry, apricot, blueberry, and pear jams work well too so when I send someone down to the canning shelves to choose a jam, I accept their choice and we go from there. I do feel obligated, however, to warn you, that it is advisable to double your tapioca pudding recipe since, with this lovely topping, everybody takes second helpings.

CRÈME FRAÎCHE :
   8 ounces heavy whipping cream
   2 tablespoons dairy sour cream *or*
      PLAIN YOGURT *[see index]*
   1/4 teaspoon freshly squeezed lemon juice

1/4 cup fruit jam—preferably homemade—or to taste

In a small mixing bowl, combine heavy cream, sour cream or yogurt, and lemon juice. Cover and allow to stand at room temperature until the mixture thickens—about 24 hours.

Add jam. Fold the jam into the thickened *crème fraîche*. Cover and refrigerate until ready to serve. Refrigerate leftovers.

Yields 10 servings
adequate for 5 people

Note: This recipe can be halved, when required.

1/10 SERVING – PROTEIN = 0.5 g.; FAT = 8.1 g.; CARBOHYDRATE = 5.6 g.;
CALORIES = 97; CALORIES FROM FAT = 76%

Paraguay

Paraguay and Uruguay are often linked as if the similar spelling of their names makes them twins. This was even the case in my college Spanish history and literature course. Land-locked Paraguay and ocean-facing Uruguay are as dissimilar to each other as are our states of Arizona and Maine. Although both have been influenced by Brazilian culture, that influence on Paraguay, coming as it did through immigration, was less subtle than it was for Uruguay which was ruled by Brazil until 1845. Both were influenced by the culture of their native peoples but only six percent of Uruguay's 3.5 million people can be classified as *mestizo* while some ninety-five percent of Paraguay's 6.6 million people are considered *mestizo;* the majority of Paraguayans are Paraguayan-born while eighty-eight percent of Uruguayans are of European origin. And, just as we see in Maine and Arizona, unique cuisines have evolved.

The settlement of *Asunción*, now the capital of Paraguay, was founded in 1537 by the Spanish explorer Juan de Salazar de Espinosa. Rather than a center of trade and commerce, the colonial province became a center for the Jesuit order of the Roman Catholic Church as it established missions in Paraguay, Brazil, Bolivia, and Argentina, but not notably in Uruguay. The Guarani profited greatly for 150 years from the guidance of the Jesuits for not only had they gained their protection from slave-hunters, schools and hospitals were set up in the *reducciones de indios* where the land was the property of the community; all worked for the common good, and all shared the profits. Literacy was a goal for the community and the Guarani society is said to have been the first society in history to achieve total literacy. Trouble began when the Portuguese, to whom territory had been ceded that included missions, tried to use the Indian labor, initiating a series of conflicts called the Guarini wars. Fearing a conflict with Portugal and mistrustful of the power of the Jesuits, the Spanish King Charles II expelled the Jesuits from the missions in 1767 at about the same time that he had suddenly expelled the Jesuits from all other areas of his realm. The Guarani left the settlement life they had learned and returned to the rural semi-nomadic life their ancestors had known.

Paraguay's isolationist reputation since its independence from Spain in 1811 can most probably be traced to its first ruler José Gaspar Rodrigues de Francia who ruled as dictator from 1814 to 1940. He created an utopian society based on Rousseau's *Social Contract*. During this period Paraguay had little contact with the rest of world. Carlos Antonio López, after a brief period when the country was ruled by a military *junta*, succeeded his uncle as dictator. Lopez, however, modernized the country, invited foreign commerce, and welcomed immigration. Paraguay's history from this period to the modern period is differently recorded and interpreted from author to author, from politician to politician. There is no official history of this country due to the fact that during the *Sauqueo de Asunción* in 1869 the Brazilian Imperial Army ransacked the Paraguayan National Archives and took the surviving contents of the archives to Rio de Janeiro where the materials were sealed and are, even today, unavailable to scholars.

The official language, used in business and commerce and spoken by ninety-two percent of the Paraguayan population, is Spanish. However, Guarani, the native language of the peoples whom the Spanish found living in this region in the sixteenth century, is spoken by ninety-eight percent of the people who call this nation home. In addition, Mennonite missionary communities who settled in the 1930s and those of German descent who emigrated from Europe and from Brazil in the twentieth century still speak German. German settlers founded towns and have promoted immigration of Germans and those of German descent from Europe, from Germany's former African colonies, and from other countries in South America. 150,000 Paraguayans are said to be of German–Brazilian descent. Some twenty-five thousand Mennonites live in the sparsely populated Paraguayan Chaco.

Paraguayan food choices seem to parallel its view of itself. Few dishes show a reaching out to the world for ingredients or inspiration, again, so different from Uruguay.

The Americas – Paraguay

Fried eggs are often served on top of a piece of grilled meat.

Vegetarians can just skip the meat and enjoy the eggs.

Orange Slices with Olive Oil

~

Winter Squash and Vegetable Soup
Sopa de Calabaza

"Beef" Soup with Noodles
So'o Yosopy

~~~~~~~~~~~~~~~~~~~~~~

Fried Eggs

Steamed or Baked Sweetpotato

Broiled Hearts of Palm
Palmitos Asados

Cheesy Cornbread
Sopa Paraguaya

~~~~~~~~~~~~~~~~~~~~~~

Coffee – Spice "Chemistry Class" Cake with Honey
Pastel con Café y Miel

Pineapple Ice Cream
Helado de Piña

PARAGUAYAN WINTER SQUASH AND VEGETABLE SOUP
Sopa de Calabaza
TPT - 42 minutes

This is one of those soups to which I turn in the winter since I usually have all the ingredients on hand. It is a casual, comforting combination of familiar flavors that warms the soul and the body especially if weather is "moving in." It is at the comfort level of the tomato stew into which we crushed crackers when I was young.

1 tablespoon butter
1 medium onion—*finely* chopped
1 medium carrot—diced
1 large garlic clove—*very finely* chopped

1/2 cup canned, *crushed* tomatoes
1 tablespoon chopped mild green *chilies*
1/4 teaspoon *jalapeño chili* sauce, or to taste
1 pound butternut squash, acorn squash, *or* pumpkin—chopped
3 cups VEGETABLE STOCK FROM SOUP *[see index] or* other vegetarian stock of choice
Freshly ground black pepper, to taste

Lime wedges

In a kettle set over *MEDIUM* heat, melt butter. Add *finely* chopped onion, diced carrot, and *very finely* chopped garlic. Sauté until onion is soft and translucent, *allowing none of the vegetables to brown.*

Add crushed tomatoes, chopped green *chilies*, *jalapeño chili* sauce, chopped squash, vegetable stock, and black pepper. Allow to cook for 30 minutes, stirring frequently.

Using a potato masher, mash the squash pieces. Turn into a heated soup tureen.

The Americas – Paraguay

PARAGUAYAN WINTER SQUASH AND VEGETABLE SOUP (cont'd)

Serve into heated soup bowls. Squeeze a lime wedge into each serving.

Yields 6 cupfuls

Note: This recipe can be doubled, when required.

1/6 SERVING (i. e., per cupful) –
PROTEIN = 1.6 g.; FAT = 2.0 g.; CARBOHYDRATE = 9.5 g.;
CALORIES = 69; CALORIES FROM FAT = 26%

PARAGUAYAN "BEEF" SOUP WITH NOODLES
So'o–Yosopy

TPT - 30 minutes

"So'o–Yosopy" is so popular in Paraguay that to leave it out of this chapter would probably have brought wrath upon my soul. Traditionally it is, of course, loaded with meat as are so many dishes in Paraguay but when it is made without meat, the texture is "so'o" different... too different. The use of a soy analogue product that mimics ground beef gives the soup the body and texture of the original. This is a good, hearty soup that satisfies on a cold winter's day.

2 tablespoons *extra virgin* olive oil
1 cup vegetarian "ground beef"
1 medium onion—*finely* chopped
1/2 green bell pepper—cored, seeded, and *finely* chopped
2 tablespoons *finely*, chopped mild green *chilies*
Dash or two *jalapeño chili* sauce

1 cup canned, *crushed* tomatoes
1 quart water
1/4 teaspoon salt, or to taste

Spaghettini spaghetti (thin spaghetti) broken into 3 sections to yield 1/2 cup

Freshly ground black pepper, to taste

In a large saucepan set over *LOW-MEDIUM* heat, heat oil. Add ground soymeat, *finely* chopped onion, green pepper, and green *chilies*, and *jalapeño chili* sauce. Sauté until onion is soft and translucent, *being careful not to allow any of ingredients to brown.*

Add crushed tomatoes, water, and salt. *Increase heat to MEDIUM* and allow the soup to come to the boil.

Add pieces of *spaghettini*. Cook, stirring frequently, for about 15 minutes, or until *pasta* is tender. Taste and season with black pepper. Turn into a heated soup tureen.

Serve into heated soup plates.

Yields 6 servings
adequate for 4 people

Note: This recipe can be doubled, when required.

1/6 SERVING – PROTEIN = 4.3 g.; FAT = 2.7 g.; CARBOHYDRATE = 11.9 g.;
CALORIES = 88; CALORIES FROM FAT = 28%

BROILED HEARTS OF PALM
Palmitos Asados

TPT - 45 minutes;
30 minutes = soaking period

I remember so well when you judged an occasion by whether a hearts of palm salad was or was not served. Hearts of palm salad is certainly not as posh to me as is this broiled vegetable dish. This is a simple and very delicious way to serve this very precious vegetable.

1 can (14 ounces) hearts of palm—well-drained

2 tablespoons freshly grated Parmesan *or pecorino Romano* cheese

Place well-drained hearts of palm segments in a pan or bowl of cold water. Allow to soak for about 30 minutes to remove the salt from the canning water. Drain well.

BROILED HEARTS OF PALM (cont'd)

Preheat broiler to 400 degree F. Prepare an *au gratin* dish by lightly coating with *high heat* lecithin spray coating.

Slice each palm heart segment in half lengthwise and place each half cut-side-up in the *au gratin* dish. Spoon the grated cheese down the length of each slice.

Broil until the cheese begins to melt and is lightly browned. Remove from the broiler.

Serve at once. Allow two halves per serving.

Yields 8 servings*

Notes: *There are usually eight segments in a 14-ounce can.

This recipe can be halved or doubled, when required.

1/8 SERVING – PROTEIN = 2.3 g.; FAT = 1.1 g.; CARBOHYDRATE = 2.6 g.;
CALORIES = 23; CALORIES FROM FAT = 43%

PARAGUAYAN CHEESY CORNBREAD
Sopa Paraguaya
TPT - 1 hour and 13 minutes

If you are looking for this recipe under breads you are apt not to find it. If you look for this recipe under soups, the odds are you will find it. Why? Well, the story that accompanies this dish relates that Governor Don Carlos Antonio López, 1841-1862, was very fond of a cheese soup thickened with corn meal. One day his cook added too much corn meal and instead of serving it as a soup, baked it and served it as a side dish. Governor López is said to have been delighted and requested the "soup," which he named "sopa' Paraguaya." It has become somewhat of a national dish and has become a traditional dish for "asados," barbecues, during Holy Week. It is a delicious vegetarian entrée.

1 medium onion—*finely* chopped
1 cup *boiling* water

2 large egg whites

6 tablespoons butter—*softened to room temperature*
3/4 cup *part-skimmed milk ricotta* cheese

1/2 cup shredded *low-moisture, part-skimmed milk mozzarella, Muenster, or Havarti* cheese
2 large egg yolks

2 cups *fine* corn meal—*masa harina*
1 cup *two-percent* milk
1/2 cup light cream *or* half and half

Preheat oven to 350 degrees F. Prepare a 9-inch-round, non-stick-coated cake pan by coating with non-stick lecithin spray coating.

In a small saucepan set over *MEDIUM* heat, combine *finely* chopped onion and *boiling* water. Boil, stirring occasionally, for 10 minutes, or until soft. Drain well. Set aside until required.

Using an electric mixer fitted with *grease-free* beaters or by hand, using a *grease-free* wire whisk, beat egg whites in a *grease-free* bowl until *stiff*, but *not dry*. Set aside until required.

Using a second mixer bowl, beat butter and *ricotta* cheese until smooth.

Add the well-drained onion, shredded cheese, and egg yolks. Beat until thoroughly incorporated, scraping down the sides of the bowl, as necessary.

Add the corn meal alternately with milk and cream. Beat until smooth.

Whisk-fold beaten egg whites *gently*, but *thoroughly*, into batter. Pour batter into prepared baking pan. Bake in preheated 350 degree oven for about 45 minutes, or until a cake tester inserted into the center comes out clean.

Serve at once. Cut into wedges to serve.

Yields 12 servings
adequate for 8-10 people

Note: This recipe can be halved and baked in an 8-inch cake pan or pie plate, if preferred.

1/12 SERVING – PROTEIN = 6.7 g.; FAT = 11.1 g.; CARBOHYDRATE = 19.0 g.;
CALORIES = 203; CALORIES FROM FAT = 49%

The Americas – Paraguay

COFFEE – SPICE "CHEMISTRY CLASS" CAKE WITH HONEY IN THE STYLE OF PARAGUAY
Pastel con Café y Miel

TPT - 1 hour and 10 minutes;
30 minutes = minimal cooling period

Paraguayans make a spice and honey cake which does not contain butter and which is flavored. by a Paraguayan cook in the southern hemisphere in the same way that my mother would have spiced a dessert for an autumn meal in the northern hemisphere. I decided to apply their seasonings to a cake in my collection that dates from the period of World War II when a very large portion of the available fresh eggs were dehydrated for shipment abroad. This cake, alternately known as "wacky cake" and "three-hole-cake," dubbed "Chemistry Class Cake" by me, is made with oil as is the cake popular in Paraguay.

3/4 cup *cold, strong* coffee—*caffeinated or decaffeinated*, as preferred
1/4 cup honey

1 1/2 cups cake flour*
1/2 cup sugar
3/4 teaspoon baking soda
1/4 teaspoon ground ginger
1/4 teaspoon ground cinnamon
1/8 teaspoon ground nutmeg
1/8 teaspoon ground cloves
Pinch salt

5 tablespoons safflower *or* sunflower oil

1 tablespoon distilled white vinegar

1 teaspoon pure vanilla extract

Confectioners' sugar *or* sweetened whipped cream, either or both, if desired

Preheat oven to 350 degrees F. Prepare an 8-inch-square baking pan, preferably non-stick-coated, by coating with non-stick lecithin spray coating.

In a measuring cup, combine cold coffee and honey. Stir to mix well. Set aside until required.

In a mixing bowl, combine flour, sugar, baking soda, ground ginger, cinnamon, nutmeg, and cloves, and a pinch of salt. Using a wire whisk, mix dry ingredients. Turn into prepared baking pan.

Using the back of a spoon, make one large and two small craters in the dry ingredients:

~ Pour oil into the large crater.

~ Pour vinegar into one of the small craters.

~ Pour vanilla extract into the remaining small crater.

~ Finally, pour cold coffee and honey mixture evenly over the ingredients in the pan.

Using a rubber spatula or wooden spoon, stir until only a few streaks of white flour remain.

Immediately, place in preheated 350 degree F. oven and bake for 30 minutes, or until a cake tester inserted in the center comes out clean. Transfer to a wire rack and allow to cool for at least 30 minutes.

Dust with confectioners' sugar, if desired.** Serve, cut into squares, directly from pan and top each serving with a dollop of whipped cream, if desired.

Leftovers will keep well at room temperature for 3-4 days, if tightly covered and well-hidden from snackers.

Notes: *Unbleached or all-purpose white flour was used by World War II and Depression era cooks but the over-all cake texture improves with the unique texture of cake flour, in my opinion.

**Sometimes we do, however, pour a tablespoonful of a coffee liqueur, such as *Kahlua*, onto the dessert plate, as one would for a *tiramisu*, before serving.

Modern, conventional mixing techniques are really not an improvement for this unorthodox recipe.

Yields 8 servings
adequate for 6 people

1/8 SERVING (without whipped cream, frosting, or liqueur) –
PROTEIN = 1.5 g.; FAT = 8.5 g.; CARBOHYDRATE = 37.2 g.;
CALORIES = 229; CALORIES FROM FAT = 33%

The Americas–**Paraguay**

PINEAPPLE ICE CREAM
Helado de Piña

TPT - 8 hours and 12 minutes;
8 hours = freezing period

When my husband and I were in graduate school, we occasionally stopped at a soda fountain that served the most delicious pineapple ice cream sodas. The soda fountain is, of course, gone . . . suburbia marches on . . . but the memory of that pineapple soda is as fresh and as refreshing as if I had tasted it last week. Pineapple ice cream is truly one of the most refreshing desserts imaginable and easy to make using this refrigerator method. Paraguayans are fond of ice cream too and since they are also fond of pineapple this ice cream seems totally appropriate. Oh . . . and crushed pineapple does not get caught in the straw.

1 cup heavy whipping cream

1 cup canned, *crushed,* juice-packed pineapple
 —*well-drained*
2/3 cup *fat-free* sweetened condensed milk
1 teaspoon pure vanilla extract

Prepare a 7 x 3 x 2-inch non-stick-coated loaf pan by placing it in the freezer until required.

Using an electric mixer fitted with *chilled* beaters or by hand, using a *chilled* wire whisk, beat heavy cream in a *chilled* bowl until stiff. Set aside.

In a large bowl, combine *well-drained* pineapple, sweetened condensed milk, and vanilla extract. Stir to blend thoroughly. *Whisk-fold* stiffly whipped cream *gently*, but *thoroughly*, into pineapple–milk mixture.

Pour mixture into chilled loaf pan. Spread evenly. Cover tightly with aluminum foil. Freeze overnight or until firm—about 8 hours.

Either scoop ice cream from pan to serve or remove entire block of ice cream from pan and slice.

Leftovers should be returned to the freezer, tightly covered.

Yields about eight 1/2-cup servings

Note: This recipe is easily doubled, when required. Use a 9 x 5 x 3-inch non-stick-coated loaf pan.

1/8 SERVING (i. e., per 1/2 cupful) –
PROTEIN = 2.7 g.; FAT = 9.8 g.; CARBOHYDRATE = 21.1 g.;
CALORIES = 183; CALORIES FROM FAT = 48%

Peru

In the Supe Valley, in the north-central coastal region of Peru, a pre-ceramic culture arose at about the same time as the pharaohs of the fourth dynasty, who built the great pyramids, were ruling Egypt. These people built the oldest civilization in the Americas, known to date, they too constructed monumental architecture with large earthwork platform mounds and sunken circular plazas as early as c. 3700 BC to 3200 BC. Their sacred city in the valley, Caral, showing habitation from 2627 BC to 2020 BC, gave rise to the designation of these peoples as the Caral civilization or the Caral–Supe civilization. They are also referenced as the Norte Chico civilization and considerably predate the c. 900 BC Chavin culture, once thought to be the first civilization cradle in the western hemisphere. Believed to have been a maritime subsistence culture, it is known that their diet included squash, beans, *lucuma* (a rarely exported native fruit), guava, *pacay* (a leguminous fruit), *camote* (sweetpotato), avocado, and *achira* (canna). Notably, there has been no evidence of a cereal dependence as with other early cultures.

Archaeological evidence indicates that there were humans in what is now Peru before the Norte Chico, as early as 9210 BC. The Norte Chico culture began its decline in about 1800 BC and was followed by the Chavin, Paracas, Mochica, Naxca, Wari, and the Chimú. It was not until the fifteenth century AD that the Incas emerged and within a century they had built the largest empire in pre-Columbian America. The end of the powerful Inca empire at the hands of the conquistadors led by Francisco Pizarro in 1532 established Spanish rule. The influence of the Spanish overshadowed the rich pre-Columbian past of this area of our hemisphere. Emancipation from Spain through the military campaigns of José de San Martin and Simón Bolívar led to a republic that struggled for national identity and economic stability. After independence, Peru saw the immigration of British, French, Germans, Italians, and, yes, Spaniards. In the 1850s Chinese immigrated and replaced the slave workers that had been the mainstay of the work force during the Spanish colonial period. Arab and Japanese immigrations have also contributed to the multi-ethnic fabric of this nation. This multiculturism is clearly apparent in Peruvian food which shows a blend of its Amerindian and Spanish past as does the culture while subtly revealing the influences of its African, Arab, Italian, Chinese, and Japanese immigrants.

The politics of Peru have been tumultuous. A period of relative stability from the 1840s through the 1860s under Ramón Castilla gave way to heavy indebtedness due to the squandering of resources. The once lucrative exportation of guano no longer filled the nation's coffers. Defeat by Chile in the so-called War of the Pacific (1879-1883) led to the loss of the provinces of Arica and Tarapacá. Political volatility, *coups*, and regime change after regime change followed the difficult period of the Great Depression, which caused the downfall of the conservative Civilista Party and the emergence of the center-left American Popular Revolutionary Alliance, which sought to bridge the philosophical gap between the Civilista and the Maoist parties. In 1975, after a *coup d'eta*, General Francisco Morales Bermúdez reorganized the government and set Peru on a democratic course establishing a representative democratic governing model but debt, inflation, political corruption, and a surge in drug trafficking have plagued this reform path and led to violence as Peru continues it struggle toward a stable democracy.

The Americas – Peru

Fried *Yuca* Root with Garlicky Lime Mayonnaise
Yuquitas Rellenas

~

Chick Pea Soup with Rice
Sopa de Garbanzos y Arroz

~

Corn and Cheese Salad
Ensalada de Choclo

Beet, Potato, and Carrot Salad
Ensalada de Remolacha y Papas y Zanahoria

~

Onion – Garlic – *Cilantro* **Salsa**
Salsa Criolla

~ ~ ~ ~ ~ ~ ~ ~ ~ ~ ~ ~ ~ ~ ~ ~ ~ ~ ~ ~

Quinoa and Vegetable Stew	or	Lima Bean and Tomato Skillet
Cocido de Quinoa y Vegetales		*Habas Verdes y Tomates*

and

Scalloped Potatoes	or	Potatoes with Peanut Sauce
Papas a la Arequipeña		*Papas con Salsa de Cachuetes*

~ ~ ~ ~ ~ ~ ~ ~ ~ ~ ~ ~ ~ ~ ~ ~ ~ ~ ~ ~

Sweetpotato Dessert Fritters
Picarones

Oven-Baked Sweet Plantains
Plantanos

over

Vanilla Ice Cream

FRIED *YUCA* ROOT WITH GARLICKY LIME MAYONNAISE
Yuquitas Rellenas
TPT - 56 minutes

Yuca, also known as sweet cassava and manioc, is the tuber of a tropical plant. Although known to most of us as the source of tapioca, it is popular as a starchy vegetable in Latin America where it is known as "yuca" in Spanish speaking countries and as "mandioca" in Brazil, where the Portuguese name for it prevails. The root, which is heavily waxed to preserve shelf life, can be found in most grocery produce departments.

Note that the uncooked juice of the yuca tuber is poisonous and that bitter cassava, as opposed to sweet cassava or yucca, is poisonous unless cooked.

**FRIED *YUCA* ROOT
WITH GARLICKY LIME MAYONNAISE** (cont'd)

PERUVIAN GARLICKY LIME MAYONNAISE:
    1/2 cup **BLENDER MAYONNAISE**
      [see index] or calorie-reduced or
      light mayonnaise*
    2 tablespoons **GARLIC OIL** *[see index]***
    2 tablespoons freshly squeezed lime
      juice
    1/4 teaspoon *jalapeño chili* sauce, or
      to taste

2 medium *yuca* roots—about 1 pound
3 quarts *boiling* water

Oil for deep-frying

Salt

In a small bowl, combine mayonnaise, garlic oil, lime juice, and *jalapeño chili* sauce. Stir to combine well. Refrigerate until required.

Using a sharp vegetable peeler, peel the waxed brown skin from the root. Cut the root in chunks about 2-3 inches long. Turn into a saucepan with *boiling* water and cook over *MEDIUM* heat for about 25-30 minutes or until pieces are tender. Remove tender pieces from the water with a skimmer. Slice in half and remove and discard tough stringy center. Slice into wedges. Pat dry and set aside until all *yuca* is cooked.

Preheat oil for deep-frying into a deep skillet to about 350-365 degrees F. Fry *yuca* pieces in a single layer, allowing them to brown before moving them in the pan or turning them over. Remove to paper toweling to drain oil from fried root pieces. Transfer to a paper toweling-lined platter.

Sprinkle with salt.

Serve at once with the prepared **GARLICKY LIME MAYONNAISE** dipping sauce.

Yields 8 servings
adequate for 4-6 people

Notes: *Homemade mayonnaise is infinitely preferable, if you have time.

       GARLIC OIL gives this sauce a phenomenal texture. If you prefer to add raw garlic, chop a garlic clove *very finely* and add it to the mayonnaise.

This recipe can be doubled, when required.

1/8 SERVING – PROTEIN = 2.0 g.; FAT = 10.6 g.; CARBOHYDRATE = 2.8 g.;
CALORIES = 169; CALORIES FROM FAT = 56%

PERUVIAN CHICK PEA SOUP WITH RICE
Sopa de Garbanzos y Arroz
TPT - 51 minutes

This soup is often allowed to thicken into a stew but with the addition of a well-flavored vegetable stock it can become a respectable soup course. We serve it with warm chunks of a good, crusty bread or with Portuguese rolls.

2 tablespoons *extra virgin* olive oil
1 medium onion—chopped
2 garlic cloves—*very finely* chopped

5 cups VEGETABLE STOCK FROM SOUP *[see index] or other vegetarian stock of choice*
1 cup canned chick peas (*garbanzos*)—well-drained, rinsed, and seed coats removed
1/2 cup canned, *diced* tomatoes
1 small yellow summer squash—peeled and diced
2 tablespoons dry long grain brown rice
1 teaspoon ground coriander
1 teaspoon ground cumin
1 teaspoon ground allspice
Salt, to taste
Freshly ground black pepper, to taste

In a kettle set over *MEDIUM* heat, heat oil. Add chopped onion and *very finely* chopped garlic. Sauté until onion is soften and translucent, *allowing neither the onion nor the garlic to brown.*

Add vegetable stock, chick peas, diced tomatoes, diced yellow squash, rice, ground coriander, cumin, and allspice, salt, and black pepper. Allow to come to the boil. Reduce heat to *LOW-MEDIUM*. Cook, stirring frequently, for 30 minutes. Taste and adjust seasoning, if necessary. Turn into a heated soup tureen.

Serve into heated soup plate.

Yields 8 cupfuls

The Americas–**Peru**

PERUVIAN CHICK PEA SOUP WITH RICE (cont'd)

Notes: This recipe can be halved, when required.

This soup freezes well.

1/8 SERVING – PROTEIN = 2.1 g.; FAT = 3.9 g.; CARBOHYDRATE = 9.2 g.;
CALORIES = 69; CALORIES FROM FAT = 51%

PERUVIAN CORN AND CHEESE SALAD
Ensalada de Choclo y Queso Fresco

TPT - 33 minutes;
30 minutes = refrigeration period

When my farmers' market has freshly picked, young corn, that is my choice for this salad. But tender, sweet, summertime-fresh corn is available for only a few months up here in the North so I use the corn I have frozen from the previous harvest season. Green, or raw, corn does give this salad a very special taste, a taste we love.

2 cups green (fresh) *or frozen* corn kernels—*well-drained*
1 small orange bell pepper—cored, seeded, and chopped*
1/3 cup chopped Italian red onion
4 ounces *fresh mozzarella* cheese—diced
2 tablespoons *finely* chopped fresh coriander (*cilantro*) leaves

2 tablespoons *extra virgin* olive oil
2 tablespoons freshly squeezed lime juice
Freshly ground black pepper, to taste

In a mixing bowl, combine corn, chopped pepper, onion, and diced *mozzarella* cheese, and *finely* chopped fresh coriander (*cilantro*). Toss to mix well.

Add olive oil, lime juice, and black pepper. Toss to coat. Turn into a serving bowl. Refrigerate for 30 minutes.

Serve chilled.

Yields 6 servings
adequate for 4 people

Notes: *Red or yellow bell peppers can be substituted, if preferred.

This recipe may be doubled or halved, when required.

1/6 SERVING – PROTEIN = 8.7 g.; FAT = 6.2 g.; CARBOHYDRATE = 23.5 g.;
CALORIES = 162; CALORIES FROM FAT = 34%

PERUVIAN BEET, POTATO, AND CARROT SALAD
Ensalada de Remolacha y Papas y Zanahoria

TPT - 24 minutes

Cooking potatoes and carrots and beets in the same water would be abhorrent to my German grandmothers. To them, potatoes should be white and carrots should be orange and beets should be in a separate bowl. My Irish-American grandmother would also never allow anything but butter to color her "murphys." It took some time for me to accept this simple, delicious warm red, root salad. It is unusual.

2 quarts *boiling* water
2 medium beets—trimmed, peeled, and cut into
   1/2-inch cubes
2 medium potatoes—peeled and cut into
   1/2-inch cubes
2 large carrots—scraped or pared and cut into
   1/4 inch slices

1 1/2 tablespoons *calorie-reduced or light* mayonnaise
Freshly ground black pepper, to taste

PERUVIAN BEET, POTATO, AND CARROT SALAD (cont'd)

In a saucepan set over *MEDIUM* heat, cook cubed beets, cubed potatoes, and carrot slices in *boiling* water until crisp-tender—about 15-20 minutes. Drain well. Turn into a mixing bowl.

Add mayonnaise. Season with black pepper. Toss gently to coat the vegetables. Turn into serving dish.

Serve warm.

Yields 6 servings
adequate for 4 people

Note: This recipe can be halved or doubled, when required.

1/6 SERVING – PROTEIN = 1.0 g.; FAT = 1.3 g.; CARBOHYDRATE = 10.1 g.;
CALORIES = 63; CALORIES FROM FAT = 19%

PERUVIAN ONION – GARLIC – *CILANTRO* SALSA
Salsa Criolla

TPT - 1 hour and 8 minutes;
1 hour = flavor development period

In the middle of the table at most Peruvian meals one finds a bowl of "salsa criolla." It compliments just about anything and is eaten as a condiment or relish. Usually made with yellow Peruvian peppers or jalapeño peppers, it can be a very fiery affair. Every cook has a version of this condiment and our version has been tempered considerably. As you build up your tolerance, add more jalapeño sauce or add very finely chopped hot peppers.

1 medium onion—halved and *thinly* sliced
1 large garlic clove—*very finely* chopped
1 orange baby bell pepper—cored, seeded, and *finely* slivered
1/4 cup *finely* chopped fresh coriander (*cilantro*) leaves

2 tablespoons freshly squeezed lime juice
1/4 teaspoon *jalapeño chili* sauce, or to taste
Salt, to taste
Freshly ground black pepper, to taste

In the mixing bowl, combine *thinly* sliced onion, *very finely* chopped garlic, *finely* slivered bell pepper, and *finely* chopped fresh coriander (*cilantro*). Toss to distribute ingredients.

In a small bowl, combine lime juice, *jalapeño* sauce, salt, and black pepper. Stir to mix well. Pour over vegetable mixture. Toss to coat the vegetables with the sauce. Cover the bowl with plastic wrap and set aside at room temperature for 1 hour before serving.

Turn into a serving bowl. Refrigerate leftovers.

Yields about 2 cupfuls
or 8 servings

Note: This sauce may be halved or doubled, when required.

1/8 SERVING (i. e., 1/4 cupful) –
PROTEIN = 0.4 g.; FAT = 0.3 g.; CARBOHYDRATE = 2.2 g.;
CALORIES = 9; CALORIES FROM FAT = 30%

The Americas–**Peru**

PERUVIAN *QUINOA* AND VEGETABLE STEW
Cocido de Quinoa y Vegetales
TPT - 1 hour and 5 minutes

Quinoa, an ancient grain cultivated by the Incas with a smoky, sesame-like taste, is a nutritional sensation. It is high in protein, containing all the essential amino acids. As such, it is a boom to vegetarian diets, especially to vegan diets, but more than that it is rich in important vitamins and minerals. The bitter saponins, with which the seeds are naturally coated and which serve as protection against bird and insect ravaging, are physically removed after harvesting. Because some of the saponins may still adhere to the seed, it is advisable to rinse the whole seeds thoroughly before cooking. Now, enjoy!

1/2 cup whole grain *quinoa*

1 cup *boiling* water

1 1/2 tablespoons *extra virgin* olive oil
2 medium onions—chopped
2 garlic cloves—*finely* chopped

1 large celery rib—sliced into 1/4-inch diagonal slices
1 medium carrot—peeled or pared and sliced into 1/4-inch diagonal slices

1 sweet green pepper—cored, seeded, and cut into 1-inch square pieces
1 small-medium zucchini—cut into 1/2-inch cubes
2 cups canned, *whole* tomatoes—coarsely chopped
1 1/2 cups VEGETARIAN BROWN STOCK [*see index*] **or other vegetarian stock of choice**
1 1/2 teaspoons ground cumin
1 teaspoon ground coriander
Pinch ground allspice
Pinch ground red pepper (cayenne)
1 teaspoon dried oregano—crushed
1/2 teaspoon chili powder

Chopped fresh coriander *(cilantro)*, for garnish

Freshly grated *pecorino Romano* cheese

Place *quinoa* in a fine sieve. Rinse well to remove any residual saponins.

In a saucepan set over *LOW-MEDIUM* heat, combine well-rinsed *quinoa* with *boiling* water. Cover and cook for about 15 minutes, or until grain is soft. Remove from heat and set aside.

Meanwhile, in a kettle, with cover, set over *MEDIUM* heat, heat oil. Sauté chopped onions and *finely* chopped garlic until onion is soft and translucent, *allowing neither the onions nor the garlic to brown.*

Add celery and carrot slices. Continue to cook, stirring frequently, for about 5 minutes.

Add green pepper squares, zucchini cubes, chopped tomatoes with canning liquid, and stock. Stir to mix well. Add ground cumin, coriander, allspice, and red pepper (cayenne), crushed oregano, and chili powder. Stir to integrate seasonings. Cover and simmer for about 15 minutes, or until vegetables are tender. Stir occasionally.

Add cooked *quinoa* and cook, uncovered, for about 5-10 minutes more.

Turn into a wide and shallow serving bowl which has been warmed. Garnish with chopped fresh coriander (*cilantro*) and serve into warmed soup plates with grated cheese.

Yields 6 servings
adequate for 4 people

Notes: This recipe may be halved, when required.

Although leftovers can be reheated, the textures of the freshly cooked vegetables are best when eaten immediately. If frozen, again, vegetable textures will suffer.

1/6 SERVING (without cheese) –
PROTEIN = 3.9 g.; FAT = 3.8 g.; CARBOHYDRATE = 18.5 g.;
CALORIES = 118; CALORIES FROM FAT = 29%

The Americas – Peru

PERUVIAN LIMA BEAN AND TOMATO SKILLET
Habas Verdes y Tomates
TPT - 22 minutes

Potatoes are the first food that comes to mind when I think of Peru because of the incredible International Potato Center and its dedication to the preservation of the potato in all its historical diversity. Even the Maoist guerrillas known at the Shining Path could not stop the scientific research project that continuously grows and harvests the potatoes in their crop bank. The staff simply limited their time to short, well-guarded periods in potato growing areas in the Andean highlands near Huancayo, and, in 1990, finally moved their research facilities to Ecuador to insure their own safety and the safety of visitors. They have duplicated the gene bank which preserves some 6,000 varieties of potato.

Lima beans are another cold climate crop that is far more diverse than just Fordhook. Here, in this popular main course vegetable skillet, the Peruvians combine lima beans with tomatoes, another food crop that has suffered because of shipping concerns and shelf life considerations, and the lack of consumer demand for flavorful fruits. It is sobering to note that only three-percent of Peru's land area is given over to growing food crop, most Peruvians live at a subsistence level, and, yet, the importance of biodiversity is recognized.

1 1/4 cups *cooked,* **fresh green lima** *or* **butter beans**

2 tablespoons canola *or* **corn oil**
1 medium onion—*finely* **chopped**

2 garlic cloves—**crushed and** *very finely* **chopped**
1/2 teaspoon chili powder

1 cup canned, *diced* **tomatoes**
1 teaspoon freshly grated *organic* **lemon zest**
1 1/2 tablespoons freshly squeezed lemon juice
2 tablespoons chopped fresh parsley
Freshly ground black pepper, to taste

In a mixing bowl, using a potato masher, mash *cooked* lima beans. Set aside briefly.

In a skillet set over *LOW-MEDIUM* heat, heat oil. Add onion and sauté until soft and translucent, *being careful not to allow onion to brown.*

Add *very finely* chopped garlic and chili powder. Cook, stirring constantly, for a minute or two.

Add the mashed beans. Stir to combine well with the sautéed onion and garlic.

Add tomatoes, lemon zest and juice, parsley, and black pepper. Cover and cook for about 10 minutes, or until heated through. Turn into a heated serving bowl. Keep warm on a warming tray until ready to serve.

Serve hot with *tortillas*, *pita* bread or other flatbread, or cornbread, or as side dish.

Yields 6 servings
adequate for 4 people

Note: This recipe can be halved or doubled, when required.

1/6 SERVING – PROTEIN = 3.8 g.; FAT = 4.6 g.; CARBOHYDRATE = 12.6 g.;
CALORIES = 106; CALORIES FROM FAT = 39%

SCALLOPED POTATOES IN THE STYLE OF PERU
Papas a la Arequipeña
TPT - 1 hour and 23 minutes

Scalloped potatoes appeared regularly on our table as I grew up and they are still a special favorite of mine and of those who gather at our table. Over the years I have added my own touches to my mom's recipe. Then I found a Peruvian recipe for scalloped potatoes which included a salty cheese like feta paired with queso blanco so I made a few more changes in my mom's recipe and developed this variation. We serve this potato dish from the southern city of Arequipa either as a vegetarian entrée or as a separate course. Peruvians, as do many South Americans, serve the potato course as a separate course prior to the main course, honoring the potato.

SCALLOPED POTATOES IN THE STYLE OF PERU (cont'd)

4 medium all-purpose potatoes *(not Idaho)*—peeled and sliced into cubes
1/2 cup *feta* cheese—cut into 1/4-inch cubes
1/2 cup *part-skimmed milk mozzarella* cheese—cut into 1/4 inch cubes
2 tablespoons chopped mild green *chilies*
3/4 teaspoon freshly ground black pepper, or to taste

1 tablespoon *extra virgin* olive oil
2 tablespoons whole wheat flour
1 1/2 cups skimmed milk

Preheat oven to 350 degrees F. Prepare a 2-quart soufflé dish or other oven-to-table casserole by coating with non-stick lecithin spray coating.

Arrange *one-half* of potato cubes in prepared baking dish. Scatter *one-half* of *feta* cheese cubes over the potatoes. Scatter *one-half* of *mozzarella* cheese over the potato–*feta* mixture. Scatter 1 tablespoonful of the chopped green *chilies* over. Grind black pepper over the top. Repeat the layering of potatoes, cheese, and green *chilies*. Set aside.

In a saucepan set over *LOW* heat, heat oil. Remove from heat and, using a wire whisk, make a *roux* by beating in flour. Return to heat and cook, stirring constantly, cook for 2 minutes, *being careful not to burn or overbrown the roux.* Remove from heat and gradually beat in milk. Return saucepan to heat and cook, stirring constantly, until thickened. Remove from heat. Pour over layered potatoes in baking dish. The potatoes should be covered. If necessary, add more milk.

Bake in preheated 350 degree F. oven for 45 minutes to 1 hour, or until potatoes are tender and sauce is thickened.

Yields 6 servings
adequate for 4 people

Notes: For variety, *finely* chopped onion may be layered with the potatoes.

This recipe may be doubled, when required.

1/6 SERVING – PROTEIN = 8.7; FAT = 4.4 g.; CARBOHYDRATE = 7.5 g.;
CALORIES = 205; CALORIES FROM FAT = 41%

PERUVIAN POTATOES WITH PEANUT SAUCE
Papas con Salsa de Cachuetes
TPT - 50 minutes

The Andean/Peruvian diet has always been simple and generally subsistence with little variety due in no small part to the lack of land and climate that welcome agriculture. Not withstanding, chilies and tomatoes, which we tend to associate closely with the cuisine of Mexico today, actually appear to have traveled north from Peru during the Spanish colonial period while, at some stage through culinary exchange, maize was introduced to Peru from Mexico. Peanuts and potatoes of many varieties pre-date contact and are still important in Peru. As in Ireland, a limited list of ingredients gets recombined and recombined to create variety. In preparing this variation of the classic Peruvian dish "Papas a la Huancaina," in which we find potatoes, peanuts, and hot chilies, a Peruvian cook would purée jalapeño, bontaka, or pequín chilies right into the sauce. About a teaspoonful of very finely chopped chili can be added, if desired. We prefer this as a spicy, but less fiery, dish to which a jalapeño hot sauce can be added at the table.

The Americas – Peru

PERUVIAN POTATOES WITH PEANUT SAUCE (cont'd)

1 1/2 teaspoons *annatto* seeds*
2 tablespoons *boiling* water

2 pounds small white or red potatoes—*unpeeled*, but well-scrubbed
2 quarts *boiling* water

1/2 cup *unsalted, additive-free, smooth* peanut butter
1 cup skimmed milk
3/4 cup chopped onion
1/4 teaspoon ground red pepper (cayenne), or to taste
Pinch salt
Freshly ground black pepper, to taste

3/4 cup *finely* shredded *queso blanco* or *Muenster* cheese**
2 large hard-cooked eggs—peeled and diced

3 tablespoons chopped fresh flat-leaved Italian parsley, for garnish
Lime wedges, for garnish

Jalapeño chili sauce—green or red, as preferred***

In a small dish, combine *annatto* seeds and 2 tablespoonfuls *boiling* water. Set aside until required.

In a large saucepan set over *MEDIUM* heat, cook *unpeeled* potatoes in the 2 quartfuls *boiling* water until tender, but *still firm*—about 25-30 minutes. Drain well.

While potatoes are boiling, in the work bowl of the food processor, fitted with steel knife, or in the container of the electric blender, combine peanut butter, milk, onion, ground red pepper (cayenne), salt, and black pepper. Process until very smooth.

Strain liquid from *annatto* seeds and add it to sauce mixture in the food processor. Process again. If necessary to achieve the desired consistency, add a bit more milk. Turn sauce into a small saucepan set over *MEDIUM* heat. Allow to heat through. Taste and adjust seasoning, if necessary.

Peel hot potatoes and halve. Put potatoes cut-side-down on a heated platter. Pour warm peanut sauce over potatoes. Sprinkle cheese over potatoes. Sprinkle diced egg over. Keep warm on warming tray until ready to serve.

When ready to serve, garnish with chopped parsley and lime wedges. Pass *jalapeño chili* sauce to accommodate individual tastes.

Yields 6 servings
adequate for 4 people

Notes: **Annatto* seeds are generally available in Hispanic or Filipino groceries but turmeric mixed with a tablespoonful of tomato purée can give the reddish hue that is characteristic of this dish.

**Muenster* cheese is an adequate substitute for the mild, soft cheese which is available in Peru.

****Jalapeño* sauce is available in Hispanic groceries, food specialty stores, and in most grocery stores throughout the Southwest.

This recipe can be halved, when required.

1/6 SERVING – PROTEIN = 13.2 g; FAT = 15.1 g; CARBOHYDRATE = 28.6 g;
CALORIES = 296; CALORIES FROM FAT = 46%

PERUVIAN SWEETPOTATO DESSERT FRITTERS
Picarones

TPT - 2 hours and 27 minutes;
1 hour = batter rising period

Years and years ago I was introduced to the work being done by a Peruvian research facility high up in the Andes to preserve heritage potatoes and other tuber varieties such as sweetpotatoes. The variety would amaze you. They have saved and annually planted wonderful potatoes, varieties that we never see, in an effort to preserve diversity just as we do when we save seeds in seed banks. They clearly recognized just what another potato famine could mean to the feeding of mankind and the importance of diversification should crop failures occur due to limiting of variety for the sake of crop yield and uniformity. The starchy sweetpotatoes which form part of the diet in Peru are a far cry from the dark orange, rich sweetpotatoes we find in our markets, but ours will do fine for these unusual and delicious fritters.

PERUVIAN SWEETPOTATO DESSERT FRITTERS (cont'd)

1 medium sweetpotato

Pinch sugar
1/4 cup *warm* water (105-115 degrees F.)
1 1/2 teaspoons (1 envelope) *preservative-free* active dry yeast*

1/4 cup *fat-free* pasteurized eggs (the equivalent of 1 egg)
1 tablespoon pure rum extract

3/4 cup unbleached white flour
1 tablespoon sugar
1/2 teaspoon ground mace
1/4 teaspoon salt

High-heat safflower *or* sunflower oil for deep-frying

2 tablespoons confectioners' sugar

Honey, pure maple syrup, jam, *or* jelly

Bake sweetpotato in a 350 degree F. oven for about 1 hour, or until soft. Scoop out sweetpotato flesh into a mixing bowl. Mash well. Using a RICER or a FOOD MILL, rice mashed sweetpotato into a clean mixing bowl. You should have about 1/2 cupful of sweetpotato purée. Set aside.

In a small bowl, dissolve the pinch of sugar in *warm* water. Sprinkle yeast over and allow to proof for about 5 minutes.

Stir yeast mixture into puréed sweetpotato. Add pasteurized eggs and rum extract. Stir well. Add flour, the 1 tablespoonful sugar, mace, and salt. Using a wooden spoon, mix well.

Cover bowl with plastic wrap and a cotton tea cloth. Allow to rise in a warm (75-80 degrees F.), draft-free place until doubled in bulk—about 1 hour.

Preheat oil for deep-frying to 365 degrees F.

Using two teaspoons, drop teaspoonfuls of batter into *hot* oil—4 or 5 at a time. *Do not crowd!* Deep-fry for about 3 minutes, turning once, until beautifully *browned and crisped*. Remove to paper toweling to drain as thoroughly as possible. Transfer to a heated serving platter and keep warm on a warming tray until all are prepared.**

Sprinkle with confectioners' sugar.

Serve with honey, pure maple syrup, jam or jelly, of choice.

Yields about 12 fritters
adequate for 4-6 people

Notes: *Some packaged dried yeast available in grocery stores contain a preservative. Natural food stores carry an additive-free dried yeast.

**Be sure that oil temperature has returned to 365 degrees F. before each batch is fried.

This recipe may be doubled, when required.

1/12 SERVING (i. e., per fritter exclusive of honey, maple syrup, jam, or jelly) –
PROTEIN = 1.6 g.; FAT = 2.8 g.; CARBOHYDRATE = 5.1 g.;
CALORIES = 71; CALORIES FROM FAT = 36%

The Americas–**Peru**

PERUVIAN OVEN-BAKED SWEET PLANTAINS
Plantanos

TPT - 22 minutes

There is really no difference botanically between plantains and the bright, yellow, sweet dessert banana, so popular in the United States. Green plantains are generally cooked and used as a starchy vegetable throughout Central and South America. When ripe, however, plantains are sweet, albeit not as sweet as are dessert bananas. Here, by the miracle of heat, the sugar is released and caramelized to create a sweet dessert.

4 *very ripe***, black plantains—peeled and sliced on the diagonal into 1/2 inch slices**
1 tablespoon *high heat* **safflower** *or* **sunflower oil**
1 1/2 cups vanilla ice cream

Preheat oven to 350-375 degrees F. Line a baking sheet with aluminum foil.

In a mixing bowl, combine the diagonal plantain slices and oil. Toss gently. Place on the foil-lined baking sheet. Bake at 350-375 degree F. for about 15 minutes, or until golden brown and tender. Turn several times. *Be careful not to allow plantain slices to burn.*

Scoop 1/4 cupful vanilla ice cream into each of six dessert dishes. Divide baked plantain slices among the dessert dish, placing them on top of the ice cream.

Serve at once while the plantain slices are still warm.

Yields 6 servings
adequate for 6 people

Note: This recipe can be halved, when required.

1/6 SERVING – PROTEIN = 2.3 g.; FAT = 3.9 g.; CARBOHYDRATE = 41 g.; CALORIES = 194; CALORIES FROM FAT = 19%

Uruguay

Uruguay means "land of painted birds" in the native Guarani language, an image that tells you much about this small but beautiful nation. The second smallest nation in South America, Uruguay, although smaller than land-locked Paraguay, has the advantage of extensive water resources. It is situated on the South Atlantic Ocean with the estuary of the Rio de la Plata to the southwest and the Uruguay River to the west. The Oriental Republic of Uruguay, a name derived from its position to the East of the Uruguay River, is a presidential republic, having gained its independence from Brazil in 1825.

Uruguay is slightly smaller than the state of Missouri and is home to about 3.5 million people, approximately eighty-eight percent of whom are of European origin. The overwhelming majority of the population lives in or in the suburbs of the capital of Montevideo. Unlike other South American nations, only about six percent of Uruguayan nationals can be categorized as *mestizo*. Small populations of emigrants from West Africa and Asia have also contributed to the diversity that is Uruguay.

There appears to have been little pre-Columbian occupation of the area we now know as Uruguay and even with the arrival of the Spanish in 1516 Uruguay was of little interest due to the lack of gold and silver. However, with the introduction of cattle those living in this region found themselves caught between the ambitions of the Spanish and the Portuguese. The Spanish founded a settlement at Soriano on the Rio Negro in 1624, the first permanent settlement in the territory, and expanded their settlements in an attempt to prevent the advancement of the Portuguese, who had fortified Colonia del Sacramento. Struggles between these colonial forces for control of the area now occupied by Argentina, Uruguay, and Brazil continued into the early nineteenth century. This was further complicated by the British, who entered the fray during their war with Spain. Uruguayan independence was hard-won but stability was challenged by reoccurring internal strife. The *Guerra Grande* raged for thirteen years, from 1839 to 1852. One of the factions was led by Giuseppe Garibaldi, the Italian revolutionary leader, who was living in exile in Uruguay and working as a mathematics teacher in Montevideo. Garibaldi was made head of Uruguayan naval forces. In the years following the *Guerra Grande* immigration, especially from Italy and Spain, increased the immigrant population from forty-eight percent to sixty-eight percent by 1868. In 1855 another civil conflict broke out precipitating The War of the Triple Alliance which continued until 1870 when both parties, tired of the constant fighting, tried to work out a settlement. Unrest and uprisings have been constant impediments to Uruguay's growth and development right up to the present but economic development has been constant and successful partially due to the very low level of corruption in government and in business. However, Uruguay is subject to the ups and downs of global economics due to its dependency upon commodity exports. The fertility of the coastal lowlands and a general terrain of rolling hills, the landscape that beckoned the Spanish and the Portuguese as they expanded their areas of influence to include grazing lands for cattle and sheep, became the source of Uruguayan success. Agricultural products are Uruguay's major export, representing eleven percent of the GNP. About fifty-percent of exports go to Argentina and Brazil whose economic rises and declines and concurrent extremes in demand for imports very directly affect Uruguay.

The diverse and adventuresome cuisine of this small nation exemplifies an adaptive and integrative microcosm evoking a diversity not unlike that of our own country, not unexpected in a nation of immigrants.

The Americas – Uruguay

Tortellini with Grated Cheese   and   **Fresh Tomato – Cream Sauce**
Salsa de Tomate con Crema

~

Chick Pea and Tomato Soup with Leeks
Sopa de Garbanzos y Tomate con Puerros

~

Beetroot and Apple Salad
Ensalada de Remolacha y Manzana (also known as *Ensalada Rusa*)

~~~~~~~~~~~~~~~~~~~~~~~~

Vegetable and Cheese Pies in the Style of Uruguay
Empanadas

Steamed Swiss Chard

~~~~~~~~~~~~~~~~~~~~~~~~

Peach Cakes with Crumbled Meringue   **Vanilla Meringues**
Postre Chajá

***Croissants* with Jam**
Bizcochos

Martín Fierro: Quince Paste with Cheese Slices
Dulce de Membrillo

White Wine and Fruit Juice Cooler
Clericó

FRESH TOMATO – CREAM SAUCE
Salsa de Tomate con Crema
TPT - about 1 hour and 8 minutes

A fresh tomato sauce with pasta is as comforting to Uruguayans of any descent as it is to Italians or to Americans of any descent. Because Uruguayans have assimilated many, many Italian dishes with the same enthusiasm as have Americans, tomato sauces with almost every variable you can think of are also found. Opinions as to what goes with what abound too. This Italian sauce is also popular in the north of Italy where it is called "sugo di pomodoro e panna." We think it is a wonderful choice as a sauce for a first course of cheese- and vegetable-filled tortellini, homemade or store-bought, or a plate of angel hair pasta.

2 cups tomato purée—preferably homemade
1 tablespoon butter
3 tablespoons *finely* chopped carrot
3 tablespoons *finely* chopped onion
3 tablespoons *finely* chopped celery
2 tablespoons *finely* chopped fresh parsley
2 teaspoons *finely* chopped fresh basil *or*
    1/4 teaspoon dried basil—crushed

3/4 cup light cream *or* half and half

In a large saucepan set over *MEDIUM* heat, combine tomato purée, butter, and *finely* chopped carrot, onion, celery, parsley, and basil. When sauce begins to simmer, reduce heat to *LOW* and gently simmer for 45 minutes. Stir frequently.

Using a FOOD MILL, purée sauce into a clean saucepan. (Reserve any residue for stock pot.)*

FRESH TOMATO – CREAM SAUCE (cont'd)

Place saucepan with puréed sauce over *LOW-MEDIUM* heat. Bring to the simmer and, stirring frequently, cook until of desired consistency. Reduce heat to *LOW*.

Using the electric blender, purée 1/2 cupful of tomato mixture with cream until smooth.

Using a wire whisk, stir puréed tomato–cream mixture into hot tomato mixture in saucepan set over *LOW* heat. Keep warm over *LOW* heat until ready to serve. *Do not allow sauce to boil!*

Yields 2 1/4 cupfuls
adequate for 4-6 people

Notes: *Sauce may be prepared to this point and refrigerated for several days before proceeding. Or, it may be frozen for future use.

This recipe may be halved or doubled, when required.

1/9 SERVING (i. e., per 1/4 cupful) –
PROTEIN = 1.3 g; FAT = 2.0 g; CARBOHYDRATE = 6.1 g;
CALORIES = 42; CALORIES FROM FAT = 43%

CHICK PEA AND TOMATO SOUP WITH LEEKS
Sopa de Garbanzos y Tomate con Puerros
TPT - 42 minutes

Meat, especially beef, is "the food of Uruguay" presenting a dilemma for a vegetarian. This wonderful skillet combination evolved in an attempt to side-step the meat in a classic Uruguayan dish called "puchero estilo murcia." The original is a complicated and rather heavy dish in which balls of a mixed vegetable, breadcrumbs, and egg combination are poached in a meat stew. The result of this experimentation provides a flavorful and nutritious side dish or, if thinned a bit with vegetable stock as is presented here, an enjoyable first course soup.

Refrigerating this soup overnight and reheating, results in an increased depth of flavor. If you have the time, do make it the day before you wish to serve it.

1 tablespoon *extra virgin* olive oil
1 large leek—*white and light green portions only*
—sliced, well-washed, and well-dried
2 garlic cloves—*very finely* chopped

1 can (15.5 ounces) chick peas (*garbanzos*)—well-drained
1 small sweetpotato—peeled and diced
1 1/2 cups canned, *diced* tomatoes with canning liquid
3 cups VEGETABLE STOCK FROM SOUP *[see index] or* other vegetarian stock of choice

Salt, to taste
Freshly ground black pepper, to taste

In a small kettle set over *MEDIUM* heat, heat olive oil. Add leek slices and *very finely* chopped garlic. Sauté until leek slices and garlic are soft and translucent, *being careful not to allow either vegetable to brown.*

Add well-drained chick peas, diced sweetpotato, tomatoes, and vegetable stock. Simmer over *LOW-MEDIUM* heat for about 30 minutes, or until sweetpotato pieces are tender. Stir frequently.

Season, to taste, with salt and pepper. Turn into a heated soup tureen.

Serve into heated soup bowls.

Yields about 6 cupfuls

Note: This recipe can be doubled, when required.

1/6 SERVING – PROTEIN = 3.8 g.; FAT = 4.2 g.; CARBOHYDRATE = 14.3 g.;
CALORIES = 84; CALORIES FROM FAT = 45%

URUGUAYAN BEETROOT AND APPLE SALAD
Ensalada de Remolacha y Manzana
(also known as *Ensalada Rusa*)

TPT - 2 hours and 11 minutes;
2 hours = marination period

I first tasted the classic Russian "salat Moscovskii" in a small hotel in Moscow while waiting for the overnight train to Saint Petersburg, then still called Leningrad. I have eaten "ensalada Rusa" from the Argentine which takes the classic Russian salad and turns it into something entirely different by adding sweetpotatoes to a classic combination dominated by beets. This version from Uruguay seems to only pay homage to the original in the fact that it is diced. Its heavy dependence on beets is more like that found in Argentina. But I suppose it does not really matter where the inspiration came from, this diced salad is really quite unique.

2 large beets—boiled, peeled and diced
1 medium potato—boiled, peeled, and diced
1 sweet apple—peeled, cored, and diced
1/2 cup diced Italian red onion
2 hard-cooked eggs—peeled and diced

Salt, to taste
Freshly ground black pepper, to taste
2 tablespoons CLASSIC FRENCH DRESSING
  [see index]

1/2 teaspoon freshly squeezed lemon juice
2 tablespoons *calorie-reduced or light* **mayonnaise**

In a large mixing bowl, combine diced beets, potato, apple, onion, and hard-cooked eggs. Toss gently to combine.

Season with salt and pepper. Add French dressing and toss gently to coat thoroughly. Cover bowl and marinate in the refrigerator for at least 2 hours, occasionally tossing to redistribute settled marinade.

Just before serving, turn salad into a fine sieve and allow to drain *very thoroughly*. (About 1 tablespoonful of marinade should drain off.) Turn drained vegetables into a large mixing bowl.

Add mayonnaise. Toss *gently*, but *thoroughly*. Turn into a serving dish. Chill until required.

Serve chilled.

Yields 6 servings
adequate for 4 people

Note: This recipe can be halved or doubled, when required.

1/6 SERVING – PROTEIN = 2.8 g.; FAT = 4.3 g.; CARBOHYDRATE = 8.6 g.;
CALORIES = 81; CALORIES FROM FAT = 48%

VEGETABLE AND CHEESE PIES IN THE STYLE OF URUGUAY
Empanadas
TPT - 47 minutes

Uruguayans have assimilated many of the dishes brought by those who have chosen to emigrate from their native lands. "Fainá," a pizza-like flat bread made from chick peas, can be traced back to Liguria, Italy. Pastas of all kinds, lasagna, ravioli, tortellini and gnocchi, called "ñoquis," are also Italian adaptations. Hot dogs, known as" panchos," are served on buns with mustard, ketchup, mayonnaise, or a salsa. "Lehmeyun" is of Armenian origin. The making of "bacalao" using dried salt cod, was brought by southern Italian, Basque, and Galician immigrants. Sauerkraut has found its way into the mainstream of this cuisine as "chucrut." "Pascualina" is an Easter specialty quite similar to "spanakopitta," the popular spinach pie of Greece. A fish pie, known locally as" empanada gallega" which was brought to Uruguay by Galician immigrants, is a perfect example of this assimilation. "Empanadas," the fish or meat or cheese pies, so popular throughout South America, are very, very popular here. Our version of this popular hand-held pie eschews the usual meat fillings and deep-frying and the addition of puff pastry contributes a welcome light contrast to the traditional heavier pastry. It is a good choice for lunch, a light supper, or as an appetizer.

VEGETABLE AND CHEESE PIES IN THE STYLE OF URUGUAY (cont'd)

1 tablespoon butter
1 1/2 cups chopped *frozen* artichoke hearts
1/2 cup diced carrot

1/2 teaspoon HERBED ITALIAN SEASONING
  MIX *(Miscuglio di Erbas Italiano)* [see index]*

1 1/2 sheets *frozen* puff pastry—brought to room temperature

About 3 ounces *low-moisture, part-skimmed milk mozzarella* cheese cut into long 1/2-once pieces
2 tablespoons *fat-free* pasteurized eggs

In a small skillet set over *MEDIUM* heat, melt butter. Add chopped artichoke hearts and diced carrot. Sauté until vegetables have softened and begin to color.

Sprinkle seasoning mixture over and continue sautéing for several minutes. Remove from heat and set aside until required.

Preheat oven to 400 degrees F. Prepare a cookie sheet by lining it with culinary parchment.

Unroll the puff pastry and cut into large circles—two circles per half sheet.** Spoon *one-sixth* of the sautéed vegetables into the center of the circle of puff pastry. Place a piece of cheese on top of the vegetables. Fold the circle over to form a half-moon. Roll and crimp edges to seal the filling in. *Be sure to seal any tears in the pastry.* Brush with the pasteurized eggs. Place on the prepared cookie sheet. Repeat until all *empanadas* have been made. Bake in preheated 400 degree F. oven for about 15 minutes, or until evenly browned. Transfer to a heated serving platter.

Serve at once.

Yields 6 individual pies

Notes: *This mixture of herbs is entirely appropriate to the cooking of Uruguay which has taken Italian cuisine to its heart.

**The scraps of puff pastry left over from cutting the circles can be gathered, wrapped in plastic wrap, and refrozen for future use.

This recipe can be increased or decreased, as required.

1/6 SERVING – PROTEIN = 9.9 g.; FAT = 21.1 g.; CARBOHYDRATE = 25.3 g.;
CALORIES = 331; CALORIES FROM FAT = 57%

URUGUAYAN PEACH CAKES WITH CRUMBLED MERINGUE
Postre Chajá

TPT - 46 minutes;
30 minutes = cake soaking period

"Postre chajá" is a unique Uruguayan dessert that looks so dramatic in bakeries that the average cook can feel rather intimidated. It was invented in Paysandú by Orlando Castellano in the late 1920s. The name of the dessert is also the name of a very strange local bird that has peculiar air pockets under its skin. It is thought that perhaps Mr. Castellano equated these air pockets with the airy meringue with which he decorated his signature cake. I make individual cakes based on the classic that are simple enough to prepare that we can enjoy them after a weekday meal.

1 cup heavy whipping cream
1 tablespoon confectioners' sugar

2/3 cup peach nectar
6 individual sponge or angel food cakes—store-bought *or* homemade

2 cups canned peach slices—well-drained

6 well-drained peach slices
6 VANILLA MERINGUE cookies [see recipe which follows]—*crumbled*

Using the electric mixer fitted with *chilled* beaters or by hand using a *chilled* wire whisk, beat heavy cream in a *chilled* bowl until soft peaks form. While continuing to beat, add confectioners' sugar. Beat until stiff peaks form. Set aside until required.

Pour peach nectar into a 9 x 9-inch baking pan. Put small cakes into the baking pan and allow them to soak up the peach nectar—about 30 minutes.

Using two spatulas, lift the cakes from the peach nectar and transfer one to each of six dessert plates. Apportion *one-sixth* of the peach slices on each serving. Cover the peaches with the prepared, sweetened whipped cream.

URUGUAYAN PEACH CAKES WITH CRUMBLED MERINGUE (cont'd)

At the very last moment, garnish each serving with one peach slice and sprinkle *one-sixth* of the crumbled vanilla meringue over the whipped cream. *Serve at once.*

Yields 6 individual servings

Note: This recipe can be increased or decreased to accommodate more or fewer diners.

1/6 SERVING – PROTEIN = 3.1 g.; FAT = 13.6 g.; CARBOHYDRATE = 39.5 g.;
CALORIES = 247; CALORIES FROM FAT = 50%

VANILLA MERINGUES
TPT - 7 hours and 10 minutes;
6 hours = in-oven cooling period

Crisp meringues can be served as cookies, used as a garnish, or prepared as dessert shells in which fruits or puddings can be served. They can be piped into shells or interesting configurations or they can be just spooned onto the baking sheet. In other words, they are useful and quite easy to prepare.

2 large egg whites

6 tablespoons *superfine* sugar
1 teaspoon pure vanilla extract

2 tablespoons *superfine* sugar

Preheat oven to 250 degrees F. Prepare a cookie sheet by lining it with culinary parchment.

Using an electric mixer fitted with *grease-free* beaters or by hand, using a *grease-free* wire whisk, beat egg whites in a *grease-free* bowl until *stiff*, but *not dry*.

Gradually, tablespoonful by tablespoonful, add the 6 tablespoonfuls sugar, *beating after each addition.**
Beat in vanilla extract. *Remove from mixer.*

Fold the remaining 2 tablespoonfuls sugar into the beaten meringue mixture. Pipe or spoon meringue onto the parchment-lined cookie sheet as shells or cookies. Bake in preheated 250 degree F. oven for 1 hour. *Turn the oven off and allow the meringues to sit in the oven undisturbed for 6 hours. Do not open oven.*

Store meringues in single layers in plastic bags or in airtight containers until required to maintain crispness. When filling shells, fill at the very last minute before serving.

Note: *To make chocolate meringues, add 4 tablespoonfuls unsweetened cocoa powder at this point. To make mocha meringues, powderize 1/2 teaspoonful freeze-dried coffee granules in a mortar with a pestle. Add this with 3 tablespoonfuls of unsweetened cocoa powder at this point.

Yields 18 small shells or cookies

1/18 SERVING – PROTEIN = 0.4 g.; FAT = 0.0 g.; CARBOHYDRATE = 6.3 g.;
CALORIES = 26; CALORIES FROM FAT = 0%

The Americas – Uruguay

CROISSANTS WITH JAM IN THE URUGUAYAN MANNER
Bizchochos
TPT - 12 minutes

The human desire for sweet must be satisfied and Uruguayans are renowned for their fondness for sweets and renowned for the many ways in which they satisfy that desire. The end result is not only an array of wonderful desserts but also bakery selections to satisfy that afternoon craving. "Bischochos" is the word for flaky pastries, among which one finds croissants, brought to Uruguay by French immigrants and wildly popular.

Per serving:
- **1 large bakery** *croissant*
- **2 teaspoons DULCE DE LECHE** [see index]*
- **1 tablespoon jam of choice**

Preheat the oven to 250 degrees F.

Starting at the highest end, slice the *croissant* in half lengthwise. Separate the two halves. Spread *dulce de leche* on one half; spread jam on the other half. Sandwich the two halves together. Place the *croissant* on a baking sheet. Bake in preheated 250 degree F. oven for about 8 minutes, or until heated through.

Serve warm.

Yields 1 serving

Notes: *If you do not make your own *dulce de leche*, several canned varieties are available in well-stocked groceries.

Of course, this recipe can be multiplied to accommodate as many diners as necessary.

1 SERVING – PROTEIN = 3.4 g.; FAT = 6.0 g.; CARBOHYDRATE = 30.5 g.; CALORIES = 212; CALORIES FROM FAT = 26%

URUGUAYAN WHITE WINE AND FRUIT JUICE COOLER
Clericó
TPT - 2 minutes

A popular drink in Uruguay, this wine cooler is a wonderful accompaniment to food. Your fruit juice choice can be your favorite juice or a juice that compliments your menu. Clericó is made in Uruguay with apple, orange, and strawberry juices. Pear or peach nectar and white grape juice are interesting as well.

6 cups white wine, of choice—*well-chilled*
2 cups fruit juice—*well chilled*

In a carafe or pitcher, combine wine and fruit juice. Using a long-handled spoon, stir to combine.

*Serve into champagne flutes.**

Yields 8 cupfuls

Notes: *A couple of slivers of fresh fruit in each glass or in the pitcher increases anticipation of the flavor to come.

This recipe can be halved or doubled, when required. A large pitcherful at each end of a dinner table, makes a dramatic presentation.

1/16 SERVING (i. e., per half-cupful; prepared with pear nectar) – PROTEIN = 0.3 g.; FAT = 0.08 g.; CARBOHYDRATE = 8.0 g.; CALORIES = 87; CALORIES FROM FAT = <1%

Venezuela

On Christopher Columbus' third voyage in 1498, the explorer of the Americas sailed close to the Orinoco Delta and along the shore as it abutted the Gulf of Paria. Columbus declared it a Paradise and named this land "Land of Grace." The following year Alonso de Ojeda explored the Venezuelan coast. Legend says that Ojeda's navigator, Amerigo Vespucci, named the region Venezuela, meaning "little Venice," because of the houses on stilts built by the natives along the coast and in the waterways. Another member of the crew, Martin Fernandez de Enciso, recorded that the native population called themselves *Veneciuela* casting question on the long-held theory of Vespucci's responsibility for the name we use today. The migration of the "first immigrants" across the land bridge from Asia as the last glacial advance receded reached western Venezuela about 15,000 years ago although archaeological evidence suggest that early peoples passed this way in the Late Pleistocene period. Radiocarbon dating is only accurate enough to date the artifacts to a period between 13,000-7,000 BC.

In 1522 the first permanent Spanish South American colony was established where the present city of Cumaná is today—a small, seaport city in northern Venezuela. Although there were attempts at colonization by Germany, the Spanish ultimately succeeded in subduing the resistant population as they pushed inland. By the early eighteenth century Venezuela became part of the Viceroyalty of New Granada. Led by Francisco de Miranda, who had fought in both the American and French revolutions, Venezuela declared independence from Spain in 1811 forming the First Venezuelan Republic. An earthquake in 1812 destroyed Caracas and in the aftermath of the devastation, the first republic fell. The war to secure the declared independence continued and a short-lived Second Venezuelan Republic was declared in 1813. In 1821 the Venezuelan cause was won under Caracas-born Simón Bolivar, who subsequently founded Gran Colombia. Ecuador and Colombia, after liberation, also joined Gran Colombia. In 1830 Venezuela became independent. Its progress through the nineteenth and twentieth centuries has been fraught with turmoil, rebellion, governmental *coups*, dictatorial leaders, and extensive corruption. Since the oil boom of the 1970s crime and drug trafficking have become increasing problems for the country which has only been a democracy since 1958. Venezuela moved more and more to the left under the leadership of Hugo Chavez, who took office in 1999, and the United Socialist Party, which he headed.

The development of oil reserves, which now accounts for about one-third of the country's GDP and about eight percent of its exports, resulted in a huge influx of emigrants from Italy, Spain, Portugal, the Middle East, Germany, Croatia, The Netherlands, and China. Between 1900 and 1958 it is estimated that more than one million emigrants from Europe relocated to Venezuela, whose population had been greatly depleted by wars. This immigration was encouraged by the government which established a colonization program supporting the new immigrants and channeling these new citizens into the work force. Almost five percent of the current population is said to have been born outside of Venezuela. The complex racial and ethnic fabric that is this country today explains and encourages a cuisine that is also excitingly complex. Venezuelans have integrated the eating habits of the many Italian immigrants and are the second largest consumers of *pasta* in the world. Here also is the opportunity to seek out the very best Italian bakery in any Venezuelan city because Venezuelans are crazy about Italian pastries, especially *cannoli*.

The Americas–**Venezuela**

Cheese *Croissants*
Cachitos

Grilled Vegetables
with
Avocado and Tomato Dipping Sauce
Guasacaca

~

St. John's Day Fruit Salad with White Corn
Ensalada de Santo Juan

Cabbage Slaw of the *Vuelta e 'Lola*   Mozzarella, Tomato, and Basil Salad
Ensalada de Vuelta e 'Lola   *Ensalada Capresse*

~

Creamy, Puréed Vegetable Soup
Puré de Vegetales

~~~~~~~~~~~~~~~~~~~~

Scrambled Eggs with Vegetables
Perico

Skillet Tomatoes and Cabbage
Tomate y Repollo en Sarten

~~~~~~~~~~~~~~~~~~~~

Chocolate Pudding   Avocado Cream
Budin de Chocolate   *Abacate con Crema*

Cannoli Pastry in the Style of Sicily
Cannoli alla Siciliano

Chocolate *Demitasse*
Toddy

Basic Chocolate Syrup

CHEESE CROISSANTS
Cachitos

TPT - 14 minutes

You do not have to bake croissants from scratch or fuss with the additive-filled crescent rolls in the dairy case to experience this popular Venezuelan appetizer/snack/sandwich. Good bakeries, donut shops, coffee shops, and in-store bakeries, will have the large croissants available for the morning coffee crowd. The advantage is not only that you will save hours of work but you can also buy just the number you need.

6 large *croissants*
3 ounces *low-moisture, part-skimmed milk mozzarella, Edam, or Gouda* cheese, as preferred—*diced* or *planed*

Preheat oven to 300 degrees F. Line a cookie sheet with culinary parchment paper.

The Americas—**Venezuela**

CHEESE *CROISSANTS* (cont'd)

Using a very sharp knife, slice each *croissant* about three-quarters of the way across. Tuck *one-sixth* of the diced or planed cheese into each *croissant* and close the *croissant* securely. Place on the cookie sheet. Bake in preheated 300 degree F. oven for about 10 minutes, or *until* the cheese begins to "ooze."

Serve at once.

Yields 6 individual servings

Note: *Any of these cheeses will substitute for the soft, fresh *queso blanco* with which this vegetarian version is made.

1/6 SERVING (per croissant) –
PROTEIN = 5.7 g.; FAT = 8.7 g.; CARBOHYDRATE = 13.6 g.;
CALORIES = 159; CALORIES FROM FAT = 49%

VENEZUELAN AVOCADO AND TOMATO DIPPING SAUCE
Guasacaca
TPT - 7 minutes

Guacamole, guacamole, guacamole . . . it seems that every party has to have a bowl of it. This is not your Tex-Mex guacamole by a long shot. There are probably as many versions of this sauce as there are cooks who make it so this cook shares her take on this very Venezuelan dipping sauce. It makes a good party dip but we especially like this version as a sauce for grilled vegetables.

1/4 cup Italian red onion—*very finely* chopped
1 garlic clove—*very finely* chopped
1 medium avocado—peeled, pitted, and chopped
1 cup canned, *diced* tomatoes—well-drained
1/2 teaspoon *jalapeño chili* sauce, or more to taste
2 teaspoons freshly squeezed lemon juice

1/3 cup *extra virgin* olive oil
1 tablespoon red wine vinegar
1/2 teaspoon MUSTARD SAUCE *[see index] or* other prepared mustard of choice
2 tablespoons *finely* chopped fresh coriander (*cilantro*) *or* parsley, if preferred

Salt, to taste

Using a food processor fitted with a steel knife, combine *very finely* chopped onion and garlic, chopped avocado, well-drained diced tomatoes, *jalapeño chili* sauce, and lemon juice. Process until ingredients are of uniform consistency, *but still chunky*.

Add oil, vinegar, mustard sauce, and *finely* chopped fresh coriander (*cilantro*), or parsley. Process again just until ingredients are integrated.

Taste and season with salt and more *jalapeño chili* sauce, if necessary. Turn into a serving bowl. Refrigerate until required. It should not be kept for more than two hours before serving or you will be risking discoloration and separation. *Leftovers will not keep well.*

Yields 2 1/2 cupfuls

Note: This recipe can be doubled, when required. If you wish to halve the recipe, as we often do, use the leftover avocado for your salad.

1/20 SERVING (i. e., about 2 tablespoonfuls) –
PROTEIN = 0.4 g.; FAT = 4.6 g.; CARBOHYDRATE = 1.5 g.;
CALORIES = 47; CALORIES FROM FAT = 88%

VENEZUELAN ST. JOHN'S DAY FRUIT SALAD WITH WHITE CORN
Ensalada de Santo Juan
TPT - 11 minutes

In the Andes the Feast of Saint John the Baptist, which corresponds to the Summer Solstice, is celebrated with an unusual and very, very delicious fruit salad. When we find an ear of white corn in the middle of June, we snatch it up. There are still oranges and grapefruits in our market and after seeking out the perfect mango and some goat cheese, we head home to gather greens from our kitchen garden. Oh yes, this is a special salad.

VENEZUELAN ST. JOHN'S DAY FRUIT SALAD WITH WHITE CORN (cont'd)

1 ear white corn—shucked and well-rinsed

1/2 red grapefruit—sectioned
1 navel orange—sectioned and chopped
1 under-ripe mango—cut into large dice

4 cups mixed greens—well-washed and dried

1 1/2 ounces goat cheese with honey—chopped into large pieces
Freshly ground black pepper, to taste

1/2 teaspoons *extra virgin* olive oil
1/2 teaspoon GARLIC–BASIL VINEGAR *[see index]*

Rub all the silk from the ear of corn. Using a very sharp knife, slice the kernels from the corn ear. Put into a small dish and set aside until required.

Set a sieve over a small bowl. Combine grapefruit sections, chopped orange, and diced mango in the sieve and allow to drain until ready to assemble the salad.

Put greens into a salad bowl or large vegetable bowl.

When ready to serve, pour combined fruits over the greens. Scatter the corn over. Scatter goat cheese pieces over and season with black pepper.

In a small dish, combine oil and vinegar. Whisk until well-mixed. Pour over salad. *Do not toss.*

Serve at once, tossing at the table.

Yields 6 servings
adequate for 4 people as a side salad
adequate for 2-3 people as entrée salad

Note: This recipe can be doubled, when required.

1/6 SERVING – PROTEIN = 2.6 g.; FAT = 2.7 g.; CARBOHYDRATE = 15.7 g.;
CALORIES = 88; CALORIES FROM FAT = 28%

CABBAGE SLAW OF THE *VUELTA E 'LOLA*
Ensalada de Vuelta e 'Lola
TPT - 12 minutes

Méridéniens, residents of the Venezuelan city of Merida, often tell the tale of two lovers whose romance ended when the young man, perhaps out of jealously, killed his love Lola. The area of the city where the buses end their runs, where the young couple walked according to legend, is still called Vuelta e 'Lola as is this salad. The cabbage is very thinly slivered into long strands to evoke Lola's hair. It is easier to tell you how to make this salad then to explain the oblique symbolism represented.

4 large leaves of red cabbage—well washed
4 large leaves of white/green cabbage—well-washed
Pinch of salt

1 tablespoon safflower *or* sunflower oil
2 teaspoons white wine vinegar
1 ounce blue-veined cheese—crumbled*

Using a very sharp knife, sliver the cabbage leaves into long, thin shreds. Work around the tough spines of the leaves. Turn into a salad bowl. You should have about five cupfuls. Sprinkle the salt over and toss.

In a small bowl, combine oil and vinegar. Whisk until well-combined. Add blue cheese. Pour the dressing over the cabbage.

Serve at once.

Yields 6 servings
adequate for 4 people

Notes: *Any blue-veined cheese can be used. Italian *Gorgonzola*, mild Danish blue cheese, and Stilton each add their own special touch to this salad.

This recipe can be halved or doubled, when required.

1/6 SERVING – PROTEIN = 1.5 g.; FAT = 3.8 g.; CARBOHYDRATE = 1.9 g.;
CALORIES = 46; CALORIES FROM FAT = 74%

The Americas–**Venezuela**

MOZZARELLA, TOMATO, AND BASIL SALAD
Ensalada Capresse

TPT - 2 hours and 18 minutes;
2 hours = marination period

"Insalata di mozzarella e pomodori," often called "insalata Capresse," is a classic Italian salad that is hugely popular wherever in the world it is introduced. In Venezuela, where all things Italian and French are explored with enthusiasm, it is called "ensalada Capresse" and is very, very popular. Using grape tomatoes, which are genuinely sweet throughout the year, means that we do not have to spend half the year waiting for the summer tomato harvest. We love to serve this as a fun "pick-up" salad or as an appetizer or as an easily eaten selection for a buffet. All the flavors of the original are there.

18 small balls of *fresh mozzarella* cheese—*mozzarella di bufala*, if available
2 tablespoons *extra virgin* olive oil
1/4 teaspoon freshly ground *white* pepper, or to taste

18 large, fresh basil leaves—well-washed and well-dried
18 grape tomatoes—well washed

Place the *fresh mozzarella* balls in a small dish. Pour olive oil over. Grind *white* pepper over. Shake the bowl to coat the *mozzarella* balls with oil and pepper. Refrigerate for at least 2 hours to allow for flavor development. Shake the bowl occasionally to insure that each ball is thoroughly coated with the oil–pepper mixture.

Using a toothpick or a cocktail pick, remove a marinated *mozzarella* ball from the oil. Wrap a basil leaf around the *mozzarella* ball. Secure it with the toothpick. Place a grape tomato on the toothpick too. Place on a serving dish. Continue until all *mozzarella* balls have been wrapped and skewered.

Serve at room temperature.

Yields 18 servings
adequate for 6 people

Note: This recipe is easily decreased or increased proportionately, when required.

1/18 SERVING – PROTEIN = 1.7 g.; FAT = 3.0 g.; CARBOHYDRATE = 2.8 g.;
CALORIES = 39; .CALORIES FROM FAT = 69%

VENEZUELAN CREAMY, PURÉED VEGETABLE SOUP
Puré de Vegetales

TPT - 57 minutes

Although a simple soup which depends little on seasoning, it does depend on the stock chosen for flavor. Venezuelans make such soups with rich meat stocks, with a stock made from goat meat favored in western areas of the country; in Llanos it might be made with a beef or wild game stock; and in the Andes one might find a similar soup made with lamb stock. This vegetarian version will profit considerably from a very rich, flavorful vegetable stock.

1 tablespoon butter
2 small onions—*finely* chopped

2 1/2 cups VEGETABLE STOCK FROM SOUP [see index] or other vegetarian stock of choice
2 medium potatoes—peeled and *shredded or finely* chopped
1 medium carrot—scraped or pared and shredded
Salt, to taste
Freshly ground black pepper, to taste

1/4 cup *two-percent* milk, more or less as necessary
1/4 cup *fat-free* pasteurized eggs (the equivalent of 1 egg)
1/4 cup *part-skimmed milk* ricotta or low-fat cottage or farmers' cheese

1/4 cup freshly shelled or frozen peas

1 avocado—peeled and sliced
1/3 cup *unsalted, roasted*, chopped *preservative-free* cashews

VENEZUELAN CREAMY, PURÉED VEGETABLE SOUP (cont'd)

In a small kettle set over *MEDIUM* heat, melt butter. Add *finely* chopped onion and sauté until onion is soft and translucent, *being careful not to allow onion to brown.*

Add vegetable stock, shredded potatoes and carrot, salt, and pepper. Cook until vegetables are tender. Remove from heat and allow to cool for about 15 minutes. Using the food processor fitted with a steel knife or the electric blender, purée the soup in batches and pour into a clean kettle or large saucepan.

In the container of the blender, combine milk, pasteurized eggs and *ricotta* or cottage cheese and process until very smooth. Add to the soup in the kettle, whisking to insure integration.

Add green peas and cook, stirring frequently, for about 5 minutes. Turn into a heated soup tureen.

Serve into heated soup cups. Float a couple of slices of avocado on each serving. Sprinkle with a few pieces of chopped cashews.

Yields 5 cupfuls

Note: This recipe can be doubled, when required.

1/6 SERVING – PROTEIN = 6.9 g.; FAT = 12.4 g.; CARBOHYDRATE = 1.9 g.;
CALORIES = 207; CALORIES FROM FAT = 54%

VENEZUELAN SCRAMBLED EGGS WITH VEGETABLES
Perico

TPT - 17 minutes

A popular breakfast dish in Venezuela, we enjoy it as the centerpiece of a light supper or for a quick and nutritious lunch. Perico is a wonderfully descriptive name which means parrot and this dish is colorful enough to evoke a parrot.

1 tablespoon corn oil *or extra virgin* olive oil, if preferred
1/2 medium red onion—*finely* chopped
2 garlic cloves—*very finely* chopped

1 red bell pepper—cored, seeded, and *finely* chopped
1 cup canned, *diced* tomatoes—well-drained— *or* the equivalent of peeled, seeded, and diced fresh tomatoes
Ground mixed peppercorns—black, red, and white—to taste

6 large *organic* eggs—lightly whisked with a fork*

In a non-stick-coated skillet set over *MEDIUM* heat, heat oil. Add *finely* chopped onion and *very finely* chopped garlic. Sauté until onion is soft and translucent, *being careful to allow neither the onion nor the garlic to brown.*

Add *finely* chopped red bell pepper and diced tomatoes. Cook, stirring frequently, until most of liquid has evaporated. Season with ground mixed peppercorns.

Add beaten eggs and cook, stirring constantly until the eggs have congealed. Turn into a heated serving bowl or onto a heated small platter.

Serve at once.

Yields 6 servings
adequate for 4 people

Notes: *Since the eggs are soft scrambled in this recipe, it is advisable to use organic eggs to avoid any possibility of *Salmonella* contamination.

This recipe can be halved, when required.

1/6 SERVING – PROTEIN = 7.3 g.; FAT = 7.7 g.; CARBOHYDRATE = 3.9 g.;
CALORIES = 113; CALORIES FROM FAT = 61%

The Americas–Venezuela

SKILLET TOMATOES AND CABBAGE
Tomate y Repollo en Sarten
TPT - 21 minutes

In the fall, when the cabbages are freshly harvested by the local truck farmers and hardened off during the cool October nights, I have always squirreled a head or two away in the refrigerator in much the same way my grandmother "put down" cabbages in the root cellar. Cabbage will keep in the cool environment through the winter. Yes, a leaf or two will have to be discarded but there is always cabbage for soups, cabbage for salads, and cabbage for skillet meals like this which are popular throughout Central and South America.

6 cups cabbage—well-washed and shredded as for slaw
1 teaspoon salt
2 quarts *boiling* water

2 tablespoons corn oil
1/4 cup chopped onion
2 garlic cloves—*very finely* chopped

12 canned, *whole* tomatoes
1/2 cup liquid in which tomatoes were canned *or* tomato purée
1/4 teaspoon ground coriander, or to taste
Freshly ground black pepper, to taste

1/2 cup chopped fresh coriander (*cilantro*)

3 tablespoons grated *pecorino Romano* cheese

In a mixing bowl, combine shredded cabbage and salt. Toss to evenly expose the cabbage to the salt. Pour *boiling* water over and allow to stand for 5 minutes. Drain well. Rinse well with cold water and drain thoroughly again. Set aside briefly.

In a large skillet set over *MEDIUM* heat, heat oil. Add chopped onion and *very finely* chopped garlic. Sauté until vegetables are soft and translucent, *being careful to allow neither the onion nor the garlic to brown.*

Add tomatoes, tomato liquid (juice or purée), and ground coriander. Reduce heat to *LOW-MEDIUM* and cook, stirring frequently, for about 5 minutes.

Add shredded cabbage. Cook, stirring frequently, for an additional 5 minutes.

Add chopped fresh coriander (*cilantro*). Turn into heated serving bowl.

Serve at once, allowing two tomatoes for each serving. Pass grated cheese.

Yields 6 servings
adequate for 4 people

Note: This recipe can be halved or doubled, when required.

1/6 SERVING – PROTEIN = 3.7 g.; FAT = 5.1 g.; CARBOHYDRATE = 12.4 g.;
CALORIES = 104; CALORIES FROM FAT = 44%

CHOCOLATE PUDDING
Budin de Chocolate
TPT - 1 hour and 27 minutes;
1 hour = chilling period

If you go to a Venezuelan restaurant or have dinner with a family in their home, do not be surprised if chocolate pudding is served; Venezuelans love chocolate pudding. This is my recipe for the ultimate comfort food. I think when you make it "from scratch," you actually feel even better!!

1/3 cup sugar
1/4 cup corn starch
1 cup *cold* skimmed milk

2/3 cup *instant* non-fat dry milk
3 tablespoons *unsweetened* cocoa powder
1 3/4 cups *boiling* water

1 tablespoon butter
1/2 teaspoon pure vanilla extract

In the top half of a double boiler, combine sugar, corn starch, and *cold* milk. Using a wire whisk, stir until corn starch is thoroughly dissolved. Place over simmering water.

Stir in dry milk powder and unsweetened cocoa. While stirring, gradually add *boiling* water. Continue cooking, stirring almost constantly with a wire whisk, until pudding is uniformly thickened. Set aside to cool slightly.

CHOCOLATE PUDDING (cont'd)

Add butter and vanilla extract, stirring to integrate thoroughly.

Divide among four sherbet glasses. Refrigerate for at least 1 hour before serving.

Garnish each serving with whipped heavy cream and grated chocolate.

Yields 4 individual servings

Notes: This recipe *can not* be doubled successfully but it can be halved, when necessary.

Occasionally, even though you are very conscientious about stirring, corn starch puddings can become lumpy. Press through a sieve into a clean saucepan and continue cooking over hot water until uniformly thickened.

1/4 SERVING (exclusive of garniture) –
PROTEIN = 7.2 g.; FAT = 3.8 g.; CARBOHYDRATE = 38.2 g.;
CALORIES = 214; CALORIES FROM FAT = 16%

AVOCADO CREAM
Abacate con Crema

TPT - 25 minutes

Avocados appear in so many dishes in Central and South America that it is not beyond imagination that you could be served a meal with avocado in every course. This dessert is a simple, but very rich, aggrandizement which is piled back into the avocado rind. It literally melts in your mouth.

1 cup heavy whipping cream

3 ripe avocados
1/4 cup confectioners' sugar
3 tablespoons freshly squeezed lime juice

Using the electric mixer fitted with *chilled* beaters or by hand using a *chilled* wire whisk, beat heavy cream in a *clean, chilled* bowl until stiff peaks form. Set aside briefly.

Slice the avocados in half *so that you can preserve the rind. Do not peel.* Remove and discard the pits. Scoop the avocado flesh into the mixing bowl of the electric mixer. Set the shells of rind aside until required.

Using the electric mixer fitted with the paddle, mash the avocado flesh and beat until fluffy. Add confectioners' sugar and lime juice and again beat until of a light and uniform consistency.

Add beaten heavy cream and machine-fold it into the avocado mixture. Apportion the mixture among the reserved rind shells.

Serve at once providing spoons to scoop the creamy avocado mixture from the shells.

Yields 6 individual servings

Note: The ingredients can be adjusted to make just two or four servings, when required.

1/6 SERVING – PROTEIN = 2.9 g.; FAT = 29.5 g.; CARBOHYDRATE = 19.1 g.;
CALORIES = 312; CALORIES FROM FAT = 85%

The Americas—**Venezuela**

CANNOLI PASTRY IN THE STYLE OF SICILY
Cannoli alla Siciliano

TPT - 48 hours and 18 minutes;
48 hours = *ricotta* draining period;
8 hours = pastry resting period

When we retired and moved to Central Pennsylvania, boxes of this and that, labeled kitchen, were being unpacked after six months in storage. My husband held up metal tubes and said, "What are these?" I quickly found a drawer spot for my cannoli tubes. A few minutes later a discolored, coffee can cover surfaced and he said, "Why didn't you just toss this before we left?" I took the template for my cannoli shells from his hand and found a spot in the same drawer.

The repertoire of ricotta recipes into which Sicilian cooks dip is almost endless. Nothing compares and is more justly celebrated, however than are cannoli pastry. The texture of this cream should be very stiff and very smooth. My first attempts as a young bride were usually unsuccessful because the filling was never quite firm enough but I was determined that we were not going to have to travel miles for the best cannolis. I finally learned to hang the ricotta in the refrigerator for several days and that secret I pass on. I often add mascarpone cheese, the sweet Italian cream cheese, to the strained ricotta to give just that hint of flavor that would be there if I had a source for ewe's milk ricotta.

2 cups *part-skimmed milk ricotta* cheese

CANNOLI SHELLS:
    2 cups unbleached white flour
    1 tablespoon sugar
    Pinch salt
    6 tablespoons white wine
    2 tablespoons *sweet* (unsalted) butter
      —*softened to room temperature*

Beaten egg white

***High-heat* safflower *or* sunflower oil**
    for deep-frying

3/4 cup confectioners' sugar
1 teaspoon pure vanilla extract

3 tablespoons *finely* chopped, *preservative-free*
  citron *or* candied orange and/or lemon peel*
2 tablespoons *finely* chopped *bittersweet* chocolate
  or *mini*-chocolate bits, if preferred

Finely ground pistachio nuts, for garnish

Place *ricotta* into a fine sieve or in a cheesecloth bag and set the sieve or hang the bag over a small bowl in the refrigerator to drain for 48 hours.

The night before the *ricotta* drainage will be completed, combine flour, sugar salt, white wine, and *softened* butter. Using a pastry blender, work the dough to form a pie crust-type dough. Gather into a ball and wrap in plastic wrap. Refrigerate overnight to allow the gluten in the flour to relax.

Heat oil for deep-frying to 350 degrees F.

Divide the dough in half; cover one half to prevent drying of the dough. Roll one portion of the dough out to a thickness of about 1/8 inch. Cut six circles from that portion.** Wrap the six circles of pastry around six *cannoli* molds. Flare the ends out slightly. Stretch the dough to overlap and seal the contact point with beaten egg white.

Deep-fry in oil heated to 350 degrees F., turning with a long handled spoon or chopsticks, until golden. *Carefully* remove to paper toweling, seam-side-down, to drain. Allow to cool for a minute or two before carefully removing metal tubes.

Prepare the next six *cannoli* shells as above.

Using the food processor fitted with steel knife or an electric mixer, beat *very well-drained ricotta* cheese until *very smooth,* scraping down the sides as necessary. Add confectioners' sugar and vanilla extract. Process until, again, *very smooth.*

Turn cheese mixture into a small mixing bowl. Add *finely* chopped citron or peel and *bittersweet* chocolate. Refrigerate until ready to serve.

When ready to serve, using a pastry bag, pipe *ricotta* filling into the prepared *cannoli* shells.

Sprinkle *finely* chopped pistachio nuts on the filling-exposed end of each *cannoli*. Place on a serving dish or platter.

Once you have filled the shells, serve at once.

Yields 12 *cannoli*

CANNOLI PASTRY IN THE STYLE OF SICILY (cont'd)

Notes: *Citron is most often treated with sulfiting agents to keep the color light and "appealing." Sulfite-free citron and citrus peels are available through mail order firms.

**After you have made the *cannoli* shells the first time you will have an idea about the size of the dough circle and can probably make a template. I use the plastic cover of a coffee can, a cover that has traveled with me all these years. The end of the pastry when rolled around the *cannoli* tube should be in from the end of the tube by about 1/2 inch.

This recipe may be halved, when required.

1/12 SERVING – PROTEIN = 6.4 g.; FAT = 5.7 g.; CARBOHYDRATE = 29.1 g.;
CALORIES = 196; CALORIES FROM FAT = 26%

CHOCOLATE *DEMITASSE*
Toddy

TPT - 10 minutes

This beverage/dessert reminds me very much of a cup of perfectly made hot chocolate I had in Nogales, Mexico, on a December morning many years ago. Maybe it was the company I was with or maybe it really was the best cup of hot chocolate ever; who knows! It is enjoyed throughout Latin America including Venezuela where there is a blending of the cuisines and customs of Latin America with those of the Italian immigrant population. It is rich, creamy, luscious and quick to prepare.

2 tablespoons *unsweetened* cocoa powder
3 tablespoons sugar
2 tablespoons *boiling* water
1/4 teaspoon pure vanilla extract

2 cups (1 pint) light cream *or* half and half *or* whole milk, if preferred

Cinnamon quill stirrers, for garnish, if desired

In a jar, measuring cup, or small bowl, combine cocoa, sugar, *boiling* water, and vanilla extract. Stir to dissolve thoroughly.* Set aside until required.

Just before serving, heat cream to *just below the boiling point. Do not boil!* Stir cocoa mixture into heated cream.

Pour into heated *demitasse* coffee pot and serve into *demitasse* cups. Garnish with cinnamon quill stirrers, if desired.

Yields 6 *demitasse* servings
adequate for 3-4 people

Notes: *If you have BASIC CHOCOLATE SYRUP [*see recipe which follows*] on hand, six or seven tablespoonfuls of the syrup may be used to prepare this beverage as a "quick dessert."

This recipe is easily doubled or tripled, when required.

1/6 SERVING – PROTEIN = 2.9 g.; FAT = 7.9 g.; CARBOHYDRATE = 11.2 g.;
CALORIES = 128; CALORIES FROM FAT = 56%

The Americas–Venezuela

BASIC CHOCOLATE SYRUP

TPT - 52 minutes;
10 minutes = first cooling period;
30 minutes = second cooling period

This syrup is a real work horse and better than any commercial chocolate syrup! Surely, you have a favorite cocoa for hot chocolate and if you use that unsweetened cocoa to make your syrup, your syrup will be, no doubt, your personal favorite.

1/2 cup *unsweetened* cocoa powder
1/2 cup sugar
1/2 cup *boiling* water

Few drops pure vanilla extract, if desired

In a non-stick-coated saucepan, set over *LOW* heat, combine cocoa powder and sugar. Stir well. Using a wire whisk, *gradually* whisk in *boiling* water. Cook, stirring frequently, until cocoa and sugar are completely dissolved.

Remove from heat. Allow to cool for about 10 minutes. Stir in vanilla extract.

Press through a fine sieve into a glass jar. Allow to cool completely, then cover and refrigerate until required.

Yields about 3/4 cupful

Note: This recipe is easily doubled.

1/12 SERVING (i. e., per tablespoonful) –
PROTEIN = 1.1 g.; FAT = 0.8 g.; CARBOHYDRATE = 11.4 g.;
CALORIES = 55; CALORIES FROM FAT = 13%

Canada

Growing up along the Southern shore of Lake Ontario and living for a year in Michigan gave me "duel citizenship" in many regards. Recipes were so interchangeable that to this day I have difficulty determining who borrowed from whom. Our heritage, our climate, our gathering on either sides of the Great Lakes, our democratic traditions, and our shared radio stations make our relationship easy and comfortable. When I lived in Rochester we visited back and forth with friends who lived in Toronto and each winter we went to Eaton's for woolen winter jackets and snow pants; when I lived in Michigan, we took the tunnel under the Detroit River just to have dinner in Windsor and my morning radio station was set to a Canadian drive-time station. Back then our currency was even interchangeable and vending machines took either Canadian or U. S. coins.

Canada represents, perhaps, what might be our system of government had the American Revolution not taken place, a parliamentary democracy and a constitutional monarchy with the British monarch as its head of state. Officially bilingual, Canada is the world's second largest country with ten provinces and three territories sharing with us the world's longest, unfortified common border. The name Canada comes from the Algonquian language, another influence shared by our two lands, and is derived from the Iroquoian word *kanata*, the word for "settlement." Until the 1950s the designation Dominion of Canada was used but with political autonomy the name changed as did the day we celebrated as Dominion Day. Canada's national holiday, since 1982, is Canada Day and is celebrated on July 1st.

Canada's Maritime provinces, especially Nova Scotia, and French-speaking Quebec still contain a minority population whose heritage can be traced to colonial America from which their Loyalist ancestors fled after the territories south of the Great Lakes and the St. Lawrence River were ceded to the United States in the Treaty of Paris in 1783. The resettlement of an estimated 50,000 Loyalists from the United States into Canada precipitated the separation of New Brunswick from Nova Scotia to accommodate the English-speaking settlers.

The menu I have chosen is an autumn menu and could easily be adapted to a Thanksgiving celebration—Canadian in October, American in November. If pumpkin or apple pies are the preferable Thanksgiving desserts for your family, they are, of course, autumn specialties in Canada as well as in the United States but since blueberries are frozen by cooks on both sides of our common border, the blueberry pudding is possible even in November. Late into the fall, when snow has already fallen, one herb can be retrieved from its winter shroud. The leaves of the sage close to the branches are still full of that divine flavor. Because this late autumn meal would still find me in my herb garden for at least a minute or two, I have chosen to include several recipes that include fresh sage, whose wonderful flavor becomes a harmonious thread in this menu that you too may find as friendly and comforting as do I.

The Americas – **Canada**

Cream of Cheddar Cheese Soup
~
Celery and Cabbage Slaw with Sour Cream

Canadian Celery Vinegar
~~~~~~~~~~~~~~~~~~~~
Wild Rice Casserole with Mushrooms and Baby Carrots
Casserole de Riz Sauvage aux Champignon et Carotti

Fried Onion Rings with Sage
Oignon Frites aux Sauge
~~~~~~~~~~~
Green Corn Pudding with Sage

Whole Wheat Baking Powder Biscuits with Sage
~~~~~~~~~~~~~~~~~~~~~
July Blueberry Pudding

Hot–Packed Blueberries

Baked Pear and Breadcrumb Pudding

Carrot – Potato – Raisin Winter Steamed Pudding

Baked Whole Wheat "Beaver Tails"

Rolled Sugar Cookies *[see index]*
Frosted with **Maple Buttercream Frosting**

CANADIAN CREAM OF CHEDDAR CHEESE SOUP
TPT - about 50 minutes

When we searched for a place to build our retirement home, I carried a list of "must have" food items and surveyed grocery stores everywhere we explored. Black Diamond Cheddar and New York State extra-sharp Cheddar were on the list. Dad had given up his favorite coffee and his Black Diamond to live in Arizona and we were not willing to do so or to have to mail order for either Cheddar.

1 tablespoon butter
2 tablespoons whole wheat flour
3 cups skimmed milk
1 garlic clove—*peeled, but left whole*

1 cup skimmed milk
6 ounces Canadian Black Diamond Cheddar cheese *or* other Cheddar cheese, of choice —diced
Pinch freshly grated nutmeg, or to taste
Pinch ground red pepper (cayenne), or to taste

1/2 cup dry white wine

1/2 cup *fat-free* pasteurized eggs (the equivalent of 1 egg)

Ground sweet paprika, for garnish

In a saucepan set over *LOW-MEDIUM* heat, melt butter. Remove from heat and, using a wire whisk, make a *roux* by beating in flour. Return to heat and, stirring constantly, cook for 2 minutes, *being careful not to burn or overbrown the roux*. Remove from heat and gradually beat in the 3 cupfuls milk. Return saucepan to heat and cook, stirring constantly, until slightly thickened. Add whole garlic clove.

In the container of the electric blender or in the work bowl of the food processor fitted with steel knife, combine the remaining 1 cupful milk, diced Cheddar cheese, nutmeg, and ground red pepper (cayenne). Process until *very smooth*.

The Americas–Canada

CANADIAN CREAM OF CHEDDAR CHEESE SOUP (cont'd)

Gradually stir cheese mixture into warmed white sauce. Continue to cook over simmering water, stirring frequently, until smooth—about 15 minutes. Remove garlic clove and set aside.

Stir in wine and continue to heat.

In a mixing bowl, using a wire whisk, beat pasteurized eggs. *Gradually, tablespoonful by tablespoonful*, stir about 1 cupful of cheese sauce into beaten eggs. Gradually add back into soup mixture in double boiler. Adjust consistency with more skimmed milk, if necessary. Heat through, but *do not allow to boil*. Taste and adjust seasoning, if necessary. Retrieve and discard garlic clove.

Turn into a heated tureen, dust with paprika, and serve into heated soup bowls.

Yields about 6 cupfuls
adequate for 4 people
as a main course offering

Notes: This soup may be halved, when required. If doubled, you must have an appropriately-sized double boiler. It is easier to make two batches, refrigerate until required, and reheat gently over water while stirring with a wire whisk.

Oven-dried French bread croutons accompany this soup well.

This soup does not freeze well.

1/6 SERVING – PROTEIN = 13.1 g.; FAT = 11.1 g.; CARBOHYDRATE = 10.4 g.;
CALORIES = 199; CALORIES FROM FAT = 50%

FRENCH CANADIAN CELERY AND CABBAGE SLAW WITH SOUR CREAM
TPT - 7 minutes

The sour cream that I remember from my childhood was so different from that which you buy "done up" in packaging in a supermarket dairy case. When we visited Grandma, she would send two or three cousins together to the Polish meat market on Joseph Avenue to get a loaf of Polish sour rye bread and a crock full of sour cream. One was entrusted with the money to pay and another carried the sour cream crock; that's why you needed two or more cousins to do this job correctly! We were admonished to mind our business and go straight to the market and back; to be careful crossing streets; not to break the crock coming and going; and not to lay the loaf of bread down on somebody's grass while we played or tied our shoes. It was serious business, as I remember. Using a wooden paddle, a great slather of fresh sour cream was scooped out of the crock by the white-coated butcher and scraped into Grandma's crock, which was then covered by a piece of waxed paper and tied with a string. The bread was wrapped in butcher's paper and tied around and around with string. We were then admonished by the market staff to go straight home to Grandma's. Fat-free sour cream is healthier for you, I guess, but it sure does not taste the same as it did when we slathered it on that wonderful bread at Grandma's kitchen table after the successful completion of our "business."

4 cups shredded cabbage
1 cup *thinly* sliced celery
4 scallions—trimmed, well-rinsed, and *thinly* sliced
1/4 cup chopped parsley

1/2 cup *fat-free* dairy sour cream
2 teaspoons chopped fresh dillweed
Pinch salt
1/4 teaspoon freshly ground *white* pepper, or to taste
1 tablespoon freshly squeezed lemon juice *or* CANADIAN CELERY VINEGAR *[see recipe which follows]*

In a mixing bowl, combine shredded cabbage, *thinly* sliced celery and scallions, and chopped parsley. Toss.

When you are ready to serve, combine sour cream, chopped dillweed, salt, *white* pepper, and lemon juice in a small bowl. Mix thoroughly. Add to vegetables and toss to coat the vegetables well. Turn into a serving bowl.

Serve at once, to preserve the crisp texture.

Yields 6 servings
adequate for 4 people

Note: This recipe may be halved or doubled, when required.

FRENCH CANADIAN CELERY AND CABBAGE SLAW WITH SOUR CREAM (cont'd)

1/8 SERVING – PROTEIN = 3.8 g.; FAT = 0.2 g.; CARBOHYDRATE = 13.3 g.;
CALORIES = 67; CALORIES FROM FAT = 3%

CANADIAN CELERY VINEGAR

TPT - 4 weeks and 14 minutes;
4 weeks = flavor development period

I discovered this in a very old Canadian cookbook, which was a revision of an even earlier cookbook. Although it had to be changed quite a bit, it is, to us, a very pleasant and fresh-tasting change during the late winter when the vinegars prepared from our summer herbs have been exhausted. And, it could not be easier to prepare. . . .

1 quart distilled white vinegar

1/2 head (about 8 ounces) celery with leaves
2 tablespoons celery seed

Sterilize two one-quart canning jars, lids, and rings.

In a saucepan set over *MEDIUM* heat, heat vinegar to the boiling point.

Remove any outside celery stalks that are less-than-perfect and trim root end. Chop into very small pieces. Divide chopped celery between the two sterilized canning jars. Pour about 1 tablespoonful of celery seed into each jar.

Pour vinegar over celery. Using a chopstick, stir leaves for about 30 seconds to start the infusion. *Cool to room temperature.* Seal the jar and place in a cool, dark place for 1 month.

Sterilize a clear, condiment bottle, or several if you are planning to give the vinegar as gifts.

Place a fine sieve over a one-quart measuring cup or mixing bowl. Strain the vinegar, discarding the celery and celery seed recovered.

Pour vinegar into sterilized condiment bottle or bottles. Cap and label.

Store at cool room temperature for up to three months.

Yields about 4 cupfuls

Note: This may be halved, when required.

1/48 SERVING (i. e., per tablespoonful) –
PROTEIN = 0.0 g.; FAT = 0.0 g.; CARBOHYDRATE = 0.7 g.;
CALORIES = 1; CALORIES FROM FAT = 0%

FRENCH CANADIAN WILD RICE CASSEROLE WITH MUSHROOMS AND BABY CARROTS

Casserole de Riz Sauvage aux Champignon et Carotti

TPT - 2 hours and 10 minutes;
30 minutes = grain soaking period

The French, while exploring the land to the north of us, encountered the grain referred to by many as Indian rice or Canada rice; the French called it "crazy oats." Wild rice is not a rice; it is the seed of a tall aquatic grass (Zizania aquatica) but rices really are also the seeds of aquatic grasses so this explanation does little to clear up the matter. Now grown commercially in Minnesota, Wisconsin, and California, it was a protected industry at one time where wild rice was still harvested in the same manner by native tribes, such as the Chippewa, who have gathered it by canoe since the 1600s. The taste of wild rice is complex making it a popular ingredient on both sides of the Great Lakes, the area to which it is native.

1 cup raw wild rice*

2 cups VEGETARIAN BROWN STOCK *[see index]* **or other vegetarian stock of choice**
1 bay leaf—halved
1 teaspoon crushed, dried thyme

1/2 pound baby carrots—trimmed and scraped, if necessary
[see next page]

FRENCH CANADIAN WILD RICE CASSEROLE WITH MUSHROOMS AND BABY CARROTS (cont'd)

2 tablespoons butter
1/2 cup chopped shallots
1 pound fresh *crimini or* baby bella mushrooms
 —trimmed, rinsed, cleaned well with a brush, and sliced
1/2 cup *thinly* sliced celery

1/4 cup chopped fresh Italian flat-leafed parsley
1 tablespoon chopped fresh tarragon
1/4 teaspoon ground black pepper, or to taste

Wash wild rice in several changes of *cool* water. Soak washed grain in *cool* water to cover for 30 minutes. Discard any kernels which float to the surface. Again, drain. Rinse again in several changes of *cool* water. Drain thoroughly.

In a saucepan with cover set over *MEDIUM-HIGH* heat, bring the 2 cupfuls of stock to the boil. Add bay leaf pieces and crushed thyme. Stir in rinsed and drained wild rice. Reduce heat to *LOW*, cover tightly, and cook *undisturbed* for about 30 minutes.

Add carrots. Uncover and allow to continue simmering at *LOW-MEDIUM* heat until most of moisture has been either absorbed or has evaporated, stirring frequently. Remove bay leaf pieces and discard.**

While the carrots are cooking, in a skillet set over *MEDIUM* heat, melt butter. Add chopped shallots, and sliced mushrooms and celery. Sauté until shallots are soft, *allowing none of the vegetables to brown.*

Add chopped parsley and tarragon, and black pepper. Stir to combine.

Stir skillet ingredients into cooked wild rice.

Turn into heated serving bowl before serving.

Yields 8 servings
adequate for 6 people

Notes: *Wild rice is an unfortunate name for this wonderful grass grain since it is confusing to the cook, new to the joys of this very American grain. Wild rice is the only grain native to North America and is far more nutritious than rice. To release its perfection of flavor and texture, it should *not* be cooked in the same manner as white and brown rices.

This recipe may be halved or doubled, when required.

1/8 SERVING – PROTEIN = 4.4 g.; FAT = 3.2 g.; CARBOHYDRATE = 19.0 g.;
CALORIES = 112; CALORIES FROM FAT = 26%

QUEBEC FRIED ONION RINGS WITH SAGE
Oignon Frites aux Sauge
TPT - 21 minutes

My mother loved the smell of fried onions cooking and she often burned her mouth as she fished onions from the skillet with a fork. Mom liked the slightly burned bits but I did not so I have always fried onions the way my grandmother suggested. Her suggestions of low burner temperature, covering, and the addition of cold water have always guided me and never failed me. Years later I learned that this steaming technique is the standard way onions are fried in Quebec. I guess I never asked . . . I love the hint of sage in these fried onions and, if you are careful, there will be no burned bits.

1 tablespoon butter

2 tablespoons *cold* water
4 large onions—peeled and sliced crosswise into
 1/2-inch rings
1 tablespoon *finely* slivered fresh sage *or*
 1 teaspoon crushed, dried sage
Pinch salt
Freshly ground black pepper, to taste

In a heavy skillet with cover, preferably a cast iron skillet, set over *LOW-MEDIUM* heat, melt butter. Add *cold* water, onion rings, *finely* slivered sage, salt, and pepper. Stir to combine. Cover and allow to cook for 8 minutes. *Remove cover.*

Increase heat to *MEDIUM-HIGH*. Cook, turning occasionally with a spatula, until golden brown. Remove to a heated platter and keep warm on a warming tray until ready to serve.

Yields 6 servings
adequate for 4 people

Note: This recipe can be halved. Doubling creates the dilemma of finding a skillet large enough and the difficulty of uneven browning.

The Americas–Canada

QUEBEC FRIED ONION RINGS WITH SAGE (cont'd)

1/6 SERVING – PROTEIN = 2.0 g.; FAT = 1.9 g.; CARBOHYDRATE = 2.0 g.;
CALORIES = 85; CALORIES FROM FAT = 20%

CANADIAN GREEN CORN PUDDING WITH SAGE
TPT - 1 hour and 5 minutes

As a child in Upstate New York, the mid-July sweet corn harvest was greatly anticipated. Although we ate most of the freshly picked corn as corn-on-the-cob, this Western Canadian specialty was often served, but not by my mother who, as I remember, reserved sage for poultry dishes. "Green corn" is simply fresh corn.

1 cup *fat-free* pasteurized eggs (the equivalent of 4 eggs)
2 cups *whole* milk

3 cups green (fresh) corn kernels, cut from cobs*
2 tablespoons butter—*melted*
2 teaspoons sugar
1 tablespoon *very finely* chopped fresh sage
Freshly ground black pepper, to taste

Preheat oven to 325 degrees F. Prepare a 1 1/2-quart soufflé dish or other oven-to-table baking dish by coating with non-stick lecithin spray coating.

In a mixing bowl, combine pasteurized eggs and milk. Beat well to combine thoroughly.

Add corn, *melted* butter, sugar, *very finely* chopped fresh sage, and black pepper. Stir to combine well. Pour mixture into prepared baking dish.

Bake in preheated 350 degree F. oven for 1 hour, or until top is firm and a cake tester, inserted into the center, comes out clean. The pudding should still "quake" when shaken slightly.

Serve hot, directly from baking dish. To serve, spoon the soft, corn pudding onto dinner plates.

Yields 4-6 servings
adequate for 4 people

Notes: *Home-frozen corn can be substituted in the winter.

This recipe may be halved, when required.

Leftovers do not reheat well.

1/6 SERVING – PROTEIN = 10.8 g.; FAT = 7.8 g.; CARBOHYDRATE = 37.3 g.;
CALORIES = 249; CALORIES FROM FAT = 28%

CANADIAN WHOLE WHEAT BAKING POWDER BISCUITS WITH SAGE FROM QUEBEC
TPT - 36 minutes

It is amazing to us how young food writers rediscover foods and subsequently tout these foods as trendy, foods that we think of as ultimate comfort foods. This observation alone gives one pause, does it not? Canadian sage biscuits are a case in point. With or without a generous slather of butter, they compliment almost any menu...and they do comfort!

1/2 cup unbleached white flour
1/2 cup whole wheat flour
2 teaspoons baking powder

2 tablespoons *cold* butter

3 tablespoons chopped fresh sage leaves—well-washed
1/3 - 1/2 cup skimmed milk

Preheat oven to 400 degrees F.

Into a large mixing bowl, sift white and whole wheat flours with baking powder.

Using a pastry blender or by pulsating the mixture in the food processor, fitted with steel knife, cut *cold* butter into dry ingredients until mixture is the consistency of coarse corn meal.

Make a well in the center, add chopped sage leaves. Pour 1/3 cupful milk into the well and stir until mixture forms a soft dough and pulls from the sides of the bowl. Add more milk, a little at a time, *only if necessary*. *(You do not want a sticky dough.)*

CANADIAN WHOLE WHEAT BAKING POWDER BISCUITS WITH SAGE FROM QUEBEC (cont'd)

Turn dough out onto a *lightly* floured surface. Lightly flour your hands and knead dough for only about 30 seconds. Pat or roll dough to an even 1/2-inch thickness. Cut with a floured 2-inch biscuit cutter. Using a spatula, transfer biscuit rounds to an *ungreased* baking sheet, spacing them at least 1 1/2 inches apart to allow for expansion and even browning.

Bake in preheated 400 degree F. oven for 12-15 minutes, or until *golden brown.*

Serve hot with butter.

Notes: When necessary, this recipe may be doubled.

For excellent CANADIAN WHOLE WHEAT BAKING POWDER BISCUITS WITH SAGE AND CHEESE FROM QUEBEC, 1/2 cupful shredded sharp Cheddar cheese, preferably Canadian Black Diamond Cheddar, may be cut into the dry ingredients with the butter.

Yields 8 biscuits

1/8 SERVING –
PROTEIN = 2.3 g.; FAT = 3.1 g.; CARBOHYDRATE = 12.1 g.;
CALORIES = 86; CALORIES FROM FAT = 32%

1/8 SERVING (CHEESE BISCUIT variation) –
PROTEIN = 4.1 g.; FAT = 5.4 g.; CARBOHYDRATE = 12.3 g.;
CALORIES = 114; CALORIES FROM FAT = 43%

JULY BLUEBERRY PUDDING IN THE STYLE OF BRITISH COLUMBIA
TPT - 1 hour and 17 minutes;
1 hour = refrigeration period

This evolved from a blueberry custard pie, popular in Vancouver where the blueberries are almost as big as our blackberries. We designated it as a July pudding because that is when the local blueberries are ripe and the last jar or two of last season's canned blueberries remain on the shelves of our fruit cellar.

1/4 cup *cold* skimmed milk
2 tablespoons corn starch

1/2 cup *fat-free* sweetened condensed milk
1/4 cup skimmed milk
1/4 cup *fat-free* pasteurized eggs (the equivalent of 1 egg or 2 egg yolks)

1/2 teaspoon pure vanilla extract

1/2 cup HOT – PACKED BLUEBERRIES *[see recipe which follows]**
1/2 cup large, fresh blueberries—well-washed and dried

In a measuring cup or small bowl, combine 1/4 cupful *cold* milk and corn starch. Using a spoon or small wire whisk, blend until corn starch is in suspension.

In a saucepan set over *LOW-MEDIUM* heat, combine sweetened condensed milk, remaining 1/4 cupful milk, and pasteurized eggs. Using a wire whisk, combine well. Cook, stirring frequently, until mixture is hot. *Reduce heat to LOW.* Add corn starch suspension. Cook, stirring constantly, until custard thickens.

Add vanilla extract. Combine thoroughly. Remove from heat.

Set a sieve over a mixing bowl. Sieve custard to eliminate any lumps. Turn smooth, sieved custard into 7-inch shallow serving bowl. Refrigerate for at least 1 hour.

Gently combine HOT – PACKED BLUEBERRIES and fresh blueberries. Spread blueberries over chilled custard.

Serve chilled.

Yields 4 servings
adequate for 3 people

Notes: *Unfortunately, there really is no substitute for my HOT – PACKED BLUEBERRIES.

This recipe can be doubled, when required. Be sure to choose a shallow serving bowl of a larger diameter.

The Americas – Canada

**JULY BLUEBERRY PUDDING
IN THE STYLE OF BRITISH COLUMBIA** (cont'd)

1/4 SERVING – PROTEIN = 5.6 g.; FAT = 0.3 g.; CARBOHYDRATE = 44.6 g.;
CALORIES = 204; CALORIES FROM FAT = 1%

HOT–PACKED BLUEBERRIES
TPT - 24 hours and 40 minutes;
24 hours = cooling period

Blueberries canned this way can be used as an ingredient for baked or refrigerated desserts, as a filling for baked goods, as a dessert with cream, or as a sauce. Freezing blueberries is easy but with just a bit more effort, the pantry presents us with this great convenience item.

2 quarts *firm* **blueberries—sorted, well-washed, and stemmed**
1 cup sugar

Sterilize nine 1/2-pint canning jars. Also sterilize lids and rings for jars.

In a kettle set over *LOW-MEDIUM* heat, combine blueberries and sugar. Cover and allow to come to the boil. Stir occasionally to prevent sticking.

Ladle into the hot, sterilized 1/2-pint canning jars. Carefully wipe lips of jars. Seal with hot, sterilized lids and rings. Process in hot-water-bath canner for 10 minutes, *timing from the moment the water reaches a full rolling boil.* Remove to surface covered with thick towels or newspapers. Allow to cool for 24 hours *undisturbed.* Check to be sure jars are sealed before labeling and storing in a dark, cool, dry place.* Loosen or remove rings before storing.

Yields nine 1/2-pint jarfuls

Note: *Any jars that do not seal can be stored in the refrigerator for about one month or resealed using a *new lid.*

1/18 SERVING (i. e., per 1/2 cupful) –
PROTEIN = 0.4 g.; FAT = 0.7 g.; CARBOHYDRATE = 43.9 g.;
CALORIES = 173; CALORIES FROM FAT = 4%

CANADIAN BAKED PEAR AND BREADCRUMB PUDDING
TPT - 1 hour and 10 minutes;
30 minutes = cooling period

We have explored many cultures in our life together and have found one extraordinary constant. There is always a use for stale bread. We have been served breakfast bread and yesterday's bread basket in so many different ways, as we have traveled, that we have become inspired by the sight of leftover bread. This is a good old-fashioned pudding that is popular in Canada and in all the states that border Canada, especially where "waste not; want not" is a mantra to be admired. It is not as fancy as a true "Charlotte," but it has all the good taste one would expect, and a good bit more.

3 cups peeled, cored and sliced ripe, *but firm,* **fresh pears—2 large pears**
3 tablespoons freshly squeezed orange juice
Pinch ground coriander
1/4 cup butter—*melted*
1/2 cup *fat-free* **pasteurized eggs (the equivalent of about 3 egg yolks)**
3 tablespoons honey
3 tablespoons *light* **brown sugar**

3 large egg whites

2 1/2 cups *fresh, coarsely–crumbed* **(BREAD MACHINE) MAPLE MULTIGRAIN BREAD**
[see index], **or bread of choice**

Light cream *or* **half and half, for garnish, if desired**

Preheat oven to 350 degrees F. Prepare a 9-inch *quiche* dish or other oven-to-table baking dish by coating with non-stick lecithin spray coating.

In a mixing bowl, combine, sliced pears, orange juice, ground coriander, *melted* butter, honey, and brown sugar. Mix *gently*, but *thoroughly*.

CANADIAN BAKED PEAR AND BREADCRUMB PUDDING (cont'd)

Using an electric mixer fitted with *grease-free* beaters or by hand, using a *grease-free* wire whisk, beat egg whites in a *grease-free* bowl until *stiff*, but *not dry*.

Fold breadcrumbs *gently*, but *thoroughly*, into the beaten egg whites.

Add egg white–breadcrumb mixture to pear mixture. Fold *gently*, but *thoroughly*. Turn into prepared *quiche* dish, spreading the mixture to the edge.

Bake in preheated 350 degree F. oven for 30 minutes, or until *puffed* and *golden brown*. Remove to a wire rack and allow to cool for 30 minutes.

Serve warm with cream, if desired.

Yields 6 servings
adequate for 4 people

1/6 SERVING (without cream) –
PROTEIN = 5.4 g.; FAT = 7.8 g.; CARBOHYDRATE = 25.6 g.;
CALORIES = 190; CALORIES FROM FAT = 37%

CANADIAN CARROT – POTATO – RAISIN WINTER STEAMED PUDDING
TPT - 2 hours

Menu variety was a daunting task for a homemaker during my childhood in the North. When food products were less available than they are now, you used what you had "put by." Fresh fruits, especially citrus fruits, and vegetables were limited; heaven knows, nothing came in from California or South America then. Periodically we visited an "orange car," a freight car loaded in Florida and dropped off on a siding down in the railroad yards to be retrieved when the train passed through heading back to the South to resupply. Egg production was reduced; nobody fooled chickens into laying with lights and music. The milk produced by cows fed only on silage was not "summer sweet" and that also meant that butter was not yellow and rich and sweet. The joy of naturally yellow, summer butter was an event I still remember.

An old magazine article turned up in cache of collected ideas in which a writer claimed that it would not be Christmas without a traditional carrot–potato–raisin pudding. I had never heard of it on my side of Lake Ontario but later found out that is was often called Ohio Pudding in the States, having evidentially made it across Lake Erie. One nineteenth-century recipe called for one cup each of grated carrot, potato, flour, suet, sugar, raisins, and currants seasoned with lots and lots of nutmeg. I set to work to honor its humble larder ingredients but, at the same time, to update it.

1/2 cup unbleached white flour
1/2 teaspoon baking powder
1/2 teaspoon baking soda
1/2 teaspoon ground cinnamon
1/2 teaspoon freshly grated nutmeg

1/4 cup butter
1/2 cup sugar

1/4 cup *fat-free* pasteurized eggs (the equivalent of 1 egg)
1/2 cup grated raw carrots
1/2 cup grated raw potatoes

3/4 cup *preservative-free dark* raisins
1/2 cup chopped *preservative-free* walnuts

Whipped cream

Prepare a 4-cup pudding mold,* suitable for steaming, by coating thoroughly with non-stick lecithin spray coating.

In a small bowl, combine flour, baking powder, baking soda, ground cinnamon and grated nutmeg. Stir together and set aside until required.

Using an electric mixer, cream butter and sugar until light and fluffy.

Add pasteurized eggs and grated raw carrot and potato. Continue beating until integrated.

While still mixing, gradually add mixed dry ingredients. Continue beating until integrated.

Using a wooden spoon, work raisins and walnuts into the stiff batter. Pack into prepared mold. Cover mold with aluminum foil and the pudding mold cover. Set mold on a rack in a kettle. Pour *boiling* water into the kettle, bringing it about halfway up the sides of the mold. Set over *LOW* heat, cover kettle, and steam in simmering water for about 1 3/4 hours. Add more *boiling* water as required.

Unmold pudding onto a serving plate.

CANADIAN CARROT – POTATO – RAISIN WINTER STEAMED PUDDING (cont'd)

Serve warm with whipped cream.**

Yields 8 servings
adequate for 6 people

Notes: *If you do not have a pudding mold, use a small mixing bowl or a 1 1/2-quart soufflé dish.

**I have had this with both a hard sauce and a brandy sauce; both sauces were complimentary.

This recipe can be doubled, if required. Use an 8-cup mold if you choose to double.

1/6 SERVING (with 2 tablespoonfuls whipped cream) –
PROTEIN = 3.3 g.; FAT = 12.3 g.; CARBOHYDRATE = 37.0 g.;
CALORIES = 273; CALORIES FROM FAT = 40%

CANADIAN BAKED WHOLE WHEAT "BEAVER TAILS"

TPT - 1 hour and 4 minutes;
30 minutes = gluten relaxation period

Whenever my mother or my grandmother baked a pie, the trimmings were rolled out into "beaver tails," or "things" as my mother chose to call them, one for each child, and one for the cook. Instead of frying them, they were baked. A generous sprinkling of cinnamon sugar was added as they came from the oven. We could hardly wait for the "tails" to cool. More traditionally, "beaver tails" are yeast-raised, fried, and sold in shops and by street vendors. Our version allows me to use my own whole wheat pie crust recipe, to avoid the lard that is usually used, and to bake instead of fry. No, they are not quite the same but they are what mothers made long before the commercial appearance of "beaver tails" and there is not a child I remember that did not love them.

Although we feel solid vegetable shortenings should be avoided, the quality of pie crusts made with oils is poor, in our opinion. There are always compromises in this life and platitudes to support them but do choose a vegetable shortening with no trans fats.

1/2 cup whole wheat flour
6 tablespoons unbleached white flour
2 tablespoons soy flour
1 tablespoon *toasted* wheat germ

2 tablespoons *cold* butter
2 tablespoons solid vegetable shortening

3-4 tablespoons *ice cold* water

2 tablespoons cinnamon sugar

Cover an area of the counter top with waxed paper. Set wire racks on waxed paper. Prepare baking sheets by lining them with culinary parchment paper.

Sift flours into a large mixing bowl. Stir in wheat germ.

Using a pastry blender, work *cold* butter and shortening into flour mixture until of the texture of coarse corn meal.

While stirring with a fork, sprinkle with *ice cold* water, 1 or 2 tablespoonfuls at a time, until mixture holds together and pulls away from the sides of the bowl. Gather into ten small balls, wrap tightly in plastic wrap, and refrigerate for about 30 minutes to allow the gluten to relax.

Preheat oven to 375 degrees F.

On a lightly floured surface, roll each ball of pastry in turn to form an elliptical shape like that of a beaver's tail. Place them on the prepared baking sheets. Bake in preheated 375 degree F. oven for 10 minutes, or until edges begin to brown. Remove baking sheets from oven and transfer pastry to wire racks.

Immediately sprinkle cinnamon sugar over the "beaver tails." Set on wire racks to cool.

Yields 10 "beaver tails"

1/10 SERVING (i. e., per "beaver tail" pastry) –
PROTEIN = 2.0 g.; FAT = 5.0 g.; CARBOHYDRATE = 11.5 g.;
CALORIES = 97; CALORIES FROM FAT = 46%

CANADIAN MAPLE BUTTERCREAM FROSTING
TPT - 20 minutes

Living close to the Canadian border for the first seventeen years of my life, I remember well the joy of maple sugar candies molded into maple leaves. The taste of maple sugar and maple syrup transport me through the years. This simple, lightly flavored frosting is pleasurable even to those who do not like to sample maple syrup "straight." It is a good frosting choice for an orange cake or to frost maple leaf sugar cookies.

1/2 cup (1 stick) butter—*softened to room temperature*
1 cup confectioners' sugar
1 teaspoon pure vanilla extract

3-4 tablespoons pure maple syrup
About 2 cups confectioners' sugar

Using an electric mixer, or food processor fitted with steel knife, or by hand, cream butter until light and fluffy. Gradually beat the 1 cupful confectioners' sugar into the creamed butter. Continue beating until smooth. Add vanilla extract. Mix well.

Beat in the remaining 2 cupfuls confectioners' sugar gradually, alternating with maple syrup, adding more of each until a smooth, spreadable consistency is achieved.

Use to frost cakes or cookies.

Yields enough to frost two 9-inch cake layers or about 24-30 cupcakes

Notes: Prepared frosting freezes well, but tends to lose flavor if frozen for more than a few days.

This recipe may be doubled, when required. It should, however, be noted that if this is being prepared by hand, a double batch is unwieldy.

1/16 SERVING (i. e., that which would be used on a two-layer slice of cake exclusive of the cake) –
PROTEIN = 0.0 g.; FAT = 5.7 g.; CARBOHYDRATE = 5.2 g.;
CALORIES = 160; CALORIES FROM FAT = 32%

1/24 SERVING (i. e., that which would be used on a cupcake exclusive of the cupcake) –
PROTEIN = 0.0 g.; FAT = 3.8 g.; CARBOHYDRATE = 3.4 g.;
CALORIES = 107; CALORIES FROM FAT = 32%

The Americas–The Native American Gift

The Spirit of the Earth

Native American foods and food habits may, perhaps, have been the greatest modifying influence on the cuisines of the Americas. The foods of the Iroquois appear on our table each week and dominate our Thanksgiving celebration here in the North. The foods of the Southwest and the exciting flavors of Tex-Mex are no longer exclusively regional. South American native foods are as much a part of food selection as are the foods of the European settlers. Chocolate had to make a detour through the courts of Europe instead of coming right up the Pan-American highway and potatoes, sweetpotatoes, squashes and other gourds, fruits like the pineapple, the avocado, the persimmon, *chili* peppers, and the tomato, corn, and peanuts, that were carried across the Atlantic and Pacific oceans from the New World, have come back to us in the foods of our immigrant ancestors. The appearance of *chipotle* peppers on the ingredient list for a sourdough cracker baked in a small bakery in the middle of Pennsylvania is a simple illustration of the migration of food ideas across our own country. We have mainstreamed Cajun food which so skillfully and excitingly combines the foods of the native peoples, the French, and the African-Americans who created a cuisine along the Gulf Coast that is unique in the world.

Waves and waves of immigrants have come to feed on the plenty of the Americas but the first immigrants, whom we refer to as Native Americans, are generally believed to have come along the edge of the receding Wisconsin glacier at the end of the last Ice Age pursuing the herds of mega-fauna. Moving from the western regions of Asia, some came across the land bridge in the vicinity of the present Aleutian Islands and made their way across the border region with Canada settling as they saw an opportunity. The extreme settlement of these travelers was at the eastern end of Long Island where archeological evidence confirms that family groups of Paleo-Indians settled as early as 12,000 years ago. Others headed south along the West Coast to our Southwest and to South America, also settling when the land and resources called.

It is estimated that fifty percent of the foods eaten today on this planet originally came from our hemisphere and yet the Spaniards still searched for gold to please their sovereign patrons. Many years ago, as we drove from Portugal into Spain, the fields of sunflowers that greeted us made me think that the gold sought by the conquistadors as they searched for the fabled Seven Cities of Cibola, the gold for which they died, was right under their noses – the sunflower and its nutritious seeds and golden oil, the corn, the pollen, the variety of nuts and drupe fruits, the melons, the squashes, and the mind-boggling variety of potatoes of all colors. No chapter in this story of our heritage which I have previously written would have been possible without the story of the foods of the Native Americans from Alaska south to the tip of South America.

The list of dishes that follows includes just a tiny number of the dishes that grace our table today whose origins can be traced to one or more of the diverse native cultures that live within the borders of, to the North of, or to the South of the land that became known as the United States of America: cranberry puddings and sauces, succotash, corn puddings and spoon breads, corn oysters, hominy and grits, cornbreads, sweetpotato breads, pumpkin and squash soups, tomato soup, Long Island's famous beach plum jam, batter-fried squash blossoms, applesauce and fruit purées, fruit honeys, fruit leathers, three-bean salad, baked beets, potatoes baked in hot ashes, bison and reindeer burgers, scrambled eggs with smoked salmon, tamales, corn-shuck- or banana-leaf-wrapped meats, fruits, and breads. These are not new or fashionably gourmet; these are gifts of the peoples who respect the land and who treasure the harvest, foods that we are revisiting.

The Americas – The Native American Gift

Appetizers

Toasted *piñon* (pine nuts or *pignoli*) nuts

Roasted Pumpkin Seeds

Baked Corn *Tortilla* Chips [see index]
Tostaditas
with

El Salvadoran Avocado, Egg, and Cheese Appetizer
[see index]
Guacamole con Huevos y Queso

Corn "Oysters"

Cheese and *Chili* Dip
with Blue Corn *Tortilla* Chips

Prickly Pear – Orange – Apple – Pineapple Punch

Salads

Mixed Greens
with
Apricot – Raspberry Salad Dressing
or
Prickly Pear *Vinaigrette*
with *Agave* **Nectar**

Nasturtium Blossoms Stuffed with Avocado

Fried Greens with "Bacon"

Purslane and Tomato Salad

Soups

Potato and Tomato Soup

Corn Chowder

Squash *Bisque*

Breads

Baking Powder Corn Meal Biscuits

Adobe Bread with Amaranth

Hazelnut Breads
with
Ersatz "Maple Syrup"

~~~~~~~~~~~~~~~~~~~~

Wild Rice and Mushroom Casserole or Vegetarian Baked Beans

Cajun Smothered Corn   or   Grilled Corn-on the-Cob   or   Pueblo-style Corn Pudding
Maquechoux

~~~~~~~~~~

Acorn Squash Baked with Honey and Hazelnut Butter

Grilled Whole Green Beans
with Sautéed Shaggy Mane or Pom Pom Mushrooms

~~~~~~~~~~

Black Beans with Green Peppers

Tortillas or Rice

~~~~~~~~~~~~~~~~~~~~

Bolivian Hot Sauce [see index]   or   Spiced Whole Cranberry Sauce
Uchu Llajwa

Lemon Jelly Infused with Fresh Herbs

Strawberry, Melon, and Black Pepper *Salsa*

The Americas – The Native American Gift

Choose Indian pudding or my pumpkin pie, your favorite pumpkin, or even pecan pie to finish off this menu and you will be again adapting that which was taught to the Europeans for survival when they arrived in this beautiful but hostile land. Roasted apples and "snow food" are snacks, given to us by the Iroquois in my area of New York State, that no one ever forgets.

~~~~~~~~~~~~~~~~~~~~~~

Indian Pudding

Iroquois Cherries in Maple Syrup

Fresh Hawaiian Pineapple Chunks
sprinkled with salt and lime juice

Cranberry and Black Walnut Sauce / Dessert

Custard Pumpkin Pie

~

Snow Food, Sweet Popcorn Clusters in the Style of the Iroquois

Apples Roasted over Coals

CORN "OYSTERS"
TPT - 28 minutes

Corn oysters and corn fritters were widely popular throughout our area of upstate New York and not just with the Iroquois tribes from whom the recipe had been learned. Fresh corn, frozen corn, canned corn, and even reconstituted dry corn kernels could be used to make the "oysters." Mom preferred to make corn fritters but when the oil had become rancid or "gone off," as they said, she made corn oysters. The batter is spooned directly onto a hot griddle and it puffs up as it cooks. To somebody the result looked like an oyster and that is presumably how this really useful vegetable side dish got its name. It was often served, as were corn fritters, with maple syrup but the syrup really hides their very real and enjoyable flavor.

About 1/2 teaspoon butter

2 egg whites

2 cups green (fresh) *or* **defrosted, frozen corn kernels**
2 egg yolks—*well-beaten*

2 tablespoons unbleached white flour
2 teaspoons whole wheat flour

1/4 teaspoon baking powder
Pinch salt
Pinch or two ground sage
Freshly ground black pepper, to taste

Melted butter

Preheat a non-stick-coated griddle or large skillet over *MEDIUM* heat. Brush lightly with butter.

Using an electric mixer fitted with *grease-free* beaters or by hand, using a *grease-free* wire whisk, beat egg whites in a *grease-free* bowl until *stiff*, but *not dry*. Set aside briefly.

In a mixing bowl, combine corn and *well-beaten* egg yolks.

In another mixing bowl, combine white and whole wheat flour, baking powder, salt, and black pepper. Stir to mix well. Add to corn mixture. Stir to mix thoroughly.

CORN "OYSTERS" (cont'd)

Add beaten egg whites. Fold gently into batter mixture. Drop by tablespoonfuls onto hot griddle, spacing each tablespoonful of "oyster" batter well apart from others. When puffed and golden, turn and brown the other side. Remove to a heated platter. Repeat until all batter has been used. *Brush the griddle with additional butter as you need it.*

Serve hot with melted butter.

Yields 6 servings—about 24 "oysters" adequate for 4-6 people

Note: This recipe can be doubled, when required.

1/24 SERVING (i. e., per "oyster" exclusive of melted butter) –
PROTEIN = 1.4 g.; FAT = 0.8 g.; CARBOHYDRATE = 5.8 g.;
CALORIES = 33; CALORIES FROM FAT = 22%

SOUTHWESTERN CHEESE AND *CHILI* DIP
TPT - 30 minutes

A recent television commercial touted a dip prepared by dumping canned vegetables and processed cheese into a bowl and then microwaving it. The family and their guests danced around manically as they dipped their chips into the dip. The following dip, from the Native American cultures of our southwestern states, might have given those people real reason to celebrate. It fills the kitchen with a wonderful aroma that lingers and the taste announces that "making from scratch" is the only way.

1 tablespoon safflower *or* sunflower oil
1 medium onion—*finely* chopped
1 garlic clove—*very finely* chopped

1 cup canned, *petite-diced* tomatoes packed in tomato purée
3 tablespoons *finely* chopped mild green *chilies*
1/2 teaspoon crushed, dried basil
1/4 teaspoon ground cumin

1 tablespoon freshly squeezed lemon juice
1/2 teaspoon *jalapeño chili* sauce, or to taste

3/4 cup shredded *extra sharp* Cheddar cheese*

Blue corn *tortilla* chips

In a large skillet set over *MEDIUM* heat, heat oil. Add *finely* chopped onion and *very finely* chopped garlic. Sauté until onion is soft and translucent, *being careful to allow neither the onion nor the garlic to brown.*

Add tomatoes with tomato purée, *finely* chopped green *chilies*, crushed basil, and ground cumin. Cook, stirring frequently, for about 15 minutes. *Remove from heat.*

Add lemon juice and *jalapeño chili* sauce. Stir to integrate thoroughly.

Add shredded cheese. Stir until cheese is melting. Turn into a serving dish. Place the dish on a plate and surround with *tortilla* chips. Set on a warming tray to keep it just slightly warm and to keep the cheese semi-liquid.

Serve at once.

Yields about 1 1/4 cupfuls

Notes: *Longhorn cheese can be substituted, if a milder cheese is desired.

This recipe can be doubled, when required.

1/20 SERVING (per tablespoonful exclusive of chips) –
PROTEIN = 0.6 g.; FAT = 1.0 g.; CARBOHYDRATE = 1.2 g.;
CALORIES = 16; CALORIES FROM FAT = 56 %

PRICKLY PEAR – ORANGE – APPLE – PINEAPPLE PUNCH
TPT - 34 minutes;
30 minutes = refrigeration period

The fruits of the Americas have provided not only the nutrition needed by early peoples but also life-sustaining liquid to those in dessert areas. Just standing in my parents' front yard in Arizona evidenced the nutritional needs of those who live in the dessert and of the prickly pear's sweet attraction. Every thick cactus paddle at the bottom of the plants had had visitors revealed by the scalloped edge and the presence of fruit only at the very top of the plant. The tunas, the fruit of the prickly pear, albeit a challenge to handle and juice, provide a sweet juice, marketed as prickly pear nectar. It can be combined with other fruit juices to give the most delicious moment of a meal.

The Americas – **The Native American Gift**

PRICKLY PEAR – ORANGE – APPLE – PINEAPPLE PUNCH (cont'd)

1 cup prickly pear nectar*
1/2 cup freshly squeezed orange juice
1/2 cup *organic, unsweetened* apple juice
1/2 cup *organic, unsweetened* pineapple juice
2 tablespoons freshly squeezed lime juice
1 tablespoon *agave* nectar

In a pitcher, combine prickly pear nectar, orange, apple, pineapple, and lime juices, and *agave* nectar. Stir to combine. Chill for at least 30 minutes to allow flavors to meld.

Serve into small brandy snifters or champagne flutes.

Notes: Cheri's prickly pear nectar is a reliable brand which is available from mail order firms and can be ordered also from online firms. Juicing prickly pear *tunas* can be a harrowing experience unless all the tiny spines have been removed, as is usually the case when you buy *tunas* in the grocery store where they are available in the fall. However, I have a pair of leather gloves specifically reserved to handle the fruit.

This recipe can be halved or doubled, when required.

Yields 6 servings
adequate for 4 people

1/6 SERVING – PROTEIN = 0.3 g.; FAT = 0.04 g.; CARBOHYDRATE = 12.0 g.;
CALORIES = 65; CALORIES FROM FAT = 1%

APRICOT – RASPBERRY SALAD DRESSING
TPT - 1 hour and 3 minutes;
1 hour = flavor development period

Having a sweet dressing with a distinctive tang that is excellent over greens in your repertoire is a must. Of course, this one is also a good choice for fruit and cheese salads too.

1/4 cup safflower *or* sunflower oil
2 tablespoons RASPBERRY VINEGAR *[see index]*
  or commercially-available, *preservative-free* raspberry vinegar
1 tablespoon freshly squeezed lime juice
3 tablespoons apricot *all-fruit* preserves

In the container of the electric blender or in the work bowl of the food processor fitted with steel knife, combine all ingredients. Process thoroughly. Turn into a cruet or bottle with tightly-fitting lid.

Set aside for about 1 hour to allow for development of flavor.

Always shake vigorously before serving. To avoid rancidity, try to prepare dressing within an hour or two of serving.

Yields about 10 tablespoonfuls

Note: This recipe is easily doubled or tripled, when required.

1/10 SERVING (i. e., per tablespoonful) –
PROTEIN = 0.0 g.; FAT = 5.6 g.; CARBOHYDRATE = 3.1 g.;
CALORIES = 62; CALORIES FROM FAT = 81%

NATIVE AMERICAN PRICKLY PEAR *VINAIGRETTE* WITH *AGAVE* NECTAR
TPT - 1 hour and 3 minutes;
1 hour = flavor development period

Prickly pear nectar can be squeezed from the fruits, known as tunas, if available and if you have heavy leather gloves to handle the fruit, or you can purchase prickly pear nectar from a mail order or online firm. I think of all the effort I have to go through to have prickly pear nectar in my Pennsylvania larder and my mother just walks out into her Arizona garden in late August and helps herself.

**NATIVE AMERICAN PRICKLY PEAR *VINAIGRETTE*
WITH *AGAVE* NECTAR** (cont'd)

1/2 cup prickly pear nectar
2 teaspoons *agave* nectar
3 tablespoons safflower *or* sunflower oil
2 tablespoons RASPBERRY VINEGAR *[see index]*
1 tablespoon freshly squeezed lime juice

In the container of the electric blender combine all ingredients. Process until thoroughly blended.

Pour puréed *vinaigrette* mixture into a jar with a tightly fitting lid or in a cruet with a tightly fitting top or cork. Set aside for about 1 hour to allow for development of flavor.

Always shake vigorously before serving. To avoid rancidity, try to prepare dressing within an hour or two of serving.

Refrigerate any leftovers.

Yields 14 tablespoonfuls

Note: This recipe may be halved or doubled, when required.

1/14 SERVING (i. e., per tablespoonful) –
PROTEIN = 0.0 g.; FAT = 0.3 g.; CARBOHYDRATE = 3.3 g.;
CALORIES = 45; CALORIES FROM FAT = 16%

NASTURTIUM BLOSSOMS STUFFED WITH AVOCADO
TPT - 30 minutes

Deep in the winter, when snow covers the herb beds and life in our gardens is rather static, I like to think of the steps from the house lined with herb- and flower-filled containers. I think about the huge pots, now empty and tucked into the garage for safekeeping, full of bright nasturtiums just waiting to be plucked for a salad. Here I sit in January with a perfectly ripened avocado that will probably become a dessert or a garnish for a salad. How I wish I had some nasturtiums to stuff.

Pinch dill seeds

2 tablespoons *reduced-calorie or light* mayonnaise
2 tablespoons *fat-free* sour cream
1 tablespoon *very finely* chopped mild green chilies
2 tablespoons chopped fresh coriander (*cilantro*)
1 tablespoon orange pulp
Pinch ground allspice
Freshly ground black pepper, to taste

1 medium, ripe avocado—peeled, pitted, and mashed
1 1/2 teaspoons freshly grated orange zest

20 perfect, *home-grown, spray-free* nasturtium blossoms—*well-washed and well-dried*

Using a mortar and pestle, grind dill seeds to a *fine* powder. Set aside.

In the mixing bowl, combine mayonnaise, sour cream, *very finely* chopped green *chilies*, chopped fresh coriander (*cilantro*), orange pulp, ground allspice, black pepper, and *finely* ground dill seeds. Process until smooth, scraping down the sides of the work bowl as necessary.

Add *mashed* avocado and grated orange zest. Thoroughly mix until all streaks of white are incorporated. Refrigerate until ready to serve.

Remove the pistil and stamen from each nasturtium blossom.

Using two spoons, put about 2 teaspoons full of the avocado stuffing into a nasturtium blossom, tucking it down into the center from which the pistil and stamen have been removed. Transfer to a chilled deviled egg dish or other chilled serving plate.

Serve at once as a salad or place each on a large cracker and serve as an appetizer.

Yields 20 servings
adequate for 4-5 people

Note: This recipe can be doubled, when required.

1/20 SERVING – PROTEIN = 0.5 g.; FAT = 2.2 g.; CARBOHYDRATE = 2.2 g.;
CALORIES = 27; CALORIES FROM FAT = 73%

The Americas—The Native American Gift

FRIED GREENS WITH "BACON"
TPT - 22 minutes

How often have you heard a Southerner evoke a" mess of greens" as pure comfort food? How did they learn to seek out the edible greens? Surely those coming from Europe and Africa could identify some of the native plants but the life-preserving guidance of those whom they found already living here must have been invaluable. This recipe is not native to our continent but our ancestors must have been very pleased to see that the native peoples, whom they met, were eating something familiar. The next question surely was, "What greens in this field are edible?" Few of us venture out now with our field guides to edible plants and key-out our botanical finds; most just depend on the grocery stores suppliers to provide us with that "mess of greens."

1 tablespoon butter
1 tablespoon *extra virgin* olive oil
1/2 cup spring ramps (wild leeks – *Allium tricoccum*) *or* scallions—trimmed, well-rinsed, and chopped
2 slices soy bacon—*finely* chopped

10 ounces spring lettuce mixture or a suitable mixture of lettuces and cooking greens —trimmed, well-rinsed, and well-dried— about 10 cups

In a non-stick-coated skillet set over *LOW-MEDIUM* heat, heat butter and oil. Add chopped ramps or scallions and *finely* chopped soy bacon. Sauté until onions begin to soften.

Add greens and continue cooking, stirring constantly, until greens are wilted. Turn out into a heated serving bowl. Keep warm on a warming tray until ready to serve.

Yields 6 servings
adequate for 4 people

Note: This recipe can be doubled, when required.

1/6 SERVING – PROTEIN = 1.2 g.; FAT = 4.1 g.; CARBOHYDRATE = 1.2 g.;
CALORIES = 47; CALORIES FROM FAT = 79%

NATIVE AMERICAN PURSLANE AND TOMATO SALAD
TPT - 16 minutes

The young, fleshy leaves of purslane or pusley (Portulaca oleracea) are an interesting addition to salads, a crop avidly cultivated in Asia, England, and in The Netherlands. Although slightly acid in taste, these leaves may be steamed like spinach and are even richer in iron than is spinach. Considered a weed by most gardeners since this green grows wild all through North America with little preference for soil conditions, purslane seeds are available from several seed companies and are often a component in more diverse mesclun mixtures. We cultivate it throughout the summer next to our mesclun rows. The older leaves can be pickled as well. There are several similar species, all of which are edible. Since there are no poisonous look-alikes, experimentation is generally a safe adventure.

5 cups purslane leaves—*very well-washed*

1 small onion—*thinly* sliced
2 ripe, *but firm*, tomatoes—chopped
3 tablespoons chopped fresh dillweed

2 tablespoons apple cider vinegar
1 tablespoon hazelnut oil, walnut oil, *or* almond oil**

Set up a steamer. Set up an ice water-bath.

Steam purslane leaves over boiling water for about 2 minutes. Plunge *immediately* into ice water to stop further cooking. Drain thoroughly.

In a mixing bowl, combine steamed purslane leaves, *thinly* sliced onion, chopped tomatoes, and dillweed. Toss gently to combine.

Add vinegar and nut oil. Again, toss gently.

Turn into a salad bowl. Refrigerate until ready to serve.

Yields 6 servings
adequate for 4 people

Notes: *Hazelnut oil, walnut oil, and almond oil are available in health food stores and in food specialty stores.

This recipe may be halved or doubled, when required.

The Americas – The Native American Gift

NATIVE AMERICAN PURSLANE AND TOMATO SALAD (cont'd)

1/6 SERVING – PROTEIN = 1.1 g.; FAT = 2.4 g.; CARBOHYDRATE = 3.8 g.;
CALORIES = 39; CALORIES FROM FAT = 55%

SOUTHWESTERN POTATO AND TOMATO SOUP
TPT - 1 hour and 14 minutes

Using the bounty of this hemisphere, Native Americans in the Southwest create a simple soup that, at once, comforts and satisfies. I have yet to sit down with a bowl of this soup and not feel good; I have always left the table feeling nourished.

8 small, ripe tomatoes—peeled and chopped
4 medium Golden Yukon potatoes—peeled, and chopped
2 small onions—sliced
1 quart *boiling* water

1/2 teaspoon *jalapeño chili* sauce, or to taste
1 Italian frying pepper *or cubanella* pepper—well-washed, cored, and sliced leaving as many seeds as possible to add to the soup
1/4 cup chopped fresh parsley
1/2 teaspoon salt

In a small kettle set over *LOW* heat, combine chopped tomatoes and potatoes, sliced onion, and *boiling* water. Partially cover and simmer for about 30-40 minutes. Stir occasionally.

Add *jalapeño chili* sauce, sliced pepper, parsley, and salt. Stir to distribute the ingredients. Cover again and allow to cook for about 30 minutes more, or until the pepper slices are cooked. Turn into a heated tureen.

Serve into heated soup plates. Accompany with warm *tortillas* or chunks of bread.

Yields 10 servings
adequate for 6 people

Notes: When required, this recipe can be doubled.

The soup can be frozen quite satisfactorily. Allow to defrost completely before reheating.

1/6 SERVING – PROTEIN = 1.9 g.; FAT = 0.3 g.; CARBOHYDRATE = 12.9 g.;
CALORIES = 62; CALORIES FROM FAT = 4%

CORN CHOWDER
TPT - 33 minutes

Corn chowder is, of course, another version of potato soup, common to so many cultures. With the addition of corn, the potato soup is home again in the Americas from whence it began its extraordinary worldwide journey. In the autumn and winter, there is nothing better.

1 medium potato—peeled and diced
3 cups *boiling* water

1 tablespoon butter
1/3 cup *finely* chopped onion
1/2 bay leaf

1/4 cup tomato purée—homemade, if possible

2 cups green (fresh) *or frozen* corn kernels
1 cup **VEGETARIAN WHITE** *or* **BROWN STOCK** *[see index]*, as preferred

1/4 teaspoon white pepper, or to taste
Pinch ground *or finely* crumbled dried sage

1 cup skimmed milk, whole milk, *or* part milk and cream, as preferred

1/4 cup chopped fresh parsley, for garnish

1/2 cup shredded (about 2 ounces) *sharp* Cheddar cheese, for garnish

CORN CHOWDER (cont'd)

In a saucepan set over *HIGH* heat, cook diced potato in *boiling* water until *crisp-tender*—about 5 minutes. Drain and rinse with *cold* water to stop further cooking. Set aside until required.

In a skillet set over *MEDIUM* heat, melt butter. Sauté *finely* chopped onion with bay leaf, until onion is soft and translucent, *being careful not to allow onion to brown*.

Add tomato purée and continue to sauté for 3-4 minutes. Remove bay leaf and discard.

Turn tomato–onion mixture into a 2-quart saucepan with corn, stock, white pepper, sage, and cooked, diced potato. Bring to the simmer over *MEDIUM-LOW* heat and simmer very gently for about 10 minutes.

Stir in milk and allow to just heat through—*do not boil!* Taste and adjust seasoning, if necessary.

Turn into heated tureen, garnish with chopped parsley and serve into heated soup bowls. Pass shredded Cheddar cheese separately.

Yields 6 servings
adequate for 4 people

Notes: This recipe is easily doubled, when required.

Since this soup freezes well, leftovers may be frozen without loss of quality.

If desired, an entirely adequate fish chowder may be created, for those at your table who eat fish, by adding about 1/2 pound firm-fleshed fish such as scrod. Chop into small pieces and add during the last 5 minutes of cooking. In this manner, you could, if desired, present two chowders on a buffet table—one meatless and the other with fish—with a minimum of extra effort.

1/6 SERVING – PROTEIN = 8.5 g.; FAT = 8.5 g.; CARBOHYDRATE = 23.2 g.;
CALORIES = 192; CALORIES FROM FAT = 40%

SQUASH *BISQUE*
TPT - 55 minutes

Squashes are beautiful vegetables, don't you think? When you are finished admiring them and decorating with them, try this beautiful, creamy, rich, elegant soup that somehow is still very "down home."

1 1/2 tablespoons butter
1/2 cup *finely* chopped onion
1/2 cup *finely* chopped carrot
1/8 teaspoon white pepper

1 cup peeled and cubed potato
1 acorn squash (about 1 pound)—peeled, seeded, and cubed
2 cups VEGETARIAN WHITE STOCK [see index]

1/2 cup light cream *or* half and half

Ground red pepper (cayenne), for garnish, if desired

In a large saucepan, with cover, set over *LOW* heat, melt butter. Add *finely* chopped onion and carrot. Sprinkle with 1/8 teaspoonful white pepper. Cover the pan with a sheet of buttered waxed paper and the cover. Cook vegetables over *LOW* heat for about 10 to 12 minutes, or until just tender, *being careful not to brown*. Discard waxed paper.

Add cubed potato and squash with vegetable stock. Simmer gently, covered, over *LOW* heat for about 30 minutes, or until the potato and squash are *very tender*.

Using a food processor, fitted with steel knife, or an electric blender, purée entire mixture. Force puréed vegetables through a sieve or through a FOOD MILL into a clean saucepan.* Stir in cream.

Cook over *LOW-MEDIUM* heat until heated through. Taste and adjust seasoning, if necessary. Turn into heated tureen and serve into heated soup cups or soup plates garnishing each serving with a sprinkling of ground red pepper (cayenne), if desired.

Yields 4-6 first course servings
adequate for 2-3 people as a
main course offering

Notes: *The purée may be refrigerated or frozen at this point. When ready to serve, heat and proceed as described above.

This recipe is easily doubled, when required.

SQUASH *BISQUE* (cont'd)

1/6 FIRST COURSE SERVING –
PROTEIN = 2.5 g.; FAT = 4.8 g.; CARBOHYDRATE = 17.3 g.;
CALORIES = 118; CALORIES FROM FAT = 37%

1/3 MAIN COURSE SERVING –
PROTEIN = 4.9 g.; FAT = 9.6 g.; CARBOHYDRATE = 34.6 g.;
CALORIES = 236; CALORIES FROM FAT = 37%

NATIVE AMERICAN BAKING POWDER CORN MEAL BISCUITS
TPT - 25 minutes

Traditionally, the women in my family made buttermilk biscuits with only white flour viewing the addition of corn as somewhat Southern, as in "corn pone," while, living all around us, the Native peoples of various tribes of the Iroquois Nation made these delicious corn meal biscuits. I often make these beautiful golden biscuits to serve with a fruit and cottage cheese salad plate or with a soup menu.

1 1/2 cups unbleached white flour
1/2 cup *fine* yellow corn meal
4 teaspoons baking powder

1 tablespoon *unfiltered, unboiled* honey
1 tablespoon pure maple syrup
2 tablespoons *cold* butter

1/3 - 1/2 cup *unsalted,* cultured buttermilk *or* skimmed milk, as preferred
1/4 cup *fat-free* pasteurized eggs (the equivalent of 1 egg)

Preheat oven to 400 degrees F.

Into a large mixing bowl, combine flour, corn meal, and baking powder. Stir to combine well.

Using a pastry blender or by pulsating the mixture in the food processor, fitted with steel knife, cut honey, maple syrup, and *cold* butter into dry ingredients until mixture is the consistency of *coarse* corn meal.

In a measuring cup or small bowl, combine 1/3 cupful buttermilk or skimmed milk and pasteurized eggs. Using a wire whisk, combine well.

Make a well in the center, pour buttermilk–egg mixture into the well and stir until mixture forms a soft dough and pulls from the sides of the bowl. Add more milk, a little at a time, *only if necessary.*

Turn dough out onto a *very lightly* floured surface. Lightly flour your hands and knead dough for only about 30 seconds. Pat or roll dough to an even 1/2-inch thickness. Cut with a floured 3-inch biscuit cutter. Using a spatula, turn each biscuit up-side-down and transfer biscuit rounds to an *ungreased* baking sheet, spacing them at least 1 1/2 inches apart to allow for expansion and even browning. *Be sure to turn the biscuits over onto the baking sheet so that the bottom surface, the surface that had to be pulled away from the surface, is now on top.* (This will give a pebbled top surface to the baked biscuits.)

Bake in preheated 400 degree F. oven for about 15 minutes, or until *golden brown.*

Serve hot with butter.

Yields 9 large biscuits

Notes: This recipe can be used to bake individual biscuits or to prepare a single round to be used as a CORN MEAL BISCUIT SHORTCAKE with berries or peaches.

When necessary, this recipe may be doubled.

1/9 SERVING (i. e., per biscuit) –
PROTEIN = 2.3 g.; FAT = 3.0 g.; CARBOHYDRATE = 14.1 g.;
CALORIES = 91; CALORIES FROM FAT = 30%

(BREAD MACHINE) NATIVE AMERICAN ADOBE BREAD WITH AMARANTH

TPT - 3 hours and 44 minutes;
2 hours = automated preparation period

Amaranth flour, although rather expensive, is available in most natural food stores. The flour is made by grinding the dried seeds of the extremely nutritious annual herb related to pigweed or lambs'-quarters. It is not, therefore, a true grain but can be used in much the same way as are grains—as a cooked cereal, in breads, and in sweet baked goods. Commercially available pastas and cereals will give you an opportunity to taste this rediscovered wonder. Believed to have been a staple in the diet of the pre-Columbian Aztecs, amaranth supplies both lysine and methionine, two essential amino acids generally absent in grains. Therefore, protein complementation is not necessary for the vegetarian when amaranth is included in a menu as "the grain." This is an updated version of a Native American classic which would traditionally be baked in a unique bee-hive oven called a horno. It is earthy, wholesome, but light. The Pueblo peoples carve spirit symbols, such as that of the squash blossom, into the top of Adobe bread loaves; you may want to try it.

1 tablespoon (1 envelope) *preservative-free* **active dried yeast***
2 cups bread flour
1/2 cup whole wheat flour
1/2 cup amaranth flour
1 1/2 tablespoons sugar
1/2 teaspoon salt
2 tablespoons butter
1 cup minus 1 tablespoon water—*heated to about 95 degrees F.*

Bring all remaining ingredients except for *warm* water to room temperature.

In the BREAD MACHINE pan, combine yeast, bread flour, whole wheat flour, amaranth flour, sugar, salt, butter, and *warm* water.**

Select MANUAL SETTING and push START.

Prepare a cookie sheet by coating with lecithin spray coating.

In 2 hours, when the automated preparation period is over, remove dough to a floured surface and knead until smooth and all trace of stickiness is gone. Divide in half and form two round loaves. Place one at each end of prepared baking sheet. Allow to rise in a warm, draft-free kitchen until doubled in volume—about 35-40 minutes.

Preheat oven to 375 degrees F.

Using a very sharp knife, *gently, without pressure,* slash 1/2-inch-deep cuts into the top of the loaf in a lattice pattern or in the shape of a squash blossom.

Bake bread in preheated oven for about 50 minutes, or until loaves "thump hollow" when tapped with your knuckles. Allow to cool completely on a wire rack before slicing into wedges to serve.

Yields two round loaves

Notes: *Some packaged dried yeast available in grocery stores contain a preservative. Natural food stores carry an additive-free dried yeast. In addition, *do not use so–called fast action yeasts.* The results will not please you.

**Be sure to follow the directions recommended by the manufacturer of your bread machine; they may be different.

Toasted, day-old adobe bread is excellent as a breakfast toast or to make croutons for *hors d'oeuvre* or soups.

1/16 SERVING (i. e., per wedge slice) –
PROTEIN = 2.9 g.; FAT = 1.8 g.; CARBOHYDRATE = 17.7 g.;
CALORIES = 99; CALORIES FROM FAT = 16%

The Americas–**The Native American Gift**

NATIVE AMERICAN HAZELNUT BREADS
TPT - 58 minutes
20 minutes = resting period

During the American Revolution, New York City and Long Island were controlled by British forces, Long Island being occupied for longer than any other area in the colonies. The division and strong feelings between Tory and Patriot families or members of the same family was deep and lasting; many Loyalists finally left the Island and either returned to England or emigrated to the Canadian Maritime Provinces, especially Nova Scotia. Long Island had been deforested by the British to provide fuel for New York City; our food stores, crops, and cattle sustained the Lobsterbacks; and our people were worn out at the end of the seven-year period. The British evacuated Boston on March 17, 1776, where their Evacuation Day is still celebrated simultaneously with St. Patrick's Day but it was some time before the British left New York City and Long Island, beginning their evacuation of New York City and Washington, DC, on November 25, 1783, and finally clearing the docks and freeing our Island on December 4th. Evacuation Day, November 25th, was celebrated as one of our young nation's first holidays until World War I, eventually supplanted by the November holidays of Armistice Day and Thanksgiving Day.

We always try to serve a dish as part of our Thanksgiving dinner that reminds us of the absolute joy of freedom, hard won and worth defending, for which we are thankful. Sometimes it is something as simple as a small pot of baked beans made from the beans we have dried from our harvest, boiled corn pudding made from dried corn, pumpkin soup, or an Indian pudding, made from winter stores. Prepared by colonial Long Islanders from a Native American recipe with the nuts dried and stored for the winter, these hazelnut skillet cakes, similar to corn oysters, accompanied meals when bread ingredients were scare. They represent another reminder to us. The corn cob-based syrup is humbling too.

1/2 cup ground *preservative-free* hazelnuts *or* hazelnut meal

2 cups *boiling* water

1/2 cup yellow corn meal
1/2 teaspoon salt

1/3 cup corn *or* safflower oil, if preferred

Pure maple syrup, FAMILY'S CHOICE PANCAKE AND WAFFLE SYRUP *[see index]*, *or* **ERSATZ MAPLE SYRUP** *[see recipe which follows]*

Turn hazelnut meal into a saucepan set over *MEDIUM* heat. Add *boiling* water and cook, stirring frequently, until the cooked nut meal is the consistency of a corn meal mush. *Remove from heat.*

Add corn meal and salt. Stir to integrate thoroughly. Allow to stand at room temperature until thick—about 20 minutes.

In a large skillet set over *MEDIUM* heat, heat oil until hot. Drop the nutmeal–corn mixture by tablespoonfuls into the hot oil. Brown on one side. Turn and flatten into a cake, using a well-oiled spatula, and brown the other side. Transfer to paper toweling to drain well.

Serve either warm or cold. If desired, these little breads can be sweetened by serving maple syrup or corn cob-based ERZATZ MAPLE SYRUP [see recipe which follows] into which they can be dunked.

Yields 16 small breads
adequate for 6-8 people

Note: This recipe can be halved or doubled, when required.

1/16 SERVING (i. e., per bread exclusive of maple syrup) –
PROTEIN = 5.7 g.; FAT = 2.2 g.; CARBOHYDRATE = 4.7 g.;
CALORIES = 82; CALORIES FROM FAT = 24%

The Americas–The Native American Gift

ERSATZ "MAPLE SYRUP"
TPT - 2 hours and 16 minutes

The harvesting of the sweet sap from the sugar maple and the black maple was taught to the colonists by the native peoples. Throughout colonial history maple syrup and maple sugar, together with molasses available via the Barbados trade, were THE family sweeteners for those living in the North. White sugar from sugar cane was "for company." Since white sugar was more expensive in the North, it is strange that this recipe, found in archival material on the eastern end of Long Island, should ever have evolved. It might have been invented to provide a sweetened syrup during the summer months when the supply of maple syrup had dwindled. It is also possible that this recipe originated in the American South and found its way to the North in the recipe collection of a relocated southern family or manumitted slave. The creator of this recipe seems to have almost anticipated the demand for the artificially flavored "pancake syrups" often made from corn syrup, which today sadly take up the greater portion of shelf space in our grocery stores. Production of maple syrup in the 1770s was approximately four times the amount produced at the time of the our Bicentennial.

No, this does not taste "exactly like genuine maple syrup," as claimed by the colonial-era author. In no way does this taste like maple syrup to us but we do offer the recipe as a historical culinary curiosity.

10 large ears of corn
4 quarts *boiling* **water**

7 cups white sugar
2 1/8 cups *dark* **brown sugar**

Sterilize 2 one-quart canning jars, lids, and rings.

Cut the kernels from the cobs and reserve for another use.* Break the corn cobs in half. Place the cobs in a large kettle set over *MEDIUM-HIGH* heat. Add *boiling* water. Allow the cobs to boil in the water for about 1 hour. Remove cob halves and discard.

Line a sieve with a cotton tea towel. Pour the liquid from the kettle through the towel into a clean kettle.

Place the kettle with the strained "corn liquid" over *MEDIUM* heat. Add white sugar and brown sugar. Cook, stirring occasionally, until the sugar is dissolved. Continue cooking until the liquid has reduced and is thickened to your liking—approximately 1 hour. *Watch carefully so that it does not become too thick or crystallize.***

Remove from heat.

Pour syrup into sterilized canning jars. Allow to cool completely. Seal and store in the refrigerator.

Use as syrup for pancakes and waffles.

Yields about 2 quartfuls

Notes: *This is a fun experiment with the cobs remaining after you have removed the kernels for freezing.

**A candy thermometer is useful in this regard.

1/112 SERVING (i. e., per tablespoonful) –
PROTEIN = 0.0 g.; FAT = 0.0 g.; CARBOHYDRATE = 16.3 g.;
CALORIES = 64; CALORIES FROM FAT = 0%

WILD RICE AND MUSHROOM CASSEROLE
TPT - 2 hours and 10 minutes;
30 minutes = grain soaking period

Wild rice is the seed of a tall aquatic grass (Zizania aquatica). It is not really a rice, although strictly speaking rices are also the seeds of aquatic grasses. Known variously as Indian rice, Canada rice, Tuscarora rice and, by French explorers, as "crazy oats," it is native to the wetland regions along the shores of the Great Lakes and their tributary rivers and streams. A closely related grass is native to areas of China and Japan. At one time the harvesting of wild rice was a protected industry, harvested by native tribes, such as the Chippewa, who have gathered it by canoe since the 1600s, and most of that available in gourmet shops was packaged in either Minnesota or Wisconsin. Today this strongly earthy, nutty-tasting grain is cultivated commercially in Minnesota, Wisconsin, and extensively also in California.

This excitingly complex casserole is the preferred main course on our Thanksgiving menu.

WILD RICE AND MUSHROOM CASSEROLE (cont'd)

1 cup dry wild rice*

Bouquet garni:
    Pinch dried thyme
    1/2 bay leaf—broken
    3 sprigs fresh parsley—chopped
    3 or 4 fresh celery leaves—chopped
2 cups VEGETARIAN BROWN STOCK *[see index] or* other vegetarian stock of choice

2 tablespoons butter
1/2 cup chopped shallots
1 pound fresh *crimini or* baby bella mushrooms
    —trimmed, rinsed, cleaned well with a brush, and sliced

Additional VEGETARIAN BROWN STOCK, if required
1/4 cup chopped fresh Italian flat-leafed parsley
1/4 cup coarsely chopped *preservative-free* pecans
1 teaspoon sweet marjoram leaves—crushed
1/4 teaspoon poultry seasoning
1/4 teaspoon ground black pepper, or to taste

Prepare a 2-quart oven casserole, with cover, by coating with non-stick lecithin spray coating.

Wash wild rice in several changes of *cool* water. Soak washed grain in *cool* water to cover for 30 minutes. Discard any kernels which float to the surface. Again, drain. Rinse again in several changes of *cool* water. Drain thoroughly.

Prepare a *bouquet garni* in a cheesecloth bag. In the bag, combine dried thyme, broken bay leaf, and chopped parsley and celery leaves. Tie tightly.

In a saucepan with cover set over *MEDIUM-HIGH* heat, bring the 2 cupfuls of stock to the boil with the *bouquet garni*. Stir in rinsed and drained wild rice. Reduce heat to *LOW,* cover tightly, and cook *undisturbed* for about 30 minutes. Remove *bouquet garni* and discard.**

Just before the end of the cooking period, in a skillet set over *MEDIUM* heat, melt butter. Add chopped shallots and sliced mushrooms. Sauté until shallots are soft, *allowing neither the shallots nor the mushrooms to brown.*

Preheat oven to 325 degrees F.

Stir sautéed vegetables into partially cooked wild rice, adding additional stock only if necessary. Add chopped parsley, chopped pecans, sweet marjoram, poultry seasoning, and black pepper. Combine thoroughly. Turn into prepared casserole. Cover tightly.

Bake, covered, in preheated 325 degree F. oven for 30 minutes. Remove cover and continue baking until stock has either been absorbed or evaporated, but *do not allow to dry!*

Turn into heated serving bowl before serving.

                              Yields 8 servings
                            adequate for 6 people

Notes: *To release its perfection of flavor and texture, wild rice should *not* be cooked in the same manner as white and brown rices.

        **The cheesecloth bag may be emptied, thoroughly washed and dried, and stored in a tightly sealed plastic bag to be reused when required again.

        This recipe may be halved or doubled, when required.

1/8 SERVING – PROTEIN = 4.7 g.; FAT = 10.1 g.; CARBOHYDRATE = 16.2 g.;
CALORIES = 168; CALORIES FROM FAT = 54%

VEGETARIAN BAKED BEANS
TPT - 8 hours and 14 minutes;
2 hours = soaking period

A Boston bean pot, whether it holds beans, a dessert, or just flowers is a symbol of comfort, a reminder of less hurried days. Narragansett and Penobscot tribes taught the Europeans how to cook beans this way. Indians of the Southwest, The Plains, and the Northwest were more apt to cook over open fires and gave us the barbecue tradition. The Northern Woodland tribes steamed meals in earthen pits and taught the colonists to cook this way. Boston baked beans are a lasting link to this traditional cooking. If you have the time, why resort to commercially-canned vegetarian baked beans. Beans cooked from scratch are so satisfying—from the moment the aroma fills the house until the last spoonful is scraped out of the bean pot. I add chopped peaches, dried fruits, chopped sun- or oven-dried tomatoes, and/or diced cheese, depending upon the whim of the moment.

1 1/2 cups (about 3/4 pound) dry pea beans
  or Great Northern beans
5 cups water

1/4 cup tomato purée
2 tablespoons bottled *chili* sauce
2 tablespoons *unsulfured* molasses
1 small onion—chopped
2 tablespoons butter—*melted*
1/4 teaspoon dry mustard
1/8 teaspoon ground ginger

Rinse dry white beans in several changes of water. Remove and discard any of poor quality. Put beans and water into a saucepan. Bring to the boil over *MEDIUM-HIGH* heat, reduce heat, and simmer for 5 minutes. Cover tightly and allow to stand at room temperature for 2 hours.*

Prepare a 1 1/2-quart bean pot by coating with non-stick lecithin spray coating.

Turn beans and liquid into a mixing bowl. Add tomato purée, *chili* sauce, chopped onion, molasses, *melted* butter, dry mustard, and ground ginger. Mix *gently*, but *thoroughly*. Turn mixture into prepared bean pot. Cover the bean pot tightly and place in a *cold oven*.

Set oven temperature at 250 degrees F., turn on, and allow beans to cook for about 6 hours. Check occasionally and add more water, only if necessary. Remove the cover for the last 30 minutes if a top crust is desired. *Be careful not to allow beans to become too dry!*

Yields 6 servings
adequate for 4 people

Note: *If more convenient, beans may be soaked overnight instead. Combine sorted, rinsed beans in water. Place in refrigerator to soak. In the morning, discard soaking water, add 3 cupfuls water to soaked beans, and proceed from *.

1/6 SERVING – PROTEIN = 13.3 g.; FAT = 4.7 g.; CARBOHYDRATE = 43.1 g.;
CALORIES = 260; CALORIES FROM FAT = 16%

CAJUN SMOTHERED CORN
Maquechoux
TPT - 40 minutes

Maquechoux is difficult to categorize. Its French name is Cajun but its origin can be traced down to the cuisines of Native American tribes who inhabited the south central United States. The dish surfaces with many interpretations, most of which incorporated either bacon or seafood. The first version I tasted was too sweet, too hot, and too salty. Our mild vegetarian rendition replaces green pepper with sweet red pepper and is best made with fresh-from-the-field corn. I do make it occasionally with corn that we have frozen but never with commercially canned or frozen corn.

8 ears fresh corn

3 tablespoons butter
3/4 cup *finely* chopped onion
1/2 cup chopped sweet red pepper
1 teaspoon sugar
1/8 teaspoon ground *white* pepper
1/8 teaspoon ground red pepper (cayenne)

1/2 cup light cream *or* half and half

1/4 cup *fat-free* pasteurized eggs (the equivalent of 1 egg)*
2 tablespoons light cream *or* half and half

CAJUN SMOTHERED CORN (cont'd)

Place a large plate on the counter top and hold an ear of corn upright in the center of the plate. Using a very sharp knife, cut the kernels from each ear of corn but cutting straight down the cob, letting the knife follow the curve of the cob. Or, place the ear in the center hole of an angel food cake pan and then cut down the cob in the same manner. Then extract as much of the "milk" from each row by pulling a potato peeler down in the same fashion.

In a large skillet set over *MEDIUM* heat, melt butter. Add corn kernels and "milk," *finely* chopped onion, chopped red pepper, sugar, *white* pepper, and ground red pepper (cayenne). Sauté for several minutes. Reduce heat to *LOW*.

Add the 1/2 cupful cream. Stir to combine. Cover and cook for about 12 minutes, *stirring frequently*.

Beat the pasteurized eggs with the remaining 2 tablespoonfuls of cream until frothy. Add to the corn and cook for a minute or two, stirring constantly.** Turn out into a heated serving bowl.

Serve at once.

Yields 6 servings
adequate for 4 people

Notes: *Since the egg is not thoroughly cooked in this dish, it is advisable to use *Salmonella*-negative pasteurized eggs.

**Note that you do not want the eggs to scramble but just to be heated through.

This recipe can be halved, when required.

1/6 SERVING – PROTEIN = 8.4 g.; FAT = 9.9 g.; CARBOHYDRATE = 45.7 g.;
CALORIES = 276; CALORIES FROM FAT = 32%

GRILLED CORN – ON – THE – COB
TPT - about 45 minutes

Not only is this a delicious way to serve corn, especially if the corn might have been picked the day before, it is a convenient method when you have lots of other things to do for a picnic. If necessary, the sauced ears may be prepared, wrapped securely, and refrigerated early in the day to ease your preparation schedule. Also it does not matter if you grill more than you need because leftover corn can be scraped from the cobs and used as an excellent omelet ingredient or filling.

3 tablespoons butter—*melted*
1/4 cup bottled *chili* sauce
5 teaspoons firmly packed *light* brown sugar
5 teaspoons distilled white vinegar

6 freshly husked, large ears of corn

Prepare a moderately hot charcoal fire of glowing coals.*

In a small bowl, combine *melted* butter, *chili* sauce, brown sugar, and vinegar.

Place each ear of corn in the middle of a square of heavy-duty aluminum foil. Brush about 1 1/2 tablespoonfuls of *chili* sauce mixture over surface of corn. Wrap ears and seal ends. Using a second square of heavy-duty aluminum foil, double wrap each ear.

When coals are *white hot*, place wrapped corn ears on the grill about 4 inches above coals. Grill for about 25-30 minutes, turning occasionally. When done, these can be set on the back of the grill for a *few* minutes until other grilled items are done.

Serve in aluminum wraps to keep them hot and moist.

Yields 6 servings
adequate for 3-6 people**

Notes: *These can also be prepared in the oven, if preferred. Bake at 375 degrees F. for about 30 minutes. Turn to keep sauce from pooling on one side only.

**It is wise to know each guest's *corn quota*. For most moderate appetites, one ear is usually sufficient. Half ears may also be prepared to accommodate smaller appetites, especially those of children.

This recipe may be halved, doubled, or tripled with ease, when required.

GRILLED CORN-ON-THE-COB (cont'd)

1/6 SERVING (i. e., per ear) –
PROTEIN = 5.0 g.; FAT = 7.1 g.; CARBOHYDRATE = 35.9 g.;
CALORIES = 204; CALORIES FROM FAT = 31%

STOVE-TOP, PUEBLO-STYLE CORN PUDDING
TPT - 30 minutes

There probably is not an American cookbook that does not have a recipe for some sort of spoon bread, a corn pudding unique to this continent. This particular version, which comes from the Pueblo peoples along the Rio Grande River, is unusual in that it also includes pumpkin and apple juice. The Pueblo depended less on the buffalo and more on what they grew. Evidence of common stores of harvested crops, including corn, wheat, pumpkins and other gourds, and dried beans, found in the abandoned pueblos of these southern plains dweller, the ancestors of today's Pueblo tribes, suggest that they too depended on "the three sisters." This casserole serves up in light, puffed spoonfuls accounting for a native reference to this dish as "corn clouds."

1 large *organic* egg white*

2 tablespoons butter
1 large garlic clove—*very finely* **chopped**

2 cups apple juice
1/4 cup canned pumpkin—*unseasoned* **and**
  unsweetened

1/2 cup *fine yellow* corn meal
1/2 cup green (fresh) *or frozen* corn kernels
1/4 teaspoon ground allspice
1/2 teaspoon *jalapeño chili* sauce, or more to
  taste
Salt, to taste
Freshly ground black pepper, to taste

***Finely* chopped fresh spring ramps, if available,**
  ***or* chives, for garnish**

Using an electric mixer fitted with *grease-free* beaters or by hand, using a *grease-free* wire whisk, beat egg white in a *grease-free* bowl until *stiff*, but *not dry*. Set aside briefly until required.

In a saucepan set over *MEDIUM* heat, melt butter. Add *very finely* chopped garlic and sauté for a couple of minutes, *being careful not to allow garlic to brown*.

Add apple juice and pumpkin purée. Stir to mix well. Allow to come to the boil. *Reduce heat to LOW.*

While stirring constantly with a wire whisk, sprinkle corn meal into the mixture in the saucepan. Add corn, ground allspice, *jalapeño chili* sauce, salt, and pepper. Stir to integrate. Cook, stirring frequently, for about 10 minutes. Remove from heat.

Whisk-fold beaten egg white *gently*, but *thoroughly*, into corn mixture. Turn into a heated serving bowl.

Serve at once. Garnish each serving with a sprinkle of *finely* chopped ramps or chives.

Yields 6 servings
adequate for 4 people

Note: *Because raw eggs present the danger of *Salmonella* poisoning, an organic egg white is specified for use in preparing this dish.

1/6 SERVING – PROTEIN = 2.6 g.; FAT = 4.4 g.; CARBOHYDRATE = 22.2 g.;
CALORIES = 134; CALORIES FROM FAT = 30%

NATIVE AMERICAN ACORN SQUASH BAKED
WITH HONEY AND HAZELNUT BUTTER
TPT - 1 hour and 32 minutes

When choosing "the three sisters" to celebrate our Thanksgiving, this is often our choice for the squash element. It is beautifully accompanied by steamed, whole green beans and cornbread to complete the threesome deemed so precious to survival by the member tribes of the Iroquois Nation.

The berries of the spicebush, a shrub native to the North American continent, provide the primary food source for the caterpillar of the Spicebush Swallowtail butterfly (Papilio troilus), a beautiful visitor to the garden and reason enough to plant a spicebush or two and share the harvest.

NATIVE AMERICAN ACORN SQUASH BAKED WITH HONEY AND HAZELNUT BUTTER (cont'd)

2 medium-large acorn squash—well-washed

1/4 cup hazelnut butter*
2 tablespoons *wildflower* honey
Ground spicebush berries** *or* ground allspice

Preheat oven to 350 degrees F.

Cut squash in half lengthwise and remove seeds. Place cut-side-down on a jelly roll pan or in a shallow baking pan with about 1/2-inch of water. Bake in preheated 350 degree F. oven for about 30 minutes, or until almost tender.

Meanwhile, in a small bowl, stir hazelnut butter into honey. Set aside.

Turn squash cut-side-up. Using a butter knife, spread hazelnut butter-honey mixture over the top edges and all over the cavity of each squash halved. Sprinkle ground spicebush berries *or* ground allspice over. Return to the oven for an additional 30 minutes.

Serve with butter, if desired.

Notes: *Hazelnut butter is available in both natural food stores and in food specialty stores. However, it is easily made at home. Process shelled hazelnuts (also called filberts) in a food processor fitted with steel knife or in an electric blender until a paste forms. Some people recommend that you blanch the shelled nuts before processing but we feel that the B-vitamins retained by not blanching are too important. Six tablespoonfuls of ground hazelnuts will yield the one-quarter cupful hazelnut butter required for this recipe.

**The red spicebush berries can be harvested from a *Lindera benzoin (formerly known as Benzoin aestivale)*, dried, and ground, if you have one growing in your yard. The spicebush is a shade-loving plant which grows well where it has a good and constant water source such as a creek bank.

This recipe is easily halved or doubled, when required

Yields 4 individual servings

1/4 SERVING – PROTEIN = 4.5 g.; FAT = 10.5 g.; CARBOHYDRATE = 26.2 g.;
CALORIES = 171; CALORIES FROM FAT = 55%

SOUTHWESTERN BLACK BEANS WITH GREEN PEPPER
TPT - 19 minutes

Sometimes referred to as puyé beans, this simple skillet bean dish is easily prepared on a stove or over an outdoor fire. Complement the leguminous proteins with rice or with bread and you have a healthy, flavorful dinner that has its origins in the Native American villages of the Southwest.

2 tablespoons peanut oil
1 Italian green frying *or* cubanella pepper
 —washed, cored, seeded, and *finely* chopped
1 small onion—*finely* chopped
1 large garlic clove—crushed and *very finely* chopped
1 bay leaf—halved
1/2 teaspoon marjoram—crushed
1/4 teaspoon freshly ground black pepper, or to taste

1 can (15.5 ounces) black beans—drained
1/4 cup water

2 tablespoons *finely* chopped onion

In a skillet set over *MEDIUM* heat, heat oil. Add *finely* chopped pepper and onion, *very finely* chopped garlic, bay leaf pieces, crushed marjoram, and black pepper. Sauté until onions are soft and translucent.

Add black beans and stir to combine. Using a wooden spoon, crush the beans gently. Add water. Stir to integrate. Cook, stirring frequently, until most of liquid has evaporated—about 8-10 minutes. Remove and discard bay leaf pieces. Turn into a heated serving dish.

Garnish with remaining 2 tablespoonfuls onion.

Serve at once.

Yields 6 servings
adequate for 4 people

Note: This recipe can be doubled, when required.

1/6 SERVING – PROTEIN = 4.6 g.; FAT = 4.0 g.; CARBOHYDRATE = 13.7 g.;
CALORIES = 98; CALORIES FROM FAT = 37%

SPICED WHOLE CRANBERRY RELISH
TPT - 40 minutes

The ancient Druids called the tart, red berry "samolus." Later people of the British Isles, who found the berries near swamps and marshes, called the same fruits marsh worts or fen berries. Settlers from Europe found the berries growing in bogs in the New World, often in close proximity to the nests of cranes. They, therefore, dubbed them "kraneberries." Long a nutritional mainstay of the Native Americans, they were preserved and dried in the fall in preparation for the long winter just as we still do today.

Commercial cranberry sauce can be so disappointing. The texture and the seasoning just are not what my grandmother made. Yes, a can in the pantry is convenient but once you have canned a few jars of this relish, what is the need for store-bought convenience; home-canned convenience is just fine with us.

3 cups sugar
1 cup distilled white vinegar
3/4 cup water
1 1/2 teaspoons ground ginger
3/4 teaspoon ground cloves
3/4 teaspoon ground cinnamon
1/4 teaspoon ground allspice

24 ounces fresh cranberries—sorted, washed, and drained

Notes: *Any jars that do not seal can be stored in the refrigerator for several months or resealed using a *NEW LID*.

This recipe can be halved, when required.

Sterilize four 1-pint jars. Also sterilize lids and rings for jars.

In a large kettle, combine sugar, vinegar, water, and ground ginger, cloves, cinnamon, and allspice. Bring to the boil over *MEDIUM* heat.

Add cranberries. Simmer for 25 minutes.

Ladle into the sterilized 1-pint canning jars, being sure that vinegar solution covers the fruit. Carefully wipe rims of jars. Seal with hot, sterilized lids and rings. Process in hot-water-bath canner for 5 minutes, *timing from the moment the water reaches a full rolling boil.* Remove to surface covered with thick towels or newspapers. Allow to cool for 24 hours *undisturbed.* Check to be sure jars are sealed before labeling and storing in a dark, cool, dry place.* Loosen or remove rings before storing.

Yields three 1-pint jarfuls

1/64 SERVING (i. e., per 2 tablespoonfuls) –
PROTEIN = 0.4 g.; FAT = 0.1 g.; CARBOHYDRATE = 10.8 g.;
CALORIES = 48; CALORIES FROM FAT = 1%

NATIVE AMERICAN LEMON JELLY INFUSED WITH FRESH HERBS
TPT - 25 hours and 16 minutes;
24 hours = cooling period

Another way to enjoy your herb harvest in the winter is to create a condiment. This one, similar to a mint jelly that I make using lemon balm, is from the files of Native American cooks. Its sweet base and savory nuances accompany so many dishes. Since herbs do not contribute natural pectin to this jelly-making process as would fruits, the jelly will not "set up" without help. Either powdered or liquid pectin must be used or you will have just a jar of herb-flavored sugar syrup. I prefer to use liquid pectin.

NATIVE AMERICAN LEMON JELLY INFUSED WITH FRESH HERBS (cont'd)

2 cups water
3/4 cup freshly squeezed lemon juice

1/4 cup *firmly-packed* fresh lemon balm (*Melissa officinalis*) leaves
1/4 cup *finely chopped* fresh chives
1/4 cup *finely chopped* fresh thyme leaves
1/4 cup *finely chopped* fresh marjoram leaves
1/4 cup *finely chopped* fresh basil leaves
2 tablespoons *finely chopped* fresh tarragon leaves
2 tablespoons finely chopped fresh fennel fronds

3 1/2 cups sugar
1 pouch (3 ounces) liquid pectin

Sterilize five 1/2-pint canning jars. Also sterilize lids and rings for jars.

In a saucepan set over *MEDIUM* heat, combine water, lemon juice, and all the *finely* chopped herb leaves. Bring to the boil. Remove from heat, cover, and allow to stand for about 20 minutes. Set a fine sieve over a large measuring cup. Pour leaves and the infusion they have formed through the sieve. Empty and wash out the sieve. Set it over a clean large non-aluminum kettle. To insure a clear jelly, line the sieve with a cotton tea towel and pour the infusion through the tea towel-lined sieve.

In a large, non-aluminum kettle, combine 2 cupfuls of the herb infusion and lemon juice. Stir in sugar. Place over *MEDIUM-HIGH* heat and bring to a *full boil*—a boil which can not be stirred down.

While stirring with a metal spoon, add fruit pectin. Continue stirring constantly while allowing mixture to return to the boil. *Boil for 1 minute. Immediately,* remove from heat. Stir and skim off all foam or it will solidify as chunks in the clear jelly

Ladle into five hot, sterilized 1/2-pint canning jars, leaving a 3/4-inch clearance to the rim of the jar. Carefully wipe lips of jars. Seal with hot, sterilized lids and rings. Process in hot-water-bath canner for 10 minutes, *timing from the moment the water reaches a full rolling boil.* Remove to surface covered with thick towels or newspapers. Allow to cool for 24 hours *undisturbed.* Check to be sure jars are sealed before labeling and storing in a dark, cool, dry place.* Loosen or remove rings before storing.

Yields five 1/2 pint jarfuls

Notes: *Any jars that do not seal can be stored in the refrigerator for about one month or resealed using a *new lid.*

This recipe can not be doubled.

1/72 SERVING (i. e., per tablespoonful) –
PROTEIN = 0.0 g.; FAT = 0.0 g.; CARBOHYDRATE = 11.2 g.;
CALORIES = 40; CALORIES FROM FAT = 0%

STRAWBERRY, MELON, AND BLACK PEPPER *SALSA*
TPT - 25 hours and 20 minutes;
24 hours = cooling period

Like any western salsa or eastern chutney, the juxtaposition of fruits and spices brings the taste buds to life. You may think that Native Americans began to use black peppercorns only after the products of the Asian spice trade spread to their culinary tradition from Europeans but a common and inexpensive substitute for black pepper comes from the seeds of a tree that is native to Central and South America called the Money Pod Tree or Rain Tree (Albizia saman or Samanea saman). It is an astounding tree that can grow to one hundred feet in height with a spread of two hundred feet. The finely chopped gingerroot that I add to this salsa is a homage to the use of wild ginger (Asarum caudatum), whose slender rhizomes were used medicinally by Native Americans of the American Northwest and southern Canada to treat infections, headaches, intestinal disorders, tuberculosis, and as a general tonic and pain reliever. This is an easy, savory preserve. It enhances almost any menu. The fruits, the black pepper, the onion, and the gingerroot . . . It is a sparkling taste.

The Americas—The Native American Gift

STRAWBERRY, MELON, AND BLACK PEPPER *SALSA* (cont'd)

2 cups white wine vinegar
2 cups sugar

8 cups well-washed, diced ripe strawberries
8 cups diced cantaloupe
2 tablespoons *finely slivered,* fresh, *organic* lime zest
1/4 cup freshly squeezed lime juice
1 cup *finely* chopped onion
2 teaspoons coarsely cracked black peppercorns
1/2 teaspoon ground allspice *or* ground spicebush berries, if available
1 1/2 teaspoons salt
2 teaspoons *finely* chopped fresh gingerroot

Sterilize six pint canning jars. Also sterilize lids and rings for jars.

In a large kettle, combine vinegar and sugar. Bring to the boil over *MEDIUM* heat. Boil for about 5 minutes until sugar is dissolved. Stir occasionally.

Add diced strawberries and cantaloupe, lime zest, lime juice, *finely* chopped onion, cracked peppercorns, ground allspice, salt, and gingerroot. Cook over *LOW* heat, uncovered, for about 25 minutes until somewhat thickened. Stir frequently.

Ladle into six sterilized pint canning jars. Carefully wipe rims of jars. Seal with hot, sterilized lids and rings. Process in hot-water-bath canner for 15 minutes, *timing from the moment the water comes to a full rolling boil.* Remove to surface covered with thick towels or newspapers. Allow to cool for 24 hours *undisturbed*. Check to be sure jars are sealed before labeling and storing in a dark, cool, dry place.* Loosen or remove rings before storing.

Yields six pint jarfuls

Note: *Any jars that do not seal can be stored in the refrigerator for several months or resealed using a *new lid.*

1/96 SERVING (i. e., 2 tablespoonfuls) –
PROTEIN = 0.2 g.; FAT = 0.08 g.; CARBOHYDRATE = 4.8 g.;
CALORIES = 27; CALORIES FROM FAT = 3%

INDIAN PUDDING
TPT - 1 hour and 55 minutes

Indian pudding is one of the few foods for which we give credit to the native people who helped us adapt to this land. A colonial American adaptation of the British "hasty pudding," which in itself evolved from an ancient porridge, Indian pudding utilized corn instead of wheat, which was more plenteous and less expensive in the Colonies. The treasured spices, held under lock and key by the mistress of the house, added something the Native Americans did not know until the coming of the Europeans. Contemporary cooks view this dish as a dessert; colonial cooks prepared it as a vegetable accompaniment to meats or as meal in itself. It is said that Abigail Adams traditionally served an Indian pudding for "Sunday night supper," as did the Theodore Roosevelts. Edith Carow Roosevelt, Teddy's Connecticut-born wife, made a version of the dish in a large crock, as traditional on Long Island as it was in New England and similar to the recipe which follows.

1 3/4 cups skimmed milk

1/4 cup *cold* skimmed milk
3 1/2 tablespoons yellow corn meal

2 tablespoons butter
2 tablespoons blackstrap molasses
2 tablespoons firmly packed *light* brown sugar
1/4 teaspoon ground ginger
1/4 teaspoon ground cinnamon
1/4 cup *preservative-free dark* raisins
1 large egg—well-beaten

1/2 cup *cold* skimmed milk

Light cream *or* vanilla ice cream

Prepare a 1-quart bean pot* by coating with non-stick lecithin spray coating or by buttering.

In a saucepan set over *MEDIUM* heat, scald 1 3/4 cupfuls milk.

Meanwhile, in the top half of a double boiler set over simmering water, combine 1/4 cupful *cold* milk and yellow corn meal. Using a wooden spoon, stir until smooth. Add scalded milk, stir thoroughly, and cook, uncovered, over simmering water for 20 minutes, or until smooth and thickened. Stir frequently.

Add butter, molasses, brown sugar, ground ginger and cinnamon, raisins, and well-beaten egg to corn meal mixture. Stir until thoroughly combined.

Turn into prepared bean pot. Pour the remaining 1/2 cupful *cold* milk over, but *do not stir it in!*

Place in the center of a *cold* oven. Bake, *uncovered*, at 300 degrees F. for 1 hour, or until set.

INDIAN PUDDING (cont'd)

*Serve warm*** with cream or with vanilla ice cream, if preferred.

Yields 5 servings
adequate for 3-4 people

Notes: *If you do not have a bean pot, this may be prepared in a 1- or 1 1/2-quart soufflé dish or other baking dish. Preheat oven to 325 degrees F. and bake pudding, uncovered, for about 50 minutes, or until set.

**If baked ahead of time and kept warm on a warming tray, the resultant pudding is of exquisite texture.

This recipe may be increased by one-half quite satisfactorily. Use 2 medium eggs and a 1 1/2-quart bean pot. Bake for about 1 1/2 hours.

1/5 SERVING – PROTEIN = 5.3 g.; FAT = 6.1 g.; CARBOHYDRATE = 26.5 g.;
CALORIES = 181; CALORIES FROM FAT = 30%

IROQUOIS CHERRIES IN MAPLE SYRUP

TPT - 35 minutes;
30 minutes = refrigeration period

It is not surprising that this simple, but very flavorful, dessert seems very comfortable and familiar to me. Its roots are in the cuisine of member tribes of the Iroquois Nation, the Haudenosaunee, "people of the long house," who lived and still live near to where I grew up. My grandmother and my mother always canned sour cherries which were used for pies, pies that I will never forget. The tartness of the cherries surrounded with sweet is a taste sensation all but lost today. Few people I know bake cherry pies and nobody I know explores the wonderfulness of sour cherries which I am still able to find at our farmers' market. This dessert gives just a hint of the possibilities.

**1 can (16-ounces) water-packed, pitted tart
   (or sour) red cherries—drained
1/4 cup white sugar
1/4 cup pure maple syrup**

In a saucepan set over *LOW-MEDIUM* heat, combine drained cherries, sugar, and maple syrup. Cook, stirring constantly, until sugar is completed dissolved. Turn into a serving dish.

Refrigerate for at least 30 minutes.

Serve chilled, with syrup spooned over each serving.

Yields 4 servings
adequate for 4 people

Note: This recipe is easily doubled, when required.

1/4 SERVING – PROTEIN = 0.0 g.; FAT = 0.0 g.; CARBOHYDRATE = 38.9 g.;
CALORIES = 156; CALORIES FROM FAT = 0%

The Americas–**The Native American Gift**

NATIVE AMERICAN CRANBERRY AND BLACK WALNUT SAUCE / DESSERT
TPT - 53 minutes;
30 minutes = refrigeration period

To label this as simply a Native American dish is an unforgivable generalization for which I apologize. It comes from the tribes that had access to cranberries and black walnuts in the Northeast—New England, New Jersey, and Long Island—and in Canada, but to give it a specific origin is impossible. Perhaps to the north the syrup from the maple harvest would have been further processed into sugar loaves; perhaps to the south the syrup would have been used for such dishes as this. Please do not try to substitute English walnuts for black walnuts. Black walnuts have a unique taste that can not be approximated so do search out someone with a black walnut tree and make a deal. Try this for a Thanksgiving dinner and watch the looks of surprise.

1 pound fresh *or* **frozen cranberries**
1/2 cup *preservative-free* **black walnut meats**
   —carefully picked over and chopped
1/4 cup *boiling* **water**
2 tablespoons *light* **brown sugar**

1/4 cup pure maple syrup

Wash cranberries thoroughly and discard any of poor quality. Drain well.

In a saucepan set over *MEDIUM* heat, combine cranberries, chopped black walnuts, *boiling* water, and brown sugar. Cook, uncovered, until cranberries pop—about 15 minutes. Stir occasionally.

Add maple syrup and allow to heat through. Remove from heat. Refrigerate for at least 30 minutes.

Turn into serving bowl or sauceboat. Serve chilled or at room temperature with grilled or roasted vegetables and other main course offerings where a sweet–tart relish will compliment.*

Yields 6 servings
adequate for 4 people

Notes: *This sauce makes an interesting dessert. Simply spoon into individual dessert dishes and top with a generous dollop of whipped cream.

If desired, a pinch of ground allspice or ground spicebush berries may be added.

When required, this dish may be doubled.

1/6 SERVING – PROTEIN = 2.3 g.; FAT = 9.1 g.; CARBOHYDRATE = 23.0 g.;
CALORIES = 179; CALORIES FROM FAT = 46%

CUSTARD PUMPKIN PIE
TPT - 1 hour and 26 minutes

Although the dates for the nationally-observed Thanksgiving celebrations in the United States and Canada differ, the choice of pumpkin/squash pie is traditional in both countries. Evaporated milk is favored over fresh milk to make pumpkin pies in the Maritime Provinces and Newfoundland, as well as in our New England states. The result is a deceptively rich texture that we are sure you will appreciate. It would not be Thanksgiving for me without this dessert, served in my family each Thanksgiving for as long as I can remember. My contribution to this was the whole wheat crust, which, we think, makes it even better.

3 large egg yolks
1 1/2 cups *canned* **pumpkin—***unseasoned*
   and *unsweetened**
3/4 cup firmly packed *light* **brown sugar**
1 teaspoon ground cinnamon
1 teaspoon ground ginger
1/4 teaspoon ground cloves
1/4 teaspoon ground nutmeg
1 teaspoon pure vanilla extract
1 1/2 cups evaporated *skimmed* **milk**

2 large egg whites

1 deep-dish 9-inch *unbaked* **WHOLE WHEAT PIE CRUST** *[see index]*

Whipped heavy cream, for garnish**

Preheat oven to 350 degrees F.

In a large mixing bowl, using a wire whisk, beat egg yolks until thick and lemon-colored. Add pumpkin purée, brown sugar, ground cinnamon, ginger, cloves, and nutmeg, and vanilla extract. Beat well. Add undiluted evaporated milk. Combine thoroughly.

CUSTARD PUMPKIN PIE (cont'd)

Using an electric mixer fitted with *grease-free* beaters or by hand using a *grease-free* wire whisk, beat egg whites in a *grease-free* bowl until soft peaks form. *Whisk-fold* beaten egg whites *gently*, but *thoroughly*, into pumpkin mixture.

Pour into prepared *unbaked* pie crust. (Any surplus may be baked in custard cups for a snack . . . or a sample!)

Bake in preheated 350 degree F. oven for about 40 minutes, or until a knife inserted into the center comes out clean. (Note that the consistency will be softer than that of other pumpkin pies.)

Cool completely before serving. After cooling to room temperature, the pie may be refrigerated, if desired.

Garnish each serving with whipped heavy cream.**

Yields 8 slices

1/8 SERVING (without whipped cream) –
PROTEIN = 8.8 g.; FAT = 8.6 g.; CARBOHYDRATE = 40.4 g.;
CALORIES = 268; CALORIES FROM FAT = 29%

Notes: *Canned pumpkin is specified because it is a thicker, more flavorful purée. Cooked, puréed, and strained fresh pumpkin may be used but we recommend that you mix it half and half with cooked, puréed, and strained fresh Golden Nugget or Acorn squash.

**A festive topping can be prepared by folding about 2 tablespoonfuls of PEAR MINCEMEAT WITH PECANS *[see index]* into 1 cupful whipped heavy cream. A few drops of rum may be added, if desired.

This recipe may be doubled for two 9-inch pies quite satisfactorily.

SNOW FOOD, SWEET POPCORN CLUSTERS IN THE STYLE OF THE IROQUOIS
TPT - 34 minutes;
20 minutes = cooling period

Popcorn has always been a sit-by-the-fire winter food in our family. When the sweet sap begins to flow in the sugar maples, the popcorn is again a treat, a treat that I learned to enjoy while growing up in upstate New York while everybody downstate was eating caramel corn. Yes, we did spoon the sticky popcorn–nut mixture onto the freshly fallen snow to cool and usually sat right there in a snowbank and ate it all.

**4 cups air–popped corn *without butter or salt*
1/4 cup *preservative-free* pecan pieces**

**1 tablespoon butter
1/4 cup pure maple syrup
1/4 teaspoon salt**

Cover a counter top area or a large bread board with waxed paper.

Prepare a shallow baking pan by coating with non-stick lecithin spray coating. Add popped corn and pecan pieces. Toss.

In a medium-sized saucepan, combine butter, maple syrup, and salt. Attach a candy thermometer to the side of the pan. Cook over *MEDIUM-HIGH* heat, stirring frequently, until mixture reaches 260 degrees F., *the hard-ball stage. Remove from heat immediately,* detach candy thermometer, and pour hot syrup in a thin stream evenly over popcorn–nut mixture. Toss to coat popcorn and nuts. *Allow to cool completely*—about 20 minutes. Turn into a serving dish.

Yields 8 servings
adequate for 4 people

Note: This recipe may be doubled, when required.

1/8 SERVING (about one-half cupful) –
PROTEIN = 1.7 g.; FAT = 5.4 g.; CARBOHYDRATE = 13.7 g.;
CALORIES = 107; CALORIES FROM FAT = 45%

APPENDIX

These are the workhorses referenced frequently in this volume.

SALAD DRESSINGS and VINEGARS

Blender Mayonnaise	675
Classic French Dressing	676
Creamy Italian Dressing	677
Danish Spiced Vinegar	677
Garlic – Basil Vinegar	678
Lemon Vinaigrette *Dijon*	678
Mixed Flower Vinegar with Oregano	679
Pear – Anise Hyssop Vinegar	679
Rosemary Vinegar	680
Spiced Orange Vinegar	680
Sweet and Tart Cranberry Vinegar	681

SAUCES - SAVORY

Fresh Marinara Sauce	682
Homemade Tomato Ketchup	683
Homemade Vegan Worcestershire – Style Sauce	683
Italian Sauce in the Hunter's Style for Vegetables and Pasta	684
Mustard Sauce	685
Tomato Mushroom Sauce	686

SAUCES - SWEET

Australian Simple Blackberry Sauce or Dessert	687
Cinnamon Syrup	687
Custard Sauce	688
Family's Choice Pancake and Waffle Syrup	688
Fresh Orange Custard Sauce	689
Lemon Sauce	689
Lemon Syrup	690
Lemon Verbena Syrup	690

SOUP STOCKS

Vegetable Stock from Soup	691
Vegetarian Stocks for Soups, Stews, and Sauces	692
Wild Mushroom Stock	694

APPENDIX of BASIC RECIPES

THIS and THAT:

Garlic Oil	694
Garlic with Thyme and Bay in Oil . .	695
Our Granola	696
Rolled Sugar Cookies	697
Seasoning Mixture for Dehydrated Soy Meat Analogue . . .	698
Wheaten Biscuit Mix	698

SALAD DRESSINGS and VINEGARS:

BLENDER MAYONNAISE
TPT - 3 minutes

I began making my own mayonnaise when we were first married. There was never a jar of commercial mayonnaise in our refrigerator for decades. Then came a national health crisis; raw eggs were spreading Salmonella infections. I abdicated. It was not until the industry responded with pasteurized eggs that homemade mayonnaise returned to our table.

1/3 cup *fat-free* pasteurized eggs—*brought to room temperature**
1/2 teaspoon salt
1/2 teaspoon dry mustard
1/4 cup vegetable oil, of choice**

3/4 cup vegetable oil, of choice

1 tablespoon freshly squeezed lemon juice—*strained*

In the dry container of the electric blender or work bowl of the food processor fitted with steel knife, place pasteurized eggs, salt, dry mustard, and 1/4 cupful oil.

With cover on blender or processor, turn on machine. *Immediately remove cover insert and very slowly add remaining 3/4 cupful of oil in a thin, steady stream.*

When mixture has *emulsified and thickened*, gradually add strained lemon juice. Turn motor off and spoon mayonnaise into a glass jar. *Store in least cold area of refrigerator* to prevent separation.

Yields about 1 1/4 cupfuls

Notes: *Because raw eggs present the danger of *Salmonella* poisoning, commercially-available pasteurized eggs are recommended for use in preparing this dish.

**We prefer to use sunflower oil when making mayonnaise. It gives a very light tasting mayonnaise.

Do not attempt to double this recipe.

If mayonnaise curdles, as it has done on occasion to all who make it, try adding a bit of the pasteurized egg product *gradually— teaspoonful by teaspoonful*. This is our preferred rescue but it can also be accomplished with a tablespoonful of water, vinegar or lemon juice, or prepared mustard if the change of flavor is desired.

VARIATIONS:
A dash of Tabasco sauce may be added, if to your taste.

Increase mustard or add prepared MUSTARD SAUCE (see *index*) or *Dijon*-styled mustard, to taste, for a MUSTARD MAYONNAISE.

Two teaspoonfuls wine vinegar may be substituted for lemon juice, if preferred, for a more classic mayonnaise.

One and two tablespoonfuls freshly squeezed orange juice may be substituted for lemon juice for a light ORANGE MAYONNAISE.

APPENDIX of BASIC RECIPES

BLENDER MAYONNAISE (cont'd)

Using a garlic press, press a clove of garlic into emulsified mayonnaise. Turn machine on briefly to integrate. Another method of making GARLIC MAYONNAISE is to include 1 or 2 tablespoonfuls of GARLIC OIL *[see index]* as part of the 1 cupful oil used. GARLIC OIL is a most useful item and can easily be prepared by refrigerating peeled garlic cloves in vegetable oil. Not only is this a way to store fresh garlic, the oil is available for any recipe where its pungency is appreciated such as in "stir-fries" and in spaghetti sauces. *Please note that garlic oil and garlic store in this manner are perishable. Do not keep for more than two weeks since mold can cause serious health problems.*

1/20 SERVING (i. e., per tablespoonful) –
PROTEIN = 0.5 g.; FAT = 11.0 g.; CARBOHYDRATE = 0.3 g.;
CALORIES = 102; CALORIES FROM FAT = 97 %

1/5 SERVING (i. e., per 1/4 cupful) –
PROTEIN = 2.0 g.; FAT = 44.0 g.; CARBOHYDRATE = 1.2 g.;
CALORIES = 408; CALORIES FROM FAT = 97%

CLASSIC FRENCH DRESSING
Vinaigrette

TPT - 1 hour and 2 minutes;
1 hour = flavor development period

This is the simple, basic French vinaigrette recipe that we have used for decades. It is all anyone really needs to bring out the taste of salad ingredients but just in case you, like I, can not leave a recipe alone, our variations are included in the notes.

1/2 cup vegetable oil, of choice
2 1/2 tablespoons red wine vinegar
1/8 teaspoon dry mustard
1/8 teaspoon freshly ground black pepper
1/8 teaspoon paprika*

In a jar with a tightly fitting lid or in a cruet with a tightly fitting top or cork, combine all ingredients. Shake vigorously and set aside for about 1 hour to allow for development of flavor. Alternately, if preferred, the electric blender or the food processor fitted with steel knife, may be used to produce a dressing which separates more slowly.

Always shake vigorously before serving.

Yields about 2/3 cupful

Notes: *The addition of paprika yields a beautifully rose-tinted dressing. It may be omitted, if preferred.

This recipe is easily doubled or tripled, when required.

Dried or fresh herbs may be added.

A fine TOMATO FRENCH DRESSING can be prepared by adding 1 tablespoonful thick tomato purée and half of a small garlic clove, *finely* chopped, to CLASSIC FRENCH DRESSING.

To prepare GARLIC FRENCH DRESSING, place a peeled garlic clove in prepared CLASSIC FRENCH DRESSING. Allow to stand for 2 days in the refrigerator. Remove and discard garlic clove. Bring to room temperature before serving.

If red wine vinegar is replaced with fresh lemon juice, an excellent LEMON FRENCH DRESSING results.

If red wine vinegar is replaced with tarragon vinegar, you have TARRAGON FRENCH DRESSING.

CLASSIC FRENCH DRESSING (cont'd)

1/10 SERVING (i. e., per tablespoonful) –
PROTEIN = trace; FAT = 8.9 g.; CARBOHYDRATE = 0.2 g.;
CALORIES = 81; CALORIES FROM FAT = 99%

CREAMY ITALIAN DRESSING
TPT - 6 minutes

This creamy Italian-style dressing is a whole lot better tasting than any bottled dressing you have ever tried. If you serve the dressing from an antique glass-topped canning jar, you will send an immediate message. When my dad visited, he always checked the canning jars in the refrigerator to see what homemade salad dressings were on the menu.

1/2 cup *calorie-reduced or light* mayonnaise
1/4 cup **PLAIN YOGURT** *[see index] or*
  commercially-available plain yogurt
1 tablespoon red wine vinegar
1 tablespoon freshly squeezed lemon juice
1 tablespoon olive oil
1 teaspoon *vegetarian* Worcestershire sauce *or*
  HOMEMADE VEGAN WORCESTERSHIRE
  –STYLE SAUCE *[see index]*
1/2 teaspoon dried oregano—crushed
1 small garlic clove—*very finely* chopped

In a mixing bowl, using a wire whisk, blend mayonnaise and yogurt thoroughly. Beat in vinegar, lemon juice, olive oil, Worcestershire sauce, crushed oregano, and *very finely* chopped garlic. Blend until smooth.

Pour into a jar and store in refrigerator until required.

Yields 1 cupful

Note: This recipe is easily doubled, when required.

1/16 SERVING (i. e., per tablespoonful) –
PROTEIN = 0.2 g.; FAT = 3.3 g.; CARBOHYDRATE = 1.0 g.;
CALORIES = 35; CALORIES FROM FAT = 85%

DANISH SPICED VINEGAR
Kryddereddike
TPT - 1 week and 5 minutes;
1 week = flavor development period

Whenever we use this vinegar to thin mayonnaise or make a vinaigrette or marinade, we can easily imagine ourselves across the Atlantic and in Denmark again. It is a unique and exciting combination of flavors.

3 1/2 cups rice wine vinegar
3 tablespoons yellow mustard seeds
1 tablespoon whole allspice
1 tablespoon *white* peppercorns
1 teaspoon dillweed seeds
1 teaspoon celery seeds
3 bay leaves—halved
3 *thin* lemon slices

Sterilize a 1-quart bottle or jar.

Put all ingredients into sterilized 1-quart bottle or jar. Cap.

Allow to stand at room temperature in a dark cupboard for 1 week to allow for both flavor and color development.

Sterilize a clear, condiment bottle.

Strain vinegar from spices into sterilized condiment bottle.

Store vinegar at cool room temperature away from light for up to a year.

Yields 3 1/2 cupfuls

Note: This recipe may be doubled or tripled or quadrupled with ease—helpful if you should want to give bottles as gifts.

1/56 SERVING (i. e., per tablespoonful) –
PROTEIN = 0.0 g.; FAT = 0.0 g.; CARBOHYDRATE = 0.0 g.;
CALORIES = 0; CALORIES FROM FAT = 0%

APPENDIX of BASIC RECIPES

GARLIC – BASIL VINEGAR

TPT - 1 week and 6 minutes;
1 week = flavor development period

The flavor or this vinegar is absolutely wonderful and it has essentially become our "house vinegar." We find adding a touch of both garlic and basil to a dish or salad using the vinegar almost as simple as making the vinegar.

2 cups distilled white vinegar
4 large garlic cloves—peeled
1 fresh basil top-floret—well-washed
1 fresh Dark Opal basil top-floret—well-washed*

Sterilize a one-quart canning jar, lid, and ring.

Pour vinegar into sterilized condiment bottle. Insert peeled garlic cloves and well-washed basil florets. Using a chopstick, stir leaves for about 30 seconds to start the infusion. Seal the jar and place in a cool, dark place for 1 week.

Sterilize a clear, condiment bottle, or several if you are planning to give the vinegar as gifts.

Place a fine sieve over a one-quart measuring cup or mixing bowl. Strain the vinegar, discarding the garlic cloves and basil recovered.

Pour vinegar into sterilized condiment bottle or bottles. Cap and label.

Store at cool room temperature for up to a year.

Yields 2 cupfuls

Notes: *Dark Opal basil *(Ocimum basilicum 'Purpurascens')* adapts well to most full sun garden settings. It is more easily grown from nursery seedlings than from seeds. This basil variety, as well as the ruffled varieties, give a purple blush to the vinegar which is most attractive.

This recipe may be doubled or tripled or quadrupled with ease—helpful if you should want to give bottles as gifts.

1/32 SERVING (i. e., per tablespoonful) –
PROTEIN = 0.0 g.; FAT = 0.0 g.; CARBOHYDRATE = 0.7 g.;
CALORIES = 1; CALORIES FROM FAT = 0%

LEMON *VINAIGRETTE DIJON*
Vinaigrette au Citron

TPT - 1 hour and 2 minutes;
1 hour = flavor development period

This classic French salad dressing compliments almost any salad no matter how simple the ingredients. I love to serve it over sliced, ripe pear slices.

6 tablespoons *extra virgin* olive oil
2 tablespoons freshly squeezed lemon juice
1/4 teaspoon *finely* and freshly grated lemon zest
1/2 teaspoon country-style *Dijon* mustard

In a jar with a tightly fitting lid or in a cruet with a tightly fitting top or cork, combine all ingredients. Shake vigorously and set aside for about 1 hour to allow for development of flavor.

Alternately, if preferred, the electric blender or the food processor fitted with steel knife, may be used to produce a dressing which separates more slowly.

Always shake vigorously before serving. To avoid rancidity, try to prepare dressing within an hour or two of serving.

Yields 6 tablespoonfuls

Note: This recipe is easily doubled or tripled, when required.

1/6 SERVING (i. e., per tablespoonful) –
PROTEIN = 0.2 g.; FAT = 8.4 g.; CARBOHYDRATE = 2.7 g.;
CALORIES = 76; CALORIES FROM FAT = 95%

APPENDIX of BASIC RECIPES

MIXED FLOWER VINEGAR WITH OREGANO
TPT - 1 week and 14 minutes;
1 week = flavor development period

I sincerely think that this is one of the most perfect vinegars I have ever evolved. The flavors are balanced perfectly; there is a subtlety that is exciting without being assertive. And, it is fun to wait for the flowers to be ready to make each year's new batch. Yes, it does border on being a perfect experience.

2 cups mixed *Borage*, chive, lavender, pansies, and nasturtium flowers—pulled from flower stems, *very* well-washed, and well-dried
3 *Calendula* flowers—pulled from flower stems, *very* well-washed, and well-dried
Petals of 4 daylilies—well-washed and well-dried
2 four-inch sprigs of Italian oregano leaves *without* flowers—*very* well-washed and well-dried
2 small thyme flower heads—*very* well-washed and well-dried
2 four-inch sprigs of Italian oregano *with* flowers—*very* well-washed and well-dried
1 small garlic clove—peeled
3 1/2 cups rice wine vinegar

Sterilize a 1-quart bottle or jar.

Pack well-washed and well-dried flowers, thyme flower heads, sprigs of oregano, and garlic clove into sterilized 1-quart bottle or jar. Pour rice wine vinegar over blossoms and herb sprigs, being sure to cover completely. Cap.

Allow to stand at room temperature in a dark cupboard for 1 week to allow for both flavor and color development.

Sterilize a clear, condiment bottle.

Strain vinegar from flowers and leaves into sterilized condiment bottle.

Store vinegar at cool room temperature away from light for up to six months.

Yields 3 1/2 cupfuls

Note: This recipe may be doubled or tripled or quadrupled with ease; helpful if you should want to give bottles as gifts

1/56 SERVING (i. e., per tablespoonful) –
PROTEIN = 0.0 g.; FAT = 0.0 g.; CARBOHYDRATE = 0.0 g.;
CALORIES = 0.0; CALORIES FROM FAT = 0%

PEAR – ANISE HYSSOP VINEGAR
TPT - 1 week and 4 minutes;
1 week = flavor development period

The taste of a simple green salad with shreds of Armenian string cheese or that of a fruit salad with crumbled feta cheese are wonderfully complicated by the flavors of a vinaigrette or a mayonnaise dressing made with this vinegar.

1 large, *ripe*, but *firm*, Bartlett pear—well-washed, peeled, cored and chopped
3 anise hyssop flower heads with leaves—well-rinsed
8 three-inch stem segments with leaves—well-rinsed
6 whole peppercorns
One 2-inch piece of a vanilla pod
2 cups white wine vinegar

Sterilize a 1-quart bottle or jar.

Put chopped pear, anise hyssop flowers heads and stem segments into sterilized 1-quart bottle or jar. Add peppercorns and vanilla pod piece. Pour white wine vinegar over, being sure to cover completely. Cap.

Allow to stand at room temperature in a dark cupboard for 1 week to allow for both flavor and color development.

Sterilize a clear, condiment bottle and a large, glass measuring cup.

Using a fine sieve or a sieve lined with culinary cheesecloth, strain vinegar from infusion elements into the measuring cup. Discard residue. Rinse sieve and cheesecloth thoroughly. Set clean sieve lined with clean cheesecloth over sterilized condiment bottle and strain the vinegar again.

APPENDIX of BASIC RECIPES

PEAR – ANISE HYSSOP VINEGAR (cont'd)

Store vinegar at cool room temperature away from light or in refrigerator for up to six months.

Yields 3 cupfuls

Note: This recipe may be doubled or tripled or quadrupled with ease—helpful if you should want to give bottles as gifts.

1/56 SERVING (i. e., per tablespoonful) –
PROTEIN = 0.0 g.; FAT = 0.0 g.; CARBOHYDRATE = 0.0 g.;
CALORIES = 0.0; CALORIES FROM FAT = 0%**

ROSEMARY VINEGAR
TPT - 72 hours and 10 minutes;
72 hours = marination period

I like rosemary, but not a lot of rosemary and, further, I do think you can ruin the whole rosemary experience when the needle pieces get stuck in your teeth. This rosemary vinegar is my favorite way to introduce the exciting flavor of this fragrant herb garden evergreen into my cooking.

1 cup distilled white vinegar

1 1/2 tablespoons fresh rosemary—well-washed and coarsely chopped
6 whole peppercorns
A small piece of bay leaf

2 whole, fresh rosemary sprigs—well-washed

In a non-aluminum saucepan, set over *MEDIUM-HIGH* heat, bring vinegar to the boil. Remove saucepan from heat.

Stir chopped rosemary, peppercorns, and bay leaf piece into hot vinegar. Pour into a clean jar*, cover, and allow to steep at room temperature for *three full days*. Shake occasionally.

Prepare a clear, condiment bottle, a fine sieve, a glass measuring cup, and a funnel by sterilizing each.

Line a fine sieve with sterile culinary cheesecloth. Strain vinegar into measuring cup. Pour vinegar through sterilized funnel into sterilized condiment bottle. Cap bottle and allow to cool to room temperature.

Insert well-washed, whole rosemary sprigs into *cooled* vinegar and recap.

Store at cool room temperature for up to a year.

Yields 1 cupful

Notes: *A pint canning jar is an ideal choice.

This recipe may be doubled or tripled or quadrupled with ease—helpful if you should want to give bottles as gifts.

1/16 SERVING (i. e., per tablespoonful) –
PROTEIN = 0.0 g.; FAT = 0.0 g.; CARBOHYDRATE = 0.7 g.;
CALORIES = 1; CALORIES FROM FAT = 0%

SWEET SPICED ORANGE VINEGAR
TPT - 1 week and 70 minutes
1 hour = cooling period;
1 week = flavor development period

This is an excellent base for a vinaigrette or a sesame dressing to serve with fruit salads.

3 1/2 cups rice wine vinegar
3 tablespoons sugar
6 whole cloves
5 whole allspice berries
1 cinnamon quill—*broken*

3 oranges—*well-washed* and *thinly* sliced

Sterilize a 1-quart bottle or jar.

In a saucepan set over *MEDIUM* heat, combine vinegar, sugar, whole cloves and allspice berries, and cinnamon quill pieces. Bring to the boil. Reduce heat to *LOW* and allow to simmer for 5 minutes. Remove from heat.

SWEET SPICED ORANGE VINEGAR (cont'd)

Add orange slices. Cover and set aside. Allow to cool at room temperature for 1 hour.

Pour spiced vinegar and *one-third* of orange slices into sterilized jar. Cap.

Allow to stand at room temperature in a dark cupboard for 1 week to allow for both flavor and color development.

Sterilize a clear, condiment bottle.

Using a fine sieve or a sieve lined with culinary cheesecloth, strain vinegar from orange slices and spices into sterilized condiment bottle.

Store vinegar at cool room temperature away from light for up to three months.

Yields 3 1/2 cupfuls

Note: This recipe may be doubled or tripled or quadrupled with ease; helpful if you should want to give bottles as gifts.

1/56 SERVING (i. e., per tablespoonful) –
PROTEIN = 0.0 g.; FAT = 0.0 g.; CARBOHYDRATE = 0.8 g.;
CALORIES = 2; CALORIES FROM FAT = 0%

SWEET AND TART CRANBERRY VINEGAR
TPT - 1 hour and 28 minutes;
30 minutes = cooling period

This is the perfect vinegar to use for a vinaigrette for salads in which dried cranberries are to be included or as the vinegar in almost any salad dressing when a cranberry dessert is planned.

1 cup fresh *or* frozen cranberries
1/2 cup sugar
1 cup *boiling* water

1 1/2 cups distilled white vinegar

3 fresh cranberries, for garnish

Sterilize a clear, condiment bottle.

Wash cranberries thoroughly and discard any of poor quality.

In a saucepan set over *LOW-MEDIUM* heat, combine washed cranberries, sugar, and *boiling* water. Simmer until quantity in pan is reduced by half—about 40 minutes.

Strain through a fine sieve into a mixing bowl. Wash sieve well. Line clean sieve with culinary cheesecloth and strain again.

Add strained cranberry juice to vinegar.

Pour cranberry vinegar into sterilized condiment bottle. Allow to cool to room temperature—about 30 minutes.

Add reserved cranberries to garnish. Cap.

Store vinegar at cool room temperature away from light for up to three months.

Yields about 4 cupfuls

Note: This recipe may be halved or doubled, when required.

1/64 SERVING (i. e., per tablespoonful) –
PROTEIN = 0.0 g.; FAT = 0.0 g.; CARBOHYDRATE = 0.0 g.;
CALORIES = 0; CALORIES FROM FAT = 0%

APPENDIX of BASIC RECIPES

SAVORY SAUCES:

FRESH *MARINARA* SAUCE
Salsa Marinara

TPT - about 2 hours and 20 minutes

If you have always wondered why a marinara sauce includes no residents of the sea, you will be interested to know that "marinara" simply means "mariners's style." It is, basically, a "sugo di pomodoro" in which garlic, onions, and the inspiration of the cook is added to tomatoes. This is our basic workhorse sauce, canned every September for our winter and spring use.

2 tablespoons *extra virgin* olive oil
1 large onion—*thinly* sliced
4 large garlic cloves—*finely* chopped

8-10 large tomatoes—peeled, seeded, and chopped
2 cups plum tomato purée—preferably homemade
1 can (6 ounces) tomato paste
1/3 cup *finely* chopped fresh, Italian flat-leafed
    parsley leaves
1 1/2 teaspoons dried oregano—crushed
1/4 teaspoon dried thyme—crushed
1/4 teaspoon freshly ground black pepper, or to taste
1 bay leaf—halved*
1 cup water

In a skillet set over *MEDIUM* heat, heat oil. Add onion slices and *finely* chopped garlic. Sauté until onion is soft and translucent, *allowing neither the onion nor the garlic to brown.*

In a kettle or large saucepan, combine chopped tomatoes, tomato purée, tomato paste, *finely* chopped parsley, crushed oregano and thyme, black pepper, bay leaf pieces, and water. Add sautéed onion and garlic. Bring to the simmer and continue to simmer, uncovered, for about 2 to 2 1/2 hours until thickened to your liking. Stir occasionally. Remove and discard bay leaf pieces.

Serve as desired or freeze in quantities appropriate to future use demands.

Yields 7-8 cupfuls

Notes: *The bay leaf pieces are most easily recovered if secured inside a tea ball during the simmering process.

This sauce may be canned using the hot-water-bath method. Process pint jars for 20 minutes from a rolling boil.

1/16 SERVING (i. e., per 1/2 cupful) –
PROTEIN = 1.2 g.; FAT = 1.5 g.; CARBOHYDRATE = 5.2 g.;
CALORIES = 36; CALORIES FROM FAT = 37%

APPENDIX of BASIC RECIPES

HOMEMADE TOMATO KETCHUP
TPT - 16 minutes

It is almost sacrilegious for a Pennsylvanian, transplanted, as am I, or not, to use the "other brand of chocolate sauce" or to make their own ketchup. My grandmother taught me to make ketchup when I was first married. It was a laborious process. There were no food processors then so the old Universal grinder was attached to the table and a kettle sat on the floor to catch the mess. We did not use commercially canned tomato products so the ketchup was made during the busy canning season of the tomato harvest. There were no electric blenders or food processors to create a smooth product; we used a sieve and wooden spoons. The only freezers we had were in the tops of refrigerators so we canned the ketchup in the cold-pack canner and stored it in the fruit cellar. Naturally, I did not have a fruit cellar in our first apartment so my first attempt at ketchup spoiled and I did not visit the process again for many, many years. This simple ketchup is a wonderfully fresh tasting sauce that is low in sugar and sodium, if you choose salt-free canned tomato products. There is no need to can it since it keeps well in the refrigerator for several months when tightly sealed in a sterilized bottle or, if preferred, it can be frozen.

2 tablespoons *extra-virgin* olive oil
1/4 cup chopped onion

1 cup *diced* tomatoes canned in purée
1 cup tomato purée
1 tablespoon tomato paste
1/2 cup *loosely-packed light* brown sugar
3 tablespoons apple cider vinegar
1/4 teaspoon dry mustard powder
1/4 teaspoon ground cinnamon
1/8 teaspoon freshly ground mixed peppercorns
 —black, white, and red
1/8 teaspoon ground cloves
1/8 teaspoon ground allspice

Prepare two bottles by sterilizing both the bottles and the tops.* Sterilize a funnel too. Set aside until required.

In a skillet set over *LOW-MEDIUM* heat, heat oil. Add chopped onion and sauté until onions are soft and translucent, *being careful not to allow onions to brown*. Turn into work bowl of the food processor.

Add diced tomatoes, tomato purée, tomato paste, *light* brown sugar, cider vinegar, dry mustard, ground cinnamon, ground mixed peppercorns, ground cloves, and ground allspice. Process until ketchup is *very* smooth. Pour into the two sterilized bottles, seal, label, and store in the refrigerator.

Yields about 2 cupfuls

Notes: *The bottles in which rice wine vinegar is marketed are perfect.

If you have the desire for a saltier ketchup, try adding celery salt. The subtle celery taste adds interest.

This ketchup can be frozen with little loss of flavor.

1/32 SERVING (i. e., per tablespoonful) –
PROTEIN = 0.2 g.; FAT = 0.7 g.; CARBOHYDRATE = 2.9 g.;
CALORIES = 18; CALORIES FROM FAT = 35%

HOMEMADE VEGAN WORCESTERSHIRE–STYLE SAUCE
TPT - 10 minutes

Fish sauces have a long history as seasoning. Garum was used in Rome and its territories to cover up the gamey or spoiled cuts of meat and almost every Asian cuisine has a fish sauce seasoning. Although Lee and Perrins did introduce a vegetarian Worcestershire sauce many years ago, they have since ceased its production now claiming that Worcestershire sauce without fish, that is anchovies, would not be their historical Worcestershire sauce. Several companies picked up the challenge and do make a sauce which substitutes adequately for Worcestershire sauce. Since we have found the commercial vegetarian versions in neither our local grocery chain stores nor in our natural food stores and the shipping and handling charged by mail order sources raises the cost of the tablespoonful needed here and there, I set out to create a worthy substitute.

APPENDIX of BASIC RECIPES

HOMEMADE VEGAN WORCESTERSHIRE–STYLE SAUCE (cont'd)

1/2 cup water
1/4 cup *tamari* soy sauce
1/4 cup brown rice syrup
3 tablespoons TAMARIND LIQUID *[see index]*
1 tablespoon apple cider vinegar
1 tablespoon unsulfured molasses
2 tablespoons tamarind concentrate*
2 teaspoons *miso***
1 teaspoon mustard powder
1 teaspoon ground ginger
1/2 teaspoon onion powder
1/2 teaspoon ground cardamom
1/4 teaspoon freshly ground black pepper
Pinch ground cloves

In the container of the electric blender, combine water, soy sauce, brown rice syrup, apple cider vinegar, molasses, tamarind concentrate, *miso*, mustard powder, ginger, onion powder, ground cardamom, black pepper, and ground cloves. Blend until smooth. Turn into saucepan with water and corn starch.

Set saucepan over *MEDIUM* heat. Cook, stirring often with a wire whisk, until sauce comes to the boil. Remove from heat. Turn into a sterilized condiment bottle. Allow to cool to room temperature before putting the top on or cork in the bottle.

Store in refrigerator and use in same quantity as you would use the commercial Worcestershire sauce.

Yields 1 1/2 cupfuls

Notes: *Tamarind concentrate is found in Asian groceries and in the international section of many well-stocked grocery stores.

**Kome miso is a mild paste made from brown rice. It is available in Asian groceries and in natural food stores. *Mugi miso* is made from soybeans, barley, seaweed, and salt. It is aged to develop flavor and is stronger in taste. *Hacho miso* is even stronger in taste since it is made from soybeans without the mellowing effect of grains. Testing different *misos* in this sauce may be the only way to determine which *miso* is more pleasing to your palate.

Although this sauce keeps well when refrigerated, it can be halved if you prefer.

1/24 SERVING (per tablespoonful) –
PROTEIN = 0.1 g.; FAT = 0.3 g.; CARBOHYDRATE = 2.8 g.;
CALORIES = 12; CALORIES FROM FAT = 23%

ITALIAN SAUCE IN THE HUNTER'S STYLE FOR VEGETABLES AND *PASTA*
Salsa di Cacciatora
TPT -1 hour

When we first married, Ray kept asking if I could learn to make the "pollo alla cacciatora" that his father loved. Since his father had died many years before, I could not ask him and so I kept searching and trying different sauces but none ever coincided with Ray's childhood memory. One day, while helping friends move, someone brought a big bucket of KFC to nourish the volunteers. Ray exclaimed, "This is my dad's chicken cacciatora." My father-in-law had evidently loved Southern fried chicken and renamed it "pollo alla cacciatora" as a joke when Ray was very small. The voluminous file of valid hunters' sauces that I had accumulated yielded this sauce, which we enjoy with vegetables, pasta, or meatless "chicken" patties. Our only homage to the hunter is the inclusion of the mushrooms, which would have had to be hunted and gathered. Although many people add rosemary to this type of sauce, we add fresh sage leaves which would have been included in the "lepre alla cacciatora," popular in Calabria where my father-in-law was born. My mother-in-law would have deplored the addition of sugar but I feel it boosts the tomato flavor. This is a fabulous, fabulous sauce!

1 tablespoon *extra virgin* olive oil
1 tablespoon butter
1 medium onion—*finely* chopped
1 large stalk celery—*finely* chopped

1 bay leaf—halved*
4 large fresh sage leaves—*finely slivered*
1 tablespoon *finely* chopped fresh basil
1 large garlic clove—*very finely* chopped
1 pound fresh Italian Roma *or* Amish Paste plum
   tomatoes—peeled, seeded, and chopped**
1/4 teaspoon sugar
1 cup dry red wine
1/2 cup WILD MUSHROOM STOCK *[see index]*
Freshly ground black pepper, to taste *[see next page]*

ITALIAN SAUCE IN THE HUNTER'S STYLE FOR VEGETABLES AND *PASTA* (cont'd)

1/4 pound fresh *crimini* mushrooms—stems removed, rinsed and cleaned well with a brush, and sliced***

1 tablespoon KNEADED FLOUR FOR THICKENING (*Buerre Manie*) [see index] —or more, as needed

2 tablespoons light cream *or* half and half

In a skillet set over *MEDIUM* heat, heat oil and butter. Add *finely* chopped onion and celery and sauté until onion is soft and translucent, *being careful not to allow the vegetables to brown.*

Add bay leaf pieces, *finely slivered* sage, *finely* chopped basil, *very finely* chopped garlic, chopped tomatoes, sugar, wine, MUSHROOM STOCK, and black pepper. Allow to come to the boil. *Reduce heat to LOW*, cover tightly, and cook, stirring frequently for 20 minutes. Remove and discard bay leaf pieces.

Add mushroom slices and allow to cook, uncovered for about 10 minutes more.

Thicken the sauce by stirring in the *buerre manie* pinch-by-pinch, until of desired consistency. *Stir constantly while thickening.*

Stir cream into sauce. Remove from heat.****

Serve over vegetables, of choice, or over *pasta*, such as *falfalle, rigatoni, fettucine,* or *pappardelle*. Freeze any leftovers for a future menu.*****

Notes: *The bay leaf pieces are most easily recovered if secured inside a tea ball during the simmering process.

  **The flavor of this sauce is unique when made with fresh tomatoes but, if you must, you can substitute drained, canned Italian-style tomatoes.

  ***Reconstituted dry mushrooms can be substituted, if desired. Be sure to remove stems, and rinse well to remove any foreign matter.

  ****Reheat over *LOW* heat. Do not allow sauce to boil or the cream will curdle.

  *****I usually make a double batch and freeze it in quantities appropriate to our menu needs.

116 SERVING (i. e., about 1/4 cupful) –
PROTEIN = 0.8 g.; FAT = 1.8 g.; CARBOHYDRATE = 2.7 g.;
CALORIES = 29; CALORIES FROM FAT = 56%

MUSTARD SAUCE

TPT - 12 hours and 23 minutes;
12 hours = mustard dissolving period

Jack Tobin on WDAF in Kansas City gave a mustard sauce recipe on the air years and years ago. It became the start of experimentation to create an additive-free mustard which duplicated the taste of Nance's Mustard, a mustard sauce whose fame has now spread far from Rochester, New York, the city of its origin. Up until the late-1970s, when I evolved this version, I had had to take a trip to Rochester to buy the taste I loved so much.

1/2 cup distilled white vinegar
1/2 cup English-style dry mustard

1/4 cup *fat-free* pasteurized eggs (the equivalent of 1 egg)
1/4 cup sugar

In a small mixing bowl, using a wire whisk, beat dry mustard into vinegar. Cover bowl with plastic wrap and leave at room temperature for 12 hours, or overnight.

Turn into a heavy saucepan and, using a wire whisk again, beat in pasteurized eggs and sugar.*

Bring just to the boil over *LOW* heat, stirring almost constantly. *This can scorch easily and must be attended carefully.* Continue cooking until mixture coats a spoon or until of desired consistency. Cool completely at room temperature—about 30 minutes.

Using a fine sieve, strain MUSTARD SAUCE into a sterilized jar with tightly fitting lid. When *completely cooled*, fasten lid and refrigerate. It keeps well for several months, if refrigerated and tightly covered.

Yields about 1/2 cupful

MUSTARD SAUCE (cont'd)

Notes: *If you are using a non-stick saucepan in which you can not use a wire whisk, beat the ingredients in a missing bowl before adding to the saucepan.

Please note that 1/2 cupful of dry mustard is much closer to 2 ounces of the product than to 4 ounces, dry weights and measures being what they are.

This recipe is easily doubled, when required.

1/8 SERVING (i. e., per tablespoonful) –
PROTEIN = 2.3 g.; FAT = 1.8 g.; CARBOHYDRATE = 9.0 g.;
CALORIES = 61; CALORIES FROM FAT = 3%

TOMATO MUSHROOM SAUCE
Salsa di Pomodori con Funghi
TPT - 2 hours and 23 minutes

This is my favorite winter red sauce for pasta. The mushrooms add a "meatiness," a substantial feel-in-the-mouth, but because of the mushrooms, the sauce must be frozen and can not be canned as can our marinara sauce and is, therefore, a bit less convenient. I started evolving this recipe in my first apartment after starting my research position at the University of Michigan, so this is the result of fifty-some years of tweaking and I still enjoy it.

1 tablespoon *extra virgin* olive oil
1 large onion—sliced
2 large garlic cloves—*finely* chopped

3 cups fresh mushroom slices—*Agaricus* or *crimini*—sliced from mushrooms that have been trimmed, rinsed, and cleaned well with a brush

4 cups Italian plum tomato purée—preferably homemade without salt
1 can (6 ounces) tomato paste
1/3 cup chopped fresh Italian flat-leafed parsley
1 tablespoon *finely* chopped fresh basil *or*
  1 teaspoon *finely* chopped, commercially-available preserved basil*
1 1/2 teaspoons dried oregano—crushed
1/4 teaspoon dried thyme—crushed
1/4 teaspoon freshly ground black pepper, or to taste
1 bay leaf—halved**
1 cup water

In a large skillet set over *MEDIUM* heat, combine oil, onion slices, and *finely* chopped garlic. Sauté until onion is soft and translucent, *allowing neither the onion nor the garlic to brown.*

Add mushroom slices and sauté for an additional 3 minutes.

In a kettle, combine tomato purée, tomato paste, chopped parsley, crushed oregano and thyme, black pepper, bay leaf pieces, and water. Add sautéed onion, garlic, and mushroom slices. Bring to the simmer. Reduce heat to *LOW* and continue to simmer, uncovered, for about 2 hours until thickened to your liking. Stir frequently. Remove and discard bay leaf pieces.

Serve as desired or freeze in quantities appropriate to future use.

Yields about 6 cupfuls

Notes: *Crushed, dried basil does not give the desired flavor complexity required for this sauce. If fresh or preserved basil is unavailable, omit basil.

**The bay leaf pieces are most easily recovered if secured inside a tea ball during the simmering process.

This recipe is easily doubled, when required.

1/12 SERVING (i. e., per 1/2 cupful) –
PROTEIN = 0.1 g.; FAT = 1.2 g.; CARBOHYDRATE = 10.5 g.;
CALORIES = 54; CALORIES FROM FAT = 20%

APPENDIX of BASIC RECIPES

SWEET SAUCES:

AUSTRALIAN SIMPLE BLACKBERRY SAUCE *OR* DESSERT
TPT - 1 hour and 15 minutes;
1 hour = chilling period

Freezing those first-of-summer large, gorgeous, delicious blackberries from the farmers' market will insure that this sauce, sometimes dessert, can refresh your spirit in the middle of the winter and remind you that it is summer in Australia.

1 1/4 teaspoons corn starch
1/2 cup *cold* water

1/4 cup sugar
1 cup blackberries—fresh, well-washed *or* frozen without sugar

Squeeze of freshly squeezed lemon juice

In a saucepan, stir cornstarch into *cold* water to form a suspension.

Place the saucepan over *MEDIUM* heat. Add sugar and cook, stirring constantly, until sugar is dissolved and sauce begins to thicken.

Add blackberries. Continue to cook, stirring constantly, until mixture is thickened—about 10 minutes.

Remove from heat. Add a squeeze of fresh lemon juice. Turn into a sauceboat or other serving dish. Refrigerate until thoroughly cooled—about 1 hour.

Serve with ice creams, cakes, dessert *crêpes*, cheese blintzes, and cheesecakes.

Yields about 1 1/4 cupfuls
or dessert for two

Notes: This recipe is easily doubled, when required.

The sauce, served with a bit of cream if desired, makes a simple dessert which really highlights the fresh blackberry taste.

1/10 SERVING (i. e., about 2 tablespoonfuls) –
PROTEIN = 0.1 g.; FAT = 0.06 g.; CARBOHYDRATE = 7.8 g.;
CALORIES = 31; CALORIES FROM FAT = 2%

1/2 SERVING –
PROTEIN = 0.5 g.; FAT = 0.3 g.; CARBOHYDRATE = 39.2 g.;
CALORIES = 155; CALORIES FROM FAT = 2%

CINNAMON SYRUP
TPT - 20 minutes

We often use this as an alternative for maple syrup on pancakes, waffles, and French toast. It is the essential sauce, as far as we are concerned, for those wonderful pastry-wrapped apple dumplings that Pennsylvanians love so well.

1/2 cup light corn syrup
1 cup sugar
1/4 cup water
1/4 teaspoon ground cinnamon

1/2 cup evaporated *skimmed* milk

In a saucepan, set over *MEDIUM* heat, mix corn syrup, sugar, water, and ground cinnamon. Bring to a full boil, stirring constantly. *Continue stirring and boiling for an additional 2 full minutes.*

Remove from heat and allow to cool for 5 minutes.

Stir in evaporated milk.

Serve warm.

Yields 1 1/2 cupfuls

Notes: This recipe may be halved, when required. It is not advisable to double this recipe. Instead, make two batches for a crowd.

Leftovers may be stored in the refrigerator and reheated in hot water, as you would for maple syrup.

1/24 SERVING (i. e., per tablespoonful) –
PROTEIN = 0.4 g.; FAT = 0.01 g.; CARBOHYDRATE = 14.7 g.;
CALORIES = 59; CALORIES FROM FAT = <1%

APPENDIX of BASIC RECIPES

CUSTARD SAUCE
Crème Anglaise

TPT - 1 hour and 37 minutes;
1 hour = chilling period

"Crème anglaise" is a wonderfully useful sauce to master and to be able to make it with fat-free pasteurized eggs makes it even more wonderful to me. This classic French sauce, often called "Crème Francaise" by French who, I think, just can not bear to have anything this delicious named for the English, is used to garnish and fill pastries and cakes and is the creamy rich base for classic desserts such as bavarois and Charlottes. The addition of arrowroot to this sauce tends to prevent clotting if the sauce is allowed to overheat and in this skimmed milk version, specifically, we find that the arrowroot thickening gives the sauce more body.

1 cup *fat-free* pasteurized eggs (the equivalent of 4 eggs)
1/4 cup sugar
1 teaspoon pure vanilla extract
1 teaspoon arrowroot flour

1 1/2 cups skimmed milk

In the mixing bowl of the electric mixer, combine pasteurized eggs, sugar, vanilla extract, and arrowroot flour. Using the electric mixer, beat mixture until thick and lemony—about 5 minutes.

Meanwhile, scald milk in a heavy saucepan over *LOW* heat.

Continue to beat egg mixture while gradually adding the hot milk. Turn into the top of a double boiler set over *simmering*, but *not boiling*, water. Cook, stirring constantly with a wire whisk, until custard has thickened—about 25 minutes.

Strain through a fine sieve into a bowl. Using a wire whisk, whisk until smooth. Chill in the refrigerator for 1 hour before serving over fruit or cereal puddings, fresh or canned fruits, or plain cake.

Yields 2 cupfuls
adequate for 6-8 servings

Notes: This recipe may be doubled, when required.

1/2 teaspoonful of cream sherry may be substituted for vanilla extract, if desired.

1/8 SERVING (i. e., per 1/4 cupful) –
PROTEIN = 4.3 g.; FAT = 0.08 g.; CARBOHYDRATE = 10.8 g.;
CALORIES = 63; CALORIES FROM FAT = 1%

FAMILY'S CHOICE PANCAKE AND WAFFLE SYRUP
TPT - 5 minutes

The multitude of variations possible make this a family favorite. Peach and apricot versions are especially delicious.

1 cup *light* corn syrup
1/3 cup all-fruit jam or preserves, of choice

In a saucepan set over *LOW* heat, combine light corn syrup and the jam or preserves that most pleases your family. Stir until heated through and of uniform consistency.

Serve immediately or refrigerate in a jar or syrup pitcher to reheat as needed.

Yields 1 1/3 cupfuls

Note: This recipe is easily halved or doubled, when required.

1/7 SERVING (i. e., about 3 tablespoonfuls) –
PROTEIN = 0.0 g.; FAT = 0.0 g.; CARBOHYDRATE = 27.0 g.;
CALORIES = 161; CALORIES FROM FAT = 0%

APPENDIX of BASIC RECIPES

FRESH ORANGE CUSTARD SAUCE
TPT - 1 hour and 30 minutes;
30 minutes = custard cooling period;
30 minutes = chilling period

Sometimes the name of a food really makes you anticipate the texture or taste. Lettuce and celery convey crunch and if you add crispy to either, it says even more. There is definitely texture to the word nut, which you feel as your teeth meet at the end of the word. Custard, to me, is another one of those words. You can roll it around on your tongue as you say it, almost tasting the texture. This custard sauce delivers the soft custard feel but with a taste that sparkles and surprises a bit.

1/2 cup *fat-free* **pasteurized eggs (the equivalent of 2 eggs)**
3 tablespoons sugar
2 tablespoons corn starch

Very finely **grated zest of 1 orange—about 1 tablespoon**
Juice of 1 large orange—strained

Juice of 1/2 lemon—strained

1/2 cup heavy whipping cream

In a mixing bowl, using a wire whisk or an electric mixer, combine pasteurized eggs, sugar, and corn starch. Beat at *MEDIUM* speed until *very thick* and lemon-colored—about 4-5 minutes.

Pour into the top half of a double boiler. Stir in grated orange zest and orange juice. Cook over *hot*, but *not boiling*, water, stirring constantly until the mixture has thickened and coats a wooden spoon.

Whisk in lemon juice. Remove from heat and set aside to cool for at least 30 minutes before proceeding.

Using an electric mixer fitted with *chilled* beaters or by hand, using a *chilled* wire whisk, beat heavy cream in a *chilled* mixing bowl until stiff.

Whisk-fold whipped cream into cooled custard mixture. Turn into serving dish. Chill in refrigerator for at least 30 minutes before serving with fruit compotes, baked fruits, dessert *crêpes*, small cakes, GINGERBREAD *[see index]*, and puddings, especially bread puddings.

Yields about 1 2/3 cupfuls
adequate for 9 servings
of 3 tablespoonfuls each

Note: This recipe is not easily doubled. It is better to make separate batches when a large quantity is required.

1/9 SERVING (i. e., 3 tablespoonfuls) –
PROTEIN = 1.7 g.; FAT = 4.4 g.; CARBOHYDRATE = 9.2 g.;
CALORIES = 83; CALORIES FROM FAT = 48%

LEMON SAUCE
TPT - 21 minutes

This is a versatile workhorse of a sauce disguised as a beautiful, delicate, soft sauce that lavishes anything it dresses. My grandmother, who loved the taste of lemon, would have really loved this sauce and I know she would have had dozens of ideas as to how to feature it.

1/4 cup sugar
2 teaspoons corn starch
1 cup *cold* **water**

1/2 cup *fat-free* **pasteurized eggs (the equivalent of 2 eggs)**
2 teaspoons freshly grated, *organic* **lemon zest***
1/4 cup freshly squeezed lemon juice
1 tablespoon butter—*softened to room temperature*

In a saucepan, combine sugar and corn starch. Using a wire whisk, stir in *cold* water. Stir until corn starch is completely in suspension. Set over *LOW* heat and cook, stirring constantly, until mixture thickens and is smooth. Remove from heat.

Using a wire whisk, beat 1/2 cupful of hot mixture into pasteurized eggs—*tablespoonful by tablespoonful*. Add to remaining hot mixture in saucepan. Using a wire whisk, combine thoroughly. Return to heat and continue to cook over *LOW* heat, stirring constantly, for about 8 minutes, or until thickened and smooth.

Add lemon zest, lemon juice, and butter. Continue to cook, stirring constantly, until butter melts.

Serve warm, room temperature, or chill and serve cold over GINGERBREAD *[see index]*, cakes, bread puddings, or over fruits such as prunes and pears.

Yields 2 cupfuls

APPENDIX of BASIC RECIPES

LEMON SAUCE (cont'd)

Notes: *If desired, you can replace a teaspoonful of freshly grated lemon zest with lime zest. It is an effective, but elusive, addition.

This recipe may be doubled, when required.

Refrigerate leftovers.

1/8 SERVING (i. e., per 1/4 cupful) –
PROTEIN = 1.5 g.; FAT = 1.4 g.; CARBOHYDRATE = 9.4 g.;
CALORIES = 55; CALORIES FROM FAT = 23%

LEMON SYRUP
TPT - 51 minutes;
30 minutes = syrup cooling period

Every year I make a dessert syrup from the lemon verbena, Aloysia triphylla, which I grow as an annual in our Zone 5 herb garden. [see recipe which follows] For several months we enjoy its lemony taste but sooner or later it is all gone. The remainder of the winter and into the spring this lemon syrup takes over. The sweet syrup has a zillion uses but I love it most with dessert pancakes, or over fresh ricotta, sliced fruits, berries, and pound cake.

1 cup sugar
6 tablespoons freshly squeezed lemon juice
1/2 cup water
2 tablespoons honey—preferably, wildflower honey
A two-inch strip of *organic* lemon zest

1/8 teaspoon pure vanilla extract

Sterilize a jelly jar, lid, and ring.

In a saucepan set over *MEDIUM-HIGH* heat, combine sugar, lemon juice, water, honey, and lemon zest. Cook, stirring constantly, until sugar is dissolved and syrup has come to the boil. Reduce heat to *MEDIUM*. Continue cooking for about 8 minutes. Syrup should be slightly thickened and the lemon fragrance should be intense. Remove from heat.

Stir in vanilla extract.

Set a funnel lined with a tea strainer or a "gold" coffee filter over the jelly jar. Strain lemon syrup into the sterilized jar, discarding the lemon zest. Allow syrup to cool to room temperature—about 30 minutes.

Seal jar and store in refrigerator until required.*

Yields about 1 1/4 cupfuls syrup

Notes: *In a sterilized jar, this syrup will keep in the refrigerator for several months.

This recipe can be halved, when required.

1/20 SERVING (per tablespoonful) –
PROTEIN = 0.01 g.; FAT = 0.0 g.; CARBOHYDRATE = 13.2 g.;
CALORIES = 51; CALORIES FROM FAT = 0%

LEMON VERBENA SYRUP
TPT - 51 minutes;
30 minutes = syrup cooling period

Lemon verbena, Aloysia triphylla, is the most truly lemon of all the "lemony herbs" and it makes a lemon syrup to die for. I love it most with sliced fruits, berries, and pound cake.

1 cup sugar
1 cup water
2 tablespoons honey—preferably, wildflower honey
2 tablespoons chopped lemon verbena leaves
A two-inch strip of *organic* lemon zest

LEMON VERBENA SYRUP (cont'd)

Sterilize two jelly jars, lids and rings.

In a saucepan set over *MEDIUM-HIGH* heat, combine sugar, water, honey, chopped lemon verbena leaves, and lemon zest. Cook, stirring constantly, until sugar is dissolved and syrup has come to the boil. Reduce heat to *MEDIUM*. Continue cooking for about 8 minutes. Syrup should be slightly thickened and the lemon fragrance should be intense. Remove from heat.

Set a funnel lined with a tea strainer or a "gold" coffee filter over the jelly jar. Strain lemon verbena syrup into the sterilized jars, discarding the spent leaves and the lemon zest. Allow syrup to cool to room temperature—about 30 minutes.

Seal jars and store in refrigerator until required.*

Yields about 1 1/4 cupfuls syrup

Notes: *In a sterilized jar, this syrup will keep in the refrigerator for several months.

This recipe can be halved, when required.

The recipe can be adapted to create dessert sauces scented with lemon balm, mint, pineapple sage, or scented geranium; basil, rosemary, sage, and thyme; roses and violets.

1/20 SERVING (per tablespoonful) –
PROTEIN = 0.01 g.; FAT = 0.0 g.; CARBOHYDRATE = 12.9 g.;
CALORIES = 50; CALORIES FROM FAT = 0%

SOUP STOCKS:

VEGETABLE STOCK FROM SOUP
TPT - 1 hour and 15 minutes

Occasionally you will find that there is a need for a stock but little in the way of soup stock ingredients on hand. This stock might well be called an emergency stock. After moving to a very rural area of Pennsylvania, we developed this during the busy autumn followed by a severe winter period during which we could not get into town to get fresh vegetables. There were, consequently, not a lot of vegetable trimmings for stock since we had not been freezing our trimmings from summer menus; those trimmings had instead become the base of our composting effort in anticipation of spring garden demands. Although this emergency stock has more fat and salt in it than our VEGETARIAN BROWN STOCK, and the tomato base may change the taste of a soup or casserole, we find it a good idea to have such a reserve. During the winter of 1995-1996 we were sure glad to have this stock in our freezer!

**2 cans (10 ounces each) condensed vegetarian
  vegetable *or* vegetarian *minestrone* soup
2 quarts water
Any vegetables accumulated in your stock bag
  for VEGETARIAN BROWN STOCK** *[see
recipe which follows]*—**coarsely chopped**

In a large kettle set over *MEDIUM* heat, combine condensed vegetable soup, water, and chopped vegetables. Stir to disperse condensed soup. Bring to the boil. Reduce heat to *LOW* and cook, stirring frequently, for about 1 hour.

Using a fine sieve, strain vegetables from stock. Discard vegetables. Strain stock through a sieve lined with culinary cheesecloth or a cotton tea towel.

VEGETABLE STOCK FROM SOUP (cont'd)

Refrigerate until ready to use or freeze in quantities appropriate for future use.

Yields about 7 cupfuls

Notes: The calories available from vegetarian stocks are almost negligible and the nutritional analyses will vary, quite naturally, with the choice of ingredients. For these reasons, we have chosen to treat these stocks merely as flavoring—omitting them from nutritional calculations but recognizing them as a food, quite rich in vitamins and minerals.

This recipe may be halved or doubled, when required.

To save space in the freezer, the stock can be canned using a hot-water-bath canner. Ladle into hot, sterilized pint or quart canning jars. Carefully wipe lips of jars. Seal with hot, sterilized lids and rings. Process in hot-water-bath canner for 10 minutes, *timing from the moment the water reaches a full rolling boil.* Remove to surface covered with thick towels or newspapers. Allow to cool for 24 hours *undisturbed.* Check to be sure jars are sealed before labeling and storing in a dark, cool, dry place. Loosen or remove rings before storing. Any jars that do not seal can be stored in the refrigerator for about one week or resealed using a *new lid.*

VEGETARIAN STOCKS for SOUPS, STEWS, and SAUCES
TPT - about 1 hour and 15 minutes

All too often restaurant dishes have to be turned down because the use of chicken, veal, and even beef stock is frequently not regarded as "a problem for vegetarians" by chefs who rarely employ vegetarian stocks. I have even encountered chefs who were incensed and claimed that their creations deserved better. Boiling an animal in a kettle hardly seems better to me. Canned vegetarian stock can, granted, be disappointing, but homemade stock, such as these, can be easily made, frozen, and used whenever stock is required.

Combine thoroughly washed trimmings from or leftovers of vegetables specified below for stock of choice. *Chop finely.* Put into a large saucepan with water to cover. Add seasonings specified. Bring to the simmer, cover, and simmer for about 1 hour—stirring and mashing occasionally.

Using a potato masher, press vegetable pieces hard against saucepan. Strain through a fine sieve lined with cheesecloth or a cotton tea towel pressing liquid from vegetable pieces using a large spoon.

Refrigerate strained stock for a maximum of 2 days or freeze in amounts convenient to use. Use as you would any stock.

APPENDIX of BASIC RECIPES

VEGETARIAN STOCKS
for **SOUPS, STEWS,** and **SAUCES** (cont'd)

For a basic stock or
WHITE STOCK:

Bean sprouts
Cauliflower
Celeriac
Celery with leaves
Cucumbers
Leeks
Mushroom stems
Onions
Parsnips
Potatoes
Scallions
Summer Squash
Turnips

For a stronger stock or
BROWN STOCK:

Any of vegetables specified for
WHITE STOCK plus,

Asparagus
Broccoli
Brussels sprouts
Cabbage
Carrots
Carrot tops
Garlic clove—unpeeled
Green beans
Lettuce leaves
Pea pods
Pumpkin
Spinach
Tomatoes
Watercress stems
Winter squash

Water from cooking any of the above vegetables, if reserved

3 sprigs fresh parsley
5 peppercorns
2 whole cloves
1/2 teaspoon salt
1 bay leaf—crumbled
Pinch dried thyme leaves—crushed
Dash mace
1/2 lemon—sliced and seeded

Remember that the percentages of each vegetable used will determine the predominating flavor of the resultant stock. The amounts of vegetables used each time stock is made will, of course, depend upon what is at hand at that moment and what is preferred. For this reason, the ingredient lists have been included without amount specification. You will arrive at a satisfactory formula by experimentation.

Also, it must be kept in mind that the seasoning of dishes using these stocks must largely be done "to taste" since each stock batch will vary somewhat. The seasoning amounts recommended here are based on vegetables and water equaling about 2 quarts.

Notes: The calories available from VEGETARIAN STOCK are almost negligible and the nutritional analyses vary, quite naturally, with the choice of ingredients. For these reasons, we have chosen to treat this stock merely as flavoring—omitting them from nutritional calculations but recognizing them as a food, quite rich in vitamins and minerals.

To save space in the freezer, the stock can be canned using a hot-water-bath canner. Ladle into hot, sterilized pint or quart canning jars. Carefully wipe lips of jars. Seal with hot, sterilized lids and rings. Process in hot-water-bath canner for 10 minutes, *timing from the moment the water reaches a full rolling boil.* Remove to surface covered with thick towels or newspapers. Allow to cool for 24 hours *undisturbed.* Check to be sure jars are sealed before labeling and storing in a dark, cool, dry place. Loosen or remove rings before storing. Any jars that do not seal can be stored in the refrigerator for about one week or resealed using a *new lid.*

APPENDIX of BASIC RECIPES

WILD MUSHROOM STOCK
TPT - 49 minutes;
45 minutes = soaking period

If an assertive, mushroom-flavored stock is appropriate to any dish, sauce, or soup, this stock is a terrific stock to have on hand. Whenever we rehydrate dried mushrooms for a recipe, the flavorful liquid that is left behind goes right into the freezer for a future menu.

1 cup mixture of *dried*, wild mushrooms—well-rinsed and brushed to remove any foreign matter
2 cups *boiling* water

Put *well-cleaned* mushrooms into a small bowl or measuring cup. Pour *boiling* water over. Weight the mushrooms down into the liquid using a small Pyrex dish. Allow to soak for at least 45 minutes. Drain thoroughly, *reserving the soaking liquid.* Strain the soaking liquid, now mushroom stock, to remove any bits of the mushrooms that remain.

Use or freeze stock. Use rehydrated mushrooms within 2 days.

Note: The calories available from vegetarian stocks, such as this, are almost negligible. For this reason, we have chosen to treat these stocks merely as flavoring—omitting them from nutritional calculations but recognizing them as a food, quite rich in vitamins and minerals.

Yields 2 cupfuls

THIS AND THAT:

GARLIC OIL
TPT - 1 hour and 20 minutes

For many, many years there was always a jar of garlic oil in my refrigerator. It was useful for so many things. Then the food safety police came along and declared garlic oil to be a dangerous brew. In 2008 the ban appeared to have lifted if you prepared it as a confit, heating the garlic in oil and refrigerating it for no more than a month or so. OK, we're back to flavor again!!

I find this to be a wonderful way to preserve the beautiful, local, organic garlic that is harvested in mid-August.

3/4 cup *extra virgin* olive oil
3/4 cup *high heat* safflower oil
24 small garlic cloves—peeled, well-washed, and well-dried

Sterilize a one-pint canning jar. Also sterilize a lid and ring for the jar.

In a large saucepan set over *VERY LOW* heat, combine olive and safflower oils. Add garlic cloves. Allow to cook until garlic is soft—about 1 hour.*

Pour garlic and oil into the sterilized jar. Seal and refrigerate. Remove garlic or oil as needed with a *clean spoon*. This will keep in the refrigerator for a month or two. **

Note: *It will take at least an hour! Do not try to hurry this along by raising the heat; do not allow the oil to boil or the garlic to brown.

APPENDIX of BASIC RECIPES

GARLIC WITH THYME AND BAY IN OIL
TPT - 2 hours;
30 minutes = cooling period

Each garlic bulb, which has grown from a single garlic clove planted the previous fall, is dug out mid-season and left to dry on the patio. Then the anticipation builds because the garlic oil and this garlic confit will be the next projects for our winter larder. Stored in the refrigerator, we will have garlic oil and herb-seasoned garlic straight through until the fall holidays. Fresh thyme and bay leaves from the garden, my favorite oils, kosher salt, a rainbow of peppercorns, and sterilized canning jars are all we need.

3 large bulbs of garlic

5 large thyme sprigs—well-washed
2 fresh bay leaves
1/2 cup *extra virgin* olive oil
1/2 cup *high-heat* safflower *or* sunflower oil

Pinch or two kosher salt
Freshly ground mixed peppercorns—white, red,
  and black—to taste

Preheat oven to 300 degrees F.

Sterilize a pint canning jar. Also sterilize a lid and ring for the jar.

Separate garlic cloves. Peel and rinse well. Put in a heavy baking casserole with cover.

Scatter thyme sprigs over the garlic cloves. Tuck bay leaves down into the garlic. Pour oils over, adding extra if garlic and herbs are not covered. Cover and bake in preheated oven for about 1 hour or until garlic is very tender. Remove from oven to a heat-resistant surface.

Season with salt and pepper and allow to cool for about 30 minutes. Remove and discard the thyme sprigs and the bay leaves.

Transfer the garlic clove and the oil to the sterilized pint canning jar. Carefully wipe lips of the jar. Seal with hot, sterilized lid and ring. Refrigerate. Remove garlic with a clean spoon each time to limit the possibility of introducing mold.

Yields one pint jarful,
about 36 cloves of garlic

Note: This recipe can be doubled, when required. Use two pint canning jars, not a quart jar, for storage to protect the confit from mold contamination.

1/36 SERVING (per clove with oil) –
PROTEIN = 2.0 g.; FAT = 5.4 g.; CARBOHYDRATE = 1.0 g.;
CALORIES = 54; CALORIES FROM FAT = 90%

APPENDIX of BASIC RECIPES

OUR GRANOLA
TPT - 2 hours and 2 minutes

In the early 1970s there was a public awakening to nutritional excellence, a path some of us had traveled just about all our lives. Most of the "thinkers" have since been put back to sleep by the wolf of commercialism in the deceptive guise of health awareness "big brotherism." Back before we let the commercials think for us, granola identified the seriously aware and we made our own granola. The big cereal companies must have feared us mightily because they quickly mobilized and capitalized on the desire of the next generation to join the awakening. The mantra on their sales office walls must have been, "Don't let them find out that they can make their own granola!"

7 cups rolled oats—quick-cooking *or* old-fashioned, *but not instant*
1 cup wheat germ—raw *or* toasted, as preferred
3/4 cup slivered, unblanched *preservative-free* **almonds**
1/2 cup chopped *preservative-free* **hazelnuts or filberts**
1/2 cup unsweetened *preservative-free* **shredded coconut**
1/2 cup millers' wheat bran
1/4 cup unsalted, *preservative-free* **sunflower seeds**

5 tablespoons butter
3 tablespoons honey
1 tablespoon blackstrap molasses
1/2 cup water

1 cup *preservative-free dark* **raisins, if desired**

1 cup chopped, *preservative-free* **dried apple, if desired**

Preheat oven to 200 degrees F.

In a large mixing bowl, combine oats, wheat germ, slivered almonds, chopped hazelnuts, shredded coconut, wheat bran, and sunflower seeds.*

In a saucepan set over *LOW* heat, melt butter. Stir in honey, molasses, and water. Continue to cook, stirring frequently, until smooth.

Pour honey–butter mixture over dry ingredients. Using either your hands or a wooden spoon, work until evenly moistened. Distribute evenly on two jelly roll pans or on two cookie sheets with sides.

Bake in preheated 200 degree F. oven for about 1 1/4 hours. Stir with a spatula every 15 minutes and shift pans from top to bottom racks (and back again) in order to allow for even browning.

Allow to cool thoroughly. Stir in raisins or chopped dried apples, if desired. Store in airtight containers in the refrigerator.

Serve with skimmed milk as a cereal or use as a topping for ice cream, yogurt, fruit desserts, and puddings or an ingredient in cookies.

Yields about twenty 1/2-cup servings
without raisins or apples

Note: *1 teaspoonful of ground cinnamon may be stirred into dry ingredients at this point for variety. This is an especially good addition if dried apples are to be included.

1/20 SERVING WITHOUT RAISINS OR APPLES (about 1/2 cupful) –
PROTEIN = 11.0 g.; FAT = 9.8 g.; CARBOHYDRATE = 37.9 g.;
CALORIES = 278; CALORIES FROM FAT = 32%

1/22 SERVING WITH RAISINS (about 1/2 cupful) –
PROTEIN = 10.1 g.; FAT = 9.0 g.; CARBOHYDRATE = 39.0 g.;
CALORIES = 280; CALORIES FROM FAT = 29%

1/22 SERVING WITH DRIED APPLE (about 1/2 cupful) –
PROTEIN = 10.1 g.; FAT = 9.0 g.; CARBOHYDRATE = 38.8 g.;
CALORIES = 269; CALORIES FROM FAT = 30%

ROLLED SUGAR COOKIES

TPT - 1 hour and 34 minutes;
30 minutes = chilling period

There is always a quantity of this dough in our freezer and a vast assortment of cookie cutters in a kitchen drawer. You just never know when you will need a few golden baked creatures to make a child happy

1 1/2 cups unbleached white flour
1 cup whole wheat flour
2 teaspoons baking powder

1/2 cup (1 stick) butter—*softened to room temperature*
3/4 cup sugar

1/2 cup *fat-free* **pasteurized eggs (the equivalent of 2 eggs)**
1 teaspoon pure vanilla extract

More unbleached white flour, as needed, during kneading and rolling

1/4 cup brown demerara sugar*

Prepare cookie sheets by lining with culinary parchment paper.**

Sift white and whole wheat flours with baking powder. Set aside.

Using the electric mixer or food processor fitted with steel knife, cream butter until light and fluffy. Add 3/4 cupful sugar and continue to cream until again light.

Add pasteurized eggs and vanilla extract. Beat until smooth.

Gradually beat in sifted ingredients until a smooth dough results. Divide dough in half. Wrap each portion tightly in plastic wrap and freeze for about 30 minutes to make dough easier to handle.***

Preheat oven to 350 degrees F.

Unwrap chilled dough and knead lightly on floured surface. Using a covered rolling pin, roll dough to about 1/8 inch thickness. Using floured cookie cutters, cut out cookies. With a spatula, transfer cookies to prepared cookie sheets. Sprinkle some of brown demerara sugar over each cookie; press granules gently into dough.

Bake one cookie sheetful at a time in preheated 350 degree F. oven for 7-8 minutes, being watchful to prevent excessive browning. Transfer to a wire rack to cool completely. Store in airtight container or plastic bag.

Yields about 60 cut-out cookies

Notes: *Brown demerara sugar is an amber, large-crystal sugar which does not melt away during baking, as do refined sugars, giving a gorgeous golden crystalline topping to baked goods. It is available from mail order baking firms.

**If not available in your grocery store or natural food store, culinary parchment paper for baking is available in food specialty and housewares' stores, and from mail order firms, where it is now even available as an unbleached, environmentally friendly product. Lining baking sheets and pans with parchment paper, instead of greasing, buttering, or oiling, not only protects your baking sheets from scorching, it encourages the even browning of cookies, scones, cakes, etc.

***If convenient, this dough may be left frozen for several months until required. Defrost in refrigerator before proceeding.

To prepare REFRIGERATOR SUGAR COOKIES instead of cut-out cookies, roll dough into 1 1/2-inch cylinders before freezing. Slice into 1/8-inch slices, press in sugar, and bake.

1/60 SERVING (i. e., per cookie) –
PROTEIN = 0.8 g.; FAT = 1.6 g.; CARBOHYDRATE = 7.6 g.;
CALORIES = 47; CALORIES FROM FAT = 31%

APPENDIX of BASIC RECIPES

SEASONING MIXTURE FOR DEHYDRATED SOY MEAT ANALOGUE
TPT - 2 minutes

So Soya+ is an unseasoned, unsalted, fat-free dehydrated meat analogue product, available by mail order from a Canadian manufacturer. Made from soy flour, it comes in convenient slices and also in a form they label as "ground." It is a rather bland product when reconstituted unless the soaking medium is seasoned. I alter the seasoning to give it more appeal using ethnic seasoning mixes. The following recipe is our basic mixture of which we add two teaspoonfuls to the two cupfuls water or stock that is used to rehydrate the soy product.

1 tablespoon salt
1 teaspoon sweet paprika*
1 teaspoon HERBED ITALIAN SEASONING MIX (*Miscuglio di Erbas Italiano*) *[see index]***
1/4 teaspoon dried onion powder
1/8 teaspoon ground cumin

In a small jelly or spice jar,*** combine salt, paprika, HERBED ITALIAN SEASONING MIX, dried onion powder, and ground cumin. Cover tightly and shake to mix thoroughly. Store in a cool, dark place.

Yields about 5 1/2 teaspoonfuls

Notes: *The Spanish export a roasted sweet paprika which is a very good choice for this mixture since it lends a unusual flavor nuance that you would not get from sweet paprika.

**Any ethnic seasoning mixture, that you might prefer and which complements your menu use, can be substituted. *[See index for seasoning mixture suggestions.]*

***Choose a small jar because the smaller the jar, the less air will come in contact with the herbs, and the longer the mix will keep its flavor.

Since the flavor on seasoning mixtures dissipates considerably due to the release of the volatile oils in crushing, I do not double this recipe. It is advisable to replace the seasoning combination after about three months.

FOOD VALUES for such herb mixtures are almost negligible.

WHEATEN BISCUIT MIX
TPT - 5 minutes

Although I do not use vegetable shortening as a rule, I would occasionally have to buy commercial biscuit mix for one recipe or another. I would use one cupful and there it would sit in the refrigerator until it turned rancid and out it would go. This convenient mix makes me feel better about putting some of those old, convenient, comfort recipes into my menu plan from time to time. The combination of baking powder and baking soda gives a good "rise," producing a light biscuit, even with the addition of the heavier whole wheat flour, and the cake flour greatly improves the texture.

3 cups cake flour
1 1/2 cups whole wheat flour
1/2 cup *non-fat* dry milk
3 tablespoons sugar
2 tablespoons baking powder
1 teaspoon baking soda

1 cup vegetable shortening *with no trans fats*

Into a large mixing bowl, sift cake and whole wheat flours, powdered milk, sugar, baking powder, salt, and baking soda.

Using a pastry blender or by pulsating the mixture in the food processor, fitted with steel knife, cut shortening into dry ingredients until mixture is the consistency of coarse corn meal. Turn into an airtight container.

Store in the refrigerator for up to 2 months or store in the freezer, tightly sealed, for up to a year. Use in any recipe calling for "Bisquick," adding *about* 1/4 cupful of liquid per cupful of biscuit mix.

Yields 6 cupfuls

Notes: When necessary, this recipe may be halved or doubled.

1/6 SERVING (i. e., per cupful) –
PROTEIN = 10.1 g.; FAT = 33.1 g.; CARBOHYDRATE = 74.6 g.;
CALORIES = 646; CALORIES FROM FAT = 46%

index

Achiote oil (Ecuador), v. II, 553
AFGHANISTAN, v. I, 637-43
ALBANIA, v. I, 3-13
ALGERIA, v. II, 3-9
amaranth, adobe bread (Native America), v. II, 660
ANDORRA, v. I, 14-21
ANGOLA, v. II, 10-16
appetizer dips and spreads
    avocado and pineapple spread (Côte d'Ivorie), v. II, 62-63
    avocado and tomato dipping sauce (Venezuela), v. II, 630
    avocado dip with lime (Sierra Leone), v. II, 226-27
    avocado dip with tomato (Zambia), v. II, 292
    black olive *tapenade* with pine nuts, v. II, 190
    cheese and *chili* dip (Native America), v. II, 653
    cheese dip with mayonnaise (Portugal), v. I, 330
    cheese spread (Croatia), v. I, 84
    cheese spread (Romania), v. I, 341
    cheese spread (Slovakia), v. I, 373
    cheese spread with garlic (Syria), v. I, 562
    chick pea dip (Turkey), v. I, 567-68
    dipping sauce (Brunei), v. II, 306-307
    dip with corn and walnuts (Mexico), v. II, 579
    dip with roasted beets and *hummus* (Israel), v. I, 494
    feta cheese spread (Romania), v. I, 341
    fenugreek and vegetable appetizer dip (Yemen), v. I, 578
    garlic dipping oil with yogurt (Eritrea), v. II, 85
    garlicky lime mayonnaise (Peru), v. II, 611-12
    garlic-walnut dipping sauce (Macedonia), v. I, 263
    garlic-yogurt sauce with *tahini* (Tunisia), v. II, 272
    goat cheese and yogurt spread (Libya), v. II, 139-40
    herbed yogurt "cheese" (Israel), v. I, 493
    lemon dipping sauce (Egypt), v. II, 80-81
    mayonnaise-cheese dip (Portugal), v. I, 330
    mung bean sauce with tomatoes and garlic (Uganda), v. II, 285-86
    mustard-soy dip (China), v. II, 325
    olive and caper *tapanade* (Panama), v. II, 597-98
    pumpkin appetizer dip (Libya), v. II, 139
    red pepper and walnut dip (Palestine), v. I, 544-45
    roasted beets and *hummus* (Israel), v. I, 494
    roasted eggplant appetizer (Lebanon), v. I, 523
    roasted eggplant *caviar* (Romania), v. I, 340-41
    roasted eggplant and pepper *caviar* (Serbia), v. I, 364-65
    spicy yogurt dipping sauce (Bangladesh), v. I, 647
    sweetpotato and black bean appetizers (Caribbean) v. II, 491
    tamarind dipping sauce (Cambodia), v. II, 316
    tomato and pepper appetizer salad (Israel), v. I 495
    tomato dipping sauce (The Gambia), v. II, 100
    vegan "chopped liver" (Israel), v. I, 493-94
    with fenugreek (Yemen), v. I, 578
    yogurt and peanut butter appetizer dip (Sudan), v. II, 252
    yogurt with green *chilies* (Palestine), v. I, 545
apples
    and beetroot salad (Uruguay), v. II, 624
    and beet salad with sour cream (Lithuania), v. I, 247
    and celeriac soup (Australia), v. II, 450
    and celery salad (Slovakia), v. I, 375
    and cheese salad (Switzerland), v. I, 410
    applesauce, v. I, 185
    applesauce with sour cream sauce (Hungary), v. I, 184
    baked dessert (Slovenia), v. I, 390
    cabbage and carrot slaw with (Ukraine), v. I, 426
    cheese-stuffed zucchini with lentils and fruit (Mexico), v. II, 583-84
    compote with *Brie* and raisins (South Africa), v. II, 243-44
    deviled beet, potato, apple, and egg salad (Estonia), v. I, 111-12
    dried, fruit salad (Uganda), v. II, 283-84
    fruit cream (Belgium), v. I, 55-56
    granola, v. II, 696
    meatballs and fruit in curry sauce (Mozambique), v. II, 183-84
    meat pies (Botswana), v. II, 21
    mixed fruit salad with *chaat masala* (India), v. I, 670
    peanut-apple crumble v. II, 469-70
    pear mincemeat with pecans (England), v. I, 441-42
    porridge with apples and oatmeal (Belarus), v. I, 41-42
    prickly pear salad with dates (Israel), v. I, 497
    pudding with breadcrumbs (Denmark), v. I, 108-109
    pudding with breadcrumbs (Russia), v. I, 359
    salad, with celery (Slovakia), v. I, 375
    salad, with onion and *feta* (Greece), v. I, 163
    savory, with sour cream (Luxembourg), v. I, 258
    slow cooker dried fruit curry (South Africa), v. II, 247-48
    soup, savory (Andorra), v. I, 17
    sweet fried (Norway), v. I, 315-16
    syrup (The Netherlands), v. I, 306
    syrup with cloves (Lebanon), v. I, 533
    uncooked applesauce (Switzerland), v. I, 419-20
    vegetable stew (Uzbekistan), v. I, 628-29
    with sauerkraut (Latvia), v. I, 235
apricots
    breaded and fried *semolina* with cranberry garnish (Slovakia), v. I, 378
    brown rice *pilaf* (Central Asia), v. I, 629-30
    chick peas with tomatoes (Yemen), v. I, 580-81
    dried, fruit salad (Uganda), v. II, 283-84
    dumplings, with mashed potatoes (Slovenia), v. I, 386
    lentil and bulgur cabbage rolls (Armenia), v. I, 592-93
    red lentil and bulgur soup (Armenia), v. I, 589-90
    salad, with mango and pineapple (Niger), v. II, 198
    sauce, for papaya and mango dessert (Tanzania), v. II, 265
    stewed fruit compote with walnuts (Armenia), v. I, 596
    tart (Austria), v. I, 31
    tea-infused dried fruits with whipped cream (Chad), v. II, 58

index

ARGENTINA, v. II, 507-13
ARMENIA, v. I, 585-99
artichokes, hearts
    and onions in tomato sauce (Armenia),
        v. I, 593-94
    cream soup (Brazil), v. II, 524
    grilled vegetable salad (Kuwait), v. I, 516
    in oil (Jordan), v. I, 505
    salad, with leeks and carrots (Turkey), v. I, 570
    salad, with preserved lemons and honey
        (Morocco), v. II, 173
    skillet stew with eggs and fava beans (Malta),
        v. I, 276-77
    summer vegetable stew (Tunisia), v. II, 276-77
    vegetable and cheese pies (Uruguay), v. II, 624-25
    vegetable *ragoût* (Lebanon), v. I, 527-28
    vegetable salad (Albania), v. I, 7
    village tossed salad (Greece), v. I, 161-62
    with angel hair *pasta*, mushrooms, and *chorizo* in
        skillet (Spain), v. I, 395
    with Irish cream and mustard sauce (Ireland),
        v. I, 200-201
artichokes, whole
    baby, sautéed with lemon and garlic (Italy),
        v. I, 225-26
    baby, with lemon dipping sauce (Egypt), v. II, 80-81
    stuffed (Italy), v. I, 218-19
asparagus
    and mushrooms with oregano and fennel oil
        (Liechtenstein), v. I, 241
    and *wonton* noodles with egg sauce (Japan),
        v. II, 364-65
    cream soup (Belgium), v. I, 48-49
    cream soup (German), v. I, 143-44
    in bitter orange sauce (Spain), v. I, 396
    rice with vegetables (Bhutan), v. I, 661-62
    salad, with capers (Romania), v. I, 343
    salad, with raspberry *vinaigrette* (Australia),
        v. II, 451
    sautéed with hazelnuts (Austria), v. I, 27
    with *fontina* (Italy), v. I, 211
AUSTRALIA (Oceania), v. II, 447-59
AUSTRIA, v. I, 22-31
avocados
    and egg salad (Colombia), v. II, 537
    and egg salad (Israel), v. I, 498
    and grapefruit salad (Somalia), v. II, 234-35
    and ice cream dessert (Indonesia), v. II, 358
    and mayonnaise salad (Ghana), v. II, 110
    and pineapple appetizer spread (Côte d'Ivoire),
        v. II, 62-63
    and pineapple salad (Central African Republics),
        v. II, 47
    and shallots in tomato soup (Australia), v. II, 449-50
    and tangerine dessert (Mozambique), v. II, 185-86
    and tomato dipping sauce (Venezuela), v. II, 630
    appetizer *guacamole* with egg and cheese (El
        Salvador), v. II, 559-60
    cream dessert (Venezuela), v. II, 635
    creamy, puréed, vegetable soup (Venezuela),
        v. II, 632-33
    dip with lime (Sierra Leone), v. II, 226-27
    dip with tomato (Zambia), v. II, 292
    fruit platter with lime *vinaigrette* (Caribbean),
        v. II, 496
    fruit salad (Central African Republics), v. II, 53
    fruit salad with citrus *vinaigrette* (Côte d'Ivoire),
        v. II, 66
    halves, with spicy dressing (Guinea), v. II, 118
    halves, stuffed with tomato salad (New Zealand),
        v. II, 463
    layered fruit salad (Cameroon), v. II, 34-35
    millet and corn salad with avocado (Central African
        Republics), v. II, 47-48
    nasturtium blossoms stuffed with avocado (Native
        America), v. II, 655
    potato and cheese soup (Ecuador), v. II, 552-53
    pudding (Western Sahara), v. II, 167-68
    salad, with cabbage and pickled red onion relish
        (Ecuador), v. II, 551
    salad, with mango, orange, and citrus dressing
        (Senegal), v. II, 219
    salad, with papaya and grapefruit (Kenya), v. II, 126
    salad, with peaches and tomato (Mozambique),
        v. II, 181
    soup, chilled (Côte d'Ivoire), v. II, 64
AZERBAIJAN, v. I, 600-609

Baking powder substitute, v. I, 305
bamboo shoots
    and greens (Uganda), v. II, 287
    rice noodle and meatball soup (Laos), v. II, 386
    stir-fried vegetables with coconut (Brunei),
        v. II, 311
    stir-fried with mushrooms (Tibet) v. II, 344
    with sesame seeds (Laos), v. II, 388-89
    wonton appetizers (China), v. II, 323-24
bananas, *see also* plantains
    and chocolate in pastry (Côte d'Ivoire), v. II, 68-69
    and deep-fried black-eyed peas (Niger),
        v. II, 199-200
    and flax cake (The Gambia), v. II, 107-108
    and lime whip (Pacific Islands), v. II, 484
    and mango salad (The Gambia), v. II, 102
    and rice curry with peanut butter (Angola), v. II, 14
    and semolina dessert (Guinea), v. II, 121-22
    and soymeat stew (Liberia), v. II, 134-35
    and sticky rice sweet (Cambodia), v. II, 321
    autumn compote (Portugal), v. I, 331
    baby, salad with peanuts (The Philippines),
        v. II, 420-21
    baked (Gabon), v. II, 52-53
    banana custard cornbread (Caribbean), v. II, 501
    banana nectar beverage dessert (Ghana), v. II, 115
    bean and celery soup (Burundi), v. II, 27-28
    biscuits (Pacific Islands – Fiji), v. II, 476-77
    cheese-stuffed zucchini with lentils and fruit
        (Mexico), v. II, 583-84
    chilled soup (Tanzania), v. II, 261-62
    dessert (Mozambique), v. II, 186
    fritters (Djibouti), v. II, 76
    fruit salad (Uganda), v. II, 283-84
    groundnut and vegetable soup (Djibouti),
        v. II, 72-73

index

bananas (cont'd)
    in aromatic sauce (Pakistan), v. **I**, 693-94
    in coconut milk (Thailand), v. **II**, 436
    ice cream (Tanzania), v. **II**, 264-65
    in pastry (Cape Verde), v. **II**, 44
    layered fruit salad (Cameroon), v. **II**, 34-35
    meatballs and fruit in curry sauce (Mozambique), v. **II**, 183-84
    omelet (São Tomé and Principe), v. **II**, 211
    papaya salad with curried island dressing (Pacific Islands – Vanuatu), v. **II**, 474
    pastry (Mauritania), v. **II**, 168
    phyllo tart (Central African Republics), v. **II**, 52
    pumpkin soup with coconut milk (Caribbean – Bahamas), v. **II**, 494
    salad, curried, with yam and hard-cooked egg (Pacific Islands), v. **II**, 475
    salad, green banana and vegetable (Costa Rica), v. **II**, 542-43
    salad, with rice (Kenya), v. **II**, 127
    slow cooker dried fruit curry (South Africa), v. **II**, 247-48
    soup, with *yucca* and coconut (Honduras), v. **II**, 573-74
    strudel (Namibia), v. **II**, 195-96
    tamarind dressing (Brunei), v. **II**, 308-309
    tropical fruit salad (Nigeria), v. **II**, 202
    vegetable and groundnut soup (Zambia), v. **II**, 292-93
    with cream, v. **II**, 289
    with mango and pineapple in mango-yogurt sauce (Oman), v. **I**, 537
    with uncooked coconut cream sauce (Pacific Islands – Cook Islands), v. **II**, 484-85
BANGLADESH, v. **I**, 644-54
barley
    and carrot pudding (Finland), v. **I**, 126-27
    and vegetable soup with sour cream (Poland), v. **I**, 322-23
    chilled soup with sour cream (Latvia), v. **I**, 233
    slow cooker vegetable soup with beans and barley (Croatia), v. **I**, 87-88
    sweet porridge (Mongolia), v. **II**, 406
    vegetable soup (Estonia), v. **I**, 112-13
    vegetable soup (Oman), v. **I**, 538
    with carrots (Belarus), v. **I**, 39
    with wild mushrooms and sage (Scotland), v. **I**, 452
basil, opal, information, v. **II**, 678 (note)
bay leaves, information, v. **I**, 334 (note)
beancurd, *see tofu*
beans, basic slow cooker preparation, v. **II**, 43-44
beans, black
    and sweetpotato appetizers (Caribbean), v. **II**, 491
    in tomato-garlic sauce (The Gambia), v. **II**, 103
    soup (The Netherlands), v. **I**, 300-301
    with green pepper (Native America), v. **II**, 667
    with rice and mango relish (Caribbean – Cuba), v. **II**, 499-500
beans, black, preserved/fermented
    lettuce wraps (Korea), v. **II**, 378
    stir-fried Chinese cabbage, peppers, and eggs (Malaysia), v. **II**, 394-95
    with roasted baby peppers (China), v. **II**, 334
beans, black-eyed peas, pigeon beans
    black-eyed peas (Namibia), v. **II**, 194-95
    and tomato soup (Liberia), v. **II**, 133
    beans in coconut milk (Chad), v. **II**, 56-57
    deep-fried with bananas (Niger), v. **II**, 199-200
    in coconut milk (Kenya), v. **II**, 127-28
    slow cooker *chili* (Uganda), v. **II**, 287-88
    with coconut and cocoa (Sierra Leone), v. **II**, 227
    with leeks and spinach in skillet (Iran), v. **I**, 479-80
beans, *borlotti*
    mixed legume soup (Morocco), v. **II**, 172-73
beans, chick peas (*garbanzos*)
    and *couscous* in vegetable soup (Angola), v. **II**, 11-12
    and Israeli *couscous* salad (Israel), v. **I**, 496
    and kale soup with peanut butter and tomatoes (Djibouti), v. **II**, 74
    and mushroom salad (Somalia), v. **II**, 235
    and potato salad (Armenia), v. **I**, 591
    and potato vegetable stew (Tunisia), v. **II**, 275-76
    and rice soup (Mongolia), v. **II**, 402-403
    and tomato soup with leeks (Uruguay), v. **II**, 623
    bread salad, with spinach, rice, and garlic-yogurt sauce with *tahini*, (Tunisia), v. **II**, 274-75
    couscous salad (Algeria), v. **II**, 4-5
    couscous salad (Mauritania), v. **II**, 162-63
    cream soup (Guatemala), v. **II**, 566-67
    curried (Nepal), v. **I**, 683-84
    dumplings in yogurt sauce (India), v. **I**, 667-68
    falafel (Jordan), v. **I**, 503
    hot yogurt soup with rice (Iran), v. **I**, 477-78
    hummus (Turkey), v. **I**, 567-68
    ground legume and spice mixture (Egypt), v. **II**, 78
    in tomato sauce (Guatemala), v. **II**, 569
    millet *couscous* with (Mauritania), v. **II**, 164-65
    mixed legume soup (Morocco), v. **II**, 172-73
    puréed cream soup with celeriac (Turkey), v. **I**, 569
    roasted beets and *hummus* (Israel), v. **I**, 494
    roasted, with nuts (Jordan), v. **I**, 503-504
    salad (Libya), v. **II**, 142
    sautéed with sage (Spain), v. **I**, 396-97
    soup, with rice (Peru), v. **II**, 612-13
    soup, with roasted red peppers and garlic (Greece), v. **I**, 165-66
    spicy, slow-cooked (Pakistan), v. **I**, 692-93
    sweet (Tunisia), v. **II**, 278
    tagliatelle with chick peas (Cyprus), v. **I**, 471
    three-bean salad with creamy dressing (Mongolia), v. **II**, 402
    tomato-black bean *vinaigrette* for *couscous* salad (Somalia), v. **II**, 234
    tomato bouillon with chick peas (Mauritania/Western Sahara), v. **II**, 164
    with fried spinach and grated cheese (Egypt), v. **II**, 81
    with groundnut butter in vegetable soup (Namibia), v. **II**, 192
    with *linguine*, red kidney beans, and seasoned soymeat (Afghanistan), v. **I**, 640
    with tomatoes and apricots (Yemen), v. **I**, 580-81

index

beans, cranberry
    bean salad with walnuts (Georgia), v. I, 615-16
    mixed legume soup (Morocco), v. II, 172-73

beans, fava, butter beans, or broad beans
    and scrambled eggs (Lebanon), v. I, 530
    artichoke skillet stew with eggs (Malta), v. I, 276-77
    bean stew with hominy and *chouriço* (Cape Verde), v. II, 42-43
    falafel (Jordan), v. I, 503
    patties (Sudan), v. II, 254-55
    salad (Malta), v. I, 275

beans, Great Northern, Navy, pea, and *cannellini*
    baked (Native America), v. II, 664
    bean and celery soup (Burundi), v. II, 27-28
    bean stew with hominy and *chouriço* (Cape Verde), v. II, 42-43
    Bosnian, v. I, 62
    chili bean soup, v. I, 283-84
    soup with pinched dumplings (Hungary), v. I, 176-77
    vegetable salad with white beans, root celery, kohlrabi, and potatoes (Czech), v. I, 96
    vegetable stew with beans and *chouriço* sausage (Angola), v. II, 13-14
    walnut and bean *pâté* with vegetable filling (France), v. I, 132-33
    white beans in tomato sauce (Albania), v. I, 10

beans, green beans
    and garlic salad (Slovenia), v. I, 387
    and potato curry (Malaysia), v. II, 393-94
    bean salad (Caribbean - Haiti), v. II, 497
    curry (Sri Lanka), v. I, 701-702
    foot long beans with black mushrooms in brown garlic sauce (China), v. II, 331
    groundnut and vegetable soup (Djibouti), v. II, 72-73
    lentil *consommé* (Lichtenstein), v. I, 239
    lentil soup with vegetables (Burundi), v. II, 28-29
    meatballs and vegetables skillet (Niger), v. II, 198-99
    Milanese *minestrone* (Italy), v. I, 222-23
    millet *couscous* with vegetables (The Gambia), v. II, 103
    niçoise salad (France), v. I, 136
    soup, with potatoes (Slovakia), v. I, 373-74
    steamed vegetable salad with sweet black sesame dressing (Brunei), v. II, 308
    stir-fried long beans and mushrooms with garlic (Laos), v. II, 388
    stir-fried vegetables with coconut (Brunei), v. II, 311
    sweet and sour bean salad (Zimbabwe), v. II, 299-300
    three-bean salad with creamy dressing (Mongolia), v. II, 402
    vegetable and groundnut soup (Zambia), v. II, 292-93
    vegetable stew (Ethiopia), v. II, 94
    vegetable stew with beer (Belgium), v. I, 49-50
    vegetables in curried coconut milk (Thailand), v. II, 434-35
    with meatballs in yogurt sauce (Bosnia), v. I, 63

beans, lima beans
    and corn custard pudding (Brazil), v. II, 526
    and rice (Cape Verde), v. II, 41
    and tomato skillet (Peru), v. II, 616
    bean and celery soup (Burundi), v. II, 27-28
    beans, carrot, and creamed corn (Oman), v. I, 539
    slow cooker vegetable stew (Botswana), v. II, 19-20
    sweet and sour bean salad (Zimbabwe), v. II, 299-300
    vegetable stew (Bolivia), v. II, 515-16
    with tomatoes and eggs (Mexico), v. II, 585

beans, mung beans
    sauce with tomatoes and garlic (Uganda), v. II, 285-86
    sprouts, curried vegetables with *tofu* (Cambodia), v. II, 319
    sprouts, dumpling soup (Korea), v. II, 371-72
    sprouts, *wonton* appetizers (China), v. II, 323-24
    sprouts, stir-fried noodles and vegetables, (Brunei), v. II, 309-10
    stir-fried vegetables with coconut (Brunei), v. II, 311

beans peanuts, including peanut butter
    and rice pudding (Zambia), v. II, 297
    and tomato sauce with garlic (The Gambia), v. II, 104
    and tomato soup (Ghana), v. II, 111
    and winter squash soup (Senegal), v. II, 216-17
    and yogurt appetizer dip (Sudan), v. II, 252
    baby banana salad (The Philippines), v. II, 420-21
    butternut squash with greens (Botswana), v. II, 22
    cabbage and carrot slaw (Pakistan), v. I, 690-91
    cabbage and green mango salad (Myanmar/ Burma), v. II, 412
    chick pea and kale soup with tomatoes (Djibouti), v. II, 74
    citrus-shallot sauce for baked *tofu* (Pacific Islands – Polynesia), v. II, 481-82
    cream of peanut butter soup (Mexico), v. II, 582
    cucumber salad with peanut-lime dressing (Central African Republics), v. II, 48-49
    dressing for *pasta* and vegetable salad (Senegal), v. II, 221
    eggplant and brown rice (Indonesia), v. II, 355
    fruit and vegetable salad (Indonesia), v. II, 354
    ground legume and spice mixture (Egypt), v. II, 78
    groundnut and vegetable soup (Djibouti), v. II, 72-73
    groundnut biscuits (Zambia), v. II, 295-96
    groundnut ice cream (Senegal), v. II, 223
    peanut-apple crumble v. II, 469-70
    peanut candy (Angola), v. II, 16
    peanut-lime dressing (Central African Republics), v. II, 48-49
    peanut macaroons (Sudan), v. II, 257-58
    potatoes with peanut sauce (Peru), v. II, 617-18
    radish and garlic relish/salad (Myanmar/Burma), v. II, 413-14
    rice curry with bananas (Angola), v. II, 14

beans, peanuts (cont'd)
- rice pudding with peanut butter cream (Togo), v. II, 269
- salad dressing (Indonesia), v. II, 354-55
- sauce for potato cakes (Ecuador), v. II, 554
- sautéed squashes with peanuts (Chad), v. II, 57-58
- slow cooker dried fruit curry (South Africa), v. II, 247-48
- soup with greens and corn (Chad), v. II, 55
- spicy sauce with ginger (Togo), v. II, 268-69
- spinach stew (Central African Republics), v. II, 51
- summer squash with peanuts and garlic (Central African Republics), v. II, 49-50
- sweetpotato and greens in vegetable soup (Zimbabwe), v. II, 300
- sweetpotatoes with gingerroot (Vietnam), v. II, 441
- toasted millet salad (Mali) v. II, 155-56
- tomato and groundnut soup (Ghana), v. II, 111
- tomato and peanut sauce with cream (Brazil), v. II, 527-28
- tomato and peanut sauce (Zambia), v. II, 294
- vegetable and groundnut soup (Zambia), v. II, 292-93
- watermelon and cucumber salad (Vietnam), v. II, 439
- with chick peas in vegetable soup (Namibia), v. II, 192
- with greens (Tanzania), v. II, 264
- with lentils (Guinea), v. II, 118-19
- with pan-grilled plantains (Nigeria), v. II, 204-205

beans, pinto
- mixed legume soup (Morocco), v. II, 172-73
- spicy bean soup with coconut milk (Djibouti), v. II, 72

beans, red kidney
- and corn casserole (Tanzania), v. II, 263
- and red peppers (Latvia), v. I, 234
- and tomatoes with plantains (Colombia), v. II, 539
- and white eggplant salad (Ethiopia), v. II, 93
- bean and celery soup (Burundi), v. II, 27-28
- bean and hominy *chili* (Somalia), v. II, 238
- bean salad (Caribbean – Haiti), v. II, 497
- *chili*, v. II, 288
- chowder of vegetables and fine noodles (Montenegro), v. I, 294-95
- coconut-bean soup with rice (Nigeria), v. II, 203-204
- layered vegetable salad (Ghana), v. II, 111-12
- noodle soup (Central Asia), v. I, 625
- red pottage (Scotland), v. I, 449
- salad, with corn and mango (Burundi), v. II, 27
- salad with eggs (Slovenia), v. I, 388-89
- slow cooker vegetable soup with beans and barley (Croatia), v. I, 87-88
- soup, curried, with coconut and basmati rice (Tanzania), v. II, 260-61
- soup, with coconut and rice (Nigeria), v. II, 203-204
- sweet and sour bean salad (Zimbabwe), v. II, 299-300
- *tacos* or *tostados* with sautéed greens and goat cheese (Panama), v. II, 600-601
- three-bean salad with creamy dressing (Mongolia), v. II, 402
- with grated cheese (El Salvador), v. II, 562
- with *linguine*, chick peas, and seasoned soymeat (Afghanistan), v. I, 640

beans, Roman
- bean and corn salad (Liechtenstein), v. I, 239
- bean salad with walnuts (Georgia), v. I, 615-16
- mixed legume soup (Morocco), v. II, 172-73
- spicy bean soup with coconut milk (Djibouti), v. II, 72

beans, vegetarian baked beans
- curried beans with sausage (Madagascar), v. II, 149
- spicy beans (Malta), v. I, 277
- with pineapple (Pacific Islands – Hawaii), v. II, 480-81

beans, yellow wax beans, three-bean salad with creamy dressing (Mongolia), v. II, 402

beets
- and apple salad (Uruguay), v. II, 624
- and apple salad with sour cream (Lithuania), v. I, 247
- and garlic salad (Greece), v. I, 162-63
- and horseradish relish (Slovakia), v. I, 379-80
- and mushroom soup (Poland), v. I, 323-24
- and spinach salad with yogurt dressing (Georgia), v. I, 618-19
- and *tahini* salad with eggs (Syria), v. I, 564
- anise-scented (Algeria), v. II, 6
- Argentine-styled Russian salad, v. II, 508-509
- bean and corn salad (Liechtenstein), v. I, 239
- chilled *borsch* (Belarus), v. I, 37
- cooked, technique recommendations, v. I, 26 (note)
- curry (Sri Lanka), v. I, 703-704
- cutlets, breaded and fried (Norway), v. I, 312
- deviled potato, apple, and egg salad (Estonia), v. I, 111-12
- dip with roasted beets, garlic, and *hummus* (Israel), v. I, 494
- Harvard (Belarus), v. I, 38-39
- in cream (Honduras), v. II, 575-76
- oven preparation technique, v. I, 26, 312
- pickled (Denmark), v. I, 104
- pink potato salad (Panama), v. II, 598-99
- red pottage (Scotland), v. I, 449
- salad, shredded (Romania), v. I, 344
- salad with cheese (Austria), v. I, 26
- salad with eggs (Belarus), v. I, 35-36
- salad with *feta* cheese (Serbia), v. I, 366-67
- salad with garlic-mayonnaise dressing (Moldova), v. I, 285
- salad, with potato and carrot (Peru), v. II, 613-14
- salad, with yogurt and mint (Iran), v. I, 478
- shredded fresh (Russia), v. I, 355
- soup (Ukraine), v. I, 426-27
- vegetable salad with hearts of palm (Brazil), v. II, 525
- vicarage, with herbs (England), v. I, 439
- with chive oil (Armenia), v. I, 595
- with chopped egg (Iceland), v. I, 189-90
- with oil and lemon (Ethiopia), v. II, 96

index

beets (cont'd)
    with tart cherry sauce and fresh herbs (Georgia), v. **I**, 617-18
    Yale, v. **I**, 39 (note)
BELARUS, v. **I**, 32-42
BELGIUM, v. **I**, 43-57
berries, *see also by name*
    and honey over pancakes (Morocco), v. **II**, 176-77
beverages
    banana nectar beverage dessert (Ghana), v. **II**, 115
    chilled coffee milk with cardamom and cinnamon (Somalia), v. **II**, 240-41
    chocolate *demitasse* (Venezuela), v. **II**, 637
    creamy cocoa cordial (São Tomé and Principe), v. **II**, 213-14
    fresh fruit refresher (Mexico), v. **II**, 587-88
    fresh pineapple drink with fresh gingerroot (Liberia), v. **II**, 132
    fruit spiders (Australia), v. **II**, 458
    hot cocoa mix, v. **I**, 220
    iced mocha (Costa Rica), v. **II**, 546
    kiwifruit *frappé* appetizer (New Zealand), v. **II**, 461-62
    limoncello, v. **II**, 473-74
    mango smoothie (Pakistan), v. **I**, 697
    mochalata cordial (São Tomé and Principe), v. **II**, 213
    orange spiced tea (Russia), v. **I**, 361
    papaya juice (Eritrea), v. **II**, 84-85
    papaya punch (Pacific Islands – Hawaii), v. **II**, 472
    passion fruit appetizer (Caribbean), v. **II**, 490
    pomegranate refresher (Morocco), v. **II**, 170-71
    prickly pear-orange-apple- pineapple punch (Native America), v. **II**, 653-54
    spiced honey tea (Central Asia), v. **I**, 634
    strawberry-rhubarb juice (Finland), v. **I**, 121-22
    tea with rosebuds (China), v. **II**, 336
    watermelon punch (Turkmenistan), v. **I**, 634
    white wine and fruit juice cooler (Uruguay), v. **II**, 627
    yogurt drink (Senegal), v. **II**, 224
    yogurt drink (Uzbekistan), v. **I**, 633
BHUTAN, v. **I**, 655-62
blackberries
    cobbler (Ireland), v. **I**, 203
    sauce or dessert (Australia), v. **II**, 687
blueberries
    and strawberry summer pudding, v. **I**, 445-46
    hot-packed, v. **II**, 646
    pudding (Canada), v. **II**, 645-46
    salad, with peaches and cantaloupe and almond syrup and *moscato* wine sauce (Macedonia), v. **I**. 264
    sauce (Lithuania), v. **I**, 250
    tossed salad with hazelnuts (England), v. **I**, 436
    Yorkshire summer pudding (England), v. **I**, 444-45
bok choy, see cabbage
BOLIVIA, v. **II**, 514-18
BOSNIA and HERTZEGOVINA, v. **I**, 58-68
BOTSWANA, v. **II**, 17-24
BRAZIL, v. **II**, 519-29

breads
    adobe bread with amaranth (Native America), v. **II**, 660
    anise toast (Italy), v. **I**, 209
    baked corn *tortilla* chips (El Salvador), v. **II**, 560
    baking powder corn meal biscuits (Native America), v. **II**, 659
    banana biscuits (Pacific Islands – Fiji), v. **II**, 476-77
    banana custard cornbread (Caribbean), v. **II**, 501
    beer biscuits (Denmark), v. **I**, 105
    Belgian waffles (Belgium), v. **I**, 56-57
    brown buttermilk scones (Ireland), v. **I**, 196-97
    buttermilk cornbread, v. **I**, 368
    cashew appetizer toasts (Brazil), v. **II**, 522-23
    colonial-style, v. **II**, 523-24
    corn meal cake (Kenya), v. **II**, 128-29
    country corn (Portugal), v. **I**, 336-37
    crostini with oil, tomato, and capers (Malta), v. **I**, 272-73
    Dutch oven unkneaded bread, v. **II**, 191
    French-style *baquettes*, v. **II**, 101-102
    fried corn flatbreads (Sudan), v. **II**, 256
    fried loaves (Botswana), v. **II**, 23
    ginger buttermilk scones (Scotland), v. **I**, 450-51
    green onion sesame skillet bread (Tibet), v. **II**, 345
    groundnut biscuits (Zambia), v. **II**, 295-96
    hazelnut breads (Native America), v. **II**, 661
    honey barley (Estonia), v. **I**, 115-16
    injera for the western kitchen, v. **II**, 92
    leek wheaten scones (Ireland), v. **I**, 197-98
    maple multigrain, v. **II**, 106-107
    oat scones (Scotland), v. **I**, 449-50
    olive oil with *hummus* and mint (Cyprus), v. **I**, 473
    pancake, quick bread, and waffle mix, v. **I**, 304-305
    parmesan toasts (Italy), v. **I**, 226
    pumpernickel, with caraway seeds (Germany), v. **I**, 150 (note)
    raisin pumpernickel (Germany), v. **I**, 150
    skillet flatbread (Somalia), v. **II**, 232
    sultan's slices (Bulgaria), v. **I**, 80
    sweetpotato biscuits (Zimbabwe), v. **II**, 301
    thyme loaves (Algeria), v. **II**, 8
    tortilla skillet (Honduras), v. **II**, 574-75
    waffles, v. **I**, 304
    wheaten biscuit mix, v. **II**, 698
    whole grain (Finland), v. **I**, 122-23
    whole wheat baking powder biscuits with sage (Canada), v. **II**, 644-45
    whole wheat hot cross buns (England), v. **I**, 446-47
    wonton skins (China), v. **II**, 324-25
    za'atar toast (Lebanon), v. **I**, 523-24
broccoli
    and potato salad with Hollandaise sauce (Brazil), v. **II**, 521
    pasta and vegetable salad with peanut butter dressing (Senegal), v. **II**, 221
    steamed vegetable salad with sweet black sesame dressing (Brunei), v. **II**, 308
    with spaghetti and garlic (Botswana), v. **II**, 22-23
BRUNEI, v. **II**, 305-13
buerre manie, v. **I**, 559
BULGARIA, v. **I**, 69-80

index

bulgur wheat
    and lentils in cabbage rolls with dried fruits (Armenia), v. I, 592-93
    and red lentil soup (Turkey), v. I, 568-69
    and red lentil soup with apricots (Armenia), v. I, 589-90
    and tomato and spinach soup with mint (Armenia), v. I, 590-91
    salad (Jordan), v. I, 504-505
BURMA, *see* **MYANMAR**
BURUNDI, v. II, 25-30

Cabbage
cabbage, *bok choy*
    almond vegetables Mandarin *mu shu* (China), v. II, 329
    and *soba* noodles with *tukpa* broth (Tibet), v. II, 340-41
    curried vegetables with *tofu* (Cambodia), v. II, 319
    red grapefruit salad with soymeat and soy sprouts (Thailand), v. II, 433-34
    soup, with clear *cilantro* stock (The Philippines), v. II, 419-20
    steamed vegetable salad with sweet black sesame dressing (Brunei), v. II, 308
    steamed with sautéed mushrooms (China), v. II, 333
    tossed salad with noodles and onion *vinaigrette* (Mongolia), v. II, 401
cabbage, Chinese, including *napa* and celery cabbage
    cabbage pickle, *kimchi* (Korea), v. II, 376-77
    dumpling soup (Korea), v. II, 371-72
    stir-fried, with peppers and eggs (Malaysia), v. II, 394-95
cabbage, red
    and black currant slaw (Finland), v. I, 125
    Christmas slaw (Iceland), v. I, 188
    sweet and sour (The Netherlands), v. I, 302-303
    sweet and sour on vegetarian reubens (Pacific Islands – Cook Islands), v. II, 478-79
    sweet and sour with sour cream (Estonia), v. I, 115
cabbage, sauerkraut
    and potato *croquettes* (Luxembourg), v. I, 256-57
    slow cooker, with apples (Latvia), v. I, 235
    vegetarian reubens (Pacific Islands – Cook Islands), v. II, 478-79
cabbage, savoy
    and potatoes (Hungary), v. I, 180
    buttered (Ireland), v. I, 202
    sautéed with fennel leaves (Romania), v. I, 345-46
    slow cooker vegetable soup with beans and barley (Croatia), v. I, 87-88
    steamed with butter and chestnuts (Lithuania), v. I, 249
cabbage, white/green
    and carrot salad with yogurt dressing (Western Sahara), v. II, 163
    and carrot slaw with peanuts (Pakistan), v. I, 690-91
    and celery with sour cream (Canada), v. II, 641-42
    and green mango salad (Myanmar/Burma), v. II, 412
    and noodle skillet (Poland), v. I, 325
    and potato pie (Luxembourg), v. I, 255-56
    and potatoes in tomato sauce (Bangladesh), v. I, 648
    bean stew with hominy and *chouriço* (Cape Verde), v. II, 42-43
    beet soup (Ukraine), v. I, 426-27
    cabbage casserole with breadcrumbs (Serbia), v. I, 369
    cabbage pickles (Nepal), v. I, 687
    cabbage rolls stuffed with lentils, bulgur and dried fruits (Armenia), v. I, 592-93
    fried with tomatoes (Moldova), v. I, 288
    glass noodle and vegetable slaw (Tibet), v. II, 341
    groundnut and vegetable soup (Djibouti), v. II, 72-73
    lentil soup with vegetables (Burundi), v. II, 28-29
    Milanese *minestrone* (Italy), v. I, 222-23
    salad, with avocado and pickled red onion relish (Ecuador), v. II, 551
    salad, with pineapple (Liberia), v. II, 133-34
    salad, with shredded carrot (Cyprus), v. I, 468
    sautéed, with carrot and onion (Mozambique), v. II, 185
    sautéed, with fennel leaves (Romania), v. I, 345-46
    scalloped with cream (Montenegro), v. I, 297
    slaw (Slovenia), v. I, 389
    slaw of the *vuelta e 'Lola*, (Venezuela), v. II, 631
    slaw with carrot, onion, and apple (Ukraine), v. I, 426
    slaw with pineapple (Cameroon), v. II, 34
    slaw with corn and dillweed (Angola), v. II, 12-13
    soup (Russia), v. I, 352
    stir-fried vegetables with coconut (Brunei), v. II, 311
    stir-fried with carrots and red pepper (Tibet), v. II, 343
    sweet browned with sausage (Denmark), v. I, 102
    tossed vegetable salad with cheese (Sudan), v. II, 252-53
    vegetable and groundnut soup (Zambia), v. II, 292-93
    vegetable slaw (El Salvador), v. II, 560-61
    vegetable soup with barley (Estonia), v. I, 112-13
    vegetable soup with oatmeal or barley (Oman), v. I, 538
    vegetable stew (Uzbekistan), v. I, 628-29
    vegetable stew with beans and *chouriço* sausage (Angola), v. II, 13-14
    with tomatoes (Venezuela), v. II, 634
cakes
    almond (Iceland), v. I, 191
    brown sugar pound cake (Costa Rica), v. II, 545-46
    buttermilk (Moldova), v. I, 289
    carrot (Switzerland), v. I, 420
    chocolate almond *torte* (Hungary), v. I, 184
    chocolate "chemistry class" cake (Bosnia), v. I, 67
    coconut (Oman), v. I, 542
    coffee-spice "chemistry class" cake with honey (Paraguay), v. II, 608
    egg sponge cake with sugar syrup (Albania), v. I, 11-12
    flax-banana (The Gambia), v. II, 107-108
    gingerbread (England), v. I, 443
    ginger cake (Nigeria), v. II, 205-206

cakes (cont'd)
    gold [Lord Baltimore], v. I, 317-18
    milk cake (Ecuador), v. II, 557
    orange (Macedonia), v. I, 269
    orange *torte* (Portugal), v. I, 338
    peach with crumbled meringue (Uruguay),
        v. II, 625-26
    semolina with *tahini* (Lebanon), v. I, 533-34
    spiced pumpkin (Liberia), v. II, 135-36
    sweet egg sponge (Guatemala), v. II, 569-70
    toasted hazelnut *torte* (Hungary), v. I, 182-83
    walnut sponge (Russia), v. I, 358
    with lemon syrup (Bosnia), v. I, 66
    yogurt (Bulgaria), v. I, 80
CAMBODIA, v. II, 314-21
CAMEROON, v. II, 31-39
CANADA, v. II, 639-49
canning and preserving, *see also* vinegars
    applesauce, v. I, 185 (note)
    brown stock, v. II, 692-93 (note)
    cabbage pickle, *kimchi* (Korea), v. II, 376-77
    corn relish, v. II, 579-80
    daikon and red radish pickles (Tibet), v. II, 346
    lemon jelly infused with fresh herbs (Native
        America), v. II, 668-69
    papaya jam (Cameroon), v. II, 33-34
    peach jam, v. I, 619
    pickled baby beets (Denmark), v. I, 104
    pickled blue plums (Poland), v. I, 326-27
    pickled eggplant with dill (Turkmenistan),
        v. I, 626-27
    pickled mustard greens (Vietnam), v. II, 442-43
    pickled red onion relish with lime juice (Ecuador),
        v. II, 552
    pineapple jam, v. II, 564
    preserved lemon conserve (Morocco), v. II, 174
    preserved mango (Cape Verde), v. II, 42
    preserved sweet and sour eggs (The Philippines),
        v. II, 419
    tomato jam (Mozambique), v. II, 180
    vegetable stock from soup, v. II, 691-92 (note)
    vegetables stocks for soups, stews and sauces,
        v. II, 692-93 (note)
    white stock, v. II, 692-93 (note)
cannoli pastry (Italy/Sicilia) (Venezuela), v. II, 636-37
CAPE VERDE, v. II, 40-44
carambola (starfruit)
    and mango appetizer with *limoncello* (Pacific
        Islands – New Guinea), v. II, 472-73
    and orange dessert (Caribbean), v. II, 505
    fruit and vegetable salad (Indonesia), v. II, 354
    fruit salad with tamarind dressing (Brunei),
        v. II, 308-309
CARIBBEAN, THE, v. II, 488-505
carrots
    almond vegetables Mandarin *mu shu* (China),
        v. II, 329
    and barley pudding (Finland), v. I, 126-27
    and cabbage salad with yogurt dressing (Western
        Sahara), v. II, 163
    and cabbage slaw with peanuts (Pakistan),
        v. I, 690-91

    and *jicama* salad with mango (Colombia),
        v. II, 538-39
    and *kumara* puréed soup with gingerroot (New
        Zealand), v. II, 465-66
    and leeks with celery sauce (Scotland), v. I, 453
    Argentine-styled Russian salad, v. II, 508-509
    artichoke salad with leeks (Turkey), v. I, 570
    baby, in wild rice casserole with mushrooms
        (Canada), v. II, 642-43
    baked lentils with cheese (Germany), v. I, 147-48
    barley and vegetable soup with sour cream (Poland),
        v. I, 322-23
    bean soup with pinched dumplings (Hungary),
        v. I, 176-77
    beetroot curry (Sri Lanka), v. I, 703-704
    beet soup (Ukraine), v. I, 426-27
    black bean soup (The Netherlands), v. I, 300-301
    braised vegetables in olive oil with rice (Saudi
        Arabia), v. I, 556
    cake (Switzerland), v. I, 420
    chick pea and potato vegetable stew (Tunisia),
        v. II, 275-76
    chowder of vegetables and fine noodles
        (Montenegro), v. I, 294-95
    collard greens and kale with potatoes and carrots
        (Montenegro), v. I, 295-96
    cream of chick pea soup (El Salvador), v. II, 566-67
    cream soup with celeriac (Finland), v. I, 123-24
    creamy, puréed, vegetable soup (Venezuela),
        v. II, 632-33
    dark vegetable stock (Thailand), v. II, 431-32
    dumpling soup (Korea), v. II, 371-72
    Flemish (Belgium), v. I, 52-53
    glass noodle and vegetable slaw (Tibet), v. II, 341
    glazed with mint (Morocco), v. II, 176
    goulash (Hungary), v. I, 177-78
    groundnut and vegetable soup (Djibouti),
        v. II, 72-73
    Irish stew, v. I, 199-200
    kohlrabi and papaya salad with tamarind dressing
        (Laos), v. II, 385
    lentil soup with vegetables (Burundi), v. II, 28-29
    macaroni and vegetables (The Gambia),
        v. II, 104-105
    Milanese *minestrone* (Italy), v. I, 222-23
    millet *couscous* with vegetables (The Gambia),
        v. II, 103
    Moscow salad (Russia), v. I, 351
    noodle soup with kidney beans (Central Asia),
        v. I, 625
    omelet on omelet (Chile), v. II, 531
    oven-roasted root vegetables with cheese (Sweden),
        v. I, 402-403
    oven-roasted root vegetables with fresh herbs and
        mushrooms (Namibia), v. II, 193-94
    pancakes with vegetables (Mauritania), v. II, 161-62
    pasta and vegetable salad with peanut butter
        dressing (Senegal), v. II, 221
    pickled vegetables (Panama), v. II, 601-602
    pilaf (Kazakhstan), v. I, 630-31
    potato-meatball soup (Latvia), v. I, 232-33
    pudding (Saudi Arabia), v. I, 559

carrots (cont'd)
- pumpkin soup with coconut milk and banana (Caribbean - Bahamas), v. II, 494
- puréed chick pea and celeriac soup (Turkey), v. I, 569
- puréed *dhal* soup (Pacific Islands – Fiji), v. II, 476
- puréed lentil soup (Somalia), v. II, 232-33
- puréed potato and sweetpotato soup (Nigeria), v. II, 203
- puréed root vegetable soup (Saudi Arabia), v. I, 555
- *quinoa* and vegetable stew (Peru), v. II, 615
- root vegetables with yogurt-dill sauce (Bulgaria), v. I, 75-76
- salad, grated (Madagascar), v. II, 147
- salad, warm with leeks and celeriac (Norway), v. I, 310-11
- salad, whole with mayonnaise-mustard sauce with capers (Belgium) v. I, 47
- salad with beets and potato (Peru), v. II, 613-14
- salad with cabbage (Cyprus), v. I, 468
- *samosa* casserole (India), v. I, 666-67
- sautéed with cabbage and onion (Mozambique), v. II, 185
- sautéed with pomegranate glaze (Macedonia), v. I, 268-69
- shredded onion and vegetable salad (Denmark), v. I, 101
- shredded with sugar and lemon (Poland), v. I, 325-26
- slaw (Kazakhstan), v. I, 627
- slaw with cabbage, onion, and apple (Ukraine), v. I, 426
- slow cooker vegetable stew (Botswana), v. II, 19-20
- slow cooker vegetable soup with beans and barley (Croatia), v. I, 87-88
- steamed pudding with potatoes and raisins (Canada), v. II, 647-48
- stewed with barley (Belarus), v. I, 39
- stir-fried vegetables with coconut (Brunei), v. II, 311
- stir-fried, with cabbage and red pepper (Tibet), v. II, 343
- summer vegetable stew (Tunisia), v. II, 276-77
- *tagine*, with onions and prunes (Western Sahara), v. II, 165-66
- tomato-squash stew (Slovenia), v. I, 383-84
- tossed vegetable salad with cheese (Sudan), v. II, 252-53
- vegetable and cheese pies (Uruguay), v. II, 624-25
- vegetable and groundnut soup (Zambia), v. II, 292-93
- vegetable pasties (New Zealand), v. II, 467
- vegetable *ragoût* (Lebanon), v. I, 527-28
- vegetable relish (Tanzania), v. II, 262-63
- vegetable salad with white beans, root celery, kohlrabi, and potatoes (Czech), v. I, 96
- vegetable slaw (El Salvador), v. II, 560-61
- vegetable soup with barley (Estonia), v. I, 112-13
- vegetable soup with fine noodles (Malta), v. I, 274
- vegetable soup with oatmeal or barley (Oman), v. I, 538
- vegetable soup with sweetpotato, greens, and peanut butter (Zimbabwe), v. II, 300
- vegetable spaghetti with grainburger (Australia), v. II, 453-54
- vegetable stew (Ethiopia), v. II, 94
- vegetable stew (Uzbekistan), v. I, 628-29
- vegetable stew with beans and *chouriço* sausage (Angola), v. II, 13-14
- vegetable stew with beer (Belgium), v. I, 49-50
- winter squash and vegetable soup (Panama), v. II, 604-605
- with angel hair *pasta*, mushrooms, and *chorizo* in skillet (Spain), v. I, 395
- with beans and creamed corn (Oman), v. I, 539
- with ginger and dill (South Africa), v. II, 247
- with ginger, lemon, and dill (Germany), v. I, 149-50
- with pineapple (Pacific Islands - Samoa), v. II, 483
- with potatoes and leeks in cream sauce (Luxembourg), v. I, 257
- yellow pea soup (Sweden), v. I, 399-400
- yellow split pea soup with meatballs (Azerbaijan), v. I, 603-604

cashews, curried (Caribbean), v. II, 492

***cassava, manioc, yucca (yuca)* root**, *see also* puddings, tapioca
- sweet fritters (Cameroon), v. II, 39
- fried, with garlicky lime mayonnaise (Peru), v. II, 611-12
- *yuca* root soup with banana and coconut (Honduras), v. II, 573-74

cauliflower
- almond vegetables Mandarin *mu shu* (China), v. II, 329
- and eggs (Myanmar/Burma), v. II, 409-10
- and noodle soup (Indonesia), v. II, 353
- and onion omelet (Georgia), v. I, 616
- breaded and fried florets (Bangladesh), v. I, 645-46
- casserole with sour cream (Croatia), v. I, 86-87
- gratin with spinach and fennel (Switzerland), v. I, 411-12
- pickled vegetables (Panama), v. II, 601-602
- pickle, with garlic (Iran), v. I, 482-83
- pudding (Portugal), v. I, 333-34
- spicy sautéed florets (Saudi Arabia), v. I, 557-58
- stir-fried, with straw mushrooms (Vietnam), v. II, 441-42
- summer vegetable stew (Tunisia), v. II, 276-77
- vegetables in curried coconut milk (Thailand), v. II, 434-35
- vegetable soup with fine noodles (Malta), v. I, 274
- whole with cheese and breadcrumbs (Estonia), v. I, 114-15
- with spicy tomato sauce (Pakistan), v. I, 695

celeriac, knob celery, celery root
- and apple soup (Australia), v. II, 450
- and leek soup (Croatia), v. I, 84-85
- and potato chowder (Switzerland), v. I, 409-10
- appetizer salad (Moldova), v. I, 282-83
- cream soup (Czech), v. I, 91-92
- cream soup with carrot (Finland), v. I, 123-24
- oven-roasted root vegetables with cheese (Sweden), v. I, 402-403

celeriac, knob celery, celery root (cont'd)
    oven-roasted root vegetables with fresh herbs and mushrooms (Namibia), v. II, 193-94
    puréed cream soup with chick peas (Turkey), v. I, 569
    salad (Hungary), v. I, 179
    salad, warm with leeks and carrots (Norway), v. I, 310-11
    salad with celery and radish, (Germany), v. I, 143
    vegetable salad with white beans, root celery, kohlrabi, and potatoes (Czech), v. I, 96
    vegetable soup with caraway (Romania), v. I, 342-43
    with creamy mustard sauce (France), v. I, 139-40

celery
    and apple salad (Slovakia), v. I, 375
    and bean soup with bananas (Burundi), v. II, 27-28
    and cabbage slaw with sour cream (Canada), v. II, 641-42
    apple and cheese salad (Switzerland), v. I, 410
    barley and vegetable soup with sour cream (Poland), v. I, 322-23
    bean salad (Caribbean – Haiti), v. II, 497
    black bean soup (The Netherlands), v. I, 300-301
    black-eyed pea and tomato soup (Liberia), v. II, 133
    cabbage salad with pineapple (Liberia), v. II, 133-34
    chick pea and potato vegetable stew (Tunisia), v. II, 275-76
    chili, v. II, 288
    cream soup with Stilton (England), v. I, 435
    eggplant relish (Australia), v. II, 455-56
    hunter's style sauce for vegetables and *pasta* (Italy), v. II, 684-85
    macaroni and vegetables (The Gambia), v. II, 104-105
    Milanese *minestrone* (Italy), v. I, 222-23
    Moscow salad (Russia), v. I, 351
    pickled with eggplant and dill (Turkmenistan), v. I, 626-27
    pink potato salad (Panama), v. II, 598-99
    pumpkin soup with coconut milk and banana (Caribbean – Bahamas), v. II, 494
    puréed *dhal* soup (Pacific Islands – Fiji), v. II, 476
    quinoa and vegetable stew (Peru), v. II, 615
    red lentil soup (Libya), v. II, 140-41
    red pottage (Scotland), v. I, 449
    salad, with apple (Slovakia), v. I, 375
    salt cod stew without the salt cod (Italy), v. I, 206-207
    sauce for sautéed leeks and carrots (Scotland), v. I, 453
    slow cooker black-eyed pea chili (Uganda), v. II, 287-88
    slow cooker vegetable soup with beans and barley (Croatia), v. I, 87-88
    slow cooker vegetable stew (Botswana), v. II, 19-20
    smoky lentils with vegetables (Panama), v. II, 599-600
    stewed carrots and barley (Belarus), v. I, 39
    stew with bananas and soymeat stew (Liberia), v. II, 134-35
    tofu "tuna"-stuffed cucumber boats (Côte d'Ivorie), v. II, 66-67
    tomato-squash soup (Algeria), v. II, 5
    vegetable *ragoût* (Lebanon), v. I, 527-28
    vegetable soup with fine noodles (Malta), v. I, 274
    vegetable stew with brown rice and soymeat (Serbia), v. I, 367-68
    vinegar (Canada), v. II, 642
    wild rice casserole with mushrooms and baby carrots (Canada), v. II, 642-43
    yellow pea soup (Sweden), v. I, 399-400
    yellow split pea soup with meatballs (Azerbaijan), v. I, 603-604

celery root, *see* celeriac
CENTRAL AFRICAN REPUBLIC (Central African Republics), v. II, 45-53
CHAD, v. II, 54-60
chayote, christophenes
    and pepper slaw (Panama), v. II, 598
    chayote, baked with onions (Caribbean – Martinique), v. II, 500-501
    pickled vegetables (Panama), v. II, 601-602
cheese and honey pastries (Malta), v. I, 279
cheese and pastry pies (Malta), v. I, 278-79
cheese, *Appenzeller*
    information, v. I, 408 (note)
    pan-fried sandwiches (Switzerland), v. I, 417
    stuffed mushroom appetizer (Switzerland), v. I, 407-408
    cheese dip with mayonnaise (Portugal), v. I, 330
cheese balls, baked in cream sauce (Tibet), v. II, 348-49
cheese, blues – Danish blue, *Gorgonzola, Stilton*
    cabbage slaw of the *vuelta e 'Lola* (Venezuela), v. II, 631
    cheese and *chili* sauce (Tibet), v. II, 347
    cheese toasts, deviled (Switzerland), v. I, 407
    chilies and cheese (Bhutan), v. I, 659-60
    cream of celery soup (England), v. I, 435
    onions with blue cheese sauce (Finland), v. I, 127
    potato slices in casserole (England), v. I, 438-39
    trahana with yogurt and cheese (Cyprus), v. I, 470
cheese, *Brie*
    compote with apples and raisins (South Africa), v. II, 243-44
    eggplant and tomato casserole (Slovakia), v. I, 377
    tossed salad with blueberries and hazelnuts (England), v. I, 436
cheese, *Caerphilly*
    glamorgan sausages (Wales), v. I, 460
    Welsh rabbit (rarebit) (Wales), v. I, 457-58
cheese, Cheddar
    baked lentils with cheese (German), v. I, 147-48
    baked oat appetizers with herbs (England), v. I, 434-35
    cheese and *chili* dip (Native America), v. II, 653
    cheese-stuffed zucchini with lentils and fruit (Mexico), v. II, 583-84
    corn chowder (Native America), v. II, 657-58
    fried, with eggs (Turkey), v. I, 570-71
    grits with cheese (Nicaragua), v. II, 591
    macaroni and cheese (England), v. I, 437-38

Cheese, Cheddar (cont'd)
    pan-fried sandwiches (England), v. I, 440
    potato and spinach *hunza* pie (New Zealand),
        v. II, 468
    puffed potato omelet (Ireland), v. I, 195-96
    shirred eggs in ramekins with cheese and onion
        sauce (Ireland), v. I, 193-94
    soup, cream (Canada), v. II, 640-41
    vegetable pasties (New Zealand), v. II, 467
    watercress omelet (Luxembourg), v. I, 253-54
    Welsh rabbit (rarebit) (Wales), v. I, 457-58
cheese *croissants* (Venezuela), v. II, 629-30
cheese, *Edam*
    braised onions with cheese (Portugal), v. I, 335
    marinated and seasoned (Norway), v. I, 310
    soup (The Netherlands), v. I, 301-302
cheese, *Emmentaler*
    apple and cheese salad (Switzerland), v. I, 410
    fondue Alice (Switzerland), v. I, 415-16
    fondue *Herren* (Switzerland), v. I, 416
    fried potato cakes (Switzerland), v. I, 413
    pan-fried sandwiches (Switzerland), v. I, 417
    vegetarian reubens (Pacific Islands – Cook Islands),
        v. II, 478-79
cheese, *feta*, including *queso fresco*
    and watermelon salad (South Africa), v. II, 244
    baby zucchini with *feta* and roasted red peppers
        (Armenia), v. I, 587-88
    baked acorn squash with rice- and cheese-stuffing
        (Bosnia), v. I, 64-65
    baked in foil (Bulgaria), v. I, 72
    baked macaroni casserole (Bolivia), v. II, 517
    baked with honey (Greece), v. I, 159-60
    beet salad (Serbia), v. I, 366-67
    cheese salad (Ethiopia), v. II, 92-93
    chilies and cheese (Bhutan), v. I, 659-60
    couscous with raisins and pine nuts (Saudi Arabia),
        v. I, 555-56
    cucumber salad (Bhutan), v. I, 657-58
    eggplant and tomato casserole (Slovakia), v. I, 377
    fried tomato and onion salad with brown rice
        (Bolivia), v. II, 516
    flatbread and cheese (Tajikistan), v. I, 631
    green onion pancakes (Mongolia), v. II, 400
    marinated appetizer (Greece), v. I, 158
    marinated *feta* and olive appetizer (Montenegro),
        v. I, 294
    mushroom casserole with sour cream (Ukraine),
        v. I, 428
    noodles with sour cream (Bosnia-Herzegovina),
        v. I, 64
    phyllo pastries (Turkey), v. I, 567
    potato and egg salad (Tunisia), v. II, 273
    potato and mushroom *momos* in *tukpa* broth
        (Bhutan), v. I, 656-57
    prickly pear salad with apricot-raspberry dressing
        (Mexico), v. II, 581
    scalloped potatoes (Peru), v. II, 616-17
    spread (Romania), v. I, 341
    spread (Slovakia), v. I, 373
    spread with garlic (Syria), v. I, 562
    stuffed frying peppers (Bulgaria), v. I, 73-74
    three-bean salad with creamy dressing (Mongolia),
        v. II, 402
    vegetable stew (Bolivia), v. II, 515-16
    village tossed salad (Greece), v. I, 161-62
    watermelon and tomato salad (Egypt), v. II, 79
cheese, fried appetizers (Lithuania), v. I, 245-46
cheese, goat (*fromage de chèvre*)
    and yogurt appetizer spread (Libya), v. II, 139-40
    red kidney bean *tacos* or *tostados* with sautéed
        greens (Panama), v. II, 600-601
    salad, with eggplant and tomato (São Tomé and
        Principe), v. II, 210-11
    St. John's Day fruit salad (Venezuela), v. II, 630-31
cheese, Gouda, braised onions with cheese (Portugal),
    v. I, 335
cheese, *Gruyère*
    apple and cheese salad (Switzerland), v. I, 410
    cheese toasts, deviled (Switzerland), v. I, 407
    fondue Alice (Switzerland), v. I, 415-16
    fondue *Herren* (Switzerland), v. I, 416
    fried potato cakes (Switzerland), v. I, 413
    fried, with eggs (Turkey), v. I, 570-71
    gratin with cauliflower, spinach, and fennel
        (Switzerland), v. I, 411-12
    open-faced sandwiches with mushrooms
        (Switzerland), v. I, 408-409
    pan-fried sandwiches (Switzerland), v. I, 417
    stuffed mushroom appetizers (Switzerland),
        v. I, 407-408
    watercress omelet (Luxembourg), v. I, 253-54
cheese, *Halloumi*
    and tomato *kebabs* (Cyprus), v. I, 471-72
    tomato salad with shredded *Halloumi* (Cyprus),
        v. I, 469
    pan-grilled, with *edamame*, peas, and red peppers
        (Australia), v. II, 453
cheese, *Havarti*
    breaded eggplant and cheese sandwiches (Armenia),
        v. I, 594-95
    macaroni and cheese (England), v. I, 437-38
cheese, homemade
    Indian *paneer* cheese (India), v. I, 676
    quark with pepper (Finland), v. I, 120-21
    ricotta, homemade (Italy), v. I, 220
    solstice cheese (Latvia), v. I, 231-32
    white soft cheese (Belgium), v. I, 45-46
cheese, *Jarlsberg*, sauce for vegetables (Norway),
    v. I, 314
cheese, *mascarpone*
    mousse (Kuwait), v. I, 519
    pineapple dessert with coconut and cream (Somalia),
        v. II, 239
cheese, *mozzarella*, Monterey Jack, and **white cheese**
    such as ***queso blanco***
    avocado, egg, and cheese appetizer (El Salvador),
        v. II, 559-60
    cheese *croissants* (Venezuela), v. II, 629-30
    cheesy cornbread (Paraguay), v. II, 607
    corn and cheese salad (Peru), v. II, 613
    fresh, melon and peach salad (New Zealand),
        v. II, 463-64
    fried corn and cheese fritters (Ecuador), v. II, 550

cheese, *mozzarella* (cont'd)
    grits with cheese (Georgia), v. I, 617
    hearts of palm salad with cheese (Ecuador),
        v. II, 550-51
    lasagne (Italy/Sicilia), v. I, 216
    mashed potatoes with cheese and garlic (France),
        v. I, 138-39
    mozzarella, tomato, and basil salad (Venezuela),
        v. II, 632
    omelet on omelet (Chile), v. II, 531
    omelets with cheese (Albania), v. I, 5
    pan-grilled Portobello mushrooms with lentils,
        escarole, tomato, and olives (Italy/Calabria),
        v. I, 205-206
    potato and cheese soup (Ecuador), v. II, 552-53
    potato cakes with peanut sauce (Ecuador), v. II, 554
    potatoes in peanut sauce (Peru), v. II, 617-18
    rice with tomatoes and hearts of palm (Costa Rica),
        v. II, 544-45
    roasted winter squash with corn and eggs (Chile),
        v. II, 532-33
    scalloped potatoes (Peru), v. II, 616-17
    skillet *lasagne* with soymeat (Italy/Sicilia) v. I, 217
    slow cooker *polenta* (Montenegro), v. I, 296-97
    squash and cheese *quesadillas* (Mexico), v. II, 580
    steamed corn- and cheese-stuffed corn husks
        (Ecuador), v. II, 549
    sweet cheese pastry (Jordan), v. I, 510
    tomato salad with garlic and cheese (Belarus),
        v. I, 35
    tortilla skillet (Honduras), v. II, 574-75
    vegetable and cheese pies (Uruguay), v. II, 624-25
cheese, *paneer*
    and red peppers in spinach sauce (India),
        v. I, 674-75
    basic recipe (India), v. I, 676
    with peas (India), v. I, 675
cheese pudding (Greece), v. I, 160-61
cheese salad (Ethiopia), v. II, 92-93
cheese, Trappist, braised onions with cheese (Portugal),
    v. I, 335
cherimoya with orange sauce (Chile), v. II, 534
cherries, dried
    pears in spiced vanilla honey with chocolate and
        cherries (Poland), v. I, 327
    stewed fruit compote with walnuts (Armenia),
        v. I, 596
cherries, sour
    beets with tart cherry sauce (Georgia), v. I, 617-18
    in maple syrup (Native America), v. II, 671
cherries, sweet
    compote from the Ardennes (Belgium), v. I, 53-54
    cream of wheat pudding (Romania), v. I, 348
    in red wine (Italy), v. I, 213
    Israeli *couscous* and chick pea salad (Israel),
        v. I, 496
    juice in strawberry-blueberry summer pudding,
        v. I, 445-46
    Yorkshire summer pudding (England), v. I, 444-45
chervil, information, v. I, 51 (note)

chestnuts
    chestnut custard ice cream (Luxembourg),
        v. I, 258-59
    chestnut purée with whipped cream (Hungary),
        v. I, 185-86
    pilaf with fruits and nuts (Azerbaijan), v. I, 609
    steamed savoy cabbage (Lithuania), v. I, 249
CHILI, v. II, 530-35
CHINA, v. II, 322-36
chive oil (Armenia), v. I, 592
cinnamon variations, v. II, 379 (note)
citrus zest, dried, v. I, 482
clarified butter, v. I, 675-76
clarified butter, *ghee* (India), v. I, 675 (note)
clarified butter, spiced *kebbeb* (Ethiopia), v. II, 95
coconut
    corn starch pudding (Nicaragua), v. II, 595
    fruit salad (Central African Republics), v. II, 53
    individual custards (South Africa), v. II, 249
    preparation, v. II, 15 (note), 182-83, 593-94
    pudding (Nicaragua), v. II, 593-94
    soup, curried, with beans and basmati rice
        (Tanzania), v. II, 260-61
    soup, with beans and rice (Nigeria), v. II, 203-204
    with rice and tomatoes (Mozambique), v. II, 182-83
    yellow coconut pudding (Angola), v. II, 15
coffeecakes
    rhubarb *streusel* (Estonia), v. I, 117-18
    stollen, German Christmas bread, v. I, 153-54
colçots (Andorra), cultivation, v. I, 14
collard greens, *see* greens, cooked
COLOMBIA, v. II, 536-40
confections
    basic almond paste for confections (Tunisia),
        v. II, 279
    cinnamon candies (Somalia), v. II, 241
    coconut brittle (The Philippines), v. II, 427
    coconut tapioca sweet (Brazil), v. II, 529
    halva with almond butter (Estonia), v. I, 118
    honey-sweetened walnuts (Georgia), v. I, 620
    peanut candy (Angola), v. II, 16
cookies
    angel food (Bosnia), v. I, 68
    beaver tails (Canada), v. II, 648
    brown sugar cut-out cookies, v. II, 29-30
    Chinese almond cookies (China), v. II, 336
    oatmeal lace cookies (Scotland), v. I, 455
    peanut macaroons (Sudan), v. II, 257-58
    ranger (Moldova), v. I, 290-91
    refrigerator, caraway (Latvia), v. I, 236-37
    rolled sugar cookies, v. II, 697
coriander (*cilantro*) in yogurt (Palestine), v. I, 548
corn, including **hominy** and **hominy grits**
    and basil puréed cream soup with tomato (Chile),
        v. II, 532
    and bean casserole (Tanzania), v. II, 263
    and bean salad (Liechtenstein), v. I, 239
    and cheese pudding (Argentina), v. II, 510-11
    and cheese salad (Peru), v. II, 613
    and cheese stuffed corn husks (Ecuador), v. II, 549
    and lima custard pudding (Brazil), v. II, 526

corn (cont'd)
- and millet salad with avocado (Central African Republics), v. II, 47-48
- and papaya salad with citrus *vinaigrette* (Togo), v. II, 268
- and plantain soup (Cameroon), v. II, 35
- and sweetpotato soup (Thailand), v. II, 430-31
- appetizer dip with corn and walnuts (Mexico), v. II, 579
- baked corn *tortilla* chips (El Salvador), v. II, 560
- baking powder corn meal biscuits (Native America), v. II, 659
- banana custard cornbread (Caribbean), v. II, 501
- bean and hominy *chili* (Somalia), v. II, 238
- bean salad with corn and mango (Burundi), v. II, 27
- bean stew with hominy and *chouriço* (Cape Verde), v. II, 42-43
- buttermilk cornbread, v. I, 368
- cheesy cornbread (Paraguay), v. II, 607
- chowder (Native America), v. II, 657-58
- corn meal cake (Kenya), v. II, 128-29
- corn meal pudding with cheese (Romania), v. I, 344-45
- corn-on-the-cob, Cambodian style, v. II, 320
- corn-on-the-cob, Kenyan style, v. II, 129-30
- country corn bread (Portugal), v. I, 336-37
- creamed, soup, with egg whites (China), v. II, 328
- creamed, with beans and carrot (Oman), v. I, 539
- cream of potato soup (Columbia), v. II, 538
- curried corn chowder (South Africa), v. II, 245
- curry with garlic and onions (Pakistan), v. I, 694-95
- custard corn meal dessert (Zimbabwe), v. II, 302
- ersatz "maple syrup" (Native America), v. II, 662
- fried flatbreads (Sudan), v. II, 256
- fried fritters with cream (Ecuador), v. II, 550
- *fufu* with yam and potato (Cameroon), v. II, 36-37
- grilled (Iraq), v. I, 490
- grilled corn-on-the-cob (Native America), v. II, 665-66
- grits with cheese (Georgia), v. I, 617
- grits with cheese (Nicaragua), v. II, 591
- groundnut and vegetable soup (Djibouti), v. II, 72-73
- hazelnut breads (Native America), v. II, 661
- Indian pudding (Native America), v. II, 670-71
- layered vegetable salad (Ghana), v. II, 111-12
- meatball and vegetable pastry bundles (Mongolia), v. II, 405
- milk soup (Botswana), v. II, 18
- millet *couscous* with vegetables (The Gambia), v. II, 103
- oysters (Native America), v. II, 652-53
- polenta with herbs (Guinea), v. II, 119-20
- pudding with sage (Canada), v. II, 644
- relish, v. II, 579-80
- salad, with *couscous* and tomato-black bean *vinaigrette* (Somalia), v. II, 234
- sesame noodle salad (Mongolia), v. II, 400-401
- slow cooker *polenta* (Montenegro), v. I, 296-97
- slow cooker vegetable stew (Botswana), v. II, 19-20
- smothered (Native America), v. II, 664-65
- snow food, sweet popcorn clusters (Native America), v. II, 673
- soup (Kuwait), v. I, 514
- soup of greens and peanut butter (Chad), v. II, 55
- soup, puréed with sweet red peppers (Mexico), v. II, 582-83
- stewed, with coconut (Ghana), v. II, 113
- stove-top pudding (Native America), v. II, 666
- sweet corn meal pudding (São Tomé and Principe), v. II, 212
- sweet hominy dessert (Panama), v. II, 602
- *tacos* or *tostados* with sautéed greens and goat cheese (Panama), v. II, 600-601
- toasted millet salad (Mali), v. II, 155-56
- vegetable and groundnut soup (Zambia), v. II, 292-93
- vegetable stew (Bolivia), v. II, 515-16
- vegetable stew (Ethiopia), v. II, 94
- vegetarian vegetable soup (Ecuador), v. II, 553
- white, in St. John's Day fruit salad (Venezuela), v. II, 630-31
- with winter squash and eggs (Chile), v. II, 532-33

COSTA RICA, v. II, 541-46
CÔTE D'IVOIRE, v. II, 61-69

couscous
- and chick peas in vegetable soup (Angola), v. II, 11-12
- Israeli *couscous* and chick pea salad with cucumber, cherries, and dates (Israel), v. I, 496
- millet *couscous* with chick peas (Mauritania), v. II, 164-65
- millet *couscous* with vegetables (The Gambia), v. II, 103
- pumpkin porridge with (Kazakhstan), v. I, 632-33
- salad, with chick peas and tomatoes (Algeria), v. II, 4-5
- salad, with chick peas and tomatoes (Mauritania), v. II, 162-63
- salad, with roasted eggplant and red pepper (Morocco), v. II, 171-72
- salad, with tomato-black bean *vinaigrette* (Somalia), v. II, 234
- sweet pudding (The Gambia), v. II, 105
- sweet pudding with raisins and pineapple (Niger), v. II, 200
- with raisins, pine nuts, and *feta* cheese (Saudi Arabia), v. I, 555-56

cranberries
- and black walnut sauce/dessert (Native America), v. II, 672
- breaded and fried *semolina* pudding (Latvia), v. I, 378
- sauce with mustard (Lithuania), v. I, 248
- spiced whole cranberry relish (Native America), v. II, 668
- sweet and tart cranberry vinegar, v. II, 681

Cream of Rice cereal
- cardamom rice pudding (Pakistan), v. I, 696-97
- *firni* (India), v. I, 677 (note)
- sweet rice and millet pudding (Mali), v. II, 158-59

Cream of Wheat cereal, *see* farina
crème fraîche (Panama), v. II, 603

CROATIA, v. I, 81-88
cucumbers
    and olive salad (Azerbaijan), v. I, 602-603
    and red onion salad (Nepal), v. I, 682
    and shallot salad (Malaysia), v. II, 392-93
    and tomato salad (Hungary), v. I, 178-79
    and tomato salad with *chaat masala* (India), v. I, 669
    and tomato salad with grated cheese (Montenegro), v. I, 295
    and watermelon salad with *hoisin*-lime dressing (Vietnam), v. II, 439
    and yogurt salad (India), v. I, 671
    bean and corn salad (Liechtenstein), v. I, 239
    boats with *tofu* "tuna" (Côte d'Ivorie), v. II, 66-67
    bread and vegetable salad (Kuwait), v. I, 515-16
    cabbage pickle, *kimchi* (Korea), v. II, 376-77
    carved cucumber flower garnishes, v. II, 585-86
    chilled soup with yogurt (Bulgaria), v. I, 74-75
    cucumber pickles (Nepal), v. I, 687
    fruit and vegetable salad (Indonesia), v. II, 354
    fruit platter with lime *vinaigrette* (Caribbean), v. II, 496
    fruit salad with tamarind dressing (Brunei), v. II, 308-309
    Israeli couscous and chick pea salad (Israel), v. I, 496
    Kirby, salad (Korea), v. II, 377-78
    layered vegetable salad (Ghana), v. II, 111-12
    millet *tabbouleh* (Lebanon), v. I, 526-27
    mixed fruit salad with *chaat masala* (India), v. I, 670
    Moscow salad (Russia), v. I, 351
    rice noodle salad with mango and sweet *cilantro* dressing (Cambodia), v. II, 318
    salad (Slovakia), v. I, 375-76
    salad, sweet and sour (Japan), v. II, 363-64
    salad, with cheese (Bhutan), v. I, 657-58
    salad, with dill and garlic mayonnaise (Ukraine), v. I, 425
    salad, with peanut-lime dressing (Central African Republics), v. II, 48-49
    salad, with pomegranate *vinaigrette* (Iran), v. I, 479
    salad, shredded, with yogurt (Sudan), v. II, 253
    salad, wilted with honey (Belarus) v. I, 34-35
    sautéed in dill butter (Russia), v. I, 356
    soup, with mango (Saudi Arabia), v. I, 554
    toasted millet salad (Mali), v. II, 155-56
    tossed vegetable salad (Azerbaijan), v. I, 606
    vegetable bread soup (Spain), v. I, 393-94
    vegetable relish (Tanzania), v. II, 262-63
    vegetable salad (Macedonia), v. I, 265
    vegetable salad with hearts of palm (Brazil), v. II, 525
    village tossed salad (Greece), v. I, 161-62
currants
    lentil and bulgur cabbage rolls (Armenia), v. I, 592-93
    meat pies (Botswana), v. II, 21
    rice- and lentil-stuffed grape leaves (Lebanon), v. I, 525
    Yorkshire summer pudding (England), v. I, 444-45

CYPRUS, v. I, 465-74
CZECH REPUBLIC, v. I, 89-98

Dandelion
    and potato salad (Slovenia), v. I, 387-88
    wilted salad (Andorra), v. I, 16-17
dates
    and orange salad (Morocco), v. II, 174
    date balls with coconut (Yemen), v. I, 582
    Israeli *couscous* and chick pea salad (Israel), v. I, 496
    prickly pear salad with apples (Israel), v. I, 497
    rice pudding (Saudi Arabia), v. I, 558
    slow cooker dried fruit curry (South Africa), v. II, 247-48
    yogurt dessert with cream, v. I, 490-91
    pilaf with fruits and nuts (Azerbaijan), v. I, 609
    sweet, with onions (South Africa), v. II, 248
DEMOCRATIC REPUBLIC OF THE CONGO (Central African Republics), v. II, 45-53
DENMARK, v. I, 99-109
desserts, *see also* puddings, pies, cakes, and individual fruit entries
    almond ball sweet (Tunisia), v. II, 278-79
    almond-pistachio sweet (Chad), v. II, 59-60
    autumn compote (Portugal), v. I, 331
    avocado cream (Venezuela), v. II, 635
    baked cheese balls in cream sauce (Tibet), v. II, 348-49
    baked cheese sweet (India), v. I, 676-77
    banana-lime whip (Pacific Islands – Cook Islands), v. II, 484
    banana, mango, and pineapple in mango-yogurt sauce (Oman), v. I, 537
    basic almond paste for confections (Tunisia), v. II, 279
    cannoli pastry (Italy/Sicily; Venezuela), v. II, 636-37
    cassava fritters (Cameroon), v. II, 39
    chick pea flour sweet (Tunisia), v. II, 278
    chocolate mousse *Kahlua*, (Switzerland), v. I, 421
    coffee ice dessert (Eritrea), v. II, 89
    cranberry and black walnut sauce/dessert (Native America), v. II, 672
    crème fraîche (Panama), v. II, 603
    croissants with jam (Uruguay), v. II, 627
    custard bread sweet (Turkey), v. I, 575
    date balls with coconut (Yemen), v. I, 582
    dried fruit compote (Tunisia), v. II, 277
    dulce de leche soufflé (Ecuador), v. II, 555-56
    fried dough balls (Nigeria), v. II, 208
    fried rice sweets (The Philippines), v. II, 425-26
    fried walnut pastries (Uzbekistan), v. I, 632
    fruit salad (Uganda), v. II, 283-84
    honey-sweetened walnuts (Georgia), v. I, 620
    mango whip (Cameroon), v. II, 37-38
    mascarpone mousse (Kuwait), v. I, 519
    Orthodox Easter *paskha* (Russia), v. I, 359-60
    palace honey bread (Egypt), v. II, 82
    "parson's" dessert (Finland), v. I, 129
    peanut-apple crumble v. II, 469-70
    pineapple pastry (El Salvador), v. II, 563

index

desserts *(cont'd)*
- puff pastry pillows with raspberry purée and peaches, v. II, 458
- puffed pastry with Argentine sweet milk (Argentina), v. II, 512
- raspberry swirl (Romania), v. I, 347
- shredded wheat in syrup (Greece), v. I, 169-70
- sour cream dessert (Nepal), v. I, 688
- squash or pumpkin in sweet syrup with walnuts (Turkey), v. I, 573-74
- stewed rhubarb with tapioca (New Zealand), v. II, 470
- sticky rice and banana sweet (Cambodia), v. II, 321
- sweet cheese pastry (Jordan), v. I, 510
- sweet coconut rice with mangoes (Cambodia), v. II, 321
- sweet egg dessert with papaya (Mozambique), v. II, 187
- sweet hominy (Panama), v. II, 602
- sweet *pasta* (Sudan), v. II, 257
- sweet *pasta* with almonds and raisins (Bangladesh), v. I, 652-53
- sweetpotato dessert fritters (Peru), v. II, 618-19
- sweet rice balls (Vietnam), v. II, 444
- sweet rice clusters (Nigeria), v. II, 207
- sweet saffron rice (Tibet), v. II, 349
- sweet scrambled eggs (Brazil), v. II, 528
- sweet wheat fritters (Ukraine), v. I, 431
- toasted semolina with honey (Algeria), v. II, 9
- vanilla meringues, v. II, 626
- yogurt with chopped dates and cream, v. I, 490-91

DJIBOUTI, v. II, 70-76

dulce de leche
- Argentine sweet milk (Argentina), v. II, 513
- preparation, v. II, 513 (Argentina); 556 (Ecuador)
- *soufflé* (Ecuador), v. II, 554-55

dumplings
- boiled (Switzerland), v. I, 414-15
- chick pea, in yogurt sauce (India), v. I, 667-68
- farina and cheese (Poland), v. I, 320-21
- pinched, in bean soup (Hungary), v. I, 176-77
- potato and mushroom *momos* in *tukpa* broth (Bhutan), v. I, 656-57
- potato-apricot (Slovenia), v. I, 386
- soup (Korea), v. II, 371-72
- with cheese and caramelized onions (Liechtenstein), v. I, 242

ECUADOR, v. II, 547-57

edamame
- with pan-grilled *Halloumi* cheese, peas, and red peppers (Australia), v. II, 453
- with *soba* noodles and vegetables in clear broth (Japan), v. II, 361-62
- salad with Armenian string cheese and chive oil (Armenia), v. I, 591-92

eggplant
- *adobo* (The Philippines), v. II, 422
- and brown rice (Indonesia), v. II, 355
- and cheese sandwiches (Armenia), v. I, 594-95
- and mushrooms with cream (Bosnia), v. I, 65-66
- and onions with yogurt (Azerbaijan), v. I, 602
- and pepper *caviar* (Serbia), v. I, 364-65
- and scallion salad (Korea), v. II, 375-76
- and tomato casserole (Slovakia), v. I, 377
- and tomato salad (Yemen), v. I, 579-80
- appetizer, with roasted red peppers (Saudi Arabia), v. I, 552-53
- baked slices (Mauritania/Western Sahara), v. II, 166-67
- baked with yogurt (Afghanistan), v. I, 642
- baked with yogurt (Iraq), v. I, 487-88
- baked with yogurt (Palestine), v. I, 547-48
- Byzantine (Greece), v. I, 167
- curry with tomatoes (Sri Lanka), v. I, 700-701
- greens and vegetables (Caribbean – Virgin Islands), v. II, 502
- *kebabs* (Greece), v. I, 166
- mixed grilled vegetables, Catalan-style (Andorra), v. I, 18
- pickled vegetables (Panama), v. II, 601-602
- pickled with dill (Turkmenistan), v. I, 626-27
- pie, roasted, in *phyllo* crust (Jordan), v. I, 506-507
- *ratatouille*, vegetable stew (France), v. I, 134-35
- *ratatouille* with puff pastry pillows (France), v. I, 135-36
- relish (Australia), v. II, 455-56
- roasted (Pacific Islands – Fiji), v. II, 481
- roasted appetizers (Lebanon), v. I, 523
- roasted appetizer spread with green peppers (Bulgaria), v. I, 71
- roasted *caviar* appetizer (Romania), v. I, 340-41
- roasted eggplant (India), v. I, 672-73
- roasted, in salad with onion dressing (Vietnam), v. II, 440
- roasted, with *couscous* and red pepper (Morocco), v. II, 171-72
- salad (China), v. II, 327-28
- salad, with herb dressing (Mongolia), v. II, 401-402
- salad, with tomato and goat cheese (São Tomé and Principe), v. II, 210-11
- spicy, with tomato and *chili* sauce (Brunei), v. II, 311-12
- steamed (Myanmar/Burma), v. II, 415
- stir-fried (Laos), v. II, 387-88
- *tagine* (Libya), v. II, 142-43
- vegetable *kebabs* with lemon (Kuwait), v. I, 518-19
- vegetable *mélange* (Malta), v. I, 275-76
- vegetable stew with brown rice and soymeat (Serbia), v. I, 367-68
- white eggplant and red kidney bean salad (Ethiopia), v. II, 93
- with tomato (Central African Republics), v. II, 50-51
- with yogurt (Palestine), v. I, 547-48

eggs
- *allioli* sauce with eggs (Andorra), v. I, 19
- almond cake (Iceland), v. I, 191
- and avocado salad (Colombia), v. II, 537
- and avocado salad (Israel), v. I, 498
- and cauliflower (Myanmar/Burma), v. II, 409-10
- and kidney bean salad (Slovenia), v. I, 388-89
- and lemon sauce (Macedonia), v. I, 267
- and lemon soup (Greece), v. I, 164-65

713

eggs (cont'd)
- and peas with curried tomato sauce (Tibet), v. II, 342-43
- and potato salad (Côte d'Ivorie), v. II, 65
- and potato salad with *feta* cheese (Tunisia), v. II, 273
- and radish salad (Tunisia), v. II, 274
- and rice (Italy), v. I, 212
- anise-scented sweet egg custard (Caribbean – Cuba), v. II, 504-505
- appetizer *guacamole* with avocado and cheese (El Salvador), v. II, 559-60
- asparagus salad with capers (Romania), v. I, 343
- baked (Belgium), v. I, 51-52
- baked honey-egg custard, v. II, 23-24
- baked macaroni casserole (Bolivia), v. II, 517
- baked pear and breadcrumb pudding (Canada), v. II, 646-47
- baked with cheese (Bulgaria), v. I, 78
- baked with rice and tomatoes (Malta), v. I, 278
- bean salad (Caribbean – Haiti), v. II, 497
- beet and *tahini* salad (Syria), v. I, 564
- beetroot and apple salad (Uruguay), v. II, 624
- beetroot salad (Belarus), v. I, 35-36
- blender Hollandaise sauce, v. II, 522
- broccoli and potato salad with Hollandaise sauce (Brazil), v. II, 521
- brown sugar pound cake (Costa Rica), v. II, 545-46
- buttermilk cake (Moldova), v. I, 289
- cake with lemon syrup (Bosnia), v. I, 66
- carrot cake (Switzerland), v. I, 420
- chocolate almond *torte* (Hungary), v. I, 184
- chocolate mousse *Kahlua* (Switzerland), v. I, 421
- coconut custard crustless pie (Colombia), v. II, 540
- coconut custards (South Africa), v. II, 249
- coffee eggs (Greece), v. I, 157-58
- coffee custards (France), v. I, 140
- corn and lima bean custard pudding (Brazil), v. II, 526
- corn oysters (Native America), v. II, 652-53
- corn pudding with sage (Canada), v. II, 644
- creamed corn soup with egg whites (China), v. II, 328
- crustless pineapple cheese pie (Ukraine), v. I, 430
- curried eggs and rice, v. I, 673-74
- curried, with green peas (Nepal), v. I, 683
- custard bread sweet (Turkey), v. I, 575
- custard pumpkin pie (Native America), v. II, 672-73
- custard sauce, v. II, 688
- dessert, with papaya (Mozambique), v. II, 187
- deviled (England), v. I, 437
- deviled beet, potato, apple, and egg salad (Estonia), v. I, 111-12
- *dulce de leche soufflé* (Ecuador), v. II, 555-56
- egg fried rice (China), v. II, 334-35
- eggnog bavarian (Germany), v. I, 151
- egg sponge cake with sugar syrup (Albania), v. I, 11-12
- fried cheese with (Turkey), v. I, 570-71
- fried on flatbread with garlic-yogurt sauce (Iran), v. I, 476-77
- *gari* with (Ghana), v. II, 113
- garlic soup (Portugal), v. I, 331-32
- individual omelets with cheese (Albania), v. I, 5
- layered vegetable salad (Ghana), v. II, 111-12
- *lecsó* omelet (Hungary), v. I, 175
- lemon curd (England), v. I, 443-44
- macaroni salad (Denmark), v. I, 107-108
- milk cake (Ecuador), v. II, 557
- mustard omelet (France), v. I, 133-34
- *niçoise* salad (France), v. I, 136
- omelet appetizers with potatoes (Belarus), v. I, 34
- omelet on omelet (Chile), v. II, 531
- omelets with parsley and scallions (Armenia), v. I, 587
- omelet with bananas (São Tomé and Principe), v. II, 211
- omelet with cauliflower and onion (Georgia), v. I, 616
- omelet with herbs (Azerbaijan), v. I, 606-607
- omelet with potato, mushroom, and onion (Belarus) v. I, 40-41
- omelet with potatoes and parsley (Algeria), v. II, 7
- omelet with roasted root vegetable filling (Sweden), v. I, 402
- omelet with sweetpotatoes (São Tomé and Principe), v. II, 211-12
- orange custards with honey and cinnamon (Portugal), v. I, 337
- orange *torte* (Portugal), v. I, 338
- peach cakes with crumbled meringue (Uruguay), v. II, 625-26
- peanut macaroons (Sudan), v. II, 257-58
- pickled (Indonesia), v. II, 352-53
- pink potato salad (Panama), v. II, 598-99
- poached with vegetarian gravy (Kenya), v. II, 124-25
- potatoes with peanut sauce (Peru), v. II, 617-18
- preserved sweet and sour (The Philippines), v. II, 419
- puffed potato-Cheddar omelet (Ireland), v. I, 195-96
- raspberry curd (Jordan), v. I, 509
- raspberry swirl dessert (Romania), v. I, 347
- rice soup with eggs and lemon (Albania), v. I, 6
- rice with onions and egg and lemon sauce (Macedonia), v. I, 266
- sauce, for asparagus and wonton noodles (Japan), v. II, 364-65
- shirred, with Cheddar and onion sauce in ramekins (Ireland), v. I, 193-94
- shirred, with vegetables (Libya), v. II, 143-44
- scrambled, v. I, 364
- scrambled with broad beans (Lebanon), v. I, 530
- scrambled with greens and mushrooms (Spain), v. I, 394
- scrambled with vegetables (Venezuela), v. II, 633
- shirred in yogurt (Lebanon), v. I, 530-31
- *smørebrød* (Denmark), v. I, 106
- *soufflé* with grated cheese (Moldova), v. I, 287
- sour cream omelet (Romania), v. I, 342
- sour cream omelets (Russia), v. I, 355
- spicy (Saudi Arabia), v. I, 554
- spinach and beet salad with yogurt dressing (Georgia), v. I, 618-19

eggs (cont'd)
    steamed cheese pudding (Czech), v. I, 91
    stuffed (Latvia), v. I, 230-31
    sweet egg sponge cakes (El Salvador), v. II, 569-70
    sweet farina omelet (Czech), v. I, 98
    sweetpotato *soufflé* (Mali), v. II, 156-57
    sweet scrambled eggs (Brazil), v. II, 528
    sweet wheat fritters (Ukraine), v. I, 431
    toasted hazelnut *torte* (Hungary), v. I, 182-83
    tomato omelet (Cyprus), v. I, 467
    tomato omelet (Greece), v. I, 168-69
    vanilla meringues (Uruguay), v. II, 626
    walnut sponge cake (Russia), v. I, 358
    watercress omelet (Luxembourg), v. I, 253-54
    white sauce (or Kampan sturgeon) (The Netherlands), v. I, 300
    with angel hair spaghetti (Malta), v. I, 273
    with beets (Iceland), v. I, 189-90
    with buckwheat noodles (Bhutan), v. I, 658-59
    with curried tomato and onion (Bangladesh), v. I, 649-50
    with curried yam and banana salad (Pacific Islands – Saipan), v. II, 475
    with fava beans (Malta), v. I, 276-77
    with greens *vinaigrette* (Senegal), v. II, 218-19
    with lima beans and tomatoes (Mexico), v. II, 585
    with stir-fried Chinese cabbage and peppers (Malaysia), v. II, 394-95
    with winter squash and eggs (Chile), v. II, 532-33
    yellow coconut pudding (Angola), v. II, 15
EGYPT, v. II, 77-82
EL SALVADOR, v. II, 558-64
endive, cream soup (Belgium), v. I, 48
ENGLAND, *see* **UNITED KINGDOM, ENGLAND**
epazote, information, v. II, 583 (note)
EQUATORIAL GUINEA (Central African Republics), v. II, 45-53
ERITREA, v. II, 83-89
escarole
    crostini, toasted bread appetizers (Italy), v. I, 222
    portobellos with lentils, escarole, tomato, and olives (Italy), v. I, 205-206
ESTONIA, v. I, 110-18
ETHIOPIA, v. II, 90-97
evaporated milk (Pakistan), v. I, 696

Farina/Cream of Wheat cereal/semolina
    and cheese dumplings (Poland), v. I, 320-21
    breaded and fried *semolina* with cranberry garnish (Slovakia), v. I, 378
    cake with lemon syrup (Bosnia), v. I, 66
    coconut cake (Oman), v. I, 542
    cream dessert with cranberry sauce (Estonia), v. I, 116-17
    croquettes (Moldova), v. I, 287-88
    custard (Greece), v. I, 171
    dessert with bananas (Guinea), v. II, 121-22
    dessert with rose water (Oman), v. I, 541
    orange wheat pudding (Israel), v. I, 499-500
    potato pudding (Lithuania), v. I, 247-48
    pudding, with coconut and spices (Madagascar), v. II, 153
    pudding, with cherries (Romania), v. I, 348
    red wheat pudding (Norway), v. I, 317
    semolina dessert with walnuts (Bulgaria), v. I, 78-79
    stewed rhubarb with (Germany), v. I, 152
    sweet omelet (Czech), v. I, 98
    sweet wheat fritters (Ukraine), v. I, 431
    toasted semolina with honey (Algeria), v. II, 9
    wheat and coconut dessert with sweet syrup (Palestine), v. I, 549-50
    whipped dessert porridge (Finland), v. I, 128
fennel
    baked (Jordan), v. I, 508-509
    blood orange salad with fennel, *pecorino*, and pomegranate (Italy), v. I, 215
    gratin with cauliflower and spinach (Switzerland), v. I, 411-12
    salad with lemon and cheese (Angola), v. II, 12
    sautéed cabbage with fennel leaves (Romania), v. I, 345-46
feta cheese, *see* cheese, *feta*
figs
    pudding (Albania), v. I, 13
    sauce (Italy), v. I, 208-209
    stuffed, with chocolate and raspberry sauce (Italy), v. I, 207-208
    tarts (Albania), v. I, 12
FINLAND, v. I, 119-29
fish sauce substitute, v. II, 320
fondue dunkables, v. I, 416
fondues
    Alice (Switzerland), v. I, 415-16
    Herren (Switzerland), v. I, 416
FRANCE, v. I, 130-40
fritters
    banana (Djibouti), v. II, 76
    curried with *chilies* (Madagascar), v. II, 150
    fried corn and cheese (Ecuador), v. II, 550
    fried with yogurt (Herzegovina), v. I, 60
    mushroom (Andorra), v. I, 20
    sweet cassava (Cameroon), v. II, 39
    sweetpotato dessert (Peru), v. II, 618-19
    sweet wheat (Ukraine), v. I, 431
frostings
    maple buttercream (Canada), v. II, 649
    orange buttercream, v. I, 269-70
    vanilla buttercream, v. I, 183
fruits, *see* by name
fruits, dried, *see* by name

GABON (Central African Republics), v. II, 45-53
GAMBIA, THE, v. II, 98-108
garlic
    allioli sauce with eggs (Andorra), v. I, 19
    and greens (Cameroon), v. II, 36
    and radish salad/relish (Myanmar/Burma), v. II, 413-14
    and papaya soup (Caribbean), v. II, 492-93
    and parsley sauce (Nicaragua), v. II, 592
    and tomato sauce for black beans (The Gambia), v. II, 103
    and tomatoes in mung bean sauce (Uganda), v. II, 285-86

garlic (cont'd)
    and yogurt sauce with *tahini* (Tunisia), v. II, 272
    avocado soup (Côte d'Ivorie), v. II, 64
    baked eggplant with yogurt (Afghanistan), v. I, 642
    baked garlic and bread pudding with cheese (Guatemala), v. II, 568-69
    braised Chinese black mushrooms with (Indonesia), v. II, 356-57
    brown rice pilaf (Central Asia), v. I, 629-30
    "chicken" stew with tomato and (Sierra Leone), v. II, 227-28
    coriander sauce (Afghanistan), v. I, 641
    corn curry (Pakistan), v. I, 694-95
    curried tomato and onion with eggs (Bangladesh), v. I, 649-50
    dark vegetable stock (Thailand), v. II, 431-32
    dipping oil with yogurt (Eritrea), v. II, 85
    dip with roasted beets and *hummus* (Israel), v. I, 494
    dried mushroom condiment (Myanmar/Burma), v. II, 410
    eggplant and brown rice (Indonesia), v. II, 355
    eggplant and tomato salad (Yemen), v. I, 579-80
    eggplant relish (Australia), v. II, 455-56
    falafel (Jordan), v. I, 503
    fried, with fried rice (Brazil), v. II, 526-27
    fried potato cakes (Ghana), v. II, 112
    grilled vegetable salad (Kuwait), v. I, 516
    lime marinade for *tofu* (Caribbean – Cuba), v. II, 498
    marinara sauce (Italy), v. II, 682
    mushroom *wonton* appetizers (Laos), v. II, 382-83
    oil, v. II, 694
    oven-roasted root vegetables with fresh herbs and mushrooms (Namibia), v. II, 193-94
    peanut butter and tomato sauce (The Gambia), v. II, 104
    pickle, with cauliflower (Iran), v. I, 482-83
    pineapple fried rice (Laos), v. II, 386-87
    powder, homemade, v. II, 327 (note)
    puréed *dhal* soup (Pacific Islands – Fiji), v. II, 476
    red kidney bean *tacos* or *tostados* with sautéed greens and goat cheese (Panama), v. II, 600-601
    roasted eggplant appetizer (Lebanon), v. I, 523
    roasted potato soup (Tibet), v. II, 339
    sauce (Moldova/Romania), v. I, 286
    sautéed potatoes with sumac (Lebanon), v. I, 532
    shirred eggs in yogurt (Lebanon), v. I, 530-31
    soup (Portugal), v. I, 331-32
    spaghetti with broccoli (Botswana), v. II, 22-23
    stew with bananas and soymeat stew (Liberia), v. II, 134-35
    stir-fried long beans and mushrooms with garlic (Laos), v. II, 388
    summer vegetable stew (Tunisia), v. II, 276-77
    tomato and pepper appetizer salad (Israel), v. I, 495
    tomato-coriander sauce (Laos), v. II, 384
    tomato soup with basil (The Gambia), v. II, 100-101
    vegetable stew (Uzbekistan), v. I, 628-29
    vegetable stew with beans and *chouriço* sausage (Angola), v. II, 13-14
    vegetable-stuffed zucchini (Turkey), v. I, 571
    vegetarian *tukpa* broth (Tibet), v. II, 339-40
    winter squash soup (Mozambique), v. II, 180-81
    with lentils and tomatoes (Eritrea), v. II, 88
    with mashed *tofu* (Bangladesh), v. I, 649
    with potatoes and coriander in tomato sauce (Somalia), v. II, 236
    with sautéed cabbage, carrot, and onion (Mozambique), v. II, 185
    with thyme and bay in oil, v. II, 695
GEORGIA, v. I, 610-20
GERMANY, v. I, 141-54
GHANA, v. II, 109-15
ghee (India), v. I, 675 (note)
grainburger on vegetable spaghetti (Australia), v. II, 453-54
grapefruit, including *pomelo*
    and avocado salad (Somalia), v. II, 234-35
    dessert, with yogurt (Israel), v. I, 500
    fruit and vegetable salad (Indonesia), v. II, 354
    fruit salad (Central African Republics), v. II, 53
    fruit salad with citrus *vinaigrette* (Côte d'Ivoire), v. II, 66
    pomelo salad (Cambodia), v. II, 317
    salad, with papaya and avocado (Kenya), v. II, 126
    salad, with soymeat and soy sprouts (Thailand), v. II, 433-34
    St. John's Day fruit salad (Venezuela), v. II, 630-31
    with honey (Algeria), v. II, 9
    with honey (Nicaragua), v. II, 590
grape leaf appetizer with rice and lentils (Lebanon), v. I, 525
grapes, autumn compote (Portugal), v. I, 331
granola, v. II, 696
GREAT BRITAIN, see **UNITED KINGDOM**
gravy, "without the 'Sunday Roast,'" v. II, 124-25
GREECE, v. I, 155-71
greens, cooked, including **collards**, **escarole**, and **kale**; *see also* spinach, Swiss chard, turnips, i. e., greens
    and bamboo shoots (Uganda), v. II, 287
    and vegetables (Caribbean – Virgin Islands), v. II, 502
    chick pea and kale soup with peanut butter and tomatoes (Djibouti), v. II, 74
    collard and kale with potatoes and carrots (Montenegro), v. I, 295-96
    collards in black-eyed pea and tomato soup (Liberia), v. II, 133
    escarole on toasted bread appetizers with garlic and capers (Italy), v. I, 222
    fried, with "bacon" (Native America), v. II, 656
    greens *vinaigrette* (Senegal), v. II, 218-19
    kale with onion and spices (Ethiopia), v. II, 95-96
    lentils, escarole, tomato, and olives in pan-grilled portobello mushrooms (Italy), v. I, 205-206
    pickled mustard greens (Vietnam), v. II, 442-43
    sautéed kale with cream (Sweden), v. I, 404
    soup, with peanut butter (Chad), v. II, 55
    tacos or *tostados* with red kidney beans and goat cheese (Panama), v. II, 600-601
    with butternut squash (Botswana), v. II, 22
    with garlic (Cameroon), v. II, 36
    with peanuts (Tanzania), v. II, 264

greens, cooked (cont'd)
    with sweetpotato and peanut butter in vegetable soup (Zimbabwe), v. II, 300grits, see corn
GUATAMALA, v. II, 565-70
guava cream tapioca pudding, v. II, 196
GUINEA. v. II, 116-22

Hazelnut butter, preparation, v. II, 667 (note)
hearts of palm
    and tomatoes in rice casserole (Costa Rica), v. II, 544-45
    broiled (Paraguay), v. II, 606-607
    curry (Sri Lanka), v. I, 702
    fruit platter with lime *vinaigrette* (Caribbean), v. II, 496
    salad (The Philippines), v. II, 421
    salad, with *jicama*, papaya, and lime *vinaigrette* (Pacific Islands), v. II, 474-75
    salad, with cheese (Ecuador), v. II, 550-51
    soup, cream of (Pacific Islands), v. II, 478
    vegetable salad (Brazil), v. II, 525
hominy, *see* corn
HONDURAS, v. II, 571-76
HUNGARY, v. I, 172-86

Ice creams
    avocado-ice cream dessert (Indonesia), v. II, 358
    banana (Tanzania), v. II, 264-65
    chestnut custard (Luxembourg), v. I, 258-59
    coconut (Honduras), v. II, 576
    creamsicle *sorbet*, v. II, 240
    French vanilla with star anise (Vietnam), v. II, 443-44
    ginger (Chad), v. II, 59
    green tea (Japan), v. II, 367
    groundnut (Senegal), v. II, 223
    mango (India), v. I, 678
    nutmeg (Caribbean), v. II, 502-503
    pineapple (Paraguay), v. II, 609
    plum and orange (Japan), v. II, 367-68
    vanilla with pear mincemeat (England), v. I, 440-41
ICELAND, v. I, 187-91
INDIA, v. I, 663-79
INDONESIA, v. II, 350-58
IRAN, v. I, 475-84
IRAQ, v. I, 485-91
IRELAND, v. I, 192-203
ISRAEL, v. I, 492-500
ITALY, v. I, 204-28

JAPAN, v. II, 359-68
Jarlsberg, *see* cheese, *Jarlsberg*
jicama
    and carrot salad with mango (Colombia), v. II, 538-39
    fruit and vegetable salad (Indonesia), v. II, 354
    fruit salad with tamarind dressing (Brunei), v. II, 308-309
    salad, with hearts of palm, papaya, and lime *vinaigrette* (Pacific Islands), v. II, 474-75

    salad, with sweetpotato and mango in citrus dressing (Caribbean), v. II, 494-95
JORDAN, v. I, 501-10

Kale, *see* greens, cooked *or* salads
KAZAKHSTAN (Central Asia), v. I, 622-34
kebabs, vegetable (Greece), v. I, 166
KENYA, v. II, 123-30
kiwifruit
    frappé appetizer (New Zealand), v. II, 461-62
    in mixed fruit salad with *chaat masala* (India), v. I, 670
    vinaigrette with honey (New Zealand), v. II, 465
knob celery, *see* celeriac
kohlrabi
    and papaya salad with tamarind dressing (Laos), v. II, 385
    slow cooker vegetable soup with beans and barley (Croatia), v. I, 87-88
    vegetable salad with white beans, root celery, kohlrabi, and potatoes (Czech), v. I, 96
    vegetable soup with *couscous* and chick peas (Angola), v. II, 11-12
    with butter and breadcrumbs (Czech), v. I, 95
KOREA, v. II, 369-80
KUWAIT, v. I, 511-20
KYRGYSTAN (Central Asia), v. I, 622-34

LAOS, v. II 381-90
LATVIA, v. I, 229-37
LEBANON, v. I, 521-34
lecsó in *phyllo* nest, v. I, 174
lecsó vegetable mélange (Hungary), v. I, 175-76
leeks
    and carrots with celery sauce (Scotland), v. I, 453
    and celeriac soup (Croatia), v. I, 84-85
    and potato gratin (Switzerland), v. I, 412-13
    and spinach soup with dill (Iraq), v. I, 488
    appetizer salad with celeriac (Moldova), v. I, 282-83
    artichoke salad with carrots (Turkey), v. I, 570
    baked (Albania), v. I, 8-9
    barley and vegetable soup with sour cream (Poland), v. I, 322-23
    black bean soup (The Netherlands), v. I, 300-301
    black lentil soup (Nepal), v. I, 681-82
    braised vegetables in olive oil with rice (Saudi Arabia), v. I, 556
    chick pea and tomato soup (Uruguay), v. II, 623
    cream of endive soup (Belgium), v. I, 48
    cream of sweetpotato soup (Côte d'Ivorie), v. II, 64-65
    creamy orange sauce (Wales), v. I, 461
    eggplant and brown rice (Indonesia), v. II, 355
    lentil soup (Macedonia), v. I, 263-64
    meatball and vegetable pastry bundles (Mongolia), v. II, 405
    mushroom casserole with sour cream (Ukraine), v. I, 428
    noodle and mushroom soup (Brunei), v. II, 307
    oven-roasted root vegetables with cheese (Sweden), v. I, 402-403

index

leeks (cont'd)
    oven-roasted root vegetables with fresh herbs and mushrooms (Namibia), v. II, 193-94
    pickled vegetables (Panama), v. II, 601-602
    potato and spinach pie (New Zealand), v. II, 468
    salad, warm with celeriac and carrots (Norway), v. I, 310-11
    slow cooker vegetable soup with beans and barley (Croatia), v. I, 87-88
    soup with leeks and potatoes (Luxembourg), v. I, 254-55
    stir-fried cauliflower and straw mushrooms (Vietnam), v. II, 441-42
    vegetable pasties (New Zealand), v. II, 467
    vegetable soup with caraway (Romania), v. I, 342-43
    vegetable spaghetti with grainburger (Australia), v. II, 453-54
    wheaten scones (Ireland), v. I, 197-98
    with black-eyed peas and spinach (Iran), v. I, 479-80
    with potatoes and carrots in cream sauce (Luxembourg), v. I, 257
lemon balm, information, v. I, 56 (note)
lemons
    and red onion salad (Myanmar/Burma), v. II, 413
    jelly infused with fresh herbs (Native America), v. II, 668-69
    lemon curd (England), v. I, 443-44
    limoncello, v. II, 473-74
    preserved, in conserve (Morocco), v. II, 174
    sauce, v. II, 689-90
    syrup, v. II, 690
    syrup (Bosnia), v. I, 66
    vegetable *kebabs* (Kuwait), v. I, 518-19
lentils
    and bulgur in cabbage rolls with dried fruits (Armenia), v. I, 592-93
    and fruit in cheese-stuffed zucchini (Mexico), v. II, 583-84
    and noodles (Syria), v. I, 563-64
    and *orzo* with caramelized onions (Cyprus), v. I, 469-70
    and *pasta* salad with nasturtium (Australia), v. II, 457
    and rice-stuffed grape leaves (Lebanon), v. I, 525
    and shallots in red wine and tomato sauce (France), v. I, 137-38
    and spinach salad (Libya), v. II, 141
    baked with cheese (Germany), v. I, 147-48
    black lentils and potatoes with lemon juice (Saudi Arabia), v. I, 553-54
    black lentil soup (Nepal), v. I, 681-82
    consommé (Liechtenstein), v. I, 239
    deep-fried *poppodum* chips with chutney dipping sauce (Bangladesh), v. I, 647-48
    mixed legume soup (Morocco), v. II, 172-73
    portobellos with lentil, escarole, tomato, and olives (Italy), v. I, 205-206
    puréed *dhal* soup (Pacific Islands – Fiji), v. II, 476
    puréed lentil soup (Somalia), v. II, 232-33
    red lentil and bulgur soup (Turkey), v. I, 568-69
    red lentil and bulgur soup with apricots (Armenia), v. I, 589-90
    red lentil and red onion cream soup (Ireland), v. I, 199
    red-lentil soup (Libya), v. II, 140-41
    red lentil stew with Bengali five-seed spice mixture (Bangladesh), v. I, 651
    salad (Iraq), v. I, 486-87
    slow cooker rice and (Egypt), v. II, 79-80
    smoky lentils with vegetables (Panama), v. II, 599-600
    soup (Macedonia), v. I, 263-64
    soup, puréed with potatoes (Kuwait), v. I, 513
    soup, with meatballs and rice (Cyprus), v. I, 467-68
    soup, with vegetables (Burundi), v. II, 28-29
    spiced orange lentils (South Africa), v. II, 246
    with gingerroot (Djibouti), v. II, 75
    with groundnut butter (Guinea), v. II, 119-120
    with tomato and garlic (Eritrea), v. II, 88
lettuce soup (Wales), v. I, 459
LIBERIA, v. II, 131-36
LIBYA, v. II, 137-44
LIECHTENSTEIN, v. I, 238-43
lime pickles (Sri Lanka), v. I, 706
lime pudding with sweetened condensed milk (Côte d'Ivorie), v. II, 68
lingonberries
    lingonberry cream dessert (Sweden), v. I, 404
    ruby pear salad (Sweden), v. I, 401
LITHUANIA, v. I, 244-51
lovage, information, v. I, 25 (note)
LUXEMBOURG, v. I, 252-60
lychees
    and *macapuna* balls in sweet cream (The Philippines), v. II, 425
    fruit compote with vanilla (Madagascar), v. II, 152
    in coconut milk (Myanmar/Burma), v. II, 415-16

MACEDONIA, v. I, 261-70

Macapuna balls and *lychees* in sweet cream (The Philippines), v. II, 425
MADAGASCAR, v. II, 145-53
MALAYSIA, v. II, 391-97
MALI, v. II, 154-59
MALTA, v. I, 271-79
mangoes
    and banana salad (The Gambia), v. II, 102
    and *carambola* appetizer with *limoncello* (Pacific Islands – New Guinea), v. II, 472-73
    and onion soup (Guinea), v. II, 117-18
    and papaya dessert with apricot sauce (Tanzania), v. II, 265
    and pineapple chutney (Uganda), v. II, 282-83
    and purple rice salad (Thailand), v. II, 432-33
    and rice noodle salad with sweet *cilantro* dressing (Cambodia), v. II, 318
    appetizer (Thailand), v. II, 429-30
    bean salad with corn (Burundi), v. II, 27
    black rice pudding (Brunei), v. II, 313
    fresh fruit refresher (Mexico), v. II, 587-88
    fruit and vegetable salad (Indonesia), v. II, 354

index

mangoes (cont'd)
- fruit platter with lime *vinaigrette* (Caribbean), v. **II**, 496
- fruit salad (Uganda), v. **II**, 283-84
- green, and cabbage salad (Myanmar/Burma), v. **II**, 412
- green, curried vegetables with *tofu* (Cambodia), v. **II**, 319
- ice cream (India), v. **I**, 678
- mango dice, preparation, v. **II**, 433 (note)
- mango powder (India), v. **I**, 667
- nectar, in passion fruit appetizer drink (Caribbean), v. **II**, 490
- pickled vegetables (Panama), v. **II**, 601-602
- preserved mango (Cape Verde), v. **II**, 42
- pudding (Caribbean), v. **II**, 503-504
- relish (Caribbean – Cuba), v. **II**, 499-500
- salad (Madagascar), v. **II**, 149-50
- salad, with avocado, orange and citrus dressing (Senegal), v. **II**, 219
- salad, with *jicama* and carrot (Colombia), v. **II**, 538-39
- salad, with pineapple and apricot (Niger), v. **II**, 198
- salad, with sweetpotato and *jicama* in citrus dressing (Caribbean), v. **II**, 494-95
- sauce, with yogurt (Oman), v. **I**, 537
- skewered fruits (Zambia), v. **II**, 295
- smoothie (Pakistan), v. **I**, 697
- soup, with cucumber (Saudi Arabia), v. **I**, 554
- stewed, with cloves (Liberia), v. **II**, 136
- St. John's Day fruit salad (Venezuela), v. **II**, 630-31
- whip (Cameroon), v. **II**, 37-38
- with banana and pineapple in mango yogurt sauce (Oman), v. **I**, 537
- with corn in bean salad (Burundi), v. **II**, 27
- with sweet coconut rice (Cambodia), v. **II**, 321

manioc, see cassava
marjoram, information, v. **I**, 25 (note)
MAURITANIA, v. **II**, 160-68
mayonnaise, blender, v. **II**, 675-76
mayonnaise, easy, light (Portugal), v. **I**, 330-31
melons, *see also* watermelon
- and soymeat skillet (Yemen), v. **I**, 581
- and walnut compote (Armenia), v. **I**, 598
- cantaloupe and watermelon in fresh fruit refresher (Mexico), v. **II**, 587-88
- cantaloupe, peach, and blueberry salad with almond syrup and *moscato* wine sauce (Macedonia), v. **I**, 264
- cantaloupe soup (Pacific Islands – Polynesia), v. **II**, 477
- cantaloupe with tomato and olive salad (Greece), v. **I**, 163-64
- honeydew and peach salad with fresh *mozzarella* (New Zealand), v. **II**, 463-64
- fruit platter with lime *vinaigrette* (Caribbean), v. **II**, 496
- melon soup with fresh mint (Oman), v. **I**, 537
- *salsa*, with strawberries and black pepper (Native America), v. **II**, 669-70

Mexican thickened cream, v. **II**, 581
MEXICO, v. **II**, 577-88

millet
- and corn salad with avocado (Central African Republics), v. **II**, 47-48
- and rice pudding (Mali), v. **II**, 158-59
- and yogurt pudding (Mauritania), v. **II**, 167
- *couscous* with chick peas (Mauritania), v. **II**, 164-65
- *couscous* with vegetables (The Gambia), v. **II**, 103
- *croquettes* with sour cream (Senegal), v. **II**, 220
- mushroom soup (Belarus), v. **I**, 36-37
- *tabbouleh* (Lebanon), v. **I**, 526-27
- toasted millet salad (Mali), v. **II**, 155-56

miso, information, v. **I**, 314 (note); v. **II**, 684 (note)
MOLDOVA, v. **I**, 280-91
MONGOLIA, v. **II**, 398-407
MONTENEGRO, v. **I**, 292-97
MOROCCO, v. **II**, 169-77
MOZAMBIQUE, v. **II**, 178-87

mushrooms
- and asparagus with oregano and fennel oil (Liechtenstein), v. **I**, 241
- and baby carrots in wild rice casserole (Canada), v. **II**, 642-43
- and barley soup with sour cream (Latvia), v. **I**, 233
- and beet soup (Poland), v. **I**, 323-24
- and chick pea salad (Somalia), v. **II**, 233
- and mango appetizer (Thailand), v. **II**, 429-30
- and meatballs in pastry bundles (Mongolia), v. **II**, 405
- and noodle soup with vegetables (Brunei), v. **II**, 307
- and potato *momos* in *tukpa* broth (Bhutan), v. **I**, 656-57
- and potato casserole (Czech), v. **I**, 94-95
- and shallots (Ireland), v. **I**, 201
- and wild rice casserole (Native America), v. **II**, 662-633
- barley and vegetable soup with sour cream (Poland), v. **I**, 322-23
- beancurd and mushrooms with Chinese brown sauce (China), v. **II**, 332-33
- breaded (Germany), v. **I**, 148-49
- Buddhist, with asparagus (China), v. **II**, 331-32
- casserole with sour cream (Ukraine), v. **I**, 428
- *chili*, v. **II**, 288
- Chinese black mushrooms braised with garlic (Indonesia), v. **II**, 356-57
- Chinese black mushrooms, information, v. **I**, 313 (note); **II**, 331
- Chinese black mushrooms with foot long beans in brown garlic sauce (China), v. **II**, 331
- cream soup (Germany), v. **I**, 144-45
- curried eggs and rice, v. **I**, 673-74
- deviled (Poland), v. **I**, 322
- dried, condiment (Myanmar/Burma), v. **II**, 410
- dried, in tomato sauce (Zambia), v. **II**, 294-95
- dried, stir-fried (Korea), v. **II**, 375
- dried, with *feta* cheese (Bulgaria), v. **I**, 76-77
- dumpling soup (Korea), v. **II**, 371-72
- eggplant and tomato casserole (Slovakia), v. **I**, 377
- *enoki* in curried vegetables with tofu (Cambodia), v. **II**, 319
- *enoki*, in stir-fried long beans and mushrooms with garlic (Laos), v. **II**, 388

mushrooms (cont'd)
    enoki mushroom wonton appetizers (Laos),
        v. **II**, 382-83
    fried egg noodles with (Ukraine), v. **I**, 428-29
    fritters (Andorra), v. **I**, 20
    hunter's style sauce for vegetables and *pasta* (Italy),
        v. **II**, 684-85
    kebabs (Greece), v. **I**, 166
    macaroni in spicy sauce with (Iraq), v. **I**, 489
    marinated (Greece), v. **I**, 159
    marinated salad (Romania), v. **I**, 346-47
    Moscow salad (Russia), v. **I**, 351
    omelet with potato, mushroom, and onion (Belarus),
        v. **I**, 40-41
    open-faced sandwiches (Switzerland), v. **I**, 408-409
    oven-roasted root vegetables with fresh herbs and
        mushrooms (Namibia), v. **II**, 193-94
    pâté (England), v. **I**, 433-34
    phyllo turnovers with mushroom and onion filling
        (Estonia), v. **I**, 113-14
    portobellos with lentils, escarole, tomato, and olives
        (Italy), v. **I**, 205-206
    ratatouille, vegetable stew (France), v. **I**, 134-35
    ratatouille with puff pastry pillows (France),
        v. **I**, 135-36
    rice with vegetables (Bhutan), v. **I**, 661-62
    roasted, in bread-cheese soup (Italy), v. **I**, 210-11
    salad (Finland), v. **I**, 124
    sauce (Norway), v. **I**, 313-14
    scrambled eggs with greens and (Spain), v. **I**, 394
    shiitake in clear soup with *soba* noodles and
        vegetables in (Japan), v. **II**, 361-62
    skillet with noodles and sausage (Spain), v. **I**, 395
    soup (Czech), v. **I**, 92-93
    soup with potatoes and mushrooms (Austria),
        v. **I**, 24-25
    soup with roasted millet (Belarus), v. **I**, 36-37
    stew (Bhutan), v. **I**, 660
    stewed (Russia), v. **I**, 356-57
    stir-fried with bamboo shoots (Tibet) v. **II**, 344
    straw, stir-fried with cauliflower (Vietnam),
        v. **II**, 441-42
    stuffed appetizers (Switzerland), v. **I**, 407-408
    tomato mushroom sauce (Italy), v. **II**, 686
    vegan "chopped liver", v. **I**, 493-94
    vegetables in curried coconut milk (Thailand),
        v. **II**, 434-35
    vegetable stew with beer (Belgium) v. **I**, 49-50
    vegetarian stock from *kombu* (Japan), v. **II**, 363
    warm spinach salad with mushrooms and garlic
        (Andorra), v. **I**, 15-16
    with steamed *bok choy* (China), v. **II**, 333
    wild mushroom stock, v. **II**, 694
    with barley and sage (Scotland), v. **I**, 452
    with eggplant in cream (Bosnia), v. **I**, 65-66
    with paprika (Hungary), v. **I**, 180-81
    with preserved lemons and snowpeas in broth
        (Cambodia), v. **II**, 316-17
    with steamed *bok choy* (China), v. **II**, 333
    with stir-fried spinach and *tofu* (Tibet), v. **II**, 341-42
    wonton appetizers (China), v. **II**, 323-24
mustard sauce, v. **II**, 685-86

mustard sauce, Scandinavian (Denmark), v. **I**, 102-103
mustard, uncooked (Sweden), v. **I**, 401
MYANMAR / BURMA. v. **II**, 408-16

NAMIBIA, v. **II**, 188-96
NATIVE AMERICA, v. **II**, 650-73
NEPAL, v. **I**, 680-88
NETHERLANDS, THE, v. **I**, 298-307
NEW ZEALAND (Oceania), v. **II**, 460-70
NICARAGUA, v. **II**, 589-95
NIGER, v. **II**, 197-200
NIGERIA, v. **II**, 201-208
noodles, *see also pasta*
    and cabbage skillet (Poland), v. **I**, 325
    and cauliflower soup (Indonesia), v. **II**, 353
    and cheese custard pudding (Slovakia), v. **I**, 376
    and lentils (Syria), v. **I**, 563-64
    and mushroom soup with vegetables (Brunei),
        v. **II**, 307
    and onion *vinaigrette* in tossed salad (Mongolia),
        v. **II**, 401
    buckwheat noodles (*soba*) with eggs and green
        onion (Bhutan), v. **I**, 658-59
    chowder of vegetables and fine noodles
        (Montenegro), v. **I**, 294-95
    clear soup with *soba* noodles and (Japan),
        v. **II**, 361-62
    cream of summer squash soup with (Lithuania),
        v. **I**, 246
    fried with mushrooms (Ukraine), v. **I**, 428-29
    glass noodle and vegetable slaw (Tibet), v. **II**, 341
    rice noodle and meatball soup (Laos), v. **II**, 386
    rice noodle salad with mango and sweet *cilantro*
        dressing (Cambodia), v. **II**, 318
    rolled noodle and spring onion salad (China),
        v. **II**, 326-27
    sautéed with spinach (Czech), v. **I**, 96-97
    sea broth with glass noodles (Myanmar/Burma),
        v. **II**, 411
    sesame noodle salad with corn (Mongolia),
        v. **II**, 400-401
    skillet, with cabbage (Poland), v. **I**, 325
    soba, and *bok choy* in *tukpa* broth (Tibet),
        v. **II**, 340-41
    soup, with kidney beans (Central Asia), v. **I**, 625
    stir-fried rice stick, with garlic and Thai basil
        (Thailand), v. **II**, 435
    stir-fried, with vegetables (Brunei), v. **II**, 309-10
    sweet with walnuts (Moldova), v. **I**, 290
    vegetable soup with fine noodles (Malta), v. **I**, 274
    with nuts and cheese (Austria), v. **I**, 26-27
    with onions (Pacific Islands – Solomon Islands),
        v. **II**, 483
    with sour cream and *feta* cheese (Bosnia-
        Herzegovina), v. **I**, 64
    with soymeat and yogurt-garlic sauce (Azerbaijan),
        v. **I**, 608
    wonton noodles and asparagus with egg sauce
        (Japan), v. **II**, 364-65
NORWAY, v. **I**, 308-18

Oatmeal/rolled oats
    and Cheddar baked appetizers with herbs (England), v. I, 434-35
    blue plum *streusel* tart (German), v. I, 152-53
    granola, v. II, 696
    maple multigrain bread, v. II, 106-107
    oatmeal lace cookies (Scotland), v. I, 455
    oat scones (Scotland), v. I, 449-50
    porridge with apple (Belarus), v. I, 41-42
    ranger cookies (Moldova), v. I, 290-91
    vegetable soup (Oman), v. I, 538
    yogurt *crème* with sweet oatmeal topping (Wales), v. I, 461-62

okra
    and tomato stew (Mali), v. II, 158
    breaded and deep-fried (The Gambia), v. II, 99-100
    breaded and deep-fried with tomato sauce (Cyprus), v. I, 472
    spicy fried (Bangladesh), v. I, 646-47
    with *vermicelli* and rice (Kuwait), v. I, 517

OMAN, v. I, 535-42

onions, including **scallions** and **chive buds**;
    see also leeks and shallots
    and artichokes in tomato sauce (Armenia), v. I, 593-94
    and cucumber salad (Nepal), v. I, 682
    and curried soymeat with coconut milk (Myanmar/Burma), v. II, 414
    and eggplant with yogurt (Azerbaijan), v. I, 602
    and fried tomato salad with brown rice (Bolivia), v. II, 516
    and mango soup (Guinea), v. II, 117-18
    and scallions in cream of spinach and potato soup (New Zealand), v. II, 466-67
    and soymeat (El Salvador), v. II, 561-62
    and tomato salad (Syria), v. I, 562-63
    and tomato salad (Tanzania), v. II, 262
    and tomato sauce for fried plantains (Guinea), v. II, 120
    and tomato sauce for meatballs (Costa Rica), v. II, 543
    baked macaroni casserole (Bolivia), v. II, 517
    baked red, with raspberry *vinaigrette* (Australia), v. II, 454-55
    beancurd and Chinese chive bud soup (Vietnam), v. II, 438-39
    beetroot and apple salad (Uruguay), v. II, 624
    braised with cheese (Portugal), v. I, 335
    cabbage pickle, *kimchi* (Korea), v. II, 376-77
    "chicken" stew (Gabon), v. II, 49
    "chicken" stew with tomato and garlic (Sierra Leone), v. II, 227-28
    chili, v. II, 288
    corn and lima bean custard pudding (Brazil), v. II, 526
    corn curry (Pakistan), v. I, 694-95
    cream of artichoke hearts soup (Brazil), v. II, 524
    cream of chick pea soup (El Salvador), v. II, 566-67
    cucumber and red onion salad (Nepal), v. I, 682
    curried, with onions and eggs (Bangladesh), v. I, 649-50
    dark vegetable stock (Thailand), v. II, 431-32
    deviled (England), v. I, 439
    fried onion rings (Canada), v. II, 643-44
    fried potato cakes (Ghana), v. II, 112
    fried scallion turnovers (Afghanistan), v. I, 638-39
    fried yams with (Ghana), v. II, 114
    green onion sesame skillet bread (Tibet), v. II, 345
    greens and vegetables (Caribbean – Virgin Islands), v. II, 502
    grilled corn-on-the-cob (Cambodia), v. II, 320
    grilled vegetable salad (Kuwait), v. I, 516
    hearts of palm salad (The Philippines), v. II, 421
    hunter's style sauce for vegetables and *pasta* (Italy), v. II, 684-85
    Irish stew, v. I, 199-200
    kebabs (Greece), v. I, 166
    layered vegetable salad (Ghana), v. II, 111-12
    lentils and *orzo* with caramelized onions (Cyprus), v. I, 469-70
    lentils with gingerroot (Djibouti), v. II, 75
    meatballs and fruit in curry sauce (Mozambique), v. II, 183-84
    millet *couscous* with vegetables (The Gambia), v. II, 103
    orange and white radish salad with cumin (India), v. I, 670-71
    oven-roasted root vegetables with fresh herbs and mushrooms (Namibia), v. II, 193-94
    pancakes with green onions (Mongolia), v. II, 400
    peanut butter and tomato sauce with garlic (The Gambia), v. II, 104
    pearl in cream *au gratin* with *Gruyère* sauce (Belgium) v. I, 52
    pickled red onion relish with lime juice (Ecuador), v. II, 552
    pink potato salad (Panama), v. II, 598-99
    potato and tomato soup (Native America), v. II, 657
    potato cakes with peanut sauce (Ecuador), v. II, 554
    potatoes with peanut sauce (Peru), v. II, 617-18
    puréed *dhal* soup (Pacific Islands – Fiji), v. II, 476
    red, and lemon salad in lettuce rolls (Myanmar/Burma), v. II, 413
    red kidney bean *tacos* or *tostados* with sautéed greens and goat cheese (Panama), v. II, 600-601
    roasted eggplant (India), v. I, 672-73
    salad (Czech), v. I, 94
    salad (Uzbekistan), v. I, 625-26
    salad with coconut milk (Sri Lanka), v. I, 703
    salsa, with garlic and *cilantro* (Peru), v. II, 614
    scallion and eggplant salad (Korea), v. II, 375-76
    scallions in celery and cabbage slaw with sour cream (Canada), v. II, 641-42
    scallions in egg and potato salad (Cote d'Ivorie), v. II, 65
    scallions in *hoisin* barbecue sauce (Mongolia), v. II, 404
    scallions in mango relish (Caribbean – Cuba), v. II, 499-500
    scallions in millet *tabbouleh* (Lebanon), v. I, 526-27
    scallions in mushroom *wonton* appetizers (Laos), v. II, 382-83

onions (cont'd)
- scallions in pickled mustard greens (Vietnam), v. II, 442-43
- scallions in pineapple fried rice (Laos), v. II, 386-87
- scallions in radish appetizer (China), v. II, 325-26
- scallions in rolled noodle salad (China), v. II, 326-27
- scallions in stir-fried bamboo shoots with sesame seeds (Laos), v. II, 388-89
- scallions in tomato-coriander sauce (Laos), v. II, 384
- scallions in *tortilla* skillet (Honduras), v. II, 574-75
- scallions, stir-fried with winter squash and red pepper (Australia), v. II, 448-49
- shirred eggs and vegetables (Libya), v. II, 143-44
- shredded salad with vegetables (Denmark), v. I, 101
- slow cooker black-eyed pea *chili* (Uganda), v. II, 287-88
- smoky lentils with vegetables (Panama), v. II, 599-600
- soup with cheese (Serbia), v. I, 365-66
- stew, with okra and tomato (Mali), v. II, 158
- stew, with onions (Sudan), v. II, 254
- stir-fried chive buds with beancurd in spicy sauce (Malaysia), v. II, 395
- stir-fried noodles and vegetables (Brunei), v. II, 309-10
- summer vegetable stew (Tunisia), v. II, 276-77
- sweet onions with dates (South Africa), v. II, 248
- sweet soy meatballs and caramelized onions (Slovenia), v. I, 385-86
- *tagine*, with carrots and prunes (Western Sahara), v. II, 165-66
- *tagine*, with Swiss chard and rice (Morocco), v. II, 175
- tart (Switzerland), v. I, 414
- *tofu* "tuna"-stuffed cucumber boats (Côte d'Ivorie), v. II, 66-67
- tomato and green onion salad (Zambia), v. II, 293
- tomato sauce (Bosnia-Herzegovina), v. I, 63
- tossed vegetable salad with cheese (Sudan), v. II, 252-53
- vegetable *kebabs* with lemon (Kuwait), v. I, 518-19
- vegetable *ragoût* (Lebanon), v. I, 527-28
- vegetable relish (Tanzania), v. II, 262-63
- vegetable soup with chick peas and groundnut butter (Namibia), v. II, 192
- vegetable stew with brown rice and soymeat (Serbia), v. I, 367-68
- vegetable stew (Uzbekistan), v. I, 628-29
- vegetarian vegetable (Ecuador), v. II, 553
- winter squash and vegetable soup (Paraguay), v. II, 604-605
- with baked *christophenes* (*chayote*) (Caribbean – Martinique), v. II, 500-501
- with blue cheese sauce (Finland), v. I, 127
- with noodles (Pacific Islands – Solomon Islands), v. II, 483
- with potatoes in aromatic cream sauce (India), v. I, 672
- with tomatoes (Bulgaria), v. I, 77
- yam salad with scallions (Chad), v. II, 56
- *yucca* soup (Guatemala), v. II, 567

oranges, including mandarin oranges
- and *carambola* dessert (Caribbean), v. II, 505
- and date salad (Morocco), v. II, 174
- and tomato salad (Kenya), v. II, 125-26
- blood orange salad with fennel, *pecorino*, and pomegranate (Italy), v. I, 215
- cantaloupe soup (Pacific Islands), v. II, 477
- creamsicle *sorbet*, v. II, 240
- custards with honey and cinnamon (Portugal), v. I, 337
- fruit compote with vanilla (Madagascar), v. II, 152
- fruit cream (Belgium), v. I, 55-56
- fruit salad (Uganda), v. II, 283-84
- in banana and mango salad (The Gambia), v. II, 102
- in cinnamon-orange syrup (Korea), v. II, 379
- mandarin oranges, in mixed fruit salad with *chaat masala* (India), v. I, 670
- mandarin oranges with caramelized sweetpotatoes (Pacific Islands - Hawaii), v. II, 479
- pear mincemeat with pecans (England), v. I, 441-42
- salad, with avocado, mango, and citrus dressing (Senegal), v. II, 219
- salad, with *calamarata* (Somalia), v. II, 235
- salad, with white radish and onion with cumin (India), v. I, 670-71
- Seville orange juice sauce for asparagus (Spain), v. I, 396
- St. John's Day fruit salad (Venezuela), v. II, 630-31
- sweet spiced orange vinegar, v. II, 680-81
- *torte* (Portugal), v. I, 338
- with orange flower water (Laos), v. II, 390

oregano and fennel oil (Liechtenstein), v. I, 241
oregano, information, v. II, 193 (note)

PACIFIC ISLANDS, v. II, 471-85
PAKISTAN, v. I, 689-97
PALESTINE, v. I, 543-50
PANAMA, v. II, 596-603

pancakes
- poppy seed filling for (Czech), v. I, 97
- custard dessert pancakes (Finland), v. I, 128-29
- dessert, with blueberry sauce (Lithuania), v. I, 250
- green onion pancakes with *feta* cheese (Mongolia), v. II, 400
- with berries and honey (Morocco), v. II, 176-77
- with vegetables (Mauritania), v. II, 161-62

papaya
- and garlic soup (Caribbean), v. II, 492-93
- and grilled pineapple *salsa* (Caribbean), v. II, 491-92
- and kohlrabi salad with tamarind dressing (Laos), v. II, 385
- and mango dessert with apricot sauce (Tanzania), v. II, 265
- and pineapple *salsa*, v. II, 491-92
- and tomato salad (Caribbean – Puerto Rico), v. II, 495-96
- fruit salad (Central African Republics), v. II, 53
- fruit salad with citrus *vinaigrette* (Côte d'Ivorie), v. II, 66

papaya (cont'd)
    fruit salad with tamarind dressing (Brunei), v. II, 308-309
    jam (Cameroon), v. II, 33-34
    juice (Eritrea), v. II, 84-85
    poached (Chile), v. II, 534-35
    punch (Pacific Islands – Hawaii), v. II, 472
    salad, and corn with citrus *vinaigrette* (Togo), v. II, 268
    salad, with avocado and grapefruit (Kenya), v. II, 126
    salad, with curried island dressing (Pacific Islands – Vanuatu), v. II, 474
    salad, with hearts of palm, *jicama*, and lime mayonnaise (Pacific Islands), v. II, 474-75
    steamed (Tanzania), v. II, 263-64
    sweet egg dessert (Mozambique), v. II, 187
    tropical fruit salad (Nigeria), v. II, 202
paprika cream (Hungary), v. I, 177-78
paprika, homemade, v. I, 186
PARAGUAY, v. II, 603-608
parsley
    and garlic sauce (Nicaragua), v. II, 592
    cream of celery soup with Stilton (England), v. I, 435
    cream of spinach and potato soup (New Zealand), v. II, 466-67
    curried *pasta* salad (Botswana), v. II, 19
    deep-fried (Switzerland), v. I, 418
    fried potato cakes (Ghana), v. II, 112
    marinara sauce (Italy), v. II, 682
    omelets with scallions (Armenia), v. I, 587
    potato omelet (Algeria), v. II, 7
    salad with *tahini* (Palestine), v. I, 548-49
    sauce (Ireland), v. I, 196
    tomato mushroom sauce (Italy), v. II, 686
    vegetable salad (Macedonia), v. I, 265
    vegetable soup (Moldova), v. I, 284
    vegetable soup with caraway (Romania), v. I, 342-43
    vegetable stew with beans and *chouriço* sausage (Angola), v. II, 13-14
parsnips
    bean soup and pinched dumplings (Hungary), v. I, 176-77
    oven-roasted root vegetables with fresh herbs and mushrooms (Namibia), v. II, 193-94
    root vegetables with yogurt-dill sauce (Bulgaria), v. I, 75-76
    steamed with honey-mustard glaze (The Netherlands), v. I, 303
    vegetable soup with caraway (Romania), v. I, 342-43
    vegetable spaghetti with grainburger (Australia), v. II, 453-54
passion fruit appetizer drink (Caribbean), v. II, 490
pasta, see also **couscous**
    and soymeat with *chimichuri* and herb dressing (Argentina), v. II, 509-10
    angel hair, mushrooms, and *chorizo* skillet, v. I, 395
    angel hair with caper and olive sauce (Croatia), v. I, 85-86
    angel hair with eggs (Malta), v. I, 273
    baked macaroni casserole (Bolivia), v. II, 517
    baked spaghetti with two sauces (Somalia), v. II, 236-37
    calamarata and orange salad (Somalia), v. II, 235
    egg and lemon soup (Greece), v. I, 164-65
    fettucine with browned butter and fried sage leaves (Italy), v. I, 225
    fried *calamarata* with garlic mayonnaise (Spain), v. I, 392-93
    in spicy sauce with mushrooms (Iraq), v. I, 489
    lasagne (Italy), v. I, 216
    linguine, chick peas, and red kidney beans with seasoned soymeat (Afghanistan), v. I, 640
    macaroni and cheese (England), v. I, 437-38
    macaroni and "meat" casserole) Greece), v. I, 167-68
    macaroni and vegetables (The Gambia), v. II, 104-105
    macaroni salad (Denmark), v. I, 107-108
    macaroni salad (Madagascar), v. II, 147
    macaroni salad with *pesto* and *chouriço* (Uganda), v. II, 284-85
    noodle soup (Eritrea), v. II, 86-87
    orzo and lentils with caramelized onions (Cyprus), v. I, 469-70
    orzo with spinach and tomatoes (Oman), v. I, 538-39
    ravioli with spinach and sage butter (Italy), v. I, 224
    rolled noodle and spring onion salad (China), v. II, 326-27
    salad, curried (Botswana), v. II, 19
    salad, with vegetables and peanut butter dressing (Senegal), v. II, 221
    skillet *lasagne* (Italy), v. I, 217
    skillet *lasagne* with *ravioli*, (Italy), v. I, 217 (note)
    spaghettini and vegetable spaghetti with grainburger (Australia), v. II, 453-54
    spaghettini in "beef" soup (Paraguay), v. II, 606
    spaghetti with broccoli and garlic (Botswana), v. II, 22-23
    sweet *pasta* dessert (Sudan), v. II, 257
    sweet *pasta* dessert with almonds and raisins (Bangladesh), v. I, 652-53
    tagliatelle with chick peas (Cyprus), v. I, 471
    tiny shells and lentil salad with nasturtium (Australia), v. II, 457
    tomato soup with walnuts and *vermicelli* (Georgia), v. I, 614
    vermicelli and rice with vegetables (Kuwait), v. I, 517
    vermicelli with buttered breadcrumbs (Slovenia), v. I, 382-83
pâtés
    brie almond (France), v. I, 132
    mushroom (England), v. I, 433-34
    walnut and bean, with vegetable filling (France), v. I, 132-33
peaches
    and melon salad with fresh *mozzarella* (New Zealand), v. II, 463-64

peaches (cont'd)
    and raspberry purée over puff pastry pillows,
        v. II, 458
    cakes with crumbled meringue (Uruguay),
        v. II, 625-26
    dried, fruit salad (Uganda), v. II, 283-84
    jam, v. I, 619
    lemon-peach salad dressing (Mozambique),
        v. II, 181-82
    salad, with avocado and tomato (Mozambique),
        v. II, 181
    salad, with cantaloupe and blueberry with almond
        syrup and *moscato* wine sauce (Macedonia),
        v. I, 264
    sautéed with soymeat (Iran), v. I, 480-81
peanuts, *see* beans
pears, including **Asian pears**
    and anise-hyssop vinegar, v. II, 679-80
    Asian pear in fruit and vegetable salad (Indonesia),
        v. II, 354
    autumn compote (Portugal), v. I, 331
    baked Bosc pears (Belgium), v. I, 54
    baked, with breadcrumb pudding (Canada),
        v. II, 646-47
    fruit salad (Central African Republics), v. II, 53
    fruit salad with tamarind dressing (Brunei),
        v. II, 308-309
    in honey-lavender syrup (Morocco), v. II, 177
    meatballs and fruit in curry sauce (Mozambique),
        v. II, 183-84
    mincemeat with pecans, v. I, 441-42
    mixed fruit salad with *chaat masala* (India),
        v. I, 670
    poached Asian pears with black peppercorns
        (Korea), v. II, 379-80
    riced, with potatoes (Switzerland), v. I, 417-18
    salad with lingonberries (Sweden), v. I, 401
    sliced with ice cream and fresh strawberry sauce
        (Andorra), v. I, 21
    spiced vanilla honey with chocolate and cherries
        (Poland), v. I, 327
    vanilla pear dessert (Liechtenstein), v. I, 243
    with buttered crumbs (Lithuania), v. I, 249
    with sour cream sauce (Serbia), v. I, 369-70
peas, *dal*, *dal makhani*, Beluga black lentils, red lentils; *also see* lentils
    masur dal, puréed red lentil and bulgur soup
        (Turkey), v. I, 568-69
    masur dal, red lentil and bulgur soup with apricots
        (Armenia), v. I, 589-90
    masur dal, red lentil soup (Libya), v. II, 140-41
    masur dal, red lentil stew with Bengali five-seed
        spice mixture (Bangladesh), v. I, 651
peas, green
    and eggs in curried tomato sauce (Tibet),
        v. II, 342-43
    Argentine-styled Russian salad, v. II, 508-509
    artichoke and fava bean skillet with eggs (Malta),
        v. I, 276-77
    creamy, puréed, vegetable soup (Venezuela),
        v. II, 632-33
    egg curry (Nepal), v. I, 683

    glass noodle and vegetable slaw (Tibet), v. II, 341
    Irish stew, v. I, 199-200
    macaroni and vegetables (The Gambia),
        v. II, 104-105
    Moscow salad (Russia), v. I, 351
    samosa casserole (India), v. I, 666-67
    sautéed in the pod (Sweden), v. I, 403
    simmered in tomato sauce (Macedonia), v. I, 268
    tendrils, in rice with vegetables (Bhutan),
        v. I, 661-62
    tomato, onion, and pea salad (Portugal), v. I, 332-33
    tomato soup with (Palestine), v. I, 545-46
    vegetable pasties (New Zealand), v. II, 467
    vegetable salad (Brazil), v. II, 525
    vegetable stew (Bolivia), v. II, 515-16
    with basmati rice and dill (Kuwait), v. I, 514-15
    with cheese (India), v. I, 675
    with pan-grilled *Halloumi* cheese, *edamame*, and
        red peppers (Australia), v. II, 452
    with potatoes and cabbage in tomato sauce
        (Bangladesh), v. I, 648
    with stir-fried spinach, *tofu*, and mushrooms (Tibet),
        v. II, 341-42
    yucca soup (Guatemala), v. II, 567
peas, snowpeas
    almond vegetables Mandarin *mu shu* (China),
        v. II, 329
    noodle and mushroom soup with vegetables
        (Brunei), v. II, 307
    rice noodle salad with mango and sweet *cilantro*
        dressing (Cambodia), v. II, 318
    steamed vegetable salad with sweet black sesame
        dressing (Brunei), v. II, 308
    stir-fried noodles and vegetables (Brunei),
        v. II, 309-10
    stir-fry with sweetpotatoes (Bangladesh),
        v. I, 650-51
    with preserved lemons and *shiitake* mushrooms in
        broth (Cambodia), v. II, 316-17
    with *soba* noodles and vegetables in clear soup
        (Japan), v. II, 361-62
    with stir-fried spinach *tofu* and mushrooms (Tibet),
        v. II, 341-42
peas, split green, Milanese *minestrone* (Italy),
    v. I, 222-23
peas, split yellow
    soup (Sweden), v. I, 399-400
    soup with meatballs (Azerbaijan), v. I, 603-604
peppers
    and *chayote* slaw (Panama), v. II, 598
    and eggplant *caviar* (Serbia), v. I, 364-65
    and red kidney beans (Latvia), v. I, 234
    angel hair *pasta*, mushroom, and *chorizo* skillet
        (Spain), v. I, 395
    baby, roasted with black beans (China), v. II, 334
    baby zucchini with *feta* and roasted red peppers
        (Armenia), v. I, 587-88
    bean salad with corn and mango (Burundi), v. II, 27
    "beef" soup with noodles (Paraguay), v. II, 606
    beet soup (Ukraine), v. I, 426-27
    black beans with green pepper (Native America),
        v. II, 667

peppers (cont'd)
- black beans with rice and mango relish (Caribbean – Cuba), v. II, 499-500
- black-eyed peas in coconut milk (Kenya), v. II, 127-28
- cabbage salad with pineapple (Liberia), v. II, 133-34
- cabbage slaw with pineapple (Cameroon), v. II, 34
- cheese-stuffed frying peppers (Bulgaria), v. I, 73-74
- chili, v. II, 288
- *chilies* and cheese (Bhutan), v. I, 659-60
- *chilies*, in curried fritters (Madagascar), v. II, 150
- *chilies*, in peanut butter and tomato sauce (The Gambia), v. II, 104
- *chilies* with fried potatoes and yogurt (Malaysia), v. II, 393
- *chilies* with spinach, gingerroot, and coconut (The Philippines), v. II, 422-23
- chilled chick pea soup with roasted red peppers and garlic (Greece), v. I, 165-66
- coconut-bean soup with rice (Nigeria), v. II, 203-204
- corn and cheese salad (Peru), v. II, 613
- corn and lima bean custard pudding (Brazil), v. II, 526
- curried vegetables with *tofu* (Cambodia), v. II, 319
- frying peppers, roasted and marinated (Turkey), v. I, 572
- *goulash* (Hungary), v. I, 177-78
- grilled vegetable salad (Kuwait), v. I, 516
- *lecsó* omelet (Hungary), v. I, 175
- *lecsó*, vegetable mélange (Hungary), v. I, 175-76
- *lecsó* in *phyllo* nest (Hungary), v. I, 174
- lentil soup (Macedonia), v. I, 263-64
- macaroni in spicy sauce with mushrooms (Iraq), v. I, 489
- mango-pineapple chutney (Uganda), v. II, 282-83
- mango salad with vegetables (Pakistan), v. I, 691
- marinated and seasoned *Edam* cheese (Norway), v. I, 310
- meatball and vegetable pastry bundles (Mongolia), v. II, 405
- millet *couscous* with vegetables (The Gambia), v. II, 103
- onion, garlic, and *cilantro salsa* (Peru), v. II, 614
- pancakes with vegetables (Mauritania), v. II, 161-62
- paprika cream (Hungary), v. I, 177-78
- pickled vegetables (Panama), v. II, 601-602
- *quinoa* and vegetable stew (Peru), v. II, 615
- *polenta* with herbs (Guinea), v. II, 119-20
- potato and tomato soup (Native America), v. II, 657
- prickly pear salad with apples and dates (Israel), v. I, 497
- puréed cream of chick pea and celeriac soup (Turkey), v. I, 569
- red beans with grated cheese (El Salvador), v. II, 562
- red lentil soup (Libya), v. II, 140-41
- red pepper dip (Palestine), v. I, 544-45
- rice curry with peanut butter and bananas (Angola), v. II, 14
- rice with tomatoes and coconut milk (Mozambique), v. II, 182-83
- roasted red pepper and tomato appetizer salad (Israel), v. I, 495
- roasted pepper and tomato salad (Tunisia), v. II, 272-73
- roasted red pepper and eggplant appetizer (Saudi Arabia), v. I, 552-53
- roasted red peppers, freezing in oil, v. I, 553 (note)
- roasted red peppers, preparation, v. I, 165, 497, 553
- roasted, with pan-grilled *Halloumi* cheese, *edamame*, and peas (Australia), v. II, 453
- roasted, with yogurt and pecans (Israel), v. I, 498
- salad (Hungary), v. I, 182
- salad, with *couscous* and roasted eggplant (Morocco), v. II, 171-72
- salad, with onion and tomato and garlic sauce (Moldova), v. I, 285-86
- scrambled eggs with vegetables (Venezuela), v. II, 633
- shirred eggs and vegetables (Libya), v. II, 143-44
- skewered with soymeat (Mali), v. II, 157
- slow-cooker black-eyed pea *chili* Uganda), v. II, 287-88
- slow cooker vegetable soup with beans and barley (Croatia), v. I, 87-88
- smoky lentils with vegetables (Panama), v. II, 599-600
- soup, puréed, with corn (Mexico), v. II, 582-83
- spinach stew with peanut butter (Central African Republics), v. II, 51
- stir-fried with cabbage and carrots (Tibet), v. II, 343
- stir-fried with Chinese cabbage and eggs (Malaysia), v. II, 394-95
- stir-fried with winter squash and scallions (Australia), v. II, 448-49
- summer vegetable stew (Tunisia), v. II, 276-77
- toasted millet salad (Mali), v. II, 155-56
- tomato and cucumber salad with (Hungary), v. I, 178-79
- tomato and groundnut soup (Ghana), v. II, 111
- tomato soup (India), v. I, 668-69
- tossed vegetable salad (Azerbaijan), v. I, 606
- vegetable bread soup (Spain), v. I, 393-94
- vegetable *kebabs* with lemon (Kuwait), v. I, 518-19
- vegetable *mélange* (Malta), v. I, 275-76
- vegetable *ragoût* (Lebanon), v. I, 527-28
- vegetables in curried coconut milk (Thailand), v. II, 434-35
- vegetable soup with chick peas and ground nut butter (Namibia), v. II, 192
- vegetable spaghetti with grainburger (Australia), v. II, 453-54
- vegetable stew (Ethiopia), v. II, 94
- vegetable stew (Uzbekistan), v. I, 628-29
- vegetable stew with brown rice and soymeat (Serbia), v. I, 367-68
- with cheese in spinach sauce (India), v. I, 674-75
- with sautéed cabbage, carrot, and onion (Mozambique), v. II, 185
- *yucca* soup (Guatemala), v. II, 567

PERU, v. II, 610-20

index

PHILIPPINES, THE, v. II, 417-27
***phyllo* pastry**
    Albanian spinach pie, v. I, 9-10
    banana tart (Central African Republics), v. II, 52
    cheese and pastry pies (Malta), v. I, 278-79
    fig tarts (Albania), v. I, 12
    lecsó in *phyllo* nest (Hungary), v. I, 174
    pastries with *feta* (Turkey), v. I, 567
    pastries with banana and chocolate (Côte d'Ivoire), v. II, 68-69
    pastries with *ricotta* and honey (Malta), v. I, 279
    pastries with rose water and honey (Saudi Arabia), v. I, 559-60
    pumpkin pie (Serbia), v. I, 370
    roasted eggplant pie (Jordan), v. I, 506-507
    sweet cheese pastry (Jordan), v. I, 510
    turnovers with mushroom and onion filling (Estonia), v. I, 113-14
pickled vegetables
    baby beets (Denmark), v. I, 104
    baby pepper salad (Bosnia), v. I, 61-62
    cabbage pickle (Nepal), v. I, 687
    cauliflower and garlic pickle (Iran), v. I, 482-83
    cucumber pickle (Nepal), v. I, 687
    daikon and red radish pickles (Tibet), v. II, 346
    onions (Austria), v. I, 28
    onion salad (Czech), v. I, 94
    pickled vegetables (Panama), v. II, 601-602
    potato with green *chilies* (Nepal), v. I, 686-87
    red onion relish (Ecuador), v. II, 552
    sweet and sour red cabbage with sour cream (Estonia), v. I, 115
pies and tarts
    apricot tart (Austria), v. I, 31
    banana *phyllo* tart (Central African Republics), v. II, 52
    blue plum *streusel* tart (Germany), v. I, 152-53
    cabbage and potato (Luxembourg), v. I, 255-56
    crustless coconut custard (Colombia), v. II, 540
    crustless pineapple cheese (Ukraine), v. I, 430
    custard pumpkin, v. II, 672-73
    fig tarts (Albania), v. I, 12
    fruit tart (Luxembourg), v. I, 259-60
    meat pies (Botswana), v. II, 21
    onion tart (Switzerland), v. I, 414
    potato and spinach (New Zealand), v. II, 468
    roasted eggplant in *phyllo* crust (Jordan), v. I, 506-507
    samosa (India), v. I, 666-67
    strawberry (Slovakia), v. I, 380
    vegetable and cheese (Uruguay), v. II, 624-25
    whole wheat pie crusts, v. II, 468-69
pineapple
    and avocado appetizer spread (Côte d'Ivoire), v. II, 62-63
    and avocado salad (Central African Republics), v. II, 47
    and mango chutney (Uganda), v. II, 282-83
    and mashed sweetpotatoes (Nicaragua), v. II, 593
    cabbage salad (Liberia), v. II, 133-34
    cabbage slaw (Cameroon), v. II, 34
    cheese-stuffed zucchini with lentils and fruit (Mexico), v. II, 583-84
    crustless pineapple cheese pie (Ukraine), v. I, 430
    curried island dressing (Pacific Islands – Vanuatu), v. II, 474
    dessert (Tanzania), v. II, 266
    drink with fresh gingerroot (Liberia), v. II, 132
    fresh fruit refresher (Mexico), v. II, 587-88
    fried rice (Laos), v. II, 386-87
    fried rice (Pacific Islands – Cook Islands), v. II, 480
    fruit and vegetable salad (Indonesia, v. II, 354
    fruit compote with vanilla (Madagascar), v. II, 152
    fruit cream (Belgium), v. I, 55-56
    fruit salad with citrus *vinaigrette* (Côte d'Ivorie), v. II, 66
    fruit salad with tamarind dressing (Brunei), v. II, 308-309
    grilled, and papaya *salsa* (Caribbean), v. II, 491-92
    grilled, with honey-lime glaze (Argentina), v. II, 513
    honey-pineapple *vinaigrette* (Burundi), v. II, 27
    ice cream (Paraguay), v. II, 609
    jam, v. II, 564
    layered fruit salad (Cameroon), v. II, 34-35
    meatballs and fruit in curry sauce (Mozambique), v. II, 183-84
    papaya punch (Pacific Islands - Hawaii), v. II, 472
    pineapple pastry (El Salvador), v. II, 563
    pineapple vinegar, v. II, 573
    pineapple vinegar, fermented (Honduras), v. II, 573
    salad, with mango and apricot (Niger), v. II, 198
    skewered fruits (Zambia), v. II, 295
    slices with cinnamon and ginger (Angola), v. II, 16
    sweet *couscous* pudding (Niger), v. II, 200
    sweet relish (Indonesia), v. II, 357
    tea-infused dried fruits with whipped cream (Chad), v. II, 58
    tropical fruit salad (Nigeria), v. II, 202
    with baked beans (Pacific Islands – Hawaii), v. II, 480-81
    with bananas and mango in mango-yogurt sauce (Oman), v. I, 537
    with carrots (Pacific Islands – Samoa), v. II, 483
    with coconut and cream (Somalia), v. II, 239
pine nut syndrome warning, v. I, 532 (note); v. II, 190 (note)
plantains
    and corn soup (Cameroon), v. II, 35
    baked, with cinnamon (Mexico), v. II, 586
    bean stew with hominy and *chouriço* (Cape Verde), v. II, 42-43
    fried (El Salvador), v. II, 562-63
    fufu with yam (Cameroon), v. II, 37
    mashed, with tomato and thyme (Caribbean – Dominican Republic), v. II, 499
    oven-baked dessert over ice cream (Peru), v. II, 620
    pan-grilled with peanuts (Nigeria), v. II, 204-205
    with beans and tomatoes (Colombia), v. II, 539
    with spicy tomato-onion sauce (Guinea), v. II, 120
plums and prunes
    and orange ice cream (Japan), v. II, 367-68
    autumn compote (Portugal), v. I, 331

prunes and **plums** (cont'd)
    blue plum *streusel* tart (Germany), v. I, 152-53
    carrot *pilaf* (Kazakhstan), v. I, 630-31
    cobbler (Switzerland), v. I, 419
    fruit tart (Luxembourg), v. I, 259-60
    ginger-steeped prunes (Australia), v. II, 459
    pickled (Poland), v. I, 326-27
    prunes with cardamom and almonds in red wine sauce (Ethiopia), v. II, 97
    sauce (Laos), v. II, 383-84
    slow cooker dried fruit curry (South Africa), v. II, 247-48
    stewed fruit compote with walnuts (Armenia), v. I, 596
    stewed prunes (Bulgaria), v. I, 79
    tagine with carrots and onion (Western Sahara), v. II, 165-66
    tea-infused dried fruits with whipped cream (Chad), v. II, 58
POLAND, v. I, 319-27
polenta, see corn
pomegranates
    blood orange salad with fennel, *pecorino*, and pomegranate (Italy), v. I, 215
    mixed fruit salad with *chaat masala* (India), v. I, 670
    molasses (Lebanon), v. I, 529
    pumpkin soup (Azerbaijan), v. I, 604
    refresher (Morocco), v. II, 170-71
    sautéed carrots with pomegranate glaze (Macedonia), v. I, 268-69
    sautéed soymeat and peaches (Iran), v. I, 480-81
    tossed vegetable salad (Azerbaijan), v. I, 606
    vinaigrette, for cucumber salad (Iran), v. I, 479
PORTUGAL, v. I, 328-38
potatoes
    and broccoli salad with Hollandaise sauce (Brazil), v. II, 521
    and cabbage in tomato sauce (Bangladesh), v. I, 648
    and celeriac chowder (Switzerland), v. I, 409-10
    and cheese casserole (Macedonia), v. I, 267-68
    and cheese soup (Ecuador), v. II, 552-53
    and Cheddar puffed omelet (Ireland), v. I, 195-96
    and chick pea salad (Armenia), v. I, 591
    and chick pea vegetable stew (Tunisia), v. II, 275-76
    and egg salad (Côte d'Ivoire), v. II, 65
    and green bean curry (Malaysia), v. II, 393-94
    and leek gratin (Switzerland), v. I, 412-13
    and meatballs in *tahini* sauce (Jordan), v. I, 508
    and mushroom *momos* in *tukpa* broth (Bhutan), v. I, 656-57
    and rutabaga casserole (Finland), v. I, 125-26
    and savoy cabbage (Hungary), v. I, 180
    and sauerkraut *croquettes* (Luxembourg), v. I, 256-57
    and spinach cream soup (New Zealand), v. II, 466-67
    and spinach pie (New Zealand), v. II, 468
    and tomato soup (Native America), v. II, 657
    and watercress soup (Ireland), v. I, 198
    and watercress soup with herbs (Wales), v. I, 458-59
    appetizer salad with celeriac (Moldova), v. I, 282-83

    Argentine-styled Russian salad, v. II, 508-509
    baked fries (Belgium), v. I, 45
    barley and vegetable soup with sour cream (Poland), v. I, 322-23
    beetroot and apple salad (Uruguay), v. II, 624
    beet soup (Ukraine), v. I, 426-27
    braised in aromatic cream sauce (India), v. I, 672
    cakes, fried (Ghana), v. II, 112
    cakes, fried (Switzerland), v. I, 413
    cakes with peanut sauce (Ecuador), v. II, 554
    casserole with potato slices and Stilton (England), v. I, 438-39
    casserole with shredded potato (Belarus), v. I, 38
    cheese soup (The Netherlands), v. I, 301-302
    chili bean soup, v. I, 283-84
    chowder of vegetables and fine noodles (Montenegro), v. I, 294-95
    collard greens and kale with potatoes and carrots (Montenegro), v. I, 295-96
    corn chowder (Native America), v. II, 657-58
    cream of asparagus soup (Germany), v. I, 143-44
    cream of summer squash soup with noodles (Lithuania), v. I, 246
    cream soup with corn (Colombia), v. II, 538
    creamy, puréed, vegetable soup (Venezuela), v. II, 632-33
    crushed (Nepal), v. I, 685-86
    curried corn chowder (South Africa), v. II, 245
    cutlets with cheese (Russia), v. I, 353-54
    deviled beets, potato, apple, and egg salad (Estonia), v. I, 111-12
    dumplings with apricots (Slovenia), v. I, 386
    egg roll appetizers (Belarus) v. I, 34
    fried, with yogurt and chilies (Malaysia), v. II, 393
    groundnut and vegetable soup (Djibouti), v. II, 72-73
    fufu with yam and corn (Cameroon), v. II, 36-37
    hot salad (Germany), v. I, 146
    Irish stew, v. I, 199-200
    kebabs made with mashed potatoes (Azerbaijan), v. I, 607-608
    layered vegetable salad (Ghana), v. II, 111-12
    lettuce soup (Wales), v. I, 459
    mashed with cheese and garlic (France), v. I, 138-39
    meatball and vegetable pastry bundles (Mongolia), v. II, 405
    meatballs and vegetables skillet (Niger), v. II, 198-99
    meat pies (Botswana), v. II, 21
    mixed grilled vegetables, Catalan-style (Andorra), v. 1, 18
    Moscow salad (Russia), v. I, 351
    new, with chervil (Belgium), v. I, 50-51
    new, with parsley (Belgium), v. I, 51 (note)
    niçoise salad (France), v. I, 136
    noodle soup with kidney beans (Central Asia), v. I, 625
    omelet with potato and parsley (Algeria), v. II, 7
    omelet with potato, mushroom, and onion (Belarus), v. I, 40-41
    oven-browned potato wedges (Costa Rica), v. II, 544

potatoes (cont'd)
- oven-roasted root vegetables with cheese (Sweden), v. **I**, 402-403
- oven-roasted root vegetables with fresh herbs and mushrooms (Namibia), v. **II**, 193-94
- pancakes with vegetables (Mauritania), v. **II**, 161-62
- pickle with green *chilies* (Nepal), v. **I**, 686-87
- pie, with cabbage (Luxembourg), v. **I**, 255-56
- pink potato salad (Panama), v. **II**, 598-99
- potato and mushroom casserole (Czech), v. **I**, 94-95
- potato–meatball soup (Latvia), v. **I**, 232-33
- potato milk soup (Bosnia), v. **I**, 61
- pudding (Lithuania), v. **I**, 247-48
- pudding with cheese (Iceland), v. **I**, 189
- puréed lentil soup (Somalia), v. **II**, 232-33
- puréed root vegetable soup (Saudi Arabia), v. **I**, 555
- puréed, soup, with sweetpotatoes (Nigeria), v. **II**, 203
- riced with pears (Switzerland), v. **I**, 417-18
- rice with vegetables (Bhutan), v. **I**, 661-62
- roasted, soup (Tibet), v. **II**, 339
- root vegetables with yogurt-dill sauce (Bulgaria), v. **I**, 75-76
- salad (Albania), v. **I**, 7
- salad (Germany), v. **I**, 145-46
- salad (Madagascar), v. **II**, 148
- salad, with beets and carrots (Peru), v. **II**, 613-14
- salad, with dandelions (Slovenia), v. **I**, 387-88
- salad, with eggs and *feta* cheese (Tunisia), v. **II**, 273
- salad, with mayonnaise (Turkmenistan), v. **I**, 627-28
- salt cod stew without the salt cod (Italy), v. **I**, 206-207
- *samosa* casserole (India), v. **I**, 666-67
- sautéed with sumac (Lebanon), v. **I**, 532
- scalloped (Peru), v. **II**, 616-17
- shirred eggs and vegetables (Libya), v. **II**, 143-44
- skillet cakes (Algeria), v. **II**, 6-7
- slow cooker lentil soup (Palestine), v. **I**, 546
- slow cooker vegetable soup with beans and barley (Croatia), v. **I**, 87-88
- slow cooker vegetable stew (Botswana), v. **II**, 19-20
- sorrel-potato soup (Russia), v. **I**, 352-53
- soup, puréed with lentils (Kuwait), v. **I**, 513-14
- soup with cheese (Sweden), v. **I**, 400
- soup, with mushrooms (Slovakia), v. **I**, 374
- soup, with potatoes and leeks (Luxembourg), v. **I**, 254-55
- soup, with potatoes and mushrooms (Austria), v. **I**, 24-25
- sour soup, with green beans (Slovakia), v. **I**, 373-74
- spicy with spinach (Pakistan), v. **I**, 692
- skillet cakes (Algeria), v. **II**, 6-7
- spicy crisps (Zambia), v. **II**, 291-92
- squash *bisque* (Native America), v. **II**, 658-59
- steamed pudding with carrot and raisins (Canada), v. **II**, 647-48
- stew, with onion (Sudan), v. **II**, 254
- straw, deep-fried (Ukraine), v. **I**, 424
- sugar-browned (Denmark), v. **I**, 103
- summer vegetable stew (Tunisia), v. **II**, 276-77
- twice-baked (Palestine), v. **I**, 547
- vegetable and cheese pies (Uruguay), v. **II**, 624-25
- vegetable and groundnut soup (Zambia), v. **II**, 292-93
- vegetable pasties (New Zealand), v. **II**, 467
- vegetable salad with white beans, root celery, kohlrabi, and potatoes (Czech), v. **I**, 96
- vegetable soup with barley (Estonia), v. **I**, 112-13
- vegetable soup with cabbage (Albania), v. **I**, 5-6
- vegetable soup with chick peas and groundnut butter (Namibia), v. **II**, 192
- vegetable soup with sour cream (Moldova), v. **I**, 284
- vegetable stew (Bolivia), v. **II**, 515-16
- vegetable stew (Ethiopia), v. **II**, 94
- vegetable stew (Uzbekistan), v. **I**, 628-29
- vegetarian *tukpa* broth (Tibet), v. **II**, 339-40
- vegetarian vegetable soup (Ecuador), v. **II**, 553
- with bacon in lettuce salad (Burundi), v. **II**, 26
- with bay butter (Portugal), v. **I**, 334
- with black lentils (Saudi Arabia), v. **I**, 553-54
- with cheese and garlic (France), v. **I**, 138-39
- with garlic and coriander in tomato sauce (Somalia), v. **II**, 236
- with leeks and carrots in cream sauce (Luxembourg), v. **I**, 257
- with peanut sauce (Peru), v. **II**, 617-18
- with rice (Uganda), v. **II**, 286
- with spicy tomato sauce (Oman), v. **I**, 539-40
- with *vermicelli* and rice (Kuwait), v. **I**, 517
- with yogurt curds (Uganda), v. **II**, 285
- yellow split pea soup with meatballs (Azerbaijan), v. **I**, 603-604

prickly pear cactus
- prickly pear *vinaigrette* with *agave* nectar (Native America), v. **II**, 654-55
- punch, with orange, apple, and pineapple juices (Native America), v. **II**, 653-54
- salad, with apple and dates (Israel), v. **I**, 497
- salad, with apricot-raspberry dressing (Mexico), v. **II**, 581

puddings
- almond and coconut corn starch pudding (Afghanistan), v. **I**, 643
- almond junket (China), v. **II**, 335
- anise-scented sweet egg custard (Caribbean – Cuba), v. **II**, 504-505
- apple-oatmeal porridge (Belarus), v. **I**, 41-42
- apple with breadcrumbs (Denmark), v. **I**, 108-109
- apple with breadcrumbs (Russia), v. **I**, 359
- avocado (Western Sahara), v. **II**, 167-68
- baked honey-egg custard, v. **II**, 23-24
- baked pear and breadcrumb pudding (Canada), v. **II**, 646-47
- black rice, with mangoes (Brunei), v. **II**, 313
- blueberry (Canada), v. **II**, 645-46
- bread (Panama), v. **II**, 602-603
- bread and butter, with apricot topping (Ireland), v. **I**, 202-203
- bread and butter, with coconut (The Gambia), v. **II**, 106
- cardamom rice (Pakistan), v. **I**, 696-97
- cardamom wheat (India), v. **I**, 677-78
- carrot (Saudi Arabia), v. **I**, 559
- carrot-potato-raisin (Canada), v. **II**, 647-48

index

puddings (cont'd)
    chocolate (Venezuela), v. II, 634-35
    Christmas porridge with dried fruit and wheat
        berries (Armenia), v. I, 598-99
    Christmas, with pear mincemeat (England), v. I, 442
    coconut (Nicaragua), v. II, 593-94
    coconut corn starch pudding (Nicaragua), v. II, 595
    coconut custards (South Africa), v. II, 249
    coconut-rice porridge (Myanmar/Burma), v. II, 416
    coffee cream (Oman), v. I, 540
    coffee custards (France), v. I, 140
    coffee soft egg custard (Turkey), v. I, 574-75
    cooked cream (Italy), v. I, 226-27
    corn meal (São Tomé and Principe), v. II, 212
    cranberry (Latvia), v. I, 235-36
    creamed rice with cardamom (Tibet), v. II, 347-48
    cream of wheat with cherries (Romania), v. I, 348
    custard corn meal dessert (Zimbabwe), v. II, 302
    custard rice (Lithuania), v. I, 251
    custard with saffron and rose water (Kuwait),
        v. I, 520
    eggnog bavarian (Germany), v. I, 151
    farina with coconut milk and spices (Madagascar),
        v. II, 153
    farina cream dessert with cranberry sauce (Estonia),
        v. I, 116-17
    farina with rose water (Oman), v. I, 541
    farina custard (Greece), v. I, 171
    fig (Albania), v. I, 13
    fruit cream (Belgium), v. I, 55-56
    ginger cream (Thailand), v. II, 436
    guava-cream tapioca, v. II, 196
    Indian (Native America), v. II, 670-71
    lemon curd (England), v. I, 443-44
    lime, with sweetened condensed milk (Côte
        d'Ivorie), v. II, 68
    lingonberry cream dessert (Sweden), v. I, 404
    little rice puddings (Italy), v. I, 227-28
    mango (Caribbean), v. II, 503-504
    milk (Armenia), v. I, 597
    milk rice (Senegal), v. II, 222-23
    milk rice (Sri Lanka), v. I, 706
    millet and yogurt (Mauritania), v. II, 167
    orange custards with honey and cinnamon
        (Portugal), v. I, 337
    orange farina (Israel), v. I, 499-500
    pearl tapioca, creamed (The Philippines), v. II, 424
    pumpkin porridge with *couscous* (Kazakhstan),
        v. I, 632-33
    red wheat (Norway), v. I, 317
    rhubarb mousse (Iceland), v. I, 190
    rice and millet (Mali), v. II, 158-59
    rice and peanut butter (Zambia), v. II, 297
    rice flour pudding (Ghana), v. II, 114-15
    rice flour pudding with rose water (Iran),
        v. I, 483-84
    rice, vegan almond, v. I, 270
    rice, with dates (Saudi Arabia), v. I, 558
    rice, with honey (Belarus), v. I, 42
    rice, with peanut butter cream (Togo), v. II, 269
    rice, with saffron (Belgium), v. I, 55
    ricotta, with citron and chocolate (Italy),
        v. I, 219
    sago with coconut milk (Bhutan), v. I, 662
    semolina (Nepal), v. I, 688
    semolina with bananas (Guinea), v. II, 121-22
    semolina with walnuts (Bulgaria), v. I, 78-79
    stewed rhubarb with farina (Germany), v. I, 152
    summer, strawberry-blueberry, v. I, 445-46
    sweet barley porridge (Mongolia), v. II, 406
    sweet *couscous* (The Gambia), v. II, 105
    sweet *couscous* with raisins and pineapple (Niger),
        v. II, 200
    sweetpotato (Pacific Islands - Palua), v. II, 485
    sweetpotato and coconut (Sri Lanka), v. I, 707
    sweetpotato with coconut (Zambia), v. II, 296
    sweet yogurt dessert (Bangladesh), v. I, 653
    tapioca in coconut milk with fruit (Malaysia),
        v. II, 396-97
    tapioca with cloves (Nigeria), v. II, 206
    tapioca with sweetpotatoes (Laos), v. II, 389-90
    tapioca with warm spices (Oman), v. I, 541-42
    walnut rice cream (Spain), v. I, 397
    wheat and coconut dessert in sweet syrup
        (Palestine), v. I, 549-50
    whipped cranberry-raspberry with farina and
        strawberries (Finland), v. I, 128
    whole grain with raisins (Egypt), v. II, 81-82
    yellow coconut pudding (Angola), v. II, 15
    yogurt cream whip with ginger, v. II, 406-407
    yogurt cream whip with rhubarb (Norway),
        v. I, 316-17
    yogurt *crème* mousse (Russia), v. I, 357
    Yorkshire summer pudding (England), v. I, 444-45
puff pastry
    banana pastry (Mauritania), v. II, 168
    bananas in pastry (Cape Verde), v. II, 44
    banana *strudel* (Namibia), v. II, 195-96
    black olive purée and *hummus* appetizers (Bulgaria),
        v. I, 72-73
    cheese pastry pies (Malta), v. I, 278-79
    meatball and vegetable pastry bundles (Mongolia),
        v. II, 405
    nut roll with dried fruits and chocolate (Austria),
        v. I, 29-30
    pastries with *ricotta* and honey (Malta), v. I, 279
    pillows with raspberry purée and peaches, v. II, 458
    pineapple pastry (El Salvador), v. II, 563
    poppy seed pillows (Croatia), v. I, 88
    ratatouille with puff pastry pillows (France),
        v. I, 135-36
    vegetable and cheese pies (Uruguay), v. II, 624-25
    vegetable pasties (New Zealand), v. II, 467
    with Argentine sweet milk (Argentina), v. II, 512
pumpkin
    appetizer dip (Libya), v. II, 139
    cake (Liberia), v. II, 135-36
    custard pie, v. II, 672-73
    dark vegetable stock (Thailand), v. II, 431-32
    pie in *phyllo* roll (Serbia), v. I, 370
    porridge with *couscous* (Kazakhstan), v. I, 632-33
    soup (Malta), v. I, 274-75

pumpkin (cont'd)
- soup, with coconut milk and banana (Caribbean – Bahamas), v. II, 494
- soup, with pomegranate seeds (Azerbaijan), v. I, 604
- stove-top corn pudding (Native America), v. II, 666
- sweet soy-glazed (Korea), v. II, 373
- vegetable pasties (New Zealand), v. II, 467
- vegetable soup with chick peas and groundnut butter (Namibia), v. II, 192
- with cream (Slovakia), v. I, 379

purslane
- and tomato salad (Native America), v. II, 656-57
- bread and vegetable salad (Kuwait), v. I, 515-16

Quesadillas, squash and cheese (Mexico), v. II, 580

quinoa
- and vegetable stew (Peru), v. II, 615
- with cream (Ecuador), v. II, 555

Radishes
- and egg salad (Tunisia), v. II, 274
- appetizer (China), v. II, 325-26
- cabbage pickle *kimchi* (Korea), v. II, 376-77
- *daikon* and garlic relish/salad (Myanmar/Burma), v. II, 413-14
- *daikon* and red radish pickles (Tibet), v. II, 346
- *daikon* in clear vegetable stock (Thailand), v. II, 431
- *daikon* in dark vegetable stock (Thailand), v. II, 431-32
- *daikon*, in orange and onion salad with cumin (India), v. I, 670-71
- dumpling soup (Korea), v. II, 371-72
- green banana and vegetable salad (Costa Rica), v. II, 542-43
- salad with mint (Guatemala), v. II, 568
- salad with sour cream (Poland), v. I, 324

raspberries
- curd (Jordan), v. I, 509
- dessert (Romania), v. I, 347
- purée, and peaches over puff pastry pillows, v. II, 458
- sauce for stuffed figs (Italy), v. I, 207-208
- Yorkshire summer pudding (England), v. I, 444-45

relishes, including **chutneys** and *salsas*
- beet and horseradish (Slovakia), v. I, 379-80
- corn, v. II, 579-80
- eggplant (Australia), v. II, 455-56
- mango-pineapple chutney (Uganda), v. II, 282-83
- mango relish (Caribbean – Cuba), v. II, 499-500
- onion, garlic, and *cilantro salsa* (Peru), v. II, 614
- papaya and grilled pineapple salsa (Caribbean), v. II, 491-92
- pickled red onion with lime juice (Ecuador), v. II, 552
- radish and garlic relish/salad (Myanmar/Burma), v. II, 413-14
- spiced whole cranberry (Native America), v. II, 668
- strawberry, melon, and black pepper *salsa* (Native America), v. II, 669-70
- sweet and sour onion with olives (Andorra), v. I, 19
- sweet pineapple (Indonesia), v. II, 357
- tomato and onion *sambol* (Sri Lanka), v. I, 700
- tomato and pepper appetizer salad (Israel), v. I, 495
- vegetable (Tanzania), v. II, 262-63
- vegetable *mélange* (Malta), v. I, 275-76

REPUBLIC OF THE CONGO (Central African Republics), v. II, 45-53

rhubarb
- freezing, v. I, 152 (note)
- mousse (Iceland), v. I, 190
- strawberry-rhubarb juice (Estonia), v. I, 121-22
- stewed (England), v. I, 446
- stewed, with farina (Germany), v. I, 152
- stewed, with tapioca (New Zealand), v. II, 470
- *streusel* coffeecake (Estonia), v. I, 117-18
- yogurt cream whipped pudding (Norway), v. I, 316-17

rice
- and black beans with mango relish (Caribbean – Cuba), v. II, 499-500
- and cheese-stuffed acorn squashes, v. I, 64-65
- and chick pea soup (Mongolia), v. II, 402-403
- and chick pea soup (Peru), v. II, 612-13
- and coconut porridge (Myanmar/Burma), v. II, 416
- and eggs (Italy), v. I, 212
- and lentil-stuffed grape leaves (Lebanon), v. I, 525
- and lima beans (Cape Verde), v. II, 41
- and millet pudding (Mali), v. II, 158-59
- and spinach soup (Lebanon), v. I, 526
- and *vermicelli* with vegetables (Kuwait), v. I, 517
- and yogurt soup (Georgia), v. I, 613-14
- and zucchini in tomato sauce (Madagascar), v. II, 150-51
- baked with eggs and tomatoes (Malta), v. I, 278
- balls (Botswana), v. II, 20
- banana fritters (Djibouti), v. II, 76
- basmati, in bread salad with spinach, chick peas, and garlic-yogurt sauce with *tahini* (Tunisia), v. II, 274-75
- basmati, in soup with coconut and beans (Tanzania), v. II, 260-61
- basmati, with peas and dill (Kuwait), v. I, 514-15
- black rice pudding (Brunei), v II, 313
- brown rice and eggplant (Indonesia), v. II, 355
- brown rice and garlic *pilaf* (Central Asia), v. I, 629-30
- cardamom rice pudding (Pakistan), v. I, 696-97
- carrot *pilaf* (Kazakhstan), v. I, 630-31
- coconut, with mangoes (Cambodia), v. II, 321
- creamed, with cardamom (Tibet), v. II, 347-48
- *croquettes* (Albania), v. I, 11
- curried eggs and rice, v. I, 673-74
- curry with peanut butter and bananas (Angola), v. II, 14
- custard pudding (Lithuania), v. I, 251
- fried sweets (The Philippines), v. II, 425-26
- fried, with pineapple (Pacific Islands – Cook Islands), v. II, 480
- fried, with fried garlic (Brazil), v. II, 526-27
- fried, with shallots and garlic (The Philippines), v. II, 423
- hot yogurt soup with chick peas (Iran), v. I, 477-78
- in coconut milk (Sri Lanka), v. I, 706

index

rice (cont'd)
- lettuce wraps (Korea), v. II, 378
- little rice puddings (Italy), v. I, 227-28
- Milanese *minestrone* (Italy), v. I, 222-23
- milk pudding (Armenia), v. I, 597
- milk rice pudding (Senegal), v. II, 222-23
- *pilaf* with fruits and nuts (Azerbaijan), v. I, 609
- *pilaf* with garlic (Central Asia), v. I, 629-30
- pineapple fried rice (Laos), v. II, 386-87
- pudding, vegan rice with almond milk, v. I, 270
- pudding, with dates (Saudi Arabia), v. I, 558
- pudding, with honey (Belarus), v. I, 42
- pudding, with peanut butter (Zambia), v. II, 297
- pudding, with peanut butter cream (Togo), v. II, 269
- pudding, with saffron (Belgium), v. I, 55
- pumpkin soup with pomegranate seeds (Azerbaijan), v. I, 604
- purple rice and mango salad (Thailand), v. II, 432-33
- red and white (Bhutan), v. I, 661
- rice flour pudding (Ghana), v. II, 114-15
- salad, with banana (Kenya), v. II, 127
- salad, with brown rice and fried tomato (Bolivia), v. II, 516
- slow cooker lentils and (Egypt), v. II, 79-80
- soup, with coconut and beans (Nigeria), v. II, 203-204
- soup, with eggs and lemon (Albania), v. I, 6
- soup, with meatballs and lentils (Cyprus), v. I, 467-68
- soup, with walnuts (Azerbaijan), v. I, 605
- soup, with yogurt (Azerbaijan), v. I, 605-606
- spicy rice with tomatoes (Djibouti), v. II, 75-76
- sticky, and banana sweet (Cambodia), v. II, 321
- sweet, deep-fried clusters (Nigeria), v. II, 207
- sweet egg sponge cakes (Guatemala), v. II, 569-70
- sweet rice balls (Vietnam), v. II, 444
- sweet rice cakes (Cameroon), v. II, 38-39
- sweet rice flour balls (Sierra Leone), v. II, 229
- sweet saffron rice (Tibet), v. II, 349
- *tagine*, with Swiss chard (Morocco), v. II, 175
- tomato soup (Austria) v. I, 23-24
- vegetable stew with soymeat (Serbia), v. I, 367-68
- walnut rice cream (Spain), v. I, 397
- with braised vegetables in olive oil (Saudi Arabia), v. I, 556
- with butter (Sudan), v. II, 255-56
- with coconut milk (Indonesia), v. II, 352
- with onions and egg and lemon sauce (Macedonia), v. I, 266
- with potatoes (Uganda), v. II, 286
- with tomatoes (Caribbean), v. II, 498-99
- with tomatoes and coconut milk (Sierra Leone), v. II, 228-29
- with tomatoes and coconut milk (Mozambique), v. II, 182-83
- with tomatoes and hearts of palm (Costa Rica), v. II, 544-45
- with vegetables (Bhutan), v. I, 661-62

rice, powdered, v. I, 397 (note)
roasted red peppers, preparation, v. I, 165, 497, 552-53
ROMANIA, v. I, 339-48

rosemary, information, v. II, 194 (note)
rosemary powder, v. I, 283 (note)
RUSSIA, v. I, 349-61
rutabaga
- and potato casserole (Finland), v. I, 125-26
- oven-roasted root vegetables with fresh herbs and mushrooms (Namibia), v. II, 193-94
- vegetable soup with barley (Estonia), v. I, 112-13

Sage, information, v. I, 29 (note); v. II, 194 (note)
sage leaves, fried (Italy), v. I, 225
salad burnet, information, v. II, 512 (note)
salads, dressings
- apricot-raspberry (Native America), v. II, 654
- black sesame dressing (Brunei), v. II, 308
- blender mayonnaise, v. II, 675-76
- Bruneian tamarind dressing (Brunei), v. II, 308-309
- celery seed, v. I, 436
- Central African peanut-lime dressing (Central African Republics), v. II, 48-49
- citrus dressing (Caribbean), v. II, 494-95
- citrus dressing (Senegal), v. II, 219
- citrus *vinaigrette* (Côte d'Ivorie), v. II, 66
- classic French, v. II, 676-77
- creamy Italian, v. II, 677
- curried island dressing (Pacific Islands – Vanuatu), v. II, 474
- curried mayonnaise (Pacific Islands - Saipan), v. II, 475
- garlic-mayonnaise (Moldova), v. I, 285
- garlic mayonnaise (Spain), v. I 392-93
- garlic *vinaigrette* (Luxembourg), v. I, 255
- Greek oregano *vinaigrette* (Greece), v. I. 162
- herb dressing (Mongolia), v. II, 401-402
- honey-pineapple *vinaigrette* (Burundi), v. II, 27
- kiwifruit *vinaigrette* with honey (New Zealand), v. II, 465
- lemon-peach (Mozambique), v. II, 181-82
- lemon *vinaigrette* Dijon, v. II, 678
- lime mayonnaise with hot peppers and ginger (Côte d'Ivorie), v. II, 63
- lime *vinaigrette* (Caribbean), v. II, 496
- lime *vinaigrette* with cumin (Pacific Islands), v. II, 474-75
- *nam jim* (Thailand), v. II, 433-34
- onion salad dressing (Vietnam), v. II, 440
- onion *vinaigrette* (Mongolia), v. II, 401
- peanut butter (Indonesia), v. II, 354-55
- peanut butter (West Africa), v. II, 221
- pepper *vinaigrette* (Eritrea), v. II, 87
- pomegranate *vinaigrette* (Israel), v. I, 479
- prickly pear *vinaigrette* with *agave* nectar (Native America), v. II, 654-55
- raspberry *vinaigrette* (Australia), v. II, 452
- sesame dressing (Korea), v. II, 374
- sour cream (Czech), v. I, 93
- sour cream-dill (Lithuania), v. I, 247
- summer fruit dressing (Argentina), v. II, 511
- sweet *cilantro* dressing (Cambodia), v. II, 318
- tamarind dressing (Laos), v. II, 385
- tomato-black bean vinaigrette (Somalia), v. II, 234

salads, fruit
    and vegetable salad (Indonesia), v. II, 354
    apple and cheese (Switzerland), v. I, 410
    apple with onion and *feta* (Greece), v. I, 163
    avocado and egg (Israel), v. I, 498
    avocado and grapefruit salad (Somalia), v. II, 234-35
    avocado and mayonnaise (Ghana), v. II, 110
    avocado halves stuffed with tomato salad (New Zealand), v. II, 463
    avocado halves with spicy dressing (Guinea), v. II, 118
    avocado, mango, and orange (Senegal), v. II, 219
    avocado, peach, and tomato (Mozambique), v. II, 181
    baby banana with peanuts (The Philippines), v. II, 420-21
    banana and mango (The Gambia), v. II, 102
    banana and rice (Kenya), v. II, 127
    beet and apple with sour cream (Lithuania), v. I, 247
    beetroot and apple (Uruguay), v. II, 624
    blood oranges with fennel, *pecorino*, and pomegranate (Italy), v. I, 215
    cabbage and green mango salad (Myanmar/Burma), v. II, 412
    celery and apple (Slovakia), v. I, 375
    curried yam and banana with hard-cooked eggs (Pacific Islands - Saipan), v. II, 475
    egg and avocado (Colombia), v. II, 537
    fruit platter with lime *vinaigrette* (Caribbean), v. II, 496
    fruit salad (Central African Republics), v. II, 53
    fruit salad (Uganda), v. II, 283-84
    fruit salad with citrus *vinaigrette* (Côte d'Ivoire), v. II, 66
    fruit salad with tamarind dressing (Brunei), v. II, 308-309
    hearts of palm, *jicama*, and papaya salad with lime *vinaigrette* (Pacific Islands), v. II, 474-75
    green banana and vegetable (Costa Rica), v. II, 542-43
    kohlrabi and papaya with tamarind dressing (Laos), v. II, 385
    layered fruit salad (Cameroon), v. II, 34-35
    lemon and red onion in lettuce rolls (Myanmar/Burma), v. II, 413
    mango (Madagascar), v. II, 149-50
    mango salad with vegetables (Pakistan), v. I, 691
    mango with mango-lime dressing (Bhutan), v. I, 658
    mango, pineapple, and apricot (Niger), v. II, 198
    melon and peach with fresh *mozzarella* (New Zealand), v. II, 463-64
    melon, tomato, and olive (Greece), v. I, 163-64
    mixed fruit salad with *chaat masala* (India), v. I, 670
    nasturtium blossoms stuffed with avocado (Native America), v. II, 655
    orange and date (Morocco), v. II, 174
    orange and tomato (Kenya), v. II, 125-26
    orange with *calamarata* (Somalia), v. II, 235
    papaya and corn with citrus *vinaigrette* (Togo), v. II, 268
    papaya and tomato (Caribbean - Puerto Rico), v. II, 495-96
    papaya, avocado, and grapefruit (Kenya), v. II, 126
    papaya with curried island dressing (Pacific Islands - Vanuatu), v. II, 474
    peach, cantaloupe, and blueberry with almond syrup and *moscato* wine sauce (Macedonia), v. I, 264
    pineapple and avocado (Central African Republics), v. II, 47
    pomegranate *vinaigrette* (Iran), v. I, 479
    pomelo (Cambodia), v. II, 317
    prickly pear salad (Israel), v. I, 497
    purple rice and mango (Thailand), v. II, 432-33
    red grapefruit with soymeat and soy sprouts (Thailand), v. II, 433-34
    ruby pear salad with lingonberries (Sweden), v. I, 401
    St. John's Day fruit salad (Venezuela), v. II, 630-31
    tossed with blueberries and hazelnuts (England), v. I, 436
    tropical fruit salad (Nigeria), v. II, 202
    watermelon and cucumber with *hoisin*-lime dressing (Vietnam), v. II, 439
    watermelon and *feta* (South Africa), v. II, 244
    watermelon, tomato and *feta* (Egypt), v. II, 79
    wilted lettuce with strawberries and smoked *Gouda* cheese (Germany), v. I, 147

salads, vegetable
    and fruit salad (Indonesia), v. II, 354
    Argentine-styled Russian salad, v. II, 508-509
    artichoke hearts with preserved lemons and honey (Morocco), v. II, 173
    artichoke with leeks and carrots (Turkey), v. I, 570
    asparagus with capers (Romania), v. I, 343
    baby pepper (Bosnia), v. I, 61-62
    bean (Caribbean - Haiti), v. II, 497
    bean salad with corn and mango (Burundi), v. II, 27
    beans and corn (Liechtenstein), v. I, 239
    beans with walnuts (Georgia), v. I, 615-16
    beet and apple with sour cream (Lithuania), v. I, 247
    beet and cheese (Austria), v. I, 26
    beet and garlic (Greece), v. I, 162-63
    beet and *tahini* with eggs (Syria), v. I, 564
    beet, potato, and carrot salad (Peru), v. II, 613-14
    beetroot and apple (Uruguay), v. II, 624
    beetroot with eggs (Belarus), v. I, 35-36
    beet with *feta* cheese (Serbia), v. I, 366-67
    beet with garlic-mayonnaise dressing (Moldova), v. I, 285
    beet with yogurt and mint (Iran), v. I, 478
    Boston lettuce and onion with sour cream dressing (Czech), v. I, 93
    bread and vegetable (Kuwait), v. I, 515-16
    bread, with spinach, rice, chick peas, and garlic-yogurt sauce with *tahini* (Tunisia), v. II, 274-75
    broccoli and potato, with Hollandaise sauce (Brazil), v. II, 521
    bulgur wheat (Jordan), v. I, 504-505
    butter bean (Malta), v. I, 275

salads, vegetable (cont'd)
    cabbage and carrot slaw with onion and apple (Ukraine), v. I, 426
    cabbage and carrot slaw with peanuts (Pakistan), v. I, 690-91
    cabbage and carrot with yogurt dressing (Western Sahara), v. II, 163
    cabbage and green mango salad (Myanmar/ Burma), v. II, 412
    cabbage pickle, *kimchi* (Korea), v. II, 376-77
    cabbage slaw (Slovenia), v. I, 389
    cabbage slaw of the *vuelta e 'Lola* (Venezuela), v. II, 631
    cabbage slaw with corn and fresh dillweed (Angola), v. II, 12-13
    cabbage slaw with pineapple (Cameroon), v. II, 34
    cabbage with avocado and pickled red onion relish (Ecuador), v. II, 551
    cabbage with pineapple (Liberia), v. II, 133-34
    cabbage with shredded carrot (Cyprus), v. I, 468
    carrot slaw (Kazakhstan), v. I, 627
    cauliflower and garlic pickle (Iran), v. I, 482-83
    celeriac (Hungary), v. I, 179
    celeriac appetizer (Moldova), v. I, 282-83
    and apple salad (Slovakia), v. I, 375
    celery and apple salad (Slovakia), v. I, 375
    celery and cabbage slaw with sour cream (Canada), v. II, 641-42
    celery, celeriac, and radish (Germany), v. I, 143
    chayote and pepper slaw (Panama), v. II, 598
    chick pea (Libya), v. II, 142
    Christmas red cabbage slaw (Iceland), v. I, 188
    corn and cheese (Peru), v. II, 613
    couscous with chick peas (Algeria), v. II, 4-5
    couscous with chick peas and tomatoes (Mauritania), v. II, 162-63
    couscous with roasted eggplant and red pepper (Morocco), v. II, 171-72
    couscous with tomato-black bean *vinaigrette* (Somalia), v. II, 234
    cucumber (Slovakia), v. I, 375-76
    cucumber and olive (Azerbaijan), v. I, 602-603
    cucumber and red onion (Nepal), v. I, 682
    cucumber and shallot (Laos), v. II, 392-93
    cucumber and tomato with *chaat masala*, (India), v. I, 669
    cucumber and yogurt (India), v. I, 671
    cucumber with cheese (Bhutan), v. I, 657-58
    cucumber with dill and garlic mayonnaise (Ukraine), v. I, 425
    cucumber, with peanut-lime dressing (Central African Republics), v. II, 48-49
    cucumber with pomegranate *vinaigrette* (Iran), v. I, 479
    cucumber with yogurt (Sudan), v. II, 253
    curried *pasta* (Botswana), v. II, 19
    curried yam and banana with hard-cooked eggs (Pacific Islands – Saipan), v. II, 475
    deviled beet, potato, apple, and egg (Estonia), v. I, 111-12

    edamame with string cheese and chive oil (Armenia), v. I, 591-92
    egg and potato (Côte d'Ivorie), v. II, 65
    eggplant (China), v. II, 327-28
    eggplant and tomato (Yemen), v. I, 579-80
    eggplant and tomato with goat cheese (São Tomé and Principe), v. II, 210-11
    eggplant, with herb dressing (Mongolia), v. II, 401-402
    fennel with lemon and cheese (Angola), v. II, 12
    fried pepper, onion, and tomato with garlic sauce (Moldova), v. I, 285-86
    fried tomatoes and onions with brown rice (Bolivia), v. II, 516
    glass noodle and vegetable slaw (Tibet), v. II, 341
    grated carrot (Madagascar), v. II, 147
    green banana and vegetable (Costa Rica), v. II, 542-43
    green bean and garlic (Slovenia), v. I, 387
    greens *vinaigrette* (Senegal), v. II, 218-19
    grilled vegetable salad (Kuwait), v. I, 516
    hearts of palm (The Philippines), v. II, 421
    hearts of palm, *jicama*, and papaya salad with lime *vinaigrette* (Pacific Islands), v. II, 474-75
    hearts of palm with cheese (Ecuador), v. II, 550-51
    hot asparagus, with raspberry *vinaigrette* (Australia), v. II, 451
    hot potato (Germany), v. I, 146
    Israeli *couscous* and chick pea with cucumber, cherries, and dates (Israel), v. I, 496
    jicama and carrot with mango (Colombia), v. II, 538-39
    kidney beans with eggs (Slovenia), v. I, 388-89
    Kirby cucumber (Korea), v. II, 377-78
    kohlrabi and papaya with tamarind dressing (Laos), v. II, 385
    layered vegetable salad (Ghana), v. II, 111-12
    lentil and *pasta* salad with nasturtium (Australia), v. II, 457
    lentil and spinach (Libya), v. II, 141
    lettuce with potatoes and bacon (Burundi), v. II, 26
    macaroni (Denmark), v. I, 107-108
    macaroni (Madagascar), v. II, 147
    macaroni with *pesto* and *chouriço* (Uganda), v. II, 284-85
    marinated dried mushrooms with herbs (Romania), v. I, 346-47
    mesclún with shaved macadamia nuts (Australia), v. II, 451
    millet and corn salad with avocado (Central African Republics), v. II, 47-48
    mixed greens with sugar and lemon (Denmark), v. I, 101
    Moscow salad (Russia), v. I, 351
    mozzarella, tomato, and basil (Venezuela), v. II, 632
    millet *tabbouleh* (Lebanon), v. I, 526-27
    mushroom (Finland), v. I, 124
    mushroom and chick pea (Somalia), v. II, 233
    niçoise (France), v. I, 136
    onion salad (Czech), v. I, 94
    onion salad with coconut milk (Sri Lanka), v. I, 703

index

salads, vegetable (cont'd)
    parsley with *tahini* (Palestine), v. I, 548-49
    pasta and vegetable salad with peanut butter
        dressing (Senegal), v. II, 221
    pepper (Hungary), v. I, 182
    pink potato salad (Panama), v. II, 598-99
    potato (Albania), v. I, 7-8
    potato (Germany), v. I, 145-46
    potato (Madagascar), v. II, 148
    potato and chick pea (Armenia), v. I, 591
    potato with dandelions (Slovenia), v. I, 387-88
    potato and egg with *feta* cheese (Tunisia),
        v. II, 273
    potato with mayonnaise (Turkmenistan),
        v. I, 627-28
    prickly pear with apricot-raspberry dressing
        (Mexico), v. II, 581
    purslane and tomato (Native America), v. II, 656-57
    radish and egg (Tunisia), v. II, 274
    radish and garlic relish/salad (Myanmar/Burma),
        v. II, 413-14
    radish with mint (Guatemala), v. II, 568
    radish with sour cream (Poland), v. I, 324
    red cabbage and black currant slaw (Finland),
        v. I, 125
    red onion (Uzbekistan), v. I, 625-26
    rice noodle and spring onion (China), v. II, 326-27
    roasted eggplant with onion dressing (Vietnam),
        v. II, 440
    roasted frying peppers (Croatia), v. I, 83
    roasted sweetpotato with macadamia nuts (New
        Zealand), v. II, 464
    roasted tomato and roasted pepper (Tunisia),
        v. II, 272-73
    rolled noodle and spring onion (China), v. II, 326-27
    sesame noodle with corn (Mongolia), v. II, 400-401
    shredded beetroot (Romania), v. I, 344
    shredded onion and vegetable (Denmark), v. I, 101
    spinach and beet with yogurt dressing (Georgia),
        v. I, 618-19
    spinach and yogurt (Kuwait), v. I, 512-13
    spinach, warm with mushrooms and garlic
        (Andorra) v. I, 15-16
    steamed eggplant and scallion (Korea), v. II, 375-76
    steamed vegetable salad with sweet black sesame
        dressing (Brunei), v. II, 308
    sweet and sour bean (Zimbabwe), v. II, 299-300
    sweet and sour cucumber (Japan), v. II, 363-64
    sweetpotato, *jicama*, and mango in citrus dressing
        (Caribbean), v. II, 494-95
    three-bean salad with creamy dressing (Mongolia),
        v. II, 402
    toasted millet (Mali), v. II, 155-56
    tofu "tuna"-stuffed cucumber boats (Côte d'Ivoire),
        v. II, 66-67
    tomato and coriander (Yemen), v. I, 579
    tomato and cucumber with grated cheese
        (Montenegro), v. I, 295
    tomato and cucumber with peppers (Hungary),
        v. I, 178-79
    tomato and green onion salad (Zambia), v. II, 293
    tomato and onion (Syria), v. I, 562-63
    tomato and onion (Tanzania), v. II, 262
    tomato and onion *sambol* (Sri Lanka), v. I, 700
    tomato and pepper appetizer salad (Israel), v. I, 495
    tomato and shredded *Halloumi* (Cyprus), v. I, 469
    tomato, onion, and pea (Portugal), v. I, 332-33
    tomato, to stuff avocado halves (New Zealand),
        v. II, 463
    tomato, with basil (The Gambia), v. II, 100-101
    tomato, with garlic and cheese (Belarus), v. I, 35
    tossed (Azerbaijan), v. I, 606
    tossed vegetables with cheese (Sudan), v. II, 252-53
    tossed, with noodles and onion *vinaigrette*
        (Mongolia), v. II, 401
    vegetable (Albania), v. I, 7
    vegetable (Madagascar), v. II, 148
    vegetable bread soup (Spain), v. I, 393-94
    vegetable *mélange* (Malta), v. I, 275-76
    vegetable relish (Tanzania), v. II, 262-63
    vegetable slaw (El Salvador), v. II, 560-61
    vegetable, with hearts of palm (Brazil), v. II, 525
    vegetable, with white beans, root celery, kohlrabi,
        and potatoes (Czech), v. I, 96
    village tossed salad (Greece), v. I, 161-62
    warm leek celeriac and carrot (Norway), v. I, 310-11
    watercress with sesame dressing (Korea), v. II, 374
    white eggplant and red kidney bean (Ethiopia),
        v. II, 93
    whole carrots with mayonnaise-mustard sauce with
        capers (Belgium), v. I, 47
    wilted cucumber with honey (Belarus), v. I, 34
    wilted dandelion (Andorra), v. I, 16-17
    yam with scallions (Chad), v. II, 56
    zucchini *vinaigrette* (Israel), v. I, 499
sandwiches
    breaded eggplant and cheese (Armenia), v. I, 594-95
    pan-fried Cheddar (England), v. I, 440
    pan-fried cheese (Switzerland), v. I, 417
    open-faced onion sandwich with eggplant spread
        (Lebanon), v. I, 523 (note)
    open-faced with mushrooms (Switzerland),
        v. I, 408-409
    quesadillas, squash and cheese (Mexico), v. II, 580
    smørbrød, open-faced (Denmark), v. I, 106-107
    vegetables and sausage (Andorra), v. I, 20-21
    vegetarian reubens (Pacific Islands – Cook
        Islands), v. II, 478-79
    Welsh rabbit (rarebit) (Wales), v. I, 457-58
SÃO TOMÉ AND PRINCIPE, v. II, 209-14
sauces , savory, including marinades
    allioli, with eggs (Andorra), v. I, 19
    blender Hollandaise, v. II, 522
    brown garlic (China), v. II, 331
    brown onion (Norway), v. I, 315
    brown sauce (China), v. II, 332-33
    caper and olive, v. I, 85-86
    celery, for sautéed leeks and carrots (Scotland),
        v. I, 453
    cheese and *chili* sauce (Tibet), v. II, 347
    cheese, for vegetables (Norway), v. I, 314
    chili and garlic sauce (Malaysia), v. II, 396
    chili and ginger (Australia), v. II, 456-57

sauces, savory (cont'd)
    chili and tomato (Bolivia), v. II, 518
    citrus shallot (Pacific Islands – Polynesia),
        v. II, 481-82
    cold watercress (Belgium), v. I, 46-47
    coriander sauce (Afghanistan), v. I, 641
    cranberry with mustard (Lithuania), v. I, 248
    cream and mustard (Ireland), v. I, 200-201
    creamed sorrel (Ireland), v. I, 194-95
    cream, with roasted shallots and thyme
        (Australia), v. II, 456
    creamy cocktail (Iceland), v. I, 188
    egg and lemon (Macedonia), v. I, 267
    garlic (Moldova/Romania), v. I, 286
    garlic and parsley (Nicaragua), v. II, 592
    garlic-walnut (Macedonia), v. I, 263
    garlic-yogurt (Iran), v. I, 476-77
    ginger and sesame (China), v. II, 330
    gravy, "without the 'Sunday Roast," v. II, 124-25
    Greek marinade, v. I, 166
    hoisin barbecue (Mongolia), v. II, 404-405
    horseradish and sour cream, uncooked (Ukraine),
        v. I, 424-25
    hunter's style (Italy), v. II, 684-85
    lime marinade for *tofu* (Caribbean – Cuba),
        v. II, 498
    marinara sauce (Italy), v. II, 682
    mayonnaise-mustard with capers (Belgium),
        v. I, 47
    mushroom (Norway), v. I, 313-14
    mustard-sour cream (Bosnia-Herzegovina),
        v. I, 60
    paprika cream (Hungary), v. I, 177-78
    parsley (Ireland), v. I, 196
    peanut butter and tomato, with garlic (The
        Gambia), v. II, 104
    pesto (Italy), v. I, 223-24
    pesto, with macadamia nuts (New Zealand),
        v. II, 462
    pine nut, with *tahini* (Lebanon), v. I, 531-32
    plum (Laos), v. II, 383-84
    polonaise (Poland), v. I, 321
    remoulade with cornichons and capers
        (Switzerland), v. I, 411
    savory forest honey with herbs (Cyprus), v. I, 474
    sour cream and onion (Latvia), v. I, 234
    sour cream with horseradish (Belarus), v. I, 40
    sour cream with horseradish (Ukraine),
        v. I, 424-25
    sweet and sour glaze (Japan), v. II, 361
    sweet sesame marinade (Korea), v. II, 372
    sweet soy sauce (Brunei), v. II, 310
    tahini (Jordan), v. I, 508
    tart cherry sauce for beets (Georgia), v. I, 617-18
    tomato and cabbage (Russia), v. I, 352 (note)
    tomato and cream (Uruguay), v. II, 622-23
    tomato and onion, for meatballs (Costa Rica),
        v. II, 543
    tomato and peanut (Zambia), v. II, 294
    tomato and peanut, with cream (Brazil),
        v. II, 527-28
    tomato-coriander (Laos), v. II, 384
    tomato mushroom (Italy), v. II, 686
    tomato, with potatoes, garlic, and coriander
        (Somalia), v. II, 236
    vegan Worcestershire-style, v. II, 683-84
    walnut and garlic (Georgia), v. I, 612-13
    with ginger and peanut butter (Togo), v. II, 268-69
    yogurt and garlic (Georgia), v. I, 612-13
    yogurt condiment with fresh coriander, garlic, and
        chilies (Tibet), v. II, 346-47
    yogurt-dill (Bulgaria), v. I, 75-76
    yogurt-garlic (Azerbaijan), v. I, 608
    yogurt-mint (Armenia), v. I, 595-96
    yogurt sauce for chick pea dumplings (India),
        v. I, 667-68
    yogurt-sour cream (Russia), v. I, 354
sauces, sweet
    apple syrup (The Netherlands), v. I, 306
    basic chocolate syrup, v. II, 638
    blackberry sauce or dessert (Australia), v. II, 687
    blueberry (Lithuania), v. I, 250
    cinnamon-orange syrup (Korea), v. I, 379
    cinnamon syrup, v. II, 687
    citrus and honey (Scotland), v. I, 454-55
    cranberry (Estonia), v. I, 116-17
    cranberry and black walnut (Native America),
        v. II, 672
    creamy cinnamon (The Netherlands), v. I, 307
    custard sauce, v. II, 688
    English cream (Scotland), v. I, 451
    ersatz "maple syrup" (Native America), v. II, 662
        fig (Italy), v. I, 208-209
    fresh orange custard sauce, v. II, 689
    honey-lemon syrup (Bosnia), v. I, 68
    lemon sauce, v. II, 689-90
    lemon syrup, v. II, 690
    lemon verbena syrup, v. II, 690-91
    mango-yogurt (Oman), v. I, 537
    mocha-cinnamon (Mexico), v. II, 587
    pancake and waffle syrup, v. II, 688
    rose water syrup (Brunei), v. II, 312-13
    rum cream (Scotland), v. I, 454
    sour cream (Hungary), v. I, 184
    sour cream and honey (Kenya), v. II, 130
    sour cream for pears (Serbia), v. I, 369-70
    sweet coffee *coulis* (Caribbean), v. II, 503
    sweet ginger syrup (Australia), v. II, 459
    toasted hazelnut-rum hard sauce (Denmark),
        v. I, 109
    toffee (England), v. I, 444
SAUDI ARABIA, v. I, 551-60
sauerkraut, *see* cabbage
sausages, *glamorgan* (Wales), v. I, 460
SCOTLAND, see UNITED KINGDOM, SCOTLAND
seasoned salt (Caribbean – St. Croix), v. II, 497
seasoning mixtures
    Bengali five-seed spice mixture (Bangladesh),
        v. I, 652
    Chinese spicing mixture, v. II, 327
    curry powder, homemade (Cambodia), v. II, 320
    East African seasoning mixture (Djibouti),
        v. II, 73-74

seasoning mixtures (cont'd)
    Egyptian ground legume and spice mixture (Egypt), v. II, 78
    Ethiopian / Eritrean seasoning mixture, v. II, 86
    French country herb (*herbes de Provence*) (France), v. I, 136-37
    garam masala (India), v. I, 678-79
    garlic powder, homemade, v. II, 327 (note)
    Georgian herbed seasoning mixture (Georgia), v. I, 615
    Greek seasoning mix (Greece), v. I, 161
    hot pepper seasoning (Madagascar), v. II, 151-52
    Indian mango powder (India), v. I, 667
    Latin American spice mix (Chile), v. II, 533
    Kuwaiti spice mixture (Kuwait), v. I, 517-18
    Mediterranean dry marinade for vegetables (Lebanon), v. I, 529
    Nepali curry mixture (Nepal), v. I, 684
    Nigerian seasoning mixture (Nigeria), v. II, 205
    North African sumac seasoning mixture (Lebanon), v. I, 524
    paprika (Hungary), v. I, 186
    Persian spice mixture for *koresh* (Iran), v. I, 481
    rose petal spice mix (Tunisia), v. II, 280
    seasoned oil and butter for Lebanese cooking (Lebanon), v. I, 528
    seasoning mixture for dehydrated meat analogue, v. II, 698
    sesame salt (Japan), v. II, 366
    South African curry powder (South Africa), v. II, 245-46
    Sri Lankan curry powder (Sri Lankan), v. I, 705
    tandoori spice mixture, *chaat masala* (India), v. I, 679
    Tunisian coriander seasoning (Tunisia), v. II, 280
    Vietnamese spicing mixture (Vietnam), v. II, 442
    Yemeni fenugreek seasoning paste (Yemen), v. I, 577-78
    Yemeni seasoning mixture (Yemen), v. I, 581-82
SENEGAL, v. II, 215-24
SERBIA, v. I, 362-70
shallots
    and avocado in tomato soup (Australia), v. II, 449-50
    and cucumber salad (Malaysia), v. II, 392-93
    citrus-shallot sauce for baked *tofu* (Pacific Islands – Polynesia), v. II, 481-82
    curried vegetables with *tofu* (Cambodia), v. II, 319
    dried mushroom condiment (Myanmar/Burma), v. II, 410
    fried potatoes with yogurt and *chilies* (Malaysia), v. II, 393
    fried rice with garlic (The Philippines), v. II, 423
    lime marinade for *tofu* (Caribbean – Cuba), v. II, 498
    mushroom and chick pea salad (Somalia), v. II, 233
    oven-roasted root vegetables with fresh herbs and mushrooms (Namibia), v. II, 193-94
    roasted, in cream sauce (Australia), v. II, 456
    salad burnet and shallot vinegar with pepper, v. II, 511-12
    sauce for spicy eggplant (Brunei), v. II, 311-12

    tomato-coriander sauce (Laos), v. II, 384
    wild rice casserole with mushrooms and baby carrots (Canada), v. II, 642-43
    with roasted mushrooms (Ireland), v. I, 201
SIERRA LEONE, v. II, 225-29
SLOVAKIA, v. I, 371-80
SLOVENIA, v. I, 381-90
slow cooker
    baked acorn squash with chutney (Indonesia), v. II, 356 (note)
    basic slow cooker bean preparation, v. II, 43-44
    bean stew with hominy and *chouriço* (Cape Verde), v. II, 42-43
    black-eyed pea *chili* (Uganda), v. II, 287-88
    braised onions with cheese (Portugal), v. I, 335
    dried fruit curry (South Africa), v. II, 247-48
    lentils and rice (Egypt), v. II, 79-80
    lentil soup with potatoes and spinach (Palestine), v. I, 546
    mixed legume soup (Morocco), v. II, 172-73
    polenta (Montenegro), v. I, 296-97
    puréed carrot and *kumara* soup with gingerroot (New Zealand), v. II, 465-66
    spicy, slow-cooked chick peas (Pakistan), v. I, 692-93
    vegetable soup with beans and barley (Croatia), v. I, 87-88
    vegetable stew (Botswana), v. II, 19-20
soba buckwheat noodles, *see* noodles
SOMALIA, v. II, 230-41
sorrel
    sauce (Ireland), v. I, 194-95
    soup, with potatoes (Russia), v. I, 352-53
soups
    barley and vegetables with sour cream (Poland), v. I, 322-23
    bean and celery with bananas (Burundi), v. II, 27-28
    beancurd and Chinese chive bud (Vietnam), v. II, 438-39
    bean with pinched dumplings (Hungary), v. I, 176-77
    bean with pinched dumplings with vegetarian franks (Hungary), v. I, 177 (note)
    "beef" with noodles (Paraguay), v. II, 606
    beet (Ukraine), v. I, 426-27
    beet and mushroom (Poland), v. I, 323-24
    black bean (The Netherlands), v. I, 300-301
    black-eyed pea and tomato (Liberia), v. II, 133
    black lentil (Nepal), v. I, 681-82
    bread-cheese (Italy), v. I, 210-11
    broth with preserved lemons, snowpeas, and *shiitake* mushrooms (Cambodia), v. II, 316-17
    brown stock, v. II, 692-93
    butternut squash with soymeat (Israel), v. I, 495
    cabbage (Russia), v. I, 352
    cabbage with clear *cilantro* stock (The Philippines), v. II, 419-20
    cantaloupe (Pacific Islands – Polynesia), v. II, 477
    cauliflower and noodle (Indonesia), v. II, 353
    celeriac and apple (Australia), v. II, 450
    celeriac and leek (Croatia), v. I, 84-85
    cheese (The Netherlands), v. I, 301-302

soups (cont'd)
    cheesy cornbread (Paraguay), v. II, 607
    chick pea and kale soup with peanut butter and tomatoes (Djibouti), v. II, 74
    chick pea and rice (Mongolia), v. II, 402-403
    chick pea and tomato with leeks (Uruguay), v. II, 623
    chick pea, with rice (Peru), v. II, 612-13
    chick pea with roasted red peppers and garlic (Greece), v. I, 165-66
    chili bean, v. I, 283-84
    chilled avocado with garlic (Côte d'Ivoire), v. II, 64
    chilled banana (Tanzania), v. II, 261-62
    chilled barley with sour cream (Latvia), v. I, 233
    chilled *borsch* (Belarus), v. I, 37
    chilled cucumber and mango soup (Saudi Arabia), v. I, 554
    chilled cucumber and yogurt (Bulgaria), v. I, 74-75
    chowder of vegetables and fine noodles (Montenegro), v. I, 294-95
    clear *cilantro* stock with garlic (The Philippines), v. II, 420
    clear vegetable stock (Thailand), v. II, 431
    clear, with *soba* noodles and vegetables (Japan), v. II, 361-62
    coconut-bean soup with rice (Nigeria), v. II, 203-204
    corn (Kuwait), v. I, 514
    corn and sweetpotato (Thailand), v. II, 430-31
    corn chowder (Native America), v. II, 657-58
    creamed corn with egg whites (China), v. II, 328
    creamed tomato with yogurt (Afghanistan), v. I, 639
    cream of artichoke hearts (Brazil), v. II, 524
    cream of asparagus (Germany), v. I, 143-44
    cream of carrot and celeriac (Finland), v. I, 123-24
    cream of celery root soup (Czech), v. I, 91-92
    cream of celery with Stilton (England), v. I, 435
    cream of cheddar cheese (Canada), v. II, 640-41
    cream of chick pea (Guatemala), v. II, 566-67
    cream of corn and basil with tomato (Chile), v. II, 532
    cream of endive (Belgium), v. I, 48
    cream of hearts of palm (Pacific Islands), v. II, 478
    cream of mushroom (Germany), v. I, 144-45
    cream of peanut butter (Mexico), v. II, 582
    cream of potato with corn (Colombia), v. II, 538
    cream of spinach and potato (New Zealand), v. II, 466-67
    cream of summer squash with noodles (Lithuania), v. I, 246
    cream of sweetpotato (Côte d'Ivoire), v. II, 64-65
    cream of white asparagus (Belgium), v. I, 48-49
    creamy baked sweetpotato (Caribbean), v. II, 493
    creamy, puréed, vegetable soup (Venezuela), v. II, 632-33
    curried coconut-bean, with brown basmati rice (Tanzania), v. II, 260-61
    curried corn chowder (South Africa), v. II, 245
    dark vegetable stock (Thailand), v. II, 431-32
    dumpling (Korea), v. II, 371-72
    egg and lemon (Greece), v. I, 164-65
    garlic (Portugal), v. I, 331-32
    greens with corn and peanut butter (Chad), v. II, 55
    groundnut and vegetable soup (Djibouti), v. II, 72-73
    hot yogurt with rice and chick peas (Iran), v. I, 477-78
    leek and potato (Luxembourg), v. I, 254-55
    lentil (Macedonia), v. I, 263-64
    lentil *consommé* (Liechtenstein), v. I, 239
    lentil, puréed with potatoes (Kuwait), v. I, 513
    lentil with vegetables (Burundi), v. II, 28-29
    lettuce (Wales), v. I, 459
    mango and onion (Guinea), v. II, 117-18
    meatball with rice and lentils (Cyprus), v. I, 467-68
    melon and fresh mint (Oman), v. I, 537
    Milanese *minestrone* (Italy), v. I, 222-23
    milk with corn (Botswana), v. II, 18
    mixed legume (Morocco), v. II, 172-73
    mushroom (Czech), v. I, 92-93
    mushroom with roasted millet (Belarus), v. I, 36-37
    noodle (Eritrea), v. II, 86-87
    noodle and mushroom with vegetables (Brunei), v. II, 307
    noodle with kidney beans (Central Asia), v. I, 625
    onion, with cheese (Serbia), v. I, 365-66
    papaya and garlic (Caribbean), v. II, 492-93
    plantain and corn (Cameroon), v. II, 35
    potato and celeriac chowder (Switzerland), v. I, 409-10
    potato and cheese (Ecuador), v. II, 552-53
    potato and meatball (Latvia), v. I, 232-33
    potato and mushroom (Austria), v. I, 24-25
    potato and tomato soup (Native America), v. II, 657
    potato and watercress with herbs (Wales), v. I, 458-59
    potato milk (Bosnia), v. I, 61
    potato with cheese (Sweden), v. I, 400
    pumpkin (Malta), v. I, 274-75
    pumpkin with coconut milk and banana (Caribbean – Bahamas), v. II, 494
    pumpkin with pomegranate seeds (Azerbaijan), v. I, 604
    puréed banana, *yuca*, and coconut (Honduras), v. II, 573-74
    puréed carrot and *kumara* with gingerroot (New Zealand), v. II, 465-66
    puréed celeriac and leek (Croatia), v. I, 84-85
    puréed corn, with sweet red peppers (Mexico), v. II, 582-83
    puréed cream of chick pea and celeriac (Turkey), v. I, 569
    puréed cream of corn and basil soup with tomato (Chile), v. II, 532
    puréed *dhal* (Pacific Islands - Fiji), v. II, 476
    puréed lentil soup (Somalia), v. II, 232-33
    puréed potato and sweetpotato (Nigeria), v. II, 203
    puréed root vegetable (Saudi Arabia), v. I, 555
    red lentil (Libya), v. II, 140-41
    red lentil and bulgur (Turkey), v. I, 568-69
    red lentil and bulgur with apricots (Armenia), v. I, 589-90
    red lentil and red onion (Ireland), v. I, 199
    rice noodle and meatball soup (Laos), v. II, 386

soups (cont'd)
- red pottage (Scotland), v. I, 449
- rice with yogurt (Azerbaijan), v. I, 605-606
- roasted potato (Tibet), v. II, 339
- savory apple (Andorra), v. I, 17
- sea broth, v. II, 411
- sea broth with glass noodles (Myanmar/Burma), v. II, 411
- slow cooker lentil, with potatoes and spinach (Palestine), v. I, 546
- slow cooker vegetable with beans and barley (Croatia), v. I, 87-88
- sorrel-potato (Russia), v. I, 352-53
- sour green bean and potato (Slovakia), v. I, 373-74
- spicy bean soup with coconut milk (Djibouti), v. II, 72
- spinach and rice (Lebanon), v. I, 526
- spinach, with leeks and dill (Iraq), v. I, 488
- squash *bisque* (Native America), v. II, 658-59
- tomato (India), v. I, 668-69
- tomato and groundnut (Ghana), v. II, 111
- tomato and spinach with bulgur wheat and mint (Armenia), v. I, 590-91
- tomato and squash (Algeria), v. II, 5
- tomato bouillon with chick peas (Mauritania/Western Sahara), v. II, 164
- tomato with avocado and shallots (Australia), v. II, 449-50
- tomato with basil (The Gambia), v. II, 100-101
- tomato with brown rice (Austria), v. I, 23-24
- tomato with green peas (Palestine), v. I, 545-46
- tomato with walnuts and *vermicelli* (Georgia), v. I, 614
- *tukpa* vegetarian broth with soba noodles and *bok choy* (Tibet), v. II, 340-41
- vegetable and groundnut soup (Zambia), v. II, 292-93
- vegetable bread soup (Spain), v. I, 393-94
- vegetable stock from soup, v. II, 691-92
- vegetable stocks for soups, stews and sauces, v. II, 692-93
- vegetable *tukpa* broth (Tibet), v. II, 339-40
- vegetable, with barley (Estonia), v. I, 112-13
- vegetable, with cabbage (Albania), v. I, 5-6
- vegetable, with caraway (Romania), v. I, 342-43
- vegetable, with chick peas and groundnut butter (Namibia), v. II, 192
- vegetable, with *couscous* and chick peas (Angola), v. II, 11-12
- vegetable, with fine noodles (Malta), v. I, 274
- vegetable with oatmeal or barley (Oman), v. I, 538
- vegetable with peanut butter, sweetpotato, and greens (Zimbabwe), v. II, 300
- vegetable, with sour cream (Moldova), v. I, 284
- vegetarian stock from *kombu* (Japan), v. II, 363
- vegetarian *tukpa* broth (Tibet), v. II, 339-40
- vegetarian vegetable (Ecuador), v. II, 553
- walnut and rice (Azerbaijan), v. I, 605
- watercress and potato (Ireland), v. I, 198
- white stock, v. II, 692-93
- wild mushroom stock, v. 694
- winter squash and peanuts (Senegal), v. II, 216-17
- winter squash and vegetable (Paraguay), v. II, 604-605
- winter squash with garlic (Mozambique), v. II, 180-81
- yellow pea (Sweden), v. I, 399-400
- yellow split pea with meatballs (Azerbaijan), v. I, 603-604
- yogurt and bread (Yemen), v. I, 578-79
- yogurt with rice (Georgia), v. I, 613-14
- *yucca* (Guatemala), v. II, 567

SOUTH AFRICA, v. II, 242-49

soybean sprouts
- dumpling soup (Korea), v. II, 371-72
- fruit and vegetable salad (Indonesia), v. II, 354
- red grapefruit salad with soymeat and (Thailand), v. II, 433-34

soy meat analogue products, bacon
- beans and tomatoes with plantains (Colombia), v. II, 539
- bean stew with hominy and *chouriço* (Cape Verde), v. II, 42-43
- corn and sweetpotato soup (Thailand), v. II, 430-31
- fried greens with bacon (Native America), v. II, 656
- Irish stew, v. I, 199-200
- mushroom soup (Czech), v. I, 92-93
- slow cooker vegetable soup with beans and barley (Croatia), v. I, 87-88
- smoky lentils with vegetables (Panama), v. II, 599-600
- with potatoes in lettuce salad (Burundi), v. II, 26-27

soy meat analogue products, *chorizo* sausage (*chouriço*)
- bean stew with hominy and *chouriço* (Cape Verde), v. II, 42-43
- savory bread with vegetables and sausage (Andorra), v. I, 20-21
- skillet, with angel hair and mushrooms (Spain), v. I, 395
- with *pesto* in macaroni salad (Uganda), v. II, 284-85

soy meat analogue products, ground
- "beef" soup with noodles (Paraguay), v. II, 606
- fried meat (Honduras), v. II, 572
- macaroni and meat casserole (Greece), v. I, 167-68
- meat pies (Botswana), v. II, 21
- noodles with soymeat and yogurt-garlic sauce (Azerbaijan), v. I, 608
- skillet *lasagne* (Italy), v. I, 217
- twice-baked potatoes (Palestine), v. I, 547
- vegetable stew (Uzbekistan), v. I, 628-29
- with *chimichuri* and herb seasoning over *pasta* (Argentina), v. II, 509-10
- with *linguine*, chick peas, and red kidney beans (Afghanistan), v. I, 640

soy meat analogue products, meatballs
- and caramelized onions (Slovenia), v. I, 385-86
- and fruit in curry sauce (Mozambique), v. II, 183-84
- and green beans in yogurt sauce (Bosnia), v. I, 63
- and vegetable pastry bundles (Mongolia), v. II, 405
- and rice noodle soup (Laos), v. II, 386
- and vegetables skillet (Niger), v. II, 198-99
- in *tahini* sauce with potatoes (Jordan), v. I, 508

index

soy meat analogue products, meatballs (cont'd)
    potato-meatball soup (Latvia), v. **I**, 232-33
    soup with rice and lentils (Cyprus), v. **I**, 467-68
    with garlic and yogurt curds (Albania) v. **I**, 8
    tomatoes, wheat berries, and yogurt (Armenia), v. **I**, 588-89
    with sweet and sour glaze (Japan), v. **II**, 361
    with tomato and onion sauce (Costa Rica), v. **II**, 543
    yellow split pea soup (Azerbaijan), v. **I**, 603-604

soy meat analogue products, sausages, breakfast links
    in sweet wine sauce (Slovenia), v. **I**, 384-85
    kidney bean salad with eggs (Slovenia), v. **I**, 388-89
    with curried beans (Madagascar), v. **II**, 149 with lemon (Greece), v. **I**, 157
    with sweet browned cabbage (Denmark), v. **I**, 102

soy meat analogue products, strips, nuggets, or tempeh
    and banana stew (Liberia), v. **II**, 134-35
    and melon skillet (Yemen), v. **I**, 581
    "chicken" stew (Gabon), v. **II**, 49
    broth with preserved lemons, snowpeas, and *shiitake* mushrooms (Brunei), v. **II**, 316-17
    butternut squash with soymeat (Israel), v. **I**, 495
    "chicken" stew with tomato and garlic (Sierra Leone), v. **II**, 227-28
    curried, with onions and coconut milk (Myanmar/ Burma), v. **II**, 414
    deviled beet, potato, apple, and egg salad (Estonia), v. **I**, 111-12
    goulash (Hungary), v. **I**, 177-78
    grapefruit salad with soymeat and soy sprouts (Thailand), v. **II**, 433-34
    Irish stew, v. **I**, 199-200
    mushroom stew (Bhutan), v. **I**, 660
    pan-grilled soymeat brochettes (Cameroon), v. **II**, 32-33
    puréed butternut squash soup (Israel), v. **I**, 495-96
    sautéed with spices and peaches (Iran), v. **I**, 480-81
    skewered with peppers (Mali), v. **II**, 157
    vegetable *ragoût* (Lebanon), v. **I**, 527-28
    vegetable stew with beer (Belgium), v. **I**, 49-50
    vegetable stew with brown rice (Serbia), v. **I**, 367-68
    with coconut milk (Sri Lanka), v. **I**, 705
    with onions (El Salvador), v. **II**, 561-62

SPAIN, v. **I**, 391-97
spicebush, information, v. **II**, 667 (note)
spiced sugar, v. **II**, 505
spinach
    and beet salad with yogurt dressing (Georgia), v. **I**, 618-19
    and lentil salad (Libya), v. **II**, 141
    and potato cream soup (New Zealand), v. **II**, 466-67
    and potato pie (New Zealand), v. **II**, 468
    and rice soup (Lebanon), v. **I**, 526
    and spicy potatoes (Pakistan), v. **I**, 692
    and tomato soup with bulgur wheat and mint (Armenia), v. **I**, 590-91
    and tomatoes with *orzo* (Oman), v. **I**, 538-39
    and yogurt salad (Kuwait), v. **I**, 512-13
    avocado and mayonnaise salad (Ghana), v. **II**, 110

    bread salad, with rice, chick peas, and garlic-yogurt sauce with *tahini* (Tunisia), v. **II**, 274-75
    cheese and peppers in spinach sauce (India), v. **I**, 674-75
    dumpling soup (Korea), v. **II**, 371-72
    fried with chick peas and grated cheese (Egypt), v. **II**, 81
    garnish for stir-fried cauliflower and straw mushrooms (Vietnam), v. **II**, 441-42
    gratin with cauliflower and fennel (Switzerland), v. **I**, 411-12
    greens and vegetables (Caribbean – Virgin Islands), v. **II**, 502
    Israeli *couscous* and chick pea salad (Israel), v. **I**, 496-97
    macaroni salad (Denmark), v. **I**, 107-108
    noodle and mushroom soup with vegetables (Brunei), v. **II**, 307
    omelet with herbs (Azerbaijan), v. **I**, 606-607
    pie (Albania), v. **I**, 9-10
    ravioli with spinach and sage butter (Italy), v. **I**, 224
    rice noodle and meatball soup (Laos), v. **II**, 386
    salad, warm with mushrooms and garlic (Andorra), v. **I**, 15-16
    sesame (Korea), v. **II**, 373-74
    skewered with peppers (Mali), v. **II**, 157
    slow cooker lentil soup (Palestine), v. **I**, 546
    soup, with leeks and dill (Iraq), v. **I**, 488
    stew with peanut butter (Central African Republics), v. **II**, 51
    stir-fried, with *tofu* and mushrooms (Tibet), v. **II**, 341-42
    tossed salad with blueberries and hazelnuts (England), v. **I**, 436
    vegetables in curried coconut milk (Thailand), v. **II**, 434-35
    with black-eyed peas and leeks in skillet (Iran), v. **I**, 479-80
    with gingerroot and *chilies* in coconut milk (The Philippines), v. **II**, 422-23
    with sautéed noodles (Czech), v. **I**, 96-97
    wonton appetizers (China), v. **II**, 323-24

squashes, summer
    and cheese *quesadillas* (Mexico), v. **II**, 580
    and tomato stew (Slovenia), v. **I**, 383-84
    and tomatoes with pumpkin seeds (Nicaragua), v. **II**, 591-92
    baby zucchini with *feta* and roasted red peppers (Armenia), v. **I**, 587-88
    cheese-stuffed zucchini with lentils and fruit (Mexico), v. **II**, 583-84
    chick pea soup with rice (Peru), v. **II**, 612-13
    chowder of vegetables and fine noodles (Montenegro), v. **I**, 294-95
    cream soup with noodles (Lithuania), v. **I**, 246
    custard casserole (Saudi Arabia), v. **I**, 557
    green squash with warm *vinaigrette* (Kenya), v. **II**, 129
    in vegetable soup with *couscous* and chick peas (Angola), v. **II**, 11-12

index

squashes, summer (cont'd)
    kebabs (Greece), v. **I**, 166
    meatball and vegetable pastry bundles (Mongolia), v. **II**, 405
    Milanese *minestrone* (Italy), v. **I**, 222-23
    omelet on omelet (Chile), v. **II**, 531
    quinoa and vegetable stew (Peru), v. **II**, 615
    ratatouille, vegetable stew (France), v. **I**, 134-35
    ratatouille with puff pastry pillows (France), v. **I**, 135-36
    salad, with *couscous* and roasted eggplant and red pepper (Morocco), v. **II**, 171-72
    sautéed, with peanuts (Chad), v. **II**, 57-58
    summer squash with *crème* (Hungary), v. **I**, 181
    vegetable *kebabs* with lemon (Kuwait), v. **I**, 518-19
    vegetarian vegetable soup (Ecuador), v. **II**, 553
    with peanuts and garlic (Central African Republics), v. **II**, 49-50
    zucchini and rice in tomato sauce (Madagascar), v. **II**, 150-51
    zucchini *vinaigrette* (Israel), v. **I**, 499
    zucchini with vegetable stuffing (Turkey), v. **I**, 571
squashes, winter
    acorn, baked with chutney (Indonesia), v. **II**, 356
    acorn, baked with honey and hazelnut butter (Native America), v. **II**, 666-67
    acorn, baked with tomato stuffing (Norway), v. **I**, 311-12
    and tomato soup (Algeria), v. **II**, 5
    bean stew with hominy and *chouriço* (Cape Verde), v. **II**, 42-43
    butternut squash soup with soymeat (Israel), v. **I**, 495-96
    dark vegetable stock (Thailand), v. **II**, 431-32
    lentil soup (Macedonia), v. **I**, 263-64
    pumpkin pie in *phyllo* roll (Serbia), v. **I**, 370
    rice and cheese-stuffed acorn squashes (Bosnia), v. **I**, 64-65
    roasted, with corn and eggs (Chile), v. **II**, 532-33
    slow cooker vegetable stew (Botswana), v. **II**, 19-20
    squash *bisque* (Native America), v. **II**, 658-59
    squash or pumpkin dessert in sweet syrup with walnuts (Turkey), v. **I**, 573-74
    stir-fried with red pepper and scallions (Australia), v. **II**, 448-49
    sweet soy-glazed pumpkin or squash (Korea), v. **II**, 373
    vegetable pasties (New Zealand), v. **II**, 467
    vegetable soup with fine noodles (Malta), v. **I**, 274
    vegetable stew (Bolivia), v. **II**, 515-16
    winter squash and peanut soup (Senegal), v. **II**, 216-17
    winter squash and vegetable soup (Paraguay), v. **II**, 604-605
    winter squash in sweet vegetable stock (Japan), v. **II**, 362-63
    winter squash soup with garlic (Mozambique), v. **II**, 180-81
    with greens (Botswana), v. **II**, 22

strawberries
    and blueberry summer pudding, v. **I**, 445-46
    fresh fruit refresher (Mexico), v. **II**, 587-88
    fruit compote with vanilla (Madagascar), v. **II**, 152
    pears with ice cream and fresh strawberry sauce (Andorra), v. **I**, 21
    salsa, with melon and black pepper (Native America), v. **II**, 669-70
    strawberry-rhubarb juice (Finland), v. **I**, 121-22
    tart (Slovakia), v. **I**, 380
    whipped cranberry-raspberry with farina and wilted lettuce salad with smoked *Gouda* cheese (Germany), v. **I**, 147
    Yorkshire summer pudding (England), v. **I**, 444-45
SRI LANKA, v. **I**, 698-707
SUDAN, v. **II**, 250-58
SWEDEN, v. **I**, 398-404
sweetpotatoes and yams
    and black bean appetizers (Caribbean), v. **II**, 491
    and coconut pudding (Sri Lanka), v. **I**, 707
    and corn soup (Thailand), v. **II**, 430-31
    and snowpea stir-fry (Bangladesh), v. **I**, 650-51
    and tomato stew (Côte d'Ivoire), v. **II**, 67
    and vegetables (Caribbean – Virgin Islands), v. **II**, 502
    Argentine-styled Russian salad, v. **II**, 508-509
    bean stew with hominy and *chouriço* (Cape Verde), v. **II**, 42-43
    biscuits (Zimbabwe), v. **II**, 301
    broth with preserved lemons, snowpeas, and *shiitake* mushrooms (Brunei), v. **II**, 316-17
    caramelized with mandarin oranges (Pacific Islands – Hawaii), v. **II**, 479
    chick pea and tomato soup with leeks (Uruguay), v. **II**, 623
    cream of sweetpotato soup (Côte d'Ivoire), v. **II**, 64-65
    creamy soup (Caribbean), v. **II**, 493
    croquettes (Senegal), v. **II**, 221-22
    dessert fritters (Peru), v. **II**, 618-19
    fried (Guinea), v. **II**, 121
    fried, with onions (Ghana), v. **II**, 114
    fufu, with plantain (Cameroon), v. **II**, 37
    fufu, with white potato and corn (Cameroon), v. **II**, 36-37
    greens and vegetables (Caribbean – Virgin Islands), v. **II**, 502
    lentil soup with vegetables (Burundi), v. **II**, 28-29
    mashed, with pineapple (Nicaragua), v. **II**, 593
    omelet (São Tomé and Principe), v. **II**, 211-12
    pudding (Pacific Islands – Palua), v. **II**, 485
    pudding, with coconut (Zambia), v. **II**, 296
    puréed carrot and *kumara* (sweetpotato) soup with gingerroot (New Zealand), v. **II**, 465-66
    puréed, soup, with potato (Nigeria), v. **II**, 203
    roasted, salad, with macadamia nuts (New Zealand), v. **II**, 464
    salad. curried, with banana and hard-cooked egg (Pacific Islands – Saipan), v. **II**, 475
    salad, with *jicama* and mango in citrus dressing (Caribbean), v. **II**, 494-95
    salad, with scallions (Chad), v. **II**, 56

index

sweetpotatoes and yams (cont'd)
  soufflé (Mali), v. II, 156-57
  spicy with coconut milk (Sri Lanka), v. I, 704
  stir-fry with snowpeas (Bangladesh), v. I, 650-51
  tagine, with carrots and onion (Western Sahara), v. II, 165-66
  tapioca pudding with (Laos), v. II, 389-90
  vegetable soup with *couscous* and chick peas (Angola), v. II, 11-12
  with gingerroot (Vietnam), v. II, 441
  with greens and peanut butter in vegetable soup (Zimbabwe), v. II, 300
Swiss chard, *tagine*, with rice (Morocco), v. II, 175
SWITZERLAND, v. I, 405-21
SYRIA, v. I, 561-64

TAJIKISTAN (Central Asia), v. I, 622-34
tamarind liquid (Cambodia), v. II, 316
tangerine, dessert, with avocado (Mozambique), v. II, 185-86
TANZANIA, v. II, 259-66
tarragon, information, v. I, 408 (note)
tart crust and *streusel* topping (Germany), v. I, 152-53
tarts, *see* pies
THAILAND, v. II, 428-36
TIBET, v. II, 337-49
tofu (**soy beancurd**)
  and Chinese chive bud soup (Vietnam), v. II, 438-39
  and mushrooms with Chinese brown sauce (China), v. II, 332-33
  baked with citrus-shallot sauce (Pacific Islands – Polynesia), v. II, 481-82
  broiled, with sweet Korean sesame marinade (Korea), v. II, 372
  broiled, with two *miso* sauces (Japan), v. II, 365-66
  deep-fried, with *chili* and garlic sauce (Malaysia), v. II, 396
  deep-fried, with Chinese ginger and sesame sauce (China), v. II, 330
  fried *tofu* with dipping sauce (Brunei), v. II, 306-307
  mashed with garlic (Bangladesh), v. I, 649
  stir-fried (Nepal), v. I, 685
  tea-smoked with ginger (Mongolia), v. II, 403-404
  tofu "tuna"-stuffed cucumber boats (Côte d'Ivorie), v. II, 66-67
  with chive buds in spicy sauce (Malaysia), v. II, 395
  with curried vegetables (Cambodia), v. II, 319
  with stir-fried spinach and mushrooms (Tibet), v. II, 341-42
TOGO, v. II, 267-69
tomatoes
  and avocado dip (Zambia), v. II, 292
  and avocado dipping sauce (Venezuela), v. II, 630
  and beans with plantains (Colombia), v. II, 539
  and black-eyed pea soup (Liberia), v. II, 133
  and chick pea soup with leeks (Uruguay), v. II, 623
  and *chili* sauce for spicy eggplant (Brunei), v. II, 311-12
  and coriander salad (Yemen), v. I, 579
  and coriander sauce (Laos), v. II, 384
  and cream sauce (Uruguay), v. II, 622-23
  and cucumber salad with *chaat masala* (India), v. I, 669
  and cucumber salad with grated cheese (Montenegro), v. I, 295
  and cucumber salad with peppers (Hungary), v. I, 178-79
  and eggplant (Central African Republics), v. II, 50-51
  and eggplant casserole (Slovakia), v. I, 377
  and eggplant salad (Yemen), v. I, 579-80
  and garlic in mung bean sauce (Uganda), v. II, 285-86
  and garlic sauce for black beans (The Gambia), v. II, 103
  and green onion salad (Zambia), v. II, 293
  and groundnut soup (Ghana), v. II, 111
  and hearts of palm in rice casserole (Costa Rica), v. II, 544-45
  and lima beans (Peru), v. II, 616
  and mashed plantains (Caribbean – Dominican Republic), v. II, 499
  and mushroom sauce (Italy), v. II, 686
  and okra stew (Mali), v. II, 158
  and onion salad (Syria), v. I, 562-63
  and onion salad (Tanzania), v. II, 262
  and onion *sambol* (Sri Lanka), v. I, 700
  and onion sauce for fried plantains (Guinea), v. II, 120
  and onion sauce for meatballs (Costa Rica), v. II, 543
  and orange salad (Kenya), v. II, 125-26
  and papaya salad (Caribbean – Puerto Rico), v. II, 495-96
  and peanut butter sauce with garlic (The Gambia), v. II, 104
  and peanut sauce (Zambia), v. II, 294
  and peanut sauce with cream (Brazil), v. II, 527-28
  and potato soup (Native America), v. II, 657
  and purslane salad (Native America), v. II, 656-57
  and red pepper appetizer salad (Israel), v. I, 495
  and rice (Caribbean), v. II, 498-99
  and rice with coconut milk (Sierra Leone), v. II, 228-29
  and sautéed cabbage, carrot, and onion (Mozambique), v. II, 185
  and squash soup (Algeria), v. II, 5
  and squash stew (Slovenia), v. I, 383-84
  and spinach with bulgur wheat and meat (Armenia), v. I, 590-91
  and spinach with *orzo* (Oman), v. I, 538-39
  and summer squash with pumpkin seeds (Nicaragua), v. II, 591-92
  and sweetpotato stew (Côte d'Ivoire), v. II, 67
  and wheat berries, meatballs, and yogurt (Armenia), v. I, 588-89
  baby potatoes in spicy sauce (Oman), v. I, 539-40
  baked (Palestine), v. I, 549
  baked fennel (Jordan), v. I, 508-509
  baked spaghetti with two sauces (Somalia), v. II, 236-37
  baked with rice and eggs (Malta), v. I, 278
  bean and hominy *chili* (Somalia), v. II, 238

tomatoes (cont'd)
   bean stew with hominy and *chouriço* (Cape Verde), v. II, 42-43
   "beef" soup with noodles (Paraguay), v. II, 606
   bouillon with chick peas (Mauritania/Western Sahara), v. II, 164
   bread and vegetable salad (Kuwait), v. I, 515-16
   broccoli and potato salad with Hollandaise sauce (Brazil), v. II, 521
   butternut squash soup with soymeat (Israel), v. I, 495-96
   cabbage salad with pineapple (Liberia), v. II, 133-34
   cabbage slaw with pineapple (Cameroon), v. II, 34
   cabbage soup (Russia), v. I, 352
   caper and olive sauce (Croatia), v. I, 85-86
   cauliflower in spicy sauce (Pakistan), v. I, 695
   cheese and *chili* dip (Native America), v. II, 653
   cheese-stuffed appetizers (Moldova), v. I, 282
   cheese with peas (India). v. I, 675
   "chicken" stew with garlic and (Sierra Leone), v. II, 227-28
   chick pea and kale soup with peanut butter (Djibouti), v. II, 74
   chick pea and potato stew (Tunisia), v. II, 275-76
   chili, v. II, 288
   chili and ginger sauce (Australia), v. II, 456-57
   chilies and cheese (Bhutan), v. I, 659-60
   chili sauce (Bolivia), v. II, 518
   coconut-bean soup with rice (Nigeria), v. II, 203-204
   condiment (Madagascar), v. II, 151
   corn soup (Kuwait), v. I, 514
   couscous salad with chick peas and tomatoes (Mauritania), v. II, 162-63
   creamed tomato soup with yogurt (Afghanistan), v. I, 639
   cream of corn and basil soup (Chile), v. II, 532
   curried coconut-bean soup with basmati rice (Tanzania), v. II, 260-61
   curried sauce, with eggs and peas (Tibet), v. II, 342-43
   curried, with onions and eggs (Bangladesh), v. I, 649-50
   dark vegetable stock (Thailand), v. II, 431-32
   dipping sauce (The Gambia), v. II, 100
   dried mushrooms in tomato sauce (Zambia), v. II, 294-95
   eggplant and tomato salad (Yemen), v. I, 579-80
   eggplant curry (Sri Lanka), v. I, 700-701
   eggplant *tagine* (Libya), v. II, 142-43
   fenugreek and vegetable appetizer dip (Yemen), v. I, 578
   fried, with onions and brown rice (Bolivia), v. II, 516
   gari with eggs (Ghana), v. II, 113
   grape tomato, salad with green bananas and vegetables (Costa Rica), v. II, 542-43
   green tomato relish (Somalia), v. II, 238-39
   groundnut and vegetable soup (Djibouti), v. II, 72-73
   hearts of palm salad with cheese (Ecuador), v. II, 550-51
   hunter's style sauce for vegetables and *pasta* (Italy), v. II, 684-85
   jam (Mozambique), v. II, 180
   kebabs (Greece), v. I, 166
   kebabs, with *Halloumi* cheese (Cyprus), v. I, 471-72
   ketchup, homemade, v. II, 683
   layered fruit salad (Cameroon), v. II, 34-35
   layered vegetable salad (Ghana), v. II, 111-12
   macaroni and vegetables (The Gambia), v. II, 104-105
   macaroni in spicy sauce with mushrooms (Iraq), v. I, 489
   marinara sauce (Italy), v. II, 682
   meatballs and vegetables skillet (Niger), v. II, 198-99
   millet and corn salad with avocado (Central African Republics), v. II, 47-48
   millet *tabbouleh* (Lebanon), v. I, 526-27
   mixed legume soup (Morocco), v. II, 172-73
   omelet (Cyprus), v. I, 467
   oven-dried, v. II, 217-18
   pancakes with vegetables (Mauritania), v. II, 161-62
   papaya and corn salad with citrus *vinaigrette* (Togo), v. II, 268
   potatoes and cabbage in tomato sauce (Bangladesh), v. I, 648
   pumpkin appetizer dip (Libya), v. II, 139
   puréed lentil soup (Somalia), v. II, 232-33
   puréed potato and sweetpotato soup (Nigeria), v. II, 203
   quinoa and vegetable stew (Peru), v. II, 615
   red lentil and bulgur soup with apricots (Armenia), v. I, 589-90
   red lentil soup (Libya), v. II, 140-41
   red pottage (Scotland), v. I, 449
   rice and coconut milk (Mozambique), v. II, 182-83
   rice with potatoes (Uganda), v. II, 286
   roasted eggplant (India), v. I, 672-73
   roasted eggplant pie in *phyllo* crust, v. I, 506-507
   roasted, with roasted pepper salad (Tunisia), v. II, 272-73
   salad, grape tomato, with *mozzarella* and basil (Venezuela), v. II, 632
   salad stuffing for avocado halves (New Zealand), v. II, 463
   salad, with avocados and peaches (Mozambique), v. II, 181
   salad, with eggplant and goat cheese (São Tomé and Principe), v. II, 210-11
   salad, with garlic and cheese (Belarus), v. I, 35
   salad, with onions and peas (Portugal), v. I, 332-33
   salad, with shredded *Halloumi* (Cyprus), v. I, 469
   salad, with watermelon and *feta* (Egypt), v. II, 79
   sauce for breaded and deep-fried okra (Cyprus), v. I, 472
   sauce for zucchini and rice (Madagascar), v. II, 150-51
   sauce, with potatoes, garlic, and coriander (Somalia), v. II, 236
   scrambled eggs with vegetables (Venezuela), v. II, 633
   shirred eggs and vegetables (Libya), v. II, 143-44

tomatoes (cont'd)
    slow cooker black-eyed pea *chili* (Uganda), v. II, 287-88
    soup (India), v. I, 668-69
    soup, with avocado and shallots (Australia), v. II, 449-50
    soup, with basil (The Gambia), v. II, 100-101
    soup, with green peas (Palestine), v. I, 545-46
    soup, with walnuts and *vermicelli* (Georgia), v. I, 614
    spicy bean soup with coconut milk (Djibouti), v. II, 72
    spicy rice (Djibouti), v. II, 75-76   spicy sauce with ginger and peanut butter (Togo), v. II, 268-69
    spinach stew with peanut butter (Central African Republics), v. II, 51
    stewed tomatoes (Jordan), v. I, 506
    stew with bananas and soymeat (Liberia), v. II, 134-35
    stew with potatoes and onions (Sudan), v. II, 254
    summer vegetable stew (Tunisia), v. II, 276-77
    tagliatelle with chick peas (Cyprus), v. I, 471
    toasted millet salad (Mali), v. II, 155-56
    tortilla skillet (Honduras), v. II, 574-75
    tossed vegetable salad (Azerbaijan), v. I, 606
    tossed vegetable salad with cheese (Sudan), v. II, 252-53
    twice-baked potatoes (Palestine), v. I, 547
    vegetable and groundnut soup (Zambia), v. II, 292-93
    vegetable bread soup (Spain), v. I, 393-94
    vegetable relish (Tanzania), v. II, 262-63
    vegetable salad (Macedonia), v. I, 265
    vegetable soup with *couscous* and chick peas (Angola), v. II, 11-12
    vegetable soup with oatmeal or barley (Oman), v. I, 538
    vegetable soup with peanut butter, sweetpotato, and greens (Zimbabwe), v. II, 300
    vegetable stew (Bolivia), v. II, 515-16
    vegetable stew (Uzbekistan), v. I, 628-29
    vegetable stew with beans and *chouriço* sausage (Angola), v. II, 13-14
    vegetable stew with brown rice and soymeat (Serbia), v. I, 367-68
    vegetarian *tukpa* broth (Tibet), v. II, 339-40
    village tossed salad (Greece), v. I, 161-62
    with angel hair *pasta*, mushrooms, and *chorizo* in skillet (Spain), v. I, 395
    with artichokes and onions (Armenia), v. I, 593-94
    with cabbage (Venezuela), v. II, 634
    with chick peas and apricots (Yemen), v. I, 580-81
    with fried cabbage (Moldova), v. I, 288
    with lentils and garlic (Eritrea), v. II, 88
    with lima beans and eggs (Mexico), v. II, 585
    with *vermicelli* and rice (Kuwait), v. I, 517
    zucchini with vegetable stuffing (Turkey), v. I, 571
    yucca soup (Guatemala), v. II, 567
trahana with yogurt and *Gorgonzola* (Cyprus), v. I, 470
TUNISIA, v. II, 270-80
TURKEY, v. I, 565-75

TURKMENISTAN (Central Asia), v. I, 622-34
turnips, Canadian/rutabaga, *see* rutabaga
turnips, French
    cheese soup (The Netherlands), v. I, 301-302
    oven-roasted root vegetables with cheese (Sweden), v. I, 402-403
    puréed root vegetable soup (Saudi Arabia), v. I, 555
    slow cooker vegetable stew (Botswana), v. II, 19-20
    vegetable stew (Uzbekistan), v. I, 628-29

UGANDA, v. II, 281-89
UKRAINE, v. I, 422-31
UNITED KINGDOM, ENGLAND, v. I, 432-47
UNTED KINGDOM, SCOTLAND, v. I, 448-55
UNITED KINGDOM, WALES, v. I, 456-62
URUGUAY, v. II, 621-27
UZBEKISTAN (Central Asia), v. I, 622-34

Vanilla extract, homemade, v. II, 426
vanilla sugar (Belgium), v. I, 54
vanilla yogurt, v. I, 573 (note)
vegetables, frozen mixed, puréed vegetable soup with sour cream (Moldova), v. I, 284
VENEZUELA, v. II, 628-38
VIETNAM, v. II, 437-44
Vietnamese mint, information, v. II, 385 (note)
vinegars
    Canadian celery vinegar
        recipe, v. II, 642;
        applications, v. I, 311; v. II, 641
    Danish spiced vinegar
        recipe, v. II, 677-78;
        application, v. I, 310-11
    garlic – basil vinegar
        recipe, v. II, 678;
        applications, v. I, 7-8, 71, 83, 143, 162-63, 346-47, 373-74, 387, 389, 515-16, 591;
        v. II, 171-72, 210-11, 457, 499, 502, 537, 550-51, 598, 630-31
    lovage-chive vinegar
        recipe, v. I, 240;
        applications, v. I, 143, 239
    mixed flower vinegar with oregano
        recipe, v. II, 679;
        applications, v. I, 136, 162-63, 499, 518-19;
        v. II, 463-64
    oregano flower vinegar
        recipe, v. I, 265-66;
        applications, v. I, 161-62, 265; v. II, 598
    pear-anise hyssop vinegar
        recipe, v. II, 679-80;
        application, v. II, 463-64
    pineapple vinegar, v. II, 573
    pineapple vinegar, fermented (Honduras), v. II, 573
    raspberry vinegar
        recipe, v. II, 452;
        applications, v. II, 452, 454-55, 463-64, 465, 581, 654, 654-55, 675
    rosemary vinegar
        recipe, v. II, 680;
        application, v. I, 591

vinegars (cont'd)
- sage vinegar
    - recipe, v. **I**, 28-29;
    - applications, v. **I**, 28, 387-88, 388-89
- salad burnet and shallot vinegar with pepper
    - recipe, v. **II**, 511-12;
    - application, v. **II**, 511
- spicy nasturtium flower vinegar
    - recipe, v. **I**, 240;
    - applications, v. **I**, 239
- sweet and tart cranberry vinegar
    - recipe, v. **II**, 681;
    - applications, v. **I**, 188; v. **II**, 465
- sweet spiced orange vinegar
    - recipe, v. **II**, 680-81;
    - applications, v. **II**, 465

Waffles, v. **I**, 304
waffles (Belgium), v. **I**, 56-57
WALES, see **UNITED KINGDOM, WALES**
walnuts, honey-sweetened (Georgia), v. **I**, 620
watermelon
- and cucumber salad with *hoisin*-lime dressing (Vietnam), v. **II**, 439
- fresh fruit refresher (Mexico), v. **II**, 587-88
- punch (Turkmenistan), v. **I**, 634
- salad, with *feta* (South Africa), v. **II**, 244
- salad, with tomato and *feta* (Egypt), v. **II**, 79

watercress
- and potato soup (Ireland), v. **I**, 198
- and potato soup with herbs (Wales), v. **I**, 458-59
- broiled *tofu* with two *miso* sauces (Japan), v. **II**, 365-66
- cold sauce (Belgium), v. **I**, 46-47
- omelet (Luxembourg), v. **I**, 253-54
- roasted eggplant salad with onion dressing (Vietnam), v. **II**, 440
- salad, with sesame dressing (Korea), v. **II**, 374

WESTERN SAHARA, v. **II**, 160-68

wheat berries
- Christmas porridge (Armenia), v. **I**, 598-99
- with tomatoes and meatballs with yogurt (Armenia), v. **I**, 588-89

whey, buttermilk cornbread, v. **I**, 368
whey, information, v. **I**, 232 (note)
wild rice
- and mushroom casserole (Native America), v. **II**, 663
- casserole with mushrooms and baby carrots (Canada), v. **II**, 642-43
- *pilaf* with fruits and nuts (Azerbaijan), v. **I**, 609

winter savory, information, v. **II**, 194 (note)
Worcestershire-style sauce, v. **II**, 683-84

Yams, *see* sweetpotatoes
YEMEN, v. **I**, 576-82
yogurt, v. **I**, 572-73
yogurt *crème*, v. **I**, 654
- English cream (Scotland), v. **I**, 451
- herbed appetizer (Israel), v. **I**, 493
- sweet yogurt dessert (Bangladesh), v. **I**, 653
- with sweet oatmeal topping (Wales), v. **I**, 461-62
- yogurt sweet ("curds and treacle") (Sri Lanka), v. **I**, 707
- yogurt with green *chilies* (Palestine), v. **I**, 545

yogurt marinade (Afghanistan), v. **I**, 640-41
yuca (*yucca*) root, *see* cassava

ZAMBIA, v. **II**, 290-97
ZIMBABWE, v. **II**, 298-302

about the author

Born in Rochester New York, at the beginning of World War II, Mrs. Spinzia has seen a dramatic change in the eating habits of Americans extending from the days of rationing to the days of fast foods. Her travels have exposed her to the world beyond our shores and her journals have preserved her observations. From Rochester her family moved to Long Island where she did her undergraduate and graduate work, married, and taught biology at Adelphi University. It was at this point that the Spinzias chose to become vegetarians and the journals expanded to recipe research. After their daughter was grown, the Spinzias began to teach courses on Long Island history. They write and speak, jointly and separately, on a variety of Long Island-related subjects including the North Shore and South Shore estates, Louis Comfort Tiffany and the stained-glass windows of Tiffany Studios, the Vanderbilts of Long Island, Long Island's maritime heritage, women of Long Island, and Long Island's socialite spies. Together they have published seven books and numerous articles on Long Island-related subjects. Articles and sample pages from their books can be found at the Spinzias' website, spinzialongislandestates.com.

Judith Spinzia now resides in central Pennsylvania with her husband of over fifty years and frequent co-author. They share their beautiful flower and herb gardens with three cats.